D0551951

COMPACT ATLAS Britain

Contents

II **Route planning maps** with key to map pages

VIII **Key to road map symbols**

2 **Road maps at 3.3 miles to 1 inch**

289 **Index** to road maps of Great Britain

www.philips-maps.co.uk

First published in 2006 by Philip's
a division of Octopus Publishing Group Ltd
Endeavour House, 189 Shaftesbury Avenue
London WC2H 8JY
An Hachette UK Company
www.hachette.co.uk

Fifth edition 2013
First impression 2013

ISBN 978-1-84907-269-4

Cartography by Philip's

Data for the speed cameras provided by **PocketGPSWorld.com** Ltd.

Information for National Parks, Areas of Outstanding Natural Beauty, National Trails and Country Parks in Wales supplied by the Countryside Council for Wales.

Information for National Parks, Areas of Outstanding Natural Beauty, National Trails and Country Parks in England supplied by Natural England.

Data for Regional Parks, Long Distance Footpaths and Country Parks in Scotland provided by Scottish Natural Heritage.

Gaelic name forms used in the Western Isles provided by Comhairle nan Eilean.

Data for the National Nature Reserves in England provided by Natural England.

Data for the National Nature Reserves in Wales provided by Countryside Council for Wales. Darparwyd data'n ymwneud â Gwarchodfeydd Natur Cenedlaethol Cymru gan Gyngor Cefn Gwlad Cymru.

Information on the location of National Nature Reserves in Scotland was provided by Scottish Natural Heritage.

Data for National Scenic Areas in Scotland provided by the Scottish Executive Office. Crown copyright material is reproduced with the permission of the Controller of HMSO and the Queen's Printer for Scotland. Licence number C02W0003960.

Printed in China

*Independent research survey, from research carried out by Outlook Research Limited, 2005/06.

Key to Map Pages

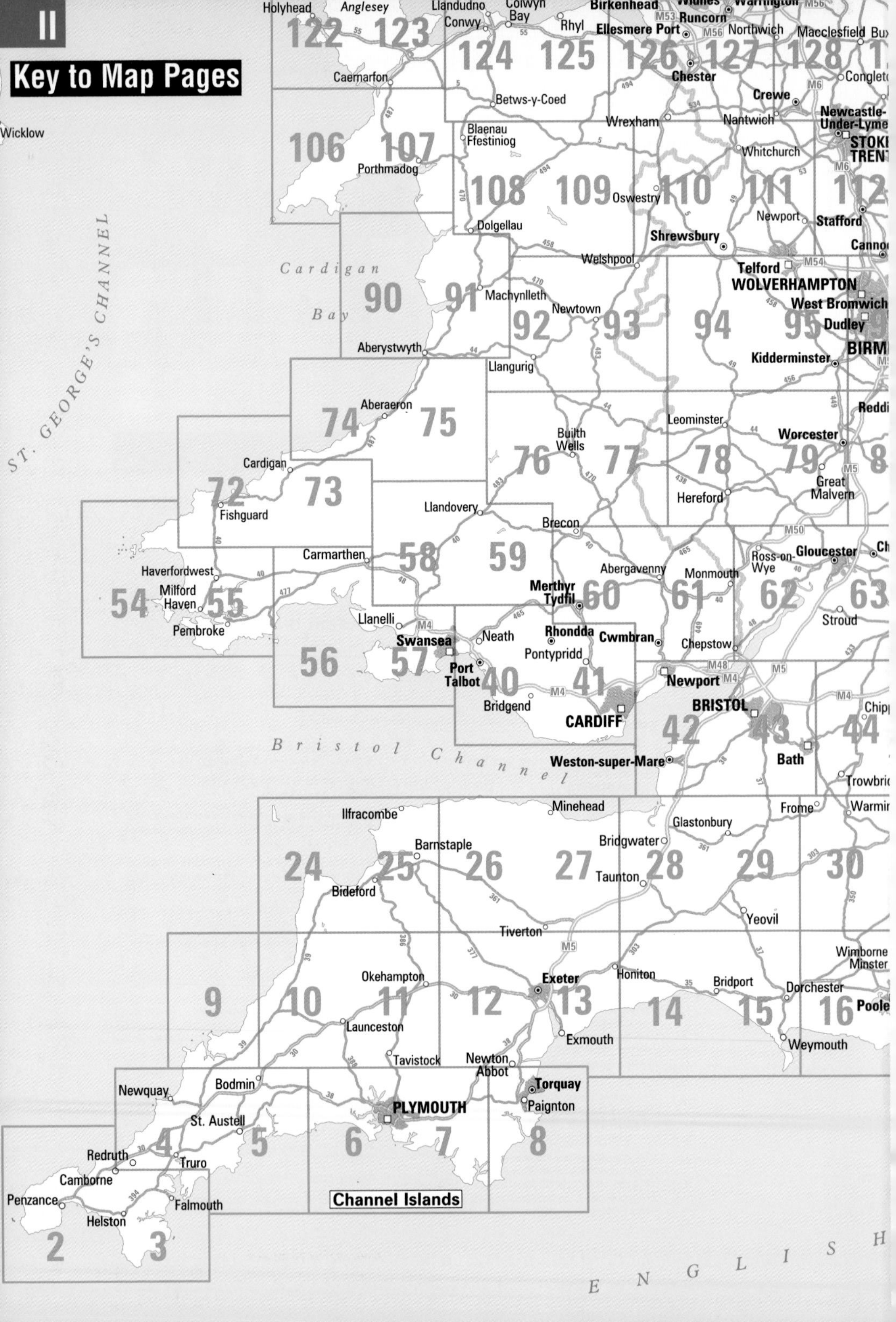

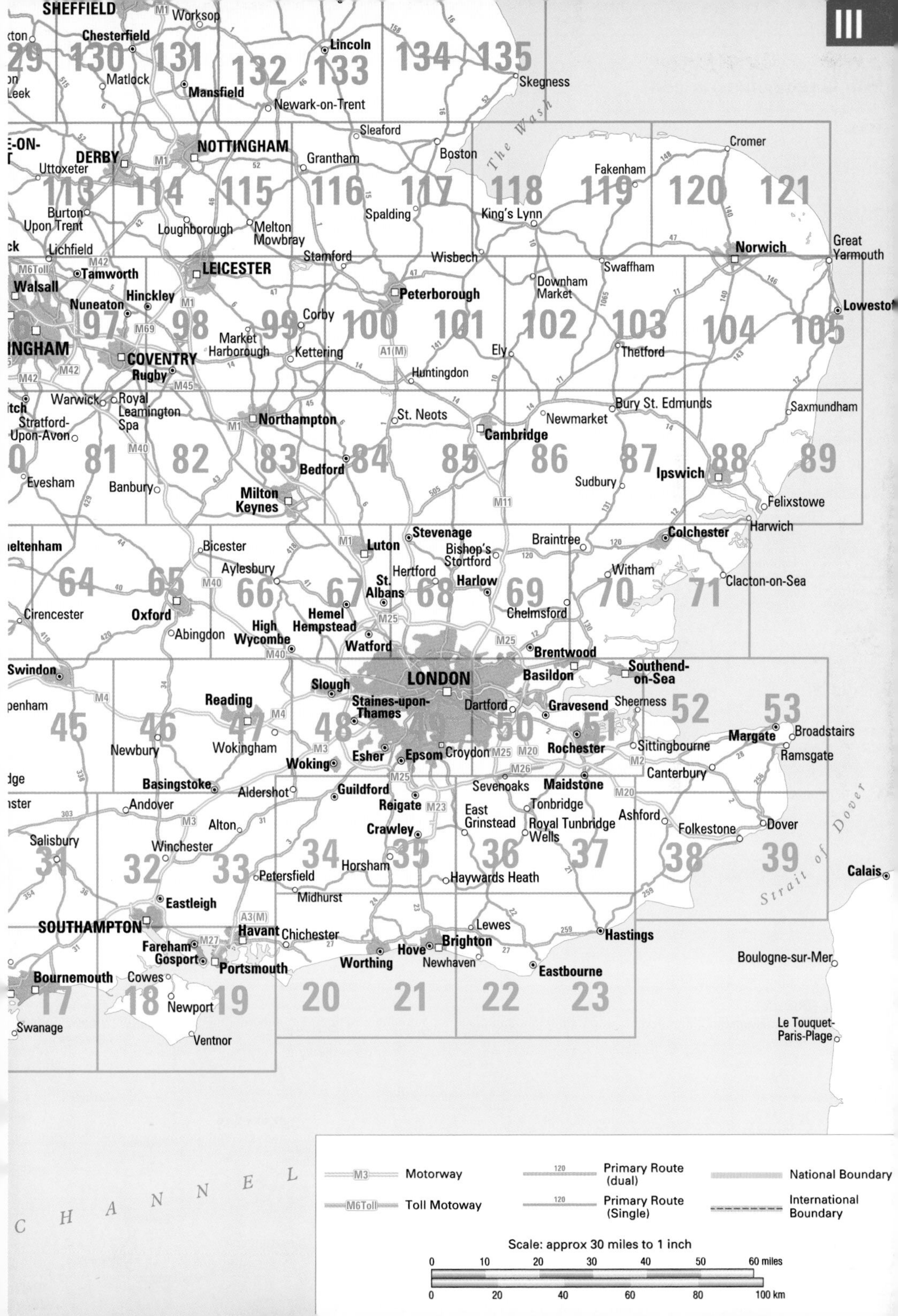
III
SHEFFIELD
Worksop
Chesterfield
Lincoln
129 130 131 132 133 134 135
Skegness
Matlock
Mansfield
Leek
Newark-on-Trent
The Wash
Sleaford
Boston
NOTTINGHAM
DERBY
Grantham
Cromer
Uttoxeter
Fakenham
113 114 115 116 117 118 119 120 121
Burton Upon Trent
Loughborough
Melton Mowbray
Spalding
King's Lynn
Lichfield
Stamford
Wisbech
Norwich
Great Yarmouth
LEICESTER
Tamworth
Swaffham
Walsall
Peterborough
Downham Market
Nuneaton
Hinckley
Lowestoft
97 98 99 100 101 102 103 104 105
Corby
Market Harborough
Kettering
Ely
Thetford
COVENTRY
Rugby
Huntingdon
Warwick
Royal Leamington Spa
Stratford-Upon-Avon
Northampton
St. Neots
Cambridge
Newmarket
Bury St. Edmunds
Saxmundham
81 82 83 84 85 86 87 88 89
Bedford
Ipswich
Evesham
Banbury
Milton Keynes
Sudbury
Felixstowe
Harwich
Colchester
Cheltenham
Stevenage
Luton
Braintree
Bicester
Bishop's Stortford
Aylesbury
Hertford
Harlow
Witham
Clacton-on-Sea
64 65 66 67 68 69 70 71
St. Albans
Cirencester
Oxford
Hemel Hempstead
Chelmsford
Abingdon
High Wycombe
Watford
Brentwood
Swindon
Slough
LONDON
Basildon
Southend-on-Sea
Reading
Staines-upon-Thames
Dartford
Gravesend
Sheerness
45 46 47 48 49 50 51 52 53
Margate
Broadstairs
Newbury
Wokingham
Esher
Epsom
Croydon
Rochester
Sittingbourne
Ramsgate
Woking
Canterbury
Basingstoke
Aldershot
Guildford
Sevenoaks
Maidstone
Andover
Reigate
East Grinstead
Tonbridge
Ashford
Alton
Royal Tunbridge Wells
Folkestone
Dover
Salisbury
Winchester
Crawley
Strait of Dover
31 32 33 34 35 36 37 38 39
Horsham
Petersfield
Haywards Heath
Calais
Midhurst
Eastleigh
SOUTHAMPTON
Havant
Chichester
Lewes
Hastings
Fareham
Gosport
Portsmouth
Hove
Brighton
Worthing
Newhaven
Eastbourne
Boulogne-sur-Mer
Bournemouth
Cowes
17 18 19 20 21 22 23
Newport
Swanage
Ventnor
Le Touquet-Paris-Plage
CHANNEL
M3 Motorway
M6Toll Toll Motoway
120 Primary Route (dual)
120 Primary Route (Single)
National Boundary
International Boundary
Scale: approx 30 miles to 1 inch
0 10 20 30 40 50 60 miles
0 20 40 60 80 100 km

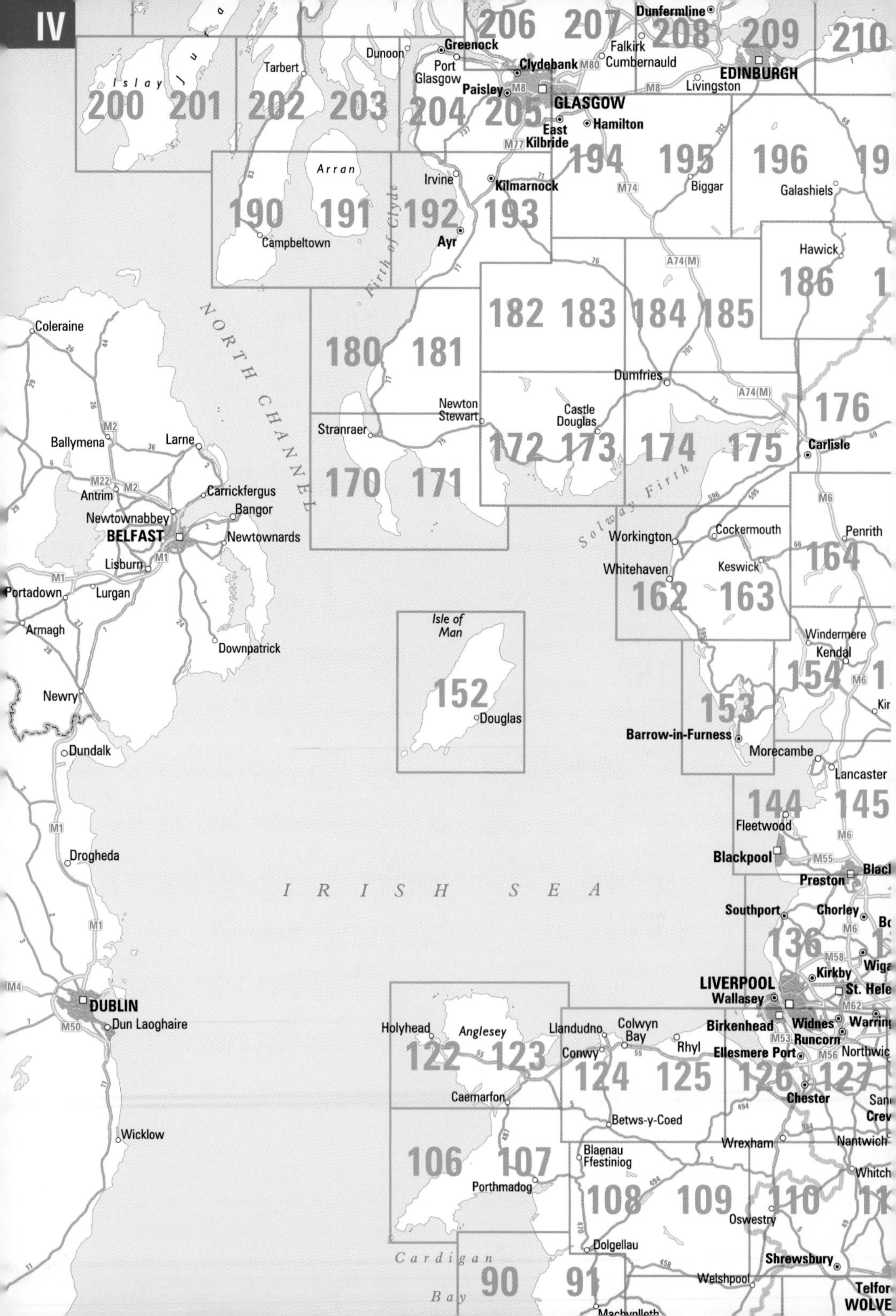
IV
Islay
Jura
200
201
Tarbert
202
203
Dunoon
Greenock
Port Glasgow
204
Paisley
205
Clydebank
GLASGOW
East Kilbride
Hamilton
206
207
Dunfermline
Falkirk
Cumbernauld
208
209
EDINBURGH
Livingston
210
Arran
190
Campbeltown
191
Firth of Clyde
192
Irvine
Ayr
193
Kilmarnock
194
195
Biggar
196
Galashiels
Hawick
186
NORTH CHANNEL
180
181
182
183
184
185
Dumfries
176
Newton Stewart
Stranraer
170
171
Castle Douglas
172
173
174
175
Carlisle
Solway Firth
Workington
Cockermouth
Whitehaven
Keswick
162
163
Penrith
164
Coleraine
Ballymena
Larne
Antrim
Carrickfergus
Newtownabbey
Bangor
BELFAST
Newtownards
Lisburn
Portadown
Lurgan
Armagh
Downpatrick
Newry
Dundalk
Drogheda
Isle of Man
152
Douglas
153
Barrow-in-Furness
Windermere
Kendal
154
Morecambe
Lancaster
144
145
Fleetwood
Blackpool
Preston
IRISH SEA
Southport
Chorley
136
Kirkby
LIVERPOOL
Wallasey
Birkenhead
Widnes
Runcorn
Ellesmere Port
Northwich
Chester
DUBLIN
Dun Laoghaire
Wicklow
Holyhead
Anglesey
122
123
Llandudno
Colwyn Bay
Conwy
Rhyl
124
125
126
127
Caernarfon
Betws-y-Coed
Wrexham
Nantwich
Blaenau Ffestiniog
106
107
Porthmadog
108
109
110
Oswestry
Dolgellau
Shrewsbury
Cardigan Bay
90
91
Welshpool
Telford
WOLVE

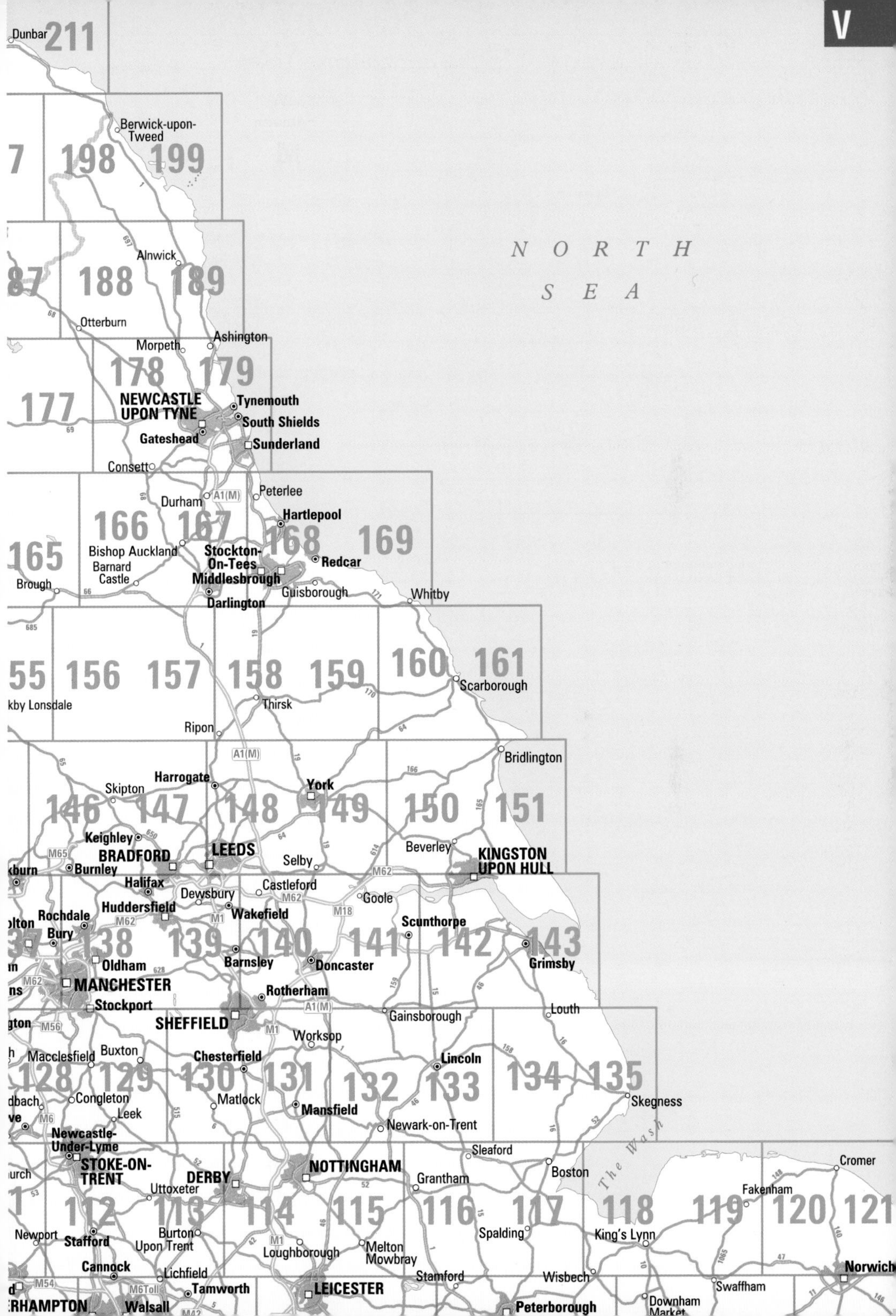
Dunbar
211
Berwick-upon-Tweed
198
199
NORTH SEA
Alnwick
188
189
Otterburn
Ashington
Morpeth
178
179
177
NEWCASTLE UPON TYNE
Tynemouth
South Shields
Gateshead
Sunderland
Consett
Peterlee
Durham
A1(M)
Hartlepool
166
167
168
169
165
Bishop Auckland
Stockton-On-Tees
Redcar
Barnard Castle
Middlesbrough
Brough
Guisborough
Whitby
Darlington
156
157
158
159
160
161
Scarborough
Thirsk
Ripon
A1(M)
Bridlington
Harrogate
Skipton
York
146
147
148
149
150
151
Keighley
BRADFORD
LEEDS
Beverley
KINGSTON UPON HULL
M65
Burnley
Selby
M62
Halifax
Castleford
Dewsbury
M62
Goole
Huddersfield
Rochdale
M62
M1
Wakefield
M18
Scunthorpe
Bury
138
139
140
141
142
143
Oldham
Barnsley
Doncaster
Grimsby
M62
MANCHESTER
Rotherham
Stockport
A1(M)
Gainsborough
Louth
M56
SHEFFIELD
M1
Worksop
Macclesfield
Buxton
Chesterfield
Lincoln
128
129
130
131
132
133
134
135
Congleton
Matlock
Mansfield
Skegness
Leek
M6
Newark-on-Trent
The Wash
Newcastle-Under-Lyme
STOKE-ON-TRENT
Sleaford
NOTTINGHAM
DERBY
Boston
Cromer
Grantham
Uttoxeter
Fakenham
112
113
114
115
116
117
118
119
120
121
Newport
Burton Upon Trent
Spalding
King's Lynn
Stafford
M1
Loughborough
Melton Mowbray
Cannock
Lichfield
Wisbech
Norwich
M54
M6Toll
Stamford
Swaffham
Walsall
Tamworth
LEICESTER
Downham Market
Peterborough

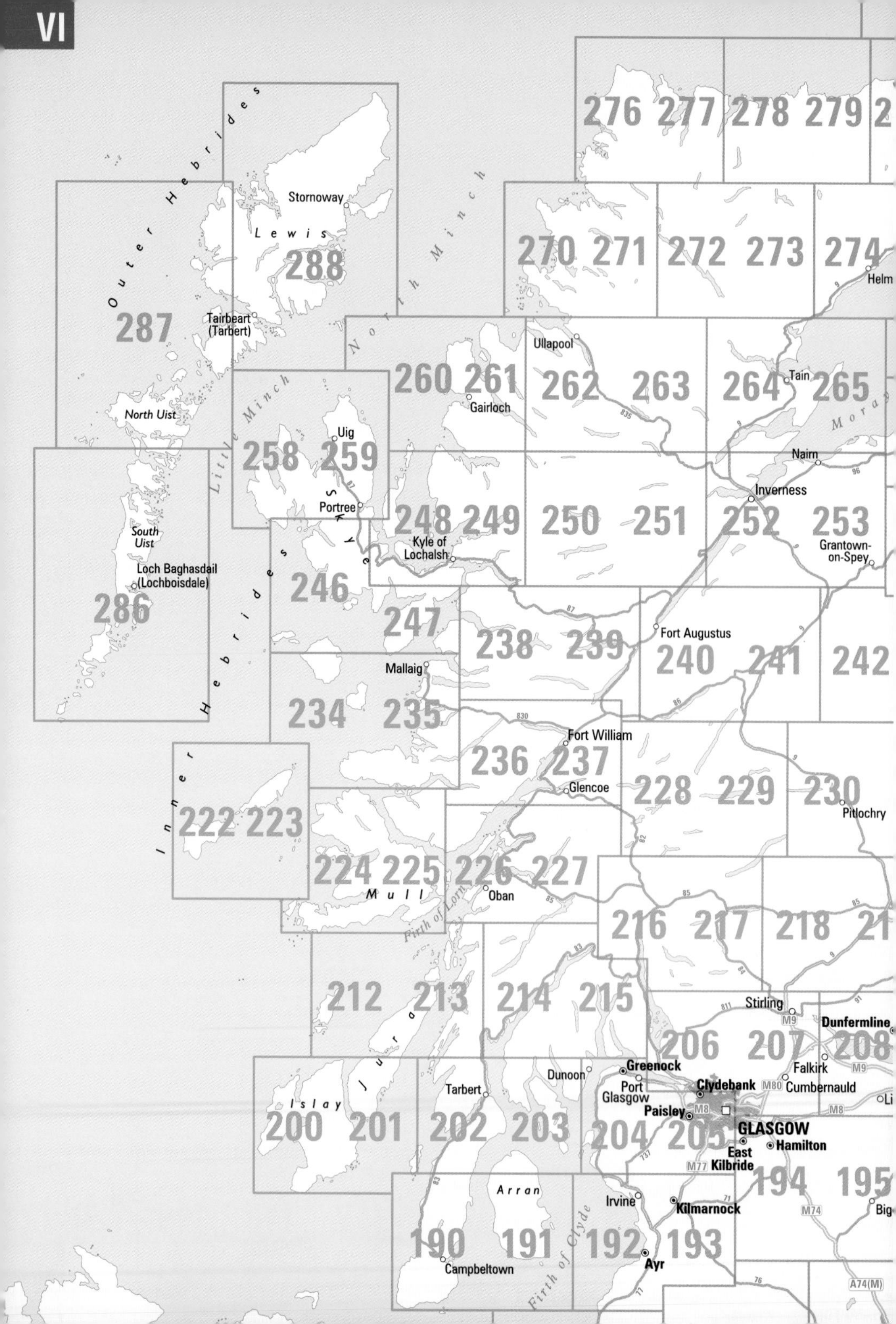
Outer Hebrides
North Minch
Little Minch
Inner Hebrides
Stornoway
Lewis
288
287
Tairbeart
(Tarbert)
North Uist
South Uist
Loch Baghasdail
(Lochboisdale)
286
276 277 278 279
270 271 272 273 274
Helm
Ullapool
260 261
Gairloch
262 263
264
Tain
265
Moray
258 259
Uig
Skye
Portree
248 249
Kyle of
Lochalsh
250 251
Nairn
Inverness
252 253
Grantown-
on-Spey
246
247
238 239
Fort Augustus
240 241 242
Mallaig
234 235
Fort William
236 237
Glencoe
228 229 230
Pitlochry
222 223
224 225 226 227
Mull
Oban
Firth of Lorn
216 217 218
212 213 214 215
Jura
Stirling
Dunfermline
206 207 208
Falkirk
Greenock
Port
Glasgow
Dunoon
Clydebank
Cumbernauld
Tarbert
Islay
Paisley
GLASGOW
Hamilton
200 201 202 203 204 205
East
Kilbride
194 195
Arran
Irvine
Kilmarnock
Big
190 191 192 193
Campbeltown
Firth of Clyde
Ayr

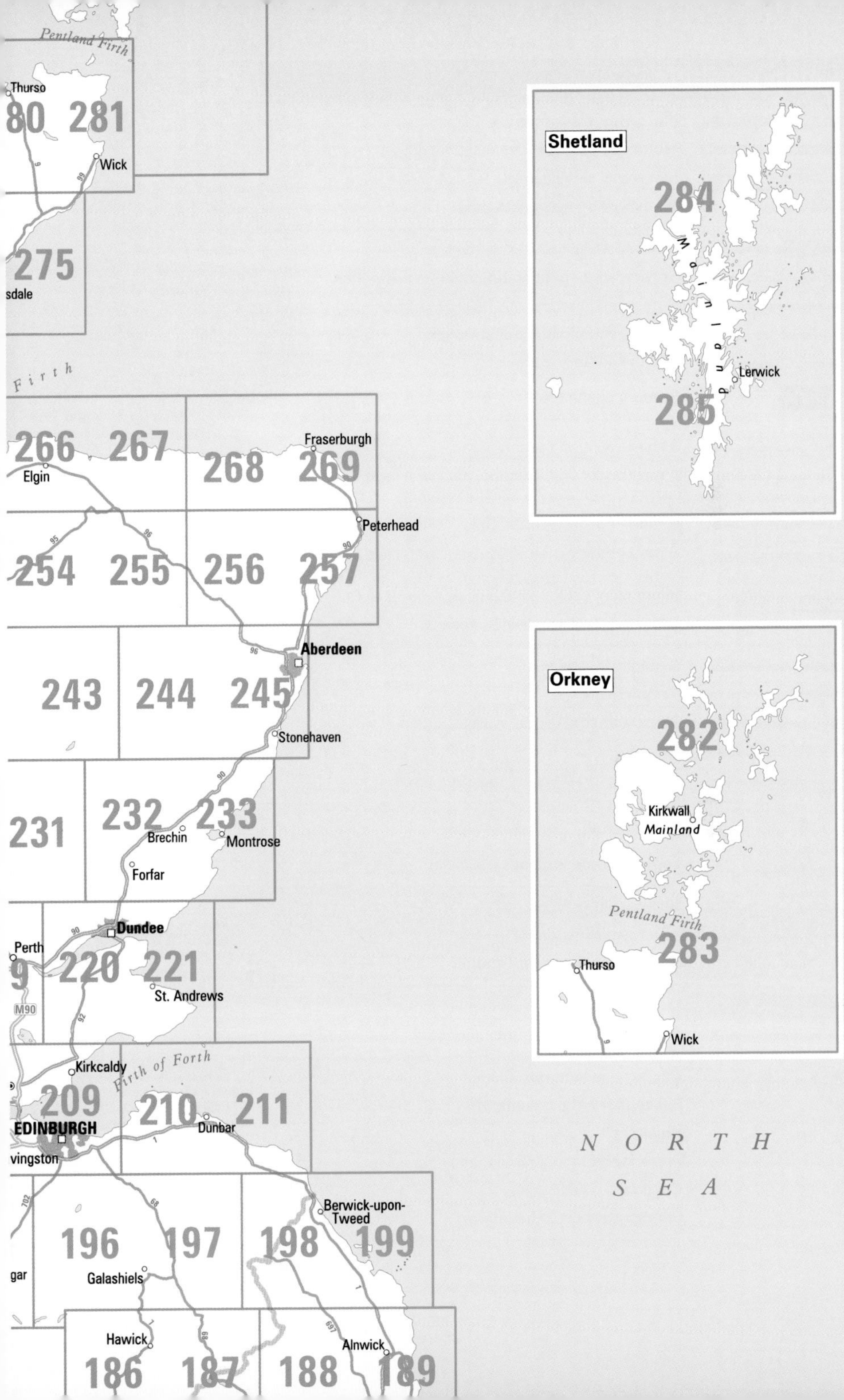

Pentland Firth
Thurso
80 281
Wick
275
sdale
Firth
266 267
Elgin
268 269
Fraserburgh
Peterhead
254 255
256 257
Aberdeen
243 244 245
Stonehaven
231 232 233
Brechin
Montrose
Forfar
Dundee
Perth
9 220 221
St. Andrews
M90
Kirkcaldy
Firth of Forth
209 210 211
EDINBURGH
Dunbar
vingston
196 197 198 199
Berwick-upon-Tweed
gar
Galashiels
Hawick
186 187 188 189
Alnwick

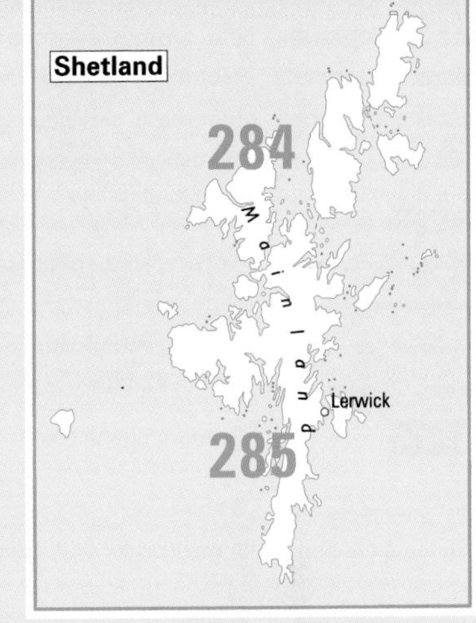

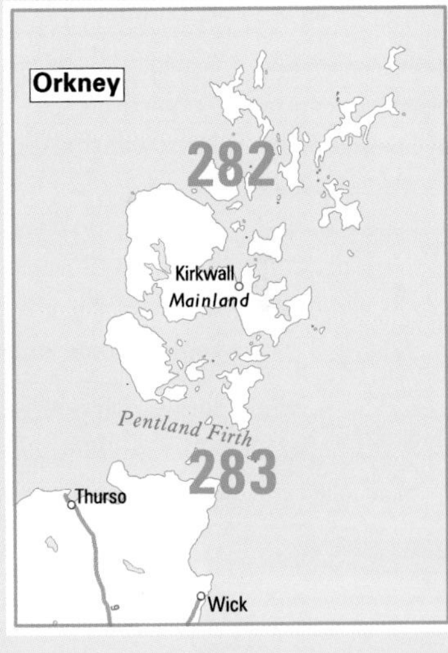

N O R T H
S E A

Road map symbols

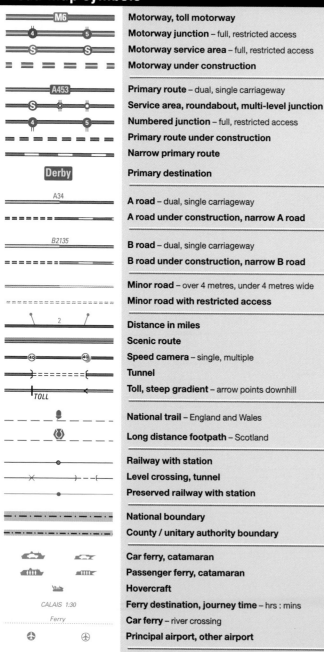

(M6) **Motorway, toll motorway**

Motorway junction – full, restricted access

Motorway service area – full, restricted access

Motorway under construction

(A453) **Primary route** – dual, single carriageway

Service area, roundabout, multi-level junction

Numbered junction – full, restricted access

Primary route under construction

Narrow primary route

(Derby) **Primary destination**

(A34) **A road** – dual, single carriageway

A road under construction, narrow A road

(B2135) **B road** – dual, single carriageway

B road under construction, narrow B road

Minor road – over 4 metres, under 4 metres wide

Minor road with restricted access

---

(2) **Distance in miles**

Scenic route

(40) **Speed camera** – single, multiple

Tunnel

(TOLL) **Toll, steep gradient** – arrow points downhill

National trail – England and Wales

Long distance footpath – Scotland

Railway with station

Level crossing, tunnel

Preserved railway with station

National boundary

County / unitary authority boundary

Car ferry, catamaran

Passenger ferry, catamaran

Hovercraft

(CALAIS 1:30) **Ferry destination, journey time** – hrs : mins

(Ferry) **Car ferry** – river crossing

Principal airport, other airport

Relief

Feet	metres
3000	914
2600	792
2200	671
1800	549
1400	427
1000	305
0	0

Speed Cameras

Fixed camera locations are shown using the (40) symbol.

In congested areas the (40) symbol is used to show that there are two or more cameras on the road indicated.

Due to the restrictions of scale the camera locations are only approximate and cannot indicate the operating direction of the camera. Mobile camera sites, and cameras located on roads not included on the mapping are not shown. Where two or more cameras are shown on the same road, drivers are warned that this may indicate that a SPEC system is in operation. These cameras use the time taken to drive between the two camera positions to calculate the speed of the vehicle.

Road map symbols

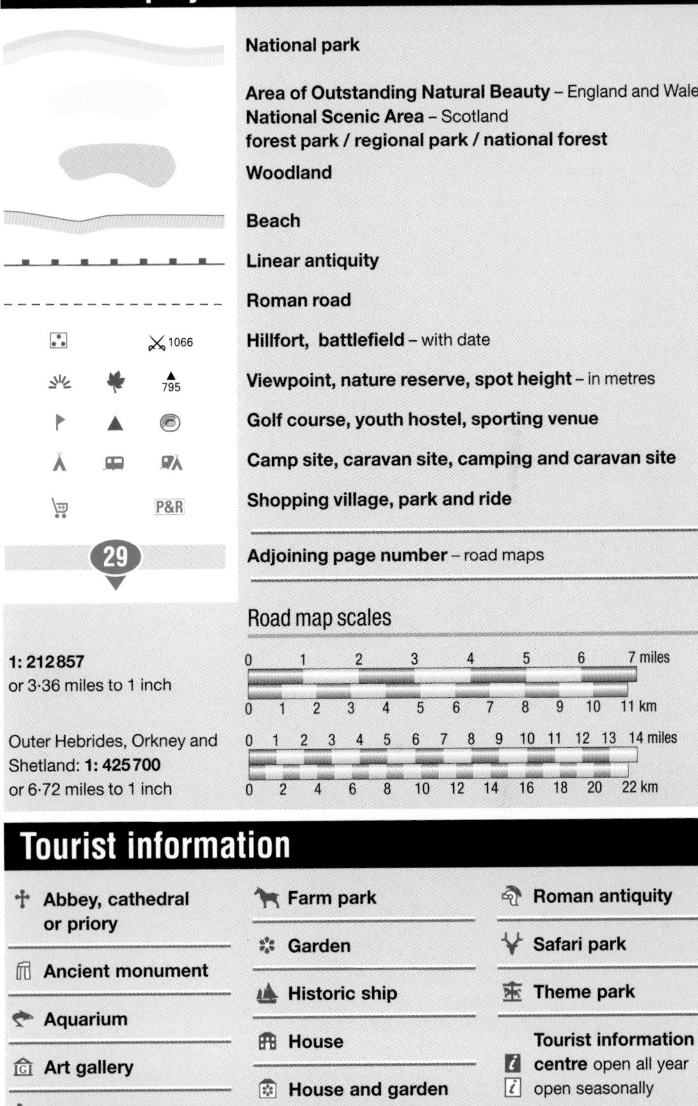

Tourist information

- Abbey, cathedral or priory
- Ancient monument
- Aquarium
- Art gallery
- Bird collection or aviary
- Castle
- Church
- Country park
  - England and Wales
  - Scotland
- Farm park
- Garden
- Historic ship
- House
- House and garden
- Motor racing circuit
- Museum
- Picnic area
- Preserved railway
- Race course
- Roman antiquity
- Safari park
- Theme park
- Tourist information centre open all year
  - open seasonally
- Zoo
- Other place of interest

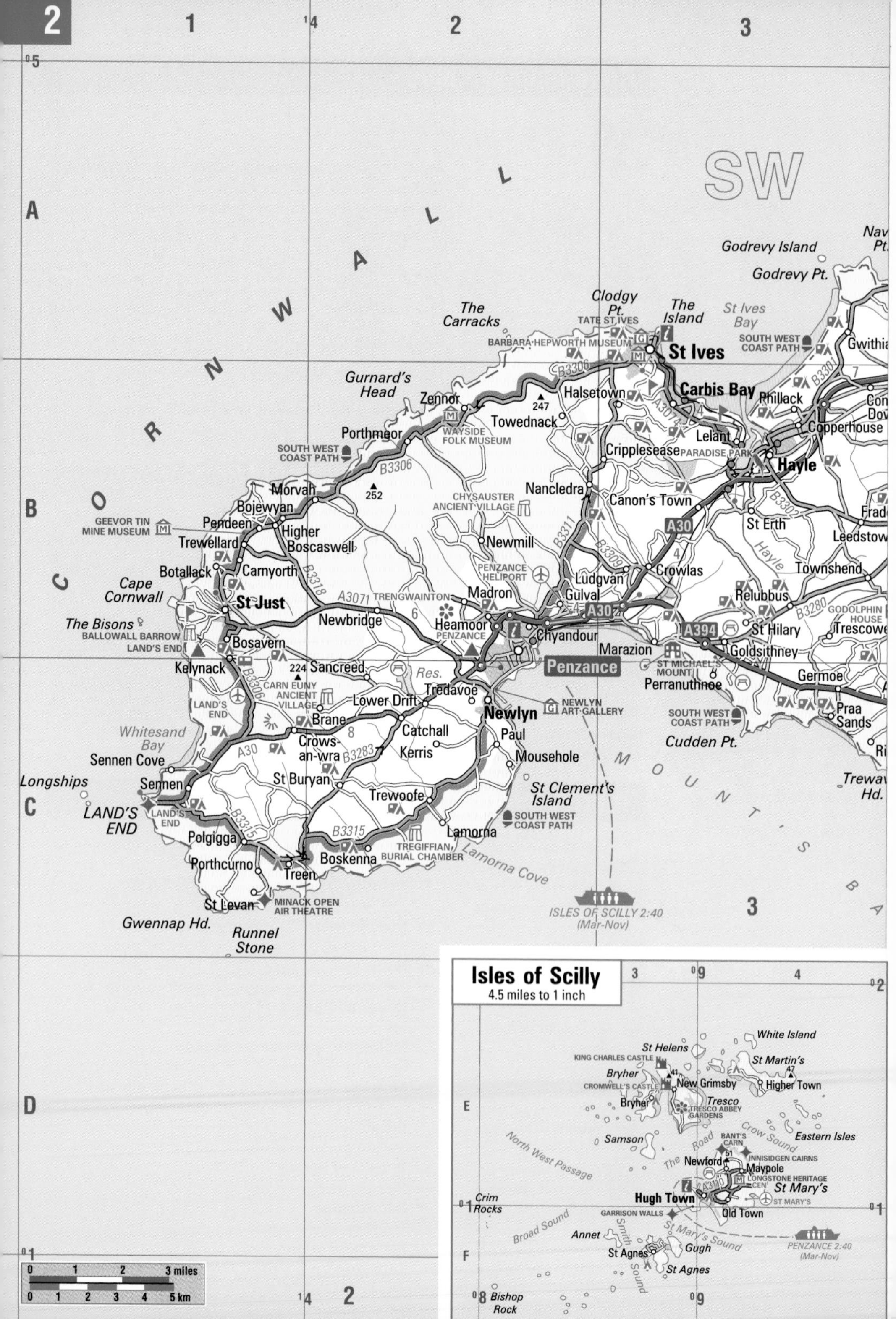
CORNWALL
SW
St Ives
Carbis Bay
Hayle
Penzance
Newlyn
St Just
LAND'S END
Zennor
Porthmeor
Morvah
Pendeen
Bojewyan
Higher Boscaswell
Trewellard
Botallack
Carnyorth
Cape Cornwall
The Bisons
Kelynack
Bosavern
Sennen Cove
Sennen
Longships
Polgigga
Porthcurno
Treen
St Levan
Gwennap Hd.
Runnel Stone
Boskenna
Lamorna
Lamorna Cove
Mousehole
Paul
St Clement's Island
Sancreed
Newbridge
Madron
Heamoor
Gulval
Chyandour
Ludgvan
Crowlas
Marazion
Perranuthnoe
Goldsithney
St Hilary
Relubbus
Townshend
Germoe
Praa Sands
Cudden Pt.
St Erth
Leedstown
Lelant
Copperhouse
Phillack
Gwithian
Godrevy Island
Godrevy Pt.
St Ives Bay
The Island
Clodgy Pt.
The Carracks
Gurnard's Head
Towednack
Halsetown
Cripplesease
Nancledra
Canon's Town
Newmill
Tredavoe
Lower Drift
Brane
Catchall
Kerris
Crows-an-wra
St Buryan
Trewoofe
Whitesand Bay
MOUNT'S BAY
TATE ST IVES
BARBARA HEPWORTH MUSEUM
SOUTH WEST COAST PATH
WAYSIDE FOLK MUSEUM
CHYSAUSTER ANCIENT VILLAGE
GEEVOR TIN MINE MUSEUM
PENZANCE HELIPORT
TRENGWAINTON
BALLOWALL BARROW
CARN EUNY ANCIENT VILLAGE
ST MICHAEL'S MOUNT
NEWLYN ART GALLERY
TREGIFFIAN BURIAL CHAMBER
MINACK OPEN AIR THEATRE
GODOLPHIN HOUSE
PARADISE PARK
ISLES OF SCILLY 2:40 (Mar-Nov)
Isles of Scilly
4.5 miles to 1 inch
St Helens
White Island
St Martin's
Higher Town
KING CHARLES CASTLE
CROMWELL'S CASTLE
Bryher
New Grimsby
Tresco
TRESCO ABBEY GARDENS
Eastern Isles
Samson
North West Passage
Crow Sound
The Road
BANT'S CARN
INNISIDGEN CAIRNS
Newford
Maypole
LONGSTONE HERITAGE CEN
St Mary's
Hugh Town
Old Town
GARRISON WALLS
Crim Rocks
Broad Sound
Annet
Smith Sound
St Mary's Sound
St Agnes
Gugh
Bishop Rock
PENZANCE 2:40 (Mar-Nov)
0 1 2 3 miles
0 1 2 3 4 5 km

St Agnes Hd.
St Agnes
Trevellas
Mithian
Goonbell
Callestick
CORNISH CYDER FARM
St Allen
Trispen
St Erme
Ladock
Marazanvose
Allet
A30
A39
Porthtowan
Mount Hawke
Three Burrows
Blackwater
Shortlanesend
Tresillian
Probus
Portreath
Mawla
P&R
A390
Truro
Kenwyn
Tresawle
CATHEDRAL
Merther
TOLGUS MILL
CORNISH GOLD
PORTREATH
TEHIDY
Illogan
Scorrier
Chacewater
Threemilestone
ROYAL CORNWALL MUS
CORNISH MINES & ENGINES
St Day
Baldhu
Kea
St Clement
Ruan Lanihorne
Roscroggan
Redruth
Twelve Heads
Bissoe
Malpas
Kehelland
Pool
Cambrea
Carharrack
Playing Place
Old Kea
St Michael Penkevil
Lamorran
Tuckingmill
GWENNAP PIT
Carnon Downs
Treworga
A30
Carnkie
Gwennap
Trelissick
Philleigh
CAMBORNE
Lanner
Penpol
Roseworthy
TREVITHICK COTTAGE
SHIRE HORSE FARM
Perranarworthal
Devoran
Feock
TRELISSICK
Ferry
Treworlas
Four Lanes
Barripper
Troon
Ponsanooth
Carnhell Green
Penhalvaen
Stithians
Burnthouse
Trewithian
Gerrans Bay
Stithians Res.
Mylor Bridge
St Just in Roseland
Praze-an-Beeble
Penmarth
Carrick Roads
Gerrans
Portscatho
Crowan
Burras
Penryn
A394
Flushing
Carnkie
Drym
Releath
Rame
Longdowns
Mabe Burnthouse
Falmouth
St Mawes
Greeb Pt.
Porkellis
ART GALLERY
NATIONAL MARITIME
Bohortha
POLDARK MINE
Godolphin Cross
Nancegollan
Budock Water
PENDENNIS CASTLE
Wendron
Seworgan
Treverva
Pendennis Pt.
Zone Pt.
Crowntown
Penjerrick
Falmouth Bay
Constantine
HELSTON RAILWAY
Sithney
Mawnan Smith
SOUTH WEST COAST PATH
Breage
Trewennack
Porth Navas
GLENDURGAN
Rosemullion Hd.
Helston
Helford Passage
TREBAH
Mawnan
Helford River
Gweek
NATIONAL SEAL SANCTUARY
FLAMBARDS EXPERIENCE
Helford
St Anthony-in-Meneage
Porthleven
The Loe
Mawgan
Manaccan
Nare Pt.
Porthleven Sands
Garras
St Martin
TRELOWARREN
HALLIGGYE FOGOU
Porthallow
Berepper
Newtown
Tregidden
Gunwalloe
Porthoustock
Cury
Cross Lanes
St Keverne
Manacle Pt.
The Manacles
Traboe
Lowland Pt.
Goonhilly Downs
Mullion
Penhale
Trelan
Coverack
THE LIZARD
COVERACK
Mullion Cove
Chynhalls Pt.
Mullion Island
Gwenter
Kuggar
Black Hd.
Predannack Wollas
St Ruan
Ruan Minor
Vellan Hd.
Cadgwith
Grade
SOUTH WEST COAST PATH
Lizard
Kynance Cove
Hot Pt.
LIZARD
LIZARD POINT
C O R N W A L L

4
1
2
3
4
A
B
C
D
SW
Park Hd.
Penrose
St Ervan
Rumford
St Issey
Tredinnick
St Jidgey
CREALY GREAT ADVENTURE PARK
St Eval
Trenance
Berryl's Pt.
Trevarrian
St Mawgan
CORNISH BIRDS OF PREY CENTRE
Talskiddy
WATERGATE BAY
Tregurrian
NEWQUAY
St Columb Major
Towan Hd.
Newquay Bay
Porth
St Columb Minor
Fistral Bay
Pentire
NEWQUAY ZOO
Trebudannon
Colan
CASTLE AN DINAS
SPRINGFIELDS FUN & PONY CENTRE
Ruthvoes
Kelsey Hd.
BLUE REEF AQUARIUM
West Pentire
Crantock
Newquay
Quintrell Downs
Mountjoy
Trevarren
Lane
Indian Queens
Penhale Pt.
HOLYWELL BAY FUN PARK
Kestle Mill
St Columb Road
Fraddon
Holywell
Carines
DAIRY LAND FARM WORLD
Penhale
St Dennis
TRERICE
St Enoder
Ligger or Perran Bay
Cubert
Penhale Sands
St Newlyn East
Gummow's Shop
Retew
Mount
Rejerrah
LAPPA VALLEY STEAM RAILWAY
Summercourt
Treviscoe
SOUTH WEST COAST PATH
Rose
PERRAN ROUND
Brighton
Trethosa
Perranporth
PERRANPORTH
Newlyn Downs
Mitchell
Goonhavern
Bolingey
Carland Cross
Trelassick
St Stephen
Perranzabuloe
Zelah
St Agnes Hd.
Trevellas
New Mills
Coombe
St Agnes
Mithian
St Allen
Callestick
Trispen
St Erme
Ladock
Grampound Road
CORNISH CYDER FARM
Marazanvose
Goonbell
Allet
Porthtowan
Mount Hawke
Shortlanesend
Probus
Grampound
TREWITHEN
Three Burrows
Tresillian
Creed
Blackwater
P&R
Truro
Kenwyn
Mawla
Tresawle
CATHEDRAL
Merther
Tregony
Portreath
TOLGUS MILL
CORNISH GOLD
Scorrier
Chacewater
Threemilestone
ROYAL CORNWALL MUS
Illogan
St Clement
CORNISH MINES & ENGINES
St Day
Baldhu
Kea
Ruan Lanihorne
Twelve Heads
Malpas
Redruth
Bissoe
Playing Place
Old Kea
St Michael Penkevil
Lamorran
Pool
Tuckingmill
Cambrea
Carharrack
GWENNAP PIT
Carnon Downs
Carnkie
Gwennap
Treworga
CAMBORNE
Lanner
Trelissick
Philleigh
Perranarworthal
Penpol
Portloe
SHIRE HORSE FARM
Troon
Four Lanes
Devoran
Feock
TRELISSICK
Ferry
Veryan
Treworlas
Ponsanooth
Carne
Penhalvaen
Gerrans Bay
Stithians
Burnthouse
Trewithian
Nare Hd.
St Just in Roseland
Mylor Bridge
Stithians Res.
Carrick Roads
Penmarth
Burras
Gerrans
Portscatho
Carnkie
Penryn
Flushing
Rame
Longdowns
Mabe Burnthouse
Falmouth
Greeb Pt.
Releath
Porkellis
St Mawes
ART GALLERY
NATIONAL MARITIME
Bohortha
POLDARK MINE
Budock Water
PENDENNIS CASTLE
Wendron
Seworgan
Treverva
Pendennis Pt.
Zone Pt.
Penjerrick
Falmouth Bay
Constantine
Mawnan Smith
SOUTH WEST COAST PATH
Porth Navas
GLENDURGAN
Rosemullion Hd.
A30
A39
A390
A392
A394
A3075
A3058
A3076
A3047
A393
A3078
B3276
B3274
B3279
B3275
B3285
B3284
B3277
B3298
B3301
B3280
B3297
B3289
B3292
0 1 2 3 miles
0 1 2 3 4 5 km

5
Bodmin
Bodmin Forest
Lostwithiel
St Austell
Fowey
Looe
Mevagissey
Par
St Blazey
Lanlivery
Luxulyan
Bugle
Roche
Lanivet
St Lawrence
Nanstallon
Ruthernbridge
Withiel
Washaway
Burlawn
Helland
Cardinham
Millpool
Maidenwell
Warleggan
St Neot
Mount
Ley
Commonmoor
St Cleer
Dobwalls
Doublebois
East Taphouse
West Taphouse
St Pinnock
Braddock
Herodsfoot
St Keyne
Trewidland
Duloe
Sandplace
Muchlarnick
Pelynt
West Looe
Porthallow
Polperro
Talland Bay
Lansallos
Trenewan
Lanteglos Highway
Penpoll
St Veep
Lanreath
Bocaddon
Couch's Mill
Lerryn
Milltown
Golant
Tywardreath
Penpillick
Trebyan
Sweethouse
Redmoor
Lockengate
Bilberry
Stenalees
Penwithick
Trethurgy
Carclaze
Boscoppa
Holmbush
Charlestown
Polkerris
Menabilly
Bodinnick
Polruan
Porthpean
Polgooth
Sticker
Hewas Water
Trewoon
St Mewan
Carthew
Nanpean
Foxhole
High Street
Hensbarrow Downs
Trezaise
Tregoss
Belowda
Victoria
Tregonetha
St Wenn
Rosenannon
ST AUSTELL BAY
Gribbin Hd.
Black Hd.
Pencarrow Hd.
Trenarren
Pentewan
Mevagissey Bay
St Ewe
Kestle
Portmellon
Chapel Pt.
Gorran Churchtown
Gorran Haven
Trevarrick
St Michael Caerhays
Boswinger
Penare
Dodman Pt.
Veryan Bay
SX
BODMIN TOWN MUSEUM
BODMIN AND WENFORD RAILWAY
LANHYDROCK HOUSE
RESTORMEL CASTLE
EDEN PROJECT
WHEAL MARTYN CHINA CLAY HERITAGE CENTRE
SHIPWRECK & HERITAGE CENTRE
ST AUSTELL BREWERY
ST CATHERINE'S CASTLE
SOUTH WEST COAST PATH
THE LOST GARDENS OF HELIGAN
WORLD OF MODEL RAILWAYS
CARNGLAZE SLATE CAVERNS
KING DONIERT'S CIRCLE
GOLITHA FALLS
HERITAGE MUSEUM
ST.BREOCK DOWNS MONOLITH
PENCARROW HOUSE
A30
A38
A390
A391
A389
A3082
B3268
B3269
B3274
B3273
B3359
B3254
Cornwall
4
5
6
7
A
B
C
D

THE HURLERS STONE CIRCLES
Minions
369
CARADON HILL
Siblyback Lake
10
Pensilva
Trevigro
Golberdon
Haye
Kelly Bray
333
KIT HILL
TOLL
Gunnislake
St Ann's Chapel
11
Albaston
Higher Walreddon
Horrabridge
Commonmoor
Darite
Callington
Harrowbarrow
DUPATH WELL HOUSE
GOLITHA FALLS
TRETHEVY QUOIT
KING DONIERT'S CIRCLE
Tremar
St Cleer
Gang
A390
St Ive
Newbridge
COTEHELE
St Dominick
Calstock
Buckland Monachorum
TAMAR VALLEY
CARNGLAZE SLATE CAVERNS
B3254
Merrymeet
162
Bere Alston
BUCKLAND ABBEY
Dobwalls
Pengover Green
St Mellion
Weir Quay
Lopwell
Doublebois
Liskeard
Quethiock
A388
St Pinnock
A38
Pillaton
Bere Ferrers
Menheniot
Blunts
Cargreen
Hatt
Landulph
MAGNIFICENT MUSIC MACHINES
Botusfleming
Tamerton Foliot
Herodsfoot
St Keyne
70
Tideford Cross
Landrake
SALTASH SERVICES
5
B3251
50
A38
Trewidland
B3252
Tideford
40
Trematon
B3271
TOLL
B3373
CROWNHILL FORT
B3413
Saltash
Plymouth
Duloe
Trerule Foot
B3249
St Erney
B3254
Widegates
A387
Hessenford
St Stephens
MARY NEWMAN'S COTTAGE
St Budeaux
A374
St Germans
Sandplace
B3253
Polbathic
ANTONY HOUSE
P&R
MERCHANT'S HOUSE
Morval
B3247
St. Germans R.
Muchlarnick
Sheviock
A374
Ferry
Pelynt
St Martin
Seaton
Torpoint
Devonport
Crafthole
Antony
MONKEY SANCTUARY
Looe
East Looe
Downderry
Portwrinkle
ROYAL CITADEL
OLD GUILDHALL
St John
Cremyll
West Looe
Looe Bay
SOUTH WEST COAST PATH
B3247
MOUNT EDGCUMBE
Portballow
Freathy
Millbrook
Drake's I.
Whitsand Bay
MOUNT EDGCUMBE
St George's or Looe I.
Talland Bay
Kingsand
The Sound
Polperro
HERITAGE MUSEUM
Cawsand
Bovisand Bay
Rame
Penlee Pt.
Heybrook Bay
Rame Hd.
Great Mew Stone
C
ROSCOFF 6:00 (Feb-Nov)
SANTANDER 20:00 (Mar-Nov)
ST MALO 9:15 (Nov-Mar)
0 1 2 3 miles
0 1 2 3 4 5 km
1
2
3
Guernsey
5 miles to 1 inch
POOLE 3:00 (Apr-Oct)
WEYMOUTH 2:10
PORTSMOUTH 7:00
L'Ancresse Bay
Le Plomb
Grand Havre
La Fontenelle
GUERNSEY
SARK 0:45
St Sampson
SHELL BEACH
Cobo Bay
L'Islet
Herm
Vazon Bay
Le Villocq
Belle Greve Bay
Lihou I.
BEAU SEJOUR CENTRE
MUSEUM & ART GALLERY
St Peter Port
0:20
Mont Saint
Jethou
Rocquaine Bay
VICTOR HUGO'S HOUSE
CASTLE CORNET
THE LITTLE CHAPEL
Carmel
Fort George
Pleinmont Pt.
GUERNSEY
ST. HELIER 2:00
Mouilpied
La Planque
Le Planel
Moulin Huet Bay
St Martin's Pt.
ST. HELIER 1:00
ST. MALO 3:00
Pointe de la Moye
Icart Pt.
DIELETTE 1:15
CARTERET 1:30 (Apr-Oct)
ALDERNEY 1:00
Jersey
5 miles to 1 inch
Plémont Pt.
Grosnez Pt.
Sorel Pt.
Ronez Pt.
St John's Bay
Belle Hougue Pt.
CARTERET 1:00
NORTH COAST VISITOR CENTRE
St John's
136
Bouley Bay
Tour de Rozel
St Mary's
Trinity
Rozel
JERSEY
St Ouens
La Coupe Pt.
DURRELL WILDLIFE CONSERVATION TRUST (ZOO)
KEMPT TOWER VISITOR CENTRE
Carrefour Selous
St Martin's
St Ouen's Bay
St Peter's
St Catherine's Bay
LA HOUGUE BIE
MONT ORGUEIL CASTLE
Five Oaks
Gorey
Red Houses
St Aubin
JERSEY MUSEUM
Grouville
Corbière Pt.
St Brelade
St Helier
Royal Bay of Grouville
SARK 1:00 (Apr-Oct)
St Aubin's Bay
St Clements
St Brelades Bay
ELIZABETH CASTLE
FORT REGENT LEISURE CENTRE
Noirmont Pt.
La Rocque Pt.
ST. PETER PORT 1:00
WEYMOUTH 3:25
POOLE 4:30 (Apr-Oct)
Le Nez Pt.
St Clements Bay
GRANVILLE 1:10
ST. PETER PORT 1:00 (Apr-Oct)
CARTERET 2:00
ST. PETER PORT 2:00
PORTSMOUTH 8:00
ST. MALO 1:20

DARTMOOR NATIONAL PARK
Whiteworks
Poundsgate
RIVER DART ADVENTURES
Ashburton
Walkhampton
Holne
515
RYDER'S HILL
Burrator Res.
PAPERWEIGHT CENTRE
Dousland
Sheepstor
Yelverton
Meavy
BUCKFAST ABBEY
Buckfast
Woodland
Forder Grn.
Buckfastleigh
Landscove
BUCKFAST BUTTERFLIES & DARTMOOR OTTER SANCTUARY
UPPER PLYM VALLEY
Clearbrook
Plym
Dean
A384
493
475
SHELL TOP
Shaugh Prior
Ugborough Moor
Dean Prior
PENNYWELL FARM & WILDLIFE CENTRE
Dartington
DARTINGTON CIDER PRESS CENTRE
Shinner
464
Didworthy
Bickleigh
DENDLES WOOD
Wotter
Lee Moor
Roborough
311
Rattery
A385
Cott
CASTLE
P&R
Plym
Forest
South Brent
Tigley
Drakeland Corner
Lutton
Cornwood
Harford
371
UGBOROUGH BEACON
Cheston
Belsford
DARTMOOR ZOOLOGICAL PARK
229
Avonwick
Lincombe
Harberton
A381
Eggbuckland
Sparkwell
Bittaford
PLYM VALLEY RAILWAY
B3213
Diptford
Harbertonford
Plympton
Lee Mill
Ivybridge
North Huish
Ugborough
Erme
Crabadon
SALTRAM
A38
Curtisknowle
B3196
A3121
Westlake
Halwell
A379
Elburton
Brixton
118
Yelmpton
Yealm
Ermington
Brownston
Moreleigh
A3122
WOODLANDS LEISURE PARK
Hooe
Modbury
Avon
Woodford
Staddiscombe
Holbeton
Millcombe
Down Thomas
Luson
B3392
Knighton
B3186
Loddiswell
Woodleigh
East Allington
Wembury
Newton Ferrers
Battisborough Cross
St Ann's Chapel
Aveton Gifford
Wembury Bay
Mothecombe
Kingston
Noss Mayo
Worswell
SOUTH WEST COAST PATH
Ringmore
Bigbury
SORLEY TUNNEL ADVENTURE WORLDS
Goveton
Stoke Pt.
Churchstow
SX
Bigbury on Sea
West Alvington
Sherford
Burgh I.
Kingsbridge
Bantham
Buckland
BIGBURY BAY
South Milton
Frogmore
Chillington
Thurlestone
Charleton
Woolston
Kernborough
Galmpton
South Pool
Malborough
Hope
Bolt Tail
Kellaton
Bolberry
Salcombe
East Portlemouth
Soar
SALCOMBE
South Allington
OVERBECKS MUSEUM AND GARDEN
East Prawle
Bolt Hd.
Prawle Pt.
SOUTH DEVON
Alderney
5 miles to 1 inch
DIELETTE 0:45
ST. PETER PORT 1:00
(Apr-Oct)
Quesnard Pt.
Brehou
Braye
Longis Bay
Clonque Bay
St Anne
ALDERNEY
Telegraph Bay

NEWTON ABBOT
Combeinteignhead
SHALDON WILDLIFE TRUST
SOUTH WEST COAST PATH
West Ogwell
Netherton
Stokeinteignhead
Wolborough
East Ogwell
BABBACOMBE BAY
Woodland
Denbury
Abbotskerswell
Coffinswell
Maidencombe
Kingskerswell
Forder Grn.
Barton
Torbryan
Ipplepen
North Whilborough
Watcombe
Landscove
Broadhempston
MODEL VILLAGE
Babbacombe
Shiphay
Compton
Torquay
Staverton
Torre
KENT'S CAVERN PREHISTORIC CAVES
Cockington
Wellswood
Hope's Nose
Dartington
Littlehempston
Marldon
Hollicombe
Shinner's Bridge
Torbay
Blagdon
Cott
Totnes
Berry Pomeroy
Paignton
Tigley
Collaton St Mary
TORBAY
Belsford
TOR BAY
Harberton
Goodrington
Ashprington
Stoke Gabriel
Brixham
Berry Head
Harbertonford
Galmpton
Churston Ferrers
Tuckenhay
Cornworthy
St Mary's Bay
Crabadon
Washbourne
Dittisham
Sharkham Pt.
Halwell
Allaleigh
Capton
Hillhead
SX SY
Moreleigh
Dartmouth
Woodford
Blackawton
Kingswear
Scabbacombe Hd.
Millcombe
Warfleet
COLETON FISHACRE
Bowden
Mew Stone
East Allington
Stoke Fleming
Blackpool
Strete
Goveton
SOUTH WEST COAST PATH
Harleston
Slapton
Sherford
Kingsbridge
Frittiscombe
Slapton Sands
Stokenham
Frogmore
Chillington
START BAY
Torcross
Kernborough
Beeson
South Pool
Beesands
Kellaton
East Portlemouth
Hallsands
South Allington
START POINT
East Prawle
Lannacombe Bay
Prawle Pt.
SOUTH DEVON
0 1 2 3 miles
0 1 2 3 4 5 km

SR
SS
SW
SX
CORNWALL
Fire Beacon Pt.
BOSCASTLE
Trevalga
CASTLE
Tintagel Hd.
OLD POST OFFICE
TINTAGEL
Bossiney
Tintagel
Treknow
Trewarmett
B3263
Start Pt.
Trebarwith
Treligga
SOUTH WEST COAST PATH
Delabole
Valley Truckle
Port Isaac Bay
B3314
Helstone
Port Isaac
Port Gaverne
B3267
St Teath
Pentire Pt.
Port Quin Bay
Port Quin
New Polzeath
LONG CROSS
Trelights
Pendoggett
Treveighan
Gulland Rock
Padstow Bay
Polzeath
St Endellion
Trelill
A39
Michaelstow
Trebetherick
Gunver Hd.
St Minver
TREVOSE HEAD
Crugmeer
Pityme
Trewethern
St Kew
St Tudy
PRIDEAUX PLACE
Trevone
Chapel Amble
B3314
Rock
St Kew Highway
Constantine Bay
Constantine Bay
NATIONAL LOBSTER HATCHERY
Padstow
Camel
TREYARNON
Treyarnon
St Merryn
Shop
Bodieve
Trevanson
B3266
St Mabyn
SOUTH WEST COAST PATH
Little Petherick
Whitecross
Wadebridge
Porthcothan
B3276
St Breock
Egloshayle
A389
PENCARROW HOUSE
Camel
Helland
Park Hd.
Penrose
St Ervan
Rumford
St Issey
A389
Tredinnick
A39
Burlawn
St Jidgey
Washaway
Bodmin Forest
CREALY GREAT ADVENTURE PARK
ST BREOCK DOWNS MONOLITH
St Eval
A30
Trenance
A
B
C
D
4
5
6
10
308

BUDE
BAY
Kilkhampton
Coombe
Stibb
Alfardisworthy
Soldon Cross
Poughill
Flexbury
Hersham
Grimscott
Dunsdon
Holsworthy Beacon
Bude Haven
Bude
Stratton
1643
Launcells
Pancrasweek
Chilsworthy
Upton
Marhamchurch
Derril
Bridgerule
Derriton
Pyworthy
Chasty
162
Widemouth Bay
Widemouth Sand
Budd's Titson
Leworthy
Millook
Coppathorne
Dizzard Pt.
Poundstock
South West Coast Path
Tregole
Treskinnick Cross
Whitstone
St Gennys
Trewint
Week St Mary
North Tamerton
Cambeak
Crackington Haven
Rosecare
Penhallam
Jacobstow
Tetcott
Lana
Wainhouse Corner
Luffincott
Tresparrett Posts
West Curry
South Wheatley
Fire Beacon Pt.
260
Beeny
Maxworthy
Marshgate
Bennacott
Northcott
Boscastle
Tresparrett
Canworthy Water
Boyton
Brazacott
Otterham
256
Lesnewth
Warbstow
Trevalga
Trelash
Tamar Otter & Wildlife Centre
Langdon
Bossiney
Tintagel
Tremaine
North Petherwin
Bridgetown
Hallworthy
Treneglos
Davidstow
308
Yeolmbridge
Trewarmett
Tresmeer
Tremail
Egloskerry
Langore
Trewassa
The Arthurian Centre
Cornwall at War
Tregeare
Trebarwith
Cold Northcott
St Stephen's
Hidden Valley Discovery Park
Piper's Pool
Launceston
Davidstow Moor
Delabole
St Clether
Laneast
Trethorne Leisure Farm
Tregadillett
Castle
Camelford
Valley Truckle
Crowdy Res.
Trewen
Daw's House
Helstone
Polyphant
South Petherwin
St Teath
High Moor
400 Rough Tor
Altarnun
Lewannick
Treveighan
420 Brown Willy
Trewint
369
Lezant
Michaelstow
Codda
Congdon's Shop
331 Garrow Tor
St Breward
Trebullett
Trebartha
Treburley
St Tudy
Row
Museum of Smuggling
Bolventor
Coad's Green
North Hill
Bradford
BODMIN MOOR
Bray Shop
Wenfordbridge
396 Kilmar Tor
Bathpool
Dozmary Pool
Blisland
Henwood
Linkinhorne
St Mabyn
Temple
Rilla Mill
South Hill
342
Colliford Lake
Upton Cross
Camel
Helland
The Hurlers Stone Circles
Minions
369 Caradon Hill
Golberdon
268
Siblyback Lake
Millpool
Maidenwell
Pensilva
Trevigro
Commonmoor
Darite
Warleggan
Golitha Falls
Trethevy Quoit
King Doniert's Stone
Tremar
Gang
St Neot
A39
A30
A395
A3072
A388
B3254
B3263
B3262
B3266
B3267
B3314
B3257
Tamar
Inny
Ottery
Strat
Deer
Claw
0 1 2 3 miles
0 1 2 3 4 5 km

11
Venn Green
Milton Damerel
Buckland Filleigh
Merton
Huish
Dolton
Hollocombe
Dowland
Petrockstow
Torridge
Shebbear
Thornbury
Meeth
Iddesleigh
Winkleigh
Woodacott
Bradford
A386
A388
A3124
Sheepwash
Broadwood Kelly
Cookbury
Black Torrington
Holemoor
Monkokehampton
Bondleigh
Highampton
Hatherleigh
A3072
B3217
olsworthy
Brandis Corner
Whimble
Hollacombe
Graddon Moor
Honeychurch
Exbourne
Chilla
WINSFORD WALLED GARDEN
Lew
Jacobstowe
A3079
Halwill Junction
Sampford Courtenay
Halwill
Beaworthy
Northlew
Inwardleigh
Clawton
Oak Cross
Patchacott
Ashbury
DARTMOOR RAILWAY
Quoditch
Folly Gate
Taw Green
BROADBURY
B3215
Okehampton
Ashwater
A30
Eworthy
Henford
Sticklepath
FINCH FOUNDRY
Carey
Germansweek
Boasley Cross
Thorndon Cross
Belstone
Virginstow
Roadford Res.
OKEHAMPTON (Dartmoor)
East Panson
CASTLE
Okehampton Camp
SOURTON CROSS SERVICES
Meldon
Grinacombe Moor
BRACKEN TOR
Bratton Clovelly
Okehampton Common
550 COSDON HILL
Taw
Gridley Corner
619 YES TOR
Sourton
Broadwoodwidger
Bridestowe
BLACK-A-TOR COPSE
621 HIGH WILLHAYS
Thrushel
Bridestowe and Sourton Common
Cross Green
Thrushelton
585
566 OKEMENT HILL
DINGLE'S FAIRGROUND HERITAGE CENTRE
Stowford
Lewdown
262
Shortacombe
Liftondown
Portgate
Lewtrenchard
Lydford
604 HANGINGSTONE HILL
Lifton
Tinhay
LYDFORD
DARTMOOR
Coryton
LYDFORD GORGE
SX
Lawhitton
North Brentor
Black Down
Willsworthy
604 CUT HILL
537 SITTAFORD TOR
Kelly
Chillaton
DARTMOOR
Tamar
Bradstone
Horndon
Milton Abbot
Dunterton
Mary Tavy
546 ROUGH TOR
B3362
Cudliptown
Rezare
NATIONAL
FOREST
Peter Tavy
Lamerton
539 GT. MIS TOR
WISTMAN'S WOOD
Sydenham Damerel
Wilminstone
Tavy
Merrivale
PREHISTORIC SETTLEMENT
Two Bridges
Stoke Climsland
Horsebridge
B3357
Rundlestone
Tavistock
HIGH MOORLAND VISITOR CENTRE
Luckett
Latchley
Downgate
Princetown
W. Dart
A390
Chilsworthy
Whitchurch
Sampford Spiney
Hexworthy
Gulworthy
B3257
TOLL
Gunnislake
Grenofen
333 KIT HILL
Kelly Bray
St Ann's Chapel
B3212
PARK
Higher Walreddon
KIT HILL
Drakewalls
Whiteworks
Callington
Albaston
Harrowbarrow
Horrabridge
Walkhampton
DUPATH WELL HOUSE
COTEHELE
Buckland Monachorum
THE GARDEN HOUSE
PAPERWEIGHT CENTRE
Dousland
Burrator Res.
St Dominick

Hollocombe
Wembworthy
B3042
192
Eastington
Black Dog
Puddington
Winkleigh
Brushford
Coldridge
Nymet Rowland
Lapford
Morchard Bishop
Woolfardisworthy
Poughill
Upham
A3124
B3220
174
Kennerleigh
Stockleigh English
Broadwood Kelly
A377
Oldborough
Cheriton Fitzpaine
West Leigh
Taw
Ash Bullayne
East Village
Bondleigh
East Leigh
Down St Mary
Zeal Monachorum
Newbuildings
Stockleigh Pomeroy
B3217
Honeychurch
204
Copplestone
Sandford
Upton Hellions
Exbourne
13
SS
Knowle
5
North Tawton
Bow
THE COLLEGIATE CHURCH OF THE HOLY CROSS
Shobrooke
Sampford Courtenay
A3072
Yeo
Coleford
Nymet Tracey
Crediton
11
Colebrooke
Itton
B3215
Hillerton
Yeoford
Uton
Hookway
DARTMOOR RAILWAY
D
e
Venny Tedburn
Newton St Cyres
Taw Green
Spreyton
SX
6
Hittisleigh
B
Sticklepath
South Tawton
Tedburn St Mary
FINCH FOUNDRY
South Zeal
14
Whitestone
Belstone
Whiddon Down
70
A30
Cheriton Bishop
Crockernwell
550
COSDON HILL
A382
Drewsteignton
Longdown
B3212
Throwleigh
CASTLE DROGO
Wonson
Sandypark
Teign
Gidleigh
Easton
Murchington
Dunsford
B3193
B3206
7
566
Chagford
Bridfordmills
Teigncombe
356
Doccombe
315
604
HANGINGSTONE HILL
Frenchbeer
B3212
Moretonhampstead
Bridford
Doddiscombsleigh
Christow
Higher Ashton
C
DARTMOOR
Lettaford
THE MINIATURE PONY CENTRE
North Bovey
Lower Ashton
9
A382
537
SITTAFORD TOR
CANONTEIGN FALLS
Trusham
A38
DARTMOOR
12
B3212
GRIMSPOUND
Manaton
Lustleigh
11
POSTBRIDGE INFORMATION CENTRE
529
HAMELDOWN TOR
Water
Bovey
Hennock
546
ROUGH TOR
Postbridge
EAST DARTMOOR WOODS & HEATHS
Bovey Tracey
Chudleigh
NATIONAL
HOUND TOR
Chudleigh Knighton
FOREST
Bellever
Widecombe in the Moor
Bonehill
Haytor Vale
Brimley
UGBROOKE HOUSE
WISTMAN'S WOOD
BELLEVER (Dartmoor)
E. Dart
CRAFT CENTRE
Ideford
B3387
HAYTOR INFORMATION CENTRE
Ilsington
Heathfield
B3193
B3357
473
RIPPON TOR
Liverton
STOVER
Preston
D
431
Coldeast
TRAGO MILLS
Ponsworthy
Sigford
4
3
A382
Teigngrace
Princetown
W. Dart
Dartmeet
Buckland in the Moor
Kingsteignton
Hexworthy
Bickington
5
Highweek
NEWTON ABBOT
Poundsgate
A383
PARK
Dart
RIVER DART ADVENTURES
A38
NEWTON ABBOT
Whiteworks
BRADLEY
West Ogwell
7
8
Ashburton
East Ogwell
Wolborough
Holne
PRICKLY BALL HEDGEHOG HOSPITAL
DECOY
0 1 2 3 miles
0 1 2 3 4 5 km
HILL
4
Woodland
Denbury
Abbotskerswell
BUCKFAST ABBEY

Tiverton
Cullompton
Honiton
Ottery St Mary
Sidford
Sidmouth
Budleigh Salterton
Exmouth
Topsham
Dawlish
Teignmouth
BLACKDOWN HILLS
EAST DEVON
Exeter International
Exeter Services
Cullompton Services
Killerton House
Bickleigh Castle
Bickleigh Mill
Devon Railway Centre
Fursdon House
Diggerland
Escot Park
Crealy Adventure Park
Bicton Park
Otterton Mill
A La Ronde
Powderham Castle
Dawlish Warren
Exmouth Model Railway
World of Country Life
Fairlynch Arts Centre and Museum
South West Coast Path
Dorset & East Devon Coast World Heritage Site
Shaldon Wildlife Trust
Ladram Bay
Danger Pt.
Straight Pt.
Babbacombe Bay
SY
SX

Bolham Water
Smeatharpe
BLACKDOWN
HILLS
Newcott
Marsh
Whitestaunton
Combe St Nicholas
Cricket Malherbie
Chillington
St George
Cudworth
Chaffcombe
Wadeford
Crewkerne
Cricket St Thomas
Hewish
Howley
Yarcombe
Wambrook
Chard
Upottery
Rawridge
Luppitt
Beacon
Whatley
Wayford
Winsham
Forton
Tatworth
Clapton
South Chard
Drimpton
FORDE ABBEY AND GARDENS
Stockland
Furley
Millhayes
Chardstock
Wick
Monkton
Membury
Tytherleigh
Thorncombe
Burstock
Alston
Holditch
Heathstock
Churchill
Cotleigh
Ham
Dalwood
Smallridge
Birdsmoorgate
Hawkchurch
THE CRAFT AND DESIGN CENTRE
Bettiscombe
Marshalsea
Wilmington
Honiton
Offwell
BURROW FARM
Weycroft
Marshwood
Pilsdon
Axminster
Shute
Kilmington
SHUTE BARTON
Church Green
Northleigh
Wootton Fitzpaine
Whitchurch Canonicorum
Broad Oak
Farway
Whitford
Ryall
EAST DEVON
Musbury
Morcombelake
Colyton
Southleigh
Broad Down
Charmouth
Symondsbury
Uplyme
Colyford
Combpyne
Lyme Regis
CHARMOUTH HERITAGE COAST CENTRE
Chideock
BLACKBURY CAMP
Rousdon
AQUARIUM
DINOSAURLAND
Eype
Seatown
Harcombe
Axmouth
SEATON TRAMWAY
SOUTH WEST COAST PATH
BEER QUARRY CAVES
BEER
AXMOUTH TO LYME REGIS UNDERCLIFFS
Weston
Vicarage
Seaton
Charlton Bay
Beer
MARINE HOUSE
Seaton Bay
SOUTH WEST COAST PATH
LYME BAY
Salcombe Regis
Branscombe
DORSET & EAST DEVON COAST WORLD HERITAGE SITE
Beer Hd.
A303
A30
A35
A358
A375
A3052
B3162
B3167
B3165
B3164
B3261
B3172
B3174
28
13
30
C
D
0 1 2 3 miles
0 1 2 3 4 5 km

4
5
6
7
Hardington Mandeville
Haselbury Plucknett
Ryme Intrinseca
Beer Hackett
Holwell
Crouch Hill
A37
29
Closworth
Pendomer
North Perrott
Hardington Marsh
182
Holnest
Leigh
B3146
Glanvilles Wootton
B3143
Pulham
Lydden
Halstock
Melbury Osmond
Chetnole
Hermitage
A352
Middlemarsh
South Perrott
West Chelborough
Melbury Sampford
Melbury Bubb
Westfields
Duntish
Mosterton
Chedington
Corscombe
Hilfield
Lyon's Gate
Mappowder
A
238
Evershot
Buckland Newton
A3066
Holywell
Batcombe
Minterne Magna
MINTERNE HOUSE & GARDENS
265
Higher A
Alton Pancras
Melcom Bingh
261
Up Cerne
Frome St Quintin
Rampisham
18
B3163
A356
17
CERNE ABBAS GIANT
Plush
Beaminster
Dorset
Up Sydling
Cerne Abbas
16
Stoke Abbott
Wraxall
Cattistock
Sydling St Nicholas
Piddletrenthide
12
Mapperton
MAPPERTON
Hooke
Chilfrome
Toller Porcorum
Maiden Newton
Nether Cerne
White Lackington
Melplash
North Poorton
HOG CLIFF
Godmanstone
Piddlehinton
Salwayash
West Milton
Toller Fratrum
B3162
A3066
Powerstock
A37
A356
Forston
Dottery
Nettlecombe
Wynford Eagle
Charlton Down
B3142
135
DORSET
Frampton
Puddletown
B
Bradpole
Eggardon Down
252
Grimstone
A352
Brit
Loders
West Compton
Muckleford
Stratton
B3143
Uploders
Bridport
Askerswell
Compton Valence
Charminster
4
HARDY'S COTTAGE GARDEN
Bradford Peverell
Walditch
Kingston Russell
A35
Dorchester
Bothenhampton
170
14
Winterbourne Abbas
Stinsford
THE TUTANKHAMUN EXHIBITION
Kingston Maurward
Shipton Gorge
Chilcombe
Long Bredy
Litton Cheney
NINE STONES
A35
THE DINOSAUR MUSEUM
MILITARY MUSEUM
West Stafford
Burton Bradstock
POOR LOT BARROWS
LITTON CHENEY
Winterbourne Steepleton
Martinstown
MAIDEN CASTLE
P&R
Littlebredy
B3159
Whitcombe
132
Black Down
Winterborne Monkton
Winterborne Herringston
Swyre
Puncknowle
VALLEY OF STONES
HARDY MONUMENT
West Knighton
KINGSTON RUSSELL STONE CIRCLE
West Bexington
B3157
A354
Broadmayne
Portesham
SOUTH WEST COAST PATH
A352
DORSET & EAST DEVON COAST WORLD HERITAGE SITE
Abbotsbury
ABBOTSBURY CHILDREN'S FARM
8
SUB TROPICAL GARDENS
Upwey
WHITE HORSE
Poxwell
C
Rodden
96
Bincombe
13
ST CATHERINES CHAPEL
SWANNERY
Broadwey
Littlemoor
Preston
A353
Upton
SOUTH WEST COAST PATH
Nottington
Overcombe
Osmington
TOLL
Langton Herring
JORDAN HILL ROMAN TEMPLE
B3157
Radipole
Osmington Mills
CHESIL BEACH
BENNETTS WATER GARDENS
SEA LIFE
Ringstead Bay
Chickerell
Melcombe Regis
16
Westham
Weymouth
Charlestown
WEYMOUTH BAY
B3156
NOTHE FORT
BREWER'S QUAY AND TIMEWALK
Rodwell
Wyke Regis
Portland Harbour
GUERNSEY 2:10
JERSEY 3:25
ST. MALO 7:30
SY
A354
WEYMOUTH & PORTLAND NATIONAL SAILING ACADEMY
D
6
PORTLAND
PORTLAND CASTLE
Fortuneswell
West Bay
130
Grove
Easton
Weston
PORTLAND
MUSEUM
Southwell
Bill of Portland

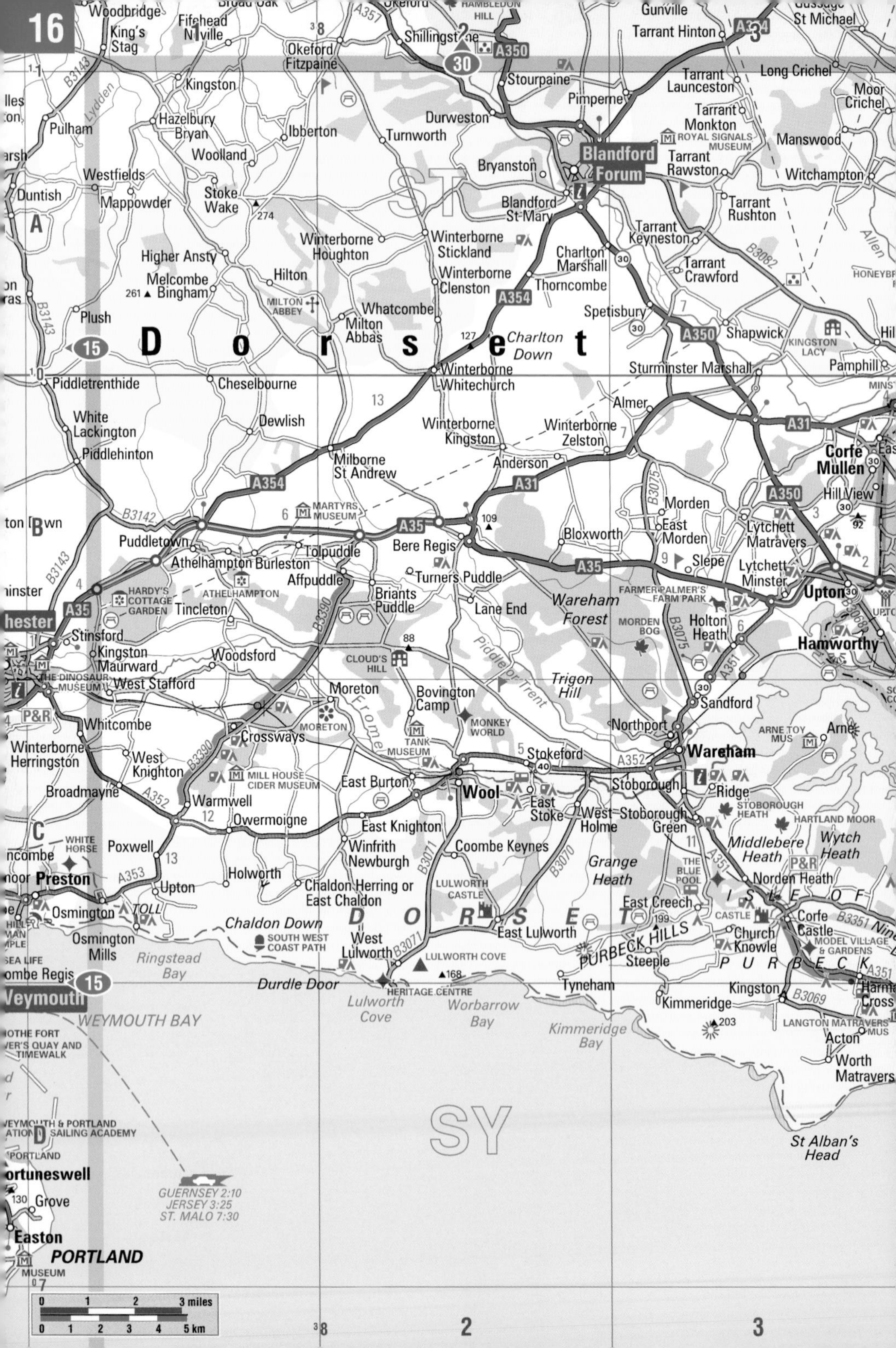
Woodbridge
King's Stag
Fifehead Neville
Okeford Fitzpaine
Shillingstone
HAMBLEDON HILL
A350
30
Gunville
Tarrant Hinton
A354
Gussage St Michael
Kingston
Stourpaine
Pimperne
Tarrant Launceston
Long Crichel
Moor Crichel
B3143
Lydden
Pulham
Hazelbury Bryan
Ibberton
Turnworth
Durweston
Tarrant Monkton
ROYAL SIGNALS MUSEUM
Manswood
Woolland
Blandford Forum
Tarrant Rawston
Witchampton
Westfields
Mappowder
Stoke Wake
274
Bryanston
Blandford St Mary
Tarrant Rushton
Duntish
A
Higher Ansty
Winterborne Houghton
Winterborne Stickland
Charlton Marshall
Tarrant Keyneston
B3082
Allen
Melcombe Bingham
261
Hilton
Winterborne Clenston
Thorncombe
Tarrant Crawford
HONEYBR
MILTON ABBEY
Whatcombe
Milton Abbas
Spetisbury
Plush
Shapwick
KINGSTON LACY
15
Dorset
127
Charlton Down
Sturminster Marshall
Pamphill
Piddletrenthide
Cheselbourne
Winterborne Whitechurch
13
Almer
White Lackington
Dewlish
Winterborne Kingston
Winterborne Zelston
A31
Corfe Mullen
Piddlehinton
Milborne St Andrew
Anderson
A354
B3075
Morden
East Morden
Hill View
MARTYRS MUSEUM
109
Lytchett Matravers
B3142
A35
Bere Regis
Bloxworth
92
Puddletown
Athelhampton
Burleston
Tolpuddle
Slepe
Lytchett Minster
Affpuddle
Turners Puddle
B3143
HARDY'S COTTAGE GARDEN
ATHELHAMPTON
Briants Puddle
FARMER PALMER'S FARM PARK
Wareham Forest
Upton
Tincleton
Lane End
Holton Heath
MORDEN BOG
Hamworthy
Stinsford
B3390
88
Kingston Maurward
Woodsford
CLOUD'S HILL
Piddle or Trent
Trigon Hill
THE DINOSAUR MUSEUM
West Stafford
Moreton
Bovington Camp
Sandford
A351
P&R
Whitcombe
Frome
MONKEY WORLD
Northport
MORETON
TANK MUSEUM
ARNE TOY MUS
Arne
Crossways
Winterborne Herringston
West Knighton
Stokeford
Wareham
B3390
MILL HOUSE CIDER MUSEUM
A352
Broadmayne
East Burton
Wool
Stoborough
Ridge
A352
Warmwell
East Stoke
West Holme
Stoborough Green
STOBOROUGH HEATH
12
Owermoigne
East Knighton
HARTLAND MOOR
C
WHITE HORSE
Poxwell
B3070
B3071
Winfrith Newburgh
Coombe Keynes
Middlebere Heath
Wytch Heath
Preston
A353
Holworth
Grange Heath
THE BLUE POOL
Norden Heath
Upton
Chaldon Herring or East Chaldon
LULWORTH CASTLE
Osmington
TOLL
East Creech
199
CASTLE
Corfe Castle
B3351
ISLE OF PURBECK
Chaldon Down
DORSET
Osmington Mills
SOUTH WEST COAST PATH
West Lulworth
East Lulworth
PURBECK HILLS
Church Knowle
MODEL VILLAGE & GARDENS
SEA LIFE
Ringstead Bay
B3071
LULWORTH COVE
Steeple
Weymouth
168
Tyneham
Kingston
A351
Durdle Door
HERITAGE CENTRE
B3069
Harmans Cross
Lulworth Cove
Worbarrow Bay
Kimmeridge
WEYMOUTH BAY
203
LANGTON MATRAVERS MUS
Kimmeridge Bay
Acton
NOTHE FORT
QUAY AND TIMEWALK
Worth Matravers
SY
WEYMOUTH & PORTLAND SAILING ACADEMY
D
PORTLAND
St Alban's Head
Fortuneswell
GUERNSEY 2:10
JERSEY 3:25
ST. MALO 7:30
130
Grove
Easton
PORTLAND
MUSEUM
0 1 2 3 miles
0 1 2 3 4 5 km
2
3

Verwood
Ringwood
Ferndown
Wimborne Minster
Bournemouth
Poole
CHRISTCHURCH
Boscombe
Highcliffe
New Milton
Barton on Sea
Milford on Sea
Brockenhurst
Christchurch Bay
Hengistbury Head
POOLE BAY
Poole Harbour
Brownsea I.
Sandbanks
Studland
Swanage
Peveril Pt.
Durlston Head
Tilly Whim Caves
The Foreland
The Needles
Alum Bay
NEW FOREST NATIONAL PARK
SZ
GUERNSEY 3:00
JERSEY 4:30
(Apr-Oct)
ST. MALO 7:30
CHERBOURG 2:30
(May-Sept)

Minstead
Newtown
Marsh
Woodlands
Ashurst
Eling
SOUTHAMPTON
LONGDOWN FARM
Pooksgreen
NEW FOREST WILDLIFE PARK
Marchwood
MARITIME MUS
Northam
TOLL
Itchen
Sholing
Thornhill
Woolston
Old Netley
NETLEY ABBEY
Netley
Bursledon
Lowford
Hound
Hamble
MANOR FARM
Burridge
Curbridge
WHITELEY VILLAGE
Swanwick
Lower Swanwick
HOLLY HILL WOODLAND PARK
Park Gate
Locks Heath
ABBEY
Warsash
Titchfield
Newtown
ROYAL VICTORIA
Hamble-le-Rice
ST ANDREWS
SOUTHAMPTON WATER
Emery Down
Lyndhurst
NEW FOREST CENTRE
REPTILIARY
Clayhill
Bank
NEW FOREST NATIONAL PARK
Denny Lodge
Dibden
Hythe
Dibden Purlieu
Buttsash
Hardley
Holbury
Fawley
Ashlett
Beaulieu Heath
Lymington
New Park
Balmerlawn
Hill Top
PALACE HO
NATIONAL MOTOR MUS
ABBEY
Beaulieu
Blackfield
CALSHOT CASTLE
CALSHOT ACTIVITY CENTRE
Calshot
Langley
TITCHFIELD HAVEN
Stubbington
Hill Head
Lee-on-the-So
Brockenhurst
Setley
Hatchet Gate
East Boldre
Beaulieu Heath
Bucklers Hard
MARITIME MUSEUM
EXBURY
Exbury
LEPE
Lepe
Stone Pt.
0:25
0:55
Battramsley
Bull Hill
Wootton
Sway
Boldre
Pilley
SPINNERS
Norleywood
Portmore
East End
Needs Ore Pt.
THE SOLENT
Golden Hill
Mount Pleasant
Hordle
Buckland
Walhampton
LYMINGTON
Pennington
Waterford
Woodside
Ashley
Milton
Everton
Downton
Lymore
BRAXTON
Lower Pennington
0:35
KEYHAVEN & PENNINGTON MARSHES
Keyhaven
Milford on Sea
HURST CASTLE
Sconce Pt.
FORT VICTORIA
ISLAND PLANETARIUM
Norton
Yarmouth
Colwell Bay
Totland
Totland Bay
TOTLAND BAY
Pound Green
Norton Green
Freshwater
Freshwater Bay
Alum Bay
The Needles
THE NEEDLES PARK
THE NEEDLES OLD BATTERY
Freshwater Bay
Afton
Cowes
MARITIME MUSEUM
East Cowes
OSBORNE HOUSE
Osborn
Gurnard Bay
Gurnard
Rew Street
Northwood
Thorness Bay
Whippingham
Medina
Newtown Bay
NEWTOWN HARBOUR
Porchfield
Parkhurst
Parkhurst Forest
Fishbou
Wootton Bridge
Hamstead
OLD TOWN HALL
Newtown
COLEMANS FARM PARK
BUTTERFLY WORLD
Wootto Commo
Cranmore
Thorley Street
Ningwood
Shalfleet
Gunville
Hunny Hill
Carisbrooke
NEWPORT
ROMAN VILLA
Staplers
Downe
Wellow
Newbridge
CALBOURNE WATER MILL
Clatterford
CARISBROOKE CASTLE
Shide
CHESSELL POTTERY BARNS
Calbourne
Isle of Wight
ARRETON MANOR
Bowcombe
Blackwater
MARITIME
Merstone
Shalcombe
Brighstone Forest
Gatcombe
Horringfo
Hulverstone
Brook
Mottistone
Chillerton
Rookley
AMAZON WORLD
Moortown
Shorwell
Branst
NATURAL HISTORY CENTRE
The Undercliff
Brighstone
BRIGHSTONE
Limerstone
Kingston
Godshill
Thorncross
Yafford
MODEL VILLAGE
Little Atherfield
Brighstone Bay
Roud
Chale Green
Pyle
Atherfield Pt.
Stenbury Down
HERITAGE
Chale
Whitwell
Chale Bay
ST CATHERINE'S ORATORY
Blackgang
Niton
Blackgang Chine
BLACKGANG CHINE
St Law
The Un
St Catherine's Point
0 1 2 3 miles
0 1 2 3 4 5 km

Wickham
Hundred Acres
Denmead
Cowplain
FOREST OF BERE
Rowlands Castle
Stoughton
Walderton
BOW HILL
STANSTED PARK
North Boarhunt
SOUTHWICK BREWHOUSE
Southwick
Waterlooville
TAUNTON
Leigh Park
Funtley
Boarhunt
FORT NELSON
Ports Down
Purbrook
Stockheath
Westbourne
Funtington
Woodmancote
Woodend
West Stoke
Mid Lavant
East Ashling
Summersdale
West Ashling
Wallington
Wymering
Bedhampton
HAVANT
Warblington
Hermitage
Hambrook
Nutbourne
Fareham
Portchester
P&R
Drayton
Cosham
Emsworth
Southbourne
Broadbridge
Fishbourne
Chichester
Fleetlands
PORTCHESTER CASTLE
Langstone
Hilsea
FARLINGTON MARSHES
Northney
Chidham
Bosham
BOSHAM WALK
FISHBOURNE PALACE
Peel Common
Bridgemary
Portsmouth
Thorney
North Hayling
CHICHESTER HARBOUR
Apuldram
FORT BROCKHURST
Portsmouth Harbour
Brockhurst
North End
Langstone Harbour
Stoke
West Thorney
Donnington
Hunston
Hardway
EXPLOSION
GUNWHARF QUAYS
DICKENS BIRTHPLACE
Fleet
West Itchenor
1642 LIVING HISTORY VILLAGE
HMS VICTORY, MARY ROSE
PORTSMOUTH
HAYLING ISLAND
Chichester Harbour
Shipton Green
Portsea
CATHEDRAL
Fratton
West Town
Birdham
GOSPORT
Milton
FORT
Eastney
ROYAL MARINES MUSEUM
SUBMARINE
South Hayling
Eastoke
Acre Street
West Wittering
Somerley
Highleigh
Stokes Bay
Alverstoke
BLUE REEF AQUARIUM
Southsea
SOUTHSEA CASTLE
EAST HAYLING LIGHT RAILWAY
East Wittering
EARNLEY BUTTERFLIES AND GARDENS
Earnley
Bracklesham
Gilkicker Pt.
SOLENT
SPITHEAD
Norton
RYDE
Selsey
TOLL
Nettlestone Pt.
SEAVIEW WILDLIFE ENCOUNTER
Binstead
BRICKFIELDS
Elmfield
Seaview
Havenstreet
Nettlestone
WALTZING WATERS
ISLE OF WIGHT STEAM RAILWAY
St Helens
Bembridge
Foreland
Brading
Steyne Cross
Lane End
WINDMILL
Hillway
ROMAN VILLA
Alverstone
MORTON MANOR
DINOSAUR ISLE
Whitecliff Bay
Newchurch
Yaverland
Culver Cliff
ISLE OF WIGHT ZOO
Sandown
Winford
Lake
Apse Heath
Sandown Bay
Shanklin
SHANKLIN CHINE
Whiteley Bank
Wroxall
Luccombe Village
Luccombe Chine
Dunnose
Bonchurch
Ventnor
BOTANIC GARDEN & VISITOR CENTRE
SZ
CAEN 6:00
LE HAVRE 8:00
ST. MALO 9:30
BILBAO 24:00
SANTANDER 24:00 (Mar-Nov)
GUERNSEY 7:00
JERSEY 8:00
CHERBOURG 3:00 (April-Nov)
0:10
0:40
0:20
4
5
6
7
B
C
D

Trotton
Minsted
A272
Midhurst
South Ambersham
Selham
Tillington
Petworth
Byworth
Bedham
Bridge
North Heath
Gay Street
Codmore Hill
34
West Lavington
Elsted
Didling
Bepton
Treyford
235
248
LINCH DOWN
Cocking
Heyshott
Graffham
Duncton
Fittleworth
Coates
Stopham
Nutbourne
West Chiltington
Pulborough
Marehill
Hardham
Wiggonholt
Coldwaltham
West Sussex
SOUTH DOWNS WAY
East Lavington
Barlavington
Sutton
Watersfield
Greatham
B2141
Marden
A285
A283
B2138
A29
255
Bignor
ROMAN VILLA
Rackham
Cootham
Chilgrove
East Marden
SOUTH DOWNS NATIONAL PARK
Bury
Amberley
PARHAM
Storrington
Singleton
Charlton
Upwaltham
West Burton
West Dean
WEST DEAN GARDENS
East Dean
KINGLEY VALE
245
B2139
WEALD AND DOWNLAND OPEN AIR MUSEUM
Houghton
AMBERLEY MUS
KITHURST HILL
213
A286
GOODWOOD
STANE STREET
206
BOW HILL
Walderton
ST. ROCHE'S HILL
Madehurst
North Stoke
19
14
South Stoke
Eartham
167
HARROW HILL
Woodend
West Stoke
East Lavant
Mid Lavant
GOODWOOD HOUSE
Arundel Park
Burpham
Halnaker
Strettington
Slindon
Offham
East Ashling
Summersdale
Westerton
Boxgrove
Fontwell
THE WILDFOWL AND WETLANDS CENTRE
ARUNDEL
West Ashling
B2146
B2178
A27
Arundel
Patching
Tangmere
AVIATION MUS
DENMANS
Walberton
Crossbush
Chichester
CATH
Westhampnett
Aldingbourne
Norton
Nyton
FONTWELL PARK
Eastergate
MUSEUM AND HERITAGE CENTRE
Hammerpot
Bosham
BOSHAM WALK
Fishbourne
FISHBOURNE PALACE
Oving
Woodgate
Westergate
B2233
Tortington
A284
Poling
Angmering
Lyminster
Barnham
A259
Hangleton
Apuldram
PALLANT HOUSE
Colworth
Yapton
Ford
Wick
Donnington
Merston
Shripney
Climping
Bilsham
Rustington
East Preston
B2187
Hunston
North Mundham
Runcton
North Bersted
Flansham
B2145
B2201
B2132
West Itchenor
SUSSEX FALCONRY CENTRE
South Mundham
South Bersted
LITTLEHAMPTON
Kingston Gorse
Shipton Green
B2179
B2166
Birdham
Street End
Nyetimber
Felpham
Middleton-on-Sea
HARBOUR PARK
Acre Street
Somerley
Highleigh
Sidlesham
Rose Green
Aldwick
SOUTHCOAST WORLD
Bognor Regis
B2198
EARNLEY BUTTERFLIES AND GARDENS
Pagham
Earnley
Bracklesham
Norton
Church Norton
Selsey
SELSEY BILL
SZ
A
B
C
D
0 1 2 3 miles
0 1 2 3 4 5 km

West Grinstead
Kent Street
Wineham
Twineham
BURGESS HILL
Wivelsfield
Wivelsfield Green
Chailey
Broomer's Corner
Dial Post
Partridge Green
Goose Green
Spear Hill
Sayers Common
JUMPING COURSE
DITCHLING COMMON
South Street
Thakeham
Ashington
West End
Blackstone
Albourne
Hurstpierpoint
Hurst Wickham
Plumpton Green
WASHBROOKS FARM CENTRE
Ashurst
Henfield
Hassocks
Keymer
Ditchling
DITCHLING MUSEUM
Chiltington
East Chiltington
Woodmancote
Streat
Westmeston
Rock
Wiston
Clayton
Cooksbridge
Washington
Small Dole
Plumpton
Offham
Pyecombe
Fulking
Poynings
DITCHLING BEACON
MT. HARRY
Steyning
Bramber
Edburton
Saddlescombe
STANMER PARK
Upper Beeding
TRULEIGH HILL
DEVIL'S DYKE
Wallands Park
Stanmer
ST MARY'S HOUSE
Findon
Botolphs
Patcham
Coldean
Falmer
Brighton and Hove
Mile Oak
Westdene
Withdean
Kingston near Lewes
Coombes
High Salvington
North Lancing
Portslade
West Blatchington
PRESTON MANOR
Moulsecoomb
Bevendean
CASTLE HILL
Preston
Salvington
Kingston by Sea
Southwick
Woodingdean
SHOREHAM
Sompting
Lancing
SHOREHAM-BY-SEA
Portslade-by-Sea
MUS & ART GAL
ROYAL PAVILION
Broadwater
HOVE
Kemp Town
Ovingdean
South Lancing
East Worthing
BRIGHTON
BRIGHTON SEA LIFE
Telscombe
Saltdean
MARLIPINS MUSEUM
Rottingdean
Worthing
Goring-by-Sea
West Worthing
VOLK'S ELECTRIC RAILWAY
BRIGHTON MARINA
Telscombe Cliffs
Peacehaven
TQ
TV
A24
A23
A27
A280
A283
A281
A2037
A273
A270
A259
A2032
A275
B2116
B2135
B2139
B2133
B2117
B2112
B2113
B2036
B2123
35
22

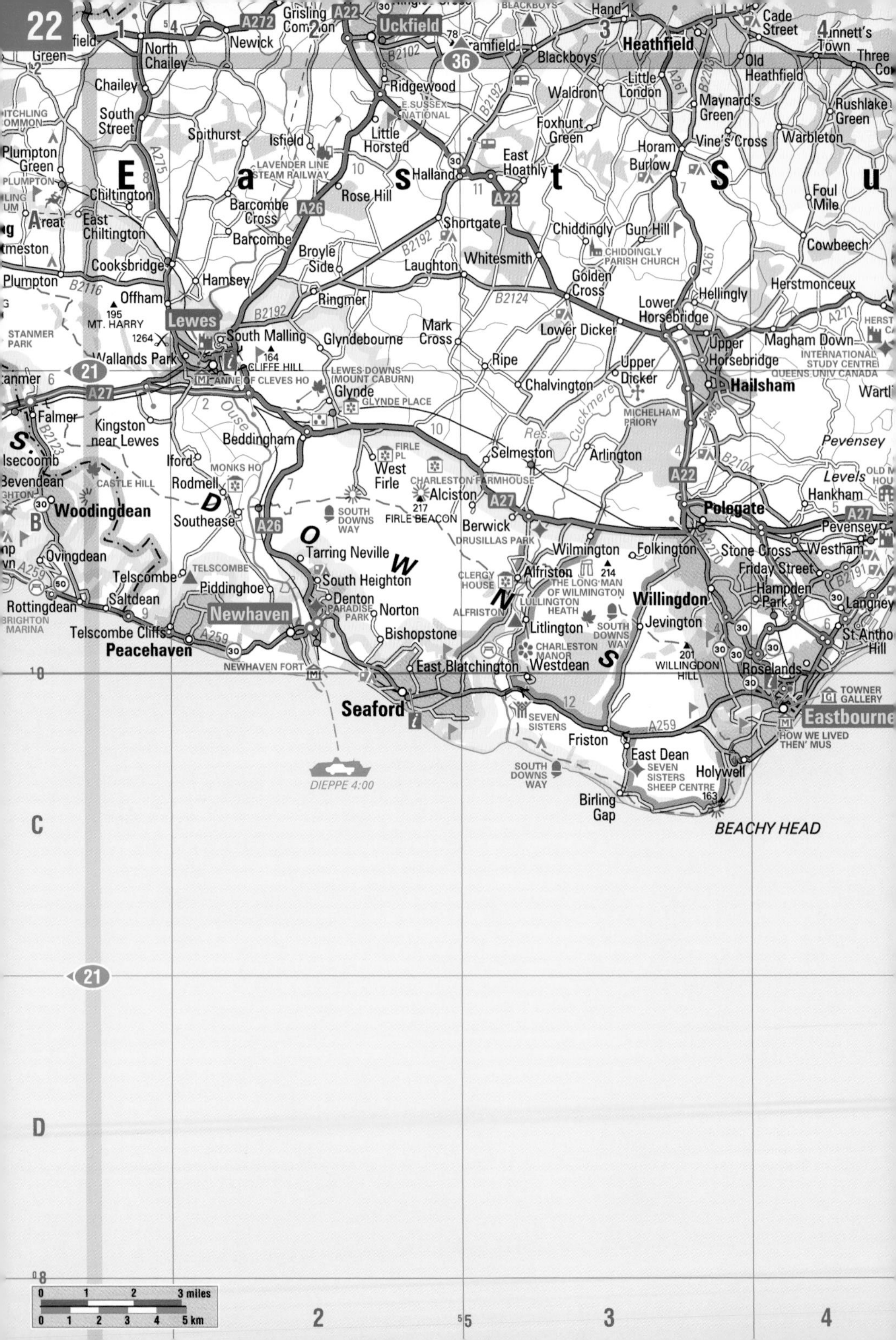
Newick
North Chailey
Grisling Common
A272
A22
Uckfield
Framfield
36
Blackboys
Hand
Heathfield
Cade Street
Old Heathfield
Three Cups
Chailey
South Street
Spithurst
Isfield
Ridgewood
E.SUSSEX NATIONAL
Little Horsted
Waldron
Little London
Maynard's Green
Rushlake Green
Plumpton Green
PLUMPTON
LAVENDER LINE STEAM RAILWAY
Halland
East Hoathly
Foxhunt Green
Horam
Vine's Cross
Warbleton
Burlow
Chiltington
East Chiltington
Barcombe Cross
Barcombe
Rose Hill
Shortgate
Foul Mile
Chiddingly
Gun Hill
CHIDDINGLY PARISH CHURCH
Cowbeech
Cooksbridge
Broyle Side
Laughton
Whitesmith
Golden Cross
Herstmonceux
Plumpton
Hamsey
Offham
Ringmer
Lower Horsebridge
Hellingly
195 MT. HARRY
Lewes
STANMER PARK
South Malling
Glyndebourne
Mark Cross
Lower Dicker
Upper Horsebridge
Magham Down
Wallands Park
164 CLIFFE HILL
ANNE OF CLEVES HO
LEWES DOWNS (MOUNT CABURN)
Ripe
Upper Dicker
INTERNATIONAL STUDY CENTRE QUEENS UNIV CANADA
Chalvington
Hailsham
Glynde
GLYNDE PLACE
A27
Falmer
Kingston near Lewes
MICHELHAM PRIORY
Beddingham
FIRLE PL
Selmeston
Arlington
Pevensey Levels
Iford
MONKS HO
West Firle
CHARLESTON FARMHOUSE
Alciston
217 FIRLE BEACON
Hankham
Polegate
Rodmell
CASTLE HILL
Woodingdean
Bevendean
Southease
SOUTH DOWNS WAY
Berwick
DRUSILLAS PARK
Pevensey
Westham
Stone Cross
Ovingdean
Tarring Neville
Wilmington
Folkington
Friday Street
Telscombe
TELSCOMBE
Piddinghoe
South Heighton
CLERGY HOUSE
Alfriston
214 THE LONG MAN OF WILMINGTON
Hampden Park
Langney
Rottingdean
Saltdean
Newhaven
Denton
PARADISE PARK
Norton
LULLINGTON HEATH
Willingdon
Jevington
BRIGHTON MARINA
Telscombe Cliffs
Peacehaven
A259
Bishopstone
Litlington
CHARLESTON MANOR
St Anthony's Hill
NEWHAVEN FORT
East Blatchington
Westdean
201 WILLINGDON HILL
Roselands
Seaford
SEVEN SISTERS
Friston
TOWNER GALLERY
Eastbourne
HOW WE LIVED THEN' MUS
East Dean
SEVEN SISTERS SHEEP CENTRE
Holywell
DIEPPE 4:00
Birling Gap
163
BEACHY HEAD
East Sussex
South Downs
0 1 2 3 miles
0 1 2 3 4 5 km

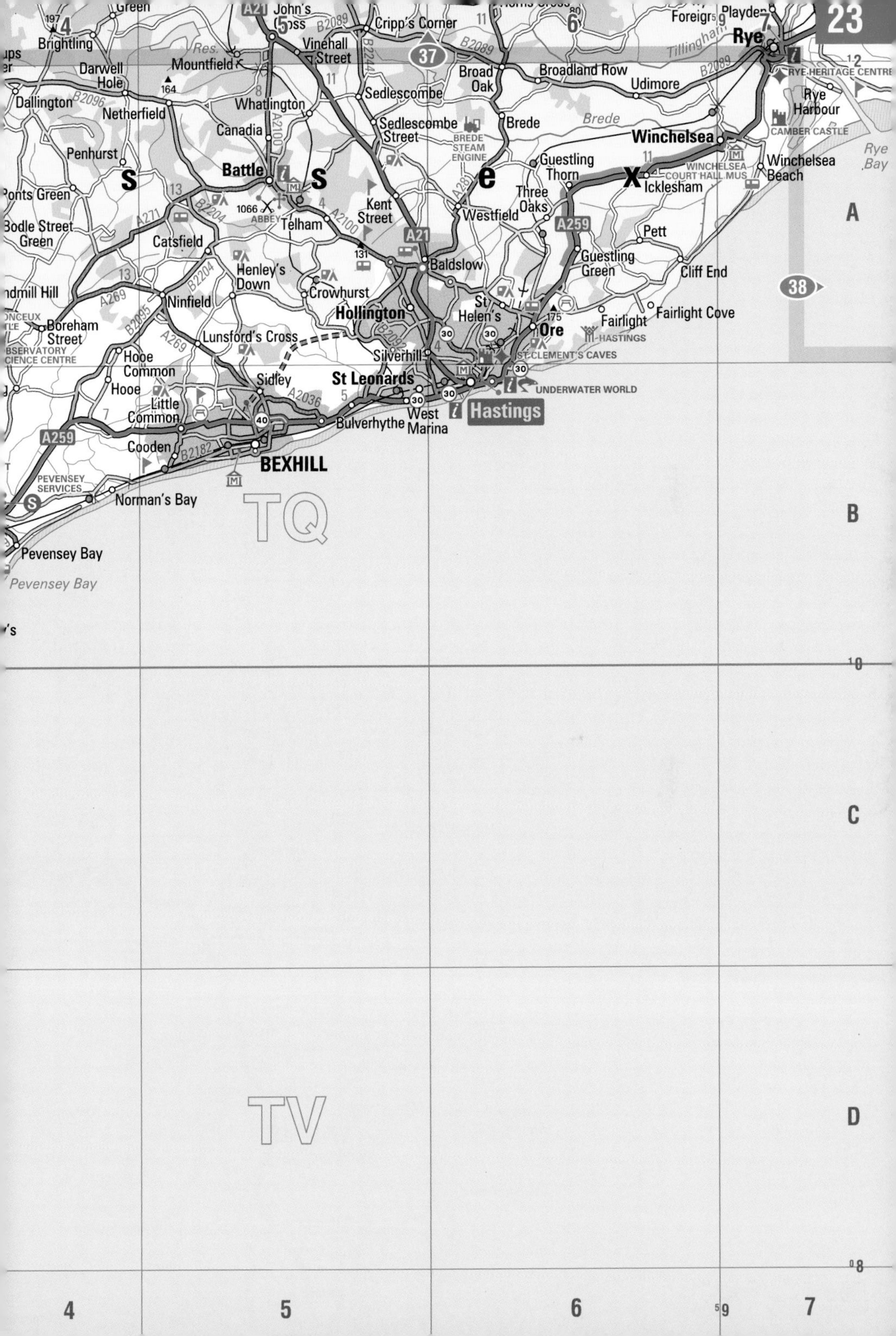
Brightling
Mountfield
Darwell Hole
Dallington
Netherfield
Whatlington
Canadia
Penhurst
Battle
1066 ABBEY
Telham
Ponts Green
Bodle Street Green
Catsfield
Henley's Down
Crowhurst
Ninfield
Boreham Street
OBSERVATORY SCIENCE CENTRE
Lunsford's Cross
Hooe Common
Hooe
Little Common
Sidley
Cooden
BEXHILL
PEVENSEY SERVICES
Norman's Bay
Pevensey Bay
John's Cross
Vinehall Street
Cripp's Corner
Sedlescombe
Sedlescombe Street
BREDE STEAM ENGINE
Kent Street
Baldslow
Hollington
Silverhill
St Leonards
Bulverhythe
West Marina
Hastings
UNDERWATER WORLD
ST CLEMENT'S CAVES
HASTINGS
Ore
St Helen's
Westfield
Broad Oak
Brede
Broadland Row
Udimore
Guestling Thorn
Three Oaks
Guestling Green
Fairlight
Fairlight Cove
Cliff End
Pett
Icklesham
Winchelsea
WINCHELSEA COURT HALL MUS
Winchelsea Beach
Rye
RYE HERITAGE CENTRE
Rye Harbour
CAMBER CASTLE
Rye Bay
Playden
Tillingham
A21
A2100
A271
A269
A259
A28
A2036
B2089
B2244
B2096
B2204
B2095
B2092
B2182
37
38
TQ
TV
A
B
C
D
4
5
6
7

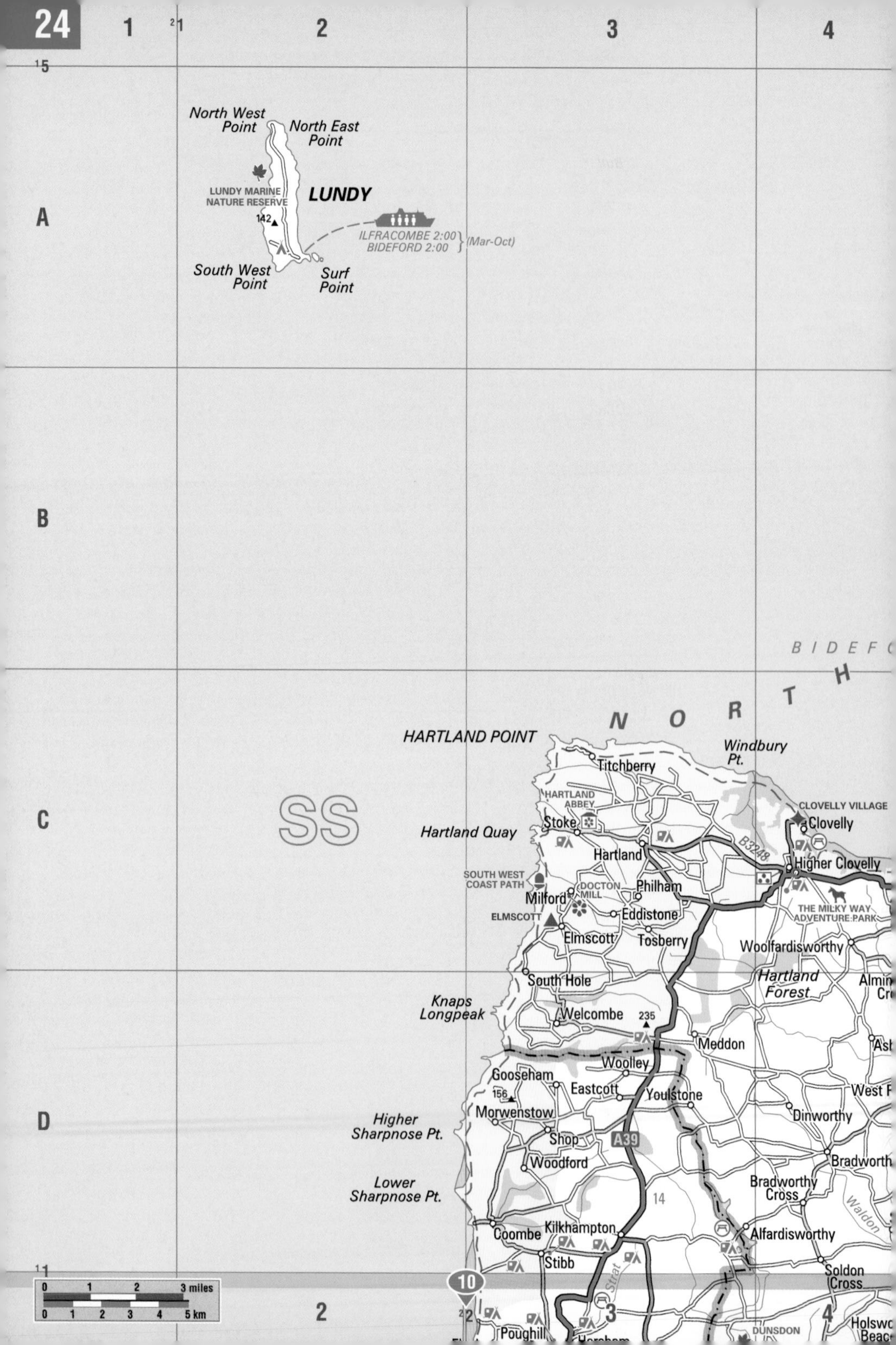
1
2
3
4
5
North West Point
North East Point
LUNDY MARINE NATURE RESERVE
LUNDY
142
ILFRACOMBE 2:00
BIDEFORD 2:00
(Mar-Oct)
South West Point
Surf Point
A
B
BIDEF
N O R T H
C
D
HARTLAND POINT
SS
Titchberry
Windbury Pt.
HARTLAND ABBEY
CLOVELLY VILLAGE
Clovelly
Stoke
Hartland Quay
Hartland
B3248
Higher Clovelly
SOUTH WEST COAST PATH
DOCTON MILL
Philham
Milford
THE MILKY WAY ADVENTURE PARK
ELMSCOTT
Eddistone
Elmscott
Tosberry
Woolfardisworthy
South Hole
Hartland Forest
Knaps Longpeak
Welcombe
235
Meddon
Woolley
Gooseham
Eastcott
Youlstone
156
Morwenstow
Dinworthy
Higher Sharpnose Pt.
Shop
A39
Woodford
Bradworthy
Lower Sharpnose Pt.
Bradworthy Cross
14
Waldon
Coombe
Kilkhampton
Alfardisworthy
Stibb
Strat
Soldon Cross
0 1 2 3 miles
0 1 2 3 4 5 km
10
Poughill
DUNSDON

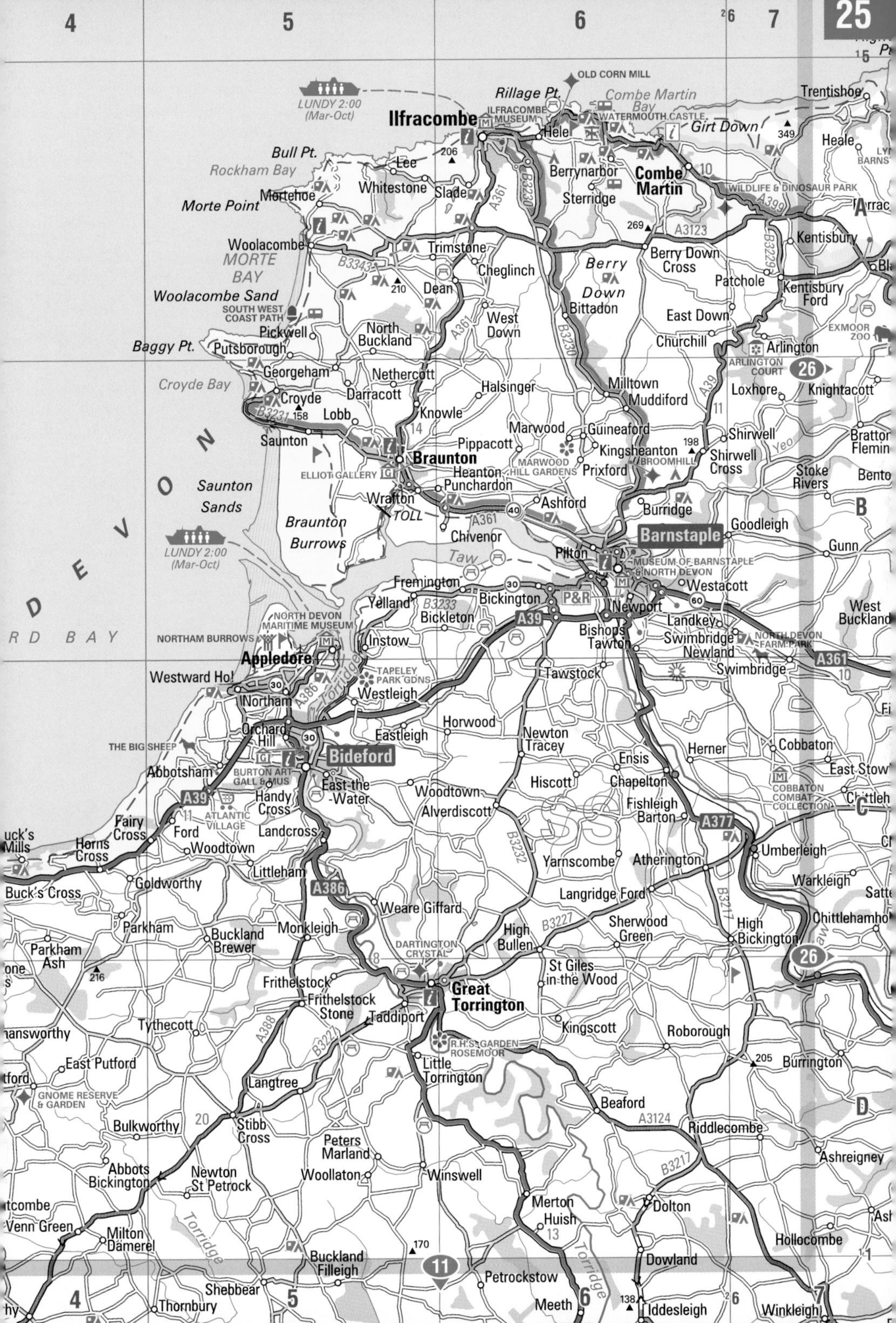
4
5
6
7
LUNDY 2:00 (Mar-Oct)
OLD CORN MILL
Rillage Pt.
Combe Martin Bay
Ilfracombe
ILFRACOMBE MUSEUM
Hele
WATERMOUTH CASTLE
Girt Down
Trentishoe
Heale
349
Bull Pt.
Lee
206
Rockham Bay
Whitestone
Slade
A361
B3230
Berrynarbor
Combe Martin
10
WILDLIFE & DINOSAUR PARK
A399
Mortehoe
Morte Point
Sterridge
269
A3123
Kentisbury
Woolacombe
Trimstone
Berry Down Cross
B3229
MORTE BAY
B3343
Cheglinch
Berry Down
Patchole
Kentisbury Ford
Woolacombe Sand
210
Dean
Bittadon
SOUTH WEST COAST PATH
West Down
East Down
EXMOOR ZOO
Pickwell
North Buckland
B3230
Churchill
Arlington
Baggy Pt.
Putsborough
ARLINGTON COURT
26
Georgeham
Nethercott
Milltown
Loxhore
Knightacott
Croyde Bay
Croyde
Darracott
Halsinger
Muddiford
158
Lobb
Knowle
A39
11
B3231
14
Marwood
Guineaford
Shirwell
Saunton
Pippacott
Kingsheanton
198
Shirwell Cross
Yeo
Braunton
MARWOOD HILL GARDENS
Prixford
BROOMHILL
Stoke Rivers
ELLIOT GALLERY
Heanton Punchardon
Saunton Sands
Wrafton
Ashford
Burridge
TOLL
40
A361
B
Braunton Burrows
Chivenor
Barnstaple
Goodleigh
LUNDY 2:00 (Mar-Oct)
Taw
Pilton
Gunn
MUSEUM OF BARNSTAPLE & NORTH DEVON
Fremington
30
Westacott
Yelland
B3233
Bickington
P&R
Newport
60
West Buckland
Bickleton
A39
Landkey
NORTH DEVON MARITIME MUSEUM
Bishops Tawton
Swimbridge
NORTH DEVON FARM PARK
NORTHAM BURROWS
Instow
7
Newland
DEVON
RD BAY
Appledore
Torridge
TAPELEY PARK GDNS
Tawstock
Swimbridge
A361
10
Westward Ho!
30
Westleigh
Northam
A386
Orchard Hill
Eastleigh
Horwood
Newton Tracey
THE BIG SHEEP
30
Bideford
Herner
Cobbaton
Ensis
East Stowford
Abbotsham
BURTON ART GALL & MUS
East-the-Water
Hiscott
Chapelton
COBBATON COMBAT COLLECTION
A39
Handy Cross
Woodtown
Alverdiscott
Fishleigh Barton
ATLANTIC VILLAGE
SS
C
Fairy Cross
11
Ford
Landcross
A377
Buck's Mills
Horns Cross
Woodtown
B3232
Yarnscombe
Atherington
Umberleigh
Littleham
Goldworthy
Warkleigh
Buck's Cross
A386
Langridge Ford
Weare Giffard
B3217
Parkham
B3227
Chittlehamholt
Monkleigh
High Bickington
Buckland Brewer
Sherwood Green
Parkham Ash
High Bullen
DARTINGTON CRYSTAL
216
8
26
St Giles in the Wood
Frithelstock
Great Torrington
Frithelstock Stone
Taddiport
Tythecott
Kingscott
A388
Roborough
B3227
R.H.S. GARDEN ROSEMOOR
205
Burrington
East Putford
Little Torrington
GNOME RESERVE & GARDEN
Langtree
Beaford
D
A3124
Riddlecombe
Bulkworthy
20
Stibb Cross
Peters Marland
Ashreigney
Abbots Bickington
Newton St Petrock
B3217
Woollaton
Winswell
Merton
Dolton
Venn Green
Huish
Milton Damerel
13
Torridge
Hollocombe
170
Buckland Filleigh
Dowland
Torridge
11
Petrockstow
Shebbear
138
4
5
6
Thornbury
Meeth
Iddesleigh
Winkleigh
7

26
Highveer Pt.
Woody Bay
Foreland Pt.
Lynmouth Bay
CLIFF RAILWAY
Lynmouth
Lynton
Countisbury
Hurlst Pt
Porlock Bay
Trentishoe
Martinhoe
WATERSMEET HOUSE
Brendon
Malmsmead
CULBONE HILL
413
TOLL
Porlock Weir
Bossington
349
Heale
LYNTON AND BARNSTAPLE RLY
Barbrook
East Ilkerton
Cheriton
Oare
B3225
Porlock
WILDLIFE & DINOSAUR PARK
Martinhoe Cross
West Lyn
Furzehill
B3223
E X M O O R
Parracombe
A399
Shallowford
Brendon Common
HAWKCOMBE WOODS
Holnicote Estate
B3229
Kentisbury
EXMOOR FOREST
465
Patchole
Blackmoor Gate
Challacombe Common
Pinkworthy Pond
DUNKERY BEACON
Kentisbury Ford
487
THE DUNKERY & HORNER WOOD
PINKERY
25
EXMOOR ZOO
B3358
Exe Plain
519
Arlington
ARLINGTON COURT
Challacombe
Exe
N A T I O N A L
329
Shoulsbarrow Common
Simonsbath
B3223
Edgcott
B3224
Loxhore
Knightacott
Leworthy
Exford
EXFORD
Shirwell
Bratton Fleming
Yeo
Bray
Barle
Shirwell Cross
Stoke Rivers
Benton
A399
Lydcott
493
443
HORSEN HILL
Withypool
Withypool Common
13
B
Goodleigh
Brayford
North Radworthy
WINSFORD HILL
Gunn
265
High Bray
North Heasley
P A R K
426
Charles
Liscombe
West Buckland
Heasley Mill
South Radworthy
TARR STEPS
East Buckland
NORTH DEVON FARM PARK
Dane's Brook
377
Hawkridge
224
Molland Common
Swimbridge
10
A361
Twitchen
North Molton
Anstey Common
Filleigh
Mole
Molland
West Anstey
Cobbaton
SS
East Anstey
QUINCE HONEY FARM
60
East Stowford
B3227
Yeo
Yeo Mill
COBBATON COMBAT COLLECTION
Chittlehampton
B3226
South Molton
Bish Mill
Newtown
B3227
Oldways End
C
Umberleigh
Clapworthy
173
Bishops Nympton
Ash Mill
Knowstone
Roachill
Warkleigh
Satterleigh
George Nympton
Alswear
Mariansleigh
Rose Ash
17
B3217
Chittlehamholt
High Bickington
Taw
25
Romansleigh
Meshaw
A361
King's Nympton
238
Creacombe
STOODLEIGH BEACON
301
A377
Rackenford
Cadbury Barton
B3137
205
Burrington
26
Week
Elstone
Dart
Queen Dart
Lutworthy
Little Dart
D
Templeton Bridge
B3096
Chulmleigh
West Worlington
East Worlington
Witheridge
Ashreigney
Cheldon
Drayford
Nomansland
Templeton
B3042
Chawleigh
Thelbridge Barton
Washford Pyne
B3137
Cruwys Morchard
Ashley
Pennymoor
B3042
Dalch
Black Dog
Hollocombe
Filleigh
Puddington
Way Village
0 1 2 3 miles
0 1 2 3 4 5 km
12
Wembworthy
Eastington
Morchard Bishop
Woolfardisworthy
Winkleigh
Coldridge
Lapford
Upham

4
5
6
30
31
15
BRIDGWATER
BAY
ST
SOUTH WEST COAST PATH
SELWORTHY BEACON
308
Allerford
Selworthy
Woodcombe
Minehead
WEST SOMERSET RAILWAY
BUTLINS
A39
Periton
Alcombe
Luccombe
Marsh Street
MINEHEAD
DOLL MUS
Blue Anchor Bay
Wootton Courtenay
DUNKERY VINEYARD
Dunster
MILL & YARN MARKET
DUNSTER CASTLE
Cowbridge
Timberscombe
Carhampton
Blue Anchor
Old Cleeve
MARKET HOUSE MUS
Watchet
B3191
West Quantoxhead
East Quantoxhead
Lilstock
Kilton
Burton
Kilve
Stringston
A
TROPIQUARIA
Withycombe
Bilbrook
Washford
Williton
Staple
Holford
28
Nether Stowey
A396
BRENDON
CROYDON HILL
365
FOREST
CLEEVE ABBEY
Rodhuish
Sampford Brett
Bicknoller
QUANTOCK
COLERIDGE COTTAGE
Cutcombe
Wheddon Cross
Luxborough
Roadwater
Yard
B3188
Vellow
358
Over Stowey
423
LYPE HILL
Kingsbridge
290
Monksilver
B3190
Stogumber
WEST SOMERSET RAILWAY
A358
B3224
Crowcombe
QUANTOCK FOREST
BRENDON HILLS
Treborough
412
Elworthy
Lower Vexford
Flaxpool
384
B
HILLS
Exton
B3224
Willett
Lydeard St Lawrence
West Bagborough
Bridgetown
Withiel Florey
Clatworthy Res.
Tolland
16
Brompton Regis
Brompton Ralph
B3224
East Combe
Combe Florey
Cothelstone
27
Wimbleball Lake
Clatworthy
Tarr
Cushuish
A396
Ash Priors
Bishops Lydeard
355
HADDON HILL
Upton
Huish Champflower
Langley Marsh
Maundown
B3188
Fitzhead
B3222
HEYDON HILL
338
Wiveliscombe
Halse
A358
40
Barle
B3222
Bury
B3190
Skilgate
Chipstable
VALE OF TAUNTON DEANE
Preston Bowyer
B3227
Heathfield
Milverton
Hillcommon
Norton Fitzwarren
Brushford
Waterrow
Oake
C
Morebath
Petton
B3227
Hillfarance
Exebridge
267
Bathealton
B3187
239
Shillingford
East Nynehead
Bradford-on-Tone
Bampton
Clayhanger
Langford Budville
Nynehead
SHEPPY'S CIDER
A38
6
Kittisford
Runnington
Staple
Appley
COTHAY
Thorne
Wellington
West Buckland
TAUNTON DEANE SERVICES
Oakford
Ashbrittle
St Margaret
Rockwell Green
Huntsham
Holywell Lake
26
28
Cove
Hockworthy
286
9
Stoodleigh
Holcombe Rogus
Sampford Arundel
Angersleigh
Wrangway
Ford Street
8
EXE VALLEY
Westleigh
M5
BLACKDOWN HILLS
East Mere
Nicholashayne
Burlescombe
60
Washfield
Chevithorne
Whitnage
Clayhidon
KNIGHTSHAYES COURT
A38
Uplowman
7
Bolham
Rosemary Lane
D
Chettiscombe
A361
Appledore
Calverleigh
27
Culm Valley
Culmstock
BLACKDOWN
Stapley
TIVERTON CASTLE
Halberton
Sampford Peverell
Uffculme
Cowleymoor
COLDHARBOUR MILL
B3391
Hemyock
TIVERTON SERVICES
258
HACKPEN HILL
GRAND WESTERN CANAL
Cotteylands
Tiverton
Craddock
Bolham Water
B3440
237
Smithincott
HILLS
Ash Thomas
Ashill
5
4
Abbey
Smeatharpe
Willand
13
DIGGERLAND
Well Town
Blackborough
A396
CULLOMPTON SERVICES
Cadeleigh
Butterleigh
Sheldon
Dunkeswell

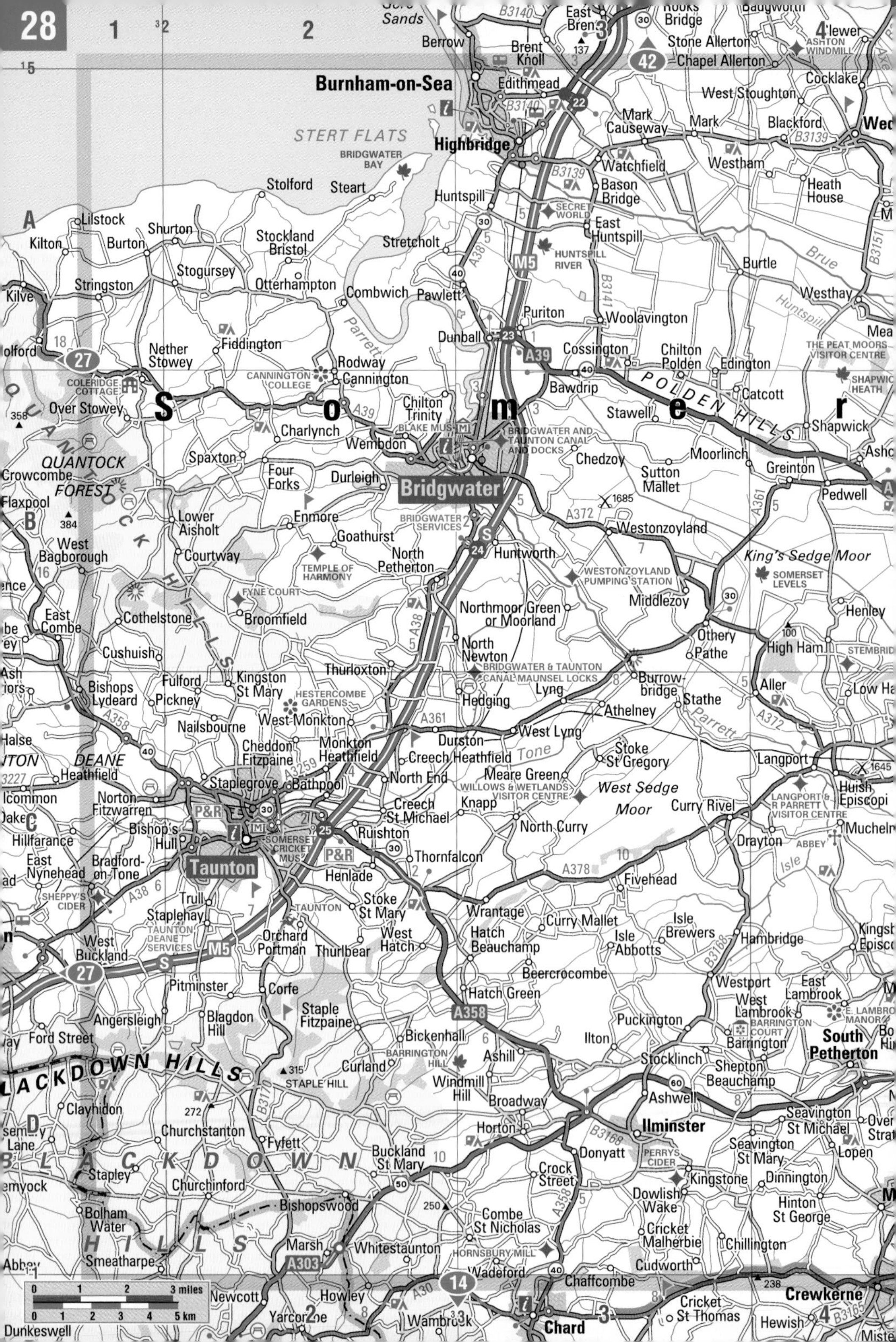
Burnham-on-Sea
Berrow
Brent Knoll
East Brent
Stone Allerton
Chapel Allerton
Badgworth
Rooks Bridge
Lower Weare
Ashton Windmill
Edithmead
Cocklake
West Stoughton
Mark Causeway
Mark
Blackford
Wedmore
Highbridge
Stert Flats
Bridgwater Bay
Watchfield
Westham
Stolford
Steart
Huntspill
Bason Bridge
Heath House
Secret World
East Huntspill
Huntspill River
Lilstock
Kilton
Burton
Shurton
Stockland Bristol
Stretcholt
Stogursey
Otterhampton
Burtle
Brue
Kilve
Stringston
Combwich
Pawlett
Puriton
Woolavington
Westhay
Parrett
Dunball
Cossington
Chilton Polden
Edington
The Peat Moors Visitor Centre
Holford
Nether Stowey
Fiddington
Rodway
Cannington
Cannington College
Coleridge Cottage
Bawdrip
Polden Hills
Catcott
Shapwick Heath
Over Stowey
Somerset
Chilton Trinity
Stawell
Shapwick
Charlynch
Blake Mus
Wembdon
Bridgwater and Taunton Canal and Docks
Quantock Forest
Crowcombe
Spaxton
Four Forks
Durleigh
Bridgwater
Chedzoy
Sutton Mallet
Moorlinch
Greinton
Ashcott
Pedwell
Flaxpool
Lower Aisholt
Enmore
Bridgwater Services
Westonzoyland
West Bagborough
Goathurst
Huntworth
Courtway
Temple of Harmony
North Petherton
King's Sedge Moor
Somerset Levels
Quantock Hills
Fyne Court
Westonzoyland Pumping Station
Middlezoy
Henley
East Combe
Cothelstone
Broomfield
Northmoor Green or Moorland
Othery
High Ham
Pathe
Stembridge
Cushuish
North Newton
Thurloxton
Bridgwater & Taunton Canal: Maunsel Locks
Burrowbridge
Bishops Lydeard
Fulford
Kingston St Mary
Hestercombe Gardens
Pickney
Hedging
Lyng
Stathe
Aller
Low Ham
Athelney
Halse
Nailsbourne
West Monkton
Durston
West Lyng
Deane
Heathfield
Cheddon Fitzpaine
Monkton Heathfield
Creech Heathfield
Tone
Stoke St Gregory
Langport
Huish Episcopi
Staplegrove
Bathpool
North End
Meare Green
Willows & Wetlands Visitor Centre
West Sedge Moor
Curry Rivel
Langport & R Parrett Visitor Centre
Norton Fitzwarren
Creech St Michael
Knapp
Muchelney
Hillfarance
Bishop's Hull
Somerset Cricket Mus
Ruishton
North Curry
Drayton
Abbey
Taunton
Thornfalcon
Isle
East Nynehead
Bradford-on-Tone
Henlade
Fivehead
Sheppy's Cider
Trull
Stoke St Mary
Wrantage
Staplehay
Taunton Deane Services
Orchard Portman
Thurlbear
West Hatch
Hatch Beauchamp
Curry Mallet
Isle Abbotts
Isle Brewers
Hambridge
Kingsbury Episcopi
West Buckland
Beercrocombe
Westport
East Lambrook
Pitminster
Corfe
Hatch Green
West Lambrook
E. Lambrook Manor
Staple Fitzpaine
Blagdon Hill
Puckington
Barrington Court
Angersleigh
Ford Street
Bickenhall
Ilton
Barrington
South Petherton
Barrington Hill
Ashill
Stocklinch
Blackdown Hills
Staple Hill
Curland
Windmill Hill
Shepton Beauchamp
Ashwell
Clayhidon
Broadway
Seavington St Michael
Horton
Ilminster
Hemyock
Churchstanton
Fyfett
Donyatt
Seavington St Mary
Lopen
Buckland St Mary
Crock Street
Perrys Cider
Kingstone
Dinnington
Stapley
Churchinford
Dowlish Wake
Hinton St George
Bishopswood
Bolham Water
Combe St Nicholas
Cricket Malherbie
Chillington
Marsh
Whitestaunton
Smeatharpe
Hornsbury Mill
Cudworth
Wadeford
Chaffcombe
Crewkerne
Newcott
Howley
Cricket St Thomas
Yarcombe
Wambrook
Chard
Hewish
Dunkeswell
0 1 2 3 miles
0 1 2 3 4 5 km

Wells
Glastonbury
Street
Shepton Mallet
Evercreech
Bruton
Castle Cary
Wincanton
Somerton
Yeovil
Sherborne
Milborne Port
Draycott
Rodney Stoke
Priddy
Emborough
Green Ore
Binegar
Gurney Slade
Ashwick
Stratton on the Fosse
Holcombe
Highbury
Coleford
Mells
Vobster
Little Green
Westbury-sub-Mendip
Wookey Hole
Wookey Hole Caves & Papermill
Ebbor Gorge
Easton
West Horrington
East Horrington
Oakhill
Nettlebridge
Stoke St Michael
Leigh upon Mendip
Whatley
Chantry
Nunney
Nunney Castle
Theale
Wookey
Henton
Burcott Mill
The Bishop's Palace
Dinder
Croscombe
Dulcote
Downside
Downhead
Heale
Dean
East Cranmore
West Cranmore
Leighton
Trudoxhill
Westhay Moor
Coxley
Polsham
Godney
Worminster
Wootton Vineyard
West Compton
East Compton
Doulting
East Somerset Railway
Southway
North Wootton
Pilton
Cannard's Grave
Prestleigh
Chesterblade
Wanstrow
Whitelake
Ham Wall
Pilton Manor Vineyard
Stoney Stratton
Westcombe
Upton Noble
Batcombe
Northover
Glastonbury Tor
Abbey
West Pennard
Edgarley
Pylle
East Pennard
Milton Clevedon
Clarks Village
West Bradley
Ditcheat
Lamyatt
North Brewham
South Brewham
Walton
Overleigh
Shoe Mus
Parbrook
Wraxall
Butleigh Wootton
Ham Street
Alhampton
Baltonsborough
Hardway
Alfred's Tower
Hornblotton Green
Sutton
Ansford
Cole
Redlynch
Stoney Stoke
Butleigh
Southwood
Pitcombe
Compton Dundon
Dundon
Brue
Barton St David
West Lydford
East Lydford
Alford
Shepton Montague
Penselwood
Kingweston
Lovington
Tower Mill
Littleton
Keinton Mandeville
Lydford-on-Fosse
Hadspen Garden
Charlton Musgrove
Leigh Common
Galhampton
Bratton Seymour
Wincanton
Charlton Adam
Babcary
North Barrow
Yarlington
Bayford
Pitney
Charlton Mackerell
Haynes Motor Mus
North Cadbury
Lytes Cary Manor
South Barrow
Holton
Cucklington
Cary Fitzpaine
Sparkford
Maperton
Lattiford
Kingsdon
South Cadbury
Compton Pauncefoot
Blackford
North Cheriton
South Cheriton
Long Sutton
Podimore
West Camel
Queen Camel
Horsington
Northover
Bridgehampton
Fleet Air Arm Mus
Sutton Montis
Corton Denham
Charlton Horethorne
Abbas Combe
Yeo
Long Load
Ilchester
Yeovilton
Limington
Chilton Cantelo
Marston Magna
Sandford Orcas Manor House
Stowell
Templecombe
Stapleton
Rimpton
Yenston
Ash
Ashington
Adber
Sandford Orcas
Milborne Wick
Henstridge Ash
Coat
Tintinhull
Tintinhull Garden
Treasurer's Ho
Yeovil Marsh
Mudford
Poyntington
Henstridge
Hurst
Chilthorne Domer
Montacute House
Trent
Oborne
Stalbridge
Stoke sub Hamdon
Stoke-sub-Hamdon Priory
Preston Plucknett
Nether Compton
Sherborne Old Castle
Goathill
Purse Caundle
Montacute
Over Compton
Stalbridge Weston
Norton sub Hamdon
Odcombe
Brympton
Ham Hill
Sherborne Castle
North Wootton
Haydon
Stourton Caundle
Chiselborough
West Coker
Alweston
Bishop's Caundle
West Chinnock
Barwick
Bradford Abbas
North Coker
Stoford
Thornford
Folke
East Coker
East Chinnock
Hardington Moor
Lillington
Longburton
Holwell
Woodbridge
Hardington Mandeville
Ryme Intrinseca
Beer Hackett
Haselbury Plucknett
Closworth
Yetminster
Crouch Hill
King's Stag
Pendomer
North Perrott
Hardington Marsh
Holnest
Leigh
Glanvilles Wootton
Pulham
Blackmoor Vale

Buckland Dinham
Lullington
Beckington
Rudge
BRATTON CAMP & WHITE HORSE
230
Littleton Down
Oldford
A36
Westbury Leigh
44
Westbury
Mells
Great Elm
Dilton Marsh
Summer Down
West Lavington Down
Vobster
Little Green
Clink
Berkley
Upton Scudamore
A350
Whatley
Frome
A3098
Chapmanslade
Corsley
Wilt
Leigh upon Mendip
Chantry
The Butts
NUNNEY CASTLE
A362
WARMINSTER SERVICES
Warminster
SAL
Downhead
Nunney
Corsley Heath
245
A36
A
A361
Tytherington
West Woodlands
Bugley
WARMINSTER DEWEY MUSEUM
Boreham
LONGLEAT
Leighton
Trudoxhill
Bishopstrow
B3414
Chitterne
Norton Bavant
Heytesbury
B390
Crockerton
Frome
Shear Cross
Horningsham
Sutton Veny
Knook
P
Wanstrow
29
Witham Friary
Tytherington
Upton Lovell
188
Longbridge Deverill
Corton
A36
Codford St Peter
Codford St Mary
Upton Noble
Gare Hill
Bruton Forest
284
Maiden Bradley
Boyton
Sherrington
Batcombe
Monkton Deverill
Brixton Deverill
A350
Stockton
257
B3092
Wylye
A359
Kilmington
North Brewham
Kingston Deverill
CRANBORNE
Great Ridge
Norton Ferris
South Brewham
Pertwood
B
Hardway
ALFRED'S TOWER
STOURHEAD
246
WHITE SHEET HILL
B3095
Keysley Down
Chicklade
A303
Stourton
STOURTON HOUSE
60
Berwick St Leonard
Fonthill Bishop
B3089
Stoney Stoke
13
Hindon
Chilmark
B3081
Penselwood
Zeals
Mere
West Knoyle
Queen Oak
BUSH FARM BISON CENTRE
The Green
Fonthill Gifford
Ridge
Teffont Evias
Charlton Musgrove
Leigh Common
Bourton
CHASE
Chicksgrove
WINCANTON
Barrow Street
East Knoyle
237
Huntingford
Tisbury
Bayford
Wincanton
A303
Stoke Trister
Milton on Stour
A350
Newtown
Hatch
193
Sutton Mandeville
Sedgehill
Cucklington
Gillingham
Elm Hill
Swallowcliffe
Lattiford
Wyke
Ham Common
Semley
OLD WARDOUR CASTLE
Ansty
PRESCOMBE DOWN
North Cheriton
AND WEST
Buckhorn Weston
Motcombe
Donhead St Andrew
242
WHITE SHEET HILL
West End
South Cheriton
C
Horsington
B3092
B3081
244
Knap Corner
Donhead St Mary
Milkwell
A30
Abbas Combe
Kington Magna
West Stour
Ivy Cross
Berwick St John
Alvediston
VALE
A30
East Stour
210
Shaftesbury
Ludwell
Templecombe
10
Charlton
Woodminton
Fifehead Magdalen
Cann
A357
Yenston
Stour Provost
Stour Row
Cann Common
277
Win Green
Henstridge Ash
Henstridge Marsh
Guy's Marsh
WILTSHIRE
Todber
Melbury Abbas
Melbury Down
Henstridge
Pillwell
Tollard Royal
CHASE
Milborne Port
29
Marnhull
Margaret Marsh
Purse Caundle
Stalbridge
Bedchester
Compton Abbas
Ashmore
Woodcutts
Stalbridge Weston
East Orchard
Stour
B3092
Hinton St Mary
West Orchard
Fontmell Magna
LARMER TREE GARDENS
B3081
Sixpenny Handley
Stourton Caundle
D
B3091
Manston
Sutton Waldron
Dean
Sturminster Newton
Farnham
Bishop's Caundle
Lydlinch
MILL
FIDDLEFORD MANOR
Hammoon
Iwerne Minster
Fiddleford
Iwerne Courtney or Shroton
Stubhampton
Cashmoor
BLACKMORE
CRANBORNE
Newton
Child Okeford
Chettle
CHETTLE HOUSE
Broad Oak
Holwell
Woodbridge
Fifehead Neville
HAMBLEDON HILL
Tarrant Gunville
Gussage St Michael
King's Stag
A357
Shillingstone
Tarrant Hinton
A354
Hill
Okeford Fitzpaine
A350
DOWNS
Long Crichel
16
Stourpaine
Tarrant Launceston
Moor Crichel
Pimperne
Durweston
Tarrant Monkton
Pulham
Ibberton
Turnworth
0 1 2 3 miles
0 1 2 3 4 5 km

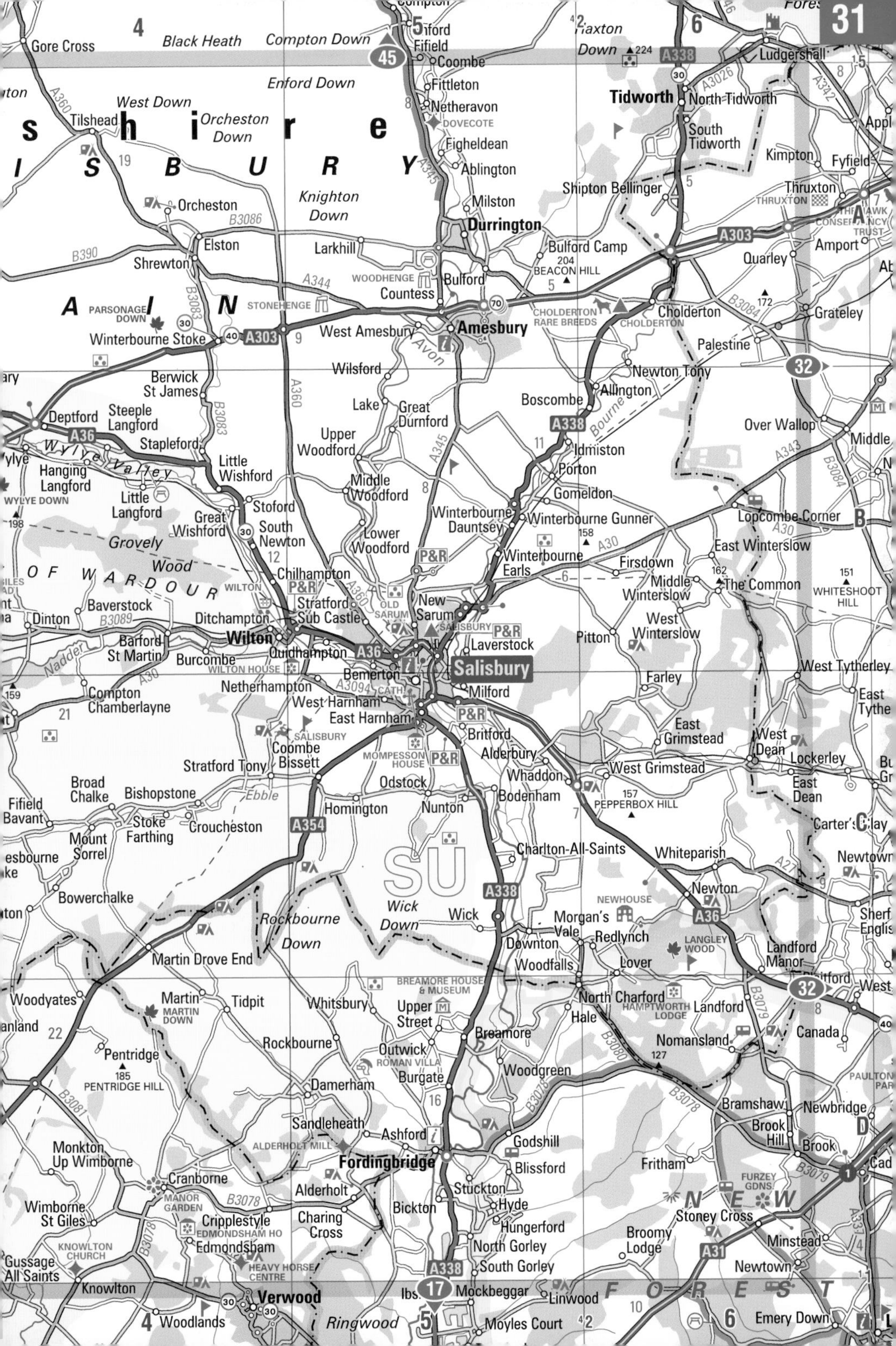
Gore Cross
Black Heath
Compton Down
Enford
Fifield
Coombe
Haxton
Down
224
A338
Ludgershall
Enford Down
Fittleton
Netheravon
DOVECOTE
West Down
Tilshead
Orcheston
Down
Tidworth
North Tidworth
South
Tidworth
Figheldean
Ablington
Kimpton
Fyfield
Shipton Bellinger
Thruxton
THRUXTON
Knighton
Down
Milston
Orcheston
B3086
Durrington
Elston
Larkhill
Bulford Camp
204
BEACON HILL
A303
Amport
Quarley
B390
Shrewton
A344
WOODHENGE
Bulford
Countess
STONEHENGE
PARSONAGE
DOWN
CHOLDERTON
RARE BREEDS
CHOLDERTON
Cholderton
B3084
172
Grateley
West Amesbury
Amesbury
Winterbourne Stoke
A303
Avon
Palestine
Wilsford
Berwick
St James
Newton Tony
Allington
Boscombe
Lake
Great
Durnford
A360
A338
Deptford
Steeple
Langford
Bourne
Over Wallop
A36
Upper
Woodford
A345
Middle
Stapleford
Idmiston
Wylye
Wylye
Valley
Hanging
Langford
Little
Wishford
Porton
A343
Middle
Woodford
Gomeldon
Little
Langford
WYLYE DOWN
198
Stoford
Great
Wishford
Winterbourne
Dauntsey
Winterbourne Gunner
Lopcombe Corner
A30
South
Newton
158
Grovely
Wood
Lower
Woodford
Winterbourne
Earls
A30
Firsdown
East Winterslow
OF WARDOUR
Chilhampton
P&R
162
WILTON
Middle
Winterslow
The Common
151
WHITESHOOT
HILL
Baverstock
Stratford
Sub Castle
OLD
SARUM
New
Sarum
Dinton
B3089
Ditchampton
West
Winterslow
Barford
St Martin
Wilton
SALISBURY
P&R
Laverstock
Pitton
Nadder
Burcombe
Quidhampton
A36
Salisbury
WILTON HOUSE
West Tytherley
Bemerton
A3094
Farley
159
Netherhampton
CATH
Milford
East
Tythe
Compton
Chamberlayne
West Harnham
East Harnham
P&R
East
Grimstead
West
Dean
A30
SALISBURY
Britford
Coombe
Bissett
Alderbury
Lockerley
MOMPESSON
HOUSE
P&R
Whaddon
West Grimstead
East
Dean
Stratford Tony
Broad
Chalke
Bishopstone
Odstock
Bodenham
157
PEPPERBOX HILL
Fifield
Bavant
Ebble
Homington
Nunton
Stoke
Farthing
Croucheston
A354
Carter's Clay
Mount
Sorrel
Charlton-All-Saints
Whiteparish
Newtown
SU
A27
Bowerchalke
Newton
A338
NEWHOUSE
Rockbourne
Down
Wick
Down
Wick
Morgan's
Vale
Redlynch
A36
LANGLEY
WOOD
Landford
Manor
Downton
Martin Drove End
Woodfalls
Lover
BREAMORE HOUSE
& MUSEUM
32
Woodyates
Martin
MARTIN
DOWN
Tidpit
Whitsbury
Upper
Street
North Charford
HAMPTWORTH
LODGE
Landford
Hale
B3079
22
Breamore
Canada
B3080
Nomansland
Pentridge
185
PENTRIDGE HILL
Rockbourne
Outwick
ROMAN VILLA
127
Burgate
Woodgreen
Damerham
B3081
16
B3078
B3078
Bramshaw
Newbridge
Brook
Hill
Sandleheath
Ashford
Brook
Godshill
Monkton
Up Wimborne
ALDERHOLT MILL
Fordingbridge
Blissford
Fritham
B3079
Cranborne
MANOR
GARDEN
Alderholt
Stuckton
FURZEY
GDNS
B3078
NEW
Wimborne
St Giles
Cripplestyle
EDMONDSHAM HO
Charing
Cross
Bickton
Hyde
Stoney Cross
B3078
Hungerford
KNOWLTON
CHURCH
Edmondsham
Broomy
Lodge
Minstead
Gussage
All Saints
North Gorley
HEAVY HORSE
CENTRE
A338
South Gorley
A31
Newtown
Knowlton
Verwood
17
Ibs.
Mockbeggar
Linwood
FOREST
Woodlands
Ringwood
Moyles Court
10
Emery Down

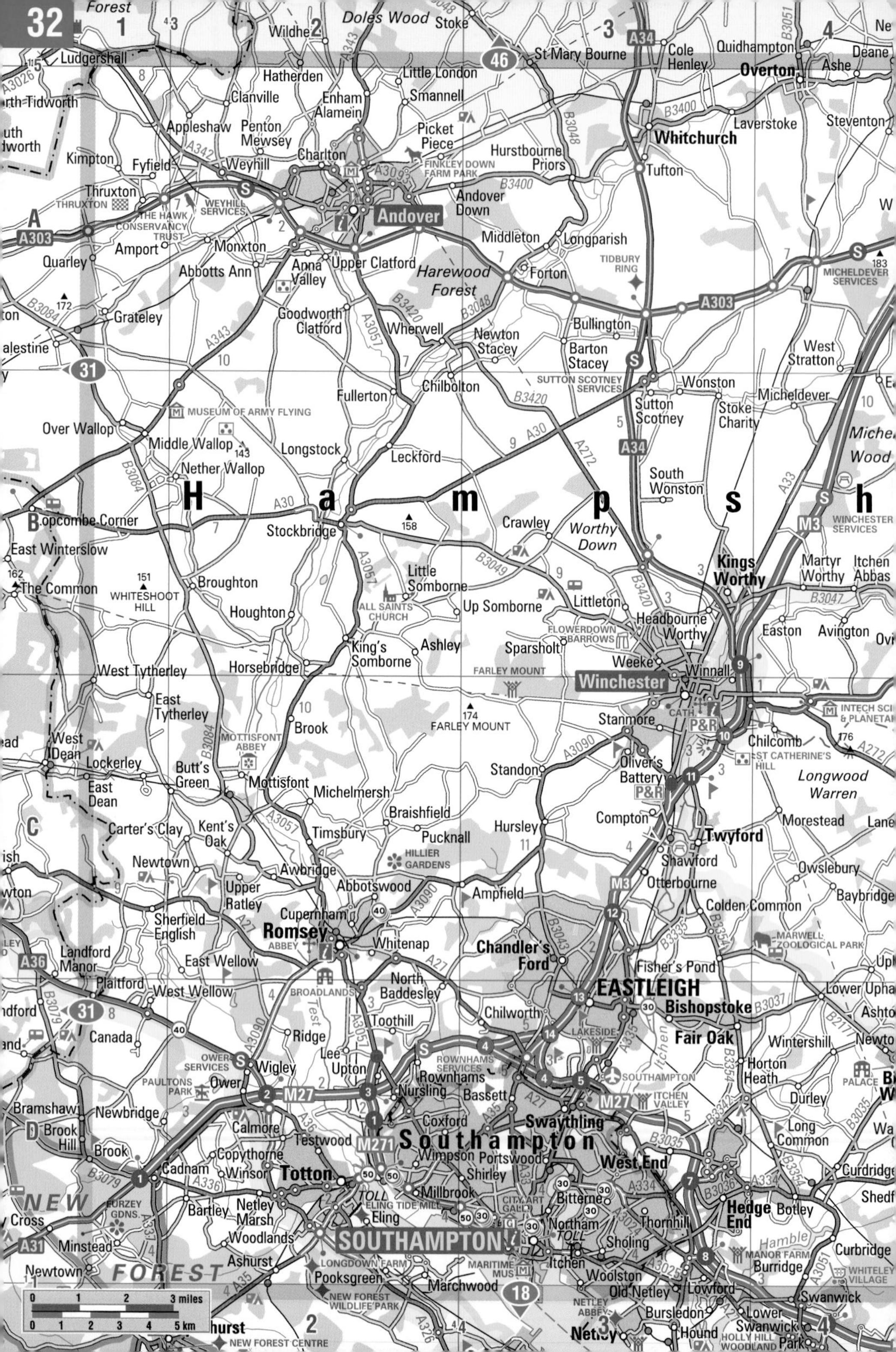
Forest
Doles Wood
Stoke
Ludgershall
Wildhern
St Mary Bourne
Cole Henley
Quidhampton
Overton
Ashe
Deane
Hatherden
Little London
Smannell
Enham Alamein
Clanville
Tidworth
Appleshaw
Penton Mewsey
Picket Piece
Charlton
Kimpton
Fyfield
Weyhill
Finkley Down Farm Park
Hurstbourne Priors
Whitchurch
Laverstoke
Steventon
Tufton
Thruxton
Weyhill Services
The Hawk Conservancy Trust
Andover
Andover Down
Middleton
Longparish
Amport
Monxton
Quarley
Abbotts Ann
Anna Valley
Upper Clatford
Harewood Forest
Forton
Tidbury Ring
Micheldever Services
Grateley
Goodworth Clatford
Wherwell
Newton Stacey
Bullington
Barton Stacey
West Stratton
Palestine
Fullerton
Chilbolton
Sutton Scotney Services
Sutton Scotney
Wonston
Stoke Charity
Micheldever
Museum of Army Flying
Over Wallop
Middle Wallop
Nether Wallop
Longstock
Leckford
Micheldever Wood
South Wonston
H a m p s h
Lopcombe Corner
Stockbridge
Crawley
Worthy Down
Winchester Services
East Winterslow
The Common
Whiteshoot Hill
Broughton
Houghton
Little Somborne
All Saints Church
Up Somborne
Littleton
Kings Worthy
Martyr Worthy
Itchen Abbas
Flowerdown Barrows
Headbourne Worthy
Easton
Avington
West Tytherley
Horsebridge
King's Somborne
Ashley
Sparsholt
Farley Mount
Weeke
Winnall
Winchester
Intech Science Centre & Planetarium
East Tytherley
Brook
Stanmore
Cath.
P&R
Chilcomb
St Catherine's Hill
West Dean
Mottisfont Abbey
Lockerley
Butt's Green
East Dean
Mottisfont
Michelmersh
Standon
Oliver's Battery
Longwood Warren
Carter's Clay
Kent's Oak
Braishfield
Timsbury
Pucknall
Hursley
Compton
Twyford
Morestead
Newtown
Hillier Gardens
Shawford
Owslebury
Awbridge
Upper Ratley
Abbotswood
Ampfield
Otterbourne
Baybridge
Cupernham
Colden Common
Sherfield English
Romsey
Abbey
Whitenap
Chandler's Ford
Fisher's Pond
Marwell Zoological Park
Landford Manor
East Wellow
Plaitford
West Wellow
Broadlands
North Baddesley
Eastleigh
Bishopstoke
Lower Upham
Canada
Toothill
Chilworth
Fair Oak
Wintershill
Ridge
Lakeside
Ower Services
Wigley
Lee
Upton
Rownhams Services
Rownhams
Southampton
Horton Heath
Paultons Park
Ower
Nursling
Bassett
Itchen Valley
Durley
Bramshaw
Newbridge
Coxford
Swaythling
Brook Hill
Calmore
Testwood
Southampton
Long Common
Brook
Copythorne
Wimpson
Portswood
West End
Curdridge
Cadnam
Winsor
Totton
Shirley
New Forest
Furzey Gdns.
Bartley
Netley Marsh
Eling Tide Mill
Millbrook
City Art Gall.
Bitterne
Thornhill
Hedge End
Botley
Cross
Eling
Northam
Minstead
Woodlands
Southampton
Sholing
Curbridge
Newtown
Ashurst
Longdown Farm
Maritime Mus.
Itchen
Manor Farm
Burridge
Forest
Pooksgreen
Woolston
Whiteley Village
Marchwood
Old Netley
Lowford
New Forest Wildlife Park
Netley Abbey
Bursledon
Swanwick
Lower Swanwick
Ashurst
New Forest Centre
Netley
Hound
Holly Hill Woodland Park
Park
0 1 2 3 miles
0 1 2 3 4 5 km

NORTH DOWNS
SOUTH DOWNS NATIONAL PARK
Farnham
Alton
Petersfield
Bordon
Liphook
New Alresford
Horndean
Waterlooville
Wickham
Shirrell Heath
Odiham
Church Crookham
Micheldever Forest
FOREST OF BERE
Meon Valley
Winslade
Herriard
Preston Candover
Four Marks
East Tisted
Selborne
Chawton
Liss
Rowlands Castle
West Meon
East Meon
Clanfield
Hambledon
Droxford
Cheriton
Rogate
Midhurst
Emsworth
Westbourne
Funtington
Waltham
Kingsley
Sleaford
Headley
Grayshott
Whitehill
Greatham
Petersfield
Chalton
Compton
South Harting
Stoughton
Wivelrod
Medstead
Bentworth
Lasham
Froyle
Bentley
Crondall
Long Sutton
Well
Dippenhall

Sandhurst
CAMBERLEY
Yateley
Frogmore
York Town
Yateley Common
Blackwater
Hawley
Frimley
Fox Lane
Farnborough Green
Cove
West Heath
St Michael's Abbey
Fleet
Pondtail
Farnborough Airport
FARNBOROUGH
Church Crookham
ALDERSHOT
Long Valley
Heath End
Hog Hatch
Badshot Lea
Upper Hale
Farnham
Dippenhall
Wrecclesham
The Bourne
Rowledge
Spreakley
Bucks Horn Oak
Frensham
Millbridge
Old Kiln Mus
Tilford
Waverley Abbey
Frensham Common
Rushmoor
Churt
Sleaford
Arford
Lindford
Headley
Bordon
Standford
Hindhead
Grayshott
Beacon Hill
Gibbet Hill
Bramshott
Conford
Shottermill
Hammer
Liphook
Longmoor Camp
Camelsdale
Linchmere
Kingsley Green
Hollycombe Steam Collection
Langley
Forest
Liss
Rake
Milland
Black Down
Fernhurst
Lurgashall
Henley
Lickfold
Borden
Rogate
Chithurst
Iping
Woolbeding
Easebourne
Lodsworth
Dumpford
Trotton
Stedham
Halfway Bridge
Upperton
Petworth Ho
Nyewood
Minsted
Midhurst
South Ambersham
Selham
Tillington
Petworth
Byworth
West Lavington
Heyshott
Trevford
Fittleworth
Coates
Stopham
Pulborough
Nutbourne
Marehill
West Chiltington
Lightwater
West End
Chobham
Woodham
Byfleet
West Byfleet
Brooklands Mus
Donkey Town
Chobham Ridges
Castle Green
Cheapside
Bisley
Knaphill
Horsell
WOKING
Wisley
RHS Garden Wisley
Pyrford
Deepcut
Brookwood
St John's
Old Woking
Ripley
Frimley Green
Mayford
Send Marsh
Ockham
Mytchett
Basingstoke Canal Centre
Pirbright
Send
Burntcommon
Fox Corner
Sutton Green
Worplesdon
East Horsley
West Horsley
Ash Vale
Willey Green
Pitch Place
Slyfield
Burpham
Clandon Park
West Clandon
Hatchlands Park
Stoughton
Wyke
Normandy
Wood Street
Dapdune Wharf
Merrow
East Clandon
Ash
Brickfields
Flexford
Newland's Corner
Wanborough
Tongham
Hogs Back
Onslow Village
Guildford
Gomshall
Albury
Shere
Runfold
Seale
Puttenham
Littleton
Compton
Shalford
Chilworth
The Sands
Loseley Ho
Blackheath
Brook
Sutton
Shackleford
Hurtmore
Wonersh
Farley Green
Norney
Farncombe
Bramley
Peper Harow
Eashing
Shamley Green
Elstead
Godalming
Godalming Mus
Hurt Wood
Milford
Thorncombe Street
Grafham
Tuesley
Winkworth Arboretum
Thursley
Wheelerstreet
Rowly
Ewhurst
Hydestile
Hascombe
Bowlhead Green
Witley
Cranleigh
Wormley
Hambledon
Brook
Sandhills
Oakhurst Cottage
Loxhill
Hindhead
Combe Common
Dunsfold
Chiddingfold
Ellen's Green
Alfold Crossways
Grayswood
Ramster Garden
Alfold
Haslemere
Alfold Bars
Tisman's Common
Bucks
Ramsnest Common
Loxwood
Park St
Fisherstreet
Plaistow
Ifold
The Haven
Northchapel
Mackerel's Common
Roundstreet Common
Ebernoe Common
Newpound Common
Balls Cross
Kirdford
Wisborough Green
Billingshurst
Strood Green
Parbrook
Adversane
Arun
Broadford Bridge
Bedham
North Heath
Codmore Hill
Gay Street
SURREY
SOUTH DOWNS
NORTH DOWNS
SURREY HILLS
0 1 2 3 miles
0 1 2 3 4 5 km

WORLD OF ADVENTURES
Belmont
Purley
Sanderstead
Farleigh
Cobham
Oxshott
EPSOM
ASHTEAD COMMON
Woodmansterne
Hamsey Green
Stoke D'Abernon
Wood Field
BANSTEAD
Kenley
Coulsdon
Warlingham
Downside
Great Burgh
Burgh Heath
Chipstead
Whyteleafe
Leatherhead Common
Ashtead
EPSOM DOWNS
Old Coulsdon
Tatsfield
COBHAM SERVICES
Fetcham
Leatherhead
Tadworth
Kingswood
Hooley
Woldingham
Little Bookham
Walton on the Hill
Chaldon
CATERHAM
Effingham
Great Bookham
BOCKETTS FARM PARK
Headley
Lower Kingswood
WALTON HEATH
Titsey
POLESDEN LACEY
Mickleham
Merstham
Limpsfield
Westhumble
BOX HILL
Brewer Street
Godstone
Oxted
TANNERS HATCH
Church Town
Ranmore Common
Dorking
Buckland
Redhill
Nutfield
Tandridge
Pixham
Betchworth
Bletchingley
GODSTONE FARM
Brockham
Reigate
Earlswood
South Nutfield
NORTH DOWNS WAY
Crowhurst Lane End
Westcott
Strood Green
Doversgreen
Ridge Green
REDHILL
South Godstone
Wotton
Sidlow
Salfords
Crowhurst
North Holmwood
Leigh
Abinger Common
Outwood
Blindley Heath
HAXTED WATERMILL
Nalderswood
South Holmwood
Horne
Meath Green
Lingfield
Holmbury St Mary
Coldharbour
Parkgate
Norwood Hill
Weatherhill
Smallfield
LEITH HILL
Beare Green
Hookwood
Horley
LINGFIELD PARK
Newdigate
GATWICK AIRPORT
Newchapel
Charlwood
Burstow
Felcourt
Forest Green
LONDON GATWICK
Capel
Ockley
Clark's Green
Copthorne
Felbridge
Walliswood
County Oak
Ifield
Three Bridges
East Grinstead
Oakwoodhill
Rusper
Crawley Down
Kingsfold
Lambs Green
Sunnyside
IFIELD WATERMILL
Pound Hill
Worth
Crawley
Turners Hill
Saint Hill
Broadfield
Rowhook
Faygate
Tilgate
Selsfield Common
Warnham
BUCHAN
Pease Pottage
PEASE POTTAGE SERVICES
TILGATE
Balcombe Lane
West Hoathly
Sharpthorne
Strood Green
Broadbridge Heath
Roffey
Colgate
PRIEST HOUSE
Tilgate Forest Row
St Leonard's Forest
THE HIGH BEECHES
WAKEHURST PLACE
Slinfold
Horsham
Balcombe
WINGS MUS
Highbrook
Handcross
NYMANS GARDEN
Ashfold Crossways
Ardingly
Horsted Keynes
Itchingfield
Mannings Heath
Staplefield
Five Oaks
Southwater Street
Monk's Gate
Slaugham
Barns Green
Lower Beeding
Brook Street
BORDE HILL GARDEN
THE BLUEBELL RAILWAY
Nuthurst
Slough Green
Southwater
LEONARDSLEE LAKES & GARDENS
Warninglid
Whitemans Green
HEAVEN FARM
Lindfield
Brooks Green
Copsale
Crabtree
Cuckfield
HAYWARDS HEATH
Coneyhurst
Maplehurst
Ansty
Scayne's Hill
Bolney
Coolham
COOLHAM AIRFIELD D-DAY MEMORIAL
Shipley
Cowfold
West Grinstead
Whitehall
Kent Street
Wivelsfield
Wivelsfield Green
Broomer's Corner
Wineham
Hickstead
North Chailey
Partridge Green
BURGESS HILL
Chailey
Goose Green
Dial Post
JUMPING COURSE
Sayers Common
DITCHLING COMMON
South Street
Spear
M25
M23
A23
A24
A22
A25
A264
A272
A243
A240
A217
A281
A29
B2036
B2028
B2110
B2115
B2114
B2116
B2135
B2139

Leaves Green
Downe
Darwin Museum
Badger's Mount
Halstead
M25
Shoreham
Fairseat
M20
Hamsey Green
Farleigh
Biggin Hill
50
Biggin Hill
Cudham
Knockholt Pound
Otford
Warlingham
Knockholt
Kemsing
Wrotham
Heaverham
South Street
Chevening
M26
Borough Green
Tatsfield
North Downs Way
Dunton Green
Seal
Platt
Woldingham
Chipstead
Riverhead
Ightham
Clacket Lane Services
Great Comp
Crouch
A
Titsey
Brasted
Sundridge
Sevenoaks
Stone Street
Claygate Cross
A22
M25
Westerham
Quebec Ho
Knole
Ivy Hatch
Plaxtol
Limpsfield
Brasted Chart
Cross Keys
Ightham Mote
Old Soar Manor
Squerryes Court
The Chart
Dunk's Green
Limpsfield Chart
Whitley Row
Oxted
Emmetts
Underriver
West Peckham
Church Town
Chartwell
Ide Hill
Shipbourne
Crockham Hill
Toy's Hill
Sevenoaks Weald
Oakhurst
Coldharbour
Tandridge
Broadview Garden
Godstone Farm
35
Pittswood
Pootings
Hadlow
Hildenborough
Higham Wood
Crowhurst Lane End
Marlpit Hill
Four Elms
Hilden Park
South Godstone
Golden Green
Crowhurst
Crouch House Green
Chiddingstone Causeway
Medway
Tonbridge Castle
How Green
Bough Beech
Leigh
Brook Street
TONBRIDGE
Blindley Heath
Haxted Watermill
Edenbridge
Chiddingstone Castle
Five Oak Green
B
Hever
Chiddingstone
Tudeley
Lingfield
Marsh Green
Hever Castle and Gardens
Penshurst Place
Haysden
All Saints Church
Penshurst
Bidborough
Lingfield Park
Markbeech
Newchapel
Dormansland
Chiddingstone Hoath
Southborough
High Brooms
Greathed Manor
Speldhurst
Felcourt
Pembury
Cowden
Mus & Art Gall
Lullenden
Hammerwood
Fordcombe
Rusthall
Felbridge
Blackham
ROYAL TUNBRIDGE WELLS
Blackwell
Ashurst
Langton Green
East Grinstead
Hammerwood Park
Hawkenbury
Lamberhurst Quarter
Crawley Down
Spa Valley Railway
Sunnyside
Ashurstwood
Groombridge
Bells Yew Green
Saint Hill
Standen
Forest Row
Forest Way
Hartfield
Eridge Green
Frant
C
Withyham
Upper Hartfield
Lye Green
West Hoathly
Coleman's Hatch
Wood's Green
Friar's Gate
Boarshead
Sharpthorne
Priest House
Mark Cross
Durgates
Wych Cross
Crowborough
Bestbeech Hill
Highbrook
Chelwood Gate
Ashdown Forest Llama Park
Riseden
ASHDOWN FOREST
Poundfield
Town Row
Tidebrook
Horsted Keynes
Chelwood Common
Jarvis Brook
Rotherfield
E. Sussex
Nutley
Duddleswell
Danehill
Coggins Mill
Mayfield
Cackle Street
Fairwarp
High Hurstwood
Butcher's Cross
Heaven Farm
Lindfield
Sheffield Green
Splayne's Green
Hadlow Down
Five Ashes
Rother
HAYWARDS HEATH
Maresfield
Pound Green
Sheffield Park
Fletching
Bluebell Railway
Scayne's Hill
Buxted
Burwash Weald
Ringles Cross
Cross in Hand
Broad Oak
Grisling Common
Blackboys
Cade Street
Wivelsfield Green
North Chailey
Newick
Uckfield
Framfield
Heathfield
Punnett's Town
Blackboys
Old Heathfield
22
Ridgewood
Little London
Waldron
Maynard's Green
Rushlake Green
Foxhunt
0 1 2 3 miles
0 1 2 3 4 5 km

Snodland
Birling
Ryarsh
Addington
West Malling
Offham
Kent Street
King's Hill
Wateringbury
Nettlestead Green
Nettlestead
Hale Street
Beltring
Paddock Wood
Brenchley
Petteridge
Lamberhurst
Cousley Wood
Bewl Water
Wallcrouch
Stonegate
Witherenden Hill
Etchingham
Burwash
Brightling
Darwell Hole
Dallington
Netherfield
Kit's Coty House
Leybourne Lake
New Hythe
Leybourne
Eccles
The Friars
Aylesford
Ditton
East Malling
Manor Park
British Legion Village
Sandling
Mus of Kent Life
Boxley
Tyland Barn
White Horse Wood
Stockbury
Detling
Thurnham
Maidstone
East Barming
Tovil
Teston
Bearsted
Shepway
Otham
Stoneacre
Roseacre
Newnham Court
East Farleigh
West Farleigh
Loose
Boughton Monchelsea
Langley
Langley Heath
Coxheath
Yalding
Yalding Organic Gdn
Hunton
Linton
Benover
Laddingford
Chainhurst
Whitbread Hop Farm
Queen Street
Collier Street
Claygate
Castle Hill
Horsmonden
Hazel Street
Goudhurst
Finchcocks
Scotney Castle
Kilndown
Bedgebury Pinetum
Bedgebury Forest
Three Leg Cross
Flimwell
Union Street
Ticehurst
Pashley Manor Gardens
Swiftsden
Hurst Green
Northbridge Street
Robertsbridge
Bateman's
Oxley's Green
Mountfield
Salehurst
Rother Valley Rly
Staple Cross
John's Cross
Cripp's Corner
Vinehall Street
Whatlington
Sedlescombe
Chart Corner
Chart Sutton
Boughton Monchelsea Place
Rabbit's Cross
Cross-at-Hand
Milebush
Marden
Marden Beech
Marden Thorn
Farm Mus
Staplehurst
Iden Croft Herbs
Knox Bridge
Winchet Hill
Curtisden Green
Collier's Green
Cranbrook Common
Sissinghurst Castle
Iden Green
Wilsley Pound
Cranbrook Museum
Union Mill
Sissinghurst
Cranbrook
Hartley
Gill's Green
Iden Green
High Street
Hawkhurst
Horns Corner
The Moor
Four Throws
Sandhurst
Linkhill
Sandhurst Cross
Bodiam
Great Dixter
Northiam
Ewhurst Green
Millcorner
Horns Cross
Broad Oak
Brede
Broadland Row
Udimore
Hucking
Broad Street
Bearsted Maidstone Services
Hollingbourne
Eyhorne Street
Leeds
Leeds Castle
Broomfield
Kingswood
Warmlake
Sutton Valence
Ulcombe
Grafty Green
Southernden
Hawkenbury
Headcorn
Sinkhurst Green
Frittenden
Lashenden
Smarden Bell
Three Chimneys
Standen
Biddenden
Biddenden Vineyard
East End
Benenden
Parkgate
Kent & East Sussex Railway
Tenterden
Dingleden
Rolvenden
Colonel Stephens Railway Museum
Rolvenden Layne
Newenden
Rother Levels
Farm World
Beckley
Four Oaks
Clayhill
Peasmarsh
Rye Foreign
Playden
Rye
Rye Harbour
Rye Heritage Centre
Tillingham
Bredgar
South Green
Bredgar & Wormshill Lt Rly
Bicknor
Swanton Street
Wormshill
Frinsted
Tunstall
Milstead
Doddington Place
Doddington
Wichling
West Street
North Downs Way
Harrietsham
Warren Street
Lenham
Sandway
Lenham Heath
Charing Heath
Boughton Malherbe
Egerton
Egerton Forstal
Little Chart
Pluckley
Pluckley Thorne
Maltman's Hill
Smarden
Haffenden Quarter
Wissenden
Bethersden
Tanden
High Halden
St Michael's
Woodchurch
Leigh Green
Brook Street
Reading Street
Small Hythe
Smallhythe Place
Appledore Heath
Isle of Oxney
Appledore
Stone
Peening Quarter
Wittersham
Ham Green
The Stocks
Iden
Houghton Green
East Guldeford
Headcorn
Kent
Downs
TQ

KENT DOWNS
Molash
Petham
Kingston
Upper Hardres Court
Lenham Heath
A252
Challock
NORTH DOWNS WAY
52
Godmersham
Charing
Charing Heath
M20
Bilting
Sole Street
Bossingham
Derringstone
Westwell Leacon
Boughton Aluph
A28
Crundale
Waltham
Westwell
A251
ELHAM VALLEY VINEYARD
Boughton Lees
Hassell Street
Stelling Minnis
Little Chart
Ram Lane
Goat Lees
Wye
WYE CROWN
Bodsham
Lyminge Forest
Pluckley
Hothfield
A20
WYE
Elmsted
Pluckley Thorne
Kennington
Brook
Hastingleigh
Elham
GODINTON HOUSE
A2070
Lymbridge Green
Maltman's Hill
Great Chart
Ashford
Hinxhill
Brabourne
B2068
Rhodes Minnis
Ottinge
ASHFORD
Willesborough Lees
Wissenden
Willesborough
Sevington
Stowting
KENT BATTLE OF BRITAIN MUSE
Brabourne Lees
Lyminge
Bethersden
37
A28
Stubbs Cross
Kingsnorth
Mersham
Smeeth
Postling
Etchinghill
Paddlesw
STOP 24 SERVICES
CHANNEL TUNNEL
Tanden
Shadoxhurst
Cheeseman's Green
Sellindge
Sellindge Lees
Beachborough
Stanford
Newington
E. Stour
High Halden
Bromley Green
Aldington Frith
Clap Hill
M20
11A
12
Henghurst
Aldington
Newingreen
Bonnington
Pedlinge
ELHAM VALLEY RLY MUS
Cheriton
Shirkoak
Court-at-Street
Lympne
A261
Saltwood
Orlestone
HAM STREET WOODS
PORT LYMPNE WILD ANIMAL PARK AND GARDENS
Woodchurch
SOUTH OF ENGLAND RARE BREEDS CEN
Ruckinge
B2067
Bilsington
Military Canal
BROCKHILL
Hythe
West Hythe
Brook Street
Kenardington
Hamstreet
Palmarsh
Warehorne
Royal
Burmarsh
B2080
Newchurch
A259
Reading Street
Appledore Heath
A2070
ROMNEY, HYTHE AND DYMCHURCH RAILWAY
HORNE'S PLACE CHAPEL
Snave
SMALLHYTHE PLACE
ISLE OF OXNEY
Appledore
ROMNEY MARSH
Dymchurch
MARTELLO TOWER
St Mary in the Marsh
Stone
Snargate
Brenzett
Ivychurch
The Stocks
AERONAUTICAL MUSEUM
ROMNEY WARREN
St Mary's Bay
Ham Green
B2082
TQ
Brookland
A259
Old Romney
Littlestone on Sea
Iden
Houghton Green
A259
New Romney
Romney Sands
Walland Marsh
B2075
Greatstone on Sea
Playden
East Guldeford
Lydd
LYDD (LONDON ASHFORD)
Rye
Lydd on Sea
Denge Marsh
RYE HERITAGE CENTRE
Camber
LYDD INTERNATIONAL RACEWAY
Rye Harbour
DUNGENESS
Denge Beach
CAMBER CASTLE
Rye Bay
DUNGENESS POWER STATION & INFORMATION CENTRE
DUNGENESS
THE OLD LIGHTHOUSE
Winchelsea Beach
37
End
Cove
0 1 2 3 miles
0 1 2 3 4 5 km

Nonington
Snowdown
Tilmanstone
Elvington
Northbourne
Great Mongeham
53
Deal Castle
Walmer
Walmer Castle and Gardens
The Downs
Womenswold
Barfrestone
East Kent Rly
Woolage Green
Eythorne
East Studdal
Sutton
Ripple
Ringwould
Kingsdown
A2
Coxhill
Shepherdswell
West Langdon
A256
East Langdon
Martin
Martin Mill
A258
Denton
Lydden
Wootton
Coldred
Whitfield
Guston
St Margaret's at Cliffe
A260
Selsted
Lydden Temple Ewell
St John's Commandery
Temple Ewell
The Bay Museum
St Margaret's Bay
West Cliffe
The Pines Garden
Swingfield Street
Ewell Minnis
Crabble Corn Mill
Buckland
Swingfield Minnis
Alkham
Roman Painted House
White Cliffs
South Foreland
Calais 1:30
Dunkerque 2:00
Densole
Drellingore
Maxton
Castle & Hellfire Corner
Farthingloe
West Hougham
Hawkinge
Dover
Aycliff
De Bradelei Wharf
A20
B2011
Capel le Ferne
Samphire Hoe
East Cliff & Warren
East Wear Bay
Folkestone
Rotunda
Cliff Lift
Sandgate
Channel Tunnel
English Channel
TR
A
B
C
D
4
5
6
4
5
6

Climaen gwyn
Ynys-meudwy
Rhyd-y-fro
Pontardawe
Glantawe Riverside Park
Rhyd-y-gwin
Craig-cefn-parc
Trebanos
Rhyd-y-pandy
Faerdre
Alltwen
Gellinudd
Rhôs
Cilybebyll
Mynydd March-Hywel
Crynant
Morfa Glas
Rheola Forest
Sarn Helen
Vale of Neath
Cwm Nedd
Blaengwrach
Cwmgwrach
Rhigos
Cwm-hwnt
Cefn Coed Colliery Mus
383
Resolven Mtn.
Resolven
Neath
Melincourt
Clydach
Ynystawe
Pant-lasau
Glais
Cilfrew
Aberdulais
Falls
Clyne
Blaenrhondda
Port Talbot
Tynewydd
Bryn-coch
Heol-las
Rhydding
Birchgrove
Neath Abbey
Tonna
Cadoxton-Juxta-Neath
Neath Museum
Glyncorrwg
Morriston
Skewen
Llansamlet
Pentre-dwr
(Castell-Nedd
Port Talbot)
Treherbert
Blaen-gwynfi
Aber-gwynfi
Cwm-parc
Neath
(Castell-Nedd)
Cimla
Duffryn
Visitor Centre
Cymer
Croeserw
Cwm
Bon-y-maen
Llandarcy
Swansea
(Abertawe)
Foxhole
Crymlyn Bog and Pant-y-sais
Plantasia
Port Tennant
Briton Ferry
Gnoll
Pontrhydyfen
South Wales Miners Museum
Caerau
568
Werfa
Foel y Dyffryn
366
Dyffryn
Spelter
Afan Forest Park
Nant-y-moel
Baglan
Pwll-y-glaw
Brynbryddan
Bryn
Blaengarw
Swansea Museum
National Waterfront Museum
Mynydd Dinas
528
Cwmafan
Nantyffyllon
Wyndham
Price Town
Pontycymer
Maesteg
Garth
Cwmfelin
Aberavon
Swansea Bay
Port Talbot
Goybre
Ogmore Vale
Llangynwyd
Pont Rhyd-y-cyff
Taibach
344
Mynydd Margam
Bridgend
Lewistown
Pant-yr-awel
Bae Abertawe
Margam
Groes
319
Moel Ton-Mawr
Bettws
Llangeinor
Margam
Margam Abbey and Stones Museum
(Pen-y-bont ar Ogwr)
C
Coytrahen
Bryngarw
Brynmenyn
Tondu
Bryncethin
Bedford
Kenfig Hill
Cefn Cross
Aberkenfig
Sarn
Sarn Park Services
Bridgend
Kenfig
Mawdlam
Kenfig Pool and Dunes
Kenfig Burrows
North Cornelly
Pyle
(Y Pîl)
Cefn Cribbwr
Pen-y-fai
Pendre
Coity
Coity Castle
Bridgend
(Pen-y-bont ar Ogwr)
South Cornelly
Newcastle
Laleston
Coychurch
Royal Porthcawl
Tythegston
Treoes
Nottage
Newton
Merthyr Mawr
Corntown
Hutchwns
Clevis
Ogmore Castle
Ewenny
Porthcawl
Merthyr Mawr Warren
Ogmore
Coney Beach
Ogmore-by-Sea
St Brides Major
Colwinston
D
SS
Tusker Rock
Penuchadre
Southerndown
Glenmorgan Heritage Coast Centre
Wales Coast Path
Wick
Broughton
17
Monknash
Marcross
Nash Pt.
Trwyn yr As
St Donat's
E
0 1 2 3 miles
0 1 2 3 4 5 km
A
B
1
2
3
4
28

Hirwaun
A465
Gellideg
Pen-yr-Heolgerrig
Merthyr Tydfil
(Merthyr Tudful)
Pontlottyn
Abertysswg
Waunlwyd
East
Cwmtillery
Abertillery
(Abertyleri)
Tre-Gibbon
YNYSFACH ENGINE HOUSE HERITAGE CENTRE
Fochriw
60
New Tredegar
(Tredegar Newydd)
FESTIVAL PARK
Cwm
Penywaun
Trecynon
Llwydcoed
Pentrebach
448
PARC CWM DARREN
Tirphil
Man-moel
Talywain
Cwmdare
ABERDARE
(ABERDÂR)
Abercanaid
Troedyrhiw
Aber-nant
491
Hollybush
Aberbeeg
DARE VALLEY
Cwmbach
Deri
St Illtyd
Bedlinog
Cwmfelin
P&R
Markham
PEN-Y-FAN POND
Brynithel
Cwm
Rhondda
Aberaman
Aberfan
ABERBARGOED GRASSLANDS
Trinant
Llanhilleth
(Llanhiledd)
Cwmaman
MOUNTAIN ASH
(ABERPENNAR)
Merthyr Vale
Bargoed
(Bargod)
Argoed
61
Cynon
A4059
A470
TAF BARGOED
Gilfach
Pengam
Oakdale
Crumlin
(Crymlyn)
Maerdy
Treorchy
(Treorci)
Ferndale
Penrhiwceiber
Treharris
Trelewis
Gelligaer
Blackwood
(Coed Duon)
Newbridge
Pentre
A4233
St Gwynno Forest
LLANCAIACH FAWR MANOR
Nelson
Pontllanfraith
RHONDDA
Taff
Ynysboeth
Lanfach
Ton-Pentre
Ystrad
Tylorstown
Abercynon
331
Hengoed
Ebbw Vale
Abercarn
Gelli
Pont-y-gwaith
Wattstown
A472
Maesycwmmer
Wyllie
Cwmcarn
Llwynypia
327
Ynysybwl
B4273
A4054
Ystrad-mynach
Rhymney Valley
FOREST
Clydach Vale
Trealaw
Ynyshir
Ynysddu
Cwm felin fach
Pontywaun
CLYDACH VALE
RHONDDA HERITAGE PARK
385
Crosskeys
Tonypandy
Porth
Glyncoch
Cilfynydd
B4251
Risca
(Rhisga)
Penygraig
A4058
Trehafod
Caerphilly
Sirhowy Valley
SIRHOWY VALLEY
Trebanog
PONTYPRIDD
325
Senghenydd
Abertridwr
Llanbradach
345
Evanstown
(Rhondda
Glyntaff
Bedwas
Machen
Gilfach Goch
Bryn Golau
Treforest
A468
Lower Machen
Hendreforgan
Tonyrefail
Pen-y-coedcae
Rhydyfelin
(Caerffili)
Penyrheol
B4600
Glynogwr
Cynon Taf)
Trecenydd
CAERPHILLY
(CAERFFILI)
Rudry
A4093
Hawthorn
Rhiwderin
Castellau
Upper Church Village
Llantwit Fardre
Nantgarw
303
MYNYDD MAENDY
Coedely
A4119
Beddau
Church Village
274
Thornhill
Michaelston-y-Fedw
MODEL HOUSE CENTRE
A473
Efail Isaf
CARDIFF GATE SERVICES
PARC CEFN ONN
Brynna
B4595
A470
Llanharan
Talbot Green
Llantrisant
Taff's Well
CASTELL COCH
Lisvane
A48(M)
Tongwynlais
29
Llanedeyrn
Bryncae
Dolau
Cross Inn
Llanishen
Pontyclun
Creigiau
Pentyrch
32
Rhiwbina
B4562
Llanilid
29A
Cyncoed
Brynsadler
FOREST FARM
Whitchurch
St Mellons
Llanharry
M4
Miskin
Groes-faen
Capel Llanilltern
Radyr
Llanrumney
35
Talygarn
34
33
Cardiff
Rumney
LLANERCH VINEYARD
CARDIFF WEST SERVICES
Birchgrove
Heath
Craig Penllyn
Vale
A4222
St Brides super Ely
A4232
NATIONAL HISTORY MUSEUM
(Caerdydd)
Llandaff
Cathays
Roath
Newton
Ely (Elai)
St Fagans
Canton
CARDIFF
Llansannor
Ystradowen
Peterston super-Ely
St George's
Ely
MILLENNIUM STADIUM
NAT MUS OF WALES
Maendy
Welsh St Donats
Pendoylan
Michaelston-super-Ely
A4232
CARDIFF
Penllyn
Aberthin
Caerau
Butetown
Cowbridge
(Y Bont-Faen)
of
A48
St Nicholas
Leckwith
Grangetown
(CAERDYDD)
Llanblethian
137
St Hilary
Bonvilston
Michaelston-le-Pit
CARDIFF BAY VISITOR CENTRE
TECHNIQUEST
42
Llandough
Glamorgan
Llantrithyd
A4226
St Lythans
Wallston
Wenvoe
Llandough
Cogan
CARDIFF BAY BARRAGE
Llanmihangel
St Mary Church
OLD BEAUPRE CASTLE
DYFFRYN GARDENS
St Andrews Major
TURNER HOUSE GALLERY
Sigingstone
(Bro
Walterston
Dinas Powys
PENARTH
Flemingston
Moulton
A4050
A4231
Cadoxton
Llanmaes
Eglwys-Brewis
Llanbethêry
Llancarfan
Colcot
Merthyr Dyfan
COSMESTON LAKES
Lower Penarth
Morgannwg)
WELSH HAWKING CENTRE
Penmark
A4055
MEDIEVAL VILLAGE
Sully
Lavernock Pt.
Trwyn Larnog
Llantwit Major
(Llanilltud Fawr)
Boverton
St Athan
A4226
B4267
CARDIFF (MAES AWYR CAERDYDD-CYMRU)
PORTHKERRY
BARRY
(Y BARRI)
Sully Island
Ynys Sili
Gileston
East Aberthaw
Rhoose
(Y Rhws)
Porthkerry
Barry Island
BARRY ISLAND PLEASURE PARK
Breaksea Pt.
Trwyn Breaksea
Flat Holm
A
B
C
D
E
4
5
6
7

42
Risca
(Rhisga)
Machen
Lower Machen
Rogerstone
Rudry
Rhiwderin
Pentre-poeth
Bassaleg
Michaelston-y-Fedw
Castleton
Coedkernew
Marshfield
Blacktown
St Brides Wentlooge
Peterstone Wentlooge
Lisvane
Llanedeyrn
St Mellons
Llanrumney
Rumney
Newton
CARDIFF
(CAERDYDD)
CARDIFF BAY VISITOR CENTRE
CARDIFF BAY BARRAGE
TURNER HOUSE GALLERY
PENARTH
Lavernock Pt.
Flat Holm
Steep Holm
Brean Down
Malpas
Bettws
Caerleon
Christchurch
Maindee
Newport
(Casnewydd)
Liswerry
Duffryn
TREDEGAR HOUSE
FOURTEEN LOCKS
WALES NATIONAL VELODROME
Newport
(Casnewydd)
Pye Corner
Nash
Goldcliff
Whitson
NEWPORT WETLANDS
Usk (Wysg)
Cat's Ash
Llanbeder
Penhow
PENHOW WOODLANDS
Langstone
Llanmartin
Llanwern
Wilcrick
Bishton
Llandevenny
Magor
MAGOR SERVICES
St Bride's Netherwent
Caerwent
Crick
Highmoor Hill
Llanfihangel-Rogiet
Rogiet
Caldicot
Undy
Summerleaze
Redwick
Caldicot Level
WALES COAST PATH
TOLL
M4
M48
M5
ABER HAFREN
MOUTH OF THE SEVERN
ST
Battery Pt.
Portishead
West Hill
Redcliff Bay
Sheepway
Weston-in-Gordano
Clapton-in-Gordano
Walton-in-Gordano
GORDANO VALLEY
Clevedon
CLEVEDON COURT
Stone-edge Batch
Tickenham
Nailsea
West End
East End
Farleigh
North Somerset
Kenn
Kingston Seymour
North End
Claverham
Yatton
Chelvey
Brockley
West Town
Cleeve
Sand Pt.
Sand Bay
Wick St Lawrence
Bourton
Hewish
Puxton
Congresbury
Wrington
Kewstoke
Worle
Milton
Weston-super-Mare
NORTH SOMERSET MUSEUM
Weston Bay
SEAQUARIUM
HELICOPTER MUS
West Wick
Locking
Hutton
Uphill
Banwell
COURT FARM
Brinsea
Lower Langford
Churchill
Sandford
Burrington
Star
Shipham
BLEADON HILL
Christon
Bleadon
Winscombe
Sidcot
Brean
Compton Bishop
Loxton
Cross
Charterhouse
KING JOHN'S HUNTING LODGE
BERROW FLATS
BREAN LEISURE PARK
Lympsham
Eastertown
Lower Weare
Axbridge
Cheddar Res.
Cheddar
CHEDDAR CAVE & GORGE
Biddisham
Weare
SEDGEMOOR SERVICES
Gore Sands
East Brent
Rooks Bridge
Badgworth
Clewer
Berrow
Brent Knoll
Stone Allerton
Chapel Allerton
ASHTON WINDMILL
Draycott
Rodney Stoke
Burnham-on-Sea
Edithmead
West Stoughton
Cocklake
Mark Causeway
Mark
Blackford
Wedmore
0 1 2 3 miles
0 1 2 3 4 5 km

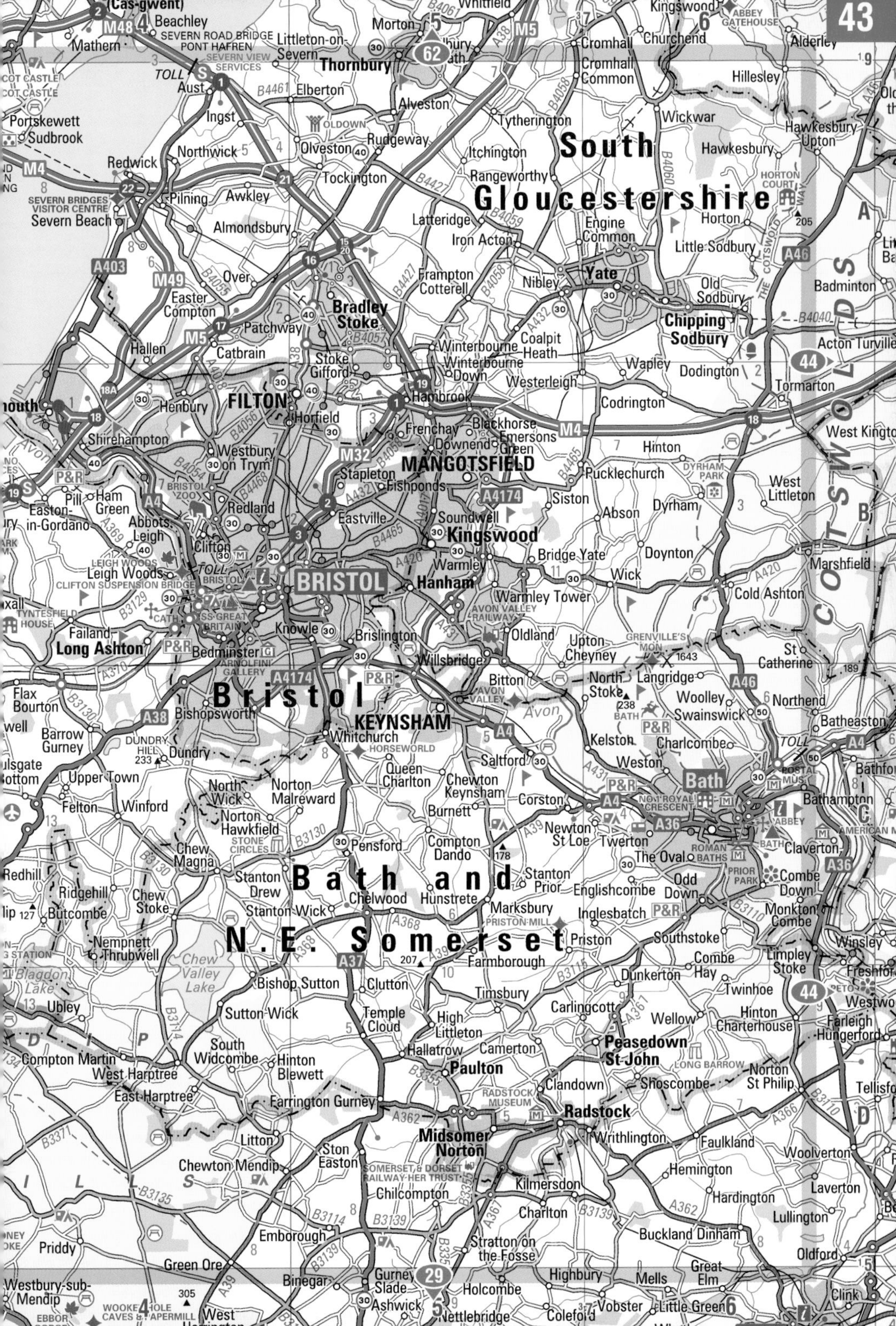

(Cas-gwent)
Beachley
Mathern
SEVERN ROAD BRIDGE
PONT HAFREN
SEVERN VIEW
SERVICES
TOLL
Aust
Littleton-on-Severn
Thornbury
Morton
Whitfield
Kingswood
ABBEY
GATEHOUSE
Cromhall
Churchend
Alderley
Cromhall Common
Hillesley
Elberton
Alveston
Ingst
Portskewett
Sudbrook
OLDOWN
Tytherington
Wickwar
Hawkesbury Upton
Hawkesbury
Olveston
Rudgeway
Itchington
South
Gloucestershire
Northwick
Redwick
Tockington
Rangeworthy
HORTON COURT
SEVERN BRIDGES
VISITOR CENTRE
Severn Beach
Pilning
Awkley
Almondsbury
Latteridge
Iron Acton
Engine Common
Horton
Little Sodbury
Over
Frampton Cotterell
Nibley
Yate
Old Sodbury
Badminton
Easter Compton
Bradley Stoke
Patchway
Chipping Sodbury
Hallen
Catbrain
Stoke Gifford
Winterbourne
Coalpit Heath
Winterbourne Down
Westerleigh
Wapley
Dodington
Acton Turville
Tormarton
Henbury
FILTON
Horfield
Hambrook
Codrington
Shirehampton
Frenchay
Blackhorse
Downend
Emersons Green
Hinton
West Kington
Westbury on Trym
MANGOTSFIELD
Pucklechurch
DYRHAM PARK
Stapleton
Fishponds
West Littleton
BRISTOL ZOO
Ham Green
Pill
Easton-in-Gordano
Redland
Siston
Abson
Dyrham
Abbots Leigh
Eastville
Soundwell
Kingswood
Clifton
Bridge Yate
Doynton
LEIGH WOODS
Leigh Woods
CLIFTON SUSPENSION BRIDGE
BRISTOL
Warmley
Hanham
Wick
Marshfield
Cold Ashton
TYNTESFIELD HOUSE
Warmley Tower
AVON VALLEY RAILWAY
SS GREAT BRITAIN
Failand
Long Ashton
Bedminster
Knowle
Brislington
Oldland
Upton Cheyney
GRENVILLE'S MON
1643
St Catherine
ARNOLFINI GALLERY
Willsbridge
Bitton
North Stoke
Langridge
Flax Bourton
Bristol
AVON VALLEY
Woolley
Northend
Swainswick
Bishopsworth
KEYNSHAM
BATH
Batheaston
Barrow Gurney
DUNDRY HILL
233
Dundry
Whitchurch
HORSEWORLD
Kelston
Charlcombe
Bathford
Upper Town
Queen Charlton
Chewton Keynsham
Saltford
Weston
POSTAL MUS.
Bath
North Wick
Norton Malreward
Corston
NO. 1 ROYAL CRESCENT
Bathampton
Felton
Winford
Norton Hawkfield
Burnett
Newton St Loe
Twerton
ABBEY
AMERICAN M
STONE CIRCLES
Chew Magna
Pensford
Compton Dando
178
ROMAN BATHS
Claverton
Redhill
Stanton Drew
Bath and
N.E. Somerset
Stanton Prior
The Oval
Englishcombe
Odd Down
PRIOR PARK
Combe Down
Ridgehill
Chew Stoke
Butcombe
127
Chelwood
Hunstrete
Stanton Wick
Marksbury
PRISTON MILL
Inglesbatch
Monkton Combe
Nempnett Thrubwell
Priston
Southstoke
Winsley
Chew Valley Lake
Blagdon Lake
207
Farmborough
Combe Hay
Limpley Stoke
Freshford
Bishop Sutton
Clutton
Dunkerton
Twinhoe
Timsbury
Ubley
Sutton Wick
Temple Cloud
Carlingcott
Wellow
High Littleton
Hinton Charterhouse
Farleigh Hungerford
Westwood
Compton Martin
South Widcombe
Hinton Blewett
Hallatrow
Camerton
Peasedown St John
West Harptree
Paulton
LONG BARROW
Norton St Philip
East Harptree
RADSTOCK MUSEUM
Clandown
Shoscombe
Tellisford
Farrington Gurney
Radstock
Litton
Midsomer Norton
Writhlington
Faulkland
Woolverton
Ston Easton
Chewton Mendip
SOMERSET & DORSET RAILWAY HER TRUST
Hemington
Kilmersdon
Chilcompton
Hardington
Laverton
Charlton
Lullington
Emborough
Buckland Dinham
Priddy
Stratton on the Fosse
Oldford
Green Ore
Great Elm
Binegar
Gurney Slade
Highbury
Mells
Westbury-sub-Mendip
305
WOOKEY HOLE
CAVES & PAPERMILL
EBBOR GORGE
Ashwick
Holcombe
Vobster
Coleford
Little Green
Clink
West Horrington
Nettlebridge
Whatley
COTSWOLDS
THE COTSWOLD WAY
Avon
M4
M5
M32
M48
M49
A4
A38
A36
A37
A46
A403
A4174
B4040
189
205
238

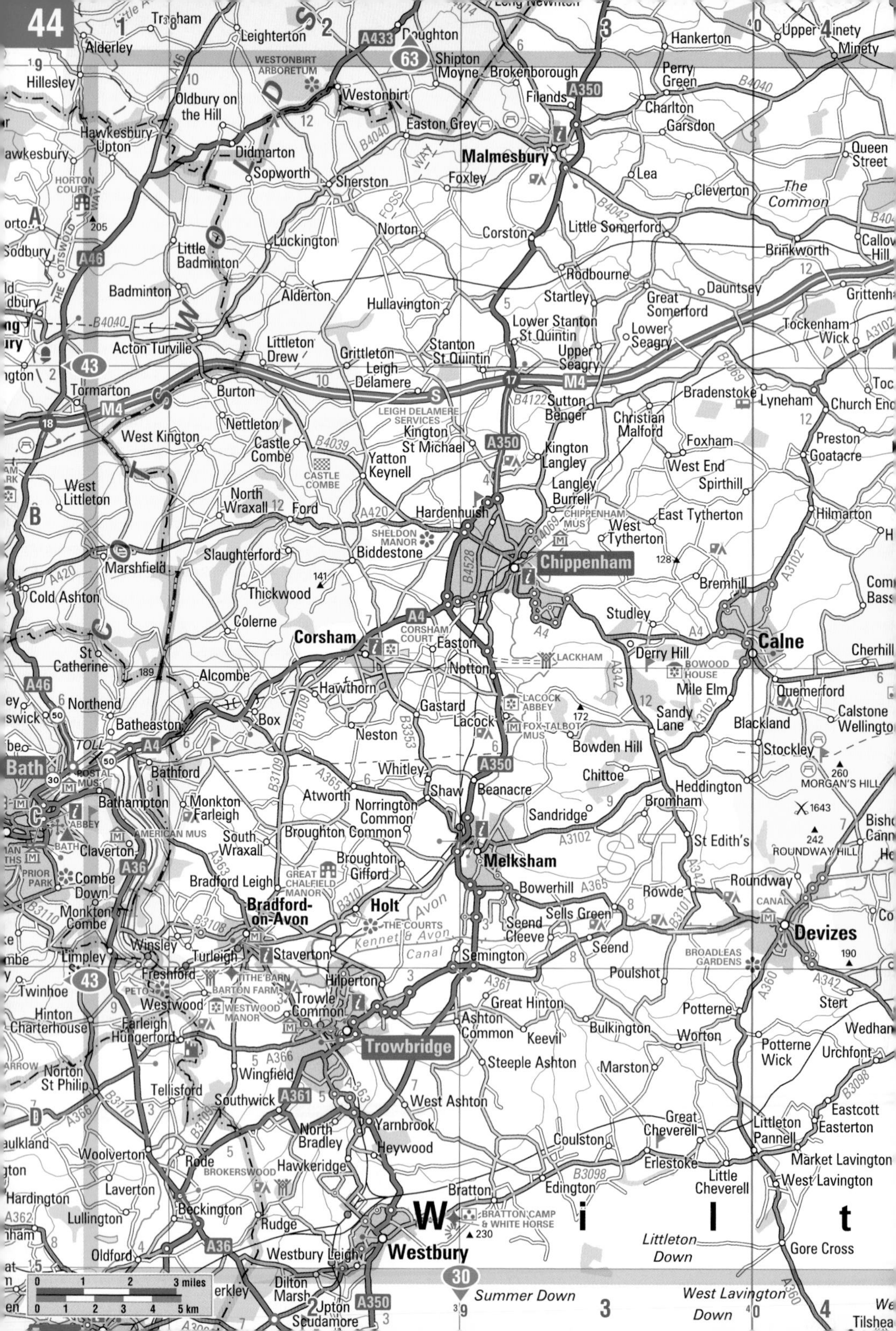
Alderley
Tresham
Leighterton
Doughton
Long Newnton
Hankerton
Upper Minety
Minety
Hillesley
Westonbirt Arboretum
Shipton Moyne
Brokenborough
Perry Green
Oldbury on the Hill
Westonbirt
Filands
Charlton
Hawkesbury Upton
Hawkesbury
Easton Grey
Garsdon
Didmarton
Malmesbury
Queen Street
Sopworth
Sherston
Foxley
Lea
Horton Court
Cleverton
The Common
Luckington
Norton
Corston
Little Somerford
Sodbury
Little Badminton
Brinkworth
Callow Hill
Rodbourne
Badminton
Alderton
Dauntsey
Hullavington
Startley
Great Somerford
Grittenham
Lower Stanton St Quintin
Lower Seagry
Tockenham Wick
Acton Turville
Littleton Drew
Grittleton
Stanton St Quintin
Upper Seagry
Leigh Delamere
Tormarton
Burton
Sutton Benger
Bradenstoke
Lyneham
Church End
Leigh Delamere Services
Nettleton
Kington St Michael
Christian Malford
West Kington
Castle Combe
Yatton Keynell
Kington Langley
Foxham
Preston
Goatacre
West End
Langley Burrell
Spirthill
West Littleton
North Wraxall
Ford
Hardenhuish
East Tytherton
Hilmarton
Chippenham Mus
West Tytherton
Sheldon Manor
Marshfield
Slaughterford
Biddestone
Chippenham
Bremhill
Cold Ashton
Thickwood
Studley
Colerne
Corsham
Corsham Court
Easton
Calne
St Catherine
Derry Hill
Cherhill
Notton
Lackham
Alcombe
Bowood House
Hawthorn
Mile Elm
Northend
Gastard
Lacock Abbey
Quemerford
Batheaston
Box
Lacock
Sandy Lane
Blackland
Calstone Wellington
Neston
Fox Talbot Mus
Bowden Hill
Stockley
Bath
Postal Mus
Bathford
Whitley
Chittoe
Heddington
Morgan's Hill
Bathampton
Atworth
Shaw
Beanacre
Monkton Farleigh
Norrington Common
Sandridge
Bromham
Abbey
American Mus
Broughton Common
Bishops Cannings
South Wraxall
St Edith's
Roundway Hill
Claverton
Melksham
Broughton Gifford
Prior Park
Combe Down
Great Chalfield Manor
Bradford Leigh
Bowerhill
Rowde
Roundway
Monkton Combe
Bradford-on-Avon
Holt
Sells Green
The Courts
Seend Cleeve
Devizes
Kennet & Avon Canal
Winsley
Seend
Limpley Stoke
Turleigh
Staverton
Semington
Broadleas Gardens
Freshford
Tithe Barn
Barton Farm
Poulshot
Twinhoe
Hilperton
Trowle Common
Westwood
Westwood Manor
Great Hinton
Stert
Hinton Charterhouse
Potterne
Farleigh Hungerford
Ashton Common
Keevil
Bulkington
Wedhampton
Worton
Trowbridge
Potterne Wick
Urchfont
Steeple Ashton
Norton St Philip
Wingfield
Marston
Tellisford
Southwick
West Ashton
Eastcott
Great Cheverell
Littleton Pannell
Easterton
Yarnbrook
North Bradley
Woolverton
Heywood
Coulston
Market Lavington
Rode
Hawkeridge
Erlestoke
Brokerswood
Little Cheverell
West Lavington
Laverton
Bratton
Edington
Hardington
Lullington
Beckington
Bratton Camp & White Horse
Rudge
Wilt
Littleton Down
Oldford
Westbury Leigh
Westbury
Gore Cross
Dilton Marsh
Berkley
Summer Down
West Lavington Down
Upton Scudamore
Tilshead
0 1 2 3 miles
0 1 2 3 4 5 km

Chelworth Green
Broad Blunsdon
Purton Stoke
SWINDON AND CRICKLADE RAILWAY
Blunsdon St Andrew
Stanton Fitzwarren
STANTON PARK
Watchfield
Longcot
Baulking
Shrivenham
Uffington
VALE OF WHITE HORSE
South Marston
West Challow
Purton
Widham
Haydon Wick
Penhill
Upper Stratton
Woolstone
Kingston Lisle
Sparsholt
Dogridge
Stratton St Margaret
Compton Beauchamp
Bourton
Lydiard Green
Lydiard Millicent
Pinehurst
Gorse Hill
Rodbourne Cheney
UFFINGTON CASTLE
WHITEHORSE HILL
WAYLAND'S SMITHY
Letcombe
LYDIARD PARK
STEAM
Ashbury
Hook
Rodbourne
Walcot
Kingston Warren
Idstone
Hinton Parva
Swindon
Bishopstone
The Marsh
SWINDON
Royal Wootton Bassett
Coate
COATE WATER
Wanborough
ASHDOWN HOUSE
LAMBOURN DOWNS
North Wroughton
Liddington
Wroughton
Upper Lambourn
Elcombe
Badbury
Chiseldon
Broadtown Lane
Lambourn
Broad Town
Baydon
Uffcott
Upper Upham
BARBURY CASTLE
CLYFFE PYPARD
Clyffe Pypard
Broad Hinton
Eastbury
Woodsend
Aldbourne
MEMBURY SERVICES
Clevancy
MARLBOROUGH DOWNS
Winterbourne Bassett
HACKPEN HILL
Southend
Ogbourne St George
Preston
Berwick Bassett
Ogbourne St Andrew
Whittonditch
WINDMILL HILL
Winterbourne Monkton
Ramsbury
Rockley
Yatesbury
THE RIDGEWAY
Ogbourne Maizey
FYFIELD DOWN
AVEBURY MANOR
Avebury
Chilton Foliat
Mildenhall
Axford
STONE CIRCLE
W KENNETT AVENUE
Fyfield
Marlborough
Kennet
Hungerford
SILBURY HILL
Beckhampton
Manton
Froxfield
West Kennett
West Overton
Lockeridge
LONG BARROW
East Kennett
THE SANCTUARY
Savernake Forest
CHISBURY CHAPEL
Chisbury
Cadley
Clench Common
Little Bedwyn
TAN HILL
Bagshot
Great Bedwyn
MILK HILL
Durley
PEWSEY DOWNS
Huish
Allington
Wootton Rivers
Shalbourne
Stanton St Bernard
West Stowell
Oare
Crofton
Ham
All Cannings
Stibb Green
CROFTON BEAM ENGINES
Alton Priors
New Mill
Eastcourt
WILTON WINDMILL
Honey Street
Wilton
Rivar
Wilcot
Burbage
Pewsey
Easton Royal
West Grafton
East Grafton
Marten
Woodborough
Milton Lilbourne
Beechingstoke
Bottlesford
Southcott
Wexcombe
Oxenwood
Manningford Bruce
Patney
HENGE
Hilcott
Tidcombe
Linkenholt
Chirton
Marden
North Newnton
Manningford Bohune
Fosbury
Vernham Street
Wilsford
Pewsey Down
HAYDOWN HILL
Vernham Dean
Charlton
Brunton
Aughton
Rushall
Upavon
Collingbourne Kingston
Lower Everleigh
Upper Chute
Chute Standen
Sunton
Cadley
Everleigh
West Chisenbury
East Chisenbury
Collingbourne Ducis
Lower Chute
Tangley
Compton
Collingbourne Forest
Black Heath
Compton Down
Enford
Fifield
Haxton Down
Wildhern
Coombe
Ludgershall
Hatherden
Enford Down
Fittleton
Tidworth
North Tidworth
Clanville
Orcheston
Netheravon
DOVECOTE
Penton
Appleshaw
VALE OF PEWSEY
NORTH WESSEX DOWNS
Swindon
Wiltshire
M4
A419
A346
A4
A338
A342
A345
A361
A420
A4361
A3102
A4259
A3026
B4000
B4001
B4005
B4006
B4019
B4040
B4192
B4507
B4508
B4553
B4587
B4534
B4696
B3087

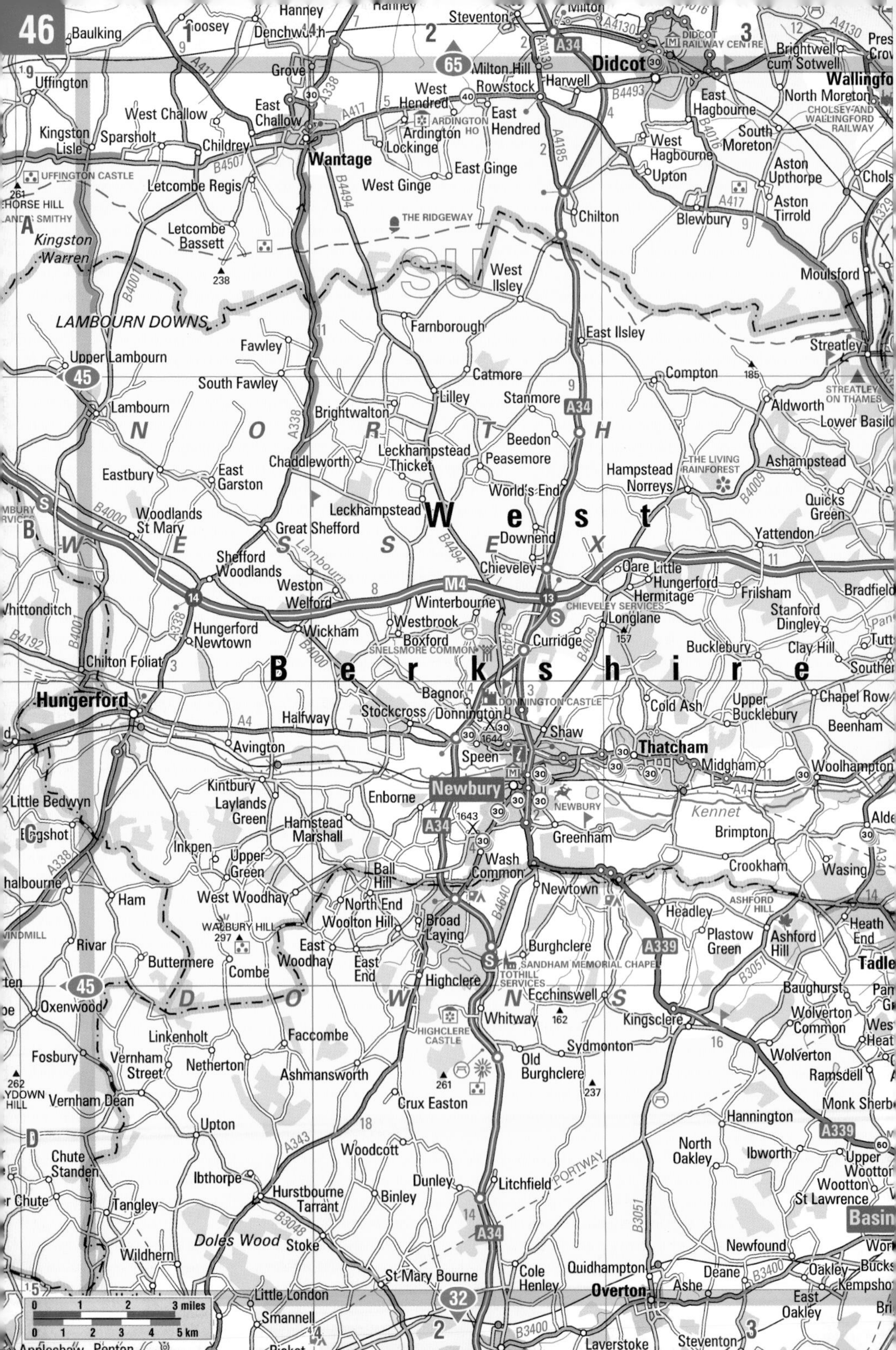
Baulking
Goosey
Hanney
Denchworth
Steventon
Milton
Didcot
Uffington
Grove
Milton Hill
Harwell
Brightwell-cum-Sotwell
Wallingford
West Challow
East Challow
West Hendred
Rowstock
East Hendred
Ardington
ARDINGTON HO
East Hagbourne
North Moreton
CHOLSEY AND WALLINGFORD RAILWAY
DIDCOT RAILWAY CENTRE
Kingston Lisle
Sparsholt
Childrey
Wantage
Lockinge
West Hagbourne
South Moreton
UFFINGTON CASTLE
Letcombe Regis
West Ginge
East Ginge
Upton
Aston Upthorpe
Aston Tirrold
Chilton
Blewbury
THE RIDGEWAY
Kingston Warren
Letcombe Bassett
238
SU
West Ilsley
Moulsford
LAMBOURN DOWNS
Farnborough
East Ilsley
Upper Lambourn
Fawley
Streatley
South Fawley
Catmore
Compton
185
Lambourn
Lilley
Stanmore
STREATLEY ON THAMES
Aldworth
Lower Basildon
Brightwalton
Beedon
Eastbury
Chaddleworth
Leckhampstead Thicket
Peasemore
Hampstead Norreys
THE LIVING RAINFOREST
Ashampstead
East Garston
World's End
Quicks Green
Woodlands St Mary
Leckhampstead
Great Shefford
West
Downend
Yattendon
Shefford Woodlands
Chieveley
Oare
Little Hungerford
Hermitage
Frilsham
Bradfield
Weston
Welford
Winterbourne
CHIEVELEY SERVICES
Stanford Dingley
Whittonditch
Hungerford Newtown
Wickham
Westbrook
Boxford
Longlane
157
Curridge
Bucklebury
Clay Hill
SNELSMORE COMMON
Berkshire
Chilton Foliat
Hungerford
Bagnor
DONNINGTON CASTLE
Cold Ash
Upper Bucklebury
Chapel Row
Halfway
Stockcross
Donnington
Shaw
Beenham
Avington
Speen
Thatcham
Midgham
Woolhampton
Kintbury
Laylands Green
Newbury
Enborne
NEWBURY
Kennet
Little Bedwyn
Hamstead Marshall
Brimpton
Aldermaston
Inkpen
Upper Green
Greenham
Eggshot
Wash Common
Crookham
Wasing
Ball Hill
West Woodhay
Ham
North End
Newtown
Headley
ASHFORD HILL
Heath End
WALBURY HILL
297
Woolton Hill
Broad Laying
Plastow Green
Ashford Hill
Rivar
East Woodhay
Burghclere
SANDHAM MEMORIAL CHAPEL
Buttermere
Combe
East End
Highclere
TOTHILL SERVICES
Tadley
Ecchinswell
Baughurst
Oxenwood
Whitway
162
Kingsclere
Wolverton Common
Linkenholt
Faccombe
HIGHCLERE CASTLE
Sydmonton
Fosbury
Vernham Street
Netherton
Old Burghclere
Wolverton
Ramsdell
Ashmansworth
261
237
262
Vernham Dean
Crux Easton
Monk Sherborne
Upton
Hannington
Woodcott
North Oakley
Ibworth
Chute Standen
Upper Wootton
Ibthorpe
Hurstbourne Tarrant
Dunley
Litchfield
PORTWAY
Wootton St Lawrence
Tangley
Binley
Basingstoke
Doles Wood
Stoke
Newfound
Wildhern
Cole Henley
Quidhampton
Deane
Oakley
Kempshott
St Mary Bourne
Ashe
Little London
Overton
East Oakley
Smannell
Laverstoke
Steventon
Penton
0 1 2 3 miles
0 1 2 3 4 5 km

Benson
Ewelme
Greenfield
Turville Heath
Turville
Fingest
Bolter End
Lane End
M40
Booker
Crowmarsh Gifford
Cookley Green
Pishill
65
Skirmett
Frieth
WYCOMBE AIR PARK
P&R
A404
Flackwell Heath
Little Marlow
Wooburn Green
Russell's Water
Park Corner
NUFFIELD PLACE
STONOR
Stonor
Rockwell End
Lower Woodend
Marlow Bottom
Bovingdon Green
Well End
A4130
A4074
Nuffield
Nettlebed
Fawley
Hambleden
Bourne End
North Stoke
Middle Assendon
Bix
Lower Assendon
Greenlands
Mill End
Marlow
Cookham Dean
Cookham
Ipsden
MAHARAJAH'S WELL
Highmoor Cross
Medmenham
Bisham
B4009
GREYS COURT
Aston
Remenham
Remenham Hill
THE THAMES PATH
Hurley
Windsor
South Stoke
Checkendon
Stoke Row
Satwell
Shepherd's Green
Park Corner
Woodcote
Rotherfield Greys
Henley-on-Thames
A4130
Pinkneys Grn.
Furze Platt
Burchett's Green
Maidenhead
Cray's Pond
Rotherfield Peppard
Harpsden
RIVER & ROWING MUSEUM
Warren Row
Goring
B4526
Goring Heath
Sonning Common
Knowl Hill
48
Bray Wick
A404(M)
BASILDON PARK
BEALE PARK
ST BARTHOLOMEW'S
Whitchurch Hill
Cane End
Kidmore End
Lower Shiplake
Shiplake
Wargrave
Littlewick Green
Woodlands Park
Binfield Hth.
White Waltham
WHITE WALTHAM
Hare Hatch
Stud Grn.
Holyport
Whitchurch
TOLL
Mapledurham
MAPLEDURHAM
Tokers Green
Dunsden Green
A4155
Thames
Maidenhead
Pangbourne
Upper Basildon
Purley
Emmer Green
Play Hatch
Sonning Eye
Ruscombe
Waltham St Lawrence
Touchen End
B478
Charvil
Twyford
B3024
Paley Street
Tidmarsh
Reading
Caversham
Sonning
Shurlock Row
M4
Sulham
Woodley
Whistley Green
Jealott's Hill
Hawthorn Hill
Tilehurst
DINTON PASTURES
Hurst
Reading
A3290
P&R
North Street
Englefield
Moss End
Warfield
Theale
Calcot Row
A33
MUS. OF ENGLISH RURAL LIFE
Earley
Binfield
B3034
Newell Grn.
Burleigh
Winnersh
Whitley
P&R
A329(M)
Emmbrook
Popeswood
A4
Ufton Nervet
Sheffield Bottom
READING SERVICES
Burghfield
M4
Sindlesham
Shinfield
A329
WOKINGHAM
Bracknell
Bullbrook
Sulhamstead
Burghfield Hill
Threemile Cross
A327
Arborfield
Arborfield Cross
Eastheath
Easthampstead
Aldermaston Wharf
Burghfield Common
Grazeley
Barkham
Wokingham
Bracknell
Padworth
Wokefield Park
Spencers Wood
The Throat
A322
Farley Hill
Arborfield Garrison
CALIFORNIA
THE LOOK OUT DISCOVERY CENTRE
Mortimer
Swallowfield
Wick Hill
B3430
B3348
Forest
SURREY HILL
Stratfield Mortimer
Beech Hill
Riseley
Finchampstead
Crowthorne
Mortimer West End
Pamber Heath
ROMAN TOWN
Silchester
Stratfield Saye
STRATFIELD SAYE HOUSE
WELLINGTON
Eversley
Little Sandhurst
48
Bagshot
West End Green
Bramshill
Eversley Cross
TRILAKES
Sandhurst
CAMBERLEY
Fair Oak Green
Heckfield
CASTLE BOTTOM
Yateley
Little London
Stratfield Turgis
Turgis Green
Hazeley
Bramshill Forest
BLACKBUSHE
YATELEY COMMON
Frogmore
York Town
Bramley
Hound Green
Mattingley
Blackwater
Hawley
Frimley
Pamber End
Sherfield on Loddon
Hartley Westpall
Hartfordbridge
Fox Lane
THE VYNE
Lyde Green
West Green
Hartley Wintney
FLEET SERVICES
Farnborough Green
Frimley Green
Church End
Rotherwick
A323
M3
Cove
Sherborne St John
A33
Phoenix Green
West Heath
ST MICHAEL'S ABBEY
Chineham
Popley
Newnham
Hook
Winchfield
Fleet
Pondtail
FARNBOROUGH AIRPORT
FARNBOROUGH
Daneshill
Oakridge
Dogmersfield
Old Basing
Long Valley
Basingstoke
P&R
South View
North Warnborough
Crookham Village
South Ham
Hatch
Up Nately
Church Crookham
ALDERSHOT
Ash Vale
Mapledurwell
Greywell
Odiham
A287
Mill Lane
Ewshot
Heath End
Ash
33
Badshot Lea
Crondall
Hog Hatch
Upper Hale
Tongham
Cliddesden
Upton Grey
Tunworth
M3

Loudwater
Forty Green
Jordans
Chalfont Common
Northwood
Hatch End
Beaconsfield
Chalfont St Peter
Harefield
Flackwell Heath
Little Marlow
Wooburn Green
Pinner
Ruislip Common
HARROW
Gerrards Cross
Denham Green
Eastcote
Well End
Wooburn
Hedgerley
Ruislip
Rayners Lane
Bourne End
Cores End
Hedsor
Tatling End
Cookham Dean
Cookham
Fulmer
Denham
Ickenham
Farnham Common
Stoke Poges
Cookham Rise
Iver Heath
Uxbridge
Northolt
Windsor
Park Corner
Burnham
Farnham Royal
Wexham Street
Stoke Green
Hillingdon
Furze Platt
Taplow
Yeading
Greenford
Cowley
Maidenhead
Slough
SLOUGH
George Green
Iver
Yiewsley
Hayes
Southall
Bray Wick
Bray
Dorney
Eton Wick
Upton
Langley
Richings Park
West Drayton
Woodlands Park
Holyport
Boveney
Eton
Harmondsworth
Sipson
Harlington
Cranford
Heston
White Waltham
Stud Grn.
Maidenhead
Fifield
Datchet
Colnbrook
Longford
Paley Street
Touchen End
Oakley Green
WINDSOR
Poyle
Horton
HEATHROW AIRPORT
HOUNSLOW
Windsor
Old Windsor
Wraysbury
Stanwell Moor
Stanwell
West Bedfont
East Bedfont
Hawthorn Hill
Jealott's Hill
Forest
WINDSOR
Cranbourne
Maiden's Green
Winkfield
Moss End
Warfield
Hythe End
Feltham
Newell Grn.
Winkfield Row
Woodside
GREAT PARK
Englefield Green
EGHAM
Staines-upon-Thames
Ashford
Hanworth
Burleigh
Bullbrook
Virginia Water
Thorpe
Laleham
Littleton
Hampton
Ascot
Sunninghill
Sunbury-on-Thames
Bracknell
South Ascot
Sunningdale
Broomhall
Shepperton
West Molesey
Bracknell
Lyne
CHERTSEY
Walton-on-Thames
Forest
Crowthorne
Windlesham
Addlestone
Ottershaw
WEYBRIDGE
Hersham
Bagshot
Burrowhill
New Haw
Lightwater
Chobham
Woodham
Byfleet
Whiteley Village
CAMBERLEY
West End
West Byfleet
Cobham
York Town
Donkey Town
Castle Green
Cheapside
Stoke D'Abernon
Chobham Ridges
Bisley
Knaphill
Horsell
Wisley
Frimley
WOKING
Pyrford
Downside
St John's
Deepcut
Brookwood
Old Woking
Ripley
Martyr's Green
Farnborough Green
Frimley Green
Mayford
Ockham
Fetcham
Cove
West Heath
Mytchett
Pirbright
Send Marsh
Send
Little Bookham
Fox Corner
Burntcommon
FARNBOROUGH
Sutton Green
Effingham
East Horsley
Worplesdon
West Horsley
Ash Vale
Willey Green
Pitch Place
Slyfield
Burpham
West Clandon
ALDERSHOT
Wyke
Normandy
Stoughton
Merrow
East Clandon
Ranmore Common
Wood Street
Newland's Corner
Wanborough
Guildford
Onslow Village
Gomshall
Abinger
Albury
Hogs Back
0 1 2 3 miles
0 1 2 3 4 5 km

Edgware
Harrow Weald
Mill Hill
Wood Green
Woodford
Finchley
Hornsey
Tottenham
Barking
Wealdstone
Kingsbury
Greenhill
Hendon
Walthamstow
Vestry House Mus
Fryent
Wanstead
Greater London
Harrow Sch
Harrow on the Hill
Golders Green
Highgate
Leytonstone
Seven Kings
Hampstead
Stoke Newington
Leyton
Ilford
Wembley
Cricklewood
Keats Ho
Forest Gate
Manor Park
Hackney
Willesden
Camden
Islington
Olympic Stadium
East Ham
Alperton
Harlesden
Kilburn
Bethnal Green
Stratford
Perivale
North Circular Road
Lord's
Regents Park
St Pancras
Shoreditch
West Ham
Finsbury
Holborn
Beckton
Ealing
Madame Tussaud's
Poplar
City
Paddington
Hyde Park
Oxford
Tate Modern
London City
Hanwell
Acton
Kensington
Nat Gall
Tower
North Woolwich
Woolwich Ferry
Holland Park
Nat History/Science Mus
Westminster
Southwark
Bermondsey
Blackwall Tunnel
Chiswick
Earls Court
Tate
Lambeth
Woolwich
Plumstead
Chelsea
Hammersmith
Cutty Sark
Greenwich
Deptford
Kew
Kew Br.
Peckham
Charlton
Syon Ho
Kew Gdns
National Archives
Battersea
Fulham
Maritime Mus
Kidbrooke
New Cross
Putney
Mortlake
Camberwell
Clapham
Lewisham
Richmond
Brixton
Dulwich
Hither Green
Dulwich Pic Gall
S. Circ. Road
Eltham
Roehampton
Wandsworth
Ham Ho
Richmond Park
New Eltham
Catford
Horniman Mus
Twickenham
Richmond Park
Wimbledon
Wimbledon Common
Balham
Streatham
Grove Park
Mottingham
Ham
Kingston Vale
Tennis Mus
Upper Tooting
West Norwood
Sydenham
Chislehurst
Crystal Palace
London
Merton
Penge
Bromley
Bushy Park
Wimbledon
Raynes Park
South Norwood
Beckenham
Hampton Court
Kingston upon Thames
Morden
Mitcham
Thornton Heath
Bickley
Petts Wood
Elmers End
Thames Ditton
New Malden
Surbiton
Selhurst
Eden Park
West Wickham
Bromley Common
Hayes
St Helier
Addiscombe
Long Ditton
Tolworth
Worcester Park
Hackbridge
Shirley
Croydon
Hook
Whitehall
Carshalton
Keston
Cheam
Beddington
Addington
Chessington
Sutton
Wallington
Farnborough
Horton
South Croydon
New Addington
Chessington World of Adventures
Ewell
High Elms
Belmont
Selsdon
Leaves Green
Downe
Purley
Sanderstead
Darwin Mus
Epsom
Ashtead Common
Woodmansterne
Hamsey Green
Farleigh
Biggin Hill
Wood Field
Great Burgh
Banstead
Kenley
Coulsdon
Warlingham
Whyteleafe
Ashtead
Epsom Downs
Burgh Heath
Chipstead
South Street
Old Coulsdon
Tatsfield
Leatherhead
Tadworth
Hooley
Kingswood
Woldingham
Chaldon
Caterham
Clacket Lane Services
Walton on the Hill
Lower Kingswood
Headley
Titsey
Bocketts Farm Park
Surrey
Walton Heath
Westerham
Limpsfield
Mickleham
Merstham
Brewer Street
Godstone
Limpsfield Chart
Oxted
Squerryes Court
Box Hill
Church Town
Crockham Hill
Buckland
Redhill
Nutfield
Tandridge
Pixham
Bletchingley
Godstone Farm
Betchworth
Brockham
Earlswood
Reigate
South Nutfield
Crowhurst Lane End
Marlpit Hill
Strood
Doversgreen
Ridge Green
M1
M25
M23
A22
A23
A24
A25
A40
A406
A205
A232
A21
A3
A4
A2
A13
A12
A11
A102
A503
A1400

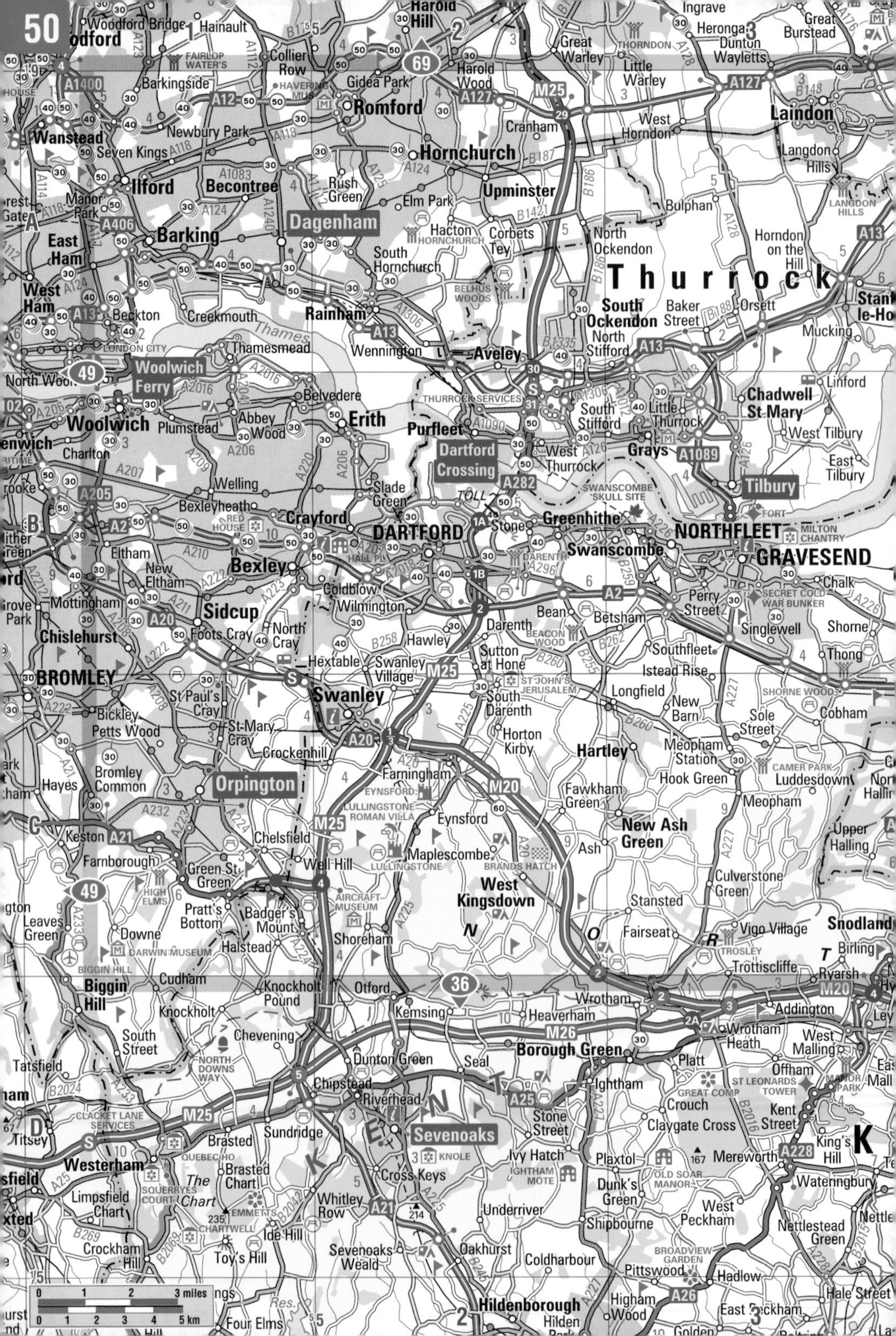
Woodford Bridge
Hainault
Harold Hill
Ingrave
Great Burstead
Herongate
Dunton Wayletts
Great Warley
Little Warley
Thorndon
Fairlop Waters
Collier Row
Barkingside
Havering Mus
Gidea Park
Romford
Harold Wood
Laindon
West Horndon
Cranham
Wanstead
Seven Kings
Newbury Park
Hornchurch
Langdon Hills
Ilford
Becontree
Rush Green
Elm Park
Upminster
Manor Park
Bulphan
East Ham
Barking
Dagenham
Hacton
Hornchurch
Corbets Tey
North Ockendon
Horndon on the Hill
West Ham
South Hornchurch
Belhus Woods
Thurrock
Beckton
Creekmouth
Rainham
South Ockendon
Baker Street
Orsett
North Stifford
Mucking
London City
Thamesmead
Wennington
Aveley
Thames
North Woolwich
Woolwich Ferry
Belvedere
Thurrock Services
Linford
Chadwell St Mary
Woolwich
Plumstead
Abbey Wood
Erith
Purfleet
South Stifford
Little Thurrock
West Tilbury
Charlton
Grays
Dartford Crossing
West Thurrock
East Tilbury
Welling
Tilbury
Slade Green
Swanscombe Skull Site
Bexleyheath
Red House
Crayford
Dartford
Stone
Greenhithe
Northfleet
Milton Chantry
Fort
Eltham
Hall Pl
Darenth
Swanscombe
Gravesend
Bexley
New Eltham
Coldblow
Chalk
Mottingham
Sidcup
Wilmington
Bean
Betsham
Perry Street
Secret Cold War Bunker
Chislehurst
Foots Cray
North Cray
Hawley
Darenth
Beacon Wood
Singlewell
Shorne
Sutton at Hone
Southfleet
Thong
Bromley
Hextable
Swanley Village
St John's Jerusalem
Istead Rise
Swanley
South Darenth
Longfield
Shorne Woods
Bickley
St Paul's Cray
New Barn
Cobham
Petts Wood
St Mary Cray
Horton Kirby
Sole Street
Crockenhill
Hartley
Meopham Station
Camer Park
Hayes
Bromley Common
Farningham
Hook Green
Luddesdown
Orpington
Eynsford
Fawkham Green
Meopham
Lullingstone Roman Villa
Eynsford
Keston
Chelsfield
Maplescombe
New Ash Green
Upper Halling
Farnborough
Well Hill
Ash
Green St Green
Lullingstone
Brands Hatch
Culverstone Green
High Elms
Aircraft Museum
West Kingsdown
Pratt's Bottom
Badger's Mount
Stansted
Leaves Green
Downe
Shoreham
Fairseat
Vigo Village
Snodland
Darwin Museum
Halstead
Trosley
Birling
Biggin Hill
Trottiscliffe
Ryarsh
Biggin Hill
Cudham
Knockholt Pound
Otford
Kemsing
Wrotham
Addington
Knockholt
Heaverham
Wrotham Heath
West Malling
South Street
Chevening
Borough Green
Dunton Green
North Downs Way
Platt
Tatsfield
Seal
Offham
Chipstead
Ightham
St Leonards Tower
Great Comp
Riverhead
Crouch
Clacket Lane Services
Stone Street
Claygate Cross
Kent Street
Titsey
Brasted
Sundridge
Sevenoaks
Kings Hill
Westerham
Quebec Ho
Knole
Ivy Hatch
Plaxtol
Mereworth
Brasted Chart
Ightham Mote
Wateringbury
The Chart
Cross Keys
Old Soar Manor
Squerryes Court
Dunk's Green
Limpsfield Chart
Whitley Row
Emmetts
Underriver
West Peckham
Chartwell
Shipbourne
Nettlestead Green
Ide Hill
Broadview Garden
Crockham Hill
Toy's Hill
Sevenoaks Weald
Oakhurst
Coldharbour
Pittswood
Hadlow
Hildenborough
Higham Wood
Hale Street
Four Elms
East Peckham
Res.
0 1 2 3 miles
0 1 2 3 4 5 km

RAYLEIGH
Stroud Green
Stambridge
Great Stambridge
Gore
Potton Island
OLD HOUSE
Rochford
Nevendon
North Benfleet
Basildon
Bowers Gifford
Pitsea
Vange
Thundersley
Daws Heath
Hadleigh
Eastwood
SOUTHEND
Barling
Havengore Island
Little Wakering
Great Wakering
Prittlewell
PRIORY
Southend-on-Sea
Bournes Green
Hope's Grn.
South Benfleet
WAT TYLER
HADLEIGH CASTLE
Leigh on Sea
CEN MUS & PLANETARIUM
Southchurch
North Shoebury
Winter Gardens
BEECROFT
Thorpe Bay
Westcliff-on-Sea
LEIGH
ADVENTURE ISLAND
Southend-on-Sea
SEA LIFE CENTRE
Cambridge Town
Shoeburyness
Shoeburyness
Fobbing
Corringham
CANVEY ISLAND
CANVEY ISLAND
Coryton
Leigh Beck
Thames Haven
London Gateway
port under construction)
TQ
THAMES ESTUARY
52
Halstow Marshes
St Mary's Marshes
Allhallows-on-Sea
Allhallows
St Mary Hoo
Lower Stoke
Grain
Isle of Grain
Cliffe
Cooling
HIGH HALSTOW
High Halstow
Stoke
Sheerness
Church Street
North Street
West Minster
Halfway Houses
Minster
Cliffe Woods
Medway
Medway
Queenborough
ABBEY
Eastchurch
Higham
Wainscott
Chattenden
Hoo St.Werburgh
UPNOR CASTLE
Upnor
DICKENS WORLD
HISTORIC DOCKYARD
Chetney Marshes
Rushenden
TEMPLE MANOR
Frindsbury
ISLE OF SHEPPEY
Strood
Brompton
Grange
Ham Green
ELMLEY
ROCHESTER
RIVERSIDE
CATH.
CHATHAM
Gillingham
Upchurch
Lower Halstow
Iwade
Luton
Kemsley
The Swale
Rainham
Breach
SITTINGBOURNE & KEMSLEY LT RLY
Wayfield
MEDWAY (Rochester)
CAPSTONE
ROCHESTER FARM
Moor Street
Bobbing
Milton Regis
MILTON CREEK
Wouldham
Wigmore
Newington
Conyer
Halling
Hempstead
Walderslade
Hartlip
MUS.
SITTINGBOURNE
Uplees
BUCKMORE PARK
Blue Bell Hill
Borden
Bapchild
Barrow Green
MEDWAY SERVICES
Teynham
Burham
Oad Street
Bredhurst
Faversham
KIT'S COTY HOUSE
Stockbury
Tunstall
Highsted
Rodmersham
LEYBOURNE LAKE
Eccles
Lynsted
OSPRINGE MAISON
Ospringe
WHITE HORSE WOOD
South Green
Bredgar
TYLAND BARN
THE FRIARS
Aylesford
Boxley
BREDGAR & WORMSHILL LT RLY
Swanton Street
Bicknor
Milstead
DODDINGTON PLACE
Newnham
Sandling
MUS OF KENT LIFE
Detling
Thurnham
Hucking
Frinsted
British Legion Village
Broad Street
Wormshill
Doddington
Eastling
Sheldwich
BELMONT
NEWNHAM COURT
BEARSTED MAISTONE SERVICES
Wichling
Throwley
Maidstone
Roseacre
Hollingbourne
East Barming
Tovil
Bearsted
Eyhorne Street
West Street
Kent
DOWNS
Shepway
STONEACRE
NORTH DOWNS WAY
Stalisfield Green
Leaveland
East Farleigh
Otham
Leeds
Harrietsham
Warren Street
West Farleigh
LEEDS CASTLE
Broomfield
Loose
Boughton Monchelsea
Langley
Langley Heath
Lenham
Sandway
Coxheath
Kingswood
Lenham Heath
Warmlake
Hunton
Linton
Chart Corner
Sutton Valence
BOUGHTON MONCHELSEA PLACE
Chart Sutton
Charing
YALDING ORGANIC GDN
Grafty Green
Boughton Malherbe
Charing Heath
Benover
Ulcombe
Westwell

1
2
3
FOULNESS ISLAND
Potton Island
Havengore Island
MAPLIN SANDS
71
Barling
Little Wakering
Great Wakering
A1159
B1017
Sea
Bournes Green
North Shoebury
A13
Thorpe Bay
SEA LIFE CENTRE
B1016
Cambridge Town
Shoeburyness
Shoeburyness
51
TQ
Sheerness
B
West Minster
A250
Halfway Houses
Minster
ABBEY
B2008
73
Warden Pt.
Warden
Rushenden
A2500
Eastchurch
B2231
Leysdown-on-Sea
A249
ISLE OF SHEPPEY
ELMLEY
Isle of Harty
THE SWALE
Shell Ness
HERNE BAY
WHITSTABLE
Tankerton
Swalecliffe
MUSEUM & GALLERY
A2990
Greenhill
Herne
Chestfield
Seasalter
South Street
Kemsley
The Swale
SITTINGBOURNE & KEMSLEY LT RLY
MILTON CREEK
C
SITTINGBOURNE
Conyer
Uplees
Barrow Green
Bapchild
Teynham
Oare
Graveney
CHART GUNPOWDER MILLS
Yorkletts
A290
Calcott
Tunstall
Highsted
Rodmersham
Faversham
Goodnestone
FLEUR DE LIS HERITAGE CENTRE
A299
Dargate
Honey Hill
Broadoak
A291
Lynsted
OSPRINGE MAISON DIEU
Ospringe
Preston
FARMING WORLD
Hernhill
MOUNT EPHRAIM
BLEAN WOODS
Blean
Tyler Hill
Sturry
Hales Place
Fordwich
M2
51
Boughton Street
Dunkirk
Rough Common
P&R
Canterbury
Milstead
DODDINGTON PLACE
Newnham
North Street
A2
South Street
Harbledown
ST AUGUSTINE'S ABBEY
Frinsted
Doddington
Eastling
A251
Sheldwich
BELMONT
Oversland
Chartham Hatch
CANTERBURY TALES
Thanington
ROMAN MUS
CANTERBURY
A2050
Wichling
KENT
Throwley
Selling
A28
Old Wives Lees
Chartham
D
Badlesmere
Shottenden
Shalmsford Street
Nackington
Bridge
Stalisfield Green
Leaveland
Chilham
Street End
Lower Hardres
NORTH DOWNS WAY
Warren Street
DOWNS
A252
Garlinge Green
Bishopsbourne
B2068
Lenham
Molash
Petham
Kingston
A20
Upper Hardres Court
Lenham Heath
A252
Challock
NORTH DOWNS WAY
Godmersham
38
Sole Street
Bossingham
Derringstone
3 miles
5 km
Westwell
Boughton Aluph
Crundale
Waltham
ELHAM VALLEY VINEYARD

TR
Margate
Cliftonville
Foreness Pt.
THE SHELL GROTTO
TURNER CONTEMPORARY
Kingsgate
NORTH FORELAND
LIGHTHOUSE
Westgate on Sea
Birchington
Minnis Bay
RECULVER
RECULVER TOWERS AND ROMAN FORT
Reculver
Hillborough
QUEX HOUSE
Isle of Thanet
SPITFIRE AND HURRICANE MEM
Northdown
St Peter's
BROADSTAIRS
BLEAK HOUSE
DICKENS HOUSE MUSEUM
Northwood
Dumpton
Newington
Ramsgate
MARITIME MUSEUM
OOSTENDE 4:00
BOULOGNE 1:15
Acol
St Nicholas at Wade
WINDMILL
Boyden Gate
Sarre
Monkton
Minster
Manston
KENT INTERNATIONAL
Way
Cliffsend
Pegwell
PEGWELL BAY
SANDWICH & PEGWELL BAY
Pegwell Bay
ST. AUGUSTINE'S CROSS
Hoath
Chislet
Upstreet
Stour
West Stourmouth
East Stourmouth
Grove
STODMARSH
Preston
Westmarsh
Ware
RICHBOROUGH CASTLE
Stodmarsh
Elmstone
Hoaden
AMPHITHEATRE
Great Stonar
WINGHAM WILDLIFE PARK
Ickham
Littlebourne
Wingham
Guilton
Ash
Sandwich
Sandwich Bay
TOLL
ROYAL ST. GEORGE'S
Marshborough
Woodnesborough
Stone Cross
Bramling
Staple
Worth
Gore
Goodnestone
GOODNESTONE PARK
Eastry
Ham
Finglesham
Adisham
Knowlton
Chillenden
Aylesham
Betteshanger
Sholden
MARITIME AND LOCAL HISTORY MUSEUM
DEAL
DEAL CASTLE
THE DOWNS
Easole Street
Nonington
Northbourne
Snowdown
Tilmanstone
Elvington
Great Mongeham
Walmer
WALMER CASTLE AND GARDENS
Womenswold
Barfrestone
EAST KENT RLY
Woolage Green
Eythorne
East Studdal
Sutton
Ringwould
Kingsdown
A28
A299
A253
A256
A257
A258
A255
A254
B2052
B2190
B2050
B2046

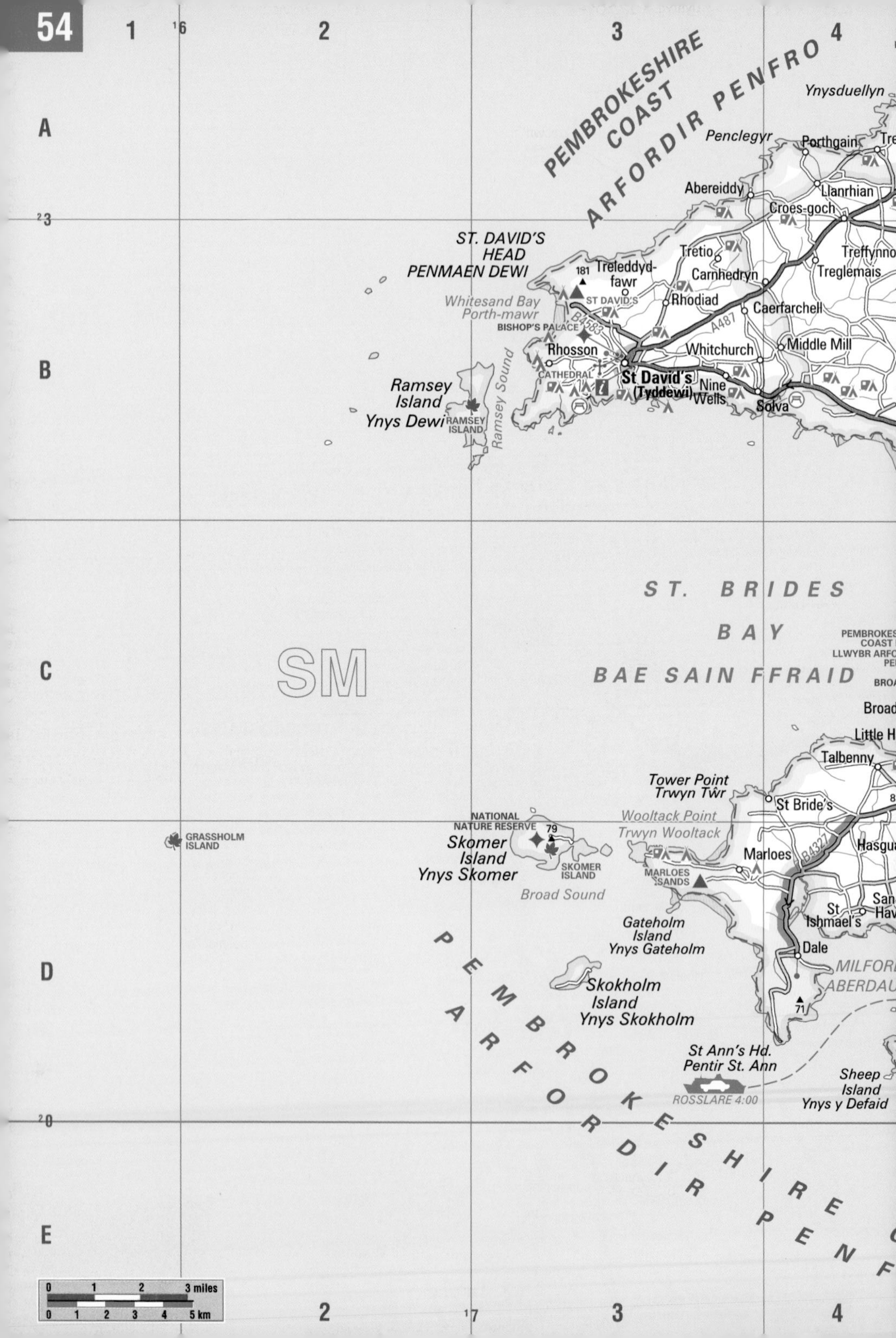
1
2
3
4
A
B
C
D
E
PEMBROKESHIRE COAST
ARFORDIR PENFRO
Ynysduellyn
Penclegyr
Porthgain
Abereiddy
Llanrhian
Croes-goch
ST. DAVID'S HEAD
PENMAEN DEWI
Tretio
Treffynnon
181
Treleddyd-fawr
Carnhedryn
Treglemais
Whitesand Bay
Porth-mawr
ST DAVID'S
Rhodiad
Caerfarchell
BISHOP'S PALACE
B4583
A487
Rhosson
Whitchurch
Middle Mill
CATHEDRAL
St David's
(Tyddewi)
Nine Wells
Solva
Ramsey Island
Ynys Dewi
RAMSEY ISLAND
Ramsey Sound
ST. BRIDES BAY
BAE SAIN FFRAID
SM
Broad
Little H
Talbenny
Tower Point
Trwyn Tŵr
St Bride's
Wooltack Point
Trwyn Wooltack
NATIONAL NATURE RESERVE
79
Skomer Island
Ynys Skomer
SKOMER ISLAND
GRASSHOLM ISLAND
Marloes
MARLOES SANDS
B4327
Broad Sound
St Ishmael's
Gateholm Island
Ynys Gateholm
Dale
Skokholm Island
Ynys Skokholm
71
St Ann's Hd.
Pentir St. Ann
ROSSLARE 4:00
Sheep Island
Ynys y Defaid
0 1 2 3 miles
0 1 2 3 4 5 km

Fishguard
(Abergwaun)
Manorowen
St Nicholas
PEMBROKESHIRE COAST PATH
TREGWYNT WOOLLEN MILL
Llanychaer
72
CARNINGLI
Cilgwyn
Crosswell
Pontygl
Brynberian
Scleddau
Granston
Pontfaen
MYNYDD PRESELI
Trecwn
Mathry
Newbridge
CORSYDD LLANGLOFFAN
Castlemorris
468
536
FOEL-CWMCERWYN
New Inn
Rosebush
Little Newcastle
Puncheston
Castlebythe
Letterston
Treddiog
164
Llanreithan
Welsh Hook
St Dogwells
Tufton
Henry's Moat
Maenclochog
Llandeloy
Wolf's Castle
Pont-yr-hafod
Llangolman
Glandy Cross
Ambleston
Woodstock
Hayscastle
Rinaston
Wallis
New Moat
Brimaston
Hayscastle Cross
LLYS-Y-FRAN RESERVOIR
73
Triffleton
Mountain Water
Treffgarne
Llys-y-frân
Llanycefn
Spittal
178
DUDWELL MT.
Leweston
SCOLTON MANOR
Walton East
Pen-ffordd
Pembrokeshire
(Sir Benfro)
Llandissilio
Roch
Wolfsdale
Clarbeston
Bletherston
Roch Gate
Rudbaxton
Clarbeston Road
Camrose
Llanfallteg
Nolton Haven
Simpson Cross
Keeston
Gelli
Clunderwen
PEMBROKE MOTOR MUSEUM
Tangiers
Pelcomb Cross
Nolton
Crundale
Wiston
LLAWHADEN CASTLE
Bethesda
Lambston
Haverfordwest
(Hwlffordd)
Slade
Pelcomb Bridge
Llawhaden
Robeston Wathen
Portfield Gate
CASTLE MUSEUM AND ART GALLERY
The Rhos
Narberth
(Arberth)
Haroldston West
Dreenhill
Uzmaston
Blackpool
WILSON MUSEUM
Crinow
Merlin's Bridge
Millin Cross
PICTON CASTLE & GARDENS
BLUE LAGOON
HERONS BROOK
Broadway
Pope Hill
Boulston
Minwear
Cross Hands
Walton West
OAKWOOD
Templeton
Cold Blow
Princes Gate
North Johnston
Freystrop
Landshipping
108
Walwyn's Castle
Hook
Ludchurch
Tiers Cross
Landshipping Quay
Martletwy
Johnston
Longstone
Robeston Cross
Llangwm
Black Tar
Yerbeston
FOLLY FARM
Reynalton
Thornton
Rosemarket
Hill Mountain
Port Lion
Loveston
Thomas Chapel
Stepaside
Steynton
Herbrandston
Houghton
Cresswell Quay
Begelly
Milford Haven
(Aberdaugleddau)
Honeyborough
Lawrenny
Cresselly
Jeffreyston
Kilgetty
West Williamston
Broadmoor
Hakin
Waterston
Neyland
Burton
Llanstadwell
UPTON CASTLE GARDENS
Carew Newton
East Williamston
56
Saundersfoot
Pembroke Dock
(Doc Penfro)
TOLL
Redberth
Cosheston
Carew
CAREW CASTLE
Broadfield
Angle
Angle Bay
Bae Angle
PEMBROKE DOCK SUNDERLAND TRUST
Milton
Sageston
New Hedges
Pwllcrochan
Pennar
Carew Cheriton
TENBY DINOSAUR PARK
TUDOR MERCHANT
Rhoscrowther
Pembroke
(Penfro)
MANOR HOUSE WILDLIFE PARK
Monkton
LAMPHEY BISHOP'S PALACE
Tenby
(Dinbych-y-Pysgod)
Hundleton
St Florence
Gumfreston
Lamphey
71
Maiden Wells
Penally
Hodgeston
Jameston
Castlemartin
St Twynnells
Freshwater East
Giltar Pt.
Lydstep
Caldey Sound
Warren
St Petrox
Cheriton or Stackpole Elidor
MANORBIER CASTLE
Manorbier
MANORBIER
Trewent Pt.
Trwyn Trewent
Merrion
Stackpole
Old Castle Hd.
STACKPOLE
ELEGUG STACKS
PEMBROKESHIRE COAST PATH
LLWYBR ARFORDIR PENFRO
Bosherston
Stackpole Hd.
Pen Stackpole
The Wash
St Govan's Hd./Pen St Gofan
SN
A40
A487
A4076
A477
A478
A4075
A4115
A4139
B4313
B4329
B4331
B4327
B4341
B4325
B4322
B4318
B4320
B4319
B4584
B4586
B4314
B4316

Llandissilio
Henllan Amgoed
Meidrim
Merthyr
Carmarthen (Caerfyrddin)
Llanfallteg
Llangynin
Clunderwen
Cwmfelin Boeth
Sarnau
Llanllwch
Bethesda
Bancyfelin
CORS GOCH, LLANLLWCH
Pwll-trap
A40
Llanddewi Velfrey
Whitland
Trevaughan
Backe
Afon Taf
St Clears (Sanclêr)
Llangynog
Llangain
Afon Cywyn
Crinow
Lampeter Velfrey
Llwyn-y-brain
Llanddowror
Morfa Bach
Afon Tywi
Tavernspite
A477
Halfpenny Furze
Llanybri
Cold Blow
Princes Gate
Red Roses
Llandawke
DYLAN THOMAS BOATHOUSE
Llansteffan
Ludchurch
Llanteg
Llansadurnen
Laugharne
CASTLE
Ferryside
Brook
Broadway
Marros
MUSEUM OF SPEED
Broadlay
FOLLY FARM
Thomas Chapel
Stepaside
COLBY WOODLAND GARDEN
Pendine
East Marsh
Llansaint
Begelly
Kilgetty
Amroth
Pendine Sands
Traeth Pentywyn
Saundersfoot
East Williamston
Broadfield
New Hedges
TENBY DINOSAUR PARK
TUDOR MERCHANT'S HOUSE
ARFORDIR PENFRO
SN
CARMARTHEN
Pembrey Forest
Gumfreston
Tenby (Dinbych-y-Pysgod)
Penally
BAY
Giltar Pt.
Caldey Sound
BAE CAERFYRDDIN
Caldey Island Ynys Bŷr
Chapel Pt. Trwyn Capel
SS
Burry Holms
Rhoss Bay
Bae Rhoss
Worms Head Penrhyn-Gŵyr
0 1 2 3 miles
0 1 2 3 4 5 km

Tanerdy
White Mill
Pont-ar-gothi
Felindre
Dryslwyn
Llandeilo
Ffairfach
Abergwili
Nantgaredig
Llanegwad
ABERGLASNEY
Cilsan
CARMARTHEN
B4300
58
Llanarthne
Afon Tywi
GELLI AUR
Llangunnor
Capel Dewi
Golden Grove
Trapp
CARREG CENNEN CASTLE & FARM
Pensarn
Nantycaws
B4310
THE NATIONAL BOTANIC GARDEN OF WALES
Penrhiwgoch
A476
Temple Bar
Milo
A483
Llandyfan
BLACK MOUNTAIN
A48
Llanddarog
Maesybont
B4297
CARMEL
Carmel
Pentre-Gwenlais
Dre-fach
Croesyceiliog
Idole
Cwmisfael
Porthyrhyd
LLYN LLECH OWAIN
272
Llandybie
Bancycapel
B4306
Gwendraeth Fach
Foel-gastell
Gorslas
B4556
Caer-bryn
Twynmynydd
Llangendeirne
Cefneithin
Pen-y-groes
Tir-y-dail
Glanaman
Afon Aman
A484
262
Crwbin
Drefach
Cwm-y-glo
Morfa
Saron
A474
Garnant
Pontantwn
Bancffosfelen
Cwm-mawr
Cross Hands
Pontamman
Ammanford
Betws (Rhydaman)
59
Gwaun-Cae-Gurwen
B4309
Pontyberem
Tumble
Penybanc
Pantyffynnon
Meinciau
Pentre
Cwmgwili
Capel Hendre
Tycroes
B4317
B4306
Four Roads
Pont-Henri
Greynor
Garnswllt
374
KIDWELLY INDUSTRIAL MUSEUM
Mynyddygarreg
Pontyates
284
Llannon
Llwyn-teg
B4297
Loughor (Llwchwr)
Mynydd y Gwair
Kidwelly (Cydweli)
Cynheidre
Sylen
A476
PONT ABRAHAM SERVICES
276
GRAIG FAWR
Carway
FFOS LAS
Llanedi
Sardis
Pentrebach
B4308
Five Roads
Horeb
Lliedi Resrs.
B4306
193
Fforest
Trimsaran
Pontarddulais
Pontardawe
Rhyd-y-gwin
Craig-cefn-parc
Hendy
Cwm-Dulais
Pinged
Waun-y-clyn
Allt
Felindre
Rhyd-y-pandy
Cwmbach
Felinfoel
A4138
Llangennech
Faerdre
Pembrey
Achddu
A484
Pwll
Furnace
Dafen
Waungron
Pontlliw
Clydach
B4297
B4296
M4
SWANSEA SERVICES
Ynystawe
Burry Port (Porth Tywyn)
Sandy
Bryn
Grovesend
Pant-lasau
Heol-las
MILLENNIUM COASTAL PARK DISCOVERY CENTRE
Llanelli
Llwynhendy
Bynea
Yspitty
Penllergaer
A4240
Llangyfelach
Machynys
Morfa
WILDFOWL AND WETLANDS TRUST
Loughor
Gorseinon
A484
Morriston
Whiteford Pt.
Trwyn Whiteford
Llanrhidian Sands
Traeth Llanrhidian
Pen-clawdd
Gowerton
B4620
Fforest-fach
P&R
Cadle
Landore
Llansamlet
WHITEFORD
Crofty
Blue Anchor
Waunarlwydd
Pentre-chwyth
Cwm
Bon-y-maen
Wernffrwd
Llanmorlais
Three Crosses
B4296
Dunvant
Cwmdu
Foxhole
Swansea (Abertawe)
PLANTASIA
Port Tennant
Cheriton
Landimore
Swansea (Abertawe)
Killay
Sketty
A4118
Llanmadoc
186
WEOBLEY CASTLE
B4295
Brynmill
SWANSEA MUSEUM
Burry Green
Llanrhidian
Llethrid
B4271
SWANSEA
Upper Killay
CLYNE VALLEY
NATIONAL WATERFRONT MUSEUM
40
Llangennith
GOWER
Burry
Reynoldston
Ilston
A4118
131
Mayals
A4067
Black Pill
THE BEACON 193
Lunnon
GOWER HERITAGE CENTRE
Kittle
Bishopston
SWANSEA
West Cross
SWANSEA BAY
Llanddewi
Knelston
186
Parkmill
Pennard
Manselfield
LOVESPOON GALLERY
OYSTERMOUTH CASTLE
BAY
Rhossili
Scurlage
Penrice
Nicholaston
Penmaen
Oldway
Newton
The Mumbles (Y Mwmbwls)
BAE ABERTAWE
Middleton
GOWER COAST
B4247
A4118
OXWICH
Southgate
Oxwich Bay
Bae Oxwich
Mumbles Hd.
Trwyn yr Mwmbwls
Pilton Green
Horton
Oxwich
OXWICH CASTLE
Pwlldu Hd.
Pen Pwlldu
Overton
Port-Eynon
PORT EYNON
Port Eynon Bay
Bae Port Eynon
Port Eynon Pt.
Trwyn Port Eynon
A
B
C
D
4
5
6

Carmarthenshire
(Sir Gaerfyrddin)
Brechfa Forest
Mynydd Pencarreg
Pont-siân
Cwmsychpant
Pentre-bâch
Ram
Llanycrwys
Tregroes
Rhydowen
Dre-fach
Alltyblaca
Pencarreg
Parc-y-rhôs
Ffarmers
Ffaldybrenin
Prengwyn
Brynteg
Llanybydder
Rhuddlan
Glan-Duar
Ty Mawr
Harford
Capel Dewi
ROCK MILL WOOLLEN MILL
Maesycrugiau
Esgairdawe
Llandre
Llandysul
Llanfihangel-ar-arth
Aber-Giâr
Pumsaint
DOLAUCOTHI GOLD MINES
Llanllwni
Caio
Bancyffordd
Rhydcymerau
Crugybar
Llidiad Nénog
New Inn
Pencader
Llansawel
Gwyddgrug
Dolgran
Edwinsford
Gwernogle
Abergorlech
Afon Cothi
MYNYDD RHOS-WEN
TALLEY ABBEY
Talley
CYNROS
Cwm-byr
Nant-y-ffin
Pen-y-garn
Waunclunda
Alltwalis
Llansadwrn
Cwmdu
Halfway
Felindre
Brechfa
Llanllawddog
Ashfield
Soar
Hermon
Pontarsais
Horeb
Llanfynydd
Pant-glas
Capel Isaac
Manordeilo
Salem
Cwmifor
Rhydargaeau
GWILI RAILWAY
Pant-teg
Pantgwyn
Bethlehem
Felingwm uchaf
Felingwm isaf
Pen-y-banc
Rhosmaen
Peniel
Llanfihangel-uwch-Gwili
Pentrefelin
Bronwydd Arms
Capel Gwyn
Broad Oak
Court Henry
DINEFWR PARK
Llangathen
Pontbren Araeth
VALE OF TYWI
DYFFRYN TYWI
Ffynnon ddrain
White Mill
Pont-ar-gothi
Cilsan
Llandeilo
Tanerdy
Nantgaredig
Felindre
ABERGLASNEY
Abergwili
Llanegwad
Dryslwyn
Ffairfach
CARMARTHEN
Llangunnor
Capel Dewi
Llanarthne
Afon Tywi
GELLI AUR
Golden Grove
Pensarn
Nantycaws
THE NATIONAL BOTANIC GARDEN OF WALES
Penrhiwgoch
Trapp
CARREG CENNEN CASTLE & FARM
Temple Bar
Milo
Cwmffrwd
Llanddarog
Maesybont
CARMEL
Llandyfan
Croesyceiliog
Carmel
Pentre-Gwenlais
Dre-fach
Idole
Cwmisfael
Porthyrhyd
LLYN LLECH OWAIN
Llandybie
Bancycapel
Foel-gastell
Twynmynydd
Gwendraeth Fach
Llangendeirne
Cefneithin
Gorslas
Caer-bryn
Glanaman
Pen-y-groes
Crwbin
Drefach
Cwm-y-glo
Tir-y-dail
Pontantwn
Morfa
Saron
Garnant
Cross Hands
Pontamman
Bancffosfelen
Cwm-mawr
Ammanford
Betws (Rhydaman)
Tumble
Penybanc
Pontyberem
Capel Hendre
Pantyffynnon
Meinciau
Pentre
Cwmgwili
Tycroes
Four Roads
Pont-Henri
Greynor
KIDWELLY INDUSTRIAL MUSEUM
Pontyates
Garnswllt
Mynyddygarreg
Llannon
Cynheidre
Llwyn-têg
Mynydd y Gwair
Kidwelly (Cydweli)
Sylen
PONT ABRAHAM SERVICES
Llanedi
GRAIG FAWR
Carway
FFOS LAS
Sardis
Five Roads
Horeb
Lliedi Resrs.
Pentrebach
Trimsaran
Fforest
Pontarddulais
Hendy
Cwm-Dulais
Rhyd-y-gwin
Craig-cefn-parc
0 1 2 3 miles
0 1 2 3 4 5 km

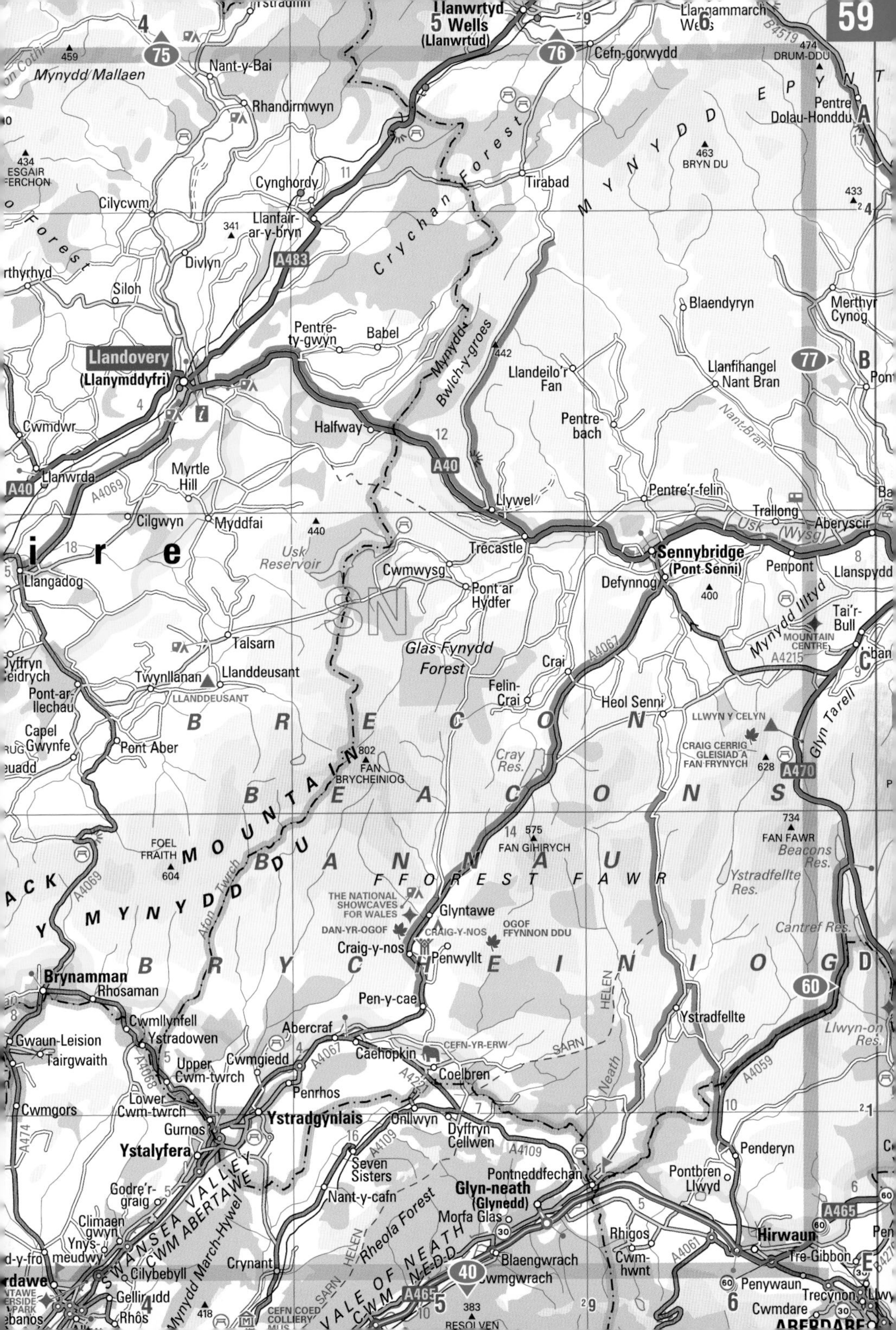
Llanwrtyd Wells
(Llanwrtud)
Llangammarch Wells
Mynydd Mallaen
Nant-y-Bai
Cefn-gorwydd
Rhandirmwyn
DRUM-DDU
ESGAIR FERCHON
Cynghordy
Tirabad
Crychan Forest
MYNYDD EPYNT
Pentre
Dolau-Honddu
BRYN DU
Cilycwm
Llanfair-ar-y-bryn
Divlyn
Siloh
Blaendyryn
Merthyr Cynog
Pentre-ty-gwyn
Babel
Mynydd Bwlch-y-groes
Llandovery
(Llanymddyfri)
Llandeilo'r Fan
Llanfihangel Nant Bran
Cwmdwr
Halfway
Pentre-bach
Nant-Brân
Llanwrda
Myrtle Hill
Llywel
Pentre'r-felin
Trallong
Cilgwyn
Myddfai
Aberyscir
Usk (Wysg)
Usk Reservoir
Trecastle
Sennybridge
(Pont Senni)
Penpont
Llanspydd
Llangadog
Cwmwysg
Defynnog
Pont ar Hydfer
Mynydd Illtyd
Tai'r-Bull
MOUNTAIN CENTRE
SN
Talsarn
Glas Fynydd Forest
Dyffryn Ceidrych
Twynllanan
Llanddeusant
LLANDDEUSANT
Crai
Pont-ar-llechau
Felin-Crai
Heol Senni
LLWYN Y CELYN
Glyn Tarell
Capel Gwynfe
Pont Aber
CRAIG CERRIG GLEISIAD A FAN FRYNYCH
Cray Res.
FAN BRYCHEINIOG
BRECON BEACONS
BANNAU BRYCHEINIOG
BLACK MOUNTAIN
FOEL FRAITH
FAN GIHIRYCH
FAN FAWR
Beacons Res.
Afon Twrch
FFOREST FAWR
Ystradfellte Res.
THE NATIONAL SHOWCAVES FOR WALES
Glyntawe
Y MYNYDD DU
DAN-YR-OGOF
CRAIG-Y-NOS
OGOF FFYNNON DDU
Cantref Res.
Craig-y-nos
Penwyllt
Brynamman
Rhosaman
Pen-y-cae
Llwyn-on Res.
Cwmllynfell
Ystradfellte
Gwaun-Leision
Ystradowen
Abercraf
Tairgwaith
Upper Cwm-twrch
Cwmgiedd
Caehopkin
CEFN-YR-ERW
SARN HELEN
Coelbren
Neath
Penrhos
Lower Cwm-twrch
Cwmgors
Ystradgynlais
Onllwyn
Gurnos
Dyffryn Cellwen
Penderyn
Ystalyfera
Seven Sisters
SWANSEA VALLEY
CWM ABERTAWE
Pontneddfechan
Pontbren Llwyd
Godre'r-graig
Nant-y-cafn
Glyn-neath
(Glynedd)
Climaen gwyn
Morfa Glas
Rhigos
Hirwaun
Ynys-meudwy
Rheola Forest
Mynydd March-Hywel
Blaengwrach
Cwm-hwnt
Tre-Gibbon
Cilybebyll
Crynant
VALE OF NEATH
CWM NEDD
Cwmgwrach
Penywaun
Gellinudd
CEFN COED COLLIERY MUS
RESOLVEN
Trecynon
Cwmdare
Rhôs
ABERDARE
A40
A483
A4069
A4067
A4215
A470
A4068
A474
A4109
A4221
A4059
A4061
A465
B4519
75
76
77
60
40

60
Trallong
Battle
Aberyscir
Brecon
(Aberhonddu)
Cathedral
Brecon Gaer Roman Fort
Llanfaes
Penpont
Llanspyddid
Mynydd Illtyd
Tai'r-Bull
Mountain Centre
Libanus
Brecknock Museum and Art Gallery
South Wales Borderers
Llechfaen
Llanywern
Llanfihangel Tal-y-llyn
Llandefaelog-tre'r-graig
Tredomen
Trefecca
Howell House
Trefeinon Open Farm
Pengenffordd
Mynydd Troed
Llangors
Llangorse Lake
Llangasty Talyllyn
Cathedine
Talyllyn
Llanhamlach
Llanfrynach
Pencelli
Scethrog
Trebinshwn House
Llansantffraed
Cwmrhos
Cwmdu
Bwlch
Cross Oak
Talybont-on-Usk
Aber-Village
Gaer
Tretower Castle & Court
Tretower
Pen Cerig-Calch
Coed-yr-ynys
Glyn Tarell
Brecon Beacons
Pen y Fan
Fan Fawr
Beacons Res.
Ystradfellte Res.
Neuadd Reservoirs
Talybont Res.
Danywenallt
Llangynidr
Crickhowell
Ffawyddog
Llangattock
Abercynafon
Cantref Res.
Garn Caws
Craig y Cilau
Mynydd Llangynidr
Mynydd Llangattock
Nant-ddu
Garwnant Visitor Centre
Pontsticill Reservoir
Llwyn-on Res.
Brecon Mountain Railway
Pontsticill
Trefil
Garnlydan
Rassau
Blackrock
Clydach
Llanelly
Cwm Clydach
Llanelly Hill
Bryn Bach
Tafarnau-bach
Beaufort
Brynmawr
Dukestown
Sirhowy
Nantyglo
Princetown
Vaynor
Penderyn
Cefn-coed-y-cymmer
Dowlais
Castle Mus & Art Gall
Llechryd
Tredegar
Ebbw Vale
(Glyn Ebwy)
Coalbrookvale
Pontypool & Blaenavon Rly
Big Pit Mining Museum
Georgetown
Rhymney
(Rhymni)
Briery Hill
Blaina
Coity Mountain
Hirwaun
Gellideg
Pen-yr-Heolgerrig
Merthyr Tydfil
(Merthyr Tudful)
Pontlottyn
Waunlwyd
Festival Park
East Bank
Tre-Gibbon
Fochriw
Abertysswg
Cwmtillery
Abertillery
(Abertyleri)
Ynysfach Engine House Heritage Cen.
Penywaun
Trecynon
Llwydcoed
Pentrebach
New Tredegar
(Tredegar Newydd)
Cwm
Manmoel
Cwmdare
Aberdare
(Aberdâr)
Dare Valley
Aber-nant
Abercanaid
Troedyrhiw
Tirphil
Hollybush
Aberbeeg
St Illtyd
Cwmbâch
Deri
Rhondda
Aberaman
Bedlinog
Cwmfelin
Markham
Pen-y-Fan Pond
Brynithel
Llanhilleth
Aberfan
Aberbargoed Grasslands
Trinant
Cwmaman
Mountain Ash
(Aberpennar)
Merthyr Vale
Bargoed
(Bargod)
Argoed
Swffryd
Cynon
Taf Bargoed
Gilfach
Maerdy
Penrhiwceiber
Treorchy
(Treorci)
Ferndale
St Gwynno Forest
Treharris
Trelewis
Gelligaer
Pengam
Oakdale
Blackwood
(Coed Duon)
Crumlin
(Crymlyn)
Newbridge
Pentre
Llancaiach Fawr Manor
Rhondda
Taff
Ynysboeth
Nelson
Pontllanfraith
Ystrad
Tylorstown
Abercynon
Hengoed
Lanfach
Ton-Pentre
Gelli
Pont-y-gwaith
Wattstown
Ystrad-mynach
Maesycwmmer
Wyllie
Abercarn
Cwmcarn
Llwynypia
Clydach Vale
Ynysybwl
Rhymney Valley
Sirhowy
Ynysddu
Cwm felin fach
Pontywaun
Crosskeys
Trealaw
Ynyshir
Rhondda Heritage Park
Tonypandy
Penygraig
Porth
Glyncoch
Cilfynydd
Caerphilly
Trehafod
Trebanog
Pontypridd
Senghenydd
Abertridwr
Llanbradach
Sirhowy Valley
Machen
Glyntaff
Bedwas
Treforest
Rhydyfelin
(Caerffili)
Penyrheol
Lower Machen
Tonyrefail
Hendreforgan
0 1 2 3 miles
0 1 2 3 4 5 km

Monmouthshire
(Sir Fynwy)
Abergavenny
(Y Fenni)
Monmouth
(Trefynwy)
Usk
(Brynbuga)
Caerleon
(Caerllion)
Cwmbran
(Cwmbrân)
PONTYPOOL
(PONT-Y-PŴL)
Newport
Caldicot
Blaenavon
Abersychan
Raglan
Pontrilas
Grosmont
Skenfrith
Llanthony
Pandy
Longtown
Chepstow Pk. Wood
Wormbridge
Kilpeck
Much Dewchurch
Wormelow Tump
Abbey Dore
Ewyas Harold
Llangarron
Marstow
Whitchurch
Symonds Yat
Dixton
Trellech
Llandogo
Tintern Parva
Shirenewton
Caerwent
Penhow
St Arvans
Mathern
Portskewett

Dewchurch
Carey
Ballingham
Falcon
Crossway
Lyne Down
Dymock
Ryton
Redmarley D'Abitot
Playley Green
78
79
Fawley Chapel
Penalt
How Caple
ST MARY'S CHURCH
Kempley
Fishpool
Poolhill
Staunton
Corse
Hoarwithy
Llandinabo
Red Rail
King's Caple
Foy
Hole-in-the-Wall
Brand Green
Leadon
Harewood End
Sellack
Upper Grove Common
Brampton Abbotts
Upton Bishop
Phocle Green
Crow Hill
Upleadon
Pencoyd
ROSS SPUR SERVICES
Gorsley
Michaelchurch
St Owens Cross
Bridstow
Peterstow
Rudhall
Linton
Bromsash
Kilcot
Newent
Hartpury
St Weonards
Tretire
Ross-on-Wye
Aston Ingham
THE INT CENTRE FOR BIRDS OF PREY
Malswick
CANDLEMAKERS
Weston under Penyard
Aston Crews
Clifford's Mesne
Kent's Green
Highleadon
Three Ashes
Tudorville
Glewstone
Hom Green
Coughton
Pontshill
Lea
Tibberton
Taynton
Rudford
Lassington
Llangarron
Pencraig
Llancloudy
Walford
Hope Mansell
Glasshouse Hill
Highnam Green
61
Marstow
Goodrich
Llangrove
Kerne Bridge
Mitcheldean
Longhope
Huntley
Bulley
Highnam
WYE VALLEY BUTTERFLY ZOO
JUBILEE MAZE
Whitchurch
WHITCHURCH SERVICES
Welsh Bicknor
WELSH BICKNOR
Ruardean
Drybrook
Birdwood
Churcham
Oakle Street
Ganarew
Greater Doward
Lower Lydbrook
Ruardean Woodside
Blaisdon
Symonds Yat
Upper Lydbrook
Nailbridge
Northwood Green
Elmore Back
Minsterworth
LADY PARK WOOD
English Bicknor
Brierley
Flaxley
Westbury-on-Severn
Farleys End
FIDDLER'S ELBOW
Dixton
Christchurch
Edge End
Bilson Green
Cinderford
Littledean
Elton
Longney
NELSON MUS
Monmouth
Berry Hill
Five Acres
FOREST
OF
DEAN
WESTBURY COURT
LITTLEDEAN HALL
Boxbush
Hardwicke
Wyesham
Staunton
Mile End
COLLIERY
BEECHENHURST LODGE
Ruspidge
Newnham
Rodley
Penallt
Coleford
Broadwell
Upper Soudley
DEAN HERITAGE CENTRE
WORKING FARM
Arlingham
Mitchel Troy
Redbrook
G W R MUSEUM
IRON MINES
Coalway
Fretherne
Saul
Upper Framilode
HIGHBURY WOOD
Newland
Milkwall
Moreton Valence
OFFA'S DYKE PATH
CAVES
Ellwood
Parkend
Awre
Whitminster
Pen-twyn
Clearwell
G
I
O
U
Hoop
Stowe Green
Trow Green
Yorkley
Viney Hill
Blakeney
The Noose
Frampton on Severn
Whitebrook
Whitecroft
Pillowell
River Severn
Trellech
Bream
The Eaves
OFFA'S DYKE
St Briavels
DEAN FOREST RAILWAY & MUSEUM
WWT SLIMBRIDGE WETLAND CENTRE
Eastington
Llandogo
ST BRIAVELS
Purton
Cambridge
Leonard Stanley
Parkhouse
Coldharbour
Lydney
Newerne
Slimbridge
Moorend
Frocester
Catbrook
Hewelsfield
Sharpness
Halmore
Gossington
Aylburton
Newtown
Coaley
OLD STA.
Tintern Parva
Brockweir
Wanswell
Breadstone
TINTERN ABBEY
Netherend
Alvington
Lower Cam
The Quarry
Nympsfield
Chapel Hill
Woolaston
Brookend
Berkeley
BERKELEY CASTLE
Cam
ULEY TUMULUS
Tidenham Chase
Stinchcombe
Dursley
Wibdon
Stroat
Ham
DR JENNER'S HOUSE
Woodmancote
St Arvans
Boughspring
Bevington
Woodcroft
Tidenham
Shepperdine
Hill
Woodford
Stone
Nibley Green
North Nibley
CHEPSTOW
Tutshill
STUART CRYSTAL VISITOR CENTRE
OLDBURY POWER STATION & VISITOR CENTRE
MICHAELWOOD SERVICES
Mounton
Sedbury
Rockhampton
Falfield
Tortworth
Pwllmeyric
Chepstow (Cas-gwent)
Oldbury-on-Severn
Charfield
Wotton-under-Edge
Beachley
Whitfield
Kingswood
ABBEY GATEHOUSE
Mathern
SEVERN ROAD BRIDGE PONT HAFREN
Morton
Littleton-on-Severn
Milbury Heath
Cromhall
Churchend
Alderley
SEVERN VIEW SERVICES
Thornbury
43
Cromhall Common
Hillesley
Elberton
Alveston
Wickwar
Portskewett
Ingst
Tytherington
A49
A449
M50
A4137
A40
A4136
A48
A466
A4151
M5
A38
M48
A417
A4135
B4024
B4215
B4221
B4222
B4224
B4234
B4228
B4226
B4227
B4231
B4432
B4066
B4058
B4059
B4060
B4061
B4461
B4071
B4235
B4293
B4521
B4348
0 1 2 3 miles
0 1 2 3 4 5 km

Forthampton
Eldersfield
Walton Cardiff
Fiddington
Oxenton
Alstone
Didbrook
Hailes Abbey
Cutsdean
Corse Lawn
Chaceley
79
Deerhurst
Odda's Chapel
Tredington
Stoke Orchard
80
Dixton
Gretton
Greet
Hailes
Ford
Farmcote
Gotherington
Bishop's Cleeve
279
274
Langley Hill
Winchcombe Pottery
Winchcombe
Sudeley Castle and Gardens
Temple
Tirley
Apperley
Hardwicke
Woodmancote
Railway Mus
299
Hasfield
Coombe Hill
Elmstone Hardwicke
Cleeve Hill
Belas Knap Long Barrow
Kineton
Ashleworth
Leigh
M5
Southam
Severn
10
Swindon
Cheltenham
The Cotswold Way
Charlton Abbots
Guiting Power
86
Norton
Boddington
Uckington
P&R
Staverton
Arle
Gallery & Museum
Prestbury
Battledown
Hawling
Sandhurst
Down Hatherley
Staverton Bridge
Golden Valley
Sandfields
Brockhampton
Nature in Art
Twigworth
Gloucestershire
Cheltenham
Charlton Kings
Sevenhampton
Maisemore
Parton
Longford
Lansdown
Up Hatherley
Whittington
Syreford
Over Bridge
Longlevens
Holst's Birthplace
A40
32
Notgrove Long Barrow
Cath
Churchdown
Badgeworth
Leckhampton
Dowdeswell
Andoversford
Docks
Gloucester Waterways Museum
Gloucester
Barnwood
Hucclecote
Shurdington
A436
Shipton Solers
Shipton
Hazleton
A417
Crickley Hill
Ullenwood
298
Hempsted
Matson
Brockworth
Bentham
Coberley
Withington
Compton Abdale
A40
Hampnett
A38
Tuffley
Upton St Leonard's
Great Witcombe
Cowley
Cotswold Countryside Collection
Cassey Compton
Robinswood Hill
Prinknash Abbey & Bird Park
Villa
Cotswold
Birdlip
Colesbourne
Chedworth Roman Villa
Yanworth
Whaddon
Cranham
Brimpsfield
Elkstone
267
Chedworth
Brookthorpe
Cotswold Commons and Beechwoods
Churn
Fossebridge
Coln St Dennis
Rococo Gardens
Sheepscombe
Whiteway
Syde
Haresfield
Harescombe
The Camp
Winstone
Rendcomb
Foss Cross
Coln Rogers
Painswick
Miserden
Woodmancote
Calmsden
Winson
Miserden Park
255
Duntisbourne Abbots
Duntisbourne Leer
North Cerney
A429
Pitchcombe
Whiteshill
Slad
Sudgrove
Randwick
Bagendon
Arlington
Bisley
Edgeworth
Duntisbourne Rouse
Stonehouse
Stroud
Ebley
Eastcombe
Bournes Green
Daglingworth
Baunton
Barnsley
King's Stanley
Rodborough
Chalford
Oakridge
Oakley Wood
Sapperton
Stratton
Thrupp
Brownshill
Ampney Crucis
Ampney St Mary
Woodchester
Brimscombe
Frampton Mansell
Cirencester
Littleworth
Amberley
Hyde
A419
Cirencester Lock Up
Nympsfield Long Barrow
Woodchester Park
Coates
Chesterton
Roman Amphitheatre
Preston
Ampney St Peter
Windsoredge
Minchinhampton
Harnhill
Nailsworth
Box
Tarlton
Source of the Thames
Siddington
Driffield
Whiteway
Cherington
64
Horsley
191
Avening
Rodmarton
Ewen
South Cerney
Trull House Gardens
Kemble
Kingscote
Shorncote
Res.
Cotswold Water Park
Poole Keynes
Keynes
Cerney Wick
Culkerton
Tetbury Upton
Neigh Bridge
Chavenage House
Ashley
Somerford Keynes
Ashton Keynes
North Meadow
A4135
Chelworth
Cricklade
Beverston
A429
Chedglow
Oaksey
Crudwell
Tetbury
Eastcourt
Swill Brook
Leigh
Long Newnton
Chelworth Green
Leighterton
A433
Doughton
Hankerton
Upper Minety
Minety
Westonbirt Arboretum
Shipton Moyne
Brokenborough
44
Perry Green
Purton Stoke
Oldbury on the Hill
Westonbirt
Filands
Charlton
Key
Purton

STANWAY HOUSE
1
2
A424
SEZINCOTE
WELLINGTON AVIATION MUSEUM
the Heath
Little Compton
3
Compton
Great Rollright
4
HAILES ABBEY
80
dean
Ford
Sezincote
81
CHASTLETON HOUSE
A3400
WINCHCOMBE
Farmcote
Longborough
Evenlode
A44
ROLLRIGHT STONES
B4077
Condicote
Donnington
A429
Chastleton
Salford
Over Norton
221
SUDELEY CASTLE GARDENS
Temple Guiting
Broadwell
Adlestrop
Cornwell
299
COTSWOLD FARM PARK
Upper Swell
Stow-on-the-Wold
A436
Chipping Norton
Kineton
Lower Swell
Oddington
Daylesford
COTSWOLDS
Barton
B4068
Maugersbury
A
Guiting Power
STOW-ON-THE-WOLD
B4450
Kingham
Churchill
A361
Lidstone
Hawling
Naunton
Upper Slaughter
Bledington
Sarsden
Brockhampton
Lower Slaughter
50
Wyck Rissington
Icomb
THE OLD MILL
Chadlington
Spelsbury
A436
13
8
Sevenhampton
MODEL VILLAGE
Westcote
Bruern Abbey
Lyneham
NOTGROVE LONG BARROW
Notgrove
Bourton-on-the-Water
250
Salperton
Idbury
Cold Aston
BIRDLAND PARK & GARDENS
Little Rissington
Upper Rissington
Chilson
63
Clapton-on-the-Hill
Fifield
11
Ascott-under-Wychwood
6
Hazleton
A429
Windrush
Milton under Wychwood
Shipton-under-Wychwood
WYCHWOOD FOREST
Turkdean
Great Rissington
A424
O
X
A40
10
186
Compton Abdale
Hampnett
Farmington
B4437
COTSWOLD COUNTRYSIDE COLLECTION
B
Cassey Compton
Sherborne
Great Barrington
Leafield
B4022
Yanworth
Northleach
Taynton
A361
Fordwells
CHEDWORTH ROMAN VILLA
Windrush
Eastington
9
Fulbrook
Asthall Leigh
Little Barrington
Chedworth
LODGE PARK
A40
Burford
Swinbrook
Fossebridge
Asthall
Minster Lovell
Coln St Dennis
60
B4047
MINSTER LOVELL HALL AND DOVECOTE
10
B4425
7
Foss Cross
50
Aldsworth
Signet
B4020
Charterville Allotments
Coln Rogers
Westwell
STREET
Winson
Holwell
Shilton
B4477
Curbridge
A429
Ablington
Leach
Bradwell Grove
COTSWOLD WILDLIFE PARK
Brize Norton
Arlington
AKEMAN
A361
A4095
Ducklington
Bibury
Carterton
ARLINGTON ROW
Eastleach Turville
BRIZE NORTON
Lew
C
Barnsley
Coln
Coln St Aldwyn's
Eastleach Martin
8
Hatherop
Filkins
Alvescot
Black Bourton
Quenington
Fyfield
Broughton Poggs
Kencot
B4020
B4425
Broadwell
Aston
Ampney Crucis
Ampney St Mary
Southrop
Bampton
Little Faringdon
Langford
Weald
12
Clanfield
10
Ampney St Peter
Poulton
Milton End
A417
11
63
Fairford
Grafton
Harnhill
Meysey Hampton
Horcott
Radcot
Driffield
Lechlade-on-Thames
B4449
Carswell Marsh
CHIMNEY MEADOWS
7
Kelmscot
Whelford
Marston Meysey
Inglesham
Eaton Hastings
South Cerney
KELMSCOTT MANOR
Dunfield
6
Res.
Buscot
A4095
Littleworth
Down Ampney
Kempsford
BUSCOT PARK
8
50
Cerney Wick
A417
Latton
Thames
Upper Inglesham
A419
D
Castle Eaton
Faringdon
Hatford
Ashton Keynes
NORTH MEADOW
THE THAMES PATH
Hannington Wick
158
BADBURY HILL
A361
GREAT BARN
Cricklade
Coleshill
Shellingford
Great Coxwell
Little Coxwell
Hannington
B4019
Leigh
Highworth
Fernham
Chelworth Green
Ray
4
50
VALE OF WHITE HORSE
B4040
SWINDON AND CRICKLADE RAILWAY
Broad Blunsdon
B4019
B4000
B4508
9
A420
B4508
Baulking
Purton Stoke
A361
Stanton Fitzwarren
9
Severnhampton
Longcot
Blunsdon St Andrew
STANTON PARK
Watchfield
45
Shrivenham
Uffington
2
P&R
Haydon
Penhill
South Marston
3
4
West
Purton
0 1 2 3 miles
0 1 2 3 4 5 km

Swerford
Hempton
Deddington
Souldern
Cottisford
Newton Purcell
Nether Worton
Baynard's Green
Hardwick
Hethe
Chetwode
Great Tew
Over Worton
Duns Tew
North Aston
Fritwell
Fringford
Little Tew
Ledwell
Somerton
Fewcott
Stoke Lyne
Heythrop
Sandford St Martin
Middle Aston
Ardley
CHERWELL VALLEY SERVICES
Middle Barton
Upper Heyford
Stratton Audley
Church Enstone
Westcott Barton
Steeple Aston
Lower Heyford
Bucknell
Gagingwell
Caversfield
Steeple Barton
Caulcott
Woodfield
Enstone
Cleveley
ROUSHAM HOUSE
Middleton Stoney
Highfield
Bicester
Kiddington
Launton
Taston
Over Kiddington
Glympton
Chesterton
BICESTER VILLAGE
Tackley
Kirtlington
Ambrosden
Blackthorn
Charlbury
Wootton
Wendlebury
Weston-on-the-Green
Lower Arncott
Stonesfield
Fawler
Bunkers Hill
Bletchingdon
Merton
Upper Arncott
Piddington
NORTH LEIGH ROMAN VILLA
Woodstock
Shipton on Cherwell
Charlton on Otmoor
Combe
BLENHEIM PALACE
LONDON OXFORD
Thrupp
Murcott
Ramsden
Hampton Poyle
Oddington
BOARSTALL TOWER
Boarstall
East End
Bladon
Begbroke
Kidlington
Islip
Brill
North Leigh
Long Hanborough
Noke
Hailey
New Yatt
Freeland
Church Hanborough
Yarnton
Horton-cum-Studley
Woodeaton
Beckley
Oakley
Witney
Barnard Gate
Cassington
OXFORD SERVICES
South Leigh
Eynsham
Wolvercote
Elsfield
High Cogges
Swinford
Summertown
Marston
Stanton St John
Forest Hill
COGGES MANOR FARM MUS
Wytham
THE OXFORD STORY
Barton
Farmoor
ASHMOLEAN MUS
Headington
Ickford
Farmoor Reservoir
Botley
UNIVERSITY
Holton
Waterperry
WATERPERRY GARDENS
Sutton
BOTANIC GARDEN
Wheatley
Waterstock
Hardwick
Stanton Harcourt
North Hinksey
Oxford
SHOTOVER
West End
New Hinksey
Horspath
Yelford
CONDUIT HOUSE
Cowley
OXFORD SERVICES
Cumnor
Chawley
South Hinksey
Iffley
Great Milton
Brighthampton
Standlake
Eaton
Cuddesdon
Northmoor
Bessels Leigh
Boars Hill
Kennington
Littlemore
Denton
Wootton
Garsington
Shifford
THE THAMES PATH
Appleton
Foxcombe Hill
Sandford on Thames
Little Milton
Thames or Isis
Lamborough Hill
Sunningwell
Toot Baldon
Duxford
ST KATHERINE'S
Longworth
Netherton
Cothill
Nuneham Courtenay
Marsh Baldon
Chislehampton
Hinton Waldrist
Fyfield
Tubney
COTHILL
Radley
Stadhampton
Kingston Bagpuize
Shippon
COUNTY HALL
KINGSTON BAGPUIZE
Southmoor
Chalgrove
Drayton St Leonard
Frilford
ABINGDON
Pusey
Garford
Marcham
Caldecott
Clifton Hampden
Berinsfield
Newington
Burcot
Brightwell Baldwin
Charney Bassett
Culham
Dorchester
PENDON MUS
Long Wittenham
DORCHESTER ABBEY
Berrick Salome
Lyford
Drayton
Sutton Courtenay
Appleford
Warborough
Roke
West Hanney
East Hanney
Little Wittenham
Shillingford
Milton
Steventon
Benson
Goosey
Denchworth
DIDCOT RAILWAY CENTRE
Brightwell cum Sotwell
Preston Crowmarsh
Milton Hill
Didcot
Grove
Harwell
Wallingford
Crowmarsh Gifford
West Hendred
Rowstock
East Hagbourne
North Moreton
CHOLSEY AND WALLINGFORD RAILWAY
East Challow
East Hendred
ARDINGTON HO
South
Oxford
AKEMAN STREET
SP
SU
WHITE HORSE

Buckingham
Winslow
Aylesbury
Thame
Haddenham
Princes Risborough
Chinnor
High Wycombe
Wendover
Weston Turville
Aston Clinton
Waddesdon
Brill
Boarstall
Long Crendon
Watlington
Stokenchurch
West Wycombe
Marsh Gibbon
Steeple Claydon
Middle Claydon
East Claydon
Botolph Claydon
Quainton
Whitchurch
Wing
Stewkley
Swanbourne
Great Horwood
Little Horwood
Padbury
Adstock
Addington
Hillesden
Twyford
Poundon
Charndon
Calvert
Edgcott
Grendon Underwood
Blackthorn
Kingswood
Ludgershall
Piddington
Westcott
Wotton Underwood
Dorton
Ashendon
Upper Pollicott
Chilton
Chearsley
Cuddington
Stone
Dinton
Westlington
Bishopstone
Ford
Stoke Mandeville
Kimble Wick
Great Kimble
Little Kimble
Ellesborough
Monks Risborough
Askett
Owlswick
Kingsey
Towersey
Longwick
Ilmer
Bledlow
Saunderton
Henton
Emmington
Sydenham
Tetsworth
Great Haseley
Little Haseley
Tiddington
Moreton
Waterperry
Waterstock
Ickford
Worminghall
Shabbington
Oakley
Little London
Easington
Postcombe
Crowell
Kingston Blount
Aston Rowant
Lewknor
Adwell
South Weston
Stoke Talmage
Shirburn
Pyrton
Cuxham
Brightwell Baldwin
Chalgrove
Newington
Stadhampton
Chislehampton
Berrick Salome
Warborough
Roke
Benson
Ewelme
Britwell Salome
Christmas Common
Northend
Greenfield
Turville Heath
Turville
Ibstone
Cadmore End
Bolter End
Fingest
Lane End
Frieth
Skirmett
Pishill
Stonor
Russell's Water
Park Corner
Cookley Green
Rockwell End
Marlow Bottom
Little Marlow
Wooburn
Flackwell Heath
Booker
Downley
Hughenden Valley
Naphill
Walters Ash
Bradenham
Lacey Green
Loosley Row
Speen
Bledlow Ridge
Radnage
The City
Great Hampden
Little Hampden
Dunsmore
Upper North Dean
Cryers Hill
Great Kingshill
Little Kingshill
Prestwood
Butler's Cross
Nash Lee
Terrick
North Lee
Halton
Buckland
Bierton
Hulcott
Rowsham
Wingrave
Weedon
Hardwick
Aston Abbotts
Cublington
Creslow
Pitchcott
Oving
North Marston
Granborough
Hoggeston
Dunton
Mursley
Drayton Parslow
North End
South End
Newton Longville
Stoke Hammond
Long Marston
Puttenham
Upper Winchendon
Lower Winchendon
Southcourt
Townsend
Aston Sandford
Meadle
Pitch Green
Great Milton
Little Milton
Denton
Holton
Launton
Stratton Audley
Fringford
Chetwode
Preston Bissett
Barton Hartshorn
Lower Arncott
Upper Arncott
Winslow Hall
Claydon House
Quainton Windmill
Buckinghamshire Railway Centre
Waddesdon Manor
Akeman Street
Boarstall Tower
Brill Windmill
Nether Winchendon House
Waterperry Gardens
Rycote Chapel
Oxford Services
Chinnor & Princes Risborough Railway
Manor House
West Wycombe Caves
West Wycombe Park
Hughenden Manor
Wycombe Air Park
The Ridgeway
Aston Rowant
St. Katherine's
0 1 2 3 miles
0 1 2 3 4 5 km

Great Brickhill
Woburn Abbey
Tingrith
Harlington
Barton-le-Clay
Pirton
Milton Bryan
Sharpenhoe
Hexton
Knocking Hoe
Kings Wood
Stockgrove Park
Potsgrove
Battlesden
Toddington Services
Sundon Hills
Barton Hills
Hitchin
Toddington
Streatley
Upper Sundon
Charlton
Heath and Reach
Lower Sundon
Lilley
Great Offley
Gosmore
St Ippolyts
Hockliffe
Tebworth
Chalton
Galley Hill
Leighton Buzzard
Eggington
Wingfield
Sundon Park
Limbury
Tilsworth
Preston
Leighton Buzzard Railway
Stanbridge
Houghton Regis
Luton
Stopsley
Wardown Park Mus
Cockernhoe Green
King's Walden
Leagrave
Billington
Mead Open Fm
Lower End
Dunstable
Biscot
Hart Hill
Breachwood Green
St Paul's Walden
Ledburn
Eaton Green
Totternhoe
The Guided Busway
Luton
Church End
Priory Church of St Peter
Farley Hill
London Luton
Whitwell
Slapton
Eaton Bray
Dunstable Downs
Stockwood Craft Mus
Edlesborough
Kensworth
Caddington
Peter's Green
Horton
Kimpton
Whipsnade
Slip End
Codicote
Ivinghoe Aston
Kensworth Common
Whipsnade Wild Animal Park
Woodside Farm and Wildfowl Park
East Hyde
Blackmore End
Ivinghoe
Dagnall
Studham
Markyate
Kinsbourne Green
Batford
Shaw's Corner
Pitstone Green
Pitstone
Jockey End
Flamstead
Ringshall
Trowley Bottom
Harpenden
Marshall's Heath
Wheathampstead
Tring Wharf
Little Gaddesden
Ashridge Park
Hatching Green
Drayton Beauchamp
New Mill
Aldbury
Redbourn
Tring
Great Gaddesden
Toll
Water End
Childwick Green
Sandridge
Stanborough Park
Nettleden
Wigginton
Piccotts End
Jersey Farm
Hastoe
Northchurch
Potten End
Old Gorhambury House
Townsend
Marshalswick
Berkhamsted Castle
The Galleria
Berkhamsted
Gadebridge
St Albans
Fleetville
Roman Theatre of Verulamium
Cholesbury
Bourne End
Buckland Common
Boxmoor
Hemel Hempstead
St Stephens
The Camp
Ashley Green
Colney Heath
Sopwell
Bellingdon
Abbey
Lee Clump
Whelpley Hill
Felden
Chiswell Green
London Colney
Chartridge
Gdns of the Rose
Bedmond
Lye Green
Bovingdon
Future Gdns/Butterfly World
Primrosehill
Botley
Bovingdon Green
Kings Langley
De Havilland Aircraft Heritage Cen
South Heath
Leyhill
Chesham
Chipperfield
Abbots Langley
Bricket Wood
Colney Street
Shenleybury
Great Missenden
Flaunden
Radlett
Shenley
Hyde Heath
Chesham Bois
Latimer
Sarratt
Aldenham
Green Street
Little Missenden
Chenies
Chenies Manor Ho
Letchmore Heath
Holmer Green
Amersham
Little Chalfont
Chorleywood
Watford
Borehamwood
Croxley Green
Aldenham
Elstree
Penn Street
Coleshill
Chiltern Open Air Mus
Rickmansworth
Oxhey
Bushey
Winchmore Hill
Chalfont St Giles
South Oxhey
Bushey Heath
Penn
Milton's Cottage
Rickmansworth Aquadrome
Knotty Green
Seer Green
Maple Cross
Eastbury
Stanmore
Forty Green
Bekonscot Model Village
Jordans
Chalfont Common
Batchworth Heath
Edgware
Loudwater
Bishop's Wood
Northwood
Hatch End
Harrow Weald
Beaconsfield
Chalfont St Peter
Harefield
Wealdstone
Bayhurst Wood
Ruislip Woods
Pinner
Ruislip Common
Harrow
Greenhill
Kingsbury
Beaconsfield Services
Gerrards
Denham Green
M1
M25
M40
A5
A41
A505
A414
A405
A413
A355
A6
83
84
68
48

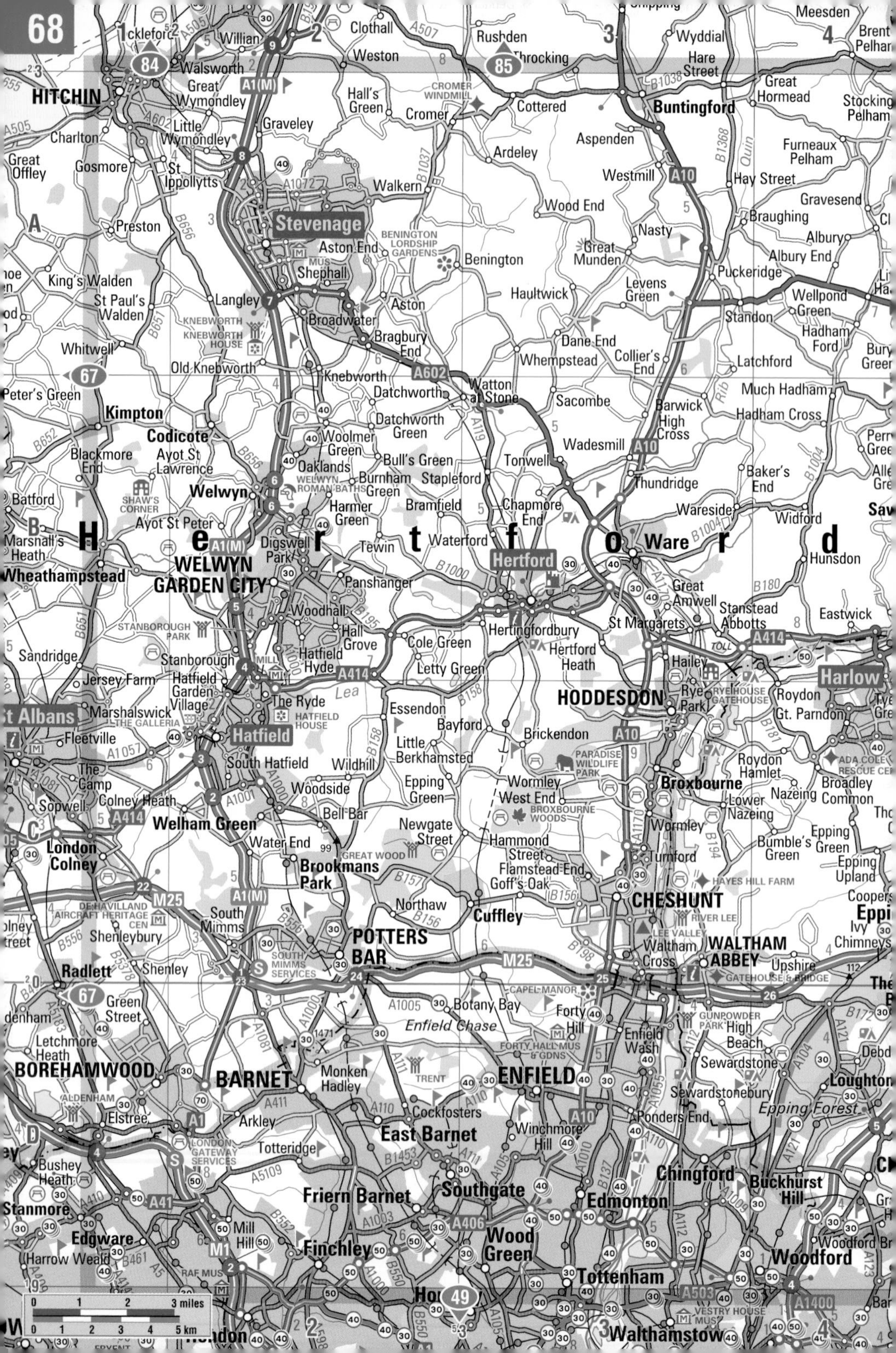

84
85
67
49
Ickleford
Willian
Clothall
Rushden
Throcking
Wyddial
Meesden
Brent Pelham
Weston
Hare Street
Walsworth
HITCHIN
Great Wymondley
Little Wymondley
Hall's Green
Cromer
CROMER WINDMILL
Cottered
Buntingford
Great Hormead
Stocking Pelham
Charlton
Graveley
Ardeley
Aspenden
Furneaux Pelham
Great Offley
Gosmore
St Ippollytts
Walkern
Westmill
Hay Street
Gravesend
Wood End
Braughing
Preston
Stevenage
Aston End
BENINGTON LORDSHIP GARDENS
Benington
Nasty
Albury
Great Munden
Albury End
King's Walden
Shephall
Puckeridge
St Paul's Walden
Langley
Haultwick
Levens Green
Wellpond Green
Broadwater
Aston
Standon
KNEBWORTH HOUSE
Bragbury End
Dane End
Hadham Ford
Whitwell
Old Knebworth
Whempstead
Collier's End
Latchford
Knebworth
Watton at Stone
Datchworth
Sacombe
Much Hadham
Peter's Green
Kimpton
Datchworth Green
Barwick
Hadham Cross
Codicote
Woolmer Green
High Cross
Blackmore End
Ayot St Lawrence
Oaklands
Bull's Green
Wadesmill
Tonwell
Baker's End
Welwyn
WELWYN ROMAN BATHS
Burnham Green
Stapleford
Thundridge
Batford
SHAW'S CORNER
Harmer Green
Bramfield
Chapmore End
Wareside
Widford
Ayot St Peter
Marshall's Heath
H e r t f o r d
Digswell Park
Tewin
Waterford
Hertford
Ware
Hunsdon
Wheathampstead
WELWYN GARDEN CITY
Panshanger
Great Amwell
Woodhall
Stanstead Abbotts
Eastwick
Sandridge
STANBOROUGH PARK
Hall Grove
Cole Green
Hertingfordbury
St Margarets
Hertford Heath
Stanborough
Hatfield Hyde
Letty Green
Hailey
Harlow
Jersey Farm
Hatfield Garden Village
The Ryde
Lea
Essendon
HODDESDON
Rye Park
RYE HOUSE GATEHOUSE
Roydon
St Albans
Marshalswick
THE GALLERIA
HATFIELD HOUSE
Bayford
Brickendon
Gt. Parndon
Fleetville
Hatfield
Little Berkhamsted
PARADISE WILDLIFE PARK
The Camp
South Hatfield
Wildhill
Roydon Hamlet
ADA COLE RESCUE CENTRE
Colney Heath
Woodside
Epping Green
Wormley West End
Broxbourne
Broadley Common
Sopwell
Bell Bar
BROXBOURNE WOODS
Lower Nazeing
Nazeing
Welham Green
Newgate Street
Wormley
London Colney
Water End
Hammond Street
Epping Green
Bumble's Green
GREAT WOOD
Turnford
Epping Upland
Brookmans Park
Flamstead End
Goff's Oak
HAYES HILL FARM
Northaw
CHESHUNT
Coopersale
DE HAVILLAND AIRCRAFT HERITAGE CEN
South Mimms
Cuffley
RIVER LEE
Epping
Shenleybury
POTTERS BAR
LEE VALLEY
WALTHAM ABBEY
Ivy Chimneys
Radlett
Shenley
SOUTH MIMMS SERVICES
Waltham Cross
Upshire
Green Street
CAPEL MANOR
GATEHOUSE & BRIDGE
Botany Bay
Forty Hill
GUNPOWDER PARK
Letchmore Heath
Enfield Chase
High Beach
Enfield Wash
FORTY HALL MUS & GDNS
Debden
BOREHAMWOOD
Monken Hadley
Sewardstone
BARNET
TRENT
ENFIELD
Loughton
ALDENHAM
Sewardstonebury
Elstree
Arkley
Cockfosters
Ponders End
Epping Forest
East Barnet
Winchmore Hill
Totteridge
Bushey
LONDON GATEWAY SERVICES
Bushey Heath
Southgate
Chingford
Buckhurst Hill
Friern Barnet
Edmonton
Stanmore
Mill Hill
Edgware
Wood Green
Woodford Bridge
Harrow Weald
Finchley
Woodford
RAF MUS
Tottenham
Walthamstow
VESTRY HOUSE MUS
Hendon
A1(M)
A505
A507
A602
A10
A414
A1
M25
M1
A41
A406
A503
0 1 2 3 miles
0 1 2 3 4 5 km

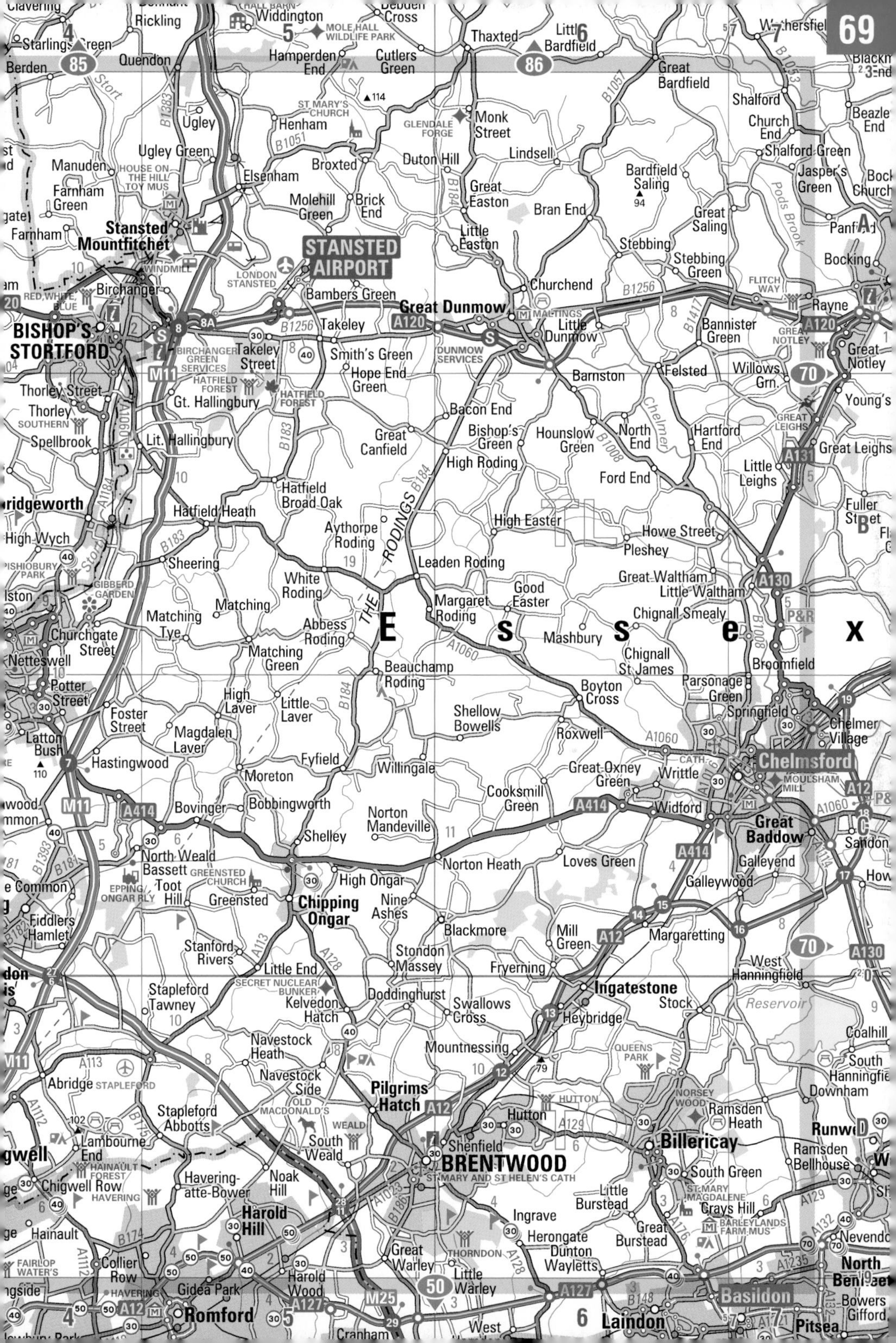

69
Rickling
Widdington
Mole Hall Wildlife Park
Cross
Thaxted
Bardfield
Starling's Green
Berden
Quendon
Hamperden End
Cutlers Green
Great Bardfield
Shalford
Stort
St Mary's Church
Henham
Glendale Forge
Monk Street
Church End
Beazle End
Ugley
Ugley Green
Broxted
Duton Hill
Lindsell
Shalford Green
Manuden
House on the Hill Toy Mus
Elsenham
Bardfield Saling
Jasper's Green
Farnham Green
Molehill Green
Brick End
Great Easton
Bran End
Great Saling
Pods Brook
Farnham
Stansted Mountfitchet
Stansted Airport
Little Easton
Stebbing
Stebbing Green
Bocking
Windmill
London Stansted
Churchend
Flitch Way
Red, White, Blue
Birchanger
Bambers Green
Great Dunmow
Maltings
Rayne
Bishop's Stortford
Takeley
Little Dunmow
Bannister Green
Great Notley
Birchanger Green Services
Takeley Street
Smith's Green
Dunmow Services
Felsted
Willows Grn.
Hatfield Forest
Hope End Green
Barnston
Thorley Street
Gt. Hallingbury
Bacon End
Young's
Thorley
Southern
Great Canfield
Bishop's Green
Hounslow Green
North End
Hartford End
Great Leighs
Chelmer
Spellbrook
Lit. Hallingbury
High Roding
Ford End
Little Leighs
Hatfield Broad Oak
Fuller Street
Hatfield Heath
Aythorpe Roding
High Easter
Howe Street
High Wych
The Rodings
Pleshey
Sheering
Leaden Roding
Gibberd Garden
White Roding
Good Easter
Great Waltham
Little Waltham
Matching
Margaret Roding
Chignall Smealy
Matching Tye
Abbess Roding
Churchgate Street
Mashbury
E s s e x
Matching Green
Chignall St James
Broomfield
Netteswell
Beauchamp Roding
Boyton Cross
Parsonage Green
Potter Street
High Laver
Little Laver
Shellow Bowells
Springfield
Chelmer Village
Foster Street
Roxwell
Magdalen Laver
Latton Bush
Hastingwood
Fyfield
Chelmsford
Willingale
Great Oxney Green
Writtle
Cath
Moulsham Mill
Moreton
Cooksmill Green
Bobbingworth
Bovinger
Widford
Norton Mandeville
Great Baddow
Sandon
Shelley
North Weald Bassett
Greensted Church
Norton Heath
Loves Green
Galleyend
Epping Ongar Rly
Toot Hill
High Ongar
Galleywood
Common
Greensted
Chipping Ongar
Nine Ashes
Fiddlers Hamlet
Blackmore
Mill Green
Margaretting
Stanford Rivers
Stondon Massey
Fryerning
West Hanningfield
Little End
Secret Nuclear Bunker
Ingatestone
Stock
Stapleford Tawney
Kelvedon Hatch
Doddinghurst
Swallows Cross
Reservoir
Heybridge
Coalhill
Navestock Heath
Mountnessing
Queens Park
South Hanningfield
Abridge
Stapleford
Navestock Side
Downham
Pilgrims Hatch
Old Macdonald's
Hutton
Norsey Wood
Ramsden Heath
Stapleford Abbotts
Weald
Lambourne End
South Weald
Shenfield
Billericay
Ramsden Bellhouse
Hainault Forest
Brentwood
St Mary and St Helen's Cath
Chigwell Row
Havering-atte-Bower
Noak Hill
South Green
Havering
Little Burstead
St Mary Magdalene
Crays Hill
Harold Hill
Ingrave
Hainault
Great Burstead
Barleylands Farm Mus
Herongate
Great Warley
Thorndon
Dunton Wayletts
Collier Row
Fairlop Water's
Harold Wood
Little Warley
North Benfleet
Gidea Park
Basildon
Havering
Romford
Laindon
Bowers Gifford
Cranham
West
Pitsea
M11
A120
A414
A12
A127
M25
A130
A131
A1060
A128
A129
B1256
B184
B183
B1008

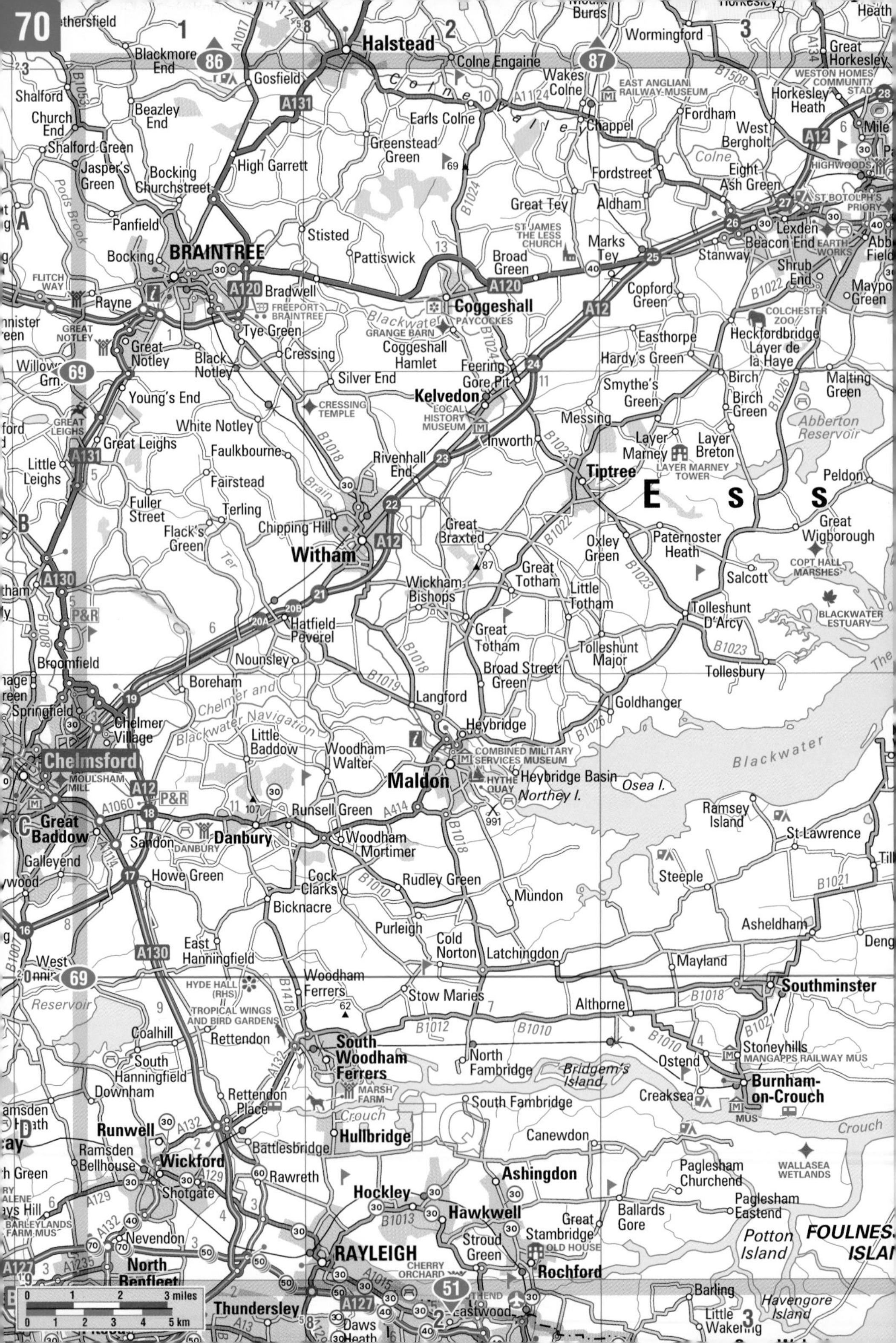

Halstead
Bures
Wormingford
Great Horkesley
Blackmore End
86
87
Colne Engaine
Wakes Colne
EAST ANGLIAN RAILWAY MUSEUM
WESTON HOMES COMMUNITY STAD
Gosfield
Colne Valley
Horkesley Heath
Shalford
Beazley End
Earls Colne
Chappel
Fordham
West Bergholt
Church End
Greenstead Green
Colne
Shalford Green
Jasper's Green
Bocking Churchstreet
High Garrett
Fordstreet
Eight Ash Green
HIGHWOODS
Great Tey
Aldham
ST BOTOLPH'S PRIORY
Panfield
Stisted
ST JAMES THE LESS CHURCH
Marks Tey
Lexden
Beacon End
EARTH WORKS
Bocking
BRAINTREE
Pattiswick
Broad Green
Stanway
Shrub End
FLITCH WAY
Rayne
Bradwell
Coggeshall
Copford Green
Maypole Green
FREEPORT BRAINTREE
PAYCOCKES
COLCHESTER ZOO
Great Notley
Tye Green
Blackwater
GRANGE BARN
Easthorpe
Heckfordbridge
Layer de la Haye
Cressing
Coggeshall Hamlet
Hardy's Green
Black Notley
Feering
Gore Pit
Birch
Malting Green
Willows Grn.
69
Silver End
Kelvedon
Smythe's Green
Birch Green
Young's End
CRESSING TEMPLE
LOCAL HISTORY MUSEUM
Messing
Abberton Reservoir
GREAT LEIGHS
White Notley
Layer Marney
Layer Breton
Great Leighs
Faulkbourne
Inworth
LAYER MARNEY TOWER
Little Leighs
Rivenhall End
Tiptree
Peldon
Fairstead
Brain
E s s
Fuller Street
Terling
Great Braxted
Great Wigborough
Flack's Green
Chipping Hill
Oxley Green
Paternoster Heath
COPT HALL MARSHES
Witham
Great Totham
Salcott
Ter
Wickham Bishops
Little Totham
BLACKWATER ESTUARY
Hatfield Peverel
Great Totham
Tolleshunt D'Arcy
Broomfield
Nounsley
Tolleshunt Major
Tollesbury
Boreham
Broad Street Green
Langford
Goldhanger
Springfield
Chelmer and Blackwater Navigation
Chelmer Village
Heybridge
Little Baddow
Woodham Walter
COMBINED MILITARY SERVICES MUSEUM
Blackwater
Chelmsford
Maldon
HYTHE QUAY
Heybridge Basin
Osea I.
Northey I.
MOULSHAM MILL
Runsell Green
Ramsey Island
Great Baddow
Sandon
Danbury
Woodham Mortimer
St Lawrence
Galleyend
Howe Green
Cock Clarks
Rudley Green
Steeple
Bicknacre
Mundon
Purleigh
Asheldham
East Hanningfield
Cold Norton
Latchingdon
West Hanningfield
Mayland
Woodham Ferrers
HYDE HALL (RHS)
Reservoir
Stow Maries
Southminster
TROPICAL WINGS AND BIRD GARDENS
Althorne
Coalhill
Rettendon
South Woodham Ferrers
North Fambridge
Stoneyhills
MANGAPPS RAILWAY MUS
South Hanningfield
Bridgemarsh Island
Ostend
Burnham-on-Crouch
Downham
MARSH FARM
Rettendon Place
South Fambridge
Creeksea
Crouch
Runwell
Hullbridge
Canewdon
Crouch
Ramsden Bellhouse
Wickford
Battlesbridge
Paglesham Churchend
WALLASEA WETLANDS
Shotgate
Rawreth
Ashingdon
Hockley
Hawkwell
Paglesham Eastend
Great Stambridge
Ballards Gore
Nevendon
Stroud Green
OLD HOUSE
Potton Island
FOULNESS ISLAND
North Benfleet
RAYLEIGH
CHERRY ORCHARD
Rochford
Barling
Thundersley
51
Eastwood
Little Wakering
Havengore Island
Daws Heath
0 1 2 3 miles
0 1 2 3 4 5 km

Langham
Dedham
MUSEUM
Lawford
Mistley
Manningtree
Bradfield
Wrabness
Parkeston
HARWICH REDOUBT FORT
Upper Dovercourt
Dovercourt
Ramsey
A12
87
88
A120
B1352
B1029
A137
Ardleigh
Bradfield Heath
B1035
Horsleycross Street
Horsley Cross
Little Bromley
Great Bromley
Little Oakley
Great Oakley
Wix
Stone's Green
Tendring Green
Little Bentley
B1414
A1232
Fox Street
Crockleford Heath
Colchester
Elmstead Market
Hare Green
Balls Green
Beaumont
A
Horsey Island
The Naze
HAMFORD WATER
Tendring
B1035
Thorpe Green
Thorpe-le-Soken
Kirby-le-Soken
MARITIME MUSEUM
Walton-on-the-Naze
Wivenhoe Cross
A133
BETH CHATTO GDNS
Old Heath
BOURNE MILL
Blackheath
B1028
Wivenhoe
Frating Green
Great Bentley
Weeley
Weeley Heath
B1033
B1027
Rowhedge
Alresford
Aingers Green
Kirby Cross
B1336
Frinton-on-Sea
Fingringhoe
Thorrington
Row Heath
CLACTON VILLAGE
Little Clacton
Abberton
Langenhoe
B1029
River Colne
St Osyth Heath
Great Holland
HOLLAND HAVEN
B1032
B1025
Brightlingsea
ST OSYTH PRIORY
St Osyth
B1027
Great Clacton
Holland-on-Sea
Clacton-on-Sea
Mersea Island
East Mersea
CUDMORE GROVE
Point Clear
Blue Row
COLNE ESTUARY
Jaywick
West Mersea
MERSEA ISLAND MUSEUM
Colne Pt.
Virley Channel
Nass
B
Sales Pt.
ST PETERS ON THE WALL
Bradwell Waterside
Bradwell on Sea
TM
C
DENGIE
Ray Sand
Montsale
Deal Hall
Foulness Sand
Foulness Pt.
TR
D
Courtsend
Churchend
MAPLIN SANDS
52
53
4
5
6

SM
ROSSLARE 3:30
PEMBROKESHIRE COAST
ARFORDIR PENFRO
Cemaes Head
Pen Cemaes
Strumble Head
Pen Caer
Dinas Head
Newport Bay
Bae Trefdraeth
Fishguard Bay
Bae Abergwaun
Goodwick (Wdig)
Fishguard (Abergwaun)
Newport (Trefdraeth)
Penbwchdy
PEMBROKESHIRE COAST PATH
LLWYBR ARFORDIR PENFRO
TREGWYNT WOOLLEN MILL
MYNYDD PRESE
FOEL-CWMCERWYN
CARNINGLI
CASTELL HENLLYS FORT
TY CANOL
CORSYDD LLANGLOFFAN
LLYS-Y-FRAN RESERVOIR
SCOLTON MANOR
DUDWELL MT.
PEMBROKE MOTOR MUSEUM
LAWHADEN CASTLE
Pembrokeshire
(Sir Benfro)
Moylgrove
Monington
Glanrhyd
Pontgareg
Nevern
Felindre Farchog
Berry Hill
Parrog
Brynhenllan
Dinas Cross
Lower Town
Llanwnda
Tresinwen
Trefasser
Dyffryn
Manorowen
St Nicholas
Granston
Abercastle
Mathry
Castlemorris
Penparc
Newbridge
Scleddau
Llanychaer
Trecwn
Pontfaen
Cilgwyn
Crosswell
Pontyglasier
Brynberian
New Inn
Rosebush
Puncheston
Castlebythe
Little Newcastle
Letterston
Treddiog
Llanreithan
Llandeloy
Welsh Hook
Wolf's Castle
St Dogwells
Tufton
Henry's Moat
Maenclochog
Llangolman
Glandy Cross
Pont-yr-hafod
Trefgarn Owen
Hayscastle
Hayscastle Cross
Brimaston
Ambleston
Rinaston
Wallis
Woodstock
New Moat
Efailwen
Triffleton
Treffgarne
Mountain Water
Spittal
Llys-y-frân
Walton East
Llanycefn
Penycwm
Newgale
Leweston
Pen-ffordd
Llandissilio
Roch
Roch Gate
Wolfsdale
Rudbaxton
Clarbeston
Clarbeston Road
Bletherston
Camrose
Llanfall
Clunderwen
Gelli
Tangiers
Pelcomb Cross
Crundale
Cippyn
POPPIT SANDS
St Dogmaels
PWLL DERI
NEWPORT
A40
A487
A4329
B4313
B4329
B4331
B4330
B4582
A478
Afon Nevern
W. Cleddau
E. Cleddau
G. Cleddau
Res.
55
19
14
15
16
213
191
347
468
536
164
178
197
0 1 2 3 miles
0 1 2 3 4 5 km

73
4
5
6
7
74
New Quay
(Ceinewydd)
Cei-bach
Maen-y-groes
Gilfachrheda
Cwmtudu
Cwmtydu
Cross Inn
Llanarth
Nanternis
Caerwedros
Ynys-Lochtyn
SN
A487
Blaencelyn
Llwyndafydd
Synod Inn
Llangrannog
Pontgarreg
Plwmp
Penbryn
Pentregat
Tresaith
Penmorfa
Brynhoffnant
Parcllyn
MWNT
Felinwynt
Aberporth
Sarnau
Talgarreg
Gwbert
Blaenannerch
ABERPORTH WEST WALES AIRPORT
Tan-y-groes
Y Ferwig
Glynarthen
Capel Cynon
RHOS LLAWR CWRT
Bwlch-y-fadfa
Tremain
Blaenporth
Penparc
Rhydlewis
Cardigan
Aberteifi
CASTLE
Bettws Ifan
Hawen
Ffostrasol
Bridgend
Pantgwyn
Beulah
Maesymeillion
Pont-siân
Llangoedmor
Ponthirwaun
Penrhiw-pâl
Coed-y-bryn
Tregroes
Bryngwyn
Brongest
Troedyraur
Maesllyn
COEDMOR
Llechryd
Llandygwydd
Capel Tygwydd
Croes-lan
Prengwyn
Pen-y-bryn
CILGERRAN CASTLE
Cilgerran
Horeb
Bridell
Carreg-wen
Cwm-cou
Llandyfriog
Aber-banc
Penrhiw-llan
ROCK MILL WOOLLEN MILL
Llantood
CORACLE CENTRE & FLOUR MILL
TEIFI VALLEY RAILWAY
Llandysul
Rhos-hill
Abercych
Cenarth
Newcastle Emlyn
(Castell Newydd Emlyn)
Pentrecagal
Henllan
Llanfihangel-ar-arth
Newchapel
CLYNFYW
Aber-Arad
NATIONAL WOOL MUSEUM
Llangeler
Drefach
Pentre-cwrt
Bancyffordd
Cilwendeg
Penrherber
Boncath
BRO MEIGAN GARDENS
CHEESE FARM
Felindre
Saron
Drefelin
Llanfair-Nant-Gwyn
Blaenffos
Cwmhiraeth
Cwmpengraig
Bwlchygroes
Cwmcych
Capel Iwan
Rhôs
Star
Clydey
MOELFRE
Penygroes
Dolgran
Cwmorgan
Tanglwst
Crymych
Tegryn
Hermon
Bryn-Iwan
Cwmduad
Pentre-galar
Llanfyrnach
Hen-feddau fawr
Trelech
Dinas
Llanpumsaint
Glandwr
Afon Taf
Hebron
Cynwyl Elfed
Blaen-y-coed
Blaen-waun
Pen-y-bont
WELSH CHOCOLATE FARM
Llanglydwen
Cwmbach
Llanwinio
Afon Duad
Cefn-y-pant
Talog
GWILI RAILWAY
Pant-y-Caws
Cwmfelin Mynach
Ty-hen
Bwlchnewydd
Maesgwynne
Cross-hands
Newchurch
Bronwydd Arms
Peniel
Llanboidy
Gellywen
Abernant
Dyffryn
Ffynnon ddrain
Hiraeth
Tre-vaughan
Tanerdy
Henllan Amgoed
Meidrim
Merthyr
Carmarthen
(Caerfyrddin)
Abergwili
Llangynin
56
Sarnau
A40
Llangunnor
Cwmfelin Boeth
Llanllwch
CORS GOCH LLANLLWCH
Johnstown
Pensarn
Bancyfelin
A48
58
A484
A486
A478
A475
B4548
B4570
B4333
B4334
B4321
B4338
B4342
B4459
B4476
B4336
B4332
B4571
B4299
B4298
B4301
A485

1
2
3
A
B
C
D
New Quay
(Ceinewydd)
Aberarth
Aberaeron
Monac
Llansan
Ffos-y-ffin
LLANERCH
Cei-bach
Llwyncelyn
Oakford
Ciliau Aeron
Maen-y-groes
Gilfachrheda
Cwmtudu
Cwmtydu
Cross Inn
Llanarth
Nanternis
Caerwedros
Dihewyd
Ynys-Lochtyn
Blaencelyn
Llwyndafydd
Mydroilyn
Synod Inn
Llangrannog
Pontgarreg
Caledrhydiau
Penbryn
Plwmp
Tresaith
Penmorfa
Pentregat
Parcllyn
Aberporth
Brynhoffnant
Talgarreg
Gorsgoch
Felinwynt
Sarnau
ABERPORTH WEST WALES AIRPORT
Blaenannerch
Tan-y-groes
Glynarthen
Capel Cynon
RHOS LLAWR CWRT
Bwlch-y-fadfa
Castell-Howell
Aber
Tremain
Blaenporth
Penparc
Rhydlewis
Ffostrasol
Bettws Ifan
Hawen
Beulah
Maesymeillion
Pont-siân
Cwmsychp
Pantgwyn
Penrhiw-pâl
Coed-y-bryn
Llangoedmor
Ponthirwaun
Bryngwyn
Brongest
Troedyraur
Tregroes
Rhydc
Llanwenog
COEDMOR
Llechryd
Llandygwydd
Capel Tygwydd
Maesllyn
Croes-lan
Prengwyn
Brynte
CILGERRAN CASTLE
Cilgerran
Carreg-wen
Cwm-cou
Llandyfriog
Aber-banc
Horeb
Capel Dewi
ROCK MILL WOOLLEN MILL
Maesycrugiau
CORACLE CENTRE & FLOUR MILL
Cenarth
Penrhiw-llan
TEIFI VALLEY RAILWAY
Llandysul
Abercych
Rhos-hill
Newcastle Emlyn
(Castell Newydd Emlyn)
Pentrecagal
Henllan
Llanfihangel-ar-arth
Aber-Arad
NATIONAL WOOL MUSEUM
Llangeler
Drefach
Penrherber
Felindre
Pentre-cwrt
Boncath
Cilwendeg
CHEESE
Saron
Bancyffordd
CASTLE
A487
A486
A484
A475
B4334
B4321
B4338
B4342
B4333
B4570
B4571
B4459
B4476
B4336
73
58
0 1 2 3 miles
0 1 2 3 4 5 km

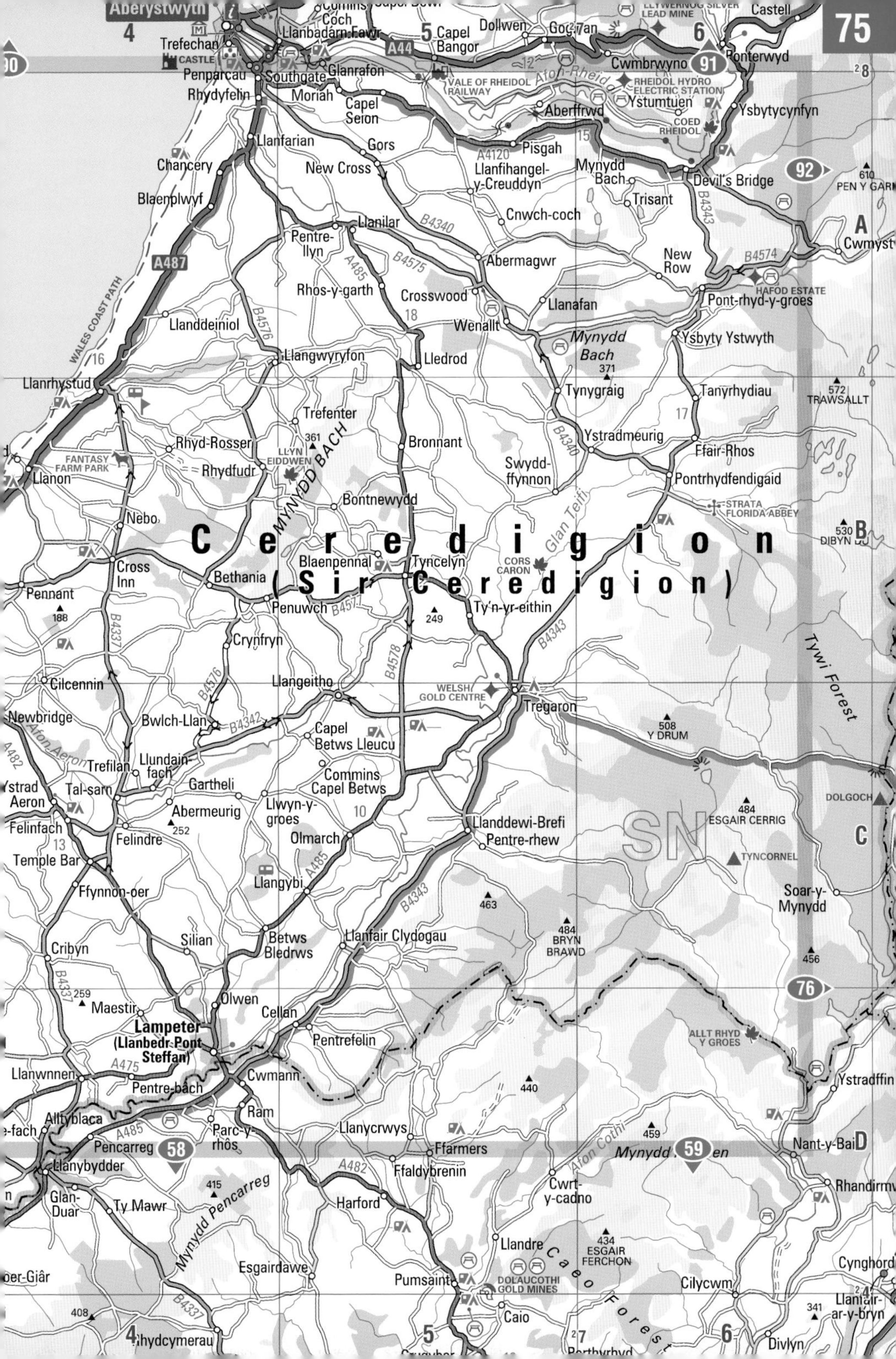

Ceredigion
(Sir Ceredigion)
Aberystwyth
Trefechan
Penparcau
Southgate
Rhydyfelin
Llanbadarn Fawr
Capel Bangor
Dollwen
Goginan
Cwmbrwyno
Ponterwyd
Castell
Glanrafon
Moriah
Capel Seion
VALE OF RHEIDOL RAILWAY
Afon Rheidol
RHEIDOL HYDRO ELECTRIC STATION
Ystumtuen
Aberffrwd
COED RHEIDOL
Ysbytycynfyn
Llanfarian
Gors
Pisgah
Chancery
New Cross
Llanfihangel-y-Creuddyn
Mynydd Bach
Trisant
Devil's Bridge
PEN Y GARN
Blaenplwyf
Cnwch-coch
Llanilar
Pentre-llyn
Abermagwr
New Row
Cwmystwyth
HAFOD ESTATE
Pont-rhyd-y-groes
Rhos-y-garth
Crosswood
Llanafan
Wenallt
Ysbyty Ystwyth
WALES COAST PATH
Llanddeiniol
Llangwyryfon
Lledrod
Tynygraig
Tanyrhydiau
TRAWSALLT
Llanrhystud
Trefenter
Ystradmeurig
Bronnant
Ffair-Rhos
Rhyd-Rosser
LLYN EIDDWEN
MYNYDD BACH
FANTASY FARM PARK
Llanon
Rhydfudr
Swydd-ffynnon
Pontrhydfendigaid
STRATA FLORIDA ABBEY
Bontnewydd
Nebo
DIBYN DU
Glan Teifi
Blaenpennal
Tyncelyn
CORS CARON
Cross Inn
Bethania
Pennant
Penuwch
Ty'n-yr-eithin
Crynfryn
Tywi Forest
Cilcennin
Llangeitho
WELSH GOLD CENTRE
Tregaron
Newbridge
Afon Aeron
Bwlch-Llan
Capel Betws Lleucu
Y DRUM
Trefilan
Llundain-fach
Commins Capel Betws
Ystrad Aeron
Tal-sarn
Gartheli
DOLGOCH
Abermeurig
Llwyn-y-groes
ESGAIR CERRIG
Felinfach
Felindre
Olmarch
Llanddewi-Brefi
Pentre-rhew
SN
Temple Bar
TYNCORNEL
Ffynnon-oer
Llangybi
Soar-y-Mynydd
Cribyn
Silian
Betws Bledrws
Llanfair Clydogau
BRYN BRAWD
Maestir
Olwen
Cellan
Lampeter
(Llanbedr Pont Steffan)
Pentrefelin
ALLT RHYD Y GROES
Llanwnnen
Cwmann
Pentre-bach
Ystradffin
Alltyblaca
Ram
Parc-y-rhôs
Llanycrwys
Pencarreg
Ffarmers
Afon Cothi
Mynydd ... en
Nant-y-Bai
Llanybydder
Ffaldybrenin
Cwrt-y-cadno
Rhandirmwyn
Glan-Duar
Ty Mawr
Mynydd Pencarreg
Harford
Llandre
ESGAIR FERCHON
Caeo Forest
Esgairdawe
Pumsaint
DOLAUCOTHI GOLD MINES
Cilycwm
Cynghordy
Llanfair-ar-y-bryn
Caio
Rhydcymerau
Porthyrhyd
Dinlyn

Rhayader
(Rhaeadr Gwy)
WELSH ROYAL CRYSTAL
Gaufron
Llansantffraed Cwmdeuddwr
THE GIGRIN FARM RED KITE FEEDING CENTRE
Elan Village
Garreg-ddu Res.
Penygarreg Res.
Craig-goch Res.
CLAERWEN
Claerwen Reservoir
Afon Claerwen
Caban-coch Res.
Llanwrthwl
Nant-glas
Argoed
Llanyre
MOEL HYWEL
572 TRAWSALLT
530 DIBYN DU
STRATA FLORIDA ABBEY
Pontrhydfendigaid
Ffair-Rhos
Ffanyrhydiau
GEIFAS
537 DRUM-DDU
Newbridge on Wye
Disserth
645 DRYGARN FAWR
532 BRYN CRWN
DOLGOCH
484 ESGAIR CERRIG
TYNCORNEL
Tywi Forest
500
NANT IRFON
Llyn Brianne Res.
Soar-y-Mynydd
456
Abergwesyn
Llanafan-fawr
CORS Y LLYN
Pentre-llwyn-llŵyd
Troed-rhiwdalar
Cwmbach
Builth Road
Cilmery
Beulah
Llanfechan
Garth
Tyn-y-graig
487
Cwm Irfon
Mynydd Trawsnant
CAMBRIAN WOOLLEN MILL
Llanwrtyd
Llanwrtyd Wells
(Llanwrtud)
Llangammarch Wells
Irfon
441
Maesmynis
Ystradffin
Nant-y-Bai
Rhandirmwyn
Cefn-gorwydd
474 DRUM-DDU
Pentre Dolau-Honddu
MYNYDD EPYNT
463 BRYN DU
Crychan Forest
Tirabad
Cynghordy
Llanfair-ar-y-bryn
341
Divlyn
433
Upper Chapel
Blaendyryn
Merthyr Cynog
423
Lower Chapel
Honddu
Pentre-ty-gwyn
Babel
Mynydd Bwlch-y-groes
442
Llandeilo'r Fan
Llanfihangel Nant Bran
Nant Bran
Pont-faen
Pwllgloyw
Sarnau
Llandovery
(Llanymddyfri)
Halfway
Pentre-bach
Myrtle Hill
Llywel
Pentre'r-felin
Trallong
Battle
Aberyscir
BRECON GAER ROMAN FORT
Usk (Wysg)
Trecastle
Sennybridge
(Pont Senni)
Penpont
Cwmwysg
A470
A44
A483
A40
B4518
B4358
B4519
B4520
A4081
75
92
59
SN
P
O
0 1 2 3 miles
0 1 2 3 4 5 km

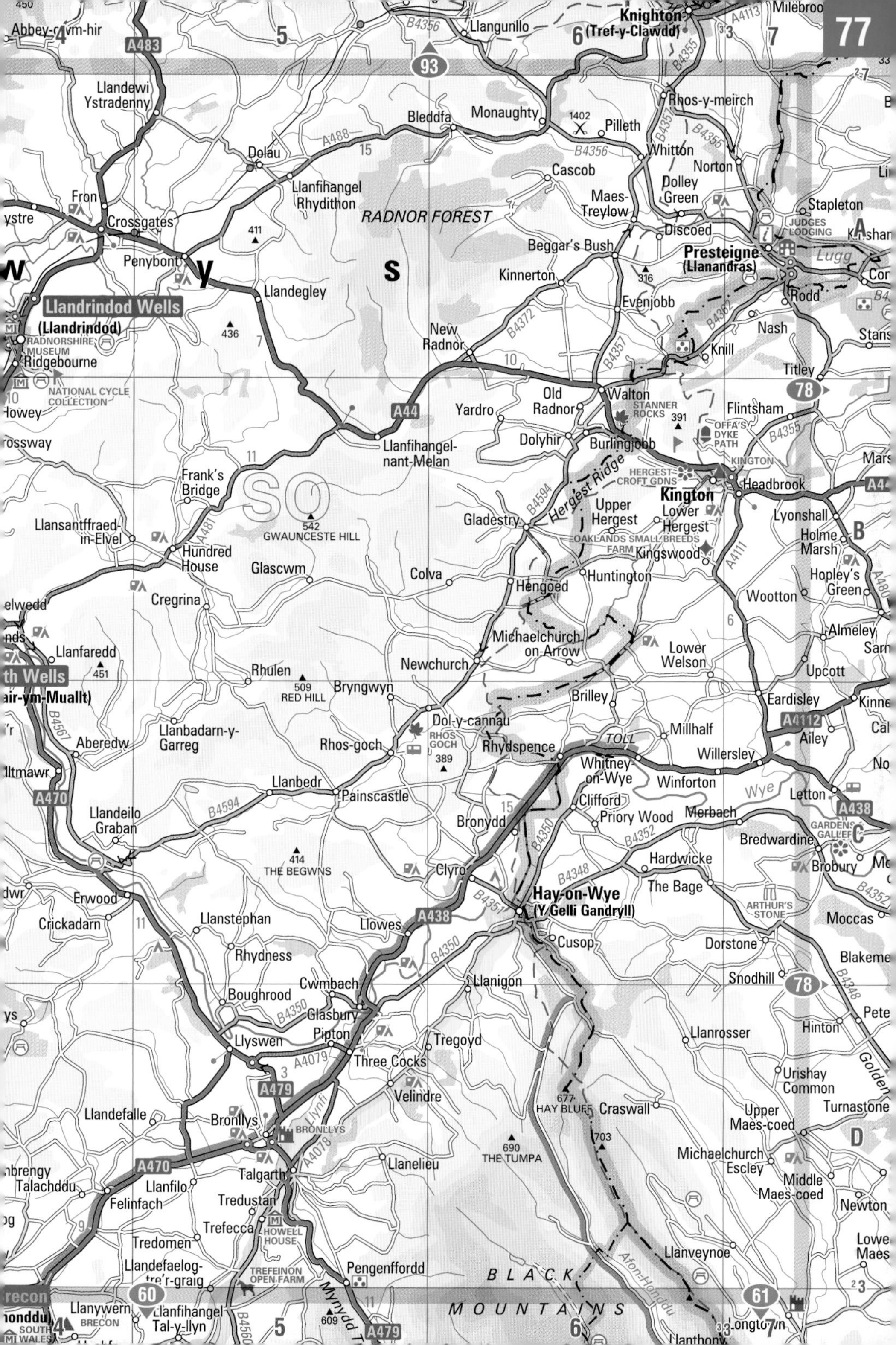
Abbey-cwm-hir
A483
B4356
Llangunllo
93
Knighton
(Tref-y-Clawdd)
A4113
B4355
Llandewi
Ystradenny
Bleddfa
Monaughty
1402
Pilleth
Rhos-y-meirch
A488
15
B4356
Whitton
B4357
B4355
Dolau
Cascob
Norton
Llanfihangel
Rhydithon
Maes-
Treylow
Dolley
Green
Fron
Crossgates
RADNOR FOREST
Stapleton
JUDGES
LODGING
411
Discoed
Beggar's Bush
Presteigne
(Llanandras)
Lugg
Penybont
Kinnerton
316
Rodd
Llandegley
Evenjobb
Llandrindod Wells
(Llandrindod)
RADNORSHIRE
MUSEUM
436
New
Radnor
B4372
B4362
Nash
Ridgebourne
B4357
Knill
10
NATIONAL CYCLE
COLLECTION
Titley
Old
Radnor
Walton
78
STANNER
ROCKS
391
Yardro
A44
Flintsham
OFFA'S
DYKE
PATH
B4355
Dolyhir
Burlingjobb
Llanfihangel-
nant-Melan
KINGTON
HERGEST
CROFT GDNS
Hergest Ridge
Headbrook
11
Frank's
Bridge
SO
Kington
B4594
Upper
Hergest
Lower
Hergest
Lyonshall
Gladestry
542
GWAUNCESTE HILL
Llansantffraed-
in-Elvel
A481
OAKLANDS SMALL BREEDS
FARM
Kingswood
Holme
Marsh
B
Hundred
House
A4111
Glascwm
Colva
Hengoed
Huntington
Hopley's
Green
Cregrina
Wootton
6
Michaelchurch-
on-Arrow
Almeley
Llanfaredd
451
Lower
Welson
Rhulen
509
RED HILL
Newchurch
Upcott
Bryngwyn
Eardisley
Brilley
B4567
Llanbadarn-y-
Garreg
Dol-y-cannau
Aberedw
RHOS
GOCH
Millhalf
A4112
Ailey
Rhos-goch
389
Rhydspence
TOLL
Willersley
Whitney-
on-Wye
A470
Llanbedr
Winforton
Painscastle
Wye
Letton
Clifford
Llandeilo
Graban
B4594
15
Priory Wood
Merbach
A438
Bronydd
B4352
B4350
Bredwardine
GARDENS
C
414
THE BEGWNS
Hardwicke
Clyro
B4348
Brobury
Hay-on-Wye
(Y Gelli Gandryll)
The Bage
Erwood
B4351
ARTHUR'S
STONE
Crickadarn
11
Llanstephan
Llowes
A438
Moccas
Cusop
Dorstone
Rhydness
B4350
Llanigon
Snodhill
78
B4348
Cwmbach
Boughrood
B4350
Glasbury
Hinton
Pipton
Llanrosser
Llyswen
Tregoyd
Three Cocks
A4079
3
Urishay
Common
A479
Velindre
677
HAY BLUFF
Craswall
Llynfi
Upper
Maes-coed
Turnastone
Llandefalle
Bronllys
BRONLLYS
703
D
A4078
690
THE TUMPA
Michaelchurch
Escley
A470
Llanelieu
Middle
Maes-coed
Talgarth
Llanfilo
Felinfach
Tredustan
Newton
9
Trefecca
HOWELL
HOUSE
Afon Honddu
Tredomen
Llanveynoe
Llandefaelog-
tre'r-graig
TREFEINON
OPEN FARM
Pengenffordd
BLACK
60
61
MOUNTAINS
Llanywern
Llanfihangel
Tal-y-llyn
BRECON
B4560
609
Mynydd
11
A479
Longtown
4
5
6
7

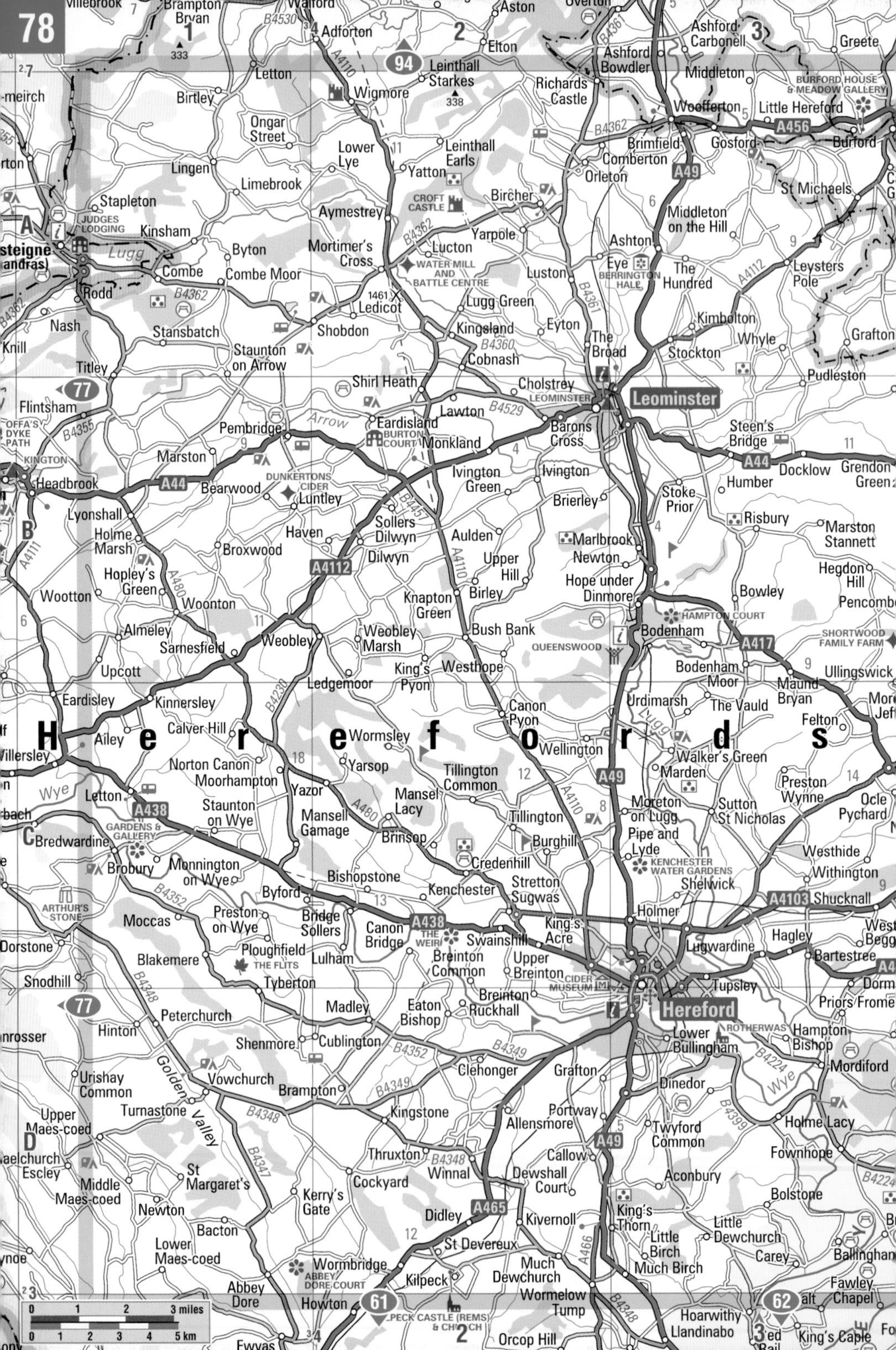
Brampton Bryan
Walford
Aston
Overton
Adforton
Elton
Ashford Carbonell
Greete
Letton
Leinthall Starkes
Ashford Bowdler
Middleton
Wigmore
Richards Castle
Birtley
Burford House & Meadow Gallery
Woofferton
Little Hereford
Ongar Street
Brimfield
Gosford
Burford
Lower Lye
Leinthall Earls
Comberton
Lingen
Yatton
Orleton
Limebrook
Croft Castle
Bircher
St Michaels
Stapleton
Aymestrey
Middleton on the Hill
Judges Lodging
Kinsham
Yarpole
Ashton
Presteigne (Llanandras)
Byton
Mortimer's Cross
Lucton
Eye
The Hundred
Leysters Pole
Lugg
Water Mill and Battle Centre
Berrington Hall
Combe
Combe Moor
Luston
Rodd
Ledicot
Lugg Green
Kimbolton
Nash
Shobdon
Kingsland
Eyton
The Broad
Whyle
Grafton
Stansbatch
Knill
Staunton on Arrow
Cobnash
Stockton
Titley
Shirl Heath
Cholstrey
Pudleston
Flintsham
Leominster
Lawton
Offa's Dyke Path
Pembridge
Arrow
Eardisland
Barons Cross
Steen's Bridge
Burton Court
Monkland
Kington
Marston
Ivington Green
Ivington
Docklow
Grendon Green
Headbrook
Bearwood
Dunkertons Cider
Humber
Luntley
Brierley
Stoke Prior
Lyonshall
Sollers Dilwyn
Risbury
Marston Stannett
Holme Marsh
Haven
Aulden
Marlbrook
Broxwood
Dilwyn
Newton
Hegdon Hill
Hopley's Green
Upper Hill
Hope under Dinmore
Wootton
Knapton Green
Birley
Bowley
Pencombe
Woonton
Hampton Court
Almeley
Weobley Marsh
Bush Bank
Bodenham
Shortwood Family Farm
Sarnesfield
Weobley
Queenswood
Upcott
Ledgemoor
King's Pyon
Westhope
Bodenham Moor
Ullingswick
Eardisley
Maund Bryan
Kinnersley
Canon Pyon
Urdimarsh
The Vault
Ailey
Calver Hill
Wormsley
Wellington
Felton
H e r e f o r d s
Willersley
Walker's Green
Norton Canon
Yarsop
Tillington Common
Marden
Preston Wynne
Moorhampton
Letton
Wye
Yazor
Mansel Lacy
Moreton on Lugg
Sutton St Nicholas
Ocle Pychard
Staunton on Wye
Mansell Gamage
Tillington
Gardens & Gallery
Bredwardine
Brinsop
Burghill
Pipe and Lyde
Westhide
Brobury
Monnington on Wye
Credenhill
Kenchester Water Gardens
Withington
Arthur's Stone
Bishopstone
Stretton Sugwas
Shelwick
Byford
Kenchester
Holmer
Shucknall
Moccas
Preston on Wye
Bridge Sollers
Canon Bridge
The Weir
Swainshill
King's Acre
Hagley
Dorstone
Blakemere
Ploughfield
Lulham
Breinton Common
Upper Breinton
Lugwardine
Bartestree
Snodhill
The Flits
Tyberton
Cider Museum
Tupsley
Dormington
Breinton
Madley
Eaton Bishop
Ruckhall
Hereford
Priors Frome
Hinton
Peterchurch
Rotherwas
Lower Bullingham
Hampton Bishop
Shenmore
Cublington
Mordiford
Urishay Common
Vowchurch
Clehonger
Grafton
Golden Valley
Brampton
Dinedor
Turnastone
Kingstone
Portway
Allensmore
Twyford Common
Holme Lacy
Upper Maes-coed
Callow
Fownhope
Michaelchurch Escley
Thruxton
Winnal
Middle Maes-coed
St Margaret's
Cockyard
Dewsall Court
Aconbury
Bolstone
Kerry's Gate
Newton
Didley
Kivernoll
King's Thorn
Little Dewchurch
Bacton
Little Birch
Lower Maes-coed
St Devereux
Much Birch
Carey
Ballingham
Wormbridge
Abbey Dore Court
Much Dewchurch
Kilpeck
Fawley Chapel
Abbey Dore
Howton
Wormelow Tump
Kilpeck Castle (Rems) & Church
Hoarwithy
Llandinabo
Orcop Hill
Ewyas
King's Caple
0 1 2 3 miles
0 1 2 3 4 5 km

Nash
Neen Sollars
Mamble
Clows Top
Rock
Stourport on Severn
WORCESTERSHIRE COUNTY MUSEUM
A456
95
Areley Kings
Hartlebury
WHITLENGE GDNS
Boraston
Frith Common
Astley Cross
Waresley
Elmley Lovett
A443
Lindridge
Pensax
Dunley
Crossway Green
Newnham Bridge
Eardiston
B4202
Lincomb
Cutnall Green
Lower Rochford
Stockton on Teme
Abberley
Astley
B4196
Tenbury Wells
Upper Rochford
B4204
Orleton
Abberley Hill
A451
Noutard's Green
A449
Dunhampton
Hanley William
Stanford on Teme
Stanford Bridge
Great Witley
Sytchampton
Doverdale
Hampton Lovett
Hanley Child
B4203
Oldfield
Broad Heath
WITLEY COURT
Uphampton
Shrawley
276
Ombersley
Droitwich Spa
Kyre Magna
Stoke Bliss
Sapey Common
Little Witley
Holt Fleet
A4133
Upper Sapey
Shelsley Walsh
Shelsley Beauchamp
Holt Heath
Holt
Salwarpe
Bank Street
B4214
Sweet Green
Clifton upon Teme
70
Worcester
Green
High Lane
Harpley
B4197
Sinton Green
Grimley
Hawford
80
Collington
Martley
Wichenford
Moseley
Martin Hussingtree
Thornbury
Tedstone Wafer
A443
Fernhill Heath
Edvin Loach
183
B4204
Shoulton
Claines
Hindlip
Tedstone Delamere
Hallow
Edwyn Ralph
Horsham
Berrow Green
Lower Broadheath
Astwood
P&R
Whitbourne
ELGAR'S BIRTHPLACE
TUDOR HOUSE
Warndon
Bredenbury
Bromyard Downs
BROCKHAMPTON ESTATE
Broad Green
Upper Broadheath
GUILDHALL
HERITAGE CENTRE
Knightwick
Lulsley
Broadwas
A44
Worcester
B4636
Red Hill
Bromyard
Linley Green
Alfrick
Brockamin
Leigh
Rushwick
St John's
Spetchley
LEIGH COURT BARN
Cherry Orchard
Whittington
Stanford Bishop
Alfrick Pound
Bransford
Teme
1651
ROYAL WORCESTER PORCELAIN
Little Cowarne
Munderfield Row
B4220
Suckley
Bowling Green
A4440
Norton
Powick
Acton Beauchamp
Leigh Sinton
Pole Elm
Littleworth
Munderfield Stocks
Acton Green
Longley Green
A4103
A449
Stanbrook
Hatfield
Callow End
Stoke Lacy
Storridge
Newland
Kempsey
A465
Evesbatch
Stony Cross
Madresfield
Bishops Frome
Fromes Hill
Stifford's Bridge
Malvern Link
Pirton
Much Cowarne
Ridgeway Cross
Cradley
M5
Kerswell Grn.
Westfield
Great Malvern
Severn
Lower Egleton
Castle Frome
West Malvern
Clifton
High Green
Norbridge
Mathon
425
B4211
B4220
Guarlford
Rhydd
A38
Ham Green
B4232
Severn Stoke
CROOME PARK
Stanley Hill
Upper Wyche
Lower Wyche
Hanley Swan
Stretton Grandison
B4214
THREE COUNTIES SHOWGROUND
Kinnersley
Dunstall Common
Frome
Canon Frome
Bosbury
Colwall Stone
B4208
B4209
Hanley Castle
Earl's Croome
Coddington
B4218
Yarkhill
Malvern Wells
Holly Grn.
A417
Staplow
Colwall Green
Baughton
Tarrington
Upton upon Severn
Munsley
Little Malvern
MALVERN HILLS
Naunton
Trumpet
Wellington Heath
339
Welland
A4104
80
Upper Strensham
Alder's End
A449
Bradlow
264
Pixley
Newbridge Green
A4172
Ripple
Woolhope Cockshoot
Aylton
Ledbury
Castlemorton
Queenhill
Putley
Hollybush
B4208
Eastnor
EASTNOR
Birts Street
Little Marcle
A438
Longdon
Puckrup
M50
Camer's Green
Rye Street
Woolhope
Preston
Shuthonger
Rushall
B4216
A417
Sledge Green
Donnington
Brown's End
Bushley
HELLEN'S MANOR
Sollers Hope
Bromsberrow Hth.
Long Green
Newtown
Much Marcle
Pendock
Tewkesbury
Falcon
Broom's Green
Ryton
Forthampton
ABBEY
B4024
Playley Green
Eldersfield
Crossway
Lyne Down
Redmarley D'Abitot
B4211
Dymock
ST MARY'S CHURCH
B4208
Corse Lawn
Chaceley
1471
How Caple
ODDA'S CHAPEL
Kempley
62
Staunton
63
Deerhurst
A449
Fishpool
M50
B4215
Poolhill
Tredington
Hole-in-the-Wall
Leadon
Corse
B4211
Tirley
Apperley
A38

Rushock
A448
Sidemoor
Bromsgrove
96
Rowney Green
Branson's Cross
Wood End
UMBERSLADE FARM
A442
Elmley Lovett
Charford
Finstall
Tardebigge
A441
Beoley
B4101
Tanworth-in-Arden
A435
Crossway Green
M5
Aston Fields
FORGE MILL NEEDLE MUS
Holt End
Gorcott Hill
Cutnall Green
Elmbridge
AVONCROFT MUS OF HISTORIC BUILDINGS
A448
Redditch
A4023
WEBBS OF WYCHBOLD
Stoke Prior
ARROW VALLEY
Ullenhall
Dunhampton
Upton Warren
Woodgate
Webheath
Ipsley
Oldberrow
Doverdale
Hampton Lovett
Wychbold
Bentley
Headless Cross
Mappleborough Green
Oldfield
FOSTERS GREEN MEADOWS
Crabbs Cross
Morton Bagot
A
A38
B4091
Droitwich Spa
HANBURY HALL
Hanbury
Woolmere Green
Ham Green
Hunt End
A441
A448
Studley
A4133
B4092
Shelfield
Salwarpe
Witton
Hadzor
B4090
B4090
Astwood Bank
Sambourne
COUGHTON COURT
Little Alne
Worcester
Hawford
Shernal Green
Bradley Green
Feckenham
Coughton
Great Alne
79
Martin Hussingtree
New End
King's Coughton
B4089
Fernhill Heath
Oddingley
Stock Wood
B4092
Holberrow Green
B4090
Alne
Hindlip
Himbleton
Stock Green
Cookhill
Alcester
Walcote
P&R
Astwood
Sale Green
Tibberton
Huddington
Dormston
A422
Overley Green
Haselor
TUDOR HOUSE
Warndon
GUILDHALL
Inkberrow
A435
A46
Billesley
Crowle
Grafton Flyford
Arrow
Exhall
Kington
Abbots Morton
RAGLEY HALL
B
Bredicot
Broughton Hackett
Weethley Gate
Wixford
Temple Grafton
B4636
WORCESTER WOODS
Flyford Flavell
Red Hill
A422
North Piddle
Ardens Grafton
B439
Cherry Orchard
Spetchley
Churchill
Upton Snodsbury
Abberton
Rous Lench
Dunnington
Iron Cross
Broom
Whittington
White Ladies Aston
A4440
Naunton Beauchamp
Ab Lench
Church Lench
B4088
A46
B4082
Norton
Egdon
Bishampton
Salford Priors
Bidford-on-Avon
Barton
Littleworth
A44
Peopleton
Atch Lench
Abbots Salford
Marlcliff
Hatfield
Stoulton
Pinvin
Throckmorton
Harvington Cross
Harvington
Cleeve Prior
Dorsington
Avon
B4084
Drake's Broughton
Norton
B4510
North Littleton
Pirton
Wadborough
A44
Lenchwick
Pebworth
Kerswell Grn.
EVESHAM COUNTRY PARK
Wyre Piddle
Lower Moor
Fladbury
Middle Littleton
M5
Pershore
Charlton
Offenham
South Littleton
Broad Marston
High Green
ABBEY
Wick
B4085
CROOME PARK
Besford
A4104
Cropthorne
A4184
A46
Aldington
Honeybourne
DOMESTIC FOWL TRUST
C
Severn Stoke
B4084
Evesham
Kinnersley
Dunstall Common
Defford
Avon
Little Comberton
Bengeworth
Bretforton
B4035
Hanley Castle
Earl's Croome
Birlingham
B4084
Hampton
THE FLEECE INN
Badsey
B4080
Fairfield
Holly Grn.
Baughton
STRENSHAM SERVICES (Northbound Only)
Great Comberton
Bricklehampton
Netherton
Eckington
Wickhamford
VALE OF EVESHAM
Elmley Castle
A44
Weston-Sub-Edge
Lower Strensham
BREDON HILL
B4632
STRENSHAM SERVICES (Southbound Only)
293
BREDON HILL
Naunton
Kersoe
Hinton on the Green
Willersey
Saintbury
Upper Strensham
Bredon's Norton
Ashton under Hill
Childswickham
79
Sedgeberrow
Ripple
BREDON BARN
Overbury
A46
Queenhill
Kemerton
CONDERTON POTTERY
Conderton
Aston Somerville
Broadway
Twyning Green
Bredon
B4081
M50
Puckrup
Twyning
A38
SILK CENTRE
Dumbleton
Kinsham
Wormington
Buckland
Shuthonger
B4079
Beckford
ALDERTON HILL
B4078
Laverton
D
BROADWAY TOWER
316
B4080
Northway
A46
Great Washbourne
205
Isbourne
Bushley
SNOWSHILL MANOR
Stanton
SNOWSHILL LAVENDER
A438
Alderton
Snowshill
COTSWOLDS
Newtown
Teddington
Aston Cross
Toddington
GLOUCESTERSHIRE WARWICKSHIRE STEAM RAILWAY
Tewkesbury
Ashchurch
ABBEY
A435
Stanway
Walton Cardiff
Alstone
B4077
1471
Oxenton
Fiddington
STANWAY HOUSE
B4632
Dixton
ODDA'S CHAPEL
Greet
Didbrook
Cutsdean
Deerhurst
M5
Gretton
HAILES ABBEY
Hailes
63
Gotherington
274
WINCHCOMBE POTTERY
Farmcote
Ford
64
Stoke Orchard
Bishop's Cleeve
279
LANGLEY HILL
Winchcombe
B4077
SUDELEY CASTLE AND GARDENS
0 1 2 3 miles
0 1 2 3 4 5 km

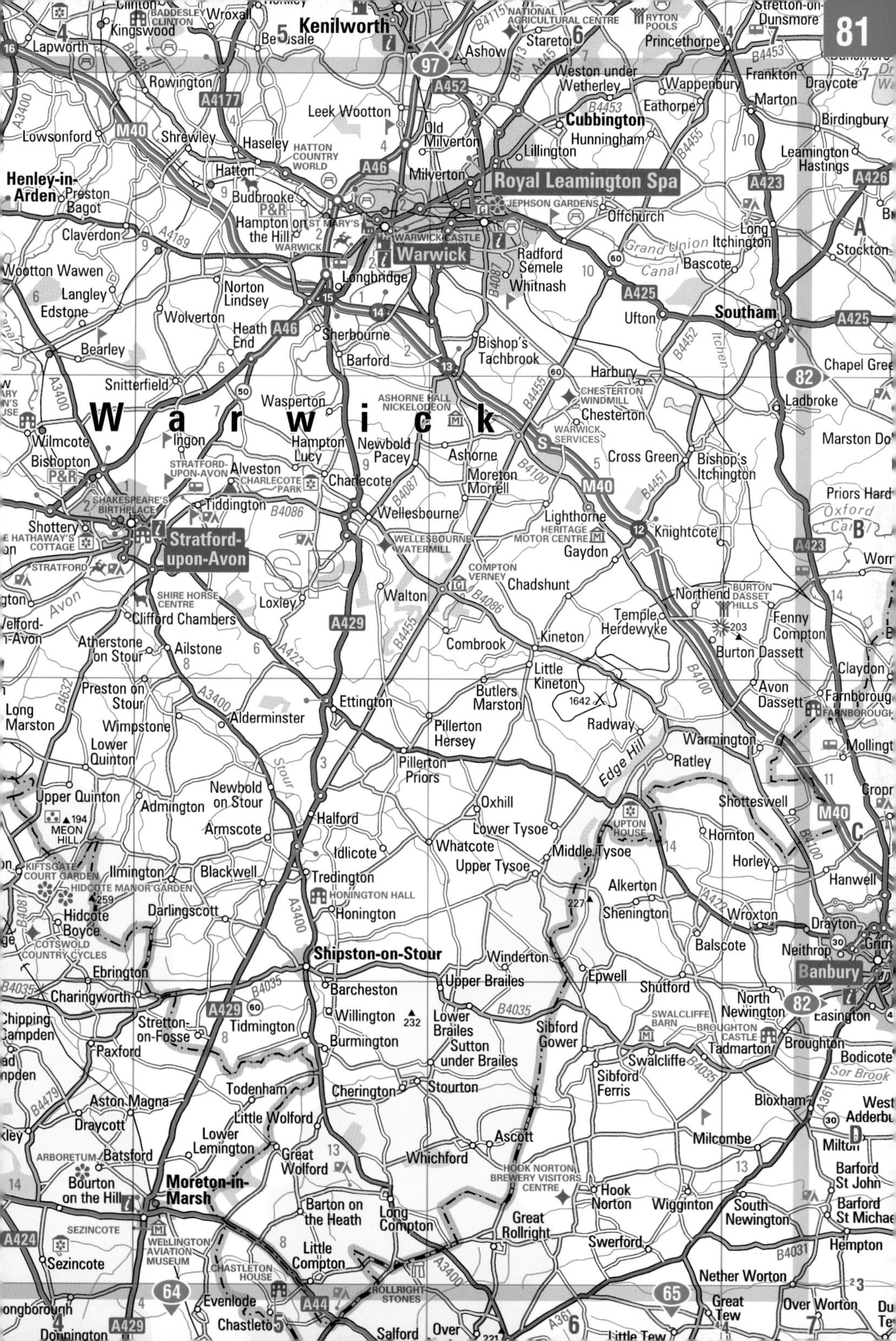
81
Kenilworth
Baddesley Clinton
Wroxall
Kingswood
Lapworth
Stretton-on-Dunsmore
National Agricultural Centre
Ryton Pools
Stareton
Princethorpe
Ashow
Rowington
Leek Wootton
Weston under Wetherley
Wappenbury
Frankton
Draycote
Marton
Eathorpe
Cubbington
Old Milverton
Hunningham
Birdingbury
Lowsonford
Shrewley
Haseley
Hatton Country World
Lillington
Leamington Hastings
Henley-in-Arden
Preston Bagot
Hatton
Milverton
Royal Leamington Spa
Budbrooke
Jephson Gardens
Offchurch
Claverdon
Hampton on the Hill
St Mary's
Warwick Castle
Warwick
Radford Semele
Long Itchington
Stockton
Wootton Wawen
Norton Lindsey
Longbridge
Whitnash
Grand Union Canal
Bascote
Langley
Edstone
Wolverton
Heath End
Sherbourne
Ufton
Southam
Bearley
Barford
Bishop's Tachbrook
Harbury
Chapel Green
Snitterfield
Wasperton
Ashorne Hall Nickelodeon
Chesterton Windmill
Chesterton
Ladbroke
Warwick
Wilmcote
Ingon
Hampton Lucy
Newbold Pacey
Ashorne
Warwick Services
Marston Doles
Bishopton
Stratford-upon-Avon
Alveston
Charlecote Park
Charlecote
Moreton Morrell
Cross Green
Bishop's Itchington
Priors Hardwick
Shakespeare's Birthplace
Tiddington
Wellesbourne
Lighthorne
Oxford Canal
Shottery
Anne Hathaway's Cottage
Stratford-upon-Avon
Wellesbourne Watermill
Heritage Motor Centre
Gaydon
Knightcote
Stratford
Compton Verney
Chadshunt
Northend
Burton Dassett Hills
Avon
Loxley
Walton
Temple Herdewycke
Fenny Compton
Shire Horse Centre
Clifford Chambers
Welford-on-Avon
Atherstone on Stour
Ailstone
Combrook
Kineton
Burton Dassett
Claydon
Little Kineton
Preston on Stour
Ettington
Butlers Marston
Avon Dassett
Farnborough
Long Marston
Alderminster
Pillerton Hersey
Radway
Wimpstone
Lower Quinton
Warmington
Mollington
Pillerton Priors
Edge Hill
Ratley
Stour
Upper Quinton
Newbold on Stour
Admington
Oxhill
Shotteswell
Meon Hill
Armscote
Halford
Lower Tysoe
Upton House
Hornton
Whatcote
Middle Tysoe
Kiftsgate Court Garden
Ilmington
Blackwell
Idlicote
Upper Tysoe
Horley
Hidcote Manor Garden
Tredington
Alkerton
Hanwell
Honington Hall
Hidcote Boyce
Darlingscott
Honington
Shenington
Wroxton
Drayton
Cotswold Country Cycles
Balscote
Neithrop
Shipston-on-Stour
Winderton
Ebrington
Epwell
Banbury
Barcheston
Upper Brailes
Shutford
Charingworth
North Newington
Swalcliffe Barn
Easington
Chipping Campden
Stretton-on-Fosse
Tidmington
Willington
Lower Brailes
Sibford Gower
Broughton Castle
Paxford
Burmington
Sutton under Brailes
Tadmarton
Broughton
Bodicote
Swalcliffe
Sibford Ferris
Sor Brook
Todenham
Cherington
Stourton
Aston Magna
Bloxham
West Adderbury
Draycott
Little Wolford
Lower Lemington
Ascott
Milcombe
Milton
Arboretum
Batsford
Great Wolford
Whichford
Bourton on the Hill
Moreton-in-Marsh
Hook Norton Brewery Visitors Centre
Hook Norton
Barford St John
Barton on the Heath
Long Compton
Wigginton
South Newington
Barford St Michael
Sezincote
Great Rollright
Wellington Aviation Museum
Little Compton
Swerford
Hempton
Chastleton House
Rollright Stones
Nether Worton
Evenlode
Great Tew
Over Worton
Longborough
Chastleton
Salford
Over
Little Tew
Donnington
M40
A46
A452
A4177
A3400
A4189
A425
A423
A426
A429
A422
A44
A424
A361
B4035
B4100
B4455
B4086
B4087
B4451
B4452
B4453
B4632
B4081
B4479
B4031
82
97
64
65

North
Daventry
Southam
Banbury
Brackley
Middleton Cheney
Dunchurch
Kilsby
Crick
West Haddon
Coton
COTON MANOR
Ravensthorpe
Bourton on Dunsmore
Thurlaston
Barby
Frankton
Draycote
Draycote Water
DRAYCOTE WATER
Marton
Kites Hardwick
Birdingbury
Watford
WATFORD GAP SERVICES
East Haddon
Ashby St Ledgers
Woolscott
Leamington Hastings
Willoughby
Long Buckby
Holdenby
HOLDENBY AND FALCONRY CENTRE
Grandborough
Braunston
Welton
Broadwell
Sawbridge
Great Brington
Long Itchington
Stockton
Nethercote
DAVENTRY
Daventry Res
Whilton
Little Brington
ALTHORP
Flecknoe
Norton
Lower Shuckburgh
Brockhall
Nobottle
DAVENTRY MUS
Staverton
Napton on the Hill
Harpole
Dodford
Flore
Chapel Green
Upper Catesby
Upper Weedon
Upper Heyford
Ladbroke
Badby
Newnham
Nene
Weedon Bec
Nether Heyford
Marston Doles
Hellidon
Church Stowe
Everdon
OLD DAIRY FARM COUNTRY SHOPPING & CRAFT CENTRE
Bugbrooke
Bishop's Itchington
Priors Marston
Charwelton
Upper Stowe
Priors Hardwick
Oxford Canal
Preston Capes
Farthingstone
Litchborough
Pattishall
Wormleighton
Upper Boddington
Byfield
Grimscote
Eastcote
Boddington Reservoir
Hinton
Woodford Halse
Maidford
Cold Higham
Astcote
BURTON DASSETT HILLS
Fenny Compton
Lower Boddington
Tiffield
Burton Dassett
GRANARY MUSEUM OF BYGONES
CANONS ASHBY HOUSE
Adstone
Duncote
Claydon
Aston le Walls
Eydon
Canons Ashby
Blakesley
Avon Dassett
Farnborough
FARNBOROUGH HALL
Cherwell
Moreton Pinkney
Woodend
Greens Norton
Chipping Warden
CATANGER LLAMA TREKKING
Woodend Green
Bradden
Mollington
Weston
Slapton
Wardington
Culworth
Weedon Lois
Abthorpe
Shotteswell
Cropredy
Upper Wardington
Sulgrave
Wappenham
Great Bourton
SULGRAVE MANOR
Hornton
Williamscott
Thorpe Mandeville
Silverstone
Horley
Helmdon
Hanwell
Chacombe
Marston St Lawrence
SILVERSTONE
Wroxton
Greatworth
Syresham
Drayton
Thenford
Balscote
Grimsbury
Crowfield
Neithrop
Overthorpe
Halse
Radstone
Biddlesden
Lillingstone Dayrell
Warkworth
North Newington
Whitfield
Farthinghoe
BROUGHTON CASTLE
Easington
STOWE SCHOOL AND GARDENS
Tadmarton
Broughton
Upper Astrop
Turweston
Dadford
Bodicote
Newbottle
Sor Brook
Shalstone
Bloxham
West Adderbury
Astrop
Hinton-in-the-Hedges
Buffler's Holt
Chackmore
King's Sutton
Charlton
Westbury
East Adderbury
Great Ouse
Milton
Evenley
Water Stratford
Radclive
Barford St John
Croughton
Mixbury
Finmere
South Newington
Barford St Michael
Aynho
Tingewick
Clifton
Hempton
Souldern
Cottisford
Barton Hartshorn
Deddington
Newton Purcell
Nether Worton
Preston Bissett
North Aston
Fritwell
Baynard's Green
Hardwick
Chetwode
Hethe
Somerton
Fringford
Stoke Lyne
Hillesden
Cherwell
M45
M1
M40
A45
A361
A5
A423
A426
A425
A428
A422
A43
A421
A4421
A413
A4260
B4037
B4525
B4100
B4031
B5385
0 1 2 3 miles
0 1 2 3 4 5 km

Walgrave
Hannington
Little Harrowden
Great Harrowden
Irthlingborough
Brixworth
Spratton
Holcot
Hardwick
Chelveston
Higham Ferrers
Caldecott
Pitsford Reservoir
Brixworth
Pitsford
Sywell
Wellingborough
Chichele College
Warmonds Hill
N'Thampton & Lamport Railway
Chapel Brampton
Mears Ashby
Little Irchester
Rushden
Knuston
Newton Bromswold
Moulton
Overstone
Sywell Reservoir
Wilby
Heritage Centre
Irchester
Little Wymington
Boughton
Harlestone
Boothville
New Barton
Great Doddington
Narrow Gauge Railway Mus
Wymington
Kingsthorpe
Kingsley Park
Ecton
Earls Barton
Farndish
Queen's Park
Weston Favell
Little Billing
Great Billing
Podington
Wollaston
Souldrop
Dallington
Billing Aquadrome
Strixton
Hinwick
Santa Pod Raceway
Duston
Northampton
Little Houghton
Cogenhoe
Whiston
Grendon
Upton
Far Cotton
Brafield-on-the-Green
Castle Ashby
Sharnbrook
Great Houghton
Denton
Easton Maudit
Bozeat
Odell
Hunsbury Hill
Hardingstone
Yardley Hastings
Harrold
Felmersham
Harrold-Odell
Wootton
Chellington
Pavenham
Collingtree
Yardley Chase
Hackleton
Carlton
Milton Malsor
Quinton
Horton
Piddington
Warrington
Lavendon
West End
Stevington
Oakley
Blisworth
Courteenhall
Cold Brayfield
Turvey
Stevington Windmill
Grand Union Canal
Salcey Forest
Roade
Eakley Lanes
Weston Underwood
Olney
Clifton Reynes
Newton Blossomville
Bromham
Canal Museum
Hartwell
Ravenstone
Emberton
Shutlanger
Stoke Bruerne
Ashton
Stoke Goldington
Box End
Towcester
Stoke Park Pavilions
Long Street
Stagsden
Milton Keynes
Filgrave
Tyringham
Great Ouse
Alderton
Grafton Regis
Hanslope
Tathall End
Gayhurst
Sherington
Hardmead
Astwood
Chicheley Hall
Chicheley
Paulerspury
North Crawley
Castlethorpe
Lathbury
Bourne End
Yardley Gobion
Potterspury
Newport Pagnell
Newport Pagnell Services
Upper Shelton
Haversham
Broad Green
Great Linford
Gullivers Land
Lower Shelton
Whittlewood Forest
Cosgrove
Cranfield
New Bradwell
Willen
Moulsoe
Old Stratford
Stony Stratford
Wolverton
Milton Keynes
P&R
St Lawrence's
Lillingstone Lovell
Deanshanger
Passenham
Bradwell
Broughton
Salford
Lidlington
Millbrook
Wicken
Calverton
Milton Keynes National Hockey
Woolstone
Milton Keynes Village
Leckhampstead
Upper Weald
Woughton on the Green
Brogborough
Beachampton
Loughton
Shenley Church End
Wavendon
Aspley Guise
Ridgmont
Maids Moreton
Thornton
Simpson
Walton
Woburn Sands
Husborne Crawley
Shenley Brook End
Bow Brickhill
Aspley Heath
Whaddon
Bletchley
Wild Animal Kingdom
Buckingham
Nash
Bletchley Park
Fenny Stratford
Woburn
Woburn
Eversholt
Tattenhoe
Thornborough
Far Bletchley
Church End
Woburn Abbey
Singleborough
Little Brickhill
Tingrith
Padbury
Great Horwood
Little Horwood
Newton Longville
Great Brickhill
Milton Bryan
Adstock
Chase
Ouse
Drayton Parslow
Stoke Hammond
King's Wood
Potsgrove
Addington
Winslow Hall
Mursley
Stockgrove Park
Battlesden
Toddington
Heath
A6
A45
A509
A508
A43
A5199
A5076
A4500
A428
A5123
A422
A5
A421
A4146
A507
A4012
A5130
A413
A510
B571
B526
B5388
B565
B4034
B4033
M1
99
84
66
67
SP

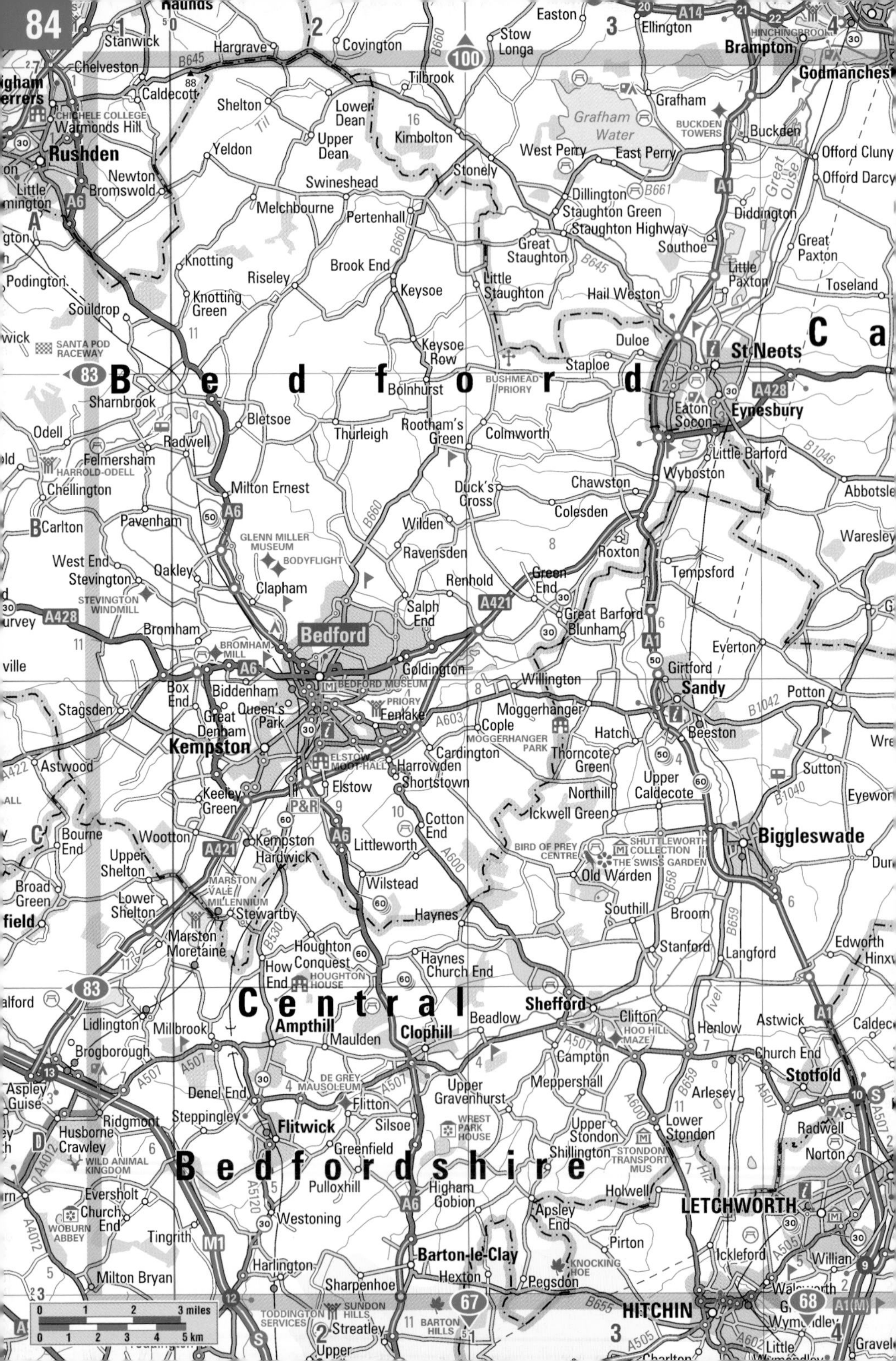

Raunds
Stanwick
Chelveston
Hargrave
Covington
Easton
Stow Longa
Ellington
A14
Brampton
HINCHINGBROOKE
Godmanchester
B645
Caldecott
Tilbrook
Shelton
Lower Dean
Upper Dean
Kimbolton
Grafham
Grafham Water
BUCKDEN TOWERS
Buckden
CHICHELE COLLEGE
Warmonds Hill
Rushden
Yeldon
Newton Bromswold
Swineshead
Stonely
West Perry
East Perry
Offord Cluny
Offord Darcy
Great Ouse
Melchbourne
Pertenhall
Dillington
B661
Staughton Green
Staughton Highway
Diddington
A1
A6
B660
Great Staughton
Southoe
Great Paxton
Little Paxton
Toseland
Knotting
Riseley
Brook End
B645
Keysoe
Little Staughton
Hail Weston
Podington
Knotting Green
Souldrop
Keysoe Row
Duloe
St Neots
SANTA POD RACEWAY
83
Bedford
BUSHMEAD PRIORY
Staploe
Bolnhurst
Sharnbrook
Eaton Socon
Eynesbury
A428
Odell
Bletsoe
Thurleigh
Rootham's Green
Colmworth
Radwell
Felmersham
HARROLD-ODELL
Little Barford
B1046
Wyboston
Chellington
Milton Ernest
Duck's Cross
Chawston
Colesden
Abbotsley
Carlton
Pavenham
Wilden
Waresley
GLENN MILLER MUSEUM
BODYFLIGHT
Ravensden
Roxton
Tempsford
West End
Stevington
Oakley
Clapham
Renhold
Green End
STEVINGTON WINDMILL
Salph End
A421
Great Barford
Blunham
A428
Bromham
Bedford
BROMHAM MILL
Goldington
Everton
Girtford
Sandy
Potton
Willington
BEDFORD MUSEUM
PRIORY
Fenlake
Box End
Biddenham
Great Denham
Queen's Park
Moggerhanger
Cople
MOGGERHANGER PARK
A603
Stagsden
Kempston
Hatch
Beeston
B1042
Cardington
Thorncote Green
Astwood
ELSTOW MOOT HALL
Harrowden
Shortstown
Elstow
Sutton
Keeley Green
P&R
Northill
Upper Caldecote
Cotton End
Ickwell Green
B1040
Eyeworth
Bourne End
Wootton
Kempston Hardwick
A421
Littleworth
BIRD OF PREY CENTRE
SHUTTLEWORTH COLLECTION
THE SWISS GARDEN
Old Warden
Biggleswade
Upper Shelton
Wilstead
A600
B658
Broad Green
Lower Shelton
MARSTON VALE MILLENNIUM
Stewartby
Haynes
Southill
Broom
B530
Marston Moretaine
Houghton Conquest
Stanford
B659
Langford
Edworth
Haynes Church End
How End
HOUGHTON HOUSE
Central
Shefford
Clifton
Ivel
Henlow
Astwick
Lidlington
Millbrook
Ampthill
Maulden
Clophill
Beadlow
HOO HILL MAZE
A507
Campton
Brogborough
Church End
Stotfold
Aspley Guise
A507
DE GREY MAUSOLEUM
Upper Gravenhurst
Meppershall
Arlesey
Denel End
Flitton
A600
Ridgmont
Steppingley
Husborne Crawley
Flitwick
Silsoe
WREST PARK HOUSE
Upper Stondon
Lower Stondon
Radwell
Greenfield
Shillington
STONDON TRANSPORT MUS
Norton
WILD ANIMAL KINGDOM
Bedfordshire
Pulloxhill
Higham Gobion
Holwell
A4012
A5120
Eversholt
Church End
WOBURN ABBEY
Westoning
Apsley End
LETCHWORTH
Tingrith
M1
Pirton
Ickleford
A505
Harlington
Barton-le-Clay
KNOCKING HOE
Willian
Milton Bryan
Hexton
Pegsdon
Sharpenhoe
67
SUNDON HILLS
TODDINGTON SERVICES
Streatley
BARTON HILLS
B655
HITCHIN
68
A1(M)
Wymondley
A505
A602
Little
Graveley
0 1 2 3 miles
0 1 2 3 4 5 km

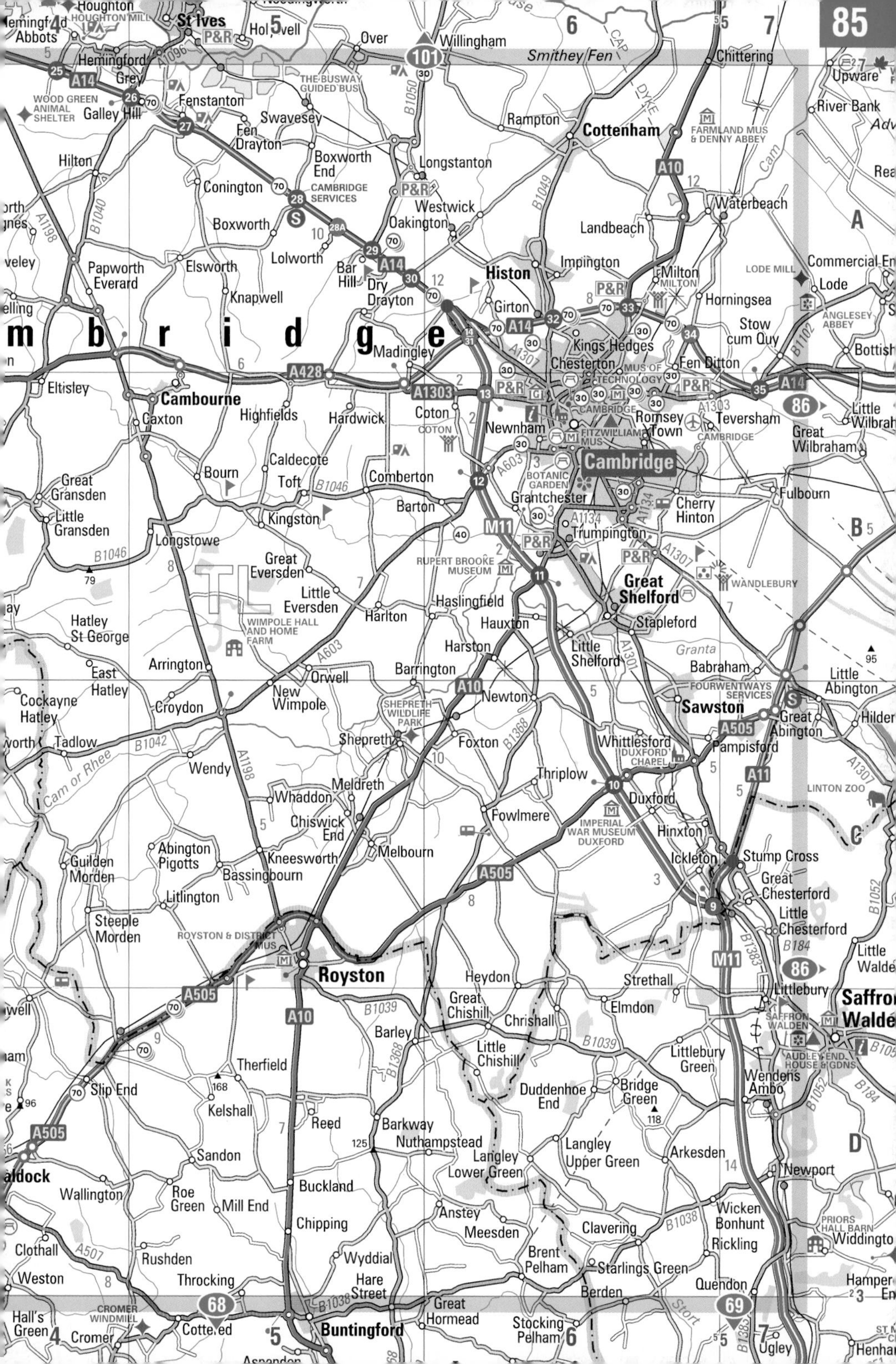
Houghton
HOUGHTON MILL
Hemingford Abbots
St Ives
P&R
Holywell
Over
101
Willingham
Smithey Fen
Chittering
Upware
Hemingford Grey
A1096
A14
THE BUSWAY GUIDED BUS
B1050
WOOD GREEN ANIMAL SHELTER
Galley Hill
Fenstanton
Swavesey
Rampton
Cottenham
FARMLAND MUS & DENNY ABBEY
River Bank
CAR DYKE
Fen Drayton
Boxworth End
Longstanton
Hilton
Conington
CAMBRIDGE SERVICES
Westwick
A10
Cam
B1049
Waterbeach
B1040
A1198
Boxworth
Oakington
Landbeach
Papworth Everard
Elsworth
Lolworth
Bar Hill
Dry Drayton
Histon
Impington
Milton
MILTON
LODE MILL
Commercial End
Lode
Knapwell
Girton
Horningsea
ANGLESEY ABBEY
Cambridge
Madingley
Kings Hedges
Stow cum Quy
B1102
Bottisham
A1307
Chesterton
MUS OF TECHNOLOGY
Fen Ditton
A428
Eltisley
Cambourne
A1303
Caxton
Highfields
Hardwick
Coton
COTON
CAMBRIDGE
Newnham
Romsey Town
Teversham
86
Little Wilbraham
Great Wilbraham
FITZWILLIAM MUS
Caldecote
Bourn
A603
BOTANIC GARDEN
Great Gransden
Toft
B1046
Comberton
Grantchester
Cherry Hinton
Fulbourn
Little Gransden
Kingston
Barton
A1134
M11
Trumpington
Longstowe
B1046
Great Eversden
RUPERT BROOKE MUSEUM
Great Shelford
WANDLEBURY
TL
Little Eversden
Harlton
Haslingfield
Hauxton
Stapleford
Hatley St George
WIMPOLE HALL AND HOME FARM
Harston
Little Shelford
A1301
Granta
Babraham
Little Abington
East Hatley
Arrington
Orwell
Barrington
FOURWENTWAYS SERVICES
Newton
Cockayne Hatley
Croydon
New Wimpole
SHEPRETH WILDLIFE PARK
Sawston
Great Abington
Hildersham
A505
Tadlow
B1042
Shepreth
Foxton
B1368
Whittlesford
Pampisford
DUXFORD CHAPEL
Cam or Rhee
Wendy
Thriplow
A11
Meldreth
LINTON ZOO
Whaddon
Fowlmere
Duxford
Chiswick End
IMPERIAL WAR MUSEUM DUXFORD
Hinxton
Abington Pigotts
Guilden Morden
Kneesworth
Melbourn
Ickleton
Stump Cross
Bassingbourn
Great Chesterford
Litlington
Little Chesterford
B1052
Steeple Morden
ROYSTON & DISTRICT MUS
B184
B1383
Little Walden
Royston
Heydon
Strethall
Littlebury
Saffron Walden
Great Chishill
Elmdon
SAFFRON WALDEN
Chrishall
B1039
Barley
Little Chishill
Littlebury Green
AUDLEY END HOUSE & GDNS
Therfield
Duddenhoe End
Bridge Green
Wendens Ambo
Slip End
Kelshall
Reed
Barkway
Nuthampstead
Langley Upper Green
Langley Lower Green
Arkesden
Baldock
Sandon
Wallington
Roe Green
Mill End
Buckland
Newport
Chipping
Anstey
Meesden
Clavering
B1038
Wicken Bonhunt
Rickling
PRIORS HALL BARN
Widdington
Clothall
A507
Rushden
Wyddial
Brent Pelham
Starlings Green
Weston
Throcking
Hare Street
Berden
Quendon
Hamperden End
68
Great Hormead
Stort
69
Hall's Green
CROMER WINDMILL
Cromer
Cottered
Buntingford
Stocking Pelham
Ugley
Henham

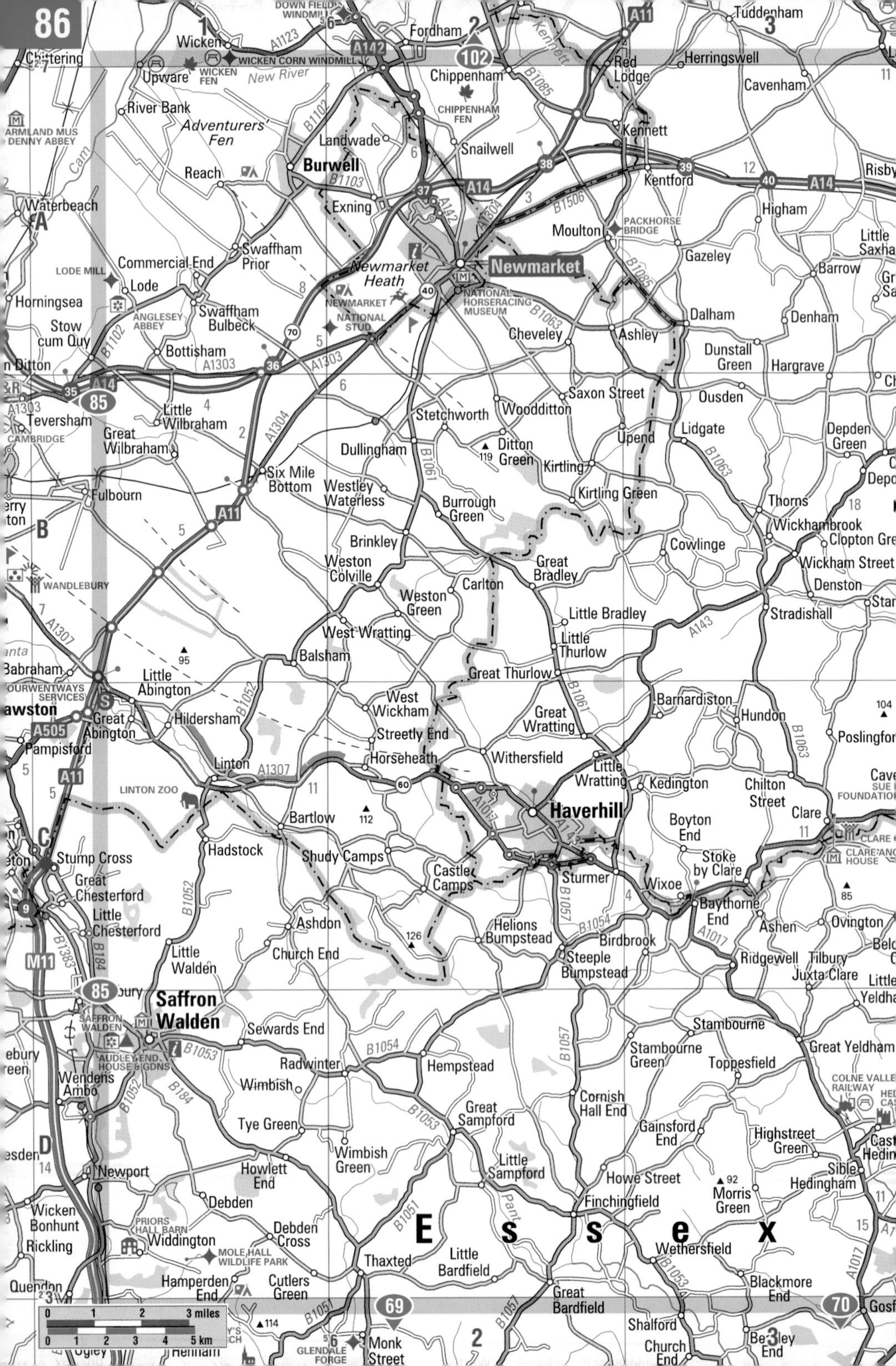
DOWN FIELD WINDMILL
Wicken
Chittering
WICKEN CORN WINDMILL
Upware
WICKEN FEN
New River
Fordham
A1123
A142
102
Chippenham
CHIPPENHAM FEN
Kennett
B1085
A11
Tuddenham
Red Lodge
Herringswell
Cavenham
River Bank
Adventurers' Fen
FARMLAND MUS DENNY ABBEY
Cam
B1102
Landwade
Burwell
B1103
Snailwell
Kennett
Kentford
Reach
Exning
A14
A1304
B1506
Moulton
PACKHORSE BRIDGE
Higham
Risby
Waterbeach
A
Swaffham Prior
Commercial End
LODE MILL
Lode
Newmarket Heath
Newmarket
NEWMARKET
NATIONAL HORSERACING MUSEUM
NATIONAL STUD
Gazeley
Barrow
Little Saxham
Horningsea
Stow cum Quy
ANGLESEY ABBEY
Swaffham Bulbeck
Bottisham
A1303
B1063
Cheveley
Ashley
Dalham
Denham
Dunstall Green
Hargrave
Ditton
Teversham
CAMBRIDGE
Great Wilbraham
Little Wilbraham
85
Saxon Street
Woodditton
Stetchworth
Ousden
Lidgate
Depden Green
Dullingham
Ditton Green
Upend
Kirtling
B1061
Six Mile Bottom
Westley Waterless
Burrough Green
Kirtling Green
Fulbourn
Thorns
Wickhambrook
Clopton Green
B
Brinkley
Cowlinge
Weston Colville
Great Bradley
Carlton
Wickham Street
Denston
WANDLEBURY
Weston Green
Little Bradley
Stradishall
A1307
West Wratting
Little Thurlow
A143
Balsham
Great Thurlow
Babraham
Little Abington
FOURWENTWAYS SERVICES
Sawston
Great Abington
Hildersham
B1052
West Wickham
Great Wratting
Barnardiston
Hundon
Poslingford
A505
Pampisford
Streetly End
Horseheath
Withersfield
Little Wratting
Kedington
Chilton Street
Clare
Linton
LINTON ZOO
Bartlow
Haverhill
Boyton End
Stoke by Clare
CLARE CASTLE
CLARE ANCIENT HOUSE
C
Stump Cross
Hadstock
Shudy Camps
Castle Camps
Sturmer
Wixoe
Baythorne End
Great Chesterford
Little Chesterford
B1057
B1054
Ashen
Ovington
Ashdon
Helions Bumpstead
Birdbrook
A1017
Ridgewell
Tilbury Juxta Clare
Church End
Steeple Bumpstead
Little Walden
M11
B1383
B184
Saffron Walden
SAFFRON WALDEN
AUDLEY END HOUSE & GDNS
Sewards End
Stambourne
Stambourne Green
Great Yeldham
B1053
Radwinter
B1054
Hempstead
Toppesfield
Wendens Ambo
Wimbish
COLNE VALLEY RAILWAY
Tye Green
Great Sampford
Cornish Hall End
Gainsford End
Highstreet Green
D
Newport
Howlett End
Wimbish Green
Little Sampford
Howe Street
Morris Green
Sible Hedingham
Debden
Finchingfield
Wicken Bonhunt
PRIORS HALL BARN
Widdington
Debden Cross
B1051
E s s e x
Rickling
MOLE HALL WILDLIFE PARK
Thaxted
Little Bardfield
Wethersfield
Quendon
Hamperden End
Cutlers Green
Great Bardfield
Blackmore End
69
70
0 1 2 3 miles
0 1 2 3 4 5 km
GLENDALE FORGE
Monk Street
Shalford
Church End
Beazley End

West Stow
Ingham
Ampton
Great Livermere
Walsham le Willows
Cranmer Green
Gislingham
Culford
A134
Ixworth
103
Langham
Four Ashes
Wickham Street
ABBEY (REM)
A143
Crownland
Westhorpe
Wickham Skeith
A1101
Timworth Green
Conyers Green
Stowlangtoft
Badwell Ash
Long Thurlow
Finningham
Hunston
Wyverstone
Thwaite
Fornham All Saints
Fornham St Martin
B1106
Pakenham
A1088
Stanton Street
Great Ashfield
Wyverstone Street
Bacton
Cotton
Great Barton
Earl's Green
Brockford Street
Ford's Green
Thurston
Norton
Bacton Green
Canham's Green
Mendlesham
Westley
Bury St Edmunds
Elmswell
Haughley Green
Ward Green
CATHEDRAL AND ABBEY RUINS
Tostock
B1113
Gipping
Mendlesham Green
A14
Wetherden
Blackthorpe
Beyton
Horringer
A134
Rushbrooke
Rougham
Hessett
Woolpit
HAUGHLEY PARK
Haughley
Middlewood Green
Saxham Street
Drinkstone
WOOLPIT BYGONES MUSEUM
Rougham Green
Drinkstone Green
Thorney Green
Stonham
Suffolk
Sicklesmere
Bradfield St George
Harleston
B1066
Little Welnetham
Rattlesden
Buxhall Fen Street
Forward Green
A143
Hawstead
Great Welnetham
Bradfield St Clare
Gedding
Poystreet Green
MUSEUM OF EAST ANGLIAN LIFE
Stowmarket
Creeting St Mary
Whepstead
REDE HALL
Bradfield Combust
BRADFIELD WOODS
Felsham
Buxhall
Great Finborough
Combs Ford
Gipping
Hoggard's Green
Cross Green
Hightown Green
High Street Green
Combs
Great Green
Moats Tye
BEACON HILL SERV
Brockley Green
Lawshall
Cockfield
Thorpe Green
Little Finborough
Battisford
Needham Market
Brettenham
Battisford Tye
Thorpe Morieux
Charles Tye
Ringshall
NEEDHAM LAKE
Hartest
Shimpling Street
TL
B1115
Cross Green
WATTISHAM AIRFIELD MUSEUM
Barking
B1078
Barking Tye
Baylham
Boxted
Shimpling
Alpheton
A1141
Hitcham
Wattisham
Ringshall Stocks
Willisham Tye
Preston St Mary
Kettlebaston
Great Bricett
Blakenham
Stanstead
A134
GUILDHALL
Brett
Bildeston
Nedging Tye
Offton
Little Blakenham
Lavenham
KENTWELL HALL
Bridge Street
Monks Eleigh
Chelsworth
Naughton
Glemsford
Somersham
B1066
B1065
High Street
Brent Eleigh
A1092
Semer
Ash Street
Elmsett
Flowton
MELFORD HALL
B1115
Milden
Whatfield
Pentlow
Long Melford
B1071
Little Waldingfield
Lindsey
A1141
Aldham
Acton
ST JAMES'S CHAPEL
Foxearth
B1064
Great Waldingfield
WOLVES WOOD RSPB RESERVE
A1071
Burstall
Borley
Kersey
A134
B1115
Hintlesham
Mill Green
Sudbury
Edwardstone
Hadleigh
Chattisham
Groton
Coles Green
Ballingdon
Great Cornard
Newton
Boxford
Belchamp Walter
Bulmer
GAINSBOROUGH'S HO
A1071
Layham
Mace Green
Stone Street
Calais Street
A131
Middleton
Little Cornard
Whitestreet Green
B1070
Raydon
Great Wenham
Capel St Mary
Bulmer Tye
A134
Gestingthorpe
Henny Street
Assington
Shelley
Polstead
B1058
B1068
Holton St Mary
Great Henny
Twinstead
Harrow Street
Stoke-by-Nayland
Wickham St Paul
Twinstead Green
Lamarsh
B1508
Honey Tye
B1087
Dedham Vale
Higham
East Bergholt
Great Maplestead
Alphamstone
Bures Green
Thorington Street
B1068
Stratford St Mary
Little Maplestead
Bures
Nayland
A12
Boxted
Dedham
BRIDGE COTTAGE
Pebmarsh
Stour
Little Horkesley
Boxted Cross
SIR ALFRED MUNNINGS ART MUSEUM
Mount Bures
Boxted Heath
Dedham Heath
Lawford
Langham
Halstead
Wormingford
A134
B1029
A137
Great Horkesley
Manningtree
Colne Engaine
Wakes Colne
70
WESTON HOMES COMMUNITY STAD
71
EAST ANGLIAN RAILWAY MUSEUM
B1508
Horkesley Heath
Ardleigh
Earls Colne
Fordham
A12
Mile End
A120
Little Bromley
Chappel
88

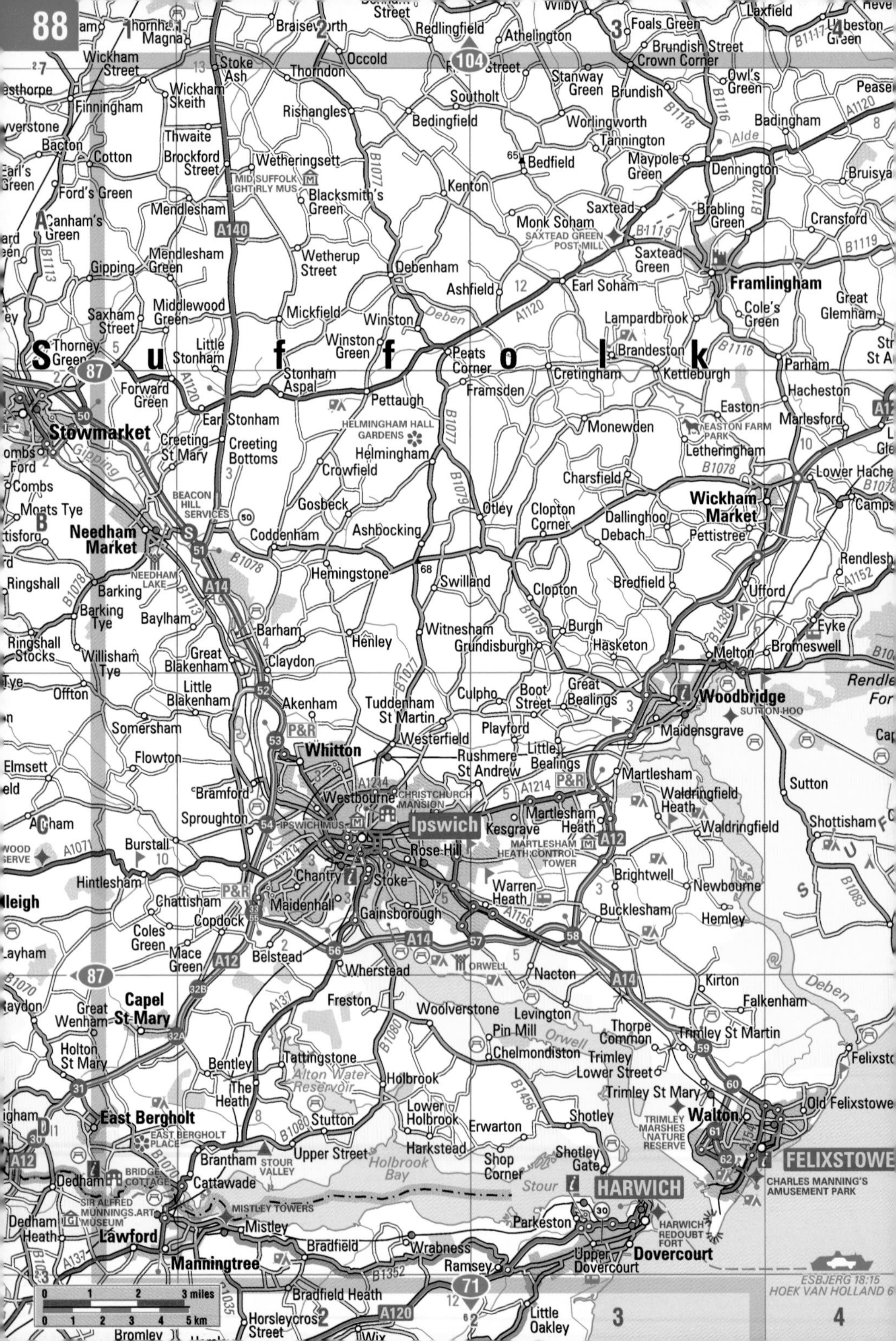
88
Thornham Magna
Braiseworth
Redlingfield
Athelington
Foals Green
Laxfield
Ubbeston Green
Wickham Street
Stoke Ash
Occold
Thorndon
Brundish Street
Crown Corner
Owl's Green
Westhorpe
Finningham
Wickham Skeith
Rishangles
Southolt
Bedingfield
Stanway Green
Brundish
Peasenhall
Wyverstone
Thwaite
Worlingworth
Tannington
Badingham
Bacton
Cotton
Brockford Street
Wetheringsett
Bedfield
Maypole Green
Dennington
Bruisyard
Earl's Green
Ford's Green
MID SUFFOLK LIGHT RLY MUS
Blacksmith's Green
Kenton
Saxtead
Brabling Green
Mendlesham
Canham's Green
Monk Soham
SAXTEAD GREEN POST MILL
Cransford
Mendlesham Green
Wetherup Street
Debenham
Saxtead Green
Gipping
Framlingham
Ashfield
Earl Soham
Great Glemham
Middlewood Green
Mickfield
Winston
Deben
Lampardbrook
Cole's Green
Saxham Street
Thorney Green
Little Stonham
Winston Green
Peats Corner
Brandeston
Parham
Suffolk
Stonham Aspal
Framsden
Cretingham
Kettleburgh
Hacheston
Forward Green
Pettaugh
Easton
Marlesford
Stowmarket
Earl Stonham
HELMINGHAM HALL GARDENS
Monewden
EASTON FARM PARK
Creeting St Mary
Creeting Bottoms
Helmingham
Letheringham
Combs Ford
Gipping
Crowfield
Charsfield
Lower Hacheston
Combs
BEACON HILL SERVICES
Gosbeck
Otley
Clopton Corner
Dallinghoo
Wickham Market
Campsea
Moats Tye
Needham Market
Coddenham
Ashbocking
Debach
Pettistree
NEEDHAM LAKE
Hemingstone
Swilland
Clopton
Bredfield
Rendlesham
Ringshall
Barking
Ufford
Barking Tye
Baylham
Witnesham
Burgh
Eyke
Ringshall Stocks
Willisham Tye
Barham
Henley
Grundisburgh
Hasketon
Melton
Bromeswell
Great Blakenham
Claydon
Offton
Little Blakenham
Akenham
Tuddenham St Martin
Culpho
Boot Street
Great Bealings
Woodbridge
Rendlesham Forest
SUTTON HOO
Somersham
Westerfield
Playford
Maidensgrave
Whitton
Rushmere St Andrew
Little Bealings
Flowton
Elmsett
Martlesham
Westbourne
CHRISTCHURCH MANSION
Waldringfield Heath
Sutton
Bramford
Sproughton
IPSWICH MUS
Ipswich
Kesgrave
Martlesham Heath
Waldringfield
Shottisham
Aldham
Burstall
Rose Hill
MARTLESHAM HEATH CONTROL TOWER
Hintlesham
Chantry
Stoke
Warren Heath
Brightwell
Newbourne
Hadleigh
Chattisham
Maidenhall
Gainsborough
Bucklesham
Hemley
Copdock
Coles Green
Layham
Mace Green
Belstead
Wherstead
ORWELL
Nacton
Kirton
Raydon
Capel St Mary
Great Wenham
Freston
Woolverstone
Levington
Falkenham
Pin Mill
Orwell
Thorpe Common
Trimley St Martin
Holton St Mary
Tattingstone
Chelmondiston
Trimley Lower Street
Felixstowe
Bentley
Alton Water Reservoir
Holbrook
Trimley St Mary
The Heath
East Bergholt
Stutton
Lower Holbrook
Erwarton
Shotley
TRIMLEY MARSHES NATURE RESERVE
Walton
Old Felixstowe
EAST BERGHOLT PLACE
Upper Street
Harkstead
Shotley Gate
FELIXSTOWE
Brantham
STOUR VALLEY
Holbrook Bay
Shop Corner
Dedham
BRIDGE COTTAGE
Cattawade
Stour
HARWICH
CHARLES MANNING'S AMUSEMENT PARK
SIR ALFRED MUNNINGS ART MUSEUM
MISTLEY TOWERS
Parkeston
HARWICH REDOUBT FORT
Dedham Heath
Lawford
Mistley
Bradfield
Wrabness
Manningtree
Ramsey
Upper Dovercourt
Dovercourt
ESBJERG 18:15
HOEK VAN HOLLAND
Bradfield Heath
Horsleycross Street
Bromley
Wix
Little Oakley
0 1 2 3 miles
0 1 2 3 4 5 km

Dunwich
Forest
DUNWICH UNDERWATER EXPLORATION EXHIBITION
Dunwich
105
High Street
Hemp Green
Sibton
Darsham
Yoxford
Westleton
WESTLETON HEATH
MINSMERE RSPB NATURE RESERVE
Middleton Moor
Middleton
Rotten End
A12
B1122
North Green
Theberton
Eastbridge
Curlew Green
Kelsale
B1121
Carlton
LEISTON ABBEY
Saxmundham
B1119
Leiston
Sizewell
Knodishall
Benhall Street
Sternfield
Aldringham
Benhall Green
Coldfair Green
B1069
B1353
Friston
Thorpeness
Farnham
Gromford
A1094
SNAPE MALTINGS
Snape
NORTH WARREN RSPB NATURE RESERVE
Aldeburgh
Blaxhall
Iken
Aldeburgh Bay
High Street
Tunstall
Tunstall Forest
B1078
Sudbourne
Alde
TM
Chillesford
Butley
B1084
ORFORD CASTLE
Orford
Orford Ness
ORFORDNESS-HAVERGATE
Butley High Corner
Andrew
Boyton
Stores Corner
Hollesley Bay
Shingle Street
4
5
6
7
A
B
C
D

1
2
3
4
A
B
C
D
107
74
75
SH
SN
CARDIGAN BAY
BAE
CEREDIGION
Tal-y-bont
Plas-canol
Llanaber
Cutiau
A496
Barmouth
(Abermaw)
RNLI LIFEBOAT MUSEUM
Afon Mawddach
BARMOUTH BAY
The Bar
Arthog
FAIRBOURNE STEAM RAILWAY
BAE BERMO
Fairbourne
Friog
Llwyngwril
A493
Llangelynin
Rhoslefain
Llanegryn
Peniarth
Llanfendigaid
309
Tonfanau
Bryncrug
Pandy
Rhyd-yr-onen
TALYLLYN RAILWAY
Tywyn
Caethle
WALES COAST PATH
279
Aberdovey
Aberdovey Bar
Bae Aberdyfi
DYFI
Ynyslas
B4353
Llancynfelyn
BORTH
Borth
Upper Borth
Dôl-y-Bont
Llandre
Pen-y-garn
B4572
Bow Street
ARTS CENTRE
NATIONAL LIBRARY
Clarach
CLIFF RAILWAY
148
Plas Gogerddan
A4159
Aberystwyth
Comins Coch
Capel
P&R
Llanbadarn Fawr
Trefechan
CASTLE
Penparcau
Southgate
Glanrafon
Rhydyfelin
Moriah
0 1 2 3 miles
0 1 2 3 4 5 km

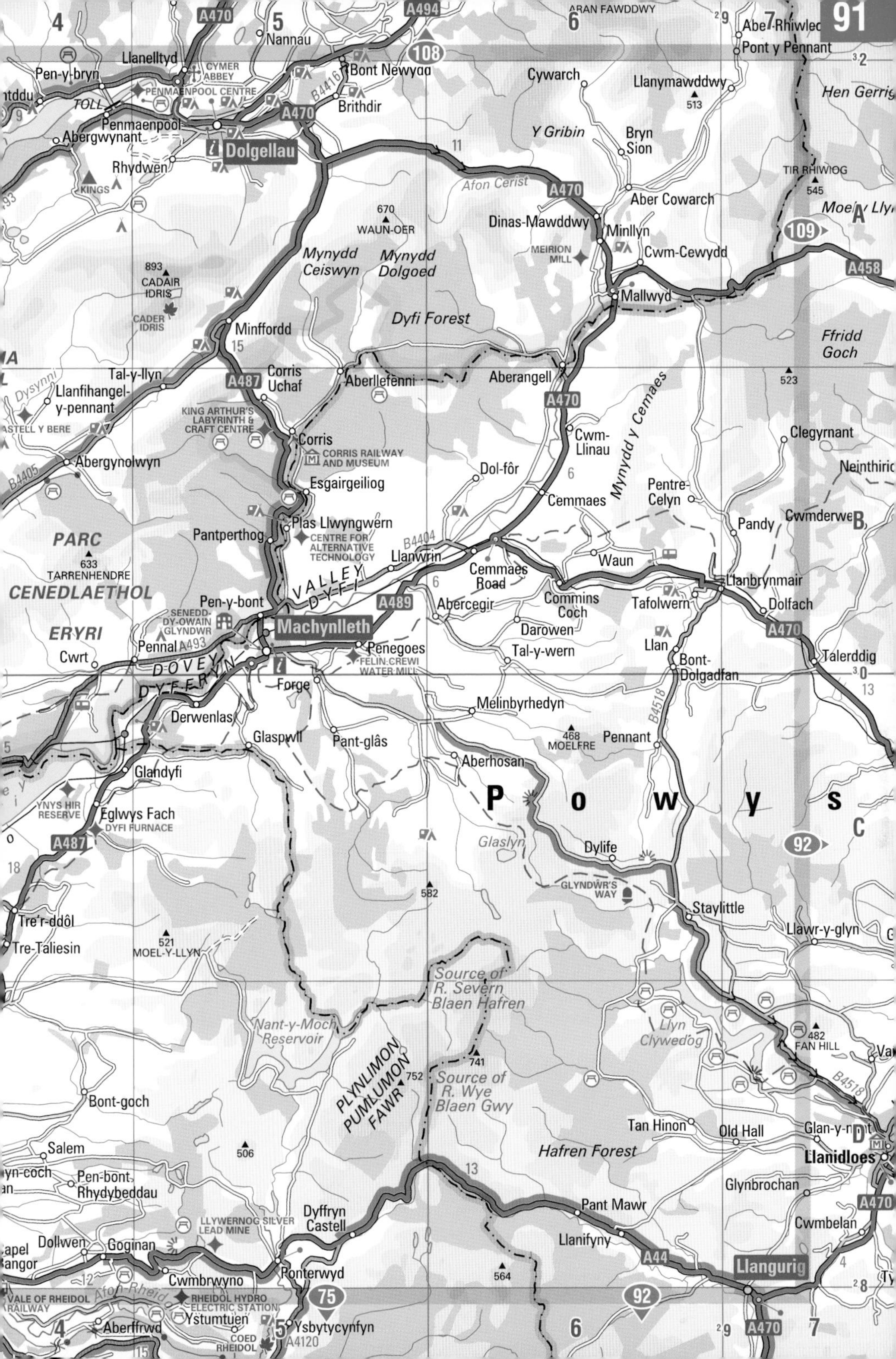
Nannau
Llanelltyd
Pen-y-bryn
CYMER ABBEY
PENMAENPOOL CENTRE
TOLL
Penmaenpool
Abergwynant
Dolgellau
Rhydwen
KINGS
Bont Newydd
Brithdir
ARAN FAWDDWY
Abe Rhiwlech
Pont y Pennant
Cywarch
Llanymawddwy
513
Hen Gerrig
Y Gribin
Bryn Sion
TIR RHIWIOG
545
Afon Cerist
Aber Cowarch
Moel y Llyn
670
WAUN-OER
Dinas-Mawddwy
Minllyn
MEIRION MILL
Cwm-Cewydd
Mynydd Ceiswyn
Mynydd Dolgoed
893
CADAIR IDRIS
CADER IDRIS
Mallwyd
Dyfi Forest
Ffridd Goch
Minffordd
Tal-y-llyn
Dysynni
Llanfihangel-y-pennant
CASTELL Y BERE
Corris Uchaf
Aberllefenni
Aberangell
523
KING ARTHUR'S LABYRINTH & CRAFT CENTRE
Corris
CORRIS RAILWAY AND MUSEUM
Mynydd y Cemaes
Cwm-Llinau
Clegyrnant
Abergynolwyn
Esgairgeiliog
Dol-fôr
Neinthirion
Pentre-Celyn
Cemmaes
PARC
633
TARRENHENDRE
Pantperthog
Plas Llwyngwern
CENTRE FOR ALTERNATIVE TECHNOLOGY
Llanwrin
Pandy
Cwmderwen
Waun
Llanbrynmair
CENEDLAETHOL
VALLEY DYFI
Cemmaes Road
Pen-y-bont
SENEDD-DY-OWAIN GLYNDWR
Abercegir
Commins Coch
Tafolwern
Dolfach
ERYRI
Machynlleth
Darowen
Llan
Cwrt
Pennal
DOVEY
DYFFRYN
Penegoes
FELIN CREWI WATER MILL
Tal-y-wern
Bont-Dolgadfan
Talerddig
Forge
Melinbyrhedyn
Derwenlas
Glaspwll
Pant-glâs
468
MOELFRE
Pennant
Aberhosan
Glandyfi
YNYS HIR RESERVE
Eglwys Fach
DYFI FURNACE
P o w y s
Glaslyn
Dylife
582
GLYNDWR'S WAY
Staylittle
Tre'r-ddôl
Tre-Taliesin
521
MOEL-Y-LLYN
Llawr-y-glyn
Source of R. Severn Blaen Hafren
Nant-y-Moch Reservoir
Llyn Clywedog
482
FAN HILL
741
752
PLYNLIMON PUMLUMON FAWR
Source of R. Wye Blaen Gwy
Bont-goch
Tan Hinon
Old Hall
Glan-y-nant
Salem
506
Hafren Forest
Llanidloes
Pen-bont Rhydybeddau
Glynbrochan
Dyffryn Castell
Pant Mawr
LLYWERNOG SILVER LEAD MINE
Cwmbelan
Dollwen
Goginan
Llanifyny
Capel Bangor
Cwmbrwyno
Ponterwyd
564
Llangurig
VALE OF RHEIDOL RAILWAY
Afon Rheidol
RHEIDOL HYDRO ELECTRIC STATION
Aberffrwd
Ystumtuen
COED RHEIDOL
Ysbyty Cynfyn
A470
A494
A487
A489
A493
A458
A44
A4120
B4416
B4405
B4404
B4518
108
109
92
75

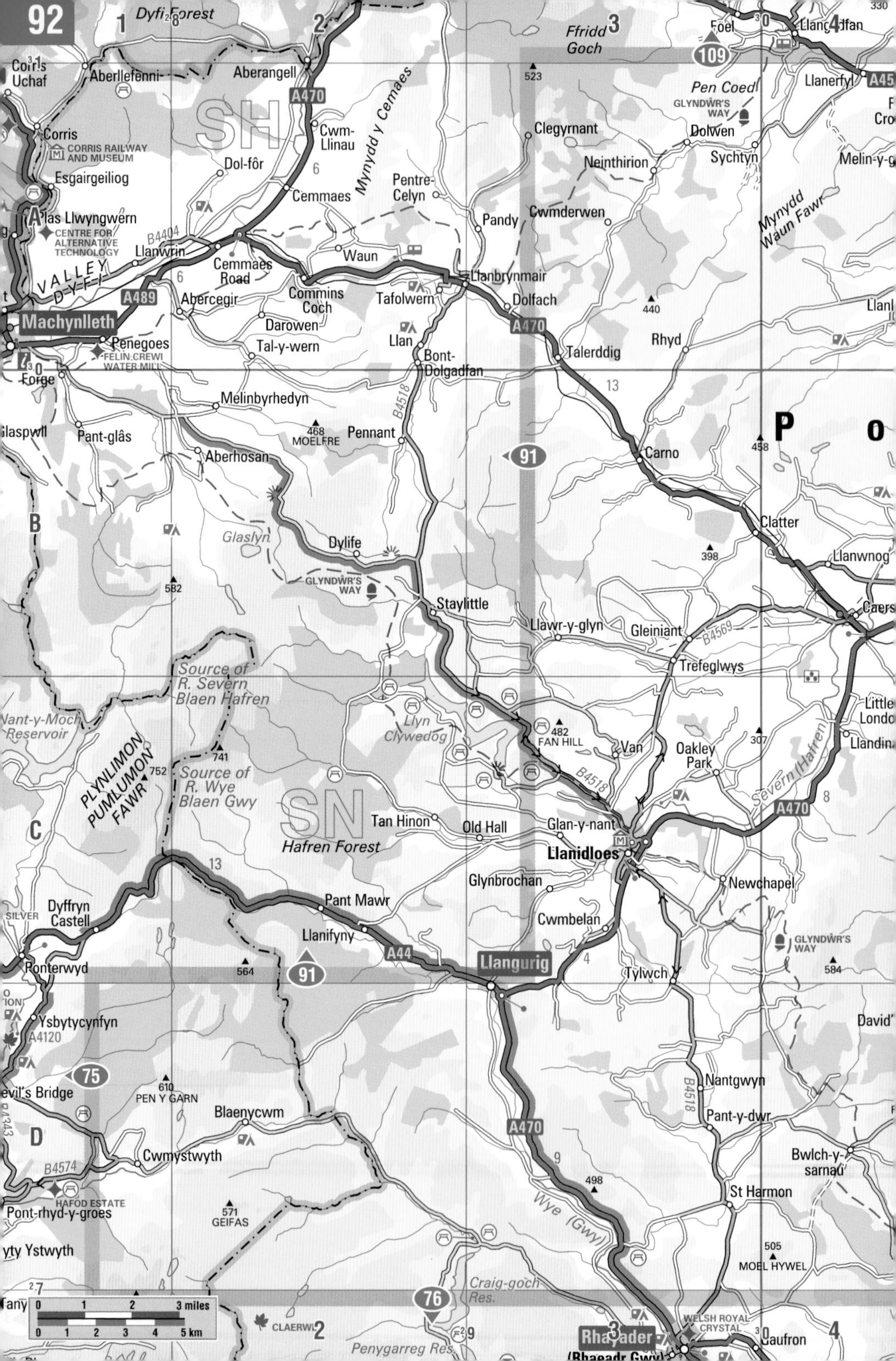
Dyfi Forest
Corris Uchaf
Aberllefenni
Aberangell
Ffridd Goch
Foel
Llangadfan
Llanerfyl
A470
SH
Cwm-Llinau
Mynydd y Cemaes
523
Pen Coed
GLYNDŴR'S WAY
Corris
CORRIS RAILWAY AND MUSEUM
Dol-fôr
Clegyrnant
Dolwen
Sychtyn
Esgairgeiliog
Neinthirion
Melin-y-g
Pentre-Celyn
Cemmaes
Plas Llwyngwern
CENTRE FOR ALTERNATIVE TECHNOLOGY
Pandy
Cwmderwen
Mynydd Waun Fawr
B4404
Llanwrin
Waun
Cemmaes Road
VALLEY DYFI
Llanbrynmair
A489
Abercegir
Commins Coch
Tafolwern
Dolfach
440
Machynlleth
Darowen
Penegoes
FELIN CREWI WATER MILL
Tal-y-wern
Llan
Talerddig
Rhyd
Bont-Dolgadfan
Forge
13
Melinbyrhedyn
B4518
Glaspwll
Pant-glâs
468
MOELFRE
Pennant
P
O
458
Aberhosan
91
Carno
Clatter
Glaslyn
Dylife
398
Llanwnog
582
GLYNDŴR'S WAY
Staylittle
Caersws
Llawr-y-glyn
Gleiniant
B4569
Trefeglwys
Source of R. Severn Blaen Hafren
Little London
Nant-y-Moch Reservoir
Llyn Clywedog
482
FAN HILL
307
Van
Oakley Park
Llandinam
741
PLYNLIMON PUMLUMON FAWR
752
Source of R. Wye Blaen Gwy
B4518
Severn (Hafren)
SN
A470
Tan Hinon
Old Hall
Glan-y-nant
8
C
Hafren Forest
Llanidloes
13
Glynbrochan
Newchapel
Pant Mawr
Dyffryn Castell
SILVER
Cwmbelan
Llanifyny
GLYNDŴR'S WAY
A44
Llangurig
4
Ponterwyd
564
91
Tylwch
584
Ysbytycynfyn
A4120
David's
75
Nantgwyn
Devil's Bridge
610
PEN Y GARN
Blaenycwm
B4518
Pant-y-dwr
D
A470
Cwmystwyth
Bwlch-y-sarnau
B4574
9
498
HAFOD ESTATE
Pont-rhyd-y-groes
571
GEIFAS
St Harmon
Wye (Gwy)
Ystwyth
505
MOEL HYWEL
Craig-goch Res.
76
0 1 2 3 miles
0 1 2 3 4 5 km
CLAERWEN
2
Rhayader (Rhaeadr Gwy)
WELSH ROYAL CRYSTAL
Gaufron
4
Penygarreg Res.

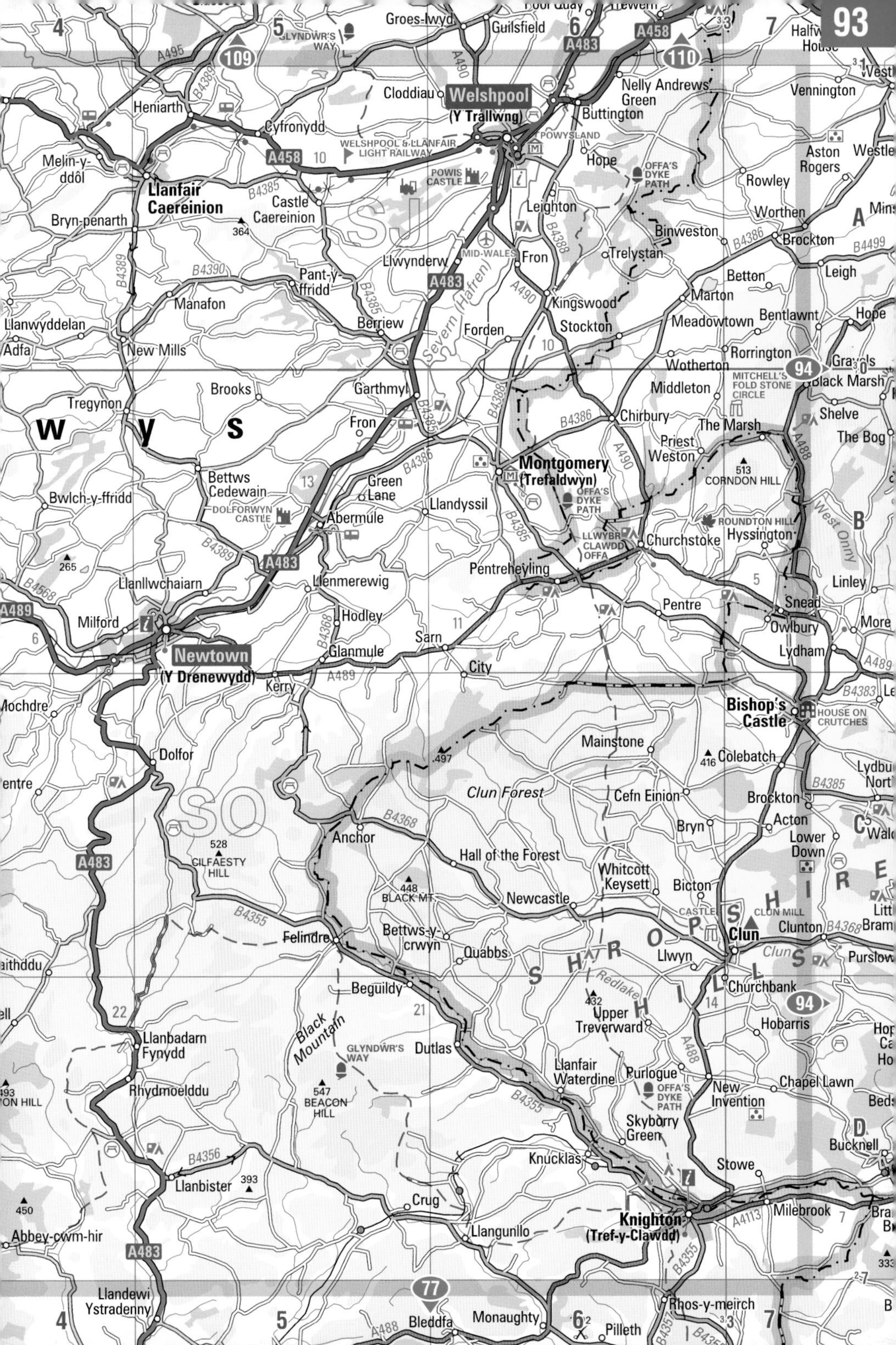

Welshpool
(Y Trallwng)
Llanfair
Caereinion
Montgomery
(Trefaldwyn)
Newtown
(Y Drenewydd)
Bishop's
Castle
Clun
Knighton
(Tref-y-Clawdd)
Guilsfield
Groes-lwyd
Cloddiau
Heniarth
Cyfronydd
Melin-y-
ddôl
Buttington
Nelly Andrews
Green
Vennington
Aston
Rogers
Rowley
Worthen
Brockton
Hope
Leighton
Binweston
Trelystan
Fron
Kingswood
Stockton
Marton
Betton
Leigh
Meadowtown
Bentlawnt
Rorrington
Wotherton
Middleton
Chirbury
Priest
Weston
The Marsh
Black Marsh
Shelve
The Bog
Castle
Caereinion
Bryn-penarth
Llwynderw
Pant-y-
ffridd
Manafon
Berriew
Forden
Llanwyddelan
Adfa
New Mills
Brooks
Garthmyl
Tregynon
Fron
Bettws
Cedewain
Bwlch-y-ffridd
Green
Lane
Llandyssil
Abermule
Churchstoke
Hyssington
Pentreheyling
Llanllwchaiarn
Llanmerewig
Hodley
Milford
Sarn
Glanmule
City
Kerry
Pentre
Snead
Owlbury
Lydham
Linley
More
Mochdre
Dolfor
Mainstone
Colebatch
Clun Forest
Cefn Einion
Brockton
Acton
Lower
Down
Bryn
Anchor
Hall of the Forest
Whitcott
Keysett
Bicton
Newcastle
Felindre
Bettws-y-
crwyn
Quabbs
Llwyn
Clunton
Purslow
Beguildy
Churchbank
Upper
Treverward
Hobarris
Llanbadarn
Fynydd
Dutlas
Llanfair
Waterdine
Purlogue
New
Invention
Chapel Lawn
Rhydmoelddu
Skyborry
Green
Bucknell
Knucklas
Stowe
Llanbister
Crug
Milebrook
Llangunllo
Abbey-cwm-hir
Llandewi
Ystradenny
Bleddfa
Monaughty
Pilleth
Rhos-y-meirch
SJ
SO
W Y S
S H R O P S H I R E
GLYNDWR'S WAY
WELSHPOOL & LLANFAIR LIGHT RAILWAY
POWIS CASTLE
POWYSLAND
OFFA'S DYKE PATH
MID-WALES
MITCHELL'S FOLD STONE CIRCLE
CORNDON HILL
ROUNDTON HILL
DOLFORWYN CASTLE
LLWYBR CLAWDD OFFA
HOUSE ON CRUTCHES
CILFAESTY HILL
BLACK MT.
BEACON HILL
CASTLE
CLUN MILL
Black Mountain
Severn (Hafren)
West Onny
Redlake
Clun
A458
A483
A490
A495
A489
A488
A4113
B4385
B4389
B4390
B4388
B4386
B4499
B4368
B4355
B4356
B4383
B4568
109
110
94
77

A458
Rowton
Halfway House
Vattlesborough Heath
Yockleton
Nox
Hortonlane
Cruckton
Porthill
Meole Brace
Preston
Emstrey
Attingham Park
Norton
A5
110
111
Westbury
Vennington
Stoney Stretton
Edge
Cruckmeole
Lea
Hanwood
Bayston Hill
P&R
Atcham
Wroxeter
Wroxeter Roman City
Upping
Farley
Hinton
Annscroft
Plealey
Great Lyth
Lyth Hill
170
Cross Houses
Donnington
Eaton
Constantine
Aston Rogers
Westley
B4387
Asterley
Rowley
Longden
Berrington
Bridge
Cantlop
Dryton
Minsterley
Pontesbury
Oaks
Condover
A Worthen
B4386
Brockton
B4499
320
Wrentnall
Stapleton
Pitchford
Cound
A458
Golding
Cressage
Great Ryton
Betton
Leigh
Ploxgreen
Habberley
Church Pulverbatch
Pulverbatch
Dorrington
Acton Pigott
Snailbeach
A488
A49
Frodesley
Acton Burnell
Langley Chapel and Gatehouse
Harley
Bentlawnt
Hope
Crowsnest
Rorrington
93
Gravels
314
Longnor
Ruckley
Kenley
Mitchell's Fold Stone Circle
Black Marsh
Stiperstones
Pennerley
Picklescott
Woolstaston
Leebotwood
Church Preen
Stretton Westwood
Hughley
Shelve
The Marsh
The Bog
Ratlinghope
Shropshire
Presthope
513
Corndon Hill
Stiperstones
Bridges
Long Mynd
Enchmarsh
Plaish
Bourton
Coldyeld
Bridges Long Mynd
All Stretton
459
Cardington
Easthope
B4378
Roundton Hill
Hyssington
West Onny
East Onny
516
Church Stretton
Gretton
East Wall
Brockton
Wall Bank
Longville in the Dale
Weston
A489
Linley
Norbury
Wentnor
B4370
B4371
Hope Bowdler
Wall under Heywood
Rushbury
Wilderhope Manor
Wilderhope
Shipton
Snead
Owlbury
More
Little Stretton
Hills
B3485
Lydham
Asterton
Minton
Acton Scott
Ticklerton
Hatton
Stanton Long
The Long Mynd
Myndtown
Marshbrook
Working Farm
Eaton
Broadstone
Ape Dale
Wenlock Edge
Corve Dale
Bishop's Castle
House on Crutches
B4383
Lea
Eaton
Choulton
Whittingslow
Holdgate
Eyton
Plowden
Woolston
Harton
Middlehope
416
Colebatch
Lydbury North
Horderley
Upper Affcot
Alcaston
Munslow
Tugford
Aston Munslow
Abdon
B4385
Wistanstow
540
Brockton
Edgton
Strefford
Westhope
Diddlebury
Upper Heath
Brown Clee Hill
Acton
Cheny Longville
Corfton
Boulden
Lower Down
Walcot
Lower Dinchope
Peaton
Clee St Margaret
Hopesay
Sibdon Carwood
Newington
Halford
B4368
Kempton
Aston on Clun
Craven Arms
Seifton
Great Sutton
Clun Mill
Little Brampton
Stokesay
Culmington
321
Stoke St Milborough
Clun
Clunton
B4368
B4367
294
Norton
Hayton's Bent
Stokesay Castle
Broome
Vernolds Common
Cleedownton
Purslow
Clunbury
Teme
B4365
B4364
Churchbank
Hopton Cangeford
Twitchen
Brandhill
Onibury
Hobarris
Stanton Lacy
Hopton Castle
Abcott
Clungunford
Wootton
Bitterley
Hoptonheath
Shelderton
306
Bromfield
Ludlow
Middleton
533
Chapel Lawn
Marlow
Henley
A4117
New Invention
Bedstone
Todding
A4113
Snitton
Farden
Cleehill
Kinton
D
Ludlow
Knowbury
Bucknell
Leintwardine
Stowe
Buckton
Downton on the Rock
Ludford
Hope Bagot
Teme
Milebrook
Brampton Bryan
Walford
Burrington
Aston
Overton
Caynham
Whitton
B4530
Adforton
B4361
Ashford Carbonell
Greete
333
Elton
Ashford Bowdler
Letton
Leinthall Starkes
78
Richards Castle
Middleton
Burford House & Meadow Gallery
Wigmore
Woofferton
Little Hereford
Ongar Street
B4362
A456
A4110
0 1 2 3 miles
0 1 2 3 4 5 km

95
Wellington
Hadley
Ketley
Arleston
Ketley Bank
Oakengates
Crackleybank
Priorslee
TELFORD SERVICES
Sheriffhales
Weston under Lizard
WESTON PARK
Wheaton Aston
Kiddemore Green
Bishop's Wood
Brewood
Aston
The Rock
Lawley
Telford
THE WREKIN
Horsehay
Dawley
TELFORD WONDERLAND
Haughton
Shifnal
Tong Norton
BOSCOBEL HOUSE & THE ROYAL OAK
Tong
WHITE LADIES PRIORY
CHILLINGTON HALL
Coven
Longwood
Little Wenlock
TELFORD STEAM RAILWAY
Stirchley
The Wyke
RAF MUSEUM
Leighton
Little Dawley
ROSEHILL HO
Buildwas
Coalbrookdale
Halesfield
Kemberton
Albrighton
Codsall Wood
M54
BUILDWAS ABBEY
MUS OF IRON
MUS OF THE GORGE
Madeley
DAVID AUSTIN ROSES
Brockton
Ironbridge
TOLLHOUSE MUS
BLISTS HILL
Grindle
Ryton
Oaken
Codsall
Fordhouse
BENTHALL HALL
Benthall
JACKFIELD TILE MUS
Coalport
Boningale
Oxley
Homer
Wyke
Broseley
Sutton Maddock
Beckbury
Wergs
Much Wenlock
Norton
Burnhill Green
Tettenhall
Willey
Stockton
Stableford
Badger
Pattingham
WIGHTWICK MANOR
Perton
Ackleton
Rudge
Wolverhampton
Callaughton
Nordley
Astley Abbotts
Chesterton
Trescott
Bradmore
Lower Penn
Penn
Acton Round
Haughton
Worfield
Shipley
Cross Lane Head
Hilton
Seisdon
MORVILLE HALL
CLIFF RAILWAY
Hopstone
Trysull
Aston Eyre
Morville
Tasley
Roughton
Claverley
Wombourne
Sedg
Monkhopton
Morville Heath
STANMORE
Heathton
BAGGERIDGE
Lower Netchwood
Bridgnorth
Blakeley
HIMLEY HALL
Upton Cressett
Farmcote
Himley
Gornal
Oldbury
WATERMILL
Danesford
WOLVERHAMPTON HALFPENNY GREEN
Halfpenny Green
Swindon
Chetton
Quatford
HIGHGATE COMMON
Middleton Priors
Eardington
Bobbington
Wall Heath
DUDMASTON
Ditton Priors
Glazeley
Quatt
Six Ashes
Kingswinford
Chelmarsh
Tuckhill
Four Ashes
Neenton
BROADFIELD HOUSE GLASS MUS
Cleobury North
Middleton Scriven
Sutton
Res.
Enville
Hampton
Hampton Loade
Sidbury
Wordsley
Amblecote
Billingsley
Birdsgreen
Stourton
Woodhill
Alveley
Potter's Cross
Aston Botterell
Highley
Chorley
SEVERN VALLEY
Romsley
Kinver
Stourbridge
Loughton
Stottesdon
RAYS FARM COUNTRY MATTERS
Kingsford
KINGSFORD
Whittington
Wheathill
Blakeshall
Shatterford
BODENHAM ARBORETUM & EARTH CENTRE
Farlow
Oreton
Kinlet
Caunsall
Upper Arley
Cookley
Hagley
Silvington
Trimpley
Churchill
Catherton
Pound Green
Low Habberley
Wolverley
Cleeton St Mary
Buttonoak
Franche
Blakedown
Neen Savage
SEVERN VALLEY RAILWAY
Hopton Wafers
WYRE FOREST
Wyre Forest
Wribbenhall
Blakebrook
Kidderminster
Cleobury Mortimer
Bewdley
Hints
Far Forest
WEST MIDLAND
Stone
Lem Hill
Fingerpost
COTTAGE GARDEN
HARVINGTON HALL
Mustow Green
Coreley
Pound Bank
Ribbesford
Callow Hill
Milson
Bayton
BLACKSTONE MEADOWS
Upper Mitton
Wilden
Shenstone
Bliss Gate
Nash
Neen Sollars
Mamble
Clows Top
Rock
Stourport on Severn
WORCESTERSHIRE COUNTY MUS
Rushock
Areley Kings
Hartlebury
WHITLENGE GDNS
Frith Common
Boraston
Astley Cross
Waresley
Elmley Lovett
Newnham Bridge
Lindridge
Eardiston
Pensax
Dunley
Crossway Green
Cutnall
Severn
Worfe
Borle Brook
Rea Brook
Stour
A5
A41
A442
A458
A454
A449
A456
A4169
A464
A4117
A443
A451
A491
A450
B4379
B4375
B4376
B4373
B4176
B4368
B4364
B4555
B4363
B4199
B4201
B4190
B4195
B4194
B4202
111
112
96
79

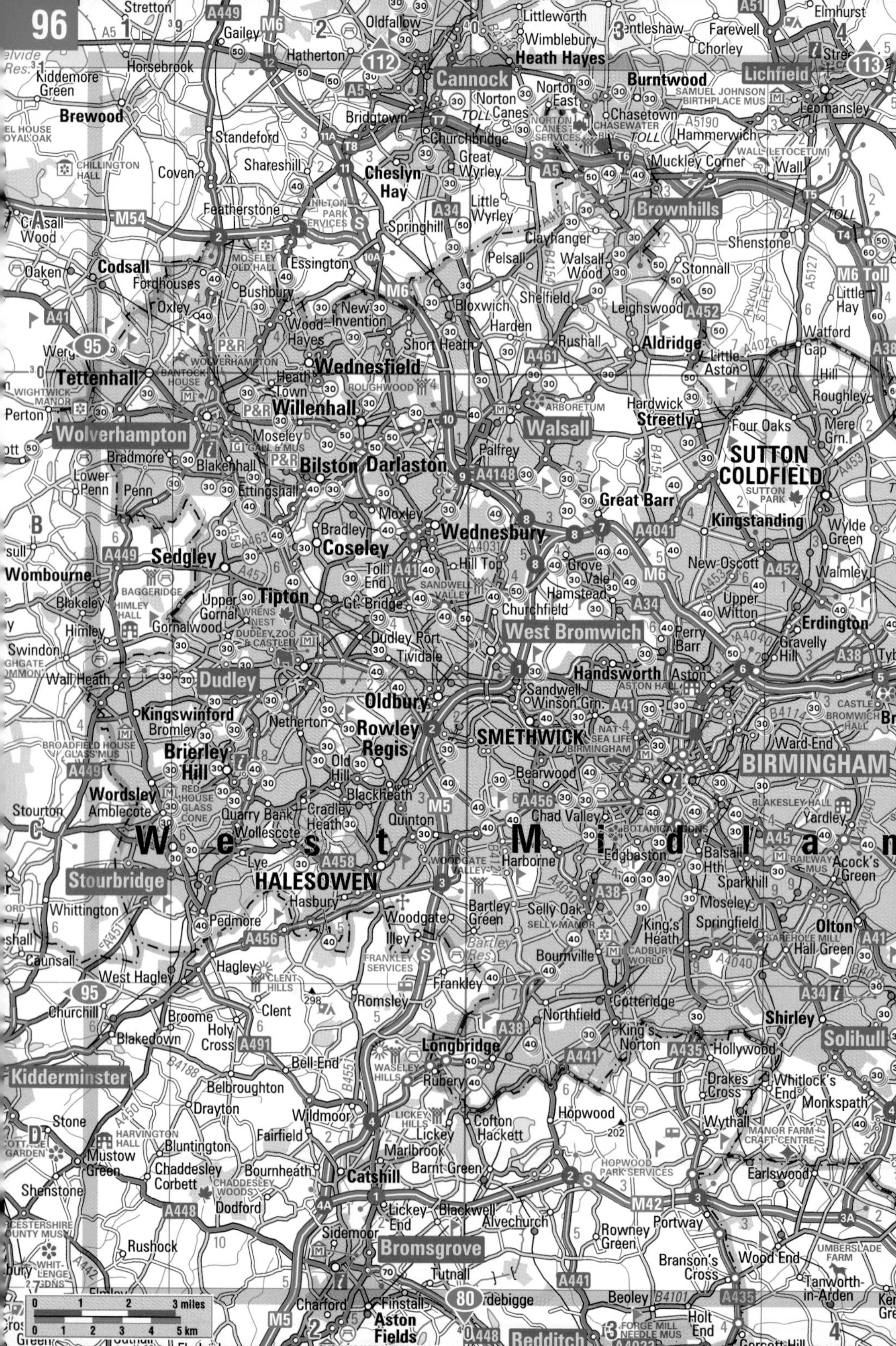
Stretton
Gailey
Oldfallow
Littleworth
Wimblebury
Gentleshaw
Farewell
Chorley
Elmhurst
Hatherton
Heath Hayes
Horsebrook
Kiddemore Green
Cannock
Lichfield
Brewood
Norton Canes
Burntwood
Chasetown
Hammerwich
Leomansley
Bridgtown
Churchbridge
Samuel Johnson Birthplace Mus
Chillington Hall
Standeford
Great Wyrley
Norton Canes Services
Muckley Corner
Wall (Letocetum)
Wall
Coven
Shareshill
Cheslyn Hay
Little Wyrley
Brownhills
Featherstone
Hilton Park Services
Springhill
Clayhanger
Shenstone
Codsall
Oaken
Moseley Old Hall
Essington
Pelsall
Walsall Wood
Stonnall
Fordhouses
Bushbury
Shelfield
Leighswood
Little Hay
Oxley
New Invention
Bloxwich
Wood Hayes
Short Heath
Harden
Rushall
Aldridge
Watford Gap
Wergs
Wolverhampton
Wednesfield
Little Aston
Tettenhall
Bantock House
Heath Town
Roughwood
Hill
Wightwick Manor
Roughley
Perton
Willenhall
Arboretum
Hardwick
Streetly
Four Oaks
Walsall
Moseley
Mere Grn.
Bradmore
Gall & Mus
Bilston
Darlaston
Palfrey
Sutton Coldfield
Lower Penn
Blakenhall
Penn
Ettingshall
Sutton Park
Great Barr
Moxley
Kingstanding
Wylde Green
Bradley
Wednesbury
Coseley
Sedgley
Hill Top
New Oscott
Wombourne
Toll End
Grove Vale
Walmley
Baggeridge
Sandwell Valley
Hamstead
Blakeley
Himley Hall
Upper Gornal
Tipton
Gt. Bridge
Churchfield
Upper Witton
Erdington
Himley
Wrens Nest
Gornalwood
Dudley Zoo & Castle
Dudley Port
West Bromwich
Perry Barr
Gravelly Hill
Swindon
Tividale
Handsworth
Aston
Wall Heath
Dudley
Aston Hall
Sandwell
Winson Grn.
Oldbury
Castle Bromwich Hall
Kingswinford
Netherton
Rowley Regis
Smethwick
Bromley
Broadfield House Glass Mus
Nat. Sea Life Birmingham
Ward End
Brierley Hill
Old Hill
Bearwood
Birmingham
Wordsley
Red House Glass Cone
Blackheath
Blakesley Hall
Stourton
Amblecote
Quarry Bank
Cradley Heath
Quinton
Chad Valley
Yardley
Wollescote
Botanical Gdns
West Midlands
Lye
Harborne
Edgbaston
Balsall Hth.
Railway Mus
Acock's Green
Stourbridge
Halesowen
Woodgate Valley
Sparkhill
Hasbury
Whittington
Woodgate
Bartley Green
Selly Oak
Moseley
Pedmore
Selly Manor
King's Heath
Springfield
Olton
Sarehole Mill
Illey
Bartley Res.
Hall Green
Caunsall
Frankley Services
Bournville
Cadbury World
Hagley
Clent Hills
West Hagley
Frankley
Churchill
Clent
Romsley
Cotteridge
Northfield
Shirley
Broome
Holy Cross
Blakedown
Longbridge
King's Norton
Hollywood
Solihull
Kidderminster
Bell End
Waseley Hills
Rubery
Drakes Cross
Whitlock's End
Belbroughton
Drayton
Hopwood
Monkspath
Stone
Wildmoor
Lickey Hills
Cofton Hackett
Wythall
Harvington Hall
Fairfield
Lickey
Manor Farm Craft Centre
Cottage Garden
Mustow Green
Bluntington
Marlbrook
Hopwood Park Services
Chaddesley Corbett
Bournheath
Barnt Green
Earlswood
Shenstone
Catshill
Chaddesley Woods
Dodford
Lickey End
Blackwell
Alvechurch
Portway
Worcestershire County Mus
Sidemoor
Rowney Green
Rushock
Bromsgrove
Branson's Cross
Wood End
Umberslade Farm
Whitlenge Gdns
Tutnall
Tanworth-in-Arden
Charford
Finstall
Tardebigge
Beoley
Holt End
Aston Fields
Forge Mill Needle Mus
Redditch
Gorcott Hill
0 1 2 3 miles
0 1 2 3 4 5 km

Tamworth
Atherstone
Nuneaton
Hinckley
Bedworth
Coventry
Kenilworth
Coleshill
Ibstock
Market Bosworth
Burbage
Dorridge
Elford
Haunton
Clifton Campville
Chilcote
Appleby Magna
Swepstone
Newton Burgoland
Snarestone
Polesworth
Wilnecote
Fazeley
Drayton Bassett
Kingsbury
Water Orton
Minworth
Curdworth
Meriden
Balsall Common
Knowle
Hampton in Arden
Fillongley
Corley
Keresley
Bulkington
Wolvey
Brinklow
Binley
Baginton
Stoneleigh
Bubbenhall
Ryton-on-Dunsmore
Wolston
Stretton-on-Dunsmore
Princethorpe
Wappenbury
Weston under Wetherley
Leek Wootton
Honiley
Wroxall
Kingswood
Lapworth
Rowington
Shrewley
M42
M6
M6Toll
M69
M40
A5
A444
A45
A46
A452
A47
97
113
114
98
81

Ellistown
Leicester Services
Markfield
Bradgate Park & Swithland Wood
Cropston
Railway
Syston
Thurcaston
Watermead
114
115
Ibstock
Stanton under Bardon
Field Head
Newtown Linford
Bradgate House Ruins
Birstall
Barkby
South Croxton
Battram
Thurmaston
Bagworth
Anstey
Castle Hill
National Space Science Centre
Beeby
Nailstone
Thornton
Groby
Gorse Hill City Farm
Belgrave Hall
Hungarton
Barton in the Beans
Ratby
Glenfield
Leicester
Keyham
Barlestone
Botcheston
Eco House
New Humberstone
Scraptoft
Carlton
Newtown Unthank
William Carey
Bushby
Market Bosworth
Tropical Bird Gardens
Kirby Muxloe
Cath
Leicester
Thurnby
Newbold Verdon
Desford
Braunstone Town
Mus & Art Gall
Evington
Houghton on the Hill
Leicester Forest East
City
Stoughton
Cadeby
The Gas Museum
Botanic Gardens
Bosworth Heritage & Country Park
97
Peckleton
Leicester Forest East Services
Stoneygate
Gaulby
Mallory Park
Kirkby Mallory
Aylestone
Knighton
Oadby
Leicester
Sutton Cheney
Little Stretton
Enderby
Glen Parva
Brock's Hill
Stapleton
Thurlaston
Wigston
Great Glen
Dadlington
Narborough
Blaby
South Wigston
Newton Harcourt
Burton Overy
Earl Shilton
Stoke Golding
Barwell
Huncote
Whetstone
Elmesthorpe
Littlethorpe
Sence
Burbage Common & Woods
Croft
Countesthorpe
Kibworth Harcourt
Hinckley
Stoney Stanton
Cosby
Kilby
The Nooks
Sutton in the Elms
Kibworth Beauchamp
Sapcote
Primethorpe
Peatling Magna
Fleckney
Sketchley
Arnesby
Smeeton Westerby
Aston Flamville
Broughton Astley
Saddington
Burbage
Willoughby Waterleys
Sharnford
Dunton Bassett
Ashby Magna
Shearsby
Burton Hastings
Frolesworth
Leire
Bruntingthorpe
Mowsley
Gumley
Smockington
Claybrooke Magna
Peatling Parva
Laughton
Claybrooke Parva
Ashby Parva
Copston Magna
Gilmorton
Wolvey
Wibtoft
Ullesthorpe
Walton
Lubenham
Kimcote
Theddingworth
Bitteswell
Willey
Lutterworth
De Bradelei
Shilton
Withybrook
Misterton
Husbands Bosworth
Cross in Hand
Swift
Walcote
North Kilworth
Ansty
Monks Kirby
Cotesbach
Sibbertoft
Oxford Canal
Pailton
Churchover
Gibbet Hill
South Kilworth
Sulby Reservoir
Stretton under Fosse
Shawell
Stanford Res.
Welford
Naseby Field
97
Coombe Abbey
Easenhall
Swinford
Stanford on Avon
Stanford Hall
Brinklow
Harborough Magna
Naseby Res.
Binley Woods
King's Newnham
Newbold on Avon
Newton
Catthorpe
Bretford
Long Lawford
Church Lawford
Lilbourne
Clay Coton
Cold Ashby
Brandon
Clifton upon Dunsmore
Yelvertoft
Thornby
Wolston
New Bilton
Ryton-on-Dunsmore
Ryton Organic Gardens
Bilton
Rugby
Hillmorton
Winwick
Guilsborough
Stretton-on-Dunsmore
Crick
West Haddon
Coton
Coton Manor
Holl
Dunchurch
Kilsby
Ravensthorpe
Bourton on Dunsmore
Thurlaston
Barby
Frankton
Draycote Water
Watford
Kites Hardwick
Ashby St Ledgers
Watford Gap Services
East Haddon
Woolscott
Holdenby
Leics
Northants
M1
M6
M69
M45
A5
A6
A14
A45
A46
A47
A50
A426
A428
A563
A4303
A4304
A5199
B4114
B581
B582
B585
B4669
B4428
B4112
B4455
B4029
B4065
B4109
B5414
B4429
B4038
B4453
B5385
0 1 2 3 miles
0 1 2 3 4 5 km

Rutland
Folville
Thorpe Satchville
Pickwell
Cold Overton
Langham
Exton
Barnsdale Gardens
Falconry Centre
Burley
Twyford
Burrough on the Hill
Burrough Hill
Barleythorpe
Oakham
Whitwell
Tickencote
Empingham
Marefield
Owston
Knossington
Egleton
Upper Hambleton
Rutland Water
Lowesby
Cold Newton
Braunston-in-Rutland
Brooke
Normanton
Tinwell
Tilton on the Hill
Halstead
Manton
Edith Weston
Ketton
Lyndon
North Luffenham
Aston on the Hill
Chater
Skeffington
Loddington
Ridlington
Preston
Wing
Pilton
Illesdon
Belton in Rutland
Ayston
South Luffenham
Collyweston
Tugby
East Norton
Glaston
Morcott
Duddington
Norton
Rolleston
Allexton
Wardley
Barrowden
Tixover
Uppingham
Bisbrooke
Wakerley
Noseley
Goadby
Seaton
Horninghold
Stockerston
Stoke Dry
Lyddington
Harringworth
Welland
Hallaton
Bede House
Laxton
Stonton Wyville
Glooston
Cranoe
Blaston
Eyebrook Reservoir
Thorpe by Water
Blatherwycke
Apethorpe
Slawston
Gretton
Bulwick
Church Langton
Welham
Medbourne
Great Easton
Caldecott
Kirby Hall
East Langton
Thorpe Langton
Drayton
Bringhurst
Rockingham
Rockingham Castle
Deene
Deene Park
Deenethorpe
Weston by Welland
Ashley
Cottingham
Rockingham Forest
Foxton Locks
Great Bowden
Sutton Bassett
Middleton
East Carlton
Little Weldon
Corby
Great Weldon
Upper Benefield
Lower Benefield
Market Harborough
Dingley
Stoke Albany
Wilbarston
East Carlton
Stanion
Brampton Ash
Little Bowden
Little Oakley
Great Oakley
Pipewell
Harper's Brook
Brigstock
Hill Farm Herbs
Lyveden New Bield
Fermyn Woods
East Farndon
Braybrooke
Wadenhoe
Great Oxendon
Desborough
Rushton Triangular Lodge
Rushton
Newton
Geddington
Eleanor Cross
Sudborough
Aldwincle
Clipston
Arthingworth
Rothwell
Weekley
Boughton House
Grafton Underwood
Lowick
Harrington
Warkton
Kelmarsh
Orton
Slipton
Islip
Thrapston
Loddington
Thorpe Malsor
Kettering
Barton Seagrave
Cranford St Andrew
Cranford St John
Twywell
Woodford
Haselbech
Maidwell
Draughton
Great Cransley
Wicksteed Park
Denford
Mawsley
Broughton
Burton Latimer
Great Addington
Ringstead
Cottesbrooke
Cottesbrooke Hall and Gdns.
Lamport
Lamport Hall
Old
Pytchley
Isham
Little Addington
Scaldwell
Walgrave
Orlingbury
Finedon
Stanwick Lakes
Creaton
Little Harrowden
Hannington
Great Harrowden
Irthlingborough
Stanwick
Brixworth
Holcot
Chelveston
Spratton
Hardwick
Wellingborough
Higham Ferrers
Caldecott
Pitsford Reservoir
Sywell
Chichele College
SK
SP
A606
A1
A6003
A47
A43
A6121
B672
B664
A6
A427
A6116
A6014
B670
B669
B576
A508
A14
A4300
A510
A509
A45
B574
B571
A5199
B6047
115
116
100
83

Peterborough
Stamford
Market Deeping
Deeping St James
Crowland
Empingham
Oundle
Yaxley
Sawtry
Thrapston
Raunds
Huntingdon
Brampton
Godmanchester
Wansford
Stibbington
Sutton
Ailsworth
Castor
Longthorpe
Orton Longueville
Orton Waterville
Alwalton
Chesterton
Elton
Fotheringhay
Nassington
Yarwell
Sibson
Water Newton
Haddon
Morborne
Norman Cross
Folksworth
Stilton
Caldecote
Denton
Lutton
Glatton
Conington
Holme
Polebrook
Ashton
Barnwell St Andrew
Barnwell All Saints
Hemington
Luddington in the Brook
Thurning
Great Gidding
Little Gidding
Steeple Gidding
Winwick
Clopton
Wigsthorpe
Pilton
Wadenhoe
Achurch
Aldwincle
Thorpe Waterville
Titchmarsh
Islip
Lowick
Slipton
Twywell
Woodford
Denford
Ringstead
Stanwick
Chelveston
Hargrave
Covington
Keyston
Bythorn
Molesworth
Brington
Old Weston
Leighton Bromswold
Catworth
Spaldwick
Easton
Stow Longa
Ellington
Barham
Woolley
Alconbury
Alconbury Weston
Buckworth
Upton
Hamerton
Coppingford
Little Stukeley
Great Stukeley
Abbots Ripton
Wennington
Wood Walton
Church End
Farcet
Stanground
Old Fletton
Fengate
Newark
Dogsthorpe
Walton
Gunthorpe
Eye Green
Eye
Newborough
Peakirk
Glinton
Northborough
Maxey
Deeping Gate
West Deeping
Tallington
Uffington
Barholm
Towngate
Frognall
Belmesthorpe
Ryhall
Little Casterton
Great Casterton
Tickencote
Northfields
Tinwell
Ketton
Easton on the Hill
Collyweston
Duddington
Wittering
Thornhaugh
Pilsgate
Barnack
Bainton
Ufford
Southorpe
Helpston
Etton
Werrington
Marholm
Upton
Wakerley
King's Cliffe
Blatherwycke
Apethorpe
Woodnewton
Bulwick
Deenethorpe
Southwick
Glapthorn
Cotterstock
Tansor
Eaglethorpe
Warmington
Upper Benefield
Lower Benefield
Stoke Doyle
Tilbrook
Shelton
Lower Dean
Grafham
South Luffenham
Greatford
Huntingdon
Farcet Fen
Whittlesey Mere
Holme Fen
Woodwalton Fen
Monks Wood
Upwood Meadows
Bedford Levels
Rockingham Forest
Nene Valley Railway
Ferry Meadows
Railworld
Longthorpe Tower
Flag Fen Bronze Age Excavation
Crown Lakes
Peterborough Services
Elton Hall
Castle Site
Southwick Hall
Barnwell
Lyveden New Bield
Fermyn Woods
Hamerton Zoo Park
Hinchingbrooke
Stanwick Lakes
Burghley
Barnack Hills and Holes
Sacrewell Farm & Country Centre
Castor Hanglands
Collyweston Great Wood
Bedford Purlieus
Tolethorpe Hall Rutland Open Air Theatre
Sibson
A1
A1(M)
A14
A15
A16
A43
A45
A47
A605
A606
A6121
A1139
A1175
A427
A6116
A141
B660
B662
B663
B645
B671
B1043
B1090
B1091
B1443
B1525
B1166
116
117
99
84
0 1 2 3 miles
0 1 2 3 4 5 km

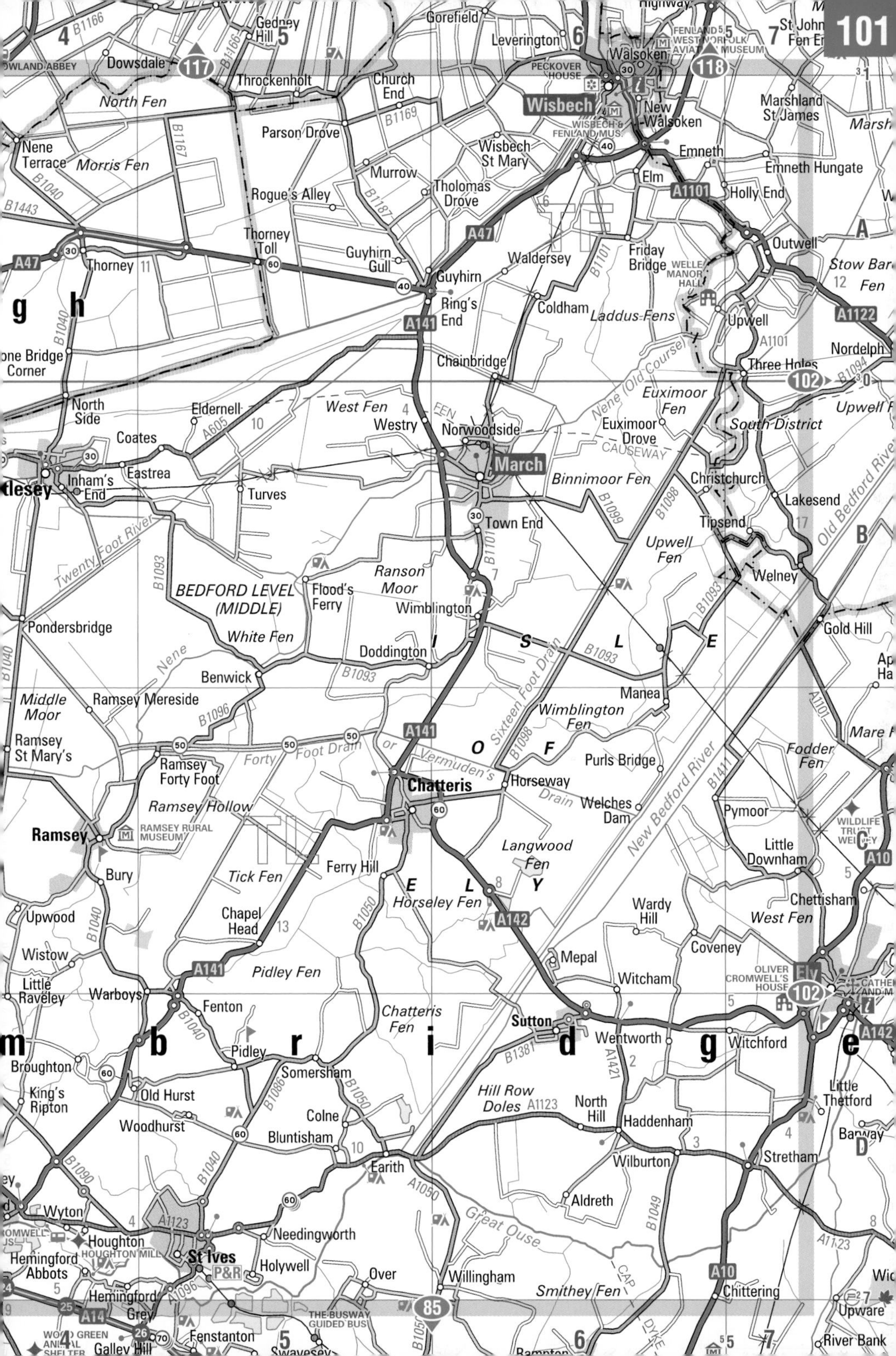

Gedney Hill
Gorefield
Leverington
Walsoken
FENLAND & WEST NORFOLK AVIATION MUSEUM
St John's Fen End
CROWLAND ABBEY
Dowsdale
117
118
Throckenholt
Church End
PECKOVER HOUSE
Wisbech
North Fen
B1169
New Walsoken
Marshland St James
Parson Drove
WISBECH & FENLAND MUS.
Nene Terrace
Morris Fen
B1167
Murrow
Wisbech St Mary
Emneth
Emneth Hungate
B1040
B1443
Rogue's Alley
Tholomas Drove
Elm
A1101
Holly End
B1187
Thorney Toll
A47
Outwell
A47
Thorney
Guyhirn Gull
Guyhirn
Waldersey
Friday Bridge
WELLE MANOR HALL
Stow Bardolph Fen
Ring's End
Coldham
Laddus Fens
Upwell
A1122
A141
Stone Bridge Corner
Chainbridge
A1101
Nordelph
Three Holes
102
B1094
North Side
Eldernell
West Fen
Westry
Nene (Old Course)
Euximoor Fen
Upwell Fen
A605
Norwoodside
Euximoor Drove
South District
Coates
CAUSEWAY
Whittlesey
Inham's End
Eastrea
March
Binnimoor Fen
Christchurch
Turves
Town End
B1099
B1098
Lakesend
Old Bedford River
Twenty Foot River
Tipsend
Upwell Fen
B1093
Ranson Moor
Flood's Ferry
Welney
BEDFORD LEVEL (MIDDLE)
Wimblington
B1093
Pondersbridge
White Fen
Gold Hill
I S L E
Doddington
B1093
Sixteen Foot Drain
Manea
Nene
Benwick
B1040
Middle Moor
Ramsey Mereside
Wimblington Fen
B1096
A1101
Ramsey St Mary's
A141
Mare Fen
Forty Foot Drain
or Vermuden's Drain
O F
Purls Bridge
Fodder Fen
Ramsey Forty Foot
Horseway
Chatteris
B1411
Welches Dam
New Bedford River
Pymoor
Ramsey Hollow
WILDLIFE TRUST WELNEY
Ramsey
RAMSEY RURAL MUSEUM
Langwood Fen
Little Downham
A10
Bury
Ferry Hill
Tick Fen
E L Y
Horseley Fen
Chettisham
Upwood
Chapel Head
A142
Wardy Hill
West Fen
B1050
Wistow
Mepal
Coveney
Pidley Fen
A141
Little Raveley
Warboys
Witcham
OLIVER CROMWELL'S HOUSE
Ely
102
Fenton
Chatteris Fen
Sutton
Wentworth
B1040
Witchford
A142
Pidley
B1381
A1421
Cambridge
Broughton
Somersham
King's Ripton
Old Hurst
Hill Row Doles
A1123
North Hill
Little Thetford
B1086
Colne
B1050
Haddenham
Woodhurst
Bluntisham
Barway
Wilburton
Stretham
Earith
B1090
B1040
A1050
Aldreth
Wyton
Great Ouse
A1123
B1049
Needingworth
Houghton
CROMWELL MUS
Hemingford Abbots
HOUGHTON MILL
St Ives
A1123
P&R
Holywell
Over
Willingham
CAP
A10
Smithey Fen
Hemingford Grey
A1096
Chittering
A14
THE BUSWAY GUIDED BUS
85
Upware
Wicken
WOOD GREEN ANIMAL SHELTER
Fenstanton
Galley Hill
Swavesey
B1050
Rampton
DYKE
River Bank

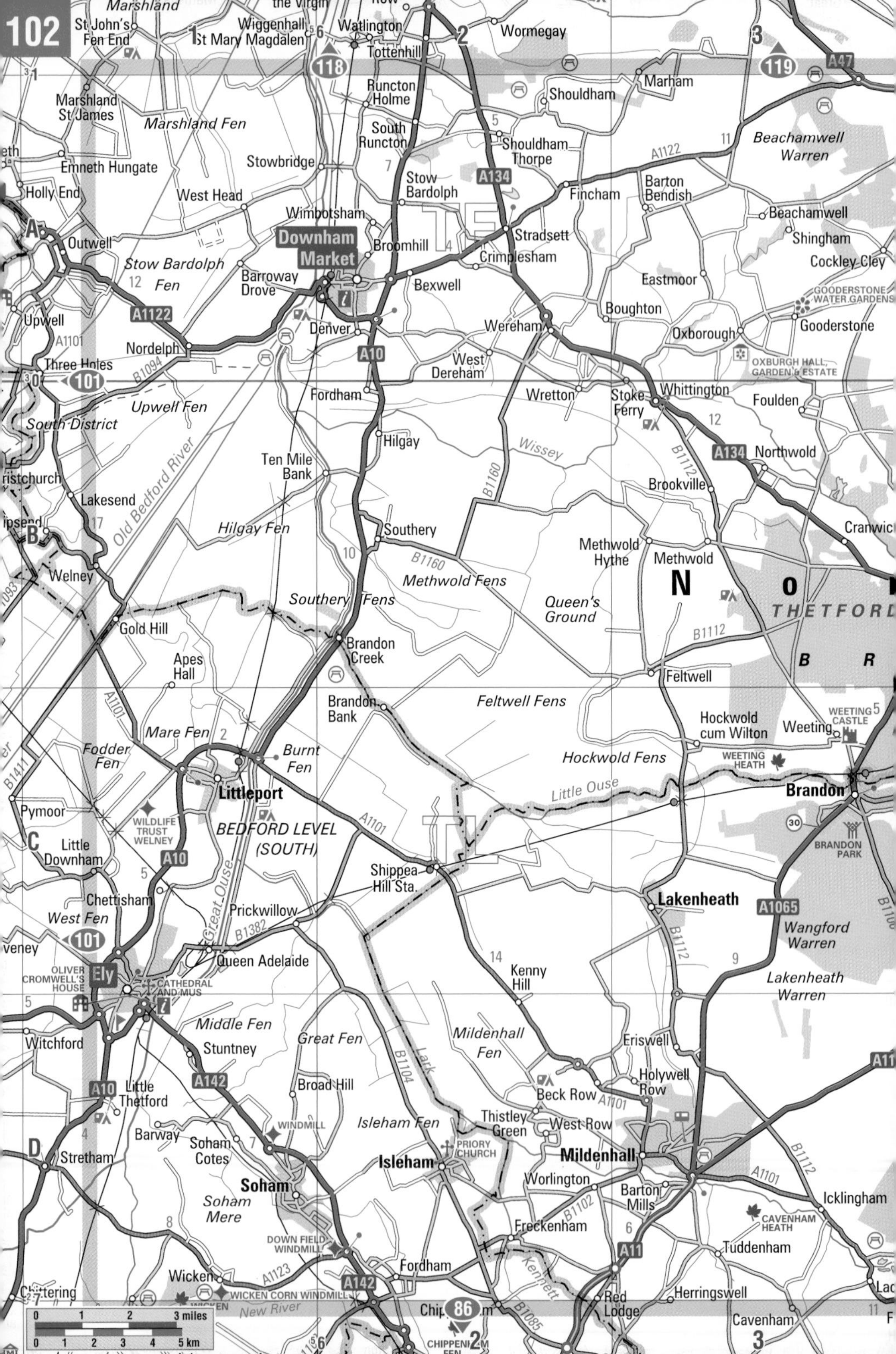
Marshland
St John's Fen End
Wiggenhall St Mary Magdalen
Watlington
Tottenhill
Wormegay
118
119
A47
Marham
Shouldham
Runcton Holme
Marshland St James
Marshland Fen
South Runcton
Shouldham Thorpe
Beachamwell Warren
A1122
Emneth Hungate
Stowbridge
Stow Bardolph
A134
Fincham
Barton Bendish
Holly End
West Head
Wimbotsham
Beachamwell
Shingham
Downham Market
Stradsett
Outwell
Broomhill
Crimplesham
Cockley Cley
Stow Bardolph Fen
Barroway Drove
Bexwell
Eastmoor
GOODERSTONE WATER GARDENS
Boughton
Upwell
Denver
Wereham
Oxborough
Gooderstone
A1101
Nordelph
West Dereham
OXBURGH HALL, GARDEN & ESTATE
Three Holes
A10
B1094
101
Fordham
Wretton
Stoke Ferry
Whittington
Foulden
Upwell Fen
South District
Hilgay
Wissey
A134
Northwold
Ten Mile Bank
B1160
B1112
Christchurch
Brookville
Lakesend
Old Bedford River
Southery
Cranwich
Hilgay Fen
Methwold Hythe
Methwold
Welney
B1160
Methwold Fens
N
O
THETFORD
Southery Fens
Queen's Ground
Gold Hill
Brandon Creek
B1112
B
R
Apes Hall
Feltwell
A1101
Brandon Bank
Feltwell Fens
Hockwold cum Wilton
Weeting
WEETING CASTLE
Mare Fen
Burnt Fen
WEETING HEATH
Fodder Fen
Hockwold Fens
Little Ouse
Brandon
B1411
Littleport
Pymoor
WILDLIFE TRUST WELNEY
BEDFORD LEVEL (SOUTH)
A1101
BRANDON PARK
C
Little Downham
A10
Shippea Hill Sta.
Chettisham
Prickwillow
Lakenheath
A1065
West Fen
Great Ouse
B1382
Wangford Warren
Queen Adelaide
Kenny Hill
Lakenheath Warren
OLIVER CROMWELL'S HOUSE
Ely
CATHEDRAL AND MUS
Middle Fen
Witchford
Mildenhall Fen
Eriswell
Stuntney
Great Fen
A142
Holywell Row
Broad Hill
B1104
Lark
Beck Row
A1101
A10
Little Thetford
Thistley Green
West Row
WINDMILL
Isleham Fen
Barway
Soham Cotes
PRIORY CHURCH
Mildenhall
D
Stretham
Isleham
A1101
B1112
Worlington
Soham
Barton Mills
Icklingham
Soham Mere
B1102
CAVENHAM HEATH
Freckenham
DOWN FIELD WINDMILL
A11
Tuddenham
Wicken
A1123
Fordham
Kennett
WICKEN CORN WINDMILL
A142
Red Lodge
Herringswell
Chittering
New River
86
B1085
Cavenham
CHIPPENHAM FEN
3 miles
5 km

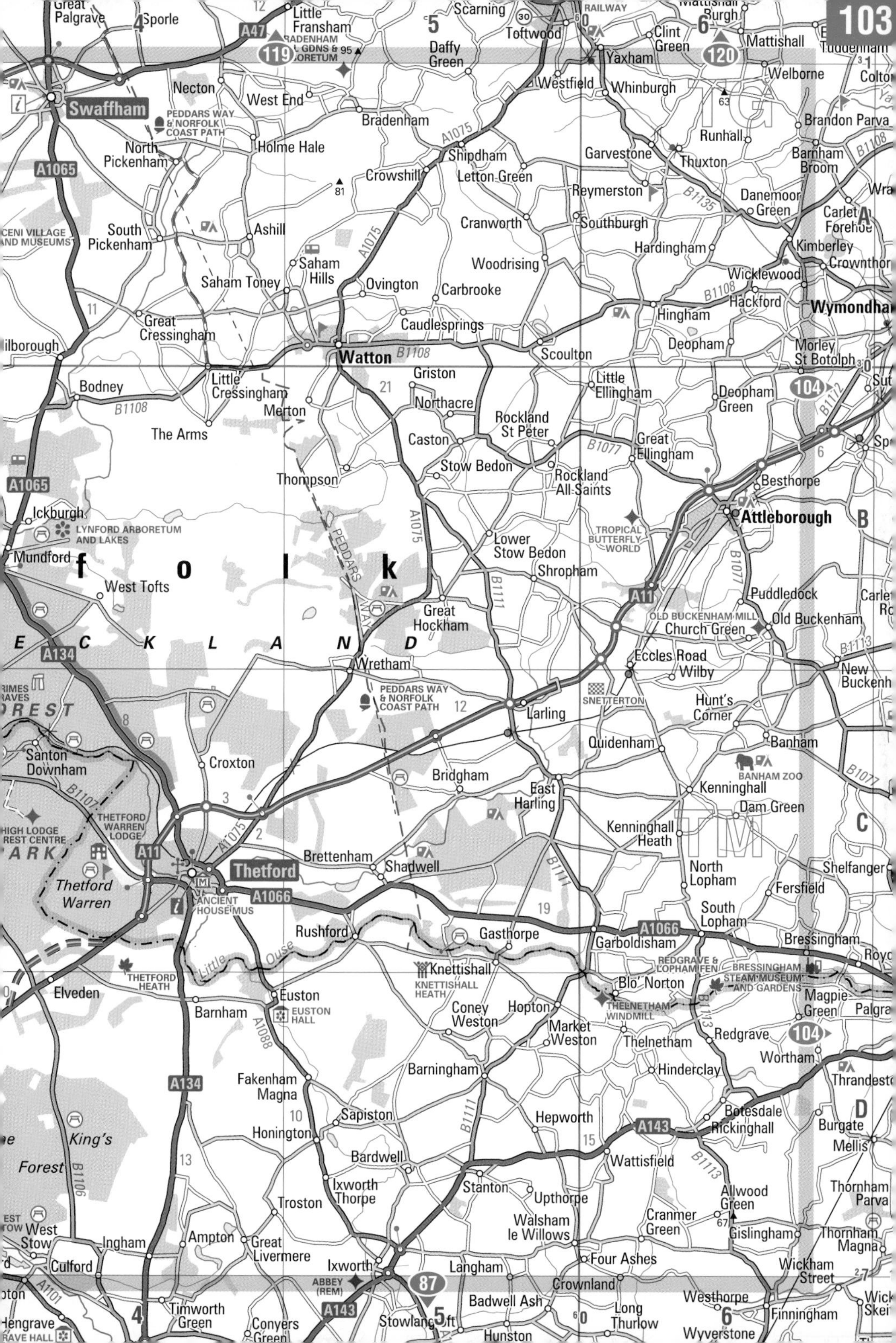
Great Palgrave
Sporle
Little Fransham
Scarning
Toftwood
RAILWAY
Mattishall Burgh
Clint Green
Mattishall
Tuddenham
A47
119
BRADENHAM GDNS & ARBORETUM
Daffy Green
Yaxham
120
Welborne
Colton
Necton
West End
Westfield
Whinburgh
Swaffham
PEDDARS WAY & NORFOLK COAST PATH
Bradenham
TG
Brandon Parva
North Pickenham
Holme Hale
A1075
Shipdham
Garvestone
Runhall
Thuxton
Barnham Broom
B1108
A1065
Crowshill
Letton Green
Reymerston
B1135
Danemoor Green
Carleton Forehoe
ICENI VILLAGE AND MUSEUMS
South Pickenham
Ashill
Cranworth
Southburgh
Hardingham
Kimberley
Saham Hills
Woodrising
Wicklewood
Crownthorpe
Saham Toney
Ovington
Carbrooke
B1108
Hackford
Wymondham
Great Cressingham
Caudlesprings
Hingham
Deopham
Morley St Botolph
Hilborough
Watton
B1108
Scoulton
Griston
Little Ellingham
104
Bodney
Little Cressingham
Merton
Northacre
Rockland St Peter
Deopham Green
B1172
B1108
The Arms
Caston
Great Ellingham
B1077
Stow Bedon
Rockland All Saints
Besthorpe
Thompson
A1065
Attleborough
Ickburgh
LYNFORD ARBORETUM AND LAKES
TROPICAL BUTTERFLY WORLD
Lower Stow Bedon
Mundford
f o l k
PEDDARS WAY
Shropham
B1077
West Tofts
B1111
A11
Puddledock
Great Hockham
OLD BUCKENHAM MILL
Old Buckenham
Church Green
E C K L A N D
A134
Eccles Road
Wilby
B1113
New Buckenham
Wretham
GRIMES GRAVES
FOREST
PEDDARS WAY & NORFOLK COAST PATH
SNETTERTON
Larling
Hunt's Corner
Quidenham
Banham
Santon Downham
Croxton
Bridgham
BANHAM ZOO
B1077
B1107
East Harling
Kenninghall
THETFORD WARREN LODGE
Dam Green
HIGH LODGE FOREST CENTRE
A1075
Kenninghall Heath
TM
PARK
A11
Brettenham
Shadwell
North Lopham
Shelfanger
Thetford Warren
Thetford
B1111
Fersfield
ANCIENT HOUSE MUS
A1066
South Lopham
Rushford
A1066
Gasthorpe
Garboldisham
Bressingham
Roydon
Little Ouse
REDGRAVE & LOPHAM FEN
BRESSINGHAM STEAM MUSEUM AND GARDENS
THETFORD HEATH
Knettishall
KNETTISHALL HEATH
Blo' Norton
Elveden
Euston
EUSTON HALL
Coney Weston
Hopton
THELNETHAM WINDMILL
Magpie Green
Palgrave
Barnham
A1088
Market Weston
Thelnetham
B1113
Redgrave
104
Wortham
Barningham
Hinderclay
Thrandeston
A134
Fakenham Magna
Botesdale
Rickinghall
Sapiston
B1111
Hepworth
Burgate
King's
Honington
A143
Mellis
Forest
Bardwell
Wattisfield
B1113
B1106
Ixworth Thorpe
Stanton
Upthorpe
Allwood Green
Thornham Parva
Troston
Walsham le Willows
Cranmer Green
West Stow
Ampton
Ingham
Great Livermere
Gislingham
Thornham Magna
Four Ashes
Culford
Ixworth
Langham
Wickham Street
ABBEY (REM)
87
Crownland
A1101
Westhorpe
Wickham Skeith
Ampton
A143
Badwell Ash
Long Thurlow
Finningham
Hengrave
HENGRAVE HALL
Timworth Green
Conyers Green
Stowlangtoft
Hunston
Wyverstone

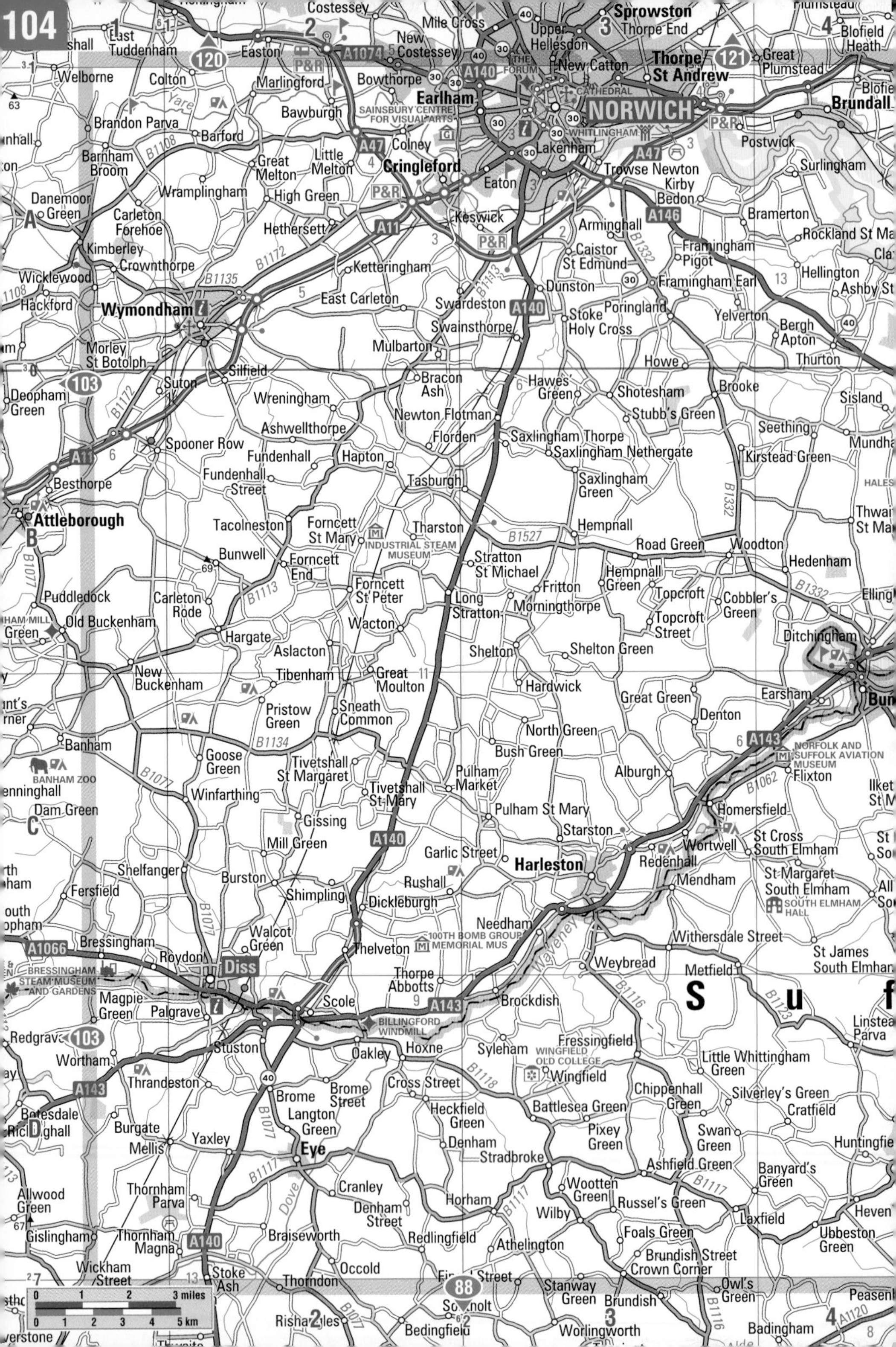

Costessey
Mile Cross
Sprowston
Thorpe End
East Tuddenham
Easton
New Costessey
Upper Hellesdon
New Catton
Thorpe St Andrew
Great Plumstead
Blofield Heath
Welborne
Colton
Marlingford
Bowthorpe
Earlham
THE FORUM
CATHEDRAL
NORWICH
Brundall
Brandon Parva
Bawburgh
SAINSBURY CENTRE FOR VISUAL ARTS
WHITLINGHAM
Barford
Colney
Lakenham
Postwick
Barnham Broom
Great Melton
Little Melton
Cringleford
Eaton
Trowse Newton
Surlingham
Danemoor Green
Wramplingham
High Green
Kirby Bedon
Carleton Forehoe
Hethersett
Keswick
Arminghall
Bramerton
Rockland St Mary
Kimberley
Crownthorpe
Caistor St Edmund
Framingham Pigot
Wicklewood
Ketteringham
Framingham Earl
Hellington
Hackford
Wymondham
East Carleton
Swardeston
Dunston
Poringland
Ashby St Mary
Stoke Holy Cross
Yelverton
Swainsthorpe
Bergh Apton
Morley St Botolph
Mulbarton
Howe
Thurton
Silfield
Suton
Bracon Ash
Hawes' Green
Shotesham
Brooke
Deopham Green
Wreningham
Newton Flotman
Stubb's Green
Sisland
Ashwellthorpe
Saxlingham Thorpe
Seething
Spooner Row
Florden
Saxlingham Nethergate
Fundenhall
Hapton
Kirstead Green
Besthorpe
Fundenhall Street
Tasburgh
Saxlingham Green
Attleborough
Tacolneston
Forncett St Mary
INDUSTRIAL STEAM MUSEUM
Tharston
Hempnall
Bunwell
Forncett End
Stratton St Michael
Road Green
Woodton
Hedenham
Puddledock
Carleton Rode
Forncett St Peter
Long Stratton
Fritton
Hempnall Green
Topcroft
Cobbler's Green
Old Buckenham
Wacton
Morningthorpe
Topcroft Street
Hargate
Aslacton
Shelton
Shelton Green
Ditchingham
New Buckenham
Tibenham
Great Moulton
Hardwick
Pristow Green
Sneath Common
Great Green
Denton
Earsham
Banham
BANHAM ZOO
North Green
Goose Green
Bush Green
NORFOLK AND SUFFOLK AVIATION MUSEUM
Tivetshall St Margaret
Pulham Market
Alburgh
Flixton
Winfarthing
Tivetshall St Mary
Pulham St Mary
Homersfield
Dam Green
Gissing
Starston
St Cross South Elmham
Mill Green
Garlic Street
Harleston
Redenhall
Wortwell
Shelfanger
Burston
Rushall
Mendham
St Margaret South Elmham
Fersfield
Shimpling
Dickleburgh
SOUTH ELMHAM HALL
Needham
Walcot Green
100TH BOMB GROUP MEMORIAL MUS
Withersdale Street
Bressingham
Roydon
Diss
Thelveton
Weybread
St James South Elmham
BRESSINGHAM STEAM MUSEUM AND GARDENS
Thorpe Abbotts
Metfield
Magpie Green
Palgrave
Scole
Brockdish
BILLINGFORD WINDMILL
Linstead Parva
Redgrave
Wortham
Stuston
Oakley
Hoxne
Syleham
Fressingfield
WINGFIELD OLD COLLEGE
Wingfield
Little Whittingham Green
Thrandeston
Brome
Brome Street
Cross Street
Chippenhall Green
Silverley's Green
Cratfield
Langton Green
Heckfield Green
Battlesea Green
Botesdale
Rickinghall
Burgate
Mellis
Yaxley
Eye
Denham
Stradbroke
Pixey Green
Swan Green
Huntingfield
Ashfield Green
Banyard's Green
Thornham Parva
Cranley
Horham
Wootten Green
Allwood Green
Denham Street
Wilby
Russel's Green
Laxfield
Heveningham
Gislingham
Thornham Magna
Braiseworth
Redlingfield
Athelington
Foals Green
Ubbeston Green
Brundish Street
Crown Corner
Wickham Street
Stoke Ash
Occold
Thorndon
Stanway Green
Brundish
Owl's Green
Peasenhall
Rishangles
Bedingfield
Worlingworth
Badingham
Yare
Waveney
Dove
S u f
0 1 2 3 miles
0 1 2 3 4 5 km

Acle
North Burlingham
Stokesby
Candlemaker Workshop
Wildlife Gardens
Caister
West End
Great Yarmouth
Great Denes
Bure
Yarmouth
A47
Damgate
Lingwood
Beighton
Tunstall
THE BROADS
Halvergate Marshes
Runham
Breydon Water
Moulton St Mary
South Burlingham
Halvergate
Great Yarmouth
Sea Life Great Yarmouth
Cobholm Island
Buckenham
Hassingham
Freethorpe
Wickhampton
Burgh Castle
Southtown
Elizabethan House, Maritime
Nelson/Tolhouse Museums
Exhibition Galleries
Amazonia-World of Reptiles
Pleasure Beach
Southwood
Cantley
Limpenhoe
Berney Arms Windmill
Bradwell
Gorleston-on-Sea
Yare
Pettitts Animal Adventure Park
Belton
A143
TG
Langley Street
Reedham
Hardley Street
Redwings Horse Sanctuary
A12
Ferry
St Olaves Priory
Fritton
Hopton on Sea
Chedgrave
Chet
Lower Thurlton
The Dell
Lound
Loddon
Thurlton
Thorpe
Somerleyton Hall
B1074
Blundeston
Stubbs Green
Hales
B1136
Herringfleet
Corton
Raveningham
Haddiscoe
Somerleyton
Pleasurewood Hills Leisure Park
Raveningham Gardens
Maypole Green
A12
Lowestoft and East Suffolk Maritime Museum
Toft Monks
A146
Oulton
A1117
Normanstone
Kirby Cane
Stockton
Wheatacre
Burgh St Peter
B1375
Aldeby
A146
Heritage/Visitor Centre
A143
Oulton Broad
Lowestoft Museum
Lowestoft
Kirby Row
Carlton Marshes Nature Reserve
Geldeston
Gillingham
Kirkley
Broome
Waveney
Beccles
A146
B1062
Shipmeadow
Barnby
Mettingham
Worlingham
Carlton Colville
Pakefield
Barsham
North Cove
Mutford
Gisleham
Ringsfield
B1127
Ilketshall St Andrew
Ringsfield Corner
Hulver Street
Rushmere
Kessingland
Ellough
Henstead
B1437
Kessingland Beach
A144
A145
Africa Alive
Benacre
Ilketshall St Lawrence
Redisham
Sotterley
B1127
Shadingfield
Stone Street
West End
TM
Cox Common
Wrentham
Benacre
Brampton
Stoven
Clay Common
Frostenden
Covehithe
Mill Common
South Cove
Spexhall
Uggeshall
Cove Bottom
Westhall
f o l k
Broadway
Wangford
B1124
B1127
Chediston
A145
Reydon Smear
B1126
Holton
Reydon
A1095
Halesworth
Blyford
B1123
Hen Reedbed Nature Reserve
Southwold Museum
Southwold
Wenhaston
Blyth
Blackheath
Blythburgh
B1387
Thorington
Walpole
Walberswick
Bramfield
B1125
Suffolk Coast
A12
A144
Sibton Green
SUFFOLK COAST AND HEATHS
Dunwich
High Street
Dunwich Underwater Exploration Exhibition
Hemp Green
Forest
Dunwich
Darsham
Sibton
89
Yoxford
Westleton Heath
Westleton
Middleton Moor
Minsmere RSPB Nature Reserve
A
B
C
D
4
5
6
7
121

1
2
3
A
B
C
D
122
CAERNARFON BAY
BAE CAERNARFON
SH
LLEYN
PENRHYN LLYN
Clyn
Gyrn-go
Bryn-yr-eryr
Trefor
564
YR EIFL
Llan
WALES COAST PATH
B4417
6
Llithfaen
Carreg Ddu
Porth Dinllaen
Pistyll
Llwyndyrys
Morfa Nefyn
Nefyn
LLEYN HISTORICAL MARITIME MUSEUM
Fron
B4354
Edern
Tan-y-graig
Rhos-fawr
Porth Ysgadan
B4417
Glanrhyd
Rhos-y-llan
CORS GEIRCH
Boduan
A497
A499
Llannor
Tudweiliog
BODVEL HALL ADVENTURE PARK
Efailnewydd
Dinas
14
Rhyd-y-clafdy
Denio
Pwllheli
Porth Golmon
Garnfadryn
B4415
South Beach
Bryn-mawr
Llaniestyn
Penrhos
Pen-y-graig
Llangwnnadl
Rhedyn
Sarn Meyllteyrn
7
Penrhyn Mawr
Pen-y-groeslon
B4413
Llanbedrog
Ty-hen
Botwnnog
Nanhoron
Bryncroes
Mynytho
Trwyn Llanbedrog
Methlem
Rhydlios
Llandegwning
304
MYNYDD RHIW
PLAS-YN-RHIW
St Tudwal's Road
Angorfa St Tudwal
Capel Carmel
Rhoshirwaun
Llawrdref Bellaf
Llangian
A499
Rhiw
Abersoch
191
B4413
Porth Neigwl or Hell's Mouth
Llanengan
St Tudwal's Island East
Ynys St Tudwal Dwyrain
Uwchmynydd
Llanfaelrhys
Sarn Bach
Aberdaron
Bwlchtocyn
Marchroes
Bodermid
St Tudwal's Island West
Ynys St Tudwal Gorllewin
Bardsey Sound
Swnt Enlli
Pen-y-cil
Cilan Uchaf
Trwyn Cilan
167
YNYS ENLLI
Bardsey Island
Ynys Enlli
0 1 2 3 miles
0 1 2 3 4 5 km

Caernarfon
Bar
Abermenai Pt.
Trwyn Abermenai
Caeathro
Ceunant
Llyn Padarn
Dinorwic
Pont Pen-y-benglog
Llyn Ogwen
Pont Rh
WELSH HIGHLAND RAILWAY
POWER OF WALES
INIGO JONES TUD SLATEWORK
LLANBERIS LAKE RAILWAY
PADARN
Llanfaglan
Croesywaun
Groes
123
Llanberis
SLATE MUS
IDWAL COTTAGE
Saron
Bontnewydd
Waunfawr
DOLBADARN
Llyn Peris
Nant Peris
CWM IDWAL
CAERNARFON AIR MUSEUM
Glan-rhyd
Rhostryfan
Morfa Dinlle
Llanwnda
A4085
726
A4086
Pass of Llanberis
999 GLYDER FAWR
Cape
Dinas Dinlle
Ffrwd
Rhosgadfan
Betws-Garmon
Llandwrog
Penyffridd
GLYNLLIFON
Groeslon
Fron
SNOWDON RANGER
SNOWDON MOUNTAIN RAILWAY
SNOWDON SUMMIT VISITOR CENTRE (HAFOD ERYRI)
PEN-Y-PASS
Pen-y-Gwryd Hotel
Llyn Cwellyn
A487
A499
Carmel
Cilgwyn
S N O W D O N I A
124
1085 SNOWDON YR WYDDFA
Llyn Llydaw
Penygroes
Nantlle
B4418
Talysarn
Rhyd-Ddu
Pontllyfni
YR WYDDFA
Llyn Gwynant
Tan-yr-allt
Llanllyfni
Ffridd-Uchaf
747
Garnedd
DOLWYDDE
N A T I O N A L
Nebo
734
Bethania
A498
BRYN GWYNANT
Tainlon
Beddgelert Forest
Nantgwynant
Nasareth
Capel Uchaf
Llyn Dinas
A470
WELSH HIGHLAND RLY
SYGUN COPPER MINE
Pass of Aberglaslyn
Afon Dwyfor
Pant-glas
Beddgelert
P A R K
G w y n e d d
509 BWLCH MAWR
Upper Clynnog
Dafarn Faig
782 MOEL HEBOG
Rhiwbryfdir
Nantmor
Tanygrisiau
Bryncir
Croesor
770 MOELWYN MAWR
Llanfihangel-y-pennant
Tyddyn-mawr
Cenin
Pen-sarn
HAFOD GARREGOG
Glan- Dwyfach
Garndolbenmaen
Dolbenmaen
MOEL-DDU 552
FFESTINIOG POWER STATION
COED CYMERAU
A496
Llecheiddior
A4085
Tan-lan
COEDYDD MAENTWROG
Golan
Rhyd-y-sarn
Rhyd
BRYNKIR WOOLLEN MILL
Afon Glaslyn
Garreg
Prenteg
Pencaenewydd
Rhoslan
A487
Penmorfa
COED TREMADOG
B4410
Llanfrothen
Tan-y-bwlch
CEUNANT CYNFAL
Llangybi
B4411
FFESTINIOG RLY
Maentwrog
Tremadog
Pentrefelin
Llanarmon
Gellilydan
COED CAMLYN
Llanystumdwy
Porthmadog
POTTERY
Penrhyndeudraeth
CEUNANT LLENNYRCH
A470
Ffôr
Chwilog
A497
TOLL
TRAWSFYNYDD NUCLEAR POWER STATION
NARTH FAWR MEDIEVAL HOUSE
MARITIME MUSEUM
Minffordd
Cilfor
Portmeirion
COED Y RHYGEN
Criccieth
LLOYD GEORGE MEMORIAL MUSEUM
THE ROPEWORKS
Morfa Bychan
Borth-y-Gest
PORTMEIRION
Caerwych
Llyn Trawsfynydd
HAVEN
Traeth Bach
Talsarnau
MORFA HARLECH
Ynys
108
Glan-y-wern
Eisingrug
g yr Imbill
623 MOEL YSGYFARNOGOD
TREMADOG BAY
BAE TREMADOG
Morfa Harlech
A496
Glyn-cywarch
B4573
PARC
Afon Eden
Harlech
CENEDLAETHOL
ERYRI
Llanfair
LLANFAIR SLATE CAVERNS
RHINOG
720 RHINOG FAWR
Llandanwg
Pen-sarn
Pen-y-bont
Pentre-Gwynfryn
COED Y BRENIN VISITOR CENTRE
Llanbedr
Morfa Dyffryn
WALES COAST PATH
754 Y LLETHR
MORFA DYFFRYN
Coed Ystumgwern
Llanenddwyn
Dyffryn Ardudwy
750 DIFFWYS
Llanddwywe
Cors-y-Gedol
Blaen-y-c
Tal-y-bont
A496
Pen-y-bryn
90
Plas-canol
4
5
Llanaber
Caerdeo
Bontddu
TOLL

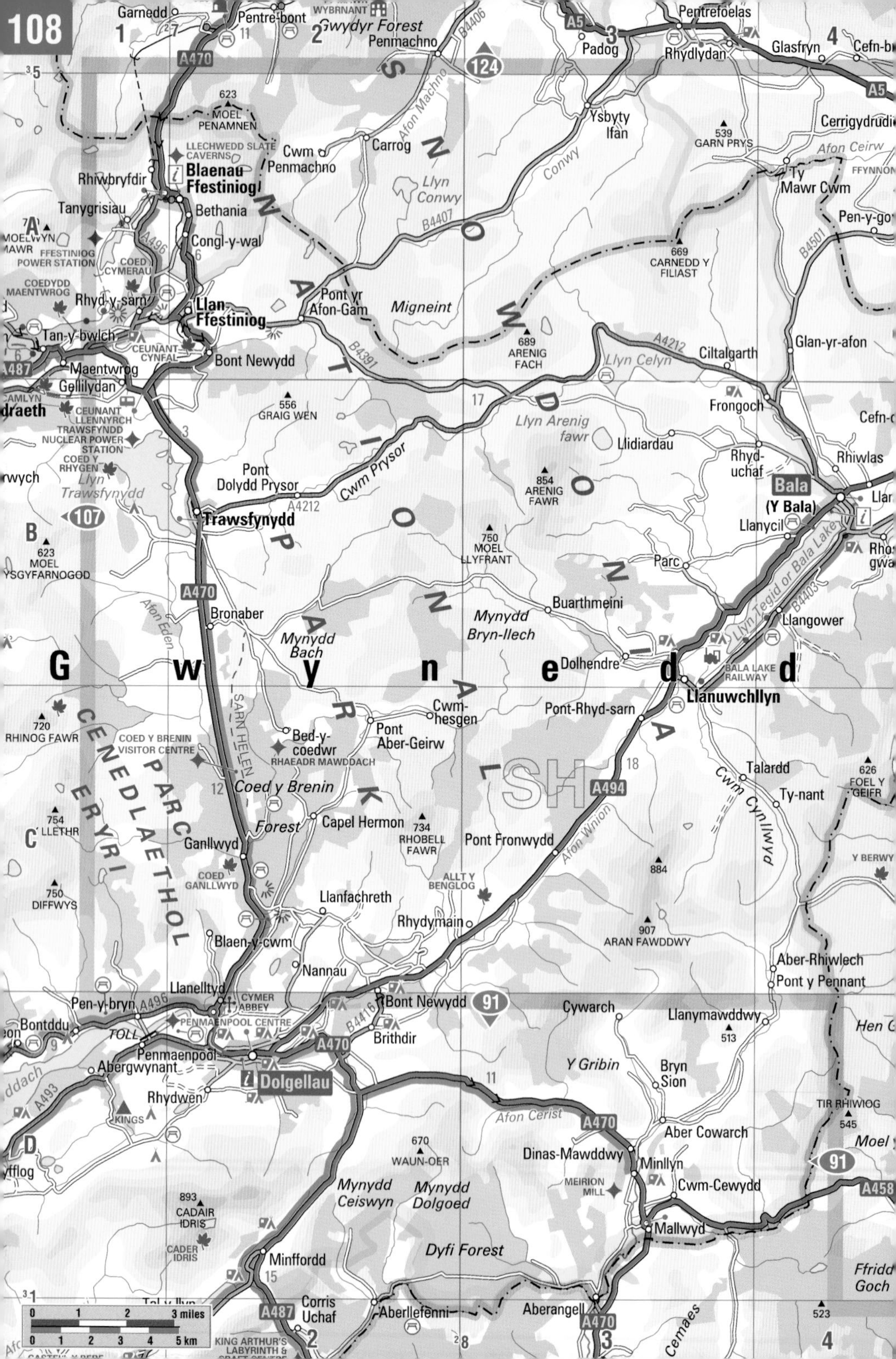
Garnedd
Pentre-bont
WYBRNANT
Gwydyr Forest
Penmachno
A5
Padog
Pentrefoelas
Rhydlydan
Glasfryn
Cefn-b
A470
124
623
MOEL PENAMNEN
Afon Machno
Ysbyty Ifan
Cerrigydrudi
539
GARN PRYS
LLECHWEDD SLATE CAVERNS
Blaenau Ffestiniog
Cwm Penmachno
Carrog
Conwy
Afon Ceirw
Ty Mawr Cwm
FFYNNON
Rhiwbryfdir
Tanygrisiau
Bethania
Llyn Conwy
B4407
Pen-y-go
MOELWYN MAWR
FFESTINIOG POWER STATION
Congl-y-wal
A496
669
CARNEDD Y FILIAST
B4501
COED CYMERAU
COEDYDD MAENTWROG
Rhyd-y-sarn
Llan-Ffestiniog
Pont yr Afon-Gam
Migneint
Tan-y-bwlch
CEUNANT CYNFAL
689
ARENIG FACH
A4212
Ciltalgarth
Glan-yr-afon
A487
Maentwrog
Bont Newydd
B4391
Llyn Celyn
Gellilydan
556
GRAIG WEN
17
Frongoch
draeth
CEUNANT LLENNYRCH
TRAWSFYNYDD NUCLEAR POWER STATION
Llyn Arenig fawr
Cefn-d
Llidiardau
COED Y RHYGEN
Llyn Trawsfynydd
Pont Dolydd Prysor
Cwm Prysor
854
ARENIG FAWR
Rhyd-uchaf
Rhiwlas
Bala
(Y Bala)
Llan
107
Trawsfynydd
A4212
750
MOEL LLYFRANT
Llanycil
623
MOEL YSGYFARNOGOD
Parc
Rho gwa
A470
Bronaber
Afon Eden
Buarthmeini
Mynydd Bryn-llech
Llyn Tegid or Bala Lake
B4403
Llangower
Mynydd Bach
Dolhendre
BALA LAKE RAILWAY
G w y n e d d
Llanuwchllyn
720
RHINOG FAWR
SARN HELEN
Cwm-hesgen
Pont-Rhyd-sarn
COED Y BRENIN VISITOR CENTRE
Bed-y-coedwr
Pont Aber-Geirw
RHAEADR MAWDDACH
CENEDLAETHOL
PARC
ERYRI
SNOWDONIA NATIONAL PARK
Coed y Brenin Forest
SH
A494
18
Talardd
626
FOEL Y GEIFR
Ty-nant
Cwm Cynllwyd
754
LLETHR
Capel Hermon
734
RHOBELL FAWR
Pont Fronwydd
Afon Wnion
Ganllwyd
Y BERWY
COED GANLLWYD
884
750
DIFFWYS
ALLT Y BENGLOG
Llanfachreth
Rhydymain
907
ARAN FAWDDWY
Blaen-y-cwm
Nannau
Aber-Rhiwlech
Pont y Pennant
Llanelltyd
CYMER ABBEY
Pen-y-bryn
A496
Bont Newydd
91
Cywarch
Llanymawddwy
Bontddu
TOLL
PENMAENPOOL CENTRE
B4416
Brithdir
513
Hen G
Penmaenpool
A470
Abergwynant
Dolgellau
Y Gribin
Bryn Sion
A493
Rhydwen
11
KINGS
TIR RHIWIOG
545
Afon Cerist
A470
Aber Cowarch
Moel
670
WAUN-OER
Dinas-Mawddwy
Minllyn
91
MEIRION MILL
Cwm-Cewydd
A458
Mynydd Ceiswyn
Mynydd Dolgoed
893
CADAIR IDRIS
CADER IDRIS
Mallwyd
Dyfi Forest
Minffordd
15
Ffridd Goch
Corris Uchaf
Aberllefenni
Aberangell
523
A487
A470
Cemaes
0 1 2 3 miles
0 1 2 3 4 5 km
KING ARTHUR'S LABYRINTH & CRAFT CENTRE

Pentre-llyn cymmer
Derwen
Rhyd-y-meudwy
Pen-y-stryt
OFFA'S DYKE PATH
Llanfihangel Glyn Myfyr
Llanelidan
Bryn Saith Marchog
CYRN Y BRAIN
LLWYBR CLAWDD OFFA
Melin-y-Wig
A494
B5105
B5429
A525
A542
Bryneglwys
Maesyrychen Mtn.
Pentredwr
Eglwyseg Mountain
Ruabon Mountain
Bettws Gwerfil Goch
Gwyddelwern
A5104
Morfydd
Llantysilio Mountain
Llandynan
Rhewl
ELISEG'S PILLAR
VALLE CRUCIS ABBEY
LLANGOLLEN MOTOR MUS
Ty-nant
Dinmael
Maerdy
A5
Llangwm
B5437
LLANGOLLEN RAILWAY
Carrog
Dee (Dyfrdwy)
CANAL EXHIBITION CENTRE
Garth
Tai-mawr
Glan-yr-afon
Druid
GLASSBLOBBERY
Corwen
Llidiart-y-parc
Glyndyfrdwy
Llangollen
Wenallt
Cynwyd Forest
Cynwyd
LLANGOLLEN EXHIBITION CENTRE
PLAS NEWYDD
Sarnau
Bethel
Llandderfel
B4402
B4401
MOEL FFERNA
CHWAREL WYNNE MINE & MUSEUM
Glyn Ceiriog
Pontfadog
B4500
Plas Nantyr
Tyn-y-celyn
Llwynmawr
Llandrillo
Pale
Cefn Coch
Pandy
B4579
BERWYN
Pentre
BRYN DU
B4391
Pennant
Tregeiriog
Llechrydau
Craignant
Aber-Hirnant
Blaen-y-Cwm
Llanarmon Dyffryn Ceiriog
Rhiwlas
Pont Cwm Pydew
Tyn-y-fedwen
MOEL SYCH
Tyn-y-ffridd
Cefn Canol
Aberhirnant Forest
Llangadwaladr
PISTYLL RHAEADR
Tan-y-pistyll
Rhydycroesau
OFFA'S DYKE PATH
LLWYBR CLAWDD OFFA
Tai-bach
Llansilin
Moelfre
Tyn-y-coed
B4580
Pencraig
Cefn Coch
Llanrhaeadr-ym-Mochnant
Trefonen
Pennant Melangell
Llangynog
SJ
Treflach
B4396
Llangedwyn
Nantmawr
Alltforgan
Penybontfawr
Pen-y-bont
Penygarnedd
Afon Tanat
Porth-y-waen
Hirnant
Rhos-y-brithdir
B4393
Lake Vyrnwy
Ty-uchaf
Llanyblodwel
Bwlchyddar
Abernaint
Llansantffraid-ym-Mechain
Llanfechain
Blaen-y-cwm
Llanymynech
Llanfyllin
Llanwddyn
Abertridwr
A490
POWYS
Tycrwyn
Ddôl-Cownwy
Llanfihangel-yng-Ngwynfa
Bwlch-y-cibau
Waen Fach
Deuddwr
Dyfnant Forest
Main
Sarnau
Arddleen
Mynydd y Gadfa
Pont Llogel
Afon Vyrnwy (Afon Efyrnwy)
Trefnanney
Geufforddd
Wern
B4395
Meifod
Pentrebeirdd
Wern
Pontrobert
Maesgwyn-Isaf
Dolanog
B4382
Glascoed
B4392
Groes-lwyd
Pool Quay
Foel
Llangadfan
GLYNDWR'S WAY
Guilsfield
A495
A458
Llanerfyl
Pen Coed
Cloddiau
Welshpool (Y Trallwng)
Heniarth
B4389
A490

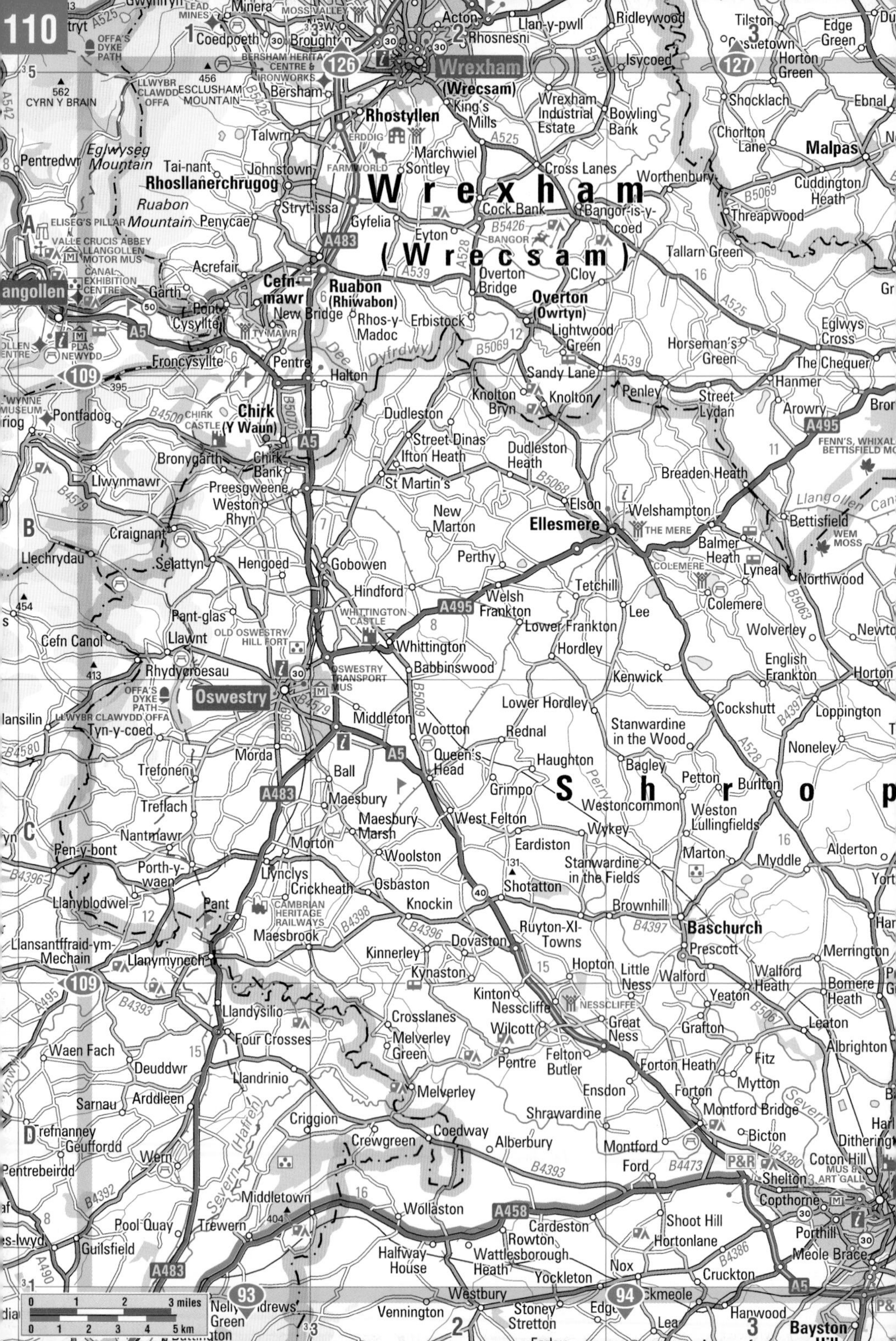
Minera
Acton
Llan-y-pwll
Ridleywood
Tilston
Edge Green
Coedpoeth
Broughton
Rhosnesni
Castletown
OFFA'S DYKE PATH
BERSHAM HERITAGE CENTRE & IRONWORKS
126
Wrexham
(Wrecsam)
Isycoed
127
Horton Green
562
CYRN Y BRAIN
LLWYBR CLAWDD OFFA
456
ESCLUSHAM MOUNTAIN
Bersham
King's Mills
Wrexham Industrial Estate
Bowling Bank
Shocklach
Ebnal
Rhostyllen
ERDDIG
Marchwiel
Chorlton Lane
Malpas
Pentredwr
Eglwyseg Mountain
Tai-nant
Johnstown
FARMWORLD
Sontley
Cross Lanes
Worthenbury
Cuddington Heath
Rhosllanerchrugog
Wrexham
Stryt-issa
Cock Bank
Bangor-is-y-coed
Threapwood
Ruabon Mountain
Penycae
Gyfelia
Eyton
BANGOR
ELISEG'S PILLAR
VALLE CRUCIS ABBEY
LLANGOLLEN MOTOR MUS
(Wrecsam)
Tallarn Green
Acrefair
CANAL EXHIBITION CENTRE
Cefn-mawr
Ruabon
(Rhiwabon)
Overton Bridge
Cloy
Overton
(Owrtyn)
Llangollen
Garth
Pont Cysyllte
New Bridge
Rhos-y-Madoc
Erbistock
Lightwood Green
Eglwys Cross
TY MAWR
PLAS NEWYDD
Dee (Dyfrdwy)
Horseman's Green
The Chequer
Froncysyllte
Pentre
Halton
Sandy Lane
109
395
Knolton Bryn
Knolton
Penley
Hanmer
Street Lydan
Arowry
WYNNE MUSEUM
Pontfadog
Chirk
CHIRK CASTLE
(Y Waun)
Dudleston
Street Dinas
Dudleston Heath
FENN'S, WHIXALL & BETTISFIELD MOSSES
Bronygarth
Chirk Bank
Ifton Heath
Llwynmawr
St Martin's
Breaden Heath
Preesgweene
Weston Rhyn
New Marton
Elson
Welshampton
Llangollen Canal
Ellesmere
THE MERE
Bettisfield
Craignant
Selattyn
Hengoed
Gobowen
Perthy
Balmer Heath
WEM MOSS
Llechrydau
COLEMERE
Lyneal
Northwood
Hindford
Tetchill
Welsh Frankton
454
Pant-glas
WHITTINGTON CASTLE
Lee
Colemere
Llawnt
OLD OSWESTRY HILL FORT
Lower Frankton
Wolverley
Newton
Cefn Canol
Whittington
Hordley
English Frankton
413
Rhydycroesau
OSWESTRY TRANSPORT MUS
Babbinswood
Kenwick
Horton
OFFA'S DYKE PATH
Oswestry
Llansilin
LLWYBR CLAWDD OFFA
Tyn-y-coed
Middleton
Lower Hordley
Cockshutt
Loppington
Wootton
Stanwardine in the Wood
Rednal
Noneley
Trefonen
Morda
Queen's Head
Haughton
Ball
Bagley
Petton
Burlton
Shrop
Grimpo
Maesbury
Westoncommon
Treflach
Weston Lullingfields
Maesbury Marsh
West Felton
Nantmawr
Wykey
Morton
Eardiston
Marton
Pen-y-bont
Woolston
131
Stanwardine in the Fields
Myddle
Alderton
Porth-y-waen
Llynclys
Llanyblodwel
Osbaston
Crickheath
Shotatton
Pant
CAMBRIAN HERITAGE RAILWAYS
Knockin
Brownhill
Baschurch
Ruyton-XI-Towns
Llansantffraid-ym-Mechain
Maesbrook
Dovaston
Prescott
Merrington
Kinnerley
Llanymynech
Hopton
Little Ness
Walford
Walford Heath
Kynaston
Bomere Heath
Kinton
Nesscliffe
NESSCLIFFE
Yeaton
Llandysilio
Crosslanes
Great Ness
Grafton
Leaton
Wilcott
Four Crosses
Melverley Green
Albrighton
Waen Fach
Pentre
Felton Butler
Forton Heath
Fitz
Deuddwr
Llandrinio
Ensdon
Forton
Mytton
Sarnau
Arddleen
Melverley
Montford Bridge
Severn
Criggion
Shrawardine
Drefnanney
Coedway
Bicton
Geufforddd
Crewgreen
Alberbury
Montford
Dithering
Wern
Pentrebeirdd
Ford
Coton Hill
Severn (Hafren)
Shelton
Middletown
Wollaston
Copthorne
404
A458
Shoot Hill
Pool Quay
Trewern
Cardeston
Hortonlane
Porthill
Guilsfield
Halfway House
Rowton
Wattlesborough Heath
Nox
Meole Brace
Yockleton
Cruckton
0 1 2 3 miles
0 1 2 3 4 5 km
93
Westbury
94
Nelly Andrews Green
Vennington
Stoney Stretton
Edge
Hanwood
Bayston Hill

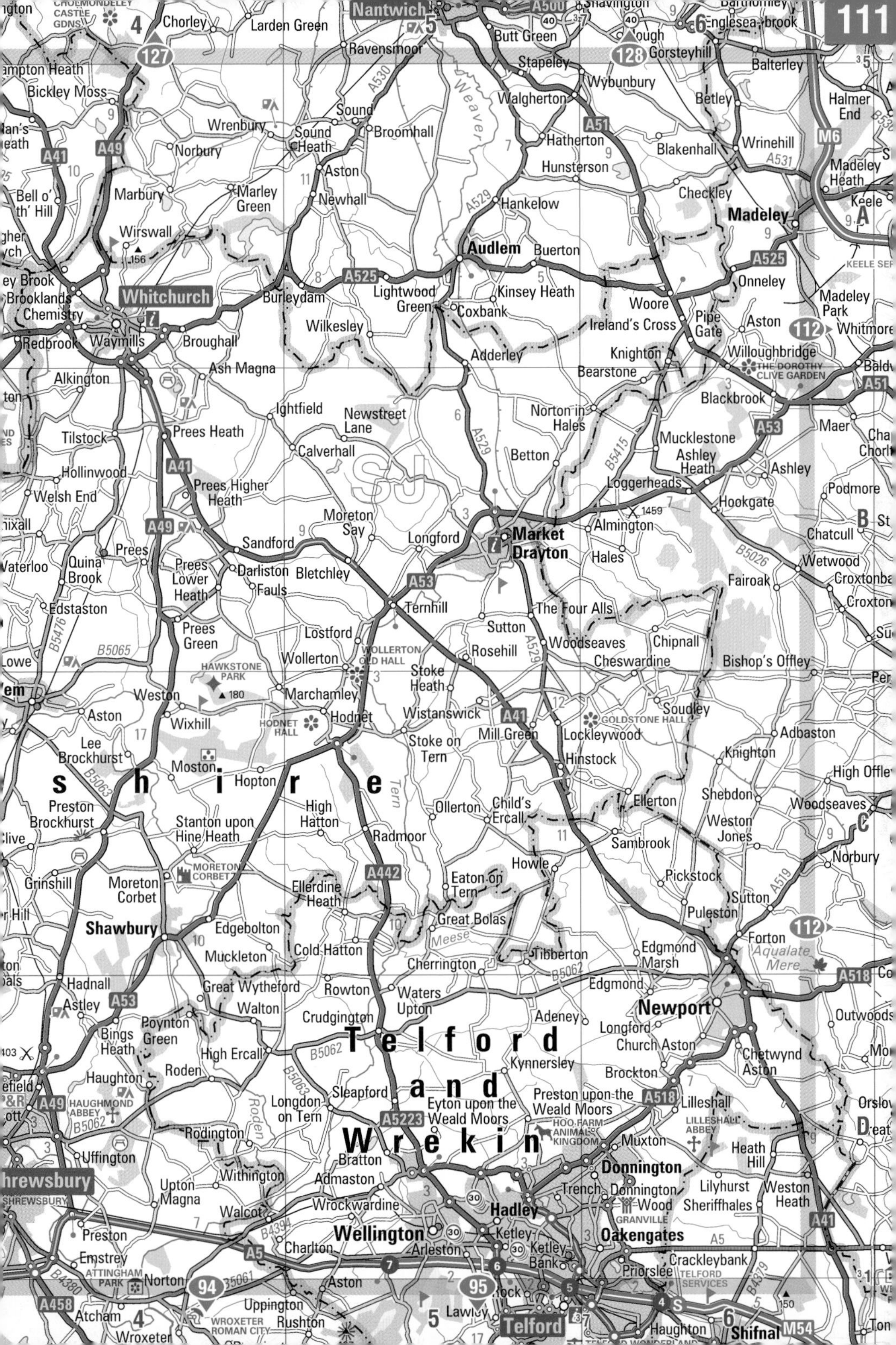
Nantwich
Chorley
Larden Green
Ravensmoor
Butt Green
Stapeley
Wybunbury
Walgherton
Gorsteyhill
Balterley
Betley
Halmer End
Wrinehill
Blakenhall
Hatherton
Hunsterson
Checkley
Madeley
Madeley Heath
Keele
Bickley Moss
Wrenbury
Sound
Sound Heath
Broomhall
Norbury
Aston
Newhall
Marbury
Marley Green
Hankelow
Weaver
Wirswall
Audlem
Buerton
Kinsey Heath
Woore
Onneley
Madeley Park
Whitchurch
Burleydam
Lightwood Green
Coxbank
Ireland's Cross
Pipe Gate
Whitmore
Brooklands
Chemistry
Waymills
Broughall
Redbrook
Wilkesley
Adderley
Knighton
Willoughbridge
THE DOROTHY CLIVE GARDEN
Ash Magna
Bearstone
Blackbrook
Alkington
Ightfield
Newstreet Lane
Norton in Hales
Maer
Tilstock
Prees Heath
Calverhall
Mucklestone
Ashley Heath
Betton
Hollinwood
Prees Higher Heath
Loggerheads
Ashley
Welsh End
Moreton Say
Hookgate
Podmore
Prees
Sandford
Longford
Market Drayton
Almington
Chatcull
Quina Brook
Prees Lower Heath
Darliston
Fauls
Bletchley
Hales
Wetwood
Croxtonbank
Edstaston
Ternhill
The Four Alls
Fairoak
Prees Green
Lostford
Sutton
Woodseaves
Chipnall
Wollerton
WOLLERTON OLD HALL
Rosehill
Cheswardine
Bishop's Offley
HAWKSTONE PARK
Stoke Heath
Weston
Wixhill
Marchamley
Hodnet
HODNET HALL
Wistanswick
Mill Green
Lockleywood
GOLDSTONE HALL
Soudley
Adbaston
Aston
Lee Brockhurst
Moston
Hopton
Stoke on Tern
Hinstock
Knighton
High Offley
Preston Brockhurst
Stanton upon Hine Heath
High Hatton
Radmoor
Ollerton
Child's Ercall
Ellerton
Shebdon
Weston Jones
Woodseaves
Sambrook
Norbury
Grinshill
Moreton Corbet
MORETON CORBET
Ellerdine Heath
Eaton on Tern
Howle
Pickstock
Sutton
Shawbury
Edgebolton
Great Bolas
Puleston
Forton
Muckleton
Cold Hatton
Meese
Tibberton
Edgmond Marsh
Aqualate Mere
Cherrington
Hadnall
Great Wytheford
Rowton
Waters Upton
Edgmond
Astley
Walton
Crudgington
Adeney
Newport
Outwoods
Poynton Green
Bings Heath
High Ercall
Telford and Wrekin
Longford
Church Aston
Chetwynd Aston
Haughton
Roden
Kynnersley
Brockton
HAUGHMOND ABBEY
Sleapford
Longdon on Tern
Eyton upon the Weald Moors
Preston upon the Weald Moors
HOO FARM ANIMAL KINGDOM
Lilleshall
LILLESHALL ABBEY
Rodington
Uffington
Bratton
Muxton
Donnington
Heath Hill
Shrewsbury
Upton Magna
Withington
Admaston
Trench
Donnington Wood
Lilyhurst
Sheriffhales
Weston Heath
Wrockwardine
Hadley
GRANVILLE
Walcot
Preston
Wellington
Ketley
Oakengates
Charlton
Arleston
Ketley Bank
Crackleybank
Emstrey
ATTINGHAM PARK
Norton
Priorslee
TELFORD SERVICES
Aston
Atcham
Uppington
Lawley
Wroxeter
WROXETER ROMAN CITY
Rushton
Telford
Haughton
Shifnal
A49
A41
A525
A530
A529
A51
A53
A531
M6
B5415
B5026
A442
A519
A518
B5062
B5063
A5223
B4394
A5
B4380
A458
B4379
M54
B5065
B5476

Tunstall
Red Street
Audley
Balterley
Burslem
Bradeley
Baddeley Green
Cheddleton
Bagnall
Basford Green
Ipstones
Stoke-on-Trent
Longport
Chesterton
Alsagers Bank
Bradwell
Wolstanton
May Bank
Milton
Abbey Hulton
Bucknall
Werrington
Wetley Rocks
Cellarhead
Consall
Foxt
Froghall
Whiston
Halmer End
Wrinehill
Knutton
Silverdale
Madeley Heath
Hanley
Kingsley
Blakeley Lane
Kingsley Holt
Oakamoor
Keele
Newcastle-under-Lyme
Madeley
Boothen
Fenton
Trent Vale
Clayton
Longton
Weston Coyney
Dilhorne
Cheadle
Onneley
Madeley Park
Whitmore
Hanford
Trentham
Dresden
Meir
Blythe Bridge
Caverswall
Forsbrook
Freehay
Aston
Willoughbridge
Hanchurch
Lightwood
Draycott in the Moors
Mobberley
Baldwin's Gate
Rough Close
Meir Heath
Blackbrook
Stableford
Beech
Tittensor
Barlaston
Cresswell
Upper Tean
Lower Tean
Checkley
Maer
Chapel Chorlton
Knenhall
Fulford
Ashley
Cranberry
Moddershall
Upper Leigh
Podmore
Oulton
Middleton Green
Lower Leigh
Church Leigh
Hookgate
Swynnerton
Meaford
Cotwalton
Hilderstone
Standon
Chatcull
Cotes
Stone
Dods Leigh
Wetwood
Millmeece
Walton
Dayhills
Garshall Green
Field
Fairoak
Croxtonbank
Slindon
Yarnfield
Little Stoke
Milwich
Coton Hill
Croxton
Coton
Gratwich
Sugnall
Sturbridge
Norton Bridge
Aston-By-Stone
Fradswell
Bishop's Offley
Pershall
Burston
Sandon
Eccleshall
Chebsey
Yarlet
Whitgreave
Gayton
Grindley
Adbaston
Marston
Salt
Weston
Stowe-by-Chartley
Knighton
Wootton
Great Bridgeford
Drointon
High Offley
Ellenhall
Hopton
Woodseaves
Holmcroft
Hixon
Newton
Lawnhead
Seighford
Ingestre
Stafford
Norbury
Knightley Dale
Ranton
Coton Clanford
Tixall
Great Haywood
Admaston
Doxey
Derrington
Forebridge
Sutton
Long Compton
Weeping Cross
Milford
Little Haywood
Gnosall
Whitecross
Colwich
Forton
Moss Pit
Walton on the Hill
Haughton
Coton
Gnosall Heath
Newport
Allimore Green
Coppenhall
Acton Trussell
Brocton
Outwoods
Apeton
Bradley
Dunston
Etchinghill
Moreton
Chetwynd Aston
Church Eaton
Bednall
Levedale
Slitting Mill
High Onn
Orslow
Mitton
Longridge
Cannock Chase
Great Chatwell
Penkridge
Pye Green
Heath Hill
Whiston
Brineton
Marston
Congreve
Huntington
Hazelslade
Weston Heath
Blymhill
Lapley
Hednesford
Wheaton Aston
Stretton
Oldfallow
Littleworth
Gailey
Wimblebury
Weston under Lizard
Hatherton
Heath Hayes
Horsebrook
Kiddemore Green
Cannock
Bishop's Wood
Brewood
Bridgtown
Norton Canes
Shifnal
SJ
0 1 2 3 miles
0 1 2 3 4 5 km

113
New Street
Waterfall
DOVEDALE
Carsington Res.
Ilam
ILAM HALL
ILAM
Waterhouses
Thorpe
Fenny Bentley
Hognaston
Beighton Hill
Ambergate
129
130
Calton
Kniveton
Kirk Ireton
Shottle
Belper Lane End
Cauldon
Blore
Atlow
Biggin
DERWENT VALLEY VISITOR CEN
Idridgehay
Mount Pleasant
Swinscoe
Mapleton
Hulland Ward
Hillcliff Lane
Blackbrook
Shottlegate
Cotton
Weaver Hills
Ashbourne
Hulland
Cowers Lane
Belper
Turnditch
Stanton
Mayfield
Bradley
Cross o' th' hands
Hazelwood
Ramshorn
Wootton
Church Mayfield
Clifton
Windley
Farley
Derby
ALTON TOWERS
Osmaston
Ellastone
Snelston
Weston Underwood
Duffield
Alton
Wyaston
Mugginton
Quixhill
Norbury
Brailsford
DARLEY MOOR
Shirley
Ednaston
Kedleston
Flaxholme
Roston
Denstone
Yeaveley
Rodsley
Hollington
Quarndon
Greatgate
Rocester
BENTLEY FIELDS OPEN FARM
KEDLESTON HALL
114
Croxden
Cubley Common
Great Cubley
Alkmonton
Hollington Grove
Kirk Langley
Allestree
Marston Montgomery
Thurvaston
Mackworth
Combridge
Longlane
Waldley
Longford
Lees
Langley Common
Beamhurst
Crakemarsh
Radbourne
Longfordlane
Stramshall
Somersal Herbert
Boylestone
HERITAGE CENTRE
Trusley
CITY MUS & ART GALL
Uttoxeter
Doveridge
Oaks Green
SK
Dalbury
Mickleover
Littleover
Normanton
Church Broughton
Sutton on the Hill
Burnaston
Foston
UTTOXETER
Sudbury
Etwall
Marchington
Scropton
Hatton
Hilton
Findern
SUDBURY HALL
Marston on Dove
Stenson
Kingstone
Gorsty Hill
Draycott in the Clay
TUTBURY
Tutbury
Egginton
Twyford
Marchington Woodlands
Willington
Barrow upon Trent
Hanbury
Rolleston-on-Dove
Repton
Stretton
Ingleby
Newborough
Hanbury Woodend
Anslow Gate
Anslow
Milton
Abbots Bromley
NEEDWOOD
Needwood
Horninglow
Newton Solney
FOREST
Rangemore
Shobnall
BASS MUS
Winshill
Bretby
Foremark Res.
Hoar Cross
Newchurch
THE
Burton upon Trent
Tatenhill
Stapenhill
Upper Midway
Lower Midway
Hartshorne
Branston
BRANSTON
Newhall
Colton
Hadley End
Woodlane
Dunstall
NATIONAL
Swadlincote
Woodville
Blithbury
Hamstall Ridware
Church Gresley
Hill Ridware
Morrey
Yoxall
Woodhouses
Barton-under-Needwood
Walton-on-Trent
Castle Gresley
Mount Pleasant
Blackfordby
Caldwell
Norris Hill
FOREST
Armitage
Handsacre
King's Bromley
Rosliston
Linton
Ashby-de-la-Zouch
Orgreave
Alrewas
Moira
NATIONAL MEMORIAL ARBORETUM
Coton in the Elms
Overseal
HEART OF THE NATIONAL FOREST
Longdon
Rileyhill
Donisthorpe
Longdon Green
Fradley
Croxall
Oakthorpe
Edingale
Lullington
Netherseal
Measham
Elmhurst
Farewell
Chorley
Streethay
Harlaston
Chilcote
Elford
Haunton
Clifton Campville
Lichfield
Burntwood
SAMUEL JOHNSON BIRTHPLACE MUS
96
97
No Man's Heath
Appleby Magna
Swepstone
Leomansley
Whittington
Thorpe Constantine
Appleby Parva
Snarestone
A523
A52
A515
A517
A50
A516
A38
A511
A5132
A444
A513
A51
A42
B5035
B5023
B5032
B5033
B5031
B5030
B5013
B5017
B5234
B5016
B5014
B5020
B5008
B5006
B5493
Trent

Ambergate
Toadmoor
Heage
Net Heage
130
RIPLEY
Riddings
Ironville
MIDLAND RAILWAY CENTRE
Jacksdale
Bagthorpe
FELLEY PRIORY
New Brinsley
Underwood
131
Newstead
Linby
Papplewick
PAPPLEWICK PUMPING ST
A617
B6011
Belper Lane End
Shottle
DERWENT VALLEY VISITOR CEN
Broadholme
Marehay
Codnor
Cross Hill
Brinsley
M1
HUCKNALL
ridgehay
Mount Pleasant
Far Laund
A38
Loscoe
Aldercar
Moorgreen
Westville
BESTWOOD
Blackbrook
Openwoodgate
Denby
HEANOR
D.H. LAWRENCE BIRTHPLACE MUS
Eastwood
Bestwood Village
Shottlegate
DE BRADELEI
Cowers Lane
Belper
Kilburn
Horsley Woodhouse
Marlpool
Watnall
A60
Hazelwood
Milford
Shipley
A610
Nuthall
Bulwell
Bestwood
Holbrook
Horsley
Smalley
SHIPLEY
Kimberley
Awsworth
Old Basford
Cotmanhay
Swingate
Weston Underwood
Duffield
Coxbench
Mapperley
EREWASH MUSEUM
Cossall
Nottingham
Bilborough
Mapperley Park
Kedleston
Flaxholme
Little Eaton
Stanley Common
West Hallam
ILKESTON
Strelley
CASTLE MUSEUM & GALLERY
THE TALES OF ROBIN HOOD
Quarndon
Morley
TROWELL SERVICES
City
KEDLESTON HALL
113
Allestree
Breadsall
Stanley
Kirk Hallam
Trowell
Wollaton
WOLLATON HALL
Lenton
Nott
A61
A6
Dale Abbey
Stanton-by-Dale
A52
Mackworth
Chaddesden
Bramcote
CATH
Ngley Common
Derby
Sandiacre
Stapleford
BEESTON
WEST BRIDG
Spondon
Ockbrook
Risley
Wilford
CITY MUS & ART GALL
Chilwell
Edwalt
Attenborough
City
Borrowash
Breaston
Toton
Clifton
Littleover
Normanton
A5111
Osmaston
ELVASTON CASTLE
Elvaston
Draycott
A6005
LONG EATON
Barton in Fabis
FRAMEWORK KNITTERS MUS
Ruddington
Alvaston
Thulston
Thrumpton
A453
RUSHCLIFFE
A38
Allenton
Sawley
GREAT CENTRAL RLY (NOTT'M)
Bradmore
Findern
Chellaston
Shardlow
Cavendish Bridge
Gotham
A514
A50
Stenson
Aston-on-Trent
Ratcliffe on Soar
Bunny
A5132
DERBY SOUTH (SHARDLOW) SERVICES
Twyford
Willington
Barrow upon Trent
Swarkestone
Canal
Weston-on-Trent
Hemington
Lockington
New Kingston
Castle Donington
Kingston on Soar
West Leake
East Leake
Repton
Ingleby
Stanton by Bridge
King's Newton
DONINGTON PARK
Kegworth
Milton
GRAND PRIX RACING CARS
EAST MIDLANDS
MANOR FARM
Costock
Melbourne
MELBOURNE HALL
Isley Walton
DONINGTON PARK SERVICES
Sutton Bonington
Wilson
Diseworth
Long Whatton
Rempsto
Bretby
Ticknall
A6006
Foremark Res.
CALKE Res.
B587
Tonge
A42
Normanton on Soar
Soar
Breedon on the Hill
Hathern
Hoton
CALKE ABBEY
Calke
Hartshorne
B5324
THE OLD RECTORY MUSEUM
Stanford on Soar
Lower Midway
Belton
Worthington
Cotes
B5006
FERRERS CENTRE FOR ARTS & CRAFTS
CHARNWOOD MUSEUM
THE BELL FOUNDRY MUSEUM
Woodville
ARBORETUM
Smisby
Thorpe Acre
Loughborough
Lount
Shepshed
Osgathorpe
A512
Newbold
Shelthorpe
Barrow Soa
MUSEUM
Coleorton
Thringstone
Blackfordby
Woodthorpe
Norris Hill
Res.
Nanpantan
Ashby-de-la-Zouch
Swannington
CHARNWOOD LODGE
Quorndon
A511
Whitwick
Woodhouse
Moira
HEART OF THE NATIONAL FOREST
THE
COALVILLE
Charnwood Forest
BEACON HILL
Mountsorrel
SNIBSTON DISCOVERY PARK
Greenhill
Donisthorpe
Packington
BROOMBRIGGS FARM
Woodhouse Eaves
A444
Ravenstone
Oakthorpe
NATIONAL
Bardon
Swithland
Rothley
Copt Oak
Measham
Normanton le Heath
THE MANOR HOUSE
Hugglescote
L e i c e
A42
FOREST
Ellistown
Cropston
LEICESTER SERVICES
BRADGATE PARK & SWITHLAND WOOD
Thurcaston
Swepstone
Heather
Markfield
Appleby
Stanton under Bardon
Ibstock
97
98
BRADGATE HOUSE RUINS
Birstall
Newton Burgoland
Battram
Field Head
Newtown Linford
A50
A46
0 1 2 3 miles
0 1 2 3 4 5 km

Halloughton
Park Hill
Morton
Farndon
Balderton
Barnby in the Willows
Oxton
Fiskerton
Hawton
131
132
Fenton
Thurgarton
Bleasby
East Stoke
Thorpe
Claypole
Epperstone
A6097
Woodborough
Stubton
Gonalston
Elston
Trent
Syerston
Cotham
Dry Doddington
Lowdham
Hoveringham
A46
Flintham
A1
Long Bennington
Caythorpe
Kneeton
Sibthorpe
Lambley
Shelton
Hougham
Burton Joyce
Bulcote
Gunthorpe
Staunton in the Vale
Westborough
Screveton
Hawksworth
Marston
East Bridgford
Flawborough
Gedling
Foston
Thoroton
Kilvington
Car Colston
Shelford
Carlton
Newton
Alverton
Scarrington
Stoke Bardolph
Orston
Normanton
Radcliffe on Trent
Bingham
Boundary Mills
Grantham North Services
Colwick
Saxondale
Aslockton
Allington
B692
Whatton
Bottesford
Great Gonerby
Holme Pierrepont
Harlequin
Upper Saxondale
A52
116
Elton
Easthorpe
Sedgebrook
Cropwell Butler
Sutton
Muston
Bassingfield
Tithby
Vale of Belvoir
Muston Meadows
Granby
Barrowby
Nottingham
Barnstone
Redmile
Stenwith
Earlsfield
Cotgrave
Cropwell Bishop
Barkestone-le-Vale
Tollerton
Naturescape Wild Flower Farm
Langar
Woolsthorpe by Belvoir
Owthorpe
Normanton-on-the-Wolds
Plungar
Belvoir
Belvoir Castle
Colston Bassett
Denton
Harlaxton
A606
Harston
Kinoulton
Stathern
Knipton
Stroxton
Stanton-on-the-Wolds
Harby
A607
Hickling
Hose
Eaton
Branston
Hungerton
Eastwell
Croxton Kerrial
Wyville
Widmerpool
Long Clawson
Goadby Marwood
Upper Broughton
Stoke Rochford
Saltby
Willoughby-on-the-Wolds
Skillington
Waltham on the Wolds
Nether Broughton
Wycomb
Chadwell
Stonesby
Holwell
Scalford
Sproxton
Wymeswold
Old Dalby
Wartnaby
Ab Kettleby
Buckminster
Grimston
Coston
Melton
Twinlakes Park
Saxelbye
B676
Sewstern
A6006
Six Hills
Thorpe Arnold
Melton Mowbray
Freeby
Garthorpe
Gunby
Ragdale
Shoby
Melton Carnegie Mus
Saxby
South Witham
Wyfordby
Wymondham
Asfordby
Asfordby Hill
Brentingby
Cribbs Meadow
Seagrave
Frisby on the Wreake
Burton Lazars
Stapleford
Hoby
Edmondthorpe
Kirby Bellars
Thrussington
A607
Rotherby
Wreake
Teigh
Market Overton
Ratcliffe on the Wreake
Barrow
The Living Ironstone Mus
Great Dalby
Rearsby
Little Dalby
Whissendine
Ashwell
East Goscote
Gaddesby
Queniborough
Ashby Folville
Thorpe Satchville
Burrough Hill
Pickwell
Eye
Syston
Barsby
Cold Overton
A606
B668
Twyford
Langham
Burrough on the Hill
Somerby
Burley
Barkby
98
South Croxton
99
Barleythorpe
Thurmaston
B6047
Oakham
Beeby
Marefield
Knossington
National Space

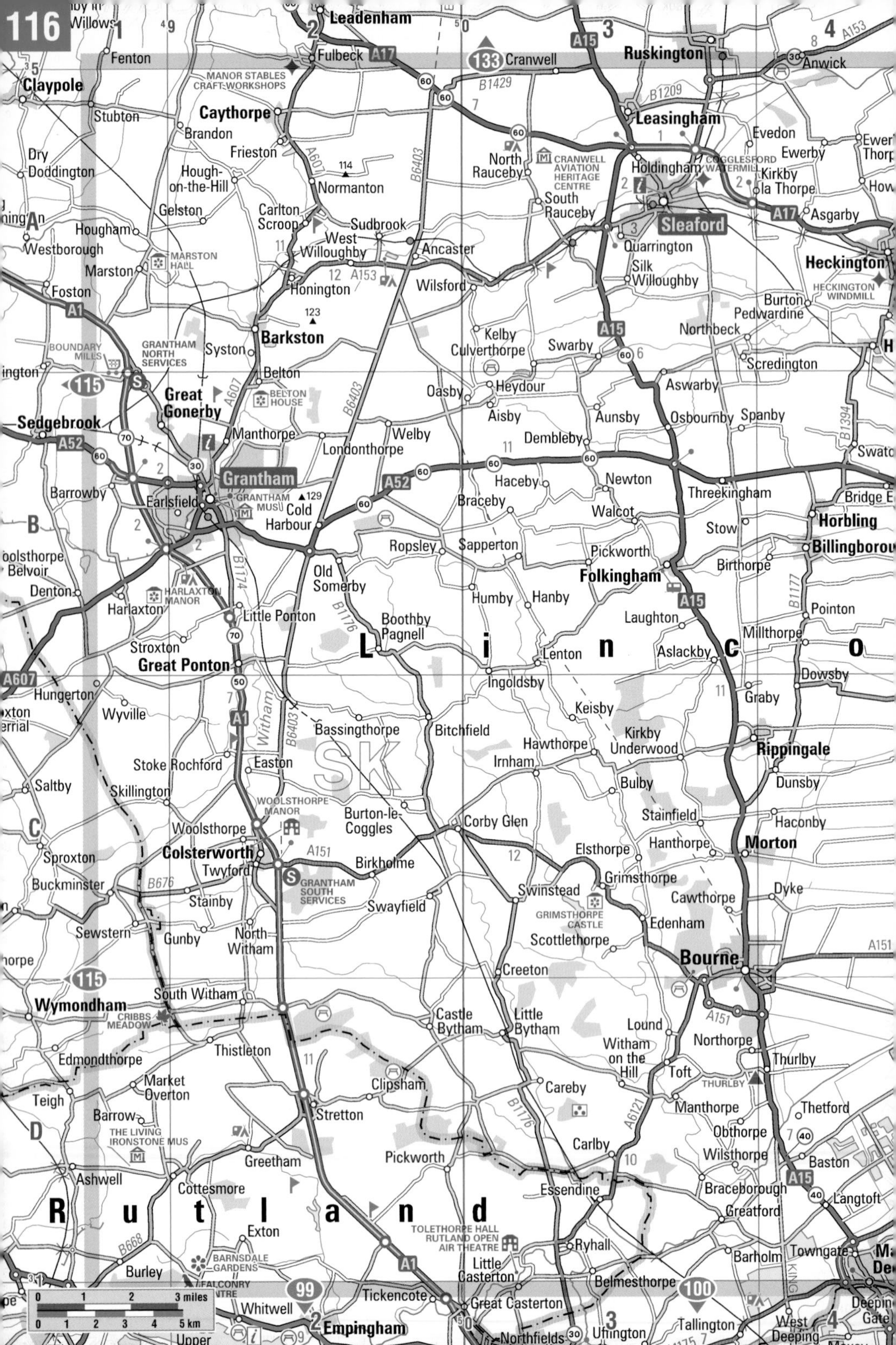
Leadenham
Fenton
Claypole
Fulbeck
A17
Cranwell
Ruskington
Anwick
MANOR STABLES
CRAFT WORKSHOPS
Caythorpe
Stubton
B1429
B1209
Leasingham
Brandon
Frieston
Evedon
Dry Doddington
Hough-on-the-Hill
A607
114
Normanton
B6403
North Rauceby
CRANWELL AVIATION HERITAGE CENTRE
Holdingham
COGGLESFORD WATERMILL
Ewerby
Kirkby la Thorpe
Gelston
Carlton Scroop
South Rauceby
Sleaford
Asgarby
Hougham
Sudbrook
West Willoughby
Ancaster
Quarrington
Westborough
MARSTON HALL
Marston
Honington
A153
Wilsford
Silk Willoughby
Heckington
HECKINGTON WINDMILL
Foston
A1
Burton Pedwardine
123
Barkston
Northbeck
A15
BOUNDARY MILLS
GRANTHAM NORTH SERVICES
Syston
Kelby
Culverthorpe
Swarby
Scredington
115
Belton
BELTON HOUSE
Oasby
Heydour
Aswarby
Great Gonerby
Aisby
Aunsby
Osbournby
Spanby
B1394
Sedgebrook
A52
Manthorpe
Welby
Londonthorpe
Dembleby
Grantham
Haceby
Newton
Threekingham
Barrowby
Earlsfield
GRANTHAM MUS
129
Cold Harbour
Braceby
Walcot
Horbling
Stow
Billingborough
Woolsthorpe by Belvoir
Ropsley
Sapperton
Pickworth
Folkingham
Birthorpe
Old Somerby
B1174
Denton
HARLAXTON MANOR
Harlaxton
Humby
Hanby
B1177
Pointon
Little Ponton
B1176
Boothby Pagnell
Laughton
Millthorpe
Stroxton
L i n c o
Lenton
Aslackby
Great Ponton
Ingoldsby
Dowsby
A607
Hungerton
Graby
Wyville
Keisby
Bassingthorpe
Bitchfield
Kirkby Underwood
Hawthorpe
Witham
Rippingale
Irnham
Stoke Rochford
Easton
SK
Saltby
Bulby
Dunsby
Skillington
WOOLSTHORPE MANOR
Burton-le-Coggles
Stainfield
Haconby
Woolsthorpe
Corby Glen
Hanthorpe
Morton
Sproxton
Colsterworth
A151
Birkholme
Elsthorpe
Twyford
Grimsthorpe
Buckminster
B676
GRANTHAM SOUTH SERVICES
Dyke
Stainby
Swinstead
Cawthorpe
GRIMSTHORPE CASTLE
Sewstern
Swayfield
Edenham
Gunby
North Witham
Scottlethorpe
Bourne
Creeton
Wymondham
South Witham
CRIBBS MEADOW
Castle Bytham
Little Bytham
Lound
Northorpe
Witham on the Hill
Thistleton
Edmondthorpe
Thurlby
Toft
THURLBY
Market Overton
Clipsham
Careby
Teigh
Thetford
Manthorpe
Barrow
Stretton
B1176
A6121
Obthorpe
THE LIVING IRONSTONE MUS
Carlby
Wilsthorpe
Baston
Pickworth
Greetham
Ashwell
Braceborough
Cottesmore
Essendine
Langtoft
Greatford
R u t l a n d
Exton
TOLETHORPE HALL
RUTLAND OPEN AIR THEATRE
Ryhall
Towngate
B668
BARNSDALE GARDENS
Barholm
Burley
FALCONRY CENTRE
Little Casterton
Belmesthorpe
KING
99
100
Tickencote
Great Casterton
Deeping Gate
Whitwell
Empingham
Northfields
Uffington
Tallington
West Deeping
Upper
0 1 2 3 miles
0 1 2 3 4 5 km

Sibsey
Frithville
Old Leake
Wrangle
Gipsey Bridge
BUBBLECAR MUSEUM
SIBSEY TRADER MILL
134
Fishtoft Drove
Holland Fen
Langrick
Anton's Gowt
Hill Dyke
Boston Long Hedges
Hurn's End
Leverton Outgate
Leverton Highgate
Leverton
Leverton Lucasgate
South Kyme Fen
Amber Hill
Frith Bank
Cowbridge
Benington
Brothertoft
HOLLAND FEN
Boston West
Boston
Haltoft End
East Heckington
Butterwick
GUILDHALL
Swineshead Bridge
Freiston
THE PEAROOM CENTRE
Hubbert's Bridge
Chain Bridge
Skirbeck
Skirbeck Quarter
Fishtoft
North End
Kirton Holme
Wyberton
Scrane End
Frampton West End
Fenhouses
Swineshead
Kirton End
Frampton
Drayton
Kirton
Sandholme
Bicker
Asperton
Skeldyke
Northorpe
Wigtoft
Seadyke
Donington
Sutterton
Bucklegate
Algarkirk
Church End
Donington South Ing
Bicker Haven
Fosdyke
TF
Quadring
Holbeach St Matthew
Westhorpe
Gosberton
Holbeach St Marks
Gosberton Clough
Dawsmere
Risegate
Surfleet Seas End
HOLBEACH MARSH
Gedney Marsh
Surfleet
Moulton Seas End
Saracen's Head
Holbeach Hurn
Crossgate
Holbeach Bank
Northgate
Halesgate
Holbeach Clough
Gedney Dyke
Pinchbeck
Lutton
Pinchbeck Bars
BAYTREE OWL CENTRE
Fleet Hargate
Chapelgate
Pinchbeck West
Weston
Holbeach
Little London
SPRINGFIELDS
Whaplode
Gedney
Spalding
Moulton
MOULTON MILL
Fleet
Long Sutton
SPRINGFIELDS SHOW GARDENS
Low Fulney
Gedney Broadgate
Pode Hole
Little London
Austendike
Clay Lake
AYSCOUGHFEE HALL
Weston Hills
Sutton Crosses
Twenty
Whaplode St Catherine
MUS OF ENTERTAINMENT
Tydd St Mary
Tongue End
Moulton Chapel
Holbeach St Johns
Sutton St James
Cowbit
Deeping Fen
Moulton Eaugate
Tydd St Giles
Deeping St Nicholas
Brotherhouse Bar
Tydd St Giles Fen
Hop Pole
Whaplode Drove
Sutton St Edmund
Fitton End
Shepeau Stow
Holbeach Drove
Gorefield
Gedney Hill
Leverington
Frognall
Dowsdale
Deeping St James
Crowland
CROWLAND ABBEY
Throckenholt
Church End
PECKOVER HOUSE
North Fen
Wisbech
Parson Drove
A16
A17
A52
A151
A1121
A1101
A1175
B1184
B1183
B1192
B1395
B1391
B1397
B1181
A152
B1356
B1180
B1357
B1359
B1168
B1165
B1390
B1166
B1167
B1169
B1525
100
101
118

Wrangle Lowgate
Friskney Flats
Wrangle
Hurn's End
Leverton Outgate
Leverton Highgate
Leverton Lucasgate
BOSTON DEEPS
LYNN DEEPS
THE WASH
NORFOLK
HOLME BIRD OBSERVATORY
Old Hunstanton
Hunstanton
SEA LIFE SANCTUARY
Heacham
Lynn Channel
SNETTISHAM NATURE RESERVE
Shepherd's Port
Holbeach St Matthew
Dawsmere
Gedney Marsh
Gedney Drove End
DERSINGHAM BOG
SANDRINGHAM
Wolferton
THE WASH
Gedney Dyke
Lutton
Guy's Head
Castle Rising
CASTLE RISING
North Wootton
Chapelgate
Terrington Marsh
Gedney
Little London
BUTTERFLY & WILDLIFE PARK
Ongar Hill
Long Sutton
South Wootton
King's Lynn
MARITIME EXHIBITION
ROYDON COMMON
Sutton Bridge
Orange Row
Clenchwarton
GUILDHALL
Gaywood
Sutton Crosses
Walpole Cross Keys
Terrington St Clement
West Lynn
Fairstead
Tydd St Mary
Hardwick
Leziate
Sutton St James
Tydd Gote
Walpole St Andrew
Hay Green
Tilney High End
Tilney All Saints
Fair Green
Tower End
Four Gotes
Walpole Marsh
Walpole St Peter
West Winch
Middleton
Tydd St Giles
Saddle Bow
North Runcton
St Giles Fen
Newton
Ingleborough
St John's Highway
Terrington St John
Tilney St Lawrence
Wiggenhall St Germans
Setchey
Blackborough End
Fitton End
West Walton
Walpole Highway
Wiggenhall St Mary the Virgin
Tottenhill Row
West Walton Highway
Marshland
Gorefield
Leverington
St John's Fen End
Wiggenhall St Mary Magdalen
Watlington
Tottenhill
Wormegay
FENLAND & WEST NORFOLK AVIATION MUSEUM
Walsoken
PECKOVER HOUSE
New Walsoken
Marshland St James
Marshland Fen
Runcton Holme
South Runcton
Shouldham
FENLAND MUS.
0 1 2 3 miles
0 1 2 3 4 5 km

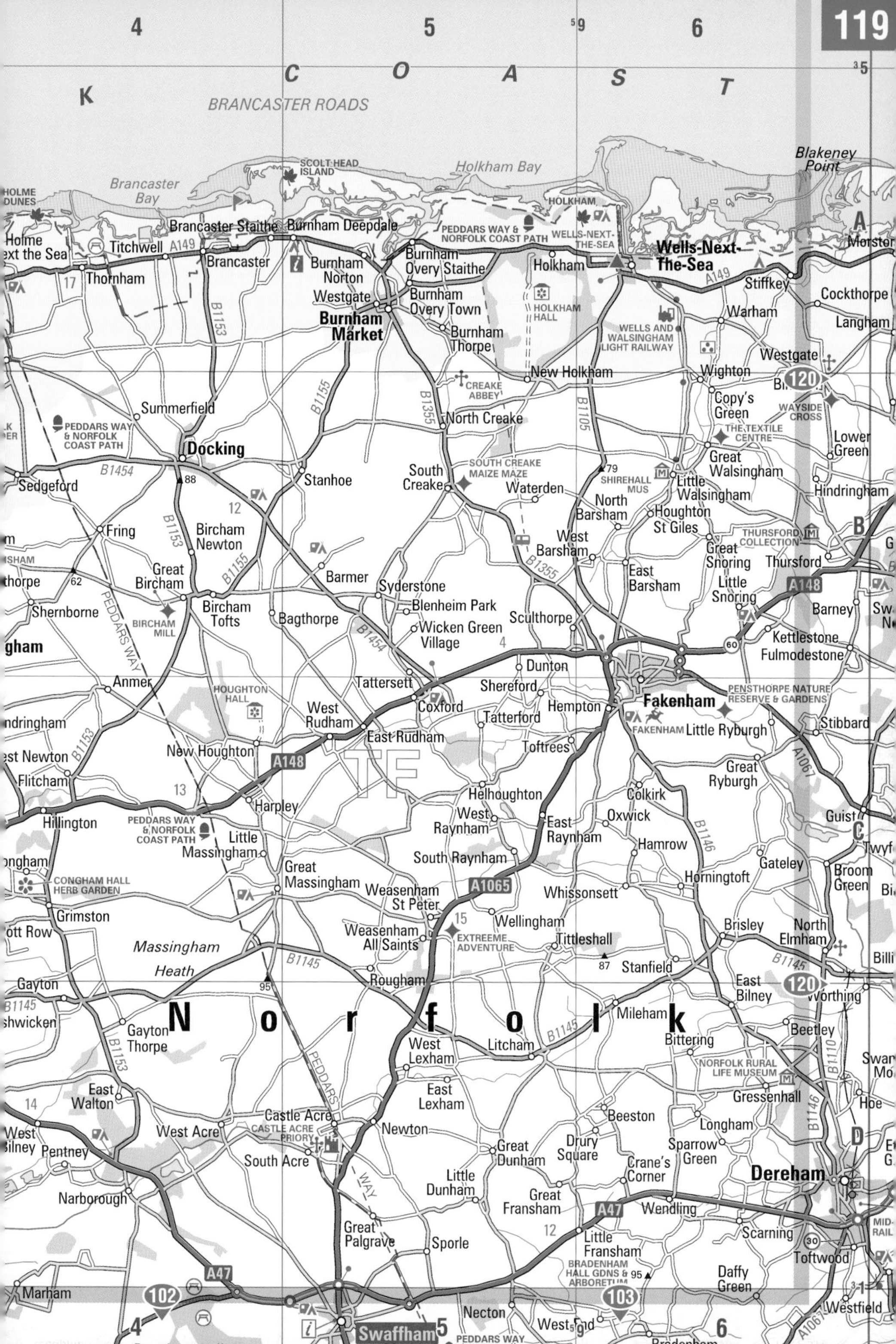
4
5
6
C O A S T
K
BRANCASTER ROADS
Holkham Bay
Blakeney Point
SCOLT HEAD ISLAND
Brancaster Bay
HOLME DUNES
HOLKHAM
Brancaster Staithe
Burnham Deepdale
PEDDARS WAY & NORFOLK COAST PATH
WELLS-NEXT-THE-SEA
Holme next the Sea
Titchwell
A149
Brancaster
Burnham Norton
Burnham Overy Staithe
Holkham
Wells-Next-The-Sea
Morston
Thornham
Westgate
Burnham Overy Town
HOLKHAM HALL
Stiffkey
Cockthorpe
Burnham Market
Burnham Thorpe
WELLS AND WALSINGHAM LIGHT RAILWAY
Warham
Langham
B1153
B1155
New Holkham
Westgate
Wighton
120
CREAKE ABBEY
Summerfield
B1355
North Creake
B1105
Copy's Green
WAYSIDE CROSS
PEDDARS WAY & NORFOLK COAST PATH
THE TEXTILE CENTRE
Lower Green
Docking
B1454
SOUTH CREAKE MAIZE MAZE
Great Walsingham
Sedgeford
88
Stanhoe
South Creake
SHIREHALL MUS
Little Walsingham
Hindringham
Waterden
North Barsham
Houghton St Giles
12
Fring
Bircham Newton
West Barsham
THURSFORD COLLECTION
Great Snoring
Thursford
Great Bircham
Barmer
B1355
East Barsham
Little Snoring
A148
62
Syderstone
Shernborne
Bircham Tofts
Blenheim Park
Barney
BIRCHAM MILL
Bagthorpe
Sculthorpe
Wicken Green Village
Kettlestone
PEDDARS WAY
4
Fulmodestone
60
Dunton
Anmer
Tattersett
Shereford
Fakenham
PENSTHORPE NATURE RESERVE & GARDENS
HOUGHTON HALL
Coxford
Hempton
West Rudham
Tatterford
FAKENHAM
Little Ryburgh
Stibbard
East Rudham
Toftrees
New Houghton
A148
Great Ryburgh
Flitcham
TF
13
Helhoughton
A1067
Colkirk
Hillington
Harpley
West Raynham
Guist
PEDDARS WAY & NORFOLK COAST PATH
Oxwick
Little Massingham
East Raynham
Hamrow
B1146
South Raynham
Gateley
CONGHAM HALL HERB GARDEN
Great Massingham
Horningtoft
Broom Green
A1065
Weasenham St Peter
Whissonsett
Grimston
15
Wellingham
Brisley
North Elmham
Weasenham All Saints
Tittleshall
EXTREEME ADVENTURE
Massingham Heath
B1145
87
Stanfield
B1145
Gayton
95
Rougham
East Bilney
120
Worthing
Mileham
N o r f o l k
Gayton Thorpe
Beetley
B11153
Bittering
West Lexham
Litcham
B1145
NORFOLK RURAL LIFE MUSEUM
B1110
PEDDARS
East Lexham
East Walton
Gressenhall
14
Hoe
B1146
Castle Acre
Beeston
CASTLE ACRE PRIORY
Newton
Longham
West Acre
West Bilney
Pentney
Drury Square
Great Dunham
Sparrow Green
South Acre
WAY
Crane's Corner
Dereham
Little Dunham
Narborough
Great Fransham
A47
Wendling
12
Great Palgrave
Scarning
Sporle
Little Fransham
30
Toftwood
A47
BRADENHAM HALL GDNS & ARBORETUM
95
Daffy Green
Marham
102
103
Westfield
Necton
4
Swaffham
5
West End
6
PEDDARS WAY
Bradenham
A1067

120
1
2
3
4
A
B
C
D
Blakeney Point
BLAKENEY
GUILDHALL
CLEY MILL
Cley next the Sea
PEDDARS WAY AND NORFOLK COAST PATH
Salthouse
MUCKLEBURGH COLLECTION
NORTH NORFOLK RAILWAY (THE POPPY LINE)
Sheringham
PRIORY MAZE & GARDENS
NORFOLK SHIRE HORSE CENTRE
Cromer
Morston
Stiffkey
Blakeney
Wiveton
Newgate
Kelling
Weybourne
SHERINGHAM PARK
SHERINGHAM
Beeston Regis
West Runton
East Runton
Cockthorpe
Warham
Langham
Glandford
N O R F O L K
Upper Sheringham
High Kelling
Bodham
A148
East Beckham
Aylmerton
Felbrigg
A149
Westgate
Wighton
119
Binham
Saxlingham
Letheringsett
Holt
Copy's Green
WAYSIDE CROSS
Field Dalling
PICTURECRAFT GALLERY
West Beckham
Gresham
FELBRIGG HALL
Crossdale Street
THE TEXTILE CENTRE
Lower Green
LETHERINGSETT WATERMILL
HOLT
BACONSTHORPE CASTLE
Great Walsingham
Bale
Sharrington
Hempstead
Baconsthorpe
Sustead
Roughton
Hindringham
Thornage
Bessingham
Hanworth
Brinton
Hunworth
Thurgarton
A140
THURSFORD COLLECTION
Stody
Edgefield
Plumstead
Matlaske
Alby Hill
Great Snoring
Gunthorpe
Aldborough
Thursford
Briningham
B1354
ALBY CRAFTS
ALBY GARDENS
Little Snoring
Edgefield Street
Little Barningham
Wickmere
Erpingham
Barney
Swanton Novers
Melton Constable
Briston
MANNINGTON GARDENS
Calthorpe
WOLTERTON PARK
Colby
STRAW MUSEUM
Kettlestone
Fulmodestone
Itteringham
Corpusty
Saxthorpe
PENSTHORPE NATURE RESERVE & GARDENS
BLICKLING HALL
Ingworth
Banningham
Thurning
Hindolveston
Blickling
Oulton
Stibbard
Wood Norton
Norton Corner
Silvergate
Dunkirk
Great Ryburgh
Guestwick
Heydon
Oulton Street
Aylsham
Guestwick Green
Wood Dalling
Burgh next Aylsham
Guist
N o r f o l
Salle
Southgate
Fengate
Twyford
Foulsham
Themelthorpe
B1145
Marsham
Gateley
Broom Green
Cawston
Little London
Bintree
FOXLEY WOOD
Reepham
Booton
Eastgate
The Heath
Buxton
Foxley
Whitwell Street
Brandiston
Brisley
North Elmham
Billingford
Bawdeswell
Haveringland
Hevingham
Stratton Strawless
East Bilney
Worthing
Sparham
ANIMAL ARK
Swannington
Waterloo
Alderford
Upgate
New Hainford
Beetley
Mill Street
Lenwade
Wensum
NORFOLK RURAL LIFE MUSEUM
Swanton Morley
Lyng
DINOSAUR ADVENTURE PARK
Felthorpe
Elsing
Morton
Attlebridge
Horsford
Newton St Faith
Gressenhall
Hoe
Woodgate
Primrose Green
Weston Longville
Thorpe Marriot
A1067
Etling Green
Weston Green
Ringland
Horsham St Faith
North Tuddenham
Taverham
Drayton
NORWICH INTERNATIONAL
Dereham
A47
Hockering
Hellesdon
Tud
MID-NORFOLK RAILWAY
Mattishall Burgh
Honingham
Costessey
Scarning
Mile Cross
Toftwood
Clint Green
Mattishall
East Tuddenham
Easton
New Costessey
Upper Hellesdon
Daffy Green
Yaxham
A1074
P&R
THE FORUM
Welborne
104
Marlingford
Bowthorpe
Earlham
Yare
Bawburgh
SAINSBURY CENTRE FOR VISUAL ARTS
Brandon Parva
0 1 2 3 miles
0 1 2 3 4 5 km

4
5
6
7
A
B
C
D
TG
Sidestrand
Trimingham
Southrepps
Gimingham
Mundesley
STOW WINDMILL
Lower Street
Trunch
Paston
Knapton
Bacton
Bradfield
Broomholm
Keswick
Walcott
Swafield
Edingthorpe
Edingthorpe Green
Witton Bridge
Happisburgh
Walsham
Spa Common
Ridlington
Crostwight
Whimpwell Green
Eccles on Sea
Happisburgh Common
EAST RUSTON OLD VICARAGE GARDEN
Lessingham
Hempstead
Honing
Sea Palling
Westwick
Bengate
East Ruston
Ingham Corner
WAXHAM GREAT BARN
Waxham
Worstead
Ingham
Dilham
Stalham
Stalham Green
Sloley
Smallburgh
NORFOLK
COAST
Hickling
MUSEUM OF THE BROADS
Sutton
Hickling Green
Scottow
Pennygate
Barton Turf
Hickling Heath
Horsey
Little Hautbois
Tunstead
Wood Street
HORSEY WINDMILL
WINTERTON DUNES
Sco Ruston
ANT BROADS AND MARSHES
Neatishead
Barton Broad
Catfield
Hickling Broad
HICKLING BROAD
WROXHAM BARNS
MARTHAM BROAD
East Somerton
Ashmanhaugh
Irstead
Coltishall
Sharp Street
Potter Heigham
West Somerton
Winterton-on-Sea
Threehammer Common
Hoveton
THE
Thurne
Martham
Belaugh
Lower Street
Bastwick
Wroxham
Ludham
Upper Street
Horning
LUDHAM MARSHES
Hemsby
Newport
HILLSIDE ANIMAL SANCTUARY
Upper Street
Repps
Rollesby
Wroxham Broad
Thurne
BURE MARSHES
Crostwick
Woodbastwick
BROADS
Ormesby St Michael
Scratby
California
Ranworth
Salhouse
Clippesby
Filby Broad
Ormesby St Margaret
FAIRHAVEN WOODLAND & WATER GARDEN
Panxworth
South Walsham
Billockby
Burgh St Margaret
CAISTER ROMAN TOWN
New Rackheath
Filby
Mautby
Caister-on-Sea
Little Plumstead
Upton
THE CANDLEMAKER WORKSHOP
Thrigby
THRIGBY HALL WILDLIFE GARDENS
West Caister
Sprowston
Hemblington
Runham
Thorpe End
Blofield Heath
North Burlingham
Stokesby
West End
Acle
GREAT YARMOUTH GREAT DENES
YARMOUTH
Thorpe St Andrew
Great Plumstead
Bure
Damgate
Blofield
Lingwood
NORWICH
Brundall
Beighton
Tunstall
Runham
Great Yarmouth
A149
B1145
B1159
B1150
A1151
B1354
A1062
B1152
B1140
A1064
A47
105

1
2
3
A
B
C
D
The Skerries
Ynysoedd y Moelrhoniaid
Carmel Head
Pen Carmel
Wilfa Head
Pen Wilfa
Cemaes Bay
Bae Cemaes
Cemlyn Bay
Bae Cemlyn
WYLFA POWER STATION AND OBSERVATION TOWER
Llanbadrig
Cemaes
Tregele
Llanfechell
Llanfairynghornwy
Isle of Anglesey (Sir Ynys Môn)
Llanfflewyn
Church Bay
Porth Swtan
Rhydwyn
Llanrhyddlad
A5025
Llanbabo
Llanfaethlu
DUBLIN 2:00
DUN LAOGHAIRE 2:00
(Apr-Sept)
DUBLIN 3:15
HOLYHEAD BAY
BAE CAERGYBI
LLYNON WINDMILL
Llanddeusant
Elim
Llanfwrog
North Stack
BREAKWATER
HOLYHEAD MOUNTAIN 220
Llaingoch
Holyhead
(Caergybi)
Llantrisant
Llanfachraeth
Carmel
South Stack
Goferydd
ELLINS TOWER RSPB RESERVE
PENRHOS FEILW STANDING STONES
Kingsland
A5
Newlands Park
Pen-llyn
Res.
Llanynghenedl
Penrhosfeilw
ANGLESEY
Bodedern
Trefor
Penrhyn Mawr
Valley
A55
Trearddur
Glan-traeth
B4545
Four Mile Bridge
Caergeiliog
Bryngwran
Llanfihangel yn Nhowyn
Gwalchmai
Holy Island
Ynys Gybi
Llanfairyneubwll
Rhoscolyn
Capel-gwyn
A4080
Ddrydwy
Cymyran Bay
Bae Cymyran
Llanfaelog
Pencarnisiog
Rhosneigr
Bryn Du
WALES COAST PATH
Bethel
Llangwyfan-isaf
Llangadwaladr
Aberffraw
Hermon
Bodorgan
NEWBOROUGH WARREN AND YNYS LLANDDWYN
Malltraeth Bay
Bae Malltraeth
Llanddwyn I.
Ynys Llanddwyn
ANGLESEY SEA ZONE
106
0 1 2 3 miles
0 1 2 3 4 5 km

Amlwch
Amlwch Port
Bull Bay Porth Llechog
Point Lynas Trwyn Eilian
Llaneilian
Pengorffwysfa
Penysarn
Nebo
Dulas
Dulas Bay Bae Dulas
Rhosybol
Tyn-y-pwll
City Dulas
Brynrefail
Moelfre
Ty-mawr
Llandyfrydog
Llanallgo
Mynydd Bodafon
Hebron
Marianglas
Bachau
Maenaddwyn
Tynygongl
Brynteg
Capel Coch
Benllech
Red Wharf Bay Traeth-coch
Red Wharf Bay
Mariandyrys
Caim
Penmon
Glan-yr-afon
Puffin Island Ynys Seiriol
Llanbedrgoch
Tregaian
Tan-y-graig
Llanddona
Llangoed
Llangwyllog
Llanddyfnan
Pentraeth
Glan Gors
Rhosmeirch
Llanfaes
Pen-y-garnedd
Talwrn
Rhoscefnhir
Llansadwrn
Beaumaris
Bodffordd
Heneglwys
Llangefni
Ceint
Penmynydd
Llandegfan
Lavan Sands Traeth Lafan
Menai Bridge (Porthaethwy)
Garth
Hirael
Bangor
Llangristiolus
Capel Mawr
Pentre Berw
Gaerwen
Llanfairpwll-gwyngyll
Coed Mawr
Llandegai
Tal-y-bont
Crymlyn
Abergwyngregyn
Aber Falls Rhaeadr Aber
Llanddaniel Fab
Glan Adda
Minffordd
Malltraeth
Llangaffo
Capel-y-graig
Glasinfryn
Llanllechid
Rachub
Brynsiencyn
Pentir
Tregarth
Bethesda
Seion
Y Felinheli
Sling
Gerlan
Dwyran
Saron
Llanddeiniolen
Braichmelyn
Rhiwlas
Bethel
Penisarwaun
Ty'n-y-maes
Waterloo Port
Llanrug
Deiniolen
Pont-rug
Clwt-y-bont
Marchlyn Mawr Res.
Caernarfon
Cwm-y-glo
Brynrefail
Llyn Padarn
Dinorwic
Caeathro
Ceunant
Abermenai Pt. Trwyn Abermenai
Llanfaglan
Llanberis
Pont Pen-y-benglog
Pont Rhyd-goch
Croesywaun
Groeslon
Llyn Peris
Llyn Ogwen
Saron
Bontnewydd
Waun
Glan-rhyd
Nant Peris
Morfa Dinlle
Rhostryfan
Capel
Penmaenm
Llanfairfe
Nant-y-p
SNOWDONIA NATIONAL PARK
PARC CENEDLAETHOL ERYRI
942 FOEL FRAS
1064 CARNEDD LLYWELYN
1044 CARNEDD DAFYDD
CORS ERDDREINIOG
CORS GOCH
THE STONE SCIENCE
CORS BODEILIO
ORIEL YNYS MON
GAOL AND COURTHOUSE
JAMES PRINGLE WEAVERS
PILI PALAS
HENBLAS COUNTRY PARK
TEGFRYN
PENRHYN
BANGOR
COEDYDD ABER
COCHWILLAN OLD HALL
BANGOR SERVICES
PLAS NEWYDD
PLAS COCH GARDEN ZOO
GREENWOOD CENTRE
SEA ZOO
BRYN BRAS CASTLE
MODEL VILLAGE
BIRD WORLD
FOEL FARM PARK
SEIONT II MARITIME MUSEUM
CASTLE & REGIMENTAL MUS
SEGONTIUM FORT
POWER OF WALES
WELSH HIGHLAND RAILWAY
INIGO JONES TUDOR SLATEWORKS
LLANBERIS LAKE RAILWAY
PADARN
SLATE MUS
IDWAL COTTAGE
CWM IDWAL
CAERNARFON AIR MUSEUM
DOLBADARN
MENAI STRAIT AFON MENAI
Afon Cefni
YNYS MÔN (Isle of Anglesey)
SH
A55
A5
A5025
A5114
A487
A4080
A4244
A545
A4086
B5111
B5110
B5108
B5109
B5420
B4419
B4421
B4366
B4409
124
107

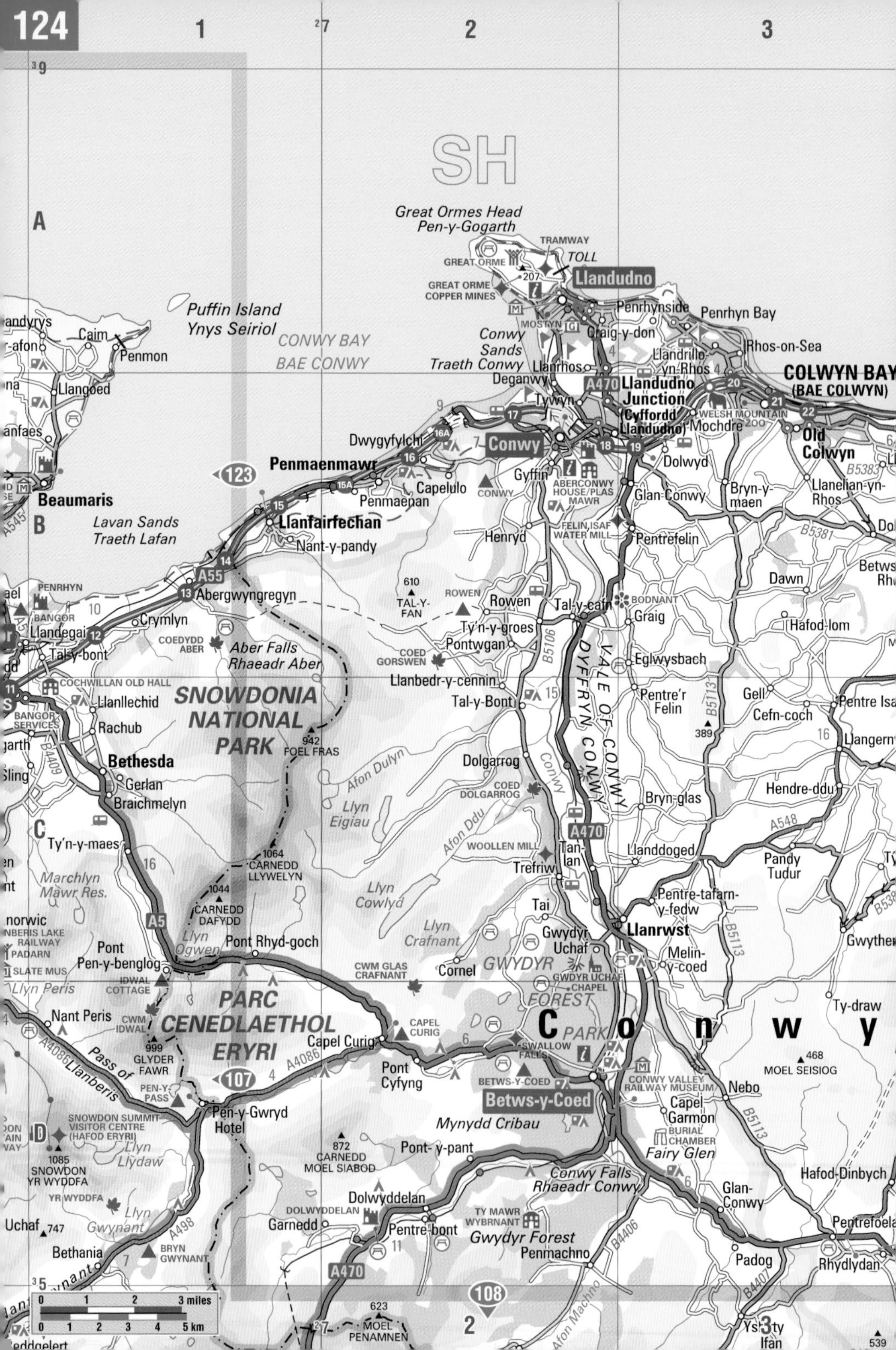

SH
Great Ormes Head
Pen-y-Gogarth
TRAMWAY
TOLL
GREAT ORME
GREAT ORME COPPER MINES
Llandudno
Penrhynside
Penrhyn Bay
Rhos-on-Sea
MOSTYN
Craig-y-don
Llandrillo-yn-Rhos
Conwy Sands
Traeth Conwy
Llanrhos
Deganwy
Tywyn
Llandudno Junction
(Cyffordd Llandudno)
COLWYN BAY
(BAE COLWYN)
WELSH MOUNTAIN ZOO
Mochdre
Old Colwyn
Puffin Island
Ynys Seiriol
CONWY BAY
BAE CONWY
Caim
Penmon
Llangoed
Beaumaris
Lavan Sands
Traeth Lafan
Dwygyfylchi
Penmaenmawr
Conwy
Capelulo
Penmaenan
Llanfairfechan
Nant-y-pandy
Gyffin
ABERCONWY HOUSE/PLAS MAWR
Dolwyd
Glan-Conwy
Bryn-y-maen
Llanelian-yn-Rhos
B5383
FELIN ISAF WATER MILL
Henryd
Pentrefelin
B5381
Dawn
A55
PENRHYN
BANGOR
Abergwyngregyn
Crymlyn
Llandegai
Tal-y-bont
610
TAL-Y-FAN
ROWEN
Rowen
Tal-y-cafn
BODNANT
Graig
Hafod-lom
COEDYDD ABER
Aber Falls
Rhaeadr Aber
COED GORSWEN
Ty'n-y-groes
Pontwgan
Eglwysbach
B5106
VALE OF CONWY
DYFFRYN CONWY
COCHWILLAN OLD HALL
Llanllechid
SNOWDONIA NATIONAL PARK
Llanbedr-y-cennin
Tal-y-Bont
Pentre'r Felin
B5113
Gell
Pentre Isa
BANGOR SERVICES
Rachub
942
FOEL FRAS
Cefn-coch
389
Llangern
B4409
Bethesda
Gerlan
Braichmelyn
Afon Dulyn
Dolgarrog
COED DOLGARROG
Conwy
Bryn-glas
Hendre-ddu
Llyn Eigiau
Afon Ddu
A470
A548
Ty'n-y-maes
1064
CARNEDD LLYWELYN
WOOLLEN MILL
Tan-lan
Llanddoged
Pandy Tudur
Marchlyn Mawr Res.
1044
CARNEDD DAFYDD
Llyn Cowlyd
Trefriw
Pentre-tafarn-y-fedw
A5
Tai
Llyn Crafnant
Gwydyr Uchaf
Llanrwst
B5113
Melin-y-coed
Gwyther
LLANBERIS LAKE RAILWAY
PADARN
SLATE MUS
Llyn Ogwen
Pont Rhyd-goch
Pont Pen-y-benglog
IDWAL COTTAGE
CWM GLAS CRAFNANT
Cornel
GWYDYR
GWYDYR UCHAF CHAPEL
FOREST PARK
Llyn Peris
Nant Peris
CWM IDWAL
PARC CENEDLAETHOL ERYRI
CAPEL CURIG
Capel Curig
Conwy
Ty-draw
468
MOEL SEISIOG
A4086
Pass of Llanberis
999
GLYDER FAWR
SWALLOW FALLS
Pont Cyfyng
BETWS-Y-COED
Betws-y-Coed
CONWY VALLEY RAILWAY MUSEUM
Nebo
PEN-Y-PASS
Pen-y-Gwryd Hotel
Capel Garmon
B5113
SNOWDON SUMMIT VISITOR CENTRE (HAFOD ERYRI)
1085
SNOWDON
YR WYDDFA
Llyn Llydaw
872
CARNEDD MOEL SIABOD
Mynydd Cribau
BURIAL CHAMBER
Fairy Glen
Pont-y-pant
Conwy Falls
Rhaeadr Conwy
Glan-Conwy
Hafod-Dinbych
YR WYDDFA
Llyn Gwynant
Dolwyddelan
DOLWYDDELAN
TY MAWR WYBRNANT
Uchaf
747
A498
Garnedd
Pentre-bont
Gwydyr Forest
Pentrefoelas
Bethania
BRYN GWYNANT
B4406
Penmachno
Padog
Rhydlydan
A470
B4407
623
MOEL PENAMNEN
Afon Machno
Ysbyty Ifan
539
0 1 2 3 miles
0 1 2 3 4 5 km

123
107
108

SJ
West Hoyle Bank
Hilbre I.
Hoylake Lifeboat Mus
West Kirby
Welsh Channel
Point of Ayr
Yr Parlwr Du
River Dee
Afon Dyfrdwy
Talacre
Gwespyr
Gronant
Ffynnongroyw
Picton
Mostyn Quay
Prestatyn
Gwaenysgor
Llanasa
Mostyn
Offa's Dyke Path
Llwybr Clawdd Offa
Seaquarium
Y-Ffrith
Rhyl
(Y Rhyl)
Meliden
Kinmel Bay
Axton
Trelogan
Glan-y-don
Abergele Roads
Angorfa Abergele
Towyn
Trelawnyd
Dyserth
Whitford
Pensarn
Rhuddlan
Greenfield
Carmel
Abergele
Cwm
Pant-y-Wacco
Gorsedd
Holywell
(Treffynnon)
Bodelwyddan
St George
Rhuallt
Pen-y-cefn
Brynford
Babell
Caerwys
Tremeirchion
St Asaph
(Llanelwy)
Glascoed
Groesffordd Marli
St Asaph Cathedral
Waen
Goleugoed
Moelfre Isaf
Afon-wen Craft and Antique Centre
Afon-wen
Ysceifiog
Pentre Halkyn
Halkyn Mountain
Lixwm
Rhes-y-cae
Vale of Clwyd
Dyffryn Clwyd
Graig
Plas-yn-Cefn
Trefnant
Bodfari
Llanfair Talhaiarn
Llannefydd
Bont-newydd
Nannerch
Bryn-nantllech
Cefn Berain
Green
Castell
Rhosesmor
Hendre
Bryn Rhyd-yr-Arian
Henllan
Clwydian Range
Bryniau Clwyd
Denbigh
(Dinbych)
Fron
Castle & Town Walls
Llangwyfan
Waen
Llansannan
Llandyrnog
Cilcain
Moel Llys-y-Coed
Pantymwyn
Gwernaffield
Groes
Tan-y-fron
Llangynhafal
Moel Famau
Loggerheads
Clwt-grugoer
Llanrhaeadr
Llanynys
Gellifor
Tafarn-y-gelyn
Bylchau
Waen
Peniel
Prion
Pentre Llanrhaeadr
Nantglyn
Saron
Hirwaen
Rhewl
Bryn Trillyn
Gorsedd Bran
Meifod
Llanbedr-Dyffryn-Clwyd
Llanferres
Craft Centre
Llanfwrog
Ruthin
(Rhuthun)
Cyffylliog
Bontuchel
Mynydd Hiraethog
Tai-Ucha
Denbighshire
(Sir Ddinbych)
Brenig Res.
Nant Uchaf
Efenechtyd
Llanarmon-yn-Ial
Graianrhyd
Llanfair-Dyffryn-Clwyd
Nilig
Pennant
Pwll-glas
Alwen Reservoir
Hafod Elwy Moor
Llyn Brenig Visitor Centre
Clocaenog
Graig-fechan
Clocaenog Forest
Clawdd-newydd
Pentre-celyn
Llandegla
Pentre-llyn cymmer
Afon Alwen
Glasfryn
Cefn-brith
Derwen
Rhyd-y-meudwy
Llanfihangel Glyn Myfyr
Llanelidan
Bryn Saith Marchog
Melin-y-Wig
Cerrigydrudion

Wallasey
Everton
LIVERPOOL
Leasowe
Seacombe
Meols
Moreton
Poulton
Bidston
HOYLAKE
HOYLAKE LIFEBOAT MUS
Edge Hill
West Hoyle Bank
Hilbre I.
Claughton
Upton
Greasby
Grange
Birkenhead
ALBERT DOCK
Toxteth
Mossley Hill
Dingle
West Kirby
Woodchurch
Frankby
Tranmere
Rock Ferry
Welsh Channel
PORT SUNLIGHT MUS
Prenton
Aigburth
Point of Ayr
Yr Parlwr Du
ARROWE
Caldy
New Ferry
Grassendale
Talacre
River Dee
Afon Dyfrdwy
BEBINGTON
LADY LEVER ART GALLERY
Thurstaston
Irby
Thingwall
Storeton
Port Sunlight
Gwespyr
Pensby
Barnston
Brimstage
WIRRAL
Bromborough
Ffynnongroyw
Picton
Llanasa
Mostyn Quay
Mostyn
Heswall
Thornton Hough
Eastham Ferry
EASTHAM
Dawpool Bank
Axton
Trelogan
Gayton
Eastham
WALES COAST PATH
Glan-y-don
Raby
Whitford
Parkgate
Hinderton
Willaston
Hooton
Greenfield
GREENFIELD VALLEY HERITAGE PARK
Holywell Bank
Gayton Sands
Neston
Childer Thornton
RIVACRE
Carmel
Little Sutton
Pant-y-Wacco
Gorsedd
Walwen
Little Neston
Overpool
Holywell
(Treffynnon)
Ness
NESS GARDENS
Great Sutton
Ben-y-cefn
Bagillt
Brynford
Burton
Ledsham
Babell
Dolphin
Two Mills
Capenhurst
Backford Cross
Caerwys
Puddington
Pentre Halkyn
Flint (Y Fflint)
AFON-WEN CRAFT AND ANTIQUE CENTRE
Ysceifiog
Mount Pleasant
Shotwick
Afon-wen
Lixwm
Halkyn Mountain
Oakenholt
Halkyn
Connah's Quay
Saughall
Mollington
Rhes-y-cae
Flint Mountain
Nannerch
Garden City
Castell
OFFA'S DYKE PATH
LLWYBR CLAWDD OFFA
Rhosesmor
Northop
Northop Hall
Shotton
Sealand
Hendre
WEPRE
Queensferry
Blacon
Rhydymwyn
Flintshire
(Sir Y Fflint)
Ewloe Grn.
Mancot
Sandycroft
Chester
Llangwyfan
Soughton
New Brighton
GREENACRES
Waen
Cilcain
Ewloe
Hawarden
(Penarlâg)
MOEL LLYS-Y-COED
Pantymwyn
Buckley
(Bwcle)
Drury
HAWARDEN
Gwernaffield
Mold
(Yr Wyddgrug)
Saltney
Llangynhafal
MOEL FAMAU
LOGGERHEADS
Mynydd Isa
Spon Green
Broughton
Bretton
Llanynys
Gellifor
Cadole
Llong
Lower Kinnerton
Tafarn-y-gelyn
Gwernymynydd
Penyffordd
Balderton
Dodleston
Hirwaen
Maeshafn
Nercwys
Higher Kinnerton
Rhewl
Pontblyddyn
Llanferres
Llanbedr-Dyffryn-Clwyd
Leeswood
Coed-Talon
CRAFT CENTRE
Hope
(Yr Hôb)
Burton Green
Pulford
Llanfwrog
Ruthin
(Rhuthun)
WAUN-Y-LLYN
Lavister
Eryrys
Treuddyn
Rossett
Caergwrle
Llanarmon-yn-Ial
Llanfynydd
Cefn-y-bedd
Marford
Graianrhyd
Llay
Llanfair-Dyffryn-Clwyd
Rhydtalog
Ffrith
Graig-fechan
Gresford
Brymbo
ALYN WATERS
Moss
Gwersyllt
Four Crosses
Bwlchgwyn
Borras Head
Pentre-celyn
Rhosrobin
Llandegla
Garden Village
Gwynfryn
Minera
LEAD MINES
MOSS VALLEY
Acton
Llan-y-pwll
Pen-y-stryt
New Broughton
Rhosnesni
Rhyd-y-meudwy
OFFA'S DYKE PATH
Coedpoeth
BERSHAM HERITAGE CENTRE & IRONWORKS
Wrexham
(Wrecsam)
Llanelidan
CYRN Y BRAIN
ESCLUSHAM MOUNTAIN
Bersham
Rhostyllen
King's Mills
Wrexham Industrial Estate
0 1 2 3 miles
0 1 2 3 4 5 km

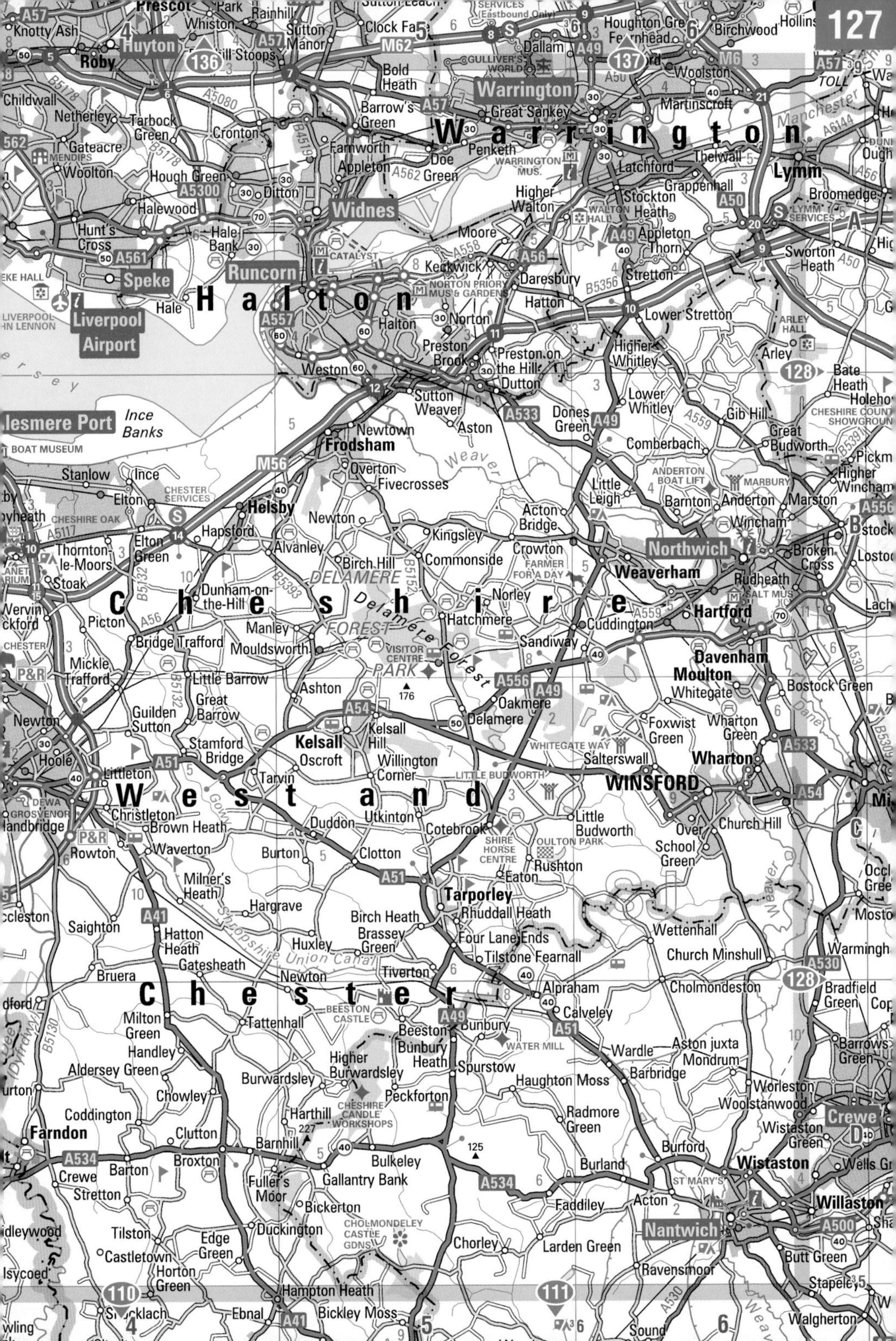
Prescot
Knotty Ash
Huyton
Roby
Whiston
Rainhill
Sutton Manor
Clock Face
Houghton Green
Fearnhead
Birchwood
Hollins
Dallam
GULLIVER'S WORLD
Bold Heath
Warrington
Woolston
Childwall
Netherley
Tarbock Green
Cronton
Barrow's Green
Great Sankey
Martinscroft
Gateacre
MENDIPS
Woolton
Farnworth
Doe Green
Penketh
Appleton
WARRINGTON MUS.
Thelwall
Lymm
Hough Green
Ditton
Latchford
Grappenhall
Broomedge
Halewood
Widnes
Higher Walton
Stockton Heath
LYMM SERVICES
Hunt's Cross
Hale Bank
Moore
WALTON HALL
Appleton Thorn
Swarton Heath
Speke
Runcorn
CATALYST
Keckwick
Daresbury
Stretton
NORTON PRIORY MUS & GARDENS
Hale
Halton
Hatton
Lower Stretton
Liverpool Airport
LIVERPOOL JOHN LENNON
Norton
ARLEY HALL
Preston Brook
Preston on the Hill
Higher Whitley
Arley
Weston
Dutton
Bate Heath
Sutton Weaver
Lower Whitley
Gib Hill
Ellesmere Port
Ince Banks
Aston
Dones Green
CHESHIRE COUNTY SHOWGROUND
BOAT MUSEUM
Newtown
Frodsham
Comberbach
Great Budworth
Weaver
Stanlow
Ince
Overton
Fivecrosses
ANDERTON BOAT LIFT
MARBURY
Higher Wincham
Elton
CHESTER SERVICES
Helsby
Little Leigh
Barnton
Anderton
Marston
CHESHIRE OAKS
Acton Bridge
Wincham
Newton
Hapsford
Kingsley
Elton Green
Thornton-le-Moors
Alvanley
Birch Hill
Commonside
Crowton
Northwich
Broken Cross
Stoak
DELAMERE
FARMER FOR A DAY
Weaverham
Rudheath
Dunham-on-the-Hill
Norley
SALT MUS.
Picton
Manley
Delamere Forest
Hatchmere
Cuddington
Hartford
Bridge Trafford
Mouldsworth
FOREST
Sandiway
CHESTER
VISITOR CENTRE
Davenham
Mickle Trafford
Little Barrow
PARK
Moulton
Ashton
Whitegate
Bostock Green
Great Barrow
Oakmere
Newton
Guilden Sutton
Kelsall
Delamere
Foxwist Green
Wharton Green
Kelsall Hill
Stamford Bridge
WHITEGATE WAY
Hoole
Oscroft
Willington Corner
Salterswall
Wharton
Littleton
Tarvin
LITTLE BUDWORTH
WINSFORD
DEWA
GROSVENOR
Christleton
Handbridge
Brown Heath
Duddon
Utkinton
Cotebrook
Little Budworth
Over
Church Hill
Rowton
Waverton
Burton
Clotton
SHIRE HORSE CENTRE
OULTON PARK
School Green
Rushton
Eaton
Milner's Heath
Tarporley
Rhuddall Heath
Eccleston
Hargrave
Birch Heath
Saighton
Hatton Heath
Brassey Green
Four Lane Ends
Wettenhall
Huxley
Gatesheath
Shropshire Union Canal
Tilstone Fearnall
Church Minshull
Bruera
Newton
Tiverton
Alpraham
Cholmondeston
Bradfield Green
Milton Green
BEESTON CASTLE
Calveley
Tattenhall
Beeston
Bunbury
Handley
Bunbury Heath
WATER MILL
Wardle
Aston juxta Mondrum
Barrows Green
Aldersey Green
Higher Burwardsley
Spurstow
Barbridge
Burwardsley
Haughton Moss
Worleston
Chowley
Peckforton
Woolstanwood
Coddington
Harthill
CHESHIRE CANDLE WORKSHOPS
Radmore Green
Crewe
Farndon
Clutton
Wistaston Green
Barnhill
Burford
Bulkeley
Burland
Wistaston
Barton
Broxton
Gallantry Bank
Crewe
Fuller's Moor
Stretton
Faddiley
Acton
ST MARY'S
Willaston
Bickerton
CHOLMONDELEY CASTLE GDNS
Nantwich
Tilston
Edge Green
Duckington
Chorley
Larden Green
Castletown
Horton Green
Ravensmoor
Butt Green
Hampton Heath
Stapeley
Stocklach
Ebnal
Bickley Moss
Sound
Walgherton
Halton
Cheshire
West and
Chester
M62
M56
M6
A57
A49
A56
A50
A533
A556
A54
A51
A41
A534
A530
A500
A5300
A561
A557
A559
136
137
128
110
111

Cadishead
Hollins Green
Partington
Ashton upon Mersey
SALE
Heaton Moor
Orford
Woolston
Warburton
Brooklands
Northenden
Martinscroft
Heatley
Mossbrow
Broadheath
Timperley
Dunham Town
Wythenshawe
GATLEY
Cheadle
Cheadle Heath
DUNHAM MASSEY
Oughtrington
Altrincham
Hale
Thelwall
Latchford
Lymm
Grappenhall
Bowdon
Little Bollington
Broomedge
Hale Barns
Bowgreen
Woodhouse Park
Cheadle Hulme
BRAMALL HALL
Stockton Heath
WALTON HALL
LYMM SERVICES
Heald Green
Appleton Thorn
MANCHESTER
Manchester Airport
Swinton Heath
High Legh
ROSTHERNE MERE
Rostherne
Ashley
Thorns Green
Styal
QUARRY BANK MILL
Handforth
Woodford
Stretton
Lower Stretton
Bucklow Hill
Hoo Green
New Mills
Morley Green
TATTON HOUSE
Mere
Dean Row
ARLEY HALL
Arley
Higher Whitley
WILMSLOW
Over Tabley
Davenport Green
Bate Heath
Lower Whitley
Holehouses
Mobberley
Knolls Green
Hough
Dones Green
Gib Hill
CHESHIRE COUNTY SHOWGROUND
Knutsford
Alderley Edge
Mottram St Andrew
Comberbach
Great Budworth
TABLEY
KNUTSFORD SERVICES
Over Knutsford
Prestbury
Pickmere
ANDERTON BOAT LIFT
MARBURY
Higher Wincham
Ollerton
Little Leigh
Barnton
Anderton
Marston
Plumley
Marthall
Nether Alderley
NETHER ALDERLEY MILL
Smithy Green
Wincham
Lostock Gralam
Over Peover
Chelford
Monks Heath
Northwich
Weaverham
Broken Cross
Lostock Green
Lower Peover
Henbury
Rudheath
SALT MUS
Swan Green
PEOVER HALL
Peover Heath
CAPESTHORNE HALL
Hartford
Lach Dennis
Cuddington
JODRELL BANK VISITOR CENTRE
Lower Pexhill
Blackden Heath
Withington Green
Davenham
Siddington
Warren
Moulton
Puddinglake
Goostrey
Gawsworth
GAWSWORTH HALL
Whitegate
Bostock Green
Lower Withington
Twemlow Green
Byley
Highlane
Foxwist Green
Wharton Green
Cranage
Marton
Gleadsmoss
Sproston Green
Holmes Chapel
Salterswall
Wharton
Swettenham
Rodeheath
WINSFORD
Sandlow Green
Newsbank
Middlewich
Hulme Walfield
Eaton
Little Budworth
Over
Church Hill
Brereton Green
Brereton Heath
BRERETON HEATH
School Green
Lower Heath
Buglawton
Occlestone Green
Bradwall Green
West Heath
Congleton
Arclid
Moston Green
Elworth
SANDBACH CROSSES
Wettenhall
Brownlow
ASTBURY MERE
Astbury
Hightown
Mossley
Warmingham
Church Minshull
Sandbach
Brookhouse Green
SANDBACH SERVICES
Brownlow Heath
Cholmondeston
Bradfield Green
Coppenhall Moss
Fourlanes End
Calveley
Wheelock
LITTLE MORETON HALL
Marsh Green
Hassall Green
Gillow Heath
Aston juxta Mondrum
Wheelock Heath
Wardle
Barrows Green
Maw Green
Thurlwood
Scholar Green
Mow Cop
MOW COP CASTLE
Barbridge
Hassall
Rode Heath
Winterley
Worleston
Church Lawton
Mount Pleasant
Woolstanwood
Haslington
Radmore Green
Crewe
Wistaston Green
Alsager
Kidsgrove
Burford
Newchapel
Radway Green
Burland
Wistaston
Wells Green
ST MARY'S
Talke
Goldenhill
Gresty Green
Acton
Willaston
Weston
FREEPORT TALKE
Faddiley
Shavington
Barthomley
Sandyford
Nantwich
Englesea-brook
Red Street
Tunstall
Bradeley
Butt Green
Hough
Ravensmoor
Gorsteyhill
Audley
Burslem
Stapeley
Balterley
Chesterton
Walgherton
Alsagers Bank
Bradwell
Halmer End
Wolstanton
ETRURIA
Ches
Ea
0 1 2 3 miles
0 1 2 3 4 5 km

PEAK DISTRICT
NATIONAL PARK
H I G H P E A K
D e r b y
S t a f f o r d
i r e
SK
138
139
130
112
113
Stockport
Bredbury
Romiley
Compstall
Chunal
FEATHERBED TOP
544
CHADKIRK COUNTRY ESTATE
Marple
Marple Bridge
Stepping Hill
Hawk Green
Mellor
Little Hayfield
Res.
Ashop
UPPER DERWENT VISITOR CENTRE
HAZEL GROVE
Thornsett
Strines
Birch Vale
Hayfield
KINDER SCOUT
636
590
THE MOORLAND CENTRE
Nether Booth
PENNINE WAY
THE PENNINE BRIDLEWAY
Edale
EDALE
Ladybower Res.
HERITAGE CENTRE
Low Leighton
Windlehurst
High Lane
Disley
New Mills
Newtown
Chinley Head
Barber Booth
MAM TOR
Noe
Aston
Poynton
Midway
LYME PARK
Furness Vale
BLACK HILL
408
451
CHESTNUT CENTRE OTTER, OWL & WILDLIFE PARK
BLUE JOHN CAVERN
517
TREAK CLIFF CAVERN
Hope
Thornhill
Wood Lanes
Bridgemont
Buxworth
Chinley
Chapel Milton
Malcoff
PEAK CAVERN
SPEEDWELL CAVERN
Castleton
Brough
PEVERIL CASTLE
Bradwell
Whaley Bridge
Whitehough
Slackhall
Perryfoot
Sparrowpit
Chapel-en-le-Frith
Horwich End
B5470
Lower Crossings
Kettleshume
Whiteley Green
Pott Shrigley
Taxal
Peak Forest
Coplow Dale
Great Hucklow
Abney
Bollington
Fernilee
Combs
Dove Holes
A623
Little Hucklow
Grindlow
Bollington Cross
Fernilee Res.
507
Peak Dale
Lane Head
Foolow
Eyam
Rainow
Upper End
Wheston
Tideswell
Litton
Burnt Bath
DERBYSHIRE DALES
Hurdsfield
Walker Barn
SHINING TOR
559
Res.
Hargatewell
Tunstead
Miller's Dale
Wardlow
Buxton
Fairfield
Wormhill
Cressbrook
Burbage
BUXTON MUS & ART GALLERY
RAVENSTOR
Little Longstone
PARADISE MILL
TEGG'S NOSE
GRIN LOW
POOLE'S CAVERN
Blackwell
Gurnett
Langley
Macclesfield Forest
Cowdale
King Sterndale
Ashford in the Water
Sutton Lane Ends
Canholes
Harpur Hill
Chelmorton
Taddington
SHUTLINGSLOE
506
Axe Edge
Oakgrove
Haddon
Wildboarclough
Brand Side
Sterndale Moor
Sheldon
Flash
Flagg
356
Allgreave
Earl Sterndale
B5055
Hollinsclough
Monyash
Over Haddon
Wincle
Danebridge
GRADBACH
Glutton Bridge
Crowdicote
Longnor
ARBOR LOW HENGE
Youlgrave
Dane
Fawfieldhead
Dove
Pilsbury
YOULGRAVE
Rushton Spencer
Newtown
Parsley Hay
Heaton
Middleton
Ryecroft Gate
385
Upper Hulme
489
380
Brund
Sheen
SHEEN
Newtown
Meerbrook
Hulme End
Hartington
THE PENNINE BRIDLEWAY
Rudyard Res.
Tittesworth Res.
HARTINGTON HALL
Heathcote
Newhaven
336
Upper Elkstone
Lower Elkstone
Biggin
Pikehall
Biddulph Moor
Rudyard
Poolend
Warslow
B5054
Ball Haye Green
Thorncliffe
BIGGIN DALE
BRINDLEY MILL AND MUS
Horton
Leek
382
Blackwood Hill
LADDEREDGE
Butterton
Wetton
Alstonefield
ALSTONEFIELD
Alsop en le Dale
Dunwood
Lowe Hill
Bradnop
Grindonmoor Gate
Hope
Endon Bank
Longsdon
Onecote
Milldale
Parwich
Ford
Dove Dale
Manifold
Horse Bridge
Grindon
Endon
Leekbrook
CHEDDLETON RAILWAY CENTRE
DEEP HAYES
FLINT MILL
Stanley
Bottom House
DOVEDALE
Tissington
Cheddleton
New Street
BLACKBROOK
Waterfall
Baddeley Green
Basford Green
CHURNET VALLEY RLY
ILAM HALL
Ilam
ILAM
Bagnall
Winkhill
Waterhouses
Thorpe
Fenny Bentley
Milton
Ipstones
Wetley Rocks
CONSALL HALL GDNS
Calton
Cauldon
Blore
Foxt
Abbey Hulton
Consall
KINGSLEY BIRD & FALCONRY
Swinscoe
Mapleton
A523
A53
A520
A54
A537
A515
A6
A5270
B5053
B6049
B6465
A5012
A6015
A624
A626
A57
A6013
A6187
A5004
A5009
A602

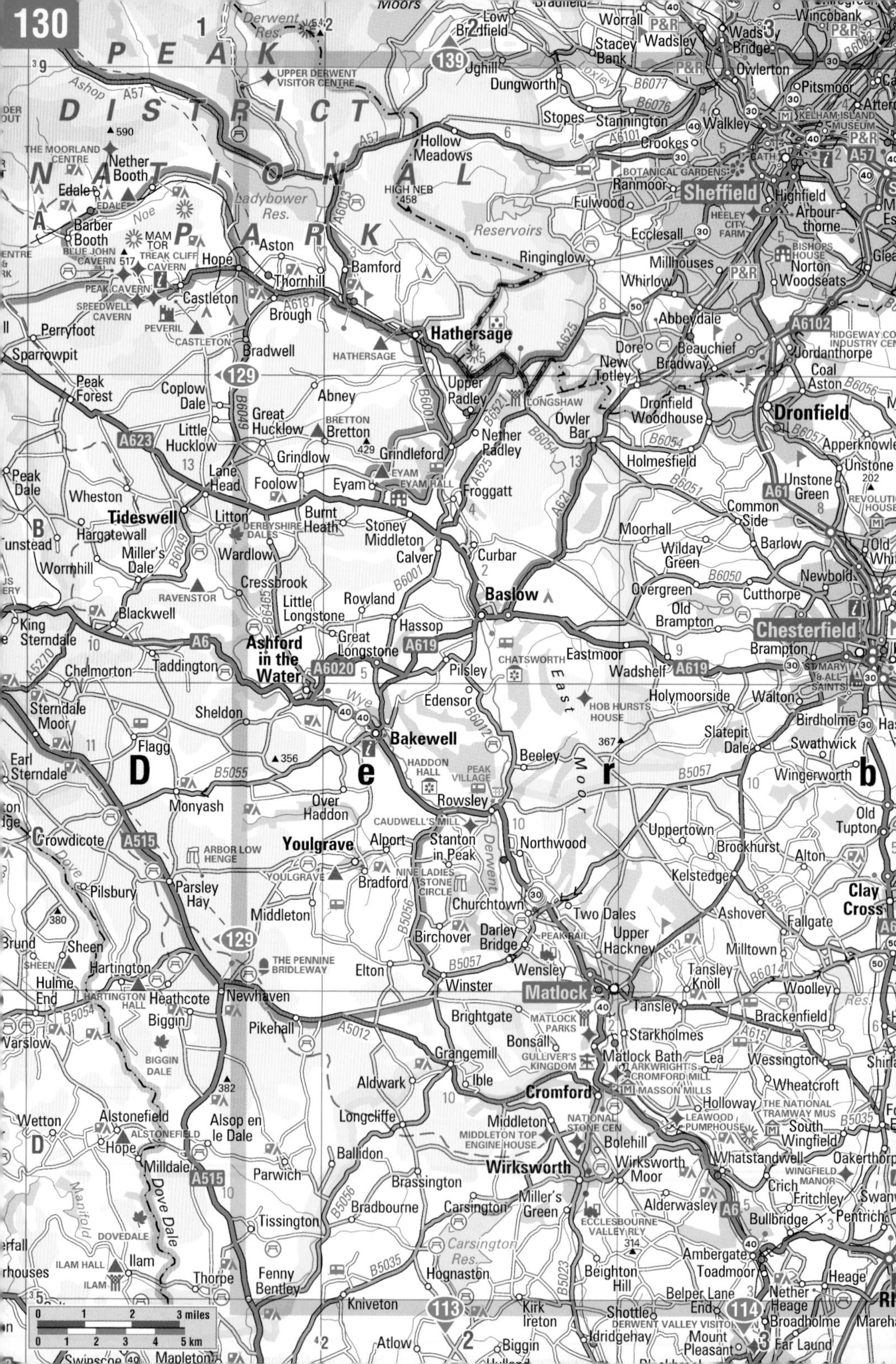
PEAK DISTRICT NATIONAL PARK
Derwent Res.
UPPER DERWENT VISITOR CENTRE
Ladybower Res.
THE MOORLAND CENTRE
Nether Booth
Edale
Barber Booth
BLUE JOHN CAVERN
MAM TOR
TREAK CLIFF CAVERN
PEAK CAVERN
SPEEDWELL CAVERN
PEVERIL
CASTLETON
Castleton
Hope
Aston
Thornhill
Bamford
Brough
Bradwell
Hathersage
HATHERSAGE
Perryfoot
Sparrowpit
Peak Forest
Coplow Dale
Great Hucklow
Little Hucklow
Abney
BRETTON
Bretton
Grindlow
Grindleford
Upper Padley
Nether Padley
LONGSHAW
Owler Bar
Eyam
EYAM HALL
Foolow
Lane Head
Froggatt
Peak Dale
Wheston
Tideswell
Hargatewall
Litton
DERBYSHIRE DALES
Burnt Heath
Stoney Middleton
Calver
Curbar
Tunstead
Miller's Dale
Wormhill
Wardlow
Cressbrook
RAVENSTOR
Blackwell
Little Longstone
Rowland
Baslow
Hassop
Great Longstone
King Sterndale
Chelmorton
Taddington
Ashford in the Water
Pilsley
CHATSWORTH
Edensor
Eastmoor
East Moor
HOB HURSTS HOUSE
Sterndale Moor
Sheldon
Bakewell
Flagg
Earl Sterndale
Monyash
Over Haddon
HADDON HALL
PEAK VILLAGE
Beeley
Rowsley
CAUDWELL'S MILL
Crowdicote
ARBOR LOW HENGE
Youlgrave
YOULGRAVE
Alport
Stanton in Peak
NINE LADIES STONE CIRCLE
Bradford
Northwood
Pilsbury
Parsley Hay
Middleton
Churchtown
Two Dales
Birchover
Darley Bridge
PEAK RAIL
Upper Hackney
Sheen
SHEEN
Hartington
HARTINGTON HALL
Hulme End
Heathcote
Newhaven
THE PENNINE BRIDLEWAY
Elton
Winster
Wensley
Matlock
Biggin
Pikehall
Brightgate
MATLOCK PARKS
Bonsall
GULLIVER'S KINGDOM
Matlock Bath
Starkholmes
Warslow
BIGGIN DALE
Grangemill
Ible
ARKWRIGHT'S CROMFORD MILL
MASSON MILLS
Aldwark
Cromford
Wetton
Alstonefield
ALSTONEFIELD
Hope
Alsop en le Dale
Longcliffe
Middleton
MIDDLETON TOP ENGINE HOUSE
NATIONAL STONE CEN
Bolehill
Milldale
Ballidon
Parwich
Wirksworth
Wirksworth Moor
Dove Dale
Manifold
Brassington
Bradbourne
Carsington
Miller's Green
Alderwasley
Tissington
DOVEDALE
Carsington Res.
ECCLESBOURNE VALLEY RLY
ILAM HALL
Ilam
ILAM
Thorpe
Fenny Bentley
Hognaston
Beighton Hill
Kniveton
Kirk Ireton
Shottle
Idridgehay
Atlow
Biggin
Belper Lane End
DERWENT VALLEY VISITOR
Mount Pleasant
Bradfield
Low Bradfield
Ughill
Dungworth
Worrall
Stacey Bank
Wadsley
Wadsley Bridge
Owlerton
Wincobank
Pitsmoor
Stopes
Stannington
Walkley
Crookes
KELHAM ISLAND MUSEUM
CATH
BOTANICAL GARDENS
Ranmoor
Sheffield
Fulwood
Hollow Meadows
HIGH NEB
Reservoirs
Ecclesall
HEELEY CITY FARM
Highfield
Arbourthorne
BISHOPS HOUSE
Norton
Woodseats
Ringinglow
Millhouses
Whirlow
Abbeydale
Beauchief
Dore
Bradway
Totley
New
Jordanthorpe
RIDGEWAY COT INDUSTRY CENTRE
Coal Aston
Dronfield
Dronfield Woodhouse
Holmesfield
Apperknowle
Unstone
Unstone Green
REVOLUTION HOUSE
Common Side
Moorhall
Barlow
Wilday Green
Newbold
Overgreen
Cutthorpe
Old Brampton
Chesterfield
Brampton
Wadshelf
ST MARY & ALL SAINTS
Holymoorside
Walton
Birdholme
Slatepit Dale
Swathwick
Wingerworth
Old Tupton
Uppertown
Brockhurst
Alton
Kelstedge
Clay Cross
Ashover
Fallgate
Milltown
Tansley Knoll
Woolley
Tansley
Brackenfield
Lea
Wessington
Wheatcroft
Holloway
THE NATIONAL TRAMWAY MUS
LEAWOOD PUMPHOUSE
South Wingfield
Whatstandwell
Oakerthorpe
WINGFIELD MANOR
Crich
Fritchley
Bullbridge
Pentrich
Ambergate
Toadmoor
Heage
Nether Heage
Broadholme
Far Laund
Loxley
Derwent
Wye
Noe
Dove
A57
A6013
A6187
A625
A6102
A61
A621
A623
A6
A619
A6020
A5270
A515
A5012
A632
A615
A6
B6049
B6001
B6521
B6054
B6051
B6050
B6465
B6012
B5055
B5057
B5056
B5054
B5035
B5023
B6036
B6014
B6077
B6076
A6101
B6057
B6056
B6082
139
129
113
114
3 miles
5 km

Harworth
Bircotes
Scaftworth
Scrooby
Hooton Levitt
Stone
Styrrup
Wickersley
Whiston
Thurcroft
Firbeck
Oldcotes
Serlby
Mattersey Thorpe
Mattersey
Brinsworth
Catcliffe
Treeton
Brampton en le Morthen
Laughton en le Morthen
Ranskill
Ulley
Aughton
Aston
Laughton Common
Dinnington
Letwell
Langold
Blyth
Torworth
Handsworth
Gildingwells
Carlton in Lindrick
Woodhouse
North Anston
Woodsetts
Barnby Moor
Sutton
Swallownest
Todwick
Beighton
Kiveton Park
South Anston
Wigthorpe
Hackenthorpe
Wales
Holbrook
Norwood
Thorpe Salvin
Gateford
West Retford
Killamarsh
Harthill
Netherthorpe
Shireoaks
Scofton
Ranby
Babworth
Rhodesia
Kilton
Spinkhill
Darfoulds
Manton
Renishaw
Worksop
Barlborough
Middle Handley
Whitwell
Hodthorpe
Mastin Moor
Clowne
Staveley
Creswell
Elkesley
Hardwick Village
Woodthorpe
Stanfree
Poolsbrook
Elmton
Holbeck
Bothamsall
Brimington
Duckmanton
Shuttlewood
Holbeck Woodhouse
Carburton
Norton
Haughton
Bevercotes
Long Duckmanton
Whaley
Whaley Thorns
Perlethorpe
Walesby
Arkwright Town
Bolsover
Cuckney
Nether Langwith
Budby
Meden Vale
Langwith
Kirton
Sutton Scarsdale
Scarcliffe
Langwith Junction
Church Warsop
Market Warsop
New Ollerton
Boughton
Palterton
Shirebrook
Edwinstowe
Ollerton
Heath
Glapwell
Holmewood
Doe Lea
New Houghton
Lidgett
Wellow
Stainsby
Old Clipstone
North Wingfield
Pleasley
Mansfield Woodhouse
Kneesall
Parkhouse Green
Hardstoft
Radmanthwaite
Clipstone
Pilsley
Teversal
Forest Town
Eakring
Skegby
Mansfield
Tibshelf
Morton
Stanton Hill
Bilsthorpe
Stonebroom
Bilsthorpe Moor
Newton
Huthwaite
Sutton in Ashfield
Rainworth
Blackwell
Hilcote
Kirklington
South Normanton
Kirkby in Ashfield
Cox Moor
White Post
Farnsfield
Alfreton
Blidworth
Edingley
Ravenshead
Haywood Oaks
Halam
Pinxton
Nuncargate
Somercotes
Annesley
Southwell
Leabrooks
Selston
Annesley Woodhouse
Riddings
Newstead
Jacksdale
Ironville
Oxton
Halloughton
Bagthorpe
Linby
New Brinsley
Papplewick
Underwood
Codnor
Brinsley
Hucknall
Calverton
Thurgarton
Epperstone
Cross Hill
Westville
Woodborough
Nottingham
SK
Sherwood Forest
Sherwood Pines Forest Park
Great Lake
Clumber Park
Creswell Crags Museum
Roche Abbey
Bolsover Castle
Hardwick Hall
Newstead Abbey
Felley Priory
Rufford
Papplewick Pumping Station
Longdale Rural Craft Centre
White Post Farm Centre
Wheelgate Park
Blyth Services
Woodall Services
Tibshelf Services
Alfreton Services
Sherwood Forest Visitors Centre
Hamlyn Lodge Cottage Industry
Beth Shalom Holocaust Centre
Barrow Hill Roundhouse Rly Ctr
Renishaw Hall Gardens
Midland Railway Centre
Burntstump
Bestwood
M1
M18
A1(M)
A1
A57
A60
A614
A616
A617
A619
A631
A632
A38
A610
A611
A6075
A6009
A620
A634
A638
A612
140
132
114
115
144

Harworth
Gainsborough
Beckingham
Blyth
RETFORD
Tuxford
East Markham
Ollerton
Boughton
Edwinstowe
Sutton on Trent
Collingham
Bilsthorpe
Southwell
Newark-on-Trent
Farndon
Balderton
Claypole
SHERWOOD FOREST
Nottingham

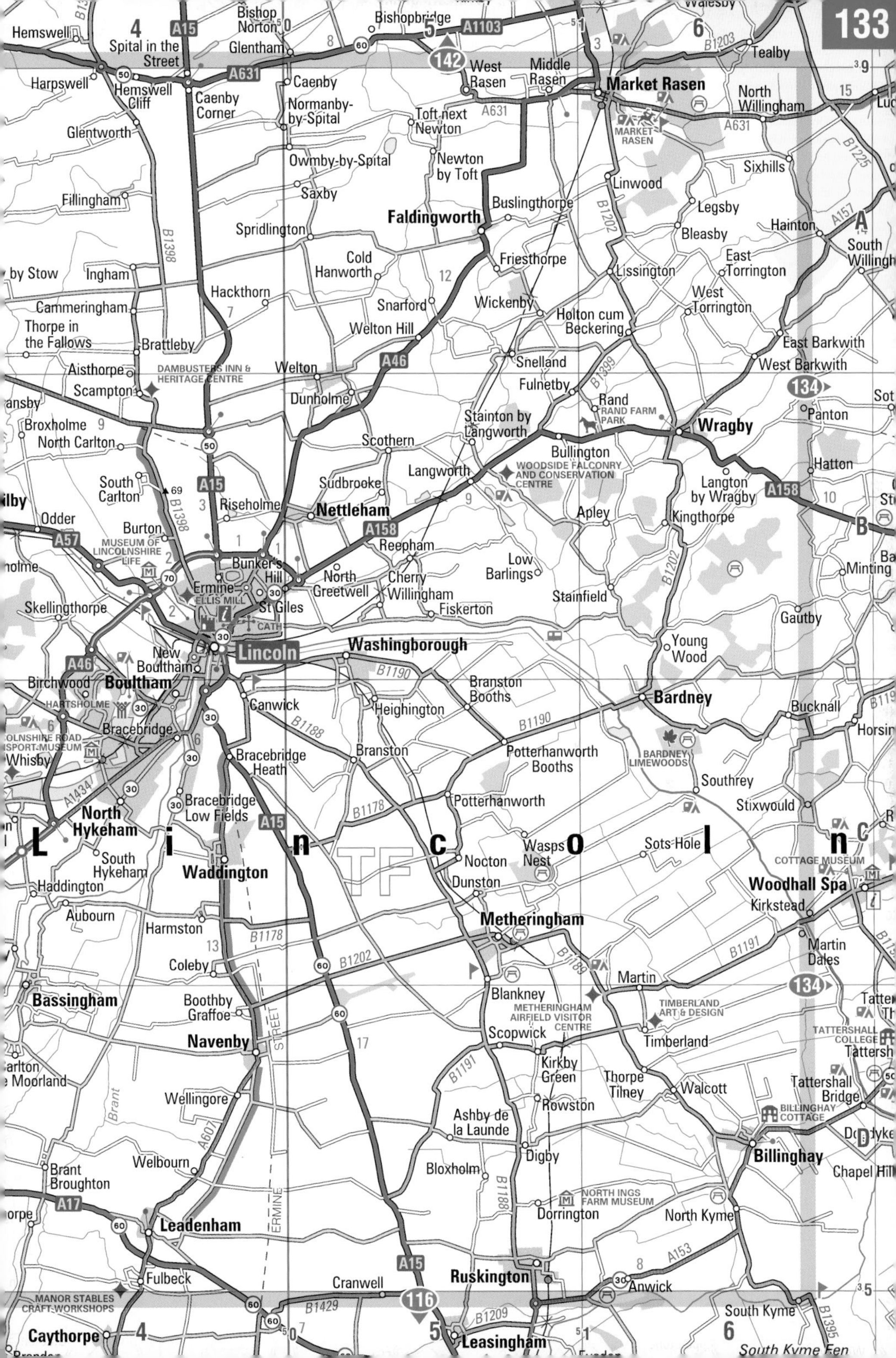
Hemswell
Bishop Norton
Bishopbridge
Walesby
Spital in the Street
Glentham
West Rasen
Middle Rasen
Market Rasen
Tealby
Harpswell
Hemswell Cliff
Caenby
Caenby Corner
Normanby-by-Spital
Toft next Newton
North Willingham
MARKET RASEN
Glentworth
Owmby-by-Spital
Newton by Toft
Sixhills
Linwood
Fillingham
Saxby
Buslingthorpe
Legsby
Faldingworth
Spridlington
Bleasby
Hainton
South Willingham
Friesthorpe
Cold Hanworth
Lissington
East Torrington
by Stow
Ingham
Hackthorn
Snarford
Wickenby
West Torrington
Cammeringham
Holton cum Beckering
Thorpe in the Fallows
Welton Hill
Brattleby
East Barkwith
West Barkwith
Aisthorpe
DAMBUSTERS INN & HERITAGE CENTRE
Welton
Snelland
Scampton
Dunholme
Fulnetby
Rand
RAND FARM PARK
Panton
Broxholme
Stainton by Langworth
Wragby
North Carlton
Scothern
Bullington
Langworth
WOODSIDE FALCONRY AND CONSERVATION CENTRE
Hatton
South Carlton
Sudbrooke
Langton by Wragby
Riseholme
Nettleham
Apley
Kingthorpe
Odder
Burton
MUSEUM OF LINCOLNSHIRE LIFE
Reepham
Bunker's Hill
Low Barlings
Minting
Ermine
ELLIS MILL
North Greetwell
Cherry Willingham
Stainfield
Skellingthorpe
St Giles
Fiskerton
Gautby
CATH
New Boultham
Lincoln
Washingborough
Young Wood
Birchwood
Boultham
HARTSHOLME
Canwick
Branston Booths
Bardney
Heighington
Bucknall
Bracebridge
Branston
Potterhanworth Booths
BARDNEY LIMEWOODS
Whisby
Bracebridge Heath
Southrey
Potterhanworth
Stixwould
North Hykeham
Bracebridge Low Fields
Nocton
Wasps Nest
Sots Hole
South Hykeham
Waddington
Dunston
COTTAGE MUSEUM
Woodhall Spa
Haddington
Kirkstead
Aubourn
Harmston
Metheringham
Martin Dales
Coleby
Martin
Bassingham
Blankney
Boothby Graffoe
METHERINGHAM AIRFIELD VISITOR CENTRE
TIMBERLAND ART & DESIGN
Navenby
Scopwick
Timberland
TATTERSHALL COLLEGE
Kirkby Green
Thorpe Tilney
Walcott
Tattershall Bridge
Wellingore
Rowston
BILLINGHAY COTTAGE
Ashby de la Launde
Digby
Billinghay
Welbourn
Bloxholm
Chapel Hill
Brant Broughton
NORTH INGS FARM MUSEUM
Dorrington
North Kyme
Leadenham
Ruskington
Anwick
Fulbeck
Cranwell
MANOR STABLES CRAFT WORKSHOPS
South Kyme
Caythorpe
Leasingham
South Kyme Fen
Lincoln
TF
A15
A1103
A631
A46
A57
A158
A15
A607
A17
A153
A1434
A157
B1398
B1202
B1399
B1190
B1188
B1178
B1191
B1189
B1429
B1209
B1395
B1203
B1225
ERMINE STREET
Brant
142
134
116

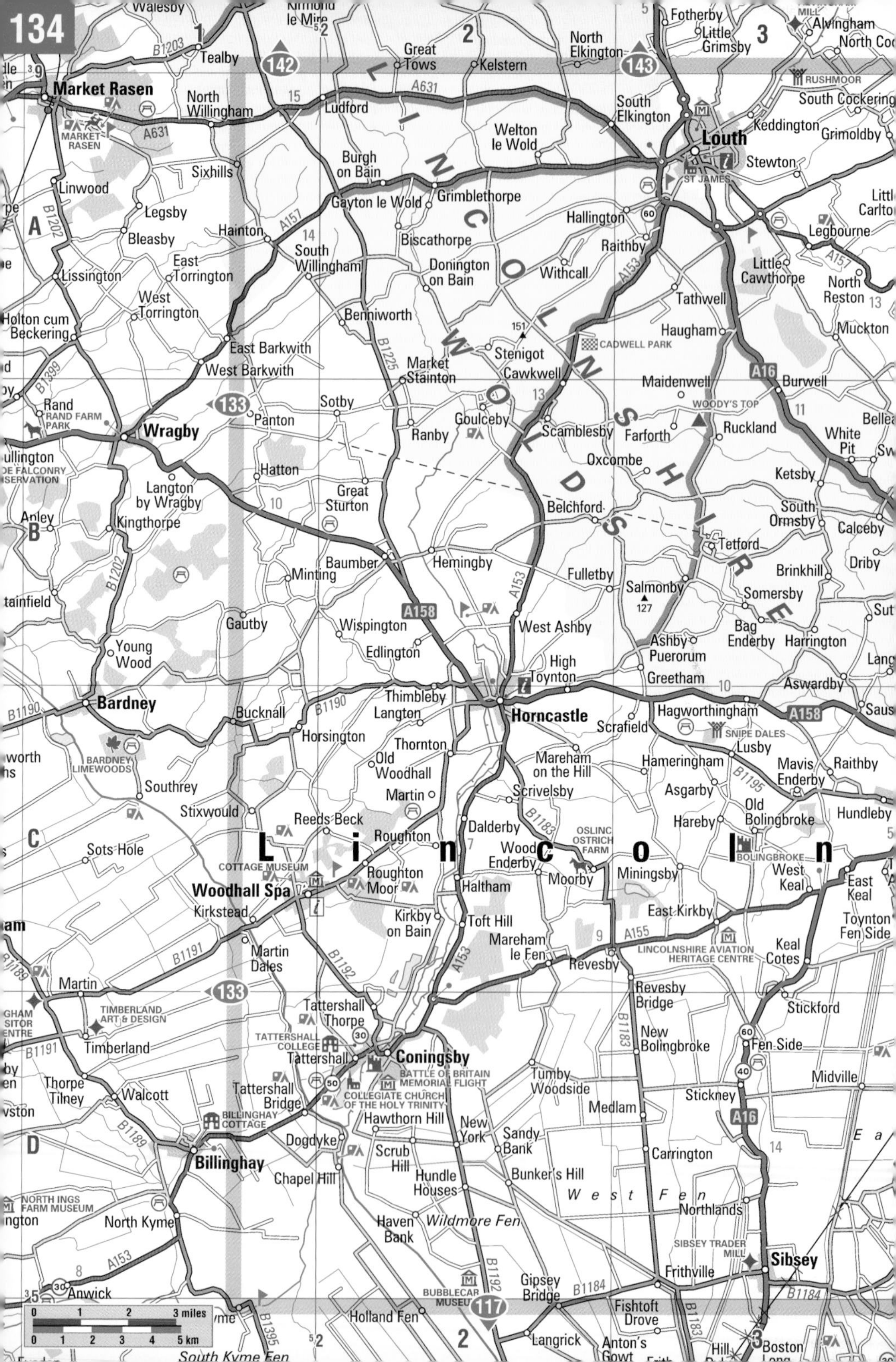

Walesby
Kirmond le Mire
Fotherby
Little Grimsby
Alvingham
North Cockerington
Tealby
Great Tows
Kelstern
North Elkington
142
143
Market Rasen
North Willingham
Ludford
South Elkington
RUSHMOOR
South Cockerington
A631
MARKET RASEN
Welton le Wold
Louth
Keddington
Grimoldby
Burgh on Bain
Stewton
Sixhills
ST JAMES
Linwood
Gayton le Wold
Grimblethorpe
Hallington
Little Carlton
Legsby
Legbourne
Bleasby
Hainton
A157
Biscathorpe
Raithby
South Willingham
Donington on Bain
Withcall
Little Cawthorpe
North Reston
Lissington
East Torrington
A153
Tathwell
West Torrington
Holton cum Beckering
Benniworth
Haugham
Muckton
East Barkwith
151
Stenigot
CADWELL PARK
West Barkwith
Market Stainton
Cawkwell
Maidenwell
Burwell
B1225
B1202
B1399
Rand
RAND FARM PARK
133
Panton
Sotby
WOODY'S TOP
Wragby
Goulceby
Ranby
Scamblesby
Farforth
Ruckland
White Pit
Oxcombe
Hatton
Ketsby
Langton by Wragby
Great Sturton
Belchford
South Ormsby
Calceby
Apley
Kingthorpe
Tetford
Baumber
Hemingby
Brinkhill
Driby
Minting
Fulletby
Salmonby
Somersby
127
A158
Gautby
Wispington
West Ashby
Bag Enderby
Harrington
Young Wood
Edlington
Ashby Puerorum
High Toynton
Greetham
Aswardby
Bardney
B1190
Thimbleby
Langton
Horncastle
Hagworthingham
Bucknall
Scrafield
Horsington
SNIPE DALES
Lusby
Thornton
Mareham on the Hill
Hameringham
Mavis Enderby
Raithby
BARDNEY LIMEWOODS
Old Woodhall
B1195
Southrey
Martin
Scrivelsby
Asgarby
Old Bolingbroke
Hundleby
Stixwould
Reeds Beck
Dalderby
Hareby
B1183
OSLINC OSTRICH FARM
Roughton
Wood Enderby
Sots Hole
L i n c o l n
COTTAGE MUSEUM
BOLINGBROKE
West Keal
East Keal
Roughton Moor
Moorby
Miningsby
Woodhall Spa
Haltham
Kirkstead
Kirkby on Bain
Toft Hill
East Kirkby
Toynton Fen Side
Mareham le Fen
A155
Martin Dales
Revesby
LINCOLNSHIRE AVIATION HERITAGE CENTRE
Keal Cotes
B1191
B1192
Martin
Revesby Bridge
Stickford
TIMBERLAND ART & DESIGN
Tattershall Thorpe
Timberland
TATTERSHALL COLLEGE
Tattershall
Coningsby
New Bolingbroke
Fen Side
BATTLE OF BRITAIN MEMORIAL FLIGHT
Thorpe Tilney
Walcott
Tattershall Bridge
COLLEGIATE CHURCH OF THE HOLY TRINITY
Tumby Woodside
Midville
Medlam
Stickney
BILLINGHAY COTTAGE
Hawthorn Hill
New York
Sandy Bank
A16
B1189
Dogdyke
Billinghay
Scrub Hill
Carrington
Chapel Hill
Hundle Houses
Bunker's Hill
West Fen
NORTH INGS FARM MUSEUM
Northlands
North Kyme
Haven Bank
Wildmore Fen
SIBSEY TRADER MILL
Sibsey
Anwick
Gipsey Bridge
B1184
Frithville
BUBBLECAR MUSEUM
117
Holland Fen
Fishtoft Drove
B1395
Langrick
Anton's Gowt
Boston
South Kyme Fen
0 1 2 3 miles
0 1 2 3 4 5 km

Saltfleetby St Clements
Saltfleetby Theddlethorpe
Saltfleetby All Saints
Theddlethorpe St Helen
Saltfleetby St Peter
Theddlethorpe All Saints
Seal Sanctuary & Nature Centre
Meers Bridge
Great Carlton
Mablethorpe
Trusthorpe
Gayton le Marsh
A1104
Strubby
Withern
A157
Thorpe
Sutton on Sea
Maltby le Marsh
B1373
Sandilands
Woodthorpe
Beesby
Claythorpe Water Mill and Wildfowl Gardens
Saleby
Hannah
Markby
Aby
A1111
Asserby
A52
Alford Windmill
Alford Manor House
Bilsby
Huttoft
Rigsby
Alford
B1449
Haugh
Anderby
On Your Marques
A1104
Farlesthorpe
Mumby
Authorpe Row
Well
Cumberworth
Ulceby
Bonthorpe
Helsey
Chapel St Leonards
Hogsthorpe
Claxby
Willoughby
A52
Sloothby
B1196
Hardy's Animal Farm
Skendleby
A1028
Ingoldmells
Fantasy Island Children's Playdrome & The Millennium Rollercoaster
Partney
Addlethorpe
Welton le Marsh
Funcoast World
Scremby
Candlesby
Orby
Orby Marsh
Ashby by Partney
Gunby Hall
A158
Burgh le Marsh
Winthorpe
Seathorne
Spilsby
Northcote Heavy Horse Centre
Bratoft
Great Steeping
Halton Holegate
Natureland Seal Sanctuary
Burgh le Marsh Windmill
Church Farm Mus
Skegness
B1195
Irby in the Marsh
The Lifeboat Station
Toynton St Peter
Little Steeping
Firsby
Thorpe Culvert
Thorpe St Peter
Croft
A52
Seacroft
Croft Marsh
Thorpe Fendykes
Wainfleet All Saints
Wainfleet Bank
Magdalen Museum
Gibraltar Point
New Leake
Wainfleet Tofts
Wainfleet St Mary
Eastville
Friskney Eaudike
Wainfleet Sand
Fen
Friskney
Wrangle Bank
Friskney Tofts
Commonside
Old Leake
Wrangle Lowgate
Friskney Flats
Wrangle
Hurn's End
Leverton Outgate
TF
143
118
4
5
6
A
B
C
D

BLACKPOOL INTERNATIONAL
Squires Gate
Westby
Wrea Green
Moss Side
Higher Ballam
Dowbridge
Lea Town
Ingol
Cadley
Fulwood
Newton
Scales
Clifton
Preston
TOY AND TEDDY BEAR MUSEUM
ROYAL LYTHAM & ST ANNES
St Annes
Lytham St Anne's
Fairhaven
Salters Bank
Ansdell
LYTHAM HALL
Lytham
Freckleton
Warton
RIBBLE STEAM RAILWAY
Bottom of Hutton
Higher Penwortham
Walton-le-Dale
Middleforth Green
Ribble
Hutton
Longton
New Longton
Lostock Hall
Faringdon
Banks Sands
Great Bank
RIBBLE MARSHES
WEST LANCASHIRE LIGHT RAILWAY
Hesketh Bank
Walmer Bridge
Midge Hall
BRITISH COMMERCIAL VEHICLE MUSEUM
Becconsall
Much Hoole
LEYLAND
Hundred End
Banks
Tarleton
Broadfield
SOUTH RIBBLE MUSEUM & EXHIBITION CENTRE
WORDEN PARK
Horse Bank
Bretherton
Crossens
Marshside
ECO VISITOR CENTRE
Southport
Sollom
Croston
Ulnes Walton
Shaw Green
Mere Brow
Churchtown
Yarrow
Holmeswood
Eccleston
Blowick
RUFFORD OLD HALL
Rufford
Birkdale
MARTIN MERE WILDFOWL AND WETLAND CENTRE
Mawdesley
Heskin Green
Brown Edge
Tarlscough
Snape Green
Bescar
New Lane
Douglas
Bispham Green
Hillside
ROYAL BIRKDALE
Scarisbrick
Wrightington Bar
Ainsdale-on-Sea
Ainsdale
Shirdley Hill
ECCLES FARM CRAFT CENTRE
Hill Dale
Burscough Bridge
Mossy Lea
Pinfold
Liverpool
Burscough
Parbold
Dangerous Corner
Woodvale
Formby Hills
AINSDALE SAND DUNES
Halsall
Leeds and
Newburgh
Appley Bridge
Shevington
Freshfield
Barton
Haskayne
ORMSKIRK
Dalton
BEACON
Roby Mill
Formby
Westhead
Stanley
Formby Pt.
Downholland Cross
Little Altcar
Aughton Park
Blaguegate
Skelmersdale
Great Altcar
Digmoor
Up Holland
Orrell
CABIN HILL
Stanley Gate
Aughton
Royal Oak
Hightown
Ince Blundell
Lydiate
Bickerstaffe
Rainford Junction
Higher End
Barrow Nook
Crawford
Maghull
Lunt
Longshaw
Little Crosby
Melling Mount
Rainford
Sefton
Netherton
Billinge
Thornton
Great Crosby
Melling
Kirkby
Crank
Garswood
BELFAST 8:00
Crosby Channel
Aintree
Moss Bank
Chadwick Green
LITHERLAND
Southdene
Waterloo
Seaforth
Orrell
DOUGLAS 4:15 (Winter Only)
DUBLIN 7:30
Fazakerley
Denton's Green
Knowsley
Bootle
Gillar's Green
St Helens
DOUGLAS 2:45 (March-Nov)
New Brighton
Walton
Norris Green
KNOWSLEY SAFARI PARK
Eccleston
Peasley Cross
CROXTETH
NEW PALACE
Kirkdale
Merseyside
Liscard
Egremont
Anfield
West Derby
Thatto Heath
WALKER GALL
Longview
Eccleston Park
Prescot
Wallasey
Everton
Rainhill
Sutton
Leasowe
Seacombe
MARITIME MUS
LIVERPOOL
Knotty Ash
Whiston
Sutton Manor
Clock Face
Moreton
Poulton
Bidston
TOLL
Edge Hill
Roby
Huyton
Rainhill Stoops
Bold Heath
TATE
ALBERT
Toxteth
Wavertree
Childwall
Netherley
Tarbock Green
Cronton
Barrow Green
Mossley
0 1 2 3 miles
0 1 2 3 4 5 km

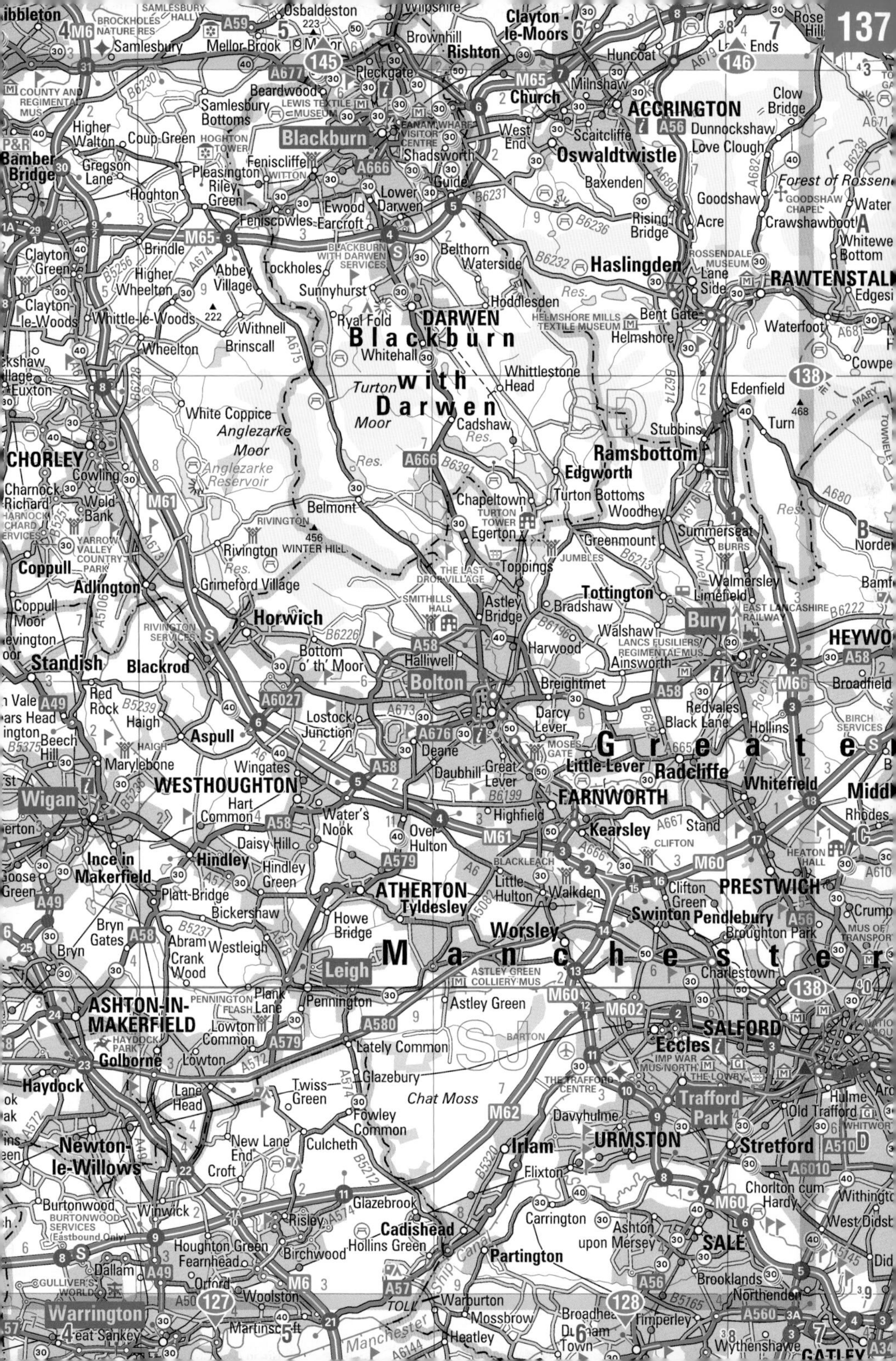

Ribbleton
Samlesbury Hall
Brockholes Nature Res
Samlesbury
Mellor Brook
Osbaldeston
Mellor
Wilpshire
Brownhill
Rishton
Clayton-le-Moors
Huncoat
Rose Hill
Ends
145
146
Pleckgate
Beardwood
Lewis Textile Museum
County and Regimental Mus
Samlesbury Bottoms
Higher Walton
Coup Green
Hoghton Tower
Blackburn
Eanam Wharf Visitor Centre
Church
Milnshaw
Accrington
Clow Bridge
West End
Scaitcliffe
Dunnockshaw
Love Clough
Oswaldtwistle
Bamber Bridge
Gregson Lane
Feniscliffe
Witton
Pleasington
Riley Green
Shadsworth
Guide
Hoghton
Lower Darwen
Ewood
Earcroft
Feniscowles
Baxenden
Forest of Rossendale
Goodshaw
Goodshaw Chapel
Water
Crawshawbooth
Rising Bridge
Acre
Whitewell Bottom
Clayton Green
Brindle
Blackburn with Darwen Services
Belthorn
Waterside
Tockholes
Haslingden
Rossendale Museum
Rawtenstall
Lane Side
Edgeside
Higher Wheelton
Abbey Village
Clayton-le-Woods
Whittle-le-Woods
Withnell
Sunnyhurst
Ryal Fold
Hoddlesden
Helmshore Mills Textile Museum
Helmshore
Bent Gate
Waterfoot
Darwen
Blackburn with Darwen
Wheelton
Brinscall
Whitehall
Res.
Whittlestone Head
Cowpe
Euxton
Turton Moor
Edenfield
138
Stubbins
Turn
White Coppice
Anglezarke Moor
Anglezarke Reservoir
Cadshaw
Ramsbottom
Edgworth
Chorley
Cowling
Charnock Richard
Weld Bank
Chapeltown
Turton Bottoms
Woodhey
Belmont
Turton Tower
Summerseat
Rivington
Winter Hill
Egerton
Greenmount
Burrs
Norden
Yarrow Valley Country Park
Coppull
Adlington
Jumbles
Toppings
The Last Drop Village
Walmersley
Limefield
Grimeford Village
Smithills Hall
Tottington
Bradshaw
Bury
East Lancashire Railway
Bamford
Coppull Moor
Horwich
Rivington Services
Astley Bridge
Walshaw
Lancs Fusiliers Regimental Mus
Heywood
Standish
Blackrod
Bottom o' th' Moor
Halliwell
Harwood
Ainsworth
Broadfield
Bolton
Breightmet
Red Rock
Haigh
Lostock Junction
Darcy Lever
Redvales
Black Lane
Birch Services
Hollins
Beech Hill
Aspull
Deane
Moses Gate
Greater Manchester
Marylebone
Wingates
Daubhill
Great Lever
Little Lever
Radcliffe
Whitefield
Middleton
Wigan
Westhoughton
Hart Common
Water's Nook
Highfield
Farnworth
Rhodes
Over Hulton
Kearsley
Stand
Clifton
Heaton Hall
Daisy Hill
Ince in Makerfield
Hindley
Hindley Green
Blackleach
Little Hulton
Walkden
Clifton Green
Prestwich
Platt Bridge
Atherton
Tyldesley
Swinton
Pendlebury
Bickershaw
Howe Bridge
Crumpsall
Bryn Gates
Abram
Westleigh
Worsley
Broughton Park
Mus of Transport
Bryn
Crank Wood
Leigh
Manchester
Charlestown
Astley Green Colliery Mus
Ashton-in-Makerfield
Pennington Flash
Plank Lane
Pennington
Astley Green
Salford
Makerfield
Lowton Common
Haydock Park
Lately Common
Barton
Eccles
Golborne
Lowton
Imp War Mus North
The Lowry
Haydock
Glazebury
The Trafford Centre
Trafford Park
Hulme
Twiss Green
Lane Head
Chat Moss
Old Trafford
Fowley Common
Davyhulme
Newton-le-Willows
New Lane End
Culcheth
Irlam
Urmston
Stretford
Croft
Flixton
Chorlton cum Hardy
Withington
Burtonwood
Winwick
Glazebrook
Burtonwood Services (Eastbound Only)
Risley
Carrington
Cadishead
Ashton upon Mersey
West Didsbury
Houghton Green
Birchwood
Hollins Green
Sale
Fearnhead
Partington
Dallam
Gulliver's World
Orford
Brooklands
Woolston
Warburton
Northenden
Warrington
Great Sankey
Martinscroft
Mossbrow
Broadheath
Timperley
Heatley
Dunham Town
Wythenshawe
Gatley
Manchester Ship Canal
TOLL
127
128
SD
SJ
M6
M61
M65
M66
M60
M602
M62
A59
A677
A666
A56
A680
A682
A671
A6238
A681
A674
A675
A6
B5256
B6228
B5251
A673
A5106
A58
A6027
A676
A665
A667
A579
A580
A572
A574
A578
A577
B5237
B5239
B5375
B5238
A49
A50
A57
A6144
A5145
A5103
A560
A34
A6010
B5165
B5320
B5212
B6226
B6391
B6213
B6196
B6199
B6214
B6232
B6236
B6231
B6230
B6222
B6292
A676
A679

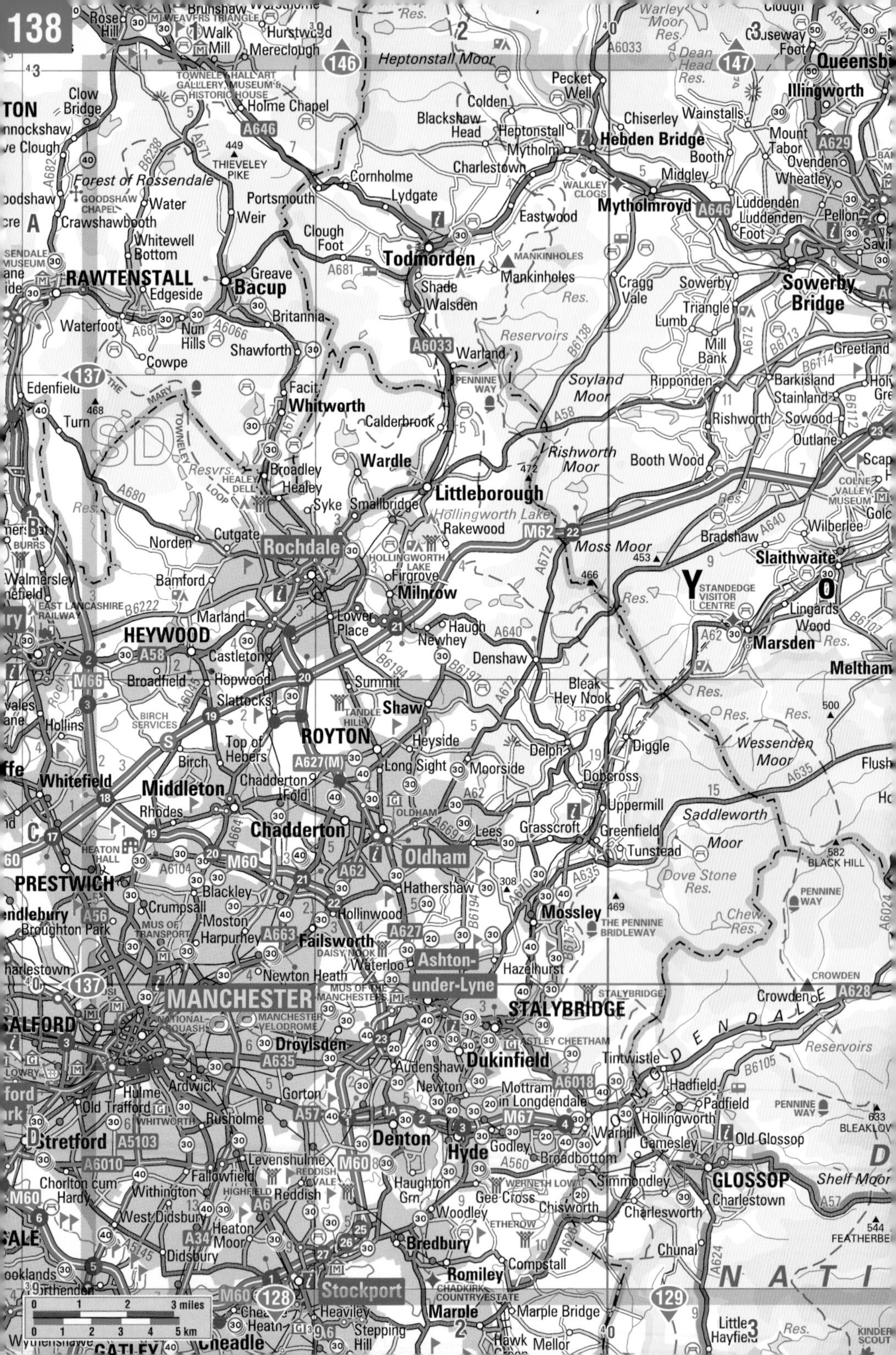

Heptonstall Moor
146
147
Queensbury
Illingworth
Causeway Foot
Warley Moor Res.
Dean Head Res.
Pecket Well
A6033
Brunshaw
Rose Hill
Walk Mill
Hurstwood
Mereclough
TOWNELEY HALL ART GALLERY, MUSEUM & HISTORIC HOUSE
Holme Chapel
Clow Bridge
Colden
Blackshaw Head
Heptonstall
Hebden Bridge
Chiserley
Wainstalls
Mount Tabor
Ovenden
Booth
Midgley
Wheatley
Luddenden
Luddenden Foot
Pellon
Mytholm
Charlestown
Mytholmroyd
WALKLEY CLOGS
Eastwood
A646
A629
Forest of Rossendale
THIEVELEY PIKE
449
GOODSHAW CHAPEL
Water
Crawshawbooth
Portsmouth
Cornholme
Lydgate
Weir
Clough Foot
Whitewell Bottom
Todmorden
MANKINHOLES
Mankinholes
Cragg Vale
Sowerby
Sowerby Bridge
Triangle
Lumb
RAWTENSTALL
Bacup
Greave
Edgeside
Shade
Walsden
Waterfoot
Nun Hills
Britannia
Shawforth
Cowpe
A681
A6066
A6033
Warland
Reservoirs
Mill Bank
Greetland
Soyland Moor
Ripponden
Barkisland
Stainland
Edenfield
THE MARY TOWNELEY LOOP
Facit
Whitworth
PENNINE WAY
137
468
Turn
Calderbrook
Rishworth
Sowood
Outlane
SD
Wardle
Rishworth Moor
Booth Wood
472
Broadley
Healey
HEALEY DELL
Resvrs.
A680
Littleborough
Syke
Smallbridge
Hollingworth Lake
Rakewood
M62
Moss Moor
COLNE VALLEY MUSEUM
Wilberlee
Bradshaw
A640
Slaithwaite
Norden
Cutgate
Rochdale
HOLLINGWORTH LAKE
Firgrove
453
466
BURRS
Walmersley
Bamford
Milnrow
STANDEDGE VISITOR CENTRE
Y
O
Lingards Wood
EAST LANCASHIRE RAILWAY
B6222
HEYWOOD
Marland
Lower Place
Haugh
Newhey
A640
A62
Marsden
Meltham
Castleton
A58
M66
Broadfield
Hopwood
B6194
B6197
Summit
Denshaw
Bleak Hey Nook
500
Slattocks
BIRCH SERVICES
Hollins
Shaw
TANDLE HILL
A672
Res.
Wessenden Moor
ROYTON
Heyside
Diggle
Delph
Top of Hebers
Birch
A627(M)
Long Sight
Moorside
Dobcross
A635
Whitefield
Middleton
Chadderton Fold
A62
Uppermill
Saddleworth Moor
Rhodes
OLDHAM LAKE
A669
Lees
Grasscroft
Greenfield
Chadderton
Oldham
Tunstead
HEATON HALL
M60
A6104
A6104
582
BLACK HILL
PRESTWICH
Blackley
Hathershaw
308
Dove Stone Res.
Crumpsall
Hollinwood
A670
PENNINE WAY
Moston
Mossley
469
THE PENNINE BRIDLEWAY
Chew Res.
A6024
Broughton Park
MUS OF TRANSPORT
Harpurhey
A663
Failsworth
A627
B6194
B6175
A56
DAISY NOOK
Waterloo
Ashton-under-Lyne
Hazelhurst
137
Newton Heath
MUS OF THE MANCHESTERS
MANCHESTER
STALYBRIDGE
CROWDEN
Crowden
A628
SALFORD
NATIONAL SQUASH
MANCHESTER VELODROME
Droylsden
ASTLEY CHEETHAM
LONGDENDALE
Reservoirs
A635
Audenshaw
Dukinfield
Tintwistle
B6105
LOWRY
Ardwick
Gorton
Newton
Mottram in Longdendale
A6018
Hadfield
Padfield
Hulme
Old Trafford
WHITWORTH
Rusholme
A57
M67
Hollingworth
PENNINE WAY
633
BLEAKLOW
Stretford
A5103
Denton
Hyde
Godley
Warhill
Gamesley
Old Glossop
A6010
Levenshulme
REDDISH VALE
M60
A560
Broadbottom
Simmondley
GLOSSOP
Shelf Moor
Chorlton cum Hardy
Fallowfield
Withington
HIGHFIELD
Reddish
Haughton Grn
WERNETH LOW
Gee Cross
Charlestown
A57
West Didsbury
A6
Woodley
Chisworth
Charlesworth
Heaton Moor
ETHEROW
544
FEATHERBED
SALE
A34
A5145
Didsbury
Bredbury
Chunal
A624
Compstall
Romiley
NATI
Brooklands
Northenden
Stockport
CHADKIRK COUNTRY ESTATE
M60
128
129
Cheadle Heath
Heaviley
Marple
Marple Bridge
Stepping Hill
Little Hayfield
Res.
KINDER SCOUT
Wythenshawe
GATLEY
Cheadle
Hawk Green
Mellor
0 1 2 3 miles
0 1 2 3 4 5 km

West Yorkshire
South Yorkshire
PEAK DISTRICT NATIONAL PARK
HOPE FOREST
Halifax
Huddersfield
Dewsbury
Wakefield
Barnsley
BRIGHOUSE
BATLEY
MORLEY
OSSETT
HOLMFIRTH
Cleckheaton
Heckmondwike
Liversedge
Mirfield
Horbury
Elland
Rothwell
Middleton
Normanton
Birstall
Darton
Royston
Penistone
Stocksbridge
Chapeltown
Hoyland
Worsbrough
Dodworth
Skelmanthorpe
Denby Dale
Clayton West
Crigglestone
Midhope Moors
Howden Moors
Broomhead Moor
Bradfield Moors
Wharncliffe Wood
UPPER DERWENT VISITOR CENTRE

148
149
Kippax
Ledston Luck
Ledsham
Lumby
South Milford
Monk Fryston
Hambleton
Thorpe Willoughby
Brayton
Swillington
Woodlesford
Great Preston
Ledston
Hillam
Gateforth
Burn
Selby Canal
Oulton
Allerton Bywater
Fairburn
Burton Salmon
Birkin
YORKSHIRE GARDEN WORLD
West Haddlesey
Chapel Haddlesey
Methley
Mickletown
New Fryston
Brotherton
Aire
Temple Hirst
Hirst Courtney
CASTLEFORD
Ferrybridge
Sutton
Beal
Kellington
Bottom Boat
Altofts
Whitwood
JUNCTION 32
Kellingley
Eggborough
Hensall
Normanton
North Featherstone
PONTEFRACT
Knottingley
Gowdall
Snaith
Wakefield
Woodhouse
Ackton
Pontefract
FERRYBRIDGE SERVICES
High Eggborough
Featherstone
Chequerfield
Cridling Stubbs
Whitley
Great Heck
Warmfield
Sharlston Common
Snydale
Darrington
Purston Jaglin
Womersley
Pollington
Balne
Aire and Calder Navigation
Sandal Magna
139
Sharlston
West Hardwick
East Hardwick
High Ackworth
Wentbridge
Little Smeaton
Walden Stubbs
Went
Crofton
Foulby
Walton
ANGLERS
Wragby
NOSTELL PRIORY
Low Ackworth
Kirk Smeaton
Sykehouse
Fenwick
Wintersett Res.
Ryhill
Fitzwilliam
Ackworth Moor Top
Thorpe Audlin
BARNSDALE BAR SERVICES
Norton
Badsworth
Kinsley
Havercroft
Upton
Wrangbrook
Campsall
CAMPSALL
Fosterhouses
Moss
Far Bank
Notton
South Hiendley
Felkirk
Hemsworth
North Elmshall
Instoneville
Sutton
Askern
Haywood
Braithwaite
Royston
Skelbrooke
Burghwallis
Owston
Thorpe in Balne
Kirk Bramwith
Shafton
Brierley
Moorthorpe
South Elmsall
South Kirkby
Hampole
Skellow
Carcroft
Carlton
Grimethorpe
Adwick le Street
Barnby Dun
Monk Bretton
Cudworth
HOWELL WOOD
Clayton
Hooton Pagnell
Toll Bar
Almholme
Kirk Sandall
Barnsley
Great Houghton
Brodsworth
HIGHFIELDS
Woodlands
Arksey
MONK BRETTON PRIORY
Ardsley
Thurnscoe
Thurnscoe East
BRODSWORTH HALL
Bentley
Edenthorpe
Kendray
Little Houghton
Scawsby
MUSEUM & ART GALLERY
Armthorpe
NETHERWOOD
Darfield
Billingley
Hickleton
Marr
CUSWORTH
Wheatley
Nutwell
DONCASTER
Goldthorpe
MELTON WOOD
Newton
Intake
Wombwell
Barnburgh
Bolton upon Dearne
CUSWORTH HALL MUSEUM
Doncaster
Worsbrough
MILL MUSEUM
South
Sprotbrough
Hyde Park
Cantley
Platts Common
Broomhill
Harlington
Bessacarr
Birdwell
Jump
Brampton
Adwick upon Dearne
High Melton
Balby
LAKESIDE VILLAGE
Hoyland
Elsecar
ELSECAR HERITAGE CENTRE
Wath upon Dearne
Mexborough
Cadeby
Warmsworth
AEROVENTURE
Swinton
Old Denaby
Denaby Main
New Edlington
Loversall
Rossington
Harley
Conisbrough
CONISBROUGH/IVANHOE
Wentworth
Upper Haugh
Kilnhurst
Old Edlington
New Rossington
Nether Haugh
Rawmarsh
Hooton Roberts
Clifton
Wadworth
ST LEGER HORSE PARK
Thorpe Hesley
Thrybergh
THRYBERGH
Ravenfield
Greasbrough
Micklebring
Braithwell
Dalton
Stainton
Spital Hill
Ecclesfield
Y
o
r
k
s
Kimberworth
Rotherham
CLIFTON PARK
Bramley
Hellaby
Maltby
Tickhill
Harworth
Parson Cross
Shiregreen
MAGNA SCIENCE ADVENTURE CENTRE
Wincobank
Broom
Wickersley
Hooton Levitt
Bircotes
Tinsley
Moorgate
Styrrup
Brinsworth
Whiston
131
Stone
ROCHE ABBEY
Oldcotes
Serlby
BLYTH SERVICES
Catcliffe
ULLEY
Brampton en
0 1 2 3 miles
0 1 2 3 4 5 km

Wressle
Brind
North Howden
A614
Portington
Hive
38
West End
A63
149
150
Cavil
Sandholme
Newsholme
Eastrington
Scalby
Newport
Ellerker
HOWDEN MINSTER
Derwent
B1230
Gilberdyke
Barmby on the Marsh
Howden
M62
Staddlethorpe
Market Weighton Canal
Elloughton
Long Drax
Asselby
Knedlington
Kilpin Pike
Balkholme
Broomfleet
Drax
Boothferry
37
Kilpin
Ouse
Camblesforth
A645
Newland
Laxton
Skelton
Hook
Airmyn
Saltmarshe
Blacktoft
Faxfleet
Whitton
36
Yokefleet
Carlton
Goole
THE YORKSHIRE WATERWAYS MUSEUM
Reedness
Ousefleet
BLACKTOFT SANDS RSPB
East Cowick
Rawcliffe
Rawcliffe Bridge
Old Goole
Swinefleet
Whitgift
Little Reedness
JULIAN'S BOWER (TURF MAZE)
Winteringham
Alkborough
Dutch River
Adlingfleet
Walcot
West Halton
Trent
A161
142
Goole Fields
Fockerby
Garthorpe
Coleby
Winterton
SE
Burton Stather
B1430
Thealby
M18
Burton upon Stather
Goole Moors
Luddington
NORMANBY HALL
Roxby
Normanby
Eastoft
Don
Moorends
HUMBERHEAD PEATLANDS
Thorne Waste or Moors
Flixborough
B1392
B
Appleby
Amcotts
Flixborough Stather
Dragonby
Fishlake
Crowle
A1077
Thorne
Stainforth & Keadby Canal
Windsor
Canal Side
Wike Well End
B1216
Santon
Ealand
Keadby
Gunness
Crosby
APPLEBY FRODINGHAM RLY PRESERVATION SOC
Frodingham
Stainforth
A18
Scunthorpe
Hatfield
Hatfield Chase
Burringham
Althorpe
M181
Brumby
A1029
A1146
M180
B1450
Woodhouse
Derrythorpe
Ashby
Broughton
Hatfield Woodhouse
Sandtoft
THE TROLLEYBUS MUSEUM AT SANDTOFT
Grey Green
Westgate
Yaddlethorpe
West End
Beltoft
Bottesford
Belton
A614
East Butterwick
Church Town
Thorne
Hatfield Moors
West Butterwick
ISLE OF AXHOLME
C
Messingham
Epworth
OLD RECTORY
Wroot
Epworth Turbary
A159
B1400
Manton
B1398
Low Burnham
Susworth
GAINSTHORPE DESERTED MEDIEVAL VILLAGE
Auckley
Kelfield
Scotterthorpe
Owston Ferry
Scotter
Blaxton
Upperthorpe
Laughton Forest
Haxey
East Lound
Kirton in Lindsey
Finningley
B1396
Westwoodside
East Ferry
Scotton
ROBIN HOOD AIRPORT DONCASTER SHEFFIELD
Craiselound
Wildsworth
B1206
Northorpe
Laughton
Idle
Grayingham
Misson
Misterton
West Stockwith
Blyton
B1205
D
Austerfield
East Stockwith
Pilham
Eau
Blyborough
Newington
SK
Bawtry
Aisby
Willoughton
Walkerith
A159
Walkeringham
Morton
Gringley on the Hill
Gainsborough
Corringham
Everton
Scaftworth
GAINSBOROUGH OLD HALL
Hemswell
A631
Scrooby
Cuckoo Hill
Spital in the Street
132
Beckingham
Mattersey Thorpe
Wiseton
Springthorpe
Harpswell
Mattersey
B1403
Hemswell Cliff

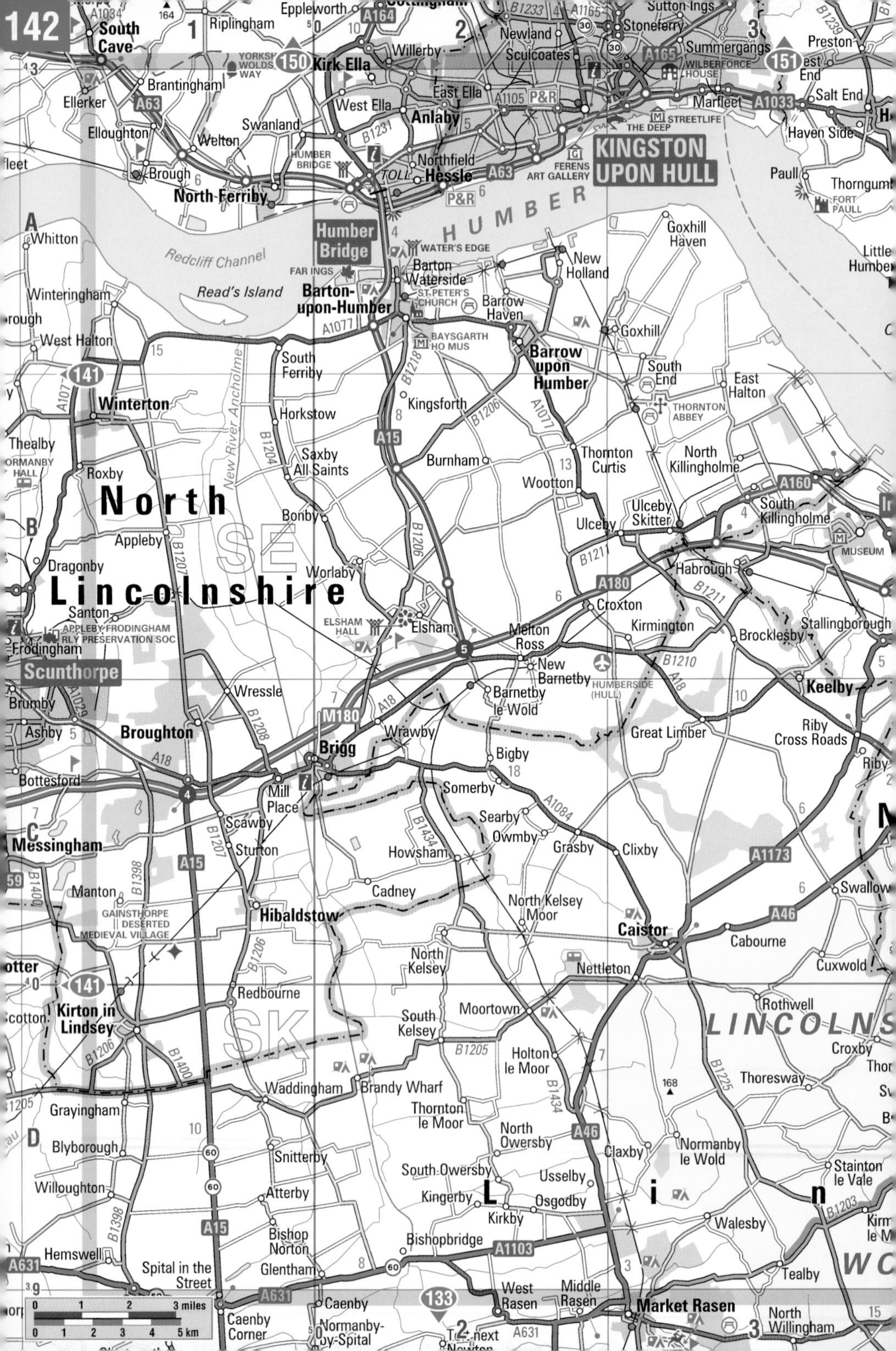
South Cave
Riplingham
Eppleworth
Kirk Ella
Willerby
Newland
Sculcoates
Stoneferry
Sutton Ings
Summergangs
Preston
WILBERFORCE HOUSE
Brantingham
Ellerker
East Ella
West Ella
Anlaby
Marfleet
Salt End
Swanland
Ellough ton
Welton
Brough
North Ferriby
HUMBER BRIDGE
Northfield
Hessle
THE DEEP
STREETLIFE
FERENS ART GALLERY
KINGSTON UPON HULL
Haven Side
Paull
FORT PAULL
HUMBER
Whitton
Humber Bridge
WATER'S EDGE
Redcliff Channel
Read's Island
FAR INGS
Barton Waterside
Barton-upon-Humber
ST PETER'S CHURCH
Barrow Haven
New Holland
Goxhill Haven
Winteringham
West Halton
BAYSGARTH HO MUS
Goxhill
South Ferriby
Barrow upon Humber
South End
East Halton
THORNTON ABBEY
Winterton
Horkstow
Kingsforth
Thealby
NORMANBY HALL
Roxby
Saxby All Saints
Burnham
Thornton Curtis
Wootton
North Killingholme
South Killingholme
North Lincolnshire
Bonby
Ulceby
Ulceby Skitter
Appleby
Dragonby
Worlaby
Habrough
MUSEUM
Lincolnshire
Croxton
Kirmington
Santon
APPLEBY-FRODINGHAM RLY PRESERVATION SOC
Frodingham
ELSHAM HALL
Elsham
Melton Ross
Brocklesby
Stallingborough
Scunthorpe
New Barnetby
HUMBERSIDE (HULL)
Brumby
Wressle
Barnetby le Wold
Keelby
Ashby
Broughton
Wrawby
Brigg
Great Limber
Riby Cross Roads
Riby
Bottesford
Bigby
Mill Place
Somerby
Messingham
Scawby
Searby
Owmby
Grasby
Clixby
Sturton
Howsham
Manton
Cadney
GAINSTHORPE DESERTED MEDIEVAL VILLAGE
Hibaldstow
North Kelsey Moor
Caistor
Cabourne
Swallow
North Kelsey
Nettleton
Cuxwold
Redbourne
Kirton in Lindsey
Moortown
Rothwell
South Kelsey
LINCOLNSHIRE
Croxby
Holton le Moor
Thoresway
Waddingham
Brandy Wharf
Grayingham
Thornton le Moor
North Owersby
Blyborough
Snitterby
Claxby
Normanby le Wold
South Owersby
Stainton le Vale
Willoughton
Atterby
Usselby
Kingerby
Osgodby
Kirkby
Bishop Norton
Walesby
Bishopbridge
Hemswell
Spital in the Street
Glentham
Tealby
West Rasen
Middle Rasen
Market Rasen
Caenby
Caenby Corner
Normanby-by-Spital
North Willingham
0 1 2 3 miles
0 1 2 3 4 5 km

Elstronwick
Tunstall
Burton Pidsea
Roos
North End
151
Waxholme
Owthorne
Withernsea
Rimswell
Burstwick
Halsham
East End
Camerton
Ryehill
Keyingham
Ottringham
Hollym
Winestead
Holmpton
Patrington
Out Newton
Welwick
Weeton
Sunk Island
Skeffling
Easington
Kilnsea
TA
SPURN
SPURN HEAD
ROTTERDAM 10:45
ZEEBRUGGE 13:15
Grimsby
Pyewipe
Healing
West Marsh
Great Coates
CLEETHORPES
Old Clee
FISHING HERITAGE CENTRE
MOUTH OF THE HUMBER
CLEETHORPES COAST LIGHT RAILWAY
PLEASURE ISLAND THEME PARK
Nunsthorpe
Laceby
Bradley
Scartho
CLEETHORPES
Humberston
North East
Waltham
New Waltham
Barnoldby le Beck
WALTHAM WINDMILL
Holton le Clay
Lincolnshire
Tetney Lock
Brigsley
Beelsby
Ashby cum Fenby
North Cotes
Hatcliffe
Tetney
Waithe
East Ravendale
Grainsby
Marshchapel
Donna Nook
TF
Eskham
Wragholme
North Thoresby
Grainthorpe
Wold Newton
Fulstow
North Somercotes
LINCOLNSHIRE WOLDS RLY
DONNA NOOK
Ludborough
Covenham St Bartholomew
Conisholme
Skidbrooke North End
South Somercotes
Saltfleet
North Ormsby
Covenham St Mary
Binbrook
Utterby
Yarburgh
Skidbrooke
ALVINGHAM MILL
Fotherby
Saltfleetby St Clements
Alvingham
Little Grimsby
North Cockerington
SALTFLEETBY THEDDLETHORPE
North Elkington
Great Tows
Kelstern
Saltfleetby All Saints
Theddlethorpe St Helen
RUSHMOOR
134
135
South Cockerington
South Elkington
Keddington
Grimoldby
Welton
A180
A16
A18
A46
A1098
B1219
A1031
B1201
B1203
A631
B1200
B1242
B1362
A1033
B1445

Barrow-in-Furness
Hawcoat
BOW BRIDGE
Newbarns
FURNESS ABBEY
GLEASTON WATERMILL
Baycliff
Aldingham
Dendron
Yarlside
Newbiggin
Leece
Roosebeck
North Scale
CUSTOM HO
THE DOCK MUSEUM
Vickerstown
Barrow Island
A5087
Biggar
Rampside
Roa Island
Foulney Island
South End
Piel Island
Isle of Walney
South End Point
South Channel
MORECAMBE
BAY
153
154
Morecambe
Sandylands
White Lund
Heysham
A589
A683
Middleton
Glasson
Sunderland Pt.
Shoulder of Lune
Lune
Cockerham Sands
Braides
DOUGLAS 3:15
Knott End-on-Sea
Fleetwood
Rossall Point
FREEPORT FLEETWOOD
B5270
Preesall
Pilling Lane
Pilling
Dam Side
Stake Pool
A588
Eagland Hill
Stalmine
Staynall
Wyre
MARSH MILL-IN-WYRE
WYRE ESTUARY
A587
Cleveleys
Trunnah
Hambleton
Out Rawcliffe
Moss Edge
Anchorsholme
Thornton
Norbreck
Little Eccleston
TOLL
A584
Skippool
Little Singleton
Bispham
Carleton
Great Eccleston
Blackpool
Warbreck
North Shore
A586
Poulton-le-Fylde
Singleton
Elswick
Queenstown
B5266
Normoss
Thistleton
B5269
A585
Layton
Staining
Esprick
BLACKPOOL TOWER
SEA LIFE CENTRE
LOUIS TUSSAUD'S WAXWORKS
ZOO PARK
Great Marton
B5260
Corner Row
Weeton
M55
South Shore
BLACKPOOL PLEASURE BEACH
Hawes Side
Mereside
Little Plumpton
Great Plumpton
Wesham
Common Edge
A583
Kirkham
Squires Gate
Westby
B5261
B5140
B5259
BLACKPOOL INTERNATIONAL
Moss Side
Wrea Green
Newton
Higher Ballam
136
TOY AND TEDDY BEAR MUSEUM
ROYAL LYTHAM & ST ANNES
LYTHAM HALL
Ansdell
Annes
Lytham St Anne's
Warton
0 1 2 3 miles
0 1 2 3 4 5 km

Millhead
Carnforth
Capernwray
Melling
Wrayton
Burton in Lonsdale
Over Kellet
Gressingham
Tatham
Wennington
Low Bentham
High Bentham
Newby
Hornby
Nether Kellet
Wray
Mewith Head
Keasden
Wenning
Aughton
Farleton
Claughton
Bolton Town End
Slyne
Bare
Halton
Caton Green
Caton
Brookhouse
Caton Moor
Salter
Goodber Common
Lowgill
Hindburn
Tatham Fells
Burn Moor
Skerton
MARITIME MUS
Crossgill
ASHTON MEMORIAL
Haylot Fell
Catlow Fell
Aldcliffe
LEISURE PARK
CITY
Scotforth
Clougha
Quernmore
561
WARD'S STONE
Mallowdale Fell
544
WHITE HILL
Lee Fell
F O R E S T
Tarnbrook Fell
Croasdale Fell
Stocks Reservoir
Conder Green
Tarnbrook
Galgate
Smith Green
Ortner
Lee
Abbeystead
Wyre
SD
Marshaw
Trough of Bowland
WHINS BROW
476
Dolphinholme
LANCASTER(FORTON) SERVICES
Hawthornthwaite Fell
O F
Slaidburn
SLAIDBURN
Forton
Street
Sykes
478
FELL TOP
Hollins Lane
Hareden
Newton
Lane Ends
Sykes Fell
Dunsop Bridge
Easington Fell
Scorton
Bleasdale Moors
B O W L A N D
Cabus
Oakenclough
Whitewell
510
FAIR SNAPE FELL
Garstang
Calder Vale
Bleasdale
Cow Ark
Grindleton
West Bradford
THE FIG TREE FAIRTRADE VISITOR CENTRE
Nateby
Bowgreave
Calder
Brock
Hodder
Waddington
Churchtown
Catterall
BEACON FELL
Chipping
Bashall Eaves
Clitheroe
Claughton
Walker Fold
Whitechapel
Low Moor
St Michael's on Wyre
Hesketh Lane
Bilsborrow
Inglewhite
Longridge Fell
Myerscough
Cuddy Hill
Knowle Green
New Row
Great Mitton
Barrow
Barton
Goosnargh
Longridge
Hurst Green
ST SAVIOUR'S CHURCH
Little Town
Old Langho
WHALLEY ABBEY
Whalley
Catforth
CHINGLE HALL
Haighton Green
Ribchester
Billington
Woodplumpton
Broughton
MUS OF CHILDHOOD
ROMAN MUSEUM
Grimsargh
Ribble
Langho
Lower Bartle
Higher Bartle
Copster Green
Great Harwood
Sharoe Green
Cottam
Lancaster Canal
Balderstone
Salesbury
Fulwood
SAMLESBURY HALL
Osbaldeston
Wilpshire
Lea Town
Ingol
Cadley
Ribbleton
BROCKHOLES NATURE RES
223
Clayton-le-Moors
Samlesbury
Mellor Brook
Mellor
Brownhill
Rishton
Clifton
Preston
Pleckgate
RIBBLE STEAM RAILWAY
COUNTY AND REGIMENTAL MUS
Samlesbury Bottoms
LEWIS TEXTILE MUSEUM
Church
Higher Walton
L a n c a s h i r e
M6
A65
A683
A59
A666
A677
M65
B6254
B6480
B6478
B6243
B6245
B6246
B5269
B5411
B6241
B6230
B5272
A588
A586
A6
A671
A680
154
155
146
136
137

INGLEBOROUGH SHOW CAVE
GAPING GILL
BRIDLEWAY
Ribblesdale
Darnbrook Fell
Kettlewell
Arncliffe
Hawkswick
662 FOUNTAINS FELL
PENNINE WAY
155
156
Newby
Wharfe
Helwith Bridge
Clapham
Austwick
Feizor
Wenning
Keasden
Lawkland
Little Stainforth
Stainforth
YORKSHIRE DALES FALCONRY AND CONSERVATION CENTRE
Stackhouse
WATERSHED MILL VISITOR CENTRE
Langcliffe
Eldroth
Giggleswick
GIGGLESWICK SCHOOL CHAPEL
Settle
Burn Moor
Wham
Catlow Fell
145
Mearbeck
Rathmell
HORSES HEALTH FARM
RIBBLESDALE
Long Preston
Wigglesworth
Tosside
Gisburn Forest
Stocks Reservoir
Grunsagill
Knotts
Slaidburn
SLAIDBURN
Newton
Lane Ends
Easington Fell
Holden
Forest Becks
Bolton-by-Bowland
Paythorne
Halton West
Nappa
Hellifield
Ribble
North Yorks
MALHAM TARN
Malham Tarn
THE SETTLE LOOP
MALHAM COVE
547 KIRKBY FELL
MALHAM
Malham
Hanlith
Kirkby Malham
Airton
Calton
Winterburn
Hetton
Otterburn
Bell Busk
Coniston Cold
Eshton
Flasby
Gargrave
Bank Newton
PENNINE WAY
219
Newsholme
Horton
Broughton
East Marton
West Marton
Kilnsey
KILNSEY PARK
Coniston
Bordley
NEW HOUSE FARM, MALHAM
Threshfield
Linton
Threapland
Cracoe
Rylstone
Thorlby
SKIPTON
Carleton
Elslack
Cononley
Thornton-in-Craven
EARBY
Earby
388
Lothersdale
Glusburn
Lane Ends
Cowling
New Road Side
Gisburn
Bracewell
Lane End
Coates
Barnoldswick
Salterforth
Kelbrook
Hey
Foulridge
Colne Edge
Blacko
Roughlee
PENDLE HERITAGE CENTRE
Barrowford
COLNE
Laneshaw Bridge
Winewall
Wycoller
WYCOLLER
Trawden
BRITISH IN INDIA MUS
NELSON
THE FOREST OF TRAWDEN
Little Marsden
Brierfield
THE PENNINE BRIDLEWAY
517 BOULSWORTH HILL
PENNINE WAY
443
KEIGHLEY MOOR
Haworth Moor
Wadsworth Moor
Walshaw Dean Res.
Widdop Res.
Heptonstall Moor
Haggate
Harle Syke
Burnley Lane
Burnley
Brunshaw
Worsthorne
WEAVERS TRIANGLE
Walk Mill
Hurstwood
Mereclough
TOWNELEY HALL ART GALLERY, MUSEUM & HISTORIC HOUSE
Holme Chapel
Colden
Blackshaw
Pecket Well
138
137
ACCRINGTON
Clow Bridge
Lane Ends
Huncoat
Rose Hill
Rose Grove
Habergham
Hapton
Padiham
GAWTHORPE HALL
Read
Altham
Simonstone
TRAPP FORGE
Higham
Fence
Sabden
THE FOREST OF PENDLE
Newchurch
Barley
557 PENDLE HILL
Sawley
ABBEY
Grindleton
West Bradford
Chatburn
Downham
Twiston
Rimington
Newby
Worston
Waddington
Clitheroe
CLITHEROE CASTLE MUSEUM
Low Moor
Pendleton
Great Mitton
Barrow
Wiswell
Whalley
WHALLEY ABBEY
Billington
Langho
Great Harwood
Clayton-le-Moors
Rishton
Wilpshire
A65
A682
A59
A629
A56
A6068
A671
A680
A678
A679
A666
A646
M65
B6480
B6479
B6478
B6160
B6265
B6251
B6252
B6383
B6246
0 1 2 3 miles
0 1 2 3 4 5 km

Moor
Stean Moor
onistone Moor
Bouthwaite
Dallowgill Moor
Dallow
Low Grantley
Winksley
157
Ramsgill
Gouthwaite Res.
Grantley
Studley Roger
ST MARY'S
STUDLEY ROYAL WATER GARDEN
FOUNTAINS ABBEY
Aldfield
Risplith
Eavestone
N I D D E R D A L E
t h
h i r e
Heathfield Moor
Wath
Pateley Moor
Sawley
B6265
Hebden Moor
Grimwith Res.
NIDDERDALE MUSEUM
Pateley Bridge
Markington
Grassington
UPPER WHARFEDALE MUSEUM
Greenhow Hill
Bewerley
Wilsill
Glasshouses
BRIMHAM ROCKS
Bishop Thornton
Hebden
STUMP CROSS CAVERNS
Low Laithe
New York
Dacre Banks
Summer Bridge
Shaw Mills
Bedlam
Thorpe
Burnsall
PARCEVALL HALL GARDENS
Pockstones Moor
B6165
Burnt Yates
Ripley
RIPLEY CASTLE
A61
B6160
Skyreholme
Dacre
Appletreewick
Padside
Darley Head
Birstwith
Clint
148
Nidd
Upper Barden Res.
Drebley
Barden Fell
Thruscross Res.
Thornthwaite
Darley
Hampsthwaite
Killinghall
West End
Kettlesing Bottom
Forest
Barden Scale
Lower Barden Res.
B6451
Moor
BOLTON ABBEY ESTATE
Bolton Abbey
Blubberhouses
A59
Kettlesing Head
MERCER ART GALLERY
KILLINGHALL MOOR
Harrogate
Eastby
Halton East
Hill End
Pace Gate
Fewston
Fewston Res.
RHS GARDEN HARLOW CARR
EMBSAY & BOLTON ABBEY STEAM RLY
BUFFERS
Hazlewood
Bland Hill
Beckwithshaw
Harlow Hill
Swinsty Res.
Timble
Rossett Green
Bolton Bridge
Beamsley
SE
Jack Hill
Draughton
A65
Langbar
Brackenthwaite
Pannal
B6161
B6160
Addingham
North Rigton
Lindley Green
Lindley Wood Res.
Low Bradley
A6034
Middleton
Denton
Braythorn
Cringles
Askwith
Clifton
Farnley
Stainburn
R O M B A L D
ILKLEY
B6382
Weston
Huby
Weeton
Farnhill
Newall
Leathley
A658
Dunkeswick
Kildwick
Silsden
Burley in Wharfedale
Otley
Pool
Castley
A629
Eastburn
Ilkley Moor
M O O R
A659
Arthington
Steeton
Menston
CHEVIN FOREST PARK
Bramhope
Sutton-in-Craven
CLIFFE CASTLE
Riddlesden
EAST RIDDLESDEN HALL
East Carlton
Old Bramhope
Eccup
Keighley
Utley
East Morton
Guiseley
Braithwaite
Micklethwaite
Hawksworth
Yeadon
A660
Eccup Res.
LEEDS BRADFORD INTERNATIONAL
Laycock
Knowle Park
Thwaites
Crossflatts
Cookridge
YORK GATE GARDEN
Alwoodley
Goose Eye
Thwaites Brow
Eldwick
BRACKEN HALL COUNTRYSIDE CENTRE
Baildon
A6038
Esholt
Rawdon
Tinshill
Holt Park
Moor Allerton
Exley Head
VINTAGE RAILWAY CARRIAGE MUS
Adel
Oakworth
B6143
Ingrow
BINGLEY
A657
A658
Apperley Bridge
A65
Horsforth
Dockroyd
Lees
BRONTE PARSONAGE MUS
HAWORTH
B6429
Harden
1853 GALLERY
Saltaire
Meanwood
Cottingley
A650
Idle
A6120
Haworth
Cullingworth
Wilsden
B6146
Moorhead
SHIPLEY
Calverley
Rodley
Hawksworth
Headingley
PENISTONE HILL
Marsh
Frizinghall
Eccleshill
BRADFORD IND MUS
KIRKSTALL ABBEY
Lingbob
CARTWRIGHT HALL ART GALLERY
Farsley
Bramley
Kirkstall
Woodh
KEIGHLEY AND WORTH VALLEY RAILWAY
Oxenhope
A629
B6144
Heaton
Undercliffe
B6157
Stanningley
CITY ART GALL
Manningham
Thornbury
A647
Burley
Denholme
CATH
Well Heads
Allerton
A647
LEEDS INDUSTRIAL MUS
B6141
Bradford
Swinnow Moor
Armley
A6033
B6145
Laisterdyke
B6154
Holbeck
Denholme Clough
Thornton
Lidgett Green
Little Horton
PUDSEY
Farnley
Wortley
Warley Moor Res.
Clayton
Great Horton
Bowling
Holme Wood
A6110
A644
West Bowling
Causeway Foot
Mountain
NAT MEDIA MUSEUM
BOLLING HALL
New Farnley
Beeston
Dean Head Res.
A647
Tong
A58
A62
Queensbury
138
Bierley
139
A650
Churwell
Illingworth
Buttershaw
Wibsey
M621
Ambler Thorn
Drighlington
Chiserley
Wainstalls
Shelf
Low Moor
Birkenshaw
A651
Gildersome
A653
A6036
M606
Adwalton

148
Ripon
Bishopton
THE COURTHOUSE
RIPON CATHEDRAL
Copt Hewick
Bridge Hewick
Norton-le-Clay
Raskelf
Easingwold
Studley Roger
N.
Y
O
Marton-le-Moor
Brafferton
Helperby
158
Aldfield
ST MARY'S
STUDLEY ROYAL WATER GARDEN
FOUNTAINS ABBEY
RIPON
Littlethorpe
Skelton-on-Ure
Kirby Hill
NEWBY HALL
Park Hill
Sawley
Langthorpe
Boroughbridge
ALDBOROUGH ROMAN TOWN
Aldborough
Tholthorpe
Myton-on-Swale
Flawith
Alne
Bishop Monkton
Roecliffe
Markington
Minskip
Lower Dunsforth
Cross Lane
Wormald Green
Burton Leonard
Copgrove
Aldwark
Tollerton
Grafton
Upper Dunsforth
Youlton
Bishop Thornton
South Stainley
Marton
TOLL
Mills
Bedlam
Staveley
Linton-on-Ouse
Great Ouseburn
Little Ouseburn
Brearton
Burnt Yates
Ripley
RIPLEY CASTLE
Nidd
Farnham
Ferrensby
Arkendale
Clint
147
Scotton
Scriven
Coneythorpe
Thorpe Underwood
Newton on Ouse
Hampsthwaite
Killinghall
KNARESBOROUGH CASTLE & COURTHOUSE MUSEUM
ALLERTON PARK
Flaxby
Allerton Mauleverer
Knaresborough
Whixley
Nun Monkton
BENINGBROUGH HALL
Beningbrough
Green Hammerton
New Park
Starbeck
MOTHER SHIPTON'S CAVE
Goldsborough
Hopperton
Moor Monkton
MERCER ART GALLERY
KILLINGHALL MOOR
Forest Lane Head
Woodlands
Harrogate
RHS GARDEN HARLOW CARR
Kirk Hammerton
Nether Poppleton
Upper Poppleton
PLUMPTON ROCKS
Walshford
Cattal
Hunsingore
MARSTON MOOR
Harlow Hill
Oatlands
Little Ribston
Tockwith
1644
Hessay
Rossett Green
Follifoot
Cowthorpe
Long Marston
Rufforth
Brackenthwaite
Pannal
SPOFFORTH CASTLE
Spofforth
North Deighton
Bickerton
WETHERBY SERVICES
Hutton Wandesley
Spacey Houses
Kirk Deighton
North Rigton
Bilton in Ainsty
Braythorn
Kirkby Overflow
Sicklinghall
WETHERBY
Walton
Askham Bryan
Stainburn
Wetherby
Angram
Huby
Weeton
Netherby
Chapel Hill
Linton
Wighill
Healaugh
Askham Richard
Dunkeswick
Collingham
Bilbrough
Castley
Harewood
Thorp Arch
Catterton
Boston Spa
Newton Kyme
Arthington
HAREWOOD HOUSE
Weardley
East Keswick
Clifford
Bramhope
Bardsey
East Rigton
Bramham
Tadcaster
Eccup
Wike
Scarcroft
BRAMHAM PARK
Stutton
Kirkby Wharfe
Bolton Percy
Eccup Res.
Scarcroft Hill
Thorner
Ulleskelf
Alwoodley
Shadwell
P&R
Moor Allerton
Adel
Roundhay
Towton
Potterton
Meanwood
Chapel Allerton
Wellington Hill
Barwick in Elmet
Scholes
Church Fenton
1461
Headingley
Potternewton
Aberford
Saxton
Seacroft
LOTHERTON HALL
Kirkstall
Woodhouse
Harehills
Manston
Barkston
Biggin
Burley
Sheepscar
Whitkirk
Old Micklefield
Sherburn in Elmet
Little Fenton
LEEDS INDUSTRIAL MUS
Armley
Halton
GARFORTH
Garden Village
LEEDS
HOME FARM
Colton
Newthorpe
STEETON HALL GATEWAY
Holbeck
Wortley
Farnley
Hunslet
TEMPLE NEWSAM HOUSE
New Micklefield
South Milford
Hambleton
THWAITE MILLS INDUSTRIAL MUS
Beeston
TEMPLE NEWSAM
Kippax
Ledston Luck
Monk Fryston
New Farnley
Swillington
Lumby
Woodlesford
Great Preston
Ledsham
140
139
Rothwell
Haigh
Oulton
Ledston
Hillam
Aire
Wharfe
Ouse
Nidd
DERE STREET
A61
A59
A658
A659
A660
A6120
A64
A58
A63
A1(M)
M1
A168
A6055
A661
A19
A162
A656
A642
A62
A6110
A647
B6265
B6165
B6161
B6164
B1224
B1217
B1222
B1223
0 1 2 3 miles
0 1 2 3 4 5 km

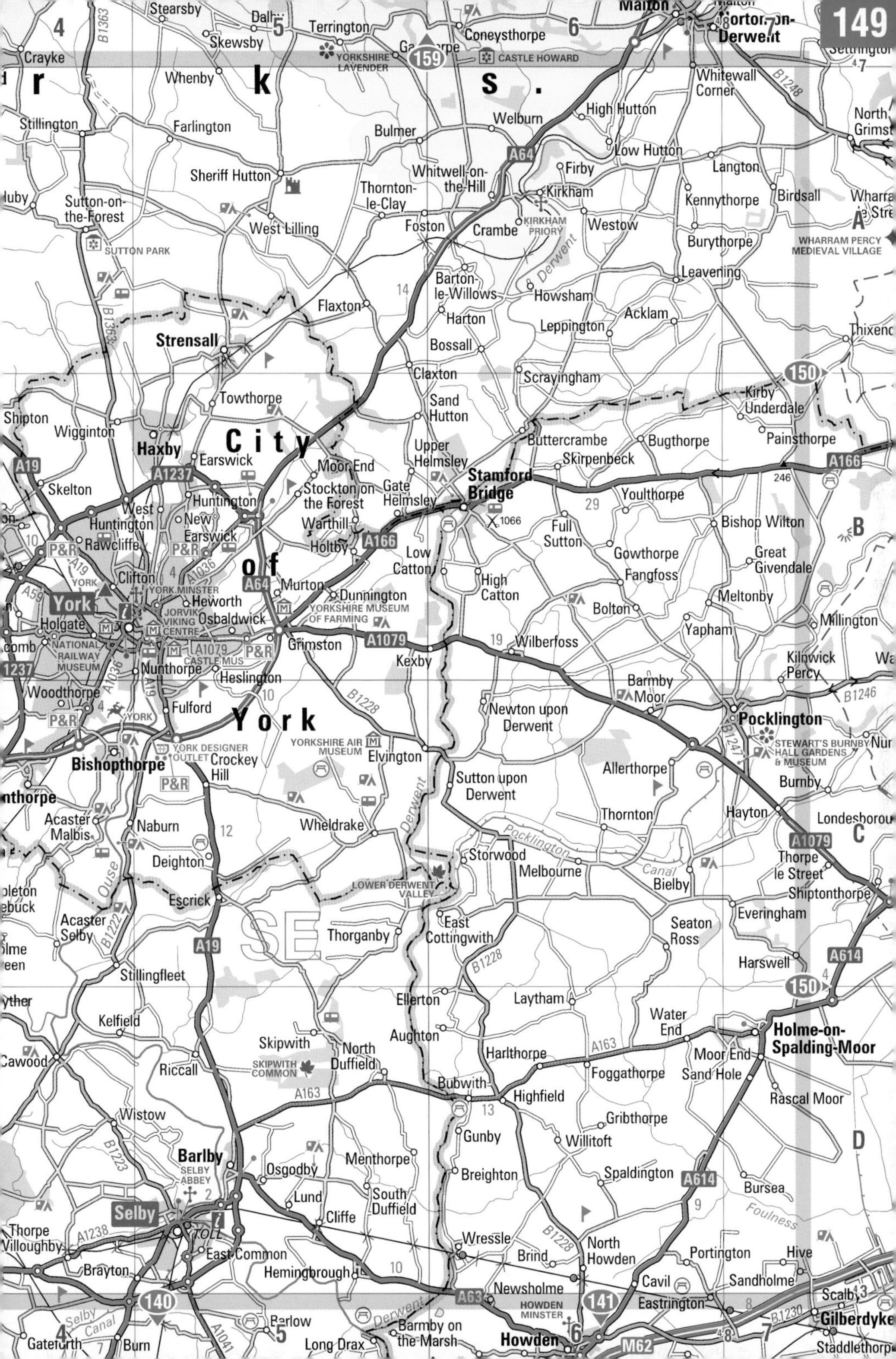

Stearsby
Dalby
Terrington
Coneysthorpe
Malton
Norton-on-Derwent
Crayke
Skewsby
YORKSHIRE LAVENDER
159
CASTLE HOWARD
Whenby
Whitewall Corner
B1248
B1363
r
k
s
.
High Hutton
Welburn
Stillington
Farlington
Bulmer
North Grimston
A64
Low Hutton
Langton
Firby
Sheriff Hutton
Whitwell-on-the-Hill
Thornton-le-Clay
Kirkham
Kennythorpe
Birdsall
Sutton-on-the-Forest
Westow
KIRKHAM PRIORY
West Lilling
Foston
Crambe
Burythorpe
WHARRAM PERCY MEDIEVAL VILLAGE
SUTTON PARK
R. Derwent
Leavening
Barton-le-Willows
Howsham
14
Flaxton
Acklam
Harton
Leppington
Strensall
Thixendale
Bossall
Claxton
Scrayingham
150
Towthorpe
Sand Hutton
Kirby Underdale
Shipton
Wigginton
City
Buttercrambe
Bugthorpe
Painsthorpe
Haxby
Upper Helmsley
Earswick
Skirpenbeck
A166
Moor End
A19
A1237
Stamford Bridge
246
Skelton
Stockton on the Forest
Gate Helmsley
Youlthorpe
Huntington
29
West Huntington
New Earswick
Warthill
1066
Full Sutton
Bishop Wilton
Holtby
10
Rawcliffe
P&R
A166
Low Catton
Gowthorpe
Great Givendale
of
Fangfoss
A19
YORK
Clifton
A1036
A59
YORK MINSTER
A64
Murton
High Catton
York
Heworth
Dunnington
Meltonby
Bolton
JORVIK VIKING CENTRE
YORKSHIRE MUSEUM OF FARMING
Millington
Holgate
Osbaldwick
Grimston
A1079
19
Wilberfoss
Yapham
NATIONAL RAILWAY MUSEUM
A1079
Kexby
Kilnwick Percy
CASTLE MUS
Nunthorpe
Heslington
1237
A1036
A19
Barmby Moor
B1246
Woodthorpe
10
B1228
Newton upon Derwent
Pocklington
4
YORK
Fulford
York
B1247
STEWART'S BURNBY HALL GARDENS & MUSEUM
YORKSHIRE AIR MUSEUM
Bishopthorpe
YORK DESIGNER OUTLET
Crockey Hill
Elvington
Allerthorpe
Sutton upon Derwent
Burnby
Hayton
Londesborough
Acaster Malbis
Naburn
Derwent
Wheldrake
Thornton
12
A1079
Deighton
Storwood
Pocklington Canal
Thorpe le Street
Melbourne
Bielby
Ouse
LOWER DERWENT VALLEY
Shiptonthorpe
Escrick
Acaster Selby
B1222
SE
East Cottingwith
Everingham
Seaton Ross
Thorganby
A19
B1228
A614
Harswell
Stillingfleet
150
4
Ellerton
Laytham
Water End
Kelfield
Holme-on-Spalding-Moor
Skipwith
Aughton
A163
Moor End
Sand Hole
North Duffield
Harlthorpe
Foggathorpe
Cawood
Riccall
SKIPWITH COMMON
A163
Bubwith
Rascal Moor
13
Highfield
Gribthorpe
Wistow
Gunby
Willitoft
B1223
Menthorpe
Barlby
Osgodby
Breighton
Spaldington
A614
SELBY ABBEY
2
Lund
South Duffield
Bursea
Selby
9
Foulness
Cliffe
Thorpe Willoughby
A1238
TOLL
B1228
North Howden
Wressle
Brayton
East Common
Brind
Portington
Hive
Hemingbrough
10
Sandholme
Cavil
Newsholme
A63
Eastrington
Scalby
140
HOWDEN MINSTER
141
8
13
B1230
Selby Canal
Barlow
Derwent
Gilberdyke
A1041
Barmby on the Marsh
Howden
6
4
Gateforth
Burn
5
Long Drax
M62
7
Staddlethorpe
A
B
C
D
4
5
6
7

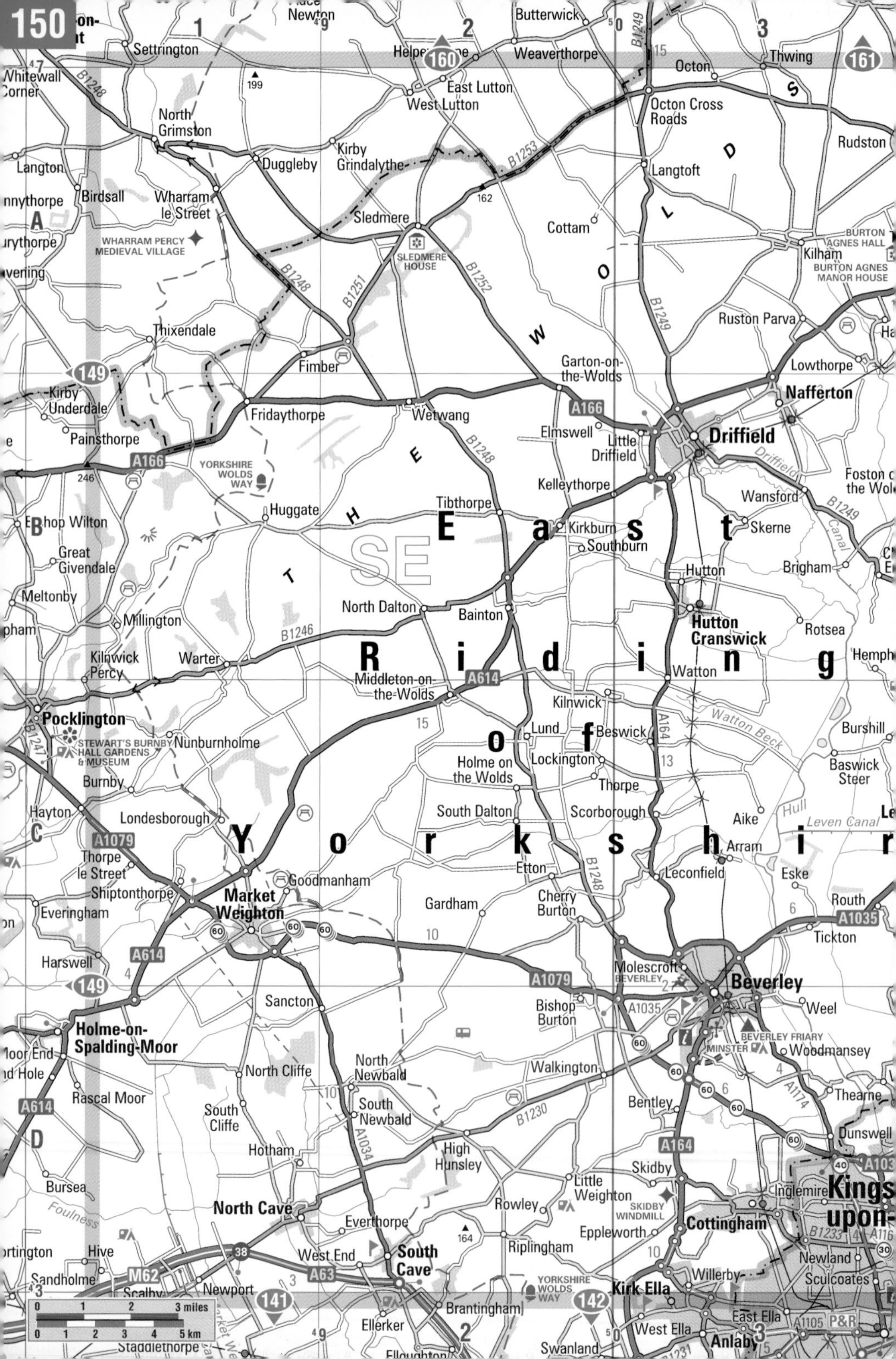
East Riding of Yorkshire
THE WOLDS
SE
Settrington
Whitewall Corner
North Grimston
Langton
Birdsall
Wharram le Street
Duggleby
Kirby Grindalythe
Sledmere
SLEDMERE HOUSE
WHARRAM PERCY MEDIEVAL VILLAGE
Thixendale
Fimber
Kirby Underdale
Fridaythorpe
Wetwang
Painsthorpe
YORKSHIRE WOLDS WAY
Huggate
Bishop Wilton
Great Givendale
Meltonby
Millington
Kilnwick Percy
Warter
Pocklington
STEWART'S BURNBY HALL GARDENS & MUSEUM
Nunburnholme
Burnby
Hayton
Londesborough
Thorpe le Street
Shiptonthorpe
Everingham
Market Weighton
Goodmanham
Harswell
Holme-on-Spalding-Moor
Rascal Moor
Sancton
North Cliffe
South Cliffe
Hotham
North Cave
Bursea
Foulness
Hive
Sandholme
Newport
M62
A63
West End
Everthorpe
South Cave
Ellerker
Brantingham
North Newbald
South Newbald
High Hunsley
Rowley
Riplingham
Walkington
Bishop Burton
Gardham
Etton
Cherry Burton
South Dalton
Holme on the Wolds
Lund
Kilnwick
Middleton-on-the-Wolds
North Dalton
Bainton
Tibthorpe
Kirkburn
Southburn
Garton-on-the-Wolds
Elmswell
Little Driffield
Driffield
Kelleythorpe
Hutton
Hutton Cranswick
Watton
Beswick
Lockington
Thorpe
Scorborough
Leconfield
Arram
Aike
Molescroft
Beverley
BEVERLEY FRIARY
MINSTER
Weel
Woodmansey
Thearne
Dunswell
Bentley
Skidby
SKIDBY WINDMILL
Little Weighton
Eppleworth
Cottingham
Kirk Ella
West Ella
Willerby
Anlaby
East Ella
Swanland
Kingston upon Hull
Newland
Sculcoates
Inglemire
Butterwick
Weaverthorpe
East Lutton
West Lutton
Helperthorpe
Octon
Thwing
Octon Cross Roads
Langtoft
Cottam
Rudston
BURTON AGNES HALL
Kilham
BURTON AGNES MANOR HOUSE
Ruston Parva
Lowthorpe
Nafferton
Wansford
Skerne
Brigham
Rotsea
Foster
Burshill
Baswick Steer
Eske
Routh
Tickton
Watton Beck
Driffield Canal
Leven Canal
Hull
A166
A614
A1079
A1035
A164
A1034
A1174
B1248
B1249
B1251
B1252
B1253
B1246
B1247
B1230
149
160
161
141
142
0 1 2 3 miles
0 1 2 3 4 5 km

FLAMBOROUGH HEAD
Flamborough
Grindale
Boynton
Sewerby
SEWERBY HALL AND GARDENS
BONDVILLE MODEL VILLAGE
PRIORY
BAYLE MUSEUM
Bridlington
OLD PENNY MEMORIES
West Hill
Hilderthorpe
Bessingby
Carnaby
Haisthorpe
BRIDLINGTON BAY
PARK ROSE BIRD OF PREY CENTRE
Burton Agnes
Fraisthorpe
Gransmoor
Barmston
Great Kelk
Lissett
Gembling
Ulrome
SKIPSEA CASTLE
Skipsea
Beeford
Skipsea Brough
Dunnington
Bewholme
Atwick
North Cliff
Hornsea
Hornsea Mere
HORNSEA MUSEUM
FREEPORT HORNSEA
Hornsea Bridge
Brandesburton
Seaton
Sigglesthorne
Catwick
Goxhill
Rolston
Mappleton
Little Hatfield
Great Hatfield
Great Cowden
Rise
Arnold
Withernwick
New Ellerby
Skirlaugh
Aldbrough
Marton
West Newton
East Newton
Old Ellerby
BURTON CONSTABLE HALL
Flinton
Garton
Grimston
Swine
Coniston
Sproatley
Humbleton
Fitling
Hilston
Thirtleby
Ganstead
Bransholme
Sutton on Hull
Bilton
Lelley
Owstwick
Tunstall
Elstronwick
Sutton Ings
Stoneferry
Preston
Burton Pidsea
North End
Roos
Summergangs
WILBERFORCE HOUSE
West End
Saltend
Waxholme
Marfleet
Hedon
Rimswell
Owthorne
Withernsea
STREETLIFE
TA
A165
A614
A1033
B1255
B1259
B1249
B1242
B1244
B1243
B1238
B1240
B1239
B1237
B1362
161
142
143
P&R

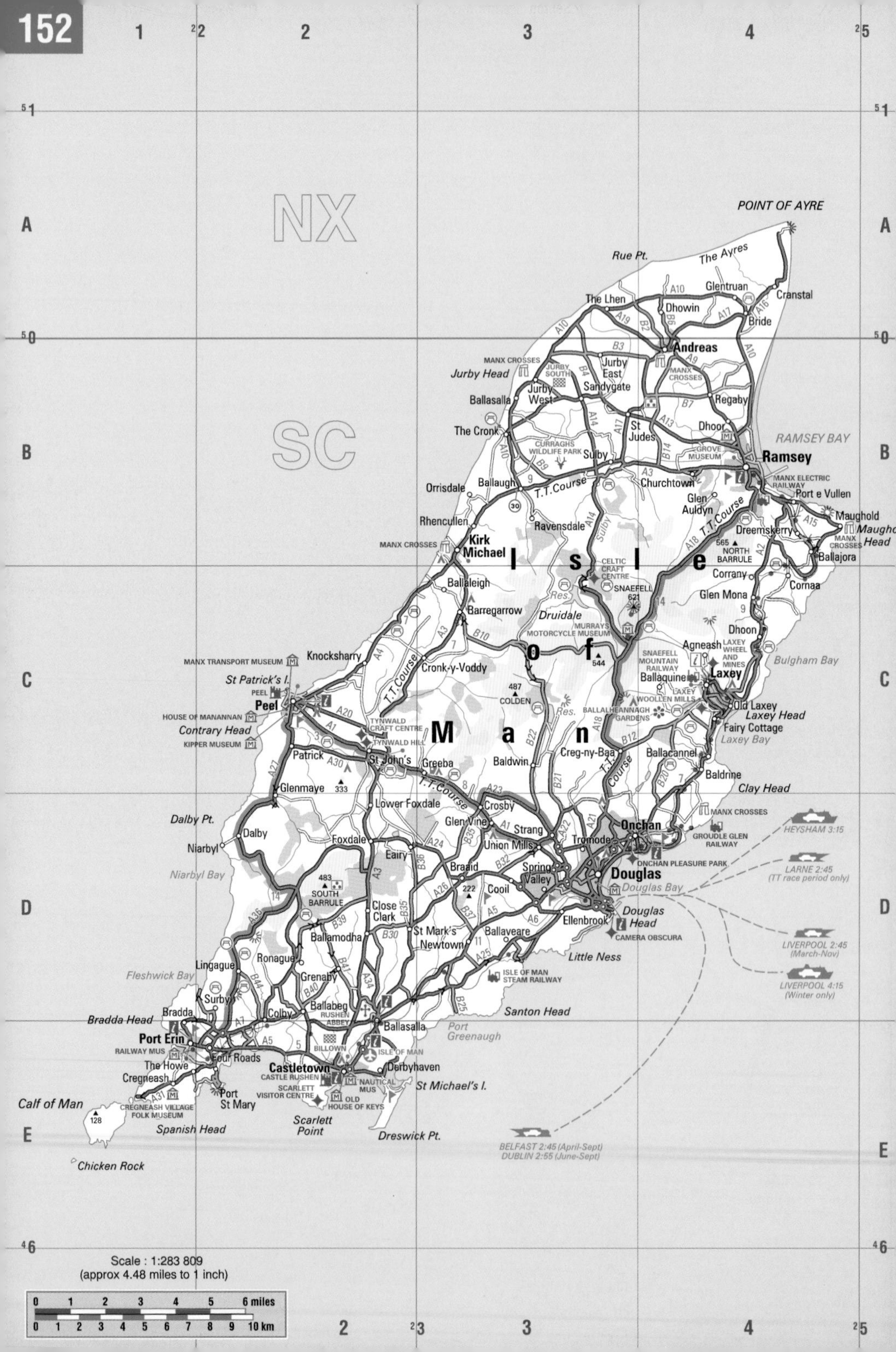

NX
SC
Isle of Man
POINT OF AYRE
Rue Pt.
The Ayres
Glentruan
Cranstal
The Lhen
Dhowin
Bride
Andreas
MANX CROSSES
Jurby Head
JURBY SOUTH
Jurby East
Jurby West
Sandygate
Ballasalla
Regaby
The Cronk
St Judes
Dhoor
RAMSEY BAY
CURRAGHS WILDLIFE PARK
GROVE MUSEUM
Sulby
Ramsey
Orrisdale
Ballaugh
T.T. Course
Churchtown
MANX ELECTRIC RAILWAY
Port e Vullen
Glen Auldyn
Rhencullen
Ravensdale
Maughold
Maughold Head
Dreemskerry
Kirk Michael
565 NORTH BARRULE
Ballajora
CELTIC CRAFT CENTRE
Corrany
Ballaleigh
SNAEFELL 621
Cornaa
Glen Mona
Barregarrow
Druidale
MURRAYS MOTORCYCLE MUSEUM
Dhoon
Agneash
LAXEY WHEEL AND MINES
MANX TRANSPORT MUSEUM
Knocksharry
544
SNAEFELL MOUNTAIN RAILWAY
Bulgham Bay
Cronk-y-Voddy
Laxey
St Patrick's I.
PEEL
Ballaquine
LAXEY WOOLLEN MILLS
487 COLDEN
Peel
Res.
BALLALHEANNAGH GARDENS
Old Laxey
HOUSE OF MANANNAN
TYNWALD CRAFT CENTRE
Laxey Head
Contrary Head
TYNWALD HILL
Fairy Cottage
Laxey Bay
KIPPER MUSEUM
Patrick
St John's
Creg-ny-Baa
Ballacannel
Greeba
Baldwin
Baldrine
Glenmaye
333
Clay Head
Lower Foxdale
Crosby
MANX CROSSES
Dalby Pt.
Glen Vine
Strang
Onchan
HEYSHAM 3:15
Dalby
Niarbyl
Union Mills
Tromode
GROUDLE GLEN RAILWAY
Foxdale
Eairy
Niarbyl Bay
Braaid
Spring Valley
ONCHAN PLEASURE PARK
LARNE 2:45 (TT race period only)
483 SOUTH BARRULE
222
Cooil
Douglas
Douglas Bay
Close Clark
Douglas Head
St Mark's
Ballaveare
Ellenbrook
CAMERA OBSCURA
Ballamodha
Newtown
LIVERPOOL 2:45 (March-Nov)
Little Ness
Ronague
Lingague
Grenaby
ISLE OF MAN STEAM RAILWAY
LIVERPOOL 4:15 (Winter only)
Fleshwick Bay
Surby
Bradda
Colby
Ballabeg
RUSHEN ABBEY
Ballasalla
Santon Head
Bradda Head
Port Greenaugh
Port Erin
BILLOWN
RAILWAY MUS
Four Roads
ISLE OF MAN
The Howe
Castletown
Derbyhaven
Cregneash
CASTLE RUSHEN
NAUTICAL MUS
St Michael's I.
Port St Mary
SCARLETT VISITOR CENTRE
OLD HOUSE OF KEYS
Calf of Man
CREGNEASH VILLAGE FOLK MUSEUM
128
Spanish Head
Scarlett Point
Dreswick Pt.
BELFAST 2:45 (April-Sept)
DUBLIN 2:55 (June-Sept)
Chicken Rock
Scale : 1:283 809
(approx 4.48 miles to 1 inch)
0 1 2 3 4 5 6 miles
0 1 2 3 4 5 6 7 8 9 10 km

Seascale
Santon Bridge
Eskdale Green
Beckfoot
Boot
Eskdale
Hardknott Pass
Wrynose Pass
Cockley Beck
FURNESS FELLS
Holmrook
Drigg
Irt
Mite
Esk
Saltcoats
RAVENGLASS AND ESKDALE RAILWAY & MUS
BATHHOUSE
Ravenglass
MUNCASTER CASTLE & WORLD OWL CENTRE
Devoke Water
Birker Fell
649 HARTER FELL
Seathwaite Tarn
CONISTON COPPERMINES
CONISTON HOLLY HOW
801 THE OLD MAN OF CONISTON
Bowmanstead
Woodend
Hall Dunnerdale
Seathwaite
Ulpha Fell
Duddon
529 CAW
Broad Oak
Newbiggin
Lane End
572 WHITFELL
Ulpha
Hoses
Torver
Coniston Water
A595
Corney Fell
A593
Stub Place
Corney
Broughton Mills
A5084
Hycemoor
Selker Bay
Water Yeat
Blawith
High Nibthwaite
Duddon Bridge
Lower Hawthwaite
Bootle
Broughton in Furness
Lowick Bridge
Black Combe
600
Hallthwaites
DUDDON MOSSES
Foxfield
Grizebeck
Lowick Green
A5092
Gawthwaite
Whitbeck
The Green
333
B5281
The Hill
Kirkby-in-Furness
Beck Side
Penny Bridge
Whicham
Silecroft
A5093
Broughton Beck
Greenodd
Arrad Foot
Kirksanton
Millom
MILLOM DISCOVERY CENTRE
Soutergate
Mansriggs
A590
LAUREL & HARDY MUS
Haverigg
DUDDON SANDS
A595
Ulverston
Askam in Furness
Ireleth
Pennington
Swarthmoor
Lindal in Furness
A5087
SOUTH LAKES WILD ANIMAL PARK
SD
SANDSCALE HAWS
Great Urswick
Dalton-in-Furness
A590
DALTON CASTLE
Stainton with Adgarley
Little Urswick
NORTH WALNEY
Scales
Baycliff
BARROW (WALNEY ISLAND)
Hawcoat
BOW BRIDGE
Newton
GLEASTON WATERMILL
Ormsgill
FURNESS ABBEY
Barrow-in-Furness
Newbarns
87
Dendron
Gleaston
Aldingham
North Scale
CUSTOM HO
Newbiggin
Leece
THE DOCK MUSEUM
Vickerstown
Barrow Island
A5087
Roosebeck
Biggar
Rampside
Roa Island
Foulney Island
South Channel
South End
Piel Island
Isle of Walney
South End Point
0 1 2 3 miles
0 1 2 3 4 5 km

LAKE DISTRICT NATIONAL PARK
Cumb
163
164
153
144
145
A591
A592
A593
A5092
A5084
A590
A6
A65
A5074
B5343
B5286
B5285
B5284
B5281
B5278
B5277
B5271
B5282
B6385
B6384
A6070
M6
HIGH WHITE STONES
762
Easedale Tarn
GRASMERE THORNEY HOW
GRASMERE BUTHARLYP HOWE
DOVE COTTAGE AND WORDSWORTH MUSEUM
Stickle Tarn
Grasmere
Langdale Pikes
Chapel Stile
Rydal
RYDAL MOUNT
Rydal Water
ELTERWATER
LANGDALE
Elterwater
Little Langdale
Ambleside
Clappersgate
Waterhead
ROMAN FORT
AMBLESIDE
Troutbeck
TOWNEND
Skelwith Bridge
Brathay
Wrynose Pass
Cockley Beck
322
BROCKHOLE - NAT PK VISITOR CENTRE
WINDERMERE
HOLEHIRD GARDENS
Low Wray
Troutbeck Bridge
FURNESS FELLS
Seathwaite Tarn
CONISTON COPPERMINES
CONISTON HOLLY HOW
801
THE OLD MAN OF CONISTON
Coniston
Bowmanstead
Outgate
HAWKSHEAD COURTHOUSE
Hawkshead Hill
High Wray
Colthouse
WINDERMERE STEAMBOATS & MUS.
Windermere
Bowness-on-Windermere
BEATRIX POTTER GALLERY
Hawkshead
Esthwaite Water
GONDOLA
BRANTWOOD
HAWKSHEAD
THE WORLD OF BEATRIX POTTER
Near Sawrey
Ferney Green
Grizedale
GRIZEDALE FOREST PARK VISITOR CENTRE
HILL TOP
Far Sawrey
Forest
Grizedale
GRIZEDALE FOREST PARK
Torver
Coniston Water
Storrs
Winster
Satterthwaite
Force Mills
335
FOREST SPINNERS
Water Yeat
Blawith
High Nibthwaite
FURNESS FELLS
Rusland
RUSLAND MOSS
STOTT PARK BOBBIN MILL
Finsthwaite
WINDERMERE
321
Oxen Park
Lakeside
AQUARIUM OF THE LAKES
FELL FOOT
Lowick Bridge
Lowick Green
Colton
Bouth
Staveley
Newby Bridge
LAKESIDE AND HAVERTHWAITE RAILWAY
Grizebeck
Gawthwaite
Spark Bridge
Backbarrow
333
Haverthwaite
Ayside
Penny Bridge
Broughton Beck
Greenodd
Field Broughton
Arrad Foot
Mansriggs
ROUDSEA WOOD AND MOSSES
LAUREL & HARDY MUS
Ulverston
CARTMEL
CARTMEL PRIORY
Cartmel
Pennington
HOLKER HALL
Holker
Allithwaite
Swarthmoor
CONISHEAD PRIORY & MANJUSHRI KADAMPA MEDITATION CENTRE
Cark
Flookburgh
Kents Bank
Cartmel Sands
Great Urswick
Ravenstown
LAKELAND RIDING CENTRE
Bardsea
Little Urswick
Stainton
Adgarley
Scales
Baycliff
GLEASTON WATERMILL
87
Gleaston
Aldingham
Humphrey Head Pt.
MORECAMBE BAY
Sadgill
Long Sleddale
Shap Fells
Kentmere
530
Kent
828 HIGH STREET
774 HARTER FELL
776
Kirkstone Pass
Inn
Lowbridge House
Elfhowe
Ings
Staveley
Garnett Bridge
Bowston
Burneside
LAKELAND CLIMBING CENTRE
Crook
Underbarrow
Crosthwaite
229
KENDAL
Kendal
K VILLAGE
K VILLAGE HERITAGE C
Gregg Hall
Bowland Bridge
Row
Gilpin
Brigsteer
Natland
Oxenholme
Cartmel Fell
The Howe
SIZERGH
Cotes
Sedgwick
Levens
Stainton
WHITBARROW
Sampool Bridge
Hincaster
Endmoor
Witherslack
Mill Side
High Newton
Town End
LEVENS HALL
Leasgill
Crooklands
Low Newton
Heversham
Milnthorpe
Meathop
Lindale
Storth
Beetham
HERON CORN MILL
ARNSIDE
Arnside
Grange-over-Sands
LAKELAND WILDLIFE OASIS
Holme
GAIT BARROWS
Yealand Redmayne
ARNSIDE AND SILVERDALE
Silverdale
Yealand Conyers
BURTON-IN-KENDAL SERVICES (Northbound)
LEIGHTON HALL
Warton
Warton Sands
Borwick
OLD RECTORY
Millhead
Carnforth
Over Kellet
Nether Kellet
Bolton-le-Sands
Farleton
Watchgate
Garth Row
Meal Bank
Middleshaw
Barrows Green
Gatebeck
Clawthorpe
Burton-in-Kendal
Priest Hutton
Capernwray
902
Res.
0 1 2 3 miles
0 1 2 3 4 5 km

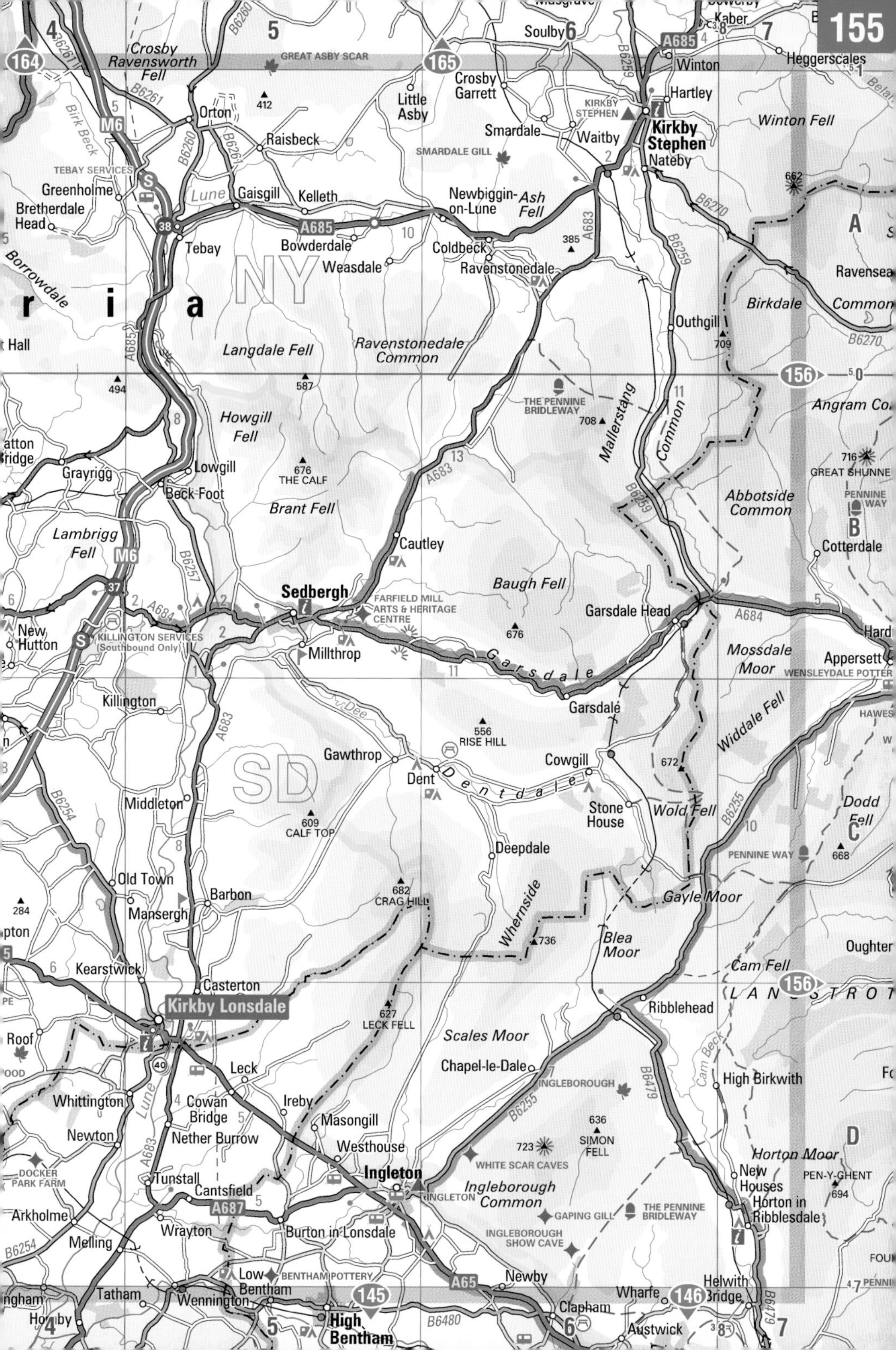
164
165
Crosby Ravensworth Fell
GREAT ASBY SCAR
412
Little Asby
Soulby
Crosby Garrett
Kaber
Winton
Heggerscales
Hartley
KIRKBY STEPHEN
Kirkby Stephen
Winton Fell
Smardale
Waitby
Nateby
SMARDALE GILL
Orton
Raisbeck
TEBAY SERVICES
Greenholme
Bretherdale Head
Gaisgill
Kelleth
Newbiggin-on-Lune
Ash Fell
Tebay
Bowderdale
Weasdale
Coldbeck
Ravenstonedale
385
Borrowdale
NY
Outhgill
Birkdale
Ravenseat
Common
Langdale Fell
Ravenstonedale Common
494
587
709
THE PENNINE BRIDLEWAY
Mallerstang Common
708
156
Angram Co
Howgill Fell
Grayrigg
Lowgill
Beck Foot
676 THE CALF
Brant Fell
716 GREAT SHUNNER
PENNINE WAY
Abbotside Common
Cotterdale
Lambrigg Fell
Cautley
Baugh Fell
Sedbergh
FARFIELD MILL ARTS & HERITAGE CENTRE
Garsdale Head
New Hutton
KILLINGTON SERVICES (Southbound Only)
Millthrop
676
Garsdale
Mossdale Moor
Appersett
WENSLEYDALE POTTER
Killington
Garsdale
Widdale Fell
HAWES
556 RISE HILL
Gawthrop
Dent
Cowgill
Dentdale
672
SD
Middleton
609 CALF TOP
Stone House
Wold Fell
Dodd Fell
Deepdale
PENNINE WAY
668
Old Town
682 CRAG HILL
Barbon
Gayle Moor
284
Mansergh
Whernside
736
Blea Moor
Oughter
Kearstwick
Casterton
Cam Fell
Kirkby Lonsdale
LECK FELL
627
Ribblehead
LANGSTROT
Roof
Scales Moor
Leck
Chapel-le-Dale
INGLEBOROUGH
High Birkwith
Whittington
Cowan Bridge
Ireby
636 SIMON FELL
Newton
Nether Burrow
Masongill
723
Westhouse
Horton Moor
DOCKER PARK FARM
WHITE SCAR CAVES
Tunstall
Cantsfield
Ingleton
Ingleborough Common
New Houses
PEN-Y-GHENT
694
INGLETON
Arkholme
Horton in Ribblesdale
Wrayton
Burton in Lonsdale
GAPING GILL
THE PENNINE BRIDLEWAY
Melling
INGLEBOROUGH SHOW CAVE
Low Bentham
BENTHAM POTTERY
Newby
Helwith Bridge
Tatham
Wennington
145
Wharfe
146
Hornby
Clapham
High Bentham
Austwick

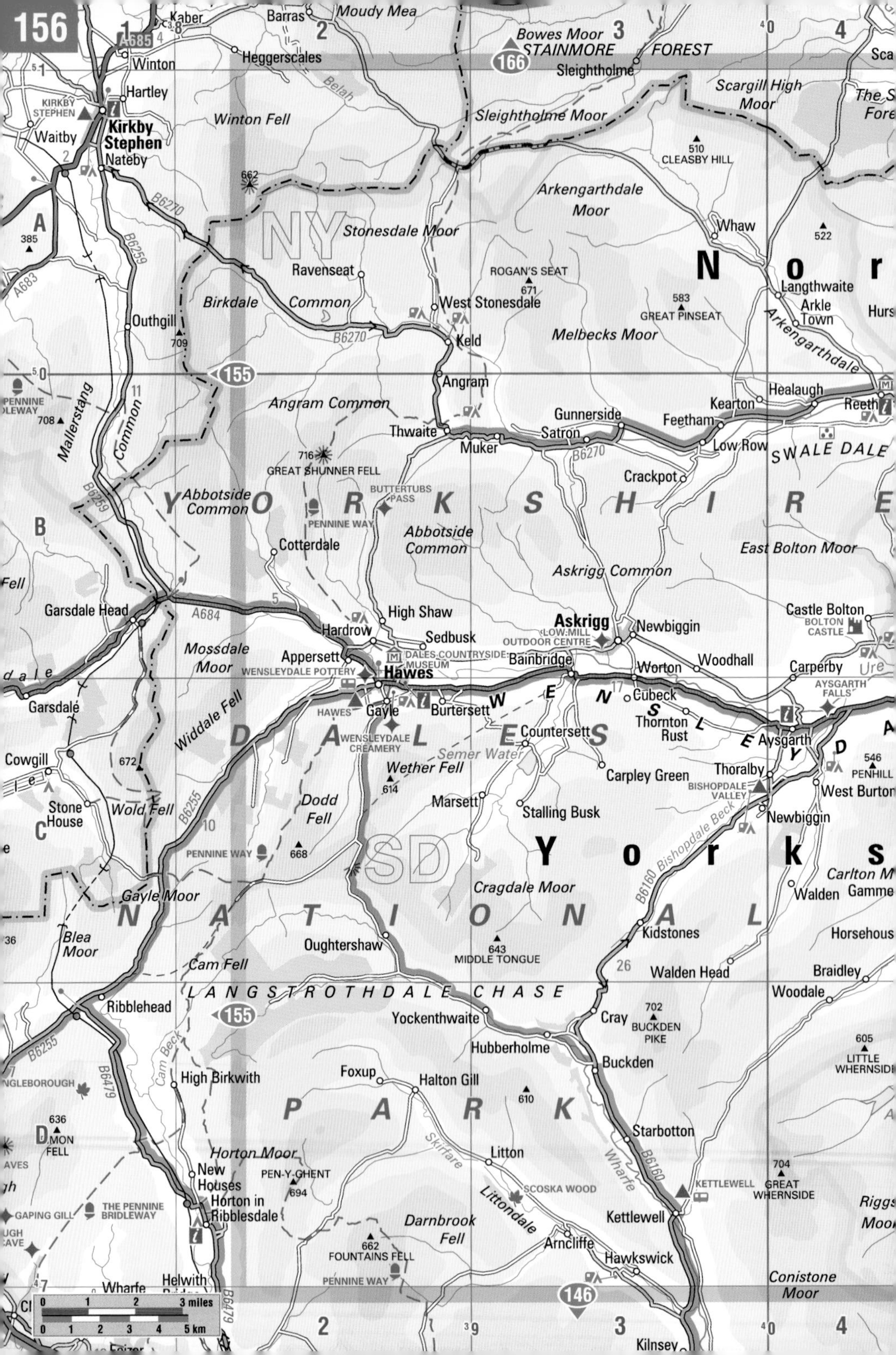
Kaber
Barras
Moudy Mea
Bowes Moor
STAINMORE FOREST
166
Sleightholme
Winton
Heggerscales
Hartley
KIRKBY STEPHEN
Kirkby Stephen
Waitby
Nateby
Belah
Winton Fell
Scargill High Moor
Sleightholme Moor
510 CLEASBY HILL
662
Arkengarthdale Moor
NY
Stonesdale Moor
Whaw
522
Ravenseat
ROGAN'S SEAT 671
Birkdale Common
West Stonesdale
583 GREAT PINSEAT
Langthwaite
Arkle Town
Arkengarthdale
Outhgill
709
B6270
Keld
Melbecks Moor
155
Angram
PENNINE BRIDLEWAY
708
Mallerstang Common
Angram Common
Gunnerside
Kearton
Healaugh
Reeth
Thwaite
Satron
Feetham
Muker
Low Row
SWALE DALE
716
GREAT SHUNNER FELL
Crackpot
BUTTERTUBS PASS
Abbotside Common
PENNINE WAY
YORKSHIRE
Abbotside Common
East Bolton Moor
Cotterdale
Askrigg Common
Garsdale Head
A684
High Shaw
Askrigg
Newbiggin
Castle Bolton
BOLTON CASTLE
LOW MILL OUTDOOR CENTRE
Hardrow
Sedbusk
Mossdale Moor
Appersett
DALES COUNTRYSIDE MUSEUM
Bainbridge
Woodhall
WENSLEYDALE POTTERY
Hawes
Worton
Carperby
Ure
Garsdale
HAWES
Gayle
Burtersett
Cubeck
AYSGARTH FALLS
WENSLEYDALE
Widdale Fell
Thornton Rust
Countersett
Aysgarth
DALES
WENSLEYDALE CREAMERY
Semer Water
546 PENHILL
Cowgill
672
Wether Fell
614
Carpley Green
Thoralby
BISHOPDALE VALLEY
West Burton
Stone House
Wold Fell
Dodd Fell
Marsett
Stalling Busk
Newbiggin
B6255
Bishopdale Beck
PENNINE WAY
668
SD
Yorks
Carlton M
Walden
Gamme
Gayle Moor
Cragdale Moor
NATIONAL
B6160
Blea Moor
Oughtershaw
Kidstones
Horsehous
643 MIDDLE TONGUE
Cam Fell
26
Walden Head
Braidley
LANGSTROTHDALE CHASE
Woodale
Ribblehead
Yockenthwaite
Cray
702 BUCKDEN PIKE
605 LITTLE WHERNSIDE
Hubberholme
Cam Beck
INGLEBOROUGH
High Birkwith
B6479
Foxup
Halton Gill
Buckden
610
636
MON FELL
PARK
Skirfare
Starbotton
Horton Moor
Litton
Wharfe
New Houses
PEN-Y-GHENT 694
704 GREAT WHERNSIDE
Riggs Moor
SCOSKA WOOD
KETTLEWELL
GAPING GILL
THE PENNINE BRIDLEWAY
Horton in Ribblesdale
Littondale
Kettlewell
Darnbrook Fell
662 FOUNTAINS FELL
Arncliffe
Hawkswick
PENNINE WAY
Conistone Moor
Wharfe
Helwith Bridge
146
0 1 2 3 miles
0 1 2 3 4 5 km
Kilnsey
A
B
C
D
1
2
3
4

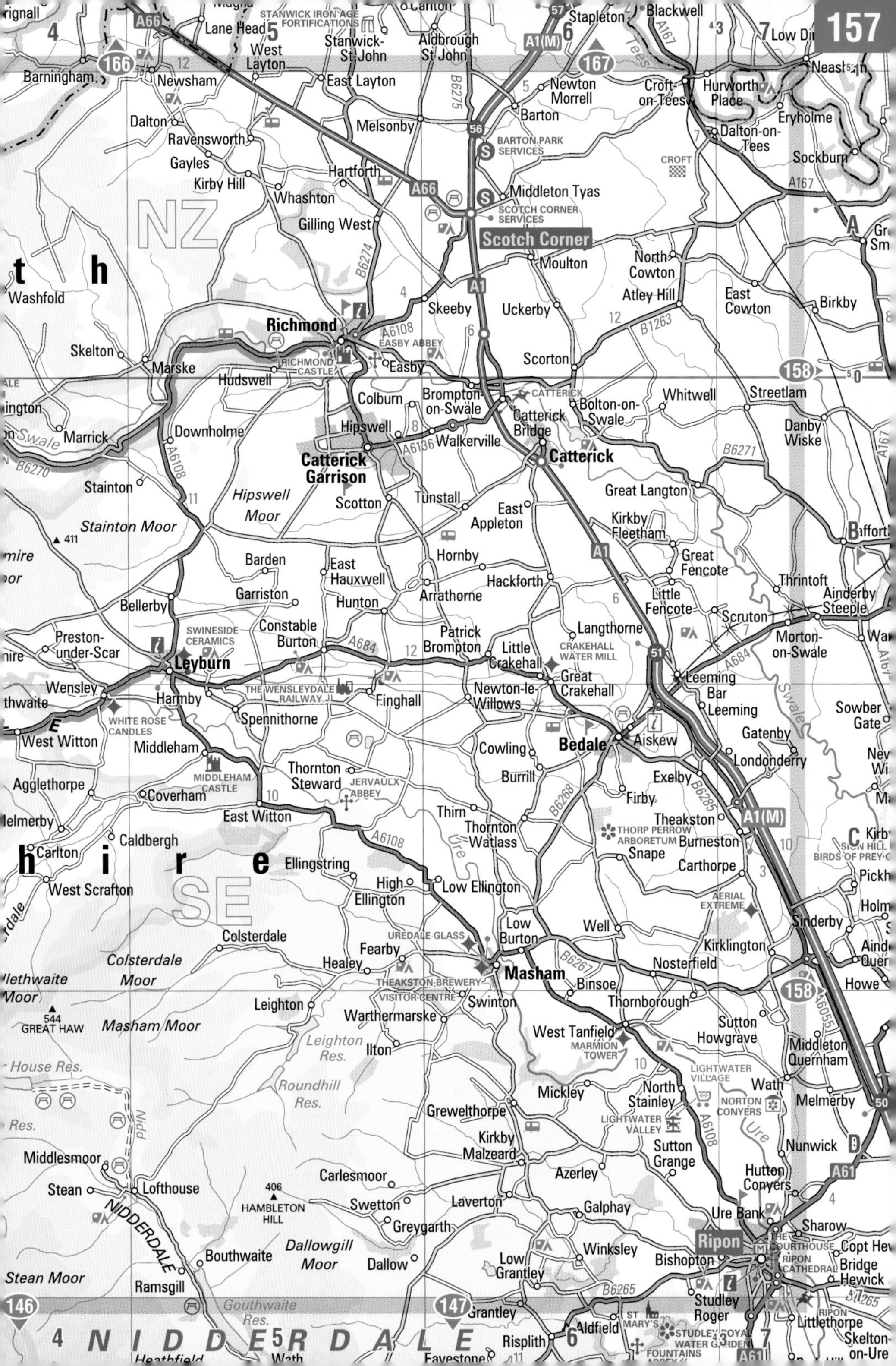
Barningham
Lane Head
STANWICK IRON AGE FORTIFICATIONS
Stanwick-St-John
Aldbrough St John
Stapleton
Blackwell
Low Dinsdale
West Layton
Newsham
East Layton
Newton Morrell
Croft-on-Tees
Hurworth Place
Neasham
Dalton
Barton
Melsonby
Ravensworth
BARTON PARK SERVICES
Dalton-on-Tees
Eryholme
Gayles
CROFT
Sockburn
Kirby Hill
Hartforth
Whashton
Middleton Tyas
SCOTCH CORNER SERVICES
Gilling West
Scotch Corner
NZ
Moulton
North Cowton
Washfold
Atley Hill
East Cowton
Birkby
Skeeby
Uckerby
Richmond
EASBY ABBEY
Skelton
RICHMOND CASTLE
Easby
Scorton
Marske
Hudswell
Colburn
Brompton-on-Swale
CATTERICK
Bolton-on-Swale
Whitwell
Streetlam
Marrick
Downholme
Hipswell
Catterick Bridge
Danby Wiske
Swale
Walkerville
Catterick
Catterick Garrison
Stainton
Hipswell Moor
Scotton
Tunstall
Great Langton
East Appleton
Stainton Moor
Kirkby Fleetham
411
Barden
East Hauxwell
Hornby
Great Fencote
Hackforth
Garriston
Thrintoft
Arrathorne
Little Fencote
Ainderby Steeple
Bellerby
Hunton
Scruton
Constable Burton
Langthorne
Preston-under-Scar
SWINESIDE CERAMICS
Patrick Brompton
Little Crakehall
CRAKEHALL WATER MILL
Morton-on-Swale
Leyburn
Great Crakehall
Leeming Bar
Wensley
THE WENSLEYDALE RAILWAY
Finghall
Newton-le-Willows
Leeming
Harmby
Spennithorne
Sowber Gate
WHITE ROSE CANDLES
West Witton
Middleham
Aiskew
Bedale
Cowling
Gatenby
Londonderry
MIDDLEHAM CASTLE
Thornton Steward
Burrill
Exelby
Agglethorpe
JERVAULX ABBEY
Coverham
Firby
East Witton
Thirn
Theakston
Thornton Watlass
THORP PERROW ARBORETUM
Melmerby
Caldbergh
Burneston
SION HILL BIRDS OF PREY CENTRE
Carlton
Snape
Carthorpe
Ellingstring
West Scrafton
High Ellington
Low Ellington
AERIAL EXTREME
SE
Sinderby
Well
Low Burton
Colsterdale
UREDALE GLASS
Kirklington
Fearby
Colsterdale Moor
Healey
Masham
Nosterfield
THEAKSTON BREWERY VISITOR CENTRE
Binsoe
Swinton
Thornborough
Leighton
544
GREAT HAW
Masham Moor
Warthermarske
West Tanfield
Sutton Howgrave
MARMION TOWER
Middleton Quernham
Leighton Res.
Ilton
LIGHTWATER VILLAGE
House Res.
Roundhill Res.
North Stainley
Wath
Mickley
NORTON CONYERS
Melmerby
Grewelthorpe
LIGHTWATER VALLEY
Res.
Nidd
Kirkby Malzeard
Sutton Grange
Nunwick
Middlesmoor
Carlesmoor
Azerley
Hutton Conyers
Stean
Lofthouse
406
HAMBLETON HILL
Swetton
Laverton
Galphay
Ure Bank
NIDDERDALE
Greygarth
Sharow
Ripon
THE COURTHOUSE
RIPON CATHEDRAL
Copt Hewick
Winksley
Bishopton
Bridge Hewick
Bouthwaite
Dallowgill Moor
Dallow
Low Grantley
Stean Moor
Ramsgill
Studley Roger
Gouthwaite Res.
Grantley
ST MARY'S
RIPON RACECOURSE
Littlethorpe
STUDLEY ROYAL WATER GARDEN
FOUNTAINS ABBEY
Aldfield
Risplith
Skelton-on-Ure
NIDDERDALE
Heathfield
Wath
Fayestone

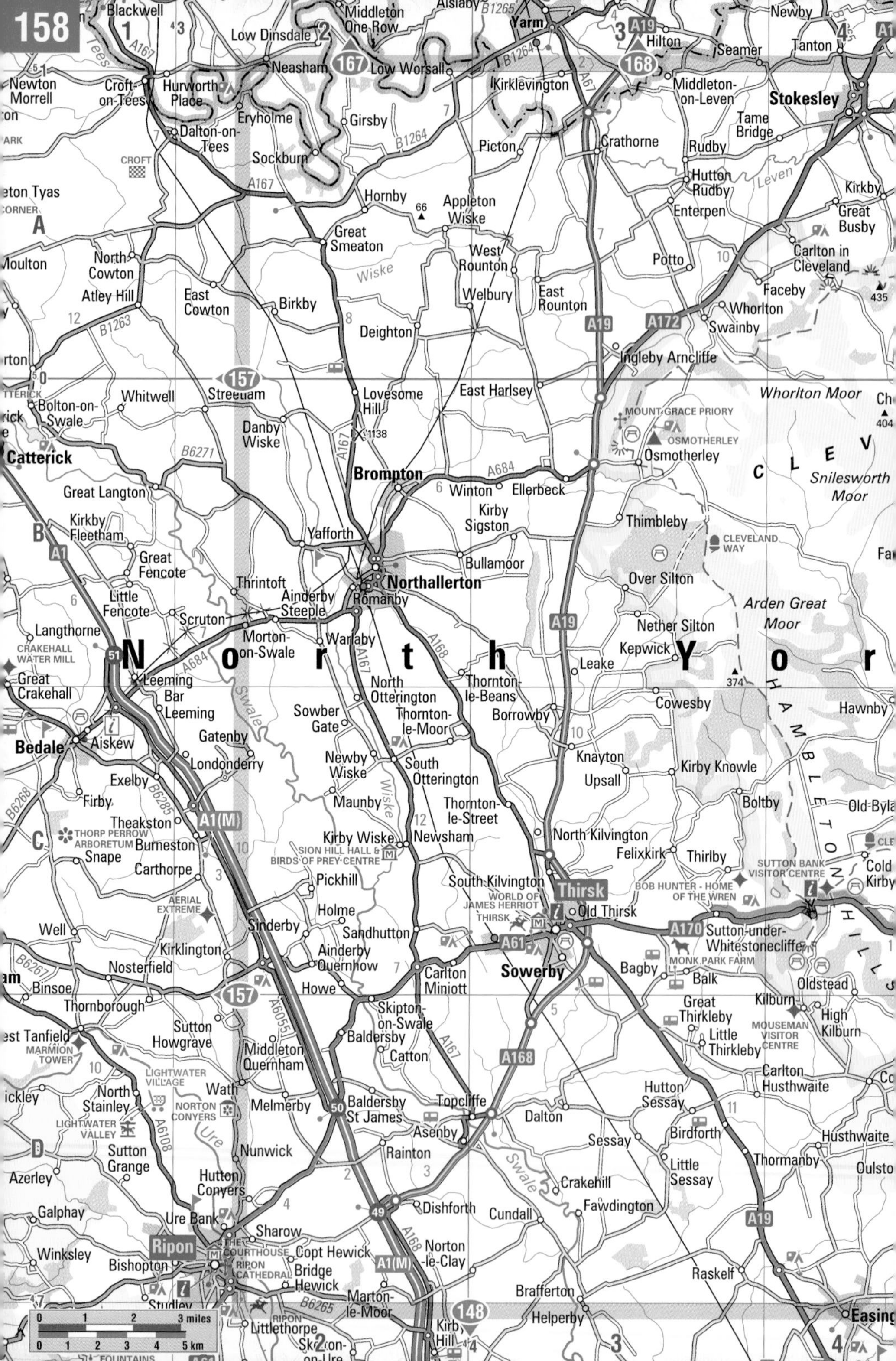
Blackwell
Middleton One Row
Aislaby
Yarm
Newby
Low Dinsdale
Hilton
Seamer
Tanton
Neasham
Low Worsall
Newton Morrell
Croft-on-Tees
Hurworth Place
Kirklevington
Middleton-on-Leven
Stokesley
Eryholme
Girsby
Dalton-on-Tees
Tame Bridge
Sockburn
Picton
Crathorne
Rudby
CROFT
Hutton Rudby
Leven
Hornby
Appleton Wiske
Enterpen
Kirkby
Great Busby
Great Smeaton
West Rounton
Potto
Carlton in Cleveland
Moulton
North Cowton
Wiske
Faceby
Atley Hill
East Cowton
Birkby
Welbury
East Rounton
Whorlton
Swainby
Deighton
Ingleby Arncliffe
Whitwell
Streetlam
Lovesome Hill
East Harlsey
Whorlton Moor
Bolton-on-Swale
Danby Wiske
MOUNT GRACE PRIORY
OSMOTHERLEY
Osmotherley
Catterick
Brompton
Winton
Ellerbeck
Great Langton
Snilesworth Moor
Kirkby Fleetham
Kirby Sigston
Thimbleby
Yafforth
CLEVELAND WAY
Great Fencote
Bullamoor
Thrintoft
Northallerton
Over Silton
Little Fencote
Ainderby Steeple
Romanby
Arden Great Moor
Scruton
Nether Silton
Langthorne
Morton-on-Swale
Warlaby
Kepwick
CRAKEHALL WATER MILL
North Yor
Leake
Great Crakehall
Leeming Bar
North Otterington
Thornton-le-Beans
Leeming
Cowesby
Hawnby
Sowber Gate
Thornton-le-Moor
Borrowby
Bedale
Aiskew
Gatenby
Knayton
Londonderry
Newby Wiske
South Otterington
Kirby Knowle
Upsall
Exelby
Firby
Maunby
Thornton-le-Street
Boltby
Theakston
HAMBLETON HILLS
THORP PERROW ARBORETUM
Burneston
Kirby Wiske
Newsham
North Kilvington
Snape
SION HILL HALL & BIRDS OF PREY CENTRE
Felixkirk
Thirlby
Carthorpe
Pickhill
South Kilvington
Thirsk
BOB HUNTER - HOME OF THE WREN
SUTTON BANK VISITOR CENTRE
AERIAL EXTREME
WORLD OF JAMES HERRIOT
Holme
Old Thirsk
Well
Sinderby
Sandhutton
Sutton-under-Whitestonecliffe
Kirklington
Ainderby Quernhow
MONK PARK FARM
Nosterfield
Carlton Miniott
Sowerby
Bagby
Balk
Binsoe
Howe
Oldstead
Thornborough
Skipton-on-Swale
Kilburn
Great Thirkleby
High Kilburn
Sutton Howgrave
Baldersby
MOUSEMAN VISITOR CENTRE
West Tanfield
Little Thirkleby
MARMION TOWER
Middleton Quernham
Catton
LIGHTWATER VILLAGE
Carlton Husthwaite
Wath
Hutton Sessay
North Stainley
Melmerby
Baldersby St James
Topcliffe
NORTON CONYERS
Dalton
LIGHTWATER VALLEY
Asenby
Birdforth
Husthwaite
Ure
Sessay
Sutton Grange
Nunwick
Rainton
Swale
Thormanby
Azerley
Hutton Conyers
Little Sessay
Crakehill
Galphay
Dishforth
Cundall
Fawdington
Ure Bank
Sharow
Ripon
THE COURTHOUSE
Copt Hewick
Norton-le-Clay
Winksley
Bishopton
RIPON CATHEDRAL
Bridge Hewick
Raskelf
Studley
Marton-le-Moor
Brafferton
Helperby
Littlethorpe
Kirby Hill
Easing
FOUNTAINS
0 1 2 3 miles
0 1 2 3 4 5 km

NORTH YORK MOORS NATIONAL PARK
CLEVELAND HILLS
HOWARDIAN HILLS
Great Ayton
Little Ayton
New Row
Commondale
Danby Low Moor
Lealholm Moor
Ugthorpe
Kildale
Kildale Moor
Easby
Battersby
Ingleby Greenhow
Castleton
Ainthorpe
Danby
THE MOORS CENTRE
Houlsyke
Lealholm
Stonegate
Westerdale
Low Garth
Street
Glaisdale
MUSEUM OF VICTORIAN SCIENCE
Egton
Egton Bridge
Grosmont
Esk Valley
Glaisdale
Westerdale Moor
Glaisdale Moor
Egton High Moor
Beck Hole
Goathland
Urra
Seave Green
Farndale Moor
COCKAYNE RIDGE
Cockayne
Wake Lady Green
Rosedale Moor
WHEELDALE MOOR ROMAN ROAD
Wheeldale Moor
Church Houses
Bilsdale East Moor
Blakey Ridge
Thorgill
Rosedale Abbey
ROSEDALE
Bransdale
Rudland Rigg
Low Mill
PICKERING MOOR
Pickering Forest
Goathland
Spaunton Moor
Cropton Forest
Hartoft End
Stape
Newton Dale
East Moors
Helmsley Moor
Skiplam Moor
RYEDALE FOLK MUSEUM
Lastingham
Levisham
Lockton
Gillamoor
Hutton-le-Hole
Spaunton
Newton-on-Rawcliffe
Fadmoor
Rievaulx Moor
Cropton
Appleton-le-Moors
NORTH YORKSHIRE MOORS RAILWAY
Carlton
Kirkbymoorside
Keldholme
Sinnington
Wrelton
Aislaby
Pockley
Kirkby Mills
Middleton
ST PETER AND ST PAUL CHURCH
Rievaulx
RIEVAULX ABBEY
HELMSLEY
Beadlam
Nawton
Welburn
Wombleton
Great Edstone
Pickering
PICKERING CASTLE
Ellerburn
Helmsley
Rye Dale
DUNCOMBE PARK
Marton
Thornton-le-Dale
Wilton
Harome
Normanby
Sproxton
Muscoates
Little Barugh
FLAMINGO LAND
Wass
Nunnington
NUNNINGTON HALL
West Ness
Salton
Great Barugh
Kirby Misperton
Ampleforth
Oswaldkirk
Stonegrave
East Ness
Brawby
High Marishes
Low Marishes
Gilling East
South Holme
Butterwick
Little Habton
Great Habton
Ryton
Scampston
SCAMPSTON HALL
Cawton
Hovingham
Fryton
Wykeham
Rillington
Yearsley
Wath
HOVINGHAM HALL
Slingsby
Barton-le-Street
EDEN CAMP MODERN HISTORY THEME MUSEUM
Coulton
Amotherby
Appleton-le-Street
Swinton
Broughton
Brandsby
Scackleton
Malton
Old Malton
Scagglethorpe
Stearsby
Dalby
Terrington
Norton-on-Derwent
Coneysthorpe
Skewsby
Crayke
YORKSHIRE LAVENDER
Ganthorpe
CASTLE HOWARD
Settrington
Whenby
Whitewall Corner
High Hutton
Stillington
Farlington
Welburn
A170
A171
A169
A64
B1257
B1363
B1248
168
169
160
149

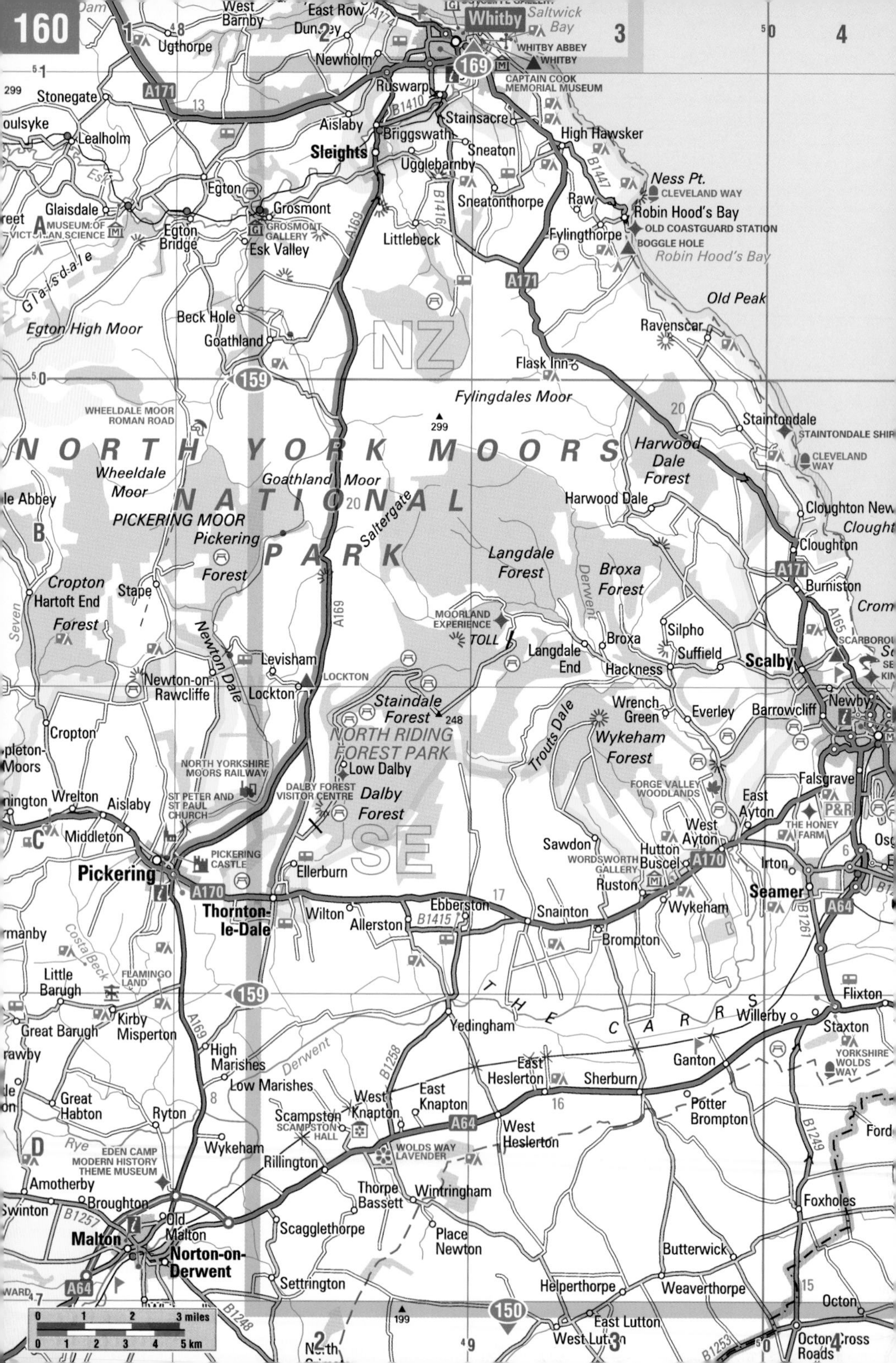
Whitby
Saltwick Bay
WHITBY ABBEY
WHITBY
CAPTAIN COOK MEMORIAL MUSEUM
West Barnby
East Row
Dunsley
Ugthorpe
Newholm
Ruswarp
Stonegate
Lealholm
Aislaby
Briggswath
Stainsacre
High Hawsker
Sleights
Sneaton
Ugglebarnby
Egton
Glaisdale
MUSEUM OF VICTORIAN SCIENCE
Egton Bridge
Grosmont
GROSMONT GALLERY
Esk Valley
Littlebeck
Sneatonthorpe
Raw
Ness Pt.
CLEVELAND WAY
Robin Hood's Bay
OLD COASTGUARD STATION
Fylingthorpe
BOGGLE HOLE
Robin Hood's Bay
Old Peak
Glaisdale
Egton High Moor
Beck Hole
Goathland
NZ
Ravenscar
Flask Inn
Fylingdales Moor
WHEELDALE MOOR ROMAN ROAD
299
Staintondale
STAINTONDALE SHIRE
CLEVELAND WAY
NORTH YORK MOORS NATIONAL PARK
Wheeldale Moor
Goathland Moor
Harwood Dale Forest
Harwood Dale
le Abbey
PICKERING MOOR
Pickering Forest
Saltergate
Langdale Forest
Broxa Forest
Cloughton Newlands
Cloughton
Burniston
Cropton Forest
Hartoft End
Stape
Newton Dale
MOORLAND EXPERIENCE
TOLL
Langdale End
Broxa
Silpho
Suffield
Hackness
Scalby
SCARBOROUGH
Levisham
LOCKTON
Lockton
Newton-on-Rawcliffe
Staindale Forest
248
Wrench Green
Everley
Barrowcliff
Newby
Cropton
NORTH RIDING FOREST PARK
Low Dalby
Trouts Dale
Wykeham Forest
Appleton-le-Moors
NORTH YORKSHIRE MOORS RAILWAY
DALBY FOREST VISITOR CENTRE
Dalby Forest
FORGE VALLEY WOODLANDS
Falsgrave
Wrelton
Aislaby
ST PETER AND ST PAUL CHURCH
East Ayton
THE HONEY FARM
West Ayton
Middleton
Sawdon
Hutton Buscel
WORDSWORTH GALLERY
Irton
PICKERING CASTLE
SE
Pickering
Ellerburn
Ruston
Seamer
Thornton-le-Dale
Wilton
Ebberston
Snainton
Wykeham
Allerston
Brompton
Normanby
Costa Beck
Little Barugh
FLAMINGO LAND
THE CARRS
Great Barugh
Kirby Misperton
Yedingham
Willerby
Flixton
Staxton
High Marishes
Derwent
East Heslerton
Ganton
YORKSHIRE WOLDS WAY
Low Marishes
Sherburn
Great Habton
West Knapton
East Knapton
Potter Brompton
Ryton
Scampston
SCAMPSTON HALL
West Heslerton
Ford
Rye
EDEN CAMP MODERN HISTORY THEME MUSEUM
Wykeham
WOLDS WAY LAVENDER
Rillington
Amotherby
Thorpe Bassett
Wintringham
Foxholes
Broughton
Swinton
Old Malton
Scagglethorpe
Malton
Place Newton
Butterwick
Norton-on-Derwent
Settrington
Helperthorpe
Weaverthorpe
Octon
199
East Lutton
West Lutton
Octon Cross Roads
0 1 2 3 miles
0 1 2 3 4 5 km

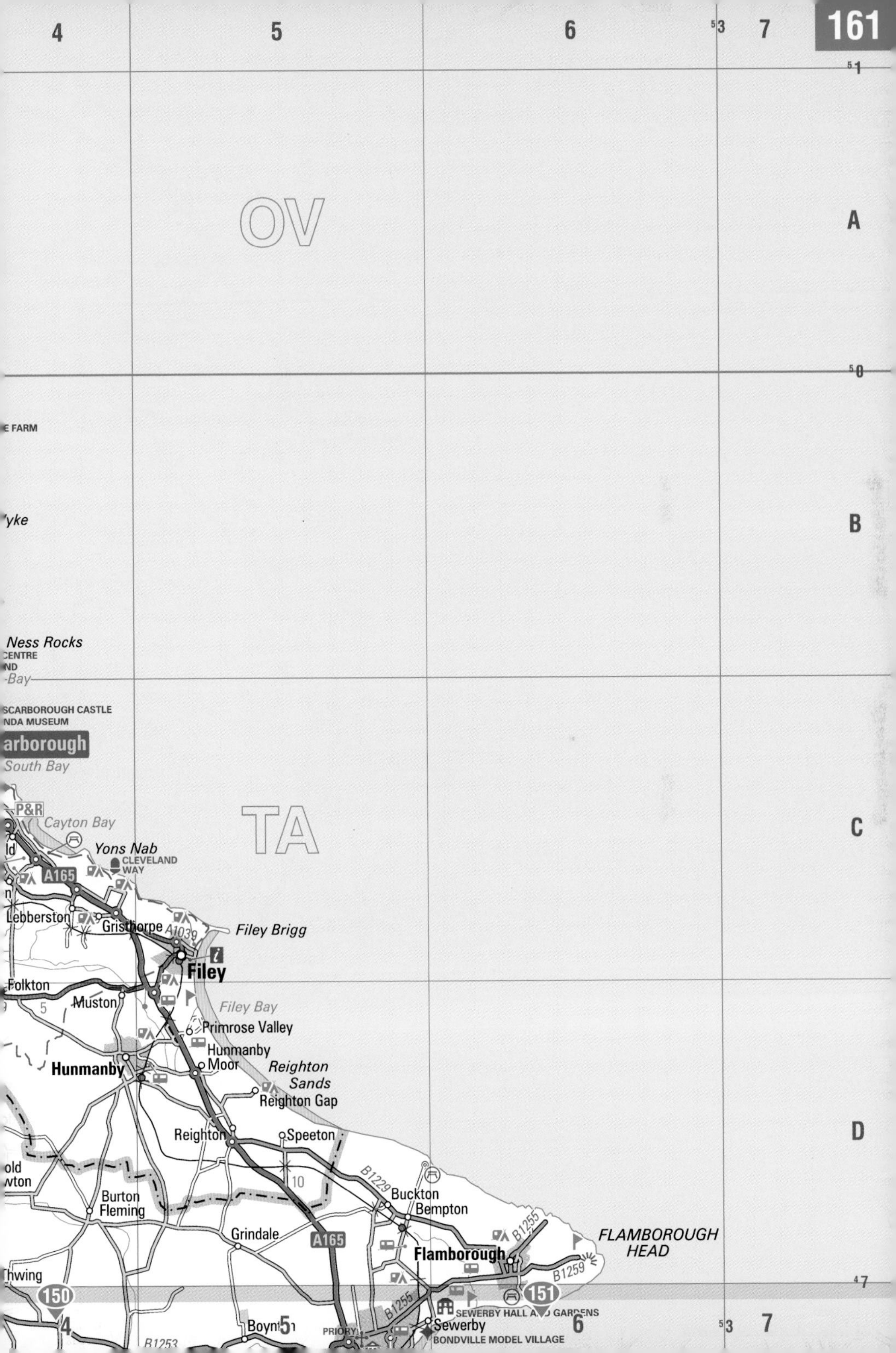
4
5
6
7
OV
TA
A
B
C
D
E FARM
Ness Rocks
CENTRE
-Bay
SCARBOROUGH CASTLE
NDA MUSEUM
arborough
South Bay
P&R
Cayton Bay
Yons Nab
CLEVELAND WAY
A165
Lebberston
Gristhorpe
A1039
Filey Brigg
Filey
Folkton
Muston
Filey Bay
Primrose Valley
Hunmanby
Hunmanby Moor
Reighton Sands
Reighton Gap
Reighton
Speeton
B1229
Buckton
Bempton
Burton Fleming
Grindale
Flamborough
B1255
FLAMBOROUGH HEAD
B1259
Thwing
150
151
SEWERBY HALL AND GARDENS
Sewerby
BONDVILLE MODEL VILLAGE
PRIORY
Boynton
B1253

173
174
153
NX
Allonby Bay
Allerby
Crosscanonby
Crosby
MARYPORT MARITIME MUSEUM
Maryport
Dearham
Flimby
Dovenby
Broughton Moor
Standingstone
Great Broughton
Little Brough
Siddick
Camerton
Derwent
Seaton
Great Clifton
North Side
Bridgefoot
Workington
Stainburn
Greysouth
HELENA THOMPSON MUS
Little Clifton
Westfield
Eaglesfiel
Mossbay
Deanscales
Marron
Winscales
Harrington
High Harrington
Dean
Branthwaite
Distington
Ullock
Lowca
Pica
Moresby
Keekle
247
Parton
Asby
Bransty
Moresby Parks
Arlecdon
THE RUM STORY
WALK MILL
Rowrah
HIGH LEYS
Kirkland
Whitehaven
Frizington
HAIG COLLIERY MINING MUSEUM
Ehen
Hensingham
Saltom Bay
Cleator Moor
Mirehouse
Ennerdale Bridge
ST BEES HEAD
Sandwith
Moor Row
Wath Brow
Rottington
Cleator
LONGLANDS LAKE
St Bees
Wilton
Egremont
Coulderton
Thornhill
Middletown
Haile
Calder
322
Nethertown
Beckermet
Calder Bridge
Braystones
High Sellafield
SELLAFIELD VISITORS CENTRE
Welling
Calder Hall
Gosforth
Seascale
Holmrook
Drigg
Irt
A596
A595
A594
A5086
B5300
B5294
B5295
B5345
B5344
3 miles
5 km

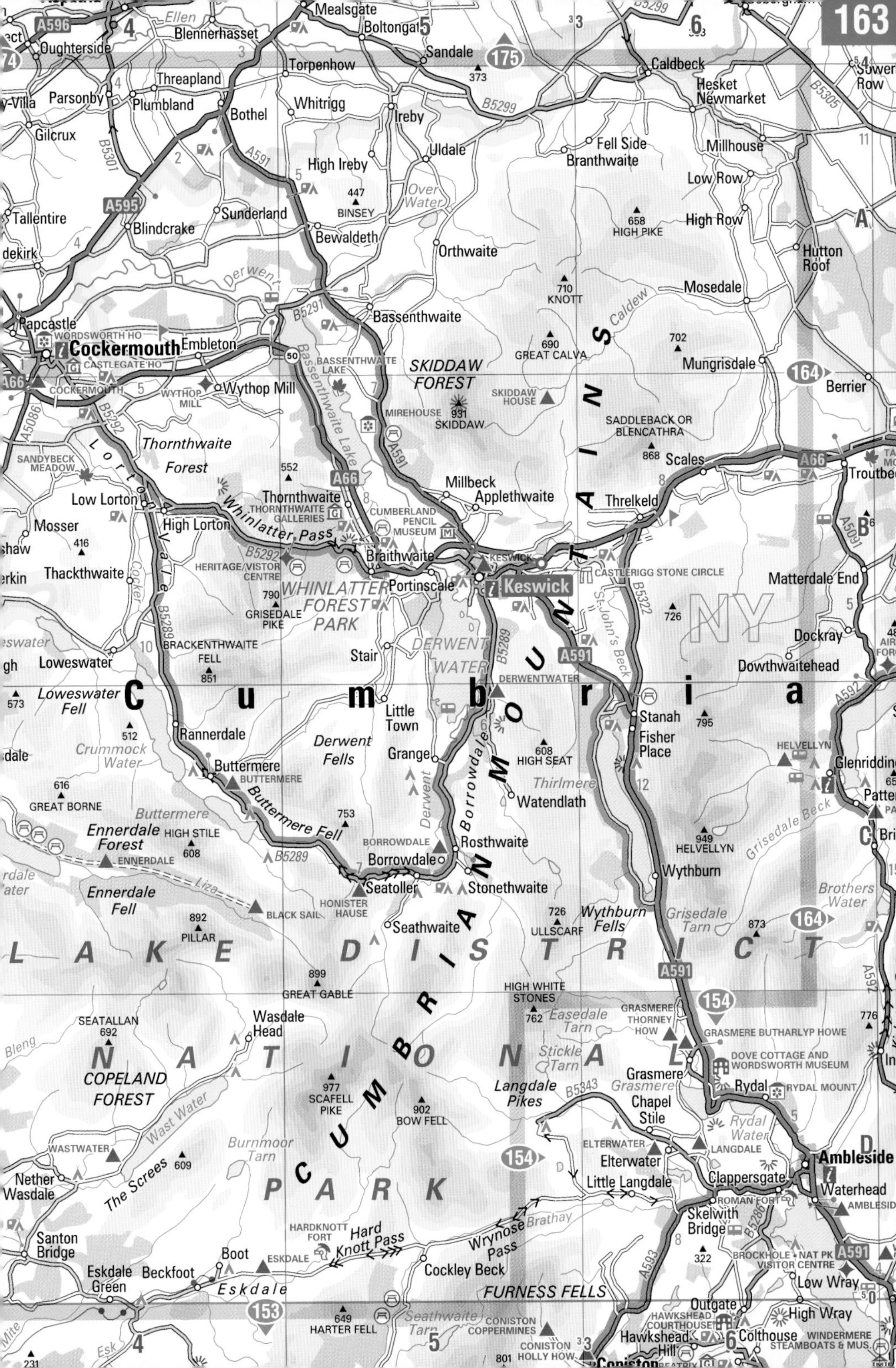
Mealsgate
Boltongate
Ellen
Blennerhasset
Oughterside
Sandale
175
Caldbeck
Hesket Newmarket
Torpenhow
Threapland
Parsonby
Plumbland
Bothel
Whitrigg
Ireby
B5299
Gilcrux
B5301
A591
Uldale
Fell Side
Branthwaite
Millhouse
High Ireby
Low Row
447
BINSEY
Over Water
A595
Tallentire
Sunderland
Blindcrake
Bewaldeth
658
HIGH PIKE
High Row
Orthwaite
Hutton Roof
Derwent
710
KNOTT
Mosedale
B5291
Bassenthwaite
Caldew
Papcastle
WORDSWORTH HO
Cockermouth
Embleton
CASTLEGATE HO
690
GREAT CALVA
702
Mungrisdale
BASSENTHWAITE LAKE
SKIDDAW FOREST
164
Berrier
A66
COCKERMOUTH
WYTHOP MILL
Wythop Mill
SKIDDAW HOUSE
MIREHOUSE
931
SKIDDAW
SADDLEBACK OR BLENCATHRA
A5086
B5292
Bassenthwaite Lake
Thornthwaite Forest
868
Scales
SANDYBECK MEADOW
Lorton Vale
552
A591
Millbeck
Applethwaite
Troutbeck
Low Lorton
Thornthwaite
THORNTHWAITE GALLERIES
Threlkeld
Mosser
High Lorton
Whinlatter Pass
CUMBERLAND PENCIL MUSEUM
416
Braithwaite
KESWICK
A5091
Thackthwaite
HERITAGE/VISITOR CENTRE
Portinscale
Keswick
CASTLERIGG STONE CIRCLE
Matterdale End
WHINLATTER FOREST PARK
790
GRISEDALE PIKE
B5322
726
NY
Cocker
B5289
BRACKENTHWAITE FELL
851
DERWENT WATER
St. John's Beck
Dockray
Loweswater
Stair
A591
Dowthwaitehead
DERWENTWATER
Cumbria
573
Loweswater Fell
Little Town
A592
512
Rannerdale
Derwent Fells
Stanah
795
Fisher Place
Crummock Water
Grange
608
HIGH SEAT
HELVELLYN
Glenridding
Buttermere
BUTTERMERE
Thirlmere
616
GREAT BORNE
Watendlath
Patterdale
Buttermere
753
Buttermere Fell
Borrowdale
Grisedale Beck
Ennerdale Forest
HIGH STILE
608
BORROWDALE
Rosthwaite
949
HELVELLYN
ENNERDALE
B5289
Borrowdale
Wythburn
Liza
Seatoller
Ennerdale Fell
HONISTER HAUSE
Stonethwaite
Brothers Water
BLACK SAIL
892
PILLAR
Seathwaite
726
ULLSCARF
Wythburn Fells
Grisedale Tarn
873
LAKE DISTRICT
A591
899
GREAT GABLE
HIGH WHITE STONES
154
SEATALLAN
692
Wasdale Head
762
Easedale Tarn
GRASMERE THORNEY HOW
GRASMERE BUTHARLYP HOWE
776
Bleng
NATIONAL
CUMBRIAN MOUNTAINS
Stickle Tarn
DOVE COTTAGE AND WORDSWORTH MUSEUM
Grasmere
COPELAND FOREST
977
SCAFELL PIKE
902
BOW FELL
Langdale Pikes
B5343
Rydal
RYDAL MOUNT
Chapel Stile
Rydal Water
Wast Water
Burnmoor Tarn
ELTERWATER
Elterwater
LANGDALE
WASTWATER
154
Ambleside
609
The Screes
Nether Wasdale
PARK
Little Langdale
Clappersgate
Waterhead
ROMAN FORT
AMBLESIDE
Brathay
Skelwith Bridge
HARDKNOTT FORT
Hard Knott Pass
Wrynose Pass
B5286
Santon Bridge
322
BROCKHOLE - NAT PK VISITOR CENTRE
A591
A593
Boot
ESKDALE
Cockley Beck
Low Wray
Eskdale Green
Beckfoot
Eskdale
FURNESS FELLS
Outgate
HAWKSHEAD COURTHOUSE
High Wray
153
649
HARTER FELL
Seathwaite Tarn
CONISTON COPPERMINES
Hawkshead Hill
Colthouse
WINDERMERE STEAMBOATS & MUS.
Mite
Esk
231
CONISTON HOLLY HOW
801
Coniston

Thursby
Dalston
Cotehill
Hornsby
Cumrew
Newbiggin
Buckabank
Wreay
West Curthwaite
East Curthwaite
Holmwrangle
Croglin
Brackenthwaite
Gaitsgill
Aiketgate
Ainstable
Armathwaite
Low Hesket
High Hesket
Raughton Head
Stockdalewath
Rosley
Welton
Southwaite
SOUTHWAITE SERVICES
HIGH HEAD SCULPTURE VALLEY
Ruckcroft
Old Town
Ivegill
Low Braithwaite
Sebergham
Staffield
High Bankhill
Kirkoswald
Thomas Close
Caldbeck
Calthwaite
Sowerby Row
Hesket Newmarket
Lazonby
Lazonby Fell
Townhead
Glassonby
Hutton End
Fell Side
Branthwaite
Millhouse
Plumpton
Great Salkeld
New Rent
Brockleymoor
Little Salkeld
Low Row
Lamonby
Unthank
Skelton
HUTTON-IN-THE-FOREST
High Row
HIGH PIKE
Ellonby
Unthank End
Plumpton Head
Winskill
Hutton Roof
Langwathby
Little Blencow
Catterlen
Johnby
Laithes
Edenhall
Mosedale
Great Blencow
Newton Reigny
Fair Hill
Greystoke
Penrith
CALVA
Mungrisdale
Carleton
MAYBURGH HENGE
BROUGHAM CASTLE
Berrier
Newbiggin
Motherby
BECKSTONES ART GALLERY
Eamont Bridge
SADDLEBACK OR BLENCATHRA
Penruddock
Stainton
Scales
TARN MOSS
Troutbeck
DALEMAIN
Sockbridge
RHEGED
LILLIPUT LANE
CLIFTON HALL
Clifton
Hutton
Dacre
Tirril
Threlkeld
CLIBURN
Melkinthorpe
LAKELAND BIRD OF PREY CENTRE
CASTLERIGG STONE CIRCLE
Wreay
Pooley Bridge
Askham
Lowther
Matterdale End
Hackthorpe
Longthwaite
Watermillock
Helton
Great Strickland
Dockray
AIRA FORCE
Knotts
Whale
Dowthwaitehead
ULLSWATER
Little Strickland
Howtown
Stanah
Sandwick
LOADPOT HILL
Sleagill
Fisher Place
HELVELLYN
Bampton Grange
Bampton
Glenridding
Martindale Common
Bampton Common
Rosgill
Patterdale
PATTERDALE
Dale Head
HELVELLYN
Bridgend
Angle Tarn
Haweswater Reservoir
SHAP ABBEY
Shap
Keld
Wythburn
Hartsop
Brothers Water
Ralfland Forest
Wythburn Fells
Grisedale Tarn
HIGH STREET
HARTER FELL
Kirkstone Pass
Shap Fells
LAKE DISTRICT NATIONAL PARK
Cumbria
Inglewood Forest
0 1 2 3 miles
0 1 2 3 4 5 km

NORTH PENNINES
Alston
Nenthead
Garrigill
Allenheads
Cowshill
Wearhead
St John's Chapel
Langdon Beck
Appleby-in-Westmorland
Brough
Kirkby Stephen
Dufton
Murton
Hilton
Warcop
Melmerby
Ousby
Skirwith
Kirkland
Blencarn
Milburn
Newbiggin
Temple Sowerby
Knock
Kirkby Thore
Long Marton
Brampton
Bolton
Crackenthorpe
King's Meaburn
Colby
Burrells
Hoff
Great Ormside
Sandford
Drybeck
Great Asby
Bleatarn
Little Musgrave
Great Musgrave
Brough Sowerby
Kaber
Winton
Hartley
Soulby
Crosby Garrett
Little Asby
Orton
Barras
Heggerscales
South Stainmore
North Stainmore
Hillbeck
Harwood
Ireshopeburn
Carrshield
Coalcleugh
Spartylea
Dirt Pot
Lanehead
Nenthall
Blagill
Ayle
Raise
Bayles
Leadgate
Gamblesby
Culgaith
Harescaugh
GILDERDALE FOREST
MILBURN FOREST
LUNE FOREST
Alston Moor
Middle Fell
Dufton Fell
Murton Fell
Warcop Fell
Mickle Fell
Cronkley Fell
Widdybank Fell
Langdon Common
Ireshope Moor
Middlehope Moor
Stainmore Common
Allendale Common
893 CROSS FELL
746 BURNHOPE SEAT
685 ROUND HILL
639 VIEWING HILL
710 MELMERBY FELL
602 WATCH HILL
696 CHAPELFELL TOP
549 DOW CRAG
Cow Green Reservoir
Burnhope Reservoir
CAULDRON SNOUT
HIGH FORCE
MOOR HOUSE-UPPER TEESDALE
PENNINE WAY
MAIDEN WAY
NENTHEAD MINES HERITAGE CENTRE
NORTH OF ENGLAND LEAD MINING MUSEUM
SOUTH TYNEDALE RAILWAY
GOSSIPGATE GALLERY
EDEN VALLEY RAILWAY
BROUGH CASTLE
ACORN BANK
GREAT ASBY SCAR
A66
A686
A689
A685
B6277
B6276
B6294
B6295
B6542
B6259
B6260
NY
176
177
166
155

Blanchland
Edmundbyers
Muggleswick
Consett
Leadgate
Bridgehill
Allensford
Templetown
Castleside
Knitsley
Delves
Hunstanworth
NOOKTON FELL
Spartylea
Muggleswick Common
Horsleyhope
BOLT'S LAW
Waskerley
East Butsfield
Cornsay
Satley
HALL HILL FARM
Rookhope
ROOKHOPE NURSERIES
Middlehope Moor
Stanhope Common
COLLIER LAW
Tunstall Res.
Lanehead
NORTH
Crawleyside
Wolsingham Park Moor
High Stoop
WEARDALE
DURHAM DALES CENTRE
Stanhope
Eastgate
Westgate
St John's Chapel
Daddry Shield
WEARDALE RAILWAY
Wolsingham
Thornley
Frosterley
Durham
NY
Hill End
Wear
PENNINES
Westernhope Moor
Bollihope Common
CHAPELFELL TOP
Fir Tree
Langdon Common
Pikeston Fell
Newbiggin Common
PAWLAW PIKE
Langdon Beck
LANGDON BECK
Middleton Common
Bedburn
Redford
TOLL
Hamsterley
Forest
Ettersgill
Tees
HIGH FORCE
BOWLEES VISITOR CENTRE
Hamsterley Forest
Newbiggin
TEESDALE
Holwick
Middleton-in-Teesdale
Woodland
Woodland Fell
Morley
Howle
Butterknowle
Copley
High Lands
Hill Top
Eggleston
Lune Moor
Bowbank
EGGLESTON HALL
Mickleton
Thringarth
Cockfield
Burnt Houses
Romaldkirk
Grassholme Reservoir
RABY CASTLE
Grassholme
Kinninvie
Hunderthwaite
Lune
Selset Reservoir
Hury
Staindrop
Hunderthwaite Moor
Cotherstone
Stainton
Cleatlam
Hury Reservoir
Little Newsham
Clove Lodge
BALDERSDALE
Balderhead Reservoir
BARNARD CASTLE
Lartington
THE BOWES MUSEUM
Cotherstone Moor
Startforth
Barnard Castle
Westwick
Whorlton
Deep Dale
Deepdale Beck
Boldron
EGGLESTONE ABBEY
ROKEBY PARK
Bowes
PENNINE WAY
BOWES CASTLE
Greta Bridge
Gilmonby
Moudy Mea
Brignall
Greta
Hutton Magna
Lane Head
Bowes Moor
STAINMORE FOREST
Scargill
Sleightholme
Barningham
Newsham
Scargill High Moor
The Stang Forest
Dalton
Sleightholme Moor
0 1 2 3 miles
0 1 2 3 4 5 km

The Middles
Grange Villa
CHESTER-LE-STREET
Herrington
Doxford Park
Burdon
Annfield Plain
Craghead
Bournmoor
Newbottle
Seaton
Northlea
SEAHAM
Maiden Law
Waldridge
Chester Moor
THE ANKERS HOUSE
Fence Houses
HOUGHTON-LE-SPRING
West Lea
Burnhope
Edmondsley
WALDRIDGE FELL
Great Lumley
Colliery Row
East Rainton
Dalton-le-Dale
Lanchester
Nettlesworth
Plawsworth
West Rainton
Hetton-le-Hole
Cold Hesledon
Sacriston
BROOM HOUSE FARM
Kimblesworth
FINCHALE PRIORY
Murton
DALTON PARK
Witton Gilbert
Pity Me
Leamside
Low Moorsley
Easington Lane
Hawthorn
DIGGERLAND
Framwellgate Moor
South Hetton
Easington Colliery
Langley Park
Pittington
DURHAM LIGHT INFANTRY MUS
Carrville
Littletown
Haswell
Easington
Esh
Cornsay Colliery
Quebec
Bearpark
Durham
Sherburn
Sherburn Hill
Haswell Plough
Ushaw Moor
Broompark
DURHAM CITY
DURHAM CATH
Shotton Colliery
Esh Winning
Waterhouses
New Brancepeth
DURHAM UNIV ORIENTAL MUS
Shadforth
Ludworth
Horden
Shincliffe
Old Cassop
Thornley
PETERLEE
East Hedleyhope
Brandon
Cassop
Wheatley Hill
Shotton
CASTLE EDEN DENE
Bowburn
Quarrington
CASSOP VALE
Castle Eden
Brancepeth
DURHAM SERVICES
Hesleden
Sunderland Bridge
Quarrington Hill
Wingate
Deaf Hill
Station Town
Croxdale
Hett
Oakenshaw
Page Bank
Kelloe
Trimdon Grange
Trimdon Colliery
Hutton Henry
Helmington Row
Willington
Tudhoe
Coxhoe
Sheraton
Cornforth
Trimdon
Byers Green
Spennymoor
Ferryhill
NZ
Newfield
Middlestone Moor
THRISLINGTON
Hunwick
Ferryhill Station
Fishburn
High Grange
Binchester Blocks
BINCHESTER FORT
Kirk Merrington
Westerton
Middlestone
Mainsforth
Bishop Middleham
Witton Park
Toronto
AUCKLAND CASTLE
Coundon
Chilton Lane
Butterwick
ESCOMB CHURCH
Escomb
Leasingthorne
Chilton
HARDWICK HALL
Low Etherley
Bishop Auckland
Sedgefield
Rushyford
Eldon
Bradbury
SEDGEFIELD
Toft Hill
ST HELEN'S
Coundon Grange
Old Eldon
Shildon
Wynyard Village
Middridge
NEWTON AYCLIFFE
Mordon
West Auckland
St Helen Auckland
Thorpe Larches
LOCOMOTION N.R.M. SHILDON
WYNYARD WOODLAND
Bildershaw
Foxton
Evenwood Gate
Royal Oak
Stillington
Thorpe Thewles
Redworth
Aycliffe
Elstob
Bolam
Wackerfield
Heighington
Whitton
Stockton-on-Tees
Norton
Hilton
Great Stainton
Redmarshall
Carlton
Roseworth
Houghton-le-Side
Brafferton
Bishopton
Ingleton
Walworth Gate
Coatham Mundeville
Little Stainton
Fairfield
Killerby
Langton
Denton
Skerne
Stockton-on-Tees
Headlam
Summerhouse
Walworth
Beaumont Hill
Barmpton
Hartburn
Gainford
Harrowgate Hill
Great Burdon
Sadberge
Elton
Thornaby-on-Tees
High Coniscliffe
Darlington
Longnewton
Piercebridge
HEAD OF STEAM
PRESTON HALL MUSEUM
ROMAN BRIDGE
Low Coniscliffe
Haughton Le Skerne
Urlay Nook
Eaglescliffe
Caldwell
Manfield
DURHAM TEES VALLEY
Ingleby Barwick
Eppleby
Cleasby
Darlington
Middleton St George
Egglescliffe
Forcett
High Leven
Carlton
Stapleton
Blackwell
Aislaby
STANWICK IRON AGE FORTIFICATIONS
Middleton One Row
Yarm
Stanwick-St-John
Aldbrough St John
Tees
Low Dinsdale
Neasham
Low Worsall
East Layton
Newton Morrell
Croft-on-Tees
Hurworth Place
Kirklevington
Barton
Eryholme
Girsby
Melsonby
A1(M)
A19
A167
A690
A691
A688
A177
A181
A182
A1086
A689
A6072
A68
A66
A66(M)
A67
A135
A1044
A1027
B6313
B1404
B1285
B1287
B1284
B6532
B6312
B6301
B6296
B6302
B1280
B1283
B1432
B1281
B6300
B6299
B6286
B6288
B6287
B6291
B1278
B6282
B6444
B6275
B6279
B6280
B1265
B1264
A6076
STREET
Wear
178
179
168
157
158
h
a
m
A
B
C
D
4
5
6
7

1
2
3
4
A
B
C
D
179
167
158
159
Park
Burdon
Seaton
B1404
B1285
B1287
Northlea
SEAHAM
HOUGHTON-LE-SPRING
West Lea
Dalton-le-Dale
Hetton-le-Hole
A182
B1285
Murton
Cold Hesledon
DALTON PARK
Low Moorsley
Easington Lane
Hawthorn
South Hetton
Beacon Pt.
A19
B1432
B1283
Easington Colliery
B1280
Haswell
Easington
Haswell Plough
Shotton Colliery
A1086
B1283
Ludworth
Horden
B1280
PETERLEE
Thornley
Shotton
CASTLE EDEN DENE
Blackhall Colliery
Wheatley Hill
Blackhall Rocks
A181
CASSOP VALE
Castle Eden
B1281
High Hesleden
Hesleden
Wingate
DURHAM COAST
Deaf Hill
Station Town
Kelloe
Hart Station
Trimdon Grange
Trimdon Colliery
Hutton Henry
A1086
Sheraton
Hart
A1049
Trimdon
B1280
A179
ST HILDA'S PARISH CHURCH
B1278
High Throston
HARTLEPOOL'S MARITIME EXPERIENCE
Hartlepool Bay
Fishburn
Elwick
West Park
SUMMERHILL
Hartlepool
Hartlepool
Dalton Piercy
Rift House
A178
Butterwick
B1276
Seaton Carew
HARDWICK HALL
A689
A19
B1277
Tees Bay
Greatham
SEDGEFIELD
A689
Graythorp
Wynyard Village
Newton Bewley
Salt Scar
REDCAR
Thorpe Larches
WYNYARD WOODLAND
Wolviston
COWPEN BEWLEY
TEESMOUTH
A177
A1185
Cowpen Bewley
A178
Coatham
A1085
Foxton
BILLINGHAM ART GALLERY
REDCAR
Stillington
Thorpe Thewles
BILLINGHAM
Dormanstown
Marske-by-the-Sea
Whitton
Stockton-on-Tees
B1275
Haverton Hill
KIRKLEATHAM OLD HALL MUSEUM
A1042
B1269
Redmarshall
Norton
BILLINGHAM BECK
Port Clarence
A1085
Kirkleatham
Roseworth
TOLL
South Bank
Yearby
Bishopton
A19
A1046
North Ormesby
Grangetown
A174
New Marske
Little Stainton
Fairfield
A1027
A1046
A66
Lazenby
Wilton
A1053
Upleatham
Stockton-on-Tees
Middlesbrough
B1269
Dunsdale
DORMAN MUSEUM
Eston
TOCKETTS WATER MILL
Hartburn
Normanby
Middlesbrough
A174
A173
Sadberge
Thornaby-on-Tees
Acklam
Park End
B1380
Redcar and
A66
Elton
A1032
NATURES WORLD
A172
Ormesby
GUISBOROUGH PRIORY
FLATTS LANE WOODLAND
Longnewton
A135
PRESTON HALL MUSEUM
Marton
ORMESBY HALL
Guisborough
A171
Charltons
Urlay Nook
Eaglescliffe
CAPTAIN COOK BIRTHPLACE
Coulby Newham
A1043
GUISBOROUGH FOREST
Hutton Gate
A67
Ingleby Barwick
B1380
Stainton
Hemlington
Nunthorpe
Cleveland
DURHAM TEES VALLEY
Thornton
Hutton Village
Gisborough Moor
Middleton St George
Egglescliffe
A1044
Maltby
A173
Newton under Roseberry
High Leven
B1292
Middleton One Row
Aislaby
B1265
A19
Newby
B1365
Yarm
A172
Great Ayton
B1264
Hilton
Tanton
Seamer
New Row
Low Worsall
Little Ayton
A67
Middleton-on-Leven
Stokesley
A173
Easby
Kildale
Tame Bridge
Kildale Moor
242
329
0 1 2 3 miles
0 1 2 3 4 5 km

4
5
6
7
A
B
C
D
NZ
MINIATURE RAILWAY
Saltburn-by-the-Sea
CHRIS BIRKBECK INTERNATIONAL RALLY SCHOOL
Skinningrove
Brotton
Boulby
Carlin How
Loftus
Staithes
North Skelton
Kilton Thorpe
Easington
Port Mulgrave
Runswick Bay
Hinderwell
Lingdale
Margrove Park
Stanghow
Roxby
Runswick Bay
Kettleness
Liverton
Newton Mulgrave
Goldsborough
Moorsholm
Ellerby
B1366
Scaling
A171
A174
B1266
Lythe
Sandsend
THE DRACULA EXPERIENCE
Mickleby
East Barnby
Sandsend Wyke
SUTCLIFFE GALLERY
West Barnby
Scaling Dam Res.
East Row
Whitby
Saltwick Bay
Dunsley
Ugthorpe
WHITBY ABBEY
Commondale
Danby Low Moor
Lealholm Moor
Newholm
WHITBY
CAPTAIN COOK MEMORIAL MUSEUM
159
160
299
Ruswarp
Danby
Stonegate
B1410
Houlsyke
Aislaby
Briggswath
High Hawsker

Barnhills
Portencalzie
North Cairn
South Cairn
Corsewall
Loch Connell
Kirkcolm
Dounan Bay
Mains of Airies
Ervie
Low Salchrie
The Wig
LOCH RYAN
Cairnryan
Penwhirn Res.
Braid Fell
Main Water of Luce
Cross Water of Luce
New Luce
Knocknain
Slouchnawen Bay
Leswalt
Craigencross
Innermessan
Auchmantle
Black Loch
CASTLE KENNEDY GARDENS
White Loch
Glenstockadale
Stranraer
Aird
Castle Kennedy
Broadsea Bay
T H E R H I N
CASTLE OF ST JOHN VISITOR CENTRE
WIGTOWN DISTRICT MUSEUM
Knockglass
Soulseat Loch
GLENWHAN GARDENS
Dunragit
CASTLE OF PARK
Mark
Lochans
Black Hd.
NW
Dunskey Ho.
LITTLE WHEELS
Portpatrick
Awhirk
Stoneykirk
Torrs Warren
Luce Sands
Port of Spittal Bay
Cairngarroch
Sandhead
Sandhead Bay
Cairngarroch Bay
KIRKMADRINE STONES
Money Hd.
Clachanmore
Hole Stone Bay
ARDWELL GDNS
Ardwell
Ardwell Mains
Chapel Rossan Bay
Ardwell Pt.
Logan Mains
LOGAN BOTANIC GARDEN
Balgowan Pt.
Mull of Logan
LOGAN FISH POND MARINE LIFE CENTRE
Port Nessock or Port Logan Bay
Port Logan
Cairnywellan Hd.
Clanyard Bay
Low Clanyard
Kirkmaiden
Drummore
Laggantalluch Hd.
Cailliness Pt.
Damnaglaur
Crammag Hd.
Maryport
Cairngaan
Port Kemin
MULL OF GA
A77
A751
A75
A718
A716
B738
B798
B7043
B7077
B7084
B7042
B7065
B7041
180
257
182
164
0 1 2 3 miles
0 1 2 3 4 5 km

LAGGANGAIRN STANDING STONES
Knowe
181
WILD GOAT PARK
B7027
A714
Penkiln Burn
A712
Palnure Burn
Penninghame Forest
Artfield Fell
244
Carseriggan
Challoch
Minnigaff
MINNIGAFF
Creebridge
711
Black Loch
Newton Stewart
213
Loch Heron
Loch Ronald
Benfield
A714
Palnure
Drumphail
205
Shennanton
A75
Tarf Water
B735
B733
14
Kirkcowan
123
Baltersan
Cree
Carscreugh
Craighlaw Mains
Causeway End
172
GEM ROCK MUSEUM
Creetown
Carsegowan
Dernaglar Loch
High Mindork
Spittal
Knock Moss
Torhousemuir
Wigtown Sands
Bladnoch
TORHOUSE STONE CIRCLE
131
B7052
B7005
A747
Whitefield Loch
NX
B733
Wigtown
A75
Carsluith
SCOTLAND'S BOOK TOWN
Fell Loch
T H E
Bladnoch
Castle Loch
Culmazie
B7005
Auchenmalg
Mochrum Loch
M A C H A R S
VISITOR CENTRE
Baldoon Sands
Braehead
Kirkinner
Ravens
Culshabbin
uchenmalg Bay
Alticry
B7005
197
B7052
B7085
A746
Loch Head
Barrachan
Whauphill
CHAPEL FINIAN
B7004
Elrig
B7085
MOTE OF DRUCHTAG
75
A747
Mochrum
Sorbie
B7052
Garlieston
Milton Pt.
Airyhassen
Drumtroddan
Drummoddie
GALLOWAY HOUSE GARDENS
Port William
DRUMTRODDAN STONES
B7063
B7085
Monreith Mains
B7021
Moor of Ravenstone
B7004
Cults
C E B A Y
A746
CRUGGLETON CHURCH AND CASTLE
BARSALLOCH FORT
Barsalloch Pt.
Monreith
Bishopton
Whithorn
Port Allen
MONREITH ANIMAL WORLD, SHORE CENTRE AND MUSEUM
PRIORY AND MUSEUM
WHITHORN TRUST DISCOVERY CENTRE
Monreith Bay
Portyerrock Bay
A747
Glasserton
A746
146
FELL OF CARLETON
B7004
ST NINIAN'S CHAPEL
ST NINIAN'S CAVE
Isle of Whithorn
Port Castle Bay
Cutcloy
BURROW HEAD
OWAY
A
B
C
D
4
5
6

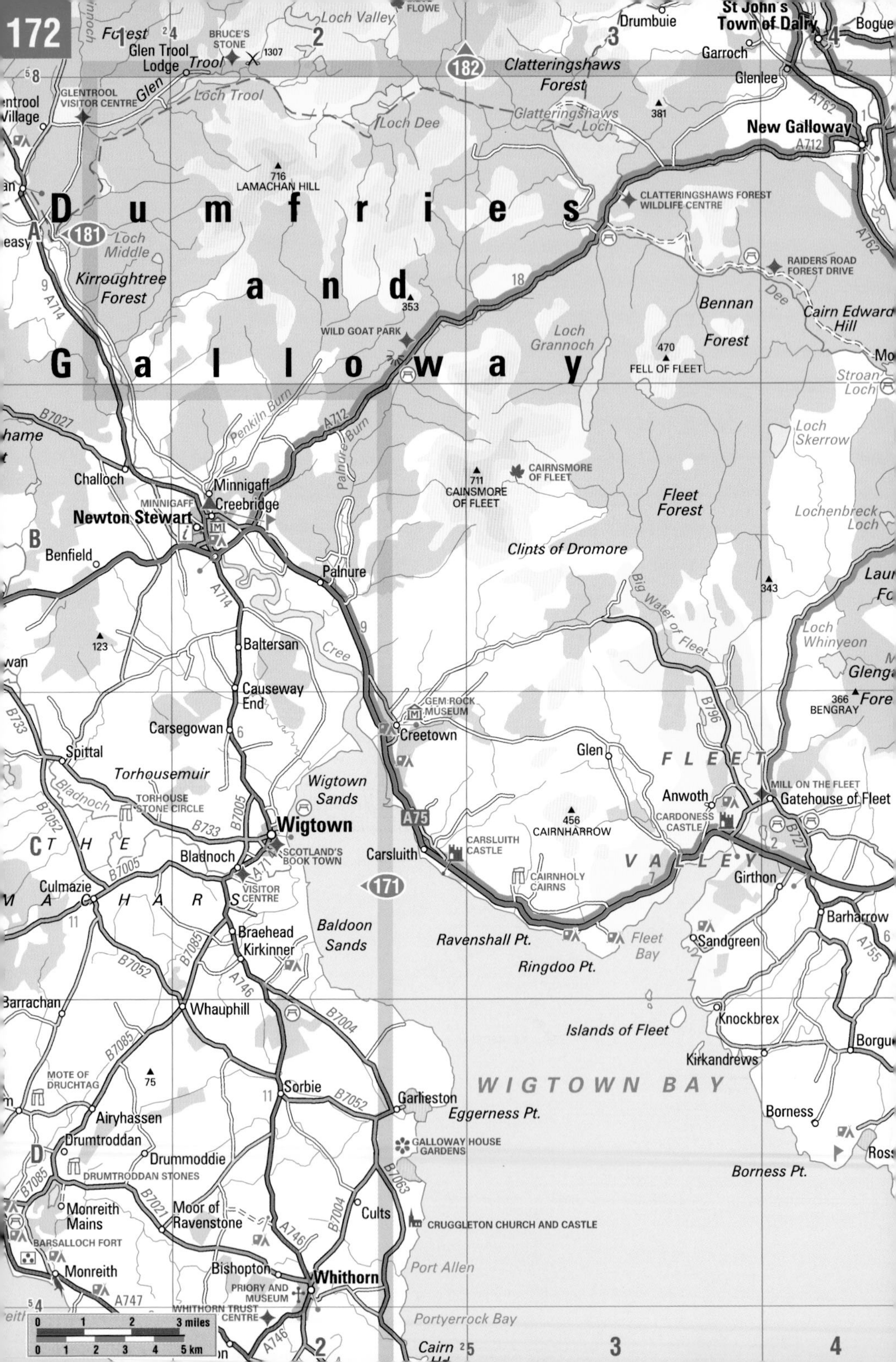
Dumfries and Galloway
Glen Trool Lodge
Bruce's Stone
Loch Valley
Loch Trool
Glentrool Visitor Centre
Glentrool Village
Clatteringshaws Forest
Clatteringshaws Loch
Loch Dee
Drumbuie
St John's Town of Dalry
Garroch
Glenlee
New Galloway
Lamachan Hill
Clatteringshaws Forest Wildlife Centre
Raiders Road Forest Drive
Loch Middle
Kirroughtree Forest
Wild Goat Park
Loch Grannoch
Fell of Fleet
Bennan Forest
Cairn Edward Hill
Stroan Loch
Loch Skerrow
Penkiln Burn
Palnure Burn
Challoch
Minnigaff
Creebridge
Newton Stewart
Benfield
Cairnsmore of Fleet
Fleet Forest
Lochenbreck Loch
Clints of Dromore
Palnure
Big Water of Fleet
Loch Whinyeon
Baltersan
Cree
Causeway End
Carsegowan
Gem Rock Museum
Creetown
Bengray
Spittal
Torhousemuir
Torhouse Stone Circle
Bladnoch
Wigtown Sands
Wigtown
Scotland's Book Town
Glen
Fleet Valley
Anwoth
Cardoness Castle
Mill on the Fleet
Gatehouse of Fleet
Cairnharrow
Carsluith
Carsluith Castle
Cairnholy Cairns
Girthon
The Machars
Culmazie
Visitor Centre
Braehead
Kirkinner
Baldoon Sands
Ravenshall Pt.
Ringdoo Pt.
Fleet Bay
Sandgreen
Barharrow
Barrachan
Whauphill
Islands of Fleet
Knockbrex
Kirkandrews
Borgue
Mote of Druchtag
Sorbie
Garlieston
Wigtown Bay
Eggerness Pt.
Airyhassen
Drumtroddan
Drummoddie
Drumtroddan Stones
Galloway House Gardens
Borness
Borness Pt.
Monreith Mains
Moor of Ravenstone
Cults
Cruggleton Church and Castle
Barsalloch Fort
Monreith
Bishopton
Whithorn
Priory and Museum
Port Allen
Whithorn Trust Centre
Portyerrock Bay
3 miles
5 km

Blackcraig
Knocklearn
Balmaclellan
Gibbshill
Corsock
Craig
Merkland
Drumrash
Parton
Loch Ken
Crossmichael
Craig
Laurieston
Loch Glentoo
Loch Bargatton
Bridge of Dee
Glengap
Ringford
Valleyfield
Twynholm
Tongland
GALLOWAY HYDRO VISITOR CENTRE
BROUGHTON HOUSE AND GARDEN
STEWARTRY MUSEUM
Kirkcudbright
St Mary's Island
Mutehill
Townhead
Balmae
Kirkcudbright Bay
Little Ross
Kirkcarswell
Dundrennan
DUNDRENNAN ABBEY
Netherlaw
Abbey Hd.
Port Mary
Orroland
Rascarrel
Rascarrel Bay
Balcary Pt.
Auchencairn
Auchencairn Bay
Hestan I.
Whinnieliggate
Gelston
Airieland
BENGAIRN
Rhonehouse or Kelton Hill
THREAVE GARDENS
KELTON MAINS OPEN FARM
THREAVE CASTLE
Townhead of Greenlaw
Castle Douglas
Carlingwark Loch
Clarebrand
Old Bridge of Urr
Haugh of Urr
MOTE OF URR
OLD BUITTLE TOWER
Dalbeattie
Barhill
Dalbeattie Forest
Palnackie
Kippford or Scaur
ORCHARDTON TOWER
MOTE OF MARK
Rockcliffe
ROUGH ISLAND
Rough I.
Castlehill Pt.
EAST STEWARTRY COAST
Barnbarroch
Colvend
Sandyhills
Portling
Drumstinchall
Caulkerbush
Mainsriddle
MERSEHEAD RSPB NATURE RESERVE
Mersehead Sands
Prestonn
SOLWAY FIRTH
Springholm
Kirkpatrick Durham
Auchenreoch Loch
Crocketford or Ninemile Bar
Milton Loch
Milton
Brooklands
Glen
Glenkiln
Glenkiln Res.
Drumpark
Shawhead
Brae
Lochfoot
Lochrutton Loch
Newtonairds
Irongray
Holywood
Newbridge
Terregles Banks
Lincluden
Maxwellto
Cargenbridge
Mabie Forest
Mabie
Loch Arthur
Lochaber Loch
Beeswing
DRUMCOLTRAN TOWER
Kirkgunzeon
LONG FELL
NATIONAL MUS OF COSTUME
New Abbey
NX

Dumfries
Locharbriggs
Newtonairds
Drumpark
Holywood
Kirkton
Tinwald
Heathhall
Irongray
Newbridge
Lincluden
Terregles Banks
The Grove
Greystone
Maxwelltown
Shawhead
Cargenbridge
Brae
Lochfoot
Lochrutton Loch
Islesteps
Kingholm Quay
Kelton
Mabie Forest
Mabie
Milton
Milton Loch
Beeswing
Loch Arthur
Lochaber Loch
Glencaple
Kirkconnell
New Abbey
Sweetheart Abbey
New Abbey Corn Mill
National Mus of Costume
Kirkconnell Flow
Lincluden College
Old Bridge House Mus
Burns House
Robert Burns Centre
Dumfries Museum & Camera Obscura
Dumfries and Galloway Aviation Mus
Lochmaben Castle
Castle Loch
Heck
Hightae
Torthorwald
Collin
Rammerscales House
Birkshaw Forest
Kettleholm
Middleshaw
Greenlea
Racks
Cleughbrae
Mouswald
Dalton
Carrutherstown
Lochar Moss
Lochar Water
Bankend
Clarencefield
Ruthwell
Ruthwell Cross
Duncan Savings Bank Museum
Cummertrees
Shearington
Blackshaw
Caerlaverock Castle
Eastpark
Bowhouse
Caerlaverock
Wildfowl and Wetland Centre
Blackshaw Bank
Nith Estuary
River Nith
Overton
Drumburn
Long Fell
Loch Kindar
Criffell
Carsethorn
Kirkbean
Arbigland Gardens
Drumstinchall
Caulkerbush
Prestonmill
Mainsriddle
Mersehead RSPB Nature Reserve
John Paul Jones Cottage Museum
Southerness
Southerness Pt.
Sandyhills
Colvend
Rockcliffe
Portling
Rough I.
Castlehill Pt.
Mersehead Sands
Barnbarroch
Solway Firth
Skinburness
Silloth
Greenrow
Causewayhead
Blitterlees
Beckfoot
Highlaws
Pelutho
Newtown
Mawbray
Holme St Cuthbert
Dubmill Pt.
Edderside
New Cowper
Allonby
Allonby Bay
Aspatria
Hayton
Prospect
Oughterside
Allerby
Crosscanonby
Crosby Villa
Parsonby
NX
A75
A76
A701
A709
A711
A710
B725
B724
B7020
B729
B793
B5300
B5301
173
184
162
0 1 2 3 miles
0 1 2 3 4 5 km

Bankshill
Kirtleton
185
Burnswark
BURNSWARK HILLFORT
GILNOCKIE TOWER
Claygate
Caulside
Waterbeck
Kirtle Water
Rowanburn
Middlebie
KIRKCONNEL CHURCHYARD
Evertown
Canonbie
Springkell
BIRRENS FORT
Milltown
Riddings
Ecclefechan
THOMAS CARLYLE'S BIRTHPLACE
Eaglesfield
Woodhouselees
Moat
Hoddomcross
Chapelknowe
SCOTS DYKE
Kirtlebridge
MERKLAND CROSS
Sark
A74(M)
Kirkpatrick-Fleming
Netherby
Easton
Brydekirk
Creca
Newton
GRETNA GREEN SERVICES
176
Charlesfield
Hollee
OLD BLACKSMITHS SHOP CENTRE
Longtown
Springfield
Gretna Green
Annan
A75
Rigg
Gretna
Kirklinton
Welldale
Shawhill
Dornock
Eastriggs
GRETNA GATEWAY
Esk
Sandysike
Smithfield
Browhouses
M6
Westlinton
Scaleby Hill
Todhills
Bowness-on-Solway
TODHILLS SERVICES
Port Carlisle
Blackford
Eden
Rockcliffe
NY
Glasson
Harker
COURSE OF HADRIAN'S WALL
Bowness Common
Drumburgh
HADRIAN'S WALL PATH
Burgh by Sands
Beaumont
Cargo
Houghton
Anthorn
Easton
Boustead Hill
Kingstown
Linstock
DRUMBURGH MOSS
Grinsdale
Kirkandrews upon Eden
Edentown
Whitrigg
Thurstonfield
Stanwix
Carlisle
Fingland
FINGLANDRIGG WOODS
Kirkbride
Moorhouse
CARLISLE
Newton Arlosh
Kirkbampton
Oughterby
TULLIE HOUSE MUS & GALL
Little Bampton
Little Orton
Botcherby
Morton
Wedholme Flow
Great Orton
Newby West
Upperby
Harraby
Seaville
Aikton
Wampool
Wiggonby
Cummersdale
Carleton
SOUTH SOLWAY MOSSES
Baldwinholme
A595
CARLISLE
Kingside Hill
Brisco
Durdar
Oulton
Waver
Kelsick
Lessonhall
Thursby
Dalston
Dundraw
Waverbridge
A596
164
Wreay
Buckabank
Blencogo
Wigton
West Curthwaite
East Curthwaite
Caldew
Bromfield
Waverton
Brackenthwaite
Gaitsgill
Waterside
Red Dial
Raughton Head
Stockdalewath
SOUTHWAITE SERVICES
Rosley
Westward
Welton
Bolton Low Houses
HIGH HEAD SCULPTURE VALLEY
Ive
Watchhill
Fletchertown
Ivegill
Low Braithwaite
Brocklebank
Mealsgate
Sebergham
Ellen
Boltongate
Blennerhasset
Roe Beck
Thomas Close
Sandale
Threapland
Torpenhow
163
Caldbeck
Sowerby Row
Hesket Newmarket
Bothel
Whitrigg
Ireby
Hutton End

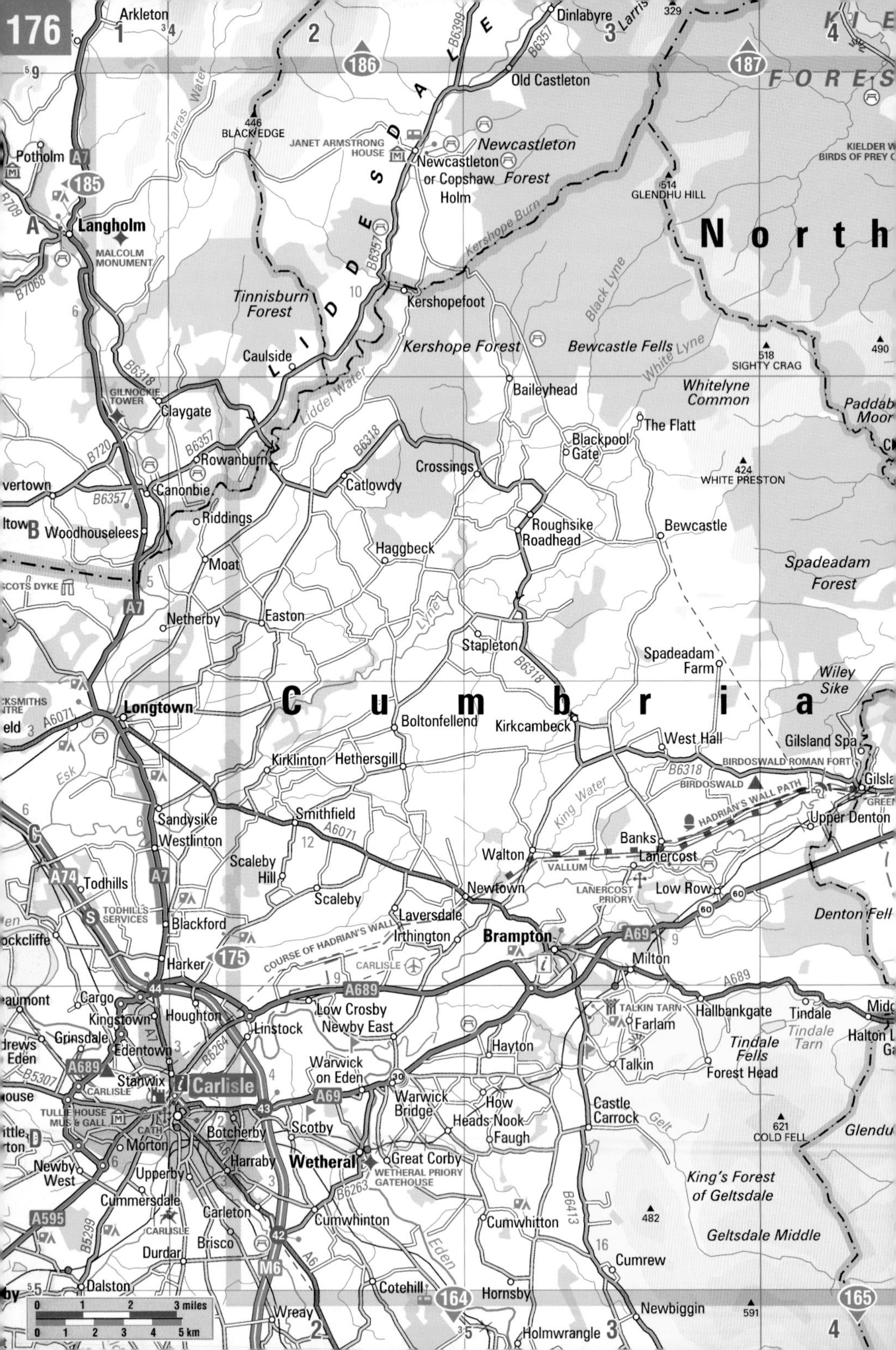
Arkleton
Dinlabyre
Larriston
186
187
LIDDESDALE
KIELDER FOREST
Old Castleton
Tarras Water
446
BLACK EDGE
JANET ARMSTRONG HOUSE
Newcastleton
Newcastleton or Copshaw Holm
Newcastleton Forest
Potholm
A7
185
B709
Langholm
MALCOLM MONUMENT
KIELDER WATER BIRDS OF PREY CENTRE
514
GLENDHU HILL
North
Kershope Burn
Black Lyne
B7068
B6357
Tinnisburn Forest
10
Kershopefoot
Kershope Forest
Bewcastle Fells
White Lyne
518
SIGHTY CRAG
490
Caulside
B6318
Liddel Water
Baileyhead
Whitelyne Common
Paddaburn Moor
GILNOCKIE TOWER
Claygate
The Flatt
B720
B6357
Rowanburn
B6318
Crossings
Blackpool Gate
424
WHITE PRESTON
Canonbie
Catlowdy
Riddings
Woodhouselees
Roughsike
Roadhead
Bewcastle
Haggbeck
Moat
SCOTS DYKE
Spadeadam Forest
Netherby
Easton
Lyne
Stapleton
Spadeadam Farm
B6318
Wiley Sike
Longtown
Cumbria
A6071
Boltonfellend
Kirkcambeck
West Hall
Gilsland Spa
Kirklinton
Hethersgill
B6318
BIRDOSWALD ROMAN FORT
BIRDOSWALD
Esk
HADRIAN'S WALL PATH
Sandysike
Smithfield
King Water
Upper Denton
Westlinton
A6071
12
Banks
Walton
Lanercost
VALLUM
A74
Todhills
Scaleby Hill
Newtown
LANERCOST PRIORY
Low Row
60
TODHILLS SERVICES
Scaleby
Laversdale
Denton Fell
Blackford
Rockcliffe
COURSE OF HADRIAN'S WALL
Irthington
Brampton
A69
9
Harker
175
CARLISLE
Milton
44
A689
A689
Cargo
Low Crosby
TALKIN TARN
Hallbankgate
Tindale
Kingstown
Houghton
Newby East
Farlam
Tindale Tarn
Halton Lea Gate
Grinsdale
Linstock
Tindale Fells
Edentown
B6264
Hayton
Talkin
Forest Head
A689
Warwick on Eden
30
B5307
Stanwix
Carlisle
A69
Warwick Bridge
How
TULLIE HOUSE MUS & GALL
43
Heads Nook
Castle Carrock
621
COLD FELL
Glendue
CATH
Botcherby
Scotby
Gelt
Morton
Faugh
Newby West
Harraby
Wetheral
Great Corby
Upperby
WETHERAL PRIORY GATEHOUSE
King's Forest of Geltsdale
B6263
B6413
Cummersdale
A595
Carleton
Cumwhinton
Cumwhitton
482
CARLISLE
Eden
B5299
Brisco
42
Geltsdale Middle
Durdar
16
A6
M6
Cumrew
Dalston
Cotehill
164
Hornsby
165
Wreay
Newbiggin
591
Holmwrangle
0 1 2 3 miles
0 1 2 3 4 5 km

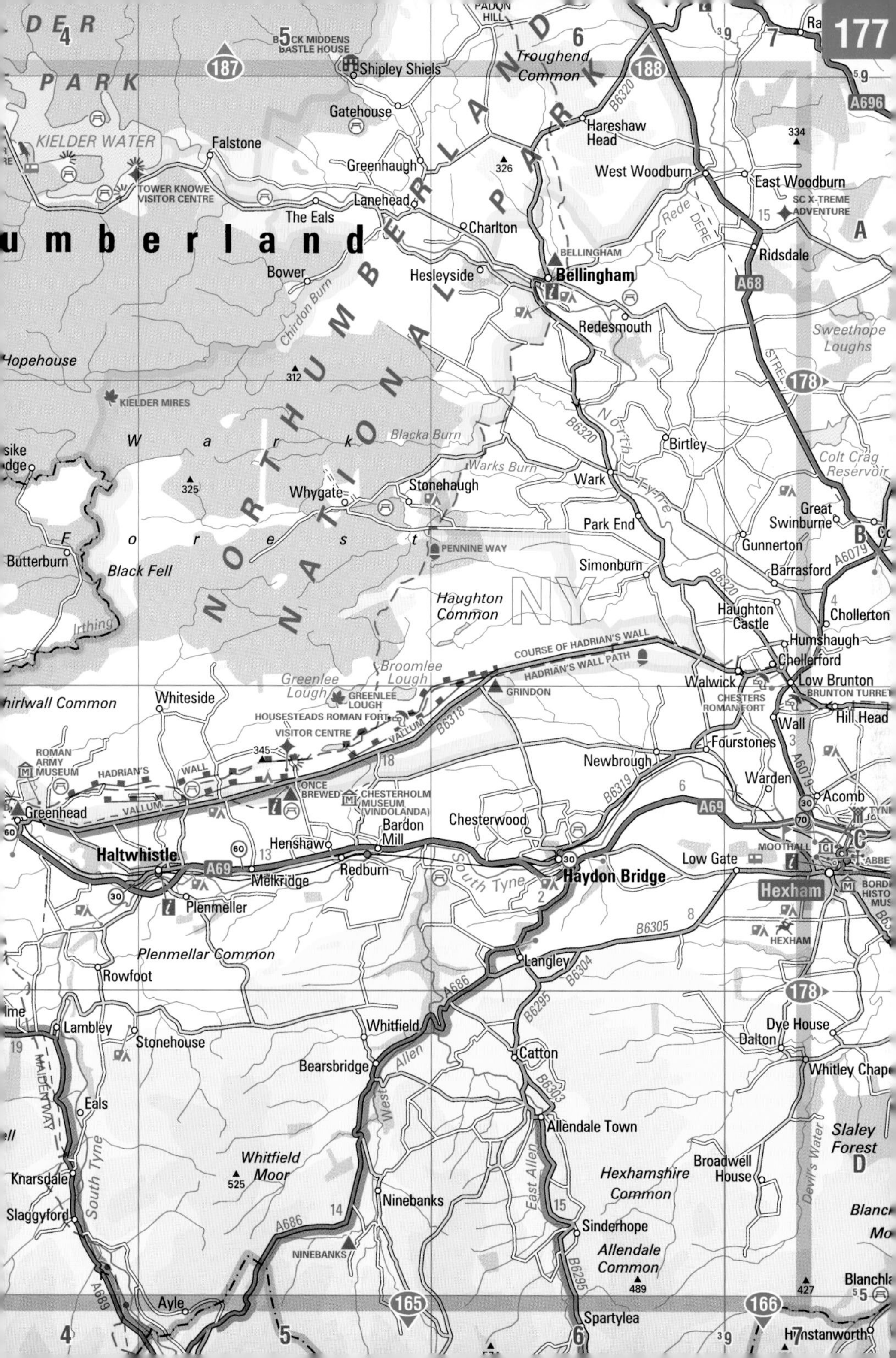
Shipley Shiels
Gatehouse
KIELDER WATER
Falstone
TOWER KNOWE VISITOR CENTRE
Greenhaugh
Lanehead
The Eals
Troughend Common
Hareshaw Head
West Woodburn
East Woodburn
SC X-TREME ADVENTURE
Ridsdale
Charlton
Northumberland
NORTHUMBERLAND NATIONAL PARK
Bower
Hesleyside
Bellingham
Redesmouth
Sweethope Loughs
Hopehouse
KIELDER MIRES
Wark Forest
Blacka Burn
Birtley
Colt Crag Reservoir
Warks Burn
Wark
Whygate
Stonehaugh
Park End
Great Swinburne
Gunnerton
Butterburn
Black Fell
PENNINE WAY
Simonburn
Barrasford
Haughton Common
Haughton Castle
Chollerton
Humshaugh
COURSE OF HADRIAN'S WALL
HADRIAN'S WALL PATH
Chollerford
Broomlee Lough
Greenlee Lough
GREENLEE LOUGH
GRINDON
Walwick
Low Brunton
BRUNTON TURRET
CHESTERS ROMAN FORT
Hill Head
Thirlwall Common
Whiteside
HOUSESTEADS ROMAN FORT
VISITOR CENTRE
Wall
Fourstones
ROMAN ARMY MUSEUM
HADRIAN'S WALL
VALLUM
Newbrough
Warden
ONCE BREWED
CHESTERHOLM MUSEUM (VINDOLANDA)
Acomb
Greenhead
Chesterwood
Bardon Mill
Henshaw
Haltwhistle
Melkridge
Redburn
South Tyne
Haydon Bridge
Low Gate
MOOTHALL
Hexham
Plenmeller
HEXHAM
Plenmellar Common
Langley
Rowfoot
Lambley
Stonehouse
Whitfield
Dye House
Dalton
Catton
Bearsbridge
Whitley Chape
West Allen
Allendale Town
Slaley Forest
Eals
Whitfield Moor
Broadwell House
Hexhamshire Common
Knarsdale
Slaggyford
Ninebanks
East Allen
Sinderhope
Allendale Common
NINEBANKS
Blanchl
Ayle
Spartylea
Hunstanworth
MAIDEN WAY
Devil's Water
NY
A68
A69
A686
A689
A6079
B6320
B6318
B6319
B6305
B6304
B6295
B6303
187
188
178
165
166

Northumberland
Raylees
Ewesley
Rothley
Shield East
Netherwitton
Stanton
188
189
A697
A1
A696
HERTERTON HOUSE GARDEN
Longwitton
Font
Pigdon
Rothley
Hart Burn
CAUSEWAY
334
B6342
East Woodburn
SC X-TREME ADVENTURE
Knowesgate
Cambo
Scots' Gap
B6343
Hartburn
Throphill
Mitford
A192
Ridsdale
A68
Kirkwhelpington
WALLINGTON
Middleton
High Angerton
Wansbeck
Meldon
Molesden
Tranwell
BOLAM LAKE
Bolam
Kirkharle
Whalton
B6524
Sweethope Loughs
DEVIL'S
Great Bavington
Capheaton
Harnham
Shilvington
Saltwick
177
Thockrington
Little Bavington
Belsay
BELSAY HALL
Ogle
Colt Crag Reservoir
Kirkheaton
KIRKLEY HALL
NORTHUMBERLAND CHEESE FARM
Hallington Reservoir
Hallington
258
Black Heddon
West Newham
Milbourne
Higham Dykes
Berwick Hill
Great Swinburne
Colwell
Gunnerton
Ryal
Ingoe
Barrasford
A6079
B6309
NY
Fenwick
Ponteland
Haughton Castle
Chollerton
Bingfield
Heugh
Dalton
Humshaugh
Matfen
Stamfordham
Pont
Darras Hall
B6545
Chollerford
Great Whittington
Ouston
Eachwick
Medburn
High Callerton
Low Brunton
BRUNTON TURRET
CHESTERS ROMAN FORT
Black Callerton
B6323
Wall
Hill Head
B6318
COURSE OF HADRIAN'S WALL
Harlow Hill
B6324
Fourstones
Halton
HADRIAN'S WALL PATH
North Walbottle
B6528
A69
Warden
AYDON CASTLE
B6321
Throckley
Acomb
Sandhoe
Aydon
Newton Hall
Horsley
Heddon-on-the-Wall
TYNE RIVERSIDE
Walbottle
TYNE GREEN
GEORGE STEPHENSON'S BIRTHPLACE
WYLAM RAILWAY MUS
Newburn
A6085
MOOTHALL
ABBEY
Corbridge
Newton
Ovingham
Wylam
Clara Vale
Ryton
B6317
Hexham
BORDER HISTORY MUS
DILSTON PHYSIC GDN
Dilston
A695
Ovington
West Wylam
Crawcrook
HEXHAM
B6305
B6306
B6307
Tyne
CHERRYBURN
Prudhoe
BLAYDON
Riding Mill
Broomhaugh
Branch End
Mickley Square
Greenside
Winlaton
Stocksfield
High Mickley
Coalburns
Painshawfield
Barlow
Broomley
Leadgate
257
High Spen
DERWENT WALK
Dye House
Dalton
New Ridley
Hedley on the Hill
Chopwell
Highfield
Slaley
Healey
HIGHLAND CATTLE CENTRE
Rowlands Gill
GIBSIDE
Byermoor
Whitley Chapel
Whittonstall
Blackhall Mill
DERWENTCOTE STEEL FURNACE
B6314
Hamsterley
Leazes
ST ANDREW'S CHURCH
Slaley Forest
Kiln Pit Hill
Newlands
High Westwood
B6310
Hobson
TANFIELD RAILWAY
Devil's Water
Ebchester
Medomsley
A692
Broadwell House
Tantobie
DERWENT RES.
Shotleyfield
Dipton
Tanfield Lea
Blanchland Moor
Shotley Bridge
STANLEY
B6278
Carterway Heads
Bridgehill
Leadgate
Catchgate
A694
B6309
B6308
B6168
POW HILL
Consett
A693
Annfield Plain
Blanchland
427
Edmundbyers
EDMUNDBYERS
166
Templetown
Iveston
Muggleswick
Allensford
Maiden Law
Castleside
Knitsley
Delves
A691
A6076
Burnhope
3 miles
5 km

Ulgham
THE SANCTUARY WILDLIFE CENTRE
Linton
Ellington
Lynemouth
189
COLLIERY MUSEUM
Beacon Pt.
Longhirst
QUEEN ELIZABETH II
Woodhorn
Ashington
Pegswood
Newbiggin-by-the-Sea
Hirst
WANSBECK
Bothal
Morpeth
North Seaton
Stakeford
Guide Post
Scotland Gate
West Sleekburn
Choppington
Cambois
Hepscott
Clifton
Bedlington Station
East Sleekburn
Bedlington
Cowpen
BLYTH
Nedderton
BEDLINGTON
Bebside
Newsham
East Hartford
New Delaval
PLESSEY WOODS
Shankhouse
Nelson Village
New Hartley
Seaton
Seaton Sluice
Cramlington
SEATON DELAVAL HALL
Southfield
East Cramlington
Seaton Delaval
Hartley
ST MARY'S LIGHTHOUSE
St Mary's or Bait I.
Brenkley
Seaton Burn
Seghill
Holywell
NZ
Dinnington
Annitsford
Dudley
Brunswick Village
Wide Open
Burradon
Backworth
Earsdon
WHITLEY BAY
Hazlerigg
NEWCASTLE
Camperdown
Monkseaton
AMSTERDAM 15:30
Killingworth
Shiremoor
Cullercoats
Marden
BLUE REEF AQUARIUM
TYNEMOUTH CASTLE & PRIORY
Tyne
Kenton
Longbenton
STEPHENSON RAILWAY MUSEUM
Tynemouth
THE RISING SUN
North Shields
ARBEIA ROMAN FORT AND MUSEUM
Gosforth
Willington
Kenton
Jesmond
WALLSEND
ROYAL QUAYS
South Shields
SOUTH SHIELDS MUSEUM
Tyne Tunnel
TOLL
NEWCASTLE UPON TYNE
Heaton
Jarrow
BEDE'S WORLD
ST PAUL'S MONASTERY
Westoe
THE LEAS AND MARSDEN ROCK
Marsden Bay
Byker
SEGEDUNUM FORT
Harton
Marsden
CASTLE KEEP
Walker
NEWCASTLE DISCOVERY
Gateshead
Hebburn
SOUTER LIGHTHOUSE
METROLAND
INTERNATIONAL STADIUM
Hedworth
Whiteleas
Cleadon
Whitburn Colliery
Dunston
Bensham
Pelaw
Boldon Colliery
Whitburn
SHIPLEY ART GAL
Felling
Boldon
Carr Hill
FULWELL WINDMILL
Low Fell
Downhill
Fulwell
Street Gate
Chowdene
Wear
Hylton Castle
Southwick
Roker
Marley Hill
Lamesley
Wrekenton
BOWES RLY
Usworth
Castletown
Monkwearmouth
NATIONAL GLASS CENTRE
Springwell
STATION MUS
ST PETER'S CHURCH
ANGEL OF THE NORTH
Blackfell
OLD HALL
South Hylton
Pallion
SUNDERLAND MINSTER
Kibblesworth
Birtley
WASHINGTON SERVICES
WASHINGTON
High Barnes
Sunderland
Pennywell
Hendon
Lambton
THE WILDFOWL & WETLANDS TRUST
BEAMISH
Ouston
Urpeth
PENSHAW MON
New Silksworth
Beamish
Perkinsville
Barley Mow
Fatfield
East Herrington
Rickleton
Penshaw
Ryhope
Pelton
Tunstall
West Pelton
Shiney Row
New Herrington
Doxford Park
RYHOPE ENGINES MUS
Grange Villa
CHESTER-LE-STREET
Bournmoor
Newbottle
Burdon
Craghead
THE ANKERS HOUSE
Fence Houses
Seaton
Northlea
Waldridge
Chester Moor
SEAHAM
167
HOUGHTON-LE-SPRING
Great Lumley
Colliery Row
West Lea
Edmondsley
East

1
2
3
A
B
C
D
E
191
192
TURNBERRY
Turnberry Bay
Brest Rocks
NW
338
Ailsa Craig
Girvan
Glendoune
Woodland Bay
A77
Kennedy's Pass
297
GREY HILL
Straid
Currarie
Lendalfoot
CARLETON CASTLE
260
Poundland
B734
Bennane Hd.
Colmonell
265
Knockdolian
Heronsford
Ballantrae Bay
B7044
Glen Tig
Water of Tig
Ballantrae
Balkissock
Downan Pt.
Auchencrosh
Arecleoch Forest
LARNE 1:00 (Mar-Oct)
439
BENERAIRD
LARNE 2:00
BELFAST 2:15
Mark
Glen App
Milleur Pt.
Miltonise
Corsewall Pt.
257
Barnhills
Portencalzie
North Cairn
South Cairn
B738
Corsewall
170
Loch Connell
Kirkcolm
Cairnryan
Penwhirn Res.
Main Water of Luce
Cross Water of Luce
Dounan Bay
Mains of Airies
Ervie
A718
Braid Fell
Low Salchrie
The Wig
B798
LOCH RYAN
New Luce
Leswalt
Craigencross
Innermessan
Auchmantle
0 1 2 3 miles
0 1 2 3 4 5 km

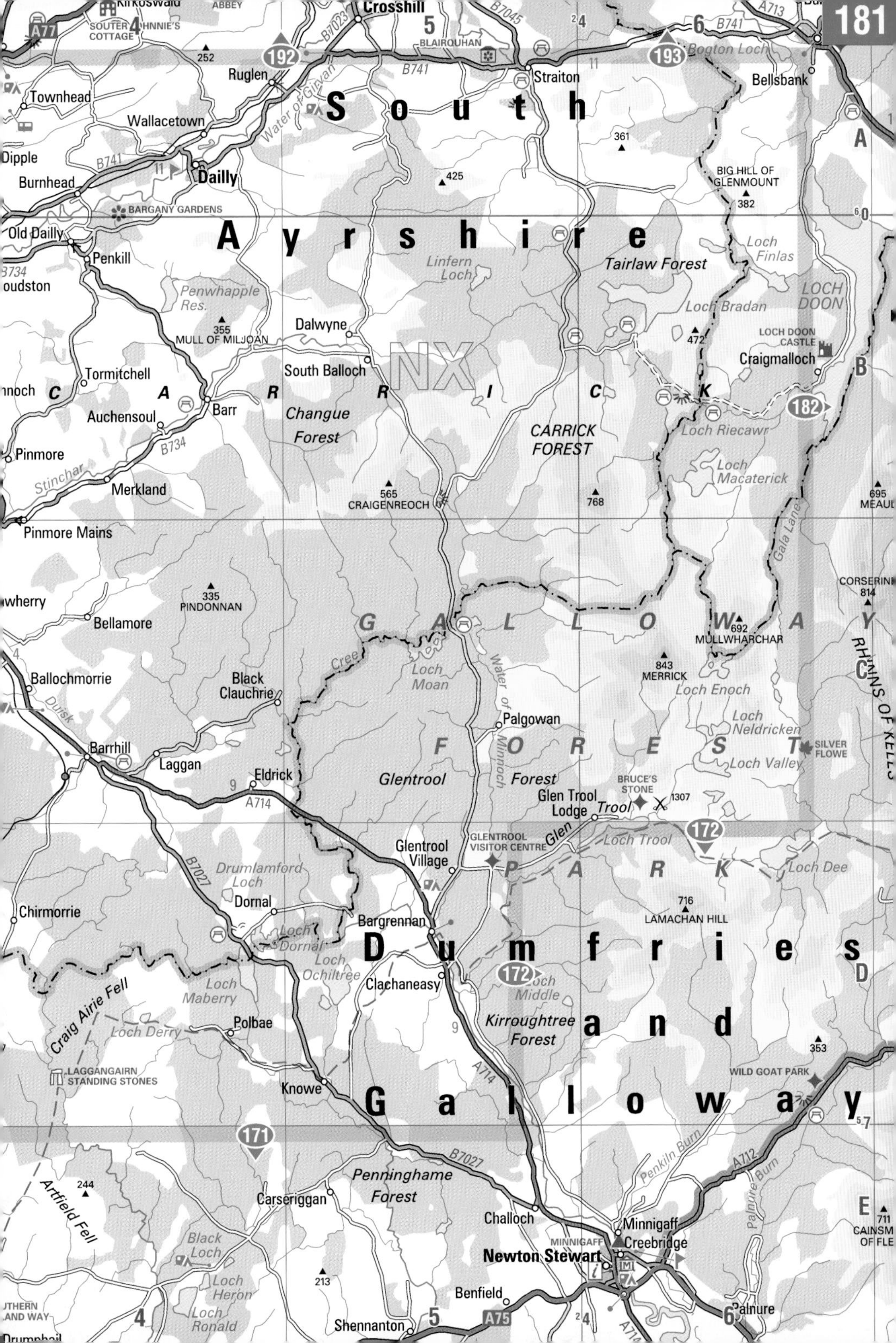
South Ayrshire
Dumfries and Galloway
CARRICK
GALLOWAY FOREST PARK
NX
Crosshill
Kirkoswald
ABBEY
SOUTER JOHNNIE'S COTTAGE
BLAIRQUHAN
Straiton
Bellsbank
Bogton Loch
Ruglen
Townhead
Wallacetown
Water of Girvan
Dipple
Dailly
Burnhead
BARGANY GARDENS
Old Dailly
Penkill
Loudston
Penwhapple Res.
MULL OF MILJOAN
Dalwyne
South Balloch
Linfern Loch
Tairlaw Forest
Loch Finlas
LOCH DOON
Loch Bradan
LOCH DOON CASTLE
Craigmalloch
BIG HILL OF GLENMOUNT
Tormitchell
Auchensoul
Barr
Pinmore
Stinchar
Merkland
Pinmore Mains
Changue Forest
CARRICK FOREST
Loch Riecawr
Loch Macaterick
CRAIGENREOCH
Gala Lane
MEAUL
CORSERINE
PINDONNAN
Bellamore
MULLWHARCHAR
MERRICK
RHINNS OF KELLS
Ballochmorrie
Cree
Loch Moan
Water of Minnoch
Loch Enoch
Loch Neldricken
Black Clauchrie
Palgowan
SILVER FLOWE
Loch Valley
Barrhill
Duisk
Laggan
Eldrick
Glentrool
Forest
BRUCE'S STONE
Glen Trool Lodge
Trool
Glen Trool
Loch Trool
Loch Dee
Glentrool Village
GLENTROOL VISITOR CENTRE
Drumlamford Loch
Dornal
Chirmorrie
Bargrennan
Loch Dornal
LAMACHAN HILL
Loch Ochiltree
Clachaneasy
Loch Middle
Loch Maberry
Craig Airie Fell
Loch Derry
Polbae
Kirroughtree Forest
LAGGANGAIRN STANDING STONES
WILD GOAT PARK
Knowe
Penkiln Burn
Palnure Burn
Artfield Fell
Penninghame Forest
Carseriggan
Challoch
Minnigaff
CAINSMORE OF FLEET
Black Loch
MINNIGAFF
Creebridge
Newton Stewart
Loch Heron
Loch Ronald
Benfield
SOUTHERN UPLAND WAY
Palnure
Shennanton
Drumphail
A77
B7023
B7045
A713
B741
B734
A714
B7027
A712
A75
192
193
182
172
171
252
361
425
382
472
355
565
768
695
814
335
692
843
1307
716
353
244
213
711

East Ayrshire
South Ayrshire
Trabboch
Ochiltree
Auchinleck
Lugar
Belston
Masonhill
Coylton
Coalhall
Joppa
Hillhead
Drongan
MACLAURIN GALLERY & ROZELLE HOUSE
Laigh Glengall
TAM O'SHANTER EXPERIENCE
Martnaham Loch
Barbieston
Sinclairston
Hayhill
Littlemill
Rankinston
Hollybush
Dalrymple
Holmhead
Logan
KEIR HARDIE STATUE
Cumnock
Netherthird
Craigens
BAIRD INSTITUTE MUSEUM
Skares
DOON VALLEY RARE BREEDS CENTRE
Pathhead
Mansfield
Connel Park
Bankglen
New Cumnock
Burnside
Dalleagles
Afton Water
Water of Coyle
Nith
Polnessan
Patna
Burnfoot
429
KILMEIN HILL
Waterside
DOON VALLEY HERITAGE MUSEUM
BENBEOCH
464
SCOTTISH INDUSTRIAL RAILWAY CENTRE
Burnton
Loch Spallander Reservoir
Aitkenhead
Doon
Dalmellington
CATHCARTSON VISITOR CENTRE
569
ENOCH HILL
BLAIRQUHAN
Straiton
Bogton Loch
Bellsbank
CAMPBELLS HILL
453
361
425
BIG HILL OF GLENMOUNT
382
Carsphairn Forest
Afton Reservoir
Tairlaw Forest
Linfern Loch
Loch Finlas
LOCH DOON
Loch Bradan
472
LOCH DOON CASTLE
Craigmalloch
Lamloch
Brockloch
797
CAIRNSMORE OF CARSPHAIRN
Loch Riecawr
CARRICK FOREST
Loch Macaterick
768
MEAUL
695
Garryhorn
Carsphairn
CAIRN AVEL
Bardennoch
Dundeugh Forest
Knowehead
Kendoon Loch
THE GLENKENS
GALLOWAY FOREST PARK
Gala Lane
Castlemaddy
Dundeugh
KENDOON
Glenhoul
Kendoon
CORSERINE
814
Loch Harrow
Forrest Lodge
Carsfad Loch
692
MULLWHARCHAR
843
MERRICK
Loch Enoch
RHINNS OF KELLS
Loch Dungeon
Water of Minnoch
Palgowan
Loch Neldricken
SILVER FLOWE
746
Millquarter
Earlstoun Loch
St John's Town of Dalry
Loch Valley
Drumbuie
Bogue
Forest
BRUCE'S STONE
1307
Glen Trool Lodge
Trool
Garroch
Clatteringshaws Forest
Glenlee
Loch Trool
Loch Dee
Clatteringshaws Loch
381
New Galloway
0 1 2 3 miles
0 1 2 3 4 5 km

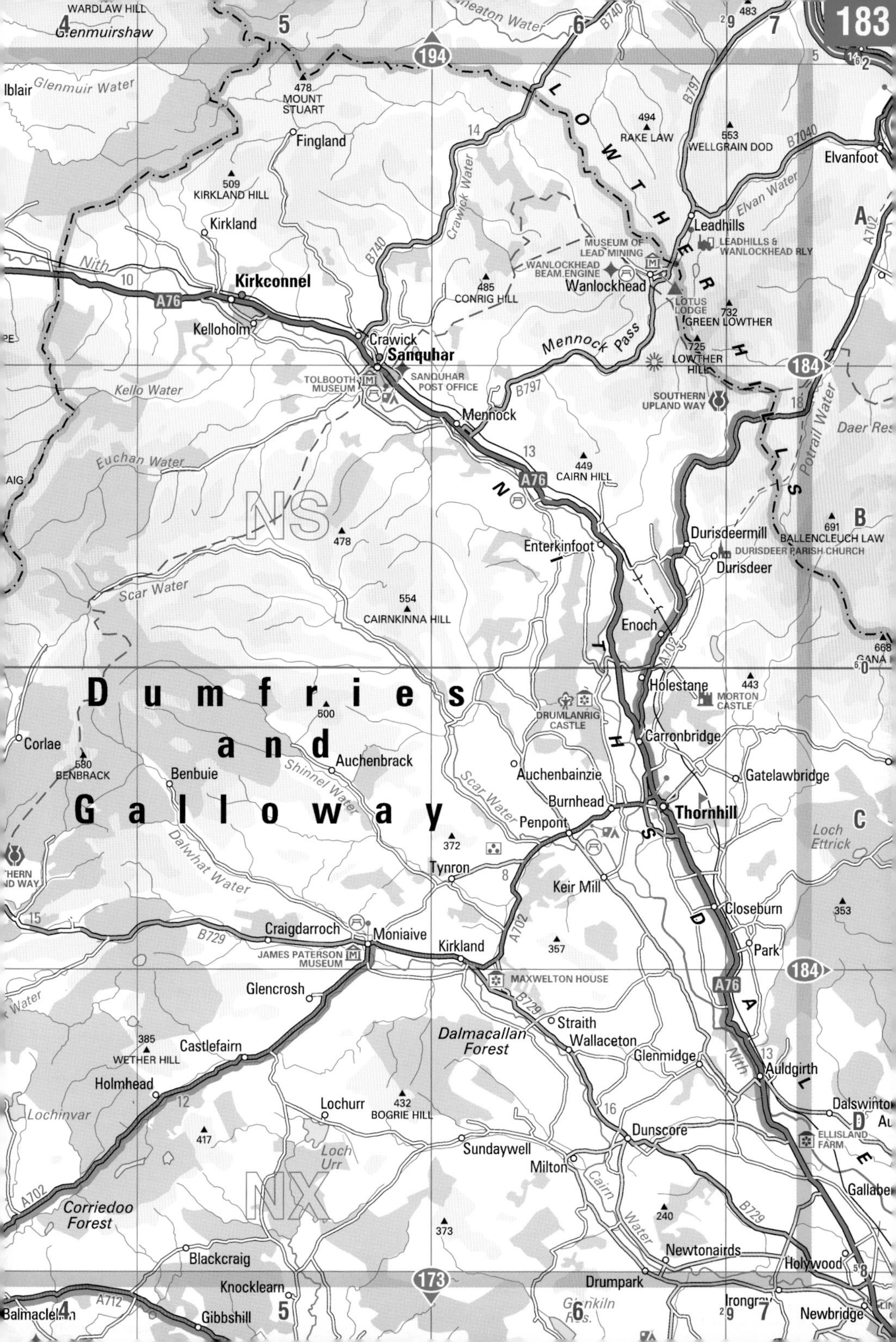

183
Dumfries and Galloway
NS
NX
194
184
173
LOWTHER HILLS
NITHSDALE
Glenmuirshaw
WARDLAW HILL
478 MOUNT STUART
Glenmuir Water
Fingland
509 KIRKLAND HILL
Kirkland
Nith
Kirkconnel
A76
Kelloholm
Crawick
Sanquhar
TOLBOOTH MUSEUM
SANQUHAR POST OFFICE
Kello Water
Mennock
Euchan Water
Crawick Water
B740
Scar Water
478
554 CAIRNKINNA HILL
500
Corlae
580 BENBRACK
Benbuie
Auchenbrack
Shinnel Water
Dalwhat Water
Scar Water
Penpont
372
Tynron
Craigdarroch
B729
Moniaive
JAMES PATERSON MUSEUM
Kirkland
Glencrosh
385 WETHER HILL
Castlefairn
Holmhead
Lochinvar
417
Lochurr
432 BOGRIE HILL
Loch Urr
Corriedoo Forest
A702
373
Blackcraig
Knocklearn
A712
Balmaclellan
Gibbshill
Meaton Water
B740
483
494 RAKE LAW
553 WELLGRAIN DOD
B797
B7040
Elvanfoot
Elvan Water
Leadhills
LEADHILLS & WANLOCKHEAD RLY
MUSEUM OF LEAD MINING
WANLOCKHEAD BEAM ENGINE
Wanlockhead
485 CONRIG HILL
LOTUS LODGE
732 GREEN LOWTHER
Mennock Pass
725 LOWTHER HILL
SOUTHERN UPLAND WAY
B797
449 CAIRN HILL
Potrail Water
Daer Res
A702
Durisdeermill
Durisdeer
DURISDEER PARISH CHURCH
691 BALLENCLEUCH LAW
Enterkinfoot
Enoch
668 GANA
Holestane
443
MORTON CASTLE
DRUMLANRIG CASTLE
Carronbridge
Auchenbainzie
Gatelawbridge
Burnhead
Thornhill
Loch Ettrick
Keir Mill
Closeburn
353
357
Park
MAXWELTON HOUSE
Straith
Wallaceton
Dalmacallan Forest
Glenmidge
Auldgirth
Dalswinton
ELLISLAND FARM
Dunscore
Sundaywell
Milton
Cairn Water
240
Gallaber
Newtonairds
Holywood
Drumpark
Irongray
Newbridge
Glenkiln Res.

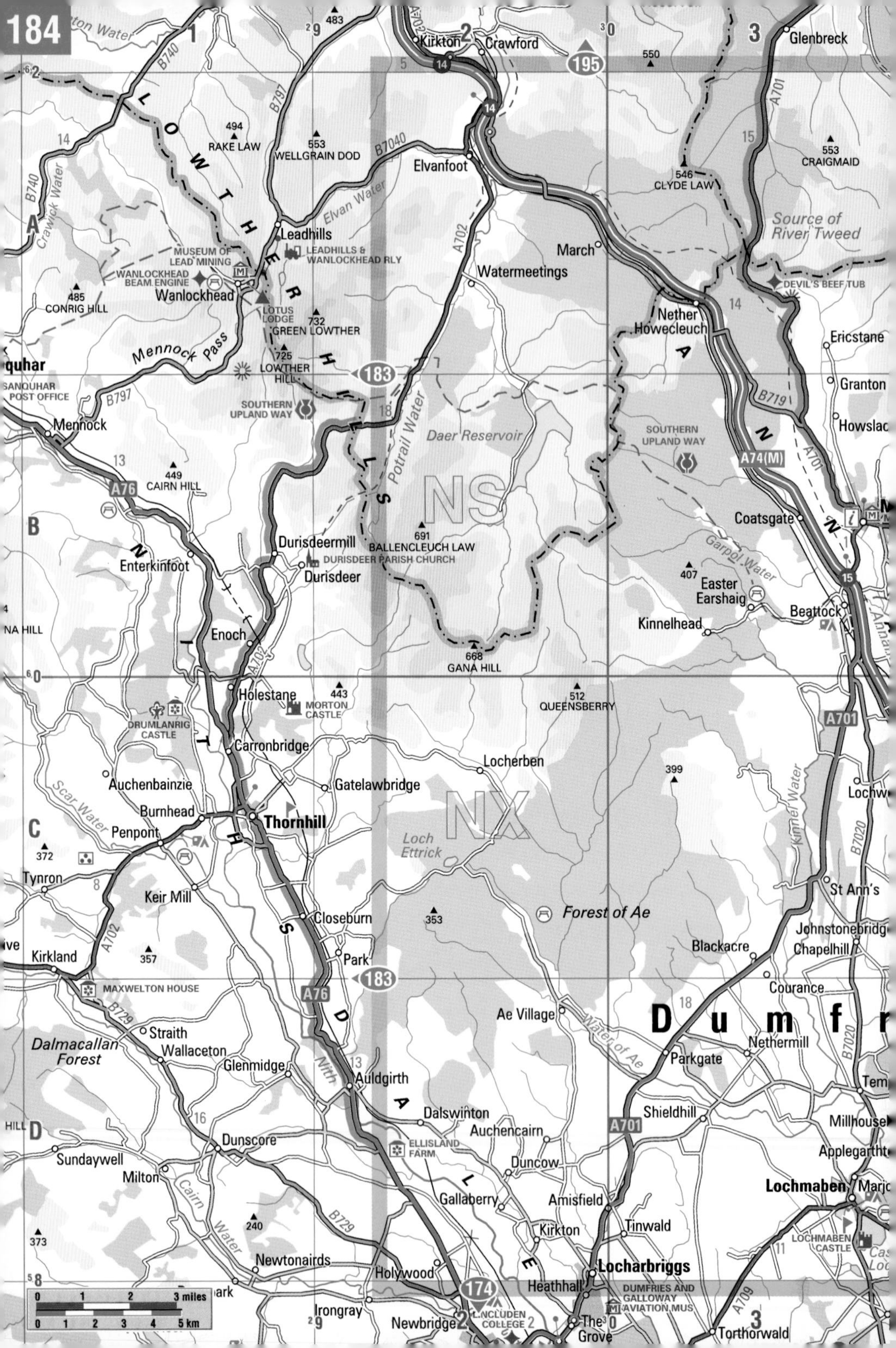

Kirkton
Crawford
195
550
Glenbreck
14
LOWTHER HILLS
494
RAKE LAW
553
WELLGRAIN DOD
B7040
Elvanfoot
553
CRAIGMAID
546
CLYDE LAW
Source of River Tweed
Elvan Water
Leadhills
MUSEUM OF LEAD MINING
LEADHILLS & WANLOCKHEAD RLY
WANLOCKHEAD BEAM ENGINE
Wanlockhead
485
CONRIG HILL
LOTUS LODGE
732
GREEN LOWTHER
725
LOWTHER HILL
Mennock Pass
March
Watermeetings
DEVIL'S BEEF TUB
Nether Howecleuch
Ericstane
Granton
183
SANQUHAR POST OFFICE
SOUTHERN UPLAND WAY
Mennock
Potrail Water
Daer Reservoir
B719
Howslac
A74(M)
449
CAIRN HILL
A76
NS
Coatsgate
Durisdeermill
691
BALLENCLEUCH LAW
DURISDEER PARISH CHURCH
Durisdeer
Enterkinfoot
Garpol Water
407
Easter Earshaig
Beattock
Kinnelhead
Enoch
668
GANA HILL
Holestane
443
MORTON CASTLE
512
QUEENSBERRY
DRUMLANRIG CASTLE
A701
Carronbridge
Locherben
399
Auchenbainzie
Gatelawbridge
NX
Scar Water
Burnhead
Thornhill
Penpont
Kinnel Water
372
Loch Ettrick
Tynron
Keir Mill
St Ann's
Closeburn
353
Forest of Ae
Johnstonebridge
Kirkland
357
Park
Blackacre
Chapelhill
MAXWELTON HOUSE
Courance
Ae Village
Water of Ae
Dumfr
Straith
Dalmacallan Forest
Wallaceton
Nethermill
Parkgate
Glenmidge
Nith
Auldgirth
Dalswinton
Shieldhill
Millhouse
Auchencairn
ELLISLAND FARM
Dunscore
Sundaywell
Milton
Duncow
Applegarth
Cairn Water
Gallaberry
Amisfield
Lochmaben
240
373
Kirkton
Tinwald
LOCHMABEN CASTLE
Newtonairds
Holywood
Locharbriggs
174
Heathhall
DUMFRIES AND GALLOWAY AVIATION MUS
Irongray
Newbridge
LINCLUDEN COLLEGE
The Grove
Torthorwald
0 1 2 3 miles
0 1 2 3 4 5 km

Megget Reservoir
Meggethead
Talla Linnfoots
195
196
THE WISS
Loch of the Lowes
Gilmanscleuch
Newburgh
Crosslee
Tushielaw
Fruid Reservoir
LOCHCRAIG HEAD
Loch Skeen
GREY MARE'S TAIL WATERFALLS
WHITE COOMB
Birkhill
Ramsey Knowe
Wardlaw
Redfordgreen
Ettrickhill
Ettrick
Ramseycleuch
Buccleuch
JAMES HOGG MONUMENT
HART FELL
SADDLE YOKE
Blackhope Burn
BLACK KNOWE
Glenkerry
Deanburnhaugh
REDCLEUCH EDGE
Craik Forest
Borthwick Water
Capplegill
Roundstonefoot
Nether Dalgliesh
Craik
Howpasley
186
RIDDELL MONUMENT
CAPEL FELL
ETTRICK PEN
Moffat Water
LOCH FELL
PIKE HILL
NT
Davington
KAGYU SAMYE LING TIBETAN CENTRE
Teviot
Wamphray Water
White Esk
Eskdalemuir Forest
Laverhay
Eskdalemuir
WISP HILL
Jamestown
Black Esk Reservoir
NY
Newton
Waterhead
Sandyford
Castle O'er Forest
Meggat Water
Ewes Water
Black Esk
Castle O'er
ANNANDALE WATER SERVICES
Dinwoodie Mains
Boreland
Georgefield
Ewes
Arkleton
Dryfe Water
Bentpath
ESKDALE
Dumfries and Galloway
HART FELL
Sibbaldbie
CALKIN RIG
CRAIGCLEUCH CASTLE COLLECTION
Potholm
Corrie Common
176
Langholm
MALCOLM MONUMENT
Paddockhole
Water of Milk
Lockerbie
Bankshill
Kirtleton
175
Burnswark
BURNSWARK HILLFORT
GILNOCKIE TOWER

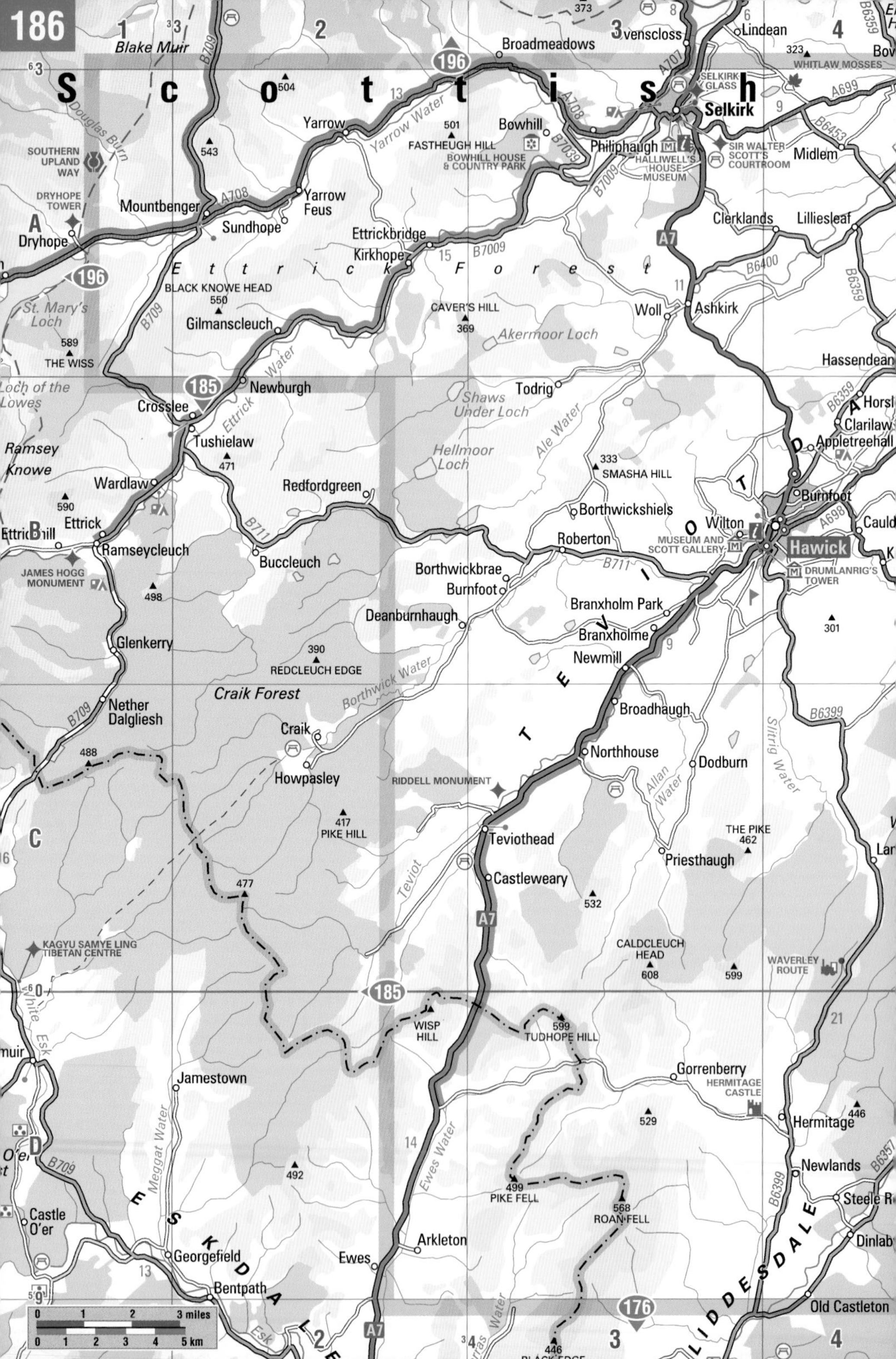
Blake Muir
Scottish
Broadmeadows
Haining/Bowhill estate area: Yarrow Water
Yarrow
Bowhill
FASTHEUGH HILL
BOWHILL HOUSE & COUNTRY PARK
Philiphaugh
Selkirk
SELKIRK GLASS
HALLIWELL'S HOUSE MUSEUM
SIR WALTER SCOTT'S COURTROOM
Lindean
WHITLAW MOSSES
Midlem
Douglas Burn
SOUTHERN UPLAND WAY
DRYHOPE TOWER
Dryhope
Mountbenger
Yarrow Feus
Sundhope
Ettrickbridge
Kirkhope
Clerklands
Lilliesleaf
Ettrick Forest
BLACK KNOWE HEAD
Gilmanscleuch
CAVER'S HILL
Akermoor Loch
Woll
Ashkirk
St. Mary's Loch
THE WISS
Hassendean
Loch of the Lowes
Newburgh
Crosslee
Ettrick Water
Todrig
Shaws Under Loch
Tushielaw
Ramsey Knowe
Hellmoor Loch
Ale Water
Horsl
Clarilaw
Appletreehall
Wardlaw
Redfordgreen
SMASHA HILL
Burnfoot
Borthwickshiels
Ettrick
Ettrick Hill
Ramseycleuch
JAMES HOGG MONUMENT
Buccleuch
Roberton
Wilton
MUSEUM AND SCOTT GALLERY
Hawick
DRUMLANRIG'S TOWER
Cauld
Borthwickbrae
Burnfoot
Deanburnhaugh
Branxholm Park
Branxholme
Glenkerry
REDCLEUCH EDGE
Newmill
Borthwick Water
Craik Forest
Nether Dalgliesh
Broadhaugh
Craik
Howpasley
Northhouse
Dodburn
Allan Water
Slitrig Water
RIDDELL MONUMENT
Teviothead
PIKE HILL
THE PIKE
Priesthaugh
Castleweary
Teviot
TEVIOTDALE
KAGYU SAMYE LING TIBETAN CENTRE
CALDCLEUCH HEAD
WAVERLEY ROUTE
White Esk
WISP HILL
TUDHOPE HILL
Gorrenberry
HERMITAGE CASTLE
Hermitage
Jamestown
Meggat Water
Ewes Water
Newlands
PIKE FELL
ROAN FELL
Castle O'er
Steele R
Arkleton
Dinlab
Georgefield
Ewes
ESKDALE
Bentpath
LIDDESDALE
Old Castleton
Esk
Tarras Water
BLACK EDGE
0 1 2 3 miles
0 1 2 3 4 5 km

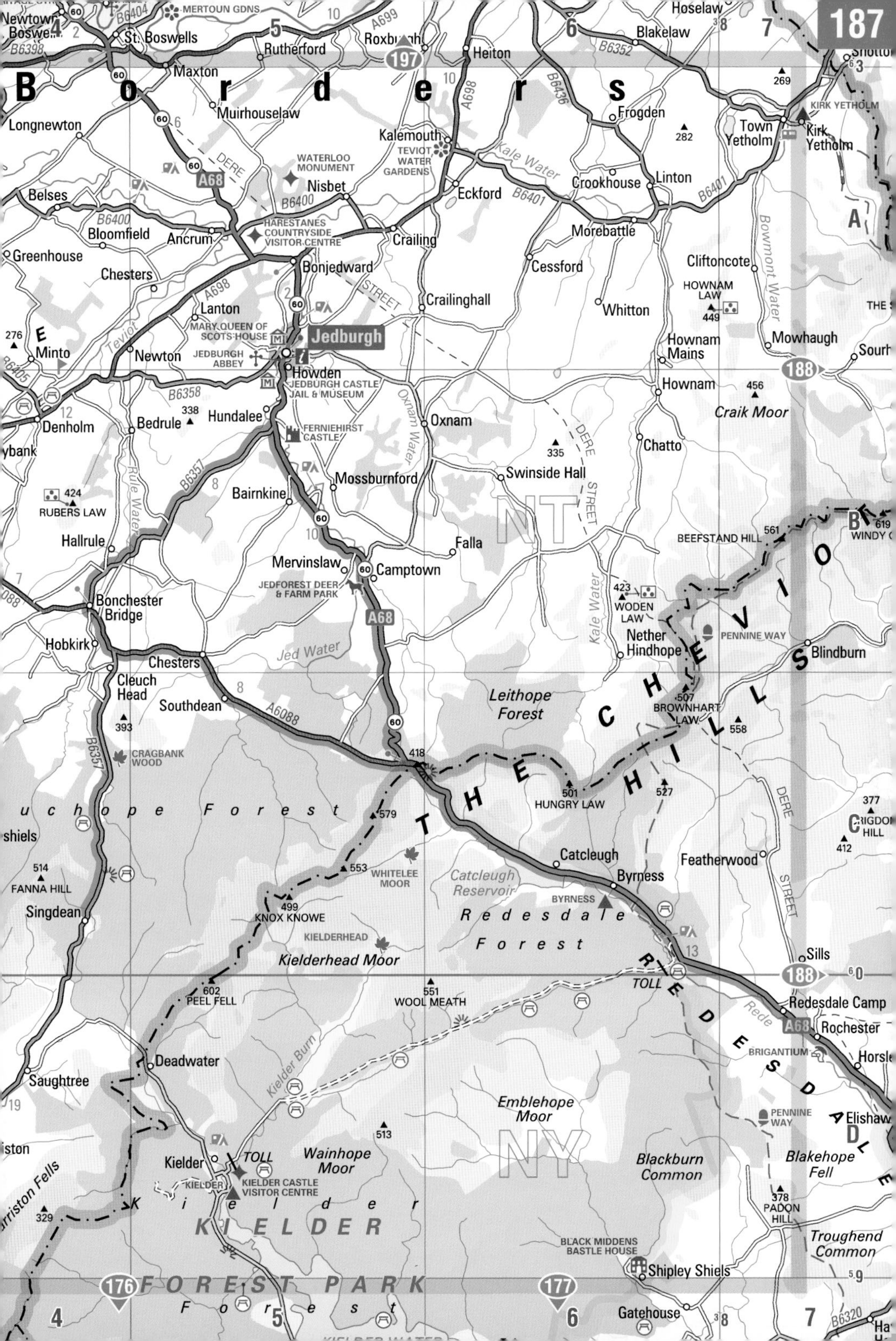
Borders
Newtown St. Boswells
St. Boswells
MERTOUN GDNS
Rutherford
Roxburgh
Hoselaw
Blakelaw
Heiton
Maxton
Muirhouselaw
Longnewton
Frogden
Kalemouth
TEVIOT WATER GARDENS
WATERLOO MONUMENT
Nisbet
Eckford
Kale Water
Crookhouse
Linton
Town Yetholm
Kirk Yetholm
KIRK YETHOLM
Belses
Bloomfield
Ancrum
HARESTANES COUNTRYSIDE VISITOR CENTRE
Crailing
Morebattle
Greenhouse
Chesters
Bonjedward
Cessford
Cliftoncote
Bowmont Water
HOWNAM LAW
Lanton
Crailinghall
Whitton
MARY QUEEN OF SCOTS HOUSE
Jedburgh
Minto
Newton
JEDBURGH ABBEY
Howden
JEDBURGH CASTLE JAIL & MUSEUM
Hownam Mains
Mowhaugh
Hownam
Craik Moor
Denholm
Bedrule
Hundalee
FERNIEHIRST CASTLE
Oxnam
Oxnam Water
Chatto
Mossburnford
Swinside Hall
Bairnkine
RUBERS LAW
Rule Water
Hallrule
Falla
NT
BEEFSTAND HILL
WINDY GYLE
Mervinslaw
Camptown
JEDFOREST DEER & FARM PARK
Bonchester Bridge
WODEN LAW
Kale Water
Hobkirk
Nether Hindhope
PENNINE WAY
Blindburn
Jed Water
Chesters
Cleuch Head
Southdean
Leithope Forest
BROWNHART LAW
THE CHEVIOT HILLS
CRAGBANK WOOD
HUNGRY LAW
Wauchope Forest
Catcleugh
Byrness
Featherwood
FANNA HILL
WHITELEE MOOR
Catcleugh Reservoir
BYRNESS
Singdean
KNOX KNOWE
Redesdale Forest
KIELDERHEAD
Kielderhead Moor
Sills
PEEL FELL
WOOL MEATH
TOLL
REDESDALE
Redesdale Camp
Rochester
BRIGANTIUM
Deadwater
Saughtree
Kielder Burn
Emblehope Moor
PENNINE WAY
Elishaw
Wainhope Moor
NY
Blackburn Common
Blakehope Fell
Kielder
TOLL
KIELDER CASTLE VISITOR CENTRE
PADON HILL
Kielder Forest
KIELDER FOREST PARK
Troughend Common
BLACK MIDDENS BASTLE HOUSE
Shipley Shiels
Gatehouse
A68
A698
A699
A6088
B6400
B6401
B6357
B6358
B6352
B6436
B6404
B6398
B6320
DERE STREET
188
197
176
177
4
5
6
7
A
B
C
D
E

Shotton
Westnewton
Lanton
Coupland
198
Newtown
West Horton
East Horton
Hazelrigg
Weetwood Hall
Ware
Kirknewton
Akeld
1402
Chatton
Greendikes
Town Yetholm
Kirk Yetholm
KIRK YETHOLM
Hethpool
College Burn
Humbleton
Wooler
WOOLER
166
537
Earle
Haugh Head
CHILLINGHAM CASTLE
Chillingham
WILD CATTLE CHILLINGHAM
Middleton Hall
Newtown
CHEVIOT HILLS
Bowmont Water
PENNINE WAY
COLD LAW
452
North Middleton
A697
Lilburn Tower
East Lilburn
Hepburn
315
South Middleton
DEVIL'S CAUSEWAY
Breamish
601
THE SCHIL
MOUNTHOOLEY
Ilderton
Old Bewick
Langleeford
Roseden
Mowhaugh
Sourhope
Harthope Burn
Roddam
B6346
726
815
AUCHOPE CAIRN
THE CHEVIOT
Wooperton
New Bewick
Egling
1464
187
456
Craik Moor
NT
569
DUNMOOR HILL
Brandon
INGRAM NATIONAL PARK CENTRE
Greensidehill
Powburn
233
Ingram
Branton
Shill Moor
Glanton
561
619
WINDY GYLE
NORTHUMBERLAND NATIONAL PARK
335
Glanton Pike
616
CUSHAT LAW
Great Ryle
Prendwick
Usway
Kidland Forest
Whittingham
Barrowburn
Alnham
Aln
Little Ryle
214
Thrunton
Blindburn
Yetlington
Scrainwood
Callaly
Thrunton Wood
501
Alwin
Biddlestone
558
Netherton
Lorbottle Hall
Shillmoor
Alwinton
Lorbottle
319
Linshiels
Burradon
377
CRIGDON HILL
High Trewhitt
DERE STREET
Coquet
Cartington
412
Harbottle
Sharperton
B6341
LADY'S WELL
Warton
Snitter
WATTY BELL'S CAIRN
361
Holystone
Flotterton
Rothbury
CRAGSIDE HOUSE
355
Caistron
Thropton
Newtown
Hepple
Whitton
NATIONAL PARK VISITOR CENTRE
Sills
Great Tosson
NY
Redesdale Camp
Rede
A68
Rochester
BRIGANTIUM
Horsley
440
TOSSON HILL
ROTHBURY FOREST
B6342
REDESDALE
274
Otterburn Camp
Forestburn Gate
PENNINE WAY
Elishaw
386
Harwood Forest
Blakehope Fell
1388
256
Otterburn
Elsdon
Fallowlees Burn
Fontburn Res.
378
PADON HILL
Raylees
Ewesley
Northumberland
Troughend Common
Old Town
Rothley Shield East
177
A696
178
HERTERTON HOUSE GARDEN
Longwitton
334
0 1 2 3 miles
0 1 2 3 4 5 km

NORTHUMBERLAND COAST
NU
NZ
Seahouses
Bradford
Bellshill
Adderstone
Lucker
Elford
North Sunderland
Beadnell
Newham Hall
Warenford
Newham
Swinhoe
Benthall
Fleetham
Beadnell Bay
Newstead
Chathill
Rosebrough
Ellingham
Preston
PRESTON TOWER
Brunton
High Newton-by-the-Sea
Low Newton-by-the-Sea
Embleton Bay
Brownyside
North Charlton
Christon Bank
Embleton
Dunstan Steads
Castle Point
DUNSTANBURGH CASTLE
West Ditchburn
South Charlton
Rock
Craster
Dunstan
Rennington
Littlemill
Howick
Shipley
HULNE PRIORY
Littlehoughton
Howick Haven
Longhoughton
ALNWICK ABBEY
Alnwick
Denwick
Boulmer
Boulmer Haven
Abberwick
Broome Park
ALNWICK
Hawkhill
Lesbury
Lemmington Hall
Bilton
Alnmouth
Alnmouth Bay
EDLINGHAM CASTLE
High Buston
Shilbottle
Low Buston
Birling
Eastfield Hall
Warkworth
Newton-on-the-Moor
Gloster Hill
Amble
Coquet I.
Coquet
Hazon
Hauxley
Swarland Estate
Guyzance
Brainshaugh
North Togston
Acklington
Radcliffe
Swarland
Togston
Broomhill
Felton
South Broomhill
LONGFRAMLINGTON GARDENS
DRURIDGE BAY
West Thirston
East Thirston
Weldon
Red Row
Eshott
Druridge Bay
West Chevington
Helm
Widdrington
Stobswood
Longhorsley
Causey Park Bridge
Widdrington Station
The Scars
Cresswell
Fenrother
Tritlington
Ellington
Ulgham
Linton
Lynemouth
THE SANCTUARY WILDLIFE CENTRE
Netherwitton
Stanton
Hebron
Longhirst
QUEEN ELIZABETH II
Ashington
Beacon Pt.
Woodhorn
CAUSEWAY
Font
A1
A697
A1068
A189
B1340
B1339
B6347
B6346
B6341
B6345
B6344
B1337
199
178
179
l a n d

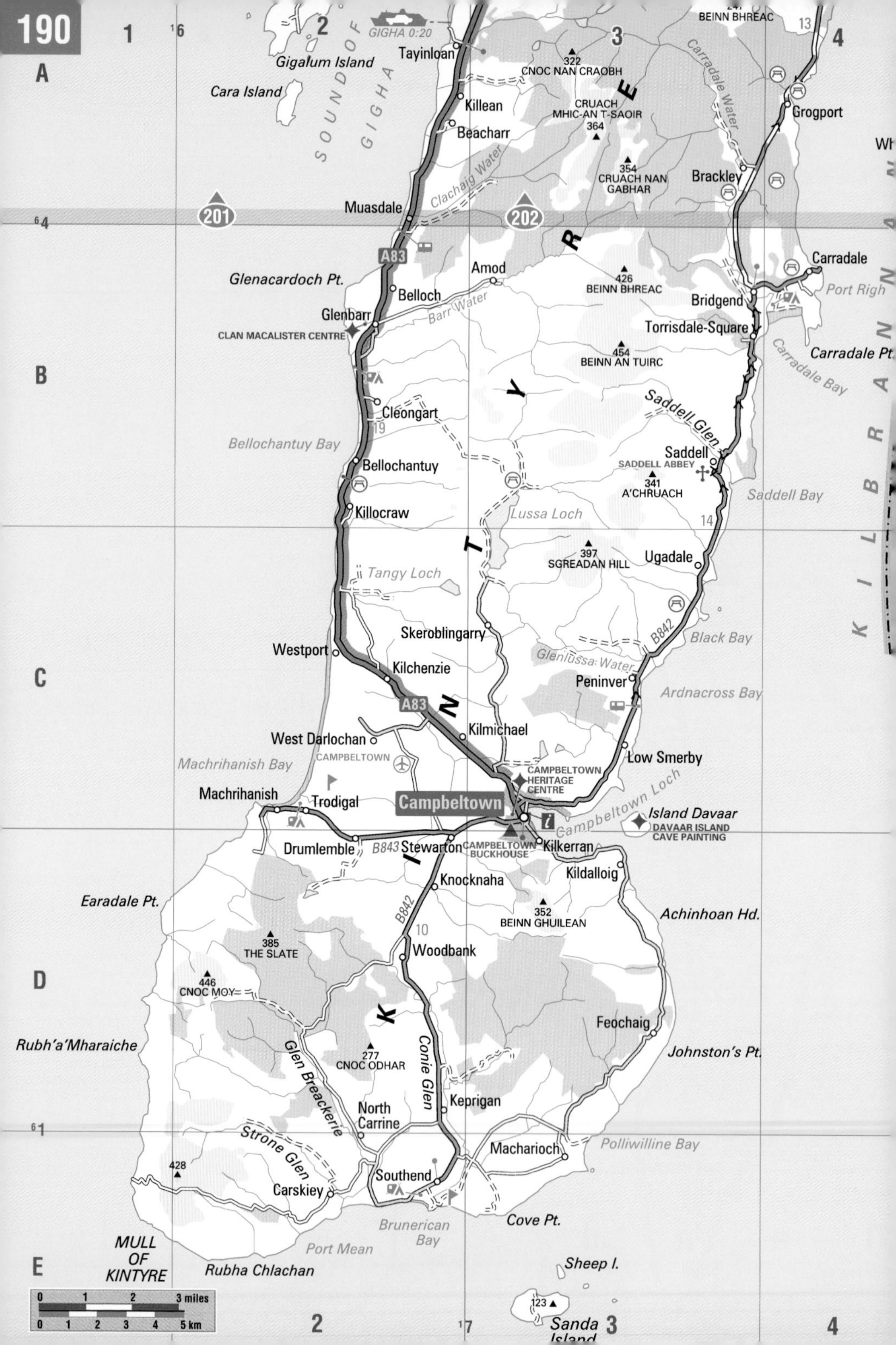

GIGHA 0:20
Tayinloan
Gigalum Island
Cara Island
SOUND OF GIGHA
Killean
Beacharr
322
CNOC NAN CRAOBH
CRUACH MHIC-AN T-SAOIR
364
354
CRUACH NAN GABHAR
BEINN BHREAC
Carradale Water
Grogport
Brackley
Clachaig Water
Muasdale
201
202
A83
Amod
426
BEINN BHREAC
Carradale
Port Righ
Glenacardoch Pt.
Belloch
Barr Water
Glenbarr
CLAN MACALISTER CENTRE
Bridgend
Torrisdale-Square
454
BEINN AN TUIRC
Carradale Pt.
Carradale Bay
Saddell Glen
Cleongart
Bellochantuy Bay
Bellochantuy
Saddell
SADDELL ABBEY
341
A'CHRUACH
Saddell Bay
Killocraw
Lussa Loch
397
SGREADAN HILL
Ugadale
Tangy Loch
Skeroblingarry
B842
Black Bay
Westport
Glenlussa Water
Kilchenzie
Peninver
Ardnacross Bay
Kilmichael
West Darlochan
CAMPBELTOWN
Low Smerby
Machrihanish Bay
CAMPBELTOWN HERITAGE CENTRE
Campbeltown Loch
Machrihanish
Trodigal
Campbeltown
Island Davaar
DAVAAR ISLAND CAVE PAINTING
Drumlemble
B843
Stewarton
CAMPBELTOWN BUCKHOUSE
Kilkerran
Kildalloig
Knocknaha
Earadale Pt.
352
BEINN GHUILEAN
Achinhoan Hd.
Woodbank
385
THE SLATE
446
CNOC MOY
Feochaig
Rubh'a'Mharaiche
277
CNOC ODHAR
Glen Breackerie
Conie Glen
Johnston's Pt.
Keprigan
North Carrine
Strone Glen
Macharioch
Polliwilline Bay
428
Southend
Carskiey
Cove Pt.
Brunerican Bay
Port Mean
MULL OF KINTYRE
Rubha Chlachan
Sheep I.
123
Sanda Island
KINTYRE
KILBRANNAN
0 1 2 3 miles
0 1 2 3 4 5 km

NORTH ISLE OF ARRAN
ARRAN
Thundergay
MEALL NAN DAMH
570
573
Pirnmill
Loch Tanna
859
Glen Sannox
NORTH SANNOX FARM PARK
A841
Sannox
Sannox Bay
Corrie
721
BEINN BHARRAIN
798
CIR MHÒR
874
GOAT FELL
BEINN TARSUINN
825
Imachar
202
203
ARDROSSAN 0:55
BRODICK
BRODICK CASTLE
ARRAN AROMATICS VISITOR CENTRE
Brodick Bay
ISLE OF ARRAN HERITAGE MUSEUM
Brodick
Strathwhillan
Glen Iorsa
Glen Rosa
Dougarie
228
Machrie Water
Glenloig
Auchagallon
Machrie Bay
B880
A'CHRUACH
512
Glen Cloy
Clauchlands Pt.
Tormore
MACHRIE MOOR STANDING STONES
503
Blairbeg
Margnaheglish
Lamlash
Lamlash Bay
Holy Island
Cordon
314
KING'S CAVE
BALMICHAEL VISITOR CENTRE
Balmichael
Torbeg
Shiskine
Drumadoon Pt.
Blackwaterfoot
Drumadoon Bay
Kilpatrick
KILPATRICK DUN
Kingscross Pt.
Kingscross
Auchencairn
458
TIGHVEIN
Knockenkelly
Whiting Bay
North Kiscadale
South Kiscadale
Largymore
Sliddery Water
Glenree
Brown Hd.
CARN BAN
Corriecravie
GLENASHDALE FALLS
Kilmory Water
Largybeg
Dippin
Dippin Head
Sliddery
Lagg
Levencorroch
Kilmory
Bennan
TORRYLINN CAIRN
Bennan Hd.
Kildonan
Sound of Pladda
Pladda
NR
NS
192
180

Seamill
Ardrossan
NORTH AYRSHIRE MUSEUM
Saltcoats
Stevenston
Kilwinning
Dalgarven
AYRSHIRE MUSEUM OF COUNTRY LIFE & COSTUME
Auchentiber
Torranyard
Chapelhill
Dykesmains
Horse Isle
BRODICK 0:55
EGLINTON
Benslie
Cunninghamhead
Girdle Toll
Perceton
Irvine
GLASGOW VENNEL MUS
Springside
Knockentiber
SCOTTISH MARITIME MUSEUM
Fullarton
Dreghorn
Irvine Bay
Drybridge
Gatehead
NS
Dundonald
DUNDONALD CASTLE
Barassie
North Bay
Muirhead
Loans
Symington
Troon
South Bay
ROYAL TROON
Lady Isle
LARNE 2:00 (March-Oct)
Monkton
GLASGOW PRESTWICK
Prestwick
Woodfield
St Quivox
Newton on Ayr
Wallacetown
Whitletts
Ayr
Seafield
Belston
Masonhill
ROBERT BURNS BIRTHPLACE MUS
Belmont
Heads of Ayr
HEADS OF AYR FARM PARK
Doonfoot
MACLAURIN GALLERY & ROZELLE HOUSE
Alloway
Laigh Glengall
BURNS NATIONAL HERITAGE PARK
TAM O'SHANTER EXPERIENCE
Fisherton
Dunure
Culroy
Minishant
Dalrymple
ELECTRIC BRAE
Culzean Bay
CULZEAN CASTLE
Whitefaulds
Maybole
COLLEGIATE CHURCH
Kirkmichael
Maidenhead Bay
CULZEAN
Aitkenhead
Maidens
Loch
TURNBERRY
Kirkoswald
CROSSRAGUEL ABBEY
Crosshill
Turnberry Bay
SOUTER JOHNNIE'S COTTAGE
Turnberry
BLAIRQUHAN
Brest Rocks
Ruglen
Townhead
Wallacetown
0 1 2 3 miles
0 1 2 3 4 5 km

Stewarton
Laighmuir
Flow Moss
205
CORSE HILL
Carnduff
JOHN HASTIE MUS.
Strathaven
M77
Waterside
Fenwick
Laigh Fenwick
246
CRINS HILL
Whitelaw
Caldermill
Calder Water
Avon Water
Wallacegill Muir
Moscow
Onthank
Knockinlaw
DEAN CASTLE
Kilmarnock
Glen Water
Stobieside
Gilmourton
Drumclog
Kype Muir
Grange
DICK INSTITUTE
Crookedholm
Hurlford
KILMARNOCK SERVICES
Galston
Greenholm
Newmilns
Darvel
A71
Rough Moss
Shortlees
MILL RIG
335
Glengavel Reservoir
194
A77
Crossroads
Sornhill
321
Craigie
A76
B744
B7037
Avon
434
WEDDER HILL
466
MIDDLEFIELD LAW
Millburn
Auchmillan
Cessnock Water
Netherwood
Mossgiel
BACHELOR'S CLUB
BURN'S HOUSE MUSEUM
Mauchline
SORN CASTLE
B743
Muirkirk
Smallburn
Kames
Tarbolton
Failford
AYR GORGE WOODLANDS
Catrine
Sorn
Ayr
Haugh
Mossblown
Crosshill
Lugar Water
Airds Moss
East
B705
Cronberry
A70
Stair
Back Rogerton
B7036
Auchinleck
Lugar
497
WARDLAW HILL
Trabboch
Ochiltree
Holmhead
Logan
Glenmuir
Glenmuirshaw
Coylton
Coalhall
KEIR HARDIE STATUE
Cumnock
182
183
Hillhead
Drongan
Netherthird
BAIRD INSTITUTE MUSEUM
Craigens
Dalblair
Ayrshire
B7046
Barbieston
Skares
DOON VALLEY RARE BREEDS CENTRE
Sinclairston
Hayhill
Littlemill
Rankinston
B730
Pathhead
Mansfield
Water of Coyle
Nith
Connel Park
Bankglen
New Cumnock
429
KILMEIN HILL
Burnside
Dalleagles
THE KNIPE
575
Burnfoot
Afton Water
Kello Water
Waterside
DOON VALLEY HERITAGE MUSEUM
BENBEOCH
464
SCOTTISH INDUSTRIAL RAILWAY CENTRE
B741
Doon
Burnton
A713
569
ENOCH HILL
700
BLACKCRAIG HILL
Euchan Water
Dalmellington
CATHCARTSON VISITOR CENTRE
Bogton Loch
Afton Reservoir
Bellsbank

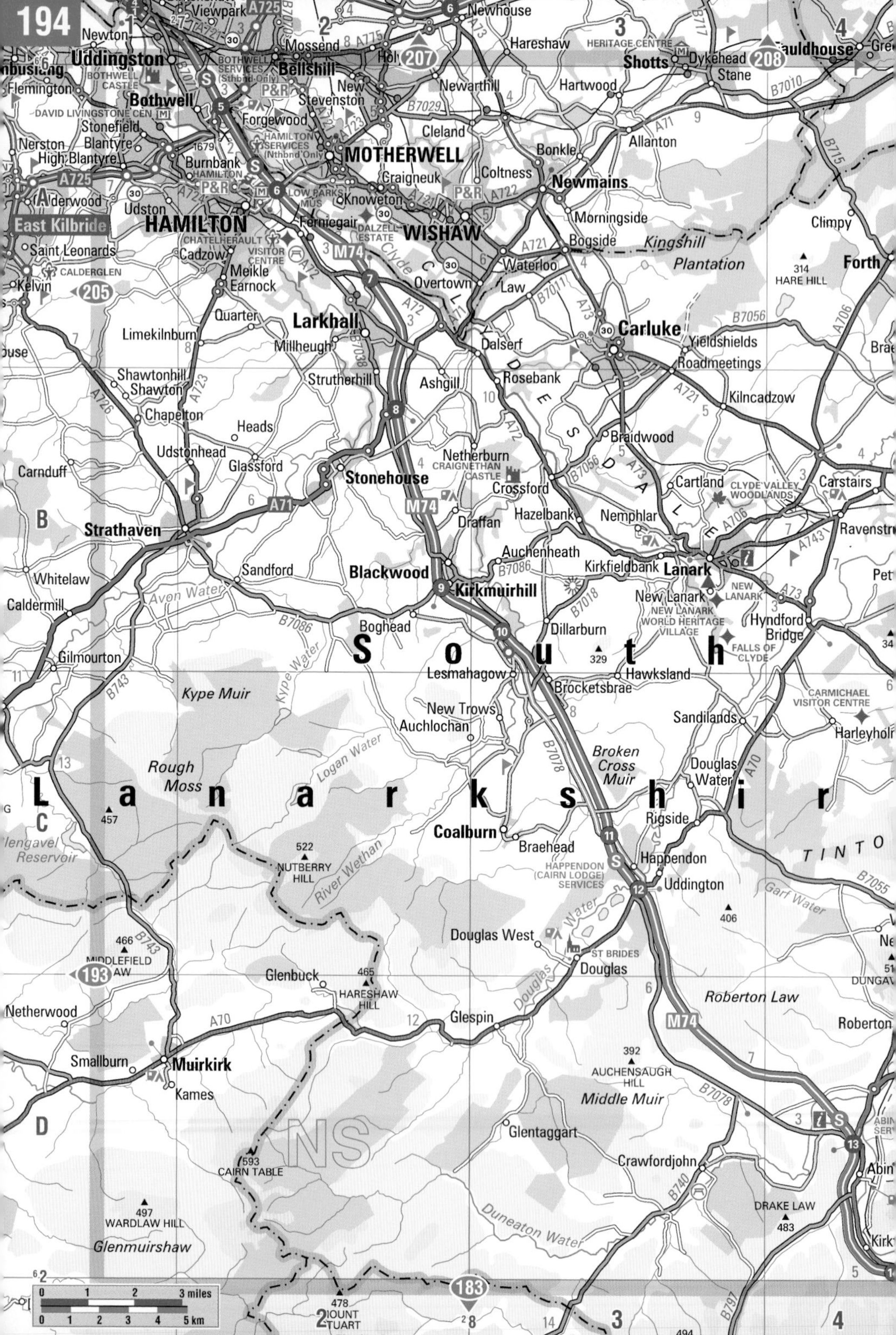
Newton
Uddingston
Flemington
Bothwell
BOTHWELL CASTLE
DAVID LIVINGSTONE CEN
Stonefield
Blantyre
Nerston
High Blantyre
A725
Alderwood
East Kilbride
Udston
HAMILTON
Saint Leonards
Cadzow
CALDERGLEN
Kelvin
205
Viewpark
Mossend
Bellshill
BOTHWELL SERVICES (Sthbnd Only)
New Stevenston
Forgewood
HAMILTON SERVICES (Nthbnd Only)
MOTHERWELL
Burnbank
Craigneuk
Knoweton
LOW PARKS MUS
Ferniegair
DALZELL ESTATE
WISHAW
CHATELHERAULT VISITOR CENTRE
Meikle Earnock
Quarter
Larkhall
Limekilnburn
Millheugh
Strutherhill
Shawtonhill
Shawton
Chapelton
Heads
Udstonhead
Glassford
Carnduff
Stonehouse
Strathaven
Whitelaw
Caldermill
Sandford
Avon Water
Blackwood
Kirkmuirhill
Boghead
Gilmourton
Kype Muir
Kype Water
Rough Moss
Logan Water
Glengavel Reservoir
457
522
NUTBERRY HILL
River Wethan
466
MIDDLEFIELD LAW
193
Glenbuck
465
HARESHAW HILL
Netherwood
A70
Smallburn
Muirkirk
Kames
NS
593
CAIRN TABLE
497
WARDLAW HILL
Glenmuirshaw
478
MOUNT STUART
183
Newhouse
Holy
207
Hareshaw
Newarthill
Cleland
Bonkle
Coltness
Newmains
HERITAGE CENTRE
Shotts
Dykehead
Stane
208
Fauldhouse
Hartwood
Allanton
Morningside
Bogside
Waterloo
Overtown
Law
Kingshill Plantation
Climpy
314
HARE HILL
Forth
Carluke
Yieldshields
Roadmeetings
Dalserf
Rosebank
Ashgill
Kilncadzow
Braidwood
Netherburn
CRAIGNETHAN CASTLE
Crossford
Hazelbank
Draffan
Cartland
CLYDE VALLEY WOODLANDS
Carstairs
Nemphlar
Ravenstruther
Auchenheath
Kirkfieldbank
Lanark
New Lanark
NEW LANARK WORLD HERITAGE VILLAGE
NEW LANARK
Hyndford Bridge
Dillarburn
FALLS OF CLYDE
329
Lesmahagow
Brocketsbrae
Hawksland
New Trows
Auchlochan
CARMICHAEL VISITOR CENTRE
Sandilands
Harleyholm
Broken Cross Muir
Douglas Water
Coalburn
Braehead
Rigside
HAPPENDON (CAIRN LODGE) SERVICES
Happendon
Uddington
TINTO
Garf Water
406
Douglas West
ST BRIDES
Douglas
Glespin
Roberton Law
Roberton
392
AUCHENSAUGH HILL
Middle Muir
Glentaggart
Crawfordjohn
DRAKE LAW
483
Duneaton Water
CLYDESDALE
South Lanarkshire
M74
A71
A72
A73
A721
A723
A726
A743
A706
B7078
B7086
B743
B740
B797
0 1 2 3 miles
0 1 2 3 4 5 km

195
PENTLAND HILLS
REGIONAL PARK
PENTLAND HILLS
Penicuik
Bents
Loganlea
Breich
Woodmuir
Plantation
359
Harperrig
Reservoir
561
EAST CAIRN
HILL
562
WEST CAIRN
HILL
579
SCALD LAW
479
519
537
Nine Mile
Burn
Howgate
North Esk
Cobbinshaw
Reservoir
Crosswood
Reservoir
Woolfords
Cottages
Tarbrax
Baddinsgill
Reservoir
Carlops
Leadburn
Auchengray
Rootpark
434
WHITE CRAIG
534
BYREHOPE
MOUNT
Cowdenburn
Whim Farm
West
Water
Reservoir
West Linton
Waterheads
North Medwin
445
BLEAK LAW
451
MENDICK HILL
B7059
A701
A702
A70
Halmyre Mains
479
WETHER LAW
Damside
Romannobridge
Eddleston
Dunsyre
Dolphinton
Mountain
Cross
South Medwin
Carnwath
Newbigging
Kaimend
Walston
516
BLACK
MOUNT
Blyth Bridge
465
Carstairs
Junction
Melbourne
Kirkurd
Drochil
Lyne Water
Eddleston Water
Elsrickle
A721
A72
B7016
Libberton
426
BLACK MELDON
407
427
WHITE
MELDON
LYNE ROMAN
CAMP
Peebles
Whitecastle
Candy Mill
571
BROUGHTON
HEIGHTS
NEIDPATH
CASTLE
Shieldhill
359
Hallyne
Kings Muir
Covington
Quothquan
Skirling
Biggar
GLADSTONE
COURT
COVENANTER'S
HOUSE
GASWORKS MUSEUM
PUPPET
THEATRE
Thankerton
549
Dreva
Forest
Stobo
Kirkton Manor
Wolfclyde
Broughton
UPPER TWEEDDALE
Causewayend
JOHN BUCHAN
CENTRE
DAWYCK
BOTANIC
GARDEN
485
Castlehill
Symington
435
Rachan Mill
B712
Bellspool
Drumelzier
Coulter
Clyde
Holms Water
676
STOB LAW
Culter Water
A73
PYKESTONE HILL
737
Manor Water
Lamington
543
BLAKEHOPE
HEAD
Langhaugh
743
DUN RIG
CULTER FELL
748
Stanhope
637
Cowgill
Upper
Reservoir
817
DOLLAR LAW
696
BLACK LAW
Crookhaugh
Culter
Waterhead
Reservoir
Hearthstane
510
688
GLENWHAPPEN RIG
NT
Tweedsmuir
569
Camps Water
Camps
Reservoir
840
BROAD LAW
Cappercleuch
Tweed
Meggethead
Megget
Reservoir
St. Mary's
Loch
Crawford
Glenbreck
Talla
Reservoir
550
Talla
Linnfoots
Loch of
the
Lowes
LOCHCRAIG
HEAD
Fruid Reservoir
A708
208
209
196
184
185

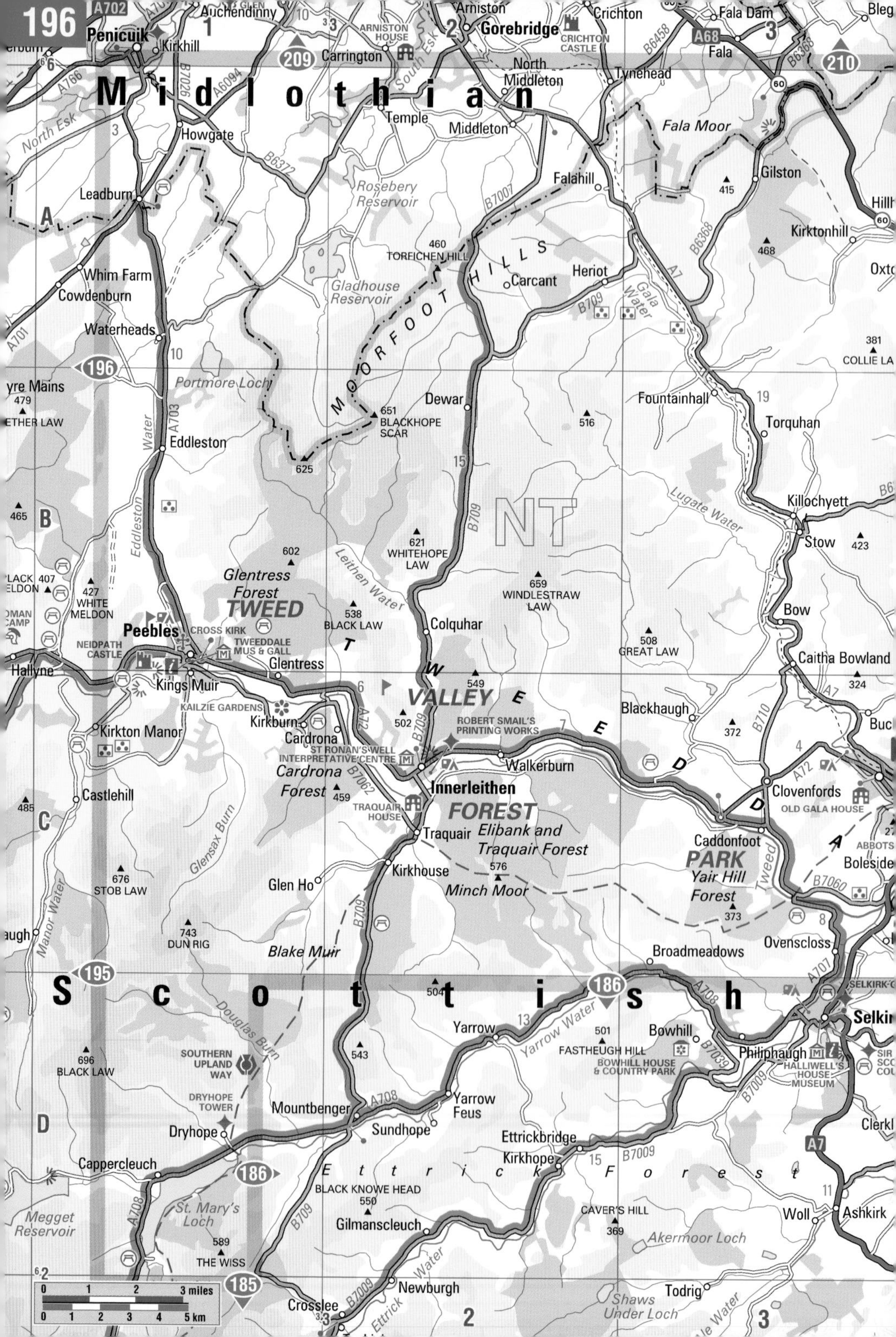

Midlothian
Penicuik
Auchendinny
Kirkhill
Carrington
ARNISTON HOUSE
Arniston
Gorebridge
Crichton
CRICHTON CASTLE
Fala Dam
Fala
North Middleton
Tynehead
Temple
Middleton
Howgate
Fala Moor
Falahill
Gilston
Leadburn
Rosebery Reservoir
Kirktonhill
TORFICHEN HILL
MOORFOOT HILLS
Heriot
Carcant
Whim Farm
Cowdenburn
Gladhouse Reservoir
Gala Water
Waterheads
COLLIE LAW
Portmore Loch
Fountainhall
Dewar
BLACKHOPE SCAR
Torquhan
ETHER LAW
Eddleston
Eddleston Water
NT
Killochyett
Lugate Water
Stow
WHITEHOPE LAW
Leithen Water
Glentress Forest
TWEED
WINDLESTRAW LAW
WHITE MELDON
BLACK LAW
Colquhar
Bow
GREAT LAW
Peebles
CROSS KIRK
TWEEDDALE MUS & GALL
NEIDPATH CASTLE
Caitha Bowland
Hallyne
Glentress
Kings Muir
VALLEY
KAILZIE GARDENS
Kirkburn
Cardrona
Blackhaugh
Kirkton Manor
ROBERT SMAIL'S PRINTING WORKS
ST RONAN'S WELL INTERPRETATIVE CENTRE
Walkerburn
Cardrona Forest
Innerleithen
Clovenfords
Castlehill
TRAQUAIR HOUSE
FOREST
OLD GALA HOUSE
Traquair
Elibank and Traquair Forest
Caddonfoot
ABBOTS
Glensax Burn
PARK
Boleside
Kirkhouse
Glen Ho
Minch Moor
Yair Hill Forest
STOB LAW
Manor Water
DUN RIG
Blake Muir
Broadmeadows
Ovenscloss
Scottish
Yarrow
Yarrow Water
Bowhill
FASTHEUGH HILL
BOWHILL HOUSE & COUNTRY PARK
Philiphaugh
HALLIWELL'S HOUSE MUSEUM
Selkirk
Douglas Burn
SOUTHERN UPLAND WAY
BLACK LAW
DRYHOPE TOWER
Mountbenger
Yarrow Feus
Sundhope
Dryhope
Ettrickbridge
Kirkhope
Cappercleuch
Ettrick Forest
BLACK KNOWE HEAD
Megget Reservoir
St. Mary's Loch
Gilmanscleuch
CAVER'S HILL
Woll
Ashkirk
Akermoor Loch
THE WISS
Ettrick Water
Newburgh
Todrig
Crosslee
Shaws Under Loch
0 1 2 3 miles
0 1 2 3 4 5 km

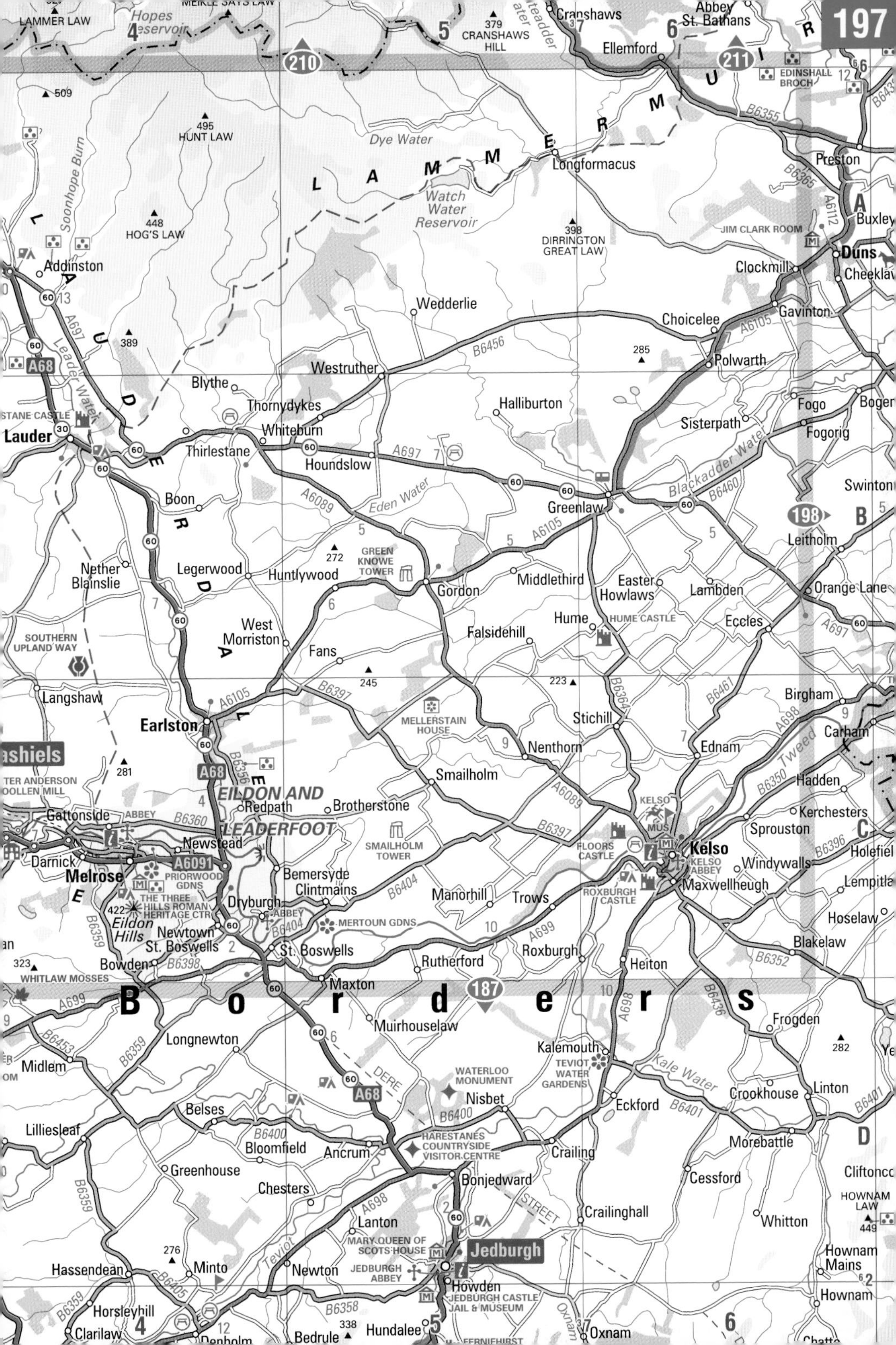

LAMMER LAW
MEIKLE SAYS LAW
Hopes Reservoir
210
379
CRANSHAWS HILL
Cranshaws
Abbey St. Bathans
Ellemford
211
EDINSHALL BROCH
509
495
HUNT LAW
Dye Water
L A M M E R M U I R
B6355
Preston
Longformacus
Soonhope Burn
448
HOG'S LAW
Watch Water Reservoir
398
DIRRINGTON GREAT LAW
B6365
A6112
Buxley
JIM CLARK ROOM
Duns
Cheeklaw
Clockmill
Addinston
A697
Leader Water
L A U D E R D A L E
Wedderlie
Choicelee
Gavinton
A6105
389
A68
B6456
285
Polwarth
Westruther
Blythe
Thornydykes
Halliburton
Fogo
Bogend
STANE CASTLE
Lauder
Whiteburn
Sisterpath
Fogorig
Thirlestane
Houndslow
A697
Blackadder Water
Swinton
Boon
Eden Water
A6089
Greenlaw
B6460
198
Leitholm
272
GREEN KNOWE TOWER
Nether Blainslie
Legerwood
Huntlywood
Gordon
Middlethird
Easter Howlaws
Lambden
Orange Lane
West Morriston
Hume
HUME CASTLE
Eccles
Falsidehill
SOUTHERN UPLAND WAY
Fans
245
223
Langshaw
B6397
B6364
B6461
Birgham
MELLERSTAIN HOUSE
Earlston
A6105
Stichill
A698
Carham
Nenthorn
Ednam
Tweed
Galashiels
281
B6356
Smailholm
B6350
Hadden
PETER ANDERSON WOOLLEN MILL
EILDON AND LEADERFOOT
KELSO
Kerchesters
Gattonside
ABBEY
Redpath
Brotherstone
MUS
Sprouston
B6360
SMAILHOLM TOWER
FLOORS CASTLE
Kelso
KELSO ABBEY
Windywalls
B6396
Holefield
Darnick
Newstead
A6091
Melrose
PRIORWOOD GDNS
Bemersyde
Clintmains
ROXBURGH CASTLE
Maxwellheugh
Lempitlaw
THE THREE HILLS ROMAN HERITAGE CTR
422
Eildon Hills
Dryburgh
ABBEY
B6404
Manorhill
Trows
Hoselaw
B6359
Newtown St. Boswells
MERTOUN GDNS
A699
Blakelaw
Bowden
B6398
St. Boswells
Rutherford
Roxburgh
Heiton
B6352
323
WHITLAW MOSSES
Maxton
187
B o r d e r s
Frogden
A699
B6453
Muirhouselaw
B6436
282
Longnewton
Kalemouth
TEVIOT WATER GARDENS
Kale Water
Midlem
WATERLOO MONUMENT
DERE
Crookhouse
Linton
A68
B6401
Belses
Nisbet
Eckford
B6401
B6400
Lilliesleaf
HARESTANES COUNTRYSIDE VISITOR CENTRE
Bloomfield
Ancrum
Crailing
Morebattle
Greenhouse
Cliftoncote
Chesters
Bonjedward
Cessford
STREET
A698
Crailinghall
HOWNAM LAW
449
Lanton
Whitton
MARY QUEEN OF SCOTS HOUSE
Jedburgh
276
Teviot
Hownam Mains
Hassendean
Minto
Newton
JEDBURGH ABBEY
B6405
Howden
Hownam
JEDBURGH CASTLE JAIL & MUSEUM
Horsleyhill
B6358
Oxnam
Clarilaw
Denholm
Bedrule
338
Hundalee
FERNIEHIRST
Oxnam

1
2
3
4
A
B
C
D
Reston
CASTLE
A1
Ayton
Burnmouth
B6438
B6437
211
Auchencrow
EDINSHALL BROCH
Prenderguest
B6355
Lintlaw
Preston
B6355
Chirnside
Lamberton Beach
Lamberton
N
O
R
T
Chirnsidebridge
A6105
Foulden
Clappers
Edrom
Whiteadder Water
FOULDEN TITHE BARN
Buxley
JIM CLARK ROOM
MANDERSTON
Allanton
Highfields
Duns
CRUMSTANE FARM PARK
Hutton
Berwick-upon-
Clockmill
Cheeklaw
Blackadder West
Paxton
B6461
BARRACKS MUSEUM & RAMPARTS
BERWICK
East Ord
Tweedmouth
Spittal
Gavinton
B6460
B6437
PAXTON HOUSE
Tweed
Choicelee
Fishwick
Loanend
Prior Park
A1167
Redshin Co
Polwarth
Sinclair's Hill
Whitsome
UNION SUSPENSION BRIDGE
A698
Horncliffe
Fogo
Bogend
Leet Water
Horndean
Thornton Park
Murton
Scremerston
Fogorig
B6461
Ladykirk
Thornton
NORHAM CASTLE
Swinton
SWINTON KIRK
Norham
West Allerdean
Chesw
M
E
R
S
E
A6112
B6470
Shoreswood
Shoresdean
DEVIL'S
CAUSEWAY
Swintonmill
Simprim
Grindon
B6460
197
Leitholm
Ancroft
NT
Felkington
B6354
Lambden
Shellacres
Berrington
Orange Lane
B6437
Duddo
Eccles
Castle Heaton
Bowsden
A697
A698
Lennel
Coldstream
HIRSEL
Cornhill-on-Tweed
HEATHERSLAW LIGHT RAILWAY
ERROL HUT SMITHY AND WOOD WORKSHOP
Barmoor Castle
Barmoor Lane End
THE HIRSEL
Etal
Lowick
B6461
Birgham
A697
HEATHERSLAW CORNMILL
B6353
A698
Carham
Wark
B6353
LADY WATERFORD HALL
Ednam
Tweed
West Learmouth
East Learmouth
Crookham
B6354
Ford
B6350
Hadden
Branxton
Kerchesters
Pressen
Flodden
Sprouston
Holefield
Kimmerston
B6396
Downham
Howtel
Windywalls
B6352
Milfield
Fenton Town
Nesbit
Lempitlaw
Mindrum
Pawston
Kilham
Glen
Doddington
Hoselaw
B6352
B6351
Lanton
Newtown
West Horton
Blakelaw
Coupland
East H
B6352
Shotton
Westnewton
Weetwood Hall
188
Kirknewton
Akeld
B6436
KIRK YETHOLM
Frogden
Humbleton
B6348
Town Yetholm
Kirk Yetholm
Hethpool
Wooler
WOOLER
Earle
Haugh Head
Crookhouse
Linton
College Burn
B6401
Middleton Hall
Newtown
Bowmont Water
B6525
PENNINE WAY
North Middleton
A697
Lilburn Tower
Morebattle
COLD LAW
Cliftoncote
South Middleton
HOWNAM LAW
THE SCHIL
MOUNTHOOLEY
Ilderton
Whitton
Langleeford
Roseden
Harthope Burn
Hownam Mains
Mowhaugh
Sourhope
Roddam
AUCHOPE CAIRN
THE CHEVIOT
Wooperton
0 1 2 3 miles
0 1 2 3 4 5 km

NU
Goswick
Emmanuel Hd.
Holy Island
(Lindisfarne)
LINDISFARNE
LINDISFARNE CASTLE
Castle Pt.
Beal
Causeway
Holy
Island
Sands
Holy
Island
HERITAGE
CENTRE
LINDISFARNE
PRIORY
Fenham
Guile
Pt.
Fenwick
East
Kyloe
Buckton
Elwick
Ross
Budle
Bay
Farne
Islands
Staple Sound
FARNE ISLANDS
Inner Sound
BAMBURGH
CASTLE
Detchant
Middleton
Budle
Bamburgh
Belford
North Hazelrigg
Easington
Waren Mill
B1342
B1340
Burton
Spindlestone
Glororum
B6349
Mousen
Bradford
B1341
Seahouses
North
Sunderland
Elford
Warenton
Bellshill
Adderstone
Lucker
Newham
Hall
Beadnell
Swinhoe
Benthall
Warenford
Greendikes
B6348
Newham
Fleetham
A1
Newstead
Beadnell
Bay
Chathill
Rosebrough
Chillingham
WILD CATTLE OF
CHILLINGHAM
Ellingham
Preston
High Newton-
by-the-Sea
Brunton
PRESTON TOWER
Low Newton-
by-the-Sea
Hepburn
Lilburn
Brownyside
Christon
Bank
Embleton Bay
North Charlton
Embleton
B6347
Dunstan Steads
Castle Point
DUNSTANBURGH
CASTLE
Old Bewick
B1339
West
Ditchburn
B6346
Harehope
South
Charlton
Rock
Craster
New
Bewick
Eglingham
B6347
B6341
Dunstan
Rennington
N
U
M
B
E
R
L
A
N
D
C
O
A
S
T

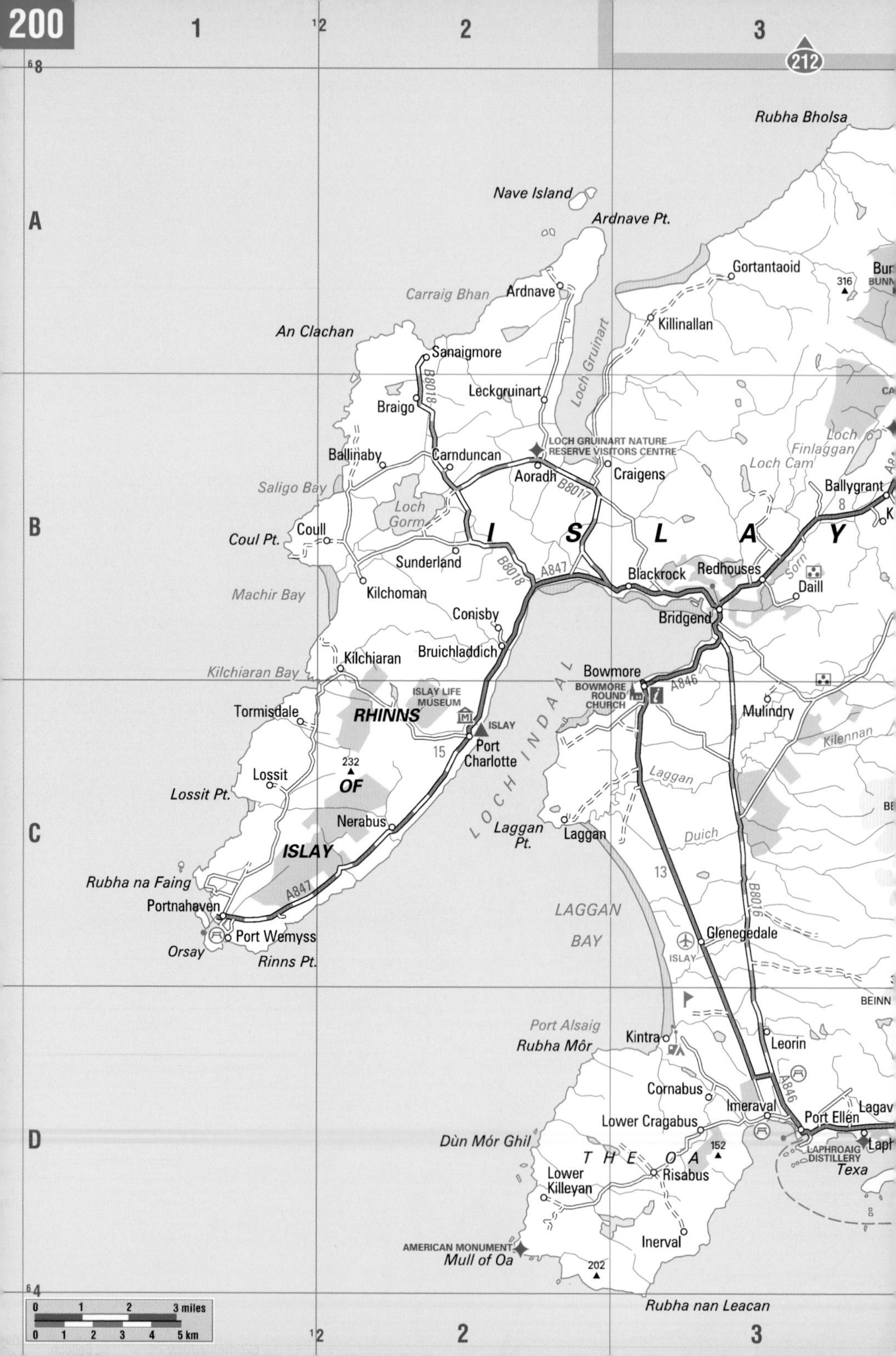
1
2
3
A
B
C
D
212
Rubha Bholsa
Nave Island
Ardnave Pt.
Ardnave
Carraig Bhan
Gortantaoid
316
Killinallan
An Clachan
Sanaigmore
Loch Gruinart
Leckgruinart
B8018
Braigo
LOCH GRUINART NATURE RESERVE VISITORS CENTRE
Loch Finlaggan
Loch Cam
Ballinaby
Carnduncan
Aoradh
Craigens
Saligo Bay
B8017
Ballygrant
8
Loch Gorm
I S L A Y
Coull
Coul Pt.
Sunderland
A847
Blackrock
Redhouses
Sorn
Daill
Machir Bay
Kilchoman
Bridgend
Conisby
Kilchiaran
Bruichladdich
Bowmore
Kilchiaran Bay
BOWMORE ROUND CHURCH
A846
ISLAY LIFE MUSEUM
Tormisdale
RHINNS
ISLAY
Mulindry
Port Charlotte
15
Kilennan
232
Lossit
OF
Laggan
Lossit Pt.
LOCH INDAAL
Nerabus
Laggan Pt.
Duich
ISLAY
13
Rubha na Faing
Portnahaven
B8016
LAGGAN BAY
Port Wemyss
Glenegedale
Orsay
Rinns Pt.
Port Alsaig
Kintra
Rubha Môr
Leorin
Cornabus
Imeraval
Lower Cragabus
Port Ellen
Dùn Mór Ghil
T H E O A
152
LAPHROAIG DISTILLERY
Texa
Lower Killeyan
Risabus
Inerval
AMERICAN MONUMENT
Mull of Oa
202
Rubha nan Leacan
0 1 2 3 miles
0 1 2 3 4 5 km

COLONSAY 1:10
(Summer Only)
4
5
6
Loch Tarbert
Tarbert
212
213
Keillmore
Rubha Lang-aoinidh
Rubha a'Mhail
Lagg
439
Loch an Aircill
Loch Lesgamaill
J U R A
785
755
PAPS OF JURA
Loch a Chnuic Bhric
15
A846
SOUND OF JURA
Eilean Môr
ST CORMAC'S CHAPEL
CHAPEL
Kilmory Bay
A
An Dùnan
Corran
JURA FOREST
Knockrome
Lowlandman's Bay
Leargybreck
Gleann Astaile
Loch na Mile
Pt. of Knap
202
Caol Ila
Port Askaig
Feolin Ferry
561
Keills
Loch Ballygrant
Keils
Craighouse
ISLE OF JURA DISTILLERY
Small Isles
Miller's Bay
Gleann Ullibh
342
BRAT BHEINN
SOUND OF ISLAY
NR
B
Kilberry Hd.
SCULPTURED STONES
Cabrach
8
267
BEINN DUBH
Rubha na Tràille
Am Fraoch Eilean
Brosdale I.
McArthur's Hd.
KENNACRAIG 2:05
Carraig Mhór
491
BEINN BHEIGEIR
Ardtalla
C
Loch Beinn Uraraidh
Claggain Bay
Eilean Garbh
West Tarbert Bay
East Tarbert Bay
Tarbert
Kintour
Ardmore Pt.
KILDALTON CHURCH AND CROSSES
Gigha Island
100
Druimyeon More
202
Eilean Craobhach
Ardminish
Ardminish Bay
Eilean a'Chuirn
KENNACRAIG 2:10
ACHAMORE GARDENS
0:20
Eilean Bhride
SOUND OF GIGHA
Ardbeg
Eilean Imersay
LAGAVULIN DISTILLERY
Tayinloan
Gigalum Island
D
Cara Island
A83
Muasdale
190
4
5
6
Glenacardoch Pt.
Belloch

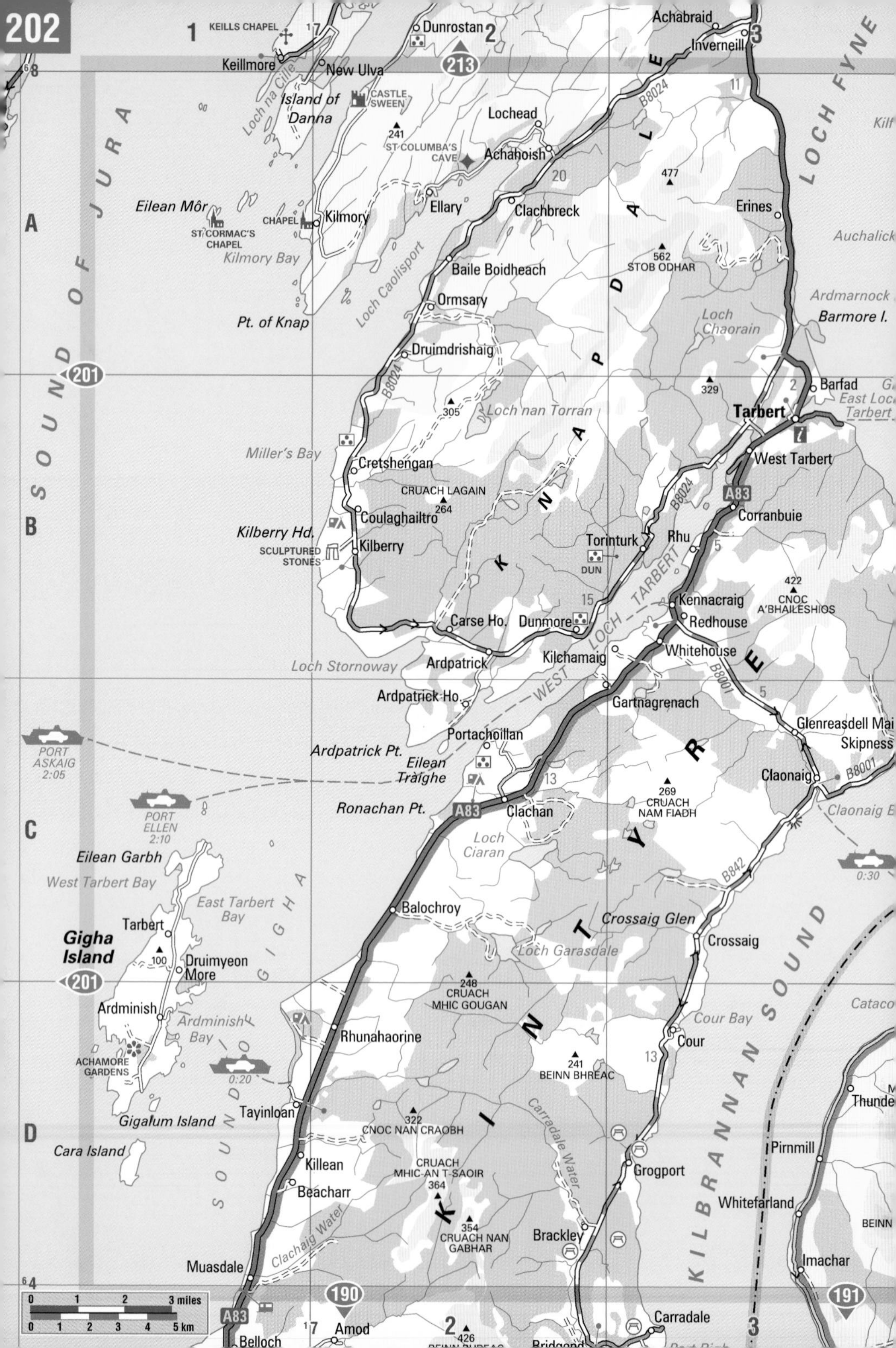
KEILLS CHAPEL
Keillmore
New Ulva
Dunrostan
213
Achabraid
Inverneill
Loch na Cille
Island of Danna
CASTLE SWEEN
241
ST COLUMBA'S CAVE
Lochead
Achahoish
B8024
LOCH FYNE
SOUND OF JURA
Eilean Mòr
ST CORMAC'S CHAPEL
CHAPEL
Kilmory
Kilmory Bay
Ellary
Clachbreck
20
477
Erines
Auchalick
Loch Caolisport
Baile Boidheach
562
STOB ODHAR
Ormsary
Pt. of Knap
Ardmarnock
Barmore I.
Loch Chaorain
Druimdrishaig
201
329
Barfad
East Loch Tarbert
Tarbert
305
Loch nan Torran
KNAPDALE
Miller's Bay
Cretshengan
West Tarbert
CRUACH LAGAIN
264
A83
Coulaghailtro
Corranbuie
Kilberry Hd.
Kilberry
SCULPTURED STONES
Torinturk
DUN
Rhu
422
CNOC A'BHAILESHIOS
Kennacraig
Redhouse
Carse Ho.
Dunmore
Loch Stornoway
Ardpatrick
Kilchamaig
Whitehouse
WEST LOCH TARBERT
B8001
Ardpatrick Ho.
Gartnagrenach
Glenreasdell Mains
Skipness
PORT ASKAIG 2:05
Portachoillan
Ardpatrick Pt.
Eilean Traighe
Claonaig
Claonaig Bay
PORT ELLEN 2:10
Ronachan Pt.
Clachan
269
CRUACH NAM FIADH
Loch Ciaran
Eilean Garbh
West Tarbert Bay
East Tarbert Bay
0:30
B842
Balochroy
Crossaig Glen
Crossaig
Gigha Island
Tarbert
100
Druimyeon More
Loch Garasdale
KINTYRE
248
CRUACH MHIC GOUGAN
SOUND OF GIGHA
Ardminish
Ardminish Bay
Rhunahaorine
Cour Bay
Cour
KILBRANNAN SOUND
ACHAMORE GARDENS
0:20
241
BEINN BHREAC
Carradale Water
Tayinloan
322
CNOC NAN CRAOBH
Gigalum Island
Cara Island
Thunderg
Grogport
Killean
CRUACH MHIC-AN T-SAOIR
364
Pirnmill
Beacharr
Whitefarland
354
CRUACH NAN GABHAR
Brackley
Clachaig Water
BEINN
Imachar
Muasdale
190
191
0 1 2 3 miles
0 1 2 3 4 5 km
A83
Amod
426
Carradale
Belloch
Bridgend

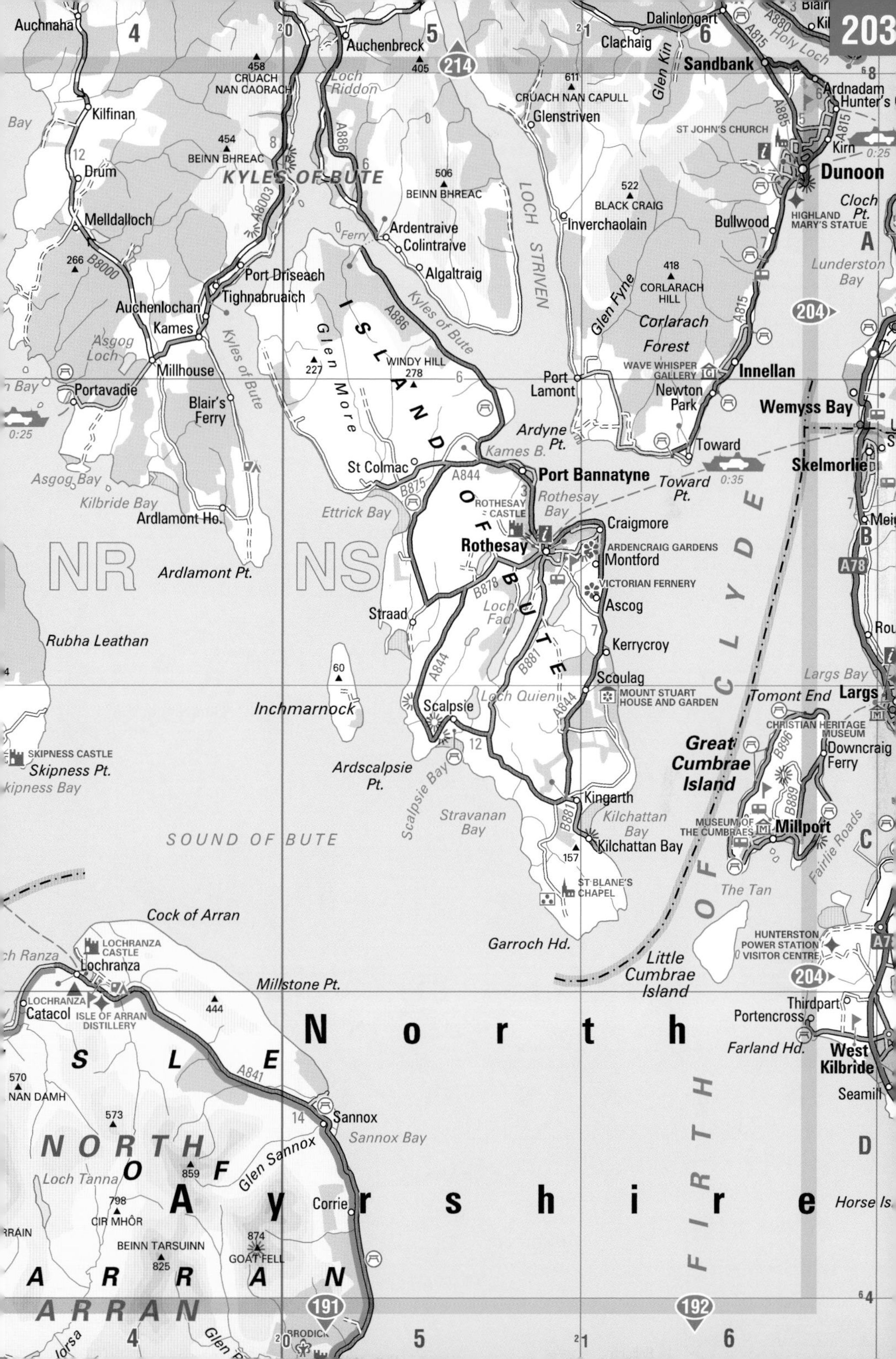

Auchnaha
Auchenbreck
405
214
Dalinlongart
Clachaig
Glen Kin
Sandbank
A815
A880
Holy Loch
458
CRUACH NAN CAORACH
Loch Riddon
611
CRUACH NAN CAPULL
Glenstriven
Ardnadam
Hunter's
Kilfinan
Bay
A886
ST JOHN'S CHURCH
A885
A815
Kirn
0:25
454
BEINN BHREAC
Drum
KYLES OF BUTE
506
BEINN BHREAC
LOCH STRIVEN
522
BLACK CRAIG
Dunoon
A8003
Cloch Pt.
HIGHLAND MARY'S STATUE
Melldalloch
Ferry
Ardentraive
Colintraive
Inverchaolain
Bullwood
266
B8000
Algaltraig
418
CORLARACH HILL
Lunderston Bay
Port Driseach
Tighnabruaich
Auchenlochan
ISLAND
Glen More
A886
Kyles of Bute
Glen Fyne
Corlarach Forest
A815
204
Kames
Asgog Loch
Kyles of Bute
227
WINDY HILL
278
WAVE WHISPER GALLERY
Innellan
Millhouse
Port Lamont
Newton Park
Bay
Portavadie
Blair's Ferry
Wemyss Bay
0:25
Ardyne Pt.
Toward
Kames B.
St Colmac
A844
Port Bannatyne
Toward Pt.
0:35
Skelmorlie
Asgog Bay
B875
OF
ROTHESAY CASTLE
Rothesay Bay
Kilbride Bay
Ettrick Bay
Ardlamont Ho.
Craigmore
Rothesay
ARDENCRAIG GARDENS
Montford
NR
NS
Ardlamont Pt.
BUTE
B878
VICTORIAN FERNERY
A78
Straad
Loch Fad
Ascog
Rubha Leathan
A844
B881
Kerrycroy
60
Scoulag
Largs Bay
Largs
Loch Quien
MOUNT STUART HOUSE AND GARDEN
Tomont End
Inchmarnock
Scalpsie
A844
CLYDE
CHRISTIAN HERITAGE MUSEUM
SKIPNESS CASTLE
Skipness Pt.
Great Cumbrae Island
B896
Downcraig Ferry
Ardscalpsie Pt.
Scalpsie Bay
Kingarth
B889
Stravanan Bay
B881
Kilchattan Bay
MUSEUM OF THE CUMBRAES
Millport
SOUND OF BUTE
157
Kilchattan Bay
Fairlie Roads
ST BLANE'S CHAPEL
The Tan
Cock of Arran
LOCHRANZA CASTLE
Lochranza
Garroch Hd.
Little Cumbrae Island
HUNTERSTON POWER STATION VISITOR CENTRE
204
Millstone Pt.
LOCHRANZA
Catacol
ISLE OF ARRAN DISTILLERY
444
Thirdpart
Portencross
North Ayrshire
Farland Hd.
West Kilbride
570
NAN DAMH
A841
Seamill
573
Sannox
Sannox Bay
NORTH
Glen Sannox
Loch Tanna
859
OF
FIRTH
798
CIR MHÒR
Corrie
Horse Is.
874
BEINN TARSUINN
825
GOAT FELL
ISLE OF ARRAN
191
192
BRODICK
Glen
Iorsa

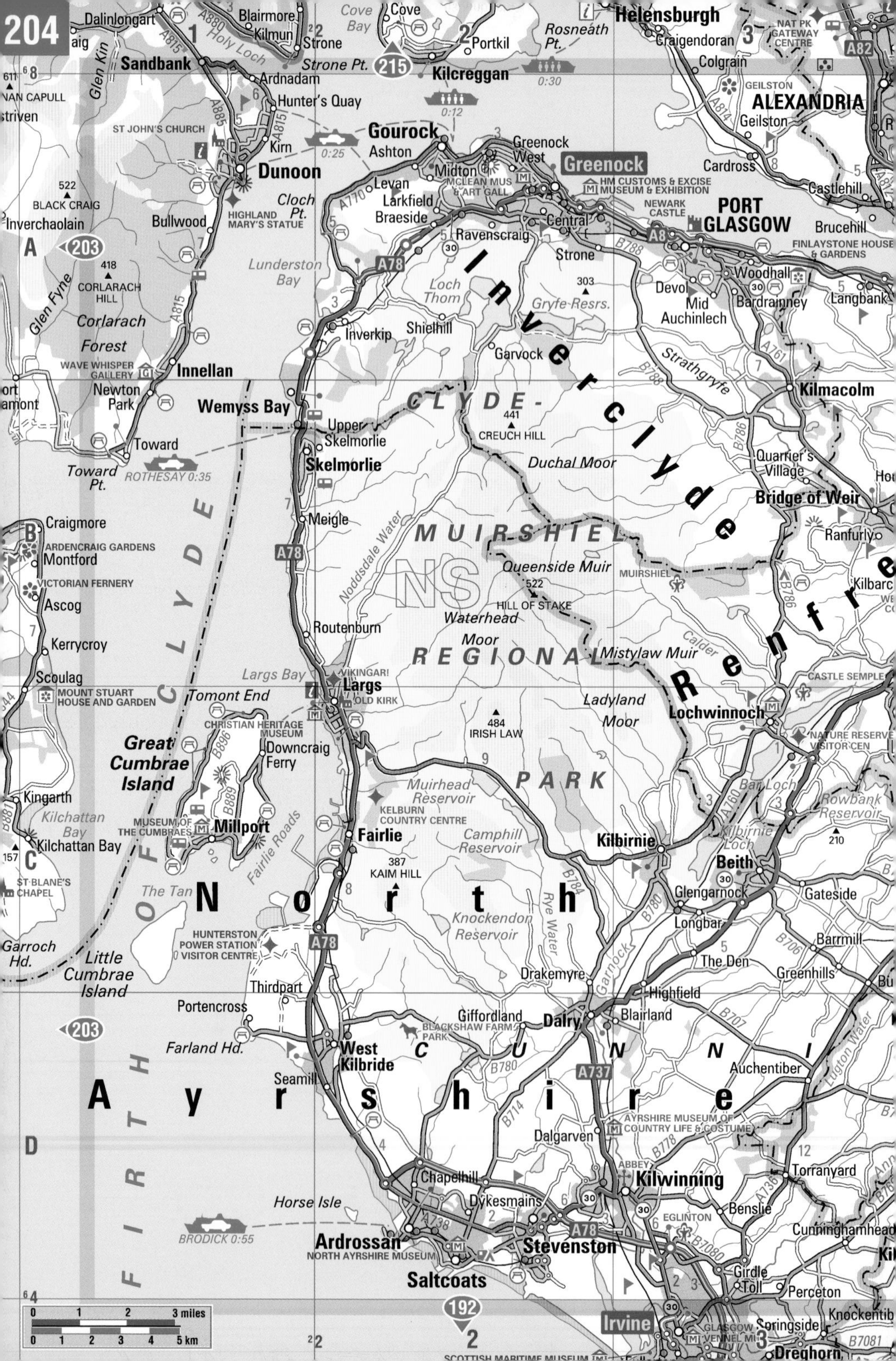

215
203
203
192

205
206
193
194
207
West
Dunbartonshire
East
Dunbartonshire
Lennoxtown
Glasgow
Renfrewshire
East
Renfrewshire
Balloch
Auchencarroch
Strathblane Hills
Blairquhosh
Blane Water
Dumbarton Muir
Resrs.
Netherton
Clachan of Campsie
Blanefield
Strathblane
Balgrochan
Bonhill
DUNCOLM
KILPATRICK HILLS
Townend
DUMBARTON
Milton
Bowling
Old Kilpatrick
DUMBARTON CASTLE
Clyde
Erskine Bridge
Duntocher
MUGDOCK
Mugdock
Milton of Campsie
Queenzieburn
Blairskaith
Birdston
ROMAN BATH HOUSE
Milngavie
LILLIE ART GALLERY
Torrance
KIRKINTILLOCH
Bardowie
WALL
ANTONINE
Cadder
Jellyhill
Waterside
Lenzie
Moodiesburn
Bridgend
BEARSDEN
Kessington
Bishopton
Rossland
Erskine
Dalmuir
Drumchapel
Bishopbriggs
Lumloch
Auchinloch
Chryston
CLYDEBANK
Lambhill
Muirhead
MUSEUM
Knightswood
Temple
Balornock
Inchinnan
Yoker
BOTANIC GDNS.
Maryhill
Springburn
Stepps
Garnkirk
RENFREW
Scotstoun
Kelvinside
ART GALL.
MUSEUM
GALLERY OF MODERN ART
CATH
Whiteinch
Partick
Garthamlock
PROVAN HALL
GLASGOW
Craigends
Govan
Riddrie
Easterhouse
GLASGOW
ABBEY
Linwood
Brookfield
Hillington
SCIENCE CENTRE
JOHNSTONE
Paisley
MUS.& ART GALL.
Cardonald
Pollokshields
PEOPLE'S PALACE
Bridgeton
Shettleston
Baillieston
Millarston
Elderslie
Pollok
POLLOK
Dalmarnock
Fullarton
Charleston
Glenburn
POLLOK HOUSE
THE BURRELL COLL.
Govanhill
Millikenpark
HAMPDEN
Rutherglen
Carmyle
GLASGOW ZOO
Newton
Foxbar
GLENIFFER BRAES
Nitshill
Cathcart
Uddingston
Howwood
Waterside
HOLMWOOD
Burnside
Cambuslang
Flemington
BOTHWELL CASTLE
Bothwell
Barrhead
Thornliebank
Castlemilk
Gateside
Auchenback
Giffnock
CATHKIN BRAES
DAVID LIVINGSTONE CEN.
Stonefield
Sheddens
Carmunnock
Nerston
Blantyre
Neilston
Clarkston
NAT. MUSEUM OF RURAL LIFE
J.HAMILTON HER.PK.
High Blantyre
Loch Libo
Newton Mearns
GREENBANK GARDEN
Busby
College Milton
Calderwood
Udston
Netherplace
Waterfoot
Thorntonhall
Uplawmoor
Peel Park
East Kilbride
HAMILTON
Hairmyres
Saint Leonards
The Murray
CALDERGLEN
Long Loch
Newlandsmuir
Kelvin
Lugton
Halket
Earn Water
Whitehills
Eaglesham
Fullwood
Gabroc Hill
Limekilnburn
Auldhouse
Dunwan Dam
Shawtonhill
Shawton
Chapelton
Kingsford
Lochgoin Reservoir
Udston
Carnduff
Stewarton
CORSE HILL
Laighmuir
Flow Moss
Strathaven
Waterside
Fenwick
Whitelaw
CRINS HILL
Laigh Fenwick
Calder Water
Caldermill
Avon Water
Onthank
Wallacegill Muir
Moscow
Gilmourton
Stobieside
Knockinlaw
DEAN CASTLE
Glen Water
Drumclog
Kilmarnock
A82
M8
M898
A8
A726
A761
M77
M80
M74
M73
A725
A71
A89
A80
A891
A807
A810
A81
A809
B8050
B822
B812
B819
A803
A806
B8023
B806
B765
A74
A730
A749
A724
B759
B766
B767
B764
A727
A77
B769
B773
A736
B762
B774
B787
B790
B789
A737
A735
B751
B778
A719
B743
B821
A879
A813
A814
A739

QUEEN ELIZABETH FOREST PARK
Loch Ard Forest
Aberfoyle
Port of Menteith
Lake of Menteith
Flanders Moss
Buchlyvie
Loch Lomond
Luss
Balmaha
Drymen
Killearn
Balfron
Helensburgh
ALEXANDRIA
Balloch
Bonhill
West Dunbartonshire
DUMBARTON
PORT GLASGOW
KILPATRICK HILLS
Milngavie
BEARSDEN
CLYDEBANK
RENFREW
Glasgow
Paisley
JOHNSTONE
Kilmacolm
Bridge of Weir
Barrhead
Renfrewshire
Erskine Bridge
Strathblane
Mugdock
Blanefield
Lochwinnoch
Howwood

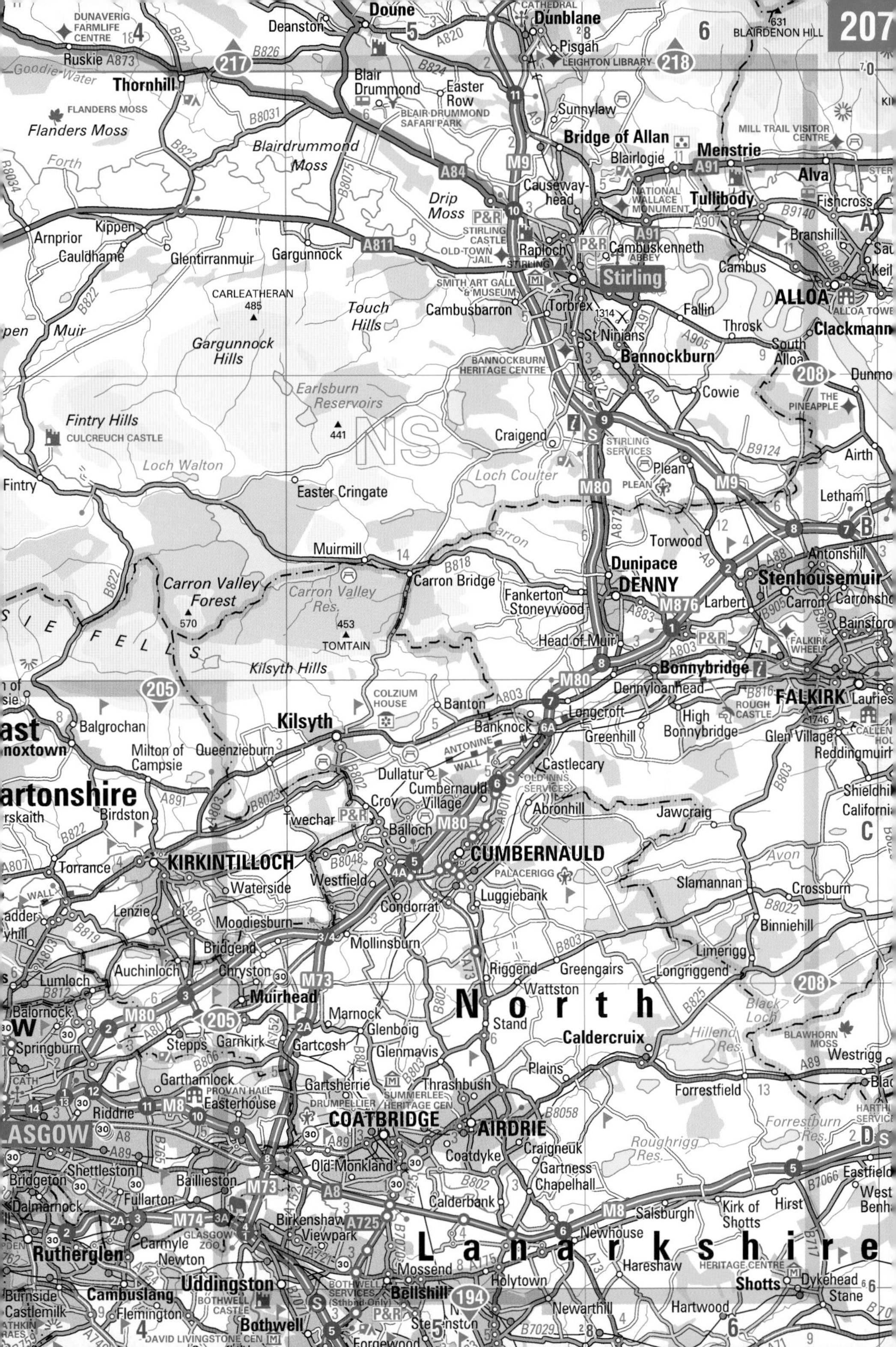
Doune
Dunblane
Deanston
DUNAVERIG FARMLIFE CENTRE
Ruskie
Thornhill
Goodie Water
FLANDERS MOSS
Flanders Moss
Blair Drummond
Easter Row
BLAIR DRUMMOND SAFARI PARK
Blairdrummond Moss
Pisgah
LEIGHTON LIBRARY
Sunnylaw
Bridge of Allan
Blairlogie
Menstrie
Alva
MILL TRAIL VISITOR CENTRE
BLAIRDENON HILL
Forth
Arnprior
Kippen
Cauldhame
Glentirranmuir
Gargunnock
Drip Moss
STIRLING CASTLE
OLD-TOWN JAIL
Raploch
Causewayhead
NATIONAL WALLACE MONUMENT
Tullibody
Fishcross
Cambuskenneth ABBEY
Cambus
Bransbill
Stirling
SMITH ART GALL & MUSEUM
ALLOA
Cambusbarron
Torbrex
Fallin
Throsk
Clackmann
CARLEATHERAN
Touch Hills
Muir
Gargunnock Hills
St Ninians
Bannockburn
BANNOCKBURN HERITAGE CENTRE
South Alloa
Dunmo
Cowie
Earlsburn Reservoirs
THE PINEAPPLE
Fintry Hills
CULCREUCH CASTLE
NS
Craigend
STIRLING SERVICES
Plean
Airth
Loch Walton
Loch Coulter
PLEAN
Fintry
Easter Cringate
Letham
Carron
Torwood
Muirmill
Carron Bridge
Dunipace
DENNY
Antonshill
Stenhousemuir
Carron Valley Forest
Carron Valley Res.
Fankerton
Stoneywood
Larbert
Carronshore
Bainsford
TOMTAIN
Head of Muir
FALKIRK WHEEL
Kilsyth Hills
Bonnybridge
FELLS
Dennyloanhead
FALKIRK
Lauries
COLZIUM HOUSE
Banton
ROUGH CASTLE
Kilsyth
Banknock
Longcroft
High Bonnybridge
Balgrochan
Milton of Campsie
Queenzieburn
Greenhill
Glen Village
Reddingmuirh
ANTONINE WALL
Castlecary
Dullatur
Cumbernauld Village
OLD INNS SERVICES
Shieldhi
Californi
Croy
Abronhill
Jawcraig
Birdston
Twechar
Balloch
Torrance
KIRKINTILLOCH
CUMBERNAULD
Avon
Westfield
PALACERIGG
Slamannan
Crossburn
Waterside
Lenzie
Condorrat
Luggiebank
Moodiesburn
Binniehill
Mollinsburn
Bridgend
Limerigg
Auchinloch
Chryston
Riggend
Greengairs
Longriggend
Lumloch
Muirhead
Wattston
Balornock
Marnock
North
Stand
Black Loch
BLAWHORN MOSS
Springburn
Stepps
Garnkirk
Gartcosh
Glenboig
Caldercruix
Hillend Res.
Westrigg
Glenmavis
Plains
Garthamlock
PROVAN HALL
Easterhouse
Gartsherrie
SUMMERLEE HERITAGE CEN
DRUMPELLIER
Thrashbush
Forrestfield
Riddrie
COATBRIDGE
AIRDRIE
Forrestburn Res.
GLASGOW
Shettleston
Old Monkland
Coatdyke
Craigneuk
Roughrigg Res.
Bridgeton
Baillieston
Gartness
Chapelhall
Eastfield
Dalmarnock
Fullarton
Calderbank
Kirk of Shotts
Hirst
Birkenshaw
Salsburgh
Newhouse
Rutherglen
Carmyle
GLASGOW ZOO
Viewpark
Lanarkshire
Newton
Mossend
Hareshaw
HERITAGE CENTRE
Uddingston
Holytown
Shotts
Dykehead
Burnside
Cambuslang
BOTHWELL SERVICES (Sthbnd Only)
Bellshill
Stane
Castlemilk
Flemington
BOTHWELL CASTLE
Newarthill
Hartwood
Bothwell
DAVID LIVINGSTONE CEN
Forgewood
Stenston
M9
M80
M876
M73
M8
M74
A84
A811
A91
A907
A905
A9
A872
A803
A88
A883
A80
A8
A89
A725
A752
A73
A71
A89
B8031
B822
B826
B824
B8075
B9140
B9124
B818
B816
B8023
B802
B8048
B803
B8022
B825
B804
B806
B765
B8058
B7066
B7029
B7070
217
218
205
208
194

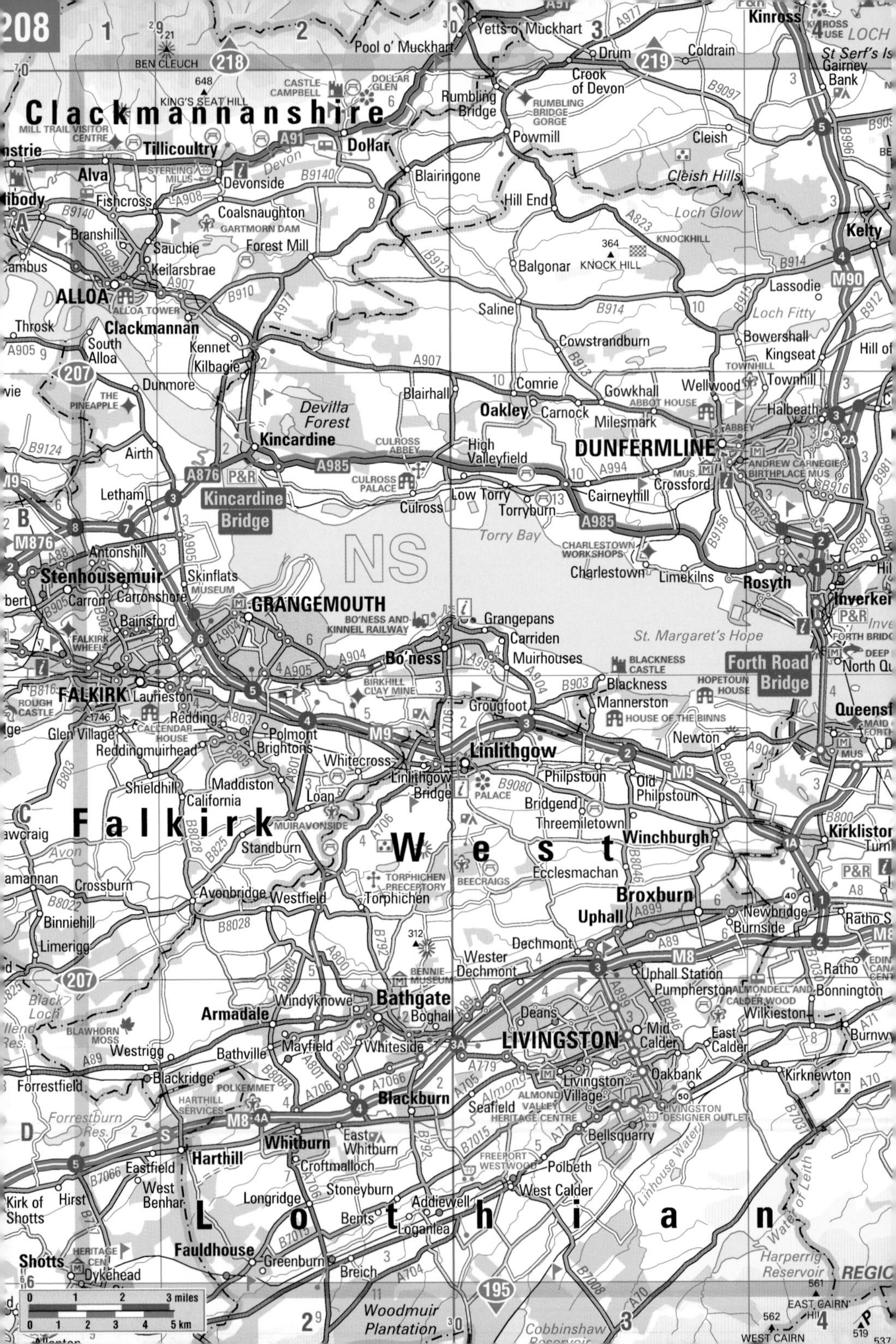
Clackmannanshire
Falkirk
West Lothian
Tillicoultry
Alva
Dollar
ALLOA
Clackmannan
Kincardine
Kincardine Bridge
DUNFERMLINE
Kinross
Kelty
Oakley
Rosyth
GRANGEMOUTH
FALKIRK
Stenhousemuir
Bo'ness
Linlithgow
Forth Road Bridge
Queensferry
Winchburgh
Broxburn
Uphall
Bathgate
Armadale
LIVINGSTON
Blackburn
Whitburn
Harthill
Fauldhouse
Shotts
Devilla Forest
Cleish Hills
Torry Bay
St. Margaret's Hope
NS
M9
M8
M90
M876
A985
A91
A907
0 1 2 3 miles
0 1 2 3 4 5 km

Markinch
Balcurvie
Scoonie
Leven
Leslie
GLENROTHES
Milton of Balgonie
Windygates
Largo Bay
Auchmuirbridge
Scotlandwell
Kinglassie
Coaltown of Balgonie
Innerleven
Methil
Buckhaven
Stenton
Thornton
Ballingry
Lochore
FIFE
Auchterderran
Cluny
East Wemyss
Coaltown of Wemyss
West Wemyss
Crosshill
Glencraig
Cardenden
Chapel
Gallatown
Lochgelly
Templehall
Dysart
RAVENSCRAIG CASTLE
Lumphinnans
Hayfield
Pathhead
KIRKCALDY ART GALLERY AND MUSEUM
Cowdenbeath
Kirkcaldy
Auchtertool
Linktown
FIFE COASTAL PATH
Donibristle
Balmule
Kinghorn
Pettycur
NT
FIRTH OF FORTH
Burntisland
ALEXANDER III MONUMENT
ABERDOUR CASTLE
Aberdour
ST BRIDGET'S CHURCH
Dalgety Bay
Inchkeith
ST COLM'S ABBEY
Inchcolm
Inchmickery
Aberlady Bay
Craigielaw
Cramond I.
Drum Sands
Gosford Bay
DALMENY HOUSE
Black Rocks
HMY BRITANNIA
LAURISTON CASTLE
Granton
Newhaven
Leith
Cramond
Cockenzie and Port Seton
SETON COLLEGIATE CHURCH
Longniddry
Davidson's Mains
ROYAL BOTANIC GARDEN
Drylaw
EDINBURGH
Prestonpans
Cramond Bridge
Barnton
MUSSELBURGH
Fisherrow Sands
INDUSTRIAL HERITAGE MUSEUM
EDINBURGH ZOO
PALACE OF HOLYROOD HOUSE
Portobello
Joppa
Musselburgh
Murrayfield
Duddingston
Gogar
Corstorphine
MURRAYFIELD
NAT. MUS. OF SCOTLAND
NEWHAILES
INVERESK LODGE GDNS
Wallyford
Tranent
Macmerry
Inveresk
Gorgie
Morningside
Craigmillar
Newcraighall
New Winton
New Town
Elphinstone
CRAIGMILLAR CASTLE
EDINBURGH SERVICES
Sighthill
Craiglockhart
ROYAL OBSERVATORY
Whitecraig
Hermiston
Colinton
Braid
Danderhall
Ormiston
Liberton
Gilmerton
Millerhill
Crossgatehall
Juniper Green
DREGHORN SERVICES
Fairmilehead
DALKEITH PARK
Pencaitland
Edinburgh
Currie
Kaimes
Dalkeith
Cousland
GLENKINCHIE DISTILLERY
MALLENY GARDEN
HILLEND SKI CENTRE
Straiton
BUTTERFLY FARM
Eskbank
HILLEND
BONALY
ALLERMUIR HILL
Loanhead
Newbattle
Peastonbank
Malleny Mills
Harlaw Reservoir
Woodhouselee
Bilston
Polton
Easthouses
Mayfield
Bonnyrigg and Lasswade
Peaston
Pathhead
PENTLAND HILLS
CASTLELAW FORT
Easter Howgate
MINING MUSEUM
VOGRIE
Threipmuir Reservoir
Glencorse Res.
Roslin
Newtongrange
Newlandrig
Humbie
Milton Bridge
ROSSLYN CHAPEL
ROSLIN GLEN
Rosewell
Tyne Water
Crichton
Fala Dam
SCALD LAW
Auchendinny
Arniston
Penicuik
ARNISTON HOUSE
Kirkhill
Gorebridge
CRICHTON CASTLE
Silverburn
Carrington
South Esk
North Middleton
Fala
Tynehead
Midlothian
Nine Mile
Temple

Largo Bay
Ruddons Pt.
St Monans
ST MONAN'S WINDMILL
ST MONAN'S CHURCH
Ardross
Elie
Earlsferry
Chapel Ness
Sauchar Pt.
221
ISLE OF MAY
Isle of May
FIRTH OF FORTH
209
Fidra
Craigleith
Bass Rock
Eyebroughy
North Berwick
SCOTTISH SEABIRD CENTRE
MUSEUM
TANTALLON CASTLE
Auldhame
DIRLETON CASTLE & GARDENS
MUIRFIELD
Dirleton
Gullane Bay
Gullane
Scoughall
West Fenton
Kingston
Whitekirk
Fenton Barns
St. Baldred's Cradle
Aberlady Bay
Aberlady
Tyne Mouth
JOHN MUIR BIRTHPLACE
Craigielaw
MYRETON MOTOR MUSEUM
Drem
THE CHESTERS FORT
East Fortune
MUSEUM OF FLIGHT
Tyninghame
JOHN MUIR
Belhaven
Dunbar
Gosford Bay
GOSFORD HOUSE
Ballencrieff
Athelstaneford
Preston
West Barns
Spittal
East Linton
Peffer Burn
Cockenzie and Port Seton
HOPETOUN MON
JANE WELSH CARLYLE MUSEUM
PRESTON MILL & PHANTASSIE DOOCOT
Biel Water
Longniddry
HAILES CASTLE
Traprain
Pitcox
Spott
Huntington
Elvingston
SETON COLLEGIATE CHURCH
Tyne
ST MARY'S COLLEGIATE CH
Luggate Burn
Stenton
Haddington
Halls
Gladsmuir
Tranent
Penston
Papple
Macmerry
East Lothian
New Town
Garvald
New Winton
Samuelston
Bolton
Dunbar Common
BRANSLY HILL
Ormiston
Carfrae
Pencaitland
East Saltoun
Gifford
Danskine
GLENKINCHIE DISTILLERY
West Saltoun
Peastonbank
Bothwell Water
Spartleton Edge
LAMMERMUIR HILLS
Gilchriston
Quarryford
Peaston
Pathhead
Long Newton
Longyester
Birns Water
Whiteadder Reservoir
Humbie
Stobshiel
Fala Dam
Blegbie
LAMMER LAW
MEIKLE SAYS LAW
Hopes Reservoir
Whiteadder Water
CRANSHAWS HILL
Fala
196
197
0 1 2 3 miles
0 1 2 3 4 5 km

4
5
6
NT
A
B
C
D
Barns Ness
East Barns
Skateraw
A1
Thorntonloch
Innerwick
COCKLAW HILL 319
DUNGLASS COLLEGIATE CHURCH
Reed Pt.
Cove
Cockburnspath
Oldhamstocks
Siccar Pt.
Wheat Stack
FAST CASTLE
ST ABB'S HEAD
St. Abb's Head
KITTIWAKE GALLERY
Lumsdaine
A1107
245
Ecclaw
Coldingham Moor
Northfield
St Abbs
Coldingham Bay
St. Abb's Haven
B6438
391 HEART LAW
SOUTHERN UPLAND WAY
Grantshouse
Huxton
Coldingham
COLDINGHAM PRIORY
Ale Water
Nether Monynut
Houndwood
Eye Water
EYEMOUTH MUSEUM
Eyemouth
Cairncross
262
Abbey St. Bathans
A6112
Reston
AYTON CASTLE
B6355
Auchencrow
B6437
Ayton
Burnmouth
Ellemford
LAMMERMUIR
197
EDINSHALL BROCH
198
Prenderguest
217
Lamberton
Lintlaw

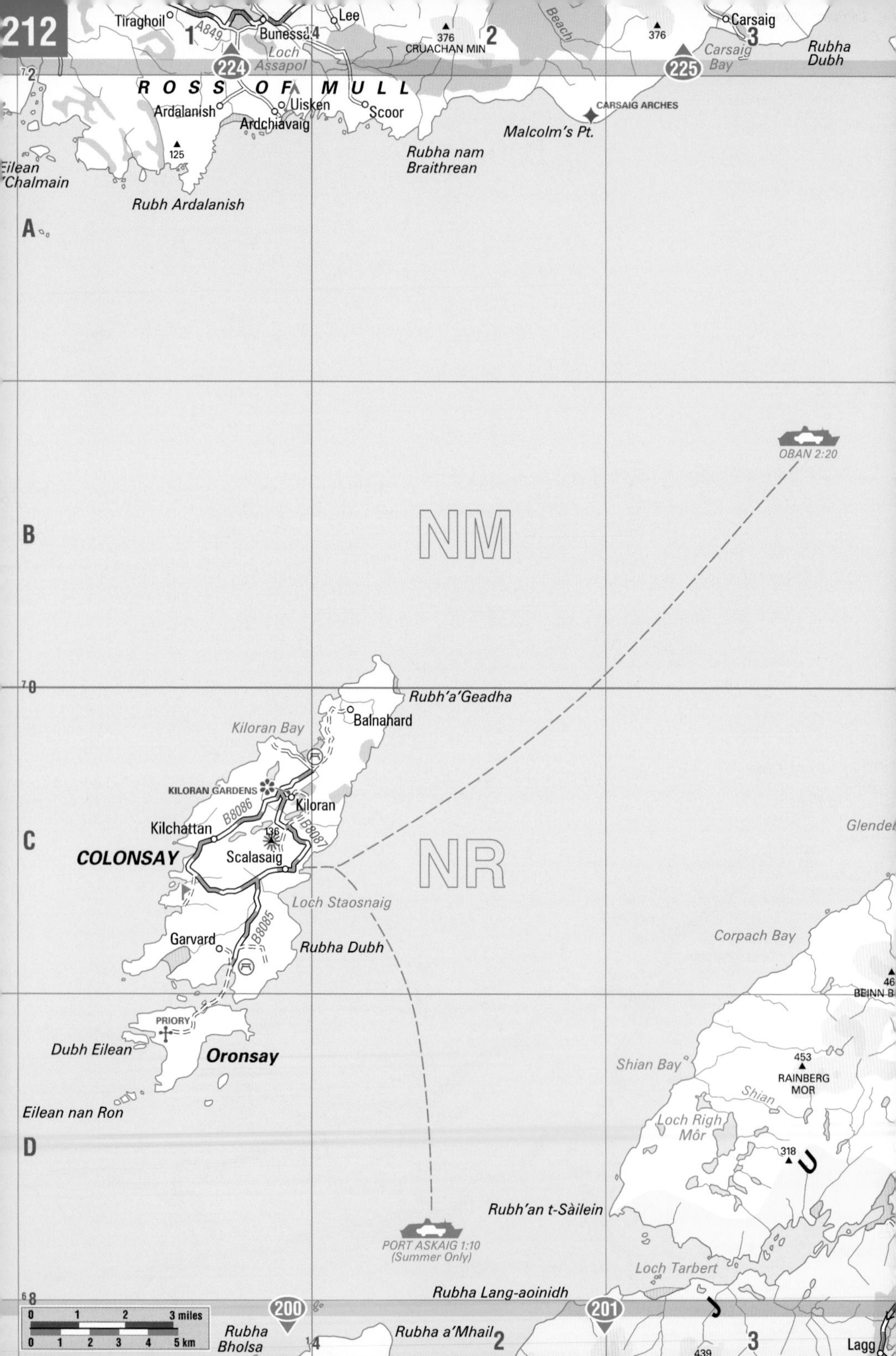
Tiraghoil
A849
Bunessan
Lee
Loch Assapol
224
376
CRUACHAN MIN
Beach
376
Carsaig
Carsaig Bay
225
Rubha Dubh
R O S S O F M U L L
Ardalanish
Uisken
Ardchiavaig
Scoor
CARSAIG ARCHES
Malcolm's Pt.
125
Rubha nam Braithrean
Eilean 'Chalmain
Rubh Ardalanish
A
B
C
D
1
2
3
14
72
70
68
OBAN 2:20
NM
NR
Rubh'a'Geadha
Balnahard
Kiloran Bay
KILORAN GARDENS
Kiloran
B8086
B8087
Kilchattan
136
Scalasaig
COLONSAY
Loch Staosnaig
Glendebadel
Corpach Bay
B8085
Garvard
Rubha Dubh
46
BEINN B
PRIORY
Dubh Eilean
Oronsay
Shian Bay
453
RAINBERG MOR
Shian
Eilean nan Ron
Loch Righ Mòr
318
Rubh'an t-Sàilein
PORT ASKAIG 1:10
(Summer Only)
Loch Tarbert
Rubha Lang-aoinidh
200
201
0 1 2 3 miles
0 1 2 3 4 5 km
Rubha Bholsa
Rubha a'Mhail
439
Lagg

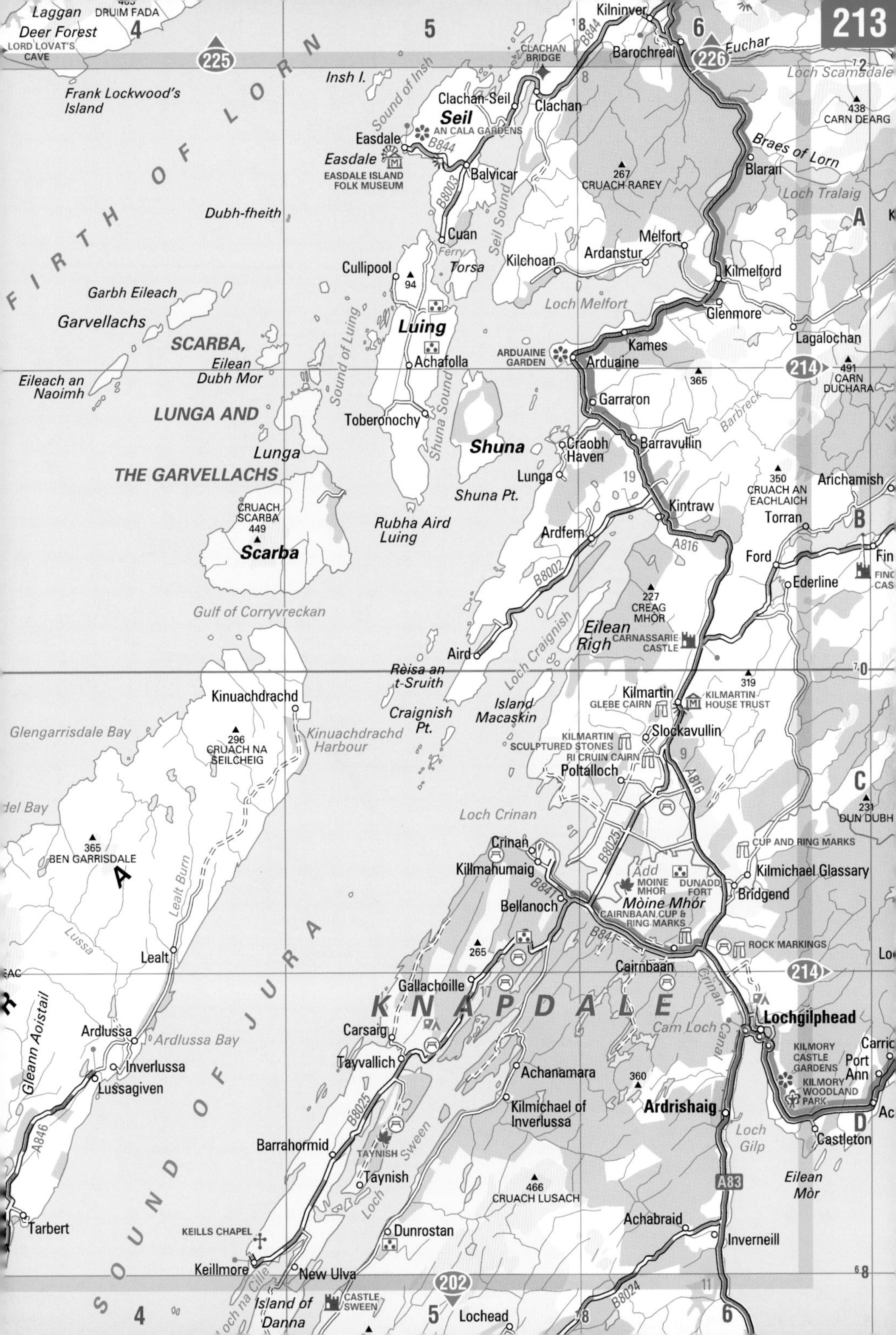

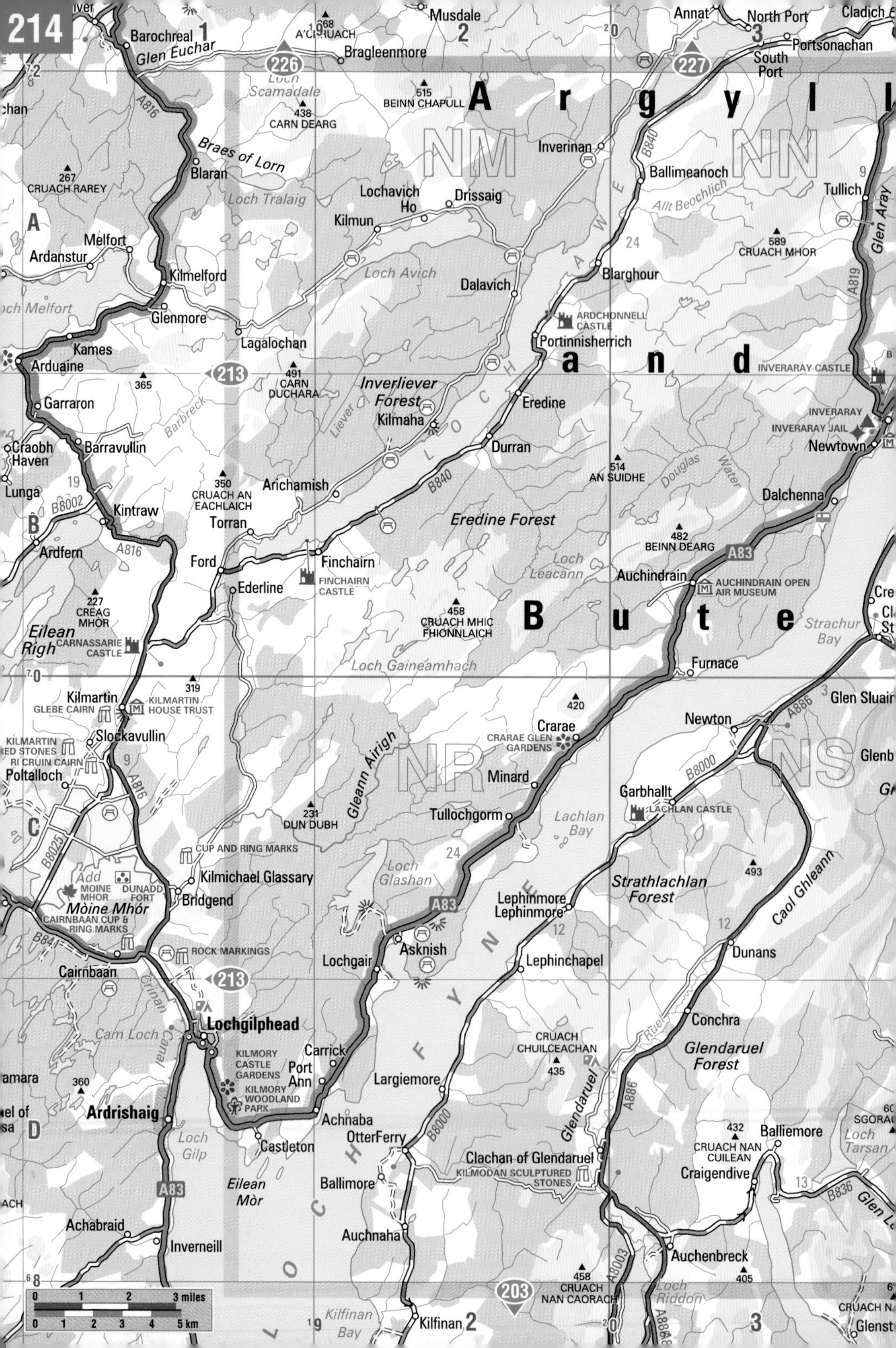
Barochreal
Glen Euchar
A'CHRUACH
Musdale
Bragleenmore
Annat
North Port
Cladich
Portsonachan
South Port
226
227
Loch Scamadale
BEINN CHAPULL
CARN DEARG
Argyll
NM
NN
Braes of Lorn
Blaran
Inverinan
Ballimeanoch
CRUACH RAREY
Loch Tralaig
Lochavich Ho
Drissaig
Allt Beochlich
Tullich
Glen Aray
Kilmun
Melfort
Ardanstur
Kilmelford
Loch Avich
Dalavich
Blarghour
CRUACH MHOR
Loch Melfort
Glenmore
ARDCHONNELL CASTLE
Portinnisherrich
Lagalochan
Kames
Arduaine
213
CARN DUCHARA
Inverliever Forest
and
INVERARAY CASTLE
Garraron
Barbreck
Liever
Kilmaha
Eredine
INVERARAY
INVERARAY JAIL
Craobh Haven
Barravullin
Durran
Newtown
Lunga
CRUACH AN EACHLAICH
Arichamish
AN SUIDHE
Douglas Water
Dalchenna
B8002
Kintraw
Torran
B840
Eredine Forest
Ardfern
A816
Ford
Finchairn
BEINN DEARG
A83
Loch Leacann
Auchindrain
AUCHINDRAIN OPEN AIR MUSEUM
Ederline
FINCHAIRN CASTLE
CREAG MHOR
CRUACH MHIC FHIONNLAICH
Bute
Eilean Righ
CARNASSARIE CASTLE
Strachur Bay
Loch Gaineamhach
Furnace
Kilmartin
KILMARTIN HOUSE TRUST
GLEBE CAIRN
Glen Sluain
Slockavullin
Crarae
CRARAE GLEN GARDENS
Newton
A886
Poltalloch
Gleann Airigh
NR
NS
Minard
B8000
Garbhallt
LACHLAN CASTLE
DUN DUBH
Tullochgorm
Lachlan Bay
B8025
CUP AND RING MARKS
Loch Glashan
Strathlachlan Forest
Moine Mhor
DUNADD FORT
Kilmichael Glassary
Bridgend
Lephinmore
Caol Ghleann
CAIRNBAAN CUP & RING MARKS
B841
ROCK MARKINGS
Asknish
Lephinchapel
Dunans
Cairnbaan
Lochgair
Crinan Canal
Cam Loch
Lochgilphead
LOCH FYNE
Conchra
KILMORY CASTLE GARDENS
Carrick
CRUACH CHUILCEACHAN
Glendaruel Forest
Port Ann
Largiemore
Glendaruel
KILMORY WOODLAND PARK
Ardrishaig
Achnaba
Loch Gilp
Castleton
OtterFerry
Clachan of Glendaruel
CRUACH NAN CUILEAN
Balliemore
Loch Tarsan
Eilean Mòr
Ballimore
KILMODAN SCULPTURED STONES
Craigendive
B836
A83
Achabraid
Auchnaha
Auchenbreck
Inverneill
A8003
CRUACH NAN CAORACH
Loch Riddon
203
Kilfinan Bay
Kilfinan
0 1 2 3 miles
0 1 2 3 4 5 km

4
5
6
227
216
Lochan Shira
Loch Stron Mor
Glen Falloch
Falls of Falloch
A82
733
TROISGEACH
Inverarnan
948
BEINN BHUIDHE
550
BEINN GHLAS
940
BEINN A'CHROIN
Ben Glas Burn
Fyne
Glen Fyne
Allt na Lairige
Brannie Burn
Shira
Glen Shira
Glenfyne Lodge
645
MAOL BREAC
Ardlui
LOCH LOMOND AND THE TROSSACHS NATIONAL PARK
Kilblaan Burn
Clachan
Loch Sloy
941
BEN VORLICH
770
Drishaig
A83
Cairndow
811
ARDKINGLAS WOODLAND GARDEN
ROB ROY'S CAVE
Stronachlachar
916
Inveruglas
Glen Kinglas
A815
Ardno
1011
BEINN IME
Inversnaid Hotel
Loch Arklet
St Catherine's
901
BEINN AN LOCHAIN
Rest and Be Thankful
B839
B828
849
WEST HIGHLAND WAY
598
Hell's Glen
565
CRUACH NAN CAPULL
Monevechadan
881
Succoth
Tarbet
Craig Rostan
LOCH LOMOND
Glen Croe
Forest
Arrochar
847
BEN DONICH
Ardgartan
Stuckgowan
Ardmay
974
BEN LOMOND
Drimsynie
Lochgoilhead
Ardgartan
703
BEINN LOCHAIN
Corrow
CNOC COINNICH
681
Ptarmigan Lodge
0:45
Blairlomond
Glen Douglas
Loch Goil
Ardgoil Forest
779
BEINN BHEULA
Invernoaden
A814
DOUNE HILL
734
Inverbeg
INVERBEG GALLERY
Rowardennan
ROWARDENNAN LODGE
596
BEINN UIRD
ARGYLL
519
THE SADDLE
Glenmallan
Rowardennan Forest
Loch Eck
Carrick Castle
CARRICK CASTLE
BEINN EICH
702
0:30
618
BEINN BHEAG
LOCH ECK
Whistlefield
Eck Forest
Portincaple
Whistlefield
Edentaggart
Glen Luss
Inchlonaig
NAT PARK CENTRE
Luss
713
BEINN CHAORACH
THISTLE BAGPIPE WORKS
LONG
Garelochhead
Bernice
659
CREACHAN MOR
593
BEINN RUISG
Aldochlay
Inchfad
741
BEINN MHOR
FOREST
206
Inchcailloch
BEINN RUADH
664
Glen Finart
GLENFINART DEER FARM
B883
STRONE HOUSE GARDENS
Glen Fruin
Faslane Port
GARE LOCH
Inchmurrin
Glenmassan
Glenfinart
Ardentinny
Coulport
Rahane
A817
Duchlage
Blairglas
Shandon
Glen Massan
BENMORE BOTANIC GARDEN
Forest
PARK
Ardpeaton
LOCH LOMOND THE TROSSACHS
Benmore
Uig
GLENARN GARDEN
THE HILL HOUSE
Arden
Clynder
202
Rhu
A818
Bannachra Muir
BALLOCH CASTLE
Ardbeg
Invereck
KILMUN ARBORETUM
LINN BOTANIC GARDENS
Rosneath
Helensburgh
Dalinlongart
A880
Blairmore
Cove Bay
Cove
Craigendoran
NAT PK GATEWAY CENTRE
Kilmun
Rosneath Pt.
Clachaig
Holy Loch
Strone
Portkil
Sandbank
Strone Pt.
Colgrain
Glen Kin
Ardnadam
204
Kilcreggan
0:30
GEILSTON
ALEXANDRIA
Hunter's Quay
0:12
A885
ST JOHN'S CHURCH
Gourock
Geilston
Bonhill
Renton
A
B
C
D

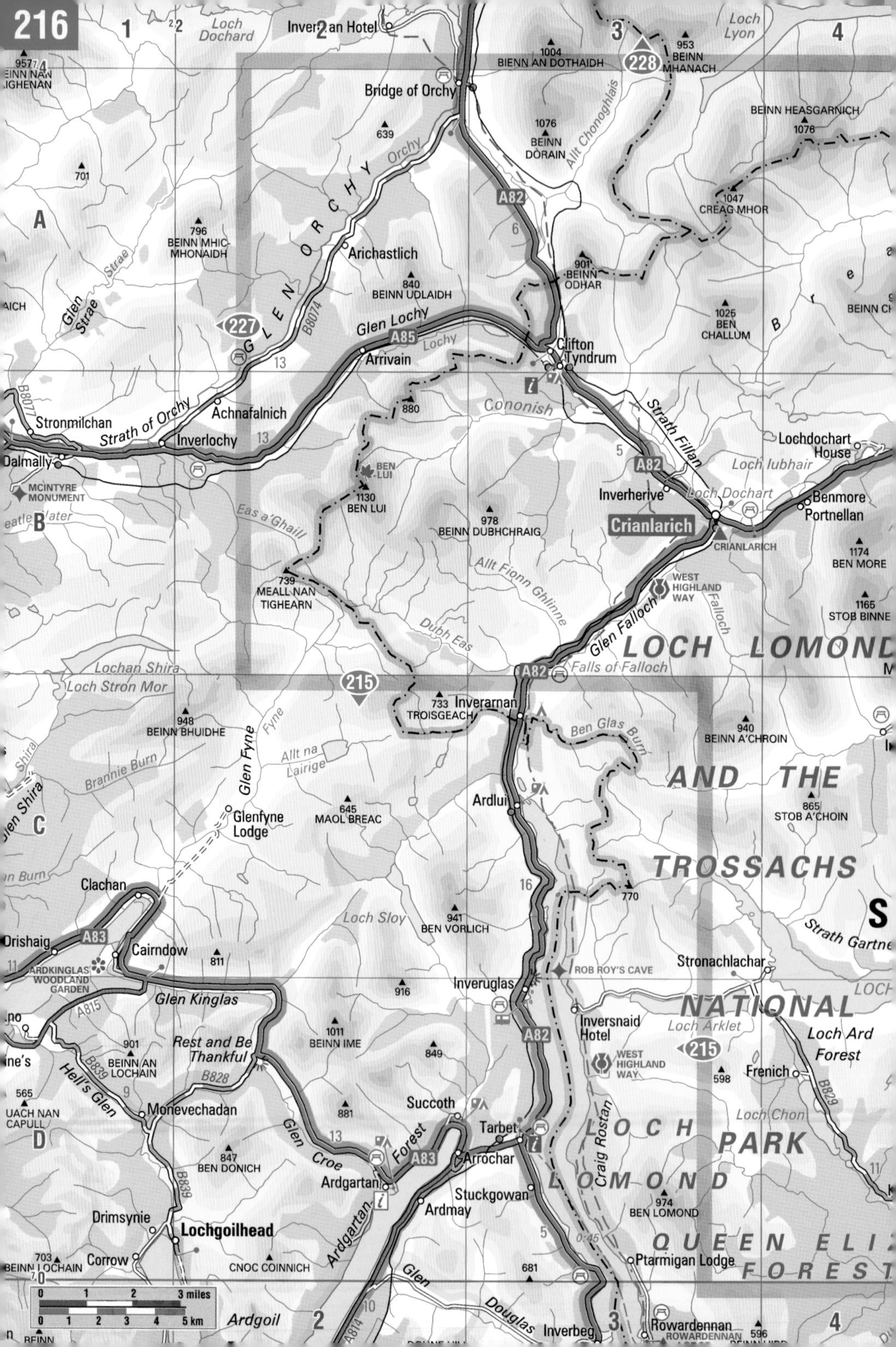
1
2
3
4
A
B
C
D
Loch Dochard
Inveroran Hotel
Loch Lyon
1004
BIENN AN DOTHAIDH
228
953
BEINN MHANACH
957
BEINN NAN AIGHENAN
Bridge of Orchy
639
BEINN HEASGARNICH
1076
1076
BEINN DORAIN
Allt Chonoghlais
701
GLEN ORCHY
Orchy
A82
1047
CREAG MHOR
796
BEINN MHIC-MHONAIDH
Arichastlich
6
901
BEINN ODHAR
840
BEINN UDLAIDH
Glen Strae
Strae
B8074
Glen Lochy
227
1025
BEN CHALLUM
BEINN CH
A85
Lochy
Clifton
Tyndrum
Arrivain
13
B8077
Stronmilchan
Achnafalnich
Strath of Orchy
Inverlochy
880
Cononish
Strath Fillan
Lochdochart House
Dalmally
13
5
A82
Loch Iubhair
MCINTYRE MONUMENT
BEN LUI
1130
BEN LUI
Inverherive
Loch Dochart
Benmore
Portnellan
Eas a'Ghaill
978
BEINN DUBHCHRAIG
Crianlarich
CRIANLARICH
1174
BEN MORE
Allt Fionn Ghlinne
739
MEALL NAN TIGHEARN
WEST HIGHLAND WAY
Falloch
1165
STOB BINNE
Dubh Eas
Glen Falloch
LOCH LOMOND
Lochan Shira
A82
Falls of Falloch
Loch Stron Mor
215
733
TROISGEACH
Inverarnan
948
BEINN BHUIDHE
Fyne
Ben Glas Burn
940
BEINN A'CHROIN
Shira
Brannie Burn
Allt na Lairige
Glen Fyne
AND THE
Ardlui
865
STOB A'CHOIN
Glenfyne Lodge
645
MAOL BREAC
TROSSACHS
16
Clachan
770
Loch Sloy
941
BEN VORLICH
Strath Gartney
A83
Cairndow
811
ROB ROY'S CAVE
Stronachlachar
ARDKINGLAS WOODLAND GARDEN
Inveruglas
916
Glen Kinglas
NATIONAL
A815
Inversnaid Hotel
Loch Arklet
Loch Ard Forest
1011
BEINN IME
A82
Rest and Be Thankful
901
BEINN AN LOCHAIN
849
WEST HIGHLAND WAY
215
Hell's Glen
B839
B828
598
Frenich
B829
565
9
Monevechadan
881
Succoth
Loch Chon
Glen Croe
13
Forest
Tarbet
Craig Rostan
LOCH
PARK
847
BEN DONICH
A83
Arrochar
Ardgartan
LOMOND
11
B839
Stuckgowan
974
BEN LOMOND
Ardgartan
Ardmay
Drimsynie
Lochgoilhead
5
0:45
QUEEN ELIZ
703
BEINN LOCHAIN
Corrow
CNOC COINNICH
681
Ptarmigan Lodge
FOREST
Glen Douglas
10
A814
0 1 2 3 miles
0 1 2 3 4 5 km
Ardgoil
Inverbeg
Rowardennan
ROWARDENNAN
596

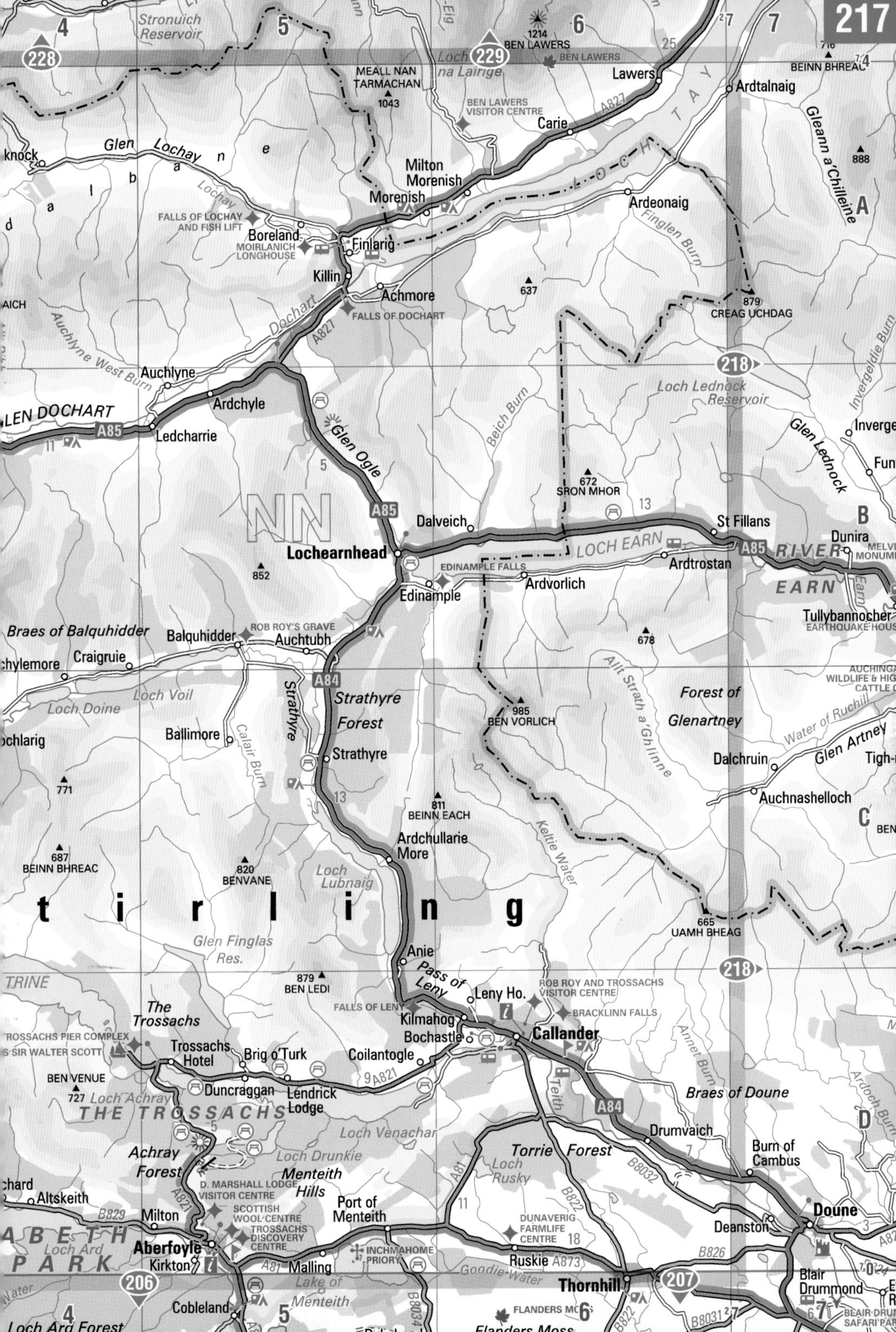

Stronuich Reservoir
BEN LAWERS
1214
MEALL NAN TARMACHAN
1043
Loch na Lairige
BEN LAWERS VISITOR CENTRE
Lawers
Ardtalnaig
BEINN BHREAC
716
Carie
A827
LOCH TAY
Glen Lochay
Breadalbane
Milton Morenish
Morenish
Ardeonaig
Gleann a'Chilleine
888
FALLS OF LOCHAY AND FISH LIFT
Boreland
MOIRLANICH LONGHOUSE
Finlarig
Finglen Burn
Killin
Achmore
637
FALLS OF DOCHART
879
CREAG UCHDAG
Auchlyne West Burn
Dochart
Auchlyne
Ardchyle
GLEN DOCHART
A85
Ledcharrie
Loch Lednock Reservoir
Invergeldie Burn
Glen Lednock
Glen Ogle
Beich Burn
NN
672
SRON MHOR
Dalveich
St Fillans
Lochearnhead
LOCH EARN
852
EDINAMPLE FALLS
Ardvorlich
Ardtrostan
Edinample
RIVER EARN
Dunira
Tullybannocher
EARTHQUAKE HOUSE
Braes of Balquhidder
Balquhidder
ROB ROY'S GRAVE
Auchtubh
678
Craigruie
A84
Strathyre
Loch Voil
Loch Doine
Strathyre Forest
Allt Strath a'Ghlinne
Forest of Glenartney
985
BEN VORLICH
Ballimore
Calair Burn
Water of Ruchill
Glen Artney
Dalchruin
Auchnashelloch
771
811
BEINN EACH
687
BEINN BHREAC
820
BENVANE
Ardchullarie More
Keltie Water
Loch Lubnaig
Stirling
665
UAMH BHEAG
Glen Finglas Res.
Anie
Pass of Leny
879
BEN LEDI
Leny Ho.
ROB ROY AND TROSSACHS VISITOR CENTRE
BRACKLINN FALLS
FALLS OF LENY
Kilmahog
Bochastle
Callander
The Trossachs
TROSSACHS PIER COMPLEX
SIR WALTER SCOTT
Trossachs Hotel
Brig o'Turk
Coilantogle
A821
Annet Burn
BEN VENUE
727
Loch Achray
Duncraggan
Lendrick Lodge
Teith
Braes of Doune
THE TROSSACHS
Loch Venachar
Drumvaich
Achray Forest
Loch Drunkie
Torrie Forest
Burn of Cambus
Menteith Hills
Loch Rusky
B8032
D. MARSHALL LODGE VISITOR CENTRE
Altskeith
Milton
B829
SCOTTISH WOOL CENTRE
TROSSACHS DISCOVERY CENTRE
Port of Menteith
B822
DUNAVERIG FARMLIFE CENTRE
Deanston
Doune
Aberfoyle
Kirkton
Loch Ard
INCHMAHOME PRIORY
Malling
A81
Ruskie
A873
B826
Lake of Menteith
Goodie Water
Thornhill
Blair Drummond
Cobleland
FLANDERS MOSS
B8031
B8034
Loch Ard Forest
Flanders Moss
BLAIR DRUMMOND SAFARI PARK
228
229
218
206
207

Perth and Kinross
NN
Lawers
Ardtalnaig
BEINN BHREAC
716
Quaich
Garrow
690
MEALL DEARG
Cablea
Braan
Carie
A827
Loch Freuchie
Glen Quaich
Amulree
Gleann a'Chilleine
888
805
MEALL NAM FUARAN
Ardeonaig
Finglen Burn
Corrymuckloch
A822
623
MEALL NAN CAORAICH
Almond
879
CREAG UCHDAG
Newton
GLEN ALMOND
Sma' Glen
931
BEN CHONZIE
Invergeldie Burn
648
MEALL TARSUINN
Loch Lednock Reservoir
Loch Turret Reservoir
Shaggie Burn
Glen Lednock
Invergeldie
Funtullich
Glen Turret
672
SRON MHOR
Monzie
350
Monzie Castle
Fowlis Wester
St Fillans
LOCH EARN
Dunira
MELVILLE MONUMENT
FALLS OF TURRET
COMRIE CROFT
Ochtertyre
Hosh
Gilmerton
STANDING STONES
Ardtrostan
A85
RIVER EARN
Earn
Lawers
Quoig
A85
Keillour
Comrie
GLENTURRET DISTILLERY
Crieff
Tullybannocher
EARTHQUAKE HOUSE
Ross
Dalginross
Lochlane
Madderty
678
B827
CRIEFF VISITORS' CENTRE
STUART CRYSTAL VISITOR CENTRE
AUCHINGARRICH WILDLIFE & HIGHLAND CATTLE CENTRE
The Balloch
B8062
Forest of Glenartney
Allt Strath a'Ghlinne
Water of Ruchill
Culloch
Torlum Wood
INNERPEFFRAY LIBRARY
STRATHEARN
Glen Artney
DRUMMOND CASTLE GARDENS
OLD CHURCH & TOWER
Kinkell Bridge
Dalchruin
Tigh-na-Blair
Ochtermuthill
Muthill
Machany Water
Auchnashelloch
533
BEN CLACH
Langside
Tullibardine
TULLIBARDINE CHAPEL
Auchterarder
A823
Glenlichorn
Knaik
B827
Garrick
Muirton
A822
665
UAMH BHEAG
BLACKHALL ROMAN CAMPS
Gleneagles Hotel
GLENEAGLES
ARDOCH ROMAN CAMP
Braco
Bullie Burn
STRATHALLAN
Blackford
Glen Eagles
BRACKLINN FALLS
Muckle Burn
Annet Burn
Greenloaning
Braes of Ogilvie
TULLIBARDINE DISTILLERY
B8033
Allan Water
Ardoch Burn
Braes of Doune
Glendevon Resvrs.
A84
Drumvaich
Kinbuck
Balhaldie
543
Torrie Forest
B8032
Burn of Cambus
Ashfield
A9
Sheriff Muir
1715
B822
Doune
Deanston
CATHEDRAL
Dunblane
A820
631
BLAIRDENON HILL
721
BEN CLEUCH
B826
B824
Pisgah
LEIGHTON LIBRARY
Blair Drummond
Easter Row
648
KING'S SEAT HILL
BLAIR DRUMMOND SAFARI PARK
0 1 2 3 miles
0 1 2 3 4 5 km

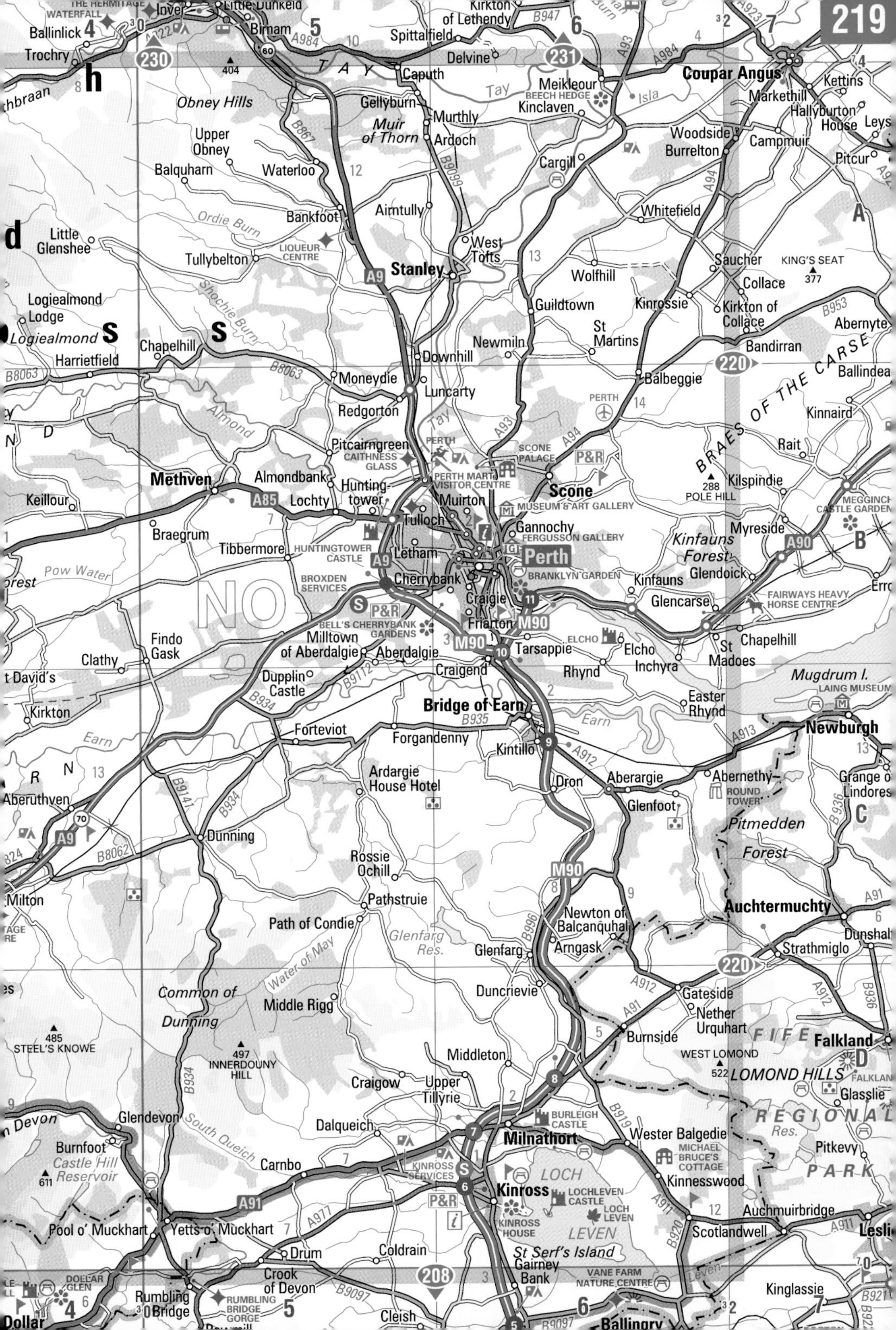
Coupar Angus
Stanley
Perth
Scone
Methven
Bridge of Earn
Newburgh
Auchtermuchty
Milnathort
Kinross
Falkland
Dollar
Bankfoot
Luncarty
Caputh
Meikleour
Kinclaven
Murthly
Woodside
Burrelton
Balbeggie
St Martins
Guildtown
Kinrossie
Saucher
Collace
Abernyte
Kinnaird
Rait
Kilspindie
Kinfauns
Glencarse
Glendoick
St Madoes
Chapelhill
Aberdalgie
Forteviot
Forgandenny
Dunning
Abernethy
Aberargie
Glenfoot
Glenfarg
Gateside
Strathmiglo
Burnside
Scotlandwell
Kinnesswood
Yetts o' Muckhart
Pool o' Muckhart
Glendevon
Rumbling Bridge
Crook of Devon
Gairney Bank
Kinglassie
BRAES OF THE CARSE
LOMOND HILLS
LOCH LEVEN
St Serf's Island
Obney Hills
Common of Dunning
Pitmedden Forest
Kinfauns Forest
Glenfarg Res.
SCONE PALACE
HUNTINGTOWER CASTLE
BRANKLYN GARDEN
FERGUSSON GALLERY
MUSEUM & ART GALLERY
BELL'S CHERRYBANK GARDENS
LOCHLEVEN CASTLE
BURLEIGH CASTLE
KINROSS HOUSE
VANE FARM NATURE CENTRE
MICHAEL BRUCE'S COTTAGE
FAIRWAYS HEAVY HORSE CENTRE
ROUND TOWER
WEST LOMOND 522
STEEL'S KNOWE 485
INNERDOUNY HILL 497
KING'S SEAT 377
POLE HILL 288
A9
A85
A90
A91
A93
A94
A912
A977
M90
B934
B9112
B935
B8062
B8063
B996
B919
B920
B953
B9099
B867
230
231
220
208

Coupar Angus
SIDLAW HILLS
Dundee
Newport-on-Tay
FIRTH OF TAY
BRAES OF THE CARSE
CARSE OF GOWRIE
Invergowrie
Newburgh
Cupar
Fife
Auchtermuchty
Falkland
Ladybank
LOMOND HILLS REGIONAL PARK
Kennoway
Markinch
Leslie
GLENROTHES
Leven
Methil
Tay Rail Bridge
Largo Bay
Kinglassie

Hayhillock
Carmyllie
Denhead of Arbilot
Hayshead
Cliffburn
The Deil's Heid
ARBROATH ABBEY
Arbroath
SIGNAL TOWER MUSEUM
CROMBIE
Arbirlot
Elliot
Kirkton of Monikie
Balmirmer
Monikie
MONIKIE
Craigton
Monikie Burn
Salmond's Muir
Wellbank
CARLUNGIE SOUTERRAIN
Muirdrum
Drumsturdy
East Haven
Newbigging
Panbride
Kellas
BARRY MILL
Barry
SOUTERRAIN ARDESTIE
Mains of Ardestie
Carnoustie
Baldovie
CARNOUSTIE
Barry Links
Monifieth
Barnhill
BROUGHTY CASTLE MUSEUM
Buddon Ness
Tayport
TENTSMUIR
Tentsmuir Forest
NO
Leuchars
LEUCHARS NORMAN CHURCH
Eden Mouth
EDEN ESTUARY CENTRE
ST ANDREWS BAY
ST ANDREWS
ST ANDREWS AQUARIUM
BRITISH GOLF MUS
St Andrews
CATH & ST RULE'S TOWER
Newpark
Brownhills
Buddo Ness
Balone
ST ANDREWS BOTANIC GARDEN
Boarhills
Babbet Ness
CRAIGTOUN
Denhead
Prior Muir
Kingsbarns
Cambo Ness
CAMBO GARDENS
Carr Brigs
Cameron Res.
Stravithie
Cameron Burn
Dunino
Tullybothy Craigs
Balcomie
Craighead
Peat Inn
Fife Ness
Radernie
Kingsmuir
CRAIL TOLBOOTH
Lathones
Lochty
SCOTLAND'S SECRET BUNKER
Crail
CRAIL MUSEUM AND HERITAGE CENTRE
Largoward
Pitcorthie
Carnbee
West Ness
Pitkierie
KELLIE CASTLE AND GARDEN
FIFE COASTAL PATH
Kilrenny
Arncroach
Anstruther Easter
SCOTTISH FISHERIES MUSEUM
Colinsburgh
Abercrombie
Pittenweem
Anstruther Wester
Kilconquhar
ST FILLAN'S CAVE
ST MONAN'S WINDMILL
St Monans
Ardross
ST MONAN'S CHURCH
Isle of May
ISLE OF MAY
Elie
Earlsferry
Chapel Ness
Sauchar Pt.
232
233
210
A
B
C
D

1
2
3
4
A
B
C
D
286
NL
NM
CASTLEBAY 2:45
(Summer only)
Feall Bay
Calgary Pt.
Gunna
Crossapol Bay
TIREE
Vaul Bay
Salum
Caolas
Rubha Dubh
Vaul
B8069
Ruaig
Balephetrish Bay
Hough Skerries
Balevullin
B8068
Gott Bay
Kenovay
Soa
R. Chraiginis
Kilkenneth
Moss
TIREE
Scarinish
B8065
Middleton
Heylipol
Heanish
Port Mor
B8065
Crossapol
Rubha Traigh an Duin
Barrapol
Loch a'Phuill
Hynish Bay
B8067
Balemartine
Rinn Thorbhais
Balephuil
141
B8066
Mannal
Balephuil Bay
Hynish
Port Snoig
0 1 2 3 miles
0 1 2 3 4 5 km

4
5
6
7
Sanna Point
Sanna Bay
Portuairk
Point of Ardnamurchan
ARDNAMURCHAN LIGHTHOUSE
Cairns of Coll
234
Eilean Mor
Rubha Mor
Sorisdale
Bousd
An Acairseid
B8072
Cliad Bay
Gallanach
Arnabost
Grishipoll
B8071
COLL
73
Loch Cliad
104
OBAN 2:55
Ardmore Bay
Quinish Pt.
Arinagour
Totronald
B8070
Loch Eatharna
Acha
Eilean Ornsay
Breachacha Castle
Friesland
Loch Breachacha
Soa
Rubha an Aird
Caliach Pt.
Sunipol
Mornish
Quinish
Mishnish
MULL THEATRE
Penmore Mill
Calgary
Dervaig
Calgary Bay
1:00
Treshnish Pt.
Ensay
342
CARN MOR
Haunn
Rubh a'Chaoil
B8073
224
Burg
Kilninian
Achleck
Fanmore
390
Treshnish Isles
Fladda
LOCH TUATH
Ballygown
EAS FORS WATERFALL
Eilean Dioghlum
Gometra
Lunga
Bearnus
313
Laggan Bay
Ulva
Ulva House
Bac Mor
Little Colonsay
Staffa
STAFFA
FINGAL'S CAVE
INCH KENNETH CHAPEL
Inch Kenneth
MACKINNON'S CAVE
Erisgeir
A
B
C
D
ARDMEANACH

COLL
Gallanach
Arinagour
Loch Cliad
Loch Eatharna
Eilean Ornsay
OBAN 2:55
TIREE 1:00
234
223
212
Ardmore Bay
Ardmore Pt.
Quinish Pt.
Glengorm Castle
MULL MUSEUM
Tobermory
Mishnish
Quinish
Rubha an Aird
Caliach Pt.
Sunipol
Mornish
Penmore Mill
MULL THEATRE
Dervaig
Achnadrish
Calgary
Calgary Bay
THE OLD BYRE HERITAGE CENTRE
Loch Frisa
Treshnish Pt.
Ensay
342 CARN MOR
Haunn
Bellart
Achnacraig
Rubh a'Chaoil
Burg
Kilninian
Achleck
Fanmore
390
Treshnish Isles
Fladda
LOCH TUATH
Ballygown
EAS FORS WATERFALL
424 BEINN NA DRISE
Eilean Dioghlum
Gometra
Lunga
Laggan Bay
Lagganulva
Oskamull
Bearnus
313
Ulva
Ulva House
Sound of Ulva
Bac Mor
LOCH NA KEAL
Little Colonsay
Eorsa
ISLE OF
INCH KENNETH CHAPEL
Inch Kenneth
Staffa
STAFFA
FINGAL'S CAVE
Balnahard
MACKINNON'S CAVE
561
Erisgeir
Glen Seilisdeir
519
BEINN NA SREINE
ARDMEANACH
Kilfinichen Bay
THE BURG
LOCH SCRIDAIN
Eilean Annraidh
MACLEAN'S CROSS
Rubha nan Cearc
100
IONA ABBEY AND CATHEDRAL
IONA HERITAGE CENTRE
Kintra
Iona
Baile Mor
Sound of Iona
ST COLUMBA EXHIBITION & WELCOME CENTRE
Loch na Lathaich
Torrans
Stac an Aoineidh
Aridhglas
Eorabus
Fionnphort
A849
Sound of Iona
Fidden
Tiraghoil
Lee
Bunessan
376 CRUACHAN MIN
Loch Assapol
Erraid
ROSS OF MULL
Ardalanish
Uisken
Scoor
Ardchiavaig
Beach
B8071
B8072
B8070
B8073
73
292
0 1 2 3 miles
0 1 2 3 4 5 km

4
5
6
clean's Nose
Ardslignish
Eilean
Mor
Glenborrodale
BEN LAGA
Laga
235
GLENCRIPESDALE
Camuschoirk
Liddesdale
Oronsay
Carna
Glencripesdale
LCHOAN 0:35
0:50
Auliston Pt.
169
516
MEALL AN
DAMHAIN
582
BEINN NAM
BEATHRACH
Lochuisg
TOBERMORY
Calve I.
TOBERMORY
DISTILLERY
0:20
Loch
Teacuis
571
BEINN IADAIN
A884
B8043
18
Loch Uisge
Drimnin
Bonnavoulin
Upper
Druimfin
M O R V E R N
Gleann Dubh
Beach
A
451
BEINN BHUIDHE
Loch Arienas
550
STITHEAN NA
RAPLAICH
739
BEINN MHEADH
A848
Acharn
Gleann Geal
MOR
Rhemore
A R O S
Ardnacross
Killundine
Claggan
rmore
B849
NM
Larachbeg
KINLOCHALINE
CASTLE
ARDTORNISH
GARDENS
Loch
Tearnait
437
BEINN A'
CHAISIL
SOUND OF MULL
10
Fiunary
Achranich
Rannoch
Savary
A884
Loch Aline
226
Loch nan
Clach
Aros
Lochaline
B
nich
Aros Mains
GLAIS BHEINN
479
AN
SLEAGHACH
513
Eignai
Rubha Mor
0:15
ARDTORNISH
CASTLE
A848
Salen
Fishnish
Bay
Ardtornish
Pt.
Pennygown
6
Killiechronan
B8035
Killbeg
A884
Camas
Gorm
Inninmore
Bay
Garbh Shlios
Kellan
Corrynachenchy
A849
8073
Gruline
412
Forsa
Garmony
Scallastle
Bay
Rubha an
Ridire
Bernera I.
Achind
5
ISLAND OF MULL
A KEAL
Knock
Java
Craignure
Bay
Kilc
Loch Bà
Scallastle
OBAN 0:45
B8035
591
BEINN
A'GHRAIG
Craignure
MULL
Glen
Cannel
766
DUN DA
GHAOITHE
Duart
Bay
Duart Pt.
DUART
CASTLE
Eilean
Musdile
C
uaig
761
BEINN TALAIDH
Lochdon
966
BEN MORE
704
CORRA-BHEINN
17
Glen More
Lussa
A849
Loch Don
Grass Pt.
B8035
Coladoir
A849
Strathcoil
226
emore
se
Aird of
Kinloch
Loch
Airdeglais
248
Kerrera
Bal
FIRTH OF LORN
BEN BUIE
717
698
CREACH BEINN
Loch
Spelve
Ardmore
Loch
Fuaron
Croggan
Rubha nan
Sailthean
Bach I.
Kinlochspelve
Pennycross
Lochbuie
Barachandroman
Rubha
Seanach
503
BEINN NA CROISE
Loch Uisg
D
Leidle
ASS
Loch Buie
Carsaig
405
DRUIM FADA
Laggan
Deer Forest
376
Rubha
Dubh
LORD LOVAT'S
CAVE
CLACHAN
BRIDGE
B844
Carsaig
Bay
212
213
Insh I.
SAIG ARCHES
Frank Lockwood's
Island
Sound of Insh
Clachan-Seil
Clachan
Seil
4
5
17
6
2

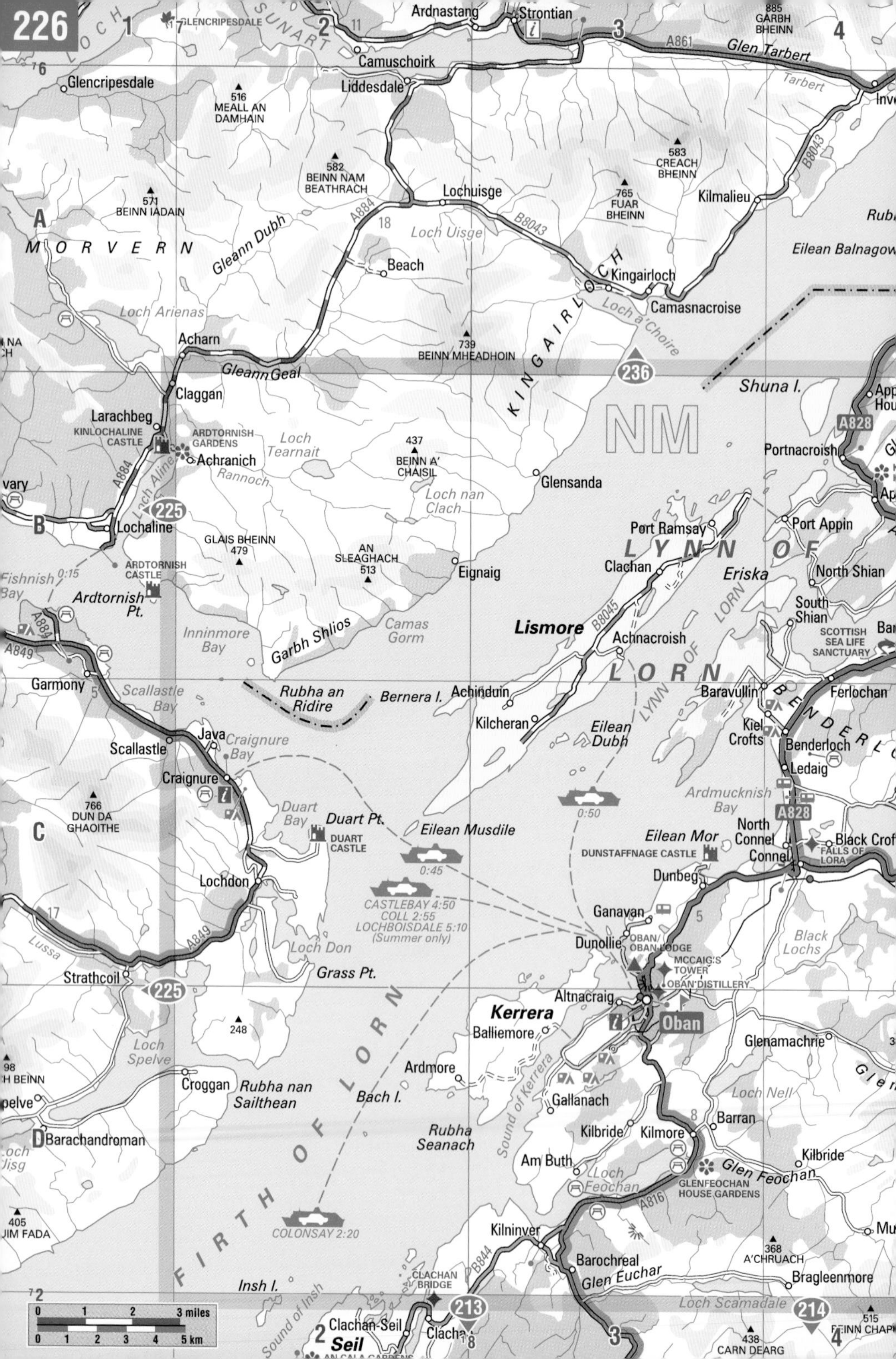
LOCH
1
GLENCRIPESDALE
SUNART
2
11
Ardnastang
Strontian
3
885
GARBH
BHEINN
4
A861
Glen Tarbert
Camuschoirk
Tarbert
Glencripesdale
Liddesdale
516
MEALL AN
DAMHAIN
583
CREACH
BHEINN
B8043
582
BEINN NAM
BEATHRACH
571
BEINN IADAIN
Lochuisge
765
FUAR
BHEINN
Kilmalieu
A
MORVERN
A884
18
Loch Uisge
B8043
Gleann Dubh
Eilean Balnagow
Beach
LOCH
Kingairloch
Loch Arienas
Camasnacroise
Loch a' Choire
Acharn
739
BEINN MHEADHOIN
KINGAIRLOCH
Gleann Geal
236
Shuna I.
Claggan
NM
A828
Larachbeg
KINLOCHALINE
CASTLE
ARDTORNISH
GARDENS
Loch
Tearnait
437
BEINN A'
CHAISIL
Portnacroish
Achranich
Rannoch
Loch Aline
Glensanda
A884
Loch nan
Clach
225
B
Lochaline
Port Ramsay
Port Appin
GLAIS BHEINN
479
LYNN OF
ARDTORNISH
CASTLE
AN
SLEAGHACH
513
Eignaig
Clachan
Eriska
North Shian
Fishnish
Bay
0:15
Ardtornish
Pt.
LYNN OF LORN
South
Shian
A884
Lismore
B8045
Inninmore
Bay
Camas
Gorm
Garbh Shlios
SCOTTISH
SEA LIFE
SANCTUARY
A849
Achnacroish
LORN
Garmony
Scallastle
Bay
Rubha an
Ridire
Bernera I.
Achinduin
Baravullin
Ferlochan
BENDERLOCH
LYNN OF LORN
Java
Craignure
Bay
Kilcheran
Eilean
Dubh
Kiel
Crofts
Scallastle
Benderloch
Ledaig
Craignure
766
DUN DA
GHAOITHE
Duart
Bay
Duart Pt.
Ardmucknish
Bay
0:50
A828
C
DUART
CASTLE
Eilean Musdile
Eilean Mor
North
Connel
Black Croft
DUNSTAFFNAGE CASTLE
FALLS OF
LORA
Connel
0:45
Lochdon
Dunbeg
CASTLEBAY 4:50
COLL 2:55
LOCHBOISDALE 5:10
(Summer only)
17
Ganavan
5
Dunollie
OBAN/
OBAN LODGE
Lussa
A849
Loch Don
Black
Lochs
MCCAIG'S
TOWER
OBAN DISTILLERY
Strathcoil
225
Grass Pt.
Altnacraig
Kerrera
Oban
248
Balliemore
Glenamachrie
Loch
Spelve
Ardmore
Sound of Kerrera
Croggan
Rubha nan
Sailthean
Bach I.
Gallanach
Loch Nell
8
Barran
D
Barachandroman
Kilbride
Kilmore
Rubha
Seanach
Kilbride
Am Buth
Loch
Feochan
Glen Feochan
GLENFEOCHAN
HOUSE GARDENS
FIRTH OF LORN
A816
405
COLONSAY 2:20
Kilninver
368
A'CHRUACH
Barochreal
B844
Glen Euchar
Bragleenmore
CLACHAN
BRIDGE
Insh I.
Sound of Insh
213
Loch Scamadale
214
515
0
1
2
3 miles
0
1
2
3
4
5 km
2
Clachan-Seil
Seil
3
438
CARN DEARG
4

Onich
North Ballachulish
Kinlochleven
THE ALUMINIUM STORY
MAM NA GUALAINN
Sallachan Pt.
LOCH LINNHE
South Ballachulish
Ballachulish
Glencoe
GLENCOE AND NORTH LORN FOLK MUSEUM
AONACH 967
GLENCOE
GLENCOE VISITOR CENTRE
Kentallen
Glenduror Forest
Glen an Fhiodh
Duror
Beinn a'Bheithir
Keil
Glen Duror
Salachan Glen
Glen Coe
Altnafeadh
BEINN A' CHRULAISTE
BEN NEVIS AND GLEN COE
BIDEAN NAM BIAN
Royal Forest
FRAOCHAIDH
SGOR NA H-ULAIDH
Dalness
Glen Etive
Alltchaorunn
Glen Creran
BEINN FHIONNLAIDH
Elleric
Fasnacloich
Invercreran
GLASDRUM WOOD
Glasdrum
BEINN CHURALAIN
Glen Ure
BEINN SGULAIRD
Creagan
Druimavuic
South Creagan
Inverchanan
Glenceitlein
STOB DUBH
CLACH LEATHAD
Allt Coire a'Chaolain
Gualachulain
STOB COIR'AN ALBANNAICH
Allt Dochard
STOB GHABHAR
BEINN TRILLEACHAN
Allt Easach
BEN STARAV
Loch Dochard
CREACH BHEINN
Abhainn Dalach
Barcaldine Forest
Allt Hallater
BEINN NAN AIGHENAN
Gleann Salach
LOCH ETIVE
BEINN MHEADHONACH
Glen Kinglass
ARDCHATTAN PRIORY
Glen Liver
BEINN MHIC-MHONAIDH
Achnacloich
ACHNACLOICH GARDEN
Bonawe
Glen Noe
GLEN ORCHY
BONAWE IRON FURNACE
INVERAWE FISHERIES AND SMOKERIES EXHIBITION
Brochroy
BEINN EUNAICH
Glen Strae
BEN CRUACHAN 1126
Taynuilt
Ichrachan
Bridge of Awe
Pass of Brander
Cruachan Reservoir
Allt Mhoille
BARGUILLEAN GARDENS
GLEN NANT
Glen Nant
Falls of Cruachan
KILCHURN CASTLE
Lochawe
Stronmilchan
Strath of Orchy
Achnafalnich
Inverlochy
Dalmally
CRUACHAN DAM VISITOR CENTRE
Loch Tromlee
Innis Chonain
MCINTYRE MONUMENT
Loch Nant
ARDANAISEIG GARDENS
Ardanaiseig
INISHAIL CHAPEL
Inishail
Teatle Water
Eas a'Ghaill
MEALL NAN TIGHEARN
Kilchrenan
Sior Loch
Annat
North Port
Cladich
Allt Fearna
Portsonachan
South Port
Cladich
Lochan Shira
Loch Stron Mor
A82 A828 A85 A819 B863 B8077 B845 B840 B8074
NN
237 228 216 214 215

Inverroy
Roybridge
Achluachrach
Murlaggan
Roughburn
Killiechonate
Spean
MONESSIE FALLS
A86
239
240
GLEN SPEAN
Fersit
Leanachan Forest
724
BEINN CHLIANAIG
Allt Loraich
1087
BEINN A'CHLACHAIR
Ardverikie Forest
The Cour
Allt Làire
Loch Ghuilbinn
1177
STOB CHOIRE CLAURIGH
1106
Allt na Lairige
Lairig Leacach
1115
STOB COIRE EASAIN
LOCH TREIG
1046
CHNO DEARG
1114
AONACH BEAG
Ossian
1234
AONACH BEAG
1094
Uisge Labhair
Creaguaineach Lodge
937
BEINN NA LAP
Corrour Shooting Lodge
Amhainn Rath
LOCH OSSIAN
Loch Ossian
Corrour Forest
237
583
952
SGOR GAIBHRE
1130
BINNEIN MOR
630
Loch Eilde Beag
MAMORE FOREST
Allt na Caim
Rannoch Forest
789
Loch Eilde Mor
906
LEUM UILLEIM
Ciaran Water
Kinlochmore
THE ALUMINIUM STORY
BLACKWATER RESERVOIR
Black Water
Leven
BEN NEVIS
Rannoch Station
B846
Altnafeadh
857
BEINN A' CHRULAISTE
Black Corries Lodge
739
STOB NA CRUAICHE
Loch Eigheach
Gaur
Coupall
Kingshouse Hotel
Loch Laidon
AND
Loch Gaineamhach
Royal Forest
GLENCOE SKI CENTRE
Etive
A82
RANNOCH MOOR
MUSEUM OF SCOTTISH SKIING AND MOUNTAINEERING
Alltchaorunn
1188
547
GLEN COE
Loch Bà
1099
CLACH LEATHAD
Bà
Loch na h-Achlaise
14
Allt Coire a'Chaolain
Water of Tulla
BLACK MOUNT
Loch an Daimh
Eas Daimh
1090
STOB GHABHAR
WEST HIGHLAND WAY
Loch Tulla
907
MEALL BUIDHE
960
STUCHD AN LOCHAIN
1081
BEINN A' CHREACHAIN
Achallader
227
Black Mount
Forest Lodge
Pubil
Cashlie
Loch Dochard
Inveroran Hotel
Loch Lyon
1004
BIENN AN DOTHAIDH
953
BEINN MHANACH
216
217
Bridge of Orchy
BEINN HEASGARNICH
0 1 2 3 miles
0 1 2 3 4 5 km

Loch Ericht Forest
Ben Alder Lodge
Loch Pattack
CREAGAN MOR
CARN NA CAIM
Cama Choire
Loch an Duin
Sronphadruig Lodge
Dail-na-Mine Forest
SRON A'CHLEIRICH
A'BHUIDHEANACH BHEAG
Ben Alder Forest
BEINN UDLAMAIN
THE SOW OF ATHOLL
Dalnaspidal Lodge
Dalnacardoch Forest
FOREST OF ATHOLL
Loch a' Bhealaich Bheithe
Corrievarkie Lodge
Dalnaspidal Forest
MEALL NA LEITREACH
Dalnacardoch Lodge
GLEN GARRY
GRAMPIAN MOUNTAINS
Talla Bheith Forest
Loch Con
Loch Errochty
Calvine
BEINN MHOLACH
Dalchalloch
Trinafour
NN
Errochty Water
GLEN ERROCHTY
Tummel Forest
SRON BHEAG
BEINN A'CHUALLAICH
Aulich Burn
Killichonan Burn
Craiganor Lodge
Kinloch Rannoch
Tummel Bridge
Dunalastair
Dunalastair Water
Bridge of Ericht
Killichonan
LOCH RANNOCH
Carie
Inverhadden
Foss
Finnart
Bridge of Gaur
Camghouran
Black Wood of Rannoch
Rannoch Forest
Loch Kinardochy
TAY FOREST PARK
SCHIEHALLION
GLENGOULANDIE DEER PARK
LOCH RANNOCH AND GLEN LYON
CARN MAIRG
MEALL A'MHUIC
CARN GORM
Keltneyburn
Appin of Dull
Dull
Camusvrachan
Invervar
ST FILLAN'S CHURCH & FORTINGALL YEW
GLEN LYON GALLERY
Innerwick
Fortingall
Taymouth Castle
Bridge of Balgie
Gallin
Glen Lyon
Kenmore
Fearnan
SCOTTISH CRANNOG CENTRE
Remony
Acharn
Falls of Acharn
LOCH TAY
Lawers Burn
BEN LAWERS
Stronuich Reservoir
Loch na Lairige
MEALL NAN TARMACHAN
BEINN BHREAC
Lawers
Ardtalnaig
BEN LAWERS VISITOR CENTRE
Quaich

1
2
3
4
A
B
C
D
241
242
229
218
219
788
UCHD A'CHLARSAIR
CARN BHA
Tarf Water
104
BEINN IU MHÒ
Loch
Dail-na-Mine Forest
816
SRON A'CHLEIRICH
Glen Bruar
1008
BEINN DEARG
879
BRAIGH SRON GHORM
Tilt
Bruar Lodge
899
Loch Loch
FOREST OF ATHOLL
Forest Lodge
TUL
Allt a' Mhuilinn
Allt a' Chireachain
ATHOLL
Glen Diridh
1120
BEINN A'GHLO
doch
Glen Tilt
975
CARN LIATH
903
BEN VUIRICH
Gleann Fearnach
A9
GLEN GARRY
Garry
Bruar Water
Falls of the Bruar
CLAN DONNACHAIDH MUSEUM
BLAIR CASTLE
Old Bridge of Tilt
Glen Girnaig
Calvine
Pitagowan
B8079
Lude House
Blair Atholl
BLAIR ATHOLL MILL
Struan
Ballentoul
NN
BLAIR ATHOLL DISTILLERY
TULACH HILL
60
470
10
B847
Errochty Water
GLEN ERROCHTY
ATHOLL COUNTRY COLLECTION
Aldclune
1689
12
Killiecrankie
KILLIECRANKIE VISITOR CENTRE
841
BEN VRACKIE
Dalnavaid
Tarvie
19
Glen Brerachan
Loch Bhac
Tummel Forest
LOCH
Bonskeid House
B8019
A924
477
Tressait
13
Queen's View
A9
641
CREAG DHUBH
PITLOCHRY
Tummel Bridge
B8019
LOCH TUMMEL
QUEEN'S VIEW CENTRE
Falls of Tummel
LINN OF TUMMEL
Moulin
Pitlochry
EDRADOUR DISTILLERY
Loch Faskally
Foss
TUMMEL
Balmore
Milton of Edradour
HYDRO-ELECTRIC VISITOR CENTRE
Loch Broom
TAY
SCOTTISH PLANT COLLECTORS GARDEN
BLAIR ATHOLL DISTILLERY VISITOR CENTRE
534
MEALL REAMHAR
Loch Kinardochy
780
FARRAGON HILL
Loch Derculich
5
Tummel
Milton of Dalcapon
FOREST PARK
Strathtay
Ballechin
B846
A827
Tay
Tulliemet
Grandtully
Edradynate
CLUNY HOUSE GARDENS
10
Little Ballinluig
Balnaguard
Logierait
Ballinluig
13
Keltney Burn
Appin of Dull
CASTLE MENZIES
Weem
ST MARY'S CHURCH
Balmacneil
Loch Ordie
Camserney
Dull
Keltneyburn
ABERFELDY DISTILLERY & DEWAR'S WORLD OF WHISKY
Kindallachan
WADE'S BRIDGE
Aberfeldy
Balnaguard Burn
Bishopric
Kincraigie
Guay
Dowally
509
DEUCHARY HILL
Falls of Moness
Loch Skiach
Taymouth Castle
BOLFRACKS GARDEN
532
B898
8
Dalguise
A827
A826
A9
Craigvinean Forest
Urlar Burn
Loch Kennard
Kenmore
566
STRATH
RIVER
SCOTTISH CRANNOG CENTRE
9
SCOTTISH HORSE REGIMENTAL MUS
Remony
LOCH TAY
Acharn
Falls of Acharn
Loch Hoil
Glen Cochill
Tombane Burn
Ballinloan Burn
CATH
Dunkeld
Little Dun
THE HERMITAGE
Inver
Birn
WATERFALL
Ballinlick
Scotston
690
MEALL DEARG
A822
Trochry
Garrow
60
404
Glen Quaich
Cablea
Strathbraan
Obney Hills
Loch
0 1 2 3 miles
0 1 2 3 4 5 km

An Socach
Loch Vrotachan
Glenshee Ski Centre
The Cairnwell
Devil's Elbow
Glas Maol
Caenlochan Forest
Carn an Tuirc
Tolmount
Broad Cairn
Lair of Aldararie
Glen Doll
Glendoll Lodge
Glendoll Forest
Braedownie
Corrie Fee
Finalty Hill
Driesh
Clova
Glen Clova
Ben Gulabin
Glenlochsie
Spittal of Glenshee
Ben Earb
Monameanach
Loch Beanie
Auchavan
Glenprosen Lodge
Glen Prosen
Balnaboth
Prosen
Glenprosen Village
Meall Uaine
Glen Shee
Duchray Hill
Badendun Hill
Dalnaglar Castle
Meikle Forter
Folda
Glenisla Forest
Cray
Enochdhu
Mount Blair
Brewlands Bridge
Backwater Res.
Glenhead Farm
Easter Lednathie
Ashintully Castle
Freuchies
Cat Law
Strathardle
Kirkmichael
Blacklunans
Kirkton of Glenisla
Bellaty
Creigh Hill
Balintore
Cairn Gibbs
Dykends
Black Water
Knock of Balmyle
Forest of Alyth
Mile Hill
NO
Loch of Lintrathen
Peel Farm Trail
Bridgend of Lintrathen
Kirkton of Kingoldrum
Loch of Kinnordy Nature Reserve
Ballintuim
Balduff Hill
Reekie Linn Waterfall
Bridge of Craigisla
Auchrannie
Netherton
Tullymurdoch
Kirkton of Airlie
Blackcraig Forest
Bamff
Forest of Clunie
Bridge of Cally
Shanzie
Craigton
Loch Benachally
Cochrage Muir
Tullyfergus
Ruthven
Ruthven House
Eassie Sculpture Stone
Lornty Burn
Middleton
Alyth
New Alyth
Riechip
Westfields of Rattray
Lornty
Balhary
Castleton
Forneth
Achalader
Blairgowrie
Kinloch
Rattray
Leitfie
Meigle Museum
Balkeerie
Eassie
Loch of Lowes
Concraigie
Loch of Clunie
Loch of Drumellie
River Ericht
Kinloch
Meigle
Kirkinch
Loch of Lowes Nature Reserve
Clunie
Craigie
Muirton of Ardblair
Rosemount
Arthurstone
Wester Denoon
Snaigow House
Kirkton of Lethendy
Lunan Burn
Ardler
Newbigging
Newtyle
Sidlaw Hills
Spittalfield
Keillor
Delvine
Coupar Angus
Tay
Caputh
Meikleour
Beech Hedge
Kettins
Markethill
Hallyburton House
Long Loch
Bonnyton
Gellyburn
Muir
Murthly
Kinclaver
Isla
Campmuir

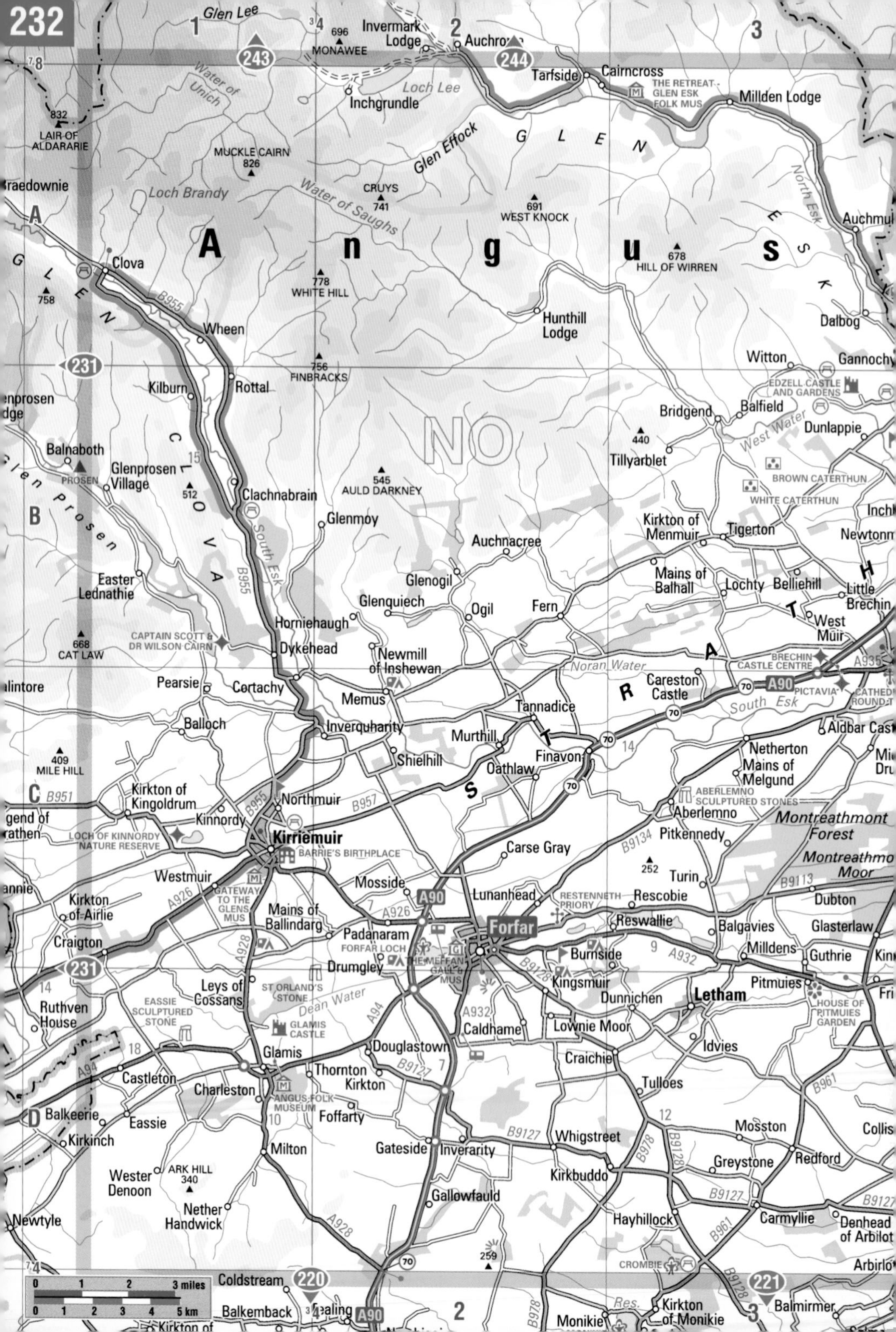
Angus
NO
Glen Lee
Invermark Lodge
Auchronie
MONAWEE
Loch Lee
Inchgrundle
Tarfside
Cairncross
THE RETREAT - GLEN ESK FOLK MUS
Millden Lodge
GLEN ESK
LAIR OF ALDARARIE
Water of Unich
MUCKLE CAIRN
Loch Brandy
Glen Effock
CRUYS
Water of Saughs
WEST KNOCK
HILL OF WIRREN
Auchmull
Braedownie
Clova
GLEN CLOVA
WHITE HILL
Hunthill Lodge
Dalbog
Wheen
FINBRACKS
Witton
Gannochy
EDZELL CASTLE AND GARDENS
Rottal
Kilburn
Glenprosen Lodge
Bridgend
Balfield
Dunlappie
West Water
Tillyarblet
Balnaboth
PROSEN
Glenprosen Village
Glen Prosen
AULD DARKNEY
BROWN CATERTHUN
WHITE CATERTHUN
Clachnabrain
South Esk
Glenmoy
Kirkton of Menmuir
Tigerton
Inchbare
Newtonmill
Auchnacree
Mains of Balhall
Lochty
Belliehill
Little Brechin
Easter Lednathie
Glenogil
Glenquiech
Ogil
Fern
West Muir
STRATHMORE
CAT LAW
CAPTAIN SCOTT & DR WILSON CAIRN
Horniehaugh
Dykehead
Newmill of Inshewan
Noran Water
BRECHIN CASTLE CENTRE
Balintore
Pearsie
Cortachy
Memus
Careston Castle
PICTAVIA
CATHEDRAL ROUND TOWER
Balloch
Inverquharity
Tannadice
Murthill
Aldbar Castle
MILE HILL
Shielhill
Oathlaw
Finavon
Netherton
Mains of Melgund
Kirkton of Kingoldrum
Northmuir
Legend of Lintrathen
Kinnordy
ABERLEMNO SCULPTURED STONES
Aberlemno
LOCH OF KINNORDY NATURE RESERVE
Kirriemuir
BARRIE'S BIRTHPLACE
Pitkennedy
Montreathmont Forest
Montreathmont Moor
Carse Gray
Westmuir
GATEWAY TO THE GLENS MUS
Mosside
Turin
Lunanhead
RESTENNETH PRIORY
Rescobie
Dubton
Kirkton of Airlie
Mains of Ballindarg
Padanaram
Forfar
Reswallie
Balgavies
Glasterlaw
Craigton
FORFAR LOCH
THE MEFFAN GALLERY & MUS
Burnside
Milldens
Guthrie
Drumgley
Kingsmuir
Leys of Cossans
ST ORLAND'S STONE
Dunnichen
Letham
Pitmuies
HOUSE OF PITMUIES GARDEN
EASSIE SCULPTURED STONE
Dean Water
Ruthven House
GLAMIS CASTLE
Caldhame
Lownie Moor
Douglastown
Glamis
Craichie
Idvies
Castleton
Thornton Kirkton
Charleston
ANGUS FOLK MUSEUM
Tulloes
Balkeerie
Eassie
Foffarty
Kirkinch
Milton
Gateside
Inverarity
Whigstreet
Mosston
Collision
Greystone
Redford
Wester Denoon
ARK HILL
Kirkbuddo
Gallowfauld
Nether Handwick
Hayhillock
Carmyllie
Denhead of Arbilot
Newtyle
CROMBIE
Arbirlot
Coldstream
Balkemback
Tealing
Monikie
Kirkton of Monikie
Balmirmer
Res.
Kirkton of
0 1 2 3 miles
0 1 2 3 4 5 km

Drumtochty Forest
Glenfarquhar Lodge
Drumtochty Castle
Cairn o' Mount
MELUNCART
525
Dellavaird
BURNS FAMILY MEMORIALS
Drumlithie
Glenbervie
Fiddes
Barras
Mill of Uras
Crawton
FOWLSHEUGH NATURE RESERVE
Crawton Bay
Pitforthie
Mondynes
Monboddo House
Roadside of Catterline
Catterline
Braidon Bay
Todhead Point
Strath Finella
Clatterin Bridge
Glensaugh
Auchenblae
Brownmuir
East Cairnbeg
Fordoun
Parkneuk
Arbuthnott
Roadside of Kinneff
Kinneff
Mains of Balnakettle
FASQUE HOUSE
Thainston
FETTERCAIRN DISTILLERY VISITOR CENTRE
Fettercairn
Howe of the Mearns
Scotston
GRASSIC GIBBON CENTRE
ARBUTHNOTT CHURCH
Mains of Allardice
ARBUTHNOTT HOUSE GARDENS
Little John's Haven
Inverbervie
Bervie Bay
Bent
Mains of Thornton
Laurencekirk
Tulloch
Meikle Strath
Inch of Arnhall
Garvock
Garvock Hill
Redford
DAMSIDE GARDEN HERBS & ARBORETUM
Benholm
Gourdon
MILL OF BENHOLM
Sauchieburn
Luthermuir
Luther Water
Edzell
Dykelands
Johnshaven
North Water Bridge
North Esk
Marykirk
Ecclesgreig
Pert
Craigo
Lochside
St Cyrus
Milton Ness
Logie Pert
Logie
Morphie
ST CYRUS
Keithock
Muirton of Ballochy
Pathhead
Trinity
Hillside
Brechin
HOUSE OF DUN
Kirkhill
Dun
CALEDONIAN RAILWAY
Montrose Basin
Bridge of Dun
Montrose
MUSEUM AND ART GALLERY
Kinnaird Castle
Barnhead
Inchbraoch
Scurdie Ness
WILLIAM LAMB MEMORIAL STUDIO
MONTROSE BASIN VISITOR CENTRE
Ferryden
Farnell
Bonnyton
Maryton
Kirkton of Craig
Carcary
Long Craig
Dunninald
Fishtown of Usan
Rossie Moor
Westerton
Boddin Pt.
Braehead of Lunan
Bolshan
Lunan
LUNAN BAY
Redcastle
Boysack
Inverkeilor
Lang Craig
Lunan Water
Chapelton
Ethie Mains
Leysmill
Cauldcots
Red Head
Ethie Castle
Drunkendub
Letham Grange
Auchmithie
Marywell
Meg's Craig
St Vigeans
ST VIGEANS MUSEUM
Hayshead
Cliffburn
The Deil's Heid
ARBROATH ABBEY
Arbroath
SIGNAL TOWER MUSEUM
Elliot
NO
A
B
C
D
4
5
6
244
245
221

Guirdil Bay
388
246
Kilmory Glen
CANNA 0:55
Kinloch Glen
Rubha na Roinne
A'Bhrideanach
Kinloch
Loch Scresort
571
ORVAL
R Ù M
KINLOCH CASTLE
Rubha Port na Caranean
RÙM
Schooner Pt.
Harris
Glen Harris
812
ASKIVAL
781
AINSHVAL
Rubha Sgorr an t-Snidhe
1:00
THE SMALL ISLES
SOUND OF RÙM
Rubha nam Meirleach
Bay of Laig
Cleadale
Rubha an Fhasaidh
Eigg
393
AN SGURR
SOUND OF EIGG
Eilean nan Each
0:35
137
Port Mor
Muck
Sanna Point
Sanna
Sanna Bay
Portuairk
Achnaha
Point of Ardnamurchan
ARDNAMURCHAN LIGHTHOUSE
Achosnich
B8007
223
Cairns of Coll
Rubha Mor
Eilean Mor
Ormsaigmore
Ormsaigbeg
An Acairseid
Kilchoan Bay
Sorisdale
Bousd
B8072
COLL
Gallanach
224
Ardmore Bay
Ardmore Pt.
0 1 2 3 miles
0 1 2 3 4 5 km

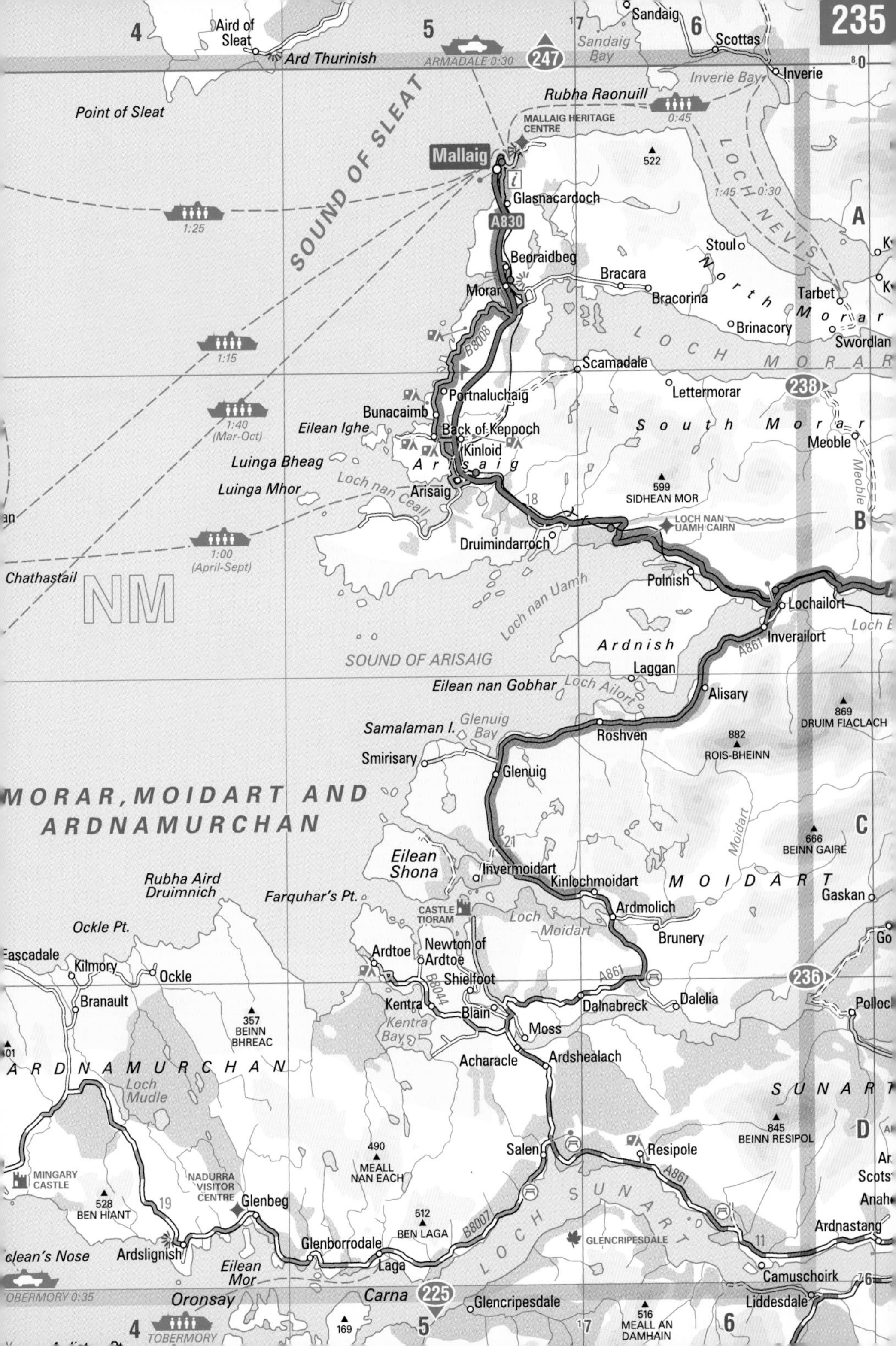

4
5
6
Aird of Sleat
Ard Thurinish
ARMADALE 0:30
247
Sandaig
Sandaig Bay
Scottas
Inverie
Inverie Bay
Point of Sleat
SOUND OF SLEAT
Rubha Raonuill
0:45
MALLAIG HERITAGE CENTRE
Mallaig
522
LOCH NEVIS
1:45
0:30
1:25
Glasnacardoch
A830
A
Stoul
Beoraidbeg
Bracara
Bracorina
North Morar
Tarbet
Morar
Brinacory
Swordlan
B8008
1:15
LOCH MORAR
Scamadale
238
Lettermorar
Portnaluchaig
Bunacaimb
1:40
(Mar-Oct)
Eilean Ighe
Back of Keppoch
South Morar
Meoble
Kinloid
Luinga Bheag
Arisaig
Loch nan Ceall
599
SIDHEAN MOR
Luinga Mhor
18
B
LOCH NAN UAMH CAIRN
Druimindarroch
1:00
(April-Sept)
Chathastail
NM
Polnish
Loch nan Uamh
Lochailort
Inverailort
A861
Ardnish
SOUND OF ARISAIG
Laggan
Eilean nan Gobhar
Loch Ailort
Alisary
869
DRUIM FIACLACH
Samalaman I.
Glenuig Bay
Roshven
882
ROIS-BHEINN
Smirisary
Glenuig
MORAR, MOIDART AND ARDNAMURCHAN
C
666
BEINN GAIRE
21
Eilean Shona
Invermoidart
Rubha Aird Druimnich
Kinlochmoidart
MOIDART
Gaskan
Farquhar's Pt.
Ardmolich
CASTLE TIORAM
Loch Moidart
Ockle Pt.
Brunery
Fascadale
Ardtoe
Newton of Ardtoe
Kilmory
Ockle
Shielfoot
A861
B8044
236
Branault
Kentra
Blain
Dalnabreck
Dalelia
Kentra Bay
357
BEINN BHREAC
Moss
Acharacle
Ardshealach
ARDNAMURCHAN
Loch Mudle
SUNART
845
BEINN RESIPOL
D
490
MEALL NAN EACH
Salen
Resipole
MINGARY CASTLE
NADURRA VISITOR CENTRE
528
BEN HIANT
19
Glenbeg
512
BEN LAGA
B8007
LOCH SUNART
GLENCRIPESDALE
Ardnastang
11
Ardslignish
Glenborrodale
Laga
Eilean Mor
Camuschoirk
TOBERMORY 0:35
Oronsay
Carna
225
Glencripesdale
Liddesdale
169
516
MEALL AN DAMHAIN
TOBERMORY

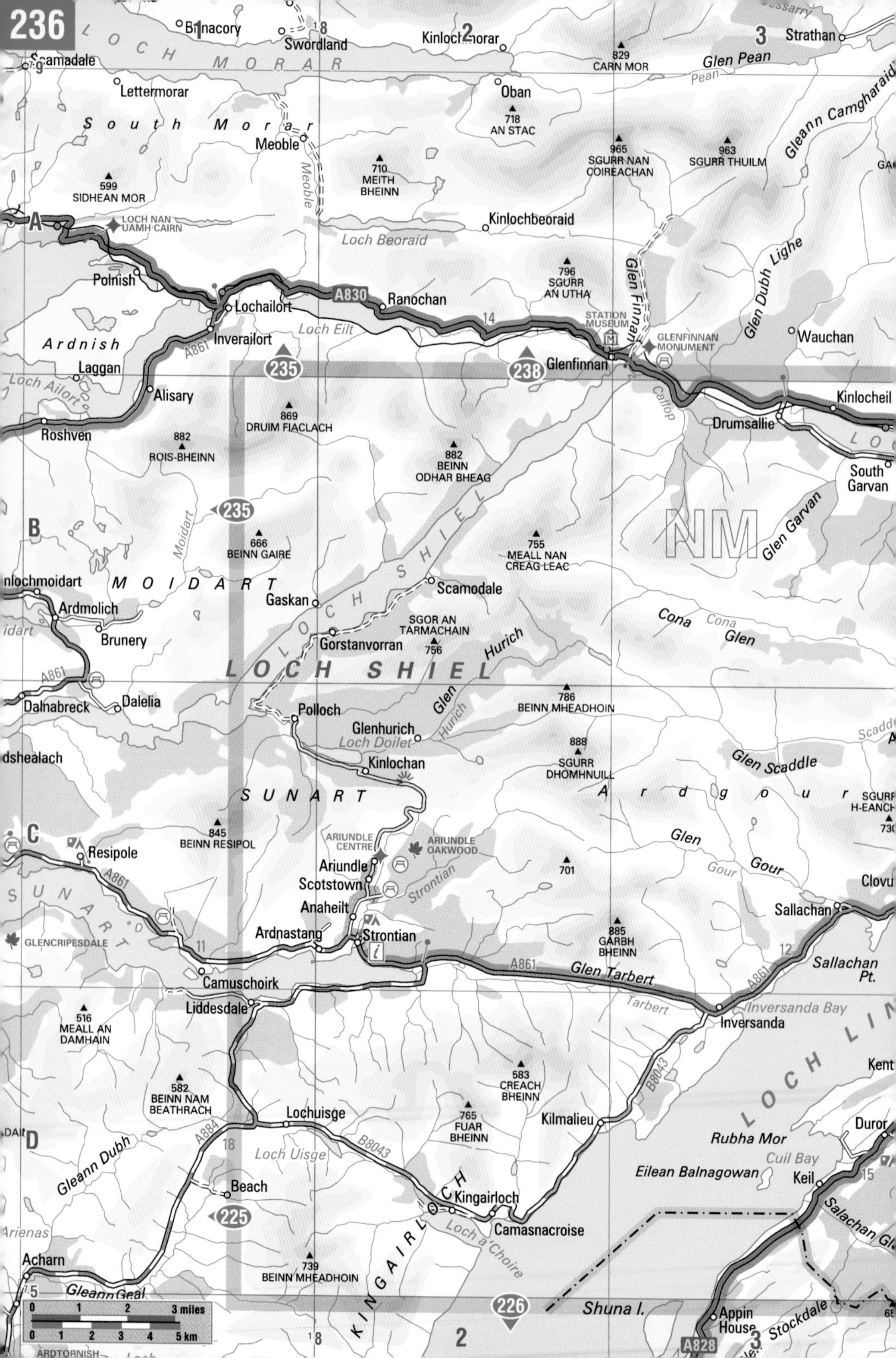
236
Bunacory
Swordland
Kinlochmorar
Strathan
Scamadale
LOCH MORAR
829
CARN MOR
Glen Pean
Pean
Lettermorar
Oban
718
AN STAC
South Morar
Meoble
Gleann Camgharaidh
965
SGURR NAN COIREACHAN
963
SGURR THUILM
710
MEITH BHEINN
599
SIDHEAN MOR
Meoble
LOCH NAN UAMH CAIRN
Kinlochbeoraid
Loch Beoraid
796
SGURR AN UTHA
Glen Finnan
Glen Dubh Lighe
Polnish
Lochailort
A830
Ranochan
Inverailort
Loch Eilt
14
STATION MUSEUM
GLENFINNAN MONUMENT
Wauchan
Ardnish
A861
235
238
Glenfinnan
Laggan
Loch Ailort
Alisary
Callop
Kinlocheil
869
DRUIM FIACLACH
Drumsallie
Roshven
882
ROIS-BHEINN
882
BEINN ODHAR BHEAG
South Garvan
Moidart
235
NM
Glen Garvan
666
BEINN GAIRE
755
MEALL NAN CREAG LEAC
Kinlochmoidart
MOIDART
Scamodale
Ardmolich
Gaskan
Cona
Cona
Glen
Brunery
Gorstanvorran
SGOR AN TARMACHAIN
756
Hurich
A861
LOCH SHIEL
Glen
Dalnabreck
Dalelia
786
BEINN MHEADHOIN
Polloch
Glenhurich
Hurich
Loch Doilet
888
SGURR DHOMHNUILL
Glen Scaddle
Kinlochan
Ardgour
SUNART
ARIUNDLE CENTRE
ARIUNDLE OAKWOOD
845
BEINN RESIPOL
Resipole
Glen
Ariundle
Gour
Gour
701
Scotstown
Strontian
A861
Anaheilt
Clovullin
Sallachan
SUNART
GLENCRIPESDALE
Ardnastang
Strontian
885
GARBH BHEINN
11
A861
Glen Tarbert
12
Sallachan Pt.
Camuschoirk
A861
Liddesdale
Tarbert
Inversanda Bay
Inversanda
516
MEALL AN DAMHAIN
Kentallen
LOCH LINNHE
582
BEINN NAM BEATHRACH
583
CREACH BHEINN
B8043
765
FUAR BHEINN
Lochuisge
Kilmalieu
Rubha Mor
Duror
A884
18
Gleann Dubh
Loch Uisge
B8043
Cuil Bay
Eilean Balnagowan
Keil
15
Beach
LOCH KINGAIRLOCH
Kingairloch
225
Camasnacroise
Salachan Glen
Arienas
Loch a'Choire
Acharn
739
BEINN MHEADHOIN
Gleann Geal
0 1 2 3 miles
0 1 2 3 4 5 km
226
Shuna I.
Appin House
Stockdale
A828
ARDTORNISH
A
B
C
D
1
2
3

LOCH ARKAIG
Ardechvie
Achnasaul
Locheil Forest
Inver Mallie
Glen Mallie
Clunes Forest
Clunes
Achnacarry
Bunarkaig
LOCH LOCHY
Letterfinlay
Altrua
Glen Gloy
PARALLEL ROADS
Upper Glenfintaig
Glen Roy
BEINN BHAN
CLAN CAMERON MUSEUM
Gairlochy
Stronaba
COIRE CEIRSLE HILL
Bohuntine
COMMANDO MEMORIAL
Kilmonivaig
GREAT GLEN WAY
Glen Loy
Gleann Suileag
Druim Fada
Glen Loy Forest
Strone
Brackletter
Highbridge
Spean Bridge
Inverroy
Roybridge
Achluachrach
Muirshearlich
Killiechonate
MONESSIE FALLS
Fassfern
A830
TOR CASTLE
TREASURES OF THE EARTH
Corpach
Banavie
NEPTUNE'S STAIRCASE LOCKS
Torlundy
Leanachan Forest
BEINN CHLIANAIG
NEVIS RANGE SKI CENTRE
Duisky
Blaich
Caol
Lochyside
INVERLOCHY CASTLE
BEN NEVIS DISTILLERY VISITOR CENTRE
Achaphubuil
Camusnagaul
Inverlochy
Claggan
Trislaig
Fort William
NN
Achintee
WEST HIGHLAND MUSEUM
STOB CHOIRE CLAURIGH
Lairig Leacach
STOB COIRE A'CHEARCAILL
Stronchreggan
Ach'an Todhair
GLEN NEVIS VISITOR CENTRE
GLEN NEVIS
Glen Nevis House
Water of Nevis
1344 BEN NEVIS
1234 AONACH BEAG
Druimarbin
Conaglen House
Blarmachfoldach
Creaguaineach Lodge
Coruanan Lodge
Inverscaddle Bay
Achriabhach
Amhainn Rath
Blar a'Chaorainn
1099 SGURR A' MHAIM
1130 BINNEIN MOR
BEINN NA GUCAIG
WEST HIGHLAND WAY
MAMORE FOREST
Loch Eilde Beag
Loch Eilde Mor
Glenrigh Forest
Corran Narrows
Inchree
Corran
Keppanach
Onich
MAM NA GUALAINN
Kinlochmore
Kinlochleven
THE ALUMINIUM STORY
BLACKWATER RESERVOIR
North Ballachulish
Loch Leven
GLENCOE AND NORTH LORN FOLK MUSEUM
Glencoe
AONACH 967
South Ballachulish
Ballachulish
A828
GLENCOE
GLENCOE VISITOR CENTRE
Glen Coe
Altnafeadh
BEINN A' CHRULAISTE
Glenduror Forest
Glen an Fhiodh
BEN NEVIS AND GLEN COE
Kingshouse Hotel
Beinn a'Bheithir
BIDEAN NAM BIAN
Royal Forest
GLENCOE SKI CENTRE
Glen Duror
MUSEUM OF SCOTTISH SKIING AND MOUNTAINEERING
FRAOCHAIDH
SGOR NA h-ULAIDH
Dalness
Glen Etive
Alltchaorunn
Glen Creran
BEINN FHIONNLAIDH
Elleric
STOB
CLACH LEATHAD

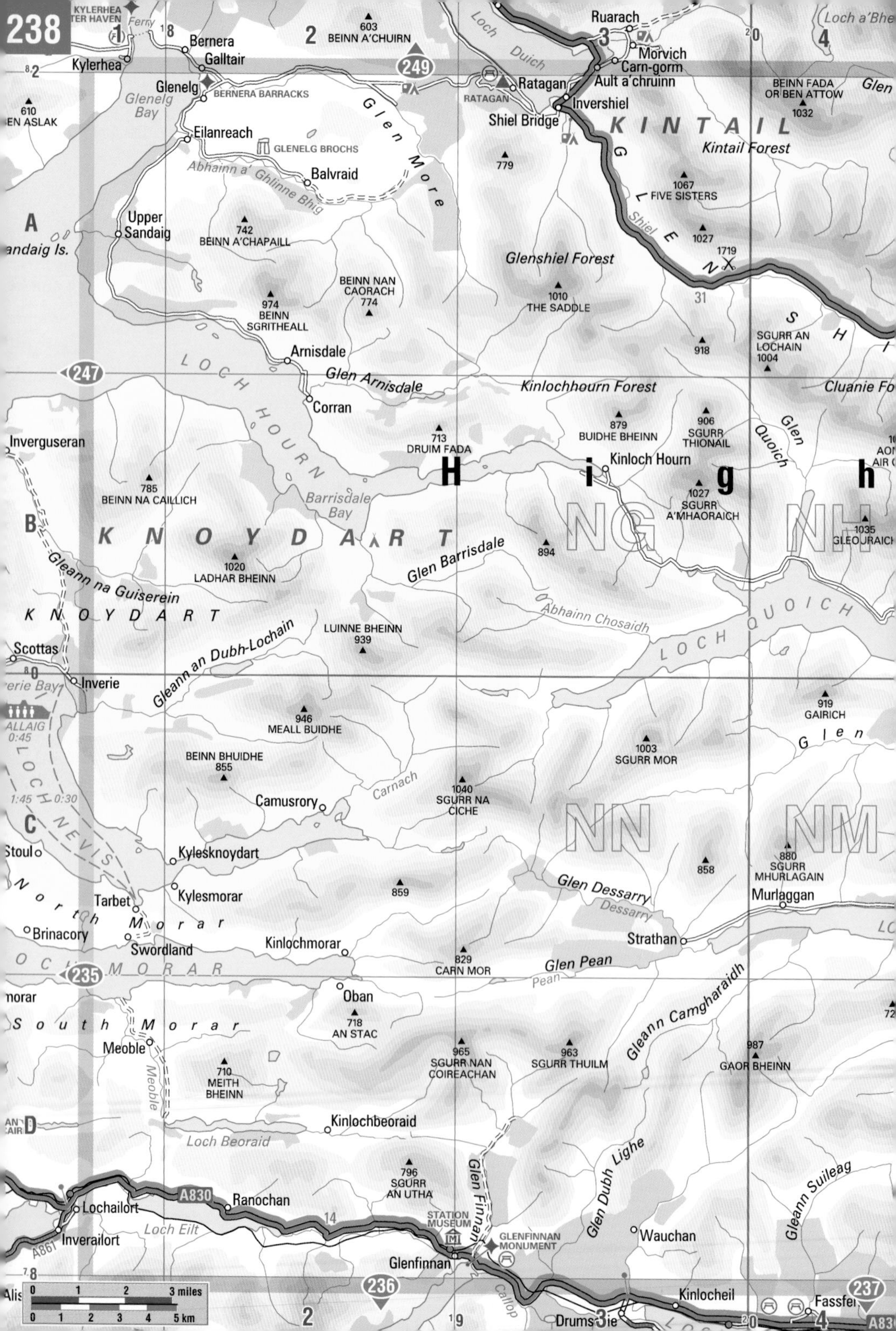

Kylerhea
Bernera
Galltair
Glenelg
Bernera Barracks
Glenelg Bay
Eilanreach
Glenelg Brochs
Balvraid
Glen More
Beinn a'Chuirn 603
249
Loch Duich
Ruarach
Morvich
Carn-gorm
Ault a'chruinn
Ratagan
Inverhiel
Shiel Bridge
Kintail
Kintail Forest
Beinn Fada or Ben Attow 1032
Five Sisters 1067
Glen Shiel
Upper Sandaig
Beinn a'Chapaill 742
Glenshiel Forest
The Saddle 1010
Beinn Sgritheall 974
Beinn nan Caorach 774
Arnisdale
Sgurr an Lochain 1004
247
Loch Hourn
Glen Arnisdale
Corran
Kinlochhourn Forest
Cluanie Forest
Druim Fada 713
Buidhe Bheinn 879
Sgurr Thionail 906
Inverguseran
Kinloch Hourn
Highland
Beinn na Caillich 785
Barrisdale Bay
Sgurr a'Mhaoraich 1027
Knoydart
Glen Barrisdale
Gleouraich 1035
Ladhar Bheinn 1020
Gleann na Guiserein
Abhainn Chosaidh
Loch Quoich
Luinne Bheinn 939
Gleann an Dubh-Lochain
Scottas
Inverie
Gairich 919
Meall Buidhe 946
Sgurr Mor 1003
Beinn Bhuidhe 855
Carnach
Sgurr na Ciche 1040
Camusrory
Loch Nevis
Stoul
Kylesknoydart
Sgurr Mhurlagain 880
Kylesmorar
Glen Dessarry
Tarbet
North Morar
Murlaggan
Brinacory
Swordland
Kinlochmorar
Strathan
Carn Mor 829
Glen Pean
Loch Morar
235
Oban
An Stac 718
South Morar
Gleann Camgharaidh
Meoble
Sgurr nan Coireachan 965
Sgurr Thuilm 963
Gaor Bheinn 987
Meith Bheinn 710
Kinlochbeoraid
Loch Beoraid
Glen Finnan
Glen Dubh Lighe
Sgurr an Utha 796
Gleann Suileag
Lochailort
A830
Ranochan
Inverailort
Loch Eilt
A861
Station Museum
Glenfinnan Monument
Wauchan
Glenfinnan
236
Kinlocheil
237
Fassfern
Callop
0 1 2 3 miles
0 1 2 3 4 5 km

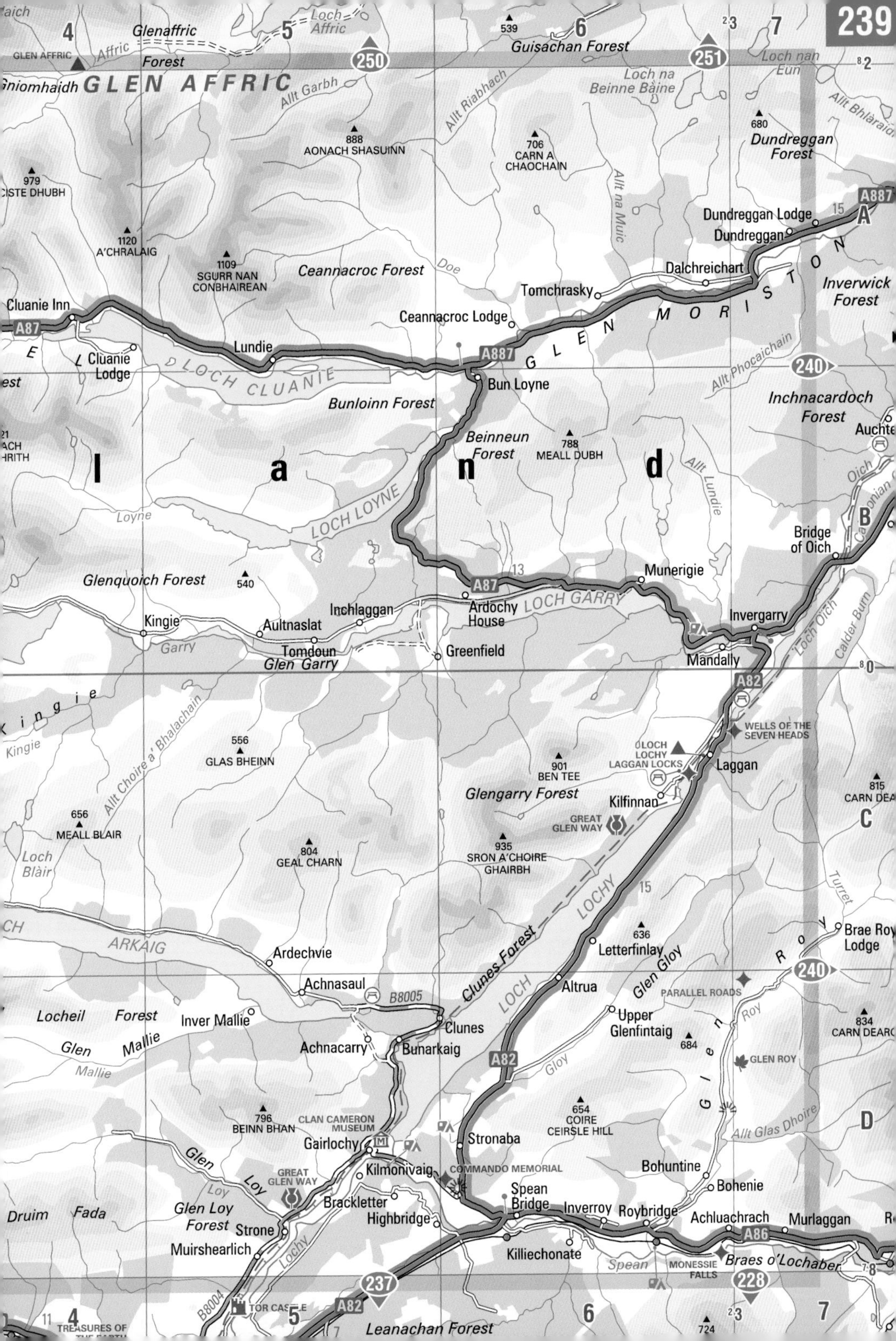
GLEN AFFRIC
Glenaffric Forest
Loch Affric
Guisachan Forest
250
251
Loch nan Eun
Loch na Beinne Bàine
Allt Garbh
Allt Riabhach
888
AONACH SHASUINN
706
CARN A CHAOCHAIN
680
Dundreggan Forest
979
1120
A'CHRALAIG
1109
SGURR NAN CONBHAIREAN
Ceannacroc Forest
Allt na Muic
A887
Dundreggan Lodge
Dundreggan
Dalchreichart
Tomchrasky
GLEN MORISTON
Inverwick Forest
Cluanie Inn
A87
Ceannacroc Lodge
Lundie
Cluanie Lodge
LOCH CLUANIE
Bun Loyne
240
Allt Phocaichain
Inchnacardoch Forest
Bunloinn Forest
Beinneun Forest
788
MEALL DUBH
Allt Lundie
LOCH LOYNE
Loyne
Bridge of Oich
Glenquoich Forest
540
13
Munerigie
Kingie
Aultnaslat
Inchlaggan
Ardochy House
LOCH GARRY
Invergarry
Garry
Tomdoun
Glen Garry
Greenfield
Mandally
A82
Loch Oich
Calder Burn
Kingie
556
GLAS BHEINN
Allt Choire a' Bhalachain
WELLS OF THE SEVEN HEADS
LOCH LOCHY
LAGGAN LOCKS
901
BEN TEE
Laggan
Glengarry Forest
Kilfinnan
815
656
MEALL BLAIR
GREAT GLEN WAY
Loch Blàir
804
GEAL CHARN
935
SRON A'CHOIRE GHAIRBH
LOCHY
Turret
ARKAIG
636
Ardechvie
Letterfinlay
Glen Gloy
Brae Roy Lodge
Achnasaul
Clunes Forest
Altrua
PARALLEL ROADS
B8005
LOCH
Glen Roy
Locheil Forest
Inver Mallie
Clunes
Upper Glenfintaig
834
Glen Mallie
Mallie
Achnacarry
Bunarkaig
684
GLEN ROY
Gloy
796
BEINN BHAN
CLAN CAMERON MUSEUM
654
COIRE CEIRSLE HILL
Allt Glas Dhoire
Gairlochy
Stronaba
Glen Loy
Loy
Kilmonivaig
COMMANDO MEMORIAL
Bohuntine
Bohenie
Spean Bridge
Inverroy
Roybridge
Achluachrach
Murlaggan
Druim Fada
Glen Loy Forest
Brackletter
Highbridge
A86
Strone
Muirshearlich
Lochy
Killiechonate
Spean
MONESSIE FALLS
Braes o'Lochaber
237
228
B8004
TOR CASTLE
A82
TREASURES OF THE EARTH
Leanachan Forest
724

Fort Augustus
Inchnacardoch Forest
Auchteraw
Glen Moriston
Levishie Forest
Levishie
Achnaconeran
Invermoriston
Falls of Moriston
Alltsigh
Creagnaneun Forest
Loch Ness
Foyers
Farigaig Forest
Lyne of Gorthleck
Wester Aberchalder
Lochgarthside
Loch Mhor
Bailebeag
Stratherrick
Whitebridge
Knockie Lodge
Loch Knockie
Portclair Forest
Portclair
Inverness 1:20 (May-Dec)
Great Glen Way
Inverwick Forest
Dundreggan Forest
Dundreggan Lodge
Dundreggan
Inchnacardoch Hotel
Glendoe Lodge
Loch Tarff
Glendoebeg
Clansman Centre
Canal Heritage Centre
Glenbrein Lodge
Garrogie Lodge
Loch Killin
Killin Lodge
Glen Brein
Glen Markie
Carn na Laraich Maoile
Burrach Mor
Allt Cam Ban
Carn Easgann Bana
Carn a'Chuilinn
Glendoe Forest
Glen Tarff
Caledonian Canal
Bridge of Oich
Newtown
Invergarry
Loch Oich
Calder Burn
Meall na h-Aisre
Culachy Forest
Wells of the Seven Heads
Laggan
Carn Dearg
Carn Leac
Corrieyairack Forest
Gairbeinn
Melgarve
Drummin
Spey
Garvamore
Geal Charn
Crathie
Loch Crunachdan
Glenshero Lodge
Strath Mashie
Brae Roy Lodge
Glen Roy
Burn of Agie
Carn Liath
Aberarder Forest
Aberarder Lodge
Cromra
Kinloch Laggan
Aberarder
Creag Meagaidh
Loch Laggan
Moy Forest
Beinn a' Chaoruinn
Moy
Moy Lodge
Lochan na h-Earba
Ardverikie Forest
Beinn Eilde
Murlaggan
Roughburn
Braes o'Lochaber
Bohenie
Geal Charn
Loch Pattack
Ben Alder Lodge
Loch Ericht
A82
A887
A86
B862
B852
251
252
239
228
229

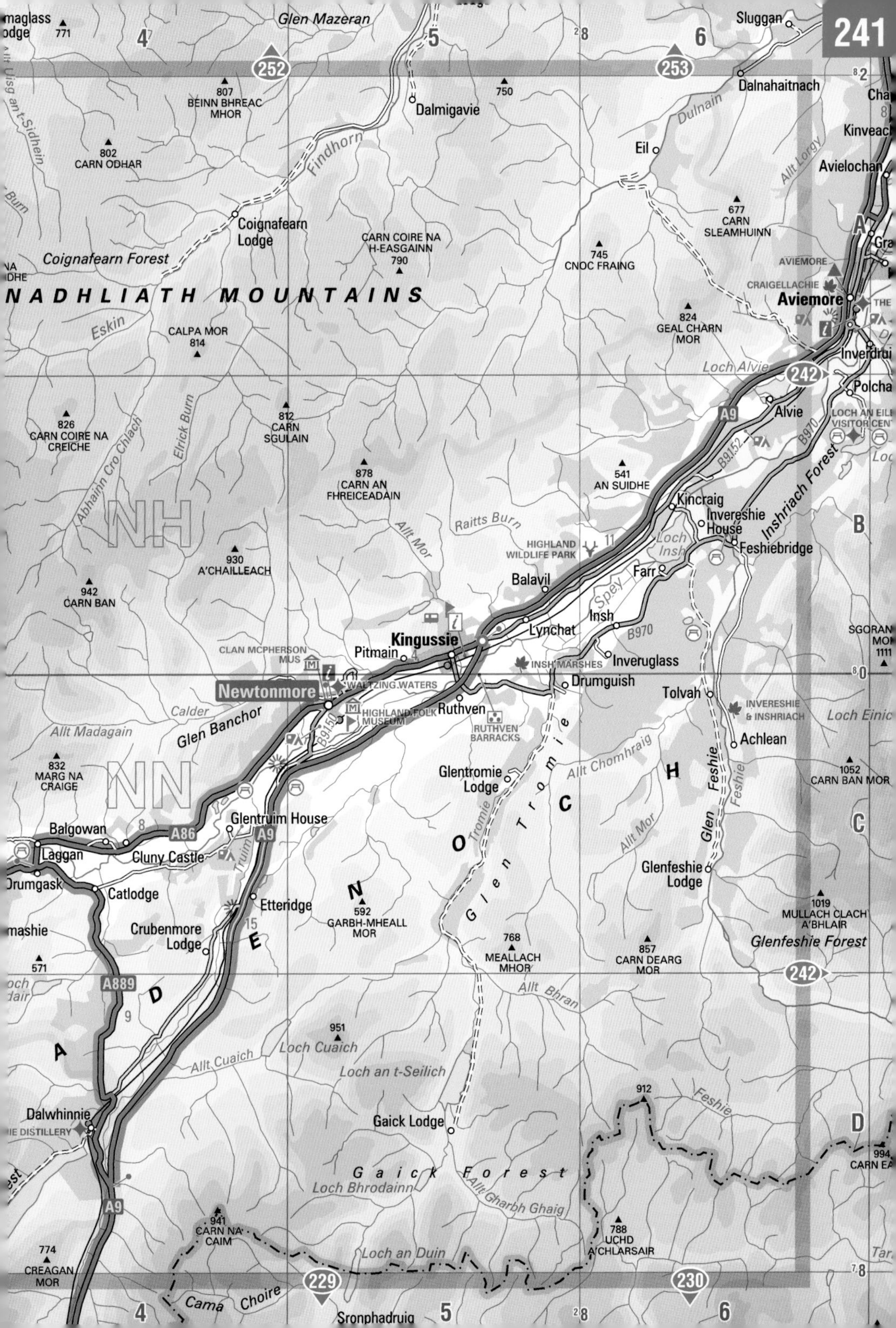

Glen Mazeran
Sluggan
771
252
253
Dalnahaitnach
807
BEINN BHREAC
MHOR
750
Dalmigavie
Dulnain
Kinveac
Eil
Allt Lorgy
802
CARN ODHAR
Findhorn
Avielochan
677
CARN
SLEAMHUINN
Coignafearn
Lodge
CARN COIRE NA
H-EASGAINN
790
745
CNOC FRAING
Coignafearn Forest
AVIEMORE
CRAIGELLACHIE
NADHLIATH MOUNTAINS
Aviemore
824
GEAL CHARN
MOR
Eskin
CALPA MOR
814
Inverdrui
Loch Alvie
242
Polcha
Elrick Burn
812
CARN
SGULAIN
A9
Alvie
826
CARN COIRE NA
CREICHE
Abhainn Cro Chlach
LOCH AN EIL
VISITOR CENT
B9152
B970
878
CARN AN
FHREICEADAIN
541
AN SUIDHE
Inshriach Forest
Kincraig
Invereshie
House
Raitts Burn
NH
Allt Mor
HIGHLAND
WILDLIFE PARK
Loch
Insh
Feshiebridge
930
A'CHAILLEACH
942
CARN BAN
Farr
Balavil
Spey
Insh
Lynchat
B970
SGORAN
1111
Kingussie
CLAN MCPHERSON
MUS
Pitmain
INSH MARSHES
Inveruglass
Newtonmore
WALTZING WATERS
Drumguish
Tolvah
INVERESHIE
& INSHRIACH
Loch Einic
Calder
HIGHLAND FOLK
MUSEUM
Ruthven
Glen Banchor
RUTHVEN
BARRACKS
Allt Madagain
B9150
Achlean
Glen Tromie
832
MARG NA
CRAIGE
NN
Glentromie
Lodge
Allt Chomhraig
H
Feshie
1052
CARN BAN MOR
C
Glentruim House
Balgowan
A86
Laggan
Cluny Castle
Truim
O
Tromie
Allt Mor
Glen
Glenfeshie
Lodge
Drumgask
Catlodge
N
Etteridge
592
GARBH-MHEALL
MOR
1019
MULLACH CLACH
A'BHLAIR
mashie
Crubenmore
Lodge
E
768
MEALLACH
MHOR
857
CARN DEARG
MOR
Glenfeshie Forest
571
A889
D
Allt Bhran
951
Loch Cuaich
A
Allt Cuaich
Loch an t-Seilich
912
Feshie
Dalwhinnie
DISTILLERY
Gaick Lodge
994
CARN EA
Gaick Forest
Loch Bhrodainn
Allt Gharbh Ghaig
941
CARN NA
CAIM
788
UCHD
A'CHLARSAIR
774
CREAGAN
MOR
Loch an Duin
229
230
Cama Choire
Sronphadruig
4
5
6

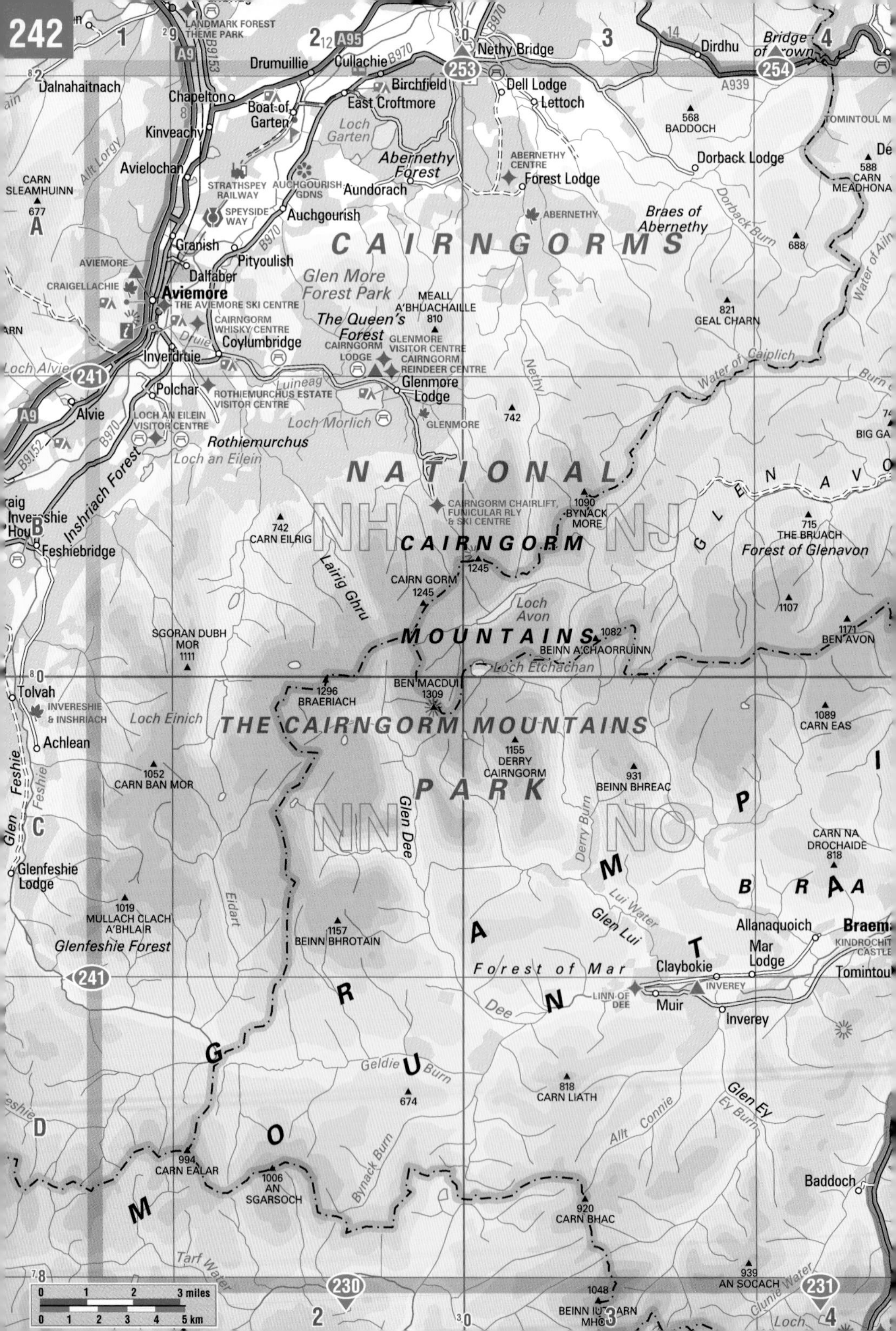

Aviemore
Nethy Bridge
Boat of Garten
Cairngorms National Park
The Cairngorm Mountains
Cairngorm Mountains
Ben Macdui 1309
Cairn Gorm 1245
Braeriach 1296
Glenmore Lodge
Coylumbridge
Rothiemurchus
Forest of Mar
Grampian Mountains
Braemar
Claybokie
Inverey
Linn of Dee
Glenfeshie Forest
Forest of Glenavon
Abernethy Forest
Glen More Forest Park
Loch Morlich
Loch an Eilein
Loch Einich
Loch Avon
Loch Etchachan
Carn Eas 1089
Ben Avon 1171
Beinn Bhrotain 1157
Carn Ealar 994
An Sgarsoch 1006
Carn Bhac 920
Carn Liath 818
An Socach 939
Derry Cairngorm 1155
Beinn Bhreac 931
Sgoran Dubh Mor 1111
Carn Ban Mor 1052
Mullach Clach a'Bhlair 1019
Glenfeshie Lodge
Feshiebridge
Inshriach Forest
Dalnahaitnach
Carrbridge
Kinveachy
Avielochan
Dorback Lodge
Forest Lodge
Dell Lodge
Lettoch
Dirdhu
Bridge of Brown
0 1 2 3 miles
0 1 2 3 4 5 km

Clashnoir
Braes of Glenlivet
Chapeltown
HILL OF THREE STONES
254
255
Tomintoul
TOMINTOUL
588
GLENLIVET ESTATE VISITOR CENTRE
804 CARN MOR
LADDER HILLS
Badenyon
Glenbuchat Lodge
Water of Buchat
Rinmore
Kildrummy
Belnacraig
KILDRUMMY CASTLE & GARDEN
658
Water of Nochty
Conglass Water
Kirkton of Glenbuchat
Blairnamarrow
718 THE SOCACH
A97
Glenkindie
Towie
LECHT SKI CENTRE
A939
Bellabeg
Forbestown
Strathdon
Glen Ernan
Ernan Water
Inverernan Ho.
A944
Candacraig Ho.
Heugh-head
792 CARN EALASAID
711
673
Boultenstone
244
Tornashean Forest
Don
Avon
Allt Tuileach
Colnabaichin
531 CRAIG OF BUNZEACH
Hillockhead
Delnadamph
Cock Bridge
Corgarff
Tornahaish
CORGARFF CASTLE
Deskry Water
Migvie
Coynach
749
Loch Builg
823 BROWN COW HILL
744
871 MORVEN
Logie Coldstone
Glen Fenzie
Milton of Logie
Glendavan Ho.
Gairnshiel Lodge
Gairn
Lary
MUIR OF DINNET
604
BURN O VAT
B976
Glen Gairn
A93
B9119
900 CULARDOCH
743 GEALLAIG HILL
Milton of Tullich
Muir of Dinnet
Bush Crathie
Coilacriech
Culsh
Bridge of Gairn
Glascorrie
CRATHIE CHURCH
Crathie
Dee
Littlemill
MCEWAN GALLERY
Ballater
Glen Tanar
BALMORAL CASTLE AND GARDENS
House of Glenmuick
529
Inver
Invergelder
Easter Balmoral
ROYAL LOCHNAGAR DISTILLERY VISITOR CENTRE
Birkhall
Girnock Burn
BRAEMAR CASTLE
Invercauld House
Mill of Sterin
Water of Tanar
GLEN TANAR
601
Glen Gelder
CLACHAN YELL
526
BRAEMAR
Aucholzie
Ballochbuie Forest
LINN OF MUICK WATERFALL
DEESIDE AND LOCHNAGAR
Forest of Glen Tanar
Auchallater
Muick
Glen Muick
BALMORAL FOREST
939 MOUNT KEEN
850 CONACHCRAIG
1150 LOCHNAGAR
GLENMUICK VISITOR CENTRE
721 FASHEILACH
Burn of Branny
Callater Burn
Spittal of Glenmuick
Glen Mark
834
Glen Callater
Loch Callater
Dubh Loch
Water of Mark
Glas-allt Shiel
1012 CAIRN BANNOCH
Loch Muick
Glen Lee
998 BROAD CAIRN
696 MONAWEE
Invermark Lodge
1019 CARN AN TUIRC
958 TOLMOUNT
231
232
Water of Unich
Loch Lee
Inchgrundle
832
A
B
C
D
4
5
6
7
8
9
10
11
12
17

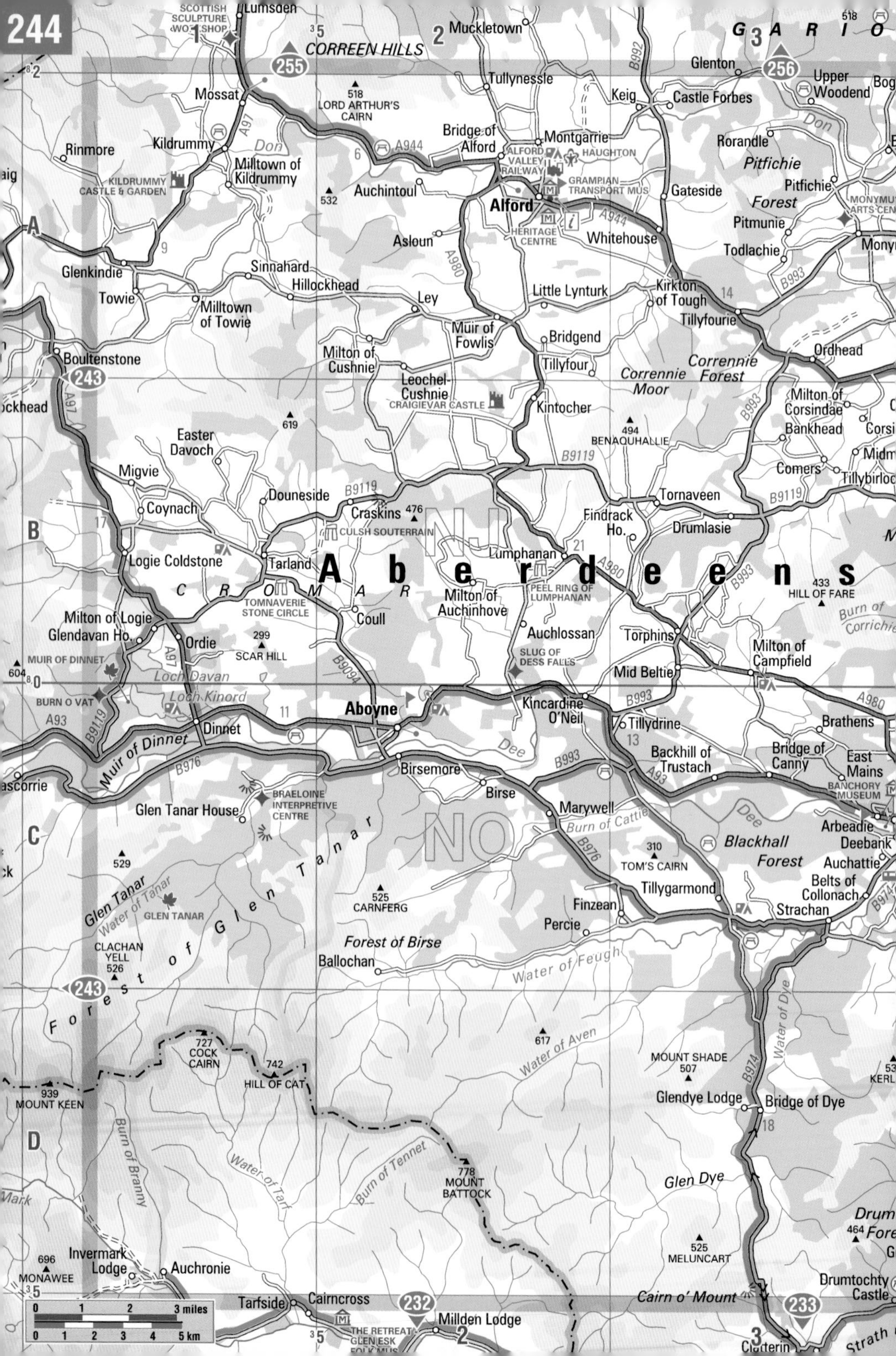
SCOTTISH SCULPTURE WORKSHOP
Lumsden
CORREEN HILLS
255
Muckletown
GARIO
256
Glenton
Upper Woodend
Tullynessle
Mossat
518
LORD ARTHUR'S CAIRN
Keig
Castle Forbes
Rinmore
Kildrummy
A97
Don
A944
Bridge of Alford
Montgarrie
Rorandle
Pitfichie
Milltown of Kildrummy
KILDRUMMY CASTLE & GARDEN
ALFORD VALLEY RAILWAY
HAUGHTON
GRAMPIAN TRANSPORT MUS
Auchintoul
532
Gateside
Pitfichie Forest
MONYMUSK ARTS CENTRE
Alford
HERITAGE CENTRE
Pitmunie
Asloun
Whitehouse
Todlachie
A980
Glenkindie
Sinnahard
Hillockhead
Little Lynturk
Kirkton of Tough
B993
Towie
Milltown of Towie
Ley
Tillyfourie
Muir of Fowlis
Bridgend
Ordhead
Milton of Cushnie
Tillyfour
Correnie Moor
Corrennie Forest
Boultenstone
243
Leochel-Cushnie
CRAIGIEVAR CASTLE
Milton of Corsindae
ockhead
Kintocher
619
494
BENAQUHALLIE
Bankhead
Easter Davoch
B9119
Migvie
Comers
Tillybirloch
Douneside
Tornaveen
Coynach
Craskins
476
Findrack Ho.
Drumlasie
CULSH SOUTERRAIN
NJ
Logie Coldstone
Tarland
Lumphanan
Aberdeenshire
CROMAR
433
HILL OF FARE
PEEL RING OF LUMPHANAN
Milton of Auchinhove
TOMNAVERIE STONE CIRCLE
Coull
Burn of Corrichie
Milton of Logie
Glendavan Ho.
Ordie
Auchlossan
Torphins
Milton of Campfield
299
SCAR HILL
MUIR OF DINNET
604
SLUG OF DESS FALLS
Mid Beltie
Loch Davan
B9094
Loch Kinord
BURN O VAT
Aboyne
Kincardine O'Neil
A980
A93
B9119
Dinnet
Tillydrine
Brathens
Muir of Dinnet
Dee
Backhill of Trustach
Bridge of Canny
East Mains
B976
Birsemore
ascorrie
BANCHORY MUSEUM
Birse
BRAELOINE INTERPRETIVE CENTRE
Glen Tanar House
Marywell
Burn of Cattie
Arbeadie
NO
Deebank
310
TOM'S CAIRN
Blackhall Forest
Auchattie
529
Belts of Collonach
Glen Tanar
Water of Tanar
GLEN TANAR
525
CARNFERG
Tillygarmond
Finzean
Strachan
Forest of Glen Tanar
Percie
Forest of Birse
CLACHAN YELL
526
Ballochan
Water of Feugh
617
Water of Dye
Water of Aven
727
COCK CAIRN
742
HILL OF CAT
MOUNT SHADE
507
939
MOUNT KEEN
B974
Glendye Lodge
Bridge of Dye
Burn of Branny
Water of Tarf
Burn of Tennet
778
MOUNT BATTOCK
Glen Dye
Mark
Drum Forest
464
696
MONAWEE
Invermark Lodge
Auchronie
525
MELUNCART
Drumtochty Castle
Tarfside
Cairncross
232
Millden Lodge
Cairn o' Mount
233
THE RETREAT GLEN ESK FOLK MUS
Clatterin
Strath
0 1 2 3 miles
0 1 2 3 4 5 km

Inverurie
Tillykerrie
Straloch
Ardo Ho.
Delfrig
Manar Ho.
Middlemuir
Port Elphinstone
Kinmuck
Middleton
Newmachar
Craigie
Causeyend
Burnhervie
Aquhythie
KINKELL CHURCH
Balbithan Ho.
Whitecairns
Belhelvie
BALMEDIE
Balmedie
Dalmadilly
Clovenstone
Balbithan
Wester Fintray
Cairnpark
Kinmundy
Grantlodge
Drumligair
Kemnay
Cottown
Kintore
Hatton of Fintray
Cothall
OLD CHURCH
Potterton
Corby Loch
Craigearn
Leylodge
Overton
Parkhill Ho.
Blackdog
Dyce
Mundurno
Lauchintilly
CASTLE FRASER
Blackburn
ABERDEEN
KIRKWALL 6:00
LERWICK 12:30
Haughs of Clinterty
Aberdeen
Stoneywood
Denmore
Achath
Lyne of Skene
East Auchronie
Bankhead
Bridge of Don
Hayton
BRIG O' BALGOWNIE
CRUICKSHANK BOTANIC GARDEN
ST MACHAR'S CATHEDRAL
Kinnernie
Dunecht
Skene Ho.
Bucksburn
City
Woodside
Old Aberdeen
Kirkton of Skene
Kittybrewster
KING'S COLLEGE VISITOR CENTRE
STONE CIRCLE
Loch of Skene
Northfield
Mastrick
Westhill
Kingswells
Aberdeen
Marionburgh
Echt
Elrick
SATROSPHERE
MARISCHAL MUSEUM
Garlogie
Cairnie
ABERDEEN
Ferryhill
GORDON HIGHLANDERS MUSEUM
Torry
Girdle Ness
South Kirkton
Mannofield
DAVID WELCH WINTER GARDENS
Nigg Bay
Leuchar Burn
Blacktop
Easter Ord
Greg Ness
Redhill
Landerberry
Ruthrieston
Kincorth
Cults
Bieldside
Garthdee
Benthoul
Contlaw
West Cullery
Milton of Murtle
Nigg
Hardgate
Craigton
Milltimber
Banchory-Devenick
Cove Bay
Charlestown
DRUM CASTLE
Peterculter
Hirn
Kirkton of Maryculter
Auchlunies
Hare Ness
Myrebird
Drumoak
Mains of Drum
Marywell
The Neuk
CRATHES CASTLE AND GARDENS
Hillside
Findon Ness
Findon
Woodside of Arbeadie
Crathes
Muirskie
Auchlee
ROYAL DEESIDE RLY
Kirkton of Durris
Woodlands
Portlethen
Banchory
Denside
Upper Burnhaugh
Downies
Cammachmore Bay
Bridge of Feugh
Cammachmore
Crossroads
Durris Forest
Borrowfield
Newtonhill
Netherley
Cookney
Muchalls
Lochton
CAIRN MON EARN
378
Bridge of Muchalls
RAEDYKES ROMAN CAMP
Union Cottage
376
MONGOUR
Mergie
Rickarton
Burn of Sheeoch
Cowie Water
Garron Pt.
Cowie
Kirktown of Fetteresso
Fetteresso Forest
Tewel
TOLBOOTH MUSEUM
Stonehaven
Castle Haven
DUNNOTTAR CASTLE
Tannachie
Carmont
New Mill
Thornyhive Bay
Mains of Dellavaird
BURNS FAMILY MEMORIALS
Drumlithie
Glenbervie
Fiddes
Mill of Uras
Barras
Crawton
Pitforthie
Crawton Bay
Monboddo House
Mondynes
Roadside of Catterline
Catterline
A90
A96
A93
A944
A947
A956
A957
A92
B979
B977
B999
B997
B993
B994
B9126
B9119
B9125
B9077
256
257
233
A
B
C
D
4
5
6

488
ABHAL BHEAG
Loch Varkasaig
Balmore
Ose
258
B885
A863
Glenmore
Loch Duagrich
Tungadal
Mugeary
Heatherfield
417
259
A87
Bracadale
Harlosh I.
Tarner I.
Ullinish
Struan
Coillore
Loch Bracadale
Wiay
Idrigill Point
MACLEOD'S MAIDENS
Oronsay
Portnalong
Fiskavaig
Rubha nan Clach
B8009
Loch Harport
439
ROINEVAL
Varragill
Glen Varragill
Fernilea
ARNAVAL
369
TALISKER DISTILLERY
Carbost
Drynoch
Crossal
A863
Gleann Oraid
Merkadale
Drynoch
Talisker Bay
Talisker
Sligachan Hotel
Eynort
Glen Brittle Forest
Eynort
Grula
445
BEINN BHREAC
459
SGURR NAN GILLEAN
964
Glen Sligachan
NG
M I N G I N I S
Loch Eynort
Brittle
Glen Brittle
SGURR A'GHREADAIDH
973
THE CU
GLENBRITTLE
CUILLIN HILLS
Glenbrittle House
Bualintur
Loch Coruisk
992
SGURR ALASDAIR
924
SGURR NAN EAG
Loch Brittle
Rubh an Dunain
Soay Sound
Soay
Mol-chlach
PRINCE
Canna
Garrisdale Pt.
A'Chill
Canna Harbour
Sanday
Rubha Shamhnan Insir
Kilmory
Sound of Canna
Guirdil Bay
Kilmory Glen
0:55
388
A'Bhrideanach
Kinloch Glen
Rubha na Roinne
234
Kinloch
Loch Scresort
571
ORVAL
R Ù M
KINLOCH CASTLE
Rubha Port
0 1 2 3 miles
0 1 2 3 4 5 km
A
B
C
D
1
2
3

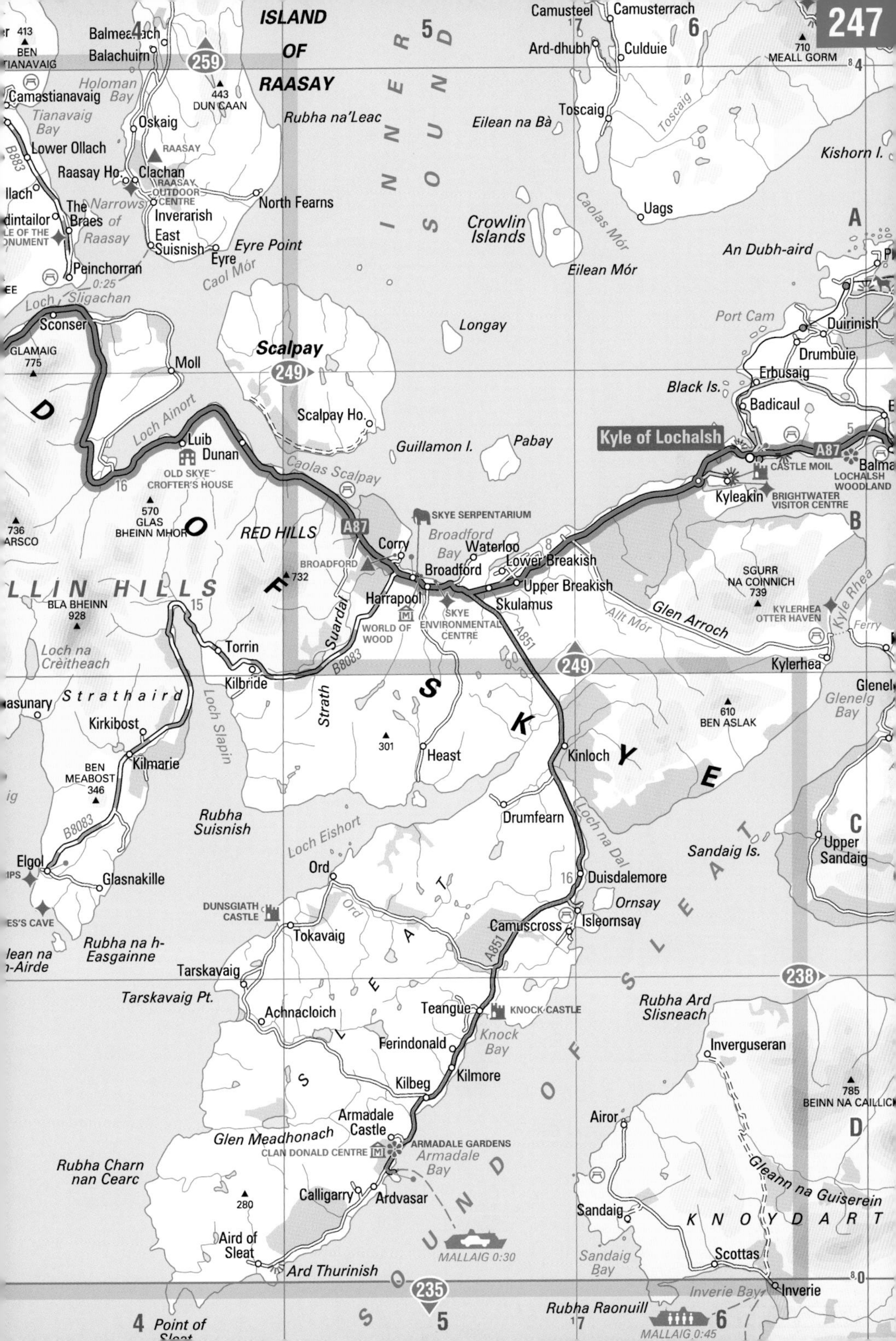
ISLAND OF RAASAY
Balmeanach
Balachuirn
259
443 DUN CAAN
Holoman Bay
Camastianavaig
Tianavaig Bay
Oskaig
Rubha na'Leac
INNER SOUND
Lower Ollach
B883
RAASAY
Raasay Ho.
Clachan
RAASAY OUTDOOR CENTRE
North Fearns
The Braes
Narrows of Raasay
Inverarish
East Suisnish
Eyre Point
Eyre
Peinchorran
Caol Mór
Loch Sligachan
Sconser
GLAMAIG 775
Moll
Scalpay
249
Loch Ainort
Luib
Dunan
OLD SKYE CROFTER'S HOUSE
Scalpay Ho.
Caolas Scalpay
570 GLAS BHEINN MHOR
736
RED HILLS
A87
CUILLIN HILLS
BLA BHEINN 928
732
BROADFORD
Corry
Harrapool
Suardal
WORLD OF WOOD
Torrin
Loch na Crèitheach
Kilbride
B8083
Strathaird
Kirkibost
Loch Slapin
Strath
BEN MEABOST 346
Kilmarie
Rubha Suisnish
Elgol
Glasnakille
Camusteel
Camusterrach
Ard-dhubh
Culduie
Toscaig
Eilean na Bà
Crowlin Islands
Caolas Mór
Eilean Mór
Uags
Longay
Guillamon I.
Pabay
SKYE SERPENTARIUM
Broadford Bay
Waterloo
Broadford
Lower Breakish
Upper Breakish
Skulamus
SKYE ENVIRONMENTAL CENTRE
A851
S K Y E
Heast
301
Kinloch
Drumfearn
Loch Eishort
Ord
DUNSGIATH CASTLE
Tokavaig
Tarskavaig
Tarskavaig Pt.
Rubha na h-Easgainne
Achnacloich
Teangue
KNOCK CASTLE
Knock Bay
Ferindonald
Kilmore
Kilbeg
SLEAT
Armadale Castle
ARMADALE GARDENS
CLAN DONALD CENTRE
Armadale Bay
Glen Meadhonach
Rubha Charn nan Cearc
280
Calligarry
Ardvasar
Aird of Sleat
Ard Thurinish
MALLAIG 0:30
235
Point of Sleat
Duisdalemore
Ornsay
Isleornsay
Camuscross
Loch na Dal
SOUND OF SLEAT
710 MEALL GORM
Kishorn I.
An Dubh-aird
Port Cam
Duirinish
Drumbuie
Erbusaig
Black Is.
Badicaul
Kyle of Lochalsh
CASTLE MOIL
LOCHALSH WOODLAND
Kyleakin
BRIGHTWATER VISITOR CENTRE
SGURR NA COINNICH 739
KYLERHEA OTTER HAVEN
Kyle Rhea
Ferry
Glen Arroch
Allt Mór
Kylerhea
610 BEN ASLAK
Glenelg Bay
Sandaig Is.
Upper Sandaig
238
Rubha Ard Slisneach
Inverguseran
785 BEINN NA CAILLICH
Airor
Gleann na Guiserein
KNOYDART
Sandaig
Sandaig Bay
Scottas
Inverie Bay
Inverie
Rubha Raonuill
MALLAIG 0:45

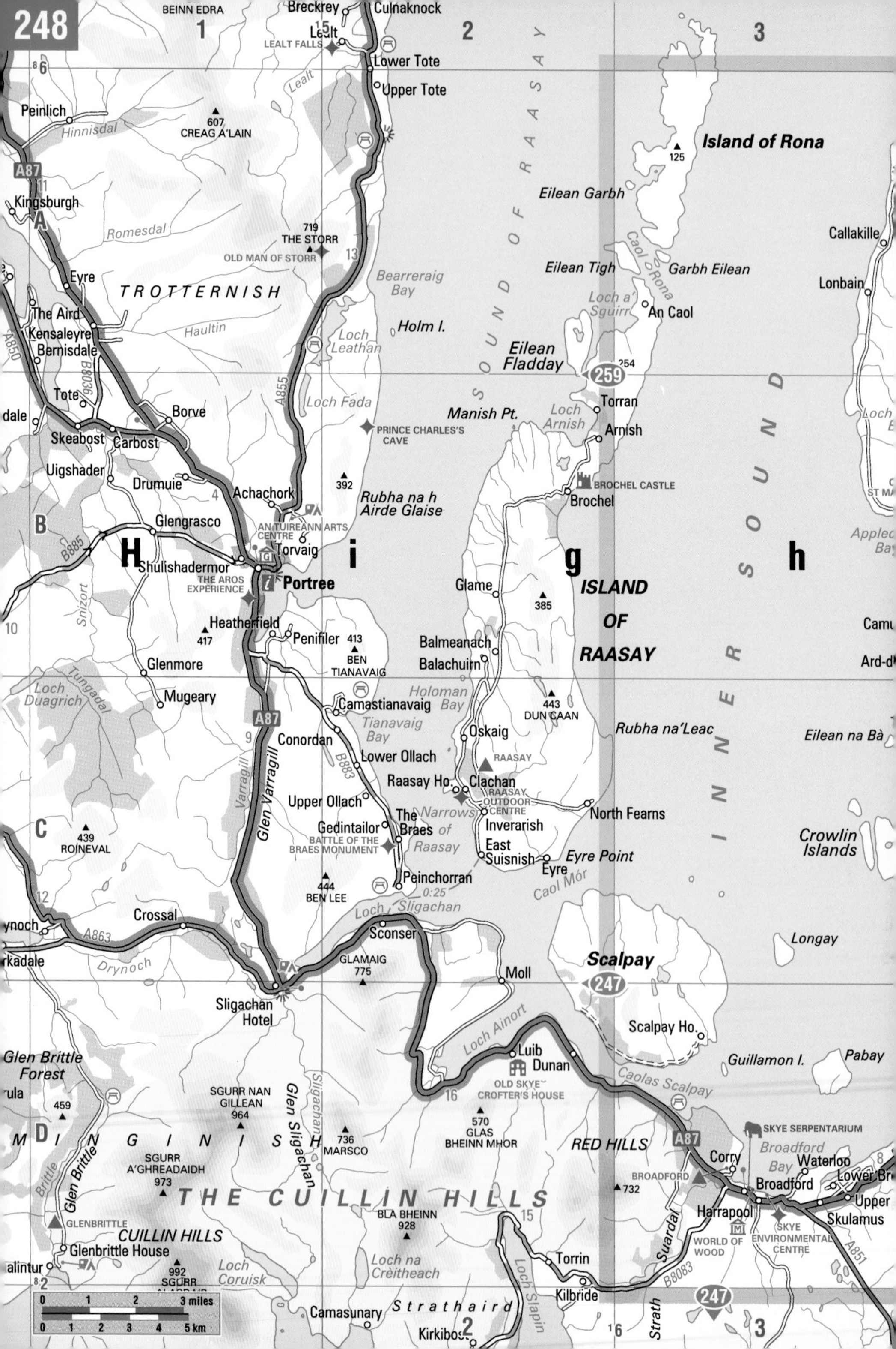

BEINN EDRA
Breckrey
Culnaknock
Lealt
LEALT FALLS
Lower Tote
Upper Tote
Lealt
Peinlich
Hinnisdal
607
CREAG A'LAIN
A87
Kingsburgh
Romesdal
719
THE STORR
OLD MAN OF STORR
Bearreraig Bay
Eyre
TROTTERNISH
The Aird
Kensaleyre
Bernisdale
Haultin
Loch Leathan
Holm I.
Loch Fada
A855
A850
B8036
Tote
Borve
dale
Skeabost
Carbost
Uigshader
Drumuie
Achachork
PRINCE CHARLES'S CAVE
392
Rubha na h Airde Glaise
B
Glengrasco
AN TUIREANN ARTS CENTRE
Torvaig
B885
H
i
g
h
Shulishadermor
THE AROS EXPERIENCE
Portree
Snizort
Heatherfield
417
Penifiler
413
BEN TIANAVAIG
Glenmore
Loch Duagrich
Tungadal
Mugeary
Holoman Bay
Camastianavaig
Tianavaig Bay
A87
Conordan
B883
Lower Ollach
Varragill
Glen Varragill
Upper Ollach
C
439
ROINEVAL
Gedintailor
The Braes
BATTLE OF THE BRAES MONUMENT
444
BEN LEE
Peinchorran
Loch Sligachan
Crossal
A863
Drynoch
rkadale
Sconser
GLAMAIG
775
Sligachan Hotel
Glen Brittle Forest
459
SGURR NAN GILLEAN
964
Glen Sligachan
Sligachan
736
MARSCO
D
MINGINISH
SGURR A'GHREADAIDH
973
THE CUILLIN HILLS
Glen Brittle
GLENBRITTLE
CUILLIN HILLS
Glenbrittle House
992
SGURR
Loch Coruisk
Loch na Crèitheach
BLA BHEINN
928
Strathaird
Camasunary
Kirkibost
Loch Slapin
Torrin
Kilbride
SOUND OF RAASAY
Island of Rona
125
Eilean Garbh
Caol Rona
Eilean Tigh
Garbh Eilean
Loch a' Sguirr
An Caol
Eilean Fladday
254
259
Torran
Manish Pt.
Loch Arnish
Arnish
BROCHEL CASTLE
Brochel
Glame
385
ISLAND OF RAASAY
Balmeanach
Balachuirn
443
DUN CAAN
Oskaig
RAASAY
Clachan
Raasay Ho.
RAASAY OUTDOOR CENTRE
Narrows of Raasay
Inverarish
North Fearns
East Suisnish
Eyre
Eyre Point
Rubha na'Leac
Caol Mór
0:25
Moll
Scalpay
247
Scalpay Ho.
Loch Ainort
Luib
Dunan
OLD SKYE CROFTER'S HOUSE
570
GLAS BHEINN MHOR
RED HILLS
Caolas Scalpay
Guillamon I.
Pabay
SKYE SERPENTARIUM
A87
Broadford Bay
Corry
BROADFORD
732
Waterloo
Broadford
Lower Br
Upper
Harrapool
Skulamus
WORLD OF WOOD
SKYE ENVIRONMENTAL CENTRE
A851
Suardal
B8083
Strath
247
INNER SOUND
Callakille
Lonbain
Applec Bay
Camu
Ard-d
Eilean na Bà
Crowlin Islands
Longay
ST M
0 1 2 3 miles
0 1 2 3 4 5 km

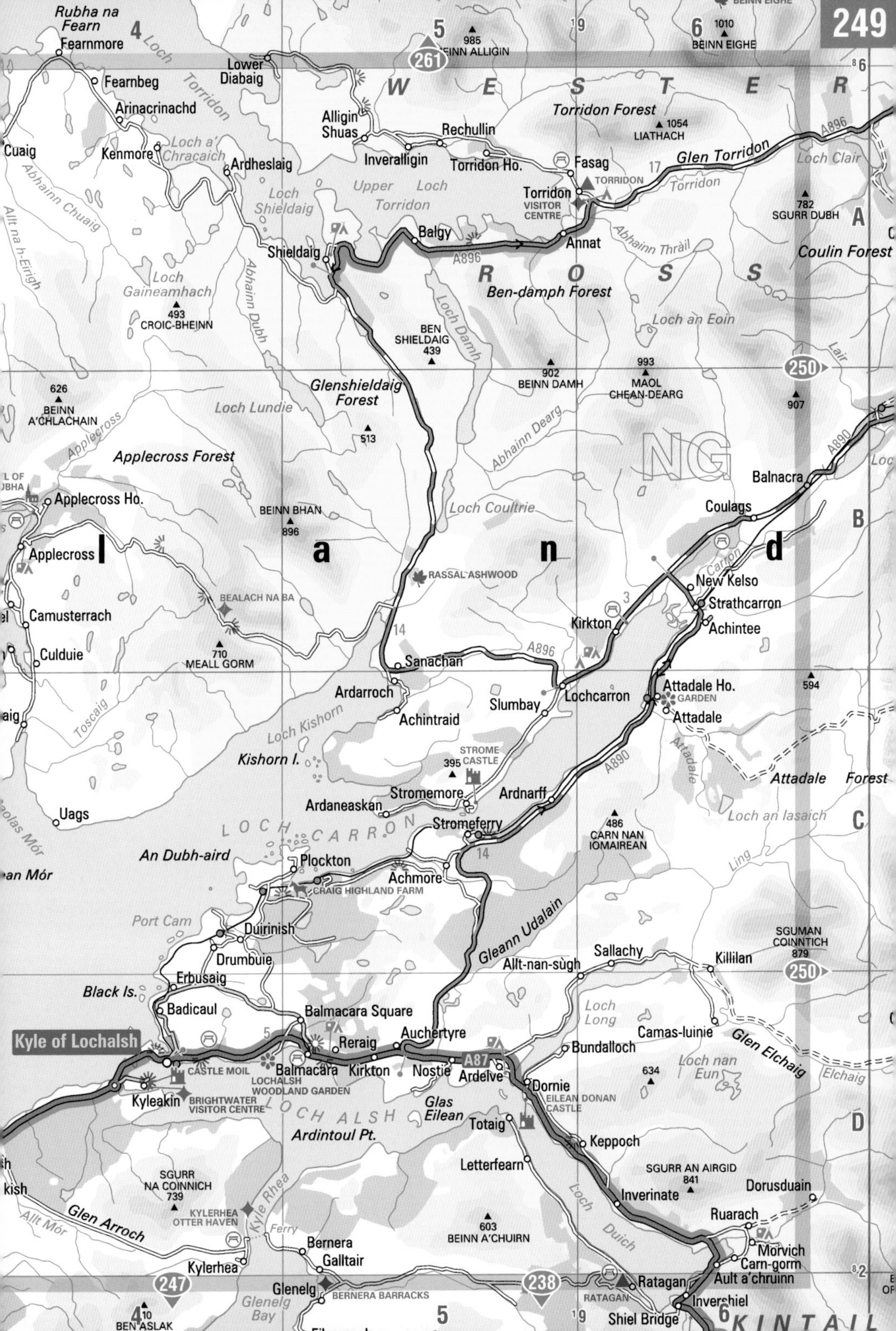

Rubha na Fearn
Fearnmore
Loch Torridon
Fearnbeg
Arinacrinachd
Cuaig
Kenmore
Loch a' Chracaich
Ardheslaig
Lower Diabaig
Alligin Shuas
Inveralligin
Rechullin
Torridon Ho.
BEINN ALLIGIN
985
BEINN EIGHE
1010
W E S T E R
R O S S
Torridon Forest
LIATHACH
1054
Fasag
Torridon
TORRIDON
VISITOR CENTRE
Glen Torridon
Loch Clair
Upper Loch Torridon
Loch Shieldaig
Shieldaig
Balgy
Annat
A896
Abhainn Thràil
SGURR DUBH
782
Coulin Forest
Abhainn Chuaig
Allt na h-Eirigh
Loch Gaineamhach
Abhainn Dubh
CROIC-BHEINN
493
Ben-damph Forest
Loch an Eoin
Loch Damh
BEN SHIELDAIG
439
BEINN DAMH
902
MAOL CHEAN-DEARG
993
907
BEINN A'CHLACHAIN
626
Loch Lundie
Glenshieldaig Forest
513
Applecross Forest
Applecross
Abhainn Dearg
NG
A890
Balnacra
Coulags
Applecross Ho.
BEINN BHAN
896
Loch Coultrie
l a n d
RASSAL ASHWOOD
New Kelso
Strathcarron
Achintee
Kirkton
BEALACH NA BA
Camusterrach
Culduie
MEALL GORM
710
Sanachan
Ardarroch
Achintraid
Slumbay
Lochcarron
Attadale Ho.
GARDEN
Attadale
594
Toscaig
Loch Kishorn
Kishorn I.
STROME CASTLE
395
Stromemore
Ardaneaskan
Ardnarff
Attadale Forest
Loch an Iasaich
Uags
LOCH CARRON
Stromeferry
CARN NAN IOMAIREAN
486
An Dubh-aird
Plockton
Achmore
CRAIG HIGHLAND FARM
Ling
Port Cam
Duirinish
Drumbuie
Gleann Udalain
Erbusaig
Black Is.
Badicaul
Allt-nan-sùgh
Sallachy
Killilan
SGUMAN COINNTICH
879
Loch Long
Balmacara Square
Camas-luinie
Glen Elchaig
Kyle of Lochalsh
Reraig
Auchertyre
Bundalloch
CASTLE MOIL
Balmacara
Kirkton
Nostie
A87
Ardelve
Dornie
Loch nan Eun
634
Elchaig
LOCHALSH WOODLAND GARDEN
EILEAN DONAN CASTLE
Kyleakin
BRIGHTWATER VISITOR CENTRE
LOCH ALSH
Glas Eilean
Ardintoul Pt.
Totaig
Keppoch
Letterfearn
SGURR AN AIRGID
841
SGURR NA COINNICH
739
Inverinate
Dorusduain
Loch Duich
Glen Arroch
Kyle Rhea
KYLERHEA OTTER HAVEN
Ruarach
Allt Mór
Ferry
BEINN A'CHUIRN
603
Bernera
Morvich
Galltair
Carn-gorm
Kylerhea
Ault a'chruinn
247
238
Glenelg
BERNERA BARRACKS
Ratagan
RATAGAN
Glenelg Bay
Inverchiel
Shiel Bridge
BEN ASLAK
KINTAIL
261
250
A B C D
4 5 6

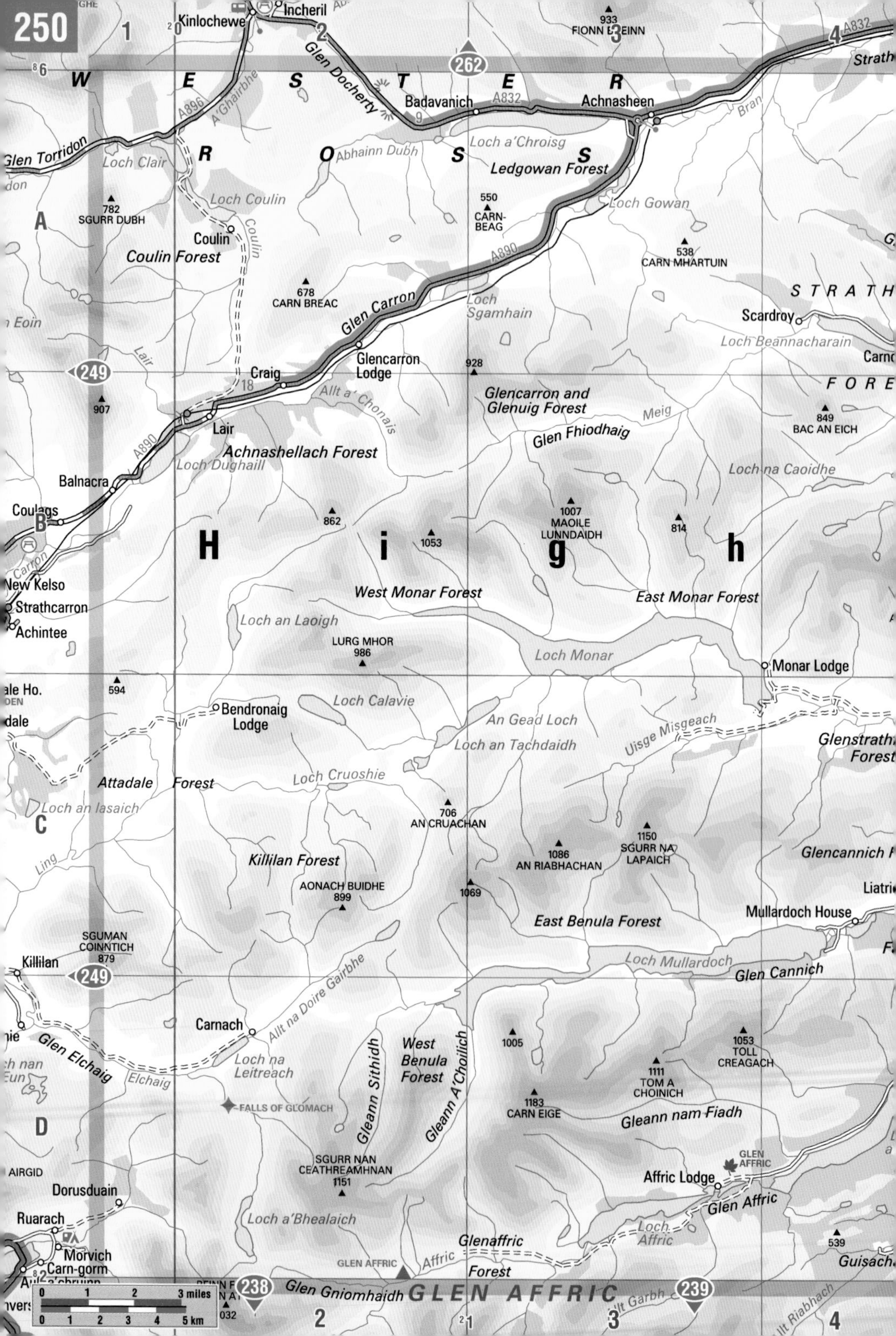

Kinlochewe
Incheril
933
FIONN BHEINN
A832
Strath
W E S T E R R O S S
262
Glen Docherty
Badavanich
A832
Achnasheen
A896
A'Ghairbhe
Bran
Glen Torridon
Loch Clair
Abhainn Dubh
Loch a'Chroisg
Ledgowan Forest
Loch Coulin
550
CARN-BEAG
Loch Gowan
782
SGURR DUBH
Coulin
Coulin Forest
A890
538
CARN MHARTUIN
678
CARN BREAC
Glen Carron
Loch Sgamhain
STRATH
Eoin
Scardroy
Loch Beannacharain
Carnc
Lair
249
Craig
Glencarron Lodge
928
FORE
907
18
Allt a' Chonais
Glencarron and Glenuig Forest
849
BAC AN EICH
Meig
Lair
Glen Fhiodhaig
A890
Achnashellach Forest
Loch Dughaill
Balnacra
Loch na Caoidhe
Coulags
862
1007
MAOILE LUNNDAIDH
814
1053
Carron
H i g h
New Kelso
Strathcarron
West Monar Forest
East Monar Forest
Achintee
Loch an Laoigh
LURG MHOR
986
Loch Monar
Monar Lodge
594
Bendronaig Lodge
Loch Calavie
An Gead Loch
Loch an Tachdaidh
Uisge Misgeach
Glenstrathfarrar Forest
Attadale Forest
Loch Cruoshie
Loch an Iasaich
706
AN CRUACHAN
Ling
1150
SGURR NA LAPAICH
1086
AN RIABHACHAN
Killilan Forest
Glencannich
AONACH BUIDHE
899
1069
East Benula Forest
Mullardoch House
SGUMAN COINNTICH
879
Killilan
249
Loch Mullardoch
Glen Cannich
Allt na Doire Gairbhe
Carnach
1005
1053
TOLL CREAGACH
Glen Elchaig
Loch na Leitreach
West Benula Forest
Gleann Sithidh
Gleann A'Choilich
1111
TOM A CHOINICH
Elchaig
FALLS OF GLOMACH
1183
CARN EIGE
Gleann nam Fiadh
AIRGID
SGURR NAN CEATHREAMHNAN
1151
GLEN AFFRIC
Affric Lodge
Dorusduain
Glen Affric
Ruarach
Loch a'Bhealaich
Loch Affric
539
Morvich
Glenaffric Forest
Carn-gorm
GLEN AFFRIC
Affric
Guisach
238
Glen Gniomhaidh
GLEN AFFRIC
239
Allt Garbh
Allt Riabhach
0 1 2 3 miles
0 1 2 3 4 5 km
1032
A B C D
1 2 3 4

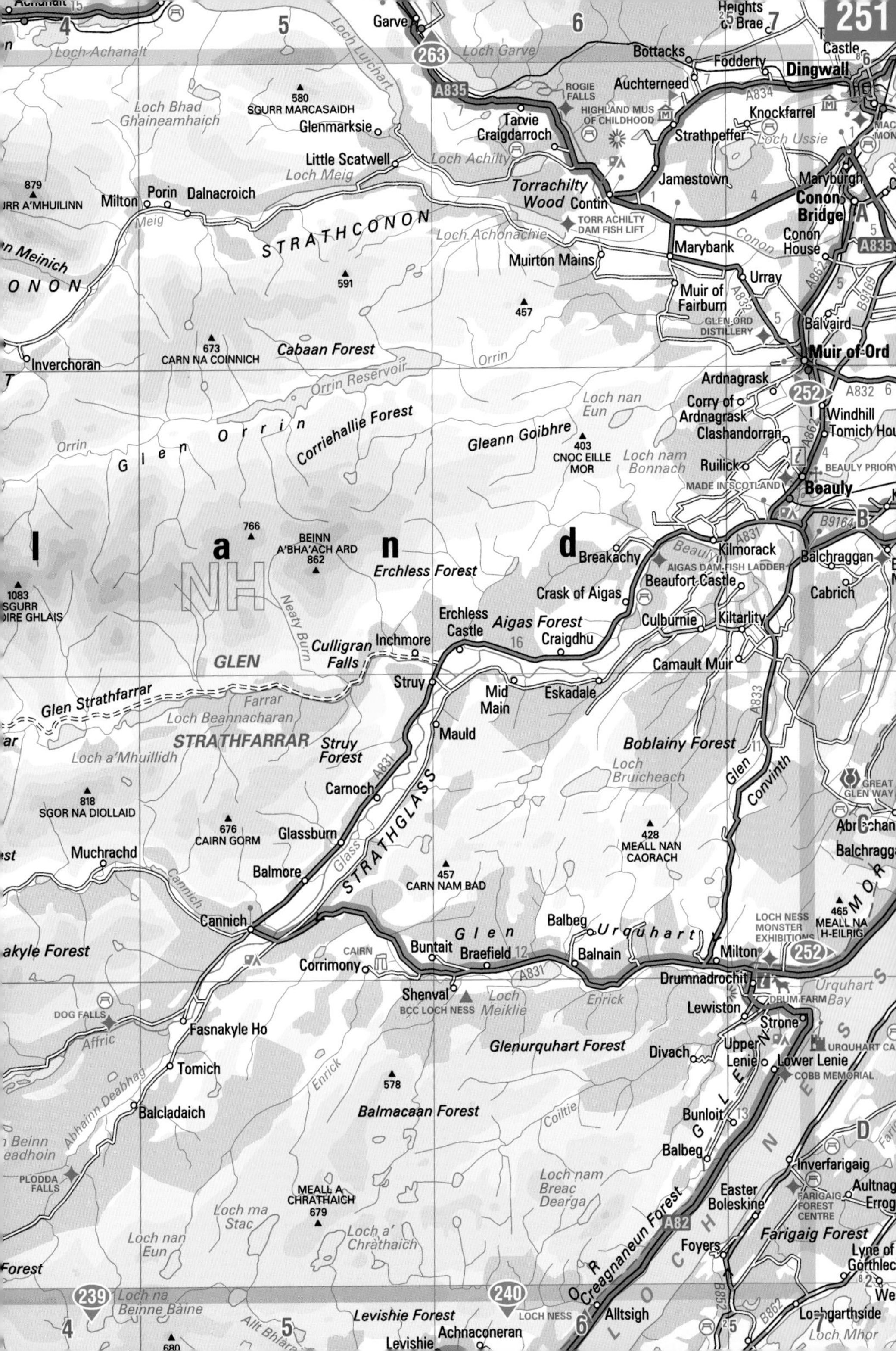
Achanalt
Garve
Heights
Brae
Castle
Loch Achanalt
Loch Luichart
263
Loch Garve
Bottacks
Fodderty
Dingwall
Auchterneed
A835
A834
ROGIE FALLS
HIGHLAND MUS OF CHILDHOOD
580
SGURR MARCASAIDH
Loch Bhad Ghaineamhaich
Tarvie
Knockfarrel
Glenmarksie
Craigdarroch
Strathpeffer
Loch Ussie
Little Scatwell
Loch Achilty
Loch Meig
879
Porin
Dalnacroich
Torrachilty Wood
Jamestown
Maryburgh
Milton
Contin
Conon Bridge
Meig
TORR ACHILTY DAM FISH LIFT
STRATHCONON
Loch Achonachie
Conon
Conon House
Marybank
A835
Muirton Mains
Urray
591
Muir of Fairburn
457
Balvaird
A832
B9169
A862
GLEN ORD DISTILLERY
673
CARN NA COINNICH
Cabaan Forest
Orrin
Muir of Ord
Inverchoran
Orrin Reservoir
Ardnagrask
252
A832
Loch nan Eun
Corry of Ardnagrask
Windhill
Tomich Hou
Corriehallie Forest
Clashandorran
Glen Orrin
Gleann Goibhre
403
CNOC EILLE MOR
Loch nam Bonnach
Ruilick
BEAULY PRIORY
MADE IN SCOTLAND
Beauly
766
B9164
BEINN A'BHA'ACH ARD
862
Beauly
A831
Kilmorack
l a n d
Breakachy
Balchraggan
NH
Erchless Forest
AIGAS DAM FISH LADDER
1083
Crask of Aigas
Beaufort Castle
Cabrich
Neaty Burn
Erchless Castle
Aigas Forest
Culburnie
Kiltarlity
Culligran Falls
Inchmore
Craigdhu
GLEN
Camault Muir
Struy
Mid Main
Eskadale
Glen Strathfarrar
Farrar
Loch Beannacharan
A833
STRATHFARRAR
Mauld
Boblainy Forest
Loch a'Mhuillidh
Struy Forest
Loch Bruicheach
A831
Glen Convinth
GREAT GLEN WAY
Carnoch
818
SGOR NA DIOLLAID
676
CAIRN GORM
Glassburn
428
MEALL NAN CAORACH
Abriachan
Muchrachd
Glass
Balchraggan
STRATHGLASS
Balmore
457
CARN NAM BAD
Cannich
465
MEALL NA H-EILRIG
LOCH NESS MONSTER EXHIBITIONS
Cannich
Balbeg
Glen Urquhart
Nakyle Forest
CAIRN
Buntait
Braefield
Balnain
Milton
252
Corrimony
A831
Drumnadrochit
Urquhart Bay
Shenval
BCC LOCH NESS
Loch Meiklie
Enrick
DRUM FARM
DOG FALLS
Lewiston
Strone
Affric
Fasnakyle Ho
Glenurquhart Forest
Upper Lenie
Divach
URQUHART CAS
Lower Lenie
Tomich
COBB MEMORIAL
Enrick
578
Abhainn Deabhag
Balcladaich
Balmacaan Forest
Coiltie
Bunloit
GLEN
Beinn Deadhoin
Balbeg
Inverfarigaig
PLODDA FALLS
Loch nam Breac Dearga
Easter Boleskine
Aultnag
FARIGAIG FOREST CENTRE
Errog
MEALL A CHRATHAICH
679
Loch ma Stac
A82
Loch a' Chràthaich
Farigaig Forest
Foyers
Creagnaneun Forest
Loch nan Eun
Lyne of Gorthleck
Forest
LOCH NESS
239
Loch na Beinne Baine
240
B852
Wes
Levishie Forest
LOCH NESS
Alltsigh
B862
Lochgarthside
Alt Bhlàra
Achnaconeran
680
Levishie
Loch Mhor

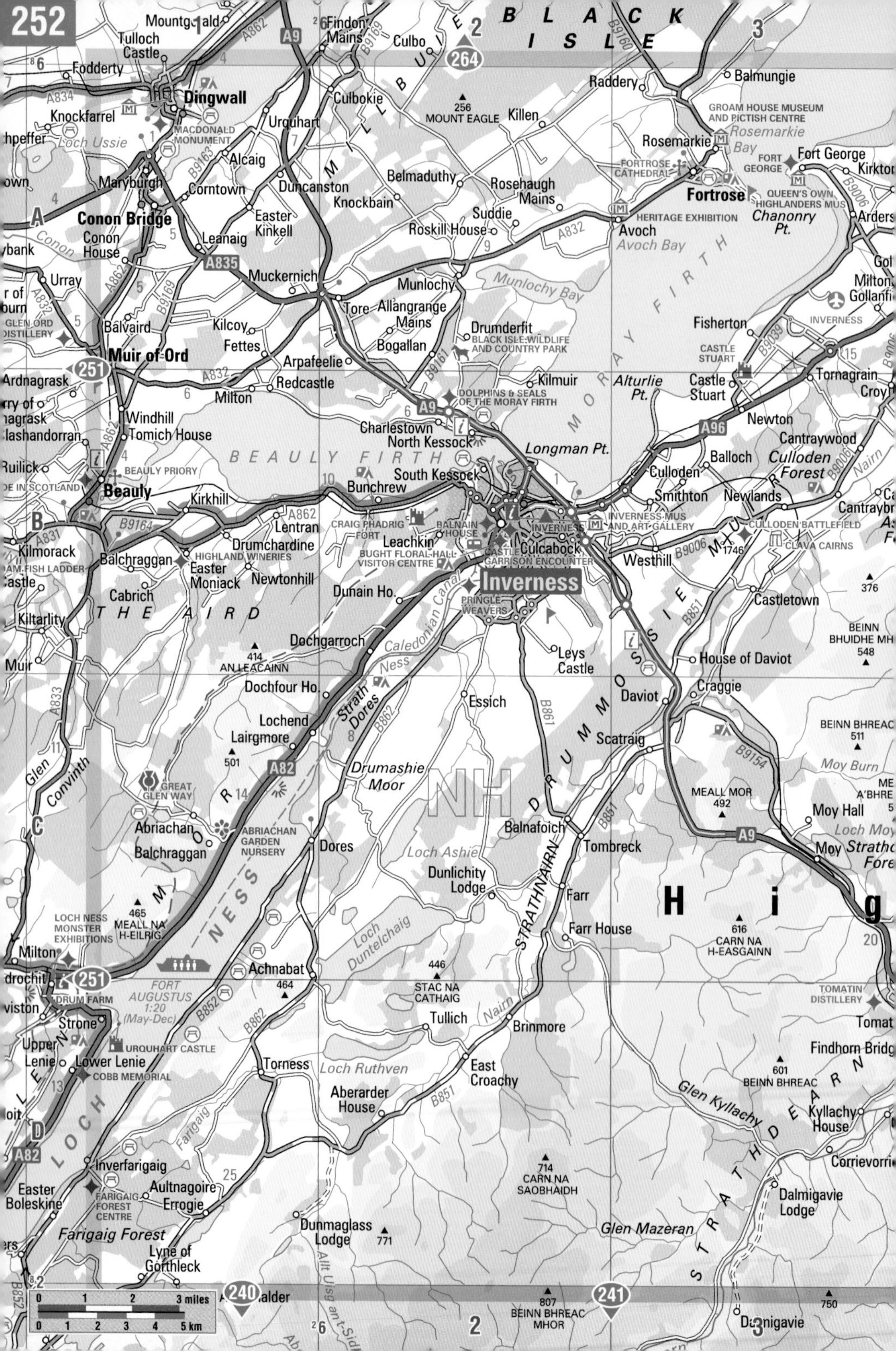
BLACK ISLE
MILLBUIE
264
Mountgerald
Tulloch Castle
Fodderty
Dingwall
Findon Mains
Culbo
Culbokie
Urquhart
256
MOUNT EAGLE
Killen
Raddery
Balmungie
GROAM HOUSE MUSEUM AND PICTISH CENTRE
Rosemarkie
Rosemarkie Bay
Knockfarrel
MACDONALD MONUMENT
Loch Ussie
Alcaig
Maryburgh
Corntown
Duncanston
Knockbain
Belmaduthy
Rosehaugh Mains
FORTROSE CATHEDRAL
FORT GEORGE
Fort George
Kirkton
Fortrose
QUEEN'S OWN HIGHLANDERS MUS
HERITAGE EXHIBITION
Conon Bridge
Conon House
Easter Kinkell
Leanaig
Suddie
Roskill House
Avoch
Avoch Bay
Chanonry Pt.
Ardersier
Urray
Muckernich
Munlochy
Munlochy Bay
MORAY FIRTH
GLEN ORD DISTILLERY
Balvaird
Kilcoy
Tore
Allangrange Mains
Drumderfit
BLACK ISLE WILDLIFE AND COUNTRY PARK
Fisherton
INVERNESS
Milton
Gollanfield
Muir of Ord
Fettes
Bogallan
Arpafeelie
CASTLE STUART
Castle Stuart
Tornagrain
Croy
251
Ardnagrask
Redcastle
Milton
Kilmuir
Alturlie Pt.
DOLPHINS & SEALS OF THE MORAY FIRTH
Windhill
Tomich House
Clashandorran
Charlestown
North Kessock
Longman Pt.
Newton
Cantraywood
BEAULY FIRTH
BEAULY PRIORY
Beauly
Ruilick
South Kessock
Bunchrew
Balloch
Culloden
Culloden Forest
Smithton
Newlands
Cantraybridge
Kirkhill
Lentran
CRAIG PHADRIG FORT
BALNAIN HOUSE
INVERNESS MUS AND ART GALLERY
CULLODEN BATTLEFIELD
CLAVA CAIRNS
Kilmorack
Balchraggan
Drumchardine
HIGHLAND WINERIES
Leachkin
BUGHT FLORAL HALL VISITOR CENTRE
CASTLE GARRISON ENCOUNTER
Culcabock
Westhill
1746
Easter Moniack
Newtonhill
Inverness
376
Cabrich
THE AIRD
Kiltarlity
Dunain Ho.
PRINGLE WEAVERS
Caledonian Canal
Castletown
BEINN BHUIDHE MHOR
548
Dochgarroch
414
AN LEACAINN
Leys Castle
House of Daviot
Muir
Dochfour Ho.
Ness
Strath Dores
Essich
Daviot
Craggie
Lochend
Lairgmore
501
DRUMMOSSIE MUIR
Scatraig
BEINN BHREAC
511
Glen Convinth
Drumashie Moor
NH
Moy Burn
GREAT GLEN WAY
MEALL MOR
492
Moy Hall
Abriachan
ABRIACHAN GARDEN NURSERY
Balchraggan
Dores
Balnafoich
Tombreck
Loch Moy
Moy
Loch Ashie
Dunlichity Lodge
Farr
LOCH NESS
465
MEALL NA H-EILRIG
LOCH NESS MONSTER EXHIBITIONS
Milton
Drumnadrochit
Loch Duntelchaig
STRATHNAIRN
Farr House
616
CARN NA H-EASGAINN
Achnabat
446
STAC NA CATHAIG
464
FORT AUGUSTUS 1:20 (May-Dec)
DRUM FARM
Lewiston
TOMATIN DISTILLERY
Tomatin
Strone
Tullich
Nairn
Brinmore
URQUHART CASTLE
Upper Lenie
Lower Lenie
COBB MEMORIAL
Torness
Loch Ruthven
East Croachy
Findhorn Bridge
601
BEINN BHREAC
Aberarder House
Glen Kyllachy
Kyllachy House
STRATHDEARN
Farigaig
Inverfarigaig
714
CARN NA SAOBHAIDH
Corrievorrie
Easter Boleskine
FARIGAIG FOREST CENTRE
Aultnagoire
Errogie
Dalmigavie Lodge
Farigaig Forest
Dunmaglass Lodge
771
Glen Mazeran
Lyne of Gorthleck
Allt Uisg an t-Sidhe
240
241
807
BEINN BHREAC MHOR
750
Dalmigavie
0 1 2 3 miles
0 1 2 3 4 5 km
A9
A862
A834
B9169
B9160
B9163
A835
A832
B9161
B9006
B9039
A96
A831
B9164
A862
B9006
B851
A833
A82
B862
B861
B851
B9154
B852
B862
B851

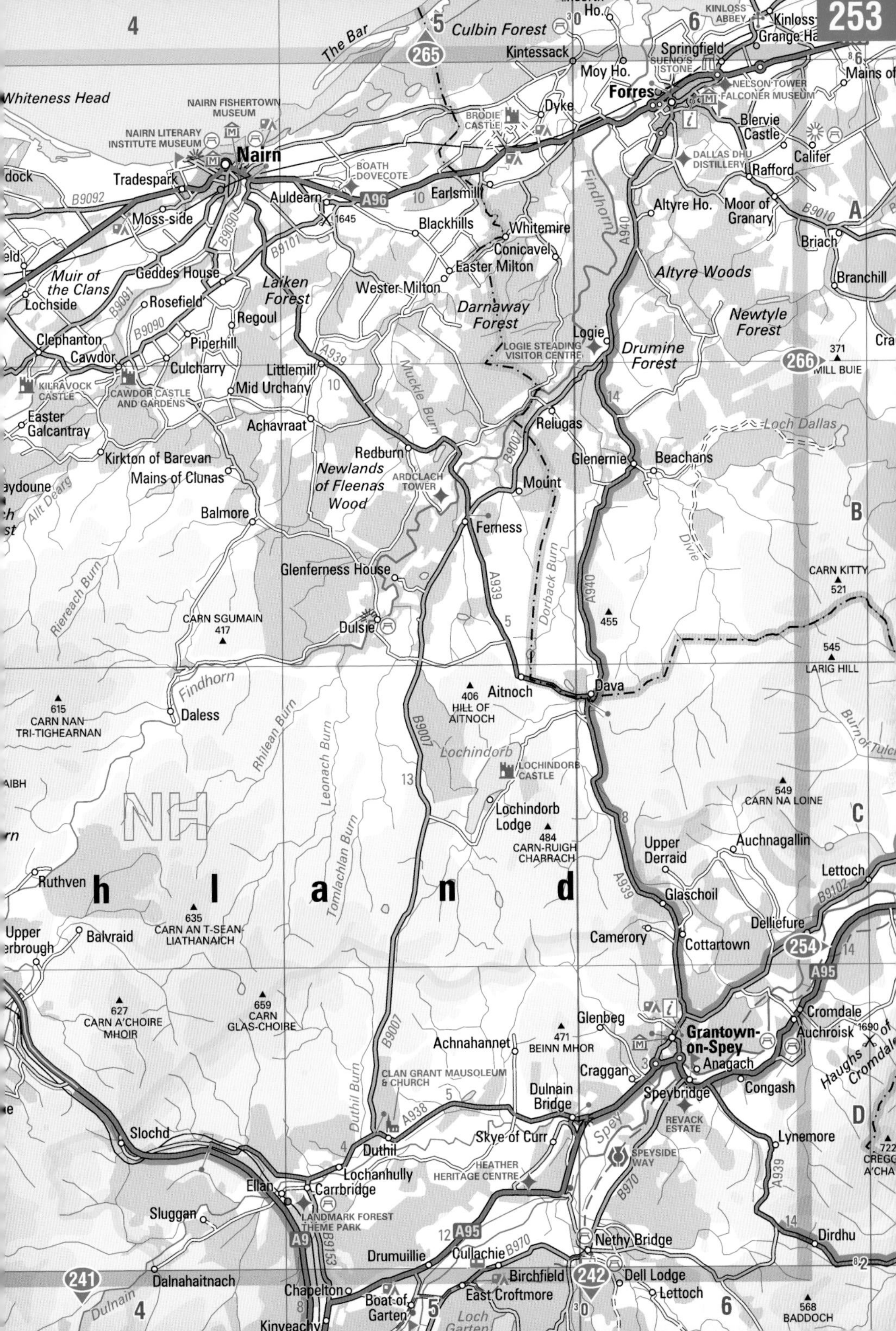

4
5
6
A
B
C
D
265
266
254
241
242
The Bar
Culbin Forest
North Ho.
Kintessack
Moy Ho.
KINLOSS ABBEY
Kinloss
Grange Hall
Springfield
SUENO'S STONE
Forres
NELSON TOWER
FALCONER MUSEUM
Mains of
Whiteness Head
NAIRN FISHERTOWN MUSEUM
NAIRN LITERARY INSTITUTE MUSEUM
Nairn
BRODIE CASTLE
Dyke
Blervie Castle
DALLAS DHU DISTILLERY
Califer
Rafford
dock
Tradespark
BOATH DOVECOTE
Auldearn
Earlsmill
A96
B9092
Moss-side
B9090
1645
Blackhills
Whitemire
Altyre Ho.
Moor of Granary
B9010
Briach
B9101
Conicavel
Easter Milton
Altyre Woods
Branchill
Muir of the Clans
Geddes House
Laiken Forest
Wester Milton
Findhorn
A940
Lochside
B9091
Rosefield
Regoul
Darnaway Forest
Newtyle Forest
Clephanton
Cawdor
Piperhill
Logie
LOGIE STEADING VISITOR CENTRE
Drumine Forest
371
MILL BUIE
KILRAVOCK CASTLE
CAWDOR CASTLE AND GARDENS
Culcharry
Littlemill
A939
Mid Urchany
Muckle Burn
Easter Galcantray
Achavraat
Relugas
Loch Dallas
Redburn
Glenernie
Beachans
Kirkton of Barevan
Mains of Clunas
Newlands of Fleenas Wood
ARDCLACH TOWER
B9007
Mount
Allt Dearg
Balmore
Ferness
Divie
Glenferness House
Dorback Burn
CARN KITTY
521
Riereach Burn
CARN SGUMAIN
417
Dulsie
455
545
LARIG HILL
Findhorn
Aitnoch
406
HILL OF AITNOCH
Dava
615
CARN NAN TRI-TIGHEARNAN
Daless
Rhilean Burn
Burn of Tulchan
Leonach Burn
Lochindorb
LOCHINDORB CASTLE
549
CARN NA LOINE
NH
Lochindorb Lodge
484
CARN-RUIGH CHARRACH
Tomlachlan Burn
Upper Derraid
Auchnagallin
Lettoch
Ruthven
h
l
a
n
d
Glaschoil
B9102
635
CARN AN T-SEAN-LIATHANAICH
Upper
Balvraid
Dellefure
Camerory
Cottartown
A95
627
CARN A'CHOIRE MHOIR
659
CARN GLAS-CHOIRE
Cromdale
Glenbeg
1690
Auchroisk
Achnahannet
471
BEINN MHOR
Grantown-on-Spey
Haughs of Cromdale
Anagach
Craggan
CLAN GRANT MAUSOLEUM & CHURCH
Congash
Dulnain Bridge
Speybridge
REVACK ESTATE
Duthil Burn
A938
Spey
Slochd
Skye of Curr
Lynemore
722
Duthil
SPEYSIDE WAY
Lochanhully
HEATHER HERITAGE CENTRE
B970
Ellan
Carrbridge
Sluggan
LANDMARK FOREST THEME PARK
A9
B9153
Nethy Bridge
Dirdhu
Drumuillie
Cullachie
Birchfield
Dalnahaitnach
Dell Lodge
Chapelton
East Croftmore
Lettoch
Boat of Garten
Loch Garten
Dulnain
Kinveachy
568
BADDOCH

Moray
Rothes
Charlestown of Aberlour
Dufftown
Craigellachie
Elchies Forest
Dallas Forest
Teindland Forest
Glenfiddich Forest
Blackwater Forest
Glenlivet Forest
HILLS OF CROMDALE
LADDER HILLS
STRATH AVON
STRATHSPEY
Tomintoul
Glenlivet
Tomnavoulin
Marypark
Archiestown
Knockando
Cromdale
Dallas
Kellas
Ben Rinnes
Glen Rinnes
Glen of Rothes
Braes of Glenlivet
Braes of Abernethy
Bridge of Brown
Bridge of Avon
Lecht Ski Centre
0 1 2 3 miles
0 1 2 3 4 5 km

255
Mains of Edingight
Deerhill
Grange Crossroads
267
Edingight Ho.
Gordonstown
Weachyburn
MILLSTONE HILL
301
KNOCK HILL
430
Blacklaw
Finnygaud
Broadrashes
Forgie
Aultmore
Crannoch
Sillyearn
Glen Barry
Knowes of Elrick
A96
Newmill
Bracobrae
Davoch of Grange
Knock
Drumnagorrach
Cranna
Aberchirder
311
Farmtown
Old Crombie
Knauchland
Mulben
Keith
STRATHISLA DISTILLERY
STRATH ISLA
A95
B9014
B9117
Marnoch
Clunie
Forest
366
Balloch Wood
265
Deveron
KEITH AND DUFFTOWN RLY
Milltown of Rothiemay
Mains of Mayen
Hillbrae
Inverkeithny
339
Ruthven
Yonder Bognie
Edintore
Glen of Coachford
Bogniebrae
344
FOURMAN HILL
Towiemore
Little Pitlurg
Coachford
Cairnie
256
Castle
Drummuir
313
THE BIN
GLENDRONACH DISTILLERY
Drumblair
Corse of Kinnoir
A96
The Bin Forest
Daugh of Cairnborrow
NORDIC SKI CENTRE
HUNTLY CASTLE
417
Lessendrum
Milltown of Auchindoun
Cairnborrow
A920
Huntly
Drumblade
Corse
Aucharnie
Torry
BRANDER MUSEUM
Brideswell
Slioch
Haugh of Glass
Deveron
259
AUCHINDOUN CASTLE
Denend
Ythanwells
STRATHBOGIE
Thomastown
487
THE SCALP
Bailiesward
Bridgend
Hillhead
Succoth
Tillathrowie
Kirkstile
Shanquhar
Bainshole
381
A96
Glens of Foudland
Ballochford
NJ
Blackburn
Tomnaven
525
Coynachie
Culdrain
467
HILL OF FOUDLAND
Clashindarroch Forest
Kirkney
Colpy
Clashindarroch Forest
Bridgend
Clashindarroch
Gartly
Largie
Inverharroch
Kirkney Water
Cults
434
KNOCKANDY HILL
Wrangham
Black Water
LEITH HALL
B992
Milton of Lesmore
Milton of Noth
Kennethmont
B9002
Oldtown
The Shevock
Aulton
Auchmair
Ardlair
Insch
Pitma
505
A941
Ardoyne
Cabrach
Belhinnie
Cottown
Rhynie
Aldunie
Clatt
Duncanstone
B9002
Wheedlemont
Kirkton
Craig Castle
Leslie
256
B9002
ST MARY'S CHURCH
Knockespock Ho.
Auchleven
721
THE BUCK
Coldwells Croft
Whitehaugh Forest
Clova
Lumsden
SCOTTISH SCULPTURE WORKSHOP
CORREEN HILLS
Muckletown
B992
Glenton
Tullynessle
243
244
518
LORD ARTHUR'S CAIRN
Mossat
Keig
Castle Forbes
Bridge of Alford
Montgarrie
Rorandle
Kildrummy
Don
A944
Rinmore
ALFORD VALLEY RAILWAY
HAUGHTON
Pitfichie
Belnacraig
Milltown of Kildrummy
KILDRUMMY CASTLE & GARDEN
Auchintoul
GRAMPIAN TRANSPORT MUS
Gateside
532
Kirkton of Glenbuchat
Alford
HERITAGE CENTRE
A944
Forest
Whitehouse
Pitmuni
Todlachie
Asloun
A980
Glenkindie
Sinnahard
A97

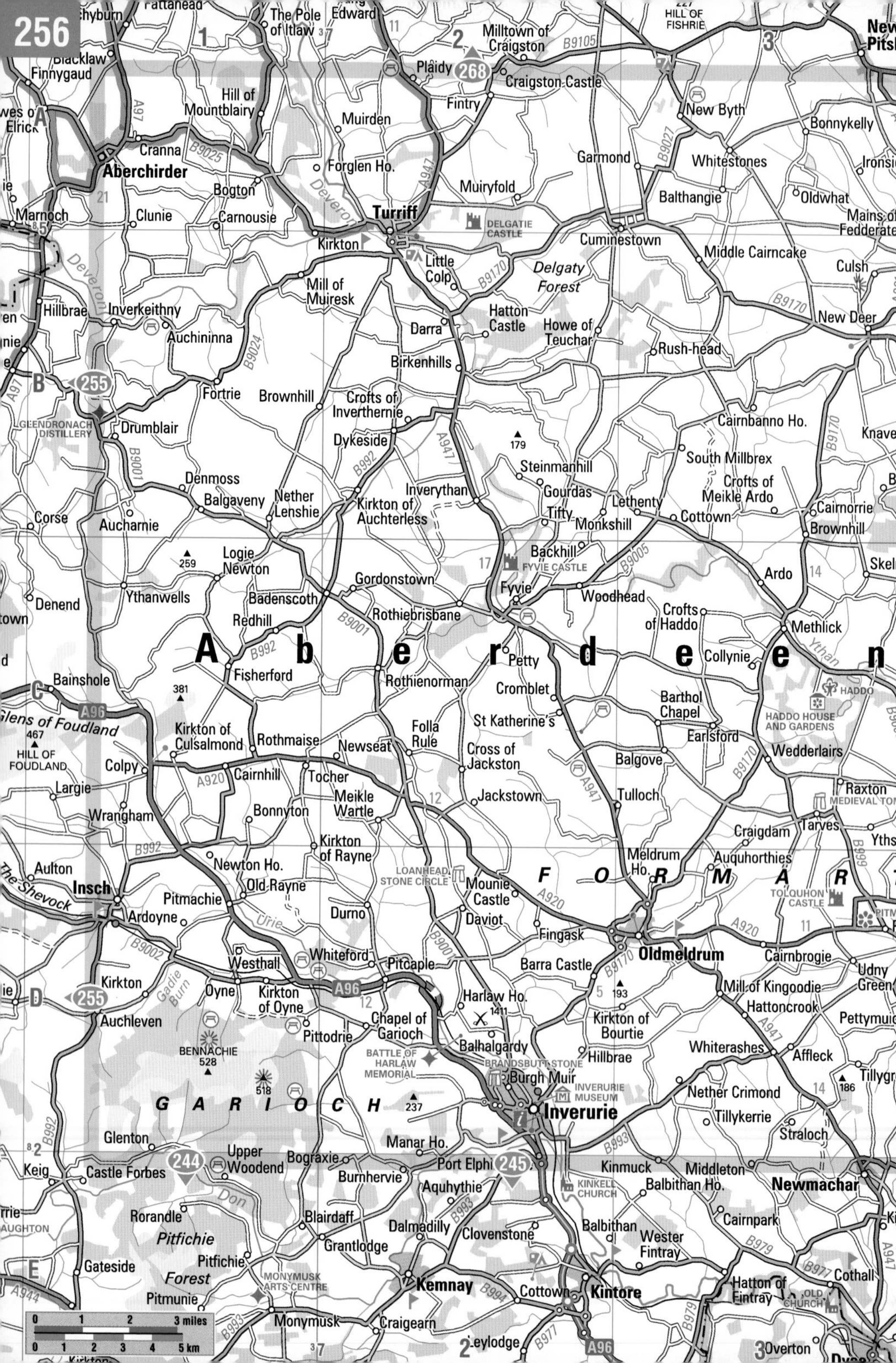
The Pole of Itlaw
Edward
Milltown of Craigston
HILL OF FISHRIE
New Pitsligo
Blacklaw
Finnygaud
Plaidy
268
Craigston Castle
Hill of Mountblairy
Fintry
New Byth
Muirden
Bonnykelly
Cranna
Aberchirder
Garmond
Whitestones
Forglen Ho.
Bogton
Muiryfold
Balthangie
Oldwhat
Marnoch
Clunie
Carnousie
Turriff
DELGATIE CASTLE
Mains of Fedderate
Kirkton
Deveron
Cuminestown
Middle Cairncake
Little Colp
Delgaty Forest
Culsh
Mill of Muiresk
Hillbrae
Inverkeithny
Auchininna
Darra
Hatton Castle
Howe of Teuchar
New Deer
Rush-head
Birkenhills
255
Fortrie
Brownhill
Crofts of Inverthernie
GLENDRONACH DISTILLERY
Drumblair
Dykeside
Cairnbanno Ho.
179
South Millbrex
Steinmanhill
Crofts of Meikle Ardo
Denmoss
Balgaveny
Nether Lenshie
Kirkton of Auchterless
Inverythan
Gourdas
Lethenty
Cairnorrie
Corse
Aucharnie
Tifty
Cottown
Monkshill
Brownhill
Backhill
Logie Newton
259
FYVIE CASTLE
Ardo
Ythanwells
Badenscoth
Gordonstown
Fyvie
Woodhead
Denend
Redhill
Rothiebrisbane
Crofts of Haddo
Methlick
Aberdeen
Petty
Collynie
Ythan
Fisherford
Rothienorman
HADDO
Bainshole
381
Cromblet
Barthol Chapel
Glens of Foudland
467
HILL OF FOUDLAND
Kirkton of Culsalmond
St Katherine's
HADDO HOUSE AND GARDENS
Rothmaise
Newseat
Folla Rule
Earlsford
Colpy
Cross of Jackston
Balgove
Wedderlairs
Cairnhill
Tocher
Largie
Jackstown
Tulloch
Raxton
Meikle Wartle
MEDIEVAL TOWER
Wrangham
Bonnyton
Tarves
Craigdam
Kirkton of Rayne
Meldrum Ho.
Auquhorthies
Aulton
Newton Ho.
LOANHEAD STONE CIRCLE
Mounie Castle
FORMARTINE
The Shevock
Insch
Old Rayne
Pitmachie
TOLQUHON CASTLE
Ardoyne
Urie
Durno
Daviot
Fingask
Cairnbrogie
Whiteford
Oldmeldrum
Westhall
Pitcaple
Barra Castle
Udny Green
Kirkton
Mill of Kingoodie
Oyne
Kirkton of Oyne
Harlaw Ho.
193
Hattoncrook
Gadie Burn
1411
Auchleven
Chapel of Garioch
Kirkton of Bourtie
Pettymuick
Pittodrie
Balhalgardy
Whiterashes
Affleck
BENNACHIE
528
BATTLE OF HARLAW MEMORIAL
BRANDSBUTT STONE
Hillbrae
Tillygreig
518
Burgh Muir
INVERURIE MUSEUM
186
Nether Crimond
GARIOCH
237
Inverurie
Tillykerrie
Glenton
Manar Ho.
Straloch
Upper Woodend
Bograxie
Port Elphinstone
Keig
244
Castle Forbes
245
Kinmuck
Middleton
Burnhervie
Balbithan Ho.
Newmachar
Aquhythie
KINKELL CHURCH
Don
Blairdaff
Rorandle
Cairnpark
Pitfichie
Dalmadilly
Clovenstone
Balbithan
Wester Fintray
Grantlodge
Pitfichie Forest
Gateside
Pitfichie
Cothall
MONYMUSK ARTS CENTRE
Kemnay
Kintore
Hatton of Fintray
Cottown
Pitmunie
OLD CHURCH
Monymusk
Craigearn
Leylodge
Overton
0 1 2 3 miles
0 1 2 3 4 5 km

Knowhead
Strichen
B9093
MORMOND HILL
Nether Park
Rattray
Blackhill
269
A90
New Leeds
Longhill
Balearn
B9093
Adziel
North Ugie Water
Leys
St Fergus Moss
Little Skillymarno
A981
Denhead
Backfolds
Kirktown
St Fergus
Scotstown Hd.
Hythie
Rora Moss
North Kirkton
Fetterangus
Rora
Forest of Deer
Toux
Lunderton
Kirkton Hd.
A950
DEER ABBEY
Dunshillock
Woodside
Ugie
Maud
U
C
H
A
N
Newseat
Inverugie
INVERUGIE CASTLE
B9029
ADEN
Mintlaw
Water
UGIE SALMON FISH HOUSE
Buchanhaven
MAUD RAILWAY MUSEUM
Old Deer
Longside
Torterston
A982
Backhill of Clackriach
ABERDEENSHIRE FARMING MUSEUM
South Ugie
Flushing
Peterhead
B9106
Stuartfield
Inverquhomery
A950
ARBUTHNOT MUSEUM & ART GALLERY
Drymuir
Keith Inch
Bulwark
Mains of Crichie
Millbreck
Hillhead of Cocklaw
PETERHEAD MARITIME
Peterhead Bay
B9030
Crichie
Nether Kinmundy
Invernettie
Nethermuir
Kinnadie
Clola
Little Dens
Sandford Bay
Skelmuir
Blackhill
Millbank
Boddam
Mains of Annochie
Buchan Ness
Auchnagatt
Backhill of Fortree
Kinknockie
Smallburn
Sandfordhill
Stirling
Moss of Cruden
Coldwells
Mains of Inkhorn
Backhill
Stoneygate
Teuchan
Longhaven
Milton Coldwells
A90
Quilquox
North Haven
A952
Auchiries
BULLERS OF BUCHAN
Hatton
Twa Havens
Muirtack
Drumwhindle
Eastertown of Auchleuchries
Cruden Bay
s
h
i
r
e
Arthrath
SLAINS CASTLE
Toll of Birness
Port Erroll
NK
A948
NJ
Bogbrae
Chapel Hill
Bay of Cruden
A975
Ythanbank
Hilton
Mains of Birness
Inverebrie
Nether Leask
Whinnyfold
Broomfield
A90
West Kinharrachie
P&R
Artrochie
Auchmacoy
Ellon
Esslemont
Kirkton of Logie Buchan
Kirktown of Slains
A920
I
N
E
VISITOR CENTRE
Collieston
Waterside
Sands of Forvie
St Catherine's Dub
Meikle Tarty
FORVIE
Tipperty
B9000
Hackley Hd. or Forvie Ness
Tarty Burn
B9000
Newburgh
Cultercullen
Foveran Burn
Foveran
Udny Station
A975
Newburgh Bar
Minnes
Tillycorthie
Rashiereive
Drums
B999
Ardo Ho.
Delfrigs
Middlemuir
Craigie
245
Causeyend
Whitecairns
Belhelvie
B977
BALMEDIE
Balmedie
Drumligair
B977
A90
Potterton
Corby Loch
Blackdog
B999
Mundurno
A
B
C
D
E
4
5
6
4
5
6

Fladda-chùain
Rubha Hu
TARBERT 1:40
LOCHMADDY 1:45
287
Lub Score
Hungladder
Borneskètaig
Kilmuir
FLORA MACDONALD'S MEMORIAL
Waterenish Point
Totscore
Kilbride Point
A855
Ascrib Islands
Idrigill
Uig Bay
Ru Chorachan
BEN GEARY 284
Geary
Ard Beag
TRUMPAN CHURCH
Trumpan
Knockbreck
Gillen
LOCH
SNIZORT
Ardmore Pt.
Lower Halistra
Upper Halistra
Hallin
WATERNISH
A87
ISLE OF SKYE
Mingay
Isay
Lyndale Pt.
Greshornish Pt.
Dunvegan Head
LOCH DUNVEGAN
Stein
Lusta
B886
Loch Bay
Loch Snizort Beag
Lyndale Ho.
Galtrigill
Loch Greshornish
Claigan
Greshornish
Treaslane
Borreraig
Uig
BORRERAIG PARK MUSEUM
327 BEINN BHREAC
Bay River
Flashader
Suladale
Husabost
Loch Pooltiel
Edinbane
An Ceannaich
Feriniquarrie
Blackhill
Lower Milovaig
Glasphein
Totaig
DUNVEGAN CASTLE
Oisgill Bay
Upper Milovaig
Lephin
B884
COLBOST FOLK MUSEUM
Colbost
Glen Bernisdale
Holmisdale
A850
GIANT ANGUS MACASKILL MUSEUM
LIGHTHOUSE
Neist Point
Skinidin
Dunvegan
Kilmuir
CRUACHAN BEINN A'CHEARCAILL 266
Hamara
Glen Dale
Lonmore
Moonen Bay
HEALABHAL MHOR 468
Roskhill
Ramasaig
Roag
Vatten
Hoe Rape
Macleod's Tables
Orbost
Loch Connan
Harlosh
488 HEALABHAL BHEAG
Ose
Loch Varkasaig
Balmore
Loch Caroy
B885
Hoe Point
A863
246
Bracadale
Geodha Mor
Harlosh I.
Tarner I.
0 1 2 3 miles
0 1 2 3 4 5 km

4
5
6
260
261
249
248
A
B
C
D
NG
Eilean Trodday
Rubha na h-Aiseig
Balmacqueen
Kilmaluag
MUSEUM OF ISLAND LIFE
Eilean Flodigarry
Flodigarry
MEALL NA SUIRAMACH
543
Digg
Staffin I.
Staffin Bay
Glashvin
THE QUIRAING
Brogaig
Stenscholl
Staffin
TROTTERNISH
Kilt Rock
KILT ROCK & MEALT FALLS
466
BIOD BUIDHE
Elishader
Maligar
Loch Mealt
Valtos
A855
Marishader
Conon
Garros
Rubha nam Brathairean
Balnaknock
611
BEINN EDRA
Breckrey
Culnaknock
Lealt
LEALT FALLS
Lower Tote
Upper Tote
Lealt
607
CREAG A'LAIN
Hinnisdal
Island of Rona
125
SOUND OF RAASAY
Eilean Garbh
719
THE STORR
OLD MAN OF STORR
Romesdal
Caol Rona
Eilean Tigh
Garbh Eilean
Callakille
Lonbain
Eyre
TROTTERNISH
Bearreraig Bay
Loch a' Sguirr
An Caol
Holm I.
Haultin
Loch Leathan
Eilean Fladday
Bernisdale
B8036
Tote
A855
Loch Fada
Torran
Manish Pt.
Loch Arnish
Arnish
Borve
Skeabost
Carbost
PRINCE CHARLES'S CAVE
INNER SOUND
Loch nan Eun
Uigshader
Drumuie
392
BROCHEL CASTLE
Brochel
Achachork
Rubha na h Airde Glaise
AN TUIREANN ARTS CENTRE
Torvaig
Glengrasco
Applecross Bay
Shulishadermor
THE AROS EXPERIENCE
Portree
Glame
385
ISLAND OF RAASAY
Snizort
Heatherfield
417
Penifiler
413
BEN TIANAVAIG
Balmeanach
Balachuirn
Camusteel
Ard-dhubh
Glenmore
Tungadal
Holoman Bay
B883
443
DUN CAAN
Mugeary
Camastianavaig
Tianavaig
A87
Toscaig

1
2
3
A
B
C
D
Garbh Eilean
Eilean Mhuire
Eilean an Tighe
Na h-Eileanan Mòra (Shiant Islands)
288
NG
259
Eilean Trodday
Rubha Hunish
Rubha na h-Aiseig
DUN TULM CASTLE
Balmacqueen
Duntulm
Kilmaluag
MUSEUM OF ISLAND LIFE
Eilean Flodigarry
Flodigarry
MEALL NA SUIRAMACH
543
Digg
Staffin Bay
Staffin I.
Kilvaxter
Glashvin
Balgown
THE QUIRAING
Brogaig
Stenscholl
Staffin
Linicro
TROTTERNISH
Kilt Rock
KILT ROCK & MEALT FALLS
A855
466
BIOD BUIDHE
Rha
Elishader
Maligar
Loch Mealt
Uig
Valtos
Marishader
Conon
Garros
Rubha nam Brathairean
UIG
Balnaknock
611
BEINN EDRA
Breckrey
Culnaknock
Island of Rona
Earlish
Lealt
LEALT FALLS
Lower Tote
Lealt
Upper Tote
0 1 2 3 miles
0 1 2 3 4 5 km

Greenstone Point
Rubha Beag
Cailleach Hd.
Bottle I.
Opinan
Rubha Mor
Mellon Udrigle
Stattic Pt.
Gruinard I.
Badluarach
Mungasdale
Gruinard Bay
Gruinard House
Achgarve
Laide
First Coast
Sand
Second Coast
Inchina
Little Gruinard
Mellon Charles
Ormiscaig
Tighnafiline
Aultbea
Drumchork
Eilean Furadh Mór
Sròn a' Gheodha Dhuibh
Camas Mór
Rubha Reidh
Loch an Draing
Cove
Isle of Ewe
296 AN CUAIDH
Loch Sguod
Loch a' Bhaid-luachraich
Melvaig
Inverasdale
LOCH EWE
Midtown
Aultgrishan
Seana Chamas
Brae
Rubha 'Ard na Bà
Loch Fada
Little Gruinard
Gruinard
Naast
Tournaig
Peterburn
Aird Dubh
INVEREWE GARDEN
680 BEINN A'CHAISGEIN BEAG
Loch Bad a'Chreamh
Port Erradale
Londubh
North Erradale
Poolewe
Loch Kernsary
Fisherfield Forest
Rubha Bàn
Big Sand
FIONN LOCH
Longa Island
Caolas Beag
CARN DEARG
Strath
Loch Tollàidh
Smithstown
GAIRLOCH HERITAGE MUSEUM
Gairloch
MEALL AN DOIREAN 420
Dubh Loch
791 BEINN AIRIGH CHARR
LOCH GAIRLOCH
Charlestown
Port Henderson
Aird
Badachro
Kerrysdale
BEINN LAIR 860
Letterewe Forest
Opinan
LOCH MAREE ISLANDS
Eilean Subhainn
Shieldaig
Kerry
Loch Bad an Sgalaig
Letterewe
South Erradale
Loch Clàir
VICTORIA FALLS
Talladale
Abhainn a' Gharbh Choire
Erradale
Redpoint
Dubh Loch
Abhainn Braigh-horrisdale
Loch Gaineamhach
WESTER ROSS
Flowerdale Forest
875 BAOSBHEINN Forest
Loch na h-Oidhche
Glen Grudie
Shieldaig
Craig
624 BEINN BHREAC
Loch a'Bhealaich
878
Kinlochewe Forest
BEINN EIGHE
Rubha na Fearn
985 BEINN ALLIGIN
1010 BEINN EIGHE
Fearnmore
Loch Torridon
Lower Diabaig
Fearnbeg
Torridon Forest
Alligin
A832
B8057
B8021
B8056
270
262
249

Carn nan Sgeir
Strathcanaird
Strath Kanaird
Strath nan Lon
Camas Mór
Isle Martin
Loch Kanaird
Cailleach Hd.
STORNOWAY 2:45
Ardmair
Rhue
Annat Bay
Rhidorroch
Stattic Pt.
Scoraig
Carnach
Rireavach
LITTLE LOCH BROOM
Morefield
Ullapool
Loch Achall
Rhidorroch Ho.
ULLAPOOL MUSEUM
Badluarach
635
BEINN GHOBHLACH
Glen Achall
East
Gruinard House
Durnamuck
Badcaul
Allt na h-Airbhe
Badrallach
A835
558
BEINN EILIDEACH
LECKMELM SHRUBBERY AND ARBORETUM
Inchina
Leckmelm
Blarnalearoch
642
MEALL DUBH
Camusnagaul
Strath Beag
Rhiroy
Ardessie
767
SAIL MHOR
Ardindrean
Ardcharnich
Dundonnell Hotel
Dundonnell
Eilean Darach
Letters
Inverlael Forest
Dundonnell House
Inverlael
LAEL FOREST GARDEN
Lael Forest
Strathnasheallag Forest
AN TEALLACH 1062
Inverbroom
Loch na Sealga
Strath More
680
BEINN A'CHAISGEIN BEAG
Dundonnell Forest
Auchindrean
889
Fisherfield Forest
Strath na Sealga
Braemore
908
BEINN DEARG MHOR
Fain
CORRIESHALLOCH GORGE
MEALL LEACACH 618
Dubh Loch
914
BEINN A' CHLAIDHEIMH
Abhainn Cuileig
Braemore Forest
Abhainn Droma
807
Lochdru
Loch a'Bhraoin
BEINN LAIR 860
Letterewe Forest
1019
MULLACH COIRE MHIC FHEARCHAIR
934
1110
SGURR MOR
Letterewe
Lochan Fada
748
GROBAN
999
A'CHAILLEACH
Loch Garbhaig
949
MEALL GORM
980
SLIOCH
Abhainn a'Chadh'Bhuidhe
Fannich Forest
WESTER ROSS
BEINN NAN RAMH 711
Fannich Lodge
692
Kinlochewe Forest
LOCH FANNICH
Glen Grudie
Heights of Kinlochewe
Leckie
Strath Chrombuill
878
Taagan
Lochrosque Forest
Kinlochewe Forest
Anancaun
Abhainn Bruachaig
BEINN EIGHE
Incheril
933
FIONN BHEINN
Kinlochewe
1010
Glen Docherty
Strath Bran
0 1 2 3 miles
0 1 2 3 4 5 km
Badavanich
Achnasheen
A832
270
271
261
250

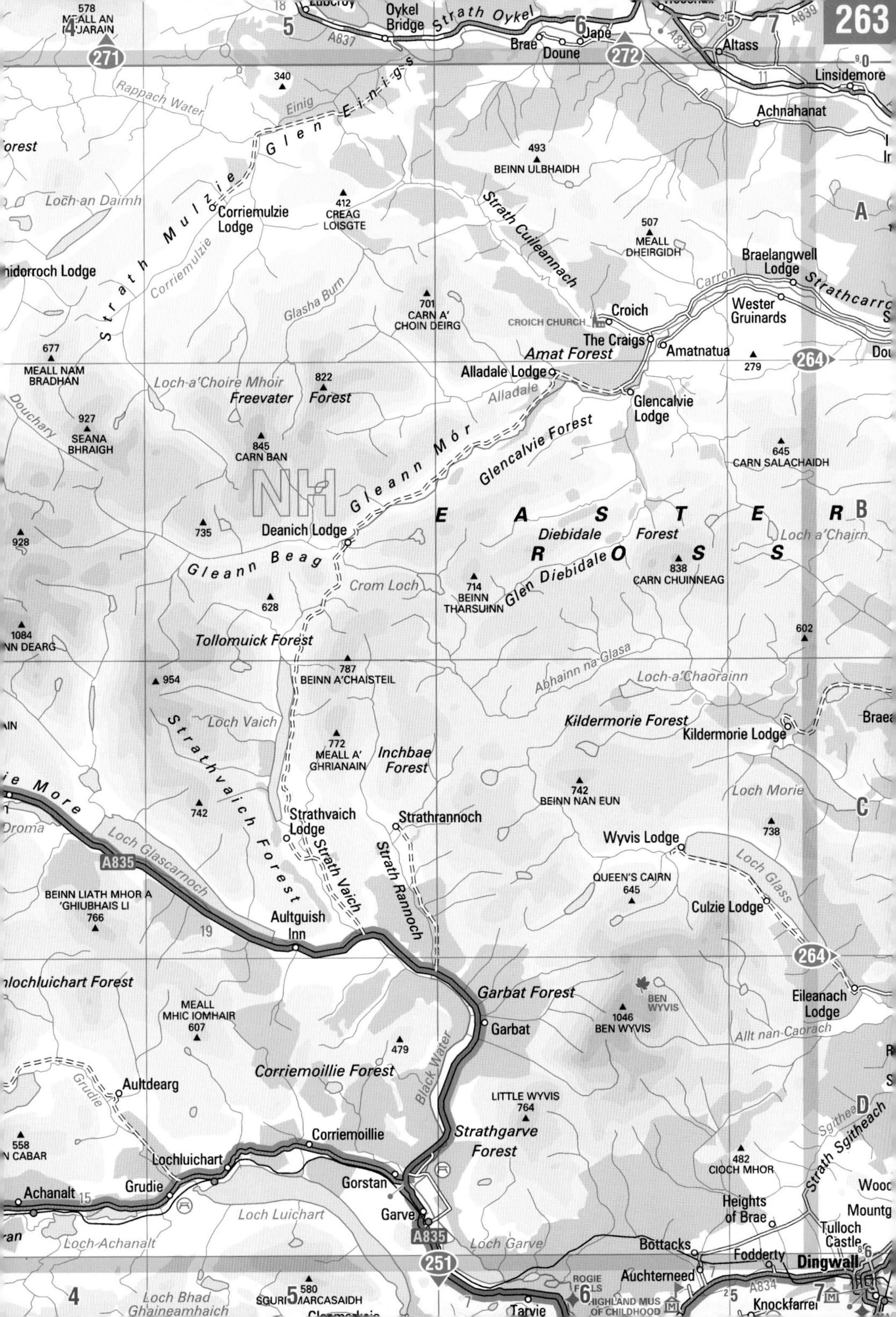
Oykel Bridge
Strath Oykel
Brae
Doune
Altass
Linsidemore
Achnahanat
Glen Einig
Rappach Water
Loch an Daimh
Strath Mulzie
Corriemulzie Lodge
Corriemulzie
Glasha Burn
BEINN ULBHAIDH
Strath Cuileannach
CREAG LOISGTE
MEALL DHEIRGIDH
Braelangwell Lodge
Strathcarron
Wester Gruinards
Carron
CARN A' CHOIN DEIRG
CROICH CHURCH
Croich
The Craigs
Amatnatua
Amat Forest
Alladale Lodge
Alladale
Glencalvie Lodge
Glencalvie Forest
MEALL NAM BRADHAN
Loch a' Choire Mhoir
Freevater Forest
Douchary
SEANA BHRAIGH
CARN BAN
CARN SALACHAIDH
Gleann Mór
NH
EASTER ROSS
Deanich Lodge
Diebidale Forest
Loch a' Chairn
Gleann Beag
Crom Loch
BEINN THARSUINN
Glen Diebidale
CARN CHUINNEAG
Tollomuick Forest
BEINN A' CHAISTEIL
Abhainn na Glasa
Loch a' Chaorainn
Strathvaich Forest
Loch Vaich
Kildermorie Forest
Kildermorie Lodge
MEALL A' GHRIANAIN
Inchbae Forest
BEINN NAN EUN
Loch Morie
Strathvaich Lodge
Strathrannoch
Strath Vaich
Strath Rannoch
Wyvis Lodge
Loch Glascarnoch
A835
QUEEN'S CAIRN
Culzie Lodge
Loch Glass
BEINN LIATH MHOR A 'GHIUBHAIS LI
Aultguish Inn
Garbat Forest
BEN WYVIS
Eileanach Lodge
Allt nan Caorach
MEALL MHIC IOMHAIR
Garbat
Corriemoillie Forest
Black Water
Aultdearg
Grudie
LITTLE WYVIS
Strathgarve Forest
Corriemoillie
Lochluichart
Gorstan
CIOCH MHOR
Strath Sgitheach
Achanalt
Grudie
Loch Luichart
Garve
Heights of Brae
Loch Achanalt
Loch Garve
Bottacks
Tulloch Castle
Fodderty
Dingwall
ROGIE FALLS
Auchterneed
A834
Loch Bhad Ghaineamhaich
SGURR MARCASAIDH
HIGHLAND MUS OF CHILDHOOD
Knockfarrel
Tarvie
271
272
264
251

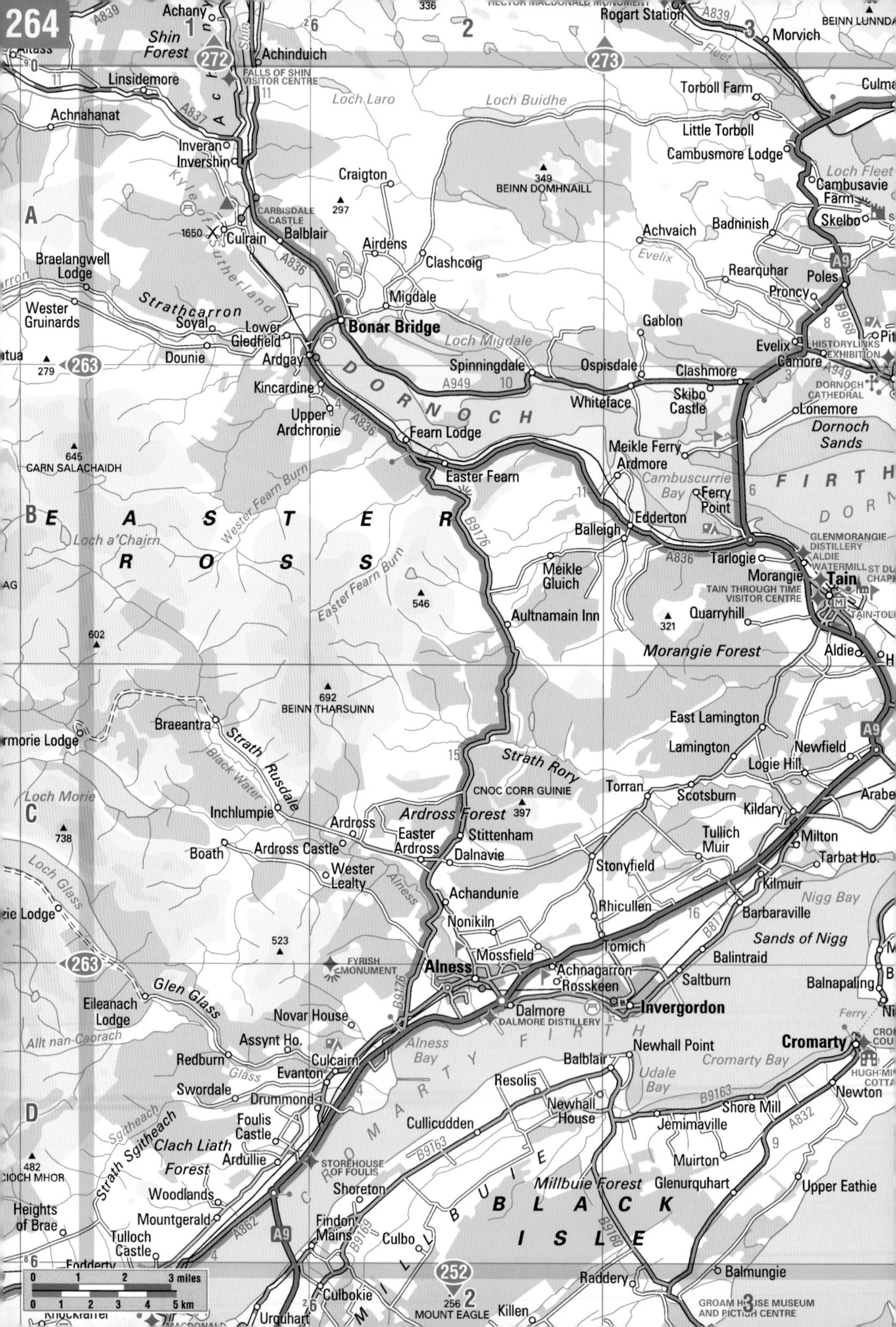
Achany
Shin Forest
Achinduich
Rogart Station
Morvich
BEINN LUNNDA
Linsidemore
FALLS OF SHIN VISITOR CENTRE
Loch Laro
Loch Buidhe
Torboll Farm
Achnahanat
Little Torboll
Inveran
Invershin
Cambusmore Lodge
Craigton
349
BEINN DOMHNAILL
Loch Fleet
Cambusavie Farm
Kyle of Sutherland
CARBISDALE CASTLE
297
Skelbo
Culrain
Balblair
Achvaich
Badninish
Airdens
Clashcoig
Evelix
Braelangwell Lodge
Rearquhar
Poles
Migdale
Proncy
Strathcarron
Wester Gruinards
Soyal
Lower Gledfield
Bonar Bridge
Gablon
Loch Migdale
Evelix
HISTORYLINKS EXHIBITION
Dounie
Ardgay
279
Spinningdale
Ospisdale
Camore
Clashmore
Kincardine
DORNOCH
Whiteface
Skibo Castle
DORNOCH CATHEDRAL
Upper Ardchronie
Lonemore
Dornoch Sands
Fearn Lodge
645
CARN SALACHAIDH
Meikle Ferry
Ardmore
Easter Fearn
Cambuscurrie Bay
Ferry Point
FIRTH
Wester Fearn Burn
EASTER ROSS
Edderton
Balleigh
Loch a'Chairn
GLENMORANGIE DISTILLERY
ALDIE WATERMILL
Meikle Gluich
Tarlogie
Morangie
Tain
TAIN THROUGH TIME VISITOR CENTRE
Easter Fearn Burn
546
Aultnamain Inn
321
Quarryhill
602
Morangie Forest
Aldie
692
BEINN THARSUINN
East Lamington
Braeantra
Strath Rusdale
Lamington
Newfield
Black Water
Strath Rory
Logie Hill
Loch Morie
CNOC CORR GUINIE
Torran
Scotsburn
Ardross Forest
397
Kildary
Inchlumpie
Ardross
Easter Ardross
Stittenham
Tullich Muir
Milton
738
Boath
Ardross Castle
Dalnavie
Tarbat Ho.
Loch Glass
Wester Lealty
Stonyfield
Kilmuir
Nigg Bay
Achandunie
Rhicullen
Barbaraville
Nonikiln
Sands of Nigg
523
Tomich
Mossfield
Balintraid
FYRISH MONUMENT
Alness
Achnagarron
Rosskeen
Saltburn
Balnapaling
Eileanach Lodge
Glen Glass
Dalmore
Invergordon
Novar House
DALMORE DISTILLERY
Ferry
Allt nan Caorach
Assynt Ho.
Alness Bay
Redburn
Culcairn
CROMARTY FIRTH
Balblair
Newhall Point
Cromarty
Cromarty Bay
Evanton
Resolis
Udale Bay
Swordale
Newhall House
Shore Mill
Newton
Drummond
Foulis Castle
Cullicudden
Jemimaville
Strath Sgitheach
Clach Liath Forest
482
Ardullie
STOREHOUSE OF FOULIS
Muirton
Millbuie Forest
Glenurquhart
Upper Eathie
Woodlands
Shoreton
BLACK ISLE
Heights of Brae
Mountgerald
Findon Mains
Culbo
Tulloch Castle
Fodderty
Raddery
Balmungie
Culbokie
256
MOUNT EAGLE
Killen
GROAM HOUSE MUSEUM AND PICTISH CENTRE
Urquhart
0 1 2 3 miles
0 1 2 3 4 5 km

Golspie
DUNROBIN CASTLE MUSEUM & GARDENS
A9
274
NH
NJ
Littleferry
Fourpenny
Embo
Embo Street
WITCHES STONE
OLD POST OFFICE VISITOR CENTRE
DORNOCH FIRTH
Whiteness Sands
Tarbat Ness
TARBAT NESS LIGHTHOUSE
Wilkhaven
Bindal
TARBAT DISCOVERY CENTRE
Portmahomack
Rockfield
Inver
Arboll
Balnagall
Tarrel
Lochslin
Loch Eye
Geanies House
B9165
Rhynie
Fearn Station
Hill of Fearn
Fearn
FEARN ABBEY
B9166
Hilton of Cadboll
Loans of Tullich
Balintore
SHANDWICK STONE
Shandwick
B9175
Ankerville
Chapelhill
Pitcalnie
Port an Righ
Nigg
203
King's Cave
Castlecraig
Sutors of Cromarty
MORAY FIRTH
266
BURGHEAD BAY
Findhorn
Lower Hempriggs
B9011
Findhorn Bay
Miltonhi
Kincorth Ho.
KINLOSS ABBEY
Kinloss
Grange Hall
A96
The Bar
Culbin Forest
Kintessack
Springfield
SUENO'S STONE
253
Moy Ho.
Forres
NELSON TOWER
FALCONER MUSEUM
Mains
Dyke
Blervie
Whiteness Head

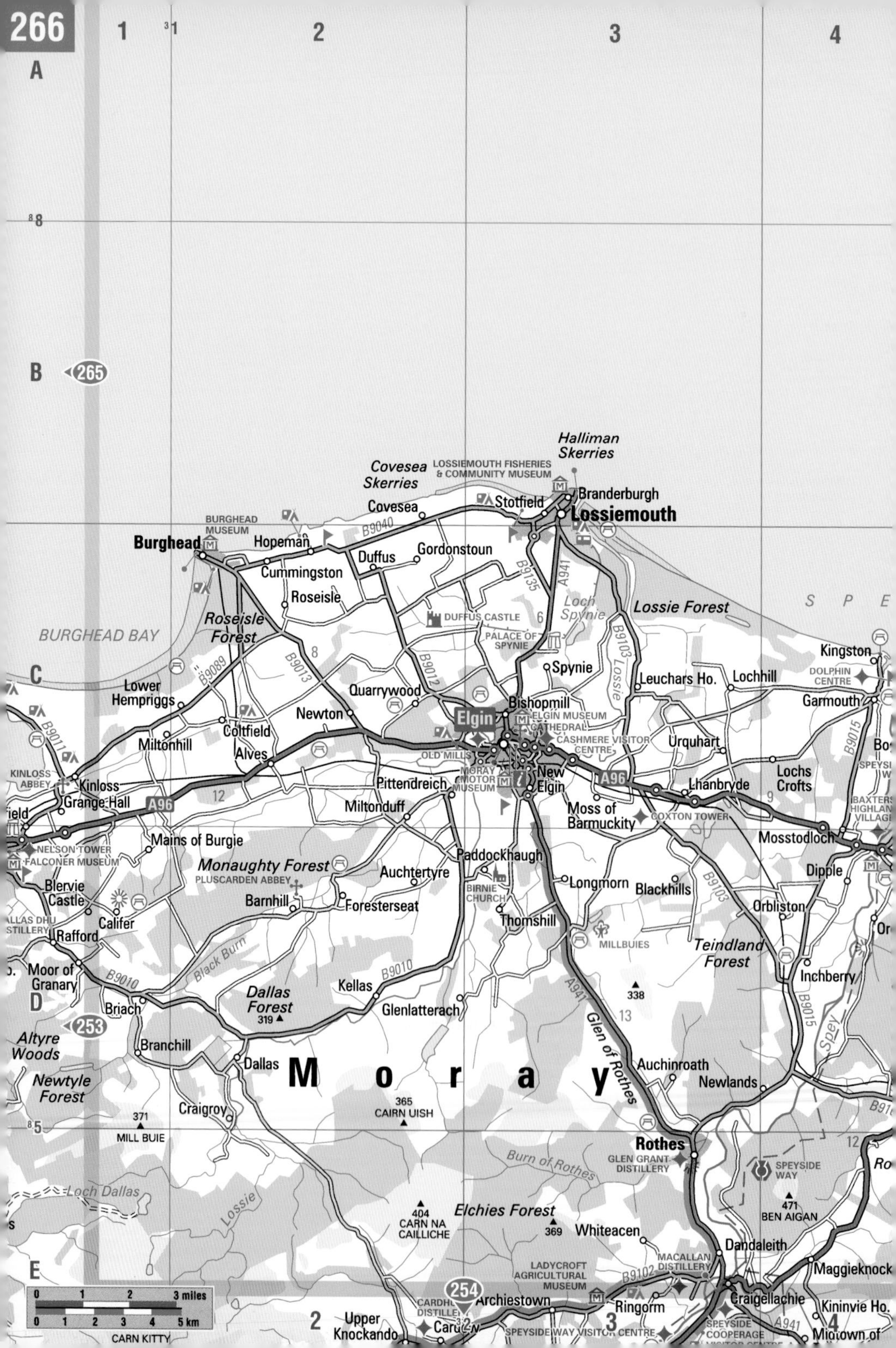

1
2
3
4
A
B
C
D
E
265
253
254
Halliman Skerries
Covesea Skerries
LOSSIEMOUTH FISHERIES & COMMUNITY MUSEUM
Branderburgh
Lossiemouth
Stotfield
Covesea
BURGHEAD MUSEUM
Burghead
Hopeman
Duffus
Gordonstoun
Cummingston
Roseisle
Roseisle Forest
BURGHEAD BAY
DUFFUS CASTLE
PALACE OF SPYNIE
Loch Spynie
Lossie Forest
S P E
Spynie
Kingston
Leuchars Ho.
Lochhill
DOLPHIN CENTRE
Garmouth
Lower Hempriggs
Quarrywood
Newton
Bishopmill
Elgin
ELGIN MUSEUM
CATHEDRAL
CASHMERE VISITOR CENTRE
Urquhart
Coltfield
Miltonhill
Alves
OLD MILLS
MORAY MOTOR MUSEUM
New Elgin
Lochs Crofts
KINLOSS ABBEY
Kinloss
Grange Hall
Pittendreich
A96
Lhanbryde
Miltonduff
Moss of Barmuckity
COXTON TOWER
BAXTERS HIGHLAND VILLAGE
Mosstodloch
Mains of Burgie
NELSON TOWER
FALCONER MUSEUM
Monaughty Forest
PLUSCARDEN ABBEY
Paddockhaugh
Auchtertyre
Longmorn
Blackhills
Dipple
Blervie Castle
Barnhill
Foresterseat
BIRNIE CHURCH
Orbliston
Califer
Thomshill
Rafford
MILLBUIES
Teindland Forest
Black Burn
Moor of Granary
B9010
Kellas
Inchberry
Dallas Forest
338
Briach
319
Glenlatterach
Glen of Rothes
Altyre Woods
Branchill
Dallas
Moray
Auchinroath
Newlands
Newtyle Forest
365 CAIRN UISH
371 MILL BUIE
Craigroy
Rothes
GLEN GRANT DISTILLERY
SPEYSIDE WAY
Burn of Rothes
Loch Dallas
Lossie
404 CARN NA CAILLICHE
Elchies Forest
369
Whiteacen
471 BEN AIGAN
Dandaleith
LADYCROFT AGRICULTURAL MUSEUM
MACALLAN DISTILLERY
Maggieknock
Craigellachie
Archiestown
Ringorm
Kininvie Ho.
Upper Knockando
SPEYSIDE WAY VISITOR CENTRE
SPEYSIDE COOPERAGE
Midtown of
CARN KITTY
0 1 2 3 miles
0 1 2 3 4 5 km
B9040
B9135
A941
B9103
B9012
B9013
B9089
B9011
B9015
B9102

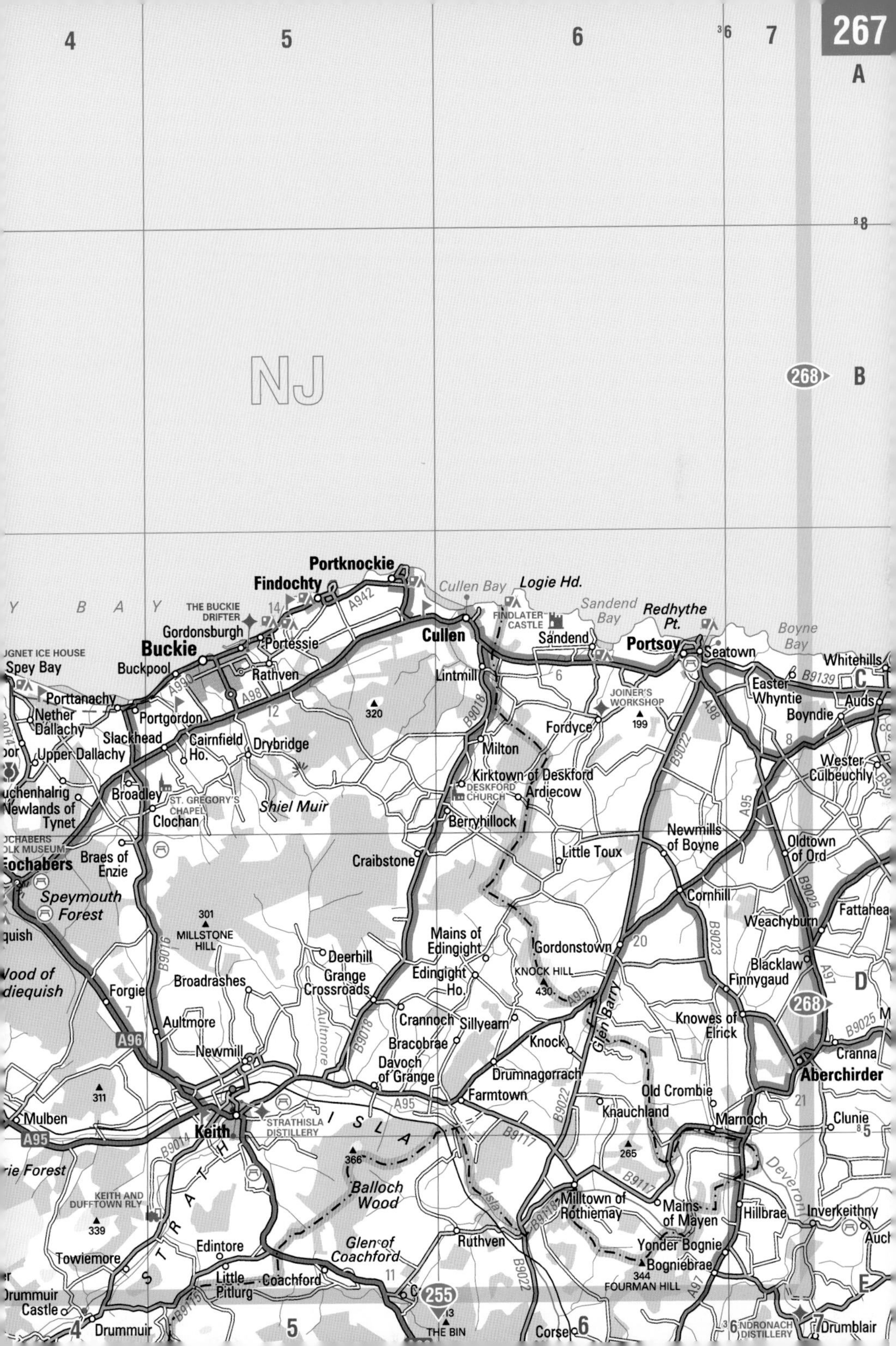
4
5
6
7
A
B
C
D
E
NJ
268
Portknockie
Findochty
Cullen Bay
Logie Hd.
Sandend Bay
Redhythe Pt.
Boyne Bay
THE BUCKIE DRIFTER
Gordonsburgh
Buckie
Portessie
Cullen
FINDLATER CASTLE
Sandend
Portsoy
Seatown
Whitehills
Spey Bay
Buckpool
Rathven
Lintmill
A942
A990
A98
B9139
Portannachy
Nether Dallachy
Portgordon
JOINER'S WORKSHOP
Easter Whyntie
Auds
Boyndie
Upper Dallachy
Slackhead
Cairnfield Ho.
Drybridge
320
Milton
Fordyce
199
B9018
B9022
Kirktown of Deskford
DESKFORD CHURCH
Ardiecow
Wester Culbeuchly
Auchenhalrig
Newlands of Tynet
Broadley
ST. GREGORY'S CHAPEL
Clochan
Shiel Muir
Berryhillock
Newmills of Boyne
A95
Oldtown of Ord
Fochabers
Braes of Enzie
Craibstone
Little Toux
Speymouth Forest
Cornhill
B9025
Fattahead
301
MILLSTONE HILL
Mains of Edingight
Gordonstown
20
Weachyburn
B9016
Deerhill
Grange Crossroads
Edingight Ho.
KNOCK HILL
430
B9023
Blacklaw
Finnygaud
Wood of Ordiequish
Broadrashes
Forgie
Aultmore
Crannoch
Sillyearn
Glen Barry
Knowes of Elrick
A97
Cranna
A96
Newmill
Bracobrae
Knock
Davoch of Grange
Drumnagorrach
Aberchirder
311
Farmtown
Old Crombie
Mulben
Keith
STRATHISLA DISTILLERY
Knauchland
Marnoch
Clunie
A95
B9014
366
B9117
265
Deveron
Balloch Wood
Milltown of Rothiemay
Mains of Mayen
Hillbrae
Inverkeithny
KEITH AND DUFFTOWN RLY
339
Isla
Edintore
Ruthven
Yonder Bognie
Glen of Coachford
Towiemore
344
Bogniebrae
FOURMAN HILL
Little Pitlurg
Coachford
11
255
Drummuir Castle
Drummuir
THE BIN
Corse
DRONACH DISTILLERY
Drumblair
STRATH ISLA
12
21
8
6
7

1
2
3
A
B
C
D
E
267
256
Troup Hd.
Pennan Hd.
Quarry Hd.
Boyne Bay
Knock Hd.
Boyndie Bay
Head of Garness
Gamrie Bay
Seatown
Whitehills
Macduff
MACDUFF MARINE AQUARIUM
Crovie
Gardenstown
Pennan
Easter Whyntie
Inverboyndie
Auds
Boyndie
Banff
BANFF MUSEUM
Easter Silverford
Dubford
Towie
New Aberdour
COLLEONARD SCULPTURE GARDEN & GALLERY
DUFF HOUSE
West Greenskares
Longmanhill
Wester Culbeuchly
Doune Park
Cushnie
231 WINDYHEADS HILL
Montcoffer Ho.
Minnonie
Ladysford
Kirktown of Alvah
Keilhill
Netherbrae
Nether Glasslaw
Oldtown of Ord
Mid Cloch Forbie
Craigmaud
Gorrachie
Greenlaw
King Edward
227 HILL OF FISHRIE
Fattahead
Weachyburn
The Pole of Itlaw
Milltown of Craigston
New Pitsligo
Blacklaw
Finnygaud
Plaidy
Craigston Castle
Hill of Mountblairy
Fintry
New Byth
Muirden
Bonnykelly
Cranna
Garmond
Whitestones
Ironside
Aberchirder
Forglen Ho.
Bogton
Muiryfold
Balthangie
Oldwhat
Clunie
Carnousie
Turriff
DELGATIE CASTLE
Mains of Fedderate
Marnoch
Deveron
Kirkton
Cuminestown
Middle Cairncake
Little Colp
Delgaty Forest
Culsh
Mill of Muiresk
Hillbrae
Inverkeithny
Hatton Castle
Howe of Teuchar
New Deer
Darra
Auchininna
Rush-head
Birkenhills
Fortrie
Brownhill
Crofts of Inverthernie
Cairnbanno Ho.
Knaven
A98
A95
A97
A947
B9139
B9121
B9025
B9023
B9031
B9105
B9027
B9170
B9024
A950
A981
A947
0 1 2 3 miles
0 1 2 3 4 5 km

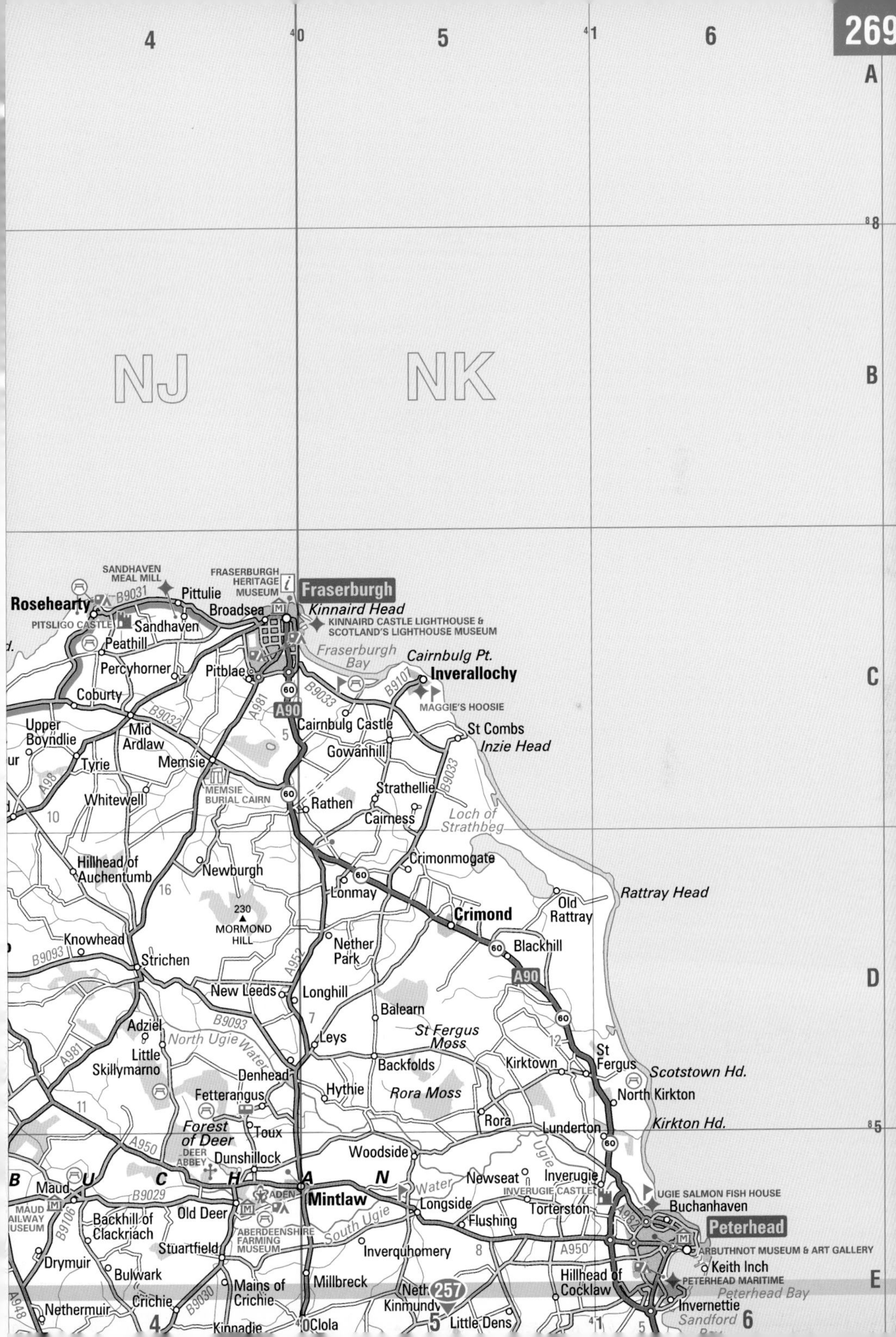
NJ
NK
Fraserburgh
Kinnaird Head
KINNAIRD CASTLE LIGHTHOUSE & SCOTLAND'S LIGHTHOUSE MUSEUM
FRASERBURGH HERITAGE MUSEUM
SANDHAVEN MEAL MILL
Rosehearty
Pittulie
Broadsea
PITSLIGO CASTLE
Sandhaven
Peathill
Percyhorner
Pitblae
Fraserburgh Bay
Cairnbulg Pt.
Inverallochy
MAGGIE'S HOOSIE
Coburty
Upper Boyndlie
Mid Ardlaw
Memsie
Tyrie
Cairnbulg Castle
St Combs
Inzie Head
Gowanhill
Strathellie
Whitewell
MEMSIE BURIAL CAIRN
Rathen
Cairness
Loch of Strathbeg
Crimonmogate
Hillhead of Auchentumb
Newburgh
Lonmay
Rattray Head
Old Rattray
Crimond
230 MORMOND HILL
Knowhead
Nether Park
Blackhill
Strichen
New Leeds
Longhill
Balearn
Adziel
North Ugie Water
Leys
St Fergus Moss
Little Skillymarno
Denhead
Backfolds
Kirktown
St Fergus
Scotstown Hd.
Fetterangus
Hythie
Rora Moss
North Kirkton
Forest of Deer
Toux
Rora
Lunderton
Kirkton Hd.
DEER ABBEY
Dunshillock
Woodside
BUCHAN
Maud
MAUD RAILWAY MUSEUM
Mintlaw
ADEN
Newseat
Inverugie
INVERUGIE CASTLE
UGIE SALMON FISH HOUSE
Buchanhaven
Backhill of Clackriach
Old Deer
Longside
Torterston
Flushing
Peterhead
ABERDEENSHIRE FARMING MUSEUM
South Ugie
Stuartfield
Inverquhomery
ARBUTHNOT MUSEUM & ART GALLERY
Drymuir
Bulwark
Millbreck
Hillhead of Cocklaw
Keith Inch
PETERHEAD MARITIME
Mains of Crichie
Crichie
Peterhead Bay
Invernettie
Nethermuir
Kinmundy
Little Dens
Sandford Bay
Kinnadie
Clola
257
A90
A952
A981
A98
A950
A982
A948
B9031
B9032
B9033
B9107
B9093
B9029
B9106
B9030

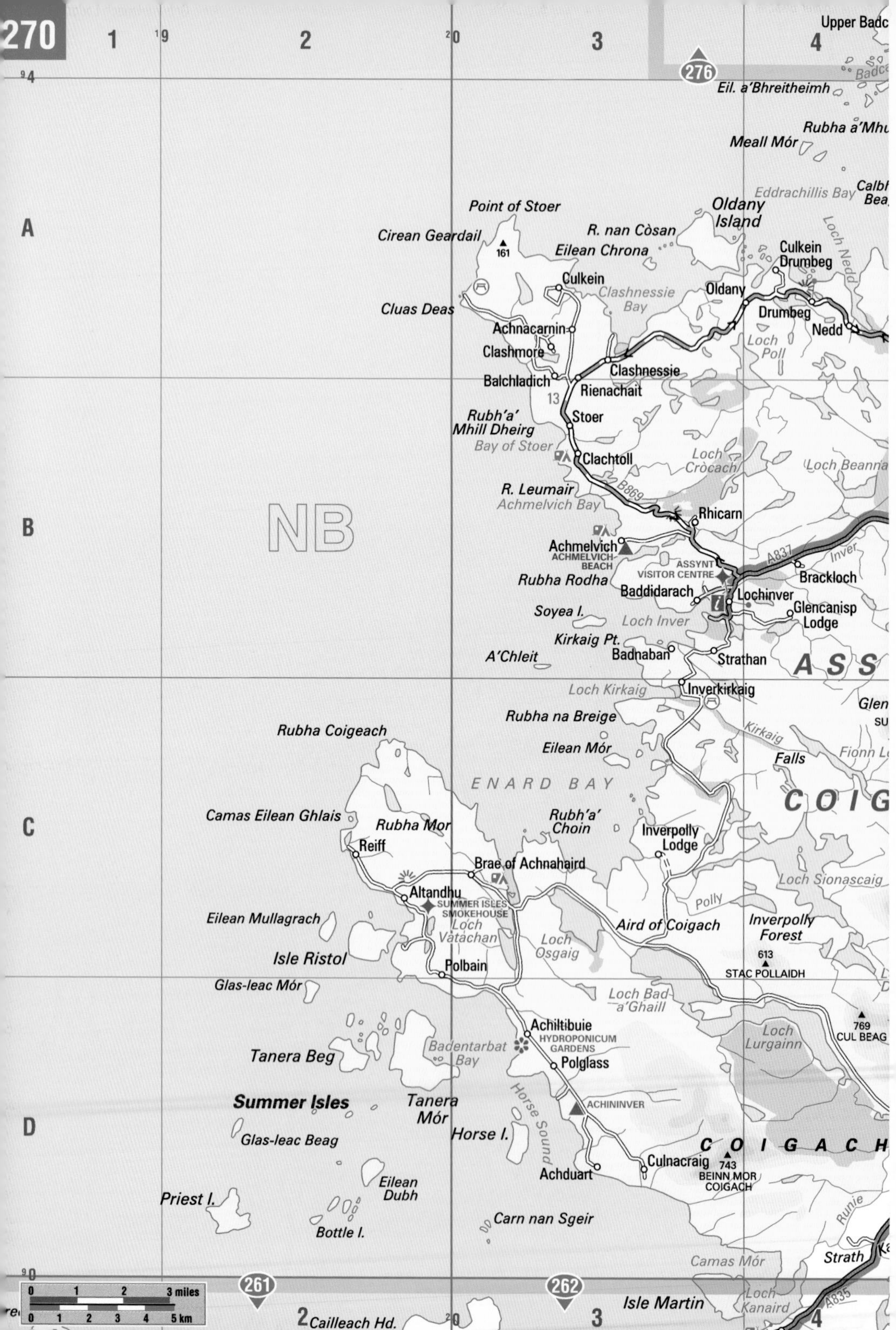

Upper Badc
276
Eil. a'Bhreitheimh
Rubha a'Mhu
Meall Mór
Eddrachillis Bay
Calbh Bea
Point of Stoer
Oldany Island
Loch Nedd
Cirean Geardail
161
R. nan Còsan
Eilean Chrona
Culkein Drumbeg
Culkein
Clashnessie Bay
Oldany
Cluas Deas
Drumbeg
Nedd
Achnacarnin
Loch Poll
Clashmore
Clashnessie
Balchladich
Rienachait
13
Rubh'a' Mhill Dheirg
Stoer
Bay of Stoer
Clachtoll
Loch Cròcach
Loch Beanna
R. Leumair
B869
Achmelvich Bay
Rhicarn
NB
Achmelvich
ACHMELVICH BEACH
A837
Inver
ASSYNT VISITOR CENTRE
Brackloch
Rubha Rodha
Baddidarach
Lochinver
Glencanisp Lodge
Soyea I.
Loch Inver
Kirkaig Pt.
Badnaban
Strathan
A'Chleit
ASS
Loch Kirkaig
Inverkirkaig
Glen
Rubha na Breige
Rubha Coigeach
Kirkaig
Falls
Eilean Mór
Fionn L
ENARD BAY
COIG
Camas Eilean Ghlais
Rubh'a' Choin
Rubha Mor
Inverpolly Lodge
Reiff
Brae of Achnahaird
Loch Sionascaig
Altandhu
SUMMER ISLES SMOKEHOUSE
Polly
Eilean Mullagrach
Loch Vatachan
Aird of Coigach
Inverpolly Forest
Loch Osgaig
Isle Ristol
613
STAC POLLAIDH
Polbain
Glas-leac Mór
Loch Bad a'Ghaill
Achiltibuie
769
CUL BEAG
HYDROPONICUM GARDENS
Loch Lurgainn
Badentarbat Bay
Tanera Beg
Polglass
Horse Sound
Summer Isles
Tanera Mór
ACHININVER
Horse I.
COIGACH
Glas-leac Beag
Culnacraig
743
BEINN MOR COIGACH
Achduart
Eilean Dubh
Priest I.
Runie
Carn nan Sgeir
Bottle I.
Strath
Camas Mór
261
262
0 1 2 3 miles
0 1 2 3 4 5 km
Loch Kanaird
A835
Isle Martin
Cailleach Hd.

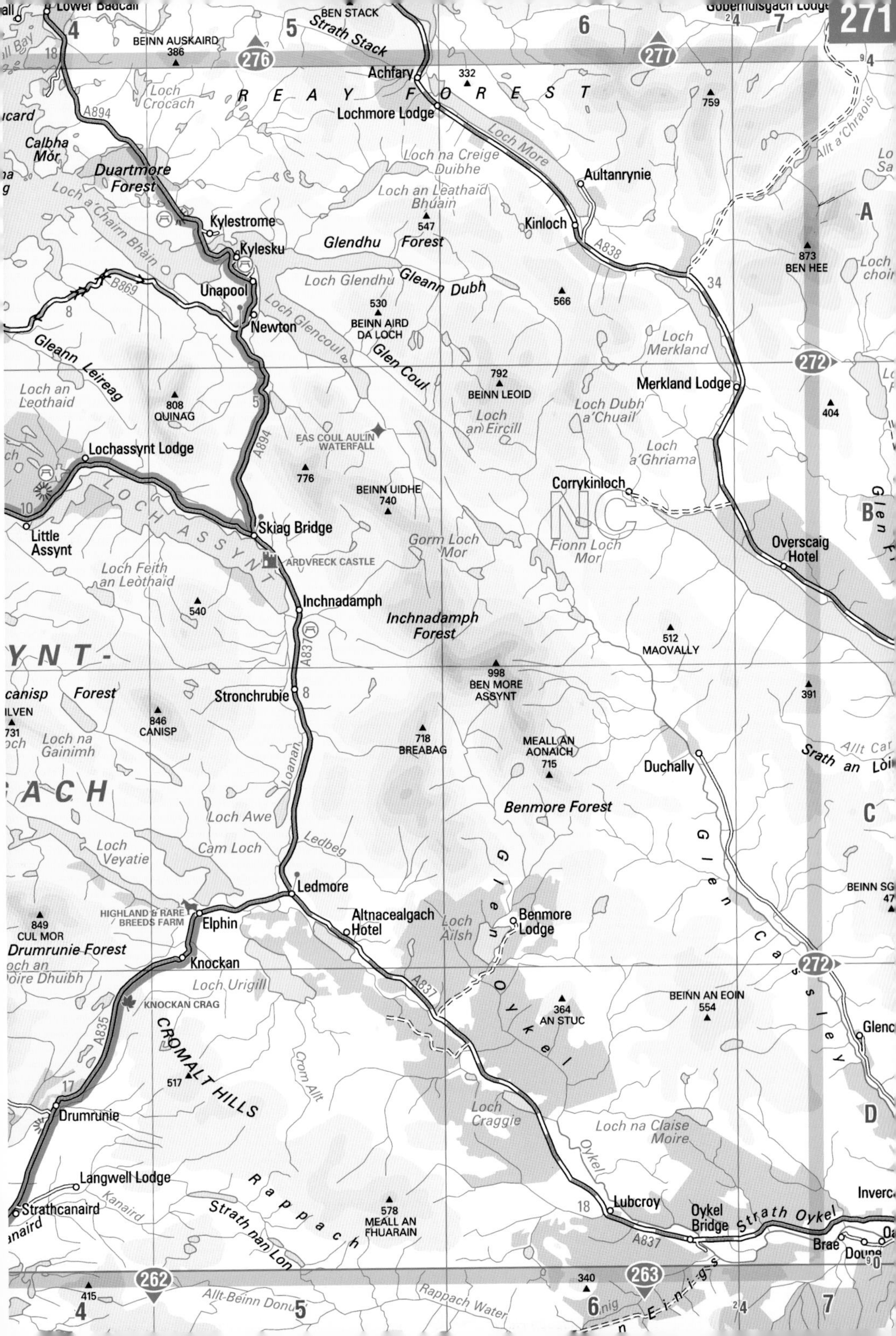

Lower Badcall
BEN STACK
Strath Stack
BEINN AUSKAIRD
386
276
277
Achfary
REAY FOREST
Lochmore Lodge
Loch Crocach
A894
Calbha Mòr
Duartmore Forest
Loch More
Loch na Creige Duibhe
Loch an Leathaid Bhuain
Aultanrynie
Kinloch
A838
Kylestrome
Kylesku
Loch a'Chairn Bhain
Glendhu Forest
Loch Glendhu
Gleann Dubh
Unapool
B869
Newton
Loch Glencoul
BEINN AIRD DA LOCH
Glen Coul
873
BEN HEE
Loch Merkland
Merkland Lodge
272
Gleann Leireag
Loch an Leothaid
808
QUINAG
BEINN LEOID
Loch an Eircill
Loch Dubh a'Chuail
EAS COUL AULIN WATERFALL
Lochassynt Lodge
Loch a'Ghriama
Corrykinloch
BEINN UIDHE
NC
LOCH ASSYNT
Skiag Bridge
Little Assynt
Gorm Loch Mor
Fionn Loch Mor
Overscaig Hotel
ARDVRECK CASTLE
Loch Feith an Leothaid
Inchnadamph
Inchnadamph Forest
A837
512
MAOVALLY
998
BEN MORE ASSYNT
Stronchrubie
Forest
846
CANISP
Loch na Gainimh
718
BREABAG
MEALL AN AONAICH
715
Duchally
Loanan
Benmore Forest
Loch Awe
Cam Loch
Loch Veyatie
Ledbeg
Glen Casslay
Ledmore
849
CUL MOR
HIGHLAND & RARE BREEDS FARM
Elphin
Altnacealgach Hotel
Loch Ailsh
Benmore Lodge
Drumrunie Forest
Knockan
Loch Urigill
Glen Oykel
KNOCKAN CRAG
364
AN STUC
BEINN AN EOIN
554
A835
CROMALT HILLS
517
Crom Allt
Drumrunie
Loch Craggie
Loch na Claise Moire
Oykel
Langwell Lodge
Rappach
Strath nan Lon
578
MEALL AN FHUARAIN
Strathcanaird
Kanaird
Lubcroy
Oykel Bridge
Strath Oykel
Brae
Doune
262
263
415
Allt-Beinn Donu
Rappach Water
340
Einig

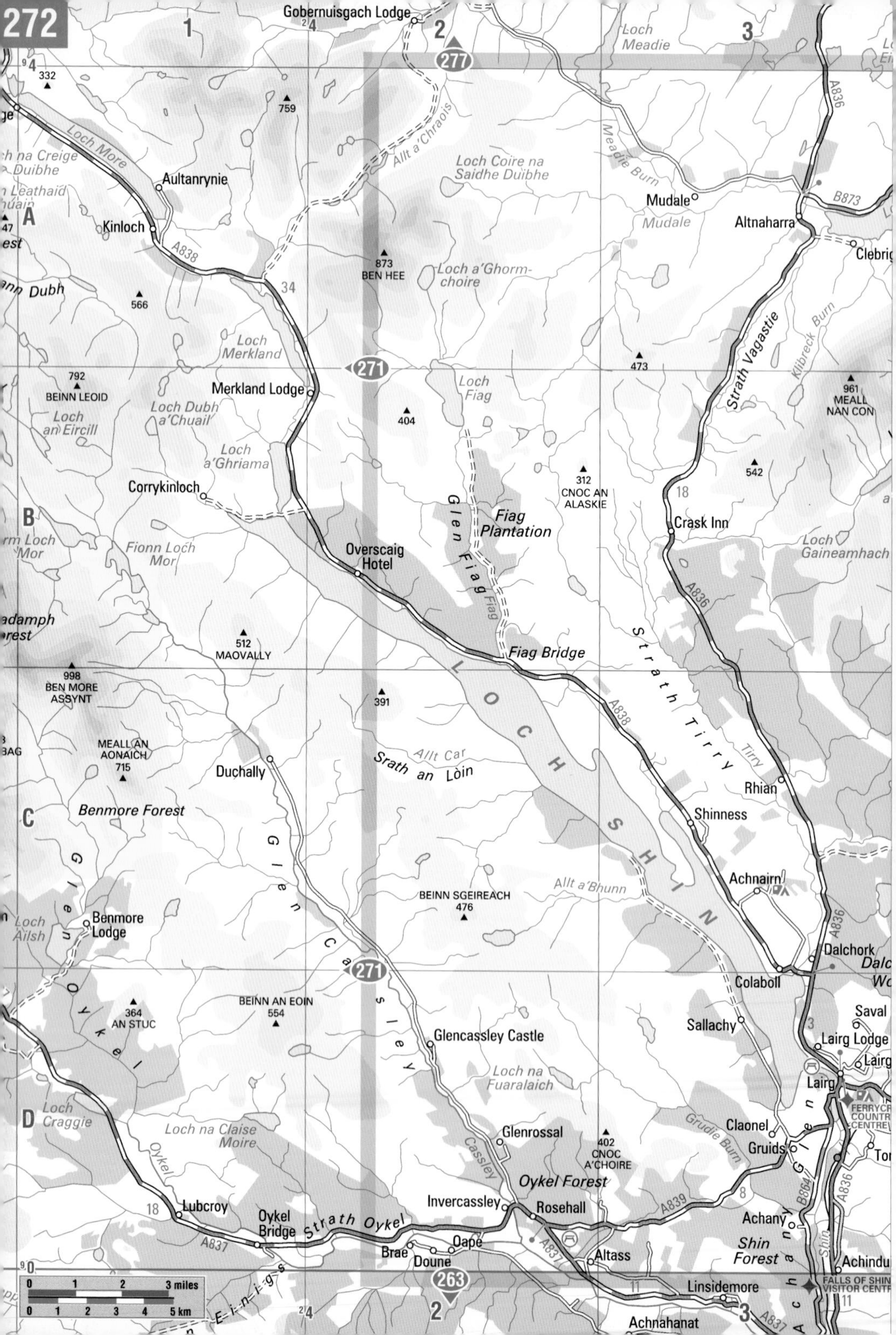
Gobernuisgach Lodge
277
271
263
Loch More
Aultanrynie
Kinloch
A838
Loch Meadie
Meadie Burn
Mudale
Altnaharra
B873
Clebrig
A836
Loch Coire na Saidhe Duibhe
Allt a'Chraois
873 BEN HEE
Loch a'Ghorm-choire
759
332
566
Loch Merkland
Merkland Lodge
792 BEINN LEOID
Loch an Eircill
Loch Dubh a'Chuail
Loch a'Ghriama
Corrykinloch
Fionn Loch Mor
Overscaig Hotel
Loch Fiag
404
473
Strath Vagastie
Klibreck Burn
961 MEALL NAN CON
542
312 CNOC AN ALASKIE
Glen Fiag
Fiag Plantation
Crask Inn
Loch Gaineamhach
512 MAOVALLY
Fiag Bridge
Strath Tirry
998 BEN MORE ASSYNT
391
LOCH SHIN
MEALL AN AONAICH 715
Allt Car
Srath an Loin
Duchally
Rhian
Shinness
Benmore Forest
Glen Cassley
Achnairn
Allt a'Bhunn
BEINN SGEIREACH 476
Glen Oykel
Loch Ailsh
Benmore Lodge
Dalchork
Colaboll
364 AN STUC
BEINN AN EOIN 554
Glencassley Castle
Sallachy
Saval
Lairg Lodge
Lairg
Loch na Fuaralaich
Loch Craggie
Loch na Claise Moire
Glenrossal
402 CNOC A'CHOIRE
Claonel
Gruids
Grudie Burn
FERRYCROFT COUNTRYSIDE CENTRE
Oykel Forest
Cassley
Oykel
Lubcroy
Oykel Bridge
Strath Oykel
Invercassley
Rosehall
A839
Achany
Glen
B864
Shin Forest
A837
Brae
Oape
Doune
Altass
Achinduich
Linsidemore
FALLS OF SHIN VISITOR CENTRE
Achnahanat
Achany Glen
Eining
0 1 2 3 miles
0 1 2 3 4 5 km

Pole Hill 294
Naver Forest
Loch Naver
Mallart
Loch Rimsdale
Loch nan Clàr
Loch Truderscaig
Loch Badanloch
Loch an Alltan Fhearna
Badanloch Lodge
Badanloch Forest
Garvault Hotel
Ben Griam More 509
Ben Griam Beg 580
Loch Druim a'Chliabhair
Achentoul Forest
Allt Airigh-dhamh
Loch an Ruathair
Loch Arichlinie
Lochside
Achentoul
Strath Beg
Kinbrace
Helmsdale
B871
B873
A897
Rimsdale Burn
Garvault Hotel
Ben Klibreck 721
Loch Choire Forest
Loch Choire Lodge
Loch Choire
Loch a'Bhealaich
Meall a'Bhata 581
Ben Armine 704
Gorm-loch Beag
Creag Mhór 713
Gorm-loch Mór
Ben Armine Forest
Borrobol Forest
Abhainn na Frithe
Altanduin
Borrobol Lodge
Creag nam Fiadh 387
Kinbrace Burn
NG
Strath Skinsdale
Skinsdale
Tuarie Burn
Craggie
Craggie Burn
Ben Armine Lodge
Strath na Seilge
Glas-loch Mor
Meallan Liath Mor 461
Dalnessie
Black Water
Brora
Loch Beannach
Balnacoil
Col-Bheinn 538
Achnaluachrach
West Langwell
Strath Brora
Gordonbush
Allt na Luibe
Loch Brora
Dalreavoch
Rhilochan
Loch Craggie
East Langwell
Farlary
Ben Horn 521
Loch Horn
Achrimsdale
East Clyne
West Clyne
Clynelish
Clynelish Distillery
Brora
Doll
Muie
Ardachu
Strath Fleet
Rogart
Pittentrail
Hector Macdonald Monument
Rogart Station
A839
Cagar Feosaig 377
Golspie Burn
Backies
Beinn Lunndaidh 466
Morvich
Fleet
A9
Dunrobin Castle Museum & Gardens
Golspie
Culmaily
Torboll Farm
Loch Cracail Mor
Loch Buidhe
Loch Laro
278
274
264

Loch Druim a'Chliabhain
580
BEN GRIAM BEG
THE FLOWS
279
Rumsdale Water
16
Garvault Hotel
509
BEN GRIAM MORE
Allt Airigh-dhamh
Achentoul Forest
373
A897
348
Glutt Lodge
Loch nan Clàr
Loch an Ruathair
Badanloch Forest
Lochside
438
Loch Badanloch
Loch Arichlinie
Knockfin Heights
Glutt Water
Badanloch Lodge
Strath Beg
Achentoul
B871
Kinbrace
318
CNOC LOCH MHADADH
328
Helmsdale
273
Kinbrace Burn
438
CNOC COIRE NA PEARNA
705
MORVEN
Borrobol Forest
Abhainn na Frithe
517
CNOC AN EIREANNAICH
Suisgill Burn
Wag
Altanduin
Borrobol Lodge
A897
NC
Langwell Fo
365
Kildonan Burn
17
387
CREAG NAM FIADH
555
CREAG SCALABSDALE
STRATH OF KILDONAN
Skinsdale
Strath Skinsdale
Kildonan Lodge
BAILE AN ÓR GOLDRUSH SITE
BEINN DUBHAIN
414
Tuarie Burn
Craggie
Craggie Burn
Helmsdale
Torrish
Kilphedir
A897
ELDRABLE HILL
417
HELMSDALE
Marrel
345
West Helmsdale
TIMESPAN
Black Water
628
BEINN DHORAIN
Glen Sletdale
Glen Loth
592
Gartymore
Portgower
Lothmore
11
Balnacoil
538
COL-BHEINN
Lothbeg
273
Gordonbush
Lothbeg Pt.
A9
Loch Brora
Dalreavoch
Rhilochan
BEN HORN
521
Achrimsdale
East Clyne
West Clyne
Farlary
Loch Horn
Clynelish
Dalchalm
CLYNELISH DISTILLERY
377
CAGAR FEOSAIG
Brora
Golspie Burn
Doll
466
BEINN LUNNDAIDH
Backies
9
A839
Morvich
DUNROBIN CASTLE MUSEUM & GARDENS
Golspie
265
0 1 2 3 miles
0 1 2 3 4 5 km

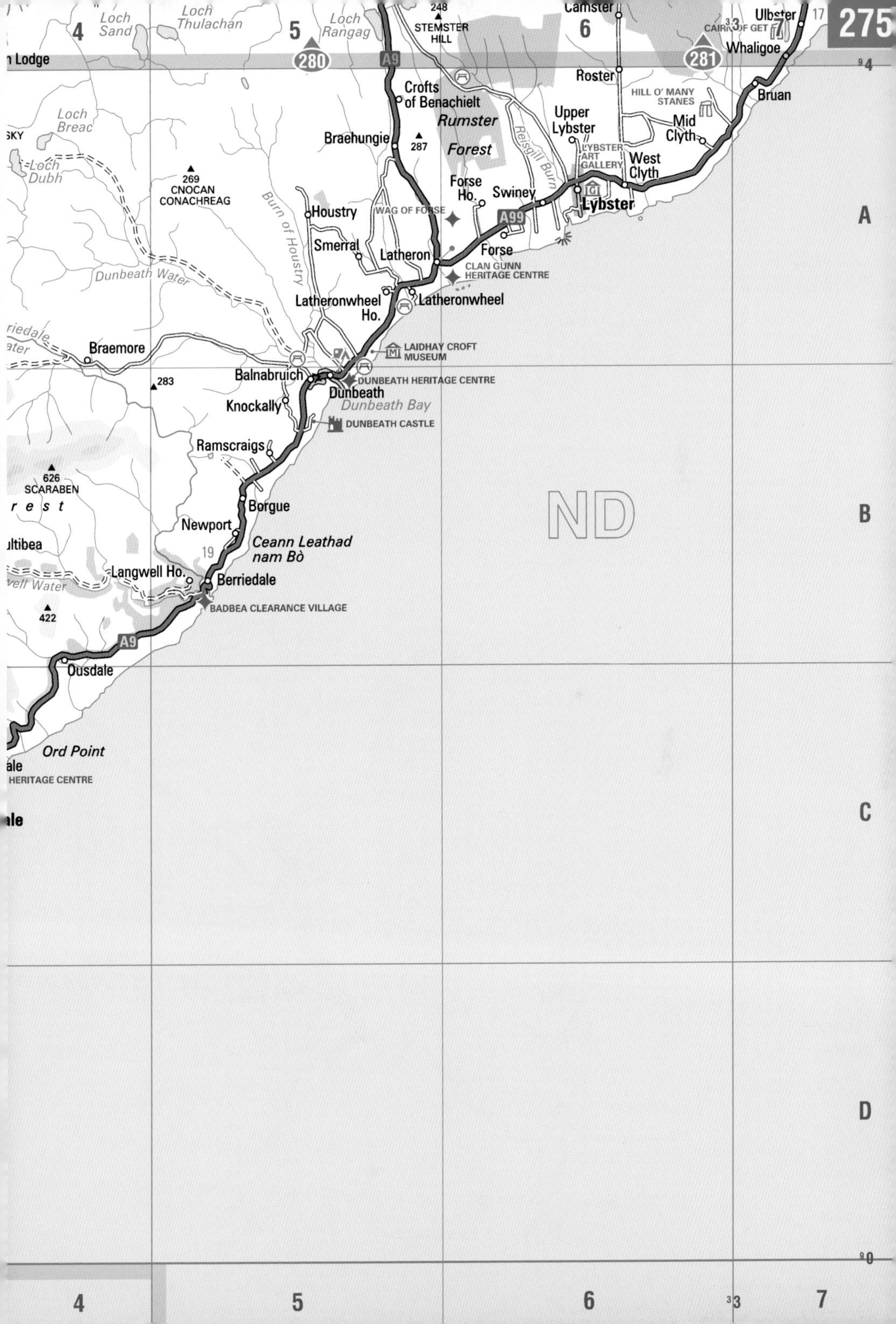

Loch Sand
Loch Thulachan
Loch Rangag
STEMSTER HILL
248
Camster
Ulbster
CAIRN OF GET
Whaligoe
280
281
A9
Lodge
Roster
Bruan
HILL O' MANY STANES
Crofts of Benachielt
Rumster Forest
Upper Lybster
Mid Clyth
Loch Breac
Loch Dubh
Braehungie
287
LYBSTER ART GALLERY
West Clyth
269
CNOCAN CONACHREAG
Forse Ho.
Swiney
Reisgill Burn
Burn of Houstry
Houstry
WAG OF FORSE
Lybster
A99
Smerral
Latheron
Forse
Dunbeath Water
CLAN GUNN HERITAGE CENTRE
Latheronwheel Ho.
Latheronwheel
Braemore
LAIDHAY CROFT MUSEUM
Balnabruich
DUNBEATH HERITAGE CENTRE
283
Dunbeath
Knockally
Dunbeath Bay
DUNBEATH CASTLE
Ramscraigs
626
SCARABEN
Borgue
ND
Newport
Ceann Leathad nam Bò
19
Langwell Ho.
Berriedale
BADBEA CLEARANCE VILLAGE
422
Ousdale
Ord Point
HERITAGE CENTRE
A
B
C
D
4
5
6
7

1
2
3
4
A
B
C
D
CAPE WRATH
Kearvaig
371
SGRIBHIS-BHEINN
Geodha Ruadh na Fola
Kearvaig
Bay of Keisgaig
Inshore
Loch Keisgaig
Geodha Ruadh
Achiem
457
FASHVEN
Am Balg
Loch Airig na Beinn
423
BEINN DEARG
Sandwood Loch
485
CREAG RIABHACH
Rubh'an Fhir Léithe
Grudie
Loch na Gainimh
Strath Shinary
332
GHLAS BHEINN
Sheigra
Balchrick
Droman
Oldshore Beg
Eilean Roin Mor
Oldshoremore
A838
521
FARRMHEALL
19
Loch Clash
Kinlochbervie
Gualin Ho.
B801
Badcall
Bagh Loch an Roin
Loch Inchard
Achriesgill
Strath Dionard
CRANS
Dionard
9
Achlyness
L. na Claise Carnaich
Loch Dughaill
Ceathramh Garbh
Rhiconich
Ardmore Pt.
A838
Rubha Ruadh
Ardmore
GANU MOR
908
Foinaven
Fanagmore
NORTH-WEST SUTHERLAND
Tarbet
Loch Laxford
Loch a'Garbh-bhaid Mór
Loch Dionar
Handa Island
Foindle
Sound of Handa
A894
Loch nam Brac
Laxford Bridge
Loch an Easain Uaine
787
ARKLE
Scourie Bay
Laxford
Scourie More
A838
Scourie
Gorm Loch
Lochstack Lodge
Rubh'Aird an t-Sionnaich
719
BEN STACK
Loch Stack
Upper Badcall
Lower Badcall
Strath Stack
BEINN AUSKAIRD
386
Badcall Bay
18
Eil. a'Bhreitheimh
270
271
Achfary
332
0 1 2 3 miles
0 1 2 3 4 5 km
Loch Crocach
REAY FOREST
Rubha a'Mhucard
A894
Lochmore Lodge

NC
Faraid Head
Balnakeil Bay
Balnakeil
BALNAKEIL CHURCH
BALNAKEIL CRAFT VILLAGE
DURNESS VISITOR CENTRE
SMOO CAVE
Durness
DURNESS
Sangomore
Leirinmore
Keoldale
Sangobeg
Kyle of Durness
Rispond
Sarsgrum
Eilean Hoan
Whiten Head
Geodh'a' Bhrideoin
Eilean Clùimhrig
Rubha Thormaid
Eilean nan Ron
Port Vasgo
Strathan
Midfield
408 BEN HUTIG
West Strathan
Talmine
Caol Raineach
Skerray
Rabbit Is.
Skinnet
Midtown
Tongue Bay
Skullomie
Coldbackie
422 MEALL MEADHONACH
LOCH ERIBOLL
Hope
A'Mhoine
A838
Portnancon
Heilam
Hope
Lochside
230
Eilean Choraidh
Achuvoldrach
TONGUE
Kirkiboll
Tongue
CASTLE VARRICH
KYLE OF TONGUE
Druim nan Cliar
772 BEINN SPIONNAIDH
Eriboll
A838
Polla
Loch Hope
A836
310
Strath Beag
30
521 AN LEAN-CHARN
Ribigill
KYLE OF TONGUE
Loch Craggie
Kinloch Lodge
Kinloch
Loch na Seilg
Loch Crocach
927 BEN HOPE
Loch a' Ghobha-Dhuibh
278
527 BEINN STUMANADH
16
764 BEN LOYAL
Loch Loyal
Loch an Dherue
FEINNE-BHEINN MOR 465
Strath More
Strathmore
Loch Loyal Lodge
Loch Haluim
557 CNOC NAN CULLEAN
Alltnacaillich
DUN DORNAIGIL BROCH
Loch Syre
Glen Golly
Loch Coulside
Inchkinloch
416
Gobernuisgach Lodge
Loch Meadie
Loch Eileanach
294 POLE HILL
271
272
759
A836
11
4
5
6
7
A
B
C
D
9

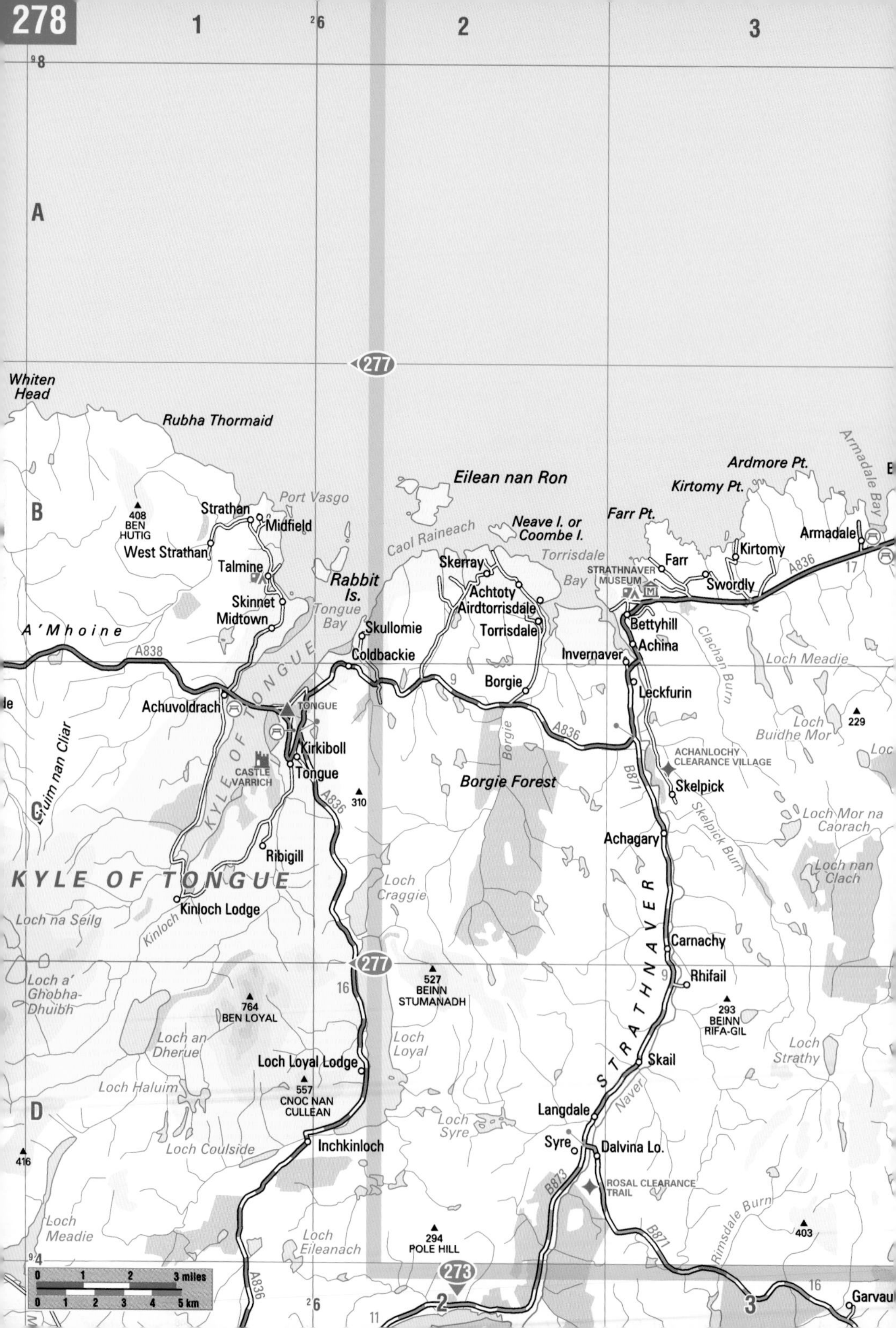

278
1
2
3
A
B
C
D
277
Whiten Head
Rubha Thormaid
Eilean nan Ron
Ardmore Pt.
Kirtomy Pt.
Armadale Bay
Port Vasgo
Neave I. or Coombe I.
Farr Pt.
408 BEN HUTIG
Strathan
Midfield
West Strathan
Talmine
Caol Raineach
Rabbit Is.
Skerray
Torrisdale Bay
Farr
Kirtomy
Armadale
A836
STRATHNAVER MUSEUM
Swordly
Skinnet
Midtown
Tongue Bay
Achtoty
Airdtorrisdale
Torrisdale
Skullomie
Bettyhill
A'Mhoine
A838
KYLE OF TONGUE
Coldbackie
Invernaver
Achina
Clachan Burn
Loch Meadie
Borgie
Leckfurin
Achuvoldrach
TONGUE
Loch Buidhe Mor
229
Kirkiboll
Tongue
CASTLE VARRICH
A836
310
Borgie
Borgie Forest
ACHANLOCHY CLEARANCE VILLAGE
Skelpick
B871
Skelpick Burn
Loch Mor na Caorach
Achagary
Ribigill
Loch nan Clach
Loch Craggie
Kinloch Lodge
Loch na Seilg
Kinloch
STRATHNAVER
Carnachy
Rhifail
Loch a' Ghobha-Dhuibh
527 BEINN STUMANADH
764 BEN LOYAL
293 BEINN RIFA-GIL
Loch an Dherue
Loch Loyal
Loch Strathy
Loch Loyal Lodge
Skail
Loch Haluim
557 CNOC NAN CULLEAN
Naver
Langdale
Loch Syre
Syre
Dalvina Lo.
Inchkinloch
Loch Coulside
416
B873
ROSAL CLEARANCE TRAIL
Rimsdale Burn
Loch Meadie
Loch Eileanach
294 POLE HILL
B871
403
273
0 1 2 3 miles
0 1 2 3 4 5 km
Garvau

NC
Strathy Point
Totegan
Strathy Bay
Aultiphurst
Lednagullin
Baligill
Strathy
Melvich Bay
Portskerra
Melvich
Bighouse
Red Pt.
Fresgoe
Sandside Ho.
Sandside Bay
Reay
A836
Isauld
Dounreay
DOUNREAY EXHIBITION CENTRE
Buldoo
A836
Achvarasdal
Achreamie
CNOC FREKEDAIN CHAMBERED CAIRN
Brims Ness
ST MARY'S CHAPEL
Crosskirk
Bridge of Forss
Spear Hd.
280
Scrabster
Thurso
THURSO
Millba
Newlands of Geise
Westfield
Shebster
Forss Water
Lieurary
B870
Golval
Bowside Lodge
Loch Akran
Sandside Burn
Loch Saorach
Broubster
Loch Calder
Calde Mains
Strathy Forest
Strathy
Meala
254
A897
Loch na Seilge
Loch Thormaid
198
Achvarasdal Burn
Shurrery
Achiemore
Upper Bighouse
Craigtown
Halladale
Dalhalvaig
Brawlbin
Shurrery Lodge
Loch Shurrery
Loch Olginey
Scots Stati
Loch Scye
Dorrery
224
Olgri
290
BEINN NAM BAD MOR
Trantlemore
Trantlebeg
STRATH HALLADALE
The Uair
Loch Tuim Ghlais
Loch Caluim
Torran Water
B870
280
Loch Meadie
Dyke
Forsinain
Loch Dubh nan Geodh
Loch nam Breac
Loch Eileanach
Loch Gaineimh
Loch na Saobhaidhe
280
SLETILL HILL
Loch Sletill
Altnabreac Station
Sleach Water
Lochmore Cottage
21
Lochdhu
Loch More
Loch Crocach
Forsinard
Forsinard Station
221
Thurso
Loch Druim a'Chliabhain
THE FLOWS
A897
Loch a' Mhuilinn
Loch Sand
580
BEN GRIAM BEG
Rumsdale Water
Dalnawillan Lodge
274
373
Hotel
348
Loch Breac

1
2
3
4
283
A
B
C
D
DUNNET HEAD
127
Briga Hd.
Scarfskerr
B855
Brough
Hunspow
The Thirl
St John's Loch
MARY ANN'S COTTAGE
Corsback
Dunnet
NATURAL HISTORY DISPLAY
DUNNET BAY
STROMNESS 1:30
Brims Ness
Spear Hd.
Holborn Hd.
Thurso Bay
Clardon Hd.
ST MARY'S CHAPEL
Crosskirk
279
Scrabster
THURSO CASTLE
THURSO FOLK MUSEUM
FLAGSTONE INTERPRETATIVE TRAIL
Castlehill
A836
16
Bridge of Forss
144
Thurso
THURSO
Millbank
Thurso East
Clardon
Murkle
Greenland
Castletown
Haimer
Sandside Bay
Dounreay
Buldoo
Achreamie
DOUNREAY EXHIBITION CENTRE
Newlands of Geise
B874
Olrig Ho.
CASTLETOWN
Tain
141
Isauld
Achvarasdal
CNOC FREKEDAIN CHAMBERED CAIRN
Geise
A9
Hilliclay
B876
Reay
Westfield
Weydale
Durran
Shebster
Forss Water
6
Lieurary
Buckies
Achingills
Sandside Burn
Achvarasdal Burn
Loch Saorach
B870
Sordale
Stemster
Bowertower
Knockdee
Loch Calder
Braal Castle
Stemster Ho.
Halcro
Broubster
Calder Mains
Roadside
Gillock
Loch Thormaid
198
Clayock
Loch Scarmclate
B874
Halkirk
A882
Shurrery
Brawlbin
Banniskirk Ho.
Loch Olginey
Scotscalder Station
Harpsdale
Loch Watten
Shurrery Lodge
Loch Shurrery
Loch Scye
Dorrery
224
Olgrinmore
176
290
BEINN NAM BAD MOR
A9
B870
Watten
Spittal
Backlass
Thurso
Loch Tuim Ghlais
Mybster
Loch of Toftingall
Loch Caluim
Torran Water
B870
Westerdale
Acharole
Burn of Acharole
279
Loch Meadie
Loch Dubh nan Geodh
Little River
Loch Eileanach
Strathmore Lodge
Loch Sletill
Loch Gaineimh
17
Camster Burn
Altnabreac Station
Sleach Water
Lochmore Cottage
Lochdhu
Loch More
Rangag
GREY CAIRNS OF CAMSTER
221
Loch Ruard
Achavanich
Thurso
248
STEMSTER HILL
Loch a' Mhuilinn
Loch Sand
Loch Thulachan
Loch Rangag
Rumsdale Water
Dalnawillan Lodge
A9
275
0 1 2 3 miles
0 1 2 3 4 5 km
348
Crofts of Benachielt

Langaton Point
Nethertown
Red Head
Island of Stroma
Mell Head
Uppertown
ST. MARGARETS HOPE 1:00
BURWICK 0:40 (May-Sept)
Muckle Skerry
Pentland Skerries
Men of Mey
St John's Pt.
Boars of Duncansby
Gills Bay
East Mey
CASTLE OF MEY
Mey
Gills
Kirkstyle
Huna
DUNCANSBY HEAD
John o' Groats
Stacks of Duncansby
Canisbay
A836
A99
Barrock
Inkstack
Brabster
Skirza
Skirza Head
Tofts
Lochend
Gill Burn
Freswick
Freswick Bay
Ness Head
BUCHOLLY CASTLE
Slickly
Reaster
Alterwall
CAITHNESS BROCH CENTRE
Auckengill
ND
Lyth
LYTH ARTS CENTRE
Sortat
Barrock Ho.
Nybster
Brough Head
Howe
Keiss
KEISS CASTLE
Mireland
Burn of Lyth
Kirk
Loch of Wester
B870
Myrelandhorn
SINCLAIR'S BAY
Killimster
Mains of Watten
B876
CASTLE SINCLAIR
CASTLE GIRNIGOE
Noss Head
Reiss
Winless
A99
Sealky Head
Wick
B874
Ackergill
Bilbster
Staxigoe
WICK HERITAGE MUS
Papigoe
Strath
A882
Wick
Broadhaven
Stirkoke Ho.
Milton
Wick Bay
Achairn Burn
Old Wick
Newton
South Hd.
CASTLE OF OLD WICK
Whiterow
Gote O'Tram
Tannach
Hempriggs House
Loch Hempriggs
Helman Hd.
HILL OF OLICLETT
Thrumster
Gansclet
Sarclet
Loch of Yarrows
Sarclet Hd.
Ulbster
CAIRN OF GET
Whaligoe
HILL O' MANY TANES
Bruan
Mid

Scale : 1:425 700
(approx 6.72 miles to 1 inch)
0 2 4 6 miles
0 2 4 6 8 10 km
Orkney
HY
North Ronaldsay
Hollandstoun
BROCH OF BURRIAN
NORTH RONALDSAY FIRTH
Papa Westray
Holm of Papa
KNAP OF HOWAR
Holland
Gayfield
Aikerness
Backaskaill
Rackwick
Pierowall
PIEROWALL CHURCH
NOLTLAND CASTLE
Broughton
Braehead
WESTRAY
NOUP HEAD
FITTY HILL
Midbea
Skelwick
Langskaill
WESTSIDE CHURCH
Rapness
Sulland
THE NORTH SOUND
KIRKWALL 1:25
WESTRAY FIRTH
Faray
Calf of Eday
Carrick Ho.
CARRICK HOUSE
Calfsound
Braeswick
Guith
Millbounds
Loth
EDAY
Backaland
Veness
Scar
Burness
Sellibister
Lettan
START PT.
Broughtown
Lady
Newark
SANDAY
Overbister
Kettletoft
Laminess
Stove
QUOYNESS CHAMBERED CAIRN
SANDAY SOUND
Papa Stronsay
Odie
Whitehall Village
Wardhill
STRONSAY
Everbay
Grobister
Kirbister
Rothiesholm
Dishes
Holland
Linga Holm
Auskerry
STRONSAY FIRTH
Edmonstone
Shapinsay
BALFOUR CASTLE
Balfour
Newlot
ABERDEEN 6:00
LERWICK 7:45
Wasbister
ROUSAY
Sourin
MIDHOWE BROCH
Eynhallow
EYNHALLOW CHURCH
Westness
KNOWE OF YARSO CAIRN
Frotoft
Brinian
Skaill
ST MAGNUS CHURCH
Egilsay
Muckle Green Holm
CUBBIE'S ROO'S CASTLE AND ST MARY'S CHAPEL
Wyre
Gairsay
BROUGH HEAD
BROUGH OF BIRSAY
EARL'S PALACE
MARWICK HEAD NATURE RESERVE
Marwick
Abune-the-Hill
The Barony
Costa
Burgar
Kirbuster
Stara
Twatt
Stenso
BROCH OF GURNESS
Redland
Tingwall
Isbister
Beaquoy
Click Mill
CLICK MILL
Scarwell
Quoyloo
Dounby
Northdyke
Skeabrae
Mirbister
Hackland
Skaill
SKAILL HOUSE
Kierfiold Ho
CORRIGALL FARM MUSEUM
Gorseness
Brough
Settiscarth
Isbister
Aith
Hestwall
Tenston
Netherbrough
Bimbister
Breck of Cruan
Yesnaby
Voy
Arion
Finstown
Work
ORKNEY MUSEUM
Craigiefield
Quholm
RING OF BRODGAR
STANDING STONES
TORMISTON MILL
MAES HOWE
Grimbister
WIRELESS MUSEUM
Kirkwall
Bridge of Waith
Clouston
Heddle
Nisthouse
ST MAGNUS CATHEDRAL
Berstane

HOY AND WEST MAINLAND
Stromness
Pier Arts Centre
Stromness Museum
Clestrain
Breckan
Murra
Graemsay
Petertown
Houton
Linksness
Hoy
Quoyness
North Hoy Nature Reserve
Scrabster 1:30
Ward Hill
Old Man of Hoy
Rackwick
Rora Head
Knap of Trowieglen
Dwarfie Stane
HOY
Lyness
Rinnigill
Bow
Little Ayre
Crockness
Wyng
Hackness
Longhope
Melsetter
Hurliness
Brims
Martello Towers
SOUTH WALLS
Scapa Flow Visitor Centre
Fara
Rysa Little
Cava
Flotta
Pan
Switha
SCAPA FLOW
Ireland
Kirbister
Cairnton
Crya
Gyre
St Nicholas Church
Hobbister
Smoogro
Swanbister
Waulkmill Lodge
Greenigoe
Tradespark
Whitecleat
Tankerness
North Halley
Deerness
Skaill
Grindigar
Gritley
Toab
Foubister
North Dawn
Norwood Museum
Upper Sanday
St Mary's
Italian Chapel
Braehead
Cornquoy
Copinsay
Fossil and Vintage Centre
Northtown
Burray
Hunda
Hillside
Burray Village
Southtown
Grimness
St. Margaret's Hope
Uppertown
Herston
Quindry
Papley
Widewall
Aikers
Sandwick
Suckquoy
Lythes
SOUTH RONALDSAY
Linklater
Dundas Ho.
Burwick
Cleat
Tomb of the Eagles and Bronze Age House
Liddel
Swona
PENTLAND FIRTH
ND
Island of Stroma
Nethertown
Uppertown
0:40 (May-Sept)
Dunnet Head
Duncansby Head
Scarfskerry
East Mey
Castle of Mey
Brough
Hunspow
Ham
Rattar
Mey
Gills
Kirkstyle
Huna
John o' Groats
Canisbay
Mary-Ann's Cottage
Corsback
Dunnet
Barrock
Dunnet Bay
Natural History Display
Stromness 1:30
St Mary's Chapel
Crosskirk
Scrabster
Thurso Castle
Folk Museum
Interpretative Trail
Castlehill
Inkstack
Brabster
Skirza
Tofts
Clardon
Murkle
Greenland
Lochend
Freswick
Dounreay
Buldoo
Bridge of Forss
Thurso
Millbank
East
Haimer
Castletown
Achreamie
Newlands of Geise
Exhibition Centre
Achvarasdal
Cnoc Freiceadain Chambered Cairn
Geise
Olrig Ho.
Tain
Reaster
Slickly
Bucholly Castle
Caithness Broch Centre
Shebster
Westfield
Lieurary
Hilliclay
Weydale
Durran
Achingills
Bowermadden
Alterwall
Lyth Arts Centre
Lyth
Sortat
Nybster
Auckengill
Forss Water
Buckies
Sordale
Knockdee
Bowertower
Barrock Ho.
Howe
Keiss
Keiss Castle
Broubster
Calder Mains
Braal Castle
Stemster Ho.
Halcro
Hastigrow
Mireland
Roadside
Gillock
Kirk
Halkirk
Clayock
North Watten
Myrelandhorn
Sinclair's Bay
Shurrery
Banniskirk Ho.
Mains of Watten
Killimster
Shurrery Lodge
Brawlbin
Scotscalder Station
Harpsdale
Dorrery
Olgrinmore
Winless
Reiss
Castle Sinclair
Castle Girnigoe
Beinn nam Bad Mor
Spittal
Backlass
Watten
Ackergill
Staxigoe
Heritage Centre
Wick
Papigoe
Broadhaven
Mybster
Bilbster
Acharole
Strath
Westerdale
Stirkoke Ho.
Milton
Old Wick
Newton
Badlipster
Castle of Old Wick
Torran Water
280
281
G
H
J
K
L
M
1
2
3
5
6
7
8

Scale : 1:425 700
(approx 6.72 miles to 1 inch)
0 2 4 6 miles
0 2 4 6 8 10 km
HO
HP
HT
HU
Shetland
UNST
YELL
MAINLAND
FETLAR
Hermaness
Hermaness Visitor Centre
Saxa Vord
The Garths
Norwick
Valsgarth
Haroldswick
Unst Boat Haven
Burrafirth
Quoys
Unst Heritage Centre
Baliasta
Buness
Baltasound
Balta
Westing
Caldback
Gloup
Greenbank
Underhoull
Cullivoe
Lund
Stonganess
Belmont
Uyeasound
Muness
Muness Castle
Clivocast
Ramnageo
South Garth
Gutcher
Uyea
Linga
The Hall
Sellafirth
North Sandwick
Colvister
Cunnister
Basta
Camb
Grimister
Windhouse
Brough Lodge
Vord Hill
Fetlar
Houbie
Hascosay
Tresta
Aith
Funzie
Interpretative Centre
Mid Yell
Colgrave Sound
Harkland
West Sandwick
Aywick
Otterswick
Swarister
West Yell
Gossabrough
Setter
Hamnavoe
Ulsta
Burravoe
Houlland
Old Haa
Brough
Copister
Bigga
Samphrey
Yell Sound
Uyea
Isbister
North Roe
South-haa
Housetter
Ronas Hill
North Collafirth
Heylor
Voe
Ollaberry
Hamnavoe
Scarff
Ure
Braehoulland
Esha Ness
Burnside
Urafirth
Eastwick
Tangwick Haa Museum
Tangwick
Hillswick
Stenness
Bardister
North Gluss
Burraland
Brough
Sullom Voe Oil Terminal
Mossbank
Sullom
Graven
Laxobigging
Nibon
Scatsta
Mangaster
Haggrister
Trondavoe
Hamnavoe
Voxter
Lunna
Isleburgh
Brae
Collafirth
Busta
Burravoe
Swining
Lunning
Skaw
Whalsay
Wethersta
Roesound
Vidlin
Gardin
Housay
Bruray
Out Skerries
Shetland
St. Magnus Bay
A968
A970
B9087
B9086
B9083
B9082
B9088
B9081
B9078
B9079
B9076
1:30
0:25
0:20

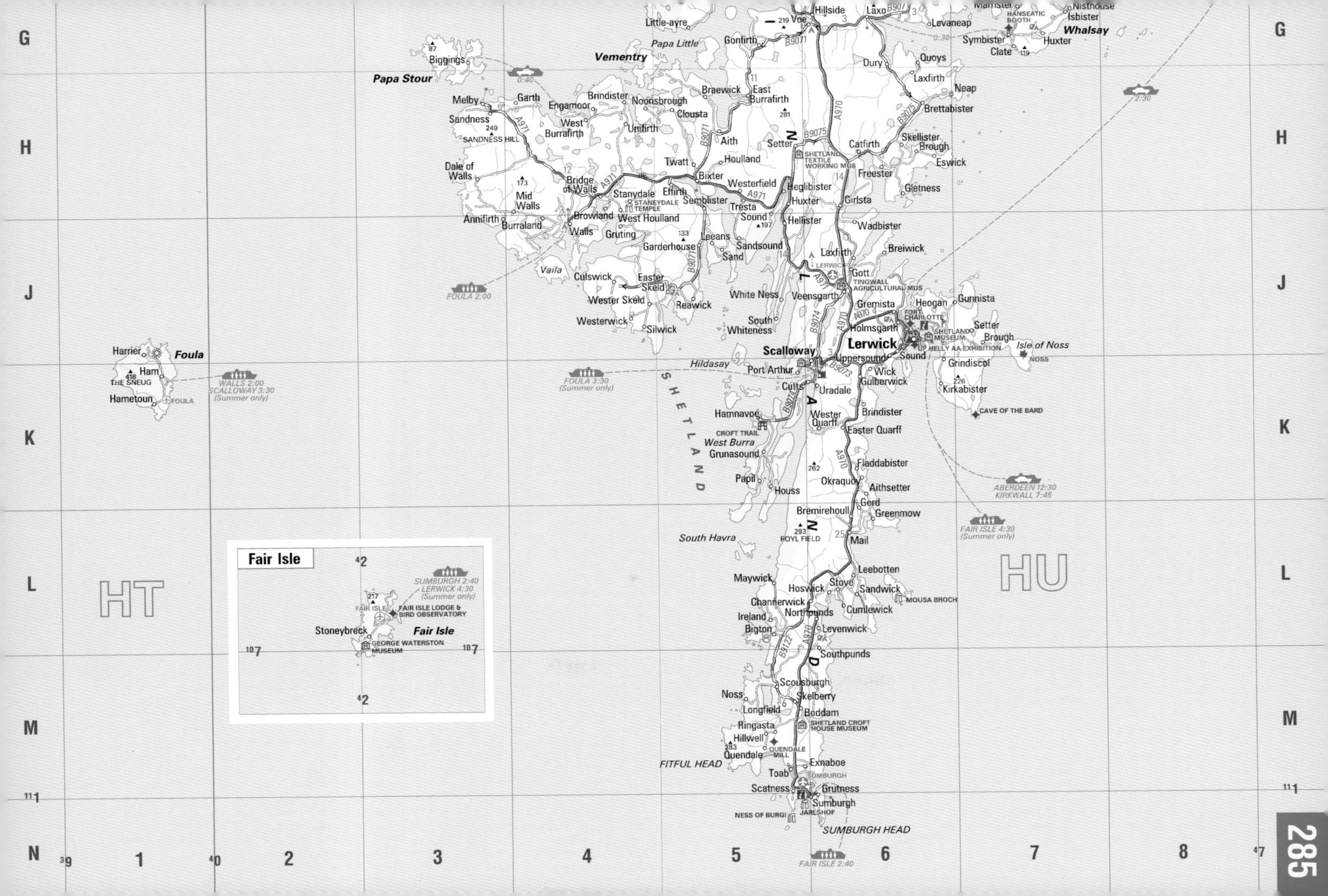
SHETLAND
Lerwick
Scalloway
Whalsay
Isle of Noss
Vementry
Papa Stour
Papa Little
Vaila
Hildasay
West Burra
South Havra
Foula
Fair Isle
FITFUL HEAD
SUMBURGH HEAD
HU
HT
Little-ayre
Voe
Hillside
Laxo
Levaneap
Symbister
Isbister
Nisthouse
Huxter
Clate
HANSEATIC BOOTH
Biggings
Gonfirth
Dury
Quoys
Laxfirth
Neap
Brettabister
Melby
Garth
Engamoor
Brindister
Noonsbrough
Braewick
East Burrafirth
Sandness
SANDNESS HILL
West Burrafirth
Clousta
Unifirth
Aith
Setter
Catfirth
Skellister
Brough
Eswick
Dale of Walls
Twatt
Houlland
SHETLAND TEXTILE WORKING MUS
Freester
Gletness
Mid Walls
Bridge of Walls
Bixter
Westerfield
Heglibister
Stanydale
STANEYDALE TEMPLE
Effirth
Semblister
Tresta
Huxter
Girlsta
Annifirth
Burraland
Browland
West Houlland
Sound
Hellister
Wadbister
Walls
Gruting
Leeans
Garderhouse
Sandsound
Sand
Laxfirth
Breiwick
LERWICK
Gott
TINGWALL AGRICULTURAL MUS
Culswick
Easter Skeld
Wester Skeld
Reawick
White Ness
Veensgarth
Gremista
Heogan
Gunnista
FORT CHARLOTTE
Westerwick
Silwick
South Whiteness
Holmsgarth
SHETLAND MUSEUM
Setter
Brough
UP HELLY AA EXHIBITION
Sound
Uppersound
Grindiscol
NOSS
Port Arthur
Cutts
Uradale
Wick
Gulberwick
Kirkabister
Hamnavoe
Wester Quarff
Brindister
Easter Quarff
CAVE OF THE BARD
CROFT TRAIL
Grunasound
Fladdabister
Papil
Houss
Okraquoy
Aithsetter
Bremirehoull
Gord
Greenmow
ROYL FIELD
Mail
Leebotten
Maywick
Hoswick
Stove
Sandwick
MOUSA BROCH
Channerwick
Northpunds
Cumlewick
Ireland
Bigton
Levenwick
Southpunds
Scousburgh
Noss
Skelberry
Longfield
Boddam
Ringasta
SHETLAND CROFT HOUSE MUSEUM
Hillwell
QUENDALE MILL
Quendale
Exnaboe
Toab
SUMBURGH
Scatness
Grutness
Sumburgh
JARLSHOF
NESS OF BURGI
Harrier
Ham
THE SNEUG
Hametoun
FOULA
Fair Isle
Stoneybreck
FAIR ISLE
FAIR ISLE LODGE & BIRD OBSERVATORY
GEORGE WATERSTON MUSEUM
A970
A971
B9071
B9075
B9073
B9074
B9122
0:30
0:40
2:30
FOULA 2:00
FOULA 3:30
(Summer only)
WALLS 2:00
SCALLOWAY 3:30
(Summer only)
ABERDEEN 12:30
KIRKWALL 7:45
FAIR ISLE 4:30
(Summer only)
FAIR ISLE 2:40
SUMBURGH 2:40
LERWICK 4:30
(Summer only)
G
H
J
K
L
M
N
1
2
3
4
5
6
7
8

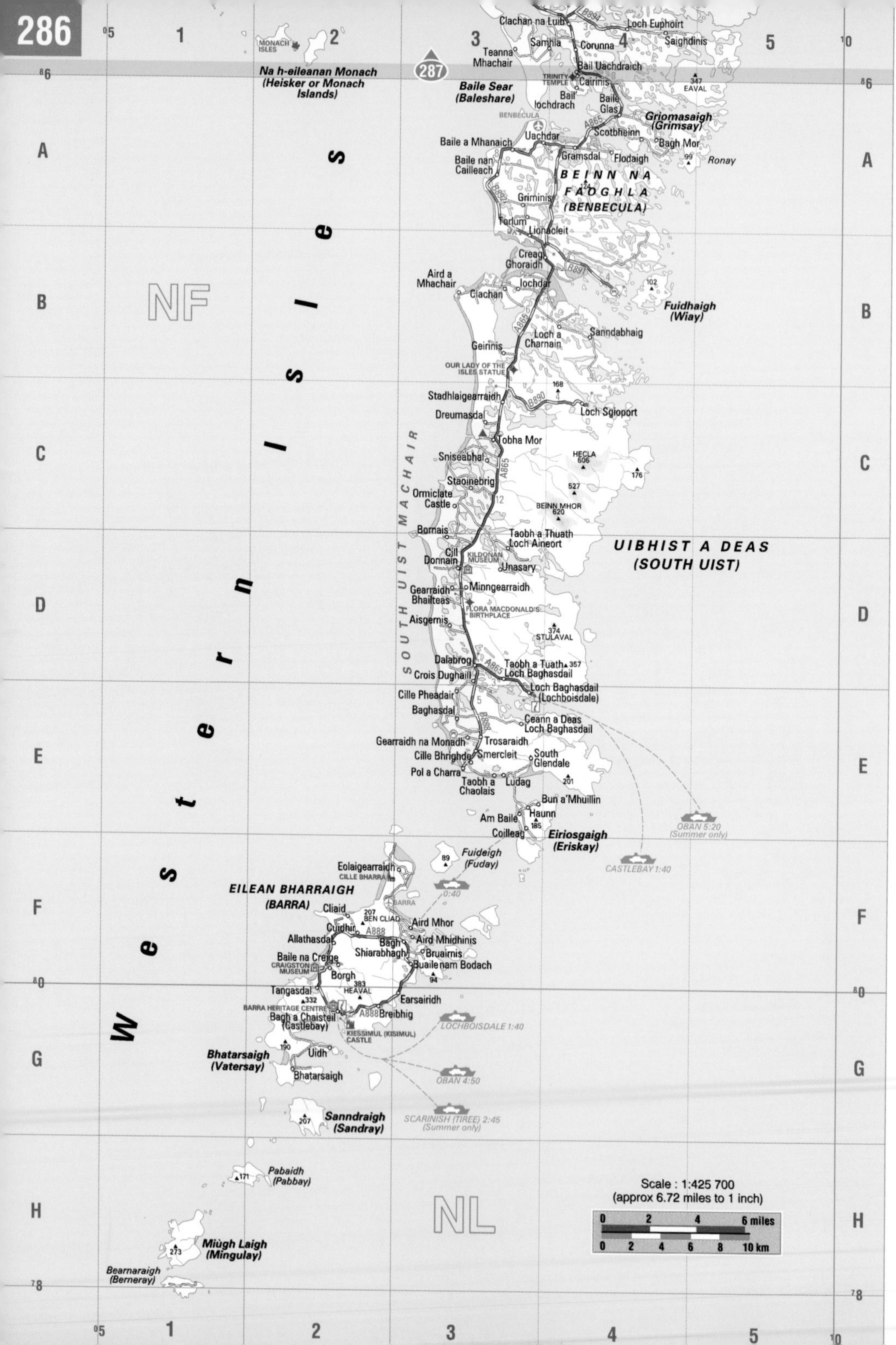
Western Isles
NF
NL
Na h-eileanan Monach (Heisker or Monach Islands)
MONACH ISLES
287
Clachan na Luib
Loch Euphoirt
Saighdinis
Samhla
Corunna
Teanna Mhachair
Bail Uachdraich
TRINITY TEMPLE
Cairinis
Baile Sear (Baleshare)
Bail Iochdrach
Baile Glas
347 EAVAL
BENBECULA
Griomasaigh (Grimsay)
Uachdar
Scotbheinn
Baile a Mhanaich
Bagh Mor
Gramsdal
Flodaigh
Ronay
Baile nan Cailleach
BEINN NA FAOGHLA (BENBECULA)
Griminis
Torlum
Lionacleit
Creag Ghoraidh
Aird a Mhachair
Iochdar
Clachan
Fuidhaigh (Wiay)
Loch a Charnain
Sanndabhaig
Geirinis
OUR LADY OF THE ISLES STATUE
Stadhlaigearraidh
Loch Sgioport
Dreumasdal
Tobha Mor
SOUTH UIST MACHAIR
Sniseabhal
HECLA 606
Staoinebrig
Ormiclate Castle
BEINN MHOR 620
Bornais
Taobh a Thuath Loch Aineort
UIBHIST A DEAS (SOUTH UIST)
Cill Donnain
KILDONAN MUSEUM
Unasary
Minngearraidh
Gearraidh Bhailteas
FLORA MACDONALD'S BIRTHPLACE
Aisgernis
374 STULAVAL
Dalabrog
Taobh a Tuath Loch Baghasdail
Crois Dughaill
Loch Baghasdail (Lochboisdale)
Cille Pheadair
Baghasdal
Ceann a Deas Loch Baghasdail
Gearraidh na Monadh
Trosaraidh
Cille Bhrighde
Smercleit
South Glendale
Pol a Charra
Taobh a Chaolais
Ludag
Bun a'Mhuillin
Am Baile
Haunn
Coilleag
Eiriosgaigh (Eriskay)
OBAN 5:20 (Summer only)
Fuideigh (Fuday)
CASTLEBAY 1:40
Eolaigearraidh
CILLE BHARRA
EILEAN BHARRAIGH (BARRA)
BARRA
0:40
Cliaid
207 BEN CLIAD
Cuidhir
Aird Mhor
Allathasdal
Aird Mhidhinis
Bagh Shiarabhagh
Baile na Creige
Bruairnis
CRAIGSTON MUSEUM
Buaile nam Bodach
Borgh
383 HEAVAL
Tangasdal
Earsairidh
BARRA HERITAGE CENTRE
Bagh a Chaisteil (Castlebay)
Breibhig
LOCHBOISDALE 1:40
KIESSIMUL (KISIMUL) CASTLE
Uidh
Bhatarsaigh (Vatersay)
Bhatarsaigh
OBAN 4:50
Sanndraigh (Sandray)
SCARINISH (TIREE) 2:45 (Summer only)
Pabaidh (Pabbay)
Miùgh Laigh (Mingulay)
Bearnaraigh (Berneray)
Scale : 1:425 700
(approx 6.72 miles to 1 inch)
0 2 4 6 miles
0 2 4 6 8 10 km

Scale : 1:425 700
(approx 6.72 miles to 1 inch)
0 2 4 6 miles
0 2 4 6 8 10 km
St. Kilda
NA
NF
Boreray
384
ST KILDA
CNOC GLAS
Soay
376
CONACHAIR
376
MULLACH BI
358
ST KILDA
St Kilda or Hirta
(Hiort)
AN CAOLAS
IRON AGE HOUSE
Crotha
Tobson
Aird Uig
BERNERA
Bhaltos
Breacleit
205
Cliobh
Timsgearraidh
Miabhig
Riof
Tacleit
Barrag
Cradhlastadh
Uigen
B8011
Crulabhig
Carnais
Cairisiadar
Eadar Dha Fhadhail
Mangurstadh
429
SUAINAVAL
288
Geisiadar
256
Islibhig
Einacleite
Breanais
574
MEALISVAL
Giosla
B8011
19
397
BEINN MHEADHONACH
Mealasta Island
308
Scarp
NB
SOUTH LEWIS,
STULAVAL
579
Huisinis
489
679
TIRGA MOR
659
ULLAVAL
Aird a' Mhu
Gobhaig
UISGNAVAL MORE
729
CLISHAM
799
Abhainn Suidhe
HARRIS AND
CEANN A TUATH NA HEARADH
Cliasmol
B887
13
LOCH A SIAR
Miabhag
Bun Abhainn Eadarra
A859
OLD WHALING STATION
559
NORTH UIST
Aird Asaig
Tarasaigh
(Taransay)
436
BEN LUSKENTYRE
Paible
Losgaintir
Tairbeart
(Tarbert)
99
467
LUSKENTYRE BEACH
288
Seilebost
A859
Borve Lodge
23
NA HEARADH
(HARRIS)
Buirgh
Kennacle
Aird Mhighe
Greosabhag
CHAIPAVAL
365
Sgarasta Mhor
386
Liceasto
Leac a Li
Geocrab
398
BLEAVAL
Cliutha
Beacrabhaic
Caolas Stocinis
Taobh Tuath
SEALLAM
Fleoideabhagh
Manais
A859
196
Pabaidh
(Pabbay)
Aird Mhighe
Fionnsbhagh
Cuidhtinis
An t-Ob
(Leverburgh)
Boirseam
Ensay
459
ROINEABHAL
Lingreabhagh
Cairminis
Srannda
NF
Eilean Bhearnaraigh
(Berneray)
Killegray
ST CLEMENT'S CHURCH
Roghadal
Ruisigearraidh
CAOLAS NA HEARADH
Boreray
Borgh
Baile
1:00
Port nan Long
Vallay
B893
Oronsay
Baile Mhic Phail
190
Scolpaig
Solas
Greinetobht
Trumaisgearraidh
SCOLPAIG TOWER
20
A865
Hermetray
Baile Mhartainn
Malacleit
180
A865
154
Taigh a Ghearraidh
Hosta
Lochportain
133
UIBHIST A TUATH
5
Hogha Gearraidh
Baile Raghaill
Loch nam Madadh
(Lochmaddy)
UIST ANIMAL VISITOR CENTRE
230
MARRIVAL
TAIGH CHEARSABHAGH
UIG 1:45
AN CAOLAS MHONACH
Ceann a Bhaigh
Claddach-knockline
A867
Paibeil
Baile Mor
(NORTH UIST)
Cladach Chireboist
250
NG
BARPA LANGASS CAIRN
8
Na h-eileanan Monach
(Heisker or Monach Islands)
Kirkibost Island
A865
B894
281
SOUTH LEE
Clachan na Luib
Loch Euphoirt
MONACH ISLES
Teanna Mhachair
Samhla
Corunna
Saighdinis
Baile Sear
(Baleshare)
TRINITY TEMPLE
Bail Uachdraich
347
EAVAL
Cairinis
286
Bail Iochdrach
Baile Glas
BENBECULA
A865
3
Griomasaigh
(Grimsay)
Scotbheinn
A
B
C
D
E
F
G
H
1
2
3
4
5

Scale : 1:425 700
(approx 6.72 miles to 1 inch)
0 2 4 6 miles
0 2 4 6 8 10 km
NB
NG
RUBHA ROBHANAIS
CHURCH OF ST MOULAG
Eòropaidh
Coig Peighinnean
HARBOUR VIEW GALLERY
Port Nis
Lional
Suainebost
Tabost
Aird Dhail
Dail bho Dheas
Cros
Dail bho Thuath
Sgiogarstaigh
Gabhsann bho Thuath
Gabhsann bho Dheas
Mealabost Bhuirgh
Cuiashader
Coig Peighinnean Bhuirgh
Bail Àrd Bhuirgh
Siadar
Siadar Iarach
TRUSHAL STONE
Siadar Uarach
Baile an Truiseil
BLACK HOUSE MUSEUM
Barabhas Iarach
Barabhas Uarach
Labost
Arnol
Brù
Barabhas
Siabost bho Thuath
Bragar
MUIRNEAG
Bail' Ur Tholastaidh
SHAWBOST NORSE MILL
SHAWBOST MUSEUM
Siabost bho Dheas
Pairc Shiaboist
Tolastadh bho Thuath
GEARRANNAN BLACKHOUSE VILLAGE
Dail Beag
Dail Mor
Na Gearrannan
Borghastan
BEINN BRAGAR
Gleann Tholàstaidh
DUN CARLOWAY BROCH
Carlabhagh
Griais
Ciribhig
Dun Charlabhaigh
Bac
AN CAOLAS
IRON AGE HOUSE
Crothair
Col
Tobson
Col Uarach
Breibhig
Great Bernera
Tolastadh a Chaolais
BEINN MHOLACH
BROAD BAY OR LOCH A TUATH
Port Nan Giuran
Aird Uig
Bhaltos
Breacleit
Tunga
Aird Thunga
Cnoc Amhlaigh
Cliobh
Port Mholair
Timsgearraidh
Miabhig
Riof
Circebost
Grianan
Newmarket
Aird
Cradhlastadh
Uigen
Tacleit
Breascleit
An Gleann Ur
Lacasdal
Sulaisiadar
Barraglom
Tobhtarol
STORNOWAY
Garrabost
EYE PENINSULA
Seisiadar
Carnais
Cairisiadar
Crulabhig
Calanais
CALANAIS VISITOR CENTRE
LEWIS LOOM CENTRE
MUSEUM NAN EILEAN
Stornoway
Mealabost
Eadar Dha Fhadhail
CALANAIS STANDING STONES
Gearraidh na h-Aibhne
Aiginis
Mangurstadh
SUAINAVAL
Geisiadar
Linsiadar
Sanndabhaig
ST COLUMBA'S
AN LANNTAIR GALLERY
An Cnoc
Pabail Uarach
Tolm
Suardail
Pabail Iarach
287
Acha Mor
Loch a' Ghainmhich
Einacleite
Islibhig
MEALISVAL
Griomsidar
Liurbost
Ben Casgro
Breanais
Giosla
ULLAPOOL 2:45
Ranais
Soval Lodge
Crosbost
BEINN MHEADHONACH
Lacasaidh
Ceos
Cromor
Gearraidh Bhaird
Baile Ailein
Cearsiadair
Sildinis
Cabharstadh
Tabost
LOCH LANGABHAT
Ceann Tarabhaigh
Marbhig
Airidh a Bhruaich
Ceann Shiphoirt
Calbost
EILEAN LEODHAIS
ISLE OF LEWIS
Taobh a' Ghlinne
Grabhair
PARK OR PAIRC
Huisinis
STULAVAL
Aline Lodge
Orasaigh
SOUTH LEWIS
Leumrabhagh
TIRGA MOR
ULLAVAL
Eisgean
Aird a' Mhulaidh
Seaforth I.
Gobhaig
UISGNAVAL MORE
BEINN MHOR
Eilean Iubhard
CLISHAM
Abhainn Suidhe
HARRIS AND
CEANN A TUATH NA HEARADH
CRIONAIG
Cliasmol
Maraig
Miabhag
Bun Abhainn Eadarra
LOCH A SIAR
OLD WHALING STATION
NORTH UIST
Aird Asaig
Reinigeadal
Tarasaigh (Taransay)
BEN LUSKENTYRE
CAOLAS NAN EILEAN
Urgha
Losgaintir
Paible
Tairbeart (Tarbert)
Carragraich
LUSKENTYRE BEACH
Caolas
Carnach
Scalpaigh
Na h-Eileanan Mòra (Shiant Islands)
Seilebost
Borve Lodge
Miabhag
Scalpay
Eilean Scalpaigh (Scalpay)
NA HEARADH (HARRIS)
Drinisiadar
Buirgh
Kennacley
Aird Mhighe
Greosabhagh
Plocrapol
Sgarasta Mhor
Scadabhagh
Liceasto
Leac a Li
UIG 1:40
Geocrab
Cliuthar
BLEAVAL
Beacrabhaic
Caolas Stocinis
Fleoideabhagh
Manais
Aird Mhighe
Ghidhtinis
An t-Ob
Fionnsbhagh
Roirseam

Index to road maps

How to use the index

Example

Thistleton Rutland **116** D2

- grid square
- page number
- county or unitary authority (only shown for duplicate names)

Abbreviations used in the index

Aberdeen **Aberdeen City**
Aberds **Aberdeenshire**
Ald **Alderney**
Anglesey **Isle of Anglesey**
Angus **Angus**
Argyll **Argyll and Bute**
Bath **Bath and North East Somerset**
Bedford **Bedford**
Bl Gwent **Blaenau Gwent**
Blackburn **Blackburn with Darwen**
Blackpool **Blackpool**
Bmouth **Bournemouth**
Borders **Scottish Borders**
Brack **Bracknell**
Bridgend **Bridgend**
Brighton **City of Brighton and Hove**
Bristol **City and County of Bristol**
Bucks **Buckinghamshire**
C Beds **Central Bedfordshire**
Caerph **Caerphilly**
Cambs **Cambridgeshire**
Cardiff **Cardiff**
Carms **Carmarthenshire**
Ceredig **Ceredigion**
Ches E **Cheshire East**
Ches W **Cheshire West and Chester**
Clack **Clackmannanshire**
Conwy **Conwy**
Corn **Cornwall**
Cumb **Cumbria**
Darl **Darlington**
Denb **Denbighshire**
Derby **City of Derby**
Derbys **Derbyshire**
Devon **Devon**
Dorset **Dorset**
Dumfries **Dumfries and Galloway**
Dundee **Dundee City**
Durham **Durham**
E Ayrs **East Ayrshire**
E Dunb **East Dunbartonshire**
E Loth **East Lothian**
E Renf **East Renfrewshire**
E Sus **East Sussex**
E Yorks **East Riding of Yorkshire**
Edin **City of Edinburgh**
Essex **Essex**
Falk **Falkirk**
Fife **Fife**
Flint **Flintshire**
Glasgow **City of Glasgow**
Glos **Gloucestershire**
Gtr Man **Greater Manchester**
Guern **Guernsey**
Gwyn **Gwynedd**
Halton **Halton**
Hants **Hampshire**
Hereford **Herefordshire**
Herts **Hertfordshire**
Highld **Highland**
Hrtlpl **Hartlepool**
Hull **Hull**
IoM **Isle of Man**
IoW **Isle of Wight**
Invclyd **Inverclyde**
Jersey **Jersey**
Kent **Kent**
Lancs **Lancashire**
Leicester **City of Leicester**
Leics **Leicestershire**
Lincs **Lincolnshire**
London **Greater London**
Luton **Luton**
M Keynes **Milton Keynes**
M Tydf **Merthyr Tydfil**
Mbro **Middlesbrough**
Medway **Medway**
Mers **Merseyside**
Midloth **Midlothian**
Mon **Monmouthshire**
Moray **Moray**
N Ayrs **North Ayrshire**
N Lincs **North Lincolnshire**
N Lanark **North Lanarkshire**
N Som **North Somerset**
N Yorks **North Yorkshire**
NE Lincs **North East Lincolnshire**
Neath **Neath Port Talbot**
Newport **City and County of Newport**
Norf **Norfolk**
Northants **Northamptonshire**
Northumb **Northumberland**
Nottingham **City of Nottingham**
Notts **Nottinghamshire**
Orkney **Orkney**
Oxon **Oxfordshire**
Pboro **Peterborough**
Pembs **Pembrokeshire**
Perth **Perth and Kinross**
Plym **Plymouth**
Poole **Poole**
Powys **Powys**
Ptsmth **Portsmouth**
Reading **Reading**
Redcar **Redcar and Cleveland**
Renfs **Renfrewshire**
Rhondda **Rhondda Cynon Taff**
Rutland **Rutland**
S Ayrs **South Ayrshire**
S Glos **South Gloucestershire**
S Lanark **South Lanarkshire**
S Yorks **South Yorkshire**
Scilly **Scilly**
Shetland **Shetland**
Shrops **Shropshire**
Slough **Slough**
Som **Somerset**
Soton **Southampton**
Staffs **Staffordshire**
Southend **Southend-on-Sea**
Stirling **Stirling**
Stockton **Stockton-on-Tees**
Stoke **Stoke-on-Trent**
Suff **Suffolk**
Sur **Surrey**
Swansea **Swansea**
Swindon **Swindon**
T&W **Tyne and Wear**
Telford **Telford and Wrekin**
Thurrock **Thurrock**
Torbay **Torbay**
Torf **Torfaen**
V Glam **The Vale of Glamorgan**
W Berks **West Berkshire**
W Dunb **West Dunbartonshire**
W Isles **Western Isles**
W Loth **West Lothian**
W Mid **West Midlands**
W Sus **West Sussex**
W Yorks **West Yorkshire**
Warks **Warwickshire**
Warr **Warrington**
Wilts **Wiltshire**
Windsor **Windsor and Maidenhead**
Wokingham **Wokingham**
Worcs **Worcestershire**
Wrex **Wrexham**
York **City of York**

A

Abbas Combe 29 C7
Abberley 79 A5
Abberton Essex 71 B4
Worcs 80 B2
Abberwick 189 B4
Abbess Roding 69 B5
Abbey 27 D6
Abbey-cwm-hir 93 D4
Abbeydale 130 A3
Abbey Dore 78 D1
Abbey Field 70 A3
Abbey Hulton 112 A3
Abbey St. Bathans 211 D4
Abbeystead 145 B5
Abbey Town 175 C4
Abbey Village 137 A5
Abbey Wood 50 B1
Abbots Bickington 25 D4
Abbots Bromley 113 C4
Abbotsbury 15 C5
Abbotsham 25 C5
Abbotskerswell 8 A2
Abbots Langley 67 C6
Abbots Leigh 43 B4
Abbotsley 84 B4
Abbots Morton 80 B3
Abbots Ripton 100 D4
Abbots Salford 80 B3
Abbotswood 32 C2
Abbotts Ann 32 A2
Abcott 94 D1
Abdon 94 C3
Aber 74 D3
Aberaeron 74 B3
Aberaman 41 A5
Aberangell 91 A6
Aber-Arad 73 C6
Aberarder 240 D2
Aberarder House 252 D2
Aberarder Lodge 240 D3
Aberargie 219 C6
Aberarth 74 B3
Aberavon 40 B2
Aber-banc 73 B6
Aberbeeg 41 A7
Abercanaid 41 A5
Abercarn 41 B7
Abercastle 55 A4
Abercegir 91 B6
Aberchirder 268 D1
Aber Cowarch 91 A6
Abercraf 59 D5
Abercrombie 221 D5
Abercych 73 B5
Abercynafon 60 B2
Abercynon 41 B5
Aberdalgie 219 B5
Aberdare Aberdâr 41 A4
Aberdaron 106 D1
Aberdeen 245 B6
Aberdesach 107 A4
Aberdour 209 B4
Aberdovey 90 C4
Aberdulais 40 A2
Aberedw 77 C4
Abereiddy 54 A3
Abererch 106 C3
Aberfan 41 A5
Aberfeldy 230 D2
Aberffraw 122 D3
Aberffrwd 75 A5
Aberford 148 D3
Aberfoyle 217 D5
Abergavenny Y Fenni 61 B4
Abergele 125 B4
Aber-Giâr 58 A2
Abergorlech 58 B2
Abergwesyn 76 B2
Abergwili 58 C1
Abergwynant 91 A4
Aber-gwynfi 40 B3
Abergwyngregyn 123 C6
Abergynolwyn 91 B4
Aber-Hirnant 109 B4
Aberhosan 91 C6
Aberkenfig 40 C3
Aberlady 210 B1
Aberlemno 232 C3
Aberllefenni 91 B5
Abermagwr 75 A5
Abermeurig 75 C4
Abermule 93 B5
Abernaint 109 C6
Abernant 73 D6
Aber-nant 41 A5
Abernethy 219 C6
Abernyte 220 A2
Aberporth 73 A5
Aber-Rhiwlech 108 C4
Abersoch 106 D3
Abersychan 61 C4
Aberthin 41 D5
Abertillery Abertyleri 41 A7
Abertridwr Caerph 41 C6
Powys 109 D5
Abertysswg 60 C3
Aberuthven 219 C4
Aber-Village 60 A3
Aberyscir 60 A1
Aberystwyth 90 D3
Abhainn Suidhe 287 D5
Abingdon 65 D5
Abinger Common 35 B4
Abinger Hammer 34 B3
Abington 194 D4
Abington Pigotts 85 C5
Ab Kettleby 115 C5
Ab Lench 80 B3
Ablington Glos 64 C2
Wilts 31 A5
Abney 130 B1
Aboyne 244 C2
Abram 137 C5
Abriachan 252 C1
Abridge 69 D4
Abronhill 207 C5
Abson 43 B6
Abthorpe 82 C3
Abune-the-Hill 282 E3
Aby 135 B4
Acaster Malbis 149 C4
Acaster Selby 149 C4
Accrington 137 A6
Acha 223 B4
Achabraid 213 D6
Achachork 259 D4
Achafolla 213 A5
Achagary 278 C3
Achahoish 202 A2
Achalader 231 D5
Achallader 228 D2
Acha Mor 288 E4
Achanalt 263 D4
Achanamara 213 D5
Achandunie 264 C2
Ach'an Todhair 237 B4
Achany 272 D3
Achaphubuil 237 B4
Acharacle 235 D5
Acharn Highld 236 D1
Perth 229 D6
Acharole 280 C4
Achath 245 A4
Achavanich 280 D3
Achavraat 253 B5
Achddu 57 B4
Achduart 270 D3
Achentoul 274 A2
Achfary 271 A5
Achgarve 261 A5
Achiemore Highld 277 B4
Highld 279 C4
A'Chill 246 D1
Achiltibuie 270 D3
Achina 278 B3
Achinduich 272 D3
Achinduin 226 C3
Achingills 280 B3
Achintee Highld 237 B5
Highld 249 B6
Achintraid 249 C5
Achlean 241 C6
Achleck 224 B3
Achluachrach 239 D6
Achlyness 276 C3
Achmelvich 270 B3
Achmore Highld 249 C5
Stirling 217 A5
Achnaba Argyll 214 D2
Argyll 226 C4
Achnabat 252 C1
Achnacarnin 270 A3
Achnacarry 239 D5
Achnacloich Argyll 227 C4
Highld 247 D4
Achnaconeran 240 A2
Achnacraig 224 B3
Achnacroish 226 B3
Achnadrish 224 A3
Achnafalnich 227 D7
Achnagarron 264 D2
Achnaha 234 D3
Achnahanat 263 A7
Achnahannet 253 D5
Achnairn 272 C3
Achnaluachrach 273 D4
Achnasaul 239 D5
Achnasheen 250 A3
Achosnich 234 D3
Achranich 226 B2
Achreamie 279 B6
Achriabhach 237 C5
Achriesgill 276 C3
Achrimsdale 274 D3
Achtoty 278 B2
Achurch 100 C2
Achuvoldrach 277 C6
Achvaich 264 A3
Achvarasdal 279 B5
Ackergill 281 C5
Acklam Mbro 168 D2
N Yorks 149 A6
Ackleton 95 B5
Acklington 189 C5
Ackton 140 A2
Ackworth Moor Top 140 B2
Acle 121 D6
Acock's Green 96 C4
Acol 53 C5
Acomb Northumb 178 C1
York 149 B4
Aconbury 78 D3
Acre 137 A6
Acrefair 110 A1
Acre Street 19 B6
Acton Ches E 127 D6
Dorset 16 D3
London 49 A5
Shrops 93 C7
Suff 87 C4
Wrex 126 D3
Acton Beauchamp 79 B4
Acton Bridge 127 B5
Acton Burnell 94 A3
Acton Green 79 B4
Acton Pigott 94 A3
Acton Round 95 B4
Acton Scott 94 C2
Acton Trussell 112 D3
Acton Turville 44 A2
Adbaston 111 C6
Adber 29 C5
Adderley 111 A5
Adderstone 199 C5
Addiewell 208 D2
Addingham 147 C4
Addington Bucks 66 A3
Kent 37 A4
London 49 C6
Addinston 197 A4
Addiscombe 49 C6
Addlestone 48 C3
Addlethorpe 135 C5
Adel 148 D1
Adeney 111 D6
Adfa 93 A4
Adforton 94 D2
Adisham 53 D4
Adlestrop 64 A3
Adlingfleet 141 A6
Adlington 137 B5
Admaston Staffs 112 C4
Telford 111 D5
Admington 81 C5
Adstock 83 D4
Adstone 82 B2
Adversane 34 D3
Advie 254 C2
Adwalton 139 A5
Adwell 66 D2
Adwick le Street 140 C3
Adwick upon Dearne 140 C2
Adziel 269 D4
Ae Village 184 D2
Affleck 256 D3
Affpuddle 16 B2
Affric Lodge 250 D3
Afon-wen 125 B6
Afton 18 C2
Agglethorpe 157 C4
Agneash 152 C4
Aigburth 126 A3
Aiginis 288 D5
Aike 150 C3
Aikerness 282 B5
Aikers 283 H5
Aiketgate 164 A2
Aikton 175 C5
Ailey 78 C1
Ailstone 81 B5
Ailsworth 100 B3
Ainderby Quernhow 158 C2
Ainderby Steeple 158 B2
Aingers Green 71 A5
Ainsdale 136 B2
Ainsdale-on-Sea 136 B2
Ainstable 164 A3
Ainsworth 137 B6
Ainthorpe 159 A6
Aintree 136 D2
Aird Argyll 213 B5
Dumfries 170 A2
Highld 261 C4
W Isles 288 D6
Aird a Mhachair 286 B3
Aird a' Mhulaidh 288 F2
Aird Asaig 288 G2
Aird Dhail 288 A5
Airdens 264 A2
Aird Mhidhinis 286 F3
Aird Mhighe W Isles 287 F5
W Isles 288 H2
Aird Mhor 286 F3
Aird of Sleat 247 D4
Airdrie 207 D5
Aird Thunga 288 D5
Airdtorrisdale 278 B2
Aird Uig 287 A5
Airidh a Bhruaich 288 F3
Airieland 173 C5
Airmyn 141 A5
Airntully 219 A5
Airor 247 D6
Airth 208 B1
Airton 146 B3
Airyhassen 171 C5
Aisby Lincs 116 B3
Lincs 141 D6
Aisgernis 286 D3
Aiskew 157 C6
Aislaby N Yorks 159 C6
N Yorks 160 A2
Stockton 168 D2
Aisthorpe 133 A4
Aith Orkney 282 F3
Shetland 284 D8
Shetland 285 H5
Aithsetter 285 K6
Aitkenhead 192 E3
Aitnoch 253 C5
Akeld 188 A2
Akeley 83 D4
Akenham 88 C2
Albaston 11 D5
Alberbury 110 D2
Albourne 21 A5
Albrighton Shrops 95 A6
Shrops 110 D3
Alburgh 104 C3
Albury Herts 68 A4
Sur 34 B3
Albury End 68 A4
Alby Hill 120 B3
Alcaig 252 A1
Alcaston 94 C2
Alcester 80 B3
Alciston 22 B3
Alcombe Som 27 A4
Wilts 44 C2
Alconbury 100 D3
Alconbury Weston 100 D3
Aldbar Castle 232 C3
Aldborough Norf 120 B3
N Yorks 148 A3
Aldbourne 45 B6
Aldbrough 151 D5
Aldbrough St John 167 D5
Aldbury 67 B5
Aldcliffe 145 A4
Aldclune 230 B3
Aldeburgh 89 B5
Aldeby 105 B5
Aldenham 67 D7
Alderbury 31 C5
Aldercar 114 A2
Alderford 120 D3
Alderholt 31 D5
Alderley 62 D3
Alderley Edge 128 B3
Aldermaston 46 C3
Aldermaston Wharf 47 C4
Alderminster 81 C5
Alder's End 79 C4
Aldersey Green 127 D4
Aldershot 34 A1
Alderton Glos 80 D3
Northants 83 C4
Shrops 110 C3
Suff 88 C4
Wilts 44 A2
Alderwasley 130 D3
Aldfield 147 A6
Aldford 127 D4
Aldham Essex 70 A3
Suff 87 C6
Aldie 264 B3
Aldingbourne 20 B2
Aldingham 154 D1
Aldington Kent 38 B2
Worcs 80 C3
Aldington Frith 38 B2
Aldochlay 206 A1
Aldreth 101 D6
Aldridge 96 A3
Aldringham 89 A5
Aldsworth 64 B2
Aldunie 255 D4
Aldwark Derbys 130 D2
N Yorks 148 A3
Aldwick 20 C2
Aldwincle 100 C2
Aldworth 46 B3
Alexandria 206 C1
Alfardisworthy 24 D3
Alfington 13 B6
Alfold 34 C3
Alfold Bars 34 C3
Alfold Crossways 34 C3
Alford Aberds 244 A2
Lincs 135 B4
Som 29 B6
Alfreton 131 D4
Alfrick 79 B5
Alfrick Pound 79 B5
Alfriston 22 B3
Algaltraig 203 A5
Algarkirk 117 B5
Alhampton 29 B6
Aline Lodge 288 F2
Alisary 235 C6
Alkborough 141 A6
Alkerton 81 C6
Alkham 39 A4
Alkington 111 B4
Alkmonton 113 B5
Alladale Lodge 263 B6
Allaleigh 8 B2
Allanaquoich 242 C4
Allangrange Mains 252 A2
Allanton Borders 198 A2
N Lanark 194 A3
Allathasdal 286 F2
All Cannings 45 C4
Allendale Town 177 D6
Allenheads 165 A6
Allensford 178 D2
Allens Green 69 B4
Allensmore 78 D2
Allenton 114 B1
Aller 28 C4
Allerby 162 A3
Allerford 27 A4
Allerston 160 C2
Allerthorpe 149 C6
Allerton Mers 127 A4
W Yorks 147 D5
Allerton Bywater 140 A2
Allerton Mauleverer 148 B3
Allesley 97 C6
Allestree 114 B1
Allet 4 C2
Allexton 99 A5
Allgreave 129 C4
Allhallows 51 B5
Allhallows-on-Sea 51 B5
Alligin Shuas 249 A5
Allimore Green 112 D2
Allington Lincs 115 A6
Wilts 31 B6
Wilts 45 C4
Allithwaite 154 D2
Alloa 208 A1
Allonby 174 D3
Alloway 192 D3
All Saints South Elmham 104 C4
All Stretton 94 B2
Allt 57 B5
Alltchaorunn 237 D5
Alltforgan 109 C4
Alltmawr 77 C4
Alltnacaillich 277 D5
Allt na h-Airbhe 262 A3
Allt-nan-sùgh 249 D6
Alltsigh 240 A2
Alltwalis 58 B1
Alltwen 40 A2
Alltyblaca 75 D4
Allwood Green 103 D6
Almeley 78 B1
Almer 16 B3
Almholme 140 C3
Almington 111 B6
Alminstone Cross 24 C4
Almondbank 219 B5
Almondbury 139 B4
Almondsbury 43 A5
Alne 148 A3
Alness 264 D2
Alnham 188 B2
Alnmouth 189 B5
Alnwick 189 B4
Alperton 49 A4
Alphamstone 87 D4
Alpheton 87 B4
Alphington 13 B4
Alport 130 C2
Alpraham 127 D5
Alresford 71 A4
Alrewas 113 D5
Alsager 128 D2
Alsagers Bank 112 A2
Alsop en le Dale 129 D6
Alston Cumb 165 A5
Devon 14 A3
Alstone 80 D2
Alstonefield 129 D6
Alswear 26 C2

Altandhu 270 C2
Altanduin 274 B2
Altarnun 10 C3
Altass 272 D2
Alterwall 281 B4
Altham 146 D1
Althorne 70 D3
Althorpe 141 C6
Alticry 171 B4
Altnabreac Station 279 D6
Altnacealgach Hotel 271 C5
Altnacraig 226 D3
Altnafeadh 237 D6
Altnaharra 272 A3
Altofts 139 A6
Alton Derbys 130 C3
Hants 33 B6
Staffs 113 A4
Alton Pancras 15 A7
Alton Priors 45 C5
Altrincham 128 A2
Altrua 239 D6
Altskeith 217 D4
Altyre Ho. 253 A6
Alva 208 A1
Alvanley 127 B4
Alvaston 114 B1
Alvechurch 96 D3
Alvecote 97 A5
Alvediston 30 C3
Alveley 95 C5
Alverdiscott 25 C6
Alverstoke 19 B5
Alverstone 19 C4
Alverton 115 A5
Alves 266 C2
Alvescot 64 C3
Alveston S Glos 43 A5
Warks 81 B5
Alvie 241 B6
Alvingham 143 D5
Alvington 62 C2
Alwalton 100 B3
Alweston 29 D6
Alwinton 188 C2
Alwoodley 148 C1
Alyth 231 D6
Amatnatua 263 A6
Am Baile 286 E3
Ambergate 130 D3
Amber Hill 117 A5
Amberley Glos 63 C4
W Sus 20 A3
Amble 189 C5
Amblecote 96 C1
Ambler Thorn 138 A3
Ambleside 154 A2
Ambleston 55 B6
Ambrosden 65 B7
Am Buth 226 D3
Amcotts 141 B6
Amersham 67 D5
Amesbury 31 A5
Amington 97 A5
Amisfield 184 D2
Amlwch 123 A4
Amlwch Port 123 A4
Ammanford Rhydaman 57 A6
Amod 190 B3
Amotherby 159 D6
Ampfield 32 C3
Ampleforth 159 D4
Ampney Crucis 63 C6
Ampney St Mary 64 C1
Ampney St Peter 64 C1
Amport 32 A1
Ampthill 84 D2
Ampton 103 D4
Amroth 56 B1
Amulree 218 A3
Anagach 253 D6
Anaheilt 236 C2
Anancaun 262 D2
An Caol 248 A3
Ancaster 116 A2
Anchor 93 C5
Anchorsholme 144 C3
An Cnoc 288 D5
Ancroft 198 B3
Ancrum 187 A5
Anderby 135 B5
Anderson 16 B2
Anderton 127 B6
Andover 32 A2
Andover Down 32 A2
Andoversford 63 B6
Andreas 152 B4
Anfield 136 D2
Angersleigh 28 D1
Angle 55 D4
An Gleann Ur 288 D5
Angmering 20 B3
Angram N Yorks 148 C4
N Yorks 156 B2
Anie 217 C5
Ankerville 265 C4
Anlaby 142 A2
Anmer 119 C4
Annan 175 B4
Annat Argyll 227 D5
Highld 249 A5
Anna Valley 32 A2
Annbank 193 C4
Annesley 131 D5
Annesley Woodhouse 131 D4
Annfield Plain 178 D3
Annifirth 285 J3
Annitsford 179 B4
Annscroft 94 A2
Ansdell 136 A2
Ansford 29 B6
Ansley 97 B5
Anslow 113 C6
Anslow Gate 113 C5
Anstey Herts 85 D6
Leics 98 A2
Anstruther Easter 221 D5
Anstruther Wester 221 D5
Ansty Hants 33 A6
Warks 97 C6
Wilts 30 C3
W Sus 35 D5
Anthill Common 33 D5
Anthorn 175 C4
Antingham 121 B4
An t-Ob Leverburgh 287 F5
Anton's Gowt 117 A5
Antonshill 208 B1
Antony 6 B3
Anwick 133 D6
Anwoth 172 C3
Aoradh 200 B2
Apes Hall 102 B1
Apethorpe 100 B2
Apeton 112 D2
Apley 133 B6
Apperknowle 130 B3
Apperley 63 A4
Apperley Bridge 147 D5
Appersett 156 B2
Appin 226 B4
Appin House 226 B4
Appleby 142 B1
Appleby-in-Westmorland 165 C4
Appleby Magna 97 A6
Appleby Parva 97 A6
Applecross 249 B4
Applecross Ho. 249 B4
Appledore Devon 25 B5
Devon 27 D5
Kent 38 C1
Appledore Heath 38 B1
Appleford 65 D6
Applegarthtown 185 D4
Appleshaw 32 A2
Applethwaite 163 B5
Appleton Halton 127 A5
Oxon 65 C5
Appleton-le-Moors 159 C6
Appleton-le-Street 159 D6
Appleton Roebuck 149 C4
Appleton Thorn 127 A6
Appleton Wiske 158 A2
Appletreehall 186 B4
Appletreewick 147 A4
Appley 27 C5
Appley Bridge 136 C4
Apse Heath 19 C4
Apsley End 84 D3
Apuldram 20 B1
Aquhythie 245 A4
Arabella 265 C4
Arbeadie 244 C3
Arbirlot 233 D4
Arboll 265 B4
Arborfield 47 C5
Arborfield Cross 47 C5
Arborfield Garrison 47 C5
Arbour-thorne 130 A3
Arbroath 233 D4
Arbuthnott 233 A5
Archiestown 254 B3
Arclid 128 C2
Ardachu 273 D4
Ardalanish 224 E2
Ardanaiseig 227 D5
Ardaneaskan 249 C5
Ardanstur 213 A6
Ardargie House Hotel 219 C5
Ardarroch 249 C5
Ardbeg Argyll 201 D4
Argyll 215 D4
Ardcharnich 262 B3
Ardchiavaig 224 E2
Ardchullarie More 217 C5
Ardchyle 217 B5
Ard-dhubh 249 B4
Arddleen 110 D1
Ardechvie 239 C5
Ardeley 68 A3
Ardelve 249 D5
Arden 206 B1
Ardens Grafton 80 B4
Ardentinny 215 D4
Ardentraive 203 A5
Ardeonaig 217 A6
Ardersier 252 A3
Ardessie 262 B2
Ardfern 213 B6
Ardgartan 215 B5
Ardgay 264 A1
Ardgour 237 C4
Ardheslaig 249 A4
Ardiecow 267 C6
Ardindrean 262 B3
Ardingly 35 D6
Ardington 46 A2
Ardlair 255 D6
Ardlamont Ho. 203 B4
Ardleigh 71 A4
Ardler 231 D6
Ardley 65 A6
Ardlui 215 A6
Ardlussa 213 D4
Ardmair 262 A3
Ardmay 215 B5
Ardminish 202 D1
Ardmolich 235 C6
Ardmore Argyll 226 D2
Highld 264 B3
Highld 276 C3
Ardnacross 225 B4
Ardnadam 203 A6
Ardnagrask 251 B7
Ardnarff 249 C5
Ardnastang 236 C2
Ardnave 200 A2
Ardno 215 B4
Ardo 256 C3
Ardoch 219 A5
Ardochy House 239 B6
Ardo Ho. 257 D4
Ardoyne 256 D1
Ardpatrick 202 B2
Ardpatrick Ho. 202 C2
Ardpeaton 215 D5
Ardrishaig 213 D6
Ardross Fife 221 D5
Highld 264 C2
Ardrossan 204 D2
Ardross Castle 264 C2
Ardshealach 235 D5
Ardsley 140 C1
Ardslignish 235 D4
Ardtalla 201 C4
Ardtalnaig 218 A2
Ardtoe 235 C5
Ardtrostan 217 B6
Arduaine 213 A5
Ardullie 264 D1
Ardvasar 247 D5
Ardvorlich 217 B6
Ardwell 170 C3
Ardwell Mains 170 C3
Ardwick 138 D1
Areley Kings 95 D6
Arford 34 C1
Argoed 41 B6
Argoed Mill 76 A3
Arichamish 214 B2
Arichastlich 216 A2
Aridhglas 224 D2
Arileod 223 B4
Arinacrinachd 249 A4
Arinagour 223 B5
Arion 282 F3
Arisaig 235 B5
Ariundle 236 C2
Arkendale 148 A2
Arkesden 85 D6
Arkholme 155 D4
Arkleton 186 D2
Arkle Town 156 A4
Arkley 68 D2
Arksey 140 C3
Arkwright Town 131 B4
Arle 63 A5
Arlecdon 162 C3
Arlesey 84 D3
Arleston 111 D5
Arley 128 A1
Arlingham 62 B3
Arlington Devon 25 A7
E Sus 22 B3
Glos 64 C2
Armadale Highld 278 B3
W Loth 208 D2
Armadale Castle 247 D5
Armathwaite 164 A3
Arminghall 104 A3
Armitage 113 D4
Armley 148 D1
Armscote 81 C5
Armthorpe 140 C4
Arnabost 223 B5
Arncliffe 156 D3
Arncroach 221 D5
Arne 16 C3
Arnesby 98 B3
Arngask 219 C6
Arnisdale 238 A2
Arnish 248 B2
Arniston Engine 209 D6
Arnol 288 C4
Arnold E Yorks 151 C4
Notts 114 A3
Arnprior 207 A4
Arnside 154 D3
Aros Mains 225 B4
Arowry 110 B3
Arpafeelie 252 A2
Arrad Foot 154 C2
Arram 150 C3
Arrathorne 157 B6
Arreton 18 C4
Arrington 85 B5
Arrivain 216 A2
Arrochar 215 B5
Arrow 80 B3
Arthington 147 C6
Arthingworth 99 C4
Arthog 90 A4
Arthrath 257 C4
Arthurstone 231 D6
Artrochie 257 C5
Arundel 20 B3
Aryhoulan 237 C4
Asby 162 B3
Ascog 203 B6
Ascot 48 C2
Ascott 81 D6
Ascott-under-Wychwood 64 B4
Asenby 158 D2
Asfordby 115 D5
Asfordby Hill 115 D5
Asgarby Lincs 116 A4
Lincs 134 C3
Ash Kent 50 C2
Kent 53 D4
Som 29 C4
Sur 34 A1
Ashampstead 46 B3
Ashbocking 88 B2
Ashbourne 113 A5
Ashbrittle 27 C5
Ash Bullayne 12 A2
Ashburton 7 A6
Ashbury Devon 11 B6
Oxon 45 A6
Ashby 141 C7
Ashby by Partney 135 C4
Ashby cum Fenby 143 C4
Ashby de la Launde 133 D5
Ashby-de-la-Zouch 114 D1
Ashby Folville 115 D5
Ashby Magna 98 B2
Ashby Parva 98 C2
Ashby Puerorum 134 B3
Ashby St Ledgers 82 A2
Ashby St Mary 104 A4
Ashchurch 80 D2
Ashcombe 13 D4
Ashcott 28 B4
Ashdon 86 C1
Ashe 32 A4
Asheldham 70 C3
Ashen 86 C3
Ashendon 66 B3
Ashfield Carms 58 C3
Stirling 218 D2
Suff 88 A3
Ashfield Green 104 D3
Ashfold Crossways 35 D5
Ashford Devon 25 B6
Hants 31 D5
Kent 38 A2
Sur 48 B3
Ashford Bowdler 94 D3
Ashford Carbonell 94 D3
Ashford Hill 46 C3
Ashford in the Water 130 C1
Ashgill 194 B2
Ash Green 97 C6
Ashill Devon 27 D5
Norf 103 A4
Som 28 D3
Ashingdon 70 D2
Ashington Northumb 179 A4
Som 29 C5
W Sus 21 A4
Ashintully Castle 231 B5
Ashkirk 186 A3
Ashlett 18 A3
Ashleworth 63 A4
Ashley Cambs 86 A2
Ches E 128 A2
Devon 26 D1
Dorset 17 A5
Glos 63 D5
Hants 17 B6
Hants 32 B2
Northants 99 B4
Staffs 111 B6
Ashley Green 67 C5
Ashley Heath Dorset 17 A5
Staffs 111 B6
Ash Magna 111 B4
Ashmanhaugh 121 C5
Ashmansworth 46 D2
Ashmansworthy 24 D4
Ash Mill 26 C2
Ashmore 30 D3
Ashorne 81 B6
Ashover 130 C3
Ashow 97 D6
Ashprington 8 B2
Ash Priors 27 C6
Ashreigney 26 D1
Ash Street 87 C6
Ashtead 35 A4
Ash Thomas 27 D5
Ashton Ches W 127 C5
Corn 3 C4
Hants 33 D4
Hereford 78 A3
Invclyd 204 A2
Northants 83 C4
Northants 100 C2
Ashton Common 44 D2
Ashton-In-Makerfield 137 D4
Ashton Keynes 63 D6
Ashton under Hill 80 D2
Ashton-under-Lyne 138 D2
Ashton upon Mersey 137 D6
Ashurst Hants 32 D2
Kent 36 C3
W Sus 21 A4
Ashurstwood 36 C2
Ash Vale 34 A1
Ashwater 11 B4
Ashwell Herts 85 D4
Rutland 115 D6
Som 28 D3
Ashwellthorpe 104 B2
Ashwick 29 A6
Ashwicken 119 D4
Ashybank 186 B4
Askam in Furness 153 C3
Askern 140 B3
Askerswell 15 B5
Askett 66 C4
Askham Cumb 164 C3
Notts 132 B2
Askham Bryan 149 C4
Askham Richard 148 C4
Asknish 214 C2
Askrigg 156 B3
Askwith 147 C5
Aslackby 116 B3
Aslacton 104 B2
Aslockton 115 B5
Asloun 244 A2
Aspatria 174 D4
Aspenden 68 A3
Asperton 117 B5
Aspley Guise 83 D6
Aspley Heath 83 D6
Aspull 137 C5
Asselby 141 A5
Asserby 135 B4
Assington 87 D5
Assynt Ho. 264 D1
Astbury 128 C3
Astcote 82 B3
Asterley 94 A1
Asterton 94 B1
Asthall 64 B3
Asthall Leigh 64 B4
Astley Shrops 111 D4
Warks 97 C6
Worcs 79 A5
Astley Abbotts 95 B5
Astley Bridge 137 B6
Astley Cross 79 A6
Astley Green 137 D6
Aston Ches E 111 A5
Ches W 127 B5
Derbys 130 A1
Hereford 94 D2
Herts 68 A2
Oxon 64 C4
Shrops 111 C4
Staffs 111 A6
S Yorks 131 A4
Telford 95 A4
W Mid 96 C3
Wokingham 47 A5

Aston Abbotts 66 A4
Aston Botterell 95 C4
Aston-By-Stone 112 B3
Aston Cantlow 80 B4
Aston Clinton 66 B4
Aston Crews 62 A2
Aston Cross 80 D2
Aston End 68 A2
Aston Eyre 95 B4
Aston Fields 80 A2
Aston Flamville 98 B1
Aston Ingham 62 A2
Aston juxta Mondrum 127 D6
Aston le Walls 82 B1
Aston Magna 81 D4
Aston Munslow 94 C3
Aston on Clun 94 C1
Aston-on-Trent 114 C2
Aston Rogers 94 A1
Aston Rowant 66 D3
Aston Sandford 66 C3
Aston Somerville 80 D3
Aston Subedge 80 C4
Aston Tirrold 46 A3
Aston Upthorpe 46 A3
Astrop 82 D2
Astwick 84 D4
Astwood M Keynes 83 C6
Worcs 79 B6
Astwood Bank 80 A3
Aswarby 116 B3
Aswardby 134 B3
Atcham 94 A3
Atch Lench 80 B3
Athelhampton 16 B1
Athelington 104 D3
Athelney 28 C3
Athelstaneford 210 C2
Atherington 25 C6
Atherstone 97 B6
Atherstone on Stour 81 B5
Atherton 137 C5
Atley Hill 157 A6
Atlow 113 A6
Attadale 249 C6
Attadale Ho. 249 C6
Attenborough 114 B3
Atterby 142 D1
Attercliffe 130 A3
Attleborough Norf 103 B6
Warks 97 B6
Attlebridge 120 D3
Atwick 151 B4
Atworth 44 C2
Aubourn 133 C4
Auchagallon 191 B4
Auchallater 243 D4
Aucharnie 256 B1
Auchattie 244 C3
Auchavan 231 B5
Auchbreck 254 D3
Auchenback 205 C5
Auchenbainzie 183 C6
Auchenblae 233 A5
Auchenbrack 183 C5
Auchenbreck 214 D3
Auchencairn Dumfries 173 C5
Dumfries 184 D2
N Ayrs 191 C6
Auchencrosh 180 D3
Auchencrow 211 D5
Auchendinny 209 D5
Auchengray 195 A4
Auchenhalrig 267 C4
Auchenheath 194 B3
Auchenlochan 203 A4
Auchenmalg 171 B4
Auchensoul 181 B4
Auchentiber 204 D3
Auchertyre 249 D5
Auchgourish 242 A2
Auchincarroch 206 B2
Auchindrain 214 B3
Auchindrean 262 B3
Auchininna 256 B1
Auchinleck 193 C5
Auchinloch 205 A6
Auchinroath 266 D3
Auchintoul 244 A2
Auchiries 257 C5
Auchlee 245 C5
Auchleven 256 D1
Auchlochan 194 C3
Auchlossan 244 B2
Auchlunies 245 C5
Auchlyne 217 B5
Auchmacoy 257 C4
Auchmair 255 D4
Auchmantle 170 A3
Auchmillan 193 C5
Auchmithie 233 D4
Auchmuirbridge 220 D2
Auchmull 232 A3
Auchnacree 232 B2
Auchnagallin 253 C6
Auchnagatt 257 B4
Auchnaha 214 D2
Auchnashelloch 218 C2
Aucholzie 243 C6
Auchrannie 231 C6
Auchroisk 253 D6
Auchronie 244 D1
Auchterarder 218 C4
Auchteraw 240 B1
Auchterderran 209 A5
Auchterhouse 220 A3
Auchtermuchty 220 C2
Auchterneed 251 A6
Auchtertool 209 A5
Auchtertyre 266 D2
Auchtubh 217 B5
Auckengill 281 B5
Auckley 140 C4
Audenshaw 138 D2
Audlem 111 A5
Audley 128 D2
Audley End 87 D4
Auds 268 C1
Aughton E Yorks 149 D6
Lancs 136 C2
Lancs 145 A5
S Yorks 131 A4
Wilts 45 D6
Aughton Park 136 C3
Auldearn 253 A5
Aulden 78 B2
Auldgirth 183 D7
Auldhame 210 B2
Auldhouse 205 C6
Ault a'chruinn 249 D6
Aultanrynie 271 A6
Aultbea 261 B5
Aultdearg 263 D4
Aultgrishan 261 B4
Aultguish Inn 263 C5
Aultibea 274 B4
Aultiphurst 279 B4
Aultmore 267 D5
Aultnagoire 252 D1
Aultnamain Inn 264 B2
Aultnaslat 239 B5
Aulton 255 D7
Aundorach 242 A2
Aunsby 116 B3
Auquhorthies 256 D3
Aust 43 A4
Austendike 117 C5
Austerfield 141 D4
Austrey 97 A5
Austwick 146 A1
Authorpe 135 A4
Authorpe Row 135 B5
Avebury 45 C5
Aveley 50 A2
Avening 63 D4
Averham 132 D2
Aveton Gifford 7 C5
Avielochan 242 A2
Aviemore 242 A1
Avington Hants 32 B4
W Berks 46 C1
Avoch 252 A3
Avon 17 B5
Avonbridge 208 C2
Avon Dassett 81 C7
Avonmouth 43 B4
Avonwick 7 B6
Awbridge 32 C2
Awhirk 170 B2
Awkley 43 A4
Awliscombe 13 A6
Awre 62 C3
Awsworth 114 A2
Axbridge 42 D3
Axford Hants 33 A5
Wilts 45 C6
Axminster 14 B2
Axmouth 14 B2
Axton 125 A6
Aycliff 39 A5
Aycliffe 167 C5
Aydon 178 C2
Aylburton 62 C2
Ayle 165 A5
Aylesbeare 13 B5
Aylesbury 66 B4
Aylesby 143 C4
Aylesford 37 A5
Aylesham 53 D4
Aylestone 98 A2
Aylmerton 120 B3
Aylsham 120 C3
Aylton 79 D4
Aymestrey 78 A2
Aynho 82 D2
Ayot St Lawrence 68 B1
Ayot St Peter 68 B2
Ayr 192 C3
Aysgarth 156 C4
Ayside 154 C2
Ayston 99 A5
Aythorpe Roding 69 B5
Ayton 211 D6
Aywick 284 E7
Azerley 157 D6

B

Babbacombe 8 A3
Babbinswood 110 B2
Babcary 29 C5
Babel 59 B5
Babell 125 B6
Babraham 85 B7
Babworth 132 A1
Bac 288 C5
Bachau 123 B4
Backaland 282 D6
Backaskaill 282 B5
Backbarrow 154 C2
Backe 56 A2
Backfolds 269 D5
Backford 127 B4
Backford Cross 126 B3
Backhill Aberds 256 C2
Aberds 257 C5
Backhill of Clackriach 257 B4
Backhill of Fortree 257 B4
Backhill of Trustach 244 C3
Backies 274 D2
Backlass 280 C4
Back of Keppoch 235 B5
Back Rogerton 193 C5
Backwell 42 C3
Backworth 179 B5
Bacon End 69 B6
Baconsthorpe 120 B3
Bacton Hereford 78 D1
Norf 121 B5
Suff 87 A6
Bacton Green 87 A6
Bacup 138 A1
Badachro 261 C4
Badanloch Lodge 273 A5
Badavanich 250 A3
Badbury 45 A5
Badby 82 B2
Badcall 276 C3
Badcaul 262 A2
Baddeley Green 129 D4
Baddesley Clinton 97 D5
Baddesley Ensor 97 B5
Baddidarach 270 B3
Baddoch 242 D4
Baddock 252 A3
Badenscoth 256 C2
Badenyon 243 A6
Badger 95 B5
Badger's Mount 50 C1
Badgeworth 63 B5
Badgworth 42 D2
Badicaul 249 D4
Badingham 88 A4
Badlesmere 52 D2
Badlipster 280 D4
Badluarach 262 A1
Badminton 44 A2
Badnaban 270 B3
Badninish 264 A3
Badrallach 262 A2
Badsey 80 C3
Badshot Lea 34 B1
Badsworth 140 B2
Badwell Ash 87 A5
Bagby 158 C3
Bag Enderby 134 B3
Bagendon 63 C6
Bagh a Chaisteil Castlebay 286 G2
Baghasdal 286 E3
Bagh Mor 286 A4
Bagh Shiarabhagh 286 F3
Bagillt 126 B2
Baginton 97 D6
Baglan 40 B2
Bagley 110 C3
Bagnall 129 D4
Bagnor 46 C2
Bagshot Sur 48 C2
Wilts 45 C7
Bagthorpe Norf 119 B4
Notts 131 D4
Bagworth 98 A1
Bagwy Llydiart 61 A6
Bail Àrd Bhuirgh 288 B5
Baildon 147 D5
Baile 287 F4
Baile Ailein 288 E3
Baile a Mhanaich 286 A3
Baile an Truiseil 288 B4
Bailebeag 240 A3
Baile Boidheach 202 A2
Baile Glas 286 A4
Baile Mhartainn 287 G2
Baile Mhic Phail 287 G3
Baile Mor Argyll 224 D1
W Isles 287 H2
Baile na Creige 286 F2
Baile nan Cailleach 286 A3
Baile Raghaill 287 G2
Baileyhead 176 B3
Bailiesward 255 C5
Baillieston 205 B6
Bail' Iochdrach 286 A4
Bail Uachdraich 287 H3
Bail' Ur Tholastaidh 288 C6
Bainbridge 156 B3
Bainsford 208 B1
Bainshole 255 C7
Bainton E Yorks 150 B2
Pboro 100 A2
Bairnkine 187 B5
Baker's End 68 B3
Baker Street 50 A3
Bakewell 130 C2
Bala Y Bala 108 B4
Balachuirn 248 B2
Balavil 241 B5
Balbeg Highld 251 C6
Highld 251 D6
Balbeggie 219 B6
Balbithan 245 A4
Balbithan Ho. 245 A5
Balblair Highld 264 A1
Highld 264 D3
Balby 140 C3
Balchladich 270 A3
Balchraggan Highld 252 B1
Highld 252 C1
Balchrick 276 C2
Balchrystie 221 D4
Balcladaich 251 D4
Balcombe 35 C6
Balcombe Lane 35 C6
Balcomie 221 C6
Balcurvie 220 D3
Baldersby 158 D2
Baldersby St James 158 D2
Balderstone 145 D6
Balderton Ches W 126 C3
Notts 132 D3
Baldhu 4 C2
Baldinnie 220 C4
Baldock 84 D4
Baldovie 221 A4
Baldrine 152 C4
Baldslow 23 A5
Baldwin 152 C3
Baldwinholme 175 C6
Baldwin's Gate 112 A1
Bale 120 B2
Balearn 269 D5
Balemartine 222 C2
Balephuil 222 C2
Balerno 209 D4
Balevullin 222 C2
Balfield 232 B3
Balfour 282 F5
Balfron 206 B3
Balfron Station 206 B3
Balgaveny 256 B1
Balgavies 232 C3
Balgonar 208 A3
Balgove 256 C3
Balgowan 241 C4
Balgown 258 B3
Balgrochan 205 A6
Balgy 249 A5
Balhaldie 218 D3
Balhalgardy 256 D2
Balham 49 B5
Balhary 231 D6
Baliasta 284 C8
Baligill 279 B4
Balintore Angus 231 C6
Highld 265 C4
Balintraid 264 C3
Balk 158 C3
Balkeerie 232 D1
Balkemback 220 A3
Balkholme 141 A5
Balkissock 180 C3
Ball 110 C2
Ballabeg 152 D2
Ballacannel 152 C4
Ballachulish 237 D4
Ballajora 152 B4
Ballaleigh 152 C3
Ballamodha 152 D2
Ballantrae 180 C2
Ballaquine 152 C4
Ballards Gore 70 D3
Ballasalla IoM 152 B3
IoM 152 D2
Ballater 243 C6
Ballaugh 152 B3
Ballaveare 152 D3
Ballcorach 254 D2
Ballechin 230 C3
Balleigh 264 B3
Ballencrieff 210 C1
Ballentoul 230 B2
Ball Haye Green 129 D4
Ball Hill 46 C2
Ballidon 130 D2
Balliemore Argyll 214 D3
Argyll 226 D3
Ballikinrain 206 B3
Ballimeanoch 214 A3
Ballimore Argyll 214 D2
Stirling 217 C5
Ballinaby 200 B2
Ballindean 220 B2
Ballingdon 87 C4
Ballinger Common 67 C5
Ballingham 78 D3
Ballingry 209 A4
Ballinlick 230 D3
Ballinluig 230 C3
Ballintuim 231 C5
Balloch Angus 232 C1
Highld 252 B3
N Lanark 207 C5
W Dunb 206 B1
Ballochan 244 C2
Ballochford 255 C4
Ballochmorrie 181 C4
Balls Cross 34 D2
Balls Green 71 A4
Ballygown 224 B3
Ballygrant 200 B3
Ballyhaugh 223 B4
Balmacara 249 D5
Balmacara Square 249 D5
Balmaclellan 173 A4
Balmacneil 230 C3
Balmacqueen 259 A4
Balmae 173 D4
Balmaha 206 A2
Balmalcolm 220 D3
Balmeanach 248 B2
Balmedie 245 A6
Balmer Heath 110 B3
Balmerino 220 B3
Balmerlawn 18 A2
Balmichael 191 B5
Balmirmer 221 A5
Balmore Highld 251 C5
Highld 253 B4
Highld 258 D2
Perth 230 C3
Balmule 209 B5
Balmullo 220 B4
Balmungie 252 A3
Balnaboth 231 B7
Balnabruaich 264 D3
Balnabruich 275 B5
Balnacoil 274 C2
Balnacra 250 B1
Balnafoich 252 C2
Balnagall 265 B4
Balnaguard 230 C3
Balnahard Argyll 212 C2
Argyll 224 C3
Balnain 251 C6
Balnakeil 277 B4
Balnaknock 259 B4
Balnapaling 264 D3
Balne 140 B3
Balochroy 202 C2
Balone 221 C4
Balornock 205 B6
Balquharn 219 A5
Balquhidder 217 B5
Balsall 97 D5
Balsall Common 97 D5
Balsall Hth. 96 C3
Balscott 81 C6
Balsham 86 B1
Baltasound 284 C8
Balterley 128 D2
Baltersan 171 A6
Balthangie 268 D3
Baltonsborough 29 B5
Balvaird 252 A1
Balvicar 213 A5
Balvraid Highld 238 A2
Highld 253 C4
Bamber Bridge 137 A4
Bambers Green 69 A5
Bamburgh 199 C5
Bamff 231 C6
Bamford Derbys 130 A2
Gtr Man 138 B1
Bampton Cumb 164 D3
Devon 27 C4
Oxon 64 C4
Bampton Grange 164 D3
Banavie 237 B5
Banbury 82 C1
Bancffosfelen 57 A4
Banchory 244 C3

Banchory-Devenick 245 B6
Bancycapel 57 A4
Bancyfelin 56 A3
Bancyffordd 73 C7
Bandirran 220 A2
Banff 268 C1
Bangor 123 C5
Bangor-is-y-coed 110 A2
Banham 103 C6
Bank 18 A1
Bankend 174 B3
Bankfoot 219 A5
Bankglen 182 A4
Bankhead
Aberdeen 245 A5
Aberds 244 B3
Bank Newton 146 B3
Banknock 207 C5
Banks Cumb 176 C3
Lancs 136 A2
Bankshill 185 D4
Bank Street 79 A4
Banningham 120 C4
Banniskirk Ho. 280 C3
Bannister Green 69 A6
Bannockburn 207 A6
Banstead 35 A5
Bantham 7 C5
Banton 207 C5
Banwell 42 D2
Banyard's Green 104 D3
Bapchild 51 C6
Barabhas 288 C4
Barabhas Iarach 288 C4
Barabhas Uarach 288 B4
Barachandroman 225 D5
Barassie 192 B3
Baravullin 226 C3
Barbaraville 264 C3
Barber Booth 129 A6
Barbieston 182 A2
Barbon 155 C5
Barbridge 127 D6
Barbrook 26 A2
Barby 98 D2
Barcaldine 227 B4
Barcheston 81 D5
Barcombe 22 A2
Barcombe Cross 22 A2
Barden 157 B5
Bardennoch 182 C3
Barden Scale 147 B4
Bardfield Saling 69 A6
Bardister 284 F5
Bardney 133 C6
Bardon 114 D2
Bardon Mill 177 C5
Bardowie 205 A5
Bardrainney 204 A3
Bardsea 154 D2
Bardsey 148 C2
Bardwell 103 D5
Bare 145 A4
Barfad 202 B3
Barford Norf 104 A2
Warks 81 A5
Barford St John 82 D1
Barford St Martin 31 B4
Barford St Michael 82 D1
Barfrestone 53 D4
Bargoed Bargod 41 B6
Bargrennan 181 D5
Barham Cambs 100 D3
Kent 53 D4
Suff 88 B2
Barharrow 172 C4
Barhill 173 B6
Bar Hill 85 A5
Barholm 116 D3
Barkby 98 A3
Barkestone-le-Vale 115 B5
Barkham 47 C5
Barking London 50 A1
Suff 87 B6
Barkingside 50 A1
Barking Tye 87 B6
Barkisland 138 B3
Barkston Lincs 116 A2
N Yorks 148 D3
Barkway 85 D5
Barlaston 112 B2
Barlavington 20 A2
Barlborough 131 B4
Barlby 149 D5
Barlestone 98 A1
Barley Herts 85 D5
Lancs 146 C2
Barley Mow 179 D4
Barleythorpe 99 A5
Barling 51 A6
Barlow Derbys 130 B3
N Yorks 140 A4
T&W 178 C3
Barmby Moor 149 C6
Barmby on the Marsh 141 A4
Barmer 119 B5
Barmoor Castle 198 C3
Barmoor Lane End 198 C4
Barmouth Abermaw 90 A4
Barmpton 167 D6
Barmston 151 B4
Barnack 100 A2
Barnacle 97 C6
Barnard Castle 166 D3
Barnard Gate 65 B5
Barnardiston 86 C3
Barnbarroch 173 C6
Barnburgh 140 C2
Barnby 105 C5
Barnby Dun 140 C4
Barnby in the Willows 132 D3
Barnby Moor 131 A6
Barnes Street 36 B4
Barnet 68 D2
Barnetby le Wold 142 C2
Barney 120 B1
Barnham Suff 103 D4
W Sus 20 B2
Barnham Broom 104 A1
Barnhead 233 C4
Barnhill Ches W 127 D4
Dundee 221 A4
Moray 266 D2
Barnhills 180 D1
Barningham Durham 166 D3
Suff 103 D5
Barnoldby le Beck 143 C4
Barnoldswick 146 C2
Barns Green 35 D4
Barnsley Glos 64 C1
S Yorks 139 C6
Barnstaple 25 B6
Barnston Essex 69 B6
Mers 126 A2
Barnstone 115 B5
Barnt Green 96 D3
Barnton Ches W 127 B6
Edin 209 C4
Barnwell All Saints 100 C2
Barnwell St Andrew 100 C2
Barnwood 63 B4
Barochreal 226 D3
Barons Cross 78 B2
Barr 181 B4
Barra Castle 256 D2
Barrachan 171 C5
Barrack 256 B3
Barraglom 288 D2
Barrahormid 213 D5
Barran 226 D3
Barrapol 222 C2
Barras Aberds 245 D5
Cumb 165 D6
Barrasford 177 B7
Barravullin 213 B6
Barregarrow 152 C3
Barrhead 205 C4
Barrhill 181 C4
Barrington Cambs 85 C5
Som 28 D3
Barripper 3 B4
Barrmill 204 C3
Barrock 281 A4
Barrock Ho. 281 B4
Barrow Lancs 146 D1
Rutland 116 D1
Suff 86 A3
Barroway Drove 102 A1
Barrowburn 188 B1
Barrowby 116 B1
Barrowcliff 160 C4
Barrowden 99 A6
Barrowford 146 D2
Barrow Green 51 C6
Barrow Gurney 43 C4
Barrow Haven 142 A2
Barrow-in-Furness 153 D3
Barrow Island 153 D2
Barrow Nook 136 C3
Barrows Green
Ches E 128 D1
Cumb 154 C4
Barrow's Green 127 A5
Barrow Street 30 B2
Barrow upon Humber 142 A2
Barrow upon Soar 114 D3
Barrow upon Trent 114 C1
Barry 221 A5
Barry Y Barri 41 E6
Barry Island 41 E6
Barsby 115 D4
Barsham 105 C4
Barston 97 D5
Bartestree 78 C3
Barthol Chapel 256 C3
Barthomley 128 D2
Bartley 32 D2
Bartley Green 96 C3
Bartlow 86 C1
Barton Cambs 85 B6
Ches W 127 D4
Glos 64 A2
Lancs 136 C2
Lancs 145 D5
N Yorks 157 A6
Oxon 65 C6
Torbay 8 A3
Warks 80 B4
Barton Bendish 102 A3
Barton Hartshorn 82 D3
Barton in Fabis 114 B3
Barton in the Beans 97 A6
Barton-le-Clay 84 D2
Barton-le-Street 159 D6
Barton-le-Willows 149 A6
Barton Mills 102 D3
Barton on Sea 17 B6
Barton on the Heath 81 D5
Barton St David 29 B5
Barton Seagrave 99 D5
Barton Stacey 32 A3
Barton Turf 121 C5
Barton-under-Needwood 113 D5
Barton-upon-Humber 142 A2
Barton Waterside 142 A2
Barugh 139 C6
Barway 102 D1
Barwell 98 B1
Barwick Herts 68 B3
Som 29 D5
Barwick in Elmet 148 D2
Baschurch 110 C3
Bascote 81 A7
Basford Green 129 D4
Bashall Eaves 145 C6
Bashley 17 B6
Basildon 51 A4
Basingstoke 47 D4
Baslow 130 B2
Bason Bridge 28 A3
Bassaleg 42 A1
Bassenthwaite 163 A5
Bassett 32 D3
Bassingbourn 85 C5
Bassingfield 115 B4
Bassingham 133 C4
Bassingthorpe 116 C2
Basta 284 D7
Baston 116 D4
Bastwick 121 D6
Baswick Steer 150 C3
Batchworth Heath 67 D6
Batcombe Dorset 15 A6
Som 29 B6
Bate Heath 128 B1
Batford 67 B7
Bath 43 C6
Bathampton 44 C1
Bathealton 27 C5
Batheaston 44 C1
Bathford 44 C1
Bathgate 208 D2
Bathley 132 D2
Bathpool Corn 10 D3
Som 28 C2
Bathville 208 D2
Batley 139 A5
Batsford 81 D4
Battersby 159 A4
Battersea 49 B5
Battisborough Cross 7 C4
Battisford 87 B6
Battisford Tye 87 B6
Battle E Sus 23 A5
Powys 76 D4
Battledown 63 A5
Battlefield 111 D4
Battlesbridge 70 D1
Battlesden 67 A5
Battlesea Green 104 D3
Battleton 27 C4
Battram 98 A1
Battramsley 18 B2
Baughton 80 C1
Baughurst 46 D3
Baulking 64 D4
Baumber 134 B2
Baunton 63 C6
Baverstock 31 B4
Bawburgh 104 A2
Bawdeswell 120 C2
Bawdrip 28 B3
Bawdsey 88 C4
Bawtry 141 D4
Baxenden 137 A6
Baxterley 97 B5
Baybridge 32 C4
Baycliff 154 D1
Baydon 45 B6
Bayford Herts 68 C3
Som 30 C1
Bayles 165 A5
Baylham 88 B2
Baynard's Green 65 A6
Bayston Hill 94 A2
Baythorn End 86 C3
Bayton 95 D4
Beach 236 D1
Beachampton 83 D4
Beachamwell 102 A3
Beachans 253 B6
Beacharr 202 D1
Beachborough 38 B3
Beachley 62 D1
Beacon 14 A1
Beacon End 70 A3
Beacon Hill 34 C1
Beacon's Bottom 66 D3
Beaconsfield 67 E5
Beacrabhaic 288 H2
Beadlam 159 C5
Beadlow 84 D3
Beadnell 189 A5
Beaford 25 D6
Beal Northumb 199 B4
N Yorks 140 A3
Beamhurst 113 B4
Beaminster 15 A4
Beamish 179 D4
Beamsley 147 B4
Bean 50 B2
Beanacre 44 C3
Beanley 188 B3
Beaquoy 282 E4
Bear Cross 17 B4
Beardwood 137 A5
Beare Green 35 B4
Bearley 81 A4
Bearnus 224 B2
Bearpark 167 A5
Bearsbridge 177 D5
Bearsden 205 A5
Bearsted 37 A5
Bearstone 111 B6
Bearwood
Hereford 78 B1
Poole 17 B4
W Mid 96 C3
Beattock 184 B3
Beauchamp Roding 69 B5
Beauchief 130 A3
Beaufort 60 B3
Beaufort Castle 251 B7
Beaulieu 18 A2
Beauly 252 B1
Beaumaris 123 C6
Beaumont Cumb 175 C6
Essex 71 A5
Beaumont Hill 167 D5
Beausale 97 D5
Beauworth 33 C4
Beaworthy 11 B5
Beazley End 70 A1
Bebington 126 A3
Bebside 179 A4
Beccles 105 B5
Becconsall 136 A3
Beckbury 95 A5
Beckenham 49 C6
Beckermet 162 D3
Beckfoot Cumb 163 D4
Cumb 174 D3
Beck Foot 155 B5
Beckford 80 D2
Beckhampton 45 C4
Beck Hole 159 A7
Beckingham
Lincs 132 D3
Notts 141 E5
Beckington 44 D2
Beckley E Sus 37 D6
Hants 17 B6
Oxon 65 B6
Beck Row 102 D2
Beck Side 153 B3
Beckton 50 A1
Beckwithshaw 147 B6
Becontree 50 A1
Bedale 157 C6
Bedburn 166 B4
Bedchester 30 D2
Beddau 41 C5
Beddgelert 107 B5
Beddingham 22 B2
Beddington 49 C6
Bedfield 88 A3
Bedford 84 B2
Bedham 34 D3
Bedhampton 19 A6
Bedingfield 88 A2
Bedlam 147 A6
Bedlington 179 A4
Bedlington Station 179 A4
Bedlinog 41 A5
Bedminster 43 B4
Bedmond 67 C6
Bednall 112 D3
Bedrule 187 B5
Bedstone 94 D1
Bedwas 41 C6
Bedworth 97 C6
Bedworth Heath 97 C6
Bed-y-coedwr 108 C2
Beeby 98 A3
Beech Hants 33 B5
Staffs 112 B2
Beech Hill
Gtr Man 137 C4
Beech Hill
W Berks 47 C4
Beechingstoke 45 D4
Beedon 46 B2
Beeford 151 B4
Beeley 130 C2
Beelsby 143 C4
Beenham 46 C3
Beeny 10 B2
Beer 14 C2
Beercrocombe 28 C3
Beer Hackett 29 D6
Beesands 8 C2
Beesby 135 A4
Beeson 8 C2
Beeston C Beds 84 C3
Ches W 127 D5
Norf 119 D6
Notts 114 B3
W Yorks 148 D1
Beeston Regis 120 A3
Beeswing 173 B6
Beetham 154 D3
Beetley 119 D6
Begbroke 65 B5
Begelly 55 D7
Beggar's Bush 77 A6
Beguildy 93 D5
Beighton Norf 105 A4
S Yorks 131 A4
Beighton Hill 130 D2
Beith 204 C3
Bekesbourne 52 D3
Belaugh 121 D4
Belbroughton 96 D2
Belchamp Otten 87 C4
Belchamp St Paul 86 C3
Belchamp Walter 87 C4
Belchford 134 B2
Belford 199 C5
Belhaven 210 C3
Belhelvie 245 A6
Belhinnie 255 D5
Bellabeg 243 A6
Bellamore 181 C4
Bellanoch 213 C5
Bellaty 231 C6
Bell Bar 68 C2
Bell Busk 146 B3
Belleau 135 B4
Bellehiglash 254 C2
Bell End 96 D2
Bellerby 157 B5
Bellever 12 D1
Belliehill 232 B3
Bellingdon 67 C5
Bellingham 177 A6
Belloch 190 B2
Bellochantuy 190 B2
Bell o' th' Hill 111 A4
Bellsbank 182 B2
Bellshill N Lanark 207 D5
Northumb 199 C5
Bellspool 195 C6
Bellsquarry 208 D3
Bells Yew Green 36 C4
Belmaduthy 252 A2
Belmesthorpe 116 D3
Belmont
Blackburn 137 B5
London 49 C5
S Ayrs 192 C3
Shetland 284 C7
Belnacraig 243 A6
Belowda 5 A4
Belper 114 A1
Belper Lane End 114 A1
Belsay 178 B3
Belses 187 A4
Belsford 7 B6
Belstead 88 C2
Belston 192 C3
Belstone 11 B7
Belthorn 137 A6
Beltinge 52 C3
Beltoft 141 C6
Belton Leics 114 C2

Belton
Lincs. 116 B2
N Lincs. 141 C5
Norf 105 A5
Belton in Rutland 99 A5
Beltring 37 B4
Belts of
Collonach 244 C3
Belvedere. 50 B1
Belvoir 115 B6
Bembridge. 19 C5
Bemersyde. 197 C4
Bemerton. 31 B5
Bempton 161 D5
Benacre 105 C6
Ben Alder
Lodge. 229 A4
Ben Armine
Lodge. 273 C5
Benbuie 183 C5
Ben Casgro 288 E5
Benderloch 226 C4
Bendronaig
Lodge. 250 C2
Benenden. 37 C6
Benfield 171 A5
Bengate 121 C5
Bengeworth. 80 C3
Benhall Green. . . . 89 A4
Benhall Street. . . . 89 A4
Benholm. 233 B6
Beningbrough. . . 148 B4
Benington Herts . . 68 A2
Lincs. 117 A6
Benllech. 123 B5
Benmore Argyll . . 215 D4
Stirling. 216 B4
Benmore Lodge . 271 C6
Bennacott 10 B3
Bennan. 191 C5
Benniworth 134 A2
Benover 37 B5
Bensham 179 C4
Benslie 204 D3
Benson 65 D7
Bent. 233 A4
Bent Gate. 137 A6
Benthall
Northumb. 189 A5
Shrops 95 A4
Bentham. 63 B5
Benthoul 245 B5
Bentlawnt 94 A1
Bentley E Yorks . . 150 D3
Hants 33 A6
Suff 88 D2
S Yorks. 140 C3
Warks. 97 B5
Worcs. 80 A2
Bentley Heath. . . . 97 D4
Benton 26 B1
Bentpath 185 C6
Bents. 208 D2
Bentworth 33 A5
Benvie. 220 A3
Benwick 101 B5
Beoley. 80 A3
Beoraidbeg 235 A5
Bepton 20 A1
Berden 69 A4
Bere Alston 6 A3
Bere Ferrers 6 A3
Berepper 3 C4
Bere Regis 16 B2
Bergh Apton 104 A4
Berinsfield. 65 D6
Berkeley. 62 D2
Berkhamsted. 67 C5
Berkley. 30 A2
Berkswell. 97 D5
Bermondsey 49 B6
Bernera 249 D5
Bernice. 215 C4
Bernisdale. 259 C4
Berrick Salome. . . 65 D7
Berriedale 275 B5
Berrier 164 C1
Berriew. 93 A5
Berrington
Northumb. 198 B4
Shrops 94 A3
Berrow 42 D2
Berrow Green 79 B5
Berry Down
Cross 25 A6
Berry Hill Glos 62 B1
Pembs 72 B3
Berryhillock. 267 C6
Berrynarbor. 25 A6
Berry Pomeroy 8 A2
Bersham. 110 A2
Berstane. 282 F5
Berwick 22 B3
Berwick Bassett . . 45 B4
Berwick Hill. 178 B3
Berwick St
James. 31 B4
Berwick St John. . 30 C3
Berwick St
Leonard 30 B3
Berwick-upon-
Tweed 198 A3
Bescar. 136 B2
Besford. 80 C2
Bessacarr. 140 C4
Bessels Leigh 65 C5
Bessingby 151 A4
Bessingham. 120 B3
Bestbeech Hill . . . 36 C4
Besthorpe Norf . . 103 B6
Notts 132 C3
Bestwood. 114 A3
Bestwood
Village 114 A3
Beswick 150 C3
Betchworth 35 B5
Bethania Ceredig . . 75 B4
Gwyn 107 A6
Gwyn 108 A2
Bethel Anglesey . . 122 C3
Gwyn 109 B4
Gwyn 123 D5
Bethersden 38 A1
Bethesda Gwyn . . 123 D6
Pembs 55 C6
Bethlehem. 58 C3
Bethnal Green. . . . 49 A6
Betley 111 A6
Betsham. 50 B3
Betteshanger 53 D5
Bettiscombe 14 B3
Bettisfield 110 B3
Betton Shrops. 93 A7
Shrops 111 B5
Bettws Bridgend . . . 40 C4
Mon 61 B4
Newport. 61 D4
Bettws Cedewain. 93 B5
Bettws Gwerfil
Goch. 109 A5
Bettws Ifan 73 B6
Bettws Newydd. . . 61 C5
Bettws-y-crwyn. . 93 C6
Bettyhill 278 B3
Betws 57 A6
Betws Bledrws . . . 75 C4
Betws-Garmon. . 107 A5
Betws-y-Coed . . 124 D2
Betws-yn-Rhos . 125 B4
Beulah Ceredig. . . . 73 B5
Powys 76 B3
Bevendean. 21 B6
Bevercotes. 132 B1
Beverley. 150 D3
Beverston. 63 D4
Bevington 62 D2
Bewaldeth 163 A5
Bewcastle 176 B3
Bewdley 95 D5
Bewerley 147 A5
Bewholme 151 B4
Bexhill. 23 B5
Bexley. 50 B1
Bexleyheath. 50 B1
Bexwell. 102 A2
Beyton 87 A5
Bhaltos 287 A5
Bhatarsaigh. 286 G2
Bibury 64 C2
Bicester 65 A6
Bickenhall 28 D2
Bickenhill. 97 C4
Bicker. 117 B5
Bickershaw 137 C5
Bickerstaffe. 136 C3
Bickerton Ches E 127 D5
N Yorks. 148 B3
Bickington Devon . 12 D2
Devon. 25 B6
Bickleigh Devon. . . . 7 A4
Devon. 13 A4
Bickleton 25 B6
Bickley 49 C7
Bickley Moss. . . . 111 A4
Bicknacre. 70 C1
Bicknoller 27 B6
Bicknor. 37 A6
Bickton. 31 D5
Bicton Shrops. 93 C6
Shrops 110 D3
Bidborough 36 B3
Biddenden. 37 C6
Biddenham 84 C2
Biddestone 44 B2
Biddisham 42 D2
Biddlesden 82 C3
Biddlestone. 188 C2
Biddulph. 128 D3
Biddulph Moor . . 129 D4
Bideford 25 C5
Bidford-on-Avon. 80 B4
Bidston. 136 D1
Bielby 149 C6
Bieldside 245 B5
Bierley IoW 18 D4
W Yorks 147 D5
Bierton 66 B4
Bigbury. 7 C5
Bigbury on Sea. . . . 7 C5
Bigby. 142 C2
Biggar Cumb. 153 D2
S Lanark. 195 C5
Biggin Derbys. . . . 113 A6
Derbys 129 D6
N Yorks. 148 D4
Biggings. 285 G3
Biggin Hill 36 A2
Biggleswade 84 C3
Bighouse 279 B4
Bighton. 33 B5
Bignor. 20 A2
Big Sand. 261 C4
Bigton. 285 L5
Bilberry. 5 A5
Bilborough 114 A3
Bilbrook. 27 A5
Bilbrough. 148 C4
Bilbster. 281 C4
Bildershaw. 167 C5
Bildeston 87 C5
Billericay 69 D6
Billesdon 99 A4
Billesley 80 B4
Billingborough . . 116 B4
Billinge. 136 C4
Billingford 120 C2
Billingham. 168 C2
Billinghay. 133 D6
Billingley 140 C2
Billingshurst 34 D3
Billingsley 95 C5
Billington C Beds . . 67 A5
Lancs 145 D7
Billockby 121 D6
Billy Row 167 B4
Bilsborrow. 145 D5
Bilsby 135 B4
Bilsham 20 B2
Bilsington 38 B2
Bilson Green 62 B2
Bilsthorpe 131 C6
Bilsthorpe
Moor. 131 D6
Bilston Midloth . . . 209 D5
W Mid 96 B2
Bilstone 97 A6
Bilting 38 A2
Bilton E Yorks 151 D4
Northumb. 189 B5
Warks. 98 D1
Bilton in Ainsty. . 148 C3
Bimbister. 282 F4
Binbrook 143 D4
Binchester
Blocks 167 B5
Bincombe. 15 C6
Bindal 265 B5
Binegar. 29 A6
Binfield. 47 B6
Binfield Hth. 47 B5
Bingfield 178 B1
Bingham. 115 B5
Bingley 147 D5
Bings Heath. 111 D4
Binham. 120 B1
Binley Hants 46 D2
W Mid 97 D6
Binley Woods 97 D6
Binniehill 207 C6
Binsoe. 157 D6
Binstead 19 B4
Binsted 33 A6
Binton. 80 B4
Bintree 120 C2
Binweston 93 A7
Birch Essex 70 B3
Gtr Man 138 C1
Bircham
Newton 119 B4
Bircham Tofts. . . 119 B4
Birchanger. 69 A5
Birchencliffe. . . . 139 B4
Bircher 78 A2
Birch Green 70 B3
Birchgrove Cardiff 41 D6
Swansea 40 B2
Birch Heath. 127 C5
Birch Hill 127 B5
Birchington 53 C4
Birchmoor. 97 A5
Birchover. 130 C2
Birch Vale 129 A5
Birchwood Lincs . 133 C4
Warr. 137 D5
Bircotes 140 D4
Birdbrook. 86 C3
Birdforth 158 D3
Birdham 20 C1
Birdholme 130 C3
Birdingbury. 82 A1
Birdlip. 63 B5
Birdsall. 149 A7
Birds Edge. 139 C5
Birdsgreen. 95 C5
Birdsmoor Gate . . 14 A3
Birdston 205 A6
Birdwell 139 C6
Birdwood. 62 B3
Birgham 198 C1
Birkby. 158 A2
Birkdale 136 B2
Birkenhead 126 A3
Birkenhills. 256 B2
Birkenshaw
N Lanark 207 D4
W Yorks 139 A5
Birkhall. 243 C6
Birkhill Angus. . . . 220 A3
Borders 185 A5
Birkholme 116 C2
Birkin 140 A3
Birley. 78 B2
Birling Kent. 50 C3
Northumb. 189 C5
Birling Gap 22 C3
Birlingham. 80 C2
Birmingham 96 C3
Birnam 230 D4
Birse 244 C2
Birsemore 244 C2
Birstall Leics. 98 A2
W Yorks 139 A5
Birstwith. 147 B6
Birthorpe 116 B4
Birtley Hereford . . . 78 A1
Northumb. 177 B6
T&W. 179 D4
Birts Street 79 D5
Bisbrooke 99 B5
Biscathorpe. 134 A2
Biscot 67 A6
Bisham 47 A6
Bishampton. 80 B2
Bish Mill. 26 C2
Bishop
Auckland. 167 C5
Bishopbridge . . . 142 D2
Bishopbriggs. . . . 205 B6
Bishop Burton. . . 150 D2
Bishop
Middleham 167 B6
Bishopmill 266 C3
Bishop
Monkton 148 A2
Bishop Norton . . 142 D1
Bishopsbourne . . . 52 D3
Bishops
Cannings. 44 C4
Bishop's Castle. . . 93 C7
Bishop's Caundle 29 D6
Bishop's Cleeve . . 63 A5
Bishops Frome . . . 79 C4
Bishop's Green. . . 69 B6
Bishop's Hull. 28 C2
Bishop's
Itchington 81 B6
Bishops Lydeard. . 27 C6
Bishops Nympton 26 C2
Bishop's Offley. . 112 C1
Bishop'S
Stortford 69 A4
Bishop's Sutton . . 33 B5
Bishop's
Tachbrook. 81 A6
Bishops Tawton . . 25 B6
Bishopsteignton. . 13 D4
Bishopstoke 32 D3
Bishopston. 57 D5
Bishopstone
Bucks 66 B4
E Sus 22 B2
Hereford 78 C2
Swindon 45 A6
Wilts. 31 C4
Bishopstrow 30 A2
Bishop Sutton. . . . 43 D4
Bishop's
Waltham 33 D4
Bishopswood 28 D2
Bishop's Wood . . . 95 A6
Bishopsworth 43 C4
Bishop
Thornton 147 A6
Bishopthorpe . . . 149 C4
Bishopton Darl. . . 167 C6
Dumfries 171 C6
N Yorks. 157 D7
Renfs 205 A4
Warks. 81 B4
Bishop Wilton. . . 149 B6
Bishton. 42 A2
Bisley Glos 63 C5
Sur 34 A2
Bispham. 144 C3
Bispham Green. . 136 B3
Bissoe. 4 C2
Bisterne Close . . . 17 A6
Bitchfield 116 C2
Bittadon 25 A6
Bittaford. 7 B5
Bittering. 119 D6
Bitterley 94 D3
Bitterne 32 D3
Bitteswell. 98 C2
Bitton 43 C5
Bix 47 A5
Bixter 285 H5
Blaby. 98 B2
Blackacre. 184 C3
Blackadder
West. 198 A2
Blackawton 8 B2
Blackborough. . . . 13 A5
Blackborough
End 118 D3
Black Bourton. . . . 64 C3
Blackboys 36 D3
Blackbrook
Derbys 114 A1
Mers. 136 D4
Staffs 111 B6
Blackburn
Aberds 245 A5
Aberds 255 C6
Blackburn. 137 A5
W Loth 208 D2
Black Callerton. . 178 C3
Black Clauchrie . 181 C4
Black Corries
Lodge. 228 C1
Blackcraig 183 D5
Black Crofts. 226 C4
Blackden Heath . 128 B2
Blackdog 245 A6
Black Dog 12 A3
Blackfell. 179 D4
Blackfield. 18 A3
Blackford Cumb. . 175 B6
Perth 218 D3
Som 28 A4
Som 29 C6
Blackfordby. 114 D1
Blackgang 18 D3
Blackhall
Colliery 168 B2
Blackhall Mill . . . 178 D3
Blackhall Rocks . 168 B2
Blackham. 36 C2
Blackhaugh 196 C3
Blackheath Essex . 71 A4
Suff 105 D5
Sur. 34 B3
W Mid 96 C2
Black Heddon . . . 178 B2
Blackhill Aberds. . 257 B5
Aberds 269 D5
Highld. 258 C3
Blackhills Highld . 253 A5
Moray. 266 D3
Blackhorse. 43 B5
Blackland. 44 C4
Black Lane. 137 C6
Blacklaw. 268 D1
Blackley 138 C1
Blacklunans. 231 B5
Black Marsh 94 B1
Blackmill 40 C4
Blackmoor. 33 B6
Blackmoor Gate . . 26 A1
Blackmore. 69 C6
Blackmore End
Essex 86 D3
Herts 67 B7
Black Mount 228 D1
Blackness. 208 C3
Blacknest. 33 A6
Black Notley 70 A1
Blacko. 146 C2
Black Pill 57 C6
Blackpool
Blackpool 144 D3
Devon. 8 C2
Pembs 55 C6
Blackpool Gate. . 176 B3
Blackridge. 208 D1
Blackrock Argyll . 200 B3
Mon 60 B4
Blackrod. 137 B5
Blackshaw 174 B3
Blackshaw
Head. 138 A2
Blacksmith's
Green. 88 A2
Blackstone. 21 A5
Black Tar 55 D5
Blackthorn. 65 B7
Blackthorpe. 87 A5
Blacktoft 141 A6
Blacktop. 245 B5
Black Torrington . 11 A5
Blacktown 42 A1
Blackwall Tunnel 49 A6
Blackwater Corn . . . 4 C2
Hants 34 A1
IoW 18 C4
Blackwaterfoot. . 191 C4
Blackwell Darl . . . 167 D5
Derbys 129 B6
Derbys 131 D4
Warks. 81 C5
Worcs. 96 D2
W Sus. 36 C1
Blackwood. 194 B2
Blackwood Coed
Duon. 41 B6
Blackwood Hill. . 129 D4
Blacon. 126 C3
Bladnoch 171 B6

Bladon 65 B5
Blaenannerch 73 B5
Blaenau Ffestiniog 108 A2
Blaenavon 61 C4
Blaencelyn 73 A6
Blaendyryn 59 B6
Blaenffos 73 C4
Blaengarw 40 B4
Blaengwrach 59 E5
Blaen-gwynfi 40 B3
Blaenpennal 75 B5
Blaenplwyf 75 A4
Blaenporth 73 B5
Blaenrhondda 40 A4
Blaen-waun 73 D5
Blaen-y-coed 73 D6
Blaenycwm 92 D2
Blaen-y-Cwm
Denb 109 B5
Gwyn 108 C2
Powys 109 C5
Blagdon N Som 43 D4
Torbay 8 A2
Blagdon Hill 28 D2
Blagill 165 A5
Blaguegate 136 C3
Blaich 237 B4
Blain 235 D5
Blaina 60 C4
Blair Atholl 230 B2
Blairbeg 191 B6
Blairdaff 244 A3
Blair Drummond 207 A5
Blairglas 206 B1
Blairgowrie 231 D5
Blairhall 208 B3
Blairingone 208 A2
Blairland 204 D3
Blairlogie 207 A6
Blairlomond 215 C4
Blairmore 215 D4
Blairnamarrow 243 A5
Blairquhosh 206 B3
Blair's Ferry 203 B4
Blairskaith 205 A5
Blaisdon 62 B3
Blakebrook 95 D6
Blakedown 96 D1
Blakelaw 197 C6
Blakeley 95 B6
Blakeley Lane 112 A3
Blakemere 78 C1
Blakeney Glos 62 C2
Norf 120 A2
Blakenhall
Ches E 111 A6
W Mid 96 B2
Blakeshall 95 C6
Blakesley 82 B3
Blanchland 178 D1
Blandford Forum 16 A2
Blandford St Mary 16 A2
Bland Hill 147 B6
Blanefield 205 A5
Blankney 133 C5
Blantyre 194 A1
Blar a'Chaorainn 237 C5
Blaran 214 A1
Blarghour 214 A2
Blarmachfoldach 237 C4
Blarnalearoch 262 A3
Blashford 17 A5
Blaston 99 B5
Blatherwycke 99 B6
Blawith 154 C1
Blaxhall 89 B4
Blaxton 141 C4
Blaydon 178 C3
Bleadon 42 D2
Bleak Hey Nook 138 C3
Blean 52 C3
Bleasby Lincs 133 A6
Notts 115 A5
Bleasdale 145 C5
Bleatarn 165 D5
Blebocraigs 220 C4
Bleddfa 77 A6
Bledington 64 A3
Bledlow 66 C3
Bledlow Ridge 66 D3
Blegbie 210 D1
Blencarn 165 B4
Blencogo 175 D4
Blendworth 33 D6
Blenheim Park 119 B5
Blennerhasset 175 D4
Blervie Castle 253 A6
Bletchingdon 65 B6
Bletchingley 35 A6
Bletchley
M Keynes 83 D5
Shrops 111 B5
Bletherston 55 B6
Bletsoe 84 B2
Blewbury 46 A3
Blickling 120 C3
Blidworth 131 D5
Blindburn 188 B1
Blindcrake 163 A4
Blindley Heath 35 B6
Blisland 10 D2
Blissford 31 D5
Bliss Gate 95 D5
Blisworth 83 B4
Blithbury 113 C4
Blitterlees 174 C4
Blockley 81 D4
Blofield 104 A4
Blofield Heath 121 D5
Blo' Norton 103 D6
Bloomfield 187 A4
Blore 113 A5
Blount's Green 113 B4
Blowick 136 B2
Bloxham 82 D1
Bloxholm 133 D5
Bloxwich 96 A2
Bloxworth 16 B2
Blubberhouses 147 B5
Blue Anchor Som 27 A5
Swansea 57 C5
Blue Row 71 B4
Blundeston 105 B6
Blunham 84 B3
Blunsdon St Andrew 45 A5
Bluntington 96 D1
Bluntisham 101 D5
Blunts 6 A2
Blyborough 142 D1
Blyford 105 D5
Blymhill 112 D2
Blyth Northumb 179 A5
Notts 131 A6
Blyth Bridge 195 B6
Blythburgh 105 D5
Blythe 197 B4
Blythe Bridge 112 A3
Blyton 141 D6
Boarhills 221 C5
Boarhunt 19 A5
Boarshead 36 C3
Boars Head 137 C4
Boars Hill 65 C5
Boarstall 66 B2
Boasley Cross 11 B5
Boath 264 C1
Boat of Garten 242 A2
Bobbing 51 C5
Bobbington 95 B6
Bobbingworth 69 C5
Bocaddon 5 B6
Bochastle 217 D6
Bocking 70 A1
Bocking Churchstreet 70 A1
Boddam Aberds 257 B6
Shetland 285 M5
Boddington 63 A4
Bodedern 122 B3
Bodelwyddan 125 B5
Bodenham
Hereford 78 B3
Wilts 31 C5
Bodenham Moor 78 B3
Bodermid 106 D1
Bodewryd 122 A3
Bodfari 125 B5
Bodffordd 123 C4
Bodham 120 A3
Bodiam 37 D5
Bodicote 82 D1
Bodieve 9 D5
Bodinnick 5 B6
Bodle Street Green 23 A4
Bodmin 5 A5
Bodney 103 B4
Bodorgan 122 D3
Bodsham 38 A3
Boduan 106 C3
Bodymoor Heath 97 B4
Bogallan 252 A2
Bogbrae 257 C5
Bogend Borders 198 B1
S Ayrs 192 B3
Boghall 208 D2
Boghead 194 B2
Bogmoor 267 C4
Bogniebrae 255 B6
Bognor Regis 20 C2
Bograxie 256 E2
Bogside 194 A3
Bogton 268 D1
Bogue 182 D4
Bohenie 239 D6
Bohortha 4 D3
Bohuntine 239 D6
Boirseam 287 F5
Bojewyan 2 B1
Bolam Durham 167 C4
Northumb 178 A2
Bolberry 7 D5
Bold Heath 127 A5
Boldon 179 C5
Boldon Colliery 179 C5
Boldre 18 B2
Boldron 166 D3
Bole 132 A2
Bolehill 130 D2
Boleside 196 C3
Bolham 27 D4
Bolham Water 27 D6
Bolingey 4 B2
Bollington 129 B4
Bollington Cross 129 B4
Bolney 35 D5
Bolnhurst 84 B2
Bolshan 233 C4
Bolsover 131 B4
Bolsterstone 139 D5
Bolstone 78 D3
Boltby 158 C3
Bolter End 66 D3
Bolton Cumb 165 C4
E Loth 210 C2
E Yorks 149 B6
Gtr Man 137 C6
Northumb 189 B4
Bolton Abbey 147 B4
Bolton Bridge 147 B4
Bolton-by-Bowland 146 C1
Boltonfellend 176 C2
Boltongate 175 D5
Bolton-le-Sands 145 A4
Bolton Low Houses 175 D5
Bolton-on-Swale 157 B6
Bolton Percy 148 C4
Bolton Town End 145 A4
Bolton upon Dearne 140 C2
Bolventor 10 D2
Bomere Heath 110 D3
Bonar Bridge 264 A2
Bonawe 227 C5
Bonby 142 B2
Boncath 73 C5
Bonchester Bridge 187 B4
Bonchurch 19 D4
Bondleigh 12 A1
Bonehill Devon 12 D2
Staffs 97 A4
Bo'ness 208 B2
Bonhill 206 C1
Boningale 95 A6
Bonjedward 187 A5
Bonkle 194 A3
Bonnavoulin 225 A4
Bonnington Edin 208 D4
Kent 38 B2
Bonnybank 220 D3
Bonnybridge 207 B6
Bonnykelly 268 D3
Bonnyrigg and Lasswade 209 D6
Bonnyton Aberds 256 C1
Angus 220 A3
Angus 233 C4
Bonsall 130 D2
Bonskeid House 230 B2
Bont 61 B5
Bontddu 91 A4
Bont-Dolgadfan 91 B6
Bont-goch 91 D4
Bonthorpe 135 B4
Bontnewydd
Ceredig 75 B5
Gwyn 107 A4
Bont-newydd 125 B5
Bont Newydd
Gwyn 108 A2
Gwyn 108 C2
Bontuchel 125 D5
Bonvilston 41 D5
Bon-y-maen 57 C6
Booker 66 D4
Boon 197 B4
Boosbeck 169 D4
Boot 163 D4
Booth 138 A3
Boothby Graffoe 133 D4
Boothby Pagnell 116 B2
Boothen 112 A2
Boothferry 141 A5
Boothville 83 A4
Booth Wood 138 B3
Bootle Cumb 153 B2
Mers 136 D2
Booton 120 C3
Boot Street 88 C3
Boquhan 206 B3
Boraston 95 D4
Borden Kent 51 C5
W Sus 34 D1
Bordley 146 A3
Bordon 33 B7
Bordon Camp 33 B6
Boreham Essex 70 C1
Wilts 30 A2
Boreham Street 23 A4
Borehamwood 68 D1
Boreland
Dumfries 185 C4
Stirling 217 A5
Borgh W Isles 286 F2
W Isles 287 F4
Borghastan 288 C3
Borgie 278 C2
Borgue Dumfries 172 D4
Highld 275 B5
Borley 87 C4
Bornais 286 D3
Bornesketaig 258 A3
Borness 172 D4
Boroughbridge 148 A2
Borough Green 36 A4
Borras Head 126 D3
Borreraig 258 C1
Borrobol Lodge 274 B2
Borrowash 114 B2
Borrowby 158 C3
Borrowdale 163 C5
Borrowfield 245 C5
Borth 90 C4
Borthwickbrae 186 B3
Borthwickshiels 186 B3
Borth-y-Gest 107 C5
Borve 259 D4
Borve Lodge 287 E5
Borwick 154 D4
Bosavern 2 B1
Bosbury 79 C4
Boscastle 10 B2
Boscombe Bmouth 17 B5
Wilts 31 B6
Boscoppa 5 B5
Bosham 19 A7
Bosherston 55 E5
Boskenna 2 C2
Bosley 129 C4
Bossall 149 A6
Bossiney 9 C6
Bossingham 38 A3
Bossington 26 A3
Bostock Green 127 C6
Boston 117 A6
Boston Long Hedges 117 A6
Boston Spa 148 C3
Boston West 117 A5
Boswinger 5 C4
Botallack 2 B1
Botany Bay 68 D2
Botcherby 175 C7
Botcheston 98 A1
Botesdale 103 D6
Bothal 179 A4
Bothamsall 131 B6
Bothel 163 A4
Bothenhampton 15 B4
Bothwell 194 A2
Botley Bucks 67 C5
Hants 32 D4
Oxon 65 C5
Botolph Claydon 66 A3
Botolphs 21 B4
Bottacks 263 D6
Bottesford Leics 115 B6
N Lincs 141 C6
Bottisham 86 A1
Bottlesford 45 D5
Bottom Boat 139 A6
Bottomcraig 220 B3
Bottom House 129 D5
Bottom of Hutton 136 A3
Bottom o' th' Moor 137 B5
Botusfleming 6 A3
Botwnnog 106 C2
Bough Beech 36 B2
Boughrood 77 D5
Boughspring 62 D1
Boughton Norf 102 A2
Northants 83 A4
Notts 131 C6
Boughton Aluph 38 A2
Boughton Lees 38 A2
Boughton Malherbe 37 B6
Boughton Monchelsea 37 A5
Boughton Street 52 D2
Boulby 169 D5
Boulden 94 C3
Boulmer 189 B5
Boulston 55 C5
Boultenstone 243 A7
Boultham 133 C4
Bourn 85 B5
Bourne 116 C3
Bourne End Bucks 48 A1
C Beds 83 C6
Herts 67 C6
Bournemouth 17 B4
Bournes Green
Glos 63 C5
Southend 51 A6
Bournheath 96 D2
Bournmoor 179 D5
Bournville 96 C3
Bourton Dorset 30 B1
N Som 42 C2
Oxon 45 A6
Shrops 94 B3
Bourton on Dunsmore 98 D1
Bourton on the Hill 81 D4
Bourton-on-the-Water 64 A2
Bousd 223 A5
Boustead Hill 175 C5
Bouth 154 C2
Bouthwaite 157 D5
Boveney 48 B2
Boverton 41 E4
Bovey Tracey 12 D3
Bovingdon 67 C6
Bovingdon Green
Bucks 47 A6
Herts 67 C6
Bovinger 69 C5
Bovington Camp 16 C2
Bow Borders 196 B3
Devon 12 A2
Orkney 283 H4
Bowbank 166 C2
Bow Brickhill 83 D6
Bowburn 167 B6
Bowcombe 18 C3
Bowd 13 B6
Bowden Borders 197 C4
Devon 8 C2
Bowden Hill 44 C3
Bowderdale 155 A5
Bowdon 128 A2
Bower 177 A5
Bowerchalke 31 C4
Bowerhill 44 C3
Bower Hinton 29 D4
Bowermadden 280 B4
Bowers Gifford 51 A4
Bowershall 208 A3
Bowertower 280 B4
Bowes 166 D2
Bowgreave 145 C4
Bowgreen 128 A2
Bowhill 186 A3
Bowhouse 174 B3
Bowland Bridge 154 C3
Bowley 78 B3
Bowlhead Green 34 C2
Bowling W Dunb 205 A4
W Yorks 147 D5
Bowling Bank 110 A2
Bowling Green 79 B6
Bowmanstead 154 B2
Bowmore 200 C3
Bowness-on-Solway 175 B5
Bowness-on-Windermere 154 B3
Bow of Fife 220 C3
Bowsden 198 B3
Bowside Lodge 279 B4
Bowston 154 B3
Bow Street 90 D4
Bowthorpe 104 A2
Box Glos 63 C4
Wilts 44 C2
Boxbush 62 B3
Box End 84 C2
Boxford Suff 87 C5
W Berks 46 B2
Boxgrove 20 B2
Boxley 37 A5
Boxmoor 67 C6
Boxted Essex 87 D6
Suff 87 B4
Boxted Cross 87 D6
Boxted Heath 87 D6
Boxworth 85 A5
Boxworth End 85 A5
Boyden Gate 53 C4
Boylestone 113 B5
Boyndie 268 C1
Boynton 151 A4
Boysack 233 D4
Boyton Corn 10 B4
Suff 89 C4
Wilts 30 B3
Boyton Cross 69 C6
Boyton End 86 C3
Bozeat 83 B6
Braaid 152 D3
Braal Castle 280 B3
Brabling Green 88 A3
Brabourne 38 A2
Brabourne Lees 38 A2
Brabster 281 B5
Bracadale 246 A2
Bracara 235 A6
Braceborough 116 D3
Bracebridge 133 C4

Bracebridge Heath 133 C4
Bracebridge Low Fields 133 C4
Braceby 116 B3
Bracewell 146 C2
Brackenfield 130 D3
Brackenthwaite
Cumb 175 D5
N Yorks 148 B1
Bracklesham 19 B7
Brackletter 239 D5
Brackley Argyll 202 D2
Northants 82 D2
Brackloch 270 B4
Bracknell 47 C6
Braco 218 D3
Bracobrae 267 D6
Bracon Ash 104 B2
Bracorina 235 A6
Bradbourne 130 D2
Bradbury 167 C6
Bradda 152 E1
Bradden 82 C3
Braddock 5 A6
Bradeley 128 D3
Bradenham Bucks 66 D4
Norf 103 A5
Bradenstoke 44 B4
Bradfield Essex 88 D2
Norf 121 B4
W Berks 47 B4
Bradfield Combust 87 B4
Bradfield Green 128 D1
Bradfield Heath 71 A5
Bradfield St Clare 87 B5
Bradfield St George 87 A5
Bradford Corn 10 D2
Derbys 130 C2
Devon 11 A5
Northumb 199 C5
W Yorks 147 D5
Bradford Abbas 29 D5
Bradford Leigh 44 C2
Bradford-on-Avon 44 C2
Bradford-on-Tone 28 C1
Bradford Peverell 15 B6
Brading 19 C5
Bradley Derbys 113 A6
Hants 33 A5
NE Lincs 143 C4
Staffs 112 D2
W Mid 96 B2
W Yorks 139 A4
Bradley Green 80 A2
Bradley in the Moors 113 A4
Bradley Stoke 43 A5
Bradlow 79 D5
Bradmore Notts 114 B3
W Mid 96 B1
Bradninch 13 A5
Bradnop 129 D5
Bradpole 15 B4
Bradshaw
Gtr Man 137 B6
W Yorks 138 B3
Bradstone 11 C4
Bradwall Green 128 C2
Bradway 130 A3
Bradwell Derbys 129 A6
Essex 70 A2
M Keynes 83 D5
Norf 105 A6
Staffs 112 A2
Bradwell Grove 64 C3
Bradwell on Sea 71 C4
Bradwell Waterside 70 C3
Bradworthy 24 D4
Bradworthy Cross 24 D4
Brae Dumfries 173 A6
Highld 261 B5
Brae
Highld 272 D2
Shetland 284 G5
Braeantra 264 C1
Braedownie 231 A6
Braefield 251 C6
Braegrum 219 B5
Braehead
Dumfries 171 B6
Orkney 282 C5
Orkney 283 G6
S Lanark 194 C3
S Lanark 195 A4
Braehead of Lunan 233 C4
Braehoulland 284 F4
Braehungie 275 A5
Braelangwell Lodge 263 A7
Braemar 243 C4
Braemore Highld 262 C3
Highld 275 A4
Brae of Achnahaird 270 C3
Brae Roy Lodge 240 C1
Braeside 204 A2
Braes of Enzie 267 D4
Braeswick 282 D7
Braewick 285 H5
Brafferton Darl 167 C5
N Yorks 158 D3
Brafield-on-the-Green 83 B5
Bragar 288 C3
Bragbury End 68 A2
Bragleenmore 226 D4
Braichmelyn 123 D6
Braid 209 D5
Braides 144 B4
Braidley 156 C4
Braidwood 194 B3
Braigo 200 B2
Brailsford 113 A6
Brainshaugh 189 C5
Braintree 70 A1
Braiseworth 104 D2
Braishfield 32 C2
Braithwaite
Cumb 163 B5
S Yorks 140 B4
W Yorks 147 C4
Braithwell 140 D3
Bramber 21 A4
Bramcote Notts 114 B3
Warks 97 C7
Bramdean 33 C5
Bramerton 104 A3
Bramfield Herts 68 B2
Suff 105 D4
Bramford 88 C2
Bramhall 128 A3
Bramham 148 C3
Bramhope 147 C6
Bramley Hants 47 D4
Sur 34 B3
S Yorks 140 D2
W Yorks 147 D6
Bramling 53 D4
Brampford Speke 13 B4
Brampton Cambs 100 D4
Cumb 165 C4
Cumb 176 C3
Derbys 130 B3
Hereford 78 D2
Lincs 132 B3
Norf 120 C4
Suff 105 C5
S Yorks 140 C2
Brampton Abbotts 62 A2
Brampton Ash 99 C4
Brampton Bryan 94 D1
Brampton en le Morthen 131 A4
Bramshall 113 B4
Bramshaw 31 D6
Bramshill 47 C5
Bramshott 34 C1
Branault 235 D4
Brancaster 119 A4
Brancaster Staithe 119 A4
Brancepeth 167 B5
Branch End 178 C2
Branchill 266 D1
Branderburgh 266 B3
Brandesburton 151 C4
Brandeston 88 A3
Brand Green 62 A3
Brandhill 94 D2
Brandis Corner 11 A5
Brandiston 120 C3
Brandon Durham 167 B5
Lincs 116 A2
Northumb 188 B3
Suff 102 C3
Warks 97 D7
Brandon Bank 102 C2
Brandon Creek 102 B2
Brandon Parva 104 A1
Brandsby 159 D4
Brandy Wharf 142 D2
Brane 2 C2
Bran End 69 A6
Branksome 17 B4
Branksome Park 17 B4
Bransby 132 B3
Branscombe 14 C1
Bransford 79 B5
Bransgore 17 B5
Branshill 208 A1
Bransholme 151 D4
Branson's Cross 96 D3
Branston Leics 115 C6
Lincs 133 C5
Staffs 113 C6
Branston Booths 133 C5
Branstone 19 C4
Bransty 162 C2
Brant Broughton 133 D4
Brantham 88 D2
Branthwaite
Cumb 162 B3
Cumb 163 A5
Brantingham 142 A1
Branton
Northumb 188 B3
S Yorks 140 C4
Branxholme 186 B3
Branxholm Park 186 B3
Branxton 198 C2
Brassey Green 127 C5
Brassington 130 D2
Brasted 36 A2
Brasted Chart 36 A2
Brathens 244 C3
Bratoft 135 C4
Brattleby 133 A4
Bratton Telford 111 D5
Wilts 44 D3
Bratton Clovelly 11 B5
Bratton Fleming 26 B1
Bratton Seymour 29 C6
Braughing 68 A3
Braunston 82 A2
Braunstone Town 98 A2
Braunston-in-Rutland 99 A5
Braunton 25 B5
Brawby 159 D6
Brawl 279 B4
Brawlbin 279 C6
Bray 48 B2
Braybrooke 99 C4
Braye Ald 7
Brayford 26 B1
Bray Shop 10 D4
Braystones 162 D3
Braythorn 147 C6
Brayton 149 D5
Bray Wick 48 B1
Brazacott 10 B3
Breach 51 C5
Breachacha Castle 223 B4
Breachwood Green 67 A7
Breacleit 288 D2
Breaden Heath 110 B3
Breadsall 114 B1
Breadstone 62 C3
Breage 3 C4
Breakachy 251 B6
Bream 62 C2
Breamore 31 D5
Brean 42 D1
Breanais 287 B4
Brearton 148 A2
Breascleit 288 D3
Breaston 114 B2
Brechfa 58 B2
Brechin 232 B3
Breckan 283 G3
Breck of Cruan 282 F4
Breckrey 259 B5
Brecon
Aberhonddu 60 A2
Bredbury 138 D2
Brede 23 A6
Bredenbury 79 B4
Bredfield 88 B3
Bredgar 51 C5
Bredhurst 51 C4
Bredicot 80 B2
Bredon 80 D2
Bredon's Norton 80 D2
Bredwardine 78 C1
Breedon on the Hill 114 C2
Breibhig W Isles 286 G2
W Isles 288 D5
Breich 208 D2
Breightmet 137 C6
Breighton 149 D6
Breinton 78 D2
Breinton Common 78 C2
Breiwick 285 J6
Bremhill 44 B3
Bremirehoull 285 L6
Brenchley 37 B4
Brendon 26 A2
Brenkley 179 B4
Brent Eleigh 87 C5
Brentford 49 B4
Brentingby 115 D5
Brent Knoll 42 D2
Brent Pelham 85 D6
Brentwood 69 D5
Brenzett 38 C2
Brereton 113 D4
Brereton Green 128 C2
Brereton Heath 128 C3
Bressingham 104 C1
Bretby 113 C6
Bretford 98 D1
Bretforton 80 C3
Bretherdale Head 155 A4
Bretherton 136 A3
Brettabister 285 H6
Brettenham Norf 103 C5
Suff 87 B5
Bretton Derbys 130 B2
Flint 126 C3
Brewer Street 35 A6
Brewlands Bridge 231 B5
Brewood 96 A1
Briach 266 D1
Briants Puddle 16 B2
Brick End 69 A5
Brickendon 68 C3
Bricket Wood 67 C7
Bricklehampton 80 C2
Bride 152 A4
Bridekirk 163 A4
Bridell 73 B4
Bridestowe 11 C6
Brideswell 255 C6
Bridford 12 C3
Bridfordmills 12 C3
Bridge 52 D3
Bridge End 116 B4
Bridgefoot
Angus 220 A3
Cumb 162 B3
Bridge Green 85 D6
Bridgehampton 29 C5
Bridge Hewick 158 D2
Bridgehill 178 D2
Bridgemary 19 A4
Bridgemont 129 A5
Bridgend Aberds 244 A2
Bridgend
Aberds 255 C6
Angus 232 B3
Argyll 190 B3
Argyll 200 B3
Argyll 214 C1
Cumb 164 D1
Fife 220 C3
Moray 255 C4
N Lanark 207 C4
Pembs 73 B4
W Loth 208 C3
Bridgend Pen-y-bont ar Ogwr 40 D4
Bridgend of Lintrathen 231 C6
Bridge of Alford 244 A2
Bridge of Allan 207 A5
Bridge of Avon 254 C2
Bridge of Awe 227 D5
Bridge of Balgie 229 D4
Bridge of Cally 231 C5
Bridge of Canny 244 C3
Bridge of Craigisla 231 C6
Bridge of Dee 173 C5
Bridge of Don 245 A6
Bridge of Dun 233 C4
Bridge of Dye 244 D3
Bridge of Earn 219 C6
Bridge of Ericht 229 C4
Bridge of Feugh 245 C4
Bridge of Forss 279 B6
Bridge of Gairn 243 C6
Bridge of Gaur 229 C4
Bridge of Muchalls 245 C5
Bridge of Oich 240 B1
Bridge of Orchy 216 A2
Bridge of Waith 282 F3
Bridge of Walls 285 H4
Bridge of Weir 204 B3
Bridgerule 10 A3
Bridges 94 B1
Bridge Sollers 78 C2
Bridge Street 87 C4
Bridgeton 205 B6
Bridgetown Corn 10 C4
Som 27 B4
Bridge Trafford 127 B4
Bridge Yate 43 B5
Bridgham 103 C5
Bridgnorth 95 B5
Bridgtown 96 A2
Bridgwater 28 B3
Bridlington 151 A4
Bridport 15 B4
Bridstow 62 A1
Brierfield 146 D2
Brierley Glos 62 B2
Hereford 78 B2
S Yorks 140 B2
Brierley Hill 96 C2
Briery Hill 60 C3
Brigg 142 C2
Briggswath 160 A2
Brigham Cumb 162 A3
E Yorks 150 B3
Brighouse 139 A4
Brighstone 18 C3
Brightgate 130 D2
Brighthampton 65 C4
Brightling 37 D4
Brightlingsea 71 B4
Brighton Brighton 21 B6
Corn 4 B4
Brighton Hill 33 A5
Brightons 208 C2
Brightwalton 46 B2
Brightwell 88 C3
Brightwell Baldwin 66 D2
Brightwell cum Sotwell 65 D6
Brignall 166 D3
Brig o'Turk 217 D5
Brigsley 143 C4
Brigsteer 154 C3
Brigstock 99 C6
Brill 66 B2
Brilley 77 C6
Brimaston 55 B5
Brimfield 78 A3
Brimington 131 B4
Brimley 12 D2
Brimpsfield 63 B5
Brimpton 46 C3
Brims 283 J3
Brimscombe 63 C4
Brimstage 126 A3
Brinacory 235 A6
Brind 149 D6
Brindister
Shetland 285 H4
Shetland 285 K6
Brindle 137 A5
Brindley Ford 128 D3
Brineton 112 D2
Bringhurst 99 B5
Brington 100 D2
Brinian 282 E5
Briningham 120 B2
Brinkhill 134 B3
Brinkley 86 B2
Brinklow 98 D1
Brinkworth 44 A4
Brinmore 252 D2
Brinscall 137 A5
Brinsea 42 C3
Brinsley 114 A2
Brinsop 78 C2
Brinsworth 131 A4
Brinton 120 B2
Brisco 175 C7
Brisley 119 C6
Brislington 43 B5
Bristol 43 B4
Briston 120 B2
Britannia 138 A1
Britford 31 C5
Brithdir 91 A5
British Legion Village 37 A5
Briton Ferry 40 B2
Britwell Salome 66 D2
Brixham 8 B3
Brixton Devon 7 B4
London 49 B6
Brixton Deverill 30 B2
Brixworth 99 D4
Brize Norton 64 C4
Broad Blunsdon 64 D2
Broadbottom 138 D2
Broadbridge 19 A7
Broadbridge Heath 35 C4
Broad Campden 81 D4
Broad Chalke 31 C4
Broadclyst 13 B4
Broadfield
Gtr Man 138 B1
Lancs 136 A4
Pembs 56 B1
W Sus 35 C5
Broadford 247 B5
Broadford Bridge 34 D3
Broad Green
C Beds 83 C6
Essex 70 A2
Worcs 79 B5
Broadhaugh 186 C3
Broadhaven 281 C5
Broad Haven 55 C4
Broadheath 128 A2
Broad Heath 79 A4
Broadhembury 13 A6
Broadhempston 8 A2
Broad Hill 102 D1
Broad Hinton 45 B5
Broadholme
Derbys 114 A1
Lincs 132 B3
Broadland Row 23 A6
Broadlay 56 B3
Broad Laying 46 C2
Broadley Lancs 138 B1
Moray 267 C4
Broadley Common 68 C4
Broad Marston 80 C4
Broadmayne 16 C1
Broadmeadows 196 C3
Broadmere 33 A5
Broadmoor 55 D6

Broadoak 52 C3
Broad Oak Carms. 58 C2
Cumb 153 A2
Dorset 14 B4
Dorset 30 D1
E Sus 23 A6
E Sus 36 D4
Hereford 61 A6
Mers 136 D4
Broadrashes 267 D5
Broadsea 269 C4
Broadstairs 53 C5
Broadstone Poole 17 B4
Shrops 94 C3
Broad Street 37 A6
Broad Street Green 70 C2
Broad Town 45 B4
Broadtown Lane 45 B4
Broadwas 79 B5
Broadwater Herts 68 A2
W Sus 21 B4
Broadway Carms 56 B2
Pembs 55 C4
Som 28 D3
Suff 105 D4
Worcs 80 D3
Broadwell Glos 62 B1
Glos 64 A3
Oxon 64 C3
Warks 82 A1
Broadwell House 177 D7
Broadwey 15 C6
Broadwindsor 14 A4
Broadwood Kelly 11 A7
Broadwoodwidger 11 C5
Brobury 78 C1
Brochel 248 B2
Brochloch 182 C3
Brochroy 227 C5
Brockamin 79 B5
Brockbridge 33 D5
Brockdam 189 A4
Brockdish 104 D3
Brockenhurst 18 A2
Brocketsbrae 194 C3
Brockford Street 88 A2
Brockhall 82 A3
Brockham 35 B4
Brockhampton
Glos 63 A6
Hereford 78 D3
Brockholes 139 B4
Brockhurst
Derbys 130 C3
Hants 19 A5
Brocklebank 175 D6
Brocklesby 142 B3
Brockley 42 C3
Brockley Green 87 B4
Brockleymoor 164 B2
Brockton Shrops 93 A7
Shrops 94 B3
Shrops 94 C1
Shrops 95 A5
Telford 111 D6
Brockweir 62 C1
Brockwood 33 C5
Brockworth 63 B4
Brocton 112 D3
Brodick 191 B6
Brodsworth 140 C3
Brogaig 259 B4
Brogborough 83 D6
Brokenborough 44 A3
Broken Cross
Ches E 128 B3
Ches W 128 B1
Bromborough 126 A3
Brome 104 D2
Brome Street 104 D2
Bromeswell 88 B4
Bromfield Cumb 175 D4
Shrops 94 D2
Bromham Bedford 84 B2
Wilts 44 C3
Bromley London 49 C7
W Mid 96 C2
Bromley Common 49 C7
Bromley Green 38 B1
Brompton Medway 51 C4
N Yorks 158 B2
N Yorks 160 C3
Brompton-on-Swale 157 B6
Brompton Ralph 27 B5
Brompton Regis 27 B4
Bromsash 62 A2
Bromsberrow Hth 79 D5
Bromsgrove 96 D2
Bromyard 79 B4
Bromyard Downs 79 B4
Bronaber 108 B2
Brongest 73 B6
Bronington 110 B3
Bronllys 77 D5
Bronnant 75 B5
Bronwydd Arms 73 D7
Bronydd 77 C6
Bronygarth 110 B1
Brook Carms 56 B2
Hants 32 C2
Hants 32 D1
IoW 18 C2
Kent 38 A2
Sur 34 B3
Sur 34 C2
Brooke Norf 104 B3
Rutland 99 A5
Brookenby 143 D4
Brookend 62 D1
Brook End 84 A2
Brookfield 205 B4
Brook Hill 31 D6
Brookhouse 145 A5
Brookhouse Green 128 C3
Brookland 38 C1
Brooklands
Dumfries 173 A6
Gtr Man 137 D6
Shrops 111 A4
Brookmans Park 68 C2
Brooks 93 B5
Brooks Green 35 D4
Brook Street Kent 36 B3
Kent 38 B1
W Sus 35 D6
Brookthorpe 63 B4
Brookville 102 B3
Brookwood 34 A2
Broom C Beds 84 C3
S Yorks 140 D2
Warks 80 B3
Worcs 96 D2
Broome Norf 105 B4
Shrops 94 C2
Broomedge 128 A2
Broome Park 189 B4
Broomer's Corner 35 D4
Broomfield
Aberds 257 C4
Essex 69 B7
Kent 37 A6
Kent 52 C3
Som 28 B2
Broomfleet 141 A6
Broom Green 120 C1
Broomhall
Ches E 111 A5
Windsor 48 C2
Broomhaugh 178 C2
Broomhill Norf 102 A2
Northumb 189 C5
S Yorks 140 C2
Broom Hill 17 A4
Broomholm 121 B5
Broomley 178 C2
Broompark 167 A5
Broom's Green 79 D5
Broomy Lodge 31 D6
Brora 274 D3
Broseley 95 A4
Brotherhouse Bar 117 D5
Brotherstone 197 C5
Brothertoft 117 A5
Brotherton 140 A2
Brotton 169 D4
Broubster 279 B6
Brough Cumb 165 D5
Derbys 130 A1
E Yorks 142 A1
Highld 280 A4
Notts 132 D3
Orkney 282 F4
Shetland 284 F6
Shetland 284 F7
Shetland 284 G7
Shetland 285 H6
Shetland 285 J7
Broughall 111 A4
Brough Lodge 284 D7
Brough Sowerby 165 D5
Broughton
Borders 195 C6
Cambs 101 D4
Flint 126 C3
Hants 32 B2
Lancs 145 D5
M Keynes 83 C5
N Lincs 142 C1
Northants 99 D5
N Yorks 146 B3
N Yorks 159 D6
Orkney 282 C5
Oxon 81 D7
V Glam 40 D4
Broughton Astley 98 B2
Broughton Beck 154 C1
Broughton Common 44 C2
Broughton Gifford 44 C2
Broughton Hackett 80 B2
Broughton in Furness 153 B3
Broughton Mills 153 A3
Broughton Moor 162 A3
Broughton Park 138 C1
Broughton Poggs 64 C3
Broughtown 282 C7
Broughty Ferry 221 A4
Browhouses 175 B5
Browland 285 H4
Brown Candover 33 B4
Brown Edge
Lancs 136 B2
Staffs 129 D4
Brown Heath 127 C4
Brownhill Aberds 256 B1
Aberds 256 B3
Blackburn 145 D6
Shrops 110 C3
Brownhills Fife 221 C5
W Mid 96 A3
Brownlow 128 C3
Brownlow Heath 128 C3
Brownmuir 233 A5
Brown's End 79 D5
Brownshill 63 C4
Brownston 7 B6
Brownyside 189 A4
Broxa 160 B3
Broxbourne 68 C3
Broxburn E Loth 210 C3
W Loth 208 C3
Broxholme 133 B4
Broxted 69 A5
Broxton 127 D4
Broxwood 78 B1
Broyle Side 22 A2
Brù 288 C4
Bruairnis 286 F3
Bruan 275 A7
Bruar Lodge 230 A2
Brucehill 206 C1
Bruera 127 C4
Bruern Abbey 64 A3
Bruichladdich 200 B2
Bruisyard 88 A4
Brumby 141 C6
Brund 129 C6
Brundall 104 A4
Brundish 88 A3
Brundish Street 104 D3
Brunery 235 C6
Brunshaw 146 D2
Brunswick Village 179 B4
Bruntcliffe 139 A5
Bruntingthorpe 98 B3
Brunton Fife 220 B3
Northumb 189 A5
Wilts 45 D6
Brushford Devon 12 A1
Som 27 C4
Bruton 29 B6
Bryanston 16 A2
Brydekirk 175 A4
Bryher Scilly 2 E3
Brymbo 126 D2
Brympton 29 D5
Bryn Carms 57 B5
Gtr Man 137 C4
Neath 40 B3
Shrops 93 C6
Brynamman 59 D4
Brynberian 72 C4
Brynbryddan 40 B2
Bryncae 41 C4
Bryncethin 40 C4
Bryncir 107 B4
Bryn-coch 40 B2
Bryncroes 106 C2
Bryncrug 90 B4
Bryn Du 122 C3
Bryneglwys 109 A6
Brynford 126 B1
Bryn Gates 137 C4
Bryn-glas 124 C3
Bryn Golau 41 C4
Bryngwran 122 C3
Bryngwyn Ceredig 73 B5
Mon 61 C5
Powys 77 C5
Brynhenllan 72 C3
Brynhoffnant 73 A6
Brynithel 41 A7
Bryn-Iwan 73 C6
Brynmawr 60 B3
Bryn-mawr 106 C2
Brynmenyn 40 C4
Brynmill 57 C6
Brynna 41 C4
Bryn-nantllech 125 C4
Bryn-penarth 93 A5
Brynrefail
Anglesey 123 B4
Gwyn 123 D5
Bryn Rhyd-yr-Arian 125 C4
Brynsadler 41 C5
Bryn Saith Marchog 125 D5
Brynsiencyn 123 D4
Bryn Sion 91 A6
Brynteg Anglesey 123 B4
Ceredig 58 A1
Bryn-y-gwenin 61 B5
Bryn-y-maen 124 B3
Bryn-yr-eryr 106 B3
Buaile nam Bodach 286 F3
Bualintur 246 B3
Buarthmeini 108 B3
Bubbenhall 97 D6
Bubwith 149 D6
Buccleuch 185 A6
Buchanhaven 257 B6
Buchanty 218 B4
Buchlyvie 206 A3
Buckabank 164 A1
Buckden Cambs 84 A3
N Yorks 156 D3
Buckenham 105 A4
Buckerell 13 A6
Buckfast 7 A6
Buckfastleigh 7 A6
Buckhaven 209 A6
Buckholm 196 C3
Buckholt 61 B7
Buckhorn Weston 30 C1
Buckhurst Hill 68 D4
Buckie 267 C5
Buckies 280 B3
Buckingham 82 D3
Buckland Bucks 66 B4
Buckland
Devon 7 C5
Glos 80 D3
Hants 18 B2
Herts 85 D5
Kent 39 A5
Oxon 64 D4
Sur 35 A5
Buckland Brewer 25 C5
Buckland Common 67 C5
Buckland Dinham 43 D6
Buckland Filleigh 11 A5
Buckland in the Moor 12 D2
Buckland Monachorum 6 A3
Buckland Newton 15 A6
Buckland St Mary 28 D2
Bucklebury 46 B3
Bucklegate 117 B6
Bucklerheads 221 A4
Bucklers Hard 18 B3
Bucklesham 88 C3
Buckley Bwcle 126 C2
Bucklow Hill 128 A2
Buckminster 116 C1
Bucknall Lincs 133 C6
Stoke 112 A3
Bucknell Oxon 65 A6
Shrops 94 D1
Buckpool 267 C5
Bucksburn 245 B5
Buck's Cross 24 C4
Bucks Green 34 C3
Buckshaw Village 137 A4
Bucks Horn Oak 33 A7
Buckskin 47 D4
Buck's Mills 25 C4
Buckton E Yorks 161 D5
Hereford 94 D1
Northumb 199 C4
Buckworth 100 D3
Budbrooke 81 A5
Budby 131 C6
Budd's Titson 10 A3
Bude 10 A3
Budlake 13 B4
Budle 199 C5
Budleigh Salterton 13 C5
Budock Water 4 D2
Buerton 111 A5
Buffler's Holt 82 D3
Bugbrooke 82 B3
Buglawton 128 C3
Bugle 5 B5
Bugley 30 A2
Bugthorpe 149 B6
Buildwas 95 A4
Builth Road 76 B4
Builth Wells Llanfair-ym-Muallt 76 B4
Buirgh 287 E5
Bulby 116 C3
Bulcote 115 A4
Buldoo 279 B5
Bulford 31 A5
Bulford Camp 31 A5
Bulkeley 127 D5
Bulkington Warks 97 C6
Wilts 44 D3
Bulkworthy 25 D4
Bullamoor 158 B2
Bullbridge 130 D3
Bullbrook 48 C1
Bulley 62 B3
Bullgill 162 A3
Bull Hill 18 B2
Bullington Hants 32 A3
Lincs 133 B5
Bull's Green 68 B2
Bullwood 203 A6
Bulmer Essex 87 C4
N Yorks 149 A5
Bulmer Tye 87 D4
Bulphan 50 A3
Bulverhythe 23 B5
Bulwark 257 B4
Bulwell 114 A3
Bulwick 99 B6
Bumble's Green 68 C4
Bun Abhainn Eadarra 288 G2
Bunacaimb 235 B5
Bun a'Mhuillin 286 E3
Bunarkaig 239 D5
Bunbury 127 D5
Bunbury Heath 127 D5
Bunchrew 252 B2
Bundalloch 249 D5
Buness 284 C8
Bunessan 224 D2
Bungay 104 C4
Bunkers Hill 65 B5
Bunker's Hill
Lincs 133 B4
Lincs 134 D2
Bunloit 251 D7
Bun Loyne 239 B6
Bunnahabhain 201 A4
Bunny 114 C3
Buntait 251 C5
Buntingford 68 A3
Bunwell 104 B2
Burbage Derbys 129 B5
Leics 98 B1
Wilts 45 C6
Burchett's Green 47 A6
Burcombe 31 B4
Burcot 65 D6
Burcott 66 A4
Burdon 179 D5
Bures 87 D5
Bures Green 87 D5
Burford Ches E 127 D6
Oxon 64 B3
Shrops 78 A3
Burg 224 B2
Burgar 282 E4
Burgate Hants 31 D5
Suff 104 D1
Burgess Hill 21 A6
Burgh 88 B3
Burgh by Sands 175 C6
Burgh Castle 105 A5
Burghclere 46 C2
Burghead 266 C2
Burghfield 47 C4
Burghfield Common 47 C4
Burghfield Hill 47 C4
Burgh Heath 35 A5
Burghill 78 C2
Burgh le Marsh 135 C5
Burgh Muir 256 D2
Burgh next Aylsham 120 C4
Burgh on Bain 134 A2
Burgh St Margaret 121 D6
Burgh St Peter 105 B5
Burghwallis 140 B3
Burham 51 C4
Buriton 33 C6
Burland 127 D6
Burlawn 9 D5
Burleigh 48 C1
Burlescombe 27 D5
Burleston 16 B1
Burley Hants 17 A6
Rutland 116 D1
W Yorks 148 D1
Burleydam 111 A5
Burley Gate 78 C3
Burley in Wharfedale 147 C5
Burley Lodge 17 A6
Burley Street 17 A6
Burlingjobb 77 B6
Burlow 22 A3
Burlton 110 C3
Burmarsh 38 B2
Burmington 81 D5
Burn 140 A3
Burnaston 113 B6
Burnbank 194 A2

Burnby 150 C1
Burncross 139 D6
Burneside 154 B4
Burness 282 C7
Burneston 157 C7
Burnett 43 C5
Burnfoot Borders 186 B3
Borders 186 B4
E Ayrs 182 B2
Perth 219 D4
Burnham Bucks 48 A2
N Lincs 142 B2
Burnham Deepdale 119 A5
Burnham Green 68 B2
Burnham Market 119 A5
Burnham Norton 119 A5
Burnham-on-Crouch 70 D3
Burnham-on-Sea 28 A3
Burnham Overy Staithe 119 A5
Burnham Overy Town 119 A5
Burnham Thorpe 119 A5
Burnhead
Dumfries 183 C6
S Ayrs 181 A4
Burnhervie 245 A4
Burnhill Green 95 A5
Burnhope 167 A4
Burnhouse 204 C3
Burniston 160 B4
Burnlee 139 C4
Burnley 146 D2
Burnley Lane 146 D2
Burnmouth 211 D6
Burn of Cambus 218 D2
Burnopfield 178 D3
Burnsall 147 A4
Burnside Angus 232 C3
E Ayrs 182 A3
Fife 219 D6
Shetland 284 F4
S Lanark 205 B6
W Loth 208 C3
Burnside of Duntrune 220 A4
Burnswark 175 A4
Burntcommon 34 A3
Burnt Heath 130 B2
Burnthouse 4 D2
Burnt Houses 166 C4
Burntisland 209 B5
Burnton 182 B2
Burntwood 96 A3
Burnt Yates 147 A6
Burnwynd 208 D4
Burpham Sur 34 A3
W Sus 20 B3
Burradon
Northumb 188 C2
T&W 179 B4
Burrafirth 284 B8
Burraland
Shetland 284 F5
Shetland 285 J4
Burras 3 B4
Burravoe
Shetland 284 F7
Shetland 284 G5
Burray Village 283 H5
Burrells 165 D4
Burrelton 220 A2
Burridge Devon 25 B6
Hants 32 D4
Burrill 157 C6
Burringham 141 C6
Burrington Devon 26 D1
Hereford 94 D2
N Som 42 D3
Burrough Green 86 B2
Burrough on the Hill 115 D5
Burrow-bridge 28 C3
Burrowhill 48 C2
Burry 57 C4
Burry Green 57 C4
Burry Port Porth Tywyn 57 B4
Burscough 136 B3
Burscough Bridge 136 B3
Bursea 149 D7
Burshill 150 C3
Bursledon 18 A3
Burslem 112 A2
Burstall 88 C1
Burstock 14 A4
Burston Norf 104 C2
Staffs 112 B3
Burstow 35 B6
Burstwick 143 A4
Burtersett 156 C2
Burtle 28 A3
Burton Ches W 126 B3
Ches W 127 C5
Dorset 17 B5
Lincs 133 B4
Northumb 199 C5
Pembs 55 D5
Som 28 A1
Wilts 44 B2
Burton Agnes 151 A4
Burton Bradstock 15 C4
Burton Dassett 81 B6
Burton Fleming 161 D4
Burton Green
W Mid 97 D5
Wrex 126 D3
Burton Hastings 97 B7
Burton-in-Kendal 154 D4
Burton in Lonsdale 155 D5
Burton Joyce 115 A4
Burton Latimer 99 D6
Burton Lazars 115 D5
Burton-le-Coggles 116 C2
Burton Leonard 148 A2
Burton on the Wolds 114 C3
Burton Overy 98 B3
Burton Pedwardine 116 A4
Burton Pidsea 151 D5
Burton Salmon 140 A2
Burton Stather 141 B6
Burton upon Stather 141 B6
Burton upon Trent 113 C6
Burtonwood 137 D4
Burwardsley 127 D5
Burwarton 95 C4
Burwash 37 D4
Burwash Common 36 D4
Burwash Weald 36 D4
Burwell Cambs 86 A1
Lincs 134 B3
Burwen 123 A4
Burwick 283 J5
Bury Cambs 101 C4
Gtr Man 137 B7
Som 27 C4
W Sus 20 A3
Bury Green 68 A4
Bury St Edmunds 87 A4
Burythorpe 149 A6
Busby 205 C5
Buscot 64 D3
Bush Bank 78 B2
Bushbury 96 A2
Bushby 98 A3
Bush Crathie 243 C5
Bushey 67 D7
Bushey Heath 67 D7
Bush Green 104 C3
Bushley 80 D1
Bushton 45 B4
Buslingthorpe 133 A5
Busta 284 G5
Butcher's Cross 36 D3
Butcombe 43 C4
Butetown 41 D6
Butleigh 29 B5
Butleigh Wootton 29 B5
Butler's Cross 66 C4
Butler's End 97 C5
Butlers Marston 81 C6
Butley 89 B4
Butley High Corner 89 C4
Butterburn 177 B4
Buttercrambe 149 B6
Butterknowle 166 C4
Butterleigh 13 A4
Buttermere
Cumb 163 C4
Wilts 46 C1
Buttershaw 139 A4
Butterstone 231 D4
Butterton 129 D5
Butterwick
Durham 167 C6
Lincs 117 A6
N Yorks 159 D6
N Yorks 160 D3
Butt Green 127 D6
Buttington 93 A6
Buttonoak 95 D5
Buttsash 18 A3
Butt's Green 32 C2
Buxhall 87 B6
Buxhall Fen Street 87 B6
Buxley 198 A2
Buxted 36 D2
Buxton Derbys 129 B5
Norf 120 C4
Buxworth 129 A5
Bwlch 60 A3
Bwlchgwyn 126 D2
Bwlch-Llan 75 C4
Bwlchnewydd 73 D6
Bwlchtocyn 106 D3
Bwlch-y-cibau 109 D6
Bwlchyddar 109 C6
Bwlch-y-fadfa 74 D3
Bwlch-y-ffridd 93 B4
Bwlchygroes 73 C5
Bwlch-y-sarnau 92 D4
Byermoor 178 D3
Byers Green 167 B5
Byfield 82 B2
Byfleet 48 C3
Byford 78 C1
Bygrave 85 D4
Byker 179 C4
Bylchau 125 C4
Byley 128 C2
Bynea 57 C5
Byrness 187 C6
Bythorn 100 D2
Byton 78 A1
Byworth 34 D2

C

Cabharstadh 288 E4
Cablea 218 A4
Cabourne 142 C3
Cabrach Argyll 201 B4
Moray 255 D4
Cabrich 252 B1
Cabus 145 C4
Cackle Street 36 D2
Cadbury 13 A4
Cadbury Barton 26 D1
Cadder 205 A6
Caddington 67 B6
Caddonfoot 196 C3
Cadeby Leics 97 A7
S Yorks 140 C3
Cadeleigh 13 A4
Cade Street 36 D4
Cadgwith 3 D5
Cadham 220 D2
Cadishead 137 D6
Cadle 57 C6
Cadley Lancs 145 D5
Wilts 45 C6
Wilts 45 D6
Cadmore End 66 D3
Cadnam 32 D1
Cadney 142 C2
Cadole 126 C2
Cadoxton 41 E6
Cadoxton-Juxta-Neath 40 B2
Cadshaw 137 B6
Cadzow 194 A2
Caeathro 123 D4
Caehopkin 59 D5
Caenby 133 A5
Caenby Corner 133 A4
Caerau Bridgend 40 B3
Cardiff 41 D6
Caér-bryn 57 A5
Caerdeon 90 A4
Caerfarchell 54 B3
Caergeiliog 122 C3
Caergwrle 126 D3
Caerleon Caerllion 61 D5
Caer Llan 61 C6
Caernarfon 123 D4
Caerphilly Caerffili 41 C6
Caersws 92 B4
Caerwedros 73 A6
Caerwent 61 D6
Caerwych 107 C6
Caerwys 125 B6
Caethle 90 C4
Caim 123 B6
Caio 58 B3
Cairinis 287 H3
Cairisiadar 287 A5
Cairminis 287 F5
Cairnbaan 213 C6
Cairnbanno Ho. 256 B3
Cairnborrow 255 B5
Cairnbrogie 256 D3
Cairnbulg Castle 269 C5
Cairncross
Angus 232 A2
Borders 211 D5
Cairndow 215 A4
Cairness 269 C5
Cairneyhill 208 B3
Cairnfield Ho. 267 C5
Cairngaan 170 D3
Cairngarroch 170 C2
Cairnhill 256 C1
Cairnie Aberds 245 B5
Aberds 255 B5
Cairnorrie 256 B3
Cairnpark 245 A5
Cairnryan 170 A2
Cairnton 283 G4
Caister-on-Sea 121 D7
Caistor 142 C3
Caistor St Edmund 104 A3
Caistron 188 C2
Caitha Bowland 196 B3
Calais Street 87 D5
Calanais 288 D3
Calbost 288 F5
Calbourne 18 C3
Calceby 134 B3
Calcot Row 47 B4
Calcott 52 C3
Caldback 284 C8
Caldbeck 163 A6
Caldbergh 157 C4
Caldecote Cambs 85 B5
Cambs 100 C3
Herts 84 D4
Northants 82 B3
Caldecott
Northants 84 A1
Oxon 65 D5
Rutland 99 B5
Calderbank 207 D5
Calder Bridge 162 D3
Calderbrook 138 B2
Caldercruix 207 D6
Calder Hall 162 D3
Calder Mains 280 C2
Caldermill 205 D6
Calder Vale 145 C5
Calderwood 205 C6
Caldhame 232 D2
Caldicot 42 A3
Caldwell Derbys 113 D6
Caldwell
N Yorks 167 D4
Caldy 126 A2
Caledrhydiau 74 C3
Calfsound 282 D6
Calgary 224 A2
Califer 266 D1
California Falk 208 C2
Norf 121 D7
Calke 114 C1
Callakille 248 A3
Callaly 188 C3
Callander 217 D6
Callaughton 95 B4
Callestick 4 B2
Calligarry 247 D5
Callington 6 A2
Callow 78 D2
Callow End 79 C6
Callow Hill Wilts 44 A4
Worcs 95 D5
Callows Grave 78 A3
Calmore 32 D2
Calmsden 63 C6
Calne 44 B4
Calow 131 B4
Calshot 18 A3
Calstock 6 A3
Calstone Wellington 44 C4
Calthorpe 120 B3
Calthwaite 164 A2
Calton N Yorks 146 B3
Staffs 129 D6
Calveley 127 D5
Calver 130 B2
Calverhall 111 B5
Calver Hill 78 C1
Calverleigh 27 D4
Calverley 147 D6
Calvert 66 A2
Calverton
M Keynes 83 D4
Notts 115 A4
Calvine 230 B2
Calvo 174 C4
Cam 62 D3
Camas-luinie 249 D6
Camasnacroise 236 D2
Camastianavaig 247 A4
Camasunary 247 C4
Camault Muir 251 B7
Camb 284 D7
Camber 38 D1
Camberley 47 C6
Camberwell 49 B6
Camblesforth 141 A4
Cambo 178 A2
Cambois 179 A5
Camborne 3 A4
Cambourne 85 B5
Cambridge Cambs 85 B6
Glos 62 C3
Cambridge Town 51 A6
Cambus 207 A6
Cambusavie Farm 264 A3
Cambusbarron 207 A5
Cambuskenneth 207 A6
Cambuslang 205 B6
Cambusmore Lodge 264 A3
Camden 49 A5
Camelford 10 C2
Camelsdale 34 C1
Camerory 253 C6
Camer's Green 79 D5
Camerton Bath 43 D5
Cumb 162 A3
E Yorks 143 A4
Camghouran 229 C4
Cammachmore 245 C6
Cammeringham 133 A4
Camore 264 A3
Campbeltown 190 C3
Camperdown 179 B4
Camp Hill 97 B6
Campmuir 220 A2
Campsall 140 B3
Campsey Ash 88 B4
Campton 84 D3
Camptown 187 B5
Camrose 55 B5
Camserney 230 D2
Camster 281 D4
Camuschoirk 235 D6
Camuscross 247 C5
Camusnagaul
Highld 237 B4
Highld 262 B2
Camusrory 238 C2
Camusteel 249 B4
Camusterrach 249 B4
Camusvrachan 229 D5
Canada 32 D1
Canadia 23 A5
Canal Side 141 B4
Candacraig Ho. 243 A6
Candlesby 135 C4
Candy Mill 195 B5
Cane End 47 B4
Canewdon 70 D2
Canford Bottom 17 A4
Canford Cliffs 17 C4
Canford Magna 17 B4
Canham's Green 87 A6
Canholes 129 B5
Canisbay 281 A5
Cann 30 C2
Cannard's Grave 29 A6
Cann Common 30 C2
Cannich 251 C5
Cannington 28 B2
Cannock 96 A2
Cannock Wood 112 D4
Canonbie 175 A6
Canon Bridge 78 C2
Canon Frome 79 C4
Canon Pyon 78 C2
Canons Ashby 82 B2
Canonstown 2 B3
Canterbury 52 D3
Cantley Norf 105 A4
S Yorks 140 C4
Cantlop 94 A3
Canton 41 D6
Cantraybruich 252 B3
Cantraydoune 252 B3
Cantraywood 252 B3
Cantsfield 155 D5
Canvey Island 51 A4
Canwick 133 C4
Canworthy Water 10 B3
Caol 237 B5
Caolas 222 C3
Caolas Scalpaigh 288 H3
Caolas Stocinis 288 H2
Caol Ila 201 A4
Capel 35 B4
Capel Bangor 91 D4
Capel Betws Lleucu 75 C5
Capel Carmel 106 D1
Capel Coch 123 B4
Capel Curig 124 D2
Capel Cynon 73 B6
Capel Dewi Carms 58 C1
Ceredig 58 A1
Ceredig 90 D4
Capel Garmon 124 D3
Capel-gwyn 122 C3
Capel Gwyn 58 C1
Capel Gwynfe 59 C4
Capel Hendre 57 A5
Capel Hermon 108 C2
Capel Isaac 58 C2
Capel Iwan 73 C5
Capel le Ferne 39 B4
Capel Llanilltern 41 C5
Capel Mawr 123 C4
Capel St Andrew 89 C4
Capel St Mary 88 D1
Capel Seion 75 A5
Capel Tygwydd 73 B5
Capel Uchaf 107 B4
Capelulo 124 B2
Capel-y-graig 123 D5
Capenhurst 126 B3
Capernwray 154 D4
Capheaton 178 A2
Cappercleuch 196 D1
Capplegill 185 B4
Capton 8 B2

Caputh 219 A5
Carbis Bay 2 B3
Carbost Highld 246 A2
Highld 259 D4
Carbrook 130 A3
Carbrooke 103 A5
Carburton 131 B6
Carcant 196 A2
Carcary 233 C4
Carclaze 5 B5
Car Colston 115 A5
Carcroft 140 B3
Cardenden 209 A5
Cardeston 110 D2
Cardiff Caerdydd 41 D6
Cardigan
Aberteifi 73 B4
Cardington
Bedford 84 C2
Shrops 94 B3
Cardinham 5 A6
Cardonald 205 B5
Cardow 254 B2
Cardrona 196 C2
Cardross 206 C1
Cardurnock 175 C4
Careby 116 D3
Careston Castle 232 C3
Carew 55 D6
Carew Cheriton 55 D6
Carew Newton 55 D6
Carey 78 D3
Carfrae 210 D2
Cargenbridge 174 A2
Cargill 219 A6
Cargo 175 C6
Cargreen 6 A3
Carham 198 C2
Carhampton 27 A5
Carharrack 4 C2
Carie Perth 217 A6
Perth 229 C5
Carines 4 B2
Carisbrooke 18 C3
Cark 154 D2
Carlabhagh 288 C3
Carland Cross 4 B3
Carlby 116 D3
Carlecotes 139 C4
Carlesmoor 157 D5
Carleton Cumb 164 C3
Cumb 176 D2
Lancs 144 D3
N Yorks 146 C3
Carleton
Forehoe 104 A1
Carleton Rode 104 B2
Carlingcott 43 D5
Carlin How 169 D5
Carlisle 175 C7
Carlops 195 A6
Carlton Bedford 83 B6
Cambs 86 B2
Leics 97 A6
Notts 115 A4
N Yorks 140 A4
N Yorks 157 C4
N Yorks 159 C5
N Yorks 167 D4
Stockton 167 C6
Suff 89 A4
S Yorks 139 B6
W Yorks 139 A6
Carlton Colville 105 C6
Carlton Curlieu 98 B3
Carlton
Husthwaite 158 D3
Carlton in
Cleveland 158 A4
Carlton in
Lindrick 131 A5
Carlton le
Moorland 133 D4
Carlton Miniott 158 C2
Carlton on
Trent 132 C2
Carlton Scroop 116 A2
Carluke 194 A3
Carmarthen
Caerfyrddin 73 D7
Carmel Anglesey 122 B3
Carms 57 A5
Carmel
Flint 125 B6
Guern 6
Gwyn 107 A4
Carmont 245 D5
Carmunnock 205 C6
Carmyle 205 B6
Carmyllie 232 D3
Carnaby 151 A4
Carnach Highld 250 D2
Highld 262 A2
W Isles 288 H3
Carnachy 278 C3
Càrnais 287 A5
Carnbee 221 D5
Carnbo 219 D5
Carnbrea 3 A4
Carnduff 205 D6
Carnduncan 200 B2
Carne 4 D4
Carnforth 154 D3
Carn-gorm 249 D6
Carnhedryn 54 B4
Carnhell Green 3 B4
Carnkie Corn 3 B4
Corn 4 D2
Carno 92 B3
Carnoch Highld 251 A4
Highld 251 C5
Carnock 208 B3
Carnon Downs 4 C2
Carnousie 268 D1
Carnoustie 221 A5
Carnwath 195 B4
Carnyorth 2 B1
Carperby 156 C4
Carpley Green 156 C3
Carr 140 D3
Carradale 190 B4
Carragraich 288 H2
Carrbridge 253 D5
Carrefour Selous
Jersey 6
Carreglefn 122 B3
Carreg-wen 73 B5
Carr Hill 179 C4
Carrick Argyll 214 D2
Fife 220 B4
Carrick Castle 215 C4
Carrick Ho. 282 D6
Carriden 208 B3
Carrington
Gtr Man 137 D6
Lincs 134 D3
Midloth 209 D6
Carrog Conwy 108 A2
Denb 109 A6
Carron Falk 208 B1
Moray 254 B3
Carronbridge 183 C6
Carron Bridge 207 B5
Carronshore 208 B1
Carrshield 165 A6
Carrutherstown 174 A4
Carrville 167 A6
Carsaig Argyll 213 D5
Argyll 225 D4
Carscreugh 171 B4
Carsegowan 171 B6
Carse Gray 232 C2
Carse Ho. 202 B2
Carseriggan 171 A5
Carsethorn 174 C2
Carshalton 49 C5
Carsington 130 D2
Carskiey 190 E2
Carsluith 171 B6
Carsphairn 182 C3
Carstairs 194 B4
Carstairs
Junction 195 B4
Carswell Marsh 64 D4
Carter's Clay 32 C2
Carterton 64 C3
Carterway
Heads 178 D2
Carthew 5 B5
Carthorpe 157 C7
Cartington 188 C3
Cartland 194 B3
Cartmel 154 D2
Cartmel Fell 154 C3
Carway 57 B4
Cary Fitzpaine 29 C5
Cascob 77 A6
Cashlie 228 D3
Cashmoor 30 D3
Cassey Compton 63 B6
Cassington 65 B5
Cassop 167 B6
Castell 125 C6
Castellau 41 C5
Castell-Howell 74 D3
Castell-y-bwch 61 D4
Casterton 155 D5
Castle Acre 119 D5
Castle Ashby 83 B5
Castle Bolton 156 B4
Castle Bromwich 96 C4
Castle Bytham 116 D2
Castlebythe 55 B6
Castle
Caereinion 93 A5
Castle Camps 86 C2
Castle Carrock 176 D3
Castlecary 207 C5
Castle Cary 29 B6
Castle Combe 44 B2
Castlecraig 265 D4
Castle
Donington 114 C2
Castle Douglas 173 B5
Castle Eaton 64 D2
Castle Eden 168 B2
Castlefairn 183 D5
Castle Forbes 244 A3
Castleford 140 A2
Castle Frome 79 C4
Castle Green 48 C2
Castle Gresley 113 D6
Castle Heaton 198 B3
Castle
Hedingham 86 D3
Castlehill
Borders 195 C7
Highld 280 B3
W Dunb 206 C1
Castle Hill 37 B4
Castle Huntly 220 B3
Castle Kennedy 170 B3
Castlemaddy 182 D3
Castlemartin 55 E5
Castlemilk
Dumfries 174 A4
Glasgow 205 C6
Castlemorris 55 A5
Castlemorton 79 D5
Castle O'er 185 C5
Castle
Pulverbatch 94 A2
Castle Rising 118 C3
Castleside 166 A3
Castle Stuart 252 B3
Castlethorpe 83 C5
Castleton Angus 232 D1
Argyll 214 D1
Derbys 129 A6
Gtr Man 138 B1
Newport 42 A1
N Yorks 159 A5
Castletown
Ches W 127 D4
Highld 252 B3
Highld 280 B3
IoM 152 E2
T&W 179 D5
Castleweary 186 C3
Castley 147 C6
Caston 103 B5
Castor 100 B3
Catacol 203 D4
Catbrain 43 A4
Catbrook 61 C7
Catchall 2 C2
Catchems Corner 97 D5
Catchgate 178 D3
Catcleugh 187 C6
Catcliffe 131 A4
Catcott 28 B3
Caterham 35 A6
Catfield 121 C5
Catfirth 285 H6
Catford 49 B6
Catforth 145 D4
Cathays 41 D6
Cathcart 205 B5
Cathedine 60 A3
Catherington 33 D5
Catherton 95 D4
Catlodge 241 C4
Catlowdy 176 B2
Catmore 46 A2
Caton 145 A5
Caton Green 145 A5
Catrine 193 C5
Cat's Ash 61 D5
Catsfield 23 A5
Catshill 96 D2
Cattal 148 B3
Cattawade 88 D2
Catterall 145 C4
Catterick 157 B6
Catterick Bridge 157 B6
Catterick
Garrison 157 B5
Catterlen 164 B2
Catterline 233 A6
Catterton 148 C4
Catthorpe 98 D2
Cattistock 15 B5
Catton Northumb 177 D6
N Yorks 158 D2
Catwick 151 C4
Catworth 100 D2
Caudlesprings 103 A5
Caulcott 65 A6
Cauldcots 233 D4
Cauldhame 207 A4
Cauldmill 186 B4
Cauldon 113 A4
Caulkerbush 174 C2
Caulside 176 A2
Caunsall 95 C6
Caunton 132 D2
Causewayend 195 C5
Causeway End 171 A6
Causeway Foot 147 D4
Causewayhead 174 C4
Causeway-head 207 A5
Causeyend 245 A6
Causey Park
Bridge 189 D4
Cautley 155 B5
Cavendish 87 C4
Cavendish
Bridge 114 C2
Cavenham 86 A3
Caversfield 65 A6
Caversham 47 B5
Caverswall 112 A3
Cavil 149 D6
Cawdor 253 B4
Cawkwell 134 B2
Cawood 149 D4
Cawsand 6 B3
Cawston 120 C3
Cawthorne 139 C5
Cawthorpe 116 C3
Cawton 159 D5
Caxton 85 B5
Caynham 94 D3
Caythorpe Lincs 116 A2
Notts 115 A4
Cayton 161 C4
Ceann a Bhaigh 287 H2
Ceannacroc
Lodge 239 A6
Ceann a Deas Loch
Baghas-
dail 286 E3
Ceann Shiphoirt 288 F3
Ceann
Tarabhaigh 288 F3
Cearsiadair 288 E4
Cefn Berain 125 C4
Cefn-brith 125 D4
Cefn Canol 110 B1
Cefn-coch 124 C3
Cefn Coch 109 C6
Cefn-coed-y-
cymmer 60 C2
Cefn Cribbwr 40 C3
Cefn Cross 40 C3
Cefn-ddwysarn 109 B4
Cefn Einion 93 C6
Cefneithin 57 A5
Cefn-gorwydd 76 C3
Cefn-mawr 110 A1
Cefn-y-bedd 126 D3
Cefn-y-pant 73 D4
Cei-bach 73 A7
Ceint 123 C4
Cellan 75 D5
Cellarhead 112 A3
Cemaes 122 A3
Cemmaes 91 B6
Cemmaes Road 91 B6
Cenarth 73 B5
Cenin 107 B4
Central 204 A2
Ceos 288 E4
Ceres 220 C4
Cerne Abbas 15 A6
Cerney Wick 63 D6
Cerrigceinwen 123 C4
Cerrigydrudion 109 A4
Cessford 187 A6
Ceunant 123 D5
Chaceley 79 D6
Chacewater 4 C2
Chackmore 82 D3
Chacombe 82 C1
Chadderton 138 C2
Chadderton
Fold 138 C1
Chaddesden 114 B1
Chaddesley
Corbett 96 D1
Chaddleworth 46 B2
Chadlington 64 A4
Chadshunt 81 B6
Chad Valley 96 C3
Chadwell 115 C5
Chadwell St Mary 50 B3
Chadwick End 97 D5
Chadwick
Green 136 D4
Chaffcombe 28 D3
Chagford 12 C2
Chailey 22 A1
Chainbridge 101 A6
Chain Bridge 117 A6
Chainhurst 37 B5
Chalbury 17 A4
Chalbury
Common 17 A4
Chaldon 35 A6
Chaldon Herring
or 16 C1
Chale 18 D3
Chale Green 18 D3
Chalfont
Common 67 D6
Chalfont St Giles 67 D5
Chalfont St Peter 67 D6
Chalford 63 C4
Chalgrove 66 D2
Chalk 50 B3
Challacombe 26 A1
Challoch 171 A5
Challock 52 D2
Chalton C Beds 67 A6
Hants 33 D6
Chalvington 22 B3
Chancery 75 A4
Chandler's Ford 32 C3
Channel Tunnel 38 B3
Channerwick 285 L6
Chantry Som 29 A7
Suff 88 C2
Chapel 209 A5
Chapel Allerton
Som 42 D3
W Yorks 148 D2
Chapel Amble 9 D5
Chapel Brampton 83 A4
Chapel Chorlton 112 B2
Chapel End 97 B6
Chapel-en-le-
Frith 129 A5
Chapelgate 117 C7
Chapel Green
Warks 82 A1
Warks 97 C5
Chapel
Haddlesey 140 A3
Chapelhall 207 D5
Chapel Head 101 C5
Chapelhill
Dumfries 184 C3
Highld 265 C4
N Ayrs 204 D2
Perth 219 A5
Perth 220 B2
Chapel Hill
Aberds 257 C5
Lincs 134 D2
Mon 62 D1
N Yorks 148 C2
Chapelknowe 175 A6
Chapel Lawn 93 D7
Chapel-le-Dale 155 D6
Chapel Milton 129 A5
Chapel of
Garioch 256 D2
Chapel Row 46 C3
Chapel St
Leonards 135 B5
Chapel Stile 154 A2
Chapelton Angus 233 D4
Devon 25 C6
Highld 242 A2
S Lanark 194 B1
Chapeltown
Blackburn 137 B6
Moray 254 D3
S Yorks 139 D6
Chapmanslade 30 A2
Chapmans Well 11 B4
Chapmore End 68 B3
Chappel 70 A2
Chard 14 A3
Chardstock 14 A3
Charfield 62 D3
Charford 80 A2
Charing 38 A1
Charing Cross 31 D5
Charing Heath 38 A1
Charingworth 81 D5
Charlbury 65 B4
Charlcombe 43 C6
Charlecote 81 B5
Charles 26 B1
Charlesfield 175 B4
Charleston
Angus 232 D1
Renfs 205 B4
Charlestown
Aberdeen 245 B6
Corn 5 B5
Derbys 138 D3
Dorset 15 D6
Fife 208 B3
Gtr Man 137 C7
Highld 252 B2
Highld 261 C5
W Yorks 138 A2
Charlestown of
Aberlour 254 B3
Charles Tye 87 B6
Charlesworth 138 D3
Charleton 7 C6
Charlton Hants 32 A2
Herts 68 A1
London 49 B7
Northants 82 D2
Northumb 177 A6
Som 43 D5
Telford 111 D4
Wilts 30 C3
Wilts 44 A3
Wilts 45 D5
Worcs 80 C3
W Sus 20 A1
Charlton Abbots 63 A6
Charlton Adam 29 C5
Charlton-All-
Saints 31 C5
Charlton Down 15 B6
Charlton
Horethorne 29 C6
Charlton Kings 63 A5
Charlton
Mackerell 29 C5
Charlton
Marshall 16 A2

Charlton Musgrove 29 C7
Charlton on Otmoor 65 B6
Charltons 168 D4
Charlwood 35 B5
Charlynch 28 B2
Charminster 15 B6
Charmouth 14 B3
Charndon 66 A2
Charney Bassett 65 D4
Charnock Richard 137 B4
Charsfield 88 B3
Chart Corner 37 A5
Charter Alley 46 D3
Charterhouse 42 D3
Charterville Allotments 64 B4
Chartham 52 D3
Chartham Hatch 52 D3
Chartridge 67 C5
Chart Sutton 37 B6
Charvil 47 B5
Charwelton 82 B2
Chasetown 96 A3
Chastleton 64 A3
Chasty 10 A4
Chatburn 146 C1
Chatcull 112 B1
Chatham 51 C4
Chathill 189 A4
Chattenden 51 B4
Chatteris 101 C5
Chattisham 88 C1
Chatto 187 B6
Chatton 188 A3
Chawleigh 26 D2
Chawley 65 C5
Chawston 84 B3
Chawton 33 B6
Cheadle Gtr Man 128 A3
Staffs 112 A4
Cheadle Heath 128 A3
Cheadle Hulme 128 A3
Cheam 49 C5
Cheapside 34 A3
Chearsley 66 B3
Chebsey 112 C2
Checkendon 47 A4
Checkley Ches E 111 A6
Hereford 78 D3
Staffs 112 B4
Chedburgh 86 B3
Cheddar 42 D3
Cheddington 67 B5
Cheddleton 129 D4
Cheddon Fitzpaine 28 C2
Chedglow 63 D5
Chedgrave 105 B4
Chedington 15 A4
Chediston 105 D4
Chedworth 63 B6
Chedzoy 28 B3
Cheeklaw 198 A1
Cheeseman's Green 38 B2
Cheglinch 25 A6
Cheldon 26 D2
Chelford 128 B3
Chellaston 114 B1
Chell Heath 128 D3
Chellington 83 B6
Chelmarsh 95 C5
Chelmer Village 70 C1
Chelmondiston 88 D3
Chelmorton 129 C6
Chelmsford 69 C7
Chelsea 49 B5
Chelsfield 50 C1
Chelsworth 87 C5
Cheltenham 63 A5
Chelveston 84 A1
Chelvey 42 C3
Chelwood 43 C5
Chelwood Common 36 D2
Chelwood Gate 36 D2
Chelworth 63 D5
Chelworth Green 64 D1
Chemistry 111 A4
Chenies 67 D6
Cheny Longville 94 C2
Chepstow Casgwent 62 D1
Chequerfield 140 A2
Cherhill 44 B4
Cherington Glos 63 D5
Warks 81 D5
Cheriton Devon 26 A2
Hants 33 C4
Kent 38 B3
Swansea 57 C4
Cheriton Bishop 12 B2
Cheriton Fitzpaine 12 A3
Cheriton or Stackpole Elidor 55 E5
Cherrington 111 C5
Cherrybank 219 B6
Cherry Burton 150 C2
Cherry Hinton 85 B6
Cherry Orchard 79 B6
Cherry Willingham 133 B5
Chertsey 48 C3
Cheselbourne 16 B1
Chesham 67 C5
Chesham Bois 67 D5
Cheshunt 68 C3
Cheslyn Hay 96 A2
Chessington 49 C4
Chester 127 C4
Chesterblade 29 A6
Chesterfield 130 B3
Chester-Le-Street 179 D4
Chester Moor 167 A5
Chesters Borders 187 A5
Borders 187 B5
Chesterton Cambs 85 A6
Cambs 100 B3
Glos 63 C6
Oxon 65 A6
Shrops 95 B5
Staffs 112 A2
Warks 81 B6
Chesterwood 177 C6
Chestfield 52 C3
Cheston 7 B5
Cheswardine 111 C6
Cheswick 198 B4
Chetnole 15 A6
Chettiscombe 27 D4
Chettisham 102 C1
Chettle 30 D3
Chetton 95 B4
Chetwode 66 A2
Chetwynd Aston 111 D6
Cheveley 86 A2
Chevening 36 A2
Chevington 86 B3
Chevithorne 27 D4
Chew Magna 43 C4
Chew Stoke 43 C4
Chewton Keynsham 43 C5
Chewton Mendip 43 D4
Chicheley 83 C6
Chichester 20 B1
Chickerell 15 C6
Chicklade 30 B3
Chicksgrove 30 B3
Chidden 33 D5
Chiddingfold 34 C2
Chiddingly 22 A3
Chiddingstone 36 B2
Chiddingstone Causeway 36 B3
Chiddingstone Hoath 36 B2
Chideock 14 B4
Chidham 19 A6
Chidswell 139 A5
Chieveley 46 B2
Chignall St James 69 C6
Chignall Smealy 69 B6
Chigwell 68 D4
Chigwell Row 69 D4
Chilbolton 32 B2
Chilcomb 32 C4
Chilcombe 15 B5
Chilcompton 43 D5
Chilcote 113 D6
Childer Thornton 126 B3
Child Okeford 30 D2
Childrey 46 A1
Child's Ercall 111 C5
Childswickham 80 D3
Childwall 127 A4
Childwick Green 67 B7
Chilfrome 15 B5
Chilgrove 20 A1
Chilham 52 D2
Chilhampton 31 B4
Chilla 11 A5
Chillaton 11 C5
Chillenden 53 D4
Chillerton 18 C3
Chillesford 89 B4
Chillingham 188 A3
Chillington Devon 8 C1
Som 28 D3
Chilmark 30 B3
Chilson 64 B4
Chilsworthy Corn 11 D5
Devon 10 A4
Chilthorne Domer 29 D5
Chiltington 22 A1
Chilton Bucks 66 B2
Durham 167 C5
Oxon 46 A2
Chilton Cantelo 29 C5
Chilton Foliat 45 B7
Chilton Lane 167 B6
Chilton Polden 28 B3
Chilton Street 86 C3
Chilton Trinity 28 B2
Chilvers Coton 97 B6
Chilwell 114 B3
Chilworth Hants 32 D3
Sur 34 B3
Chimney 65 C4
Chineham 47 D4
Chingford 68 D3
Chinley 129 A5
Chinley Head 129 A5
Chinnor 66 C3
Chipnall 111 B6
Chippenhall Green 104 D3
Chippenham Cambs 86 A2
Wilts 44 B3
Chipperfield 67 C6
Chipping Herts 85 D5
Lancs 145 C6
Chipping Campden 81 D4
Chipping Hill 70 B2
Chipping Norton 64 A4
Chipping Ongar 69 C5
Chipping Sodbury 43 A6
Chipping Warden 82 C1
Chipstable 27 C5
Chipstead Kent 36 A2
Sur 35 A5
Chirbury 93 B6
Chirk Y Waun 110 B1
Chirk Bank 110 B1
Chirmorrie 181 D4
Chirnside 198 A2
Chirnsidebridge 198 A2
Chirton 45 D4
Chisbury 45 C6
Chiselborough 29 D4
Chiseldon 45 B5
Chiserley 138 A3
Chislehampton 65 D6
Chislehurst 50 B1
Chislet 53 C4
Chiswell Green 67 C7
Chiswick 49 B5
Chiswick End 85 C5
Chisworth 138 D2
Chithurst 34 D1
Chittering 101 D6
Chitterne 30 A3
Chittlehamholt 26 C1
Chittlehampton 26 C1
Chittoe 44 C3
Chivenor 25 B6
Chobham 48 C2
Choicelee 197 A6
Cholderton 31 A6
Cholesbury 67 C5
Chollerford 177 B7
Chollerton 178 B1
Cholmondeston 127 C6
Cholsey 46 A3
Cholstrey 78 B2
Chop Gate 159 B4
Choppington 179 A4
Chopwell 178 D3
Chorley Ches E 127 D5
Lancs 137 B4
Shrops 95 C4
Staffs 113 D4
Chorleywood 67 D6
Chorlton cum Hardy 137 D7
Chorlton Lane 110 A3
Choulton 94 C1
Chowdene 179 D4
Chowley 127 D4
Chrishall 85 D6
Christchurch Cambs 101 B6
Dorset 17 B5
Glos 62 B1
Newport 42 A2
Christian Malford 44 B3
Christleton 127 C4
Christmas Common 66 D3
Christon 42 D2
Christon Bank 189 A5
Christow 12 C3
Chryston 207 C4
Chudleigh 12 D3
Chudleigh Knighton 12 D3
Chulmleigh 26 D1
Chunal 138 D3
Church 137 A6
Churcham 62 B3
Church Aston 111 D6
Churchbank 93 D7
Church Brampton 83 A4
Churchbridge 96 A2
Church Broughton 113 B6
Church Crookham 47 D6
Churchdown 63 B4
Church Eaton 112 D2
Churchend Essex 69 A6
Essex 71 D4
S Glos 62 D3
Church End Cambs 100 C4
Cambs 101 A5
C Beds 67 A5
C Beds 84 D1
C Beds 84 D3
Essex 69 A7
Essex 86 C1
E Yorks 150 B3
Hants 47 D4
Lincs 117 B5
Warks 97 B5
Warks 97 B5
Wilts 44 B4
Church Enstone 65 A4
Church Fenton 148 D4
Churchfield 96 B3
Churchgate Street 69 B4
Church Green Devon 14 B1
Norf 103 B6
Church Gresley 113 D6
Church Hanborough 65 B5
Church Hill 127 C6
Church Houses 159 B5
Churchill Devon 14 A3
Devon 25 A6
Churchill N Som 42 D3
Oxon 64 A3
Worcs 80 B2
Worcs 96 D1
Churchinford 28 D2
Church Knowle 16 C3
Church Laneham 132 B3
Church Langton 99 B4
Church Lawford 98 D1
Church Lawton 128 D3
Church Leigh 112 B4
Church Lench 80 B3
Church Mayfield 113 A5
Church Minshull 127 C6
Church Norton 20 C1
Churchover 98 C2
Church Preen 94 B3
Church Pulverbatch 94 A2
Churchstanton 28 D1
Church Stoke 93 B6
Churchstow 7 C6
Church Stowe 82 B3
Church Street 51 B4
Church Stretton 94 B2
Churchtown Derbys 130 C2
IoM 152 B4
Lancs 145 C4
Mers 136 B2
Church Town N Lincs 141 C5
Sur 35 A6
Church Village 41 C5
Church Warsop 131 C5
Churnsike Lodge 177 B4
Churston Ferrers 8 B3
Churt 34 C1
Churton 127 D4
Churwell 139 A5
Chute Standen 45 D7
Chwilog 107 C4
Chyandour 2 B2
Cilan Uchaf 106 D2
Cilcain 126 C1
Cilcennin 75 B4
Cilfor 107 C6
Cilfrew 40 A2
Cilfynydd 41 B5
Cilgerran 73 B4
Cilgwyn Carms 59 C4
Gwyn 107 A4
Pembs 72 C3
Ciliau Aeron 74 C3
Cill Donnain 286 D3
Cille Bhrighde 286 E3
Cille Pheadair 286 E3
Cilmery 76 B4
Cilsan 58 C2
Ciltalgarth 108 A3
Cilwendeg 73 C5
Cilybebyll 40 A2
Cilycwm 59 B4
Cimla 40 B2
Cinderford 62 B2
Cippyn 72 B4
Circebost 288 D2
Cirencester 63 C6
Ciribhig 288 C2
City London 49 A6
Powys 93 C6
City Dulas 123 B4
Clachaig 215 D4
Clachan Argyll 202 C2
Argyll 213 A5
Argyll 215 A4
Argyll 226 B3
Highld 248 C2
W Isles 286 B3
Clachaneasy 181 D5
Clachanmore 170 C2
Clachan na Luib 287 H3
Clachan of Campsie 205 A6
Clachan of Glendaruel 214 D2
Clachan-Seil 213 A5
Clachan Strachur 214 B3
Clachbreck 202 A2
Clachnabrain 232 B1
Clachtoll 270 B3
Clackmannan 208 A2
Clacton-on-Sea 71 B5
Cladach Chireboist 287 H2
Claddach-knockline 287 H2
Cladich 227 D5
Claggan Highld 225 B5
Highld 237 B5
Claigan 258 C2
Claines 79 B6
Clandown 43 D5
Clanfield Hants 33 D5
Oxon 64 C3
Clanville 32 A2
Claonaig 202 C3
Claonel 272 D3
Clapgate Dorset 17 A4
Herts 68 A4
Clapham Bedford 84 B2
London 49 B5
N Yorks 146 A1
W Sus 20 B3
Clap Hill 38 B2
Clappers 198 A3
Clappersgate 154 A2
Clapton 14 A4
Clapton-in-Gordano 42 B3
Clapton-on-the-Hill 64 B2
Clapworthy 26 C1
Clarach 90 D4
Clara Vale 178 C3
Clarbeston 55 B6
Clarbeston Road 55 B6
Clarborough 132 A2
Clardon 280 B3
Clare 86 C3
Clarebrand 173 B5
Clarencefield 174 B3
Clarilaw 186 B4
Clark's Green 35 C4
Clarkston 205 C5
Clashandorran 251 B7
Clashcoig 264 A2
Clashindarroch 255 C5
Clashmore Highld 264 B3
Highld 270 A3
Clashnessie 270 A3
Clashnoir 254 D3
Clate 285 G7
Clathy 219 C4
Clatt 255 D6
Clatter 92 B3
Clatterford 18 C3
Clatterin Bridge 233 A4
Clatworthy 27 B5
Claughton Lancs 145 A5
Lancs 145 C5
Mers 126 A3
Claverdon 81 A4
Claverham 42 C3
Clavering 85 D6
Claverley 95 B5
Claverton 44 C1
Clawdd-newydd 125 D5
Clawthorpe 154 D4
Clawton 11 B4
Claxby Lincs 135 B4
Lincs 142 D3
Claxton Norf 104 A4
N Yorks 149 A5
Claybokie 242 D3
Claybrooke Magna 98 C1
Claybrooke Parva 98 C1
Clay Common 105 C5
Clay Coton 98 D2
Clay Cross 130 C3
Claydon Oxon 82 B1
Suff 88 B2
Claygate Dumfries 175 A6
Kent 37 B5

Claygate Sur 49 C4
Claygate Cross 36 A4
Clayhanger Devon 27 C5
W Mid 96 A3
Clayhidon 27 D6
Clayhill E Sus 37 D6
Hants 18 A2
Clay Hill 46 B3
Clay Lake 117 C5
Clayock 280 C3
Claypole 115 A6
Clayton Staffs 112 A2
S Yorks 140 C2
W Sus 21 A5
W Yorks 147 D5
Clayton Green 137 A4
Clayton-le-Moors 146 D1
Clayton-le-Woods 137 A4
Clayton West 139 B5
Clayworth 132 A2
Cleadale 234 B3
Cleadon 179 C5
Clearbrook 7 A4
Clearwell 62 C1
Cleasby 167 D5
Cleat 283 J5
Cleatlam 166 D4
Cleator 162 C3
Cleator Moor 162 C3
Clebrig 272 A3
Cleckheaton 139 A4
Cleedownton 94 C3
Cleehill 94 D3
Clee St Margaret 94 C3
Cleethorpes 143 C5
Cleeton St Mary 95 D4
Cleeve 42 C3
Cleeve Hill 63 A5
Cleeve Prior 80 C3
Clegyrnant 91 B7
Clehonger 78 D2
Cleish 208 A3
Cleland 194 A3
Clench Common 45 C5
Clenchwarton 118 C2
Clent 96 D2
Cleobury Mortimer 95 D4
Cleobury North 95 C4
Cleongart 190 B2
Clephanton 253 A4
Clerklands 186 A4
Clestrain 283 G4
Cleuch Head 187 B4
Cleughbrae 174 A3
Clevancy 45 B4
Clevedon 42 B3
Cleveley 65 A4
Cleveleys 144 C3
Cleverton 44 A3
Clevis 40 D3
Clewer 42 D3
Cley next the Sea 120 A2
Cliaid 286 F2
Cliasmol 287 D5
Cliburn 164 C3
Click Mill 282 E4
Cliddesden 33 A5
Cliffburn 233 D4
Cliffe Medway 51 B4
N Yorks 149 D5
Cliff End 23 A6
Cliffe Woods 51 B4
Clifford Hereford 77 C6
W Yorks 148 C3
Clifford Chambers 81 B4
Clifford's Mesne 62 A3
Cliffsend 53 C5
Clifton Bristol 43 B4
C Beds 84 D3
Cumb 164 C3
Derbys 113 A5
Lancs 145 D4
Northumb 179 A4
Nottingham 114 B3
N Yorks 147 C5
Oxon 82 D1
Clifton Stirling 216 A3
S Yorks 140 D3
Worcs 79 C6
York 149 B4
Clifton Campville 113 D6
Cliftoncote 187 A7
Clifton Green 137 C6
Clifton Hampden 65 D6
Clifton Reynes 83 B6
Clifton upon Dunsmore 98 D2
Clifton upon Teme 79 A5
Cliftonville 53 B5
Climaen gwyn 59 E4
Climping 20 B3
Climpy 194 A4
Clink 30 A1
Clint 147 B6
Clint Green 120 D2
Clintmains 197 C5
Cliobh 287 A5
Clippesby 121 D6
Clipsham 116 D2
Clipston 99 C4
Clipstone 131 C5
Clitheroe 146 C1
Cliuthar 288 H2
Clive 111 C4
Clivocast 284 C8
Clixby 142 C3
Clocaenog 125 D5
Clochan 267 C5
Clock Face 136 D4
Clockmill 197 A6
Cloddiau 93 A6
Clodock 61 A5
Clola 257 B5
Clophill 84 D2
Clopton Northants 100 C2
Suff 88 B3
Clopton Corner 88 B3
Clopton Green 86 B3
Closeburn 183 C6
Close Clark 152 D2
Closworth 29 D5
Clothall 85 D4
Clotton 127 C5
Clough Foot 138 A2
Cloughton 160 B4
Cloughton Newlands 160 B4
Clousta 285 H5
Clouston 282 F3
Clova Aberds 255 D5
Angus 232 A1
Clovelly 24 C4
Clove Lodge 166 D2
Clovenfords 196 C3
Clovenstone 245 A4
Clovullin 237 C4
Clow Bridge 137 A7
Clowne 131 B4
Clows Top 95 D5
Cloy 110 A2
Cluanie Inn 239 A4
Cluanie Lodge 239 A4
Clun 93 C7
Clunbury 94 C1
Clunderwen 55 C7
Clune 252 D3
Clunes 239 D6
Clungunford 94 D1
Clunie Aberds 268 D1
Perth 231 D5
Clunton 94 C1
Cluny 209 A5
Cluny Castle 241 C4
Clutton Bath 43 D5
Ches W 127 D4
Clwt-grugoer 125 C4
Clwt-y-bont 123 D5
Clydach Mon 60 B4
Swansea 40 A1
Clydach Vale 41 B4
Clydebank 205 A4
Clydey 73 C5
Clyffe Pypard 45 B4
Clynder 215 D5
Clyne 40 A3
Clynelish 274 D2
Clynnog-fawr 107 A4
Clyro 77 C6
Clyst Honiton 13 B4
Clyst Hydon 13 A5
Clyst St George 13 C4
Clyst St Lawrence 13 A5
Clyst St Mary 13 B4
Cnoc Amhlaigh 288 D6
Cnwch-coch 75 A5
Coachford 255 B5
Coad's Green 10 D3
Coal Aston 130 B3
Coalbrookdale 95 A4
Coalbrookvale 60 C3
Coalburn 194 C3
Coalburns 178 C3
Coalcleugh 165 A6
Coaley 62 C3
Coalhall 182 A2
Coalhill 70 D1
Coalpit Heath 43 A5
Coalport 95 A4
Coalsnaughton 208 A2
Coaltown of Balgonie 209 A5
Coaltown of Wemyss 209 A6
Coalville 114 D2
Coalway 62 B1
Coat 29 C4
Coatbridge 207 D5
Coatdyke 207 D5
Coate Swindon 45 A5
Wilts 44 C4
Coates Cambs 101 B5
Glos 63 C5
Lancs 146 C2
Notts 132 A3
W Sus 20 A2
Coatham 168 C3
Coatham Mundeville 167 C5
Coatsgate 184 B3
Cobbaton 25 C7
Cobbler's Green 104 B3
Coberley 63 B5
Cobham Kent 50 C3
Sur 48 C4
Cobholm Island 105 A6
Cobleland 206 A3
Cobnash 78 A2
Coburty 269 C4
Cockayne 159 B5
Cockayne Hatley 85 C4
Cock Bank 110 A2
Cock Bridge 243 B5
Cockburnspath 211 C4
Cock Clarks 70 C2
Cockenzie and Port Seton 209 C7
Cockerham 145 B4
Cockermouth 163 A4
Cockernhoe Green 67 A7
Cockfield Durham 166 C4
Suff 87 B5
Cockfosters 68 D2
Cocking 20 A1
Cockington 8 A2
Cocklake 28 A4
Cockley Beck 163 D5
Cockley Cley 102 A3
Cockshutt 110 C3
Cockthorpe 120 A1
Cockwood 13 C4
Cockyard 78 D2
Codda 10 D2
Coddenham 88 B2
Coddington Ches W 127 D4
Hereford 79 C5
Notts 132 D3
Codford St Mary 30 B3
Codford St Peter 30 B3
Codicote 68 B2
Codmore Hill 34 D3
Codnor 114 A2
Codrington 43 B6
Codsall 95 A6
Codsall Wood 95 A6
Coedely 41 C5
Coedkernew 42 A1
Coed Mawr 123 C5
Coed Morgan 61 B5
Coedpoeth 126 D2
Coed-Talon 126 D2
Coedway 110 D2
Coed-y-bryn 73 B6
Coed-y-paen 61 D5
Coed-yr-ynys 60 A3
Coed Ystumgwern 107 D5
Coelbren 59 D5
Coffinswell 8 A2
Cofton Hackett 96 D3
Cogan 41 D6
Cogenhoe 83 A5
Cogges 65 C4
Coggeshall 70 A2
Coggeshall Hamlet 70 A2
Coggins Mill 36 D3
Coignafearn Lodge 241 A4
Coig Peighinnean 288 A6
Coig Peighinnean Bhuirgh 288 B5
Coilacriech 243 C6
Coilantogle 217 D5
Coilleag 286 E3
Coillore 246 A2
Coity 40 C4
Col 288 C5
Colaboll 272 C3
Colan 4 A3
Colaton Raleigh 13 C5
Colbost 258 D2
Colburn 157 B5
Colby Cumb 165 C4
IoM 152 D2
Norf 120 B4
Colchester 71 A4
Colcot 41 E6
Cold Ash 46 C3
Cold Ashby 98 D3
Cold Ashton 43 B6
Cold Aston 64 B2
Coldbackie 277 C7
Coldbeck 155 A6
Coldblow 50 B2
Cold Blow 55 C7
Cold Brayfield 83 B6
Coldean 21 B6
Coldeast 12 D3
Colden 138 A2
Colden Common 32 C3
Coldfair Green 89 A5
Coldham 101 A6
Cold Hanworth 133 A5
Coldharbour Glos 62 C1
Kent 36 A3
Sur 35 B4
Cold Harbour 116 B2
Cold Hatton 111 C5
Cold Hesledon 168 A2
Cold Higham 82 B3
Coldingham 211 D6
Cold Kirby 158 C4
Cold Newton 99 A4
Cold Northcott 10 C3
Cold Norton 70 C2
Cold Overton 115 D6
Coldrain 219 D5
Coldred 39 A4
Coldridge 12 A1
Coldstream Angus 220 A3
Borders 198 C2
Coldwaltham 20 A3
Coldwells 257 B6
Coldwells Croft 255 D6
Coldyeld 94 B1
Cole 29 B6
Colebatch 93 C7
Colebrook 13 A5
Colebrooke 12 B2
Coleby Lincs 133 C4
N Lincs 141 B6
Coleford Devon 12 A2
Coleford Glos 62 B1
Som 29 A6
Cole Green 68 B2
Cole Henley 46 D2
Colehill 17 A4
Coleman's Hatch 36 C2
Colemere 110 B3
Colemore 33 B6
Coleorton 114 D2
Colerne 44 B2
Colesbourne 63 B5
Colesden 84 B3
Coles Green 88 C1
Cole's Green 88 A3
Coleshill Bucks 67 D5
Oxon 64 D3
Warks 97 C5
Colestocks 13 A5
Colgate 35 C5
Colgrain 206 B1
Colinsburgh 221 D4
Colinton 209 D5
Colintraive 203 A5
Colkirk 119 C6
Collace 220 A2
Collafirth 284 G6
Collaton St Mary 8 B2
College Milton 205 C6
Collessie 220 C2
Collier Row 69 D5
Collier's End 68 A3
Collier's Green 37 C5
Collier Street 37 B5
Colliery Row 167 A6
Collieston 257 D5
Collin 174 A3
Collingbourne Ducis 45 D6
Collingbourne Kingston 45 D6
Collingham Notts 132 C3
W Yorks 148 C2
Collington 79 A4
Collingtree 83 B4
Collins Green 137 D4
Colliston 233 D4
Collycroft 97 C6
Collynie 256 C3
Collyweston 100 A1
Colmonell 180 C3
Colmworth 84 B3
Colnabaichin 243 B5
Colnbrook 48 B3
Colne Cambs 101 D5
Lancs 146 C2
Colne Edge 146 C2
Colne Engaine 87 D4
Colney 104 A2
Colney Heath 68 C2
Colney Street 67 C7
Coln Rogers 64 C1
Coln St Aldwyn's 64 C2
Coln St Dennis 64 B1
Colpy 256 C1
Colquhar 196 B2
Colsterdale 157 C5
Colsterworth 116 C2
Colston Bassett 115 B4
Coltfield 266 C2
Colthouse 154 B2
Coltishall 121 D4
Coltness 194 A3
Colton Cumb 154 C2
Norf 104 A2
N Yorks 148 C4
Staffs 113 C4
W Yorks 148 D2
Col Uarach 288 D5
Colva 77 B6
Colvend 173 C6
Colvister 284 D7
Colwall Green 79 C5
Colwall Stone 79 C5
Colwell 178 B1
Colwich 112 C4
Colwick 115 A4
Colwinston 40 D4
Colworth 20 B2
Colwyn Bay Bae Colwyn 124 B3
Colyford 14 B2
Colyton 14 B2
Combe Hereford 78 A1
Oxon 65 B5
W Berks 46 C1
Combe Common 34 C2
Combe Down 43 C6
Combe Florey 27 B6
Combe Hay 43 D6
Combeinteignhead 13 D4
Combe Martin 25 A6
Combe Moor 78 A1
Combe Raleigh 13 A6
Comberbach 127 B6
Comberton Cambs 85 B5
Hereford 78 A2
Combe St Nicholas 28 D3
Combpyne 14 B2
Combridge 113 B4
Combrook 81 B6
Combs Derbys 129 B5
Suff 87 B6
Combs Ford 87 B6
Combwich 28 A2
Comers 244 B3
Comins Coch 90 D4
Commercial End 86 A1
Commins Capel Betws 75 C5
Commins Coch 91 B6
Commondale 169 D4
Common Edge 144 D3
Commonmoor 6 A1
Commonside 127 B5
Common Side 130 B3
Compstall 138 D2
Compton Devon 8 A2
Hants 32 C3
Sur 34 B1
Sur 34 B2
W Berks 46 B3
Wilts 45 D5
W Sus 33 D6
Compton Abbas 30 D2
Compton Abdale 63 B6
Compton Bassett 44 B4
Compton Beauchamp 45 A6
Compton Bishop 42 D2
Compton Chamberlayne 31 C4
Compton Dando 43 C5
Compton Dundon 29 B4
Compton Martin 43 D4
Compton Pauncefoot 29 C6
Compton Valence 15 B5
Comrie Fife 208 B3
Perth 218 B2
Conaglen House 237 C4
Conchra 214 D3
Concraigie 231 D5
Conder Green 145 B4
Conderton 80 D2
Condicote 64 A2
Condorrat 207 C5
Condover 94 A2
Coneyhurst 35 D4
Coneysthorpe 159 D6
Coneythorpe 148 B2
Coney Weston 103 D5
Conford 33 B7
Congash 253 D6
Congdon's Shop 10 D3
Congerstone 97 A6
Congham 119 C4
Congleton 128 C3
Congl-y-wal 108 A2
Congresbury 42 C3
Congreve 112 D3
Conicavel 253 A5
Coningsby 134 D2
Conington Cambs 85 A5
Cambs 100 C3
Conisbrough 140 D3
Conisby 200 B2

Conisholme 143 D6
Coniston Cumb 154 B2
E Yorks 151 D4
Coniston Cold 146 B3
Conistone 146 A3
Connah's Quay 126 C2
Connel 226 C4
Connel Park 182 A4
Connor Downs 2 B3
Conon Bridge 252 A1
Conon House 252 A1
Cononley 146 C3
Conordan 247 A4
Consall 112 A3
Consett 178 D3
Constable Burton 157 B5
Constantine 3 C5
Constantine Bay 9 D4
Contin 251 A6
Contlaw 245 B5
Conwy 124 B2
Conyer 51 C6
Conyers Green 87 A4
Cooden 23 B5
Cooil 152 D3
Cookbury 11 A5
Cookham 48 A1
Cookham Dean 47 A6
Cookham Rise 48 A1
Cookhill 80 B3
Cookley Suff 104 D4
Worcs 95 C6
Cookley Green 66 D2
Cookney 245 C5
Cookridge 147 C6
Cooksbridge 22 A2
Cooksmill Green 69 C6
Coolham 35 D4
Cooling 51 B4
Coombe Corn 4 B4
Corn 24 D3
Hants 33 C5
Wilts 45 D5
Coombe Bissett 31 C5
Coombe Hill 63 A4
Coombe Keynes 16 C2
Coombes 21 B4
Coopersale Common 69 C4
Cootham 20 A3
Copdock 88 C2
Copford Green 70 A3
Copgrove 148 A2
Copister 284 F6
Cople 84 C3
Copley 166 C3
Coplow Dale 129 B6
Copmanthorpe 149 C4
Coppathorne 10 A3
Coppenhall 112 D3
Coppenhall Moss 128 D2
Copperhouse 2 B3
Coppingford 100 C3
Copplestone 12 A2
Coppull 137 B4
Coppull Moor 137 B4
Copsale 35 D4
Copster Green 145 D6
Copston Magna 98 C1
Copt Heath 97 D4
Copt Hewick 158 D2
Copthorne
Shrops 110 D3
Sur 35 C6
Copt Oak 114 D2
Copy's Green 119 B6
Copythorne 32 D2
Corbets Tey 50 A2
Corbridge 178 C1
Corby 99 C5
Corby Glen 116 C2
Cordon 191 B6
Coreley 95 D4
Cores End 48 A2
Corfe 28 D2
Corfe Castle 16 C3
Corfe Mullen 16 B3
Corfton 94 C2
Corgarff 243 B5
Corhampton 33 C5
Corlae 183 C4
Corley 97 C6
Corley Ash 97 C5
Corley Moor 97 C5
Cornaa 152 C4
Cornabus 200 D3
Cornel 124 C2
Corner Row 144 D4
Corney 153 A2
Cornforth 167 B6
Cornhill 267 D6
Cornhill-on-Tweed 198 C2
Cornholme 138 A2
Cornish Hall End 86 D2
Cornquoy 283 H6
Cornsay 166 A4
Cornsay Colliery 167 A4
Corntown Highld 252 A1
V Glam 40 D4
Cornwell 64 A3
Cornwood 7 B5
Cornworthy 8 B2
Corpach 237 B4
Corpusty 120 B3
Corran Highld 237 C4
Highld 238 B2
Corranbuie 202 B3
Corrany 152 C4
Corrie 203 D5
Corrie Common 185 D5
Corriecravie 191 C5
Corriemoillie 263 D5
Corriemulzie Lodge 263 A5
Corrievarkie Lodge 229 A4
Corrievorrie 252 D3
Corrimony 251 C5
Corringham
Lincs 141 D6
Thurrock 51 A4
Corris 91 B5
Corris Uchaf 91 B5
Corrour Shooting Lodge 228 B3
Corrow 215 B4
Corry 247 B5
Corrykinloch 271 B6
Corrymuckloch 218 A3
Corrynachenchy 225 B5
Corry of Ardnagrask 251 B7
Corsback 280 A4
Corscombe 15 A5
Corse Aberds 255 B7
Glos 62 A3
Corse Lawn 79 D6
Corse of Kinnoir 255 B6
Corsewall 170 A2
Corsham 44 B2
Corsindae 244 B3
Corsley 30 A2
Corsley Heath 30 A2
Corsock 173 A5
Corston Bath 43 C5
Wilts 44 A3
Corstorphine 209 C4
Cors-y-Gedol 107 D5
Cortachy 232 C1
Corton Suff 105 B6
Wilts 30 A3
Corton Denham 29 C6
Coruanan Lodge 237 C4
Corunna 287 H3
Corwen 109 A5
Coryton Devon 11 C5
Thurrock 51 A4
Cosby 98 B2
Coseley 96 B2
Cosgrove 83 C4
Cosham 19 A5
Cosheston 55 D6
Cossall 114 A2
Cossington Leics 115 D4
Som 28 A3
Costa 282 E4
Costessey 120 D3
Costock 114 C3
Coston 115 C6
Cote 64 C4
Cotebrook 127 C5
Cotehill 176 D2
Cotes Cumb 154 C3
Leics 114 C3
Staffs 112 B2
Cotesbach 98 C2
Cotgrave 115 B4
Cothall 245 A5
Cotham 115 A5
Cothelstone 28 B1
Cotherstone 166 D3
Cothill 65 D5
Cotleigh 14 A2
Cotmanhay 114 A2
Cotmaton 13 C6
Coton Cambs 85 B6
Northants 98 D3
Staffs 112 B3
Staffs 112 C2
Coton Clanford 112 C2
Coton Hill
Shrops 110 D3
Staffs 112 B3
Coton in the Elms 113 D6
Cott 8 A1
Cottam E Yorks 150 A2
Lancs 145 D5
Notts 132 B3
Cottartown 253 C6
Cottenham 85 A6
Cotterdale 156 B2
Cottered 68 A3
Cotteridge 96 D3
Cotterstock 100 B2
Cottesbrooke 99 D4
Cottesmore 116 D2
Cotteylands 27 D4
Cottingham
E Yorks 150 D3
Northants 99 B5
Cottingley 147 D5
Cottisford 82 D2
Cotton Staffs 113 A4
Suff 87 A6
Cotton End 84 C2
Cottown Aberds 245 A4
Aberds 255 D6
Aberds 256 B3
Cotwalton 112 B3
Couch's Mill 5 B6
Coughton
Hereford 62 A1
Warks 80 A3
Coulaghailtro 202 B2
Coulags 249 B6
Coulby Newham 168 D3
Coulderton 162 D2
Coulin 250 A2
Coull Aberds 244 B2
Argyll 200 B2
Coulport 215 D5
Coulsdon 35 A5
Coulston 44 D3
Coulter 195 C5
Coulton 159 D5
Cound 94 A3
Coundon Durham 167 C5
W Mid 97 C6
Coundon Grange 167 C5
Countersett 156 C3
Countess 31 A5
Countess Wear 13 C4
Countesthorpe 98 B2
Countisbury 26 A2
County Oak 35 C5
Coupar Angus 231 D6
Coup Green 137 A4
Coupland 198 C3
Cour 202 D3
Courance 184 C3
Court-at-Street 38 B2
Courteenhall 83 B4
Court Henry 58 C2
Courtsend 71 D4
Courtway 28 B2
Cousland 209 D6
Cousley Wood 37 C4
Cove Argyll 215 D5
Borders 211 C4
Devon 27 D4
Hants 34 A1
Highld 261 A5
Cove Bay 245 B6
Cove Bottom 105 D5
Covehithe 105 C6
Coven 96 A2
Coveney 101 C6
Covenham St Bartholomew 143 D5
Covenham St Mary 143 D5
Coventry 97 D6
Coverack 3 D5
Coverham 157 C5
Covesea 266 B2
Covington
Cambs 100 D2
S Lanark 195 C4
Cowan Bridge 155 D5
Cow Ark 145 C6
Cowbeech 22 A4
Cowbit 117 D5
Cowbridge Lincs 117 A6
Som 27 A4
Cowbridge Y Bont-Faen 41 D4
Cowdale 129 B5
Cowden 36 B2
Cowdenbeath 209 A4
Cowdenburn 195 A7
Cowers Lane 113 A7
Cowes 18 B3
Cowesby 158 C3
Cowfold 35 D5
Cowgill 155 C6
Cowie Aberds 245 D5
Stirling 207 B6
Cowley Devon 13 B4
Glos 63 B5
London 48 A3
Oxon 65 C6
Cowleymoor 27 D4
Cowling Lancs 137 B4
N Yorks 146 C3
N Yorks 157 C6
Cowlinge 86 B3
Cowpe 138 A1
Cowpen 179 A4
Cowpen Bewley 168 C2
Cowplain 33 D5
Cowshill 165 A6
Cowslip Green 42 C3
Cowstrandburn 208 A3
Cowthorpe 148 B3
Coxbank 111 A5
Coxbench 114 A1
Cox Common 105 C4
Coxford Norf 119 C5
Soton 32 D2
Cox Grn 48 B1
Coxheath 37 A5
Coxhill 39 A4
Coxhoe 167 B6
Coxley 29 A5
Cox Moor 131 D5
Coxwold 158 D4
Coychurch 40 D4
Coylton 193 C4
Coylumbridge 242 A2
Coynach 244 B1
Coynachie 255 C5
Coytrahen 40 C3
Crabadon 7 B6
Crabbs Cross 80 A3
Crabtree 35 D5
Crackenthorpe 165 C4
Crackington Haven 10 B2
Crackley 97 D5
Crackleybank 111 D6
Crackpot 156 B3
Cracoe 146 A3
Craddock 27 D5
Cradhlastadh 287 A5
Cradley 79 C5
Cradley Heath 96 C2
Crafthole 6 B2
Craggan 253 D6
Craggie Highld 252 C3
Highld 274 C2
Cragg Vale 138 A3
Craghead 179 D4
Crai 59 C5
Craibstone 267 D5
Craichie 232 D3
Craig Dumfries 173 A4
Dumfries 173 B4
Highld 250 B2
Craiganor Lodge 229 C5
Craig Castle 255 D5
Craig-cefn-parc 40 A1
Craigdam 256 C3
Craigdarroch
Dumfries 183 C5
Highld 251 A6
Craigdhu 251 B6
Craigearn 245 A4
Craigellachie 254 B3
Craigencross 170 A2
Craigend Perth 219 B6
Stirling 207 B5
Craigendive 214 D3
Craigendoran 215 D6
Craigends 205 B4
Craigens Argyll 200 B2
E Ayrs 182 A3
Craighat 206 B2
Craighead 221 D6
Craighlaw Mains 171 A5
Craighouse 201 B5
Craigie Aberds 245 A6
Dundee 220 A4
Perth 219 B6
Perth 231 D5
S Ayrs 193 B4
Craigiefield 282 F5
Craigielaw 210 C1
Craiglockhart 209 C5
Craigmalloch 182 C2
Craigmaud 268 D3
Craigmillar 209 C5
Craigmore 203 B6
Craignant 110 B1
Craigneuk
N Lanark 194 A2
N Lanark 207 D5
Craignure 225 C6
Craigo 233 B4
Craigow 219 D5
Craig Penllyn 41 D4
Craigrothie 220 C3
Craigroy 266 D2
Craigruie 217 B4
Craigston Castle 268 D2
Craigton
Aberdeen 245 B5
Angus 221 A5
Angus 232 C1
Highld 264 A2
Craigtown 279 C4
Craig-y-don 124 A2
Craig-y-nos 59 D5
Craik 185 B6
Crail 221 D6
Crailing 187 A5
Crailinghall 187 A5
Craiselound 141 D5
Crakehill 158 D3
Crakemarsh 113 B4
Crambe 149 A6
Cramlington 179 B4
Cramond 209 C4
Cramond Bridge 209 C4
Cranage 128 C2
Cranberry 112 B2
Cranborne 31 D4
Cranbourne 48 B2
Cranbrook Devon 13 B5
Kent 37 C5
Cranbrook Common 37 C5
Crane Moor 139 C6
Crane's Corner 119 D6
Cranfield 83 C6
Cranford 48 B4
Cranford St Andrew 99 D6
Cranford St John 99 D6
Cranham Glos 63 B4
London 50 A2
Crank 136 D4
Crank Wood 137 C5
Cranleigh 34 C3
Cranley 104 D2
Cranmer Green 103 D6
Cranmore 18 C2
Cranna 268 D1
Crannich 225 B4
Crannoch 267 D5
Cranoe 99 B4
Cransford 88 A4
Cranshaws 210 D3
Cranstal 152 A4
Crantock 4 A2
Cranwell 116 A3
Cranwich 102 B3
Cranworth 103 A5
Craobh Haven 213 B5
Crapstone 7 A4
Crarae 214 C2
Crask Inn 272 B3
Craskins 244 B2
Crask of Aigas 251 B6
Craster 189 B5
Craswall 77 D6
Cratfield 104 D4
Crathes 245 C4
Crathie Aberds 243 C5
Highld 240 C3
Crathorne 158 A3
Craven Arms 94 C2
Crawcrook 178 C3
Crawford Lancs 136 C3
S Lanark 195 D4
Crawfordjohn 194 D3
Crawick 183 A5
Crawley Hants 32 B3
Oxon 64 B4
W Sus 35 C5
Crawley Down 35 C6
Crawleyside 166 A2
Crawshawbooth 137 A7
Crawton 233 A6
Cray N Yorks 156 D3
Perth 231 B5
Crayford 50 B2
Crayke 159 D4
Crays Hill 69 D7
Cray's Pond 47 A4
Creacombe 26 D3
Creagan 227 B4
Creag Ghoraidh 286 B3
Creaguaineach Lodge 228 B2
Creaksea 70 D3
Creaton 99 D4
Creca 175 A5
Credenhill 78 C2
Crediton 12 A3
Creebridge 171 A6
Creech Heathfield 28 C2
Creech St Michael 28 C2
Creed 4 C4
Creekmouth 50 A1
Creeting Bottoms 88 B2
Creeting St Mary 88 B1
Creeton 116 C3
Creetown 171 B6
Creggans 214 B3
Cregneash 152 E1
Creg-ny-Baa 152 C3
Cregrina 77 B5
Creich 220 B3
Creigiau 41 C5
Cremyll 6 B3
Creslow 66 A4
Cressage 94 A3
Cressbrook 129 B6
Cresselly 55 D6
Cressing 70 A1
Cresswell
Northumb 189 D5
Staffs 112 B3
Cresswell Quay 55 D6
Creswell 131 B5

Cretingham 88 A3
Cretshengan 202 B2
Crewe Ches E 128 D2
Ches W 127 D4
Crewgreen 110 D2
Crewkerne 14 A4
Crianlarich 216 B3
Cribyn 75 C4
Criccieth 107 C4
Crich 130 D3
Crichie 257 B4
Crichton 209 D6
Crick Mon 61 D6
Northants 98 D2
Crickadarn 77 C4
Cricket Malherbie 28 D3
Cricket St Thomas 14 A3
Crickheath 110 C1
Crickhowell 60 B4
Cricklade 64 D2
Cricklewood 49 A5
Cridling Stubbs 140 A3
Crieff 218 B3
Criggion 110 D1
Crigglestone 139 B6
Crimond 269 D5
Crimonmogate 269 D5
Crimplesham 102 A2
Crinan 213 C5
Cringleford 104 A2
Cringles 147 C4
Crinow 56 A1
Cripplesease 2 B3
Cripplestyle 31 D4
Cripp's Corner 37 D5
Croasdale 162 C3
Crockenhill 50 C2
Crockernwell 12 B2
Crockerton 30 A2
Crocketford or Ninemile Bar 173 A6
Crockey Hill 149 C5
Crockham Hill 36 A2
Crockleford Heath 71 A4
Crockness 283 H4
Crock Street 28 D3
Croeserw 40 B3
Croes-goch 54 A4
Croes-lan 73 B6
Croesor 107 B6
Croesyceiliog Carms 57 A4
Torf 61 D5
Croes-y-mwyalch 61 D5
Croesywaun 107 A5
Croft Leics 98 B2
Lincs 135 C5
Pembs 73 B4
Warr 137 D5
Croftamie 206 B2
Croftmalloch 208 D2
Crofton Wilts 45 C6
W Yorks 140 B1
Croft-on-Tees 157 A6
Crofts of Benachielt 275 A5
Crofts of Haddo 256 C3
Crofts of Inverthernie 256 B2
Crofts of Meikle Ardo 256 B3
Crofty 57 C5
Croggan 225 D6
Croglin 164 A3
Croich 263 A6
Crois Dughaill 286 D3
Cromarty 264 D3
Cromblet 256 C2
Cromdale 253 D6
Cromer Herts 68 A2
Norf 120 A4
Cromford 130 D2
Cromhall 62 D2
Cromhall Common 43 A5
Cromor 288 E5
Cromra 240 C3
Cromwell 132 C2
Cronberry 193 C6
Crondall 33 A6
Cronk-y-Voddy 152 C3
Cronton 127 A4
Crook Cumb 154 B3
Durham 167 B4
Crookedholm 193 B4
Crookes 130 A3
Crookham Northumb 198 C3
W Berks 46 C3
Crookham Village 47 D5
Crookhaugh 195 D6
Crookhouse 187 A6
Crooklands 154 C4
Crook of Devon 219 D5
Cropredy 82 C1
Cropston 114 D3
Cropthorne 80 C2
Cropton 159 C6
Cropwell Bishop 115 B4
Cropwell Butler 115 B4
Cros 288 A6
Crosbost 288 E4
Crosby Cumb 162 A3
IoM 152 D3
N Lincs 141 B6
Crosby Garrett 155 A6
Crosby Ravensworth 165 D4
Crosby Villa 162 A3
Croscombe 29 A5
Cross 42 D3
Crossaig 202 C3
Crossal 246 A3
Crossapol 222 C2
Cross Ash 61 B6
Cross-at-Hand 37 B5
Crossburn 207 C6
Crossbush 20 B3
Crosscanonby 162 A3
Crossdale Street 120 B4
Crossens 136 B2
Crossflatts 147 C5
Crossford Fife 208 B3
S Lanark 194 B3
Crossgate 117 C5
Crossgatehall 209 D6
Crossgates Fife 208 B4
Powys 77 A4
Crossgill 145 A5
Cross Green Devon 11 C4
Suff 87 B4
Suff 87 B5
Warks 81 B6
Cross Hands 57 A5
Cross-hands 73 D4
Cross Hands 55 C6
Crosshill E Ayrs 193 C4
Fife 209 A4
S Ayrs 192 E3
Cross Hill 114 A2
Crosshouse 192 B3
Cross Houses 94 A3
Crossings 176 B3
Cross in Hand E Sus 36 D3
Leics 98 C2
Cross Inn Ceredig 73 A6
Ceredig 75 B4
Rhondda 41 C5
Crosskeys 41 B7
Cross Keys 36 A3
Crosskirk 279 A6
Cross Lane Head 95 B5
Crosslanes 110 D2
Cross Lanes Corn 3 C4
N Yorks 148 A4
Wrex 110 A2
Crosslee Borders 185 A6
Renfs 205 B4
Crossmichael 173 B5
Crossmoor 144 D4
Cross Oak 60 A3
Cross of Jackston 256 C2
Cross o' th' hands 113 A6
Crossroads Aberds 245 C4
E Ayrs 193 B4
Cross Street 104 D2
Cross Trickett's 17 A4
Crossway Hereford 79 D4
Mon 61 B6
Powys 77 B4
Crossway Green 79 A6
Crossways 16 C1
Crosswell 72 C4
Crosswood 75 A5
Crosthwaite 154 B3
Croston 136 B3
Crostwick 121 D4
Crostwight 121 C5
Crothair 288 D2
Crouch 36 A4
Croucheston 31 C4
Crouch Hill 29 D7
Crouch House Green 36 B2
Croughton 82 D2
Crovie 268 C3
Crowan 3 B4
Crowborough 36 C3
Crowcombe 27 B6
Crowdecote 129 C6
Crowden 138 D3
Crow Edge 139 C4
Crowell 66 D3
Crowfield Northants 82 C3
Suff 88 B2
Crow Hill 62 A2
Crowhurst E Sus 23 A5
Sur 36 B1
Crowhurst Lane End 36 B1
Crowland 117 D5
Crowlas 2 B3
Crowle N Lincs 141 B5
Worcs 80 B2
Crowmarsh Gifford 47 A4
Crown Corner 104 D3
Crownhill 6 B3
Crownland 103 E6
Crownthorpe 104 A1
Crowntown 3 B4
Crows-an-wra 2 C1
Crowshill 103 A5
Crowsnest 94 A1
Crowthorne 47 C6
Crowton 127 B5
Croxall 113 D5
Croxby 142 D3
Croxdale 167 B5
Croxden 113 B4
Croxley Green 67 D6
Croxton Cambs 84 A4
N Lincs 142 B2
Norf 103 C4
Staffs 112 B1
Croxtonbank 112 B1
Croxton Kerrial 115 C6
Croy Highld 252 B3
N Lanark 207 C5
Croyde 25 B5
Croydon Cambs 85 C5
London 49 C6
Crubenmore Lodge 241 C4
Cruckmeole 94 A2
Cruckton 110 D3
Cruden Bay 257 C5
Crudgington 111 D5
Crudwell 63 D5
Crug 93 D5
Crugmeer 9 D5
Crugybar 58 B3
Crulabhig 288 D2
Crumlin Crymlyn 41 B7
Crumpsall 138 C1
Crundale Kent 38 A2
Pembs 55 C5
Cruwys Morchard 26 D3
Crux Easton 46 D2
Crwbin 57 A4
Crya 283 G4
Cryers Hill 66 D4
Crymlyn 123 C6
Crymych 73 C4
Crynant 40 A2
Crynfryn 75 B4
Cuaig 249 A4
Cuan 213 A5
Cubbington 81 A6
Cubeck 156 C3
Cubert 4 B2
Cubley 139 C5
Cubley Common 113 B5
Cublington Bucks 66 A4
Hereford 78 D2
Cuckfield 35 D6
Cucklington 30 C1
Cuckney 131 B5
Cuckoo Hill 141 D5
Cuddesdon 65 C7
Cuddington Bucks 66 B3
Ches W 127 B6
Cuddington Heath 110 A3
Cuddy Hill 145 D4
Cudham 36 A2
Cudliptown 11 D6
Cudworth Som 28 D3
S Yorks 140 C1
Cuffley 68 C3
Cuiashader 288 B6
Cuidhir 286 F2
Cuidhtinis 287 F5
Culbo 264 D2
Culbokie 252 A2
Culburnie 251 B6
Culcabock 252 B2
Culcairn 264 D2
Culcharry 253 A4
Culcheth 137 D5
Culdrain 255 C6
Culduie 249 B4
Culford 103 D4
Culgaith 165 C4
Culham 65 D6
Culkein 270 A3
Culkein Drumbeg 270 A4
Culkerton 63 D5
Cullachie 253 D5
Cullen 267 C6
Cullercoats 179 B5
Cullicudden 264 D2
Cullingworth 147 D4
Cullipool 213 A5
Cullivoe 284 C7
Culloch 218 C2
Culloden 252 B3
Cullompton 13 A5
Culmaily 265 A4
Culmazie 171 B5
Culmington 94 C2
Culmstock 27 D6
Culnacraig 270 D3
Culnaknock 259 B5
Culpho 88 C3
Culrain 264 A1
Culross 208 B2
Culroy 192 D3
Culsh Aberds 243 C6
Aberds 256 B3
Culshabbin 171 B5
Culswick 285 J4
Cultercullen 257 D4
Cults Aberdeen 245 B5
Aberds 255 C6
Dumfries 171 C6
Culverstone Green 50 C3
Culverthorpe 116 A3
Culworth 82 C2
Culzie Lodge 263 C7
Cumbernauld 207 C5
Cumbernauld Village 207 C5
Cumberworth 135 B5
Cuminestown 268 D3
Cumlewick 285 L6
Cummersdale 175 C6
Cummertrees 174 B4
Cummingston 266 C2
Cumnock 193 C5
Cumnor 65 C5
Cumrew 176 D3
Cumwhinton 176 D2
Cumwhitton 176 D3
Cundall 158 D3
Cunninghamhead 204 D3
Cunnister 284 D7
Cupar 220 C3
Cupar Muir 220 C3
Cupernham 32 C2
Curbar 130 B2
Curbridge Hants 32 D4
Oxon 64 C4
Curdridge 32 D4
Curdworth 97 B4
Curland 28 D2
Curlew Green 89 A4
Currarie 180 B3
Curridge 46 B2
Currie 209 D4
Curry Mallet 28 C3
Curry Rivel 28 C3
Curtisden Green 37 B5
Curtisknowle 7 B6
Cury 3 C4
Cushnie 268 C2
Cushuish 28 B1
Cusop 77 C6
Cutcloy 171 D6
Cutcombe 27 B4
Cutgate 138 B1
Cutiau 90 A4
Cutlers Green 86 D1
Cutnall Green 80 A1
Cutsdean 80 D3
Cutthorpe 130 B3
Cutts 285 K6
Cuxham 66 D2
Cuxton 51 C4
Cuxwold 142 C3
Cwm Bl Gwent 60 C3
Denb 125 B5
Swansea 40 B1
Cwmafan 40 B2
Cwmaman 41 B5
Cwmann 75 D4
Cwmavon 61 C4
Cwmbach Carms 57 B4
Carms 73 D5
Powys 76 B4
Powys 77 D5
Cwmbâch 41 A5
Cwmbelan 92 C3
Cwmbran
Cwmbrân 61 D4
Cwmbrwyno 91 D5
Cwm-byr 58 B3
Cwmcarn 41 B7
Cwmcarvan 61 C6
Cwm-Cewydd 91 A6
Cwm-cou 73 B5
Cwmcych 73 C5
Cwmdare 41 A4
Cwmderwen 92 A3
Cwmdu Carms 58 B3
Powys 60 A3
Swansea 57 C6
Cwmduad 73 C6
Cwm-Dulais 57 B6
Cwmdwr 59 B4
Cwmfelin Bridgend 40 C3
M Tydf 41 A5
Cwmfelin Boeth 56 A1
Cwm-felin-fach 41 B6
Cwmfelin Mynach 73 D5
Cwmffrwd 57 A4
Cwm Ffrwd-oer 61 C4
Cwmgiedd 59 D4
Cwmgors 59 D4
Cwmgwili 57 A5
Cwmgwrach 40 A3
Cwm-hesgen 108 C2
Cwmhiraeth 73 C6
Cwm-hwnt 59 E6
Cwmifor 58 C3
Cwm Irfon 76 C2
Cwmisfael 57 A4
Cwm-Llinau 91 B6
Cwmllynfell 59 D4
Cwm-mawr 57 A5
Cwmorgan 73 C5
Cwm-parc 40 B4
Cwmpengraig 73 C6
Cwm Penmachno 108 A2
Cwmrhos 60 A3
Cwmsychpant 74 D3
Cwmtillery 60 C4
Cwmwysg 59 C5
Cwm-y-glo Carms 57 A5
Gwyn 123 D5
Cwmyoy 61 A4
Cwmystwyth 92 D1
Cwrt 91 B4
Cwrt-newydd 74 D3
Cwrt-y-cadno 58 A3
Cwrt-y-gollen 60 B4
Cyffylliog 125 D5
Cyfronydd 93 A5
Cymer 40 B3
Cyncoed 41 C6
Cynghordy 59 A5
Cynheidre 57 B4
Cynwyd 109 A5
Cynwyl Elfed 73 D6
Cywarch 91 A6

D

Dacre Cumb 164 C2
N Yorks 147 A5
Dacre Banks 147 A5
Daddry Shield 166 B1
Dadford 82 D3
Dadlington 97 B7
Dafarn Faig 107 B4
Dafen 57 B5
Daffy Green 103 A5
Dagenham 50 A1
Daglingworth 63 C5
Dagnall 67 B5
Dail Beag 288 C3
Dail bho Dheas 288 A5
Dail bho Thuath 288 A5
Daill 200 B3
Dailly 181 A4
Dail Mor 288 C3
Dairsie or Osnaburgh 220 C4
Daisy Hill 137 C5
Dalabrog 286 D3
Dalavich 214 A2
Dalbeattie 173 B6
Dalblair 182 A4
Dalbog 232 A3
Dalbury 113 B6
Dalby IoM 152 D2
N Yorks 159 D5
Dalchalloch 229 B6
Dalchalm 274 D3
Dalchenna 214 B3
Dalchirach 254 C2
Dalchork 272 C3
Dalchreichart 239 A6
Dalchruin 218 C2
Dalderby 134 C2
Dale 54 D4
Dale Abbey 114 B2
Dale Head 164 D2
Dalelia 235 D6
Dale of Walls 285 H3
Daless 253 C4
Dalfaber 242 A2
Dalgarven 204 D2
Dalgety Bay 209 B4
Dalginross 218 B2
Dalguise 230 D3
Dalhalvaig 279 C4
Dalham 86 A3
Dalinlongart 215 D4
Dalkeith 209 D6
Dallam 137 D4
Dallas 266 D2
Dalleagles 182 A3
Dallinghoo 88 B3
Dallington E Sus 23 A4
Northants 83 A4
Dallow 157 D5
Dalmadilly 245 A4
Dalmally 227 D6

Dalmarnock 205 B6
Dalmary 206 A3
Dalmellington 182 B2
Dalmeny 208 C4
Dalmigavie 241 A5
Dalmigavie Lodge 252 D3
Dalmore 264 D2
Dalmuir 205 A4
Dalnabreck 235 D5
Dalnacardoch Lodge 229 A6
Dalnacroich 251 A5
Dalnaglar Castle 231 B5
Dalnahaitnach 253 D4
Dalnaspidal Lodge 229 A5
Dalnavaid 230 B4
Dalnavie 264 C2
Dalnawillan Lodge 279 D6
Dalness 237 D5
Dalnessie 273 C4
Dalqueich 219 D5
Dalreavoch 273 D5
Dalry 204 D2
Dalrymple 192 D3
Dalserf 194 A3
Dalston 175 C6
Dalswinton 184 D2
Dalton Dumfries 174 A4
 Lancs 136 C3
 Northumb 177 D7
 Northumb 178 B3
 N Yorks 157 A5
 N Yorks 158 D3
 S Yorks 140 D2
Dalton-in-Furness 153 C3
Dalton-le-Dale 168 A2
Dalton-on-Tees 157 A6
Dalton Piercy 168 B2
Dalveich 217 B6
Dalvina Lo. 278 D2
Dalwhinnie 241 D4
Dalwood 14 A2
Dalwyne 181 B5
Damerham 31 D5
Damgate 105 A5
Dam Green 103 C6
Damnaglaur 170 D3
Damside 195 B6
Dam Side 144 C4
Danbury 70 C1
Danby 159 A6
Danby Wiske 158 B2
Dandaleith 254 B3
Danderhall 209 D6
Danebridge 129 C4
Dane End 68 A3
Danehill 36 D2
Danemoor Green 103 A6
Danesford 95 B5
Daneshill 47 D4
Dangerous Corner 136 B4
Danskine 210 D2
Darcy Lever 137 C6
Darenth 50 B2
Daresbury 127 A5
Darfield 140 C2
Darfoulds 131 B5
Dargate 52 C2
Darite 6 A1
Darlaston 96 B2
Darley 147 B6
Darley Bridge 130 C2
Darley Head 147 B5
Darlingscott 81 C5
Darlington 167 D5
Darliston 111 B4
Darlton 132 B2
Darnall 130 A3
Darnick 197 C4
Darowen 91 B6
Darra 256 B2
Darracott 25 B5
Darras Hall 178 B3
Darrington 140 A2
Darsham 89 A5
Dartford 50 B2
Dartford Crossing 50 B2
Dartington 8 A1
Dartmeet 12 D1
Dartmouth 8 B2
Darton 139 C6
Darvel 193 B5
Darwell Hole 23 A4
Darwen 137 A5
Datchet 48 B2
Datchworth 68 B2
Datchworth Green 68 B2
Daubhill 137 C6
Daugh of Kinermony 254 B3
Dauntsey 44 A3
Dava 253 C6
Davenham 127 B6
Davenport Green 128 B3
Daventry 82 A2
Davidson's Mains 209 C5
Davidstow 10 C2
David's Well 93 D4
Davington 185 B5
Daviot Aberds 256 D2
 Highld 252 C3
Davoch of Grange 267 D5
Davyhulme 137 D6
Dawley 95 A4
Dawlish 13 D4
Dawlish Warren 13 D4
Dawn 124 B3
Daws Heath 51 A5
Daw's House 10 C4
Dawsmere 118 B1
Dayhills 112 B3
Daylesford 64 A3
Ddôl-Cownwy 109 D5
Ddrydwy 122 C3
Deadwater 187 D5
Deaf Hill 167 B6
Deal 53 D5
Deal Hall 71 D4
Dean Cumb 162 B3
 Devon 7 A6
 Devon 25 A6
 Dorset 30 D3
 Hants 33 D4
 Som 29 A6
Deanburnhaugh 186 B2
Deane Gtr Man 137 C5
 Hants 46 D3
Deanich Lodge 263 B5
Deanland 30 D3
Dean Prior 7 A6
Dean Row 128 A3
Deans 208 D3
Deanscales 162 B3
Deanshanger 83 D4
Deanston 218 D2
Dearham 162 A3
Debach 88 B3
Debden Essex 68 D4
 Essex 86 D1
Debden Cross 86 D1
Debenham 88 A2
Dechmont 208 C3
Deddington 82 D1
Dedham 87 D6
Dedham Heath 87 D6
Deebank 244 C3
Deene 99 B6
Deenethorpe 99 B6
Deepcar 139 D5
Deepcut 34 A2
Deepdale 155 C6
Deeping Gate 100 A3
Deeping St James 100 A3
Deeping St Nicholas 117 D5
Deerhill 267 D5
Deerhurst 63 A4
Deerness 283 G6
Defford 80 C2
Defynnog 59 C6
Deganwy 124 B2
Deighton N Yorks 158 A2
 W Yorks 139 B4
 York 149 C5
Deiniolen 123 D5
Delabole 9 C6
Delamere 127 C5
Delfrigs 257 D4
Delliefure 254 C1
Dell Lodge 242 A3
Delnabo 243 A4
Delnadamph 243 B5
Delph 138 C2
Delves 166 A4
Delvine 231 D5
Dembleby 116 B3
Denaby Main 140 D2
Denbigh
 Dinbych 125 C5
Denbury 8 A2
Denby 114 A1
Denby Dale 139 C5
Denchworth 65 D4
Dendron 153 C3
Denel End 84 D2
Denend 255 C7
Denford 100 D1
Dengie 70 C3
Denham Bucks 48 A3
 Suff 86 A3
 Suff 104 D2
Denham Street 104 D2
Denhead Aberds 269 D4
 Fife 221 C4
Denhead of Arbilot 232 D3
Denhead of Gray 220 A3
Denholm 187 B4
Denholme 147 D4
Denholme Clough 147 D4
Denio 106 C3
Denmead 33 D5
Denmore 245 A6
Denmoss 256 B1
Dennington 88 A3
Denny 207 B6
Dennyloanhead 207 B6
Denny Lodge 18 A2
Denshaw 138 B2
Denside 245 C5
Densole 39 A4
Denston 86 B3
Denstone 113 A5
Dent 155 C6
Denton Cambs 100 C3
 Darl 167 D5
 E Sus 22 B2
 Gtr Man 138 D2
 Kent 39 A4
 Lincs 115 B6
 Norf 104 C3
 Northants 83 B5
 N Yorks 147 C5
 Oxon 65 C6
Denton's Green 136 D3
Denver 102 A2
Denwick 189 B5
Deopham 103 A6
Deopham Green 103 B6
Depden 86 B3
Depden Green 86 B3
Deptford London 49 B6
 Wilts 31 B4
Derby 114 B1
Derbyhaven 152 E2
Dereham 120 D1
Deri 41 A6
Derril 10 A4
Derringstone 39 A4
Derrington 112 C2
Derriton 10 A4
Derryguaig 224 C3
Derry Hill 44 B3
Derrythorpe 141 C6
Dersingham 118 B3
Dervaig 224 A3
Derwen 125 D5
Derwenlas 91 C5
Desborough 99 C5
Desford 98 A1
Detchant 199 C4
Detling 37 A5
Deuddwr 110 D1
Devauden 61 D6
Devil's Bridge 75 A6
Devizes 44 C4
Devol 204 A3
Devonport 6 B3
Devonside 208 A2
Devoran 4 D2
Dewar 196 B2
Dewlish 16 B1
Dewsbury 139 A5
Dewsbury Moor 139 A5
Dewshall Court 78 D2
Dhoon 152 C4
Dhoor 152 B4
Dhowin 152 A4
Dial Post 21 A4
Dibden 18 A3
Dibden Purlieu 18 A3
Dickleburgh 104 C2
Didbrook 80 D3
Didcot 46 A3
Diddington 84 A3
Diddlebury 94 C3
Didley 78 D2
Didling 20 A1
Didmarton 44 A2
Didsbury 138 D1
Didworthy 7 A5
Digby 133 D5
Digg 259 B4
Diggle 138 C3
Digmoor 136 C3
Digswell Park 68 B2
Dihewyd 74 C3
Dilham 121 C5
Dilhorne 112 A3
Dillarburn 194 B3
Dillington 84 A3
Dilston 178 C1
Dilton Marsh 30 A2
Dilwyn 78 B2
Dinas Carms 73 C5
 Gwyn 106 C2
Dinas Cross 72 C3
Dinas Dinlle 107 A4
Dinas-Mawddwy 91 A6
Dinas Powys 41 D6
Dinder 29 A5
Dinedor 78 D3
Dingestow 61 B6
Dingle 126 A3
Dingleden 37 C6
Dingley 99 C4
Dingwall 252 A1
Dinlabyre 186 D4
Dinmael 109 A5
Dinnet 244 C1
Dinnington Som. 28 D4
 S Yorks 131 A5
 T&W 179 B4
Dinorwic 123 D5
Dinton Bucks 66 B3
 Wilts 31 B4
Dinwoodie Mains 185 C4
Dinworthy 24 D4
Dippen 191 C6
Dippenhall 33 A7
Dipple Moray 266 D4
 S Ayrs 181 A4
Diptford 7 B6
Dipton 178 D3
Dirdhu 254 D1
Dirleton 210 B2
Dirt Pot 165 A6
Discoed 77 A6
Diseworth 114 C2
Dishes 282 E7
Dishforth 158 D2
Disley 129 A4
Diss 104 D2
Disserth 76 B4
Distington 162 B3
Ditchampton 31 B4
Ditcheat 29 B6
Ditchingham 104 B4
Ditchling 21 A6
Ditherington 111 D4
Dittisham 8 B2
Ditton Halton 127 A4
 Kent 37 A5
Ditton Green 86 B2
Ditton Priors 95 C4
Divach 251 D6
Divlyn 59 B4
Dixton Glos 80 D2
 Mon 61 B7
Dobcross 138 C2
Dobwalls 5 A7
Doccombe 12 C2
Dochfour Ho. 252 C2
Dochgarroch 252 B2
Docking 119 B4
Docklow 78 B3
Dockray 164 C1
Dockroyd 147 D4
Dodburn 186 C3
Doddinghurst 69 D5
Doddington
 Cambs 101 B5
 Kent 51 D6
 Lincs 133 B4
 Northumb 198 C3
 Shrops 95 D4
Doddiscombsleigh 12 C3
Dodford Northants 82 A3
 Worcs 96 D2
Dodington 43 A6
Dodleston 126 C3
Dods Leigh 112 B4
Dodworth 139 C6
Doe Green 127 A5
Doe Lea 131 C4
Dogdyke 134 D2
Dogmersfield 47 D5
Dogridge 45 A4
Dogsthorpe 100 A3
Dog Village 13 B4
Dolanog 109 D5
Dolau Powys 77 A5
 Rhondda 41 C4
Dolbenmaen 107 B5
Dolfach 91 B7
Dolfor 93 C5
Dol-fôr 91 B6
Dolgarrog 124 C2
Dolgellau 91 A5
Dolgran 58 B1
Dolhendre 108 B3
Doll 274 D2
Dollar 208 A2
Dolley Green 77 A6
Dollwen 91 D4
Dolphin 126 B1
Dolphinholme 145 B5
Dolphinton 195 B6
Dolton 25 D6
Dolwen Conwy 124 B3
 Powys 92 A3
Dolwyd 124 B3
Dolwyddelan 124 D2
Dôl-y-Bont 90 D4
Dol-y-cannau 77 C6
Dolyhir 77 B6
Doncaster 140 C3
Dones Green 127 B6
Donhead St Andrew 30 C3
Donhead St Mary 30 C3
Donibristle 209 B4
Donington 117 B5
Donington on Bain 134 A2
Donington South Ing 117 B5
Donisthorpe 113 D7
Donkey Town 48 C2
Donnington Glos 64 A2
 Hereford 79 D5
 Shrops 94 A3
 Telford 111 D6
 W Berks 46 C2
 W Sus 20 B1
Donnington Wood 111 D6
Donyatt 28 D3
Doonfoot 192 D3
Dorback Lodge 242 A3
Dorchester Dorset 15 B6
 Oxon 65 D6
Dordon 97 A5
Dore 130 A3
Dores 252 C1
Dorking 35 B4
Dormansland 36 B2
Dormanstown 168 C3
Dormington 78 C3
Dormston 80 B2
Dornal 181 D4
Dorney 48 B2
Dornie 249 D5
Dornoch 264 B3
Dornock 175 B5
Dorrery 279 C6
Dorridge 97 D4
Dorrington Lincs 133 D5
 Shrops 94 A2
Dorsington 80 C4
Dorstone 77 C7
Dorton 66 B2
Dorusduain 250 D1
Dosthill 97 B5
Dottery 15 B4
Doublebois 5 A6
Dougarie 191 B4
Doughton 63 D4
Douglas IoM 152 D3
 S Lanark 194 C3
Douglas & Angus 220 A4
Douglastown 232 D2
Douglas Water 194 C3
Douglas West 194 C3
Doulting 29 A6
Dounby 282 E3
Doune Highld 272 D2
 Stirling 218 D2
Doune Park 268 C2
Douneside 244 B1
Dounie 264 A1
Dounreay 279 B5
Dousland 7 A4
Dovaston 110 C2
Dove Holes 129 B5
Dovenby 162 A3
Dover 39 A5
Dovercourt 88 D3
Doverdale 79 A6
Doveridge 113 B5
Doversgreen 35 B5
Dowally 230 D4
Dowbridge 144 D4
Dowdeswell 63 B5
Dowlais 60 C2
Dowland 25 D6
Dowlish Wake 28 D3
Down Ampney 64 D2
Downcraig Ferry 204 C1
Downderry 6 B2
Downe 50 C1
Downend IoW 18 C4
 S Glos 43 B5
 W Berks 46 B2
Downfield 220 A3
Downgate 11 D4
Downham Essex 70 D1
 Lancs 146 C1
 Northumb 198 C2
Downham Market 102 A2
Down Hatherley 63 A4
Downhead 29 A6
Downhill Perth 219 A5
 T&W 179 D5
Downholland Cross 136 C2
Downholme 157 B5
Downies 245 C6
Downley 66 D4
Down St Mary 12 A2
Downside Som 29 A6
 Sur 35 A4
Down Thomas 7 B4
Downton Hants 17 B6
 Wilts 31 C5
Downton on the Rock 94 D2
Dowsby 116 C4
Dowsdale 117 D5

Dowthwaitehead 163 B6
Doxey 112 C3
Doxford 189 A4
Doxford Park 179 D5
Doynton 43 B6
Draffan 194 B2
Dragonby 141 B7
Drakeland Corner 7 B4
Drakemyre 204 C2
Drake's Broughton 80 C2
Drakes Cross 96 D3
Drakewalls 11 D5
Draughton Northants 99 D4
N Yorks 147 B4
Drax 141 A4
Draycote 98 D1
Draycott Derbys 114 B2
Glos 81 D4
Som 42 D3
Draycott in the Clay 113 C5
Draycott in the Moors 112 A3
Drayford 26 D2
Drayton Leics 99 B5
Lincs 117 B5
Norf 120 D3
Oxon 65 D5
Oxon 82 C1
Ptsmth 19 A5
Som 28 C4
Worcs 96 D2
Drayton Bassett 97 A4
Drayton Beauchamp 67 B5
Drayton Parslow 66 A4
Drayton St Leonard 65 D6
Drebley 147 B4
Dreemskerry 152 B4
Dreenhill 55 C5
Drefach Carms 57 A5
Carms 73 C6
Dre-fach Carms 57 A6
Ceredig 75 D4
Drefelin 73 C6
Dreghorn 192 B3
Drellingore 39 A4
Drem 210 C2
Dresden 112 A3
Dreumasdal 286 C3
Drewsteignton 12 B2
Driby 134 B3
Driffield E Yorks 150 B3
Glos 63 D6
Drigg 153 A1
Drighlington 139 A5
Drimnin 225 A4
Drimpton 14 A4
Drimsynie 215 B4
Drinisiadar 288 H2
Drinkstone 87 A5
Drinkstone Green 87 A5
Drishaig 215 A4
Drissaig 214 A2
Drochil 195 B6
Drointon 112 C4
Droitwich Spa 80 A1
Droman 276 C2
Dron 219 C6
Dronfield 130 B3
Dronfield Woodhouse 130 B3
Drongan 182 A2
Dronley 220 A3
Droxford 33 D5
Droylsden 138 D2
Druid 109 A5
Druidston 55 C4
Druimarbin 237 B4
Druimavuic 227 B5
Druimdrishaig 202 A2
Druimindarroch 235 B5
Druimyeon More 202 C1
Drum Argyll 203 A4
Perth 219 D5
Drumbeg 270 A4
Drumblade 255 B6
Drumblair 256 B1
Drumbuie Dumfries 182 D3
Highld 249 C4
Drumburgh 175 C5
Drumburn 174 B2
Drumchapel 205 A5
Drumchardine 252 B1
Drumchork 261 B5
Drumclog 193 B6
Drumderfit 252 A2
Drumeldrie 220 D4
Drumelzier 195 C6
Drumfearn 247 C5
Drumgask 241 C4
Drumgley 232 C2
Drumguish 241 C5
Drumin 254 C2
Drumlasie 244 B3
Drumlemble 190 D2
Drumligair 245 A6
Drumlithie 245 D4
Drummoddie 171 C5
Drummond 264 D2
Drummore 170 D3
Drummuir 255 B4
Drummuir Castle 255 B4
Drumnadrochit 251 D7
Drumnagorrach 267 D6
Drumoak 245 C4
Drumpark 183 D6
Drumphail 171 A4
Drumrash 173 A4
Drumrunie 271 D4
Drums 257 D4
Drumsallie 236 B3
Drumstinchall 173 C6
Drumsturdy 221 A4
Drumtochty Castle 244 E3
Drumtroddan 171 C5
Drumuie 259 D4
Drumuillie 253 D5
Drumvaich 217 D6
Drumwhindle 257 C4
Drunkendub 233 D4
Drury 126 C2
Drury Square 119 D6
Drybeck 165 D4
Drybridge Moray 267 C5
N Ayrs 192 B3
Drybrook 62 B2
Dryburgh 197 C4
Dry Doddington 115 A6
Dry Drayton 85 A5
Dryhope 196 D1
Drylaw 209 C5
Drym 3 B4
Drymen 206 B2
Drymuir 257 B4
Drynoch 246 A3
Dryslwyn 58 C2
Dryton 94 A3
Dubford 268 C3
Dubton 232 C3
Duchally 271 C6
Duchlage 206 B1
Duck Corner 89 C4
Duckington 127 D4
Ducklington 65 C4
Duckmanton 131 B4
Duck's Cross 84 B3
Duddenhoe End 85 D6
Duddingston 209 C5
Duddington 100 A1
Duddleswell 36 D2
Duddo 198 B3
Duddon 127 C5
Duddon Bridge 153 B3
Dudleston 110 B2
Dudleston Heath 110 B2
Dudley T&W 179 B4
W Mid 96 B2
Dudley Port 96 B2
Duffield 114 A1
Duffryn Neath 40 B3
Newport 42 A1
Dufftown 254 C4
Duffus 266 C2
Dufton 165 C4
Duggleby 150 A1
Duirinish 249 C4
Duisdalemore 247 C6
Duisky 237 B4
Dukestown 60 B3
Dukinfield 138 D2
Dulas 123 B4
Dulcote 29 A5
Dulford 13 A5
Dull 230 D2
Dullatur 207 C5
Dullingham 86 B2
Dulnain Bridge 253 D5
Duloe Bedford 84 A3
Corn 6 B1
Dulsie 253 B5
Dulverton 27 C4
Dulwich 49 B6
Dumbarton 205 A3
Dumbleton 80 D3
Dumcrieff 185 B4
Dumfries 174 A2
Dumgoyne 206 B3
Dummer 33 A4
Dumpford 34 D1
Dumpton 53 C5
Dun 233 C4
Dunain Ho. 252 B2
Dunalastair 229 C6
Dunan 247 B4
Dunans 214 C3
Dunball 28 A3
Dunbar 210 C3
Dunbeath 275 B5
Dunbeg 226 C3
Dunblane 218 D2
Dunbog 220 C2
Duncanston 252 A1
Duncanstone 255 D6
Dun Charlabhaigh 288 C2
Dunchurch 98 D1
Duncote 82 B3
Duncow 184 D2
Duncraggan 217 D5
Duncrievie 219 D6
Duncton 20 A2
Dundas Ho. 283 J5
Dundee 220 A4
Dundeugh 182 D3
Dundon 29 B4
Dundonald 192 B3
Dundonnell 262 B2
Dundonnell Hotel 262 B2
Dundonnell House 262 B3
Dundraw 175 D5
Dundreggan 239 A7
Dundreggan Lodge 240 A1
Dundrennan 173 D5
Dundry 43 C4
Dunecht 245 B4
Dunfermline 208 B3
Dunfield 64 D2
Dunford Bridge 139 C4
Dungworth 130 A2
Dunham 132 B3
Dunham-on-the-Hill 127 B4
Dunhampton 79 A6
Dunham Town 128 A2
Dunholme 133 B5
Dunino 221 C5
Dunipace 207 B6
Dunira 218 B2
Dunkeld 230 D4
Dunkerton 43 D6
Dunkeswell 13 A6
Dunkeswick 148 C2
Dunkirk Kent 52 D2
Norf 120 C4
Dunk's Green 36 A4
Dunlappie 232 B3
Dunley Hants 46 D2
Worcs 79 A5
Dunlichity Lodge 252 C2
Dunlop 205 D4
Dunmaglass Lodge 252 D1
Dunmore Argyll 202 B2
Falk 208 B1
Dunnet 280 A4
Dunnichen 232 D3
Dunninald 233 C5
Dunning 219 C5
Dunnington E Yorks 151 B4
Warks 80 B3
York 149 B5
Dunnockshaw 137 A7
Dunollie 226 C3
Dunoon 203 A6
Dunragit 170 B3
Dunrostan 213 D5
Duns 198 A1
Dunsby 116 C4
Dunscore 183 D6
Dunscroft 141 C4
Dunsdale 168 D4
Dunsden Green 47 B5
Dunsfold 34 C3
Dunsford 12 C3
Dunshalt 220 C2
Dunshillock 257 B4
Dunskey Ho. 170 B2
Dunsley 169 D6
Dunsmore 66 C4
Dunsop Bridge 145 B6
Dunstable 67 A6
Dunstall 113 C5
Dunstall Common 80 C1
Dunstall Green 86 A3
Dunstan 189 B5
Dunstan Steads 189 A5
Dunster 27 A4
Duns Tew 65 A5
Dunston Lincs 133 C5
Norf 104 A3
Staffs 112 D3
T&W 179 C4
Dunsville 140 C4
Dunswell 150 D3
Dunsyre 195 B5
Dunterton 11 D4
Duntisbourne Abbots 63 C5
Duntisbourne Leer 63 C5
Duntisbourne Rouse 63 C5
Duntish 15 A6
Duntocher 205 A4
Dunton Bucks 66 A4
C Beds 84 C4
Norf 119 B5
Dunton Bassett 98 B2
Dunton Green 36 A3
Dunton Wayletts 69 D6
Duntulm 259 A4
Dunure 192 D2
Dunvant 57 C5
Dunvegan 258 D2
Dunwich 105 D5
Dunwood 129 D4
Dupplin Castle 219 C5
Durdar 175 C7
Durgates 36 C4
Durham 167 A5
Durisdeer 183 B6
Durisdeermill 183 B6
Durkar 139 B6
Durleigh 28 B2
Durley Hants 32 D4
Wilts 45 C6
Durnamuck 262 A2
Durness 277 B5
Durno 256 D2
Duror 236 D3
Durran Argyll 214 B2
Highld 280 B3
Durrington Wilts 31 A5
W Sus 21 B4
Dursley 62 D3
Durston 28 C2
Durweston 16 A2
Dury 285 G6
Duston 83 A4
Duthil 253 D5
Dutlas 93 D6
Duton Hill 69 A6
Dutson 10 C4
Dutton 127 B5
Duxford Cambs 85 C6
Oxon 65 D4
Dwygyfylchi 124 B2
Dwyran 123 D4
Dyce 245 A5
Dye House 178 D1
Dyffryn Bridgend 40 B3
Carms 73 D6
Pembs 72 C2
Dyffryn Ardudwy 107 D5
Dyffryn Castell 91 D5
Dyffryn Ceidrych 59 C4
Dyffryn Cellwen 59 E5
Dyke Lincs 116 C4
Moray 253 A5
Dykehead Angus 232 B1
N Lanark 207 E6
Stirling 206 A3
Dykelands 233 B5
Dykends 231 C6
Dykeside 256 B2
Dykesmains 204 D2
Dylife 91 C6
Dymchurch 38 C2
Dymock 79 D5
Dyrham 43 B6
Dysart 209 A6
Dyserth 125 B5

E

Eachwick 178 B3
Eadar Dha Fhadhail 287 A5
Eagland Hill 144 C4
Eagle 132 C3
Eagle Barnsdale 132 C3
Eagle Moor 132 C3
Eaglescliffe 168 D2
Eaglesfield Cumb 162 B3
Dumfries 175 A5
Eaglesham 205 C5
Eaglethorpe 100 B2
Eairy 152 D2
Eakley Lanes 83 B5
Eakring 132 C1
Ealand 141 B5
Ealing 49 A4
Eals 177 D4
Eamont Bridge 164 C3
Earby 146 C3
Earcroft 137 A5
Eardington 95 B5
Eardisland 78 B2
Eardisley 77 C7
Eardiston Shrops 110 C2
Worcs 79 A4
Earith 101 D5
Earle 188 A2
Earley 47 B5
Earlham 104 A3
Earlish 258 B3
Earls Barton 83 A5
Earls Colne 70 A2
Earl's Croome 79 C6
Earlsdon 97 D6
Earlsferry 221 E4
Earlsfield 116 B2
Earlsford 256 C3
Earl's Green 87 A6
Earlsheaton 139 A5
Earl Shilton 98 B1
Earlsmill 253 A5
Earl Soham 88 A3
Earl Sterndale 129 C5
Earlston Borders 197 C4
E Ayrs 193 B4
Earl Stonham 88 B2
Earlswood Mon 61 D6
Sur 35 B5
Warks 96 D4
Earnley 19 B7
Earsairidh 286 G3
Earsdon 179 B5
Earsham 104 C4
Earswick 149 B5
Eartham 20 B2
Easby N Yorks 157 A5
N Yorks 159 A4
Easdale 213 A5
Easebourne 34 D1
Easenhall 98 D1
Eashing 34 B2
Easington Bucks 66 B2
Durham 168 A2
E Yorks 143 B5
Northumb 199 C5
Oxon 66 D2
Oxon 82 D1
Redcar 169 D5
Easington Colliery 168 A2
Easington Lane 167 A6
Easingwold 148 A4
Easole Street 53 D4
Eassie 232 D1
East Aberthaw 41 E5
East Adderbury 82 D1
East Allington 7 C6
East Anstey 26 C3
East Appleton 157 B6
East Ardsley 139 A6
East Ashling 19 A7
East Auchronie 245 B5
East Ayton 160 C3
East Bank 60 C4
East Barkwith 133 A6
East Barming 37 A5
East Barnby 169 D6
East Barnet 68 D2
East Barns 211 C4
East Barsham 119 B6
East Beckham 120 B3
East Bedfont 48 B3
East Bergholt 87 D6
East Bilney 119 D6
East Blatchington 22 B2
East Boldre 18 A2
Eastbourne 22 C4
East Brent 42 D2
Eastbridge 89 A5
East Bridgford 115 A4
East Buckland 26 B1
East Budleigh 13 C5
Eastburn 147 C4
East Burrafirth 285 H5
East Burton 16 C2
Eastbury London 67 D6
W Berks 46 B1
East Butsfield 166 A4
East Butterwick 141 C6
Eastby 147 B4
East Cairnbeg 233 A5
East Calder 208 D3
East Carleton 104 A2
East Carlton Northants 99 C5
W Yorks 147 C6
East Chaldon 16 C1
East Challow 46 A1
East Chiltington 21 A6
East Chinnock 29 D4
East Chisenbury 45 D5
Eastchurch 52 B1
East Clandon 34 A3
East Claydon 66 A3
East Clyne 274 D2
East Coker 29 D5
Eastcombe 63 C4
East Combe 27 B6
East Common 149 D5
East Compton 29 A6
Eastcote London 48 A4
Northants 82 B3
W Mid 97 D4
Eastcott Corn 24 D3
Wilts 44 D4
East Cottingwith 149 C6
Eastcourt Wilts 45 C6
Wilts 63 D5
East Cowes 18 B4
East Cowick 141 A4
East Cowton 157 A7

East Cramlington 179 B4
East Cranmore 29 A6
East Creech 16 C3
East Croachy 252 D2
East Croftmore 242 A2
East Curthwaite 164 A1
East Dean E Sus 22 C3
Hants 31 C6
W Sus 20 A2
East Down 25 A7
East Drayton 132 B2
East Ella 142 A2
East End Dorset 16 B3
E Yorks 143 A4
Hants 18 B2
Hants 33 C5
Hants 46 C2
Herts 69 A4
Kent 37 C6
N Som 42 B3
Oxon 65 B4
Easter Ardross 264 C2
Easter Balmoral 243 C5
Easter Boleskine 251 D7
Easter Compton 43 A4
Easter Cringate 207 B5
Easter Davoch 244 B1
Easter Earshaig 184 B3
Easter Fearn 264 B2
Easter Galcantray 253 B4
Eastergate 20 B2
Easterhouse 207 D4
Easter Howgate 209 D5
Easter Howlaws 197 B6
Easter Kinkell 252 A1
Easter Lednathie 232 B1
Easter Milton 253 A5
Easter Moniack 252 B1
Eastern Green 97 C5
Easter Ord 245 B5
Easter Quarff 285 K6
Easter Rhynd 219 C6
Easter Row 207 A5
Easter Silverford 268 C2
Easter Skeld 285 J5
Easterton 44 D4
Eastertown 42 D2
Eastertown of Auchleuchries 257 C5
Easter Whyntie 267 C7
East Farleigh 37 A5
East Farndon 99 C4
East Ferry 141 D6
Eastfield
N Lanark 208 D1
N Yorks 160 C4
Eastfield Hall 189 C5
East Fortune 210 C2
East Garston 46 B1
Eastgate Durham 166 B2
Norf 120 C3
East Ginge 46 A2
East Goscote 115 D4
East Grafton 45 C6
East Grimstead 31 C6
East Grinstead 36 C1
East Guldeford 38 C1
East Haddon 82 A3
East Hagbourne 46 A3
East Halton 142 B3
Eastham 126 A3
East Ham 50 A1
Eastham Ferry 126 A3
Easthampstead 47 C6
East Hanney 65 D5
East Hanningfield 70 C1
East Hardwick 140 B2
East Harling 103 C5
East Harlsey 158 B3
East Harnham 31 C5
East Harptree 43 D4
East Hartford 179 B4
East Harting 33 D6
East Hatley 85 B4
East Hauxwell 157 B5
East Haven 221 A5
Eastheath 47 C6
East Heckington 117 A4
East Hedleyhope 167 A4
East Hendred 46 A2
East Herrington 179 D5
East Heslerton 160 D3
East Hoathly 22 A3
Easthope 94 B3
Easthorpe Essex 70 A3
Leics 115 B6
Notts 132 D2
East Horrington 29 A5
East Horsley 34 A3
East Horton 198 C4
Easthouses 209 D6
East Huntspill 28 A3
East Hyde 67 B7
East Ilkerton 26 A2
East Ilsley 46 A2
Eastington Devon 12 A2
Glos 62 C3
Glos 64 B2
East Keal 134 C3
East Kennett 45 C5
East Keswick 148 C2
East Kilbride 205 C6
East Kirkby 134 C3
East Knapton 160 D2
East Knighton 16 C2
East Knoyle 30 B2
East Kyloe 199 C4
East Lambrook 28 D4
East Lamington 264 C3
East Langdon 39 A5
East Langton 99 B4
East Langwell 273 D5
East Lavant 20 B1
East Lavington 20 A2
East Layton 157 A5
Eastleach Martin 64 C3
Eastleach Turville 64 C2
East Leake 114 C3
East Learmouth 198 C2
Eastleigh Devon 25 C5
Hants 32 D3
East Leigh 12 A1
East Lexham 119 D5
East Lilburn 188 A3
Eastling 51 D6
East Linton 210 C2
East Liss 33 C6
East Looe 6 B1
East Lound 141 D5
East Lulworth 16 C2
East Lutton 150 A2
East Lydford 29 B5
East Mains 244 C3
East Malling 37 A5
East March 220 A4
East Marden 33 D7
East Markham 132 B2
East Marton 146 B3
East Meon 33 C5
East Mere 27 D4
East Mersea 71 B4
East Mey 281 A5
East Molesey 49 C4
Eastmoor Derbys 130 B3
Norf 102 A3
East Morden 16 B3
East Morton 147 C4
East Ness 159 D5
East Newton 151 D5
Eastney 19 B5
Eastnor 79 D5
East Norton 99 A4
East Nynehead 27 C6
East Oakley 46 D3
Eastoft 141 B6
East Ogwell 12 D3
Eastoke 19 B6
Easton Cambs 100 D3
Cumb 175 C5
Cumb 176 B2
Devon 12 C2
Dorset 15 D6
Hants 32 B4
Easton
Lincs 116 C2
Norf 120 D3
Som 29 A5
Suff 88 B3
Wilts 44 B2
Easton Grey 44 A2
Easton-in-Gordano 43 B4
Easton Maudit 83 B5
Easton on the Hill 100 A2
Easton Royal 45 C6
East Orchard 30 D2
East Ord 198 A3
East Panson 11 B4
Eastpark 174 B3
East Peckham 37 B4
East Pennard 29 B5
East Perry 84 A3
East Portlemouth 7 D6
East Prawle 8 D1
East Preston 20 B3
East Putford 25 D4
East Quantoxhead 27 A6
East Rainton 167 A6
East Ravendale 143 D4
East Raynham 119 C5
Eastrea 101 B4
East Rhidorroch Lodge 262 A4
Eastriggs 175 B5
East Rigton 148 C2
Eastrington 141 A5
East Rounton 158 A3
East Row 169 D6
East Rudham 119 C5
East Runton 120 A3
East Ruston 121 C5
Eastry 53 D5
East Saltoun 210 D1
East Sleekburn 179 A4
East Somerton 121 D6
East Stockwith 141 D5
East Stoke Dorset 16 C2
Notts 115 A5
East Stour 30 C2
East Stourmouth 53 C4
East Stowford 26 C1
East Stratton 32 B4
East Studdal 39 A5
East Suisnish 248 C2
East Taphouse 5 A6
East-the-Water 25 C5
East Thirston 189 D4
East Tilbury 50 B3
East Tisted 33 B6
East Torrington 133 A6
East Tuddenham 120 D2
East Tytherley 32 C1
East Tytherton 44 B3
East Village 12 A3
Eastville Bristol 43 B5
Lincs 135 D4
East Wall 94 B3
East Walton 119 D4
Eastwell 115 C5
East Wellow 32 C2
East Wemyss 209 A6
East Whitburn 208 D2
Eastwick Herts 68 B4
Shetland 284 F5
East Williamston 55 D6
East Winch 118 D3
East Winterslow 31 B6
East Wittering 19 B6
East Witton 157 C5
Eastwood Notts 114 A2
Southend 51 A5
W Yorks 138 A2
East Woodburn 177 A7
East Woodhay 46 C2
East Worldham 33 B6
East Worlington 26 D2
East Worthing 21 B4
Eathorpe 81 A6
Eaton Ches E 128 C3
Ches W 127 C5
Leics 115 C5
Norf 104 A3
Eaton
Notts 132 B2
Oxon 65 C5
Shrops 94 C1
Shrops 94 C3
Eaton Bishop 78 D2
Eaton Bray 67 A5
Eaton Constantine 94 A3
Eaton Green 67 A5
Eaton Hastings 64 D3
Eaton on Tern 111 C5
Eaton Socon 84 B3
Eavestone 147 A6
Ebberston 160 C2
Ebbesbourne Wake 30 C3
Ebbw Vale Glyn Ebwy 60 C3
Ebchester 178 D3
Ebford 13 C4
Ebley 63 C4
Ebnal 110 A3
Ebrington 81 D4
Ecchinswell 46 D2
Ecclaw 211 D4
Ecclefechan 175 A4
Eccles Borders 197 B6
Gtr Man 137 D6
Kent 51 C4
Ecclesall 130 A3
Ecclesfield 139 D6
Ecclesgreig 233 B5
Eccleshall 112 C2
Eccleshill 147 D5
Ecclesmachan 208 C3
Eccles on Sea 121 C6
Eccles Road 103 B6
Eccleston
Ches W 127 C4
Lancs 136 B4
Mers 136 D3
Eccleston Park 136 D3
Eccup 148 C1
Echt 245 B4
Eckford 187 A6
Eckington
Derbys 131 B4
Worcs 80 C2
Ecton 83 A5
Edale 129 A6
Edburton 21 A5
Edderside 174 D3
Edderton 264 B3
Eddistone 24 C3
Eddleston 196 B1
Edenbridge 36 B2
Edenfield 137 B6
Edenhall 164 B3
Edenham 116 C3
Eden Park 49 C6
Edensor 130 C2
Edentaggart 215 C6
Edenthorpe 140 C4
Edentown 175 C6
Ederline 214 B1
Edern 106 C2
Edgarley 29 B5
Edgbaston 96 C3
Edgcott Bucks 66 A2
Som 26 B3
Edge 94 A1
Edgebolton 111 C4
Edge End 62 B1
Edgefield 120 B2
Edgefield Street 120 B2
Edge Green 127 D4
Edge Hill 136 D2
Edgeside 138 A1
Edgeworth 63 C5
Edgmond 111 D6
Edgmond Marsh 111 C6
Edgton 94 C1
Edgware 68 D1
Edgworth 137 B6
Edinample 217 B5
Edinbane 258 C3
Edinburgh 209 C5
Edingale 113 D6
Edingight Ho. 267 D6
Edingley 131 D6
Edingthorpe 121 B5
Edingthorpe Green 121 B5
Edington Som 28 B3
Wilts 44 D3
Edintore 255 B5
Edithmead 28 A3
Edith Weston 99 A6
Edlesborough 67 B5
Edlingham 189 C4
Edlington 134 B2
Edmondsham 31 D4
Edmondsley 167 A5
Edmondthorpe 115 D6
Edmonstone 282 E6
Edmonton 68 D3
Edmundbyers 178 D2
Ednam 197 C6
Ednaston 113 A6
Edradynate 230 C2
Edrom 198 A2
Edstaston 111 B4
Edstone 81 A4
Edvin Loach 79 B4
Edwalton 114 B3
Edwardstone 87 C5
Edwinsford 58 B3
Edwinstowe 131 C6
Edworth 84 C4
Edwyn Ralph 79 B4
Edzell 232 B3
Efail Isaf 41 C5
Efailnewydd 106 C3
Efailwen 72 D4
Efenechtyd 125 D6
Effingham 35 A4
Effirth 285 H5
Efford 12 A3
Egdon 80 B2
Egerton Gtr Man 137 B6
Kent 37 B7
Egerton Forstal 37 B6
Eggborough 140 A3
Eggbuckland 7 B4
Eggington 67 A5
Egginton 113 C6
Egglescliffe 168 D2
Eggleston 166 C2
Egham 48 B3
Egleton 99 A5
Eglingham 189 B4
Egloshayle 9 D5
Egloskerry 10 C3
Eglwysbach 124 B3
Eglwys-Brewis 41 E5
Eglwys Cross 110 A3
Eglwys Fach 91 C4
Eglwyswen 73 C4
Eglwyswrw 72 C4
Egmanton 132 C2
Egremont Cumb 162 C3
Mers 136 D2
Egton 159 A7
Egton Bridge 159 A7
Eight Ash Green 70 A3
Eignaig 226 B2
Eil 241 A6
Eilanreach 238 A2
Eileanach Lodge 264 D1
Eilean Darach 262 B3
Einacleite 288 E2
Eisgean 288 F4
Eisingrug 107 C6
Elan Village 76 A3
Elberton 43 A5
Elburton 7 B4
Elcho 219 B6
Elcombe 45 A5
Eldernell 101 B5
Eldersfield 79 D6
Elderslie 205 B4
Eldon 167 C5
Eldrick 181 C4
Eldroth 146 A1
Eldwick 147 C5
Elfhowe 154 B3
Elford Northumb 199 C5
Staffs 113 D5
Elgin 266 C3
Elgol 247 C4
Elham 38 A3
Elie 221 D4
Elim 122 B3
Eling 32 D2
Elishader 259 B5
Elishaw 188 D1
Elkesley 132 B1
Elkstone 63 B5
Ellan 253 D4
Elland 139 A4
Ellary 202 A2
Ellastone 113 A5
Ellemford 211 D4
Ellenbrook 152 D3
Ellenhall 112 C2
Ellen's Green 34 C3
Ellerbeck 158 B3
Ellerburn 160 C2
Ellerby 169 D5
Ellerdine Heath 111 C5
Ellerhayes 13 A4
Elleric 227 B5
Ellerker 141 A7
Ellerton E Yorks 149 D6
Shrops 111 C6
Ellesborough 66 C4
Ellesmere 110 B3
Ellesmere Port 127 B4
Ellingham Norf 105 B4
Northumb 189 A4
Ellingstring 157 C5
Ellington Cambs 100 D3
Northumb 189 D5
Elliot 221 A6
Ellisfield 33 A5
Ellistown 114 D2
Ellon 257 C4
Ellonby 164 B2
Ellough 105 C5
Elloughton 142 A1
Ellwood 62 C1
Elm 101 A6
Elmbridge 80 A2
Elmdon Essex 85 D6
W Mid 97 C4
Elmdon Heath 97 C4
Elmers End 49 C6
Elmesthorpe 98 B1
Elmfield 19 B5
Elm Hill 30 C2
Elmhurst 113 D5
Elmley Castle 80 C2
Elmley Lovett 79 A6
Elmore 62 B3
Elmore Back 62 B3
Elm Park 50 A2
Elmscott 24 C3
Elmsett 87 C6
Elmstead Market 71 A4
Elmsted 38 A3
Elmstone 53 C4
Elmstone Hardwicke 63 A5
Elmswell E Yorks 150 B2
Suff 87 A5
Elmton 131 B5
Elphin 271 C5
Elphinstone 209 C6
Elrick 245 B5
Elrig 171 C5
Elsdon 188 D2
Elsecar 140 C1
Elsenham 69 A5
Elsfield 65 B6
Elsham 142 B2
Elsing 120 D2
Elslack 146 C3
Elson 110 B2
Elsrickle 195 B5
Elstead 34 B2
Elsted 33 D7
Elsthorpe 116 C3
Elstob 167 C6
Elston Notts 115 A5
Wilts 31 A4
Elstone 26 D1
Elstow 84 C2
Elstree 68 D1
Elstronwick 151 D5
Elswick 144 D4
Elsworth 85 A5
Elterwater 154 A2
Eltham 50 B1

Eltisley 85 B4
Elton Cambs 100 B2
Ches W 127 B4
Derbys 130 C2
Glos 62 B3
Hereford 94 D2
Notts 115 B5
Stockton 168 D2
Elton Green 127 B4
Elvanfoot 184 A2
Elvaston 114 B2
Elveden 103 D4
Elvingston 210 C1
Elvington Kent 53 D4
York 149 C5
Elwick Hrtlpl 168 B2
Northumb 199 C5
Elworth 128 C2
Elworthy 27 B5
Ely Cambs 102 C1
Cardiff 41 D6
Emberton 83 C5
Embleton Cumb 163 A4
Northumb 189 A5
Embo 265 A4
Emborough 43 D5
Embo Street 265 A4
Embsay 147 B4
Emersons Green 43 B5
Emery Down 18 A1
Emley 139 B5
Emmbrook 47 C5
Emmer Green 47 B5
Emmington 66 C3
Emneth 101 A6
Emneth Hungate 101 A7
Empingham 99 A6
Empshott 33 B6
Emstrey 111 D4
Emsworth 19 A6
Enborne 46 C2
Enchmarsh 94 B3
Enderby 98 B2
Endmoor 154 C4
Endon 129 D4
Endon Bank 129 D4
Enfield 68 D3
Enfield Wash 68 D3
Enford 45 D5
Engamoor 285 H4
Engine Common 43 A5
Englefield 47 B4
Englefield Green 48 B2
Englesea-brook 128 D2
English Bicknor 62 B1
Englishcombe 43 C6
English Frankton 110 C3
Enham Alamein 32 A2
Enmore 28 B2
Ennerdale Bridge 162 C3
Enoch 183 B6
Enochdhu 231 B4
Ensay 224 B2
Ensbury 17 B4
Ensdon 110 D3
Ensis 25 C6
Enstone 65 A4
Enterkinfoot 183 B6
Enterpen 158 A3
Enville 95 C6
Eolaigearraidh 286 F3
Eorabus 224 D2
Eòropaidh 288 A6
Epperstone 115 A4
Epping 69 C4
Epping Green Essex 68 C4
Herts 68 C2
Epping Upland 68 C4
Eppleby 167 D4
Eppleworth 150 D3
Epsom 49 C5
Epwell 81 C6
Epworth 141 C5
Epworth Turbary 141 C5
Erbistock 110 A2
Erbusaig 249 D4
Erchless Castle 251 B6
Erdington 96 B4
Eredine 214 B2
Eriboll 277 C5
Ericstane 184 A3
Eridge Green 36 C3
Erines 202 A3
Eriswell 102 D3
Erith 50 B2
Erlestoke 44 D3
Ermine 133 B4
Ermington 7 B5
Erpingham 120 B3
Errogie 252 D1
Errol 220 B2
Erskine 205 A4
Erskine Bridge 205 A4
Ervie 170 A2
Erwarton 88 D3
Erwood 77 C4
Eryholme 157 A7
Eryrys 126 D2
Escomb 167 C4
Escrick 149 C5
Esgairdawe 58 A3
Esgairgeiliog 91 B5
Esh 167 A4
Esher 48 C4
Esholt 147 C5
Eshott 189 D5
Eshton 146 B3
Esh Winning 167 A4
Eskadale 251 C6
Eskbank 209 D6
Eskdale Green 163 D4
Eskdalemuir 185 C5
Eske 150 C3
Eskham 143 D5
Esk Valley 159 A7
Esprick 144 D4
Essendine 116 D3
Essendon 68 C2
Essich 252 C2
Essington 96 A2
Esslemont 257 D4
Eston 168 D3
Eswick 285 H6
Etal 198 C3
Etchilhampton 44 C4
Etchingham 37 D5
Etchinghill Kent 38 B3
Staffs 112 D4
Ethie Castle 233 D4
Ethie Mains 233 D4
Etling Green 120 D2
Eton 48 B2
Eton Wick 48 B2
Etteridge 241 C4
Ettersgill 166 C1
Ettingshall 96 B2
Ettington 81 C5
Etton E Yorks 150 C2
Pboro 100 A3
Ettrick 185 A5
Ettrickbridge 186 A2
Ettrickhill 185 A5
Etwall 113 B6
Euston 103 D4
Euximoor Drove 101 B6
Euxton 137 B4
Evanstown 41 C4
Evanton 264 D2
Evedon 116 A3
Evelix 264 A3
Evenjobb 77 A6
Evenley 82 D2
Evenlode 64 A3
Evenwood 167 C4
Evenwood Gate 167 C4
Everbay 282 E7
Evercreech 29 B6
Everdon 82 B2
Everingham 149 C7
Everleigh 45 D6
Everley 160 C3
Eversholt 84 D1
Evershot 15 A5
Eversley 47 C5
Eversley Cross 47 C5
Everthorpe 150 D2
Everton C Beds 84 B4
Hants 18 B1
Mers 136 D2
Everton Notts 141 D4
Evertown 175 A6
Evesbatch 79 C4
Evesham 80 C3
Evington 98 A3
Ewden Village 139 D5
Ewell 49 C5
Ewell Minnis 39 A4
Ewelme 66 D2
Ewen 63 D6
Ewenny 40 D4
Ewerby 116 A4
Ewerby Thorpe 116 A4
Ewes 185 C6
Ewesley 188 D3
Ewhurst 34 B3
Ewhurst Green E Sus 37 D5
Sur 34 C3
Ewloe 126 C3
Ewloe Grn. 126 C2
Ewood 137 A5
Eworthy 11 B5
Ewshot 33 A7
Ewyas Harold 61 A5
Exbourne 11 A7
Exbury 18 B3
Exebridge 27 C4
Exelby 157 C6
Exeter 13 B4
Exford 26 B3
Exhall 80 B4
Exley Head 147 D4
Exminster 13 C4
Exmouth 13 C5
Exnaboe 285 M5
Exning 86 A2
Exton Devon 13 C4
Hants 33 C5
Rutland 116 D2
Som 27 B4
Exwick 13 B4
Eyam 130 B2
Eydon 82 B2
Eye Hereford 78 A2
Pboro 100 A4
Suff 104 D2
Eye Green 100 A4
Eyemouth 211 D6
Eyeworth 85 C4
Eyhorne Street 37 A6
Eyke 88 B4
Eynesbury 84 B3
Eynort 246 B2
Eynsford 50 C2
Eynsham 65 C5
Eype 14 B4
Eyre Highld 248 C2
Highld 259 C4
Eythorne 39 A4
Eyton Hereford 78 A2
Shrops 94 C1
Wrex 110 A2
Eyton upon the Weald Moors 111 D5

F

Faccombe 46 D1
Faceby 158 A3
Facit 138 B1
Faddiley 127 D5
Fadmoor 159 C5
Faerdre 40 A1
Failand 43 B4
Failford 193 C4
Failsworth 138 C1
Fain 262 C3
Fairbourne 90 A4
Fairburn 140 A2
Fairfield Derbys 129 B5
Stockton 168 D2
Worcs 80 C3
Worcs 96 D2
Fairford 64 C2
Fair Green 118 D3
Fairhaven 136 A2
Fair Hill 164 B3
Fairlie 204 C2
Fairlight 23 A6
Fairlight Cove 23 A6
Fairmile 13 B5
Fairmilehead 209 D5
Fairoak 111 B6
Fair Oak 32 D3
Fair Oak Green 47 C4
Fairseat 50 C3
Fairstead Essex 70 B1
Norf 118 D3
Fairwarp 36 D2
Fairy Cottage 152 C4
Fairy Cross 25 C5
Fakenham 119 C6
Fakenham Magna 103 D5
Fala 210 D1
Fala Dam 210 D1
Falahill 196 A2
Falcon 79 D4
Faldingworth 133 A5
Falfield 62 D2
Falkenham 88 D3
Falkirk 208 C1
Falkland 220 D2
Falla 187 B6
Fallgate 130 C3
Fallin 207 A6
Fallowfield 138 D1
Fallsidehill 197 B5
Falmer 21 B6
Falmouth 4 D3
Falsgrave 160 C4
Falstone 177 A5
Fanagmore 276 D2
Fangdale Beck 159 B4
Fangfoss 149 B6
Fankerton 207 B5
Fanmore 224 B3
Fannich Lodge 262 D4
Fans 197 B5
Far Bank 140 B4
Far Bletchley 83 D5
Farcet 100 B4
Far Cotton 83 B4
Farden 94 D3
Fareham 19 A4
Farewell 113 D4
Far Forest 95 D5
Farforth 134 B3
Faringdon 64 D3
Farington 136 A4
Farlam 176 D3
Farlary 273 D5
Far Laund 114 A1
Farleigh N Som 42 C3
Sur 49 C6
Farleigh Hungerford 44 D2
Farleigh Wallop 33 A5
Farlesthorpe 135 B4
Farleton Cumb 154 C4
Lancs 145 A5
Farley Shrops 94 A1
Staffs 113 A4
Wilts 31 C6
Farley Green 34 B3
Farley Hill Luton 67 A6
Wokingham 47 C5
Farleys End 62 B3
Farlington 149 A5
Farlow 95 C4
Farmborough 43 C5
Farmcote Glos 63 A6
Shrops 95 B5
Farmington 64 B2
Farmoor 65 C5
Farmtown 267 D6
Farnborough Hants 34 A1
London 50 C1
Warks 82 C1
W Berks 46 A2
Farnborough Green 34 A1
Farncombe 34 B2
Farndish 83 A6
Farndon Ches W 127 D4
Notts 132 D2
Farnell 233 C4
Farnham Dorset 30 D3
Essex 69 A4
N Yorks 148 A2
Farnham Suff 89 A4
Sur 34 B1
Farnham Common 48 A2
Farnham Green 69 A4
Farnham Royal 48 A2
Farnhill 147 C4
Farningham 50 C2
Farnley N Yorks 147 C6
W Yorks 147 D6
Farnley Tyas 139 B4
Farnsfield 131 D6
Farnworth Gtr Man 137 C6
Halton 127 A5
Farr Highld 241 B6
Highld 252 C2
Highld 278 B3
Farr House 252 C2
Farringdon 13 B5
Farrington Gurney 43 D5
Far Sawrey 154 B2
Farsley 147 D6
Farthinghoe 82 D2
Farthingloe 39 A4
Farthingstone 82 B3
Fartown 139 B4
Farway 14 B1
Fasag 249 A5
Fascadale 235 C4
Faslane Port 215 D5
Fasnacloich 227 B5
Fasnakyle Ho 251 D5
Fassfern 237 B4
Fatfield 179 D5
Fattahead 268 D1
Faugh 176 D3
Fauldhouse 208 D2
Faulkbourne 70 B1
Faulkland 43 D6
Fauls 111 B4
Faversham 52 C2
Favillar 254 C3
Fawdington 158 D3
Fawfieldhead 129 C5
Fawkham Green 50 C2
Fawler 65 B4
Fawley Bucks 47 A5
Hants 18 A3
W Berks 46 A1
Fawley Chapel 62 A1
Faxfleet 141 A6
Faygate 35 C5
Fazakerley 136 D2
Fazeley 97 A5
Fearby 157 C5
Fearn 265 C4
Fearnan 229 D6
Fearnbeg 249 A4
Fearnhead 137 D5
Fearn Lodge 264 B2
Fearnmore 261 D4
Fearn Station 265 C4
Featherstone Staffs 96 A2
W Yorks 140 A2
Featherwood 187 C7
Feckenham 80 A3
Feering 70 A2
Feetham 156 B3
Feizor 146 A1
Felbridge 35 C6
Felbrigg 120 B4
Felcourt 36 B1
Felden 67 C6
Felin-Crai 59 C5
Felindre Carms 58 B3
Carms 58 C2
Carms 59 C4
Carms 73 C6
Ceredig 75 C4
Powys 93 C5
Swansea 57 B6
Felindre Farchog 72 C4
Felinfach Ceredig 75 C4
Powys 77 D4
Felinfoel 57 B5
Felingwm isaf 58 C2
Felingwm uchaf 58 C2
Felinwynt 73 A5
Felixkirk 158 C3
Felixstowe 88 D3
Felixstowe Ferry 88 D4
Felkington 198 B3
Felkirk 140 B1
Felling 179 C4
Fell Side 163 A6
Felmersham 84 B1
Felmingham 120 C4
Felpham 20 C2
Felsham 87 B5
Felsted 69 A6
Feltham 48 B4
Felthorpe 120 D3
Felton Hereford 78 C3
Northumb 189 C4
N Som 43 C4
Felton Butler 110 D2
Feltwell 102 B3
Fenay Bridge 139 B4
Fence 146 D2
Fence Houses 179 D5
Fen Ditton 85 A6
Fen Drayton 85 A5
Fen End 97 D5
Fengate Norf 120 C3
Pboro 100 B4
Fenham 199 B4
Fenhouses 117 A5
Feniscliffe 137 A5
Feniscowles 137 A5
Feniton 13 B6
Fenlake 84 C2
Fenny Bentley 130 D1
Fenny Bridges 13 B6
Fenny Compton 81 B7
Fenny Drayton 97 B6
Fenny Stratford 83 D5
Fenrother 189 D4
Fen Side 134 D3
Fenstanton 85 A5
Fenton Cambs 101 D5
Lincs 132 B3
Lincs 132 D3
Stoke 112 A6
Fenton Barns 210 B2
Fenton Town 198 C3
Fenwick E Ayrs 205 D4
Northumb 178 B2
Northumb 199 B4
S Yorks 140 B3
Feochaig 190 D3
Feock 4 D3
Feolin Ferry 201 B4
Ferindonald 247 D5
Feriniquarrie 258 C1
Ferlochan 226 B4
Fern 232 B2
Ferndale 41 B5
Ferndown 17 A4
Ferness 253 B5
Ferney Green 154 B3
Fernham 64 D3
Fernhill Heath 79 B6
Fernhurst 34 D1
Fernie 220 C3
Ferniegair 194 A2
Fernilea 246 A2
Fernilee 129 B5
Ferrensby 148 A2
Ferring 20 B3
Ferrybridge 140 A2
Ferryden 233 C5
Ferryhill Aberdeen 245 B6
Durham 167 B5
Ferry Hill 101 C5
Ferryhill Station 167 B6
Ferry Point 264 B3
Ferryside 56 A3
Fersfield 103 C6
Fersit 228 A2
Ferwig 73 B4
Feshiebridge 241 B6
Fetcham 35 A4
Fetterangus 269 D4
Fettercairn 233 A4
Fettes 252 A1
Fewcott 65 A6

Fewston 147 B5
Ffairfach 58 C3
Ffair-Rhos 75 B6
Ffaldybrenin 58 A3
Ffarmers 58 A3
Ffawyddog 60 B4
Fforest 57 B5
Fforest-fâch 57 C6
Ffostrasol 73 B6
Ffos-y-ffin 74 B3
Ffridd-Uchaf 107 A5
Ffrith 126 D2
Ffrwd 107 A4
Ffynnon ddrain 73 D7
Ffynnongroyw 125 A6
Ffynnon-oer 75 C4
Fidden 224 D2
Fiddes 245 D5
Fiddington Glos 80 D2
Som 28 A2
Fiddleford 30 D2
Fiddlers Hamlet 69 C4
Field 112 B4
Field Broughton 154 C2
Field Dalling 120 B2
Field Head 98 A1
Fifehead Magdalen 30 C1
Fifehead Neville 30 D1
Fifield Oxon 64 B3
Wilts 45 D5
Windsor 48 B2
Fifield Bavant 31 C4
Figheldean 31 A5
Filands 44 A3
Filby 121 D6
Filey 161 C5
Filgrave 83 C5
Filkins 64 C3
Filleigh Devon 26 C1
Devon 26 D2
Fillingham 133 A4
Fillongley 97 C5
Filton 43 B5
Fimber 150 A1
Finavon 232 C2
Finchairn 214 B2
Fincham 102 A2
Finchampstead 47 C5
Finchdean 33 D6
Finchingfield 86 D2
Finchley 68 D2
Findern 113 B7
Findhorn 265 D6
Findhorn Bridge 253 D4
Findochty 267 C5
Findo Gask 219 B5
Findon Aberds 245 C6
W Sus 21 B4
Findon Mains 264 D2
Findrack Ho 244 B3
Finedon 99 D6
Fingal Street 88 A3
Fingask 256 D2
Fingerpost 95 D5
Fingest 66 D3
Finghall 157 C5
Fingland Cumb 175 C5
Dumfries 183 A5
Finglesham 53 D5
Fingringhoe 71 A4
Finlarig 217 A5
Finmere 82 D3
Finnart 229 C4
Finningham 87 A6
Finningley 141 D4
Finnygaud 267 D6
Finsbury 49 A6
Finstall 80 A2
Finsthwaite 154 C2
Finstock 65 B4
Finstown 282 F4
Fintry Aberds 268 D2
Dundee 220 A4
Stirling 207 B4
Finzean 244 C3
Fionnphort 224 D2
Fionnsbhagh 287 F5
Firbeck 131 A5
Firby N Yorks 149 A6
N Yorks 157 C6
Firgrove 138 B2
Firsby 135 C4
Firsdown 31 B6
First Coast 261 A6
Fir Tree 166 B4
Fishbourne IoW 19 B4
W Sus 20 B1
Fishburn 167 B6
Fishcross 208 A1
Fisherford 256 C1
Fisher Place 163 C6
Fisher's Pond 32 C3
Fisherstreet 34 C2
Fisherton Highld 252 A3
S Ayrs 192 D2
Fishguard Abergwaun 72 C2
Fishlake 141 B4
Fishleigh Barton 25 C6
Fishponds 43 B5
Fishpool 62 A2
Fishtoft 117 A6
Fishtoft Drove 117 A6
Fishtown of Usan 233 C5
Fishwick 198 A3
Fiskavaig 246 A2
Fiskerton Lincs 133 B5
Notts 132 D2
Fitling 151 D5
Fittleton 31 A5
Fittleworth 20 A3
Fitton End 118 D1
Fitz 110 D3
Fitzhead 27 C6
Fitzwilliam 140 B2
Fiunary 225 B5
Five Acres 62 B1
Five Ashes 36 D3
Fivecrosses 127 B5
Fivehead 28 C3
Five Oak Green 36 B4
Five Oaks Jersey 6
W Sus 34 D3
Five Roads 57 B4
Flack's Green 70 B1
Flackwell Heath 48 A1
Fladbury 80 C2
Fladdabister 285 K6
Flagg 129 C6
Flamborough 161 D6
Flamstead 67 B6
Flamstead End 68 C3
Flansham 20 B2
Flanshaw 139 A6
Flasby 146 B3
Flash 129 C5
Flashader 258 C3
Flask Inn 160 A3
Flaunden 67 C6
Flawborough 115 A5
Flawith 148 A3
Flax Bourton 43 C4
Flaxby 148 B2
Flaxholme 114 A1
Flaxley 62 B2
Flaxpool 27 B6
Flaxton 149 A5
Fleckney 98 B3
Flecknoe 82 A2
Fledborough 132 B3
Fleet Hants 19 A6
Hants 47 D6
Lincs 117 C6
Fleetham 189 A4
Fleet Hargate 117 C6
Fleetlands 19 A4
Fleetville 67 C7
Fleetwood 144 C3
Flemingston 41 D5
Flemington 205 C6
Flempton 87 A4
Fleoideabhagh 287 F5
Fletchertown 175 D5
Fletching 36 D2
Flexbury 10 A3
Flexford 34 B2
Flimby 162 A3
Flimwell 37 C5
Flint Y Fflint 126 B2
Flintham 115 A5
Flint Mountain 126 B2
Flinton 151 D5
Flintsham 77 B7
Flitcham 119 C4
Flitton 84 D2
Flitwick 84 D2
Flixborough 141 B6
Flixborough Stather 141 B6
Flixton Gtr Man 137 D6
N Yorks 160 D4
Suff 104 C4
Flockton 139 B5
Flodaigh 286 A4
Flodden 198 C3
Flodigarry 259 A4
Flood's Ferry 101 B5
Flookburgh 154 D2
Florden 104 B2
Flore 82 A3
Flotterton 188 C2
Flowton 88 C1
Flush House 139 C4
Flushing Aberds 257 B5
Corn 4 D3
Flyford Flavell 80 B2
Foals Green 104 D3
Fobbing 51 A4
Fochabers 266 D4
Fochriw 60 C3
Fockerby 141 B6
Fodderletter 254 D2
Fodderty 251 A7
Foel 109 D4
Foel-gastell 57 A5
Foffarty 232 D2
Foggathorpe 149 D6
Fogo 197 B6
Fogorig 198 B1
Foindle 276 D2
Folda 231 B5
Fole 112 B4
Foleshill 97 C6
Folke 29 D6
Folkestone 39 B4
Folkingham 116 B3
Folkington 22 B3
Folksworth 100 C3
Folkton 161 D4
Folla Rule 256 C2
Follifoot 148 B2
Folly Gate 11 B6
Fonthill Bishop 30 B3
Fonthill Gifford 30 B3
Fontmell Magna 30 D2
Fontwell 20 B2
Foolow 130 B1
Foots Cray 50 B1
Forbestown 243 A6
Force Mills 154 B2
Forcett 167 D4
Ford Argyll 214 B1
Bucks 66 C3
Devon 25 C5
Glos 64 A1
Northumb 198 C3
Shrops 110 D3
Staffs 129 D5
Wilts 44 B2
W Sus 20 B2
Fordcombe 36 B3
Fordell 209 B4
Forden 93 A6
Ford End 69 B6
Forder Grn 8 A1
Fordham Cambs 102 D2
Essex 70 A3
Norf 102 B2
Fordhouses 96 A2
Fordingbridge 31 D5
Fordon 160 D4
Fordoun 233 A5
Ford's Green 87 A6
Fordstreet 70 A3
Ford Street 27 D6
Fordwells 64 B4
Fordwich 52 D3
Fordyce 267 C6
Forebridge 112 C3
Forest 165 B6
Forest Becks 146 B1
Forestburn Gate 188 D3
Foresterseat 266 D2
Forest Gate 49 A7
Forest Green 35 B4
Forest Hall 154 A4
Forest Head 176 D3
Forest Hill 65 C6
Forest Lane Head 148 B2
Forest Lodge Argyll 228 D1
Highld 242 A3
Perth 230 A3
Forest Mill 208 A2
Forest Row 36 C2
Forestside 33 D6
Forest Town 131 C5
Forfar 232 C2
Forgandenny 219 C5
Forge 91 C5
Forge Side 60 C4
Forgewood 194 A2
Forgie 267 D4
Forglen Ho 268 D1
Formby 136 C2
Forncett End 104 B2
Forncett St Mary 104 B2
Forncett St Peter 104 B2
Forneth 231 D4
Fornham All Saints 87 A4
Fornham St Martin 87 A4
Forres 253 A6
Forrestfield 207 D6
Forrest Lodge 182 D3
Forsbrook 112 A3
Forse 275 A6
Forse Ho 275 A6
Forsinain 279 D5
Forsinard 279 D4
Forsinard Station 279 D4
Forston 15 B6
Fort Augustus 240 B1
Forteviot 219 C5
Fort George Guern 6
Highld 252 A3
Forth 194 A4
Forthampton 79 D6
Forth Road Bridge 208 C4
Fortingall 229 D6
Forton Hants 32 A3
Lancs 145 B4
Shrops 110 D3
Som 14 A3
Staffs 111 C6
Forton Heath 110 D3
Fortrie 256 B1
Fortrose 252 A3
Fortuneswell 15 D6
Fort William 237 B5
Forty Green 67 D5
Forty Hill 68 D3
Forward Green 88 B1
Fosbury 45 D7
Fosdyke 117 B6
Foss 230 C1
Foss Cross 63 C6
Fossebridge 64 B1
Fosterhouses 141 B4
Foster Street 69 C4
Foston Derbys 113 B5
Lincs 115 A6
N Yorks 149 A5
Foston on the Wolds 151 B4
Fotherby 143 D5
Fotheringhay 100 B2
Foubister 283 G6
Foulby 140 B1
Foulden Borders 198 A3
Norf 102 B3
Foulis Castle 264 D1
Foul Mile 22 A4
Foulridge 146 C2
Foulsham 120 C2
Fountainhall 196 B3
Four Ashes Staffs 95 C6
Suff 103 D6
Four Crosses Powys 93 A4
Powys 110 D1
Wrex 126 D2
Four Elms 36 B2
Four Forks 28 B2
Four Gotes 118 D1
Fourlane Ends 130 D3
Four Lane Ends 127 C5
Four Lanes 3 B4
Fourlanes End 128 D3
Four Marks 33 B5
Four Mile Bridge 122 C2
Four Oaks E Sus 37 D6
W Mid 96 B4
W Mid 97 C5
Fourpenny 265 A4
Four Roads Carms 57 B4
IoM 152 E2
Fourstones 177 C6
Four Throws 37 D5
Fovant 31 C4
Foveran 257 D4
Fowey 5 B6
Fowley Common 137 D5
Fowlis 220 A3
Fowlis Wester 218 B4
Fowlmere 85 C6
Fownhope 78 D3
Foxbar 205 B4
Foxcombe Hill 65 C5
Fox Corner 34 A2
Foxdale 152 D2
Foxearth 87 C4
Foxfield 153 B3
Foxham 44 B3
Foxhole Corn 5 B4
Swansea 57 C6
Foxholes 160 D4
Foxhunt Green 22 A3
Fox Lane 34 A1
Foxley Norf 120 C2
Wilts 44 A2
Fox Street 71 A4
Foxt 112 A4
Foxton Cambs 85 C6
Durham 167 C6
Leics 99 B4
Foxup 156 D2
Foxwist Green 127 C6
Foxwood 95 D4
Foy 62 A1
Foyers 251 D6
Fraddam 2 B3
Fraddon 4 B4
Fradley 113 D5
Fradswell 112 B3
Fraisthorpe 151 A4
Framfield 36 D2
Framingham Earl 104 A3
Framingham Pigot 104 A3
Framlingham 88 A3
Frampton Dorset 15 B6
Lincs 117 B6
Frampton Cotterell 43 A5
Frampton Mansell 63 C5
Frampton on Severn 62 C3
Frampton West End 117 A5
Framsden 88 B2
Framwellgate Moor 167 A5
Franche 95 D6
Frankby 126 A2
Frankley 96 C2
Frank's Bridge 77 B5
Frankton 98 D1
Frant 36 C3
Fraserburgh 269 C4
Frating Green 71 A4
Fratton 19 B5
Freathy 6 B3
Freckenham 102 D2
Freckleton 136 A3
Freeby 115 C6
Freehay 112 A4
Freeland 65 B5
Freester 285 H6
Freethorpe 105 A5
Freiston 117 A6
Fremington Devon 25 B6
N Yorks 156 B4
Frenchay 43 B5
Frenchbeer 12 C1
Frenich 216 D4
Frensham 34 B1
Fresgoe 279 B5
Freshfield 136 C1
Freshford 44 C1
Freshwater 18 C2
Freshwater Bay 18 C2
Freshwater East 55 E6
Fressingfield 104 D3
Freston 88 D2
Freswick 281 B5
Fretherne 62 C3
Frettenham 120 D4
Freuchie 220 D2
Freuchies 231 B6
Freystrop 55 C5
Friar's Gate 36 C2
Friarton 219 B6
Friday Bridge 101 A6
Friday Street 22 B4
Fridaythorpe 150 B1
Friern Barnet 68 D2
Friesland 223 B4
Friesthorpe 133 A5
Frieston 116 A2
Frieth 66 D3
Frilford 65 D5
Frilsham 46 B3
Frimley 34 A1
Frimley Green 34 A1
Frindsbury 51 B4
Fring 119 B4
Fringford 65 A7
Frinsted 37 A6
Frinton-on-Sea 71 A6
Friockheim 232 D3
Friog 90 A4
Frisby on the Wreake 115 D4
Friskney 135 D4
Friskney Eaudike 135 D4
Friskney Tofts 135 D4
Friston E Sus 22 C3
Suff 89 A5
Fritchley 130 D3
Fritham 31 D6
Frith Bank 117 A6
Frith Common 79 A4
Frithelstock 25 D5
Frithelstock Stone 25 D5
Frithville 134 D3
Frittenden 37 B6
Frittiscombe 8 C2
Fritton Norf 104 B3
Norf 105 A5
Fritwell 65 A6
Frizinghall 147 D5
Frizington 162 C3
Frocester 62 C3
Frodesley 94 A3
Frodingham 141 B6
Frodsham 127 B5
Frogden 187 A6
Froggatt 130 B2
Froghall 112 A4
Frogmore Devon 7 C6
Hants 34 A1
Frognall 117 D4
Frogshail 121 B4
Frolesworth 98 B2
Frome 30 A1
Frome St Quintin 15 A5
Fromes Hill 79 C4
Fron Denb 125 C5
Gwyn 106 C3
Gwyn 107 A5
Powys 77 A4
Powys 93 A6

Fron
Powys 93 B5
Froncysyllte 110 A1
Frongoch 108 B4
Frostenden 105 C5
Frosterley 166 B3
Frotoft 282 E5
Froxfield 45 C6
Froxfield Green 33 C6
Froyle 33 A6
Fryerning 69 C6
Fryton 159 D5
Fulbeck 133 D4
Fulbourn 85 B7
Fulbrook 64 B3
Fulford Som 28 C2
Staffs 112 B3
York 149 C5
Fulham 49 B5
Fulking 21 A5
Fullarton
Glasgow 205 B6
N Ayrs 192 B3
Fuller's Moor 127 D4
Fuller Street 70 B1
Fullerton 32 B2
Fulletby 134 B2
Full Sutton 149 B6
Fullwood 205 C4
Fulmer 48 A2
Fulmodestone 120 B1
Fulnetby 133 B5
Fulstow 143 D5
Fulwell 179 D5
Fulwood Lancs 145 D5
S Yorks 130 A3
Fundenhall 104 B2
Fundenhall
Street 104 B2
Funtington 19 A6
Funtley 19 A4
Funtullich 218 B2
Funzie 284 D8
Furley 14 A2
Furnace Argyll 214 B3
Carms 57 B5
Furnace End 97 B5
Furneaux Pelham 68 A4
Furness Vale 129 A5
Furzehill 26 A2
Furze Platt 48 A1
Fyfett 28 D2
Fyfield Essex 69 C5
Glos 64 C3
Hants 32 A1
Oxon 65 D5
Wilts 45 C5
Fylingthorpe 160 A3
Fyvie 256 C2

G

Gabhsann bho
Dheas 288 B5
Gabhsann bho
Thuath 288 B5
Gablon 264 A3
Gabroc Hill 205 C4
Gaddesby 115 D4
Gadebridge 67 C6
Gaer 60 A3
Gaerllwyd 61 D6
Gaerwen 123 C4
Gagingwell 65 A5
Gaick Lodge 241 D5
Gailey 112 D3
Gainford 167 D4
Gainsborough
Lincs 141 D6
Suff 88 C2
Gainsford End 86 D3
Gairloch 261 C5
Gairlochy 239 D5
Gairney Bank 208 A4
Gairnshiel
Lodge 243 B5
Gaisgill 155 A5
Gaitsgill 164 A1
Galashiels 196 C3
Galgate 145 B4
Galhampton 29 C6
Gallaberry 184 D2
Gallachoille 213 D5
Gallanach Argyll 223 A5
Argyll 226 D3
Gallantry Bank 127 D5
Gallatown 209 A5
Galley Common 97 B6
Galleyend 69 C7
Galley Hill 85 A5
Galleywood 69 C7
Gallin 229 D4
Gallowfauld 232 D2
Gallows Green 113 A4
Galltair 249 D5
Galmisdale 234 B3
Galmpton Devon 7 C5
Torbay 8 B2
Galphay 157 D6
Galston 193 B5
Galtrigill 258 C1
Gamblesby 165 B4
Gamesley 138 D3
Gamlingay 84 B4
Gammersgill 157 C4
Gamston 132 B2
Ganarew 62 B1
Ganavan 226 C3
Gang 6 A2
Ganllwyd 108 C2
Gannochy Angus 232 A3
Perth 219 B6
Gansclet 281 D5
Ganstead 151 D4
Ganthorpe 159 D5
Ganton 160 D3
Garbat 263 D6
Garbhallt 214 C3
Garboldisham 103 C6
Garden City 126 C3
Gardenstown 268 C2
Garden Village
Wrex 126 D3
W Yorks 148 D3
Garderhouse 285 J5
Gardham 150 C2
Gardin 284 G6
Gare Hill 30 A1
Garelochhead 215 C5
Garford 65 D5
Garforth 148 D3
Gargrave 146 B3
Gargunnock 207 A5
Garlic Street 104 C3
Garlieston 171 C6
Garlinge Green 52 D3
Garlogie 245 B4
Garmond 268 D3
Garmony 225 B5
Garmouth 266 C4
Garnant 58 D3
Garndiffaith 61 C4
Garndolbenmaen
107 B4
Garnedd 124 D2
Garnett Bridge 154 B4
Garnfadryn 106 C2
Garnkirk 207 D4
Garnlydan 60 B3
Garnswllt 57 B6
Garn-yr-erw 60 B4
Garrabost 288 D6
Garraron 213 B6
Garras 3 C5
Garreg 107 B6
Garrick 218 C3
Garrigill 165 A5
Garriston 157 B5
Garroch 182 D3
Garrogie Lodge 240 A3
Garros 259 B4
Garrow 230 D2
Garryhorn 182 C3
Garsdale 155 C6
Garsdale Head 155 B6
Garsdon 44 A3
Garshall Green 112 B3
Garsington 65 C6
Garstang 145 C4
Garston 127 A4
Garswood 137 D4
Gartcosh 207 D4
Garth Bridgend 40 B3
Garth
Gwyn 123 C5
Powys 76 C3
Shetland 285 H4
Wrex 110 A1
Garthamlock 205 B6
Garthbrengy 76 D4
Garthdee 245 B6
Gartheli 75 C4
Garthmyl 93 B5
Garthorpe Leics 115 C6
N Lincs 141 B6
Garth Row 154 B4
Gartly 255 C6
Gartmore 206 A3
Gartnagrenach 202 C2
Gartness
N Lanark 207 D5
Stirling 206 B3
Gartocharn 206 B2
Garton 151 D5
Garton-on-the-
Wolds 150 B2
Gartsherrie 207 D5
Gartymore 274 C4
Garvald 210 C2
Garvamore 240 C3
Garvard 212 C1
Garvault Hotel 273 A5
Garve 263 D5
Garvestone 103 A6
Garvock Aberds 233 A5
Invclyd 204 A2
Garway 61 A6
Garway Hill 61 A6
Gaskan 236 B1
Gastard 44 C2
Gasthorpe 103 C5
Gatcombe 18 C3
Gateacre 127 A4
Gatebeck 154 C4
Gate Burton 132 A3
Gateford 131 A5
Gateforth 140 A3
Gatehead 192 B3
Gate Helmsley 149 B5
Gatehouse 177 A5
Gatehouse of
Fleet 172 C4
Gatelawbridge 183 C7
Gateley 119 C6
Gatenby 158 C2
Gateshead 179 C4
Gatesheath 127 C4
Gateside Aberds 244 A3
Angus 232 D2
E Renf 205 C4
Fife 219 D6
N Ayrs 204 C3
Gathurst 136 C4
Gatley 128 A3
Gattonside 197 C4
Gatwick Airport 35 B5
Gaufron 76 A3
Gaulby 98 A3
Gauldry 220 B3
Gaunt's Common 17 A4
Gautby 134 B1
Gavinton 197 A6
Gawber 139 C6
Gawcott 82 D3
Gawsworth 128 C3
Gawthorpe 139 A5
Gawthrop 155 C5
Gawthwaite 153 B3
Gaydon 81 B6
Gayfield 282 B5
Gayhurst 83 C5
Gayle 156 C2
Gayles 157 A5
Gay Street 34 D3
Gayton Mers 126 A2
Norf 119 D4
Northants 83 B4
Staffs 112 C3
Gayton le Marsh 135 A4
Gayton le Wold 134 A2
Gayton Thorpe 119 D4
Gaywood 118 C3
Gazeley 86 A3
Geanies House 265 C4
Gearraidh
Bhailteas 286 D3
Gearraidh
Bhaird 288 E4
Gearraidh na h-
Aibhne 288 D3
Gearraidh na
Monadh 286 E3
Geary 258 B2
Geddes House 253 A4
Gedding 87 B5
Geddington 99 C5
Gedintailor 247 A4
Gedling 115 A4
Gedney 117 C7
Gedney
Broadgate 117 C7
Gedney Drove
End 118 C1
Gedney Dyke 117 C7
Gedney Hill 117 D6
Gee Cross 138 D2
Geilston 206 C1
Geirinis 286 B3
Geise 280 B3
Geisiadar 288 D2
Geldeston 105 B4
Gell 124 C3
Gelli Pembs 55 C6
Rhondda 41 B4
Gellideg 60 C2
Gellifor 125 C6
Gelligaer 41 B6
Gellilydan 107 C6
Gellinudd 40 A2
Gellyburn 219 A5
Gellywen 73 D5
Gelston Dumfries 173 C5
Lincs 116 A2
Gembling 151 B4
Gentleshaw 113 D4
Geocrab 288 H2
Georgefield 185 C5
George Green 48 A3
Georgeham 25 B5
George Nympton 26 C2
Georgetown 60 C3
Gerlan 123 D6
Germansweek 11 B5
Germoe 2 C3
Gerrans 4 D3
Gerrards Cross 48 A3
Gestingthorpe 87 D4
Geuffordd 109 D7
Gibbet Hill 98 C2
Gibbshill 173 A5
Gib Hill 127 B6
Gidea Park 50 A2
Gidleigh 12 C1
Giffnock 205 C5
Gifford 210 D2
Giffordland 204 D2
Giffordtown 220 C2
Giggleswick 146 A2
Gilberdyke 141 A6
Gilchriston 210 D1
Gilcrux 163 A4
Gildersome 139 A5
Gildingwells 131 A5
Gileston 41 E5
Gilfach 41 B6
Gilfach Goch 41 C4
Gilfachrheda 73 A7
Gillamoor 159 C5
Gillar's Green 136 D3
Gillen 258 C2
Gilling East 159 D5
Gillingham Dorset 30 C2
Medway 51 C4
Norf 105 B5
Gilling West 157 A5
Gillock 280 C4
Gillow Heath 128 D3
Gills 281 A5
Gill's Green 37 C5
Gilmanscleuch 196 D2
Gilmerton Edin. 209 D5
Perth 218 B3
Gilmonby 166 D2
Gilmorton 98 C2
Gilmourton 205 D6
Gilsland 176 C4
Gilsland Spa 176 C4
Gilston Borders 196 A3
Herts 68 B4
Gilwern 60 B4
Gimingham 121 B4
Giosla 288 E2
Gipping 87 A6
Gipsey Bridge 117 A5
Girdle Toll 204 D3
Girlsta 285 H6
Girsby 158 A2
Girtford 84 B3
Girthon 172 C4
Girton Cambs 85 A6
Notts 132 C3
Girvan 180 B3
Gisburn 146 C2
Gisleham 105 C6
Gislingham 104 D1
Gissing 104 C2
Gittisham 13 B6
Gladestry 77 B6
Gladsmuir 210 C1
Glais 40 A2
Glaisdale 159 A6
Glame 248 B2
Glamis 232 D1
Glan Adda 123 C5
Glanaman 57 A6
Glan Conwy 124 B3
Glan-Conwy 124 D3
Glandford 120 A2
Glan-Duar 58 A2
Glandwr 73 D4
Glan-Dwyfach 107 B4
Glandy Cross 72 D4
Glandyfi 91 C4
Glan Gors 123 C4
Glangrwyney 60 B4
Glanmule 93 B5
Glanrafon 90 D4
Glanrhyd Gwyn 106 C2
Pembs 72 B4
Glan-rhyd 107 A4
Glanton 188 B3
Glanton Pike 188 B3
Glan-traeth 122 C2
Glanvilles
Wootton 15 A6
Glan-y-don 125 B6
Glan-y-nant 92 C3
Glan-yr-afon
Anglesey 123 B6
Gwyn 108 A4
Gwyn 109 A5
Glan-y-wern 107 C6
Glapthorn 100 B2
Glapwell 131 C4
Glas-allt Shiel 243 D5
Glasbury 77 D5
Glaschoil 253 C6
Glascoed Denb 125 B4
Mon 61 C5
Powys 109 D6
Glascorrie 243 C6
Glascote 97 A5
Glascwm 77 B5
Glasdrum 227 B5
Glasfryn 125 D4
Glasgow 205 B5
Glashvin 259 B4
Glasinfryn 123 D5
Glasnacardoch 235 A5
Glasnakille 247 C4
Glasphein 258 D1
Glaspwll 91 C5
Glassburn 251 C5
Glasserton 171 D6
Glassford 194 B2
Glasshouse Hill 62 A3
Glasshouses 147 A5
Glasslie 220 D2
Glasson Cumb 175 B5
Lancs 144 B4
Glassonby 164 B3
Glasterlaw 232 C3
Glaston 99 A5
Glastonbury 29 B5
Glatton 100 C3
Glazebrook 137 D5
Glazebury 137 D5
Glazeley 95 C5
Gleadless 130 A3
Gleadsmoss 128 C3
Gleann
Tholàstaidh 288 C6
Gleaston 153 C3
Gleiniant 92 B3
Glemsford 87 C4
Glen Dumfries 172 C3
Dumfries 173 A6
Glenamachrie 226 D4
Glen Auldyn 152 B4
Glenbarr 190 B2
Glenbeg Highld 235 D4
Highld 253 D6
Glen Bernisdale 259 D4
Glenbervie 245 D4
Glenboig 207 D5
Glenborrodale 235 D5
Glenbranter 215 C4
Glenbreck 195 D5
Glenbrein
Lodge 240 A2
Glenbrittle
House 246 B3
Glenbuchat
Lodge 243 A6
Glenbuck 194 D2
Glenburn 205 B4
Glencalvie
Lodge 263 B6
Glencanisp
Lodge 270 B4
Glencaple 174 B2
Glencarron
Lodge 250 A2
Glencarse 219 B6
Glencassley
Castle 272 D2
Glenceitlein 227 B6
Glencoe 237 D4
Glencraig 209 A4
Glencripesdale 225 A5
Glencrosh 183 D5
Glendavan Ho. 244 B1
Glendevon 219 D4
Glendoebeg 240 B2
Glendoe Lodge 240 B2
Glendoick 220 B2
Glendoll Lodge 231 A6
Glendoune 180 B3
Glenduckie 220 C2
Glendye Lodge 244 D3
Gleneagles
Hotel 218 C4
Gleneagles
House 218 D4
Glenegedale 200 C3
Glenelg 238 A2
Glenernie 253 B6
Glenfarg 219 C6
Glenfarquhar
Lodge 245 D4
Glenferness
House 253 B5
Glenfeshie
Lodge 241 C6
Glenfield 98 A2
Glenfinnan 238 D3
Glenfoot 219 C6
Glenfyne Lodge 215 A5
Glengap 173 C4
Glengarnock 204 C3
Glengorm
Castle 224 A3
Glengrasco 259 D4
Glenhead Farm 231 B6
Glen Ho 196 C1
Glenhoul 182 D4
Glenhurich 236 C2
Glenkerry 185 A5
Glenkiln 173 A6
Glenkindie 244 A1
Glenlatterach 266 D2
Glenlee 182 D4
Glenlichorn 218 C2
Glenlivet 254 D2
Glenlochsie 231 A4
Glenloig 191 B5
Glenluce 171 B4

Glenmallan 215 C5
Glenmarksie 251 A5
Glenmassan 215 D4
Glenmavis 207 D5
Glenmaye 152 D2
Glenmidge 183 D6
Glen Mona 152 C4
Glenmore Argyll 213 A6
Highld 259 D4
Glenmore Lodge 242 B2
Glenmoy 232 B2
Glen Nevis House 237 B5
Glenogil 232 B2
Glen Parva 98 B2
Glenprosen Lodge 231 B6
Glenprosen Village 232 B1
Glenquiech 232 B2
Glenreasdell Mains 202 C3
Glenree 191 C5
Glenridding 164 D1
Glenrossal 272 D2
Glenrothes 220 D2
Glensanda 226 B3
Glensaugh 233 A4
Glenshero Lodge 240 C3
Glen Sluain 214 C3
Glenstockadale 170 A2
Glenstriven 203 A5
Glentaggart 194 D3
Glen Tanar House 244 C1
Glentham 142 D2
Glentirranmuir 207 A4
Glenton 256 D1
Glentress 196 C1
Glentromie Lodge 241 C5
Glen Trool Lodge 181 C6
Glentrool Village 181 D5
Glentruan 152 A4
Glentruim House 241 C4
Glentworth 133 A4
Glenuig 235 C5
Glenurquhart 264 D3
Glen Village 208 C1
Glen Vine 152 D3
Glespin 194 D3
Gletness 285 H6
Glewstone 62 A1
Glinton 100 A3
Glooston 99 B4
Glororum 199 C5
Glossop 138 D3
Gloster Hill 189 C5
Gloucester 63 B4
Gloup 284 C7
Glusburn 147 C4
Glutt Lodge 274 A3
Glutton Bridge 129 C5
Glympton 65 A5
Glynarthen 73 B6
Glynbrochan 92 C3
Glyn-Ceiriog 109 B7
Glyncoch 41 B5
Glyncorrwg 40 B3
Glyn-cywarch 107 C6
Glynde 22 B2
Glyndebourne 22 A2
Glyndyfrdwy 109 A6
Glyn-neath
Glynedd 59 E5
Glynogwr 41 C4
Glyntaff 41 C5
Glyntawe 59 D5
Gnosall 112 C2
Gnosall Heath 112 C2
Goadby 99 B4
Goadby Marwood 115 C5
Goatacre 44 B4
Goathill 29 D6
Goathland 160 A2
Goathurst 28 B2
Goat Lees 38 A2
Gobernuisgach Lodge 277 D5
Gobhaig 287 D5
Gobowen 110 B2
Godalming 34 B2
Godley 138 D2
Godmanchester 100 D4
Godmanstone 15 B6
Godmersham 52 D2
Godney 29 A4
Godolphin Cross 3 B4
Godre'r-graig 59 E4
Godshill Hants 31 D5
IoW 18 C4
Godstone 35 A6
Godwinscroft 17 B5
Goetre 61 C5
Goferydd 122 B2
Goff's Oak 68 C3
Gogar 209 C4
Goginan 91 D4
Golan 107 B5
Golant 5 B6
Golberdon 10 D4
Golborne 137 D5
Golcar 139 B4
Goldcliff 42 A2
Golden Cross 22 A3
Golden Green 36 B4
Golden Grove 57 A5
Goldenhill 128 D3
Golden Hill 17 B6
Golden Pot 33 A6
Golden Valley 63 A5
Golders Green 49 A5
Goldhanger 70 C3
Gold Hill 102 B1
Golding 94 A3
Goldington 84 B2
Goldsborough
N Yorks 148 B2
N Yorks 169 D6
Goldsithney 2 B3
Goldsworthy 25 C4
Goldthorpe 140 C2
Gollanfield 253 A4
Golspie 274 D2
Golval 279 B4
Gomeldon 31 B5
Gomersal 139 A5
Gomshall 34 B3
Gonalston 115 A4
Gonfirth 285 G5
Good Easter 69 B6
Gooderstone 102 A3
Goodleigh 25 B7
Goodmanham 150 C1
Goodnestone
Kent 52 C2
Kent 53 D4
Goodrich 62 B1
Goodrington 8 B2
Goodshaw 137 A7
Goodwick Wdig 72 C2
Goodworth Clatford 32 A2
Goole 141 A5
Goonbell 4 C2
Goonhavern 4 B2
Goose Eye 147 C4
Goose Green
Gtr Man 137 C4
Norf 104 C2
W Sus 21 A4
Gooseham 24 D3
Goosey 65 D4
Goosnargh 145 D5
Goostrey 128 B2
Gorcott Hill 80 A3
Gord 285 L6
Gordon 197 B5
Gordonbush 274 D2
Gordonsburgh 267 C5
Gordonstoun 266 C2
Gordonstown
Aberds 256 C2
Aberds 267 D6
Gore 53 D5
Gorebridge 209 D6
Gore Cross 44 D4
Gorefield 117 D7
Gore Pit 70 B2
Gorey Jersey 6
Gorgie 209 C5
Goring 47 A4
Goring-by-Sea 21 B4
Goring Heath 47 B4
Gorleston-on-Sea 105 A6
Gornalwood 96 B2
Gorrachie 268 D2
Gorran Churchtown 5 C4
Gorran Haven 5 C5
Gorrenberry 186 D3
Gors 75 A5
Gorsedd 125 B6
Gorse Hill 45 A5
Gorseinon 57 C5
Gorseness 282 F5
Gorsgoch 74 C3
Gorslas 57 A5
Gorsley 62 A2
Gorstan 263 D5
Gorstanvorran 236 B2
Gorsteyhill 128 D2
Gorsty Hill 113 C5
Gortantaoid 200 A3
Gorton 138 D1
Gosbeck 88 B2
Gosberton 117 B5
Gosberton Clough 117 C4
Gosfield 70 A1
Gosford 78 A3
Gosforth Cumb 162 D3
T&W 179 C4
Gosmore 68 A1
Gosport 19 B5
Gossabrough 284 E7
Gossington 62 C3
Goswick 199 B4
Gotham 114 B3
Gotherington 63 A5
Gott 285 J6
Goudhurst 37 C5
Goulceby 134 B2
Gourdas 256 B2
Gourdon 233 A6
Gourock 204 A2
Govan 205 B5
Govanhill 205 B5
Goveton 7 C6
Govilon 61 B4
Gowanhill 269 C5
Gowdall 140 A4
Gowerton 57 C5
Gowkhall 208 B3
Gowthorpe 149 B6
Goxhill E Yorks 151 C4
N Lincs 142 A3
Goxhill Haven 142 A3
Goybre 40 C2
Grabhair 288 F4
Graby 116 C3
Grade 3 D5
Graffham 20 A2
Grafham Cambs 84 A3
Sur 34 B3
Grafton Hereford 78 D2
N Yorks 148 A3
Oxon 64 C3
Shrops 110 D3
Worcs 78 A3
Grafton Flyford 80 B2
Grafton Regis 83 C4
Grafton Underwood 99 C6
Grafty Green 37 B6
Graianrhyd 126 D2
Graig Conwy 124 B3
Denb 125 B5
Graig-fechan 125 D6
Grain 51 B5
Grainsby 143 D4
Grainthorpe 143 D5
Grampound 4 C4
Grampound Road 4 B4
Gramsdal 286 A4
Granborough 66 A3
Granby 115 B5
Grandborough 82 A1
Grandtully 230 C3
Grange Cumb 163 C5
E Ayrs 193 B4
Medway 51 C4
Mers 126 A2
Perth 220 B2
Grange Crossroads 267 D5
Grange Hall 265 D6
Grange Hill 68 D4
Grangemill 130 D2
Grange Moor 139 B5
Grangemouth 208 B2
Grange of Lindores 220 C2
Grange-over-Sands 154 D3
Grangepans 208 B3
Grangetown
Cardiff 41 D6
Redcar 168 C3
Grange Villa 179 D4
Granish 242 A2
Gransmoor 151 B4
Granston 55 A4
Grantchester 85 B6
Grantham 116 B2
Grantley 147 A6
Grantlodge 245 A4
Granton Dumfries 184 B3
Edin 209 C5
Grantown-on-Spey 253 D6
Grantshouse 211 D5
Grappenhall 127 A6
Grasby 142 C2
Grasmere 154 A2
Grasscroft 138 C2
Grassendale 126 A3
Grassholme 166 C2
Grassington 147 A4
Grassmoor 131 C4
Grassthorpe 132 C2
Grateley 32 A1
Gratwich 112 B4
Graveley Cambs 84 A4
Herts 68 A2
Gravelly Hill 96 B4
Gravels 94 A1
Graven 284 F6
Graveney 52 C2
Gravesend Herts 68 A4
Kent 50 B3
Grayingham 142 D1
Grayrigg 155 B4
Grays 50 B3
Grayshott 34 C1
Grayswood 34 C2
Graythorp 168 C3
Grazeley 47 C4
Greasbrough 140 D2
Greasby 126 A2
Great Abington 86 C1
Great Addington 99 D6
Great Alne 80 B4
Great Altcar 136 C2
Great Amwell 68 B3
Great Asby 165 D4
Great Ashfield 87 A5
Great Ayton 168 D3
Great Baddow 70 C1
Great Bardfield 86 D2
Great Barford 84 B3
Great Barr 96 B3
Great Barrington 64 B3
Great Barrow 127 C4
Great Barton 87 A4
Great Barugh 159 D6
Great Bavington 178 A1
Great Bealings 88 C3
Great Bedwyn 45 C6
Great Bentley 71 A5
Great Billing 83 A5
Great Bircham 119 B4
Great Blakenham 88 B2
Great Blencow 164 B2
Great Bolas 111 C5
Great Bookham 35 A4
Great Bourton 82 C1
Great Bowden 99 C4
Great Bradley 86 B2
Great Braxted 70 B2
Great Bricett 87 B6
Great Brickhill 83 D6
Great Bridgeford 112 C2
Great Brington 82 A3
Great Bromley 71 A4
Great Broughton
Cumb 162 A3
N Yorks 158 A4
Great Budworth 127 B6
Great Burdon 167 D6
Great Burgh 35 A5
Great Burstead 69 D6
Great Busby 158 A4
Great Canfield 69 B5
Great Carlton 135 A4
Great Casterton 100 A2
Great Chart 38 A1
Great Chatwell 112 D1
Great Chesterford 85 C7
Great Cheverell 44 D3
Great Chishill 85 D6
Great Clacton 71 B5
Great Cliff 139 B6
Great Clifton 162 B3
Great Coates 143 C4
Great Comberton 80 C2
Great Corby 176 D2
Great Cornard 87 C4
Great Cowden 151 C5
Great Coxwell 64 D3
Great Crakehall 157 B6
Great Cransley 99 D5
Great Cressingham 103 A4
Great Crosby 136 D2
Great Cubley 113 B5
Great Dalby 115 D5
Great Denham 84 C2
Great Doddington 83 A5
Great Dunham 119 D5
Great Dunmow 69 A6
Great Durnford 31 B5
Great Easton
Essex 69 A6
Leics 99 B5
Great Eccleston 144 C4
Great Edstone 159 C6
Great Ellingham 103 B6
Great Elm 30 A1
Greater Doward 62 B1
Great Eversden 85 B5
Great Fencote 157 B6
Great Finborough 87 B6
Greatford 116 D3
Great Fransham 119 D5
Great Gaddesden 67 B6
Greatgate 113 A4
Great Gidding 100 C3
Great Givendale 149 B7
Great Glemham 88 A4
Great Glen 98 B3
Great Gonerby 116 B1
Great Gransden 85 B4
Great Green
Norf 104 C3
Suff 87 B5
Great Habton 159 D6
Great Hale 116 A4
Greatham Hants 33 B6
Hrtlpl 168 C2
W Sus 20 A3
Great Hampden 66 C4
Great Harrowden 99 D5
Great Harwood 146 D1
Great Haseley 66 C2
Great Hatfield 151 C4
Great Haywood 112 C3
Great Heath 97 C6
Great Heck 140 A3
Great Henny 87 D4
Great Hinton 44 D3
Great Hockham 103 B5
Great Holland 71 B6
Great Horkesley 87 D5
Great Hormead 68 A3
Great Horton 147 D5
Great Horwood 83 D4
Great Houghton
Northants 83 B4
S Yorks 140 C2
Great Hucklow 130 B1
Great Kelk 151 B4
Great Kimble 66 C4
Great Kingshill 66 D4
Great Langton 157 B6
Great Leighs 70 B1
Great Lever 137 C6
Great Limber 142 C3
Great Linford 83 C5
Great Livermere 103 D4
Great Longstone 130 B2
Great Lumley 167 A5
Great Lyth 94 A2
Great Malvern 79 C5
Great Maplestead 87 D4
Great Marton 144 D3
Great Massingham 119 C4
Great Melton 104 A2
Great Milton 66 C2
Great Missenden 66 C4
Great Mitton 145 D7
Great Mongeham 53 D5
Great Moulton 104 B2
Great Munden 68 A3
Great Musgrave 165 D5
Great Ness 110 D2
Great Notley 70 A1
Great Oakley
Essex 71 A5
Northants 99 C5
Great Offley 67 A7
Great Ormside 165 D5
Great Orton 175 C6
Great Ouseburn 148 A3
Great Oxendon 99 C4
Great Oxney Green 69 C6
Great Palgrave 119 D5
Great Paxton 84 A4
Great Plumpton 144 D3
Great Plumstead 121 D5
Great Ponton 116 B2
Great Preston 140 A2
Great Raveley 101 C4
Great Rissington 64 B2
Great Rollright 81 D6
Great Ryburgh 119 C6
Great Ryle 188 B3
Great Ryton 94 A2
Great Saling 69 A7
Great Salkeld 164 B3
Great Sampford 86 D2
Great Sankey 127 A5
Great Saxham 86 A3
Great Shefford 46 B1
Great Shelford 85 B6
Great Smeaton 158 A2
Great Snoring 119 B6
Great Somerford 44 A3
Great Stainton 167 C6
Great Stambridge 70 D2
Great Staughton 84 A3
Great Steeping 135 C4
Great Stonar 53 D5
Greatstone on Sea 38 C2
Great Strickland 164 C3
Great Stukeley 100 D4
Great Sturton 134 B2
Great Sutton
Ches W 126 B3
Shrops 94 C3
Great Swinburne 178 B1
Great Tew 65 A4
Great Tey 70 A2
Great Thurkleby 158 D3
Great Thurlow 86 B2
Great Torrington 25 D5
Great Tosson 188 C3
Great Totham
Essex 70 B2

Great Totham
Essex 70 B2
Great Tows 143 D4
Great Urswick 153 C3
Great Wakering 51 A6
Great Waldingfield 87 C5
Great Walsingham 119 B6
Great Waltham 69 B6
Great Warley 69 D5
Great Washbourne 80 D2
Great Weldon 99 C6
Great Welnetham 87 B4
Great Wenham 87 D6
Great Whittington 178 B2
Great Wigborough 70 B3
Great Wilbraham 86 B1
Great Wishford 31 B4
Great Witcombe 63 B5
Great Witley 79 A5
Great Wolford 81 D5
Greatworth 82 C2
Great Wratting 86 C2
Great Wymondley 68 A2
Great Wyrley 96 A2
Great Wytheford 111 D4
Great Yarmouth 105 A6
Great Yeldham 86 D3
Greave 138 A1
Greeba 152 C3
Green 125 C5
Greenbank 284 C7
Greenburn 208 D2
Greendikes 188 A3
Green End 84 B3
Greenfield C Beds 84 D2
Flint 126 B1
Gtr Man 138 C2
Highld 239 B6
Oxon 66 D3
Greenford 48 A4
Greengairs 207 C5
Greenham 46 C2
Green Hammerton 148 B3
Greenhaugh 177 A5
Greenhead 177 C4
Greenhill Falk 207 C6
Kent 52 C3
Leics 114 D2
London 49 A4
Greenhills 204 C3
Greenhithe 50 B2
Greenholm 193 B5
Greenholme 155 A4
Greenhouse 187 A4
Greenhow Hill 147 A5
Greenigoe 283 G5
Greenland 280 B4
Greenlands 47 A5
Green Lane 93 B5
Greenlaw Aberds 268 D1
Borders 197 B6
Greenlea 174 A3
Greenloaning 218 D3
Greenmount 137 B6
Greenmow 285 L6
Greenock 204 A2
Greenock West 204 A2
Greenodd 154 C2
Green Ore 43 D4
Greenrow 174 C4
Green St Green 50 C1
Greenside 178 C3
Greensidehill 188 B2
Greens Norton 82 C3
Greenstead Green 70 A2
Greensted 69 C5
Green Street 68 D1
Greenwich 49 B6
Greet 80 D3
Greete 94 D3
Greetham Lincs 134 B3
Rutland 116 D2
Greetland 138 A3
Gregg Hall 154 B3
Gregson Lane 137 A4
Greinetobht 287 G3
Greinton 28 B4
Gremista 285 J6
Grenaby 152 D2
Grendon Northants 83 A5
Warks 97 A5
Grendon Common 97 B5
Grendon Green 78 B3
Grendon Underwood 66 A2
Grenofen 11 D5
Grenoside 139 D6
Greosabhagh 288 H2
Gresford 126 D3
Gresham 120 B3
Greshornish 258 C3
Gressenhall 119 D6
Gressingham 145 A5
Gresty Green 128 D2
Greta Bridge 166 D3
Gretna 175 B6
Gretna Green 175 B6
Gretton Glos 80 D3
Northants 99 B5
Shrops 94 B3
Grewelthorpe 157 D6
Greygarth 157 D5
Grey Green 141 C5
Greynor 57 B5
Greysouthen 162 B3
Greystoke 164 B2
Greystone Angus 232 D3
Dumfries 174 A2
Greywell 47 D5
Griais 288 C5
Grianan 288 D5
Gribthorpe 149 D6
Gridley Corner 11 B4
Griff 97 C6
Griffithstown 61 D4
Grimbister 282 F4
Grimblethorpe 134 A2
Grimeford Village 137 B5
Grimethorpe 140 C2
Griminis 286 A3
Grimister 284 D6
Grimley 79 A6
Grimness 283 H5
Grimoldby 134 A3
Grimpo 110 C2
Grimsargh 145 D5
Grimsbury 82 C1
Grimsby 143 B4
Grimscote 82 B3
Grimscott 10 A3
Grimsthorpe 116 C3
Grimston E Yorks 151 D5
Leics 115 C4
Norf 119 C4
York 149 B5
Grimstone 15 B6
Grinacombe Moor 11 B5
Grindale 161 D5
Grindigar 283 G6
Grindiscol 285 K6
Grindle 95 A5
Grindleford 130 B2
Grindleton 146 C1
Grindley 112 C4
Grindley Brook 111 A4
Grindlow 130 B1
Grindon
Northumb 198 B3
Staffs 129 D5
Grindonmoor Gate 129 D5
Gringley on the Hill 141 D5
Grinsdale 175 C6
Grinshill 111 C4
Grinton 156 B4
Griomsidar 288 E4
Grishipoll 223 B4
Grisling Common 36 D2
Gristhorpe 161 C4
Griston 103 B5
Gritley 283 G6
Grittenham 44 A4
Grittleton 44 A2
Grizebeck 153 B3
Grizedale 154 B2
Grobister 282 E7
Groby 98 A2
Groes Conwy 125 C5
Neath 40 C2
Groes-faen 41 C5
Groesffordd Marli 125 B5
Groeslon Gwyn 107 A4
Gwyn 123 D5
Groes-lwyd 109 D7
Grogport 202 D3
Gromford 89 B4
Gronant 125 A5
Groombridge 36 C3
Grosmont Mon 61 A6
N Yorks 160 A2
Groton 87 C5
Grougfoot 208 C3
Grouville Jersey 6
Grove Dorset 15 D7
Kent 53 C4
Notts 132 B2
Oxon 65 D5
Grove Park 49 B7
Grovesend 57 B5
Grove Vale 96 B3
Grudie 263 D5
Gruids 272 D3
Gruinard House 261 A6
Grula 246 B2
Gruline 225 B4
Grunasound 285 K5
Grundisburgh 88 B3
Grunsagill 146 B1
Gruting 285 J4
Grutness 285 N6
Gt. Bridge 96 B2
Gt. Hallingbury 69 B5
Gt. Parndon 68 C4
Gualachulain 227 B6
Gualin Ho. 276 C4
Guardbridge 221 C4
Guarlford 79 C6
Guay 230 D4
Guestling Green 23 A6
Guestling Thorn 23 A6
Guestwick 120 C2
Guestwick Green 120 C2
Guide 137 A6
Guide Post 179 A4
Guilden Morden 85 C4
Guilden Sutton 127 C4
Guildford 34 B2
Guildtown 219 A6
Guilsborough 98 D3
Guilsfield 109 D7
Guilton 53 D4
Guineaford 25 B6
Guisborough 168 D4
Guiseley 147 C5
Guist 120 C1
Guith 282 D6
Guiting Power 64 A1
Gulberwick 285 K6
Gullane 210 B1
Gulval 2 B2
Gulworthy 11 D5
Gumfreston 55 D7
Gumley 98 B3
Gummow's Shop 4 B3
Gunby E Yorks 149 D6
Lincs 116 C2
Gundleton 33 B5
Gun Hill 22 A3
Gunn 26 B1
Gunnerside 156 B3
Gunnerton 177 B7
Gunness 141 B6
Gunnislake 11 D5
Gunnista 285 J7
Gunthorpe Norf 120 B2
Notts 115 A4
Pboro 100 A3
Gunville 18 C3
Gunwalloe 3 C4
Gurnard 18 B3
Gurnett 129 B4
Gurney Slade 29 A6
Gurnos 59 E4
Gussage All Saints 31 D4
Gussage St Michael 30 D3
Guston 39 A5
Gutcher 284 D7
Guthrie 232 C3
Guyhirn 101 A5
Guyhirn Gull 101 A5
Guy's Head 118 C1
Guy's Marsh 30 C2
Guyzance 189 C5
Gwaenysgor 125 A5
Gwalchmai 122 C3
Gwaun-Cae-Gurwen 59 D4
Gwaun-Leision 59 D4
Gwbert 73 B4
Gweek 3 C5
Gwehelog 61 C5
Gwenddwr 77 C4
Gwennap 4 D2
Gwenter 3 D5
Gwernaffield 126 C2
Gwernesney 61 C6
Gwernogle 58 B2
Gwernymynydd 126 C2
Gwersyllt 126 D3
Gwespyr 125 A6
Gwithian 2 A3
Gwredog 123 B4
Gwyddelwern 109 A5
Gwyddgrug 58 B1
Gwydyr Uchaf 124 C2
Gwynfryn 126 D2
Gwystre 77 A4
Gwytherin 124 C3
Gyfelia 110 A2
Gyffin 124 B2
Gyre 283 G4
Gyrn-goch 107 B4

H

Habberley 94 A1
Habergham 146 D2
Habrough 142 B3
Haceby 116 B3
Hacheston 88 B4
Hackbridge 49 C5
Hackenthorpe 131 A4
Hackford 103 A6
Hackforth 157 B6
Hackland 282 E4
Hackleton 83 B5
Hackness
N Yorks 160 B3
Orkney 283 H4
Hackney 49 A6
Hackthorn 133 A4
Hackthorpe 164 C3
Haconby 116 C4
Hacton 50 A2
Hadden 198 C1
Haddenham Bucks 66 C3
Cambs 101 D6
Haddington
E Loth 210 C2
Lincs 133 C4
Haddiscoe 105 B5
Haddon Cambs 100 B3
Ches E 129 C4
Hade Edge 139 C4
Hademore 97 A4
Hadfield 138 D3
Hadham Cross 68 B4
Hadham Ford 68 A4
Hadleigh Essex 51 A5
Suff 87 C6
Hadley 111 D5
Hadley End 113 C5
Hadlow 36 B4
Hadlow Down 36 D3
Hadnall 111 D4
Hadstock 86 C1
Hady 130 B3
Hadzor 80 A2
Haffenden Quarter 37 B6
Hafod-Dinbych 124 D3
Hafod-Iom 124 B3
Haggate 146 D2
Haggbeck 176 B2
Haggerston 198 B4
Haggrister 284 F5
Hagley Hereford 78 C3
Worcs 96 C2
Hagworthingham 134 C3
Haigh Gtr Man 137 C5
S Yorks 139 B5
Haigh Moor 139 A5
Haighton Green 145 D5
Haile 162 D3
Hailes 80 D3
Hailey Herts 68 B3
Oxon 65 B4
Hailsham 22 B3
Hail Weston 84 A3
Haimer 280 B3
Hainault 69 D4
Hainford 120 D4
Hainton 134 A1
Hairmyres 205 C6
Haisthorpe 151 A4
Hakin 55 D4
Halam 132 D1
Halbeath 208 B4
Halberton 27 D5
Halcro 280 B4
Hale Gtr Man 128 A2
Halton 127 A4
Hants 31 D5
Hale Bank 127 A4
Halebarns 128 A2
Hales Norf 105 B4
Staffs 111 B6
Halesfield 95 A5
Halesgate 117 C6
Halesowen 96 C2
Hales Place 52 D3
Hale Street 37 B4
Halesworth 105 D4
Halewood 127 A4
Halford Shrops 94 C2
Warks 81 C5
Halfpenny Furze 56 A2
Halfpenny Green 95 B6
Halfway Carms 58 B3
Carms 59 B5
W Berks 46 C2
Halfway Bridge 34 D2
Halfway House 110 D2
Halfway Houses 51 B6
Halifax 138 A3
Halket 205 C4
Halkirk 280 C3
Halkyn 126 B2
Halland 22 A2
Hallaton 99 B4
Hallatrow 43 D5
Hallbankgate 176 D3
Hall Dunnerdale 153 A3
Hallen 43 A4
Hall Green W Mid 96 C4
W Yorks 139 B6
Hall Grove 68 B2
Halliburton 197 B5
Hallin 258 C2
Halling 51 C4
Hallington Lincs 134 A3
Northumb 178 B1
Halliwell 137 B6
Hall of Tankerness 283 G6
Hall of the Forest 93 C6
Halloughton 132 D1
Hallow 79 B6
Hallrule 187 B4
Halls 210 C3
Hallsands 8 D2
Hall's Green 68 A2
Hallthwaites 153 B2
Hallworthy 10 C2
Hallyburton House 220 A2
Hallyne 195 B6
Halmer End 112 A1
Halmore 62 C2
Halmyre Mains 195 B6
Halnaker 20 B2
Halsall 136 B2
Halse Northants 82 C2
Som 27 C6
Halsetown 2 B3
Halsham 143 A4
Halsinger 25 B6
Halstead Essex 87 D4
Kent 50 C1
Leics 99 A4
Halstock 15 A5
Haltham 134 C2
Haltoft End 117 A6
Halton Bucks 66 B4
Halton 127 A5
Lancs 145 A5
Northumb 178 C1
Wrex 110 B2
W Yorks 148 D2
Halton East 147 B4
Halton Gill 156 D2
Halton Holegate 135 C4
Halton Lea Gate 176 D4
Halton West 146 B2
Haltwhistle 177 C5
Halvergate 105 A5
Halwell 8 B1
Halwill 11 B5
Halwill Junction 11 A5
Ham Devon 14 A2
Glos 62 D2
Highld 280 A4
Kent 53 D5
London 49 B4
Shetland 285 K1
Wilts 46 C1
Hambleden 47 A5
Hambledon Hants 33 D5
Sur 34 C2
Hamble-le-Rice 18 A3
Hambleton Lancs 144 C3
N Yorks 149 D4
Hambridge 28 C3
Hambrook S Glos 43 B5
W Sus 19 A6
Ham Common 30 C2
Hameringham 134 C3
Hamerton 100 D3
Hametoun 285 K1
Ham Green
Hereford 79 C5
Kent 37 D6
Kent 51 C5
N Som 43 B4
Worcs 80 A3
Hamilton 194 A2
Hammer 34 C1
Hammerpot 20 B3
Hammersmith 49 B5
Hammerwich 96 A3
Hammerwood 36 C2
Hammond Street 68 C3
Hammoon 30 D2
Hamnavoe
Shetland 284 E4
Shetland 284 E6
Shetland 284 F6
Shetland 285 K5
Hampden Park 22 B4
Hamperden End 86 D1
Hampnett 64 B1
Hampole 140 B3
Hampreston 17 B4
Hampstead 49 A5
Hampstead Norreys 46 B3
Hampsthwaite 147 B6
Hampton London 48 C4
Shrops 95 C5
Worcs 80 C3
Hampton Bishop 78 D3
Hampton Heath 110 A3
Hampton in Arden 97 C5
Hampton Loade 95 C5
Hampton Lovett 80 A1
Hampton Lucy 81 B5

Hampton on the Hill 81 A5
Hampton Poyle 65 B6
Hamrow 119 C6
Hamsey 22 A2
Hamsey Green 35 A6
Hamstall Ridware 113 D5
Hamstead IoW 18 B3
W Mid 96 B3
Hamstead Marshall 46 C2
Hamsterley Durham 166 B4
Durham 178 D3
Hamstreet 38 B2
Ham Street 29 B5
Hamworthy 16 B3
Hanbury Staffs 113 C5
Worcs 80 A2
Hanbury Woodend 113 C5
Hanby 116 B3
Hanchurch 112 A2
Handbridge 127 C4
Handcross 35 D5
Handforth 128 A3
Handley 127 D4
Handsacre 113 D4
Handsworth S Yorks 131 A4
W Mid 96 B3
Handy Cross 25 C5
Hanford 112 A2
Hanging Langford 31 B4
Hangleton 20 B3
Hanham 43 B5
Hankelow 111 A5
Hankerton 63 D5
Hankham 22 B4
Hanley 112 A2
Hanley Castle 79 C6
Hanley Child 79 A4
Hanley Swan 79 C6
Hanley William 79 A4
Hanlith 146 A3
Hanmer 110 B3
Hannah 135 B5
Hannington Hants 46 D3
Northants 99 D5
Swindon 64 D2
Hannington Wick 64 D2
Hansel Village 192 B3
Hanslope 83 C5
Hanthorpe 116 C3
Hanwell London 49 A4
Oxon 82 C1
Hanwood 94 A2
Hanworth London 48 B4
Norf 120 B3
Happendon 194 C3
Happisburgh 121 B5
Happisburgh Common 121 C5
Hapsford 127 B4
Hapton Lancs 146 D1
Norf 104 B2
Harberton 8 B1
Harbertonford 8 B1
Harbledown 52 D3
Harborne 96 C3
Harborough Magna 98 D1
Harbottle 188 C2
Harbury 81 B6
Harby Leics 115 B5
Notts 132 B3
Harcombe 13 B6
Harden W Mid 96 A3
W Yorks 147 D4
Hardenhuish 44 B3
Hardgate 245 B4
Hardham 20 A3
Hardingham 103 A6
Hardingstone 83 B4
Hardington 43 D6
Hardington Mandeville 29 D5
Hardington Marsh 15 A5
Hardley 18 A3
Hardley Street 105 A4
Hardmead 83 C6
Hardrow 156 B2
Hardstoft 131 C4
Hardway Hants 19 A5
Som 29 B7
Hardwick Bucks 66 B4
Cambs 85 B5
Norf 104 C3
Norf 118 D3
Northants 83 A5
Notts 131 B6
Oxon 65 A6
Oxon 65 C4
W Mid 96 B3
Hardwicke Glos 62 B3
Glos 63 A5
Hereford 77 C6
Hardy's Green 70 A3
Hareby 134 C3
Hareden 145 B6
Harefield 67 D6
Hare Green 71 A4
Hare Hatch 47 B6
Harehills 148 D2
Harehope 188 A3
Haresceugh 165 A4
Harescombe 63 B4
Haresfield 63 B4
Hareshaw 207 D6
Hareshaw Head 177 A6
Hare Street 68 A3
Harewood 148 C2
Harewood End 62 A1
Harford Carms 58 A3
Devon 7 B5
Hargate 104 B2
Hargatewall 129 B6
Hargrave Ches W 127 C4
Northants 100 D2
Suff 86 B3
Harker 175 B6
Harkland 284 E6
Harkstead 88 D2
Harlaston 113 D6
Harlaw Ho. 256 D2
Harlaxton 116 B1
Harlech 107 C5
Harlequin 115 B4
Harlescott 111 D4
Harlesden 49 A5
Harleston Devon 8 C1
Norf 104 C3
Suff 87 B6
Harlestone 83 A4
Harle Syke 146 D2
Harley Shrops 94 A3
S Yorks 139 D6
Harleyholm 194 C4
Harlington C Beds 84 D2
London 48 B3
S Yorks 140 C2
Harlosh 258 D2
Harlow 69 B4
Harlow Hill Northumb 178 C2
N Yorks 148 B1
Harlthorpe 149 D6
Harlton 85 B5
Harman's Cross 16 C3
Harmby 157 C5
Harmer Green 68 B2
Harmer Hill 110 C3
Harmondsworth 48 B3
Harmston 133 C4
Harnham 178 B2
Harnhill 63 C6
Harold Hill 69 D5
Haroldston West 55 C4
Haroldswick 284 B8
Harold Wood 69 D5
Harome 159 C5
Harpenden 67 B7
Harpford 13 B5
Harpham 150 A3
Harpley Norf 119 C4
Worcs 79 A4
Harpole 82 A3
Harpsdale 280 C3
Harpsden 47 A5
Harpswell 133 A4
Harpurhey 138 C1
Harpur Hill 129 B5
Harraby 175 C7
Harrapool 247 B5
Harrier 285 J1
Harrietfield 219 B4
Harrietsham 37 A6
Harrington Cumb 162 B2
Lincs 134 B3
Northants 99 C4
Harringworth 99 B6
Harris 234 A2
Harrogate 148 B2
Harrold 83 B6
Harrow 49 A4
Harrowbarrow 6 A2
Harrowden 84 C2
Harrowgate Hill 167 D5
Harrow on the Hill 49 A4
Harrow Street 87 D5
Harrow Weald 67 D7
Harston Cambs 85 B6
Leics 115 B6
Harswell 150 C1
Hart 168 B2
Hartburn Northumb 178 A2
Stockton 168 D2
Hart Common 137 C5
Hartest 87 B4
Hartfield 36 C2
Hartford Cambs 101 D4
Ches W 127 B6
Hartfordbridge 47 D5
Hartford End 69 B6
Hartforth 157 A5
Harthill Ches W 127 D5
N Lanark 208 D2
S Yorks 131 A4
Hart Hill 67 A7
Hartington 129 C6
Hartland 24 C3
Hartlebury 95 D6
Hartlepool 168 B3
Hartley Cumb 155 A6
Kent 37 C5
Kent 50 C3
Northumb 179 B5
Hartley Westpall 47 D4
Hartley Wintney 47 D5
Hartlip 51 C5
Hartoft End 159 B6
Harton N Yorks 149 A6
Shrops 94 C2
T&W 179 C5
Hartpury 62 A3
Hartshead 139 A4
Hartshill 97 B6
Hartshorne 113 C7
Hartsop 164 D2
Hart Station 168 B2
Hartwell 83 B4
Hartwood 194 A3
Harvieston 206 B3
Harvington 80 C3
Harvington Cross 80 C3
Harwell 46 A2
Harwich 88 D3
Harwood Durham 165 B6
Gtr Man 137 B6
Harwood Dale 160 B3
Harworth 140 D4
Hasbury 96 C2
Hascombe 34 B2
Haselbech 99 D4
Haselbury Plucknett 29 D4
Haseley 81 A5
Haselor 80 B4
Hasfield 63 A4
Hasguard 55 D4
Haskayne 136 C2
Hasketon 88 B3
Hasland 130 C3
Haslemere 34 C2
Haslingden 137 A6
Haslingfield 85 B6
Haslington 128 D2
Hassall 128 D2
Hassall Green 128 D2
Hassell Street 38 A2
Hassendean 186 A4
Hassingham 105 A4
Hassocks 21 A5
Hassop 130 B2
Hastigrow 281 B4
Hastingleigh 38 A2
Hastings 23 B6
Hastingwood 69 C4
Hastoe 67 C5
Haswell 167 A6
Haswell Plough 167 A6
Hatch C Beds 84 C3
Hants 47 D4
Wilts 30 C3
Hatch Beauchamp 28 C3
Hatch End 67 D7
Hatchet Gate 18 A2
Hatch Green 28 D3
Hatching Green 67 B7
Hatchmere 127 B5
Hatcliffe 143 C4
Hatfield Hereford 78 B3
Herts 68 C2
S Yorks 141 C4
Worcs 80 B1
Hatfield Broad Oak 69 B5
Hatfield Garden Village 68 C2
Hatfield Heath 69 B5
Hatfield Hyde 68 B2
Hatfield Peverel 70 B1
Hatfield Woodhouse 141 C4
Hatford 64 D4
Hatherden 46 D1
Hatherleigh 11 A6
Hathern 114 C2
Hatherop 64 C2
Hathersage 130 A2
Hathershaw 138 C2
Hatherton Ches E 111 A5
Staffs 112 D3
Hatley St George 85 B4
Hatt 6 A2
Hattingley 33 B5
Hatton Aberds 257 C5
Derbys 113 C6
Lincs 134 B1
Shrops 94 B2
Warks 81 A5
Warr 127 A5
Hatton Castle 256 B2
Hattoncrook 256 D3
Hatton Heath 127 C4
Hatton of Fintray 245 A5
Haugh E Ayrs 193 C4
Gtr Man 138 B2
Lincs 135 B4
Haugham 134 A3
Haugh Head 188 A3
Haughley 87 A6
Haughley Green 87 A6
Haugh of Glass 255 C5
Haugh of Urr 173 B6
Haughs of Clinterty 245 A5
Haughton Notts 132 B1
Shrops 95 A5,
Shrops 95 B4
Shrops 110 C2
Shrops 111 D4
Staffs 112 C2
Haughton Castle 177 B7
Haughton Grn. 138 D2
Haughton Moss 127 D5
Haultwick 68 A3
Haunn Argyll 224 B2
W Isles 286 E3
Haunton 113 D6
Hauxley 189 C5
Hauxton 85 B6
Havant 19 A6
Haven 78 B2
Haven Bank 134 D2
Haven Side 142 A3
Havenstreet 19 B4
Havercroft 140 B1
Haverfordwest Hwlffordd 55 C5
Haverhill 86 C2
Haverigg 153 C2
Havering-atte-Bower 69 D5
Haveringland 120 C3
Haversham 83 C5
Haverthwaite 154 C2
Haverton Hill 168 C2
Hawarden Penarlâg 126 C3
Hawcoat 153 C3
Hawen 73 B6
Hawes 156 C2
Hawes' Green 104 B3
Hawes Side 144 D3
Hawford 79 A6
Hawick 186 B4
Hawkchurch 14 A3
Hawkedon 86 B3
Hawkenbury Kent 36 C3
Kent 37 B6
Hawkeridge 44 D2
Hawkerland 13 C5
Hawkesbury S Glos 43 A6
Warks 97 C6
Hawkesbury Upton 44 A1
Hawkes End 97 C6
Hawk Green 129 A4
Hawkhill 189 B5
Hawkhurst 37 C5
Hawkinge 39 B4
Hawkley 33 C6
Hawkridge 26 B3
Hawkshead 154 B2
Hawkshead Hill 154 B2
Hawksland 194 C3
Hawkswick 156 D3
Hawksworth Notts 115 A5
W Yorks 147 C5
W Yorks 147 D6
Hawkwell 70 D2
Hawley Hants 34 A1
Kent 50 B2
Hawling 63 A6
Hawnby 158 C4
Haworth 147 D4
Hawstead 87 B4
Hawthorn Durham 168 A2
Rhondda 41 C6
Wilts 44 C2
Hawthorn Hill Brack 48 B1
Lincs 134 D2
Hawthorpe 116 C3
Hawton 132 D2
Haxby 149 B5
Haxey 141 C5
Haydock 137 D4
Haydon 29 D6
Haydon Bridge 177 C6
Haydon Wick 45 A5
Haye 6 A2
Hayes London 48 A4
London 49 C7
Hayfield Derbys 129 A5
Fife 209 A5
Hay Green 118 D2
Hayhill 182 A2
Hayhillock 232 D3
Hayle 2 B3
Haynes 84 C2
Haynes Church End 84 C2
Hay-on-Wye Y Gelli Gandryll 77 C6
Hayscastle 55 B4
Hayscastle Cross 55 B5
Hayshead 233 D4
Hay Street 68 A3
Hayton Aberdeen 245 B6
Cumb 174 D4
Cumb 176 D3
E Yorks 149 C7
Notts 132 A2
Hayton's Bent 94 C3
Haytor Vale 12 D2
Haywards Heath 35 D6
Haywood 140 B3
Haywood Oaks 131 D6
Hazelbank 194 B3
Hazelbury Bryan 16 A1
Hazeley 47 D5
Hazel Grove 129 A4
Hazelhurst 138 C2
Hazelslade 112 D4
Hazel Street 37 C4
Hazelton 64 B1
Hazelton Walls 220 B3
Hazelwood 114 A1
Hazlemere 66 D4
Hazlerigg 179 B4
Hazlewood 147 B4
Hazon 189 C4
Heacham 118 B3
Headbourne Worthy 32 B3
Headbrook 77 B7
Headcorn 37 B6
Headingley 148 D1
Headington 65 C6
Headlam 167 D4
Headless Cross 80 A3
Headley Hants 33 B7
Hants 46 C3
Sur 35 A5
Head of Muir 207 B6
Headon 132 B2
Heads 194 B2
Heads Nook 176 D2
Heage 130 D3
Healaugh N Yorks 148 C3
N Yorks 156 B4
Heald Green 128 A3
Heale Devon 26 A1
Som 29 A6
Healey Gtr Man 138 B1
Northumb 178 D2
N Yorks 157 C5
Healing 143 B4
Heamoor 2 B2
Heanish 222 C3
Heanor 114 A2
Heanton Punchardon 25 B6
Heapham 132 A3
Hearthstane 195 D6
Heasley Mill 26 B2
Heast 247 C5
Heath Cardiff 41 D6
Derbys 131 C4
Heath and Reach 67 A5
Heathcote 129 C6
Heath End Hants 46 C3
Sur 34 B1
Warks 81 A5
Heather 114 D1
Heatherfield 259 D4
Heathfield Devon 12 D3
E Sus 36 D3
Som 27 C6
Heathhall 174 A2
Heath Hayes 112 D4
Heath Hill 111 D6
Heath House 28 A4
Heathrow Airport 48 B3
Heathstock 14 A2
Heathton 95 B6
Heath Town 96 B2
Heatley 128 A2
Heaton Lancs 144 A4
Staffs 129 C4
T&W 179 C4
W Yorks 147 D5
Heaton Moor 138 D1
Heaverham 36 A3
Heaviley 129 A3
Heavitree 13 B4
Hebburn 179 C5
Hebden 147 A4
Hebden Bridge 138 A2
Hebron Anglesey 123 B4
Carms 73 D4
Northumb 178 A3
Heck 184 D3
Heckfield 47 C5
Heckfield Green 104 D2

Heckfordbridge 70 A3
Heckington 116 A4
Heckmondwike 139 A5
Heddington 44 C3
Heddle 282 F4
Heddon-on-the-Wall 178 C3
Hedenham 104 B4
Hedge End 32 D3
Hedgerley 48 A2
Hedging 28 C3
Hedley on the Hill 178 D2
Hednesford 112 D3
Hedon 142 A3
Hedsor 48 A2
Hedworth 179 C5
Hegdon Hill 78 B3
Heggerscales 165 D6
Heglibister 285 H5
Heighington
Darl 167 C5
Lincs 133 C5
Heights of Brae 263 D7
Heights of Kinlochewe 262 D2
Heilam 277 B5
Heiton 197 C6
Hele Devon 13 A4
Devon 25 A6
Helensburgh 215 D5
Helford 3 C5
Helford Passage 3 C5
Helhoughton 119 C5
Helions Bumpstead 86 C2
Hellaby 140 D3
Helland 10 D1
Hellesdon 120 D4
Hellidon 82 B2
Hellifield 146 B2
Hellingly 22 A3
Hellington 104 A4
Hellister 285 J5
Helm 189 D4
Helmdon 82 C2
Helmingham 88 B2
Helmington Row 167 B4
Helmsdale 274 C4
Helmshore 137 A6
Helmsley 159 C5
Helperby 148 A3
Helperthorpe 160 D3
Helpringham 116 A4
Helpston 100 A3
Helsby 127 B4
Helsey 135 B5
Helston 3 C4
Helstone 10 C1
Helton 164 C3
Helwith Bridge 146 A2
Hemblington 121 D5
Hemel Hempstead 67 C6
Hemingbrough 149 D5
Hemingby 134 B2
Hemingford Abbots 101 D4
Hemingford Grey 101 D4
Hemingstone 88 B2
Hemington Leics 114 C2
Northants 100 C2
Som 43 D6
Hemley 88 C3
Hemlington 168 D3
Hemp Green 89 A4
Hempholme 150 B3
Hempnall 104 B3
Hempnall Green 104 B3
Hempriggs House 281 D5
Hempstead Essex 86 D2
Medway 51 C4
Norf 120 B3
Norf 121 C6
Hempsted 63 B4
Hempton Norf 119 C6
Oxon 82 D1
Hemsby 121 D6
Hemswell 142 D1

Hemswell Cliff 133 A4
Hemsworth 140 B2
Hemyock 27 D6
Henbury Bristol 43 B4
Ches E 128 B3
Hendon London 49 A5
T&W 179 D6
Hendre 126 C1
Hendre-ddu 124 C3
Hendreforgan 41 C4
Hendy 57 B5
Heneglwys 123 C4
Hen-feddau fawr 73 C5
Henfield 21 A5
Henford 11 B4
Henghurst 38 B1
Hengoed Caerph 41 B6
Powys 77 B6
Shrops 110 B1
Hengrave 87 A4
Henham 69 A5
Heniarth 93 A5
Henlade 28 C2
Henley Shrops 94 D3
Som 28 B4
Suff 88 B2
W Sus 34 D1
Henley-in-Arden 81 A4
Henley-on-Thames 47 A5
Henley's Down 23 A5
Henllan Ceredig 73 B6
Denb 125 C5
Henllan Amgoed 73 D4
Henllys 61 D4
Henlow 84 D3
Hennock 12 C3
Henny Street 87 D4
Henryd 124 B2
Henry's Moat 55 B6
Hensall 140 A3
Henshaw 177 C5
Hensingham 162 C2
Henstead 105 C5
Henstridge 30 D1
Henstridge Ash 29 C7
Henstridge Marsh 30 C1
Henton Oxon 66 C3
Som 29 A4
Henwood 10 D3
Heogan 285 J6
Heol-las 40 B1
Heol Senni 59 C6
Heol-y-Cyw 40 C4
Hepburn 188 A3
Hepple 188 C2
Hepscott 179 A4
Heptonstall 138 A2
Hepworth Suff 103 D5
W Yorks 139 C4
Herbrandston 55 D4
Hereford 78 C3
Heriot 196 A2
Hermiston 209 C4
Hermitage
Borders 186 D4
Dorset 15 A6
W Berks 46 B3
W Sus 19 A6
Hermon Anglesey 122 D3
Carms 58 C3
Carms 73 C6
Pembs 73 C5
Herne 52 C3
Herne Bay 52 C3
Herner 25 C6
Hernhill 52 C2
Herodsfoot 5 A7
Herongate 69 D6
Heronsford 180 C3
Herriard 33 A5
Herringfleet 105 B5
Herringswell 102 D3
Hersden 53 C4
Hersham Corn 10 A3
Sur 48 C4
Herstmonceux 22 A4
Herston 283 H5
Hertford 68 B3
Hertford Heath 68 B3
Hertingfordbury 68 B3

Hesketh Bank 136 A3
Hesketh Lane 145 C6
Hesket Newmarket 163 A6
Heskin Green 136 B4
Hesleden 168 B2
Hesleyside 177 A6
Heslington 149 B5
Hessay 148 B4
Hessenford 6 B2
Hessett 87 A5
Hessle 142 A2
Hest Bank 145 A4
Heston 48 B4
Hestwall 282 F3
Heswall 126 A2
Hethe 65 A6
Hethersett 104 A2
Hethersgill 176 C2
Hethpool 188 A1
Hett 167 B5
Hetton 146 B3
Hetton-le-Hole 167 A6
Hetton Steads 198 C4
Heugh 178 B2
Heugh-head 243 A6
Heveningham 104 D4
Hever 36 B2
Heversham 154 C3
Hevingham 120 C3
Hewas Water 5 C4
Hewelsfield 62 C1
Hewish N Som 42 C3
Som 14 A4
Heworth 149 B5
Hexham 178 C1
Hextable 50 B2
Hexton 84 D3
Hexworthy 12 D1
Hey 146 C2
Heybridge Essex 69 D6
Essex 70 C2
Heybridge Basin 70 C2
Heybrook Bay 7 C4
Heydon Cambs 85 C6
Norf 120 C3
Heydour 116 B3
Heylipol 222 C2
Heylor 284 E4
Heysham 144 A4
Heyshott 20 A1
Heyside 138 C2
Heytesbury 30 A3
Heythrop 64 A4
Heywood
Gtr Man 138 B1
Wilts 44 D2
Hibaldstow 142 C1
Hickleton 140 C2
Hickling Norf 121 C6
Notts 115 C4
Hickling Green 121 C6
Hickling Heath 121 C6
Hickstead 35 D5
Hidcote Boyce 81 C4
High Ackworth 140 B2
Higham Derbys 130 D3
Kent 51 B4
Lancs 146 D2
Suff 86 A3
Suff 87 D6
Higham Dykes 178 B3
Higham Ferrers 83 A6
Higham Gobion 84 D3
Higham on the Hill 97 B6
Highampton 11 A5
Higham Wood 36 B3
High Angerton 178 A2
High Bankhill 164 A3
High Barnes 179 D5
High Beach 68 D4
High Bentham 145 A6
High Bickington 25 C7
High Birkwith 155 D6
High Blantyre 194 A1
High Bonnybridge 207 C6
High Bradfield 139 D5
High Bray 26 B1
Highbridge
Highld 239 D5

Highbridge
Som 28 A3
Highbrook 35 C6
High Brooms 36 B3
High Bullen 25 C6
Highburton 139 B4
Highbury 29 A6
High Buston 189 C5
High Callerton 178 B3
High Catton 149 B6
Highclere 46 C2
Highcliffe 17 B6
High Cogges 65 C4
High Coniscliffe 167 D5
High Cross Hants 33 C6
Herts 68 B3
High Easter 69 B6
High Eggborough 140 A3
High Ellington 157 C5
Higher Ansty 16 A1
Higher Ashton 12 C3
Higher Ballam 144 D3
Higher Bartle 145 D5
Higher Boscaswell 2 B1
Higher Burwardsley 127 D5
High Ercall 111 D4
Higher Clovelly 24 C4
Higher End 136 C4
Higher Kinnerton 126 C3
Higher Penwortham 136 A4
Higher Town
Scilly P02 E4
Higher Walreddon 11 D5
Higher Walton
Lancs 137 A4
Warr 127 A5
Higher Wheelton 137 A5
Higher Whitley 127 A6
Higher Wincham 128 B1
Higher Wych 110 A3
High Etherley 167 C4
Highfield E Yorks 149 D6
Gtr Man 137 C6
N Ayrs 204 C3
Oxon 65 A6
S Yorks 130 A3
T&W 178 D3
Highfields Cambs 85 B5
Northumb 198 A3
High Garrett 70 A1
Highgate 49 A5
High Grange 167 B4
High Green Norf 104 A2
S Yorks 139 D6
Worcs 80 C1
High Halden 37 C6
High Halstow 51 B4
High Ham 28 B4
High Harrington 162 B3
High Hatton 111 C5
High Hawsker 160 A3
High Hesket 164 A2
High Hesleden 168 B2
High Hoyland 139 B5
High Hunsley 150 D2
High Hurstwood 36 D2
High Hutton 149 A6
High Ireby 163 A5
High Kelling 120 A3
High Kilburn 158 D4
High Lands 166 C4
Highlane Ches E 128 C3
Derbys 131 A4
High Lane
Gtr Man 129 A4
Worcs 79 A4
High Laver 69 C5
Highlaws 174 D4
Highleadon 62 A3
High Legh 128 A2
Highleigh 20 C1
High Leven 168 D2
Highley 95 C5
High Littleton 43 D5
High Lorton 163 B4

High Marishes 159 D7
High Marnham 132 B3
High Melton 140 C3
High Mickley 178 C2
High Mindork 171 B5
Highmoor Cross 47 A5
Highmoor Hill 42 A3
Highnam 62 B3
Highnam Green 62 A3
High Newton 154 C3
High Newton-by-the-Sea 189 A5
High Nibthwaite 154 C1
High Offley 112 C1
High Ongar 69 C5
High Onn 112 D2
High Roding 69 B6
High Row 163 A6
High Salvington 21 B4
High Sellafield 162 D3
High Shaw 156 B2
High Spen 178 D3
Highsted 51 C6
High Stoop 166 A4
High Street Corn 5 B4
Kent 37 C5
Suff 87 C4
Suff 89 B5
Suff 105 D5
Highstreet Green 86 D3
High Street Green 87 B6
Hightae 174 A3
High Throston 168 B2
Hightown Ches E 128 C3
Mers 136 C2
Hightown Green 87 B5
High Toynton 134 C2
High Trewhitt 188 C3
High Valleyfield 208 B3
Highway 44 B4
Highweek 12 D3
High Westwood 178 D3
Highworth 64 D3
High Wray 154 B2
High Wych 69 B4
High Wycombe 66 D4
Hilborough 103 A4
Hilcote 131 D4
Hilcott 45 D5
Hildenborough 36 B3
Hilden Park 36 B3
Hildersham 86 C1
Hilderstone 112 B3
Hilderthorpe 151 A4
Hilfield 15 A6
Hilgay 102 B2
Hill Pembs 55 D7
S Glos 62 D2
W Mid 96 B4
Hillam 140 A3
Hillbeck 165 D5
Hillborough 53 C4
Hillbrae Aberds 255 B7
Aberds 256 D2
Hill Brow 33 C6
Hillbutts 16 A3
Hillcliffiane 113 A6
Hillcommon 27 C6
Hill Dale 136 B3
Hill Dyke 117 A6
Hillend 208 B4
Hill End Durham 166 B3
Fife 208 A3
N Yorks 147 B4
Hillerton 12 B2
Hillesden 66 A2
Hillesley 43 A6
Hillfarance 27 C6
Hillhead Aberds 255 C6
Devon 8 B3
S Ayrs 182 A2
Hill Head Hants 18 A4
Northumb 178 C1
Hillhead of Auchentumb 269 D4
Hillhead of Cocklaw 257 B5
Hillhouse 197 A4
Hilliclay 280 B3
Hillingdon 48 A3

Hillington
Glasgow 205 B5
Norf 119 C4
Hillmorton 98 D2
Hill Mountain 55 D5
Hillockhead
Aberds 243 B6
Aberds 244 A1
Hill of Beath 209 A4
Hill of Fearn 265 C4
Hill of Mountblairy 268 D1
Hill Ridware 113 D4
Hillside Aberds 245 C6
Angus 233 B5
Mers 136 B2
Orkney 283 H5
Shetland 285 G6
Hillswick 284 F4
Hill Top Durham 166 C2
Hants 18 A3
W Mid 96 B2
W Yorks 139 B6
Hill View 16 B3
Hillway 19 C5
Hillwell 285 M5
Hilmarton 44 B4
Hilperton 44 D2
Hilsea 19 A5
Hilston 151 D5
Hilton Aberds 257 C4
Cambs 85 A4
Cumb 165 C5
Derbys 113 B6
Dorset 16 A1
Durham 167 C4
Highld 264 B3
Shrops 95 B5
Stockton 168 D2
Hilton of Cadboll 265 C4
Himbleton 80 B2
Himley 96 B1
Hincaster 154 C4
Hinckley 98 B1
Hinderclay 103 D6
Hinderton 126 B3
Hinderwell 169 D5
Hindford 110 B2
Hindhead 34 C1
Hindley 137 C5
Hindley Green 137 C5
Hindlip 80 B1
Hindolveston 120 C2
Hindon 30 B3
Hindringham 120 B1
Hingham 103 A6
Hinstock 111 C5
Hintlesham 88 C1
Hinton Hants 17 B6
Hereford 78 D1
Northants 82 B2
S Glos 43 B6
Shrops 94 A2
Hinton Ampner 33 C4
Hinton Blewett 43 D4
Hinton Charterhouse 43 D6
Hinton-in-the-Hedges 82 D2
Hinton Martell 17 A4
Hinton on the Green 80 C3
Hinton Parva 45 A6
Hinton St George 28 D4
Hinton St Mary 30 D1
Hinton Waldrist 65 D4
Hints Shrops 95 D4
Staffs 97 A4
Hinwick 83 A6
Hinxhill 38 A2
Hinxton 85 C6
Hinxworth 84 C4
Hipperholme 139 A4
Hipswell 157 B5
Hirael 123 C5
Hiraeth 73 D4
Hirn 245 B4
Hirnant 109 C5

Hirst N Lanark 207 D6
Northumb 179 A4
Hirst Courtney 140 A4
Hirwaen 125 C6
Hirwaun 59 E6
Hiscott 25 C6
Histon 85 A6
Hitcham 87 B5
Hitchin 68 A1
Hither Green 49 B6
Hittisleigh 12 B2
Hive 149 D7
Hixon 112 C4
Hoaden 53 D4
Hoaldalbert 61 A5
Hoar Cross 113 C5
Hoarwithy 62 A1
Hoath 53 C4
Hobarris 93 D7
Hobbister 283 G4
Hobkirk 187 B4
Hobson 178 D3
Hoby 115 D4
Hockering 120 D2
Hockerton 132 D2
Hockley 70 D2
Hockley Heath 97 D4
Hockliffe 67 A5
Hockwold cum Wilton 102 C3
Hockworthy 27 D5
Hoddesdon 68 C3
Hoddlesden 137 A6
Hoddomcross 175 A4
Hoddom Mains 175 A4
Hodgeston 55 E6
Hodley 93 B5
Hodnet 111 C5
Hodthorpe 131 B5
Hoe Hants 33 D4
Norf 120 D1
Hoe Gate 33 D5
Hoff 165 D4
Hoggard's Green 87 B4
Hoggeston 66 A4
Hogha Gearraidh 287 G2
Hoghton 137 A5
Hognaston 130 D2
Hog Patch 34 B1
Hogsthorpe 135 B5
Holbeach 117 C6
Holbeach Bank 117 C6
Holbeach Clough 117 C6
Holbeach Drove 117 D6
Holbeach Hurn 117 C6
Holbeach St Johns 117 D6
Holbeach St Marks 117 B6
Holbeach St Matthew 117 B7
Holbeck Notts 131 B5
W Yorks 148 D1
Holbeck Woodhouse 131 B5
Holberrow Green 80 B3
Holbeton 7 B5
Holborn 49 A6
Holbrook Derbys 114 A1
Suff 88 D2
S Yorks 131 A4
Holburn 198 C4
Holbury 18 A3
Holcombe Devon 13 D4
Som 29 A6
Holcombe Rogus 27 D5
Holcot 83 A4
Holden 146 C1
Holdenby 82 A3
Holdenhurst 17 B5
Holdgate 94 C3
Holdingham 116 A3
Holditch 14 A3
Holefield 198 C2
Holehouses 128 B2
Hole-in-the-Wall 62 A2
Holemoor 11 A5
Holestane 183 C6
Holford 27 A6
Holgate 149 B4
Holker 154 D2
Holkham 119 A5
Hollacombe 11 A4
Holland Orkney 282 B5
Orkney 282 E7
Holland Fen 117 A5
Holland-on-Sea 71 B6
Hollandstoun 282 B8
Hollee 175 B5
Hollesley 89 C4
Hollicombe 8 A2
Hollingbourne 37 A6
Hollington
Derbys 113 B6
E Sus 23 A5
Staffs 113 B4
Hollington Grove 113 B6
Hollingworth 138 D3
Hollins 137 C7
Hollinsclough 129 C5
Hollins Green 137 D5
Hollins Lane 145 B4
Hollinwood
Gtr Man 138 C2
Shrops 111 B4
Hollocombe 26 D1
Holloway 130 D3
Hollowell 98 D3
Hollow Meadows 130 A2
Hollybush Caerph 41 A6
E Ayrs 182 A1
Worcs 79 D5
Holly End 101 A6
Holly Grn. 79 C6
Hollym 143 A5
Hollywood 96 D3
Holmbridge 139 C4
Holmbury St Mary 35 B4
Holmbush 5 B5
Holmcroft 112 C3
Holme Cambs 100 C3
Cumb 154 D4
Notts 132 D3
N Yorks 158 C2
W Yorks 139 C4
Holme Chapel 138 A1
Holme Green 149 C4
Holme Hale 103 A4
Holme Lacy 78 D3
Holme Marsh 78 B1
Holme next the Sea 119 A4
Holme-on-Spalding-Moor 149 D7
Holme on the Wolds 150 C2
Holme Pierrepont 115 B4
Holmer 78 C3
Holmer Green 67 D5
Holme St Cuthbert 174 D4
Holmes Chapel 128 C2
Holmesfield 130 B3
Holmeswood 136 B3
Holmewood 131 C4
Holme Wood 147 D5
Holmfirth 139 C4
Holmhead
Dumfries 183 D5
E Ayrs 193 C5
Holmisdale 258 D1
Holmpton 143 A5
Holmrook 153 A1
Holmsgarth 285 J6
Holmwrangle 164 A3
Holne 7 A6
Holnest 15 A6
Holsworthy 10 A4
Holsworthy Beacon 11 A4
Holt Dorset 17 A4
Norf 120 B2
Wilts 44 C2
Worcs 79 A6
Holt
Wrex 127 D4
Holtby 149 B5
Holt End Hants 33 B5
Worcs 80 A3
Holt Fleet 79 A6
Holt Heath 79 A6
Holton Oxon 65 C7
Som 29 C6
Suff 105 D4
Holton cum Beckering 133 A6
Holton Heath 16 B3
Holton le Clay 143 C4
Holton le Moor 142 D2
Holton St Mary 87 D6
Holt Park 147 C6
Holwell Dorset 29 D7
Herts 84 D3
Leics 115 C5
Oxon 64 C3
Holwick 166 C2
Holworth 16 C1
Holybourne 33 A6
Holy Cross 96 D2
Holyhead
Caergybi 122 B2
Holy Island 199 B5
Holymoorside 130 C3
Holyport 48 B1
Holystone 188 C2
Holytown 207 D5
Holywell Cambs 101 D5
Corn 4 B2
Dorset 15 A5
E Sus 22 C3
Northumb 179 B5
Holywell
Treffynnon 126 B1
Holywell Green 138 B3
Holywell Lake 27 C6
Holywell Row 102 D3
Holywood 184 D2
Homer 95 A4
Homersfield 104 C3
Hom Green 62 A1
Homington 31 C5
Honeyborough 55 D5
Honeybourne 80 C4
Honeychurch 12 A1
Honey Hill 52 C3
Honey Street 45 C5
Honey Tye 87 D5
Honiley 97 D5
Honing 121 C5
Honingham 120 D3
Honington Lincs 116 A2
Suff 103 D5
Warks 81 C5
Honiton 13 A6
Honley 139 B4
Hood Green 139 C6
Hooe E Sus 23 B4
Plym 7 B4
Hooe Common 23 A4
Hoo Green 128 A2
Hook E Yorks 141 A5
Hants 47 D5
London 49 C4
Pembs 55 C5
Wilts 45 A4
Hooke 15 B5
Hookgate 111 B6
Hook Green Kent 37 C4
Kent 50 C3
Hook Norton 81 D6
Hookway 12 B3
Hookwood 35 B5
Hoole 127 C4
Hooley 35 A5
Hoop 61 C7
Hoo St.Werburgh 51 B4
Hooton 126 B3
Hooton Levitt 140 D3
Hooton Pagnell 140 C2
Hooton Roberts 140 D2
Hope Derbys 129 A6
Devon 7 D5
Highld 277 C5
Powys 93 A6
Shrops 94 A1
Staffs 129 D6
Hope Yr Hôb 126 D3
Hope Bagot 94 D3
Hope Bowdler 94 B2
Hope End Green 69 A5
Hope Green 129 A4
Hopeman 266 C2
Hope Mansell 62 B2
Hopesay 94 C1
Hope's Grn. 51 A4
Hope under Dinmore 78 B3
Hopley's Green 78 B1
Hopperton 148 B3
Hop Pole 117 D4
Hopstone 95 B5
Hopton Shrops 110 C2
Shrops 111 C4
Staffs 112 C3
Suff 103 D5
Hopton Cangeford 94 C3
Hopton Castle 94 D1
Hoptonheath 94 D1
Hopton on Sea 105 A6
Hopton Wafers 95 D4
Hopwas 97 A4
Hopwood
Gtr Man 138 C1
Worcs 96 D3
Horam 22 A3
Horbling 116 B4
Horbury 139 B5
Horcott 64 C2
Horden 168 A2
Horderley 94 C2
Hordle 17 B6
Hordley 110 B2
Horeb Carms 57 B4
Carms 58 C2
Ceredig 73 B6
Horfield 43 B5
Horham 104 D3
Horkesley Heath 70 A3
Horkstow 142 B1
Horley Oxon 81 C7
Sur 35 B5
Hornblotton Green 29 B5
Hornby Lancs 145 A5
N Yorks 157 B6
N Yorks 158 A2
Horncastle 134 C2
Hornchurch 50 A2
Horncliffe 198 B3
Horndean
Borders 198 B2
Hants 33 D6
Horndon 11 D6
Horndon on the Hill 50 A3
Horne 35 B6
Horniehaugh 232 B2
Horning 121 D5
Horninghold 99 B5
Horninglow 113 C6
Horningsea 85 A6
Horningsham 30 A2
Horningtoft 119 C6
Hornsby 176 D3
Horns Corner 37 D5
Horns Cross
Devon 25 C4
E Sus 37 D6
Hornsea 151 C5
Hornsea Bridge 151 C5
Hornsey 49 A6
Hornton 81 C6
Horrabridge 7 A4
Horringer 87 A4
Horringford 18 C4
Horsebridge
Devon 11 D5
Hants 32 B2
Horse Bridge 129 D4
Horsebrook 112 D2
Horsehay 95 A4
Horseheath 86 C2
Horsehouse 156 C4
Horsell 34 A2
Horseman's Green 110 A3
Horseway 101 C6
Horsey 121 C6
Horsford 120 D3
Horsforth 147 D6
Horsham Worcs 79 B5
W Sus 35 C4
Horsham St Faith 120 D4
Horsington Lincs 134 C1
Som 29 C7
Horsley Derbys 114 A1
Glos 63 D4
Northumb 178 C2
Northumb 188 D1
Horsley Cross 71 A5
Horsleycross Street 71 A5
Horsleyhill 186 B4
Horsleyhope 166 A3
Horsley Woodhouse 114 A1
Horsmonden 37 B4
Horspath 65 C6
Horstead 121 D4
Horsted Keynes 36 D1
Horton Bucks 67 B5
Dorset 17 A4
Lancs 146 B2
Northants 83 B5
S Glos 43 A6
Shrops 110 C3
Som 28 D3
Staffs 129 D4
Swansea 57 D4
Wilts 45 C4
Windsor 48 B3
Horton-cum-Studley 65 B6
Horton Green 110 A3
Horton Heath 32 D3
Horton in Ribblesdale 155 D7
Horton Kirby 50 C2
Hortonlane 110 D3
Horwich 137 B5
Horwich End 129 A5
Horwood 25 C6
Hose 115 C5
Hoselaw 198 C2
Hoses 153 A3
Hosh 218 B3
Hosta 287 G2
Hoswick 285 L6
Hotham 150 D1
Hothfield 38 A1
Hoton 114 C3
Houbie 284 D8
Houdston 181 B3
Hough Ches E 128 B3
Ches E 128 D2
Hougham 116 A1
Hough Green 127 A4
Hough-on-the-Hill 116 A2
Houghton Cambs 101 D4
Cumb 175 C7
Hants 32 B2
Pembs 55 D5
W Sus 20 A3
Houghton Conquest 84 C2
Houghton Green
E Sus 37 D7
Warr 137 D5
Houghton-le-Side 167 C5
Houghton-Le-Spring 167 A6
Houghton on the Hill 98 A3
Houghton Regis 67 A6
Houghton St Giles 119 B6
Houlland
Shetland 284 F7
Shetland 285 H5
Houlsyke 159 A6
Hound 18 A3
Hound Green 47 D5
Houndslow 197 B5
Houndwood 211 D5
Hounslow 48 B4
Hounslow Green 69 B6
Housay 284 F8
House of Daviot 252 B3
House of Glenmuick 243 C6
Housetter 284 E5
Houss 285 K5
Houston 205 B4
Houstry 275 A5
Houton 283 G4
Hove 21 B5
Hoveringham 115 A4
Hoveton 121 D5
Hovingham 159 D5
How 176 D3
Howbrook 139 D6
How Caple 79 D4
Howden Borders 187 A5
E Yorks 141 A5
Howden-le-Wear 167 B4
Howe Highld 281 B5
Norf 104 A3
N Yorks 158 C2
Howe Bridge 137 C5
Howe Green 70 C1
Howell 116 A4
How End 84 C2
Howe of Teuchar 256 B2
Howe Street
Essex 69 B6
Essex 86 D2
Howey 77 B4
Howgate 196 A1
How Green 36 B2
Howick 189 B5
Howle Durham 166 C3
Telford 111 C5
Howlett End 86 D1
Howley 14 A2
Hownam 187 B6
Hownam Mains 187 A6
Howpasley 185 B6
Howsham
N Lincs 142 C2
N Yorks 149 A6
Howslack 184 B3
Howtel 198 C2
Howton 61 A6
Howtown 164 D2
Howwood 204 B3
Hoxne 104 D2
Hoy 283 G3
Hoylake 126 A2
Hoyland 139 C6
Hoylandswaine 139 C5
Hubberholme 156 D3
Hubbert's Bridge 117 A5
Huby N Yorks 147 C6
N Yorks 149 A4
Hucclecote 63 B4
Hucking 37 A6
Hucknall 114 A3
Huddersfield 139 B4
Huddington 80 B2
Hudswell 157 A5
Huggate 150 B1
Hugglescote 114 D2
Hughenden Valley 66 D4
Hughley 94 B3
Hugh Town Scilly 2 E4
Huish Devon 25 D6
Wilts 45 C5
Huish Champflower 27 C5
Huish Episcopi 28 C4
Huisinis 287 C4
Hulcott 66 B4
Hulland 113 A6
Hulland Ward 113 A6
Hullavington 44 A2
Hullbridge 70 D2
Hulme 138 D1
Hulme End 129 D6
Hulme Walfield 128 C3
Hulverstone 18 C2
Hulver Street 105 C5
Humber 78 B3
Humber Bridge 142 A2
Humberston 143 C5

Humbie 210 D1
Humbleton
E Yorks 151 D5
Northumb 188 A2
Humby 116 B3
Hume 197 B6
Humshaugh 177 B7
Huna 281 A5
Huncoat 146 D1
Huncote 98 B2
Hundalee 187 B5
Hunderthwaite 166 C2
Hundleby 134 C3
Hundle Houses 134 D2
Hundleton 55 D5
Hundon 86 C3
Hundred Acres 33 D4
Hundred End 136 A3
Hundred House 77 B5
Hungarton 98 A3
Hungerford Hants 31 D5
W Berks 46 C1
Hungerford Newtown 46 B1
Hungerton 116 C1
Hungladder 258 A3
Hunmanby 161 D4
Hunmanby Moor 161 D5
Hunningham 81 A6
Hunny Hill 18 C3
Hunsdon 68 B4
Hunsingore 148 B3
Hunslet 148 D2
Hunsonby 164 B3
Hunspow 280 A4
Hunstanton 118 A3
Hunstanworth 166 A2
Hunsterson 111 A5
Hunston Suff 87 A5
W Sus 20 B1
Hunstrete 43 C5
Hunt End 80 A3
Hunter's Quay 203 A6
Hunthill Lodge 232 A2
Huntingdon 100 D4
Huntingfield 104 D4
Huntingford 30 B2
Huntington
E Loth 210 C1
Hereford 77 B6
Staffs 112 D3
York 149 B5
Hunting-tower 219 B5
Huntley 62 B3
Huntly 255 C6
Huntlywood 197 B5
Hunton Kent 37 B5
N Yorks 157 B5
Hunt's Corner 103 C6
Hunt's Cross 127 A4
Huntsham 27 C5
Huntspill 28 A3
Huntworth 28 B3
Hunwick 167 B4
Hunworth 120 B2
Hurdsfield 129 B4
Hurley Warks 97 B5
Windsor 47 A6
Hurlford 193 B4
Hurliness 283 J3
Hurn 17 B5
Hurn's End 118 A1
Hursley 32 C3
Hurst N Yorks 156 A4
Som 29 D4
Wokingham 47 B5
Hurstbourne Priors 32 A3
Hurstbourne Tarrant 46 D1
Hurst Green E Sus 37 D5
Lancs 145 D6
Hurstpierpoint 21 A5
Hurst Wickham 21 A5
Hurstwood 146 D2
Hurtmore 34 B2
Hurworth Place 157 A6
Hury 166 D2
Husabost 258 C2
Husbands Bosworth 98 C3
Husborne Crawley 83 D6
Husthwaite 158 D4
Hutchwns 40 D3
Huthwaite 131 D4
Huttoft 135 B5
Hutton Borders 198 A3
Cumb 164 C2
Essex 69 D6
E Yorks 150 B3
Lancs 136 A3
N Som 42 D2
Hutton Buscel 160 C3
Hutton Conyers 158 D2
Hutton Cranswick 150 B3
Hutton End 164 B2
Hutton Gate 168 D3
Hutton Henry 168 B2
Hutton-le-Hole 159 B6
Hutton Magna 166 D4
Hutton Roof
Cumb 155 D4
Cumb 163 A6
Hutton Rudby 158 A3
Hutton Sessay 158 D3
Hutton Village 168 D3
Hutton Wandesley 148 B4
Huxley 127 C5
Huxter Shetland 285 G7
Shetland 285 H5
Huxton 211 D5
Huyton 136 D3
Hycemoor 153 B1
Hyde Glos 63 C4
Gtr Man 138 D2
Hants 31 D5
Hyde Heath 67 C5
Hyde Park 140 C3
Hydestile 34 B2
Hylton Castle 179 D5
Hyndford Bridge 194 B4
Hynish 222 D2
Hyssington 93 B7
Hythe Hants 18 A3
Kent 38 B3
Hythe End 48 B3
Hythie 269 D5

I

Ibberton 16 A1
Ible 130 D2
Ibsley 17 A5
Ibstock 114 D2
Ibstone 66 D3
Ibthorpe 46 D1
Ibworth 46 D3
Ichrachan 227 C5
Ickburgh 103 B4
Ickenham 48 A3
Ickford 66 C2
Ickham 53 D4
Ickleford 84 D3
Icklesham 23 A6
Ickleton 85 C6
Icklingham 102 D3
Ickwell Green 84 C3
Icomb 64 A3
Idbury 64 B3
Iddesleigh 11 A6
Ide 12 B3
Ideford 12 D3
Ide Hill 36 A2
Iden 37 D7
Iden Green Kent 37 C5
Kent 37 C6
Idle 147 D5
Idlicote 81 C5
Idmiston 31 B5
Idole 57 A4
Idridgehay 113 A6
Idrigill 258 B3
Idstone 45 A6
Idvies 232 D3
Iffley 65 C6
Ifield 35 C5
Ifold 34 C3
Iford 22 B2
Ifton Heath 110 B2
Ightfield 111 B4
Ightham 36 A3
Iken 89 B5
Ilam 129 D6
Ilchester 29 C5
Ilderton 188 A3
Ilford 50 A1
Ilfracombe 25 A6
Ilkeston 114 A2
Ilketshall St Andrew 105 C4
Ilketshall St Lawrence 105 C4
Ilketshall St Margaret 104 C4
Ilkley 147 C5
Illey 96 C2
Illingworth 138 A3
Illogan 3 A4
Illston on the Hill 99 B4
Ilmer 66 C3
Ilmington 81 C5
Ilminster 28 D3
Ilsington 12 D2
Ilston 57 C5
Ilton N Yorks 157 D5
Som 28 D3
Imachar 202 D3
Imeraval 200 D3
Immingham 142 B3
Impington 85 A6
Ince 127 B4
Ince Blundell 136 C2
Ince in Makerfield 137 C4
Inchbare 233 B4
Inchberry 266 D4
Inchbraoch 233 C5
Incheril 262 D2
Inchgrundle 232 A2
Inchina 261 A6
Inchinnan 205 B4
Inchkinloch 277 D6
Inchlaggan 239 B5
Inchlumpie 264 C1
Inchmore 251 B5
Inchnacardoch Hotel 240 A1
Inchnadamph 271 B5
Inch of Arnhall 233 A4
Inchree 237 C4
Inchture 220 B2
Inchyra 219 B6
Indian Queens 4 B4
Inerval 200 D3
Ingatestone 69 D6
Ingbirchworth 139 C5
Ingestre 112 C3
Ingham Lincs 133 A4
Norf 121 C5
Suff 103 D4
Ingham Corner 121 C5
Ingleborough 118 D1
Ingleby Derbys 114 C1
Lincs 132 B3
Ingleby Arncliffe 158 A3
Ingleby Barwick 168 D2
Ingleby Greenhow 159 A4
Inglemire 150 D3
Inglesbatch 43 C6
Inglesham 64 D3
Ingleton Durham 167 C4
N Yorks 155 D5
Inglewhite 145 C5
Ingliston 208 C4
Ingoe 178 B2
Ingol 145 D5
Ingoldisthorpe 118 B3
Ingoldmells 135 C5
Ingoldsby 116 B3
Ingon 81 B5
Ingram 188 B3
Ingrow 147 D4
Ings 154 B3
Ingst 43 A4
Ingworth 120 C3
Inham's End 101 B4
Inkberrow 80 B3
Inkpen 46 C1
Inkstack 281 A4
Inn 154 A3
Innellan 203 A6
Innerleithen 196 C2
Innerleven 220 D3
Innermessan 170 A2
Innerwick E Loth 211 C4
Perth 229 D4
Innis Chonain 227 D6
Insch 256 D1
Insh 241 B6
Inshore 276 B4
Inskip 145 D4
Instoneville 140 B3
Instow 25 B5
Intake 140 C3
Inver Aberds 243 C5
Highld 265 B4
Perth 230 D4
Inverailort 235 B6
Inveraldie 220 A4
Inveralligin 249 A5
Inverallochy 269 C5
Inveran 264 A1
Inveraray 214 B3
Inverarish 248 C2
Inverarity 232 D2
Inverarnan 215 A6
Inverasdale 261 B5
Inverbeg 206 A1
Inverbervie 233 A6
Inverboyndie 268 C1
Inverbroom 262 B3
Invercassley 272 D2
Invercauld House 243 C4
Inverchaolain 203 A5
Invercharnan 227 B6
Inverchoran 251 A4
Invercreran 227 B5
Inverdruie 242 A2
Inverebrie 257 C4
Invereck 215 D4
Inverernan Ho. 243 A6
Invereshie House 241 B6
Inveresk 209 C6
Inverey 242 D3
Inverfarigaig 251 D7
Invergarry 239 B7
Invergelder 243 C5
Invergeldie 218 B2
Invergordon 264 D3
Invergowrie 220 A3
Inverguseran 247 D6
Inverhadden 229 C5
Inverharroch 255 C4
Inverherive 216 B3
Inverie 247 E6
Inverinan 214 A2
Inverinate 249 D6
Inverkeilor 233 D4
Inverkeithing 208 B4
Inverkeithny 256 B1
Inverkip 204 A2
Inverkirkaig 270 C3
Inverlael 262 B3
Inverlochlarig 216 C4
Inverlochy Argyll 227 D6
Highld 237 B5
Inverlussa 213 D4
Inver Mallie 239 D5
Invermark Lodge 244 D1
Invermoidart 235 C5
Invermoriston 240 A2
Invernaver 278 B3
Inverneill 213 D6
Inverness 252 B2
Invernettie 257 B6
Invernoaden 215 C4
Inveroran Hotel 228 D1
Inverpolly Lodge 270 C3
Inverquharity 232 C2
Inverquhomery 257 B5
Inverroy 239 D6
Inversanda 236 D3
Invershiel 238 A3
Invershin 264 A1
Inversnaid Hotel 215 B6
Inverugie 257 B6
Inveruglas 215 B6
Inveruglass 241 B6
Inverurie 256 D2
Invervar 229 D5
Inverythan 256 B2
Inwardleigh 11 B6
Inworth 70 B2
Iochdar 286 B3
Iping 34 D1
Ipplepen 8 A2
Ipsden 47 A4
Ipsley 80 A3
Ipstones 129 D5
Ipswich 88 C2
Irby 126 A2
Irby in the Marsh 135 C4
Irby upon Humber 142 C3
Irchester 83 A6
Ireby Cumb 163 A5
Lancs 155 D5
Ireland Orkney 283 G4
Shetland 285 L5
Ireland's Cross 111 A6
Ireleth 153 C3
Ireshopeburn 165 B6
Irlam 137 D6
Irnham 116 C3
Iron Acton 43 A5
Ironbridge 95 A4
Iron Cross 80 B3
Irongray 173 A7
Ironmacannie 173 A4
Ironside 268 D3
Ironville 131 D4
Irstead 121 C5
Irthington 176 C2
Irthlingborough 99 D6
Irton 160 C4
Irvine 192 B3
Isauld 279 B5
Isbister Orkney 282 E3
Orkney 282 F4
Shetland 284 D5
Shetland 285 G7
Isfield 22 A2
Isham 99 D5
Isle Abbotts 28 C3
Isle Brewers 28 C3
Isleham 102 D2
Isle of Whithorn 171 D6
Isleornsay 247 C6
Islesburgh 284 G5
Islesteps 174 A2
Isleworth 49 B4
Isley Walton 114 C2
Islibhig 287 B4
Islington 49 A6
Islip Northants 100 D1
Oxon 65 B6
Istead Rise 50 C3
Isycoed 127 D4
Itchen 32 D3
Itchen Abbas 32 B4
Itchen Stoke 33 B4
Itchingfield 35 D4
Itchington 43 A5
Itteringham 120 B3
Itton 12 B1
Itton Common 61 D6
Ivegill 164 A2
Iver 48 A3
Iver Heath 48 A3
Iveston 178 D3
Ivinghoe 67 B5
Ivinghoe Aston 67 B5
Ivington 78 B2
Ivington Green 78 B2
Ivybridge 7 B5
Ivy Chimneys 68 C4
Ivychurch 38 C2
Ivy Cross 30 C2
Ivy Hatch 36 A3
Iwade 51 C6
Iwerne Courtney or Shroton 30 D2
Iwerne Minster 30 D2
Ixworth 103 D5
Ixworth Thorpe 103 D5

J

Jack Hill 147 B6
Jack in the Green 13 B5
Jacksdale 131 D4
Jackstown 256 C2
Jacobstow 10 B2
Jacobstowe 11 A6
Jameston 55 E6
Jamestown
Dumfries 185 C6
Highld 251 A6
W Dunb 206 B1
Jarrow 179 C5
Jarvis Brook 36 D3
Jasper's Green 69 A7
Java 225 C6
Jawcraig 207 C6
Jaywick 71 B5
Jealott's Hill 47 B6
Jedburgh 187 A5
Jeffreyston 55 D6
Jellyhill 205 A6
Jemimaville 264 D3
Jersey Farm 67 C7
Jesmond 179 C4
Jevington 22 B3
Jockey End 67 B6
Johnby 164 B2
John o' Groats 281 A5
John's Cross 37 D5
Johnshaven 233 B5
Johnston 55 C5
Johnstone 205 B4
Johnstonebridge 184 C3
Johnstown Carms 57 A4
Wrex 110 A2
Joppa Edin 209 C6
S Ayrs 182 A2
Jordans 67 D5
Jordanthorpe 130 A3
Jump 140 C1
Jumpers Green 17 B5
Juniper Green 209 D4
Jurby East 152 B3
Jurby West 152 B3

K

Kaber 165 D5
Kaimend 195 B4
Kaimes 209 D5
Kalemouth 187 A6
Kames Argyll 203 A4
Argyll 213 A6
E Ayrs 194 D1
Kea 4 C3
Keadby 141 B6
Keal Cotes 134 C3
Kearsley 137 C6
Kearstwick 155 C5
Kearton 156 B3
Kearvaig 276 A3
Keasden 145 A7
Keckwick 127 A5
Keddington 134 A3
Kedington 86 C3
Kedleston 113 A7
Keelby 142 B3
Keele 112 A2
Keeley Green 84 C2
Keeston 55 C5
Keevil 44 D3
Kegworth 114 C2
Kehelland 3 A4
Keig 244 A3
Keighley 147 C4
Keil 236 D3
Keilarsbrae 208 A1
Keilhill 268 D2
Keillmore 213 D4
Keillor 231 D6
Keillour 219 B4
Keills 201 B4
Keils 201 B5

Keinton Mandeville 29 B5
Keir Mill 183 C6
Keisby 116 C3
Keiss 281 B5
Keith 267 D5
Keith Inch 257 B6
Keithock 233 B4
Kelbrook 146 C3
Kelby 116 A3
Keld Cumb 164 D3
N Yorks 156 A2
Keldholme 159 C6
Kelfield N Lincs 141 C6
N Yorks 149 D4
Kelham 132 D2
Kellan 225 B4
Kellas Angus 221 A4
Moray 266 D2
Kellaton 8 D2
Kelleth 155 A5
Kelleythorpe 150 B2
Kelling 120 A2
Kellingley 140 A3
Kellington 140 A3
Kelloe 167 B6
Kelloholm 183 A5
Kelly 11 C4
Kelly Bray 11 D4
Kelmarsh 99 D4
Kelmscot 64 D3
Kelsale 89 A4
Kelsall 127 C5
Kelsall Hill 127 C5
Kelshall 85 D5
Kelsick 175 C4
Kelso 197 C6
Kelstedge 130 C3
Kelstern 143 D4
Kelston 43 C6
Keltneyburn 229 D6
Kelton 174 A2
Kelty 208 A4
Kelvedon 70 B2
Kelvedon Hatch 69 D5
Kelvin 205 C6
Kelvinside 205 B5
Kelynack 2 B1
Kemback 220 C4
Kemberton 95 A5
Kemble 63 D5
Kemerton 80 D2
Kemeys Commander 61 C5
Kemnay 245 A4
Kempley 62 A2
Kempsey 79 C6
Kempsford 64 D2
Kemps Green 96 D4
Kempshott 47 D4
Kempston 84 C2
Kempston Hardwick 84 C2
Kempton 94 C1
Kemp Town 21 B6
Kemsing 36 A3
Kemsley 51 C6
Kenardington 38 B1
Kenchester 78 C2
Kencot 64 C3
Kendal 154 B4
Kendoon 182 D4
Kendray 139 C6
Kenfig 40 C3
Kenfig Hill 40 C3
Kenilworth 97 D5
Kenknock 217 A4
Kenley London 35 A6
Shrops 94 A3
Kenmore Highld 249 A4
Perth 230 D1
Kenn Devon 13 C4
N Som 42 C3
Kennacley 288 H2
Kennacraig 202 B3
Kennerleigh 12 A3
Kennet 208 A2
Kennethmont 255 D6
Kennett 86 A2
Kennford 13 C4
Kenninghall 103 C6
Kenninghall Heath 103 C6
Kennington Kent 38 A2
Oxon 65 C6
Kennoway 220 D3
Kenny Hill 102 D2
Kennythorpe 149 A6
Kenovay 222 C2
Kensaleyre 259 C4
Kensington 49 B5
Kensworth 67 B6
Kensworth Common 67 B6
Kentallen 237 D4
Kentchurch 61 A6
Kentford 86 A3
Kentisbeare 13 A5
Kentisbury 25 A7
Kentisbury Ford 25 A7
Kentmere 154 A3
Kenton Devon 13 C4
Suff 88 A2
T&W 179 C4
Kenton Bankfoot 179 C4
Kentra 235 D5
Kents Bank 154 D2
Kent's Green 62 A3
Kent's Oak 32 C2
Kent Street E Sus 23 A5
Kent 37 A4
W Sus 35 D5
Kenwick 110 B3
Kenwyn 4 C3
Keoldale 277 B4
Keppanach 237 C4
Keppoch 249 D6
Keprigan 190 D2
Kepwick 158 B3
Kerchesters 197 C6
Keresley 97 C6
Kernborough 8 C1
Kerne Bridge 62 B1
Kerris 2 C2
Kerry 93 C5
Kerrycroy 203 B6
Kerrysdale 261 C5
Kerry's Gate 78 D1
Kersall 132 C2
Kersey 87 C6
Kershopefoot 176 A2
Kersoe 80 D2
Kerswell 13 A5
Kerswell Grn. 79 C6
Kesgrave 88 C3
Kessingland 105 C6
Kessingland Beach 105 C6
Kessington 205 A5
Kestle 5 C4
Kestle Mill 4 B3
Keston 49 C7
Keswick Cumb 163 B5
Norf 104 A3
Norf 121 B5
Ketley 111 D5
Ketley Bank 111 D5
Ketsby 134 B3
Kettering 99 D5
Ketteringham 104 A2
Kettins 220 A2
Kettlebaston 87 B5
Kettlebridge 220 D3
Kettleburgh 88 A3
Kettlehill 220 D3
Kettleholm 174 A4
Kettleness 169 D6
Kettleshume 129 B4
Kettlesing Bottom 147 B6
Kettlesing Head 147 B6
Kettlestone 119 B6
Kettlethorpe 132 B3
Kettletoft 282 D7
Kettlewell 156 D3
Ketton 100 A1
Kew 49 B4
Kew Br. 49 B4
Kewstoke 42 C2
Kexbrough 139 C6
Kexby Lincs 132 A3
York 149 B6
Key Green 128 C3
Keyham 98 A3
Keyhaven 18 B2
Keyingham 143 A4
Keymer 21 A6
Keynsham 43 C5
Keysoe 84 A2
Keysoe Row 84 A2
Keyston 100 D2
Keyworth 115 B4
Kibblesworth 179 D4
Kibworth Beauchamp 98 B3
Kibworth Harcourt 98 B3
Kidbrooke 49 B7
Kiddemore Green 95 A6
Kidderminster 95 D6
Kiddington 65 A5
Kidlington 65 B5
Kidmore End 47 B4
Kidsgrove 128 D3
Kidstones 156 C3
Kidwelly Cydweli 57 B4
Kiel Crofts 226 C4
Kielder 187 D5
Kierfiold Ho. 282 F3
Kilbagie 208 B2
Kilbarchan 205 B4
Kilbeg 247 D5
Kilberry 202 B2
Kilbirnie 204 C3
Kilbride Argyll 226 D3
Argyll 226 D4
Highld 247 B4
Kilburn Angus 232 B1
Derbys 114 A1
London 49 A5
N Yorks 158 D4
Kilby 98 B3
Kilchamaig 202 B3
Kilchattan 212 C1
Kilchattan Bay 203 C6
Kilchenzie 190 C2
Kilcheran 226 C3
Kilchiaran 200 B2
Kilchoan Argyll 213 A5
Highld 234 D3
Kilchoman 200 B2
Kilchrenan 227 D5
Kilconquhar 221 D4
Kilcot 62 A2
Kilcoy 252 A1
Kilcreggan 215 D5
Kildale 159 A5
Kildalloig 190 D3
Kildary 264 C3
Kildermorie Lodge 263 C7
Kildonan 191 C6
Kildonan Lodge 274 B3
Kildonnan 234 B3
Kildrummy 244 A1
Kildwick 147 C4
Kilfinan 203 A4
Kilfinnan 239 C6
Kilgetty 56 B1
Kilgwrrwg Common 61 D6
Kilham E Yorks 150 A3
Northumb 198 C2
Kilkenneth 222 C2
Kilkerran 190 D3
Kilkhampton 24 D3
Killamarsh 131 A4
Killay 57 C6
Killbeg 225 B5
Killean 202 D1
Killearn 206 B3
Killen 252 A2
Killerby 167 D4
Killichonan 229 C4
Killiechonate 239 D6
Killiechronan 225 B4
Killiecrankie 230 B3
Killiemor 224 C3
Killiemore House 224 D3
Killilan 249 C6
Killimster 281 C5
Killin 217 A5
Killinallan 200 A3
Killinghall 148 B1
Killington 155 C5
Killingworth 179 B4
Killin Lodge 240 B3
Killmahumaig 213 C5
Killochyett 196 B3
Killocraw 190 B2
Killundine 225 B4
Kilmacolm 204 B3
Kilmaha 214 B2
Kilmahog 217 D6
Kilmalieu 236 D2
Kilmaluag 259 A4
Kilmany 220 B3
Kilmarie 247 C4
Kilmarnock 193 B4
Kilmaron Castle 220 C3
Kilmartin 213 C6
Kilmaurs 205 D4
Kilmelford 213 A6
Kilmeny 200 B3
Kilmersdon 43 D5
Kilmeston 33 C4
Kilmichael 190 C2
Kilmichael Glassary 214 C1
Kilmichael of Inverlussa 213 D5
Kilmington Devon 14 B2
Wilts 30 B1
Kilmonivaig 239 D5
Kilmorack 251 B6
Kilmore Argyll 226 D3
Highld 247 D5
Kilmory Argyll 202 A2
Highld 235 C4
Highld 246 D2
N Ayrs 191 C5
Kilmuir Highld 252 B2
Highld 258 A3
Highld 258 D2
Highld 264 C3
Kilmun Argyll 214 A2
Argyll 215 D4
Kilncadzow 194 B3
Kilndown 37 C5
Kilnhurst 140 D2
Kilninian 224 B2
Kilninver 226 D3
Kiln Pit Hill 178 D2
Kilnsea 143 B6
Kilnsey 146 A3
Kilnwick 150 C2
Kilnwick Percy 149 B7
Kiloran 212 C1
Kilpatrick 191 C5
Kilpeck 78 D2
Kilphedir 274 C3
Kilpin 141 A5
Kilpin Pike 141 A5
Kilrenny 221 D5
Kilsby 98 D2
Kilspindie 220 B2
Kilsyth 207 C5
Kiltarlity 251 B7
Kilton Notts 131 B5
Som 27 A6
Kilton Thorpe 169 D4
Kilvaxter 258 B3
Kilve 27 A6
Kilvington 115 A5
Kilwinning 204 D3
Kimberley Norf 103 A6
Notts 114 A3
Kimber worth 140 D2
Kimblesworth 167 A5
Kimble Wick 66 C4
Kimbolton Cambs 84 A2
Hereford 78 A3
Kimcote 98 C2
Kimmeridge 16 D3
Kimmerston 198 C3
Kimpton Hants 32 A1
Herts 68 B1
Kinbrace 274 A2
Kinbuck 218 D2
Kincaple 221 C4
Kincardine Fife 208 B2
Highld 264 B2
Kincardine Bridge 208 B2
Kincardine O'Neil 244 C2
Kinclaven 219 A6
Kincorth 245 B6
Kincorth Ho. 265 D6
Kincraig 241 B6
Kincraigie 230 D3
Kindallachan 230 D3
Kineton Glos 64 A1
Warks 81 B6
Kinfauns 219 B6
Kingairloch 236 D2
Kingarth 203 C5
Kingcoed 61 C6
King Edward 268 D2
Kingerby 142 D2
Kingham 64 A3
Kingholm Quay 174 A2
Kinghorn 209 B5
Kingie 239 B5
Kinglassie 209 A5
Kingoodie 220 B3
King's Acre 78 C2
Kingsand 6 B3
Kingsbarns 221 C5
Kingsbridge Devon 7 C6
Som 27 B4
King's Bromley 113 D5
Kingsburgh 258 C3
Kingsbury London 49 A5
Warks 97 B5
Kingsbury Episcopi 28 C4
King's Caple 62 A1
Kingsclere 46 D3
King's Cliffe 100 B2
Kingscote 63 D4
Kingscott 25 D6
King's Coughton 80 B3
Kingscross 191 C6
Kingsdon 29 C5
Kingsdown 39 A5
Kingseat 208 A4
Kingsey 66 C3
Kingsfold 35 C4
Kingsford E Ayrs 205 D4
Worcs 95 C6
Kingsforth 142 B2
Kingsgate 53 B5
Kingsheanton 25 B6
King's Heath 96 C3
Kings Hedges 85 A6
King's Hill 37 A4
Kingshouse Hotel 237 D6
Kingside Hill 175 C4
Kingskerswell 8 A2
Kingskettle 220 D3
Kingsland Anglesey 122 B2
Hereford 78 A2
Kings Langley 67 C6
Kingsley Ches W 127 B5
Hants 33 B6
Staffs 112 A4
Kingsley Green 34 C1
Kingsley Holt 112 A4
Kingsley Park 83 A4
King's Lynn 118 C3
King's Meaburn 165 C4
King's Mills 110 A2
Kingsmuir Angus 232 D2
Fife 221 D5
Kings Muir 196 C1
King's Newnham 98 D1
King's Newton 114 C1
Kingsnorth 38 B2
King's Norton Leics 98 A3
W Mid 96 D3
King's Nympton 26 D1
King's Pyon 78 B2
King's Ripton 101 D4
King's Somborne 32 B2
King's Stag 30 D1
King's Stanley 63 C4
King's Sutton 82 D1
Kingstanding 96 B3
Kingsteignton 12 D3
King Sterndale 129 B5
King's Thorn 78 D3
Kingsthorpe 83 A4
Kingston Cambs 85 B5
Devon 7 C5
Dorset 16 A1
Dorset 16 D3
E Loth 210 B2
Hants 17 A5
IoW 18 C3
Kent 52 D3
Moray 266 C4
Kingston Bagpuize 65 D5
Kingston Blount 66 D3
Kingston by Sea 21 B5
Kingston Deverill 30 B2
Kingstone Hereford 78 D2
Som 28 D3
Staffs 113 C4
Kingston Gorse 20 B3
Kingston Lisle 45 A7
Kingston Maurward 15 B7
Kingston near Lewes 22 B1
Kingston on Soar 114 C3
Kingston Russell 15 B5
Kingston St Mary 28 C2
Kingston Seymour 42 C3
Kingston Upon Hull 142 A2
Kingston upon Thames 49 C4
Kingston Vale 49 B5
Kingstown 175 C6
King's Walden 67 A7
Kingswear 8 B2
Kingswells 245 B5
Kingswinford 96 C1
Kingswood Bucks 66 B2
Glos 62 D3
Hereford 77 B6
Kent 37 A6
Powys 93 A6
S Glos 43 B5
Sur 35 A5
Warks 97 D4
Kings Worthy 32 B3
Kingthorpe 133 B6
Kington Hereford 77 B6
Worcs 80 B2
Kington Langley 44 B3
Kington Magna 30 C1
Kington St Michael 44 B3
Kingussie 241 B5
Kingweston 29 B5
Kininvie Ho. 254 B4
Kinkell Bridge 218 C4
Kinknockie 257 B5
Kinlet 95 C5
Kinloch Fife 220 C2
Highld 234 A2
Highld 247 C5
Highld 271 A6
Perth 231 D5
Perth 231 D6
Kinlochan 236 C2
Kinlochard 217 D4
Kinlochbeoraid 238 D2
Kinlochbervie 276 C3
Kinlocheil 236 B3
Kinlochewe 262 D2
Kinloch Hourn 238 B3
Kinloch Laggan 240 D3
Kinlochleven 237 C5
Kinloch Lodge 277 C6
Kinlochmoidart 235 C6
Kinlochmorar 238 C2
Kinlochmore 237 C5
Kinloch Rannoch 229 C5
Kinlochspelve 225 D5
Kinloid 235 B5
Kinloss 265 D6
Kinmel Bay 125 A4
Kinmuck 256 E3
Kinmundy 245 A5
Kinnadie 257 B4

Kinnaird 220 B2
Kinnaird Castle 233 C4
Kinneff 233 A6
Kinnelhead 184 B3
Kinnell 233 C4
Kinnerley 110 C2
Kinnersley
Hereford 78 C1
Worcs 79 C6
Kinnerton 77 A6
Kinnesswood 219 D6
Kinninvie 166 C3
Kinnordy 232 C1
Kinoulton 115 B4
Kinross 219 D6
Kinrossie 219 A6
Kinsbourne Green 67 B7
Kinsey Heath 111 A5
Kinsham Hereford 78 A1
Worcs 80 D2
Kinsley 140 B2
Kinson 17 B4
Kintbury 46 C1
Kintessack 265 D5
Kintillo 219 C6
Kintocher 244 B2
Kinton Hereford 94 D2
Shrops 110 D2
Kintore 245 A4
Kintour 201 C4
Kintra Argyll 200 D3
Argyll 224 D2
Kintraw 213 B6
Kinuachdrachd 213 C5
Kinveachy 242 A2
Kinver 95 C6
Kippax 148 D3
Kippen 207 A4
Kippford or Scaur 173 C6
Kirbister Orkney 282 E7
Orkney 283 G4
Kirbuster 282 E3
Kirby Bedon 104 A3
Kirby Bellars 115 D5
Kirby Cane 105 B4
Kirby Cross 71 A6
Kirby Grindalythe 150 A2
Kirby Hill N Yorks 148 A2
N Yorks 157 A5
Kirby Knowle 158 C3
Kirby-le-Soken 71 A6
Kirby Misperton 159 D6
Kirby Muxloe 98 A2
Kirby Row 105 B4
Kirby Sigston 158 B3
Kirby Underdale 149 B7
Kirby Wiske 158 C2
Kirdford 34 D3
Kirk 281 C4
Kirkabister 285 K6
Kirkandrews 172 D4
Kirkandrews upon Eden 175 C6
Kirkbampton 175 C6
Kirkbean 174 C2
Kirk Bramwith 140 B4
Kirkbride 175 C5
Kirkbuddo 232 D3
Kirkburn Borders 196 C1
E Yorks 150 B2
Kirkburton 139 B4
Kirkby Lincs 142 D2
Mers 136 D3
N Yorks 158 A4
Kirkby Fleetham 157 B6
Kirkby Green 133 D5
Kirkby In Ashfield 131 D5
Kirkby-in-Furness 153 B3
Kirkby la Thorpe 116 A4
Kirkby Lonsdale 155 D5
Kirkby Malham 146 A2
Kirkby Mallory 98 A1
Kirkby Malzeard 157 D6
Kirkby Mills 159 C6
Kirkbymoorside 159 C5
Kirkby on Bain 134 C2
Kirkby Overflow 148 C2
Kirkby Stephen 155 A6
Kirkby Thore 165 C4
Kirkby Underwood 116 C3
Kirkby Wharfe 148 C4
Kirkcaldy 209 A5
Kirkcambeck 176 C3
Kirkcarswell 173 D5
Kirkcolm 170 A2
Kirkconnel 183 A5
Kirkconnell 174 B2
Kirkcowan 171 A5
Kirkcudbright 173 C4
Kirkdale 136 D2
Kirk Deighton 148 B2
Kirk Ella 142 A2
Kirkfieldbank 194 B3
Kirkgunzeon 173 B6
Kirk Hallam 114 A2
Kirkham Lancs 144 D4
N Yorks 149 A6
Kirkhamgate 139 A5
Kirk Hammerton 148 B3
Kirkharle 178 A2
Kirkheaton
Northumb 178 B2
W Yorks 139 B4
Kirkhill Angus 233 B4
Highld 252 B1
Midloth 209 D5
Moray 254 C3
Kirkhope 186 A2
Kirkhouse 196 C2
Kirkiboll 277 C6
Kirkibost 247 C4
Kirkinch 231 D7
Kirkinner 171 B6
Kirkintilloch 205 A6
Kirk Ireton 130 D2
Kirkland Cumb 162 C3
Cumb 165 B4
Dumfries 183 A5
Dumfries 183 C6
Kirk Langley 113 B6
Kirkleatham 168 C3
Kirklevington 158 A3
Kirkley 105 B6
Kirklington
Notts 132 D1
N Yorks 157 C7
Kirklinton 176 C2
Kirkliston 208 C4
Kirkmaiden 170 D3
Kirk Merrington 167 B5
Kirkmichael
Perth 231 C4
S Ayrs 192 E3
Kirk Michael 152 B3
Kirkmuirhill 194 B2
Kirknewton
Northumb 198 C3
W Loth 208 D4
Kirkney 255 C6
Kirk of Shotts 207 D6
Kirkoswald
Cumb 164 A3
S Ayrs 192 E2
Kirkpatrick Durham 173 A5
Kirkpatrick-Fleming 175 A5
Kirk Sandall 140 C4
Kirksanton 153 B2
Kirk Smeaton 140 B3
Kirkstall 147 D6
Kirkstead 134 C1
Kirkstile 255 C6
Kirkstyle 281 A5
Kirkton Aberds 256 D1
Aberds 268 E1
Angus 220 A4
Angus 232 D2
Borders 186 B4
Dumfries 184 D2
Fife 220 B3
Highld 249 B6
Highld 249 D5
Highld 252 A3
Highld 265 A3
Kirkton
Perth 219 C4
S Lanark 194 D4
Stirling 217 D5
Kirktonhill 196 A3
Kirkton Manor 195 C7
Kirkton of Airlie 231 C7
Kirkton of Auchterhouse 220 A3
Kirkton of Auchterless 256 B2
Kirkton of Barevan 253 B4
Kirkton of Bourtie 256 D3
Kirkton of Collace 219 A6
Kirkton of Craig 233 C5
Kirkton of Culsalmond 256 C1
Kirkton of Durris 245 C4
Kirkton of Glenbuchat 243 A6
Kirkton of Glenisla 231 B6
Kirkton of Kingoldrum 232 C1
Kirkton of Largo 220 D4
Kirkton of Lethendy 231 D5
Kirkton of Logie Buchan 257 D4
Kirkton of Maryculter 245 C5
Kirkton of Menmuir 232 B3
Kirkton of Monikie 221 A5
Kirkton of Oyne 256 D1
Kirkton of Rayne 256 D1
Kirkton of Skene 245 B5
Kirkton of Tough 244 A3
Kirktown 269 D5
Kirktown of Alvah 268 C1
Kirktown of Deskford 267 C6
Kirktown of Fetteresso 245 D5
Kirktown of Mortlach 254 C4
Kirktown of Slains 257 D5
Kirkurd 195 B6
Kirkwall 282 F5
Kirkwhelpington 178 A1
Kirk Yetholm 188 A1
Kirmington 142 B3
Kirmond le Mire 142 D3
Kirn 203 A6
Kirriemuir 232 C1
Kirstead Green 104 B3
Kirtlebridge 175 A5
Kirtleton 185 D5
Kirtling 86 B2
Kirtling Green 86 B2
Kirtlington 65 B5
Kirtomy 278 B3
Kirton Lincs 117 B6
Notts 132 C1
Suff 88 D3
Kirton End 117 A5
Kirton Holme 117 A5
Kirton in Lindsey 142 D1
Kislingbury 82 B3
Kites Hardwick 82 A1
Kittisford 27 C5
Kittle 57 D5
Kitt's Green 97 C4
Kitt's Moss 128 A3
Kittybrewster 245 B6
Kitwood 33 B5
Kivernoll 78 D2
Kiveton Park 131 A4
Knaith 132 A3
Knaith Park 132 A3
Knap Corner 30 C2
Knaphill 34 A2
Knapp Perth 220 A2
Som 28 C3
Knapthorpe 132 D2
Knapton Norf 121 B5
York 149 B4
Knapton Green 78 B2
Knapwell 85 A5
Knaresborough 148 B2
Knarsdale 177 D4
Knauchland 267 D6
Knaven 256 B3
Knayton 158 C3
Knebworth 68 A2
Knedlington 141 A5
Kneesall 132 C2
Kneesworth 85 C5
Kneeton 115 A5
Knelston 57 D4
Knenhall 112 B3
Knettishall 103 C5
Knightacott 26 B1
Knightcote 81 B6
Knightley Dale 112 C2
Knighton Devon 7 C4
Leicester 98 A2
Staffs 111 A6
Staffs 111 C6
Knighton Tref-y-Clawdd 93 D6
Knightswood 205 B5
Knightwick 79 B5
Knill 77 A6
Knipton 115 B6
Knitsley 166 A4
Kniveton 130 D2
Knock Argyll 225 C4
Cumb 165 C4
Moray 267 D6
Knockally 275 B5
Knockan 271 C5
Knockandhu 254 D3
Knockando 254 B2
Knockando Ho. 254 B3
Knockbain 252 A2
Knockbreck 258 B2
Knockbrex 172 D3
Knockdee 280 B3
Knockdolian 180 C3
Knockenkelly 191 C6
Knockentiber 192 B3
Knockespock Ho. 255 D6
Knockfarrel 251 A7
Knockglass 170 B2
Knockholt 36 A2
Knockholt Pound 36 A2
Knockie Lodge 240 A2
Knockin 110 C2
Knockinlaw 193 B4
Knocklearn 173 A5
Knocknaha 190 D2
Knocknain 170 A1
Knockrome 201 A5
Knocksharry 152 C2
Knodishall 89 A5
Knolls Green 128 B3
Knolton 110 B2
Knolton Bryn 110 B2
Knook 30 A3
Knossington 99 A5
Knott End-on-Sea 144 C3
Knotting 84 A2
Knotting Green 84 A2
Knottingley 140 A3
Knotts Cumb 164 C2
Lancs 146 B1
Knotty Ash 136 D3
Knotty Green 67 D5
Knowbury 94 D3
Knowe 181 D5
Knowehead 182 C4
Knowesgate 178 A1
Knowes of Elrick 267 D7
Knoweton 194 A2
Knowhead 269 D4
Knowle Bristol 43 B5
Knowle
Devon 12 A2
Devon 13 C5
Devon 25 B5
Shrops 94 D3
W Mid 97 D4
Knowle Green 145 D6
Knowle Park 147 C4
Knowl Hill 47 B6
Knowlton Dorset 31 D4
Kent 53 D4
Knowsley 136 D3
Knowstone 26 C3
Knox Bridge 37 B5
Knucklas 93 D6
Knuston 83 A6
Knutsford 128 B2
Knutton 112 A2
Knypersley 128 D3
Kuggar 3 D5
Kyleakin 247 B6
Kyle of Lochalsh 249 D4
Kylerhea 247 B6
Kylesknoydart 238 C2
Kylesku 271 A5
Kylesmorar 238 C2
Kylestrome 271 A5
Kyllachy House 252 D3
Kynaston 110 C2
Kynnersley 111 D5
Kyre Magna 79 A4

L

Labost 288 C3
Lacasaidh 288 E4
Lacasdal 288 D5
Laceby 143 C4
Lacey Green 66 D4
Lach Dennis 128 B2
Lackford 102 D3
Lacock 44 C3
Ladbroke 81 B7
Laddingford 37 B4
Lade Bank 134 D3
Ladock 4 B3
Lady 282 C7
Ladybank 220 C3
Ladykirk 198 B2
Ladysford 269 C4
La Fontenelle Guern 6
Laga 235 D5
Lagalochan 214 A1
Lagavulin 201 D4
Lagg Argyll 201 A5
N Ayrs 191 C5
Laggan Argyll 200 C2
Highld 235 C6
Highld 239 C6
Highld 241 C4
S Ayrs 181 C4
Lagganulva 224 B3
Laide 261 A5
Laigh Fenwick 205 D4
Laigh Glengall 192 D3
Laighmuir 205 D4
Laindon 50 A3
Lair 250 B2
Lairg 272 D3
Lairg Lodge 272 D3
Lairgmore 252 C1
Lairg Muir 272 D3
Laisterdyke 147 D5
Laithes 164 B2
Lake IoW 19 C4
Wilts 31 B5
Lakenham 104 A3
Lakenheath 102 C3
Lakesend 101 B7
Lakeside 154 C2
Laleham 48 C3
Laleston 40 D3
Lamarsh 87 D4
Lamas 120 C4
Lambden 197 B6
Lamberhurst 37 C4
Lamberhurst Quarter 37 C4
Lamberton 198 A3
Lambeth 49 B6
Lambhill 205 B5
Lambley
Northumb 177 D4
Notts 115 A4
Lamborough Hill 65 C5
Lambourn 46 B1
Lambourne End 69 D4
Lambs Green 35 C5
Lambston 55 C5
Lambton 179 D4
Lamerton 11 D5
Lamesley 179 D4
Laminess 282 D7
Lamington
Highld 264 C3
S Lanark 195 C4
Lamlash 191 B6
Lamloch 182 C3
Lamonby 164 B2
Lamorna 2 C2
Lamorran 4 C3
Lampardbrook 88 A3
Lampeter Llanbedr Pont Steffan 75 D4
Lampeter Velfrey 56 A1
Lamphey 55 D6
Lamplugh 162 B3
Lamport 99 D4
Lamyatt 29 B6
Lana 10 B4
Lanark 194 B3
Lancaster 145 A4
Lanchester 167 A4
Lancing 21 B4
Landbeach 85 A6
Landcross 25 C5
Landerberry 245 B4
Landford 31 D6
Landford Manor 31 C6
Landimore 57 C4
Landkey 25 B6
Landore 57 C6
Landrake 6 A2
Landscove 8 A1
Landshipping 55 C6
Landshipping Quay 55 C6
Landulph 6 A3
Landwade 86 A2
Lane 4 A3
Laneast 10 C3
Lane End Bucks 66 D4
Cumb 153 A2
Dorset 16 B2
Hants 33 C4
IoW 19 C5
Lancs 146 C2
Lane Ends Lancs 146 B1
Lancs 146 D1
N Yorks 146 C3
Laneham 132 B3
Lanehead
Durham 165 A6
Northumb 177 A5
Lane Head
Derbys 129 B6
Durham 166 D4
Gtr Man 137 D5
W Yorks 139 C4
Lanercost 176 C3
Laneshaw Bridge 146 C3
Lane Side 137 A6
Lanfach 41 B7
Langar 115 B5
Langbank 204 A3
Langbar 147 B4
Langburnshiels 186 C4
Langcliffe 146 A2
Langdale 278 D2
Langdale End 160 B3
Langdon 10 C4
Langdon Beck 165 B6
Langdon Hills 50 A3
Langdyke 220 D3
Langenhoe 71 B4
Langford C Beds 84 C3
Devon 13 A5
Essex 70 C2

Langford
Notts 132 D3
Oxon 64 C3
Langford Budville 27 C6
Langham Essex 87 D6
Norf 120 A2
Rutland 115 D6
Suff 103 E5
Langhaugh 195 C7
Langho 145 D7
Langholm 185 D6
Langleeford 188 A2
Langley Ches E 129 B4
Hants 18 A3
Herts 68 A2
Kent 37 A6
Northumb 177 C6
Slough 48 B3
Warks 81 A4
W Sus 33 C7
Langley Burrell 44 B3
Langley Common 113 B6
Langley Heath 37 A6
Langley Lower Green 85 D6
Langley Marsh 27 C5
Langley Park 167 A5
Langley Street 105 A4
Langley Upper Green 85 D6
Langney 22 B4
Langold 131 A5
Langore 10 C4
Langport 28 C4
Langrick 117 A5
Langridge 43 C6
Langridge Ford 25 C6
Langrigg 175 D4
Langrish 33 C6
Langsett 139 C5
Langshaw 197 C4
Langside 218 C2
Langskaill 282 C5
Langstone Hants 19 A6
Newport 61 D5
Langthorne 157 B6
Langthorpe 148 A2
Langthwaite 156 A4
Langtoft E Yorks 150 A3
Lincs 116 D4
Langton Durham 167 D4
Lincs 134 B3
Lincs 134 C2
N Yorks 149 A6
Langton by Wragby 133 B6
Langton Green
Kent 36 C3
Suff 104 D2
Langton Herring 15 C6
Langton Matravers 17 D4
Langtree 25 D5
Langwathby 164 B3
Langwell Ho. 275 B5
Langwell Lodge 271 D4
Langwith 131 C5
Langwith Junction 131 C5
Langworth 133 B5
Lanivet 5 A5
Lanlivery 5 B5
Lanner 4 D2
Lanreath 5 B6
Lansallos 5 B6
Lansdown 63 A5
Lanteglos Highway 5 B6
Lanton Borders 187 A5
Northumb 198 C3
Lapford 12 A2
Laphroaig 200 D3
La Planque Guern 6
Lapley 112 D2
Lapworth 97 D4
Larachbeg 225 B5
Larbert 207 B6
Larden Green 127 D5
Largie 255 C7
Largiemore 214 D2
Largoward 221 D4
Largs 204 C2
Largybeg 191 C6
Largymore 191 C6
Larkfield 204 A2
Larkhall 194 A2
Larkhill 31 A5
Larling 103 C5
Larriston 186 D4
Lartington 166 D3
Lary 243 B6
Lasham 33 A5
Lashenden 37 B6
Lassington 62 A3
Lassodie 208 A4
Lastingham 159 B6
Latcham 29 A4
Latchford Herts 68 A3
Warr 127 A6
Latchingdon 70 C2
Latchley 11 D5
Lately Common 137 D5
Lathbury 83 C5
Latheron 275 A5
Latheronwheel 275 A5
Latheronwheel Ho. 275 A5
Lathones 221 D4
Latimer 67 D6
Latteridge 43 A5
Lattiford 29 C6
Latton 64 D1
Latton Bush 69 C4
Lauchintilly 245 A4
Lauder 197 B4
Laugharne 56 A3
Laughterton 132 B3
Laughton E Sus 22 A3
Leics 98 C3
Lincs 116 B3
Lincs 141 D6
Laughton Common 131 A5
Laughton en le Morthen 131 A5
Launcells 10 A3
Launceston 10 C4
Launton 65 A7
Laurencekirk 233 A5
Laurieston
Dumfries 173 B4
Falk 208 C2
Lavendon 83 B6
Lavenham 87 C5
Laverhay 185 C4
Laversdale 176 C2
Laverstock 31 B5
Laverstoke 32 A3
Laverton Glos 80 D3
N Yorks 157 D6
Som 44 D1
Lavister 126 D3
Law 194 A3
Lawers Perth 217 A6
Perth 218 B2
Lawford 88 D1
Lawhitton 11 C4
Lawkland 146 A1
Lawley 95 A4
Lawnhead 112 C2
Lawrenny 55 D6
Lawshall 87 B4
Lawton 78 B2
Laxey 152 C4
Laxfield 104 D3
Laxfirth Shetland 285 H6
Shetland 285 J6
Laxford Bridge 276 D3
Laxo 285 G6
Laxobigging 284 F6
Laxton E Yorks 141 A5
Northants 99 B6
Notts 132 C2
Laycock 147 C4
Layer Breton 70 B3
Layer de la Haye 70 B3
Layer Marney 70 B3
Layham 87 C6
Laylands Green 46 C1
Laytham 149 D6
Layton 144 D3
Lazenby 168 C3
Lazonby 164 B3
Lea Derbys 130 D3
Hereford 62 A2
Lincs 132 A3
Shrops 94 A2
Shrops 94 C1
Wilts 44 A3
Leabrooks 131 D4
Leac a Li 288 H2
Leachkin 252 B2
Leadburn 196 A1
Leadenham 133 D4
Leaden Roding 69 B5
Leadgate Cumb 165 A5
Durham 178 D3
T&W 178 D3
Leadhills 183 A6
Leafield 64 B4
Leagrave 67 A6
Leake 158 B3
Leake Commonside 134 D3
Lealholm 159 A6
Lealt Argyll 213 C4
Highld 259 B5
Lea Marston 97 B5
Leamington Hastings 82 A1
Leamonsley 96 A4
Leamside 167 A6
Leanaig 252 A1
Leargybreck 201 A5
Leasgill 154 C3
Leasingham 116 A3
Leasingthorne 167 C5
Leasowe 136 D1
Leatherhead 35 A4
Leatherhead Common 35 A4
Leathley 147 C6
Leaton 110 D3
Lea Town 145 D4
Leaveland 52 D2
Leavening 149 A6
Leaves Green 49 C7
Leazes 178 D3
Lebberston 161 C4
Lechlade-on-Thames 64 D3
Leck 155 D5
Leckford 32 B2
Leckfurin 278 C3
Leckgruinart 200 B2
Leckhampstead
Bucks 83 D4
W Berks 46 B2
Leckhampstead Thicket 46 B2
Leckhampton 63 B5
Leckie 262 D2
Leckmelm 262 A3
Leckwith 41 D6
Leconfield 150 C3
Ledaig 226 C4
Ledburn 67 A5
Ledbury 79 D5
Ledcharrie 217 B5
Ledgemoor 78 B2
Ledicot 78 A2
Ledmore 271 C5
Lednagullin 278 B3
Ledsham Ches W 126 B3
W Yorks 140 A2
Ledston 140 A2
Ledston Luck 148 D3
Ledwell 65 A5
Lee Argyll 224 D3
Devon 25 A5
Hants 32 D2
Lancs 145 B5
Shrops 110 B3
Leeans 285 J5
Leebotten 285 L6
Leebotwood 94 B2
Lee Brockhurst 111 C4
Leece 153 D3
Leechpool 55 C5
Lee Clump 67 C5
Leeds Kent 37 A6
W Yorks 148 D1
Leedstown 3 B4
Leek 129 D4
Leekbrook 129 D4
Leek Wootton 81 A5
Lee Mill 7 B5
Leeming 157 C6
Leeming Bar 157 B6
Lee Moor 7 A4
Lee-on-the-Solent 19 A4
Lees Derbys 113 B6
Gtr Man 138 C2
W Yorks 147 D4
Leeswood 126 C2
Legbourne 134 A3
Legerwood 197 B4
Legsby 133 A6
Leicester 98 A2
Leicester Forest East 98 A2
Leigh Dorset 15 A6
Glos 63 A4
Gtr Man 137 C5
Kent 36 B3
Shrops 94 A1
Sur 35 B5
Wilts 63 D6
Worcs 79 B5
Leigh Beck 51 A5
Leigh Common 30 C1
Leigh Delamere 44 B2
Leigh Green 37 C7
Leigh on Sea 51 A5
Leigh Park 19 A6
Leigh Sinton 79 B5
Leighswood 96 A3
Leighterton 63 D4
Leighton N Yorks 157 D5
Powys 93 A6
Shrops 95 A4
Som 29 A7
Leighton Bromswold 100 D3
Leighton Buzzard 67 A5
Leigh upon Mendip 29 A6
Leigh Woods 43 B4
Leinthall Earls 78 A2
Leinthall Starkes 78 A2
Leintwardine 94 D2
Leire 98 B2
Leirinmore 277 B5
Leiston 89 A5
Leitfie 231 D6
Leith 209 C5
Leitholm 198 B1
Lelant 2 B3
Lelley 151 D5
Lem Hill 95 D5
Lemmington Hall 189 B4
Lempitlaw 198 C1
Lenchwick 80 C3
Lendalfoot 180 C3
Lendrick Lodge 217 D5
Lenham 37 A6
Lenham Heath 37 B7
Lennel 198 B2
Lennoxtown 205 A6
Lenton Lincs 116 B3
Nottingham 114 B3
Lentran 252 B1
Lenwade 120 D2
Leny Ho. 217 D6
Lenzie 205 A6
Leoch 220 A3
Leochel-Cushnie 244 A2
Leominster 78 B2
Leonard Stanley 63 C4
Leorin 200 D3
Lepe 18 B3
Lephin 258 D1
Lephinchapel 214 C2
Lephinmore 214 C2
Le Planel Guern 6
Leppington 149 A6
Lepton 139 B5
Lerryn 5 B6
Lerwick 285 J6
Lesbury 189 B5
Le Skerne Haughton 167 D6
Leslie Aberds 255 D6
Fife 220 D2
Lesmahagow 194 C3
Lesnewth 10 B2
Lessendrum 255 B6
Lessingham 121 C5
Lessonhall 175 C5
Leswalt 170 A2
Letchmore Heath 67 D7
Letchworth 84 D4
Letcombe Bassett 46 A1
Letcombe Regis 46 A1
Letham Angus 232 D3
Falk 208 B1
Fife 220 C3
Perth 219 B5
Letham Grange 233 D4
Lethenty 256 B3
Letheringham 88 B3
Letheringsett 120 B2
Lettaford 12 C2
Lettan 282 C8
Letterewe 261 C6
Letterfearn 249 D5
Letterfinlay 239 C6
Lettermorar 235 B6
Lettermore 224 B3
Letters 262 B3
Letterston 55 B5
Lettoch Highld 242 A3
Highld 254 C1
Letton Hereford 78 C1
Hereford 94 D1
Letton Green 103 A5
Letty Green 68 B2
Letwell 131 A5
Leuchars 221 B4
Leuchars Ho. 266 C3
Leumrabhagh 288 F4
Levan 204 A2
Levaneap 285 G6
Levedale 112 D2
Leven E Yorks 151 C4
Fife 220 D3
Levencorroch 191 C6
Levens 154 C3
Levens Green 68 A3
Levenshulme 138 D1
Levenwick 285 L6
Leverington 118 D1
Leverton 117 A7
Leverton Highgate 117 A7
Leverton Lucasgate 117 A7
Leverton Outgate 117 A7
Le Villocq Guern 6
Levington 88 D3
Levisham 160 B2
Levishie 240 A2
Lew 64 C4
Lewannick 10 C3
Lewdown 11 C5
Lewes 22 A2
Leweston 55 B5
Lewisham 49 B6
Lewiston 251 D7
Lewistown 40 C4
Lewknor 66 D3
Leworthy Devon 10 A4
Devon 26 B1
Lewtrenchard 11 C5
Lexden 70 A3
Ley Aberds 244 A2
Corn 5 A6
Leybourne 37 A4
Leyburn 157 B5
Leyfields 97 A5
Leyhill 67 C5
Leyland 136 A4
Leylodge 245 A4
Leymoor 139 B4
Leys Aberds 269 D5
Perth 220 A2
Leys Castle 252 B2
Leysdown-on-Sea 52 B2
Leysmill 233 D4
Leys of Cossans 232 D1
Leysters Pole 78 A3
Leyton 49 A6
Leytonstone 49 A6
Lezant 10 D4
Leziate 118 D3
Lhanbryde 266 C3
Liatrie 250 C4
Libanus 60 A1
Libberton 195 B4
Liberton 209 D5
Liceasto 288 H2
Lichfield 96 A4
Lickey 96 D2
Lickey End 96 D2
Lickfold 34 D2
Liddel 283 J5
Liddesdale 236 D1
Liddington 45 A6
Lidgate 86 B3
Lidget 141 C4
Lidget Green 147 D5
Lidgett 131 C6
Lidlington 84 D1
Lidstone 65 A4
Lieurary 279 B6
Liff 220 A3
Lifton 11 C4
Liftondown 11 C4
Lighthorne 81 B6
Lightwater 48 C2
Lightwood 112 A3
Lightwood Green
Ches E 111 A5
Wrex 110 A2
Lilbourne 98 D2
Lilburn Tower 188 A3
Lilleshall 111 D6
Lilley Herts 67 A7
W Berks 46 B2
Lilliesleaf 186 A4
Lillingstone Dayrell 83 D4
Lillingstone Lovell 83 C4
Lillington Dorset 29 D6
Warks 81 A6
Lilliput 17 B4
Lilstock 27 A6
Lilyhurst 111 D6
Limbury 67 A6
Limebrook 78 A1
Limefield 137 B7
Limekilnburn 194 A2
Limekilns 208 B3
Limerigg 207 C6
Limerstone 18 C3
Limington 29 C5
Limpenhoe 105 A4
Limpley Stoke 44 C1
Limpsfield 36 A2
Limpsfield Chart 36 A2
Linby 131 D5
Linchmere 34 C1
Lincluden 174 A2
Lincoln 133 B4
Lincomb 79 A6
Lincombe 7 B6
Lindale 154 C3
Lindal in Furness 153 C3
Lindean 196 C3
Lindfield 35 D6
Lindford 33 B7
Lindifferon 220 C3
Lindley 139 B4
Lindley Green 147 C6
Lindores 220 C2
Lindridge 79 A4
Lindsell 69 A6
Lindsey 87 C5
Linford Hants 17 A5
Thurrock 50 B3
Lingague 152 D2
Lingards Wood 138 B3
Lingbob 147 D4
Lingdale 169 D4
Lingen 78 A1
Lingfield 36 B1
Lingreabhagh 287 F5
Lingwood 105 A4
Linicro 258 B3

Linkenholt 46 D1
Linkhill 37 D6
Linkinhorne 10 D4
Linklater 283 J5
Linksness 283 G3
Linktown 209 A5
Linley 94 B1
Linley Green 79 B4
Linlithgow 208 C3
Linlithgow Bridge 208 C2
Linshiels 188 C1
Linsiadar 288 D3
Linsidemore 264 A1
Linslade 67 A5
Linstead Parva 104 D4
Linstock 176 D2
Linthwaite 139 B4
Lintlaw 198 A2
Lintmill 267 C6
Linton Borders 187 A6
Cambs 86 C1
Derbys 113 D6
Hereford 62 A2
Kent 37 B5
Northumb 189 D5
N Yorks 146 A3
W Yorks 148 C2
Linton-on-Ouse 148 A3
Linwood Hants 17 A5
Lincs 133 A6
Renfs 205 B4
Lionacleit 286 B3
Lional 288 A6
Liphook 34 C1
Liscard 136 D2
Liscombe 26 B3
Liskeard 6 A1
L'Islet Guern 6
Liss 33 C6
Lissett 151 B4
Liss Forest 33 C6
Lissington 133 A6
Lisvane 41 C6
Liswerry 42 A2
Litcham 119 D5
Litchborough 82 B3
Litchfield 46 D2
Lit. Hallingbury 69 B4
Litherland 136 D2
Litlington Cambs 85 C5
E Sus 22 B3
Little Abington 86 C1
Little Addington 99 D6
Little Alne 80 A4
Little Altcar 136 C2
Little Asby 155 A5
Little Assynt 271 B4
Little Aston 96 A3
Little Atherfield 18 C3
Little Ayre 283 H4
Little-ayre 285 G5
Little Ayton 168 D3
Little Baddow 70 C1
Little Badminton 44 A2
Little Ballinluig 230 C3
Little Bampton 175 C5
Little Bardfield 86 D2
Little Barford 84 B3
Little Barningham 120 B3
Little Barrington 64 B3
Little Barrow 127 B4
Little Barugh 159 D6
Little Bavington 178 B1
Little Bealings 88 C3
Littlebeck 160 A2
Little Bedwyn 45 C6
Little Bentley 71 A5
Little Berkhamsted 68 C2
Little Billing 83 A5
Little Birch 78 D3
Little Blakenham 88 C2
Little Blencow 164 B2
Little Bollington 128 A2
Little Bookham 35 A4
Littleborough
Gtr Man 138 B2
Notts 132 A3
Littlebourne 53 D4
Little Bowden 99 C4
Little Bradley 86 B2
Little Brampton 94 C1
Little Brechin 232 B3
Littlebredy 15 C5
Little Brickhill 83 D6
Little Brington 82 A3
Little Bromley 71 A4
Little Broughton 162 A3
Little Budworth 127 C5
Little Burstead 69 D6
Littlebury 85 D7
Littlebury Green 85 D6
Little Bytham 116 D3
Little Carlton
Lincs 134 A3
Notts 132 D2
Little Casterton 100 A2
Little Cawthorpe 134 A3
Little Chalfont 67 D5
Little Chart 38 A1
Little Chesterford 85 C7
Little Cheverell 44 D3
Little Chishill 85 D6
Little Clacton 71 B5
Little Clifton 162 B3
Little Colp 256 B2
Little Comberton 80 C2
Little Common 23 B5
Little Compton 81 D5
Little Cornard 87 D4
Little Cowarne 79 B4
Little Coxwell 64 D3
Little Crakehall 157 B6
Little Cressingham 103 B4
Little Crosby 136 C2
Little Dalby 115 D5
Little Dawley 95 A4
Littledean 62 B2
Little Dens 257 B5
Little Dewchurch 78 D3
Little Downham 101 C7
Little Driffield 150 B3
Little Dunham 119 D5
Little Dunkeld 230 D4
Little Dunmow 69 A6
Little Easton 69 A6
Little Eaton 114 A1
Little Eccleston 144 C4
Little Ellingham 103 B6
Little End 69 C5
Little Eversden 85 B5
Little Faringdon 64 C3
Little Fencote 157 B6
Little Fenton 148 D4
Littleferry 265 A4
Little Finborough 87 B6
Little Fransham 119 D6
Little Gaddesden 67 B5
Little Gidding 100 C3
Little Glemham 88 B4
Little Glenshee 219 A4
Little Gransden 85 B4
Little Green 29 A7
Little Grimsby 143 D5
Little Gruinard 261 B6
Little Habton 159 D6
Little Hadham 68 A4
Little Hale 116 A4
Littleham Devon 13 C5
Devon 25 C5
Little Hampden 66 C4
Littlehampton 20 B3
Little Harrowden 99 D5
Little Haseley 66 C2
Little Hatfield 151 C4
Little Hautbois 121 C4
Little Haven 55 C4
Little Hay 96 A4
Little Hayfield 129 A5
Little Haywood 112 C4
Little Heath 97 C6
Littlehempston 8 A2
Little Hereford 78 A3
Little Horkesley 87 D5
Little Horsted 22 A2
Little Horton 147 D5
Little Horwood 83 D4
Littlehoughton 189 B5
Little Houghton
Northants 83 B5
S Yorks 140 C2
Little Hucklow 129 B6
Little Hulton 137 C6
Little Humber 142 A3
Little Hungerford 46 B3
Little Irchester 83 A6
Little Kimble 66 C4
Little Kineton 81 B6
Little Kingshill 66 D4
Little Langdale 154 A2
Little Langford 31 B4
Little Laver 69 C5
Little Leigh 127 B6
Little Leighs 69 B7
Little Lever 137 C6
Little London
Bucks 66 B2
E Sus 22 A3
Hants 32 A2
Hants 47 D4
Lincs 117 C5
Lincs 118 C1
Norf 120 C3
Powys 92 C4
Little Longstone 130 B1
Little Lynturk 244 A2
Little Malvern 79 C5
Little Maplestead 87 D4
Little Marcle 79 D4
Little Marlow 47 A6
Little Marsden 146 D2
Little Massingham 119 C4
Little Melton 104 A2
Littlemill Aberds 243 C6
E Ayrs 182 A2
Highld 253 A5
Northumb 189 B5
Little Mill 61 C5
Little Milton 65 C7
Little Missenden 67 D5
Littlemoor 15 C6
Littlemore 65 C6
Little Musgrave 165 D5
Little Ness 110 D3
Little Neston 126 B2
Little Newcastle 55 B5
Little Newsham 166 D4
Little Oakley
Essex 71 A6
Northants 99 C5
Little Orton 175 C6
Little Ouseburn 148 A3
Littleover 114 B1
Little Paxton 84 A3
Little Petherick 9 D5
Little Pitlurg 255 B5
Little Plumpton 144 D3
Little Plumstead 121 D5
Little Ponton 116 B2
Littleport 102 C1
Little Raveley 101 D4
Little Reedness 141 A6
Little Ribston 148 B2
Little Rissington 64 B2
Little Ryburgh 119 C6
Little Ryle 188 B3
Little Salkeld 164 B3
Little Sampford 86 D2
Little Sandhurst 47 C6
Little Saxham 86 A3
Little Scatwell 251 A5
Little Sessay 158 D3
Little Shelford 85 B6
Little Singleton 144 D3
Little Skillymarno 269 D4
Little Smeaton 140 B3
Little Snoring 119 B6
Little Sodbury 43 A6
Little Somborne 32 B2
Little Somerford 44 A3
Little Stainforth 146 A2
Little Stainton 167 C6
Little Stanney 127 B4
Little Staughton 84 A3
Little Steeping 135 C4
Little Stoke 112 B3
Littlestone on Sea 38 C2
Little Stonham 88 A2
Little Stretton
Leics 98 A3
Shrops 94 B2
Little Strickland 164 D3
Little Stukeley 100 D4
Little Sutton 126 B3
Little Tew 65 A4
Little Thetford 102 D1
Little Thirkleby 158 D3
Littlethorpe Leics 98 B2
N Yorks 148 A2
Little Thurlow 86 B2
Little Thurrock 50 B3
Littleton Ches W 127 C4
Hants 32 B3
Perth 220 A2
Som 29 B4
Sur 34 B2
Sur 48 C3
Littleton Drew 44 A2
Littleton-on-Severn 43 A4
Littleton Pannell 44 D4
Little Torboll 264 A3
Little Torrington 25 D5
Little Totham 70 B2
Little Toux 267 D6
Littletown 167 A6
Little Town
Cumb 163 C5
Lancs 145 D6
Little Urswick 153 C3
Little Wakering 51 A6
Little Walden 86 C1
Little Waldingfield 87 C5
Little Walsingham 119 B6
Little Waltham 69 B7
Little Warley 69 D6
Little Weighton 150 D2
Little Weldon 99 C6
Little Welnetham 87 A4
Little Wenlock 95 A4
Little Whittingham Green 104 D3
Littlewick Green 47 B6
Little Wilbraham 86 B1
Little Wishford 31 B4
Little Witley 79 A5
Little Wittenham 65 D6
Little Wolford 81 D5
Littleworth
Bedford 84 C2
Glos 63 C4
Oxon 64 D4
Staffs 112 D4
Worcs 80 B1
Little Wratting 86 C2
Little Wymington 83 A6
Little Wymondley 68 A2
Little Wyrley 96 A3
Little Yeldham 86 D3
Litton Derbys 129 B6
N Yorks 156 D3
Som 43 D4
Litton Cheney 15 B5
Liurbost 288 E4
Liverpool 136 D2
Liverpool Airport 127 A4
Liversedge 139 A5
Liverton Devon 12 D3
Redcar 169 D5
Livingston 208 D3
Livingston Village 208 D3
Lixwm 125 B6
Lizard 3 D5
Llaingoch 122 B2
Llaithddu 93 C4
Llan 91 B6
Llanaber 90 A4
Llanaelhaearn 106 B3
Llanafan 75 A5
Llanafan-fawr 76 B3
Llanallgo 123 B4
Llanarmon 107 C4
Llanarmon Dyffryn Ceiriog 109 B6
Llanarmon-yn-Ial 126 D1
Llanarth Ceredig 73 A7
Mon 61 B5
Llanarthne 58 C2
Llanasa 125 A6
Llanbabo 122 B3
Llanbadarn Fawr 90 D4
Llanbadarn Fynydd 93 D5
Llanbadarn-y-Garreg 77 C5
Llanbadoc 61 C5
Llanbadrig 122 A3
Llanbeder 61 D5
Llanbedr Gwyn 107 D5
Powys 60 A4
Powys 77 C5
Llanbedr-Dyffryn-Clwyd 125 D6
Llanbedrgoch 123 B5
Llanbedrog 106 C3
Llanbedr-y-cennin 124 C2
Llanberis 123 D5
Llanbethêry 41 E5
Llanbister 93 D5
Llanblethian 41 D4
Llanboidy 73 D5
Llanbradach 41 B6
Llanbrynmair 91 B6
Llancarfan 41 D5
Llancayo 61 C5
Llancloudy 61 A6
Llancynfelyn 90 C4
Llandaff 41 D6
Llandanwg 107 D5
Llandarcy 40 B2
Llandawke 56 A2
Llanddaniel Fab 123 C4
Llanddarog 57 A5
Llanddeiniol 75 A4
Llanddeiniolen 123 D5
Llandderfel 109 B4
Llanddeusant
Anglesey 122 B3
Carms 59 C4
Llanddew 77 D4
Llanddewi 57 D4
Llanddewi-Brefi 75 C5
Llanddewi'r Cwm 76 C4
Llanddewi Rhydderch 61 B5
Llanddewi Velfrey 56 A1
Llanddoged 124 C3
Llanddona 123 C5
Llanddowror 56 A2
Llanddulas 125 B4
Llanddwywe 107 D5
Llanddyfynan 123 C5
Llandefaelog Fach 76 D4
Llandefaelog-tre'r-graig 77 E5
Llandefalle 77 D5
Llandegai 123 C5
Llandegfan 123 C5
Llandegla 126 D1
Llandegley 77 A5
Llandegveth 61 D5
Llandegwning 106 C2
Llandeilo 58 C3
Llandeilo Graban 77 C4
Llandeilo'r Fan 59 B5
Llandeloy 55 B4
Llandenny 61 C6
Llandevenny 42 A3
Llandewednock 3 D5
Llandewi Ystradenny 77 A5
Llandinabo 61 A7
Llandinam 92 C4
Llandissilio 55 B7
Llandogo 62 C1
Llandough V Glam 41 D4
V Glam 41 D6
Llandovery
Llanymddyfri 59 B4
Llandow 40 D4
Llandre Carms 58 A3
Ceredig 90 D4
Llandrillo 109 B5
Llandrillo-yn-Rhos 124 A3
Llandrindod Wells
Llandrindod 77 A4
Llandrinio 110 D1
Llandudno 124 A2
Llandudno Junction
Cyffordd Llandudno 124 B2
Llandwrog 107 A4
Llandybie 57 A6
Llandyfaelog 57 A4
Llandyfan 57 A6
Llandyfriog 73 B6
Llandyfrydog 123 B4
Llandygwydd 73 B5
Llandynan 109 A6
Llandyrnog 125 C6
Llandysilio 110 D1
Llandyssil 93 B5
Llandysul 73 B7
Llanedeyrn 41 C7
Llanedi 57 B5
Llaneglwys 77 D4
Llanegryn 90 B3
Llanegwad 58 C2
Llaneilian 123 A4
Llanelian-yn-Rhos 124 B3
Llanelidan 125 D6
Llanelieu 77 D5
Llanellen 61 B5
Llanelli 57 C5
Llanelltyd 91 A5
Llanelly 60 B4
Llanelly Hill 60 B4
Llanelwedd 76 B4
Llanenddwyn 107 D5
Llanengan 106 D2
Llanerchymedd 123 B4
Llanerfyl 92 A4
Llanfachraeth 122 B3
Llanfachreth 108 C2
Llanfaelog 122 C3
Llanfaelrhys 106 D2
Llanfaenor 61 B6
Llanfaes
Anglesey 123 C6
Powys 60 A2
Llanfaethlu 122 B3
Llanfaglan 123 D4
Llanfair 107 D5
Llanfair-ar-y-bryn 59 B5
Llanfair Caereinion 93 A5
Llanfair Clydogau 75 C5
Llanfair-Dyffryn-Clwyd 125 D6
Llanfairfechan 124 B1
Llanfair Kilgheddin 61 C5
Llanfair-Nant-Gwyn 73 C4
Llanfairpwll-gwyngyll 123 C5
Llanfair Talhaiarn 125 B4
Llanfair Waterdine 93 D6
Llanfairyneubwll 122 C3
Llanfairynghornwy 122 A3
Llanfallteg 56 A1
Llanfaredd 77 B4
Llanfarian 75 A4
Llanfechain 109 C6
Llanfechan 76 B3
Llanfechell 122 A3
Llanfendigaid 90 B3
Llanferres 126 C1
Llan Ffestiniog 108 A2
Llanfflewyn 122 B3
Llanfihangel-ar-arth 58 B1

Llanfihangel-Crucorney 61 A5
Llanfihangel Glyn Myfyr 109 A4
Llanfihangel Nant Bran 59 B6
Llanfihangel-nant-Melan 77 B5
Llanfihangel Rhydithon 77 A5
Llanfihangel Rogiet 42 A3
Llanfihangel Tal-y-llyn 60 A3
Llanfihangel-uwch-Gwili 58 C1
Llanfihangel-y-Creuddyn 75 A5
Llanfihangel-yn-Ngwynfa 109 D5
Llanfihangel yn Nhowyn 122 C3
Llanfihangel-y-pennant
Gwyn 91 B4
Gwyn 107 B5
Llanfihangel-y-traethau 107 C5
Llanfilo 77 D5
Llanfoist 61 B4
Llanfor 108 B4
Llanfrechfa 61 D5
Llanfrothen 107 B6
Llanfrynach 60 A2
Llanfwrog
Anglesey 122 B3
Denb 125 D6
Llanfyllin 109 D6
Llanfynydd Carms 58 C2
Flint 126 D2
Llanfyrnach 73 C5
Llangadfan 109 D5
Llangadog 59 C4
Llangadwaladr
Anglesey 122 D3
Powys 109 B6
Llangaffo 123 D4
Llangain 56 A3
Llangammarch Wells 76 C3
Llangan 41 D4
Llangarron 62 A1
Llangasty Talyllyn 60 A3
Llangathen 58 C2
Llangattock 60 B4
Llangattock Lingoed 61 A5
Llangattock nigh Usk 61 C5
Llangattock-Vibon-Avel 61 B6
Llangedwyn 109 C6
Llangefni 123 C4
Llangeinor 40 C4
Llangeitho 75 C5
Llangeler 73 C6
Llangelynin 90 B3
Llangendeirne 57 A4
Llangennech 57 B5
Llangennith 57 C4
Llangenny 60 B4
Llangernyw 124 C3
Llangian 106 D2
Llanglydwen 73 D4
Llangoed 123 C6
Llangoedmor 73 B4
Llangollen 109 A7
Llangolman 55 B7
Llangors 60 A3
Llangovan 61 C6
Llangower 108 B4
Llangrannog 73 A6
Llangristiolus 123 C4
Llangrove 62 B1
Llangua 61 A5
Llangunllo 93 D6
Llangunnor 57 A4
Llangurig 92 D3
Llangwm Conwy 109 A4
Mon 61 C6
Pembs 55 D5
Llangwnnadl 106 C2
Llangwyfan 125 C6
Llangwyfan-isaf 122 D3
Llangwyllog 123 C4
Llangwyryfon 75 A4
Llangybi Ceredig 75 C5
Gwyn 107 B4
Mon 61 D5
Llangyfelach 57 C6
Llangynhafal 125 C6
Llangynidr 60 B3
Llangynin 56 A2
Llangynog Carms 56 A3
Powys 109 C5
Llangynwyd 40 C3
Llanhamlach 60 A2
Llanharan 41 C5
Llanharry 41 C5
Llanhennock 61 D5
Llanhilleth
Llanhiledd 41 A7
Llanidloes 92 C3
Llaniestyn 106 C2
Llanifyny 91 D6
Llanigon 77 D6
Llanilar 75 A5
Llanilid 41 C4
Llanishen Cardiff 41 C6
Mon 61 C6
Llanllawddog 58 C1
Llanllechid 123 D6
Llanllowell 61 D5
Llanllugan 93 A4
Llanllwch 56 A3
Llanllwchaiarn 93 B5
Llanllwni 58 B1
Llanllyfni 107 A4
Llanmadoc 57 C4
Llanmaes 41 E4
Llanmartin 42 A2
Llanmihangel 41 D4
Llanmorlais 57 C5
Llannefydd 125 B4
Llannon 57 B5
Llannor 106 C3
Llanon 75 B4
Llanover 61 C5
Llanpumsaint 73 D7
Llanreithan 55 B4
Llanrhaeadr 125 C5
Llanrhaeadr-ym-Mochnant 109 C6
Llanrhian 54 A4
Llanrhidian 57 C4
Llanrhos 124 A2
Llanrhyddlad 122 B3
Llanrhystud 75 B4
Llanrosser 77 D6
Llanrothal 61 B6
Llanrug 123 D5
Llanrumney 41 C7
Llanrwst 124 C3
Llansadurnen 56 A2
Llansadwrn
Anglesey 123 C5
Carms 58 B3
Llansaint 56 B3
Llansamlet 40 B1
Llansannan 125 C4
Llansannor 41 D4
Llansantffraed
Ceredig 75 B4
Powys 60 A3
Llansantffraed Cwmdeuddwr 76 A3
Llansantffraed-in-Elvel 77 B4
Llansantffraid-ym-Mechain 109 C7
Llansawel 58 B3
Llansilin 109 C7
Llansoy 61 C6
Llanspyddid 60 A2
Llanstadwell 55 D5
Llansteffan 56 A3
Llanstephan 77 C5
Llantarnam 61 D5
Llanteg 56 A1
Llanthony 61 A4
Llantilio Crossenny 61 B5
Llantilio Pertholey 61 B5
Llantood 73 B4
Llantrisant
Anglesey 122 B3
Mon 61 D5
Rhondda 41 C5
Llantrithyd 41 D5
Llantwit Fardre 41 C5
Llantwit Major
Llanilltud Fawr 41 E4
Llanuwchllyn 108 B3
Llanvaches 61 D6
Llanvair Discoed 61 D6
Llanvapley 61 B5
Llanvetherine 61 B5
Llanveynoe 77 D7
Llanvihangel Gobion 61 C5
Llanvihangel-Ystern-Llewern 61 B6
Llanwarne 61 A7
Llanwddyn 109 D5
Llanwenog 74 D3
Llanwern 42 A2
Llanwinio 73 D5
Llanwnda Gwyn 107 A4
Pembs 72 C2
Llanwnnen 75 D4
Llanwnog 92 B4
Llanwrda 59 B4
Llanwrin 91 B5
Llanwrthwl 76 A3
Llanwrtyd 76 C2
Llanwrtyd Wells
Llanwrtud 76 C2
Llanwyddelan 93 A4
Llanyblodwel 110 C1
Llanybri 56 A3
Llanybydder 58 A2
Llanycefn 55 B6
Llanychaer 72 C2
Llanycil 108 B4
Llanycrwys 75 D5
Llanymawddwy 91 A7
Llanymynech 110 C1
Llanynghenedl 122 B3
Llanynys 125 C6
Llan-y-pwll 126 D3
Llanyre 76 A4
Llanystumdwy 107 C4
Llanywern 60 A3
Llawhaden 55 C6
Llawnt 110 B1
Llawr Dref 106 D2
Llawryglyn 92 B3
Llay 126 D3
Llechcynfarwy 122 B3
Llecheiddior 107 B4
Llechfaen 60 A2
Llechryd Caerph 60 C3
Ceredig 73 B5
Llechrydau 110 B1
Lledrod 75 A5
Llenmerewig 93 B5
Llethrid 57 C5
Llidiad Nenog 58 B2
Llidiardau 108 B3
Llidiart-y-parc 109 A6
Llithfaen 106 B3
Llong 126 C2
Llowes 77 C5
Llundain-fach 75 C4
Llwydcoed 41 A4
Llwyn 93 C6
Llwyncelyn 74 C3
Llwyndafydd 73 A6
Llwynderw 93 A6
Llwyn-du 61 B4
Llwyndyrys 106 B3
Llwyngwril 90 B3
Llwyn-hendy 57 C5
Llwynmawr 110 B1
Llwyn-têg 57 B5
Llwyn-y-brain 56 A1
Llwyn-y-groes 75 C4
Llwynypia 41 B4
Llynclys 110 C1
Llynfaes 123 C4
Llysfaen 124 B3
Llyswen 77 D5
Llysworney 41 D4
Llys-y-frân 55 B6
Llywel 59 B5
Loan 208 C2
Loanend 198 A3
Loanhead 209 D5
Loans 192 B3
Loans of Tullich 265 C4
Lobb 25 B5
Loch a Charnain 286 B4
Loch a' Ghainmhich 288 E3
Lochailort 235 B6
Lochaline 225 B5
Lochanhully 253 D5
Lochans 170 B2
Locharbriggs 184 D2
Lochassynt Lodge 271 B4
Lochavich Ho 214 A2
Lochawe 227 D6
Loch Baghasdail
Lochboisdale 286 E3
Lochbuie 225 D5
Lochcarron 249 C5
Loch Choire Lodge 273 A4
Lochdhu 279 D6
Lochdochart House 216 B4
Lochdon 225 C6
Lochdrum 263 C4
Lochead 202 A2
Lochearnhead 217 B5
Lochee 220 A3
Lochend Highld 252 C1
Highld 281 B4
Locherben 184 C2
Loch Euphoirt 287 H3
Lochfoot 173 A6
Lochgair 214 C2
Lochgarthside 240 A3
Lochgelly 209 A4
Lochgilphead 214 D1
Lochgoilhead 215 B5
Loch Head 171 C5
Lochhill 266 C3
Lochindorb Lodge 253 C5
Lochinver 270 B3
Lochlane 218 B3
Loch Loyal Lodge 277 D7
Lochluichart 263 D5
Lochmaben 184 D3
Lochmore Cottage 280 D2
Lochmore Lodge 271 A5
Loch nam Madadh
Lochmaddy 287 H4
Lochore 209 A4
Lochportain 287 G4
Lochranza 203 C4
Lochs Crofts 266 C4
Loch Sgioport 286 C4
Lochside Aberds 233 B5
Highld 253 A4
Highld 274 A2
Highld 277 C5
Lochslin 265 B4
Lochstack Lodge 276 D3
Lochton 245 C4
Lochty Angus 232 B3
Fife 221 D5
Perth 219 B5
Lochuisge 236 D1
Lochurr 183 D5
Lochwinnoch 204 C3
Lochwood 184 C3
Lochyside 237 B5
Lockengate 5 A5
Lockerbie 185 D4
Lockeridge 45 C5
Lockerley 32 C1
Locking 42 D2
Lockinge 46 A2
Lockington
E Yorks 150 C2
Lockington
Leics 114 C2
Lockleywood 111 C5
Locks Heath 18 A4
Lockton 160 B2
Lockwood 139 B4
Loddington Leics 99 A4
Northants 99 D5
Loddiswell 7 C6
Loddon 105 B4
Lode 86 A1
Loders 15 B4
Lodsworth 34 D2
Lofthouse
N Yorks 157 D5
W Yorks 139 A6
Loftus 169 D5
Logan 193 C5
Loganlea 208 D2
Logan Mains 170 C2
Loggerheads 111 B6
Logie Angus 233 B4
Fife 220 B4
Moray 253 A6
Logiealmond Lodge 219 A4
Logie Coldstone 244 B1
Logie Hill 264 C3
Logie Newton 256 C1
Logie Pert 233 B4
Logierait 230 C3
Login 73 D4
Lolworth 85 A5
Lonbain 248 A3
Londesborough 150 C1
London Colney 68 C1
Londonderry 157 C7
Londonthorpe 116 B2
Londubh 261 B5
Lonemore 264 B3
Long Ashton 43 B4
Longbar 204 C3
Long Bennington 115 A6
Longbenton 179 C4
Longborough 64 A2
Long Bredy 15 B5
Longbridge Warks 81 A5
W Mid 96 D3
Longbridge Deverill 30 A2
Long Buckby 82 A3
Longburton 29 D6
Long Clawson 115 C5
Longcliffe 130 D2
Long Common 32 D4
Long Compton
Staffs 112 C2
Warks 81 D5
Longcot 64 D3
Long Crendon 66 C2
Long Crichel 30 D3
Longcroft 207 C5
Longden 94 A2
Long Ditton 49 C4
Longdon Staffs 113 D4
Worcs 79 D6
Longdon Green 113 D4
Longdon on Tern 111 D5
Longdown 12 B3
Longdowns 4 D2
Long Drax 141 A4
Long Duckmanton 131 B4
Long Eaton 114 B2
Longfield Kent 50 C3
Shetland 285 M5
Longford Derbys 113 B6
Glos 63 A4
London 48 B3
Shrops 111 B5
Telford 111 D6
W Mid 97 C6
Longfordlane 113 B6
Longforgan 220 B3
Longformacus 197 A5
Longframlington 189 C4
Long Green 79 D6
Longham Dorset 17 B4
Norf 119 D6
Long Hanborough 65 B5
Longhaven 257 C6
Longhill 269 D4
Longhirst 179 A4
Longhope Glos 62 B2
Orkney 283 H4
Longhorsley 189 D4
Longhoughton 189 B5
Long Itchington 81 A7
Longlane Derbys 113 B6
W Berks 46 B2
Long Lawford 98 D1
Longlevens 63 A4
Longley 139 C4
Longley Green 79 B5
Long Load 29 C4
Longmanhill 268 C2
Long Marston
Herts 66 B4
N Yorks 148 B4
Warks 81 C4
Long Marton 165 C4
Long Melford 87 C4
Longmoor Camp 33 B6
Longmorn 266 D3
Long Newnton 63 D5
Longnewton
Borders 187 A4
Stockton 167 D6
Long Newton 210 D2
Longney 62 B3
Longniddry 210 C1
Longnor Shrops 94 A2
Staffs 129 C5
Longparish 32 A3
Longport 112 A2
Long Preston 146 B2
Longridge Lancs 145 D6
Staffs 112 D3
W Loth 208 D2
Longriggend 207 C6
Long Riston 151 C4
Longsdon 129 D4
Longshaw 136 C4
Longside 257 B5
Long Sight 138 C2
Longstanton 85 A5
Longstock 32 B2
Longstone 56 B1
Longstowe 85 B5
Long Stratton 104 B2
Long Street 83 C4
Long Sutton
Hants 33 A6
Lincs 118 C1
Som 29 C4
Longthorpe 100 B3
Long Thurlow 87 A6
Longthwaite 164 C2
Longton Lancs 136 A3
Stoke 112 A3
Longtown Cumb 175 B6
Hereford 61 A5
Longview 136 D3
Longville in the Dale 94 B3
Long Whatton 114 C2
Longwick 66 C3
Long Wittenham 65 D6
Longwitton 178 A2
Longwood 95 A4
Longworth 65 D4
Longyester 210 D2
Lonmay 269 D5
Lonmore 258 D2
Looe 6 B1
Loose 37 A5
Loosley Row 66 C4
Lopcombe Corner 31 B6
Lopen 28 D4
Loppington 110 C3
Lopwell 6 A3
Lorbottle 188 C3
Lorbottle Hall 188 C3
Lornty 231 D5
Loscoe 114 A2
Losgaintir 287 E5
Lossiemouth 266 B3
Lossit 200 C1
Lostford 111 B5

Lostock Gralam . 128 B1
Lostock Green . . 128 B1
Lostock Hall 136 A4
Lostock Junction 137 C5
Lostwithiel. 5 B6
Loth 282 D7
Lothbeg 274 C3
Lothersdale 146 C3
Lothmore 274 C3
Loudwater 67 D5
Loughborough . . 114 D3
Loughor 57 C5
Loughton Essex . . . 68 D4
M Keynes 83 D5
Shrops 95 C4
Lound Lincs. 116 D3
Notts 132 A1
Suff 105 B6
Lount 114 D1
Louth 134 A3
Love Clough 137 A7
Lovedean 33 D5
Lover 31 C6
Loversall 140 D3
Loves Green 69 C6
Lovesome Hill . . . 158 B2
Loveston 55 D6
Lovington 29 B5
Low Ackworth . . . 140 B2
Low Barlings 133 B5
Low Bentham . . . 145 A6
Low Bradfield . . . 139 D5
Low Bradley 147 C4
Low Braithwaite 164 A2
Lowbridge House 154 A4
Low Brunton 177 B7
Low Burnham . . . 141 C5
Low Burton 157 C6
Low Buston 189 C5
Lowca 162 B2
Low Catton 149 B6
Low Clanyard . . . 170 D3
Low Coniscliffe . . 167 D5
Low Crosby 176 D2
Low Dalby 160 C2
Lowdham 115 A4
Low Dinsdale . . . 167 D6
Lowe 111 B4
Lowe Hill 129 D4
Low Ellington . . . 157 C6
Lower Aisholt 28 B2
Lower Arncott 65 B7
Lower Ashton 12 C3
Lower Assendon . 47 A5
Lower Badcall . . 276 D2
Lower Bartle 145 D4
Lower Basildon . . 47 B4
Lower Beeding . . . 35 D5
Lower Benefield 100 C1
Lower Boddington 82 B1
Lower Brailes 81 D6
Lower Breakish . 247 B5
Lower Broadheath 79 B6
Lower Bullingham 78 D3
Lower Cam 62 C3
Lower Chapel 76 D4
Lower Chute 45 D7
Lower Cragabus 200 D3
Lower Crossings 129 A5
Lower Cumberworth . . 139 C5
Lower Cwm-twrch 59 D4
Lower Darwen . . 137 A5
Lower Dean 84 A2
Lower Diabaig . . 261 D4
Lower Dicker 22 A3
Lower Dinchope . . 94 C2
Lower Down 94 C1
Lower Drift 2 C2
Lower Dunsforth 148 A3
Lower Egleton . . . 79 C4
Lower Elkstone . . 129 D5
Lower End 67 A5
Lower Everleigh . . 45 D5
Lower Farringdon 33 B6
Lower Foxdale . . 152 D2
Lower Frankton . 110 B2
Lower Froyle 33 A6
Lower Gledfield . 264 A1
Lower Green 120 B1
Lower Hacheston. 88 B4
Lower Halistra . . 258 C2
Lower Halstow . . . 51 C5
Lower Hardres . . . 52 D3
Lower Hawthwaite . . . 153 B3
Lower Heath 128 C3
Lower Hempriggs 266 C2
Lower Hergest . . . 77 B6
Lower Heyford . . . 65 A5
Lower Higham . . . 51 B4
Lower Holbrook . . 88 D2
Lower Hordley . . 110 C2
Lower Horsebridge 22 A3
Lower Killeyan . . 200 D2
Lower Kingswood 35 A5
Lower Kinnerton 126 C3
Lower Langford . . 42 C3
Lower Largo 220 D4
Lower Leigh 112 B4
Lower Lemington 81 D5
Lower Lenie 251 D7
Lower Lydbrook . . 62 B1
Lower Lye 78 A2
Lower Machen . . . 42 A1
Lower Maes-coed 78 D1
Lower Mayland . . . 70 C3
Lower Midway . . 113 C7
Lower Milovaig . . 258 C1
Lower Moor 80 C2
Lower Nazeing . . . 68 C3
Lower Netchwood 95 B4
Lower Ollach 247 A4
Lower Penarth . . . 41 D6
Lower Penn 95 B6
Lower Pennington 18 B2
Lower Peover . . . 128 B2
Lower Pexhill . . . 128 B3
Lower Place 138 B2
Lower Quinton . . . 81 C4
Lower Rochford . . 79 A4
Lower Seagry 44 A3
Lower Shelton . . . 84 C1
Lower Shiplake . . 47 B5
Lower Shuckburgh 82 A1
Lower Slaughter . 64 A2
Lower Stanton St Quintin 44 A3
Lower Stoke 51 B5
Lower Stondon . . . 84 D3
Lower Stow Bedon 103 B5
Lower Street Norf 121 B4
Norf 121 D5
Lower Strensham 80 C2
Lower Stretton . . 127 A6
Lower Sundon . . . 67 A6
Lower Swanwick . 18 A3
Lower Swell 64 A2
Lower Tean 112 B4
Lower Thurlton . . 105 B5
Lower Tote 259 B5
Lower Town 72 C2
Lower Tysoe 81 C6
Lower Upham 32 D4
Lower Vexford . . . 27 B6
Lower Weare 42 D3
Lower Welson 77 B6
Lower Whitley . . . 127 B6
Lower Wield 33 A5
Lower Winchendon 66 B3
Lower Withington 128 C3
Lower Woodend . . 47 A6
Lower Woodford . 31 B5
Lower Wyche 79 C5
Lowesby 99 A4
Lowestoft 105 B6
Loweswater 163 B4
Low Etherley 167 C4
Low Fell 179 D4
Lowford 32 D3
Low Fulney 117 C5
Low Garth 159 A6
Low Gate 177 C7
Lowgill Cumb 155 B5
Lancs 145 A6
Low Grantley 157 D6
Low Habberley . . . 95 D6
Low Ham 28 C4
Low Hesket 164 A2
Low Hesleyhurst . . . 188 D3
Low Hutton 149 A6
Lowick Northants 100 C1
Northumb 198 C4
Lowick Bridge . . . 154 C1
Lowick Green . . . 154 C1
Low Laithe 147 A5
Lowlands 61 D4
Low Leighton . . . 129 A5
Low Lorton 163 B4
Low Marishes . . . 159 D7
Low Marnham . . . 132 C3
Low Mill 159 B5
Low Moor Lancs . . 146 C1
W Yorks 139 A4
Lowmoor Row . . . 165 C4
Low Moorsley . . . 167 A6
Low Newton 154 C3
Low Newton-by-the-Sea 189 A5
Lownie Moor 232 D2
Low Row Cumb . . . 163 A6
Cumb 176 C3
N Yorks 156 B3
Low Salchrie 170 A2
Low Smerby 190 C3
Lowsonford 81 A4
Lowther 164 C3
Lowthorpe 150 A3
Lowton 137 D5
Lowton Common 137 D5
Low Torry 208 B3
Low Worsall 158 A2
Low Wray 154 A2
Loxbeare 27 D4
Loxhill 34 C3
Loxhore 25 B7
Loxley 81 B5
Loxton 42 D2
Loxwood 34 C3
Lubcroy 271 D6
Lubenham 99 C4
Luccombe 27 A4
Luccombe Village 19 D4
Lucker 199 C5
Luckett 11 D4
Luckington 44 A2
Lucklawhill 220 B4
Luckwell Bridge . . 27 B4
Lucton 78 A2
Ludag 286 E3
Ludborough 143 D4
Ludchurch 56 A1
Luddenden 138 A3
Luddenden Foot 138 A3
Luddesdown 50 C3
Luddington N Lincs 141 B6
Warks 81 B4
Luddington in the Brook 100 C3
Lude House 230 B2
Ludford Lincs 134 A2
Shrops 94 D3
Ludgershall Bucks. 66 B2
Wilts 45 D6
Ludgvan 2 B3
Ludham 121 D5
Ludlow 94 D3
Ludwell 30 C3
Ludworth 167 A6
Luffincott 10 B4
Lugar 193 C5
Luggate Burn . . . 210 C3
Lugg Green 78 A2
Luggiebank 207 C5
Lugton 205 C4
Lugwardine 78 C3
Luib 247 B4
Lulham 78 C2
Lullenden 36 B2
Lullington Derbys 113 D6
Som 44 D1
Lulsgate Bottom . . 43 C4
Lulsley 79 B5
Lumb 138 A3
Lumby 148 D3
Lumloch 205 B6
Lumphanan 244 B2
Lumphinnans . . . 209 A4
Lumsdaine 211 D5
Lumsden 255 D5
Lunan 233 C4
Lunanhead 232 C2
Luncarty 219 B5
Lund E Yorks 150 C2
N Yorks 149 D5
Shetland 284 C7
Lunderton 269 E6
Lundie Angus 220 A2
Highld 239 A5
Lundin Links 220 D4
Lunga 213 B5
Lunna 284 G6
Lunning 284 G7
Lunnon 57 D5
Lunsford's Cross . 23 A5
Lunt 136 C2
Luntley 78 B1
Luppitt 13 A6
Lupset 139 B6
Lupton 155 C4
Lurgashall 34 D2
Lusby 134 C3
Luson 7 C5
Luss 206 A1
Lussagiven 213 D4
Lusta 258 C2
Lustleigh 12 C2
Luston 78 A2
Luthermuir 233 B4
Luthrie 220 C3
Luton Devon 13 D4
Luton 67 A6
Medway 51 C4
Lutterworth 98 C2
Lutton Devon 7 B4
Lincs 118 C1
Northants 100 C3
Lutworthy 26 D2
Luxborough 27 B4
Luxulyan 5 B5
Lybster 275 A6
Lydbury North 94 C1
Lydcott 26 B1
Lydd 38 C2
Lydden 39 A4
Lyddington 99 B5
Lydd on Sea 38 C2
Lydeard St Lawrence 27 B6
Lyde Green 47 D5
Lydford 11 C6
Lydford-on-Fosse 29 B5
Lydgate 138 A2
Lydham 94 B1
Lydiard Green 45 A4
Lydiard Millicent . 45 A4
Lydiate 136 C2
Lydlinch 30 D1
Lydney 62 C2
Lydstep 55 E6
Lye 96 C2
Lye Green Bucks . . 67 C5
E Sus 36 C3
Lyford 65 D4
Lymbridge Green 38 A3
Lyme Regis 14 B3
Lyminge 38 A3
Lymington 18 B2
Lyminster 20 B3
Lymm 128 A1
Lymore 18 B1
Lympne 38 B3
Lympsham 42 D2
Lympstone 13 C4
Lynchat 241 B5
Lyndale Ho. 258 C3
Lyndhurst 18 A2
Lyndon 99 A6
Lyne 48 C3
Lyneal 110 B3
Lyne Down 79 D4
Lyneham Oxon 64 A3
Wilts 44 B4
Lynemore 253 D6
Lynemouth 189 D5
Lyne of Gorthleck 252 D1
Lyne of Skene . . . 245 A4
Lyness 283 H4
Lyng Norf 120 D2
Som 28 C3
Lynmouth 26 A2
Lynsted 51 C6
Lynton 26 A2
Lyon's Gate 15 A6
Lyonshall 78 B1
Lytchett Matravers 16 B3
Lytchett Minster . . 16 B3
Lyth 281 B4
Lytham 136 A2
Lytham St Anne's 136 A2
Lythe 169 D6
Lythes 283 J5

M

Mabe Burnthouse . 4 D2
Mabie 174 A2
Mablethorpe 135 A5
Macclesfield 129 B4
Macclesfield Forest 129 B4
Macduff 268 C2
Mace Green 88 C2
Macharioch 190 E3
Machen 41 C7
Machrihanish . . . 190 C2
Machynlleth 91 B5
Machynys 57 C5
Mackerel's Common 34 D3
Mackworth 113 B7
Macmerry 210 C1
Madderty 219 B4
Maddiston 208 C2
Madehurst 20 A2
Madeley Staffs 111 A6
Telford 95 A4
Madeley Heath . . 112 A1
Madeley Park . . . 112 A1
Madingley 85 A5
Madley 78 D2
Madresfield 79 C6
Madron 2 B2
Maenaddwyn 123 B4
Maenclochog 55 B6
Maendy 41 D5
Maentwrog 107 B6
Maen-y-groes . . . 73 A6
Maer 112 B1
Maerdy Conwy . . . 109 A5
Rhondda 41 B4
Maesbrook 110 C1
Maesbury 110 C2
Maesbury Marsh 110 C2
Maesgwyn-Isaf . . 109 D6
Maesgwynne 73 D5
Maeshafn 126 C2
Maesllyn 73 B6
Maesmynis 76 C4
Maesteg 40 B3
Maestir 75 D4
Maes-Treylow . . . 77 A6
Maesybont 57 A5
Maesycrugiau 58 A1
Maesy cwmmer . . 41 B6
Maesymeillion . . . 73 B7
Magdalen Laver . . 69 C5
Maggieknockater 254 B4
Magham Down . . . 22 A4
Maghull 136 C2
Magor 42 A3
Magpie Green . . . 104 D1
Maiden Bradley . . 30 B2
Maidencombe 8 A3
Maidenhall 88 C2
Maidenhead 48 A1
Maiden Law 167 A4
Maiden Newton . . 15 B5
Maidens 192 E2
Maidensgrave 88 C3
Maiden's Green . . 48 B1
Maidenwell Corn . . 10 D2
Lincs 134 B3
Maiden Wells 55 E5
Maidford 82 B3
Maids Moreton . . . 83 D4
Maidstone 37 A5
Maidwell 99 D4
Mail 285 L6
Main 109 D6
Maindee 42 A2
Mainsforth 167 B6
Mains of Airies . . 170 A1
Mains of Allardice 233 A6
Mains of Annochie 257 B4
Mains of Ardestie 221 A5
Mains of Balhall 232 B3
Mains of Ballindarg 232 C2
Mains of Balnakettle 233 A4
Mains of Birness 257 C4
Mains of Burgie . 266 D1
Mains of Clunas 253 B4
Mains of Crichie 257 B4
Mains of Dalvey . 254 C2
Mains of Dellavaird 245 D4
Mains of Drum . . 245 C5
Mains of Edingight 267 D6
Mains of Fedderate 268 E3
Mains of Inkhorn 257 C4
Mains of Mayen . 255 B6
Mains of Melgund 232 C3
Mains of Thornton 233 A4
Mains of Watten 281 C4
Mainsriddle 174 C2
Mainstone 93 C6
Maisemore 63 A4
Malacleit 287 G2
Malborough 7 D6
Malcoff 129 A5
Maldon 70 C2
Malham 146 A3
Maligar 259 B4
Mallaig 235 A5
Malleny Mills 209 D4
Malling 217 D5
Malltraeth 123 D4
Mallwyd 91 A6
Malmesbury 44 A3
Malmsmead 26 A2
Malpas Ches W . . . 110 A3
Corn 4 C3
Newport 61 D5
Malswick 62 A3
Maltby Stockton . . 168 D2
S Yorks 140 D3
Maltby le Marsh 135 A4
Malting Green 70 A3
Maltman's Hill . . . 37 B7
Malton 159 D6
Malvern Link 79 C5
Malvern Wells 79 C5
Mamble 95 D4

Manaccan 3 C5
Manafon 93 A5
Manar Ho. 256 D2
Manaton 12 C2
Manby 134 A3
Mancetter 97 B6
Manchester 138 D1
Manchester Airport 128 A3
Mancot 126 C3
Mandally 239 B6
Manea 101 C6
Manfield 167 D5
Mangaster 284 F5
Mangotsfield 43 B5
Mangurstadh 287 A5
Mankinholes 138 A2
Manley 127 B5
Man-moel 41 A6
Mannal 222 C2
Mannerston 208 C3
Manningford Bohune 45 D5
Manningford Bruce 45 D5
Manningham 147 D5
Mannings Heath 35 D5
Mannington 17 A4
Manningtree 88 D1
Mannofield 245 B6
Manor 50 A1
Manorbier 55 E6
Manordeilo 58 C3
Manor Estate 130 A3
Manorhill 197 C5
Manorowen 72 C2
Manselfield 57 D5
Mansel Lacy 78 C2
Mansell Gamage 78 C1
Mansergh 155 C5
Mansfield E Ayrs 182 A4
Notts 131 C5
Mansfield Woodhouse 131 C5
Mansriggs 154 C1
Manston Dorset 30 D2
Kent 53 C5
W Yorks 148 D2
Manswood 16 A3
Manthorpe Lincs 116 B2
Lincs 116 D3
Manton N Lincs 142 C1
Notts 131 B5
Rutland 99 A5
Wilts 45 C5
Manuden 69 A4
Maperton 29 C6
Maplebeck 132 C2
Maple Cross 67 D6
Mapledurham 47 B4
Mapledurwell 47 D4
Maplehurst 35 D4
Maplescombe 50 C2
Mapleton 113 A5
Mapperley 114 A2
Mapperley Park 114 A3
Mapperton 15 B5
Mappleborough Green 80 A3
Mappleton 151 C5
Mappowder 16 A1
Maraig 288 G2
Marazanvose 4 B3
Marazion 2 B3
Marbhig 288 F5
Marbury 111 A4
March Cambs 101 B6
S Lanark 184 A2
Marcham 65 D5
Marchamley 111 C4
Marchington 113 B5
Marchington Woodlands 113 C5
Marchroes 106 D3
Marchwiel 110 A2
Marchwood 32 D2
Marcross 40 E4
Marden Hereford 78 C3
Kent 37 B5
Marden T&W 179 B5
Wilts 45 D4
Marden Beech 37 B5
Marden Thorn 37 B5
Mardy 61 B5
Marefield 99 A4
Mareham le Fen 134 C2
Mareham on the Hill 134 C2
Marehay 114 A1
Marehill 20 A3
Maresfield 36 D2
Marfleet 142 A3
Marford 126 D3
Margam 40 C2
Margaret Marsh 30 D2
Margaret Roding 69 B5
Margaretting 69 C6
Margate 53 B5
Margnaheglish 191 B6
Margrove Park 169 D4
Marham 119 D4
Marhamchurch 10 A3
Marholm 100 A3
Mariandyrys 123 B6
Marianglas 123 B5
Mariansleigh 26 C2
Marionburgh 245 B4
Marishader 259 B4
Marjoriebanks 184 D3
Mark Dumfries 170 B3
S Ayrs 180 D2
Som 28 A3
Markbeech 36 B2
Markby 135 B4
Mark Causeway 28 A3
Mark Cross E Sus 22 A2
E Sus 36 C3
Market Bosworth 97 A7
Market Deeping 116 E4
Market Drayton 111 B5
Market Harborough 99 C4
Markethill 220 A2
Market Lavington 44 D4
Market Overton 116 D1
Market Rasen 133 A6
Market Stainton 134 B2
Market Warsop 131 C5
Market Weighton 150 C1
Market Weston 103 D5
Markfield 114 D2
Markham 41 A6
Markham Moor 132 B2
Markinch 220 D2
Markington 148 A1
Marksbury 43 C5
Marks Tey 70 A3
Markyate 67 B6
Marland 138 B1
Marlborough 45 C5
Marlbrook Hereford 78 B3
Worcs 96 D2
Marlcliff 80 B3
Marldon 8 A2
Marlesford 88 B4
Marley Green 111 A4
Marley Hill 179 D4
Marley Mount 17 B6
Marlingford 104 A2
Mar Lodge 242 C3
Marloes 54 D3
Marlow Bucks 47 A6
Hereford 94 D2
Marlow Bottom 47 A6
Marlpit Hill 36 B2
Marlpool 114 A2
Marnhull 30 D1
Marnoch 267 D6
Marnock 207 D5
Marple 129 A4
Marple Bridge 129 A4
Marr 140 C3
Marrel 274 C4
Marrick 157 B4
Marrister 285 G7
Marros 56 B2
Marsden T&W 179 C5
W Yorks 138 B3
Marsett 156 C3
Marsh Devon 28 D2
W Yorks 147 D4
Marshall's Heath 67 B7
Marshalsea 14 A3
Marshalswick 67 C7
Marsham 120 C3
Marshaw 145 B5
Marsh Baldon 65 D6
Marshborough 53 D5
Marshbrook 94 C2
Marshchapel 143 D5
Marshfield Newport 42 A1
S Glos 44 B1
Marshgate 10 B2
Marsh Gibbon 66 A2
Marsh Green Devon 13 B5
Kent 36 B2
Staffs 128 D3
Marshland St James 101 A7
Marsh Lane 131 B4
Marshside 136 B2
Marsh Street 27 A4
Marshwood 14 B3
Marske 157 A5
Marske-by-the-Sea 168 C4
Marston Ches W 127 B6
Hereford 78 B1
Lincs 116 A1
Oxon 65 C6
Staffs 112 C3
Staffs 112 D2
Warks 97 B5
Wilts 44 D3
Marston Doles 82 B1
Marston Green 97 C4
Marston Magna 29 C5
Marston Meysey 64 D2
Marston Montgomery 113 B5
Marston Moretaine 84 C1
Marston on Dove 113 C6
Marston St Lawrence 82 C2
Marston Stannett 78 B3
Marston Trussell 98 C3
Marstow 62 B1
Marsworth 67 B5
Marten 45 D6
Marthall 128 B3
Martham 121 D6
Martin Hants 31 D4
Kent 39 A5
Lincs 133 D6
Lincs 134 C2
Martin Dales 134 C1
Martin Drove End 31 C4
Martinhoe 26 A1
Martinhoe Cross 26 A1
Martin Hussingtree 80 A1
Martin Mill 39 A5
Martinscroft 127 A6
Martinstown 15 C6
Martlesham 88 C3
Martlesham Heath 88 C3
Martletwy 55 C6
Martley 79 A5
Martock 29 D4
Marton Ches E 128 C3
E Yorks 151 D4
Lincs 132 A3
Mbro 168 D3
N Yorks 148 A3
N Yorks 159 C6
Shrops 93 A6
Shrops 110 C3
Warks 81 A7
Marton-le-Moor 158 D2
Martyr's Green 34 A3
Martyr Worthy 32 B4
Marwick 282 E3
Marwood 25 B6
Marybank 251 A6
Maryburgh 252 A1
Maryhill 205 B5
Marykirk 233 B4
Marylebone 137 C4
Marypark 254 C2
Maryport Cumb 162 A3
Dumfries 170 D3
Mary Tavy 11 D6
Maryton 233 C4
Marywell Aberds 244 C2
Aberds 245 C6
Angus 233 D4
Masham 157 C6
Mashbury 69 B6
Masongill 155 D5
Masonhill 192 C3
Mastin Moor 131 B4
Mastrick 245 B5
Matching 69 B5
Matching Green 69 B5
Matching Tye 69 B5
Matfen 178 B2
Matfield 37 B4
Mathern 62 D1
Mathon 79 C5
Mathry 55 A4
Matlaske 120 B3
Matlock 130 C2
Matlock Bath 130 D2
Matson 63 B4
Matterdale End 164 C1
Mattersey 132 A1
Mattersey Thorpe 132 A1
Mattingley 47 D5
Mattishall 120 D2
Mattishall Burgh 120 D2
Mauchline 193 C4
Maud 257 B4
Maugersbury 64 A3
Maughold 152 B4
Mauld 251 C6
Maulden 84 D2
Maulds Meaburn 165 D4
Maunby 158 C2
Maund Bryan 78 B3
Maundown 27 C5
Mautby 121 D6
Mavis Enderby 134 C3
Mawbray 174 D3
Mawdesley 136 B3
Mawdlam 40 C3
Mawgan 3 C5
Maw Green 128 D2
Mawla 4 C2
Mawnan 3 C5
Mawnan Smith 3 C5
Mawsley 99 D5
Maxey 100 A3
Maxstoke 97 C5
Maxton Borders 197 C5
Kent 39 A5
Maxwellheugh 197 C6
Maxwelltown 174 A2
Maxworthy 10 B3
Mayals 57 C6
May Bank 112 A2
Maybole 192 E3
Mayfield E Sus 36 D3
Midloth 209 D6
Staffs 113 A5
W Loth 208 D2
Mayford 34 A2
Mayland 70 C3
Maynard's Green 22 A3
Maypole Mon 61 B6
Scilly 2 E4
Maypole Green Essex 70 A3
Norf 105 B5
Suff 88 A3
Maywick 285 L5
Meadle 66 C4
Meadowtown 93 A7
Meaford 112 B2
Mealabost 288 D5
Mealabost Bhuirgh 288 B5
Meal Bank 154 B4
Mealsgate 175 D5
Meanwood 148 D1
Mearbeck 146 A2
Meare 29 A4
Meare Green 28 C3
Mears Ashby 83 A5
Measham 114 D1
Meath Green 35 B5
Meathop 154 C3
Meaux 150 D3
Meavy 7 A4
Medbourne 99 B4
Medburn 178 B3
Meddon 24 D3
Meden Vale 131 C5
Medlam 134 D3
Medmenham 47 A6
Medomsley 178 D3
Medstead 33 B5
Meerbrook 129 C4
Meer End 97 D5
Meers Bridge 135 A4
Meesden 85 D6
Meeth 11 A6
Meggethead 195 D6
Meidrim 73 D5
Meifod Denb 125 D5
Powys 109 D6
Meigle N Ayrs 204 B1
Perth 231 D6
Meikle Earnock 194 A2
Meikle Ferry 264 B3
Meikle Forter 231 B5
Meikle Gluich 264 B2
Meikleour 219 A6
Meikle Pinkerton 211 C4
Meikle Strath 233 A4
Meikle Tarty 257 D4
Meikle Wartle 256 C2
Meinciau 57 A4
Meir 112 A3
Meir Heath 112 A3
Melbourn 85 C5
Melbourne Derbys 114 C1
E Yorks 149 C6
S Lanark 195 B5
Melbury Abbas 30 C2
Melbury Bubb 15 A5
Melbury Osmond 15 A5
Melbury Sampford 15 A5
Melby 285 H3
Melchbourne 84 A2
Melcombe Bingham 16 A1
Melcombe Regis 15 C6
Meldon Devon 11 B6
Northumb 178 A3
Meldreth 85 C5
Meldrum Ho. 256 D3
Melfort 213 A6
Melgarve 240 C2
Meliden 125 A5
Melinbyrhedyn 91 C6
Melincourt 40 A3
Melin-y-coed 124 C3
Melin-y-ddôl 93 A4
Melin-y-grug 93 A4
Melin-y-Wig 109 A5
Melkinthorpe 164 C3
Melkridge 177 C5
Melksham 44 C3
Melldalloch 203 A4
Melling Lancs 155 D4
Mers 136 C2
Melling Mount 136 C3
Mellis 104 D2
Mellon Charles 261 A5
Mellon Udrigle 261 A5
Mellor Gtr Man 129 A4
Lancs 145 D6
Mellor Brook 145 D6
Mells 30 A1
Melmerby Cumb 165 B4
N Yorks 157 C4
N Yorks 158 D2
Melplash 15 B4
Melrose 197 C4
Melsetter 283 J3
Melsonby 157 A5
Meltham 138 B4
Melton 88 B3
Meltonby 149 B6
Melton Constable 120 B2
Melton Mowbray 115 D5
Melton Ross 142 B2
Melvaig 261 B4
Melverley 110 D2
Melverley Green 110 D2
Melvich 279 B4
Membury 14 A2
Memsie 269 C4
Memus 232 C2
Menabilly 5 B5
Menai Bridge Porthaethwy 123 C5
Mendham 104 C3
Mendlesham 88 A2
Mendlesham Green 88 A1
Menheniot 6 A1
Mennock 183 B6
Menston 147 C5
Menstrie 207 A6
Menthorpe 149 D5
Mentmore 67 B5
Meoble 238 D1
Meole Brace 110 D3
Meols 136 D1
Meonstoke 33 D5
Meopham 50 C3
Meopham Station 50 C3
Mepal 101 C6
Meppershall 84 D3
Merbach 77 C7
Mere Ches E 128 A2
Wilts 30 B2
Mere Brow 136 B3
Mereclough 146 D2
Mere Grn. 96 B4
Mereside 144 D3
Mereworth 37 A4
Mergie 245 D4
Meriden 97 C5
Merkadale 246 A2
Merkland Dumfries 173 A5
S Ayrs 181 B4
Merkland Lodge 271 B7
Merley 17 B4
Merlin's Bridge 55 C5
Merrington 110 C3
Merrion 55 E5
Merriott 28 D4
Merrivale 11 D6
Merrow 34 A3
Merrymeet 6 A1
Mersham 38 B2
Merstham 35 A5
Merston 20 B1
Merstone 18 C4
Merther 4 C3
Merthyr 73 D6
Merthyr Cynog 76 D3
Merthyr-Dyfan 41 E6
Merthyr Mawr 40 D3
Merthyr Tydfil Merthyr Tudful 60 C2
Merthyr Vale 41 B5
Merton Devon 25 D6
London 49 B5
Norf 103 B5
Oxon 65 B6
Mervinslaw 187 B5
Meshaw 26 D2
Messing 70 B2
Messingham 141 C6
Metfield 104 C3
Metheringham 133 C5
Methil 209 A6
Methlem 106 C1
Methley 140 A1
Methlick 256 C3
Methven 219 B5
Methwold 102 B3
Methwold Hythe 102 B3
Mettingham 105 C4

Mevagissey 5 C5
Mewith Head 145 A7
Mexborough 140 C2
Mey 281 A4
Meysey Hampton 64 D2
Miabhag W Isles 287 D5
W Isles 288 H2
Miabhig 287 A5
Michaelchurch 61 A7
Michaelchurch Escley 77 D7
Michaelchurch on Arrow 77 B6
Michaelston-le-Pit 41 D6
Michaelston-y-Fedw 42 A1
Michaelstow 10 D1
Michealston-super-Ely 41 D6
Micheldever 32 B4
Michelmersh 32 C2
Mickfield 88 A2
Micklebring 140 D3
Mickleby 169 D6
Mickleham 35 A4
Mickleover 113 B7
Micklethwaite 147 C5
Mickleton
Durham 166 C2
Glos 81 C4
Mickletown 140 A1
Mickle Trafford 127 C4
Mickley 157 D6
Mickley Square 178 C2
Mid Ardlaw 269 C4
Mid Auchinlech 204 A3
Midbea 282 C5
Mid Beltie 244 B3
Mid Calder 208 D3
Mid Cloch Forbie 268 D2
Mid Clyth 275 A6
Middle Assendon 47 A5
Middle Aston 65 A5
Middle Barton 65 A5
Middlebie 175 A5
Middle Cairncake 256 B3
Middle Claydon 66 A3
Middle Drums 232 C3
Middleforth Green 136 A4
Middleham 157 C5
Middle Handley 131 B4
Middlehope 94 C2
Middle Littleton 80 C3
Middle Maes-coed 78 D1
Middlemarsh 15 A6
Middle Mill 54 B4
Middlemuir 257 D4
Middle Rasen 133 A5
Middle Rigg 219 D5
Middlesbrough 168 C2
Middleshaw
Cumb 155 C4
Dumfries 174 A4
Middlesmoor 157 D4
Middlestone 167 B5
Middlestone Moor 167 B5
Middlestown 139 B5
Middlethird 197 B5
Middleton
Aberds 245 A5
Argyll 222 C2
Cumb 155 C5
Derbys 130 C1
Derbys 130 D2
Essex 87 D4
Gtr Man 138 C1
Hants 32 A3
Hereford 78 A3
Lancs 144 B4
Midloth 196 A2
Norf 118 D3
Northants 99 C5
Northumb 178 A2
Northumb 199 C5
N Yorks 147 C5
N Yorks 159 C6
Middleton
Perth 219 D6
Perth 231 D5
Shrops 93 B6
Shrops 94 D3
Shrops 110 C2
Suff 89 A5
Swansea 57 D4
Warks 97 B4
W Yorks 139 A5
Middleton Cheney 82 C1
Middleton Green 112 B3
Middleton Hall 188 A2
Middleton-in-Teesdale 166 C2
Middleton Moor 89 A5
Middleton One Row 167 D6
Middleton-on-Leven 158 A3
Middleton-on-Sea 20 B2
Middleton on the Hill 78 A3
Middleton-on-the-Wolds 150 C2
Middleton Priors 95 B4
Middleton Quernham 158 D2
Middleton St George 167 D6
Middleton Scriven 95 C4
Middleton Stoney 65 A6
Middleton Tyas 157 A6
Middletown
Cumb 162 D2
Powys 110 D2
Middle Tysoe 81 C6
Middle Wallop 32 B1
Middlewich 128 C1
Middle Winterslow 31 B6
Middle Woodford 31 B5
Middlewood Green 88 A1
Middlezoy 28 B3
Middridge 167 C5
Midfield 277 B6
Midge Hall 136 A4
Midgeholme 176 D4
Midgham 46 C3
Midgley W Yorks 138 A3
W Yorks 139 B5
Midhopestones 139 D5
Midhurst 34 D1
Mid Lavant 20 B1
Midlem 186 A4
Mid Main 251 C6
Midmar 244 B3
Midsomer Norton 43 D5
Midton 204 A2
Midtown Highld 261 B5
Highld 277 B6
Midtown of Buchromb 254 B4
Mid Urchany 253 B4
Midville 134 D3
Mid Walls 285 H4
Midway 129 A4
Mid Yell 284 D7
Migdale 264 A2
Migvie 244 B1
Milarrochy 206 A2
Milborne Port 29 D6
Milborne St Andrew 16 B2
Milborne Wick 29 C6
Milbourne 178 B3
Milburn 165 C4
Milbury Heath 62 D2
Milcombe 81 D7
Milden 87 C5
Mildenhall Suff 102 D3
Wilts 45 C6
Milebrook 93 D7
Milebush 37 B5
Mile Cross 120 D4
Mile Elm 44 C3
Mile End Essex 70 A3
Glos 62 B1
Mileham 119 D6
Mile Oak 21 B5
Milesmark 208 B3
Milfield 198 C3
Milford Derbys 114 A1
Devon 24 C3
Powys 93 B4
Staffs 112 C3
Sur 34 B2
Wilts 31 C5
Milford Haven Aberdaugleddau 55 D5
Milford on Sea 18 B1
Milkwall 62 C1
Milkwell 30 C3
Milland 34 D1
Millarston 205 B4
Millbank Aberds 257 B6
Highld 280 B3
Mill Bank 138 A3
Millbeck 163 B5
Millbounds 282 D6
Millbreck 257 B5
Millbridge 34 B1
Millbrook C Beds 84 D2
Corn 6 B3
Soton 32 D2
Millburn 193 C4
Millcombe 8 C2
Mill Common 105 C5
Millcorner 37 D6
Milldale 129 D6
Millden Lodge 232 A3
Milldens 232 C3
Mill End Bucks 47 A5
Herts 85 D5
Millerhill 209 D6
Miller's Dale 129 B6
Miller's Green 130 D2
Millgreen 111 C5
Mill Green Essex 69 C6
Norf 104 C2
Suff 87 C5
Millhalf 77 C6
Millhayes 14 A2
Millhead 154 D3
Millheugh 194 A2
Mill Hill 68 D2
Millholme 155 B4
Millhouse Argyll 203 A4
Cumb 163 A6
Millhousebridge 185 D4
Millhouse Green 139 C5
Millhouses 130 A3
Millikenpark 205 B4
Millin Cross 55 C5
Millington 150 B1
Mill Lane 47 D5
Millmeece 112 B2
Mill of Kingoodie 256 D3
Mill of Muiresk 256 B1
Mill of Sterin 243 C6
Mill of Uras 245 D5
Millom 153 B2
Millook 10 B2
Mill Place 142 C1
Millpool 10 D2
Millport 204 C1
Millquarter 182 D4
Mill Side 154 C3
Mill Street 120 D2
Millthorpe 116 B4
Millthrop 155 B5
Milltimber 245 B5
Milltown Corn 5 B6
Derbys 130 C3
Devon 25 B6
Dumfries 175 A6
Milltown of Aberdalgie 219 B5
Milltown of Auchindoun 255 B4
Milltown of Craigston 268 D2
Milltown of Edinvillie 254 B3
Milltown of Kildrummy 244 A1
Milltown of Rothiemay 255 B6
Milltown of Towie 244 A1
Milnathort 219 D6
Milner's Heath 127 C4
Milngavie 205 A5
Milnrow 138 B2
Milnshaw 137 A6
Milnthorpe 154 C3
Milo 57 A5
Milson 95 D4
Milstead 37 A7
Milston 31 A5
Milton Angus 232 D1
Cambs 85 A6
Cumb 176 C3
Derbys 113 C7
Dumfries 171 B4
Dumfries 173 A6
Dumfries 183 D6
Highld 251 A5
Highld 251 C6
Highld 252 B1
Highld 264 C3
Highld 281 C5
Moray 267 C6
Notts 132 B2
N Som 42 C2
Oxon 65 D5
Oxon 82 D1
Pembs 55 D6
Perth 219 C4
Ptsmth 19 B5
Stirling 217 D5
Stoke 129 D4
W Dunb 205 A4
Milton Abbas 16 A2
Milton Abbot 11 D5
Milton Bridge 209 D5
Milton Bryan 83 D6
Milton Clevedon 29 B6
Milton Coldwells 257 C4
Milton Combe 6 A3
Milton Damerel 25 D4
Miltonduff 266 C2
Milton End 64 C2
Milton Ernest 84 B2
Milton Green 127 D4
Miltonhill 266 C1
Milton Hill 65 D5
Miltonise 180 D3
Milton Keynes 83 D5
Milton Keynes Village 83 D5
Milton Lilbourne 45 C5
Milton Malsor 83 B4
Milton Morenish 217 A6
Milton of Auchinhove 244 B2
Milton of Balgonie 220 D3
Milton of Buchanan 206 A2
Milton of Campfield 244 B3
Milton of Campsie 205 A6
Milton of Corsindae 244 B3
Milton of Cushnie 244 A2
Milton of Dalcapon 230 C3
Milton of Edradour 230 C3
Milton of Gollanfield 252 A3
Milton of Lesmore 255 D5
Milton of Logie 244 B1
Milton of Murtle 245 B5
Milton of Noth 255 D6
Milton of Tullich 243 C6
Milton on Stour 30 C1
Milton Regis 51 C6
Milton under Wychwood 64 B3
Milverton Som 27 C6
Warks 81 A6
Milwich 112 B3
Minard 214 C2
Minchinhampton 63 C4
Mindrum 198 C2
Minehead 27 A4
Minera 126 D2
Minety 63 D6
Minffordd Gwyn 91 A5
Gwyn 107 C5
Gwyn 123 C5
Miningsby 134 C3
Minions 10 D3
Minishant 192 D3
Minllyn 91 A6
Minnes 257 D4
Minngearraidh 286 D3
Minnigaff 171 A6
Minnonie 268 C2
Minskip 148 A2
Minstead 32 D1
Minsted 34 D1
Minster Kent 51 B6
Kent 53 C5
Minsterley 94 A1
Minster Lovell 64 B4
Minsterworth 62 B3
Minterne Magna 15 A6
Minting 134 B1
Mintlaw 257 B5
Minto 187 A4
Minton 94 B2
Minwear 55 C6
Minworth 97 B4
Mirbister 282 E4
Mirehouse 162 C2
Mireland 281 B5
Mirfield 139 B5
Miserden 63 C5
Miskin 41 C5
Misson 141 D4
Misterton Leics 98 C2
Notts 141 D5
Som 15 A4
Mistley 88 D2
Mitcham 49 C5
Mitcheldean 62 B2
Mitchell 4 B3
Mitchel Troy 61 B6
Mitcheltroy Common 61 C6
Mitford 178 A3
Mithian 4 B2
Mitton 112 D2
Mixbury 82 D3
Moat 175 A7
Moats Tye 87 B6
Mobberley
Ches E 128 B2
Staffs 112 A4
Moccas 78 C1
Mochdre Conwy 124 B3
Powys 93 C4
Mochrum 171 C5
Mockbeggar 17 A5
Mockerkin 162 B3
Modbury 7 B5
Moddershall 112 B3
Moelfre Anglesey 123 B5
Powys 109 C6
Moffat 184 B3
Moggerhanger 84 C3
Moira 113 D7
Molash 52 D2
Mol-chlach 246 C3
Mold Yr Wyddgrug 126 C2
Moldgreen 139 B4
Molehill Green 69 A5
Molescroft 150 C3
Molesden 178 A3
Molesworth 100 D2
Moll 247 A4
Molland 26 C3
Mollington
Ches W 126 B3
Oxon 82 C1
Mollinsburn 207 C5
Monachty 75 B4
Monachylemore 217 C4
Monar Lodge 250 B4
Monaughty 77 A6
Monboddo House 233 A5
Mondynes 233 A5
Monevechadan 215 B4
Monewden 88 B3
Moneydie 219 B5
Moniaive 183 C5
Monifieth 221 A4
Monikie 221 A4
Monimail 220 C2
Monington 72 B4
Monk Bretton 139 C6
Monken Hadley 68 D2
Monk Fryston 140 A3
Monkhopton 95 B4
Monkland 78 B2
Monkleigh 25 C5
Monknash 40 D4
Monkokehampton 11 A6
Monkseaton 179 B5
Monks Eleigh 87 C5
Monk's Gate 35 D5
Monks Heath 128 B3
Monk Sherborne 47 D4
Monkshill 256 B2
Monksilver 27 B5
Monks Kirby 98 C1
Monk Soham 88 A3
Monkspath 96 D4
Monks Risborough 66 C4
Monk Street 69 A6
Monkswood 61 C5
Monkton Devon 14 A1
Kent 53 C4
Pembs 55 D5
S Ayrs 192 C3
Monkton Combe 44 C1
Monkton Deverill 30 B2
Monkton Farleigh 44 C2
Monkton Heathfield 28 C2
Monkton Up Wimborne 31 D4
Monkwearmouth 179 D5
Monkwood 33 B5
Monmouth Trefynwy 61 B7
Monmouth Cap 61 A5
Monnington on Wye 78 C1
Monreith 171 C5
Monreith Mains 171 C5
Montacute 29 D4
Montcoffer Ho. 268 C1
Montford Argyll 203 B6
Shrops 110 D3
Montford Bridge 110 D3
Montgarrie 244 A2
Montgomery Trefaldwyn 93 B6
Montrave 220 D3
Montrose 233 C5
Mont Saint Guern 6
Montsale 71 D4
Monxton 32 A2
Monyash 129 C6
Monymusk 244 A3
Monzie 218 B3
Monzie Castle 218 B3
Moodiesburn 207 C4
Moonzie 220 C3
Moor Allerton 148 D1
Moorby 134 C2
Moor Crichel 16 A3
Moordown 17 B4
Moore 127 A5
Moorend 62 C3
Moor End
E Yorks 149 D7
York 149 B5
Moorends 141 B4

Moorgate 140 D2
Moorgreen 114 A2
Moorhall 130 B3
Moorhampton 78 C1
Moorhead 147 D5
Moorhouse
Cumb 175 C6
Notts 132 C2
Moorlinch 28 B3
Moor Monkton 148 B4
Moor of Granary 253 A6
Moor of Ravenstone 171 C5
Moor Row 162 C3
Moorsholm 169 D4
Moorside 138 C2
Moor Street 51 C5
Moorthorpe 140 B2
Moortown Hants 17 A5
IoW 18 C3
Lincs 142 D2
Morangie 264 B3
Morar 235 A5
Morborne 100 B3
Morchard Bishop 12 A2
Morcombelake 14 B4
Morcott 99 A6
Morda 110 C1
Morden Dorset 16 B3
London 49 C5
Mordiford 78 D3
Mordon 167 C6
More 94 B1
Morebath 27 C4
Morebattle 187 A6
Morecambe 144 A4
Morefield 262 A3
Moreleigh 7 B6
Morenish 217 A5
Moresby 162 B2
Moresby Parks 162 C2
Morestead 32 C4
Moreton Dorset 16 C2
Essex 69 C5
Mers 136 D1
Oxon 66 C2
Staffs 112 D1
Moreton Corbet 111 C4
Moretonhampstead 12 C2
Moreton-in-Marsh 81 D5
Moreton Jeffries 79 C4
Moreton Morrell 81 B6
Moreton on Lugg 78 C3
Moreton Pinkney 82 C2
Moreton Say 111 B5
Moreton Valence 62 C3
Morfa Carms 57 A5
Carms 57 C5
Morfa Bach 56 A3
Morfa Bychan 107 C5
Morfa Dinlle 107 A4
Morfa Glas 59 E5
Morfa Nefyn 106 B2
Morfydd 109 A6
Morgan's Vale 31 C5
Moriah 75 A5
Morland 164 C3
Morley Derbys 114 A1
Durham 166 C4
W Yorks 139 A5
Morley Green 128 A3
Morley St Botolph 104 B1
Morningside
Edin 209 C5
N Lanark 194 A3
Morningthorpe 104 B3
Morpeth 179 A4
Morphie 233 B5
Morrey 113 D5
Morris Green 86 D3
Morriston 57 C6
Morston 120 A2
Mortehoe 25 A5
Mortimer 47 C4
Mortimer's Cross 78 A2
Mortimer West End 47 C4
Mortlake 49 B5
Morton Cumb 175 C6
Derbys 131 C4
Lincs 116 C3
Lincs 132 C3
Lincs 141 D6
Norf 120 D3
Notts 132 D2
S Glos 62 D2
Shrops 110 C1
Morton Bagot 80 A4
Morton-on-Swale 157 B7
Morvah 2 B2
Morval 6 B1
Morvich Highld 249 D6
Highld 273 D5
Morville 95 B4
Morville Heath 95 B4
Morwenstow 24 D3
Mosborough 131 A4
Moscow 205 D4
Mosedale 163 A6
Moseley W Mid 96 B2
W Mid 96 C3
Worcs 79 B6
Moss Argyll 222 C2
Highld 235 D5
S Yorks 140 B3
Wrex 126 D3
Mossat 244 A1
Mossbank 284 F6
Moss Bank 136 D4
Mossbay 162 B2
Mossblown 193 C4
Mossbrow 128 A2
Mossburnford 187 B5
Mossdale 173 A4
Moss Edge 144 C4
Mossend 207 D5
Moss End 47 B6
Mosser 163 B4
Mossfield 264 C2
Mossgiel 193 C4
Mosside 232 C2
Mossley Ches E 128 C3
Gtr Man 138 C2
Mossley Hill 126 A3
Moss of Barmuckity 266 C3
Moss Pit 112 C3
Moss-side 253 A4
Moss Side 144 D3
Mosstodloch 266 D4
Mosston 232 D3
Mossy Lea 136 B4
Mosterton 15 A4
Moston Gtr Man 138 C1
Shrops 111 C4
Moston Green 128 C2
Mostyn 125 A6
Mostyn Quay 125 A6
Motcombe 30 C2
Mothecombe 7 C5
Motherby 164 C2
Motherwell 194 A2
Mottingham 49 B7
Mottisfont 32 C2
Mottistone 18 C3
Mottram in Longdendale 138 D2
Mottram St Andrew 128 B3
Mouilpied Guern 6
Mouldsworth 127 B5
Moulin 230 C3
Moulsecoomb 21 B6
Moulsford 46 A3
Moulsoe 83 C6
Moulton Ches W 127 C6
Lincs 117 C6
Northants 83 A4
N Yorks 157 A6
Suff 86 A2
V Glam 41 D5
Moulton Chapel 117 D5
Moulton Eaugate 117 D6
Moulton St Mary 105 A4
Moulton Seas End 117 C6
Mounie Castle 256 D2
Mount Corn 4 B2
Corn 5 A6
Highld 253 B5
Mountain 147 D4
Mountain Ash
Aberpennar 41 B5
Mountain Cross 195 B6
Mountain Water 55 B5
Mountbenger 196 D2
Mount Bures 87 D5
Mount Canisp 264 C3
Mountfield 37 D5
Mountgerald 264 D1
Mount Hawke 4 C2
Mountjoy 4 A3
Mountnessing 69 D6
Mounton 61 D7
Mount Pleasant
Ches E 128 D3
Derbys 113 D6
Derbys 114 A1
Flint 126 B2
Hants 18 B1
W Yorks 139 A5
Mountsorrel 114 D3
Mount Sorrel 31 C4
Mount Tabor 138 A3
Mousehole 2 C2
Mousen 199 C5
Mouswald 174 A3
Mow Cop 128 D3
Mowhaugh 187 A7
Mowsley 98 C3
Moxley 96 B2
Moy Highld 240 D2
Highld 252 C3
Moy Hall 252 C3
Moy Ho. 265 D6
Moyles Court 17 A5
Moylgrove 72 B4
Moy Lodge 240 D2
Muasdale 202 D1
Muchalls 245 C6
Much Birch 78 D3
Much Cowarne 79 C4
Much Dewchurch 78 D2
Muchelney 28 C4
Much Hadham 68 B4
Much Hoole 136 A3
Muchlarnick 5 B7
Much Marcle 79 D4
Muchrachd 251 C4
Much Wenlock 95 A4
Muckernich 252 A1
Mucking 50 A3
Muckleford 15 B6
Mucklestone 111 B6
Muckleton 111 C4
Muckletown 255 D6
Muckley Corner 96 A3
Muckton 134 A3
Mudale 272 A3
Muddiford 25 B6
Mudeford 17 B5
Mudford 29 D5
Mudgley 28 A4
Mugdock 205 A5
Mugeary 246 A3
Mugginton 113 A6
Muggleswick 166 A3
Muie 273 D4
Muir 242 D3
Muirden 268 D2
Muirdrum 221 A5
Muirhead Angus 220 A3
Fife 220 D2
N Lanark 207 D4
S Ayrs 192 B3
Muirhouselaw 187 A5
Muirhouses 208 B3
Muirkirk 194 D1
Muirmill 207 B5
Muir of Fairburn 251 A6
Muir of Fowlis 244 A2
Muir of Ord 252 A1
Muir of Pert 220 A4
Muirshearlich 239 D5
Muirskie 245 C5
Muirtack 257 C4
Muirton Highld 264 D3
Perth 218 C4
Perth 219 B6
Muirton Mains 251 A6
Muirton of Ardblair 231 D5
Muirton of Ballochy 233 B4
Muiryfold 268 D2
Muker 156 B3
Mulbarton 104 A2
Mulben 267 D4
Mulindry 200 C3
Mullardoch House 250 C4
Mullion 3 D4
Mullion Cove 3 D4
Mumby 135 B5
Munderfield Row 79 B4
Munderfield Stocks 79 B4
Mundesley 121 B5
Mundford 103 B4
Mundham 104 B4
Mundon 70 C2
Mundurno 245 A6
Munerigie 239 B6
Muness 284 C8
Mungasdale 261 A6
Mungrisdale 163 A6
Munlochy 252 A2
Munsley 79 C4
Munslow 94 C3
Murchington 12 C1
Murcott 65 B6
Murkle 280 B3
Murlaggan
Highld 238 C4
Highld 239 D7
Murra 283 G3
Murrayfield 209 C5
Murrow 101 A5
Mursley 66 A4
Murthill 232 C2
Murthly 219 A5
Murton Cumb 165 C5
Durham 167 A6
Northumb 198 B3
York 149 B5
Musbury 14 B2
Muscoates 159 C5
Musdale 226 D4
Musselburgh 209 C6
Muston Leics 115 B6
N Yorks 161 D4
Mustow Green 95 D6
Mutehill 173 D4
Mutford 105 C5
Muthill 218 C3
Mutterton 13 A5
Muxton 111 D6
Mybster 280 C3
Myddfai 59 C4
Myddle 110 C3
Mydroilyn 74 C3
Myerscough 145 D4
Mylor Bridge 4 D3
Mynachlog-ddu 72 C4
Myndtown 94 C1
Mynydd Bach 75 A6
Mynydd-bach 61 D6
Mynydd Bodafon 123 B4
Mynydd-isa 126 C2
Mynyddygarreg 57 B4
Mynytho 106 C3
Myrebird 245 C4
Myrelandhorn 281 C4
Myreside 220 B2
Myrtle Hill 59 B4
Mytchett 34 A1
Mytholm 138 A2
Mytholmroyd 138 A3
Myton-on-Swale 148 A3
Mytton 110 D3

N

Naast 261 B5
Naburn 149 C4
Nackington 52 D3
Nacton 88 C3
Nafferton 150 B3
Na Gearrannan 288 C2
Nailbridge 62 B2
Nailsbourne 28 C2
Nailsea 42 B3
Nailstone 97 A7
Nailsworth 63 D4
Nairn 253 A4
Nalderswood 35 B5
Nancegollan 3 B4
Nancledra 2 B2
Nanhoron 106 C2
Nannau 108 C2
Nannerch 125 C6
Nanpantan 114 D3
Nanpean 5 B4
Nanstallon 5 A5
Nant-ddu 60 B2
Nanternis 73 A6
Nantgaredig 58 C1
Nantgarw 41 C6
Nant-glas 76 A3
Nantglyn 125 C5
Nantgwyn 92 D3
Nantlle 107 A5
Nantmawr 110 C1
Nantmel 76 A4
Nantmor 107 B6
Nant Peris 107 A6
Nant Uchaf 125 D5
Nantwich 127 D6
Nant-y-Bai 59 A4
Nant-y-cafn 59 E5
Nantycaws 57 A4
Nant-y-derry 61 C5
Nant-y-ffin 58 B2
Nantyffyllon 40 B3
Nantyglo 60 B3
Nant-y-moel 40 B4
Nant-y-pandy 124 B1
Naphill 66 D4
Nappa 146 B2
Napton on the Hill 82 A1
Narberth Arberth 55 C7
Narborough Leics 98 B2
Norf 119 D4
Nasareth 107 A4
Naseby 98 D3
Nash Bucks 83 D4
Hereford 77 A7
Newport 42 A2
Shrops 95 D4
Nash Lee 66 C4
Nassington 100 B2
Nasty 68 A3
Nateby Cumb 155 A6
Lancs 145 C4
Natland 154 C4
Naughton 87 C6
Naunton Glos 64 A2
Worcs 80 D1
Naunton Beauchamp 80 B2
Navenby 133 D4
Navestock Heath 69 D5
Navestock Side 69 D5
Navidale 274 C4
Nawton 159 C5
Nayland 87 D5
Nazeing 68 C4
Neacroft 17 B5
Neal's Green 97 C6
Neap 285 H7
Near Sawrey 154 B2
Neasham 167 D6
Neath Castell-Nedd 40 B2
Neath Abbey 40 B2
Neatishead 121 C5
Nebo Anglesey 123 A4
Ceredig 75 B4
Conwy 124 D3
Gwyn 107 A4
Necton 103 A4
Nedd 270 A4
Nedderton 179 A4
Nedging Tye 87 C6
Needham 104 C3
Needham Market 88 B1
Needingworth 101 D5
Needwood 113 C5
Neen Savage 95 D4
Neen Sollars 95 D4
Neenton 95 C4
Nefyn 106 B3
Neilston 205 C4
Neinthirion 92 A3
Neithrop 82 C1
Nelly Andrews Green 93 A6
Nelson Caerph 41 B6
Lancs 146 D2
Nelson Village 179 B4
Nemphlar 194 B3
Nempnett Thrubwell 43 C4
Nene Terrace 101 A4
Nenthall 165 A5
Nenthead 165 A5
Nenthorn 197 C5
Nerabus 200 C2
Nercwys 126 C2
Nerston 205 C6
Nesbit 198 C3
Ness 126 B3
Nesscliffe 110 D2
Neston Ches W 126 B2
Wilts 44 C2
Nether Alderley 128 B3
Netheravon 31 A5
Nether Blainslie 197 B4
Nether Booth 129 A6
Netherbrae 268 D2
Netherbrough 282 F4
Nether Broughton 115 C4
Netherburn 194 B3
Nether Burrow 155 D5
Netherbury 15 B4
Netherby Cumb 175 A6
N Yorks 148 C2
Nether Cerne 15 B6
Nether Compton 29 D5
Nethercote 82 A2
Nethercott 25 B5
Nether Crimond 256 D3
Nether Dalgliesh 185 B5
Nether Dallachy 267 C4
Netherend 62 C1
Nether Exe 13 A4
Netherfield 23 A5
Nether Glasslaw 268 D3
Netherhampton 31 C5
Nether Handwick 232 D1
Nether Haugh 140 D2
Nether Heage 130 D3
Nether Heyford 82 B3
Nether Hindhope 187 B6
Nether Howecleuch 184 A3
Nether Kellet 145 A5
Nether Kinmundy 257 B5
Nether Langwith 131 B5
Netherlaw 173 D5
Nether Leask 257 C5
Nether Lenshie 256 B1
Netherley Aberds 245 C5
Mers 127 A4
Nethermill 184 D3
Nether Monynut 211 D4
Nethermuir 257 B4
Nether Padley 130 B2
Nether Park 269 D5
Netherplace 205 C5
Nether Poppleton 149 B4
Netherseal 113 D6
Nether Silton 158 B3
Nether Stowey 28 B1
Netherthird 182 A3

Netherthong 139 C4
Netherthorpe 131 A5
Netherton Angus 232 C3
Devon 12 D3
Hants 46 D1
Mers 136 C2
Northumb 188 C2
Oxon 65 D5
Perth 231 C5
Stirling 205 A5
W Mid 96 C2
Worcs 80 C2
W Yorks 139 B4
W Yorks 139 B5
Nethertown
Cumb 162 D2
Highld 281 A5
Nether Urquhart 219 D6
Nether Wallop 32 B2
Nether Wasdale 163 D4
Nether Whitacre 97 B5
Netherwitton 189 D4
Netherwood 193 C6
Nether Worton 82 D1
Nethy Bridge 253 D6
Netley 18 A3
Netley Marsh 32 D2
Netteswell 69 B4
Nettlebed 47 A5
Nettlebridge 29 A6
Nettlecombe 15 B5
Nettleden 67 B6
Nettleham 133 B5
Nettlestead 37 A4
Nettlestead Green 37 A4
Nettlestone 19 B5
Nettlesworth 167 A5
Nettleton Lincs 142 C3
Wilts 44 B2
Neuadd 58 C3
Nevendon 70 D1
Nevern 72 B3
New Abbey 174 B2
New Aberdour 268 C3
New Addington 49 C6
Newall 147 C5
New Alresford 33 B4
New Alyth 231 D6
Newark Orkney 282 C8
Pboro 100 A4
Newark-on-Trent 132 D2
New Arley 97 C5
Newarthill 194 A2
New Ash Green 50 C3
New Barn 50 C3
New Barnetby 142 B2
Newbarns 153 C3
New Barton 83 A5
Newbattle 209 D6
New Bewick 188 A3
Newbiggin Cumb 153 A1
Cumb 153 D3
Cumb 164 A3
Cumb 164 C2
Cumb 165 C4
Durham 166 C2
N Yorks 156 B3
N Yorks 156 C3
Newbiggin-by-the-Sea 179 A5
Newbigging
Angus 220 A4
Angus 221 A4
S Lanark 195 B5
New-bigging 231 D6
Newbiggin-on-Lune 155 A6
New Bilton 98 D1
Newbold Derbys 130 B3
Leics 114 D2
Newbold on Avon 98 D1
Newbold on Stour 81 C5
Newbold Pacey 81 B5
Newbold Verdon 98 A1
New Bolingbroke 134 D3
Newborough
Anglesey 123 D4
Pboro 100 A4
Staffs 113 C5
Newbottle
Northants 82 D2
T&W 179 D5
New Boultham 133 B4
Newbourne 88 C3
New Bradwell 83 C5
New Brancepeth 167 A5
Newbridge Caerph 41 B7
Ceredig 75 C4
Corn 2 B2
Corn 6 A2
Dumfries 174 A2
Edin 208 C4
Hants 32 D1
IoW 18 C3
Pembs 55 A5
New Bridge 110 A1
Newbridge Green 79 D6
Newbridge-on-Usk 61 D5
Newbridge on Wye 76 B4
New Brighton
Flint 126 C2
Mers 136 D2
New Brinsley 131 D4
Newbrough 177 C6
New Broughton 126 D3
New Buckenham 104 B1
Newbuildings 12 A2
Newburgh
Aberds 257 D4
Aberds 269 D4
Borders 185 A6
Fife 220 C2
Lancs 136 B3
Newburn 178 C3
Newbury 46 C2
Newbury Park 50 A1
Newby Cumb 164 C3
Lancs 146 C2
N Yorks 155 D6
N Yorks 160 B4
N Yorks 168 D3
Newby Bridge 154 C2
Newby East 176 D2
New Byth 268 D3
Newby West 175 C6
Newby Wiske 158 C2
Newcastle Mon 61 B6
Shrops 93 C6
Newcastle Emlyn
Castell Newydd Emlyn 73 B6
Newcastleton or Copshaw Holm 176 A2
Newcastle-under-Lyme 112 A2
Newcastle Upon Tyne 179 C4
New Catton 120 D4
Newchapel Pembs 73 C5
Powys 92 C3
Staffs 128 D3
Sur 35 B6
New Cheriton 33 C4
Newchurch Carms 73 D6
IoW 19 C4
Kent 38 B2
Lancs 146 D2
Mon 61 D6
Powys 77 B6
Staffs 113 C5
New Costessey 120 D3
Newcott 14 A2
New Cowper 174 D4
Newcraighall 209 C6
New Cross Ceredig 75 A5
London 49 B6
New Cumnock 182 A4
New Deer 256 B3
New Delaval 179 B4
Newdigate 35 B4
New Duston 83 A4
New Earswick 149 B5
New Edlington 140 D3
New Elgin 266 C3
New Ellerby 151 D4
Newell Grn. 48 B1
New Eltham 50 B1
New End 80 B3
Newenden 37 D6
Newent 62 A3
Newerne 62 C2
New Farnley 147 D6
New Ferry 126 A3
Newfield Durham 167 B5
Highld 264 C3
Newford Scilly 2 E4
Newfound 46 D3
New Fryston 140 A2
Newgale 54 B4
New Galloway 172 A4
Newgate 120 A2
Newgate Street 68 C3
New Gilston 220 D4
New Grimsby Scilly 2 E3
New Hainford 120 D4
Newhall Ches E 111 A5
Derbys 113 C6
Newhall House 264 D2
Newhall Point 264 D3
Newham 189 A4
Newham Hall 189 A4
New Hartley 179 B5
Newhaven
Derbys 129 D6
Edin 209 C5
E Sus 22 B2
New Haw 48 C3
New Hedges 56 B1
New Herrington 179 D5
Newhey 138 B2
New Hinksey 65 C6
New Holkham 119 B5
New Holland 142 A2
Newholm 169 D6
New Houghton
Derbys 131 C4
Norf 119 C4
Newhouse 207 D5
New Houses 155 D7
New Humberstone 98 A3
New Hutton 155 B4
New Hythe 37 A5
Newick 36 D2
Newingreen 38 B3
Newington Kent 38 B3
Kent 51 C5
Kent 53 C5
Notts 141 D4
Oxon 65 D7
Shrops 94 C2
New Inn Carms 58 B1
Mon 61 C6
Pembs 55 A6
Torf 61 D5
New Invention
Shrops 93 D6
W Mid 96 A2
New Kelso 249 B6
New Kingston 114 C3
New Lanark 194 B3
Newland Glos 62 C1
Hull 150 D3
N Yorks 141 A4
Worcs 79 C5
Newlandrig 209 D6
Newlands
Borders 186 D4
Highld 252 B3
Moray 266 D4
Northumb 178 D2
Newland's Corner 34 B3
Newlandsmuir 205 C6
Newlands of Geise 280 B2
Newlands of Tynet 267 C4
Newlands Park 122 B2
New Lane 136 B3
New Lane End 137 D5
New Leake 135 D4
New Leeds 269 D4
New Longton 136 A4
Newlot 282 F6
New Luce 170 A3
Newlyn 2 C2
Newmachar 245 A5
Newmains 194 A3
New Malden 49 C5
Newmarket Suff 86 A2
W Isles 288 D5
New Marske 168 C4
New Marton 110 B2
New Micklefield 148 D3
Newmill Borders 186 B3
Corn 2 B2
Moray 267 D5
New Mill Aberds 245 D4
Herts 67 B5
Wilts 45 C5
W Yorks 139 C4
Newmill of Inshewan 232 B2
New Mills Ches E 128 A2
Corn 4 B3
Derbys 129 A4
Powys 93 A4
Newmills of Boyne 267 D6
Newmiln 219 A6
Newmilns 193 B5
New Milton 17 B6
New Moat 55 B6
Newnham Cambs 85 B6
Glos 62 B2
Hants 47 D5
Herts 84 D4
Kent 51 D6
Northants 82 B2
Newnham Bridge 79 A4
New Ollerton 131 C6
New Oscott 96 B3
Newpark 221 C4
New Park 148 B1
New Pitsligo 268 D3
New Polzeath 9 D5
Newport Devon 25 B6
Essex 85 D7
E Yorks 150 D1
Highld 275 B5
IoW 18 C4
Norf 121 D7
Telford 111 D6
Newport
Casnewydd 42 A2
Newport
Trefdraeth 72 C3
Newport-on-Tay 220 B4
Newport Pagnell 83 C5
Newpound Common 34 D3
Newquay 4 A3
New Quay
Ceinewydd 73 A6
New Rackheath 121 D4
New Radnor 77 A6
New Rent 164 B2
New Ridley 178 D2
New Road Side 146 C3
New Romney 38 C2
New Rossington 140 D4
New Row Ceredig 75 A6
Lancs 145 D6
N Yorks 168 D4
New Sarum 31 B5
Newsbank 128 C3
Newseat Aberds 256 C2
Aberds 257 B5
Newsham
Northumb 179 B5
N Yorks 158 C2
N Yorks 166 D4
Newsholme
E Yorks 141 A5
Lancs 146 B2
New Silksworth 179 D5
Newsome 139 B4
Newstead
Borders 197 C4
Northumb 189 A4
Notts 131 D5
New Stevenston 194 A2
New Street 129 D5
New Street Lane 111 B5
New Swanage 17 C4
Newthorpe 148 D3
Newton Argyll 214 C3
Borders 187 B2
Bridgend 40 D3
Cambs 85 C6
Cambs 118 D1
Cardiff 42 B1
Ches W 127 B5
Ches W 127 C4
Ches W 127 D5
Cumb 153 C3
Derbys 131 D4
Dorset 30 D1
Dumfries 175 A5
Dumfries 185 C4
Gtr Man 138 D2
Hereford 78 B3
Hereford 78 D1
Highld 252 B3
Highld 264 D3
Highld 271 A5
Highld 281 D5
Lancs 144 D4
Lancs 145 B6
Lancs 155 D4
Lincs 116 B3
Moray 266 C2
Norf 119 D5
Northants 99 C5
Northumb 178 C2
Notts 115 A4
Perth 218 A3
S Lanark 194 C4
S Lanark 205 B6
Staffs 112 C4
Suff 87 C5
Swansea 57 D6
S Yorks 140 C3
Warks 98 D2
Wilts 31 C6
W Loth 208 C3
Newton Abbot 12 D3
Newtonairds 183 D6
Newton Arlosh 175 C4
Newton Aycliffe 167 C5
Newton Bewley 168 C2
Newton Blossomville 83 B6
Newton Bromswold 84 A1
Newton Burgoland 97 A6
Newton by Toft 133 A5
Newton Ferrers 7 C4
Newton Flotman 104 B3
Newtongrange 209 D6
Newton Hall 178 C2
Newton Harcourt 98 B3
Newton Heath 138 C1
Newtonhill
Aberds 245 C6
Highld 252 B1
Newton Ho. 256 D1
Newton Kyme 148 C3
Newton-le-Willows
Mers 137 D4
N Yorks 157 C6
Newton Longville 83 D5
Newton Mearns 205 C5
Newtonmill 233 B4
Newtonmore 241 C5
Newton Morrell 157 A6
Newton Mulgrave 169 D5
Newton of Ardtoe 235 C5
Newton of Balcanquhal 219 C6
Newton of Falkland 220 D2
Newton on Ayr 192 C3
Newton on Ouse 148 B4
Newton-on-Rawcliffe 159 B7
Newton-on-the-Moor 189 C4
Newton on Trent 132 B3
Newton Park 203 B6
Newton Poppleford 13 C5
Newton Purcell 82 D3
Newton Regis 97 A5
Newton Reigny 164 B2
Newton St Cyres 12 B3
Newton St Faith 120 D4
Newton St Loe 43 C6
Newton St Petrock 25 D5
Newton Solney 113 C6
Newton Stacey 32 A3
Newton Stewart 171 A6
Newton Tony 31 A6
Newton Tracey 25 C6
Newton under Roseberry 168 D3
Newton upon Derwent 149 C6
Newton Valence 33 B6
New Totley 130 B3
Newtown Argyll 214 B3
Ches W 127 B5
Corn 3 C5
Cumb 174 D3
Cumb 176 C3
Derbys 129 A4
Devon 26 C2
Glos 62 C2
Glos 80 D2
Hants 18 A3
Hants 31 D6
Hants 32 C2
Hants 32 D4
Hants 33 D5
Hants 46 C2
Hereford 79 C4
Highld 240 B1
IoM 152 D3
IoW 18 B3
Northumb 188 A3
Northumb 188 C3
Northumb 198 C3
Poole 17 B4
Shrops 110 B3
Staffs 129 C4
Staffs 129 C5
Wilts 30 C3
New Town 210 C1
Newtown Y Drenewydd 93 B5
Newtown Linford 98 A2
Newtown St. Boswells 197 C4
Newtown Unthank 98 A1
New Tredegar
Tredegar Newydd 41 A6
New Trows 194 C3
Newtyle 231 D6
New Ulva 213 D5
New Walsoken 101 A6
New Waltham 143 C4
New Whittington 130 B3
New Wimpole 85 C5
New Winton 210 C1
New Yatt 65 B4
New York Lincs 134 D2
N Yorks 147 A5
Neyland 55 D5
Niarbyl 152 D2
Nibley 43 A5
Nibley Green 62 D3
Nibon 284 F5
Nicholashayne 27 D6
Nicholaston 57 D5
Nidd 148 A2
Nigg Aberdeen 245 B6
Highld 265 C4
Nigg Ferry 264 D3
Nightcott 26 C3
Nilig 125 D5
Nine Ashes 69 C5
Ninebanks 177 D5

Nine Mile Burn . . 195 A6
Nine Wells . . 54 B3
Ninfield . . 23 A5
Ningwood . . 18 C2
Nisbet . . 187 A5
Nisthouse Orkney 282 F4
  Shetland . . 285 G7
Niton . . 18 D4
Nitshill . . 205 B5
Noak Hill . . 69 D5
Noblethorpe . . 139 C5
Nobottle . . 82 A3
Nocton . . 133 C5
Noke . . 65 B6
Nolton . . 55 C4
Nolton Haven . . 55 C4
No Man's Heath
  Ches W . . 111 A4
  Warks . . 97 A5
Nomansland
  Devon . . 26 D3
  Wilts . . 31 D6
Noneley . . 110 C3
Nonikiln . . 264 C2
Nonington . . 53 D4
Noonsbrough . . 285 H4
Norbreck . . 144 C3
Norbridge . . 79 C5
Norbury Ches E . . 111 A4
  Derbys . . 113 A5
  Shrops . . 94 B1
  Staffs . . 112 C1
Nordelph . . 102 A1
Norden . . 138 B1
Norden Heath . . 16 C3
Nordley . . 95 B4
Norham . . 198 B3
Norley . . 127 B5
Norleywood . . 18 B2
Normanby
  N Lincs . . 141 B6
  N Yorks . . 159 C6
  Redcar . . 168 D3
Normanby-by-Spital . . 133 A5
Normanby by Stow . . 132 A3
Normanby le Wold . . 142 D3
Norman Cross . . 100 B3
Normandy . . 34 A2
Norman's Bay . . 23 B4
Norman's Green . . 13 A5
Normanstone . . 105 B6
Normanton
  Derby . . 114 B1
  Leics . . 115 A6
  Lincs . . 116 A2
  Notts . . 132 D2
  Rutland . . 99 A6
  W Yorks . . 140 A1
Normanton le Heath . . 114 D1
Normanton on Soar . . 114 C3
Normanton-on-the-Wolds . . 115 B4
Normanton on Trent . . 132 C2
Normoss . . 144 D3
Norney . . 34 B2
Norrington Common . . 44 C2
Norris Green . . 136 D2
Norris Hill . . 114 D1
Northacre . . 103 B5
Northallerton . . 158 B2
Northam Devon . . 25 C5
  Soton . . 32 D3
Northampton . . 83 A4
North Anston . . 131 A5
North Aston . . 65 A5
Northaw . . 68 C2
North Baddesley . 32 D2
North Ballachulish . . 237 C4
North Barrow . . 29 C6
North Barsham . . 119 B6
Northbeck . . 116 A3
North Benfleet . . 51 A4
North Bersted . . 20 B2
North Berwick . . 210 B2
North Boarhunt . . 33 D5
Northborough . . 100 A3
Northbourne . . 53 D5
North Bovey . . 12 C2
North Bradley . . 44 D2
North Brentor . . 11 C5
North Brewham . . 29 B7
Northbridge Street . . 37 D5
North Buckland . . 25 A5
North Burlingham . . 121 D5
North Cadbury . . 29 C6
North Cairn . . 180 D1
North Carlton . . 133 B4
North Carrine . . 190 E2
North Cave . . 150 D1
North Cerney . . 63 C6
Northchapel . . 34 D2
North Charford . . 31 D5
North Charlton . . 189 A4
North Cheriton . . 29 C6
Northchurch . . 67 C5
North Cliff . . 151 C5
North Cliffe . . 150 D1
North Clifton . . 132 B3
North Cockerington . . 143 D5
North Coker . . 29 D5
North Collafirth . 284 E5
North Common . . 36 D1
North Connel . . 226 C4
North Cornelly . . 40 C3
North Cotes . . 143 C5
Northcott . . 10 B4
North Cove . . 105 C5
North Cowton . . 157 A6
North Crawley . . 83 C6
North Cray . . 50 B1
North Creake . . 119 B5
North Curry . . 28 C3
North Dalton . . 150 B2
North Dawn . . 283 G5
North Deighton . 148 B2
Northdown . . 53 B5
North Duffield . . 149 D5
Northdyke . . 282 E3
North Elkington . 143 D4
North Elmham . . 120 C1
North Elmshall . . 140 B2
Northend Bath . . 44 C1
  Bucks . . 66 D3
  Warks . . 81 B6
North End Bucks . . 66 A4
  Essex . . 69 B6
  E Yorks . . 151 D5
  Hants . . 46 C2
  Lincs . . 117 A5
  N Som . . 42 C3
  Ptsmth . . 19 A5
  Som . . 28 C2
  W Sus . . 21 B4
Northenden . . 137 D7
North Erradale . . 261 B4
North Fambridge 70 D2
North Fearns . . 248 C2
North Featherstone . . 140 A2
North Ferriby . . 142 A1
Northfield
  Aberdeen . . 245 B6
  Borders . . 211 D6
  E Yorks . . 142 A2
  W Mid . . 96 D3
Northfields . . 100 A2
Northfleet . . 50 B3
North Frodingham . . 151 B4
Northgate . . 117 C4
North Gluss . . 284 F5
North Gorley . . 31 D5
North Green
  Norf . . 104 C3
  Suff . . 89 A4
North Greetwell 133 B5
North Grimston . 150 A1
North Halley . . 283 G6
North Halling . . 51 C4
North Hayling . . 19 A6
North Hazelrigg 199 C4
North Heasley . . 26 B2
North Heath . . 34 D3
North Hill Cambs 101 D6
  Corn . . 10 D3
North Hinksey . . 65 C5
North Holmwood . 35 B4
Northhouse . . 186 C3
North Howden . . 149 D6
North Huish . . 7 B6
North Hykeham . 133 C4
Northiam . . 37 D6
Northill . . 84 C3
Northington . . 33 B4
North Johnston . . 55 C5
North Kelsey . . 142 C2
North Kelsey Moor . . 142 C2
North Kessock . . 252 B2
North Killingholme . . 142 B3
North Kilvington . . 158 C3
North Kilworth . . 98 C3
North Kirkton . . 269 D6
North Kiscadale 191 C6
North Kyme . . 133 D6
North Lancing . . 21 B4
Northlands . . 134 D3
Northlea . . 179 D6
Northleach . . 64 B2
North Lee . . 66 C4
Northleigh . . 14 B1
North Leigh . . 65 B4
North Leverton with Habblesthorpe . . 132 A2
Northlew . . 11 B6
North Littleton . . 80 C3
North Lopham . . 103 C6
North Luffenham 99 A6
North Marden . . 33 D7
North Marston . . 66 A3
North Middleton
  Midloth . . 196 A2
  Northumb . . 188 A3
North Molton . . 26 C2
Northmoor . . 65 C5
Northmoor Green or Moorland . . 28 B3
North Moreton . . 46 A3
Northmuir . . 232 C1
North Mundham . . 20 B1
North Muskham 132 D2
North Newbald . 150 D2
North Newington 81 D7
North Newnton . . 45 D5
North Newton . . 28 B2
Northney . . 19 A6
North Nibley . . 62 D3
North Oakley . . 46 D3
North Ockendon . . 50 A2
Northolt . . 48 A4
Northop . . 126 C2
Northop Hall . . 126 C2
North Ormesby . 168 C3
North Ormsby . . 143 D4
Northorpe Lincs . . 116 D3
  Lincs . . 117 B5
  Lincs . . 141 D6
North Otterington . . 158 C2
Northover Som . . 29 B4
  Som . . 29 C5
North Owersby . . 142 D2
Northowram . . 139 A4
North Perrott . . 15 A4
North Petherton . . 28 B2
North Petherwin . 10 C3
North Pickenham . . 103 A4
North Piddle . . 80 B2
North Poorton . . 15 B5
Northport . . 16 C3
North Port . . 227 D5
Northpunds . . 285 L6
North Queensferry . . 208 B4
North Radworthy . 26 B2
North Rauceby . . 116 A3
Northrepps . . 120 B4
North Reston . . 134 A3
North Rigton . . 148 C1
North Rode . . 128 C3
North Roe . . 284 E5
North Runcton . . 118 D3
North Sandwick 284 D7
North Scale . . 153 D2
North Scarle . . 132 C3
North Seaton . . 179 A4
North Shian . . 226 B4
North Shields . . 179 C5
North Shoebury . . 51 A6
North Shore . . 144 D3
North Side Cumb 162 B3
  Pboro . . 101 B4
North Skelton . . 169 D4
North Somercotes . . 143 D6
North Stainley . . 157 D6
North Stainmore . . 165 D6
North Stifford . . 50 A3
North Stoke Bath . . 43 C6
  Oxon . . 47 A4
  W Sus . . 20 A3
North Street
  Hants . . 33 B5
  Kent . . 52 D2
  Medway . . 51 B5
  W Berks . . 47 B4
North Sunderland . . 199 C6
North Tamerton . . 10 B4
North Tawton . . 12 A1
North Thoresby . 143 D4
North Tidworth . . 31 A6
North Togston . . 189 C5
Northtown . . 283 H5
North Tuddenham . . 120 D2
North Walbottle 178 C3
North Walsham . 121 B4
North Waltham . . 33 A4
North Warnborough . . 47 D5
North Water Bridge . . 233 B4
North Watten . . 280 C4
Northway . . 80 D2
North Weald Bassett . . 69 C4
North Wheatley . 132 A2
North Whilborough . . 8 A2
Northwich . . 127 B6
Northwick . . 43 A4
North Wick . . 43 C4
North Willingham . . 133 A6
North Wingfield 131 C4
North Witham . . 116 C2
Northwold . . 102 B3
Northwood
  Derbys . . 130 C2
  IoW . . 18 B3
  Kent . . 53 C5
  London . . 67 D6
  Shrops . . 110 B3
Northwood Green . . 62 B3
North Woolwich . . 50 B1
North Wootton
  Dorset . . 29 D6
  Norf . . 118 C3
  Som . . 29 A5
North Wraxall . . 44 B2
North Wroughton 45 A5
Norton E Sus . . 22 B2
  Glos . . 63 A4
  Halton . . 127 A5
  Herts . . 84 D4
  IoW . . 18 C2
  Mon . . 61 B6
  Northants . . 82 A3
  Notts . . 131 B5
  Powys . . 77 A7
  Shrops . . 94 A3
  Shrops . . 94 C2
  Shrops . . 95 A5
  Stockton . . 168 C2
  Suff . . 87 A5
  S Yorks . . 140 B3
  Wilts . . 44 A2
Norton
  Worcs . . 80 B1
  Worcs . . 80 C3
  W Sus . . 20 B2
  W Sus . . 20 C1
Norton Bavant . . 30 A3
Norton Bridge . . 112 B2
Norton Canes . . 96 A3
Norton Canon . . 78 C1
Norton Corner . . 120 C2
Norton Disney . . 132 D3
Norton East . . 96 A3
Norton Ferris . . 30 B1
Norton Fitzwarren . . 28 C1
Norton Green . . 18 C2
Norton Hawkfield . . 43 C4
Norton Heath . . 69 C6
Norton in Hales . 111 B6
Norton-in-the-Moors . . 128 D3
Norton-Juxta-Twycross . . 97 A6
Norton-le-Clay . 158 D3
Norton Lindsey . . 81 A5
Norton Malreward . . 43 C5
Norton Mandeville . . 69 C5
Norton-on-Derwent . . 159 D6
Norton St Philip . . 43 D6
Norton sub Hamdon . . 29 D4
Norton Woodseats . . 130 A3
Norwell . . 132 C2
Norwell Woodhouse . . 132 C2
Norwich . . 104 A3
Norwick . . 284 B8
Norwood . . 131 A4
Norwood Hill . . 35 B5
Norwoodside . . 101 B6
Noseley . . 99 B4
Noss . . 285 M5
Noss Mayo . . 7 C4
Nosterfield . . 157 C6
Nostie . . 249 D5
Notgrove . . 64 A2
Nottage . . 40 D3
Nottingham . . 114 B3
Nottington . . 15 C6
Notton Wilts . . 44 C3
  W Yorks . . 139 B6
Nounsley . . 70 B1
Noutard's Green . . 79 A5
Novar House . . 264 D2
Nox . . 110 D3
Nuffield . . 47 A4
Nunburnholme . . 150 C1
Nuncargate . . 131 D5
Nuneaton . . 97 B6
Nuneham Courtenay . . 65 D6
Nun Hills . . 138 A1
Nun Monkton . . 148 B4
Nunney . . 30 A1
Nunnington . . 159 D5
Nunnykirk . . 188 D3
Nunsthorpe . . 143 C4
Nunthorpe Mbro . 168 D3
  York . . 149 B5
Nunton . . 31 C5
Nunwick . . 157 D7
Nupend . . 62 C3
Nursling . . 32 D2
Nursted . . 33 C6
Nutbourne W Sus . 19 A6
  W Sus . . 20 A3
Nutfield . . 35 A6
Nuthall . . 114 A3
Nuthampstead . . 85 D6
Nuthurst . . 35 D4
Nutley E Sus . . 36 D2
  Hants . . 33 A5
Nutwell . . 140 C4
Nybster . . 281 B5
Nyetimber . . 20 C1
Nyewood . . 33 C7
Nymet Rowland . . 12 A2
Nymet Tracey . . 12 A2
Nympsfield . . 63 C4
Nynehead . . 27 C6
Nyton . . 20 B2

O

Oadby . . 98 A3
Oad Street . . 51 C5
Oakamoor . . 113 A4
Oakbank . . 208 D3
Oak Cross . . 11 B6
Oakdale . . 41 B6
Oake . . 27 C6
Oaken . . 95 A6
Oakenclough . . 145 C5
Oakengates . . 111 D6
Oakenholt . . 126 B2
Oakenshaw
  Durham . . 167 B5
  W Yorks . . 139 A4
Oakerthorpe . . 130 D3
Oakes . . 139 B4
Oakfield . . 61 D5
Oakford Ceredig . . 74 C3
  Devon . . 27 C4
Oakfordbridge . . 27 C4
Oakgrove . . 129 C4
Oakham . . 99 A5
Oakhanger . . 33 B6
Oakhill . . 29 A6
Oakhurst . . 36 A3
Oakington . . 85 A6
Oaklands Herts . . 68 B2
  Powys . . 76 B4
Oakle Street . . 62 B3
Oakley Bedford . . 84 B2
  Bucks . . 66 B2
  Fife . . 208 B3
  Hants . . 46 D3
  Oxon . . 66 C3
  Poole . . 17 B4
  Suff . . 104 D2
Oakley Green . . 48 B2
Oakley Park . . 92 C3
Oakmere . . 127 C5
Oakridge Glos . . 63 C5
  Hants . . 47 D4
Oaks . . 94 A2
Oaksey . . 63 D5
Oaks Green . . 113 B5
Oakthorpe . . 113 D7
Oakwoodhill . . 35 C4
Oakworth . . 147 D4
Oape . . 272 D2
Oare Kent . . 52 C2
  Som . . 26 A3
  W Berks . . 46 B3
  Wilts . . 45 C5
Oasby . . 116 B3
Oathlaw . . 232 C2
Oatlands . . 148 B2
Oban Argyll . . 226 D3
  Highld . . 238 D2
Oborne . . 29 D6
Obthorpe . . 116 D3
Occlestone Green . . 128 C1
Occold . . 104 D2
Ochiltree . . 193 C5
Ochtermuthill . . 218 C3
Ochtertyre . . 218 B3
Ockbrook . . 114 B2
Ockham . . 34 A3
Ockle . . 235 C4
Ockley . . 35 C4
Ocle Pychard . . 78 C3
Octon . . 150 A3
Octon Cross Roads . . 150 A3
Odcombe . . 29 D5
Odd Down . . 43 C6
Oddendale . . 164 D3
Odder . . 133 B4
Oddingley . . 80 B2
Oddington Glos . . 64 A3
  Oxon . . 65 B6
Odell . . 83 B6
Odie . . 282 E7
Odiham . . 47 D5
Odstock . . 31 C5

Odstone 97 A6
Offchurch 81 A6
Offenham 80 C3
Offham E Sus 22 A1
Kent 37 A4
W Sus 20 B3
Offord Cluny 84 A4
Offord Darcy 84 A4
Offton 87 C6
Offwell 14 B1
Ogbourne Maizey 45 B5
Ogbourne St Andrew 45 B5
Ogbourne St George 45 B6
Ogil 232 B2
Ogle 178 B3
Ogmore 40 D3
Ogmore-by-Sea 40 D3
Ogmore Vale 40 B4
Okeford Fitzpaine 30 D2
Okehampton 11 B6
Okehampton Camp 11 B6
Okraquoy 285 K6
Old 99 D4
Old Aberdeen 245 B6
Old Alresford 33 B4
Oldany 270 A4
Old Arley 97 B5
Old Basford 114 A3
Old Basing 47 D4
Oldberrow 80 A4
Old Bewick 188 A3
Old Bolingbroke 134 C3
Oldborough 12 A2
Old Bramhope 147 C6
Old Brampton 130 B3
Old Bridge of Tilt 230 B2
Old Bridge of Urr 173 B5
Old Buckenham 103 B6
Old Burghclere 46 D2
Oldbury Shrops 95 B5
Warks 97 B6
W Mid 96 C2
Oldbury-on-Severn 62 D2
Oldbury on the Hill 44 A2
Old Byland 159 C4
Old Cassop 167 B6
Oldcastle Bridgend 40 D4
Mon 61 A5
Old Castleton 186 D4
Old Catton 120 D4
Old Clee 143 C4
Old Cleeve 27 A5
Old Clipstone 131 C6
Old Colwyn 124 B3
Oldcotes 131 A5
Old Coulsdon 35 A6
Old Crombie 267 D6
Old Dailly 181 B4
Old Dalby 115 C4
Old Deer 257 B4
Old Denaby 140 D2
Old Edlington 140 D3
Old Eldon 167 C5
Old Ellerby 151 D4
Oldfallow 112 D3
Old Felixstowe 88 D4
Oldfield 79 A6
Old Fletton 100 B3
Oldford 44 D1
Old Glossop 138 D3
Old Goole 141 A5
Old Hall 91 D7
Oldham 138 C2
Oldhamstocks 211 C4
Old Heath 71 A4
Old Heathfield 36 D3
Old Hill 96 C2
Old Hunstanton 118 A3
Old Hurst 101 D4
Old Hutton 155 C4
Old Kea 4 C3
Old Kilpatrick 205 A4
Old Kinnernie 245 B4
Old Knebworth 68 A2
Oldland 43 B5
Old Langho 145 D7
Old Laxey 152 C4
Old Leake 135 D4
Old Malton 159 D6
Oldmeldrum 256 D3
Old Micklefield 148 D3
Old Milton 17 B6
Old Milverton 81 A5
Old Monkland 207 D5
Old Netley 18 A3
Old Philpstoun 208 C3
Old Quarrington 167 B6
Old Radnor 77 B6
Old Rattray 269 D5
Old Rayne 256 D1
Old Romney 38 C2
Oldshore Beg 276 C2
Oldshoremore 276 C3
Old Sodbury 43 A6
Old Somerby 116 B2
Oldstead 158 C4
Old Stratford 83 C4
Old Thirsk 158 C3
Oldtown 255 D6
Old Town Cumb 155 C4
Cumb 164 A2
Northumb 188 D1
Scilly 2 E4
Oldtown of Ord 267 D7
Old Trafford 137 D7
Old Tupton 130 C3
Old Warden 84 C3
Oldway 57 D5
Oldways End 26 C3
Old Weston 100 D2
Oldwhat 268 D3
Old Whittington 130 B3
Old Wick 281 C5
Old Windsor 48 B2
Old Wives Lees 52 D2
Old Woking 34 A3
Old Woodhall 134 C2
Olgrinmore 280 C2
Oliver's Battery 32 C3
Ollaberry 284 E5
Ollerton Ches E 128 B2
Notts 131 C6
Shrops 111 C5
Olmarch 75 C5
Olney 83 B5
Olrig Ho. 280 B3
Olton 96 C4
Olveston 43 A5
Olwen 75 D4
Ombersley 79 A6
Ompton 132 C1
Onchan 152 D3
Onecote 129 D5
Onen 61 B6
Ongar Hill 118 C2
Ongar Street 78 A1
Onibury 94 D2
Onich 237 C4
Onllwyn 59 D5
Onneley 111 A6
Onslow Village 34 B2
Onthank 205 D4
Openwoodgate 114 A1
Opinan Highld 261 A5
Highld 261 C4
Orange Lane 198 B1
Orange Row 118 C2
Orasaigh 288 F4
Orbliston 266 D4
Orbost 258 D2
Orby 135 C4
Orchard Hill 25 C5
Orchard Portman 28 C2
Orcheston 31 A4
Orcop 61 A6
Orcop Hill 61 A6
Ord 247 C5
Ordhead 244 A3
Ordie 244 B1
Ordiequish 266 D4
Ordsall 132 A1
Ore 23 A6
Oreton 95 C4
Orford Suff 89 C5
Warr 137 D5
Orgreave 113 D5
Orlestone 38 B1
Orleton Hereford 78 A2
Worcs 79 A4
Orlingbury 99 D5
Ormesby 168 D3
Ormesby St Margaret 121 D6
Ormesby St Michael 121 D6
Ormiclate Castle 286 C3
Ormiscaig 261 A5
Ormiston 209 D7
Ormsaigbeg 234 D3
Ormsaigmore 234 D3
Ormsary 202 A2
Ormsgill 153 C2
Ormskirk 136 C3
Orpington 50 C1
Orrell Gtr Man 136 C4
Mers 136 D2
Orrisdale 152 B3
Orroland 173 D5
Orsett 50 A3
Orslow 112 D2
Orston 115 A5
Orthwaite 163 A5
Ortner 145 B5
Orton Cumb 155 A5
Northants 99 D5
Orton Longueville 100 B3
Orton-on-the-Hill 97 A6
Orton Waterville 100 B3
Orwell 85 B5
Osbaldeston 145 D6
Osbaldwick 149 B5
Osbaston 110 C2
Osbournby 116 B3
Oscroft 127 C5
Ose 258 D3
Osgathorpe 114 D2
Osgodby Lincs 142 D2
N Yorks 149 D5
N Yorks 161 C4
Oskaig 248 C2
Oskamull 224 B3
Osmaston Derby 114 B1
Derbys 113 A6
Osmington 16 C1
Osmington Mills 16 C1
Osmotherley 158 B3
Ospisdale 264 B3
Ospringe 52 C2
Ossett 139 A5
Ossington 132 C2
Ostend 70 D3
Oswaldkirk 159 D5
Oswaldtwistle 137 A6
Oswestry 110 C1
Otford 36 A3
Otham 37 A5
Othery 28 B3
Otley Suff 88 B3
W Yorks 147 C6
Otterbourne 32 C3
Otterburn Northumb 188 D1
N Yorks 146 B2
Otterburn Camp 188 D1
Otter Ferry 214 D2
Otterham 10 B2
Otterhampton 28 A2
Ottershaw 48 C3
Otterswick 284 E7
Otterton 13 C5
Ottery St Mary 13 B6
Ottinge 38 A3
Ottringham 143 A4
Oughterby 175 C5
Oughtershaw 156 C2
Oughterside 174 D4
Oughtibridge 139 D6
Oughtrington 128 A1
Oulston 158 D4
Oulton Cumb 175 C5
Norf 120 C3
Staffs 112 B3
Suff 105 B6
W Yorks 139 A6
Oulton Broad 105 B6
Oulton Street 120 C3
Oundle 100 C2
Ousby 165 B4
Ousdale 275 B4
Ousden 86 B3
Ousefleet 141 A6
Ouston Durham 179 D4
Northumb 178 B2
Outertown 282 F3
Outgate 154 B2
Outhgill 155 A6
Outlane 138 B3
Out Newton 143 A5
Out Rawcliffe 144 C4
Outwell 101 A7
Outwick 31 D5
Outwood Sur 35 B6
W Yorks 139 A6
Outwoods 112 D1
Ovenden 138 A3
Ovenscloss 196 C3
Over Cambs 101 D5
Ches W 127 C6
S Glos 43 A4
Overbister 282 C7
Overbury 80 D2
Overcombe 15 C6
Over Compton 29 D5
Overgreen 130 B3
Over Green 97 B4
Over Haddon 130 C2
Over Hulton 137 C5
Over Kellet 154 D4
Over Kiddington 65 A5
Over Knutsford 128 B2
Overleigh 29 B4
Overley Green 80 B3
Over Monnow 61 B7
Over Norton 64 A4
Over Peover 128 B2
Overpool 126 B3
Overscaig Hotel 271 B7
Overseal 113 D6
Over Silton 158 B3
Oversland 52 D2
Overstone 83 A5
Over Stowey 28 B1
Overstrand 120 A4
Over Stratton 28 D4
Over Tabley 128 A2
Overthorpe 82 C1
Overton Aberdeen 245 A5
Ches W 127 B5
Dumfries 174 B2
Hants 32 A4
Lancs 144 B4
N Yorks 149 B4
Shrops 94 D3
Swansea 57 D4
W Yorks 139 B5
Overton Owrtyn 110 A2
Overton Bridge 110 A2
Overtown 194 A3
Over Wallop 32 B1
Over Whitacre 97 B5
Over Worton 65 A5
Oving Bucks 66 A3
W Sus 20 B2
Ovingdean 21 B6
Ovingham 178 C2
Ovington Durham 166 D4
Essex 86 C3
Hants 33 B4
Norf 103 A5
Northumb 178 C2
Ower 32 D2
Owermoigne 16 C1
Owlbury 93 B7
Owler Bar 130 B2
Owlerton 130 A3
Owl's Green 88 A3
Owlswick 66 C3
Owmby 142 C2
Owmby-by-Spital 133 A5
Owslebury 32 C4
Owston Leics 99 A4
S Yorks 140 B3
Owston Ferry 141 C6
Owstwick 151 D5
Owthorne 143 A5
Owthorpe 115 B4
Oxborough 102 A3
Oxcombe 134 B3
Oxenholme 154 C4
Oxenhope 147 D4
Oxen Park 154 C2
Oxenton 80 D2
Oxenwood 45 D7
Oxford 65 C6
Oxhey 67 D7
Oxhill 81 C6
Oxley 96 A2
Oxley Green 70 B3
Oxley's Green 37 D4
Oxnam 187 B2
Oxshott 48 C4
Oxspring 139 C5
Oxted 36 A1
Oxton Borders 196 A3
Notts 131 D6
Oxwich 57 D4
Oxwick 119 C6
Oykel Bridge 271 D6
Oyne 256 D1

P

Pabail Iarach 288 D6
Pabail Uarach 288 D6
Pace Gate 147 B5
Packington 114 D1
Padanaram 232 C2
Padbury 83 D4
Paddington 49 A5
Paddlesworth 38 B3
Paddockhaugh 266 D3
Paddockhole 185 D5
Paddock Wood 37 B4
Padfield 138 D3
Padiham 146 D1
Padog 124 D3
Padside 147 B5
Padstow 9 D5
Padworth 47 C4
Page Bank 167 B5
Pagham 20 C1
Paglesham Churchend 70 D3
Paglesham Eastend 70 D3
Paibeil 287 H2
Paible 287 E5
Paignton 8 A2
Pailton 98 C1
Painscastle 77 C5
Painshawfield 178 C2
Painsthorpe 149 B7
Painswick 63 C4
Pairc Shiaboist 288 C3
Paisley 205 B4
Pakefield 105 B6
Pakenham 87 A5
Pale 109 B4
Palestine 31 A6
Paley Street 47 B6
Palfrey 96 B3
Palgowan 181 C5
Palgrave 104 D2
Pallion 179 D5
Palmarsh 38 B3
Palnackie 173 C6
Palnure 171 A6
Palterton 131 C4
Pamber End 47 D4
Pamber Green 47 D4
Pamber Heath 47 C4
Pamphill 16 A3
Pampisford 85 C6
Pan 283 H4
Panbride 221 A5
Pancrasweek 10 A3
Pandy Gwyn 90 B4
Mon 61 A5
Powys 91 B7
Wrex 109 B6
Pandy Tudur 124 C3
Panfield 70 A1
Pangbourne 47 B4
Pannal 148 B2
Panshanger 68 B2
Pant 110 C1
Pant-glas Carms 58 C2
Gwyn 107 B4
Pant-glâs 91 C5
Pant-glas 110 B1
Pantgwyn Carms 58 C2
Ceredig 73 B5
Pant-lasau 57 C6
Pant Mawr 91 D6
Panton 134 B1
Pantperthog 91 B5
Pant-teg 58 C1
Pant-y-Caws 73 D4
Pant-y-dwr 92 D3
Pant-y-ffridd 93 A5
Pantyffynnon 57 A6
Pantymwyn 126 C1
Pant-yr-awel 40 C4
Pant-y-Wacco 125 B6
Panxworth 121 D5
Papcastle 163 A4
Papigoe 281 C5
Papil 285 K5
Papley 283 H5
Papple 210 C2
Papplewick 131 D5
Papworth Everard 85 A4
Papworth St Agnes 85 A4
Par 5 B5
Parbold 136 B3
Parbrook Som 29 B5
W Sus 34 D3
Parc 108 B3
Parcllyn 73 A5
Parc-Seymour 61 D6
Parc-y-rhôs 75 D4
Pardshaw 162 B3
Parham 88 A4
Park 183 C7
Park Corner Oxon 47 A4
Windsor 47 A6
Parkend 62 C2
Park End Mbro 168 D3
Northumb 177 B6
Parkeston 88 D3
Parkgate Ches W 126 B2
Dumfries 184 D3
Kent 37 C6
Sur 35 B5
Park Gate 18 A4
Parkham 25 C4
Parkham Ash 25 C4
Park Hill Notts 132 D1
N Yorks 148 A2
Parkhill Ho. 245 A5
Parkhouse 61 C6
Parkhouse Green 131 C4
Parkhurst 18 B3
Parkmill 57 D5
Parkneuk 233 A5
Parkstone 17 B4
Park Street 35 C4
Parley Cross 17 B4
Parracombe 26 A1
Parrog 72 C3
Parsley Hay 129 C6
Parsonage Green 69 C7
Parsonby 163 A4
Parson Cross 139 D6
Parson Drove 101 A5
Parson's Heath 71 A4
Partick 205 B5
Partington 137 D6
Partney 135 C4
Parton Cumb 162 B2
Dumfries 173 A4
Glos 63 A4
Partridge Green 21 A4
Parwich 130 D1
Passenham 83 D4
Paston 121 B5
Patchacott 11 B5
Patcham 21 B6
Patching 20 B3
Patchole 25 A7
Patchway 43 A4

Pateley Bridge 147 A5
Paternoster Heath 70 B3
Pathe 28 B3
Pathhead Aberds 233 B5
E Ayrs 182 A4
Fife 209 A5
Midloth 209 D6
Path of Condie 219 C5
Pathstruie 219 C5
Patna 182 A2
Patney 45 D4
Patrick 152 C2
Patrick Brompton 157 B6
Patrington 143 A5
Patrixbourne 52 D3
Patterdale 164 D1
Pattingham 95 B6
Pattishall 82 B3
Pattiswick Green 70 A2
Patton Bridge 155 B4
Paul 2 C2
Paulerspury 83 C4
Paull 142 A3
Paulton 43 D5
Pavenham 84 B1
Pawlett 28 A3
Pawston 198 C2
Paxford 81 D4
Paxton 198 A3
Payhembury 13 A5
Paythorne 146 B2
Peacehaven 22 B2
Peak Dale 129 B5
Peak Forest 129 B6
Peakirk 100 A3
Pearsie 232 C1
Peasedown St John 43 D6
Peasemore 46 B2
Peasenhall 89 A4
Pease Pottage 35 C5
Peaslake 34 B3
Peasley Cross 136 D4
Peasmarsh 37 D6
Peaston 210 D1
Peastonbank 210 D1
Peathill 269 C4
Peat Inn 221 D4
Peatling Magna 98 B2
Peatling Parva 98 C2
Peaton 94 C3
Peats Corner 88 A2
Pebmarsh 87 D4
Pebworth 80 C4
Pecket Well 138 A2
Peckforton 127 D5
Peckham 49 B6
Peckleton 98 A1
Pedlinge 38 B3
Pedmore 96 C2
Pedwell 28 B4
Peebles 196 B1
Peel 152 C2
Peel Common 19 A4
Peel Park 205 C6
Peening Quarter 37 D6
Pegsdon 84 D3
Pegswood 179 A4
Pegwell 53 C5
Peinchorran 247 A4
Peinlich 259 C4
Pelaw 179 C4
Pelcomb Bridge 55 C5
Pelcomb Cross 55 C5
Peldon 70 B3
Pellon 138 A3
Pelsall 96 A3
Pelton 179 D4
Pelutho 174 D4
Pelynt 5 B7
Pemberton 137 C4
Pembrey 57 B4
Pembridge 78 B1
Pembroke
Penfro 55 D5
Pembroke Dock Doc
Penfro 55 D5
Pembury 36 B4
Penallt 61 B7
Penally 55 E7
Penalt 62 A1
Penare 5 C4
Penarth 41 D6
Pen-bont Rhydybeddau 91 D4
Penbryn 73 A5
Pencader 58 B1
Pencaenewydd 107 B4
Pencaitland 210 D1
Pencarnisiog 122 C3
Pencarreg 75 D4
Pencelli 60 A2
Pen-clawdd 57 C5
Pencoed 41 C4
Pencombe 78 B3
Pencoyd 61 A7
Pencraig Hereford 62 A1
Powys 109 C5
Pendeen 2 B1
Penderyn 59 E6
Pendine 56 B2
Pendlebury 137 C6
Pendleton 146 D1
Pendock 79 D5
Pendoggett 9 D6
Pendomer 29 D5
Pendoylan 41 D5
Pendre 40 C4
Penegoes 91 B5
Pen-ffordd 55 B6
Pengam 41 B6
Penge 49 B6
Pengenffordd 77 D5
Pengorffwysfa 123 A4
Pengover Green 6 A1
Pen-groes-oped 61 C5
Penhale Corn 3 D4
Corn 4 B4
Penhalvaen 4 D2
Penhill 45 A5
Penhow 61 D6
Penhurst 23 A4
Peniarth 90 B4
Penicuik 209 D5
Peniel Carms 58 C1
Denb 125 C5
Penifiler 259 D4
Peninver 190 C3
Penisarwaun 123 D5
Penistone 139 C5
Penjerrick 4 D2
Penketh 127 A5
Penkill 181 B4
Penkridge 112 D3
Penley 110 B3
Penllergaer 57 C6
Penllyn 41 D4
Pen-llyn 122 B3
Pen-lon 123 D4
Penmachno 124 D2
Penmaen 57 D5
Penmaenan 124 B2
Penmaenmawr 124 B2
Penmaenpool 91 A4
Penmark 41 E5
Penmarth 4 D2
Penmon 123 B6
Penmore Mill 224 A3
Penmorfa Ceredig 73 A6
Gwyn 107 B5
Penmynydd 123 C5
Penn Bucks 67 D5
W Mid 96 B1
Pennal 91 B5
Pennan 268 C3
Pennant Ceredig 75 B4
Denb 109 B5
Denb 125 D5
Powys 91 C6
Pennant Melangell 109 C5
Pennar 55 D5
Pennard 57 D5
Pennerley 94 B1
Pennington
Cumb 153 C3
Gtr Man 137 D5
Hants 18 B2
Penn Street 67 D5
Penny Bridge 154 C2
Pennycross 225 D4
Pennygate 121 C5
Pennygown 225 B4
Pennymoor 26 D3
Pennywell 179 D5
Penparc Ceredig 73 B5
Pembs 55 A4
Penparcau 90 D3
Penperlleni 61 C5
Penpillick 5 B5
Penpol 4 D3
Penpoll 5 B6
Penpont
Dumfries 183 C6
Powys 59 C6
Penrherber 73 C5
Penrhiwceiber 41 B5
Penrhiw goch 57 A5
Penrhiw-llan 73 B6
Penrhiw-pâl 73 B6
Penrhos 106 C3
Penrhôs 61 B6
Penrhos 59 D4
Penrhosfeilw 122 B2
Penrhyn Bay 124 A3
Penrhyn-coch 90 D4
Penrhyndeudraeth 107 C6
Penrhynside 124 A3
Penrice 57 D4
Penrith 164 B3
Penrose 9 D4
Penruddock 164 C2
Penryn 4 D2
Pensarn Carms 57 A4
Conwy 125 B4
Pen-sarn Gwyn 107 B4
Gwyn 107 D5
Pensax 79 A5
Pensby 126 A2
Penselwood 30 B1
Pensford 43 C5
Penshaw 179 D5
Penshurst 36 B3
Pensilva 6 A1
Penston 210 C1
Pentewan 5 C5
Pentir 123 D5
Pentire 4 A2
Pentlow 87 C4
Pentney 119 D4
Penton Mewsey 32 A2
Pentraeth 123 C5
Pentre Carms 57 A5
Powys 93 B6
Powys 93 C4
Rhondda 41 B4
Shrops 110 D2
Wrex 109 B6
Wrex 110 A1
Pentrebach
M Tydf 41 A5
Swansea 57 B6
Pentre-bâch 75 D4
Pentre-bach 59 B6
Pentrebeirdd 109 D6
Pentre Berw 123 C4
Pentre-bont 124 D2
Pentrecagal 73 B6
Pentre-celyn
Denb 125 D6
Powys 91 B6
Pentre-chwyth 57 C6
Pentre-cwrt 73 C6
Pentre Dolau-Honddu 76 C3
Pentredwr 109 A6
Pentre-dwr 40 B1
Pentrefelin Carms 58 C2
Ceredig 75 D5
Conwy 124 B3
Gwyn 107 C5
Pentrefoelas 124 D3
Pentre-galar 73 C4
Pentregat 73 A6
Pentre-Gwenlais 57 A6
Pentre Gwynfryn 107 D5
Pentre Halkyn 126 B2
Pentreheyling 93 B6
Pentre-Isaf 124 C3
Pentre Llanrhaeadr 125 C5
Pentre-llwyn-llyd 76 B3
Pentre-llyn 75 A5
Pentre-llyn cymmer 125 D4
Pentre Meyrick 41 D4
Pentre-poeth 42 A1
Pentre'r Felin 124 C3
Pentre'r-felin 59 B6
Pentre-rhew 75 C5
Pentre-tafarn-y-fedw 124 C3
Pentre-ty-gwyn 59 B5
Pentrich 130 D3
Pentridge 31 D4
Pen-twyn 61 C7
Pentyrch 41 C6
Penuchadre 40 D3
Penuwch 75 B4
Penwithick 5 B5
Penwyllt 59 D5
Penybanc 57 A6
Pen-y-banc 58 C3
Penybont 77 A5
Pen-y-bont
Carms 73 D6
Gwyn 91 B5
Gwyn 107 D6
Powys 109 C7
Penybontfawr 109 C5
Pen-y-bryn Gwyn 91 A4
Pembs 73 B4
Penycae 110 A1
Pen-y-cae 59 D5
Pen-y-cae-mawr 61 D6
Pen-y-cefn 125 B6
Pen-y-clawdd 61 C6
Pen-y-coedcae 41 C5
Penycwm 54 B4
Pen-y-fai 40 C3
Penyffordd 126 C3
Penyffridd 107 A5
Pen-y-garn Carms 58 B2
Ceredig 90 D4
Penygarnedd 109 C6
Pen-y-garnedd 123 C5
Pen-y-gop 108 A4
Penygraig 41 B4
Pen-y-graig 106 C1
Penygroes Gwyn 107 A4
Pembs 73 C4
Pen-y-groes 57 A5
Pen-y-groeslon 106 C2
Pen-y-Gwryd Hotel 107 A6
Penyrheol 41 C6
Pen-yr-heol 61 B6
Pen-yr-Heolgerrig 60 C2
Penysarn 123 A4
Pen-y-stryt 126 D1
Penywaun 41 A4
Penzance 2 B2
Peopleton 80 B2
Peover Heath 128 B2
Peper Harow 34 B2
Perceton 204 D3
Percie 244 C2
Percyhorner 269 C4
Periton 27 A4
Perivale 49 A4
Perkinsville 179 D4
Perlethorpe 131 B6
Perranarworthal 4 D2
Perranporth 4 B2
Perranuthnoe 2 C3
Perranzabuloe 4 B2
Perry Barr 96 B3
Perryfoot 129 A6
Perry Green Herts 68 B4
Wilts 44 A3
Perry Street 50 B3
Pershall 112 B2
Pershore 80 C2
Pert 233 B4
Pertenhall 84 A2
Perth 219 B6
Perthy 110 B2
Perton 95 B6
Pertwood 30 B2
Peterborough 100 B3
Peterburn 261 B4
Peterchurch 78 D1
Peterculter 245 B5
Peterhead 257 B6
Peterlee 168 A2
Petersfield 33 C6
Peter's Green 67 B7
Peters Marland 25 D5
Peterstone Wentlooge 42 A1
Peterston super-Ely 41 D5
Peterstow 62 A1
Peter Tavy 11 D6
Petertown 283 G4
Petham 52 D3
Petrockstow 11 A6
Pett 23 A6
Pettaugh 88 B2
Petteridge 37 B4
Pettinain 195 B4
Pettistree 88 B3
Petton Devon 27 C5
Shrops 110 C3
Petts Wood 50 C1
Petty 256 C2
Pettycur 209 B5
Pettymuick 257 D4
Petworth 34 D2
Pevensey 22 B4
Pevensey Bay 23 B4
Pewsey 45 C5
Philham 24 C3
Philiphaugh 186 A3
Phillack 2 B3
Philleigh 4 D3
Philpstoun 208 C3
Phocle Green 62 A2
Phoenix Green 47 D5
Pica 162 B3
Piccotts End 67 C6
Pickering 159 C6
Picket Piece 32 A2
Picket Post 17 A5
Pickhill 158 C2
Picklescott 94 B2
Pickletillem 220 B4
Pickmere 128 B1
Pickney 28 C1
Pickstock 111 C6
Pickwell Devon 25 A5
Leics 115 D5
Pickworth Lincs 116 B3
Rutland 116 D2
Picton Ches W 127 B4
Flint 125 A6
N Yorks 158 A3
Piddinghoe 22 B2
Piddington
Northants 83 B5
Oxon 66 B2
Piddlehinton 15 B7
Piddletrenthide 15 B7
Pidley 101 D5
Piercebridge 167 D5
Pierowall 282 C5
Pigdon 178 A3
Pikehall 130 D1
Pilgrims Hatch 69 D5
Pilham 141 D6
Pill 43 B4
Pillaton 6 A2
Pillerton Hersey 81 C6
Pillerton Priors 81 C5
Pilleth 77 A6
Pilley Hants 18 B2
S Yorks 139 C6
Pilling 144 C4
Pilling Lane 144 C3
Pillowell 62 C2
Pillwell 30 D1
Pilning 43 A4
Pilsbury 129 C6
Pilsdon 14 B4
Pilsgate 100 A2
Pilsley Derbys 130 B2
Derbys 131 C4
Pilton Devon 25 B6
Northants 100 C2
Rutland 99 A6
Som 29 A5
Pilton Green 57 D4
Pimperne 16 A3
Pinchbeck 117 C5
Pinchbeck Bars 117 C4
Pinchbeck West 117 C5
Pincheon Green 141 B4
Pinehurst 45 A5
Pinfold 136 B2
Pinged 57 B4
Pinhoe 13 B4
Pinkneys Grn 47 A6
Pinley 97 D6
Pin Mill 88 D3
Pinminnoch 180 B3
Pinmore 181 B4
Pinmore Mains 181 B4
Pinner 48 A4
Pinvin 80 C2
Pinwherry 180 C3
Pinxton 131 D4
Pipe and Lyde 78 C3
Pipe Gate 111 A6
Piperhill 253 A4
Piper's Pool 10 C3
Pipewell 99 C5
Pippacott 25 B6
Pipton 77 D5
Pirbright 34 A2
Pirnmill 202 D3
Pirton Herts 84 D3
Worcs 80 C1
Pisgah Ceredig 75 A5
Stirling 218 D2
Pishill 47 A5
Pistyll 106 B3
Pitagowan 230 B2
Pitblae 269 C4
Pitcairngreen 219 B5
Pitcalnie 265 C4
Pitcaple 256 D2
Pitchcombe 63 C4
Pitchcott 66 A3
Pitchford 94 A3
Pitch Green 66 C3
Pitch Place 34 A2
Pitcombe 29 B6
Pitcorthie 221 D5
Pitcox 210 C3
Pitcur 220 A2
Pitfichie 244 A3
Pitforthie 233 A6
Pitgrudy 264 A3
Pitkennedy 232 C3
Pitkevy 220 D2
Pitkierie 221 D5
Pitlessie 220 D3
Pitlochry 230 C3
Pitmachie 256 D1
Pitmain 241 B5
Pitmedden 256 D3
Pitminster 28 D2
Pitmuies 232 D3
Pitmunie 244 A3
Pitney 29 C4
Pitscottie 220 C4
Pitsea 51 A4
Pitsford 83 A4
Pitsmoor 130 A3
Pitstone 67 B5
Pitstone Green 67 B5
Pittendreich 266 C2
Pittentrail 273 D5
Pittenweem 221 D5
Pittington 167 A6
Pittodrie 256 D1
Pitton 31 B6
Pittswood 36 B4
Pittulie 269 C4
Pityme 9 D5
Pity Me 167 A5
Pityoulish 242 A2
Pixey Green 104 D3
Pixham 35 A4
Pixley 79 D4
Place Newton 160 D2
Plaidy 268 D2
Plains 207 D5
Plaish 94 B3
Plaistow 34 C3
Plaitford 32 D1
Plank Lane 137 D5
Plas-canol 90 A3

Plas Gogerddan 90 D4
Plas Llwyngwern 91 B5
Plas Nantyr 109 B6
Plastow Green 46 C3
Plas-yn-Cefn 125 B5
Platt 36 A4
Platt Bridge 137 C5
Platts Common 139 C6
Plawsworth 167 A5
Plaxtol 36 A4
Playden 37 D7
Playford 88 C3
Play Hatch 47 B5
Playing Place 4 C3
Playley Green 79 D5
Plealey 94 A2
Plean 207 B6
Pleasington 137 A5
Pleasley 131 C5
Pleckgate 145 D6
Plenmeller 177 C5
Pleshey 69 B6
Plockton 249 C5
Plocrapol 288 H2
Ploughfield 78 C1
Plowden 94 C1
Ploxgreen 94 A1
Pluckley 38 A1
Pluckley Thorne 37 B7
Plumbland 163 A4
Plumley 128 B2
Plumpton Cumb 164 B2
E Sus 21 A6
Plumpton Green 21 A6
Plumpton Head 164 B3
Plumstead London 50 B1
Norf 120 B3
Plumtree 115 B4
Plungar 115 B5
Plush 15 A7
Plwmp 73 A6
Plymouth 6 B3
Plympton 7 B4
Plymstock 7 B4
Plymtree 13 A5
Pockley 159 C5
Pocklington 149 C7
Pode Hole 117 C5
Podimore 29 C5
Podington 83 A6
Podmore 112 B1
Point Clear 71 B4
Pointon 116 B4
Pokesdown 17 B5
Pol a Charra 286 E3
Polbae 181 D4
Polbain 270 C2
Polbathic 6 B2
Polbeth 208 D3
Polchar 242 B1
Polebrook 100 C2
Pole Elm 79 C6
Polegate 22 B3
Poles 264 A3
Polesworth 97 A5
Polgigga 2 C1
Polglass 270 D3
Polgooth 5 B4
Poling 20 B3
Polkerris 5 B5
Polla 277 C4
Pollington 140 B4
Polloch 236 C1
Pollok 205 B5
Pollokshields 205 B5
Polmassick 5 C4
Polmont 208 C2
Polnessan 182 A2
Polnish 235 B6
Polperro 5 B7
Polruan 5 B6
Polsham 29 A5
Polstead 87 D5
Poltalloch 213 C6
Poltimore 13 B4
Polton 209 D5
Polwarth 197 A6
Polyphant 10 C3
Polzeath 9 D5
Pondersbridge 101 B4
Ponders End 68 D3
Pondtail 34 A1
Ponsanooth 4 D2
Ponsworthy 12 D2
Pont Aber 59 C4
Pont Aber-Geirw 108 C2
Pontamman 57 A6
Pontantwn 57 A4
Pontardawe 40 A2
Pontarddulais 57 B5
Pont-ar-gothi 58 C2
Pont ar Hydfer 59 C5
Pont-ar-llechau 59 C4
Pontarsais 58 C1
Pontblyddyn 126 C2
Pontbren Araeth 58 C3
Pontbren Llwyd 59 E6
Pont Cwm Pydew 109 B5
Pont Cyfyng 124 D2
Pont Cysyllte 110 A1
Pont Dolydd Prysor 108 B2
Pontefract 140 A2
Ponteland 178 B3
Ponterwyd 91 D5
Pontesbury 94 A1
Pontfadog 110 B1
Pontfaen 55 A6
Pont-faen 76 D3
Pont Fronwydd 108 C3
Pont-gareg 72 B4
Pontgarreg 73 A6
Pont-Henri 57 B4
Ponthir 61 D5
Ponthirwaun 73 B5
Pontllanfraith 41 B6
Pontlliw 57 B6
Pont-Llogel 109 D5
Pontllyfni 107 A4
Pontlottyn 60 C3
Pontneddfechan 59 E6
Pontnewydd 61 D4
Pont Pen-y-benglog 123 D6
Pontrhydfendigaid 75 B6
Pont Rhyd-goch 124 C1
Pont-Rhyd-sarn 108 C3
Pont Rhyd-y-cyff 40 C3
Pontrhydyfen 40 B2
Pont-rhyd-y-groes 75 A6
Pontrilas 61 A5
Pontrobert 109 D6
Pont-rug 123 D5
Ponts Green 23 A4
Pontshill 62 A2
Pont-siân 74 D3
Pontsticill 60 B2
Pontwgan 124 B2
Pontyates 57 B4
Pontyberem 57 A5
Pontyclun 41 C5
Pontycymer 40 B4
Pontyglasier 72 C4
Pont-y-gwaith 41 B5
Pont-y-pant 124 D2
Pont y Pennant 108 C4
Pontypool Pont-Y-Pl 61 C4
Pontypridd 41 C5
Pont yr Afon-Gam 108 A2
Pont-yr-hafod 55 B5
Pontywaun 41 B7
Pooksgreen 32 D2
Pool Corn 3 A4
W Yorks 147 C6
Poole 17 B4
Poole Keynes 63 D5
Poolend 129 D4
Poolewe 261 B5
Pooley Bridge 164 C2
Poolfold 128 D3
Poolhill 62 A3
Pool o' Muckhart 219 D5
Pool Quay 110 D1
Poolsbrook 131 B4
Pootings 36 B2
Pope Hill 55 C5
Popeswood 47 C6
Popham 33 A4
Poplar 49 A6
Popley 47 D4
Porchester 114 A3
Porchfield 18 B3
Porin 251 A5
Poringland 104 A3
Porkellis 3 B4
Porlock 26 A3
Porlock Weir 26 A3
Portachoillan 202 C2
Port Ann 214 D2
Port Appin 226 B4
Port Arthur 285 K5
Port Askaig 201 B4
Portavadie 203 B4
Port Bannatyne 203 B5
Portbury 43 B4
Port Carlisle 175 B5
Port Charlotte 200 C2
Portchester 19 A5
Portclair 240 A2
Port Clarence 168 C2
Port Driseach 203 A4
Port Ellen 200 D3
Port Elphinstone 256 E2
Portencalzie 180 D2
Portencross 204 D1
Port Erin 152 E1
Port Erroll 257 C5
Portesham 15 C6
Portessie 267 C5
Port e Vullen 152 B4
Port-Eynon 57 D4
Portfield Gate 55 C5
Portgate 11 C5
Port Gaverne 9 C6
Port Glasgow 204 A3
Portgordon 267 C4
Portgower 274 C4
Porth Corn 4 A3
Rhondda 41 B5
Porthallow Corn 3 C5
Corn 6 B1
Porthcawl 40 D3
Porthcothan 9 D4
Porthcurno 2 C1
Port Henderson 261 C4
Porthgain 54 A4
Porthill 110 D3
Porthkerry 41 E5
Porthleven 3 C4
Porthllechog 123 A4
Porthmadog 107 C5
Porthmeor 2 B2
Porth Navas 3 C5
Portholland 5 C4
Porthoustock 3 C6
Porthpean 5 B5
Porthtowan 3 A4
Porthyrhyd Carms 57 A5
Carms 59 B4
Porth-y-waen 110 C1
Portincaple 215 C5
Portington 149 D6
Portinnisherrich 214 A2
Portinscale 163 B5
Port Isaac 9 C5
Portishead 42 B3
Portkil 215 D5
Portknockie 267 C5
Port Lamont 203 A5
Portlethen 245 C6
Portling 173 C6
Port Lion 55 D5
Portloe 4 D4
Port Logan 170 C2
Portmahomack 265 B5
Portmeirion 107 C5
Portmellon 5 C5
Port Mholair 288 D6
Port Mor 234 C3
Portmore 18 B2
Port Mulgrave 169 D5
Portnacroish 226 B4
Portnahaven 200 C1
Portnalong 246 A2
Portnaluchaig 235 B5
Portnancon 277 B5
Port Nan Giùran 288 D6
Port nan Long 287 G3
Portnellan 216 B4
Port Nis 288 A6
Portobello 209 C6
Port of Menteith 217 D5
Porton 31 B5
Portpatrick 170 B2
Port Quin 9 C5
Port Ramsay 226 B3
Portreath 3 A4
Portree 259 D4
Port St Mary 152 E2
Portscatho 4 D3
Portsea 19 A5
Portskerra 279 B4
Portskewett 43 A4
Portslade 21 B5
Portslade-by-Sea 21 B5
Portsmouth Ptsmth 19 A5
W Yorks 138 A2
Portsonachan 227 D5
Portsoy 267 C6
Port Sunlight 126 A3
Portswood 32 D3
Port Talbot 40 B2
Porttanachy 267 C4
Port Tennant 57 C6
Portuairk 234 D3
Portway Hereford 78 D2
Worcs 96 D3
Port Wemyss 200 C1
Port William 171 C5
Portwrinkle 6 B2
Poslingford 86 C3
Postbridge 12 D1
Postcombe 66 D3
Postling 38 B3
Postwick 104 A3
Potholm 185 D6
Potsgrove 67 A5
Potten End 67 C6
Potter Brompton 160 D3
Potterhanworth 133 C5
Potterhanworth Booths 133 C5
Potter Heigham 121 D6
Potterne 44 D3
Potterne Wick 44 D4
Potternewton 148 D2
Potters Bar 68 C2
Potter's Cross 95 C6
Potterspury 83 C4
Potter Street 69 C4
Potterton Aberds 245 A6
W Yorks 148 D3
Potto 158 A3
Potton 84 C4
Pott Row 119 C4
Pott Shrigley 129 B4
Poughill Corn 10 A3
Devon 12 A3
Poulshot 44 D3
Poulton Glos 64 C2
Mers 136 D2
Poulton-le-Fylde 144 D3
Pound Bank 95 D5
Poundfield 36 C3
Pound Green E Sus 36 D3
IoW 18 C2
Worcs 95 D5
Pound Hill 35 C5
Poundland 180 C3
Poundon 66 A2
Poundsgate 12 D2
Poundstock 10 B3
Powburn 188 B3
Powderham 13 C4
Powerstock 15 B5
Powfoot 174 B4
Powick 79 B6
Powmill 208 A3
Poxwell 16 C1
Poyle 48 B3
Poynings 21 A5
Poyntington 29 D6
Poynton 129 A4
Poynton Green 111 D4
Poystreet Green 87 B5
Praa Sands 2 C3
Pratt's Bottom 50 C1
Praze 2 B3
Praze-an-Beeble 3 B4
Predannack Wollas 3 D4
Prees 111 B4
Preesall 144 C3
Prees Green 111 B4
Preesgweene 110 B1
Prees Heath 111 B4
Prees Higher Heath 111 B4
Prees Lower Heath 111 B4
Prenderguest 198 A3
Prendwick 188 B3
Prengwyn 73 B7
Prenteg 107 B5
Prenton 126 A3
Prescot 136 D3
Prescott 110 C3
Pressen 198 C2
Prestatyn 125 A5
Prestbury Ches E 129 B4
Glos 63 A5
Presteigne Llanandras 77 A7
Presthope 94 B3
Prestleigh 29 A6
Preston Borders 198 A1
Brighton 21 B6
Devon 12 D3
Dorset 15 C7
E Loth 210 C2
E Yorks 151 D4
Glos 63 C6
Glos 79 D4
Herts 68 A1
Kent 52 C2
Kent 53 C4
Lancs 136 A4
Northumb 189 A4
Rutland 99 A5
Shrops 111 D4
Wilts 44 B4
Wilts 45 B6
Preston Bagot 81 A4
Preston Bissett 66 A2
Preston Bowyer 27 C6
Preston Brockhurst 111 C4
Preston Brook 127 A5
Preston Candover 33 A5
Preston Capes 82 B2
Preston Crowmarsh 65 D7
Preston Gubbals 110 D3
Prestonmill 174 C2
Preston on Stour 81 C5
Preston on the Hill 127 A5
Preston on Wye 78 C1
Prestonpans 209 C6
Preston Plucknett 29 D5
Preston St Mary 87 B5
Preston-under-Scar 157 B4
Preston upon the Weald Moors 111 D5
Preston Wynne 78 C3
Prestwich 137 C7
Prestwick Northumb 178 B3
S Ayrs 192 C3
Prestwood 66 C4
Price Town 40 B4
Prickwillow 102 C1
Priddy 43 D4
Priesthaugh 186 C3
Priest Hutton 154 D4
Priest Weston 93 B6
Primethorpe 98 B2
Primrose Green 120 D2
Primrosehill 67 C6
Primrose Valley 161 D5
Princes Gate 56 A1
Princes Risborough 66 C4
Princethorpe 97 D7
Princetown Caerph 60 B3
Devon 11 D6
Prion 125 C5
Prior Muir 221 C5
Prior Park 198 A3
Priors Frome 78 D3
Priors Hardwick 82 B1
Priorslee 111 D6
Priors Marston 82 B1
Priory Wood 77 C6
Priston 43 C5
Pristow Green 104 C2
Prittlewell 51 A5
Privett 33 C5
Prixford 25 B6
Probus 4 C3
Proncy 264 A3
Prospect 174 D4
Prudhoe 178 C2
Ptarmigan Lodge 215 B6
Pubil 228 D3
Puckeridge 68 A3
Puckington 28 D3
Pucklechurch 43 B5
Pucknall 32 C2
Puckrup 80 D1
Puddinglake 128 C2
Puddington Ches W 126 B3
Devon 26 D3
Puddledock 103 B6
Puddletown 16 B1
Pudleston 78 B3
Pudsey 147 D6
Pulborough 20 A3
Puleston 111 C6
Pulford 126 D3
Pulham 15 A7
Pulham Market 104 C2
Pulham St Mary 104 C3
Pulloxhill 84 D2
Pumpherston 208 D3
Pumsaint 58 A3
Puncheston 55 B6
Puncknowle 15 C5
Punnett's Town 36 D4
Purbrook 19 A5
Purewell 17 B5
Purfleet 50 B2
Puriton 28 A3
Purleigh 70 C2
Purley London 49 C6
W Berks 47 B4
Purlogue 93 D6
Purls Bridge 101 C6
Purse Caundle 29 D6
Purslow 94 C1
Purston Jaglin 140 B2
Purton Glos 62 C2
Glos 62 C2
Wilts 45 A4
Purton Stoke 64 D1
Pury End 83 C4
Pusey 65 D4
Putley 79 D4
Putney 49 B5
Putsborough 25 A5
Puttenham Herts 66 B4
Sur 34 B2
Puxton 42 C3
Pwll 57 B4
Pwllcrochan 55 D5
Pwll-glas 125 D6
Pwllgloyw 76 D4
Pwllheli 106 C3
Pwllmeyric 61 D7
Pwll-trap 56 A2
Pwll-y-glaw 40 B2
Pyecombe 21 A5
Pye Corner 42 A2
Pye Green 112 D3
Pyewipe 143 B4

Pyle 18 D3
Pyle Y Pîl 40 C3
Pylle 29 B6
Pymoor 101 C6
Pyrford 34 A3
Pyrton 66 D2
Pytchley 99 D5
Pyworthy 10 A4

Q

Quabbs 93 C6
Quadring 117 B5
Quainton 66 B3
Quarley 31 A6
Quarndon 114 A1
Quarrier's Homes 204 B3
Quarrington 116 A3
Quarrington Hill 167 B6
Quarry Bank 96 C2
Quarryford 210 D2
Quarryhill 264 B3
Quarrywood 266 C2
Quarter 194 A2
Quatford 95 B5
Quatt 95 C5
Quebec 167 A4
Quedgeley 63 B4
Queen Adelaide 102 C1
Queenborough 51 B6
Queen Camel 29 C5
Queen Charlton 43 C5
Queen Dart 26 D3
Queenhill 79 D6
Queen Oak 30 B1
Queensbury 147 D5
Queensferry
Edin 208 C4
Flint 126 C3
Queen's Head 110 C2
Queen's Park
Bedford 84 C2
Northants 83 A4
Queenstown 144 D3
Queen Street Kent 37 B4
Wilts 44 A4
Queenzieburn 207 C4
Quemerford 44 C4
Quendale 285 M5
Quendon 85 D7
Queniborough 115 D4
Quenington 64 C2
Quernmore 145 B5
Quethiock 6 A2
Quholm 282 F3
Quicks Green 46 B3
Quidenham 103 C6
Quidhampton
Hants 46 D3
Wilts 31 B5
Quilquox 257 C4
Quina Brook 111 B4
Quindry 283 H5
Quinton Northants 83 B4
W Mid 96 C2
Quintrell Downs 4 A3
Quixhill 113 A5
Quoditch 11 B5
Quoig 218 B3
Quorndon 114 D3
Quothquan 195 C4
Quoyloo 282 E3
Quoyness 283 G3
Quoys Shetland 284 B8
Shetland 285 G6

R

Raasay Ho. 248 C2
Rabbit's Cross 37 B5
Raby 126 B3
Rachan Mill 195 C6
Rachub 123 D6
Rackenford 26 D3
Rackham 20 A3
Rackheath 121 D4
Racks 174 A3
Rackwick Orkney 282 C5
Orkney 283 H3
Radbourne 113 B6
Radcliffe Gtr Man 137 C6
Northumb 189 C5
Radcliffe on Trent 115 B4
Radclive 82 D3
Radcot 64 D3
Raddery 252 A3
Radernie 221 D4
Radford Semele 81 A6
Radipole 15 C6
Radlett 67 D7
Radley 65 D6
Radmanthwaite 131 C5
Radmoor 111 C5
Radmore Green 127 D5
Radnage 66 D3
Radstock 43 D5
Radstone 82 C2
Radway 81 C6
Radway Green 128 D2
Radwell Bedford 84 B2
Herts 84 D4
Radwinter 86 D2
Radyr 41 C6
Rafford 253 A6
Ragdale 115 D4
Raglan 61 C6
Ragnall 132 B3
Rahane 215 D5
Rainford 136 C3
Rainford Junction 136 C3
Rainham London 50 A2
Medway 51 C5
Rainhill 136 D3
Rainhill Stoops 136 D4
Rainow 129 B4
Rainton 158 D2
Rainworth 131 D5
Raisbeck 155 A5
Raise 165 A5
Rait 220 B2
Raithby Lincs 134 A3
Lincs 134 C3
Rake 33 C7
Rakewood 138 B2
Ram 75 D4
Ramasaig 258 D1
Rame Corn 4 D2
Corn 6 C3
Rameldry Mill Bank 220 D3
Ram Lane 38 A1
Ramnageo 284 C8
Rampisham 15 A5
Rampside 153 D3
Rampton Cambs 85 A6
Notts 132 B2
Ramsbottom 137 B6
Ramsbury 45 B6
Ramscraigs 275 B5
Ramsdean 33 C6
Ramsdell 46 D3
Ramsden 65 B4
Ramsden Bellhouse 69 D7
Ramsden Heath 69 D7
Ramsey Cambs 101 C4
Essex 88 D3
IoM 152 B4
Ramseycleuch 185 A5
Ramsey Forty Foot 101 C5
Ramsey Heights 101 C4
Ramsey Island 70 C3
Ramsey Mereside 101 C4
Ramsey St Mary's 101 C4
Ramsgate 53 C5
Ramsgill 157 D5
Ramshorn 113 A4
Ramsnest Common 34 C2
Ranais 288 E5
Ranby Lincs 134 B2
Notts 131 A6
Rand 133 B6
Randwick 63 C4
Ranfurly 204 B3
Rangag 280 D3
Rangemore 113 C5
Rangeworthy 43 A5
Rankinston 182 A2
Ranmoor 130 A3
Ranmore Common 35 A4
Rannerdale 163 C4
Rannoch Station 228 C3
Ranochan 238 D2
Ranskill 131 A6
Ranton 112 C2
Ranworth 121 D5
Raploch 207 A5
Rapness 282 C6
Rascal Moor 149 D7
Rascarrel 173 D5
Rashiereive 257 D4
Raskelf 158 D3
Rassau 60 B3
Rastrick 139 A4
Ratagan 238 A3
Ratby 98 A2
Ratcliffe Culey 97 B6
Ratcliffe on Soar 114 C2
Ratcliffe on the Wreake 115 D4
Rathen 269 C5
Rathillet 220 B3
Rathmell 146 B2
Ratho 208 C4
Ratho Station 208 C4
Rathven 267 C5
Ratley 81 C6
Ratlinghope 94 B2
Rattar 281 A4
Ratten Row 144 C4
Rattery 7 A6
Rattlesden 87 B5
Rattray 231 D5
Raughton Head 164 A1
Raunds 100 D1
Ravenfield 140 D2
Ravenglass 153 A1
Raveningham 105 B4
Ravenscar 160 A3
Ravenscraig 204 A2
Ravensdale 152 B3
Ravensden 84 B2
Ravenseat 156 A2
Ravenshead 131 D5
Ravensmoor 127 D6
Ravensthorpe
Northants 98 D3
W Yorks 139 A5
Ravenstone
Leics 114 D2
M Keynes 83 B5
Ravenstonedale 155 A6
Ravenstown 154 D2
Ravenstruther 194 B4
Ravensworth 157 A5
Raw 160 A3
Rawcliffe E Yorks 141 A4
York 149 B4
Rawcliffe Bridge 141 A4
Rawdon 147 D6
Rawmarsh 140 D2
Rawreth 70 D1
Rawridge 14 A2
Rawtenstall 137 A7
Raxton 256 C3
Raydon 87 D6
Raylees 188 D2
Rayleigh 70 D2
Rayne 70 A1
Rayners Lane 48 A4
Raynes Park 49 C5
Reach 86 A1
Read 146 D1
Reading 47 B5
Reading Street 37 C7
Reagill 165 D4
Rearquhar 264 A3
Rearsby 115 D4
Reaster 281 B4
Reawick 285 J5
Reay 279 B5
Rechullin 249 A5
Reculver 53 C4
Redberth 55 D6
Redbourn 67 B7
Redbourne 142 D1
Redbrook Mon 62 B1
Wrex 111 A4
Redburn Highld 253 B5
Highld 264 D1
Northumb 177 C5
Redcar 168 C4
Redcastle Angus 233 C4
Highld 252 B1
Redcliff Bay 42 B3
Red Dial 175 D5
Redding 208 C2
Reddingmuirhead 208 C2
Reddish 138 D1
Redditch 80 A3
Rede 87 B4
Redenhall 104 C3
Redesdale Camp 187 D7
Redesmouth 177 A6
Redford Aberds 233 A5
Angus 232 D3
Durham 166 B3
Redfordgreen 185 A6
Redgorton 219 B5
Redgrave 103 D6
Redhill Aberds 245 B4
Aberds 256 C1
N Som 42 C3
Sur 35 A5
Red Hill 79 B6
Redhouse 202 B3
Redhouses 200 B3
Red Houses Jersey 6
Redisham 105 C5
Redland Bristol 43 B4
Orkney 282 E4
Redlingfield 104 D2
Red Lodge 102 D2
Redlynch Som 29 B7
Wilts 31 C6
Redmarley D'Abitot 79 D5
Redmarshall 167 C6
Redmile 115 B5
Redmire 156 B4
Redmoor 5 A5
Rednal 110 C2
Redpath 197 C4
Redpoint 261 D4
Red Rail 62 A1
Red Rock 137 C4
Red Roses 56 A2
Red Row 189 D5
Redruth 3 A4
Red Street 128 D3
Redvales 137 C7
Red Wharf Bay 123 B5
Redwick Newport 42 A3
S Glos 43 A4
Redworth 167 C5
Reed 85 D5
Reedham 105 A5
Reedness 141 A5
Reeds Beck 134 C2
Reepham Lincs 133 B5
Norf 120 C2
Reeth 156 B4
Regaby 152 B4
Regoul 253 A4
Reiff 270 C2
Reigate 35 A5
Reighton 161 D5
Reighton Gap 161 D5
Reinigeadal 288 G3
Reiss 281 C5
Rejerrah 4 B2
Releath 3 B4
Relubbus 2 B3
Relugas 253 B5
Remenham 47 A5
Remenham Hill 47 A5
Remony 229 D6
Rempstone 114 C3
Rendcomb 63 C6
Rendham 88 A4
Rendlesham 88 B4
Renfrew 205 B5
Renhold 84 B2
Renishaw 131 B4
Rennington 189 B5
Renton 206 C1
Renwick 164 A3
Repps 121 D6
Repton 113 C7
Reraig 249 D5
Rescobie 232 C3
Resipole 235 D6
Resolis 264 D2
Resolven 40 A3
Reston 211 D5
Reswallie 232 C3
Retew 4 B4
Retford 132 A2
Rettendon 70 D1
Rettendon Place 70 D1
Revesby 134 C2
Revesby Bridge 134 C3
Rewe 13 B4
Rew Street 18 B3
Reydon 105 D5
Reydon Smear 105 D5
Reymerston 103 A6
Reynalton 55 D6
Reynoldston 57 C4
Rezare 11 D4
Rhandirmwyn 59 A4
Rhayader Rhaeadr Gwy 76 A3
Rhyd-y-foel 125 B4
Rhedyn 106 C2
Rhemore 225 A4
Rhencullen 152 B3
Rhes-y-cae 126 B1
Rhewl Denb 109 A6
Denb 125 C6
Rhian 272 C3
Rhicarn 270 B3
Rhiconich 276 C3
Rhicullen 264 C2
Rhidorroch Ho. 262 A3
Rhifail 278 D3
Rhigos 59 E6
Rhilochan 273 D5
Rhiroy 262 B3
Rhiw 106 D2
Rhiwbina 41 C6
Rhiwbryfdir 107 B6
Rhiwderin 42 A1
Rhiwlas Gwyn 108 B4
Gwyn 123 D5
Powys 109 B6
Rhodes 138 C1
Rhodesia 131 B5
Rhodes Minnis 38 A3
Rhodiad 54 B3
Rhondda 41 B4
Rhonehouse or Kelton Hill 173 C5
Rhoose Y Rhws 41 E5
Rhôs Carms 73 C6
Neath 40 A2
Rhosaman 59 D4
Rhosbeirio 122 A3
Rhoscefnhir 123 C5
Rhoscolyn 122 C2
Rhoscrowther 55 D5
Rhosesmor 126 C2
Rhos-fawr 106 C3
Rhosgadfan 107 A5
Rhosgoch 123 B4
Rhos-goch 77 C5
Rhos-hill 73 B4
Rhoshirwaun 106 D1
Rhoslan 107 B4
Rhoslefain 90 B3
Rhosllanerchrugog 110 A1
Rhosmaen 58 C3
Rhosmeirch 123 C4
Rhosneigr 122 C3
Rhosnesni 126 D3
Rhos-on-Sea 124 A3
Rhosrobin 126 D3
Rhossili 57 D4
Rhosson 54 B3
Rhostryfan 107 A4
Rhostyllen 110 A2
Rhosybol 123 B4
Rhos-y-brithdir 109 C6
Rhos-y-garth 75 A5
Rhos-y-gwaliau 108 B4
Rhos-y-llan 106 C2
Rhos-y-Madoc 110 A2
Rhos-y-meirch 77 A6
Rhu Argyll 202 B3
Argyll 215 D5
Rhuallt 125 B5
Rhuddall Heath 127 C5
Rhuddlan Ceredig 58 A1
Denb 125 B5
Rhue 262 A2
Rhulen 77 B5
Rhunahaorine 202 D2
Rhyd Gwyn 107 B6
Powys 92 A3
Rhydargaeau 58 C1
Rhydcymerau 58 B2
Rhydd 79 C6
Rhyd-Ddu 107 A5
Rhydding 40 B2
Rhydfudr 75 B4
Rhydlewis 73 B6
Rhydlios 106 C1
Rhydlydan 124 D3
Rhyd-moel-ddu 93 D4
Rhydness 77 C5
Rhydowen 74 D3
Rhyd-Rosser 75 B4
Rhydspence 77 C6
Rhydtalog 126 D2
Rhyd-uchaf 108 B4
Rhyd-wen 91 A5
Rhydwyn 122 B3
Rhyd-y-clafdy 106 C3
Rhydycroesau 110 B1
Rhydyfelin Ceredig 75 A4
Rhondda 41 C5
Rhyd-y-fro 59 E4
Rhyd-y-gwin 57 B6
Rhydymain 108 C3
Rhyd-y-meirch 61 C5
Rhyd-y-meudwy 125 D6
Rhydymwyn 126 C2
Rhyd-y-pandy 57 B6
Rhyd-yr-onen 90 B4
Rhyd-y-sarn 107 B6
Rhyl Y Rhyl 125 A5
Rhymney Rhymni 60 C3
Rhynd Fife 221 B4
Perth 219 B6
Rhynie Aberds 255 D5
Highld 265 C4
Ribbesford 95 D5
Ribblehead 155 D6
Ribbleton 145 D5
Ribchester 145 D6
Ribigill 277 C6
Riby 142 C3
Riby Cross Roads 142 C3
Riccall 149 D5
Riccarton 193 B4
Richards Castle 78 A2
Richings Park 48 B3
Richmond London 49 B4
N Yorks 157 A5
Rickarton 245 D5
Rickinghall 103 D6
Rickleton 179 D4
Rickling 85 D6
Rickmansworth 67 D6
Riddings Cumb 175 A7
Derbys 131 D4
Riddlecombe 25 D7
Riddlesden 147 C4
Riddrie 205 B6
Ridge Dorset 16 C3
Hants 32 D2
Wilts 30 B3
Ridgebourne 77 A4
Ridge Green 35 B6
Ridgehill 43 C4
Ridge Lane 97 B5
Ridgeway Cross 79 C5
Ridgewell 86 C3
Ridgewood 22 A2
Ridgmont 84 D1
Riding Mill 178 C2

Ridleywood 127 D4
Ridlington Norf . . 121 B5
Rutland 99 A5
Ridsdale 177 A7
Riechip 231 D4
Riemore 230 D4
Rienachait 270 A3
Rievaulx 159 C4
Rift House 168 B2
Rigg 175 B5
Riggend 207 C5
Rigsby 135 B4
Rigside 194 C3
Riley Green 137 A5
Rileyhill 113 D5
Rilla Mill 10 D3
Rillington 160 D2
Rimington 146 C2
Rimpton 29 C6
Rimswell 143 A5
Rinaston 55 B5
Ringasta 285 M5
Ringford 173 C4
Ringinglow 130 A2
Ringland 120 D3
Ringles Cross 36 D2
Ringmer 22 A2
Ringmore 7 C5
Ringorm 254 B3
Ring's End 101 A5
Ringsfield 105 C5
Ringsfield
Corner 105 C5
Ringshall Herts . . . 67 B5
Suff 87 B6
Ringshall Stocks . 87 B6
Ringstead Norf . . . 119 A4
Northants 100 D1
Ringwood 17 A5
Ringwould 39 A5
Rinmore 243 A7
Rinnigill 283 H4
Rinsey 2 C3
Riof 288 D2
Ripe 22 A3
Ripley Derbys 130 D3
Hants 17 B5
N Yorks 148 A1
Sur 34 A3
Riplingham 150 D2
Ripon 157 D7
Rippingale 116 C3
Ripple Kent 39 A5
Worcs 79 D6
Ripponden 138 B3
Rireavach 262 A2
Risabus 200 D3
Risbury 78 B3
Risby 86 A3
Risca Rhisga 60 D4
Rise 151 C4
Riseden 36 C4
Risegate 117 C5
Riseholme 133 B4
Riseley Bedford . . . 84 A2
Wokingham 47 C5
Rishangles 88 A2
Rishton 146 D1
Rishworth 138 B3
Rising Bridge . . . 137 A6
Risley Derbys 114 B2
Warr 137 D5
Risplith 147 A6
Rispond 277 B5
Rivar 45 C7
Rivenhall End 70 B2
River Bank 86 A1
Riverhead 36 A3
Rivington 137 B5
Roachill 26 C3
Roade 83 B4
Road Green 104 B3
Roadhead 176 B3
Roadmeetings . . . 194 B3
Roadside 280 B3
Roadside of
Catterline 233 A6
Roadside of
Kinneff 233 A6
Roadwater 27 B5
Roag 258 D2
Roa Island 153 D3
Roath 41 D6
Roberton
Borders 186 B3
S Lanark 194 D4
Robertsbridge 37 D5
Roberttown 139 A4
Robeston Cross . . 55 D4
Robeston
Wathen 55 C6
Robin Hood 139 A6
Robin Hood's
Bay 160 A3
Roborough Devon . . 7 A4
Devon 25 D6
Roby 136 D3
Roby Mill 136 C4
Rocester 113 B5
Roch 55 B4
Rochdale 138 B1
Roche 5 A4
Rochester
Medway 51 C4
Northumb 188 D1
Rochford 70 D2
Roch Gate 55 B4
Rock Corn 9 D5
Northumb 189 A5
Worcs 95 D5
W Sus 21 A4
Rockbeare 13 B5
Rockbourne 31 D5
Rockcliffe Cumb . 175 B6
Dumfries 173 C6
Rock Ferry 126 A3
Rockfield Highld . 265 B5
Mon 61 B6
Rockford 17 A5
Rockhampton 62 D2
Rockingham 99 B5
Rockland All
Saints 103 B5
Rockland St
Mary 104 A4
Rockland St
Peter 103 B5
Rockley 45 B5
Rockwell End 47 A5
Rockwell Green . . 27 C6
Rodborough 63 C4
Rodbourne
Swindon 45 A5
Wilts 44 A3
Rodbourne
Cheney 45 A5
Rodd 77 A7
Roddam 188 A3
Rodden 15 C6
Rode 44 D2
Rodeheath 128 C3
Rode Heath 128 D3
Roden 111 D4
Rodhuish 27 B5
Rodington 111 D4
Rodley Glos 62 B3
W Yorks 147 D6
Rodmarton 63 D5
Rodmell 22 B2
Rodmersham 51 C6
Rodney Stoke 42 D3
Rodsley 113 A6
Rodway 28 B2
Rodwell 15 D6
Roecliffe 148 A2
Roe Green 85 D5
Roehampton 49 B5
Roesound 284 G5
Roffey 35 C4
Rogart 273 D5
Rogart Station . . 273 D5
Rogate 33 C7
Rogerstone 42 A1
Roghadal 287 F5
Rogiet 42 A3
Rogue's Alley . . . 101 A5
Roke 66 D2
Roker 179 D6
Rollesby 121 D6
Rolleston Leics 99 A4
Notts 132 D2
Rolleston-on-
Dove 113 C6
Rolston 151 C5
Rolvenden 37 C6
Rolvenden Layne 37 C6
Romaldkirk 166 C2
Romanby 158 B2
Romannobridge 195 B6
Romansleigh 26 C2
Romford 50 A2
Romiley 138 D2
Romsey 32 C2
Romsey Town 85 B6
Romsley Shrops . . . 95 C5
Worcs 96 D2
Ronague 152 D2
Rookhope 166 A2
Rookley 18 C4
Rooks Bridge 42 D2
Roos 151 D5
Roosebeck 153 D3
Rootham's Green . 84 B3
Rootpark 195 A4
Ropley 33 B5
Ropley Dean 33 B5
Ropsley 116 B2
Rora 269 D5
Rorandle 244 A3
Rorrington 93 A7
Roscroggan 3 A4
Rose 4 B2
Roseacre Kent 37 A5
Lancs 144 D4
Rose Ash 26 C2
Rosebank 194 B3
Rosebrough 189 A4
Rosebush 55 B6
Rosecare 10 B2
Rosedale Abbey 159 B6
Roseden 188 A3
Rosefield 253 A4
Rose Green 20 C2
Rose Grove 146 D2
Rosehall 272 D2
Rosehaugh
Mains 252 A2
Rosehearty 269 C4
Rosehill 111 B5
Rose Hill E Sus 22 A2
Lancs 146 D2
Suff 88 C2
Roseisle 266 C2
Roselands 22 B4
Rosemarket 55 D5
Rosemarkie 252 A3
Rosemary Lane . . . 27 D6
Rosemount 231 D5
Rosenannon 5 A4
Rosewell 209 D5
Roseworth 168 C2
Roseworthy 3 B4
Rosgill 164 D3
Roshven 235 C6
Roskhill 258 D2
Roskill House . . . 252 A2
Rosley 175 D6
Roslin 209 D5
Rosliston 113 D6
Rosneath 215 D5
Ross Dumfries 172 D4
Northumb 199 C5
Perth 218 B2
Rossett 126 D3
Rossett Green . . . 148 B2
Rossie Ochill 219 C5
Rossie Priory 220 A2
Rossington 140 D4
Rosskeen 264 D2
Rossland 205 A4
Ross-on-Wye 62 A2
Roster 281 E4
Rostherne 128 A2
Rosthwaite 163 C5
Roston 113 A5
Rosyth 208 B4
Rothbury 188 C3
Rotherby 115 D4
Rotherfield 36 D3
Rotherfield Greys 47 A5
Rotherfield
Peppard 47 A5
Rotherham 140 D2
Rothersthorpe . . . 83 B4
Rotherwick 47 D5
Rothes 254 B3
Rothesay 203 B5
Rothiebrisbane . . 256 C2
Rothienorman . . . 256 C2
Rothiesholm 282 E7
Rothley Leics 114 D3
Northumb 178 A2
Rothley Shield
East 188 D3
Rothmaise 256 C1
Rothwell Lincs . . . 142 D3
Northants 99 C5
W Yorks 139 A6
Rothwell Haigh . . 139 A6
Rotsea 150 B3
Rottal 232 B1
Rotten End 89 A4
Rottingdean 21 B6
Rottington 162 C2
Roud 18 C4
Rougham Norf . . . 119 C5
Suff 87 A5
Rougham Green . . 87 A5
Roughburn 240 D1
Rough Close 112 B3
Rough Common . . 52 D3
Roughlee 146 C2
Roughley 96 B4
Roughsike 176 B3
Roughton Lincs . . 134 C2
Norf 120 B4
Shrops 95 B5
Roughton Moor . 134 C2
Roundhay 148 D2
Roundstonefoot 185 B4
Roundstreet
Common 34 D3
Roundway 44 C4
Rousdon 14 B2
Rous Lench 80 B3
Routenburn 204 B1
Routh 150 C3
Row Corn 10 D1
Cumb 154 C3
Rowanburn 175 A7
Rowardennan . . . 206 A1
Rowde 44 C3
Rowen 124 B2
Rowfoot 177 C4
Row Heath 71 B5
Rowhedge 71 A4
Rowhook 35 C4
Rowington 81 A5
Rowland 130 B2
Rowlands Castle . . 33 D6
Rowlands Gill . . . 178 D3
Rowledge 33 A7
Rowlestone 61 A5
Rowley E Yorks . . . 150 D2
Shrops 93 A7
Rowley Hill 139 B4
Rowley Regis 96 C2
Rowly 34 B3
Rowney Green . . . 96 D3
Rownhams 32 D2
Rowrah 162 C3
Rowsham 66 B4
Rowsley 130 C2
Rowstock 46 A2
Rowston 133 D5
Rowton Ches W . . 127 C4
Shrops 110 D2
Telford 111 D5
Roxburgh 197 C6
Roxby N Lincs 141 B7
N Yorks 169 D5
Roxton 84 B3
Roxwell 69 C6
Royal Leamington
Spa 81 A6
Royal Oak Darl . . . 167 C5
Lancs 136 C3
Royal Tunbridge
Wells 36 C3
Royal Wootton
Bassett 45 A4
Roybridge 239 D6
Roydhouse 139 B5
Roydon Essex 68 C4
Norf 104 C1
Norf 119 C4
Roydon Hamlet . . . 68 C4
Royston Herts 85 C5
Royston
S Yorks 139 B6
Royton 138 C2
Rozel Jersey 6
Ruabon
Rhiwabon 110 A2
Ruaig 222 C3
Ruan Lanihorne . . . 4 C3
Ruan Minor 3 D5
Ruarach 249 D6
Ruardean 62 B2
Ruardean
Woodside 62 B2
Rubery 96 D2
Ruckcroft 164 A3
Ruckhall 78 D2
Ruckinge 38 B2
Ruckland 134 B3
Ruckley 94 A3
Rudbaxton 55 B5
Rudby 158 A3
Ruddington 114 B3
Rudford 62 A3
Rudge Shrops 95 B6
Som 44 D2
Rudgeway 43 A5
Rudgwick 34 C3
Rudhall 62 A2
Rudheath 128 B1
Rudley Green 70 C2
Rudry 41 C6
Rudston 150 A3
Rudyard 129 D4
Rufford 136 B3
Rufforth 148 B4
Rugby 98 D2
Rugeley 112 D4
Ruglen 181 A4
Ruilick 251 B7
Ruishton 28 C2
Ruisigearraidh . . 287 F4
Ruislip 48 A3
Ruislip Common . . 48 A3
Rumbling
Bridge 208 A3
Rumburgh 104 C4
Rumford 9 D4
Rumney 41 D7
Runcorn 127 A5
Runcton 20 B1
Runcton Holme . 102 A2
Rundlestone 11 D6
Runfold 34 B1
Runhall 103 A6
Runham Norf 105 A6
Norf 121 D6
Runnington 27 C6
Runsell Green 70 C1
Runswick Bay . . . 169 D6
Runwell 70 D1
Ruscombe 47 B5
Rushall Hereford . . 79 D4
Norf 104 C2
Wilts 45 D5
W Mid 96 A3
Rushbrooke 87 A4
Rushbury 94 B3
Rushden Herts 85 D5
Northants 83 A6
Rushenden 51 B6
Rushford 103 C5
Rush Green 50 A2
Rush-head 256 B3
Rushlake Green . . 22 A4
Rushmere 105 C5
Rushmere St
Andrew 88 C3
Rushmoor 34 B1
Rushock 96 D1
Rusholme 138 D1
Rushton Ches W . . 127 C5
Northants 99 C5
Shrops 95 A4
Rushton
Spencer 129 C4
Rushwick 79 B6
Rushyford 167 C5
Ruskie 217 D6
Ruskington 133 D5
Rusland 154 C2
Rusper 35 C5
Ruspidge 62 B2
Russell's Water . . 47 A5
Russel's Green . . 104 D3
Rusthall 36 C3
Rustington 20 B3
Ruston 160 C3
Ruston Parva 150 A3
Ruswarp 160 A2
Rutherford 197 C5
Rutherglen 205 B6
Ruthernbridge 5 A5
Ruthin Rhuthun . . . 125 D6
Ruthrieston 245 B6
Ruthven Aberds . . 255 B6
Angus 231 D6
Highld 241 C5
Highld 253 C4
Ruthven House . . 231 D7
Ruthvoes 4 A4
Ruthwell 174 B3
Ruyton-XI-
Towns 110 C2
Ryal 178 B2
Ryal Fold 137 A5
Ryall 14 B4
Ryarsh 37 A4
Rydal 154 A2
Ryde 19 B4
Rye 37 D7
Ryecroft Gate . . . 129 C4
Rye Foreign 37 D6
Rye Harbour 38 D1
Ryehill 143 A4
Rye Park 68 B3
Rye Street 79 D5
Ryhall 116 D3
Ryhill 140 B1
Ryhope 179 D6
Rylstone 146 B3
Ryme Intrinseca . . 29 D5
Ryther 149 D4
Ryton Glos 79 D5
N Yorks 159 D6
Shrops 95 A5
T&W 178 C3
Ryton-on-
Dunsmore 97 D6

S

Sabden 146 D1
Sacombe 68 B3
Sacriston 167 A5
Sadberge 167 D6
Saddell 190 B3
Saddington 98 B3
Saddle Bow 118 D3
Saddlescombe . . . 21 A5
Sadgill 154 A3
Saffron Walden . . 86 D1
Sageston 55 D6
Saham Hills 103 A5
Saham Toney . . . 103 A5
Saighdinis 287 H3
Saighton 127 C4
St Abbs 211 D6
St Agnes Corn 4 B2
Scilly 2 F3
St Albans 67 C7
St Allen 4 B3
St Andrews 221 C5
St Andrew's
Major 41 D6
St Anne Ald 7
St Annes 136 A2
St Ann's 184 C3
St Ann's Chapel
Corn 11 D5
Devon 7 C5
St Anthony-in-
Meneage 3 C5
St Anthony's Hill . 22 B4
St Arvans 61 D7
St Asaph
Llanelwy 125 B5
St Athan 41 E5
St Aubin Jersey 6
St Austell 5 B5
St Bees 162 C2

St Blazey 5 B5
St Brelade Jersey 6
St Breock 9 D5
St Breward 10 D1
St Briavels 62 C1
St Bride's 54 C4
St Brides Major 40 D3
St Bride's Netherwent 42 A3
St Brides super Ely 41 D5
St Brides Wentlooge 42 A1
St Budeaux 6 B3
Saintbury 80 D4
St Buryan 2 C2
St Catherine 44 B1
St Catherine's 215 B4
St Clears Sanclêr 56 A2
St Cleer 6 A1
St Clement 4 C3
St Clements Jersey 6
St Clether 10 C3
St Colmac 203 B5
St Columb Major 4 A4
St Columb Minor 4 A3
St Columb Road 4 B4
St Combs 269 C5
St Cross South Elmham 104 C3
St Cyrus 233 B5
St David's 218 B4
St David's Tyddewi 54 B3
St Day 4 C2
St Dennis 4 B4
St Devereux 78 D2
St Dogmaels 73 B4
St Dogwells 55 B5
St Dominick 6 A3
St Donat's 40 E4
St Edith's 44 C3
St Endellion 9 D5
St Enoder 4 B3
St Erme 4 B3
St Erney 6 B2
St Erth 2 B3
St Ervan 9 D4
St Eval 4 A3
St Ewe 5 C4
St Fagans 41 D6
St Fergus 269 D5
St Fillans 217 B6
St Florence 55 D6
St Genny's 10 B2
St George 125 B4
St George's 41 D5
St Germans 6 B2
St Giles 133 B4
St Giles in the Wood 25 D6
St Giles on the Hth. 11 B4
St Harmon 92 D3
St Helena 97 A5
St Helen Auckland 167 C4
St Helens IoW 19 C5
Mers. 136 D4
St Helen's 23 A6
St Helier Jersey 6
London 49 C5
St Hilary Corn. 2 B3
V Glam 41 D5
Saint Hill 36 C1
St Illtyd 41 A7
St Ippollytts 68 A1
St Ishmael's 54 D4
St Issey 9 D5
St Ive 6 A2
St Ives Cambs 101 D5
Corn 2 A3
Dorset 17 A5
St James South Elmham 104 C4
St Jidgey 9 E5
St John 6 B3
St John's IoM 152 C2
Jersey 6
Sur 34 A2
Worcs 79 B6
St John's Chapel 166 B1
St John's Fen End 118 D2
St John's Highway 118 D2
St John's Town of Dalry 182 D4
St Judes 152 B3
St Just 2 B1
St Just in Roseland 4 D3
St Katherine's 256 C2
St Keverne 3 C5
St Kew 9 D6
St Kew Highway 9 D6
St Keyne 6 A1
St Lawrence Corn 5 A5
Essex 70 C3
IoW 18 D4
St Leonards Dorset 17 A5
E Sus 23 B5
St Leonard's 67 C5
Saint Leonards 205 C6
St Levan 2 C1
St Lythans 41 D6
St Mabyn 9 D6
St Madoes 219 B6
St Margarets 68 B3
St Margaret's 78 D1
St Margaret's at Cliffe 39 A5
St Margaret South Elmham 104 C4
St Mark's 152 D2
St Martin 6 B1
St Martins Corn 3 C5
Perth 219 A6
St Martin's Jersey 6
Shrops 110 B2
St Mary Bourne 46 D2
St Mary Church 41 D5
St Mary Cray 50 C1
St Mary Hill 41 D4
St Mary Hoo 51 B5
St Mary in the Marsh 38 C2
St Mary's Jersey 6
Orkney 283 G5
St Mary's Bay 38 C2
St Maughans 61 B6
St Mawes 4 D3
St Mawgan 4 A3
St Mellion 6 A2
St Mellons 42 A1
St Merryn 9 D4
St Mewan 5 B4
St Michael Caerhays 5 C4
St Michael Penkevil 4 C3
St Michaels 78 A3
St Michael's 37 C6
St Michael's on Wyre 145 C4
St Michael South Elmham 104 C4
St Minver 9 D5
St Monans 221 D5
St Neot 5 A6
St Neots 84 A3
St Newlyn East 4 B3
St Nicholas Pembs 72 C1
V Glam 41 D5
St Nicholas at Wade 53 C4
St Ninians 207 A5
St Osyth 71 B5
St Osyth Heath 71 B5
St Ouens Jersey 6
St Owens Cross 62 A1
St Paul's Cray 50 C1
St Paul's Walden 68 A1
St Peter Port Guern 6
St Peter's Jersey 6
Kent 53 C5
St Petrox 55 E5
St Pinnock 5 A7
St Quivox 192 C3
St Ruan 3 D5
St Sampson Guern. 6
St Stephen 4 B4
St Stephens Corn 6 B3
Herts 67 C7
St Stephen's 10 C4
St Teath 9 C6
St Thomas 13 B4
St Tudy 9 D6
St Twynnells 55 E5
St Veep 5 B6
St Vigeans 233 D4
St Wenn 5 A4
St Weonards 61 A6
Salcombe 7 D6
Salcombe Regis 13 C6
Salcott 70 B3
Sale 137 D6
Saleby 135 B4
Sale Green 80 B2
Salehurst 37 D5
Salem Carms 58 C3
Ceredig 91 D4
Salen Argyll 225 B4
Highld 235 D5
Salesbury 145 D6
Salford C Beds 83 D6
Gtr Man 137 D7
Oxon 64 A3
Salford Priors 80 B3
Salfords 35 B5
Salhouse 121 D5
Saline 208 A3
Salisbury 31 C5
Sallachan 236 C3
Sallachy Highld. 249 C6
Highld 272 D3
Salle 120 C3
Salmonby 134 B3
Salmond's Muir 221 A5
Salperton 64 A1
Salph End 84 B2
Salsburgh 207 D6
Salt 112 C3
Saltaire 147 D5
Saltash 6 B3
Saltburn 264 D3
Saltburn-by-the-Sea 169 C4
Saltby 115 C6
Saltcoats Cumb 153 A1
N Ayrs 204 D2
Saltdean 22 B1
Salt End 142 A3
Salter 145 A6
Salterforth 146 C2
Salterswall 127 C6
Saltfleet 143 D6
Saltfleetby All Saints 143 D6
Saltfleetby St Clements 143 D6
Saltfleetby St Peter 135 A4
Saltford 43 C5
Salthouse 120 A2
Saltmarshe 141 A5
Saltney 126 C3
Salton 159 D6
Saltwick 178 B3
Saltwood 38 B3
Salum 222 C3
Salvington 21 B4
Salwarpe 80 A1
Salwayash 15 B4
Sambourne 80 A3
Sambrook 111 C6
Samhla 287 H2
Samlesbury 145 D5
Samlesbury Bottoms 137 A5
Sampford Arundel 27 D6
Sampford Brett 27 A5
Sampford Courtenay 12 A1
Sampford Peverell 27 D5
Sampford Spiney 11 D6
Sampool Bridge 154 C3
Samuelston 210 C1
Sanachan 249 B5
Sanaigmore 200 A2
Sancreed 2 C2
Sancton 150 D2
Sand Highld 261 A6
Shetland 285 J5
Sandaig 247 D6
Sandale 175 D5
Sandal Magna 139 B6
Sandbach 128 C2
Sandbank 215 D4
Sandbanks 17 C4
Sandend 267 C6
Sanderstead 49 C6
Sandfields 63 A5
Sandford Cumb 165 D5
Devon 12 A3
Dorset 16 C3
IoW 18 C4
N Som 42 D3
Shrops 111 B4
S Lanark 194 B2
Sandfordhill 257 B6
Sandford on Thames 65 C6
Sandford Orcas 29 C6
Sandford St Martin 65 A5
Sandgate 38 B3
Sandgreen 172 C3
Sandhaven 269 C4
Sandhead 170 C2
Sandhills 34 C2
Sandhoe 178 C1
Sand Hole 149 D7
Sandholme E Yorks 150 D1
Lincs 117 B6
Sandhurst Brack 47 C6
Glos 63 A4
Kent 37 D5
Sandhurst Cross 37 D5
Sandhutton 158 C2
Sand Hutton 149 B5
Sandiacre 114 B2
Sandilands Lincs 135 A5
S Lanark 194 C3
Sandiway 127 B6
Sandleheath 31 D5
Sandling 37 A5
Sandlow Green 128 C2
Sandness 285 H3
Sandon Essex 70 C1
Herts 85 D5
Staffs 112 B3
Sandown 19 C4
Sandplace 6 B1
Sandridge Herts 67 B7
Wilts 44 C3
Sandringham 118 C3
Sandsend 169 D6
Sandside Ho. 279 B5
Sandsound 285 J5
Sandtoft 141 C5
Sandway 37 A6
Sandwell 96 C3
Sandwich 53 D5
Sandwick Cumb 164 D2
Orkney 283 J5
Shetland 285 L6
Sandwith 162 C2
Sandy Carms 57 B4
C Beds 84 C3
Sandy Bank 134 D2
Sandycroft 126 C3
Sandyford Dumfries 185 C5
Stoke 128 D3
Sandygate 152 B3
Sandy Haven 55 D4
Sandyhills 173 C6
Sandylands 144 A4
Sandy Lane Wilts 44 C3
Wrex 110 A2
Sandypark 12 C2
Sandysike 175 B6
Sangobeg 277 B5
Sangomore 277 B5
Sanna 234 D3
Sanndabhaig W Isles 286 B4
W Isles 288 D5
Sannox 203 D5
Sanquhar 183 B5
Santon 142 B1
Santon Bridge 163 D4
Santon Downham 103 C4
Sapcote 98 B1
Sapey Common 79 A5
Sapiston 103 D5
Sapley 100 D4
Sapperton Glos 63 C5
Lincs 116 B3
Saracen's Head 117 C6
Sarclet 281 D5
Sardis 57 B5
Sarn Bridgend 40 C4
Powys 93 B6
Sarnau Carms 56 A3
Ceredig 73 A6
Gwyn 109 B4
Powys 76 D4
Powys 110 D1
Sarn Bach 106 D3
Sarnesfield 78 B1
Sarn Meyllteyrn 106 C2
Saron Carms 57 A6
Carms 73 C6
Denb 125 C5
Gwyn 107 A4
Gwyn 123 D5
Sarratt 67 D6
Sarre 53 C4
Sarsden 64 A3
Sarsgrum 277 B4
Satley 166 A4
Satron 156 B3
Satterleigh 26 C1
Satterthwaite 154 B2
Satwell 47 A5
Sauchen 244 A3
Saucher 219 A6
Sauchie 208 A1
Sauchieburn 233 B4
Saughall 126 B3
Saughtree 187 D4
Saul 62 C3
Saundby 132 A2
Saundersfoot 56 B1
Saunderton 66 C3
Saunton 25 B5
Sausthorpe 134 C3
Saval 272 D3
Savary 225 B5
Savile Park 138 A3
Sawbridge 82 A2
Sawbridgeworth 69 B4
Sawdon 160 C3
Sawley Derbys 114 B2
Lancs 146 C1
N Yorks 147 A6
Sawston 85 C6
Sawtry 100 C3
Saxby Leics 115 D6
Lincs 133 A5
Saxby All Saints 142 B1
Saxelbye 115 C5
Saxham Street 88 A1
Saxilby 132 B3
Saxlingham 120 B2
Saxlingham Green 104 B3
Saxlingham Nethergate 104 B3
Saxlingham Thorpe 104 B3
Saxmundham 89 A4
Saxondale 115 B4
Saxon Street 86 B2
Saxtead 88 A3
Saxtead Green 88 A3
Saxthorpe 120 B3
Saxton 148 D3
Sayers Common 21 A5
Scackleton 159 D5
Scadabhagh 288 H2
Scaftworth 141 D4
Scagglethorpe 160 D2
Scaitcliffe 137 A6
Scalasaig 212 C1
Scalby E Yorks 141 A6
N Yorks 160 B4
Scaldwell 99 D4
Scaleby 176 C2
Scaleby Hill 176 C2
Scale Houses 164 A3
Scales Cumb 153 C3
Cumb 163 B6
Lancs 145 D4
Scalford 115 C5
Scaling 169 D5
Scallastle 225 C5
Scalloway 285 K6
Scalpay 288 H3
Scalpay Ho. 247 B5
Scalpsie 203 C5
Scamadale 235 A6
Scamblesby 134 B2
Scamodale 236 B2
Scampston 160 D2
Scampton 133 B4
Scapa 283 G5
Scapegoat Hill 138 B3
Scar 282 C7
Scarborough 160 C4
Scarcliffe 131 C4
Scarcroft 148 C2
Scarcroft Hill 148 C2
Scardroy 250 A4
Scarff 284 E4
Scarfskerry 281 A4
Scargill 166 D3
Scarinish 222 C3
Scarisbrick 136 B2
Scarning 119 D6
Scarrington 115 A5
Scartho 143 C4
Scarwell 282 E3
Scatness 285 M5
Scatraig 252 C3
Scawby 142 C1
Scawsby 140 C3
Scawton 158 C4
Scayne's Hill 35 D6
Scethrog 60 A3
Scholar Green 128 D3
Scholes W Yorks 139 A4
W Yorks 139 C4
W Yorks 148 D2
School Green 127 C6
Scleddau 55 A5
Scofton 131 A6
Scole 104 D2
Scolpaig 287 G2
Scone 219 B6
Sconser 247 A4
Scoonie 220 D3
Scoor 224 E3
Scopwick 133 D5
Scoraig 262 A2
Scorborough 150 C3
Scorrier 4 C2
Scorton Lancs 145 C5
N Yorks 157 A6
Sco Ruston 121 C4
Scotbheinn 286 A4
Scotby 176 D2
Scotch Corner 157 A6
Scotforth 145 B4
Scothern 133 B5
Scotland Gate 179 A4
Scotlandwell 219 D6
Scotsburn 264 C3
Scotscalder Station 280 C2
Scotscraig 220 B4
Scots' Gap 178 A2
Scotston Aberds 233 A5
Perth 230 D3
Scotstoun 205 B5
Scotstown 236 C2
Scotswood 178 C3
Scottas 247 D6
Scotter 141 C6
Scotterthorpe 141 C6
Scottlethorpe 116 C3
Scotton Lincs 141 D6
N Yorks 148 B2
N Yorks 157 B5
Scottow 121 C4
Scoughall 210 B3
Scoulag 203 C6
Scoulton 103 A5
Scourie 276 D2
Scourie More 276 D2

Scousburgh 285 M5
Scrabster 280 B2
Scrafield 134 C3
Scrainwood 188 C2
Scrane End 117 A6
Scraptoft 98 A3
Scratby 121 D7
Scrayingham 149 A6
Scredington 116 A3
Scremby 135 C4
Scremerston 198 B4
Screveton 115 A5
Scrivelsby 134 C2
Scriven 148 B2
Scrooby 141 D4
Scropton 113 B5
Scrub Hill 134 D2
Scruton 157 B6
Sculcoates 150 D3
Sculthorpe 119 B5
Scunthorpe 141 B6
Scurlage 57 D4
Seaborough 14 A4
Seacombe 136 D2
Seacroft Lincs 135 C5
W Yorks 148 D2
Seadyke 117 B6
Seafield S Ayrs 192 C3
W Loth 208 D3
Seaford 22 C2
Seaforth 136 D2
Seagrave 115 D4
Seaham 168 A2
Seahouses 199 C6
Seal 36 A3
Sealand 126 C3
Seale 34 B1
Seamer N Yorks 160 C4
N Yorks 168 D2
Seamill 204 D2
Sea Palling 121 C6
Searby 142 C2
Seasalter 52 C2
Seascale 162 D3
Seathorne 135 C5
Seathwaite
Cumb 153 A3
Cumb 163 C5
Seatoller 163 C5
Seaton Corn 6 B2
Cumb 162 A3
Devon 14 B2
Durham 179 D5
E Yorks 151 C4
Northumb 179 B5
Rutland 99 B6
Seaton Burn 179 B4
Seaton Carew 168 C3
Seaton Delaval 179 B5
Seaton Ross 149 C6
Seaton Sluice 179 B5
Seatown Aberds 267 C6
Dorset 14 B4
Seave Green 159 A4
Seaview 19 B5
Seaville 175 C4
Seavington St Mary 28 D3
Seavington St Michael 28 D4
Sebergham 164 A1
Seckington 97 A5
Second Coast 261 A6
Sedbergh 155 B5
Sedbury 62 D1
Sedbusk 156 B2
Sedgeberrow 80 D3
Sedgebrook 115 B6
Sedgefield 167 C6
Sedgeford 119 B4
Sedgehill 30 C2
Sedgley 96 B2
Sedgwick 154 C4
Sedlescombe 23 A5
Sedlescombe Street 23 A5
Seend 44 C3
Seend Cleeve 44 C3
Seer Green 67 D5
Seething 104 B4
Sefton 136 C2
Seghill 179 B4
Seifton 94 C2
Seighford 112 C2
Seilebost 287 E5
Seion 123 D5
Seisdon 95 B6
Seisiadar 288 D6
Selattyn 110 B1
Selborne 33 B6
Selby 149 D5
Selham 34 D2
Selhurst 49 C6
Selkirk 186 A3
Sellack 62 A1
Sellafirth 284 D7
Sellibister 282 C8
Sellindge 38 B2
Sellindge Lees 38 B3
Selling 52 D2
Sells Green 44 C3
Selly Oak 96 C3
Selmeston 22 B3
Selsdon 49 C6
Selsey 20 C1
Selsfield Common 35 C6
Selsted 39 A4
Selston 131 D4
Selworthy 27 A4
Semblister 285 H5
Semer 87 C5
Semington 44 C2
Semley 30 C2
Send 34 A3
Send Marsh 34 A3
Senghenydd 41 B6
Sennen 2 C1
Sennen Cove 2 C1
Sennybridge Pont Senni 59 C6
Serlby 131 A6
Sessay 158 D3
Setchey 118 D3
Setley 18 A2
Setter Shetland 284 E6
Shetland 285 H5
Shetland 285 J7
Settiscarth 282 F4
Settle 146 A2
Settrington 160 D2
Sevenhampton 63 A6
Seven Kings 50 A1
Sevenoaks 36 A3
Sevenoaks Weald 36 A3
Seven Sisters 59 E5
Severn Beach 43 A4
Severnhampton 64 D3
Severn Stoke 79 C6
Sevington 38 A2
Sewards End 86 D1
Sewardstone 68 D3
Sewardstonebury 68 D3
Sewerby 151 A4
Seworgan 4 D2
Sewstern 116 C1
Sezincote 81 D4
Sgarasta Mhor 287 E5
Sgiogarstaigh 288 A6
Shabbington 66 C2
Shackerstone 97 A6
Shackleford 34 B2
Shade 138 A2
Shadforth 167 A6
Shadingfield 105 C5
Shadoxhurst 38 B1
Shadsworth 137 A6
Shadwell Norf 103 C5
W Yorks 148 D2
Shaftesbury 30 C2
Shafton 140 B1
Shalbourne 45 C7
Shalcombe 18 C2
Shalden 33 A5
Shaldon 13 D4
Shalfleet 18 C3
Shalford Essex 69 A7
Sur 34 B3
Shalford Green 69 A7
Shallowford 26 A2
Shalmsford Street 52 D2
Shalstone 82 D3
Shamley Green 34 B3
Shandon 215 D5
Shandwick 265 C4
Shangton 99 B4
Shankhouse 179 B4
Shanklin 19 C4
Shanquhar 255 C6
Shanzie 231 C6
Shap 164 D3
Shapwick Dorset 16 A3
Som 28 B4
Shardlow 114 B2
Shareshill 96 A2
Sharlston 140 B1
Sharlston Common 140 B1
Sharnbrook 84 B1
Sharnford 98 B1
Sharoe Green 145 D5
Sharow 158 D2
Sharpenhoe 84 D2
Sharperton 188 C2
Sharpness 62 C2
Sharp Street 121 C5
Sharpthorne 35 C6
Sharrington 120 B2
Shatterford 95 C5
Shaugh Prior 7 A4
Shavington 128 D2
Shaw Gtr Man 138 C2
W Berks 46 C2
Wilts 44 C2
Shawbury 111 C4
Shawdon Hall 188 B3
Shawell 98 C2
Shawford 32 C3
Shawforth 138 A1
Shaw Green 136 B4
Shawhead 173 A6
Shawhill 175 B5
Shaw Mills 147 A6
Shawton 194 B1
Shawtonhill 194 B1
Shear Cross 30 A2
Shearington 174 B3
Shearsby 98 B3
Shebbear 11 A5
Shebdon 111 C6
Shebster 279 B6
Sheddens 205 C5
Shedfield 33 D4
Sheen 129 C6
Sheepscar 148 D2
Sheepscombe 63 B4
Sheepstor 7 A4
Sheepwash 11 A5
Sheepway 42 B3
Sheepy Magna 97 A6
Sheepy Parva 97 A6
Sheering 69 B5
Sheerness 51 B6
Sheet 33 C6
Sheffield 130 A3
Sheffield Bottom 47 C4
Sheffield Green 36 D2
Shefford 84 D3
Shefford Woodlands 46 B1
Sheigra 276 B2
Sheinton 95 A4
Shelderton 94 D2
Sheldon Derbys 129 C6
Devon 13 A6
W Mid 97 C4
Sheldwich 52 D2
Shelf 139 A4
Shelfanger 104 C2
Shelfield Warks 80 A4
W Mid 96 A3
Shelford 115 A4
Shellacres 198 B2
Shelley Essex 69 C5
Suff 87 D6
W Yorks 139 B5
Shellingford 64 D4
Shellow Bowells 69 C6
Shelsley Beauchamp 79 A5
Shelsley Walsh 79 A5
Shelthorpe 114 D3
Shelton Bedford 84 A2
Norf 104 B3
Notts 115 A5
Shelton
Shrops 110 D3
Shelton Green 104 B3
Shelve 94 B1
Shelwick 78 C3
Shenfield 69 D6
Shenington 81 C6
Shenley 68 C1
Shenley Brook End 83 D5
Shenleybury 68 C1
Shenley Church End 83 D5
Shenmore 78 D1
Shennanton 171 A5
Shenstone Staffs 96 A4
Worcs 95 D6
Shenton 97 A6
Shenval Highld 251 D6
Moray 254 D3
Shepeau Stow 117 D6
Shephall 68 A2
Shepherd's Green 47 A5
Shepherd's Port 118 B3
Shepherdswell 39 A4
Shepley 139 C4
Shepperdine 62 D2
Shepperton 48 C3
Shepreth 85 C5
Shepshed 114 D2
Shepton Beauchamp 28 D4
Shepton Mallet 29 A6
Shepton Montague 29 B6
Shepway 37 A5
Sheraton 168 B2
Sherborne Dorset 29 D6
Glos 64 B2
Sherborne St John 47 D4
Sherbourne 81 A5
Sherburn
Durham 167 A6
N Yorks 160 D3
Sherburn Hill 167 A6
Sherburn in Elmet 148 D3
Shere 34 B3
Shereford 119 C5
Sherfield English 32 C1
Sherfield on Loddon 47 D4
Sherford 8 C1
Sheriffhales 111 D6
Sheriff Hutton 149 A5
Sheringham 120 A3
Sherington 83 C5
Shernal Green 80 A2
Shernborne 119 B4
Sherrington 30 B3
Sherston 44 A2
Sherwood Green 25 C6
Shettleston 205 B6
Shevington 136 C4
Shevington Moor 136 B4
Shevington Vale 136 C4
Sheviock 6 B2
Shide 18 C3
Shiel Bridge 238 A3
Shieldaig Highld 249 A5
Highld 261 C5
Shieldhill
Dumfries 184 D3
Falk 208 C1
S Lanark 195 B5
Shielfoot 235 D5
Shielhill Angus 232 C2
Invclyd 204 A2
Shifford 65 C4
Shifnal 95 A5
Shilbottle 189 C4
Shildon 167 C5
Shillingford Devon 27 C4
Oxon 65 D6
Shillingford St George 13 C4
Shillingstone 30 D2
Shillington 84 D3
Shillmoor 188 C1
Shilton Oxon 64 C3
Warks 97 C7
Shilvington 178 A3
Shimpling Norf 104 C2
Suff 87 B4
Shimpling Street 87 B4
Shincliffe 167 A5
Shiney Row 179 D5
Shinfield 47 C5
Shingham 102 A3
Shingle Street 89 C4
Shinner's Bridge 8 A1
Shinness 272 C3
Shipbourne 36 A3
Shipdham 103 A5
Shipham 42 D3
Shiphay 8 A2
Shiplake 47 B5
Shipley Derbys 114 A2
Northumb 189 B4
Shrops 95 B6
W Sus 35 D4
W Yorks 147 D5
Shipley Shiels 187 D6
Shipmeadow 105 C4
Shippea Hill Sta 102 C2
Shippon 65 D5
Shipston-on-Stour 81 C5
Shipton Glos 63 B6
N Yorks 149 B4
Shrops 94 B3
Shipton Bellinger 31 A6
Shipton Gorge 15 B4
Shipton Green 19 A7
Shipton Moyne 44 A2
Shipton on Cherwell 65 B5
Shipton Solers 63 B6
Shiptonthorpe 150 C1
Shipton-under-Wychwood 64 B3
Shirburn 66 D2
Shirdley Hill 136 B2
Shirebrook 131 C5
Shiregreen 139 D6
Shirehampton 43 B4
Shiremoor 179 B5
Shirenewton 61 D6
Shireoaks 131 A5
Shirkoak 38 B1
Shirland 130 D3
Shirley Derbys 113 A6
London 49 C6
Soton 32 D3
W Mid 96 D4
Shirl Heath 78 B2
Shirrell Heath 33 D4
Shirwell 25 B6
Shirwell Cross 25 B6
Shiskine 191 C5
Shobdon 78 A2
Shobnall 113 C6
Shobrooke 12 A3
Shoby 115 D4
Shocklach 110 A3
Shoeburyness 51 A6
Sholden 53 D5
Sholing 32 D3
Shoot Hill 110 D3
Shop Corn 9 D4
Corn 24 D3
Shop Corner 88 D3
Shoreditch 49 A6
Shoreham 50 C2
Shoreham-By-Sea 21 B5
Shore Mill 264 D3
Shoresdean 198 B3
Shoreswood 198 B3
Shoreton 264 D2
Shorncote 63 D6
Shorne 50 B3
Shortacombe 11 C6
Shortgate 22 A2
Short Heath 96 A2
Shortlanesend 4 C3
Shortlees 193 B4
Shortstown 84 C2
Shorwell 18 C3
Shoscombe 43 D6
Shotatton 110 C2
Shotesham 104 B3
Shotgate 70 D1
Shotley 88 D3
Shotley Bridge 178 D2
Shotleyfield 178 D2
Shotley Gate 88 D3
Shottenden 52 D2
Shottermill 34 C1
Shottery 81 B4
Shotteswell 81 C7
Shottisham 88 C4
Shottle 113 A7
Shottlegate 113 A7
Shotton Durham 168 B2
Flint 126 C3
Northumb 198 C2
Shotton Colliery 167 A6
Shotts 207 D6
Shotwick 126 B3
Shouldham 102 A2
Shouldham Thorpe 102 A2
Shoulton 79 B6
Shover's Green 37 C4
Shrawardine 110 D3
Shrawley 79 A6
Shrewley Common 81 A5
Shrewsbury 110 D3
Shrewton 31 A4
Shripney 20 B2
Shrivenham 45 A6
Shropham 103 B5
Shrub End 70 A3
Shucknall 78 C3
Shudy Camps 86 C2
Shulishadermor 259 D4
Shurdington 63 B5
Shurlock Row 47 B6
Shurrery 279 C6
Shurrery Lodge 279 C6
Shurton 28 A2
Shustoke 97 B5
Shute Devon 12 A3
Devon 14 B2
Shutford 81 C6
Shuthonger 80 D1
Shutlanger 83 B4
Shuttington 97 A5
Shuttlewood 131 B4
Siabost bho Dheas 288 C3
Siabost bho Thuath 288 C3
Siadar 288 B4
Siadar Iarach 288 B4
Siadar Uarach 288 B4
Sibbaldbie 185 D4
Sibbertoft 98 C3
Sibdon Carwood 94 C2
Sibford Ferris 81 D6
Sibford Gower 81 D6
Sible Hedingham 86 D3
Sibsey 134 D3
Sibson Cambs 100 B2
Leics 97 A6
Sibthorpe 115 A5
Sibton 89 A4
Sibton Green 105 D4
Sicklesmere 87 A4
Sicklinghall 148 C2
Sid 13 C6
Sidbury Devon 13 B6
Shrops 95 C4
Sidcot 42 D3
Sidcup 50 B1
Siddick 162 A3
Siddington
Ches E 128 B3
Glos 63 D6
Sidemoor 96 D2
Sidestrand 121 B4
Sidford 13 B6
Sidlesham 20 C1
Sidley 23 B5
Sidlow 35 B5
Sidmouth 13 C6
Sigford 12 D2

Sigglesthorne 151 C4
Sighthill 209 C4
Sigingstone 41 D4
Signet 64 B3
Silchester 47 C4
Sildinis 288 F3
Sileby 114 D3
Silecroft 153 B2
Silfield 104 B2
Silian 75 C4
Silkstone 139 C5
Silkstone Common 139 C5
Silk Willoughby 116 A3
Silloth 174 C4
Sills 188 C1
Sillyearn 267 D6
Siloh 59 B4
Silpho 160 B3
Silsden 147 C4
Silsoe 84 D2
Silverburn 209 D5
Silverdale Lancs 154 D3
Staffs 112 A2
Silver End 70 B2
Silvergate 120 C3
Silverhill 23 A5
Silverley's Green 104 D3
Silverstone 82 C3
Silverton 13 A4
Silvington 95 D4
Silwick 285 J4
Simmondley 138 D3
Simonburn 177 B6
Simonsbath 26 B2
Simonstone 146 D1
Simprim 198 B2
Simpson 83 D5
Simpson Cross 55 C4
Sinclair's Hill 198 A2
Sinclairston 182 A2
Sinderby 158 C2
Sinderhope 177 D6
Sindlesham 47 C5
Singdean 187 C4
Singleborough 83 D4
Singleton Lancs 144 D3
W Sus 20 A1
Singlewell 50 B3
Sinkhurst Green 37 B6
Sinnahard 244 A1
Sinnington 159 C6
Sinton Green 79 A6
Sipson 48 B3
Sirhowy 60 B3
Sisland 104 B4
Sissinghurst 37 C5
Sisterpath 197 B6
Siston 43 B5
Sithney 3 C4
Sittingbourne 51 C5
Six Ashes 95 C5
Sixhills 133 A6
Six Hills 115 C4
Six Mile Bottom 86 B1
Sixpenny Handley 30 D3
Sizewell 89 A5
Skail 278 D3
Skaill Orkney 282 D5
Orkney 282 F3
Orkney 283 G6
Skares 182 A3
Skateraw 211 C4
Skaw 284 G7
Skeabost 259 D4
Skeabrae 282 E3
Skeeby 157 A6
Skeffington 99 A4
Skeffling 143 B5
Skegby 131 C4
Skegness 135 C5
Skelberry 285 M5
Skelbo 264 A3
Skelbrooke 140 B3
Skeldyke 117 B6
Skellingthorpe 133 B4
Skellister 285 H6
Skellow 140 B3
Skelmanthorpe 139 B5
Skelmersdale 136 C3
Skelmonae 256 C3
Skelmorlie 204 B1
Skelmuir 257 B4
Skelpick 278 C3
Skelton Cumb 164 B2
E Yorks 141 A5
N Yorks 157 A4
Redcar 169 D4
York 149 B4
Skelton-on-Ure 148 A2
Skelwick 282 C5
Skelwith Bridge 154 A2
Skendleby 135 C4
Skene Ho. 245 B4
Skenfrith 61 A6
Skerne 150 B3
Skeroblingarry 190 C3
Skerray 278 B2
Skerton 145 A4
Sketchley 98 B1
Sketty 57 C6
Skewen 40 B2
Skewsby 159 D5
Skeyton 120 C4
Skiag Bridge 271 B5
Skibo Castle 264 B3
Skidbrooke 143 D6
Skidbrooke North End 143 D6
Skidby 150 D3
Skilgate 27 C4
Skillington 116 C1
Skinburness 174 C4
Skinflats 208 B2
Skinidin 258 D2
Skinnet 277 B6
Skinningrove 169 C5
Skipness 202 C3
Skippool 144 C3
Skipsea 151 B4
Skipsea Brough 151 B4
Skipton 146 B3
Skipton-on-Swale 158 D2
Skipwith 149 D5
Skirbeck 117 A6
Skirbeck Quarter 117 A6
Skirlaugh 151 D4
Skirling 195 C5
Skirmett 47 A5
Skirpenbeck 149 B6
Skirwith 165 B4
Skirza 281 B5
Skulamus 247 B5
Skullomie 277 B7
Skyborry Green 93 D6
Skye of Curr 253 D5
Skyreholme 147 A4
Slackhall 129 A5
Slackhead 267 C5
Slad 63 C4
Slade Devon 25 A6
Pembs 55 C5
Slade Green 50 B2
Slaggyford 177 D4
Slaidburn 145 B7
Slaithwaite 138 B3
Slaley 178 D1
Slamannan 207 C6
Slapton Bucks 67 A5
Devon 8 C2
Northants 82 C3
Slatepit Dale 130 C3
Slattocks 138 C1
Slaugham 35 D5
Slaughterford 44 B2
Slawston 99 B4
Sleaford Hants 33 B7
Lincs 116 A3
Sleagill 164 D3
Sleapford 111 D5
Sledge Green 79 D6
Sledmere 150 A2
Sleightholme 166 D2
Sleights 160 A2
Slepe 16 B3
Slickly 281 B4
Sliddery 191 C5
Sligachan Hotel 246 B3
Slimbridge 62 C3
Slindon Staffs 112 B2
W Sus 20 B2
Slinfold 35 C4
Sling 123 D6
Slingsby 159 D5
Slioch 255 C6
Slip End C Beds 67 B6
Herts 85 D4
Slipton 99 D6
Slitting Mill 112 D4
Slochd 253 D4
Slockavullin 213 C6
Sloley 121 C4
Sloothby 135 B4
Slough 48 B2
Slough Green 35 D5
Sluggan 253 D4
Slumbay 249 C5
Slyfield 34 A2
Slyne 145 A4
Smailholm 197 C5
Smallbridge 138 B2
Smallburgh 121 C5
Smallburn Aberds 257 B5
E Ayrs 194 D1
Small Dole 21 A5
Smalley 114 A2
Smallfield 35 B6
Small Hythe 37 C6
Smallridge 14 A3
Smannell 32 A2
Smardale 155 A6
Smarden 37 B6
Smarden Bell 37 B6
Smeatharpe 28 D1
Smeeth 38 B2
Smeeton Westerby 98 B3
Smercleit 286 E3
Smerral 275 A5
Smethwick 96 C3
Smirisary 235 C5
Smisby 114 D1
Smithfield 176 C2
Smith Green 145 B4
Smithincott 27 D5
Smith's Green 69 A5
Smithstown 261 C4
Smithton 252 B3
Smithy Green 128 B2
Smockington 98 C1
Smoogro 283 G4
Smythe's Green 70 B3
Snaigow House 231 D4
Snailbeach 94 A1
Snailwell 86 A2
Snainton 160 C3
Snaith 140 A4
Snape N Yorks 157 C6
Suff 89 B4
Snape Green 136 B2
Snarestone 97 A6
Snarford 133 A5
Snargate 38 C1
Snave 38 C2
Snead 93 B7
Sneath Common 104 C2
Sneaton 160 A2
Sneatonthorpe 160 A3
Snelland 133 A5
Snelston 113 A5
Snettisham 118 B3
Sniseabhal 286 C3
Snitter 188 C3
Snitterby 142 D1
Snitterfield 81 B5
Snitton 94 D3
Snodhill 77 C7
Snodland 51 C3
Snowden Hill 139 C5
Snowdown 53 D4
Snowshill 80 D3
Snydale 140 B2
Soar Anglesey 122 C3
Carms 58 C3
Devon 7 D6
Soar-y-Mynydd 76 B1
Soberton 33 D5
Soberton Heath 33 D5
Sockbridge 164 C3
Sockburn 158 A2
Soham 102 D1
Soham Cotes 102 D1
Solas 287 G3
Soldon Cross 24 D4
Soldridge 33 B5
Sole Street Kent 38 A2
Kent 50 C3
Solihull 97 D4
Sollers Dilwyn 78 B2
Sollers Hope 79 D4
Sollom 136 B3
Solva 54 B3
Somerby Leics 115 D5
Lincs 142 C2
Somercotes 131 D4
Somerford 17 B5
Somerford Keynes 63 D6
Somerley 19 B7
Somerleyton 105 B5
Somersal Herbert 113 B5
Somersby 134 B3
Somersham Cambs 101 D5
Suff 88 C1
Somerton Oxon 65 A5
Som 29 C4
Sompting 21 B4
Sonning 47 B5
Sonning Common 47 A5
Sonning Eye 47 B5
Sontley 110 A2
Sopley 17 B5
Sopwell 67 C7
Sopworth 44 A2
Sorbie 171 C6
Sordale 280 B3
Sorisdale 223 A5
Sorn 193 C5
Sornhill 193 B5
Sortat 281 B4
Sotby 134 B2
Sots Hole 133 C6
Sotterley 105 C5
Soudley 111 C6
Soughton 126 C2
Soulbury 66 A4
Soulby 165 D5
Souldern 82 D2
Souldrop 84 A1
Sound Ches E 111 A5
Shetland 285 H5
Shetland 285 J6
Sound Heath 111 A5
Soundwell 43 B5
Sourhope 188 A1
Sourin 282 D5
Sourton 11 B6
Soutergate 153 B3
South Acre 119 D5
Southall 48 A4
South Allington 8 D1
South Alloa 208 A1
Southam Glos 63 A5
Warks 81 A7
South Ambersham 34 D2
Southampton 32 D3
South Anston 131 A5
South Ascot 48 C2
South Ballachulish 237 D4
South Balloch 181 B5
South Bank 168 C3
South Barrow 29 C6
South Beach 106 C3
South Benfleet 51 A4
South Bersted 20 B2
Southborough 36 B3
Southbourne Bmouth 17 B5
W Sus 19 A6
South Brent 7 A5
South Brewham 29 B7
South Broomhill 189 D5
Southburgh 103 A5
South Burlingham 105 A4
Southburn 150 B2
South Cadbury 29 C6
South Cairn 170 A1
South Carlton 133 B4
South Cave 150 D2
South Cerney 63 D6
South Chard 14 A3
South Charlton 189 A4
South Cheriton 29 C6
Southchurch 51 A6
South Cliffe 150 D1
South Clifton 132 B3
South Cockerington 134 A3
South Cornelly 40 C3
Southcott 45 D5
Southcourt 66 B4
South Cove 105 C5
South Creagan 227 B4
South Creake 119 B5
South Croxton 115 D4
South Croydon 49 C6
South Dalton 150 C2
South Darenth 50 C2
Southdean 187 C5
Southdene 136 D3
South Duffield 149 D5
Southease 22 B2
South Elkington 134 A2
South Elmsall 140 B2
Southend Argyll 190 E2
W Berks 46 B3
Wilts 45 B5
South End Bucks 66 A4
Cumb 153 D3
N Lincs 142 A3
Southend-on-Sea 51 A5
Southernden 37 B6
Southerndown 40 D3
Southerness 174 C2
South Erradale 261 C4
Southery 102 B2
South Fambridge 70 D2
South Fawley 46 A1
South Ferriby 142 A1
Southfield 179 B4
Southfleet 50 B3
South Garth 284 D7
South Garvan 236 B3
Southgate Ceredig 75 A4
London 68 D2
Norf 120 C3
Swansea 57 D5
South Glendale 286 E3
South Godstone 35 B6
South Gorley 31 D5
South Green Essex 69 D6
Kent 51 C5
South-haa 284 E5
South Ham 47 D4
South Hanningfield 70 D1
South Harting 33 D6
South Hatfield 68 C2
South Hayling 19 B6
South Hazelrigg 199 C4
South Heath 67 C5
South Heighton 22 B2
South Hetton 167 A6
South Hiendley 140 B1
South Hill 10 D4
South Hinksey 65 C6
South Hole 24 C3
South Holme 159 D5
South Holmwood 35 B4
South Hornchurch 50 A2
South Hykeham 133 C4
South Hylton 179 D5
Southill 84 C3
South Kelsey 142 D2
South Kessock 252 B2
South Killingholme 142 B3
South Kilvington 158 C3
South Kilworth 98 C3
South Kirkby 140 B2
South Kirkton 245 B4
South Kiscadale 191 C6
South Kyme 117 A4
South Lancing 21 B4
Southleigh 14 B2
South Leigh 65 C4
South Leverton 132 A2
South Littleton 80 C3
South Lopham 103 C6
South Luffenham 99 A6
South Malling 22 A2
South Marston 45 A5
South Middleton 188 A2
South Milford 148 D3
South Millbrex 256 B3
South Milton 7 C6
South Mimms 68 C2
Southminster 70 D3
South Molton 26 C2
Southmoor 65 D4
South Moreton 46 A3
South Mundham 20 B1
South Muskham 132 D2
South Newbald 150 D2
South Newington 81 D7
South Newton 31 B4
South Normanton 131 D4
South Norwood 49 C6
South Nutfield 35 B6
South Ockendon 50 A2
Southoe 84 A3
Southolt 88 A2
South Ormsby 134 B3
Southorpe 100 A2
South Otterington 158 C2
South Owersby 142 D2
Southowram 139 A4
South Oxhey 67 D7
South Perrott 15 A4
South Petherton 28 D4
South Petherwin 10 C4
South Pickenham 103 A4
South Pool 7 C6
Southport 136 B2
South Port 227 D5
Southpunds 285 L6
South Radworthy 26 B2
South Rauceby 116 A3
South Raynham 119 C5
Southrepps 121 B4
South Reston 135 A4
Southrey 133 C6
Southrop 64 C2
Southrope 33 A5
South Runcton 102 A2
South Scarle 132 C3
Southsea 19 B5
South Shian 226 B4
South Shields 179 C5
South Shore 144 D3
South Somercotes 143 D6
South Stainley 148 A2
South Stainmore 165 D6
South Stifford 50 B3
Southstoke 43 C6
South Stoke Oxon 46 A3
W Sus 20 B3
South Street E Sus 22 A1
Kent 52 C3
Kent 52 D2
London 36 A2
South Tawton 12 B1
South Thoresby 135 B4
South Tidworth 31 A6
Southtown Norf 105 A6
Orkney 283 H5
South Town 33 B5
South View 47 D4
Southwaite 164 A2
South Walsham 121 D5
Southwark 49 B6
South Warnborough 33 A6
Southwater 35 D4

Southwater Street 35 D4
Southway 29 A5
South Weald 69 D5
Southwell Dorset 15 D6
Notts 132 D1
South Weston 66 D3
South Wheatley Corn 10 B3
Notts 132 A2
South Whiteness 285 J5
Southwick Hants 19 A5
Northants 100 B2
T&W 179 D5
Wilts 44 D2
W Sus 21 B5
South Widcombe 43 D4
South Wigston 98 B2
South Willingham 134 A1
South Wingfield 130 D3
South Witham 116 D2
Southwold 105 D6
South Wonston 32 B3
Southwood Norf 105 A4
Som 29 B5
South Woodham Ferrers 70 D2
South Wootton 118 C3
South Wraxall 44 C2
South Zeal 12 B1
Soval Lodge 288 E4
Sowber Gate 158 C2
Sowerby N Yorks 158 C3
W Yorks 138 A3
Sowerby Bridge 138 A3
Sowerby Row 164 B1
Sowood 138 B3
Sowton 13 B4
Soyal 264 A1
Spacey Houses 148 B2
Spa Common 121 B4
Spadeadam Farm 176 B3
Spalding 117 C5
Spaldington 149 D6
Spaldwick 100 D3
Spalford 132 C3
Spanby 116 B3
Sparham 120 D2
Spark Bridge 154 C2
Sparkford 29 C6
Sparkhill 96 C3
Sparkwell 7 B4
Sparrow Green 119 D6
Sparrowpit 129 A5
Sparsholt Hants 32 B3
Oxon 46 A1
Spartylea 165 A6
Spaunton 159 C6
Spaxton 28 B2
Spean Bridge 239 D6
Spear Hill 21 A4
Speen Bucks 66 D4
W Berks 46 C2
Speeton 161 D5
Speke 127 A4
Speldhurst 36 B3
Spellbrook 69 B4
Spelsbury 64 A4
Spelter 40 B3
Spencers Wood 47 C5
Spennithorne 157 C5
Spennymoor 167 B5
Spetchley 80 B1
Spetisbury 16 A3
Spexhall 105 C4
Spey Bay 267 C4
Speybridge 253 D6
Speyview 254 B3
Spilsby 135 C4
Spindlestone 199 C5
Spinkhill 131 B4
Spinningdale 264 B2
Spirthill 44 B3
Spital Hill 140 D4
Spital in the Street 133 A4
Spithurst 22 A2
Spittal Dumfries 171 B5
E Loth 210 C1
Spittal Highld 280 C3
Northumb 198 A4
Pembs 55 B5
Stirling 206 B3
Spittalfield 231 D5
Spittal of Glenmuick 243 D6
Spittal of Glenshee 231 A5
Spixworth 120 D4
Splayne's Green 36 D2
Spofforth 148 B2
Spondon 114 B2
Spon End 97 D6
Spon Green 126 C2
Spooner Row 104 B1
Sporle 119 D5
Spott 210 C3
Spratton 99 D4
Spreakley 34 B1
Spreyton 12 B1
Spridlington 133 A5
Springburn 205 B6
Springfield Dumfries 175 B6
Essex 69 C7
Fife 220 C3
Moray 253 A6
W Mid 96 C3
Springhill 96 A2
Springholm 173 B6
Springkell 175 A5
Springside 192 B3
Springthorpe 132 A3
Spring Vale 139 C5
Spring Valley 152 D3
Springwell 179 D4
Sproatley 151 D4
Sproston Green 128 C2
Sprotbrough 140 C3
Sproughton 88 C2
Sprouston 197 C6
Sprowston 120 D4
Sproxton Leics 115 C6
N Yorks 159 C5
Spurstow 127 D5
Spynie 266 C3
Squires Gate 144 D3
Srannda 287 F5
Sronphadruig Lodge 229 A6
St. Abb's Haven 211 D6
Stableford Shrops 95 B5
Staffs 112 B2
Stacey Bank 139 D5
Stackhouse 146 A2
Stackpole 55 E5
Staddiscombe 7 B4
Staddlethorpe 141 A6
Stadhampton 65 D7
Stadhlaigearraidh 286 C3
Staffield 164 A3
Staffin 259 B4
Stafford 112 C3
Stagsden 84 C1
Stainburn Cumb 162 B3
N Yorks 147 C6
Stainby 116 C2
Staincross 139 B6
Staindrop 166 C4
Staines-upon-Thames 48 B3
Stainfield Lincs 116 C3
Lincs 133 B6
Stainforth N Yorks 146 A2
S Yorks 140 B4
Staining 144 D3
Stainland 138 B3
Stainsacre 160 A3
Stainsby 131 C4
Stainton Cumb 154 C4
Cumb 164 C2
Durham 166 D3
Mbro 168 D2
N Yorks 157 B5
S Yorks 140 D3
Stainton by Langworth 133 B5
Staintondale 160 B3
Stainton le Vale 142 D3
Stainton with Adgarley 153 C3
Stair Cumb 163 B5
E Ayrs 193 C4
Stairhaven 171 B4
Staithes 169 D5
Stakeford 179 A4
Stake Pool 144 C4
Stalbridge 30 D1
Stalbridge Weston 29 D7
Stalham 121 C5
Stalham Green 121 C5
Stalisfield Green 51 D6
Stallingborough 142 B3
Stalling Busk 156 C3
Stalmine 144 C3
Stalybridge 138 D2
Stambourne 86 D3
Stambourne Green 86 D3
Stamford 100 A2
Stamford Bridge Ches W 127 C4
E Yorks 149 B6
Stamfordham 178 B2
Stanah 163 C6
Stanborough 68 B2
Stanbridge C Beds 67 A5
Dorset 17 A4
Stanbrook 79 C6
Stanbury 147 D4
Stand Gtr Man 137 C6
N Lanark 207 D5
Standburn 208 C2
Standeford 96 A2
Standen 37 B6
Standford 33 B7
Standingstone 162 A3
Standish 137 B4
Standlake 65 C4
Standon Hants 32 C3
Herts 68 A3
Staffs 112 B2
Stane 194 A3
Stanfield 119 C6
Stanford C Beds 84 C3
Kent 38 B3
Stanford Bishop 79 B4
Stanford Bridge 79 A5
Stanford Dingley 46 B3
Stanford in the Vale 64 D4
Stanford-le-Hope 50 A3
Stanford on Avon 98 D2
Stanford on Soar 114 C3
Stanford on Teme 79 A5
Stanford Rivers 69 C5
Stanfree 131 B4
Stanghow 169 D4
Stanground 100 B4
Stanhoe 119 B5
Stanhope Borders 195 D6
Durham 166 B2
Stanion 99 C6
Stanley Derbys 114 A2
Durham 178 D3
Lancs 136 C3
Perth 219 A6
Staffs 129 D4
W Yorks 139 A6
Stanley Common 114 A2
Stanley Gate 136 C3
Stanley Hill 79 C4
Stanlow 127 B4
Stanmer 21 B6
Stanmore Hants 32 C3
London 67 D7
W Berks 46 B2
Stannergate 220 A4
Stanningley 147 D6
Stannington Northumb 179 B4
S Yorks 130 A3
Stansbatch 78 A1
Stansfield 86 B3
Stanstead 87 C4
Stanstead Abbotts 68 B3
Stansted 50 C3
Stansted Airport 69 A5
Stansted Mountfitchet 69 A5
Stanton Glos 80 D3
Mon 61 A5
Northumb 178 A3
Staffs 113 A5
Suff 103 D5
Stanton by Bridge 114 C1
Stanton-by-Dale 114 B2
Stanton Drew 43 C4
Stanton Fitzwarren 64 D2
Stanton Harcourt 65 C5
Stanton Hill 131 C4
Stanton in Peak 130 C2
Stanton Lacy 94 D2
Stanton Long 94 B3
Stanton-on-the-Wolds 115 B4
Stanton Prior 43 C5
Stanton St Bernard 45 C4
Stanton St John 65 C6
Stanton St Quintin 44 B3
Stanton Street 87 A5
Stanton under Bardon 114 D2
Stanton upon Hine Heath 111 C4
Stanton Wick 43 C5
Stanwardine in the Fields 110 C3
Stanwardine in the Wood 110 C3
Stanway Essex 70 A3
Glos 80 D3
Stanway Green 104 D3
Stanwell 48 B3
Stanwell Moor 48 B3
Stanwick 100 D1
Stanwick-St-John 167 D4
Stanwix 175 C7
Stanydale 285 H4
Staoinebrig 286 C3
Stape 159 B6
Stapehill 17 A4
Stapeley 111 A5
Stapenhill 113 C6
Staple Kent 53 D4
Som 27 A6
Staple Cross 37 D5
Staplefield 35 D5
Staple Fitzpaine 28 D2
Stapleford Cambs 85 B6
Herts 68 B3
Leics 115 D6
Lincs 132 D3
Notts 114 B2
Wilts 31 B4
Stapleford Abbotts 69 D5
Stapleford Tawney 69 D5
Staplegrove 28 C2
Staplehay 28 C2
Staplehurst 37 B5
Staplers 18 C4
Stapleton Bristol 43 B5
Cumb 176 B3
Hereford 78 A1
Leics 98 B1
N Yorks 167 D5
Shrops 94 A2
Som 29 C4
Stapley 28 D1
Staploe 84 A3
Staplow 79 C4
Star Fife 220 D3
Pembs 73 C5
Som 42 D3
Stara 282 E3
Starbeck 148 B2
Starbotton 156 D3
Starcross 13 C4
Stareton 97 D6
Starkholmes 130 D3
Starlings Green 85 D6
Starston 104 C3
Startforth 166 D3
Startley 44 A3
Stathe 28 C3
Stathern 115 B5
Station Town 168 B2
Staughton Green 84 A3
Staughton Highway 84 A3
Staunton Glos 62 A3
Glos 62 B1
Staunton in the Vale 115 A6
Staunton on Arrow 78 A1
Staunton on Wye 78 C1
Staveley Cumb 154 B3
Cumb 154 C2
Derbys 131 B4
N Yorks 148 A2
Staverton Devon 8 A1
Glos 63 A4
Northants 82 A2
Wilts 44 C2
Staverton Bridge 63 A4
Stawell 28 B3
Staxigoe 281 C5
Staxton 160 D4
Staylittle 91 C6
Staynall 144 C3
Staythorpe 132 D2
St. Boswells 197 C4
Stean 157 D4
Stearsby 159 D5
Steart 28 A2
Stebbing 69 A6
Stebbing Green 69 A6
Stedham 34 D1
Steele Road 186 D4
Steen's Bridge 78 B3
Steep 33 C6
Steeple Dorset 16 C3
Essex 70 C3
Steeple Ashton 44 D3
Steeple Aston 65 A5
Steeple Barton 65 A5
Steeple Bumpstead 86 C2
Steeple Claydon 66 A2
Steeple Gidding 100 C3
Steeple Langford 31 B4
Steeple Morden 85 C4
Steep Marsh 33 C6
Steeton 147 C4
Stein 258 C2
Steinmanhill 256 B2
Stelling Minnis 38 A3
Stemster 280 B3
Stemster Ho. 280 B3
Stenalees 5 B5
Stenhousemuir 207 B6
Stenigot 134 A2
Stenness 284 F4
Stenscholl 259 B4
Stenso 282 E4
Stenson 114 C1
Stenton E Loth 210 C3
Fife 209 A5
Stenwith 115 B6
Stepaside 56 B1
Stepping Hill 129 A4
Steppingley 84 D2
Stepps 205 B6
Sterndale Moor 129 C6
Sternfield 89 A4
Sterridge 25 A6
Stert 44 D4
Stetchworth 86 B2
Stevenage 68 A2
Stevenston 204 D2
Steventon Hants 32 A4
Oxon 65 D5
Stevington 84 B1
Stewartby 84 C2
Stewarton Argyll 190 D2
E Ayrs 205 D4
Stewkley 66 A4
Stewton 134 A3
Steyne Cross 19 C5
Steyning 21 A4
Steynton 55 D5
Stibb 24 D3
Stibbard 120 C1
Stibb Cross 25 D5
Stibb Green 45 C6
Stibbington 100 B2
Stichill 197 C6
Sticker 5 B4
Stickford 134 D3
Sticklepath 12 B1
Stickney 134 D3
Stiffkey 119 A6
Stifford's Bridge 79 C5
Stillingfleet 149 C4
Stillington N Yorks 149 A4
Stockton 167 C6
Stilton 100 C3
Stinchcombe 62 D3
Stinsford 15 B7
Stirchley 95 A5
Stirkoke Ho. 281 C5
Stirling Aberds 257 B6
Stirling 207 A5
Stisted 70 A1
Stithians 4 D2
Stittenham 264 C2
Stivichall 97 D6
Stixwould 134 C1
St. Margaret's Hope 283 H5
Stoak 127 B4
Stobieside 193 B6
Stobo 195 C6
Stoborough 16 C3
Stoborough Green 16 C3
Stobshiel 210 D1
Stobswood 189 D5
Stock 69 D6
Stockbridge 32 B2
Stockbury 51 C5
Stockcross 46 C2
Stockdalewath 164 A1
Stockerston 99 B5
Stock Green 80 B2
Stockheath 19 A6
Stockiemuir 206 B3
Stockingford 97 B6
Stocking Pelham 69 A4
Stockland 14 A2
Stockland Bristol 28 A2
Stockleigh English 12 A3
Stockleigh Pomeroy 12 A3
Stockley 44 C4
Stocklinch 28 D3
Stockport 138 D1
Stocksbridge 139 D5
Stocksfield 178 C2
Stockton Hereford 78 A3
Norf 105 B4
Shrops 93 A6
Shrops 95 B5
Warks 82 A1
Wilts 30 B3
Stockton Heath 127 A6
Stockton-on-Tees 168 D2
Stockton on Teme 79 A5
Stockton on the Forest 149 B5
Stock Wood 80 B3
Stodmarsh 53 C4
Stody 120 B2
Stoer 270 B3
Stoford Som 29 D5
Wilts 31 B4
Stogumber 27 B5
Stogursey 28 A2
Stoke Devon 24 C3
Hants 19 A6
Hants 46 D2
Medway 51 B5
Suff 88 C2

Stoke Abbott 15 A4
Stoke Albany 99 C5
Stoke Ash 104 D2
Stoke Bardolph 115 A4
Stoke Bliss 79 A4
Stoke Bruerne 83 C4
Stoke by Clare 86 C3
Stoke-by-Nayland 87 D5
Stoke Canon 13 B4
Stoke Charity 32 B3
Stoke Climsland 11 D4
Stoke D'Abernon 35 A4
Stoke Doyle 100 C2
Stoke Dry 99 B5
Stoke Farthing 31 C4
Stoke Ferry 102 B3
Stoke Fleming 8 C2
Stokeford 16 C2
Stoke Gabriel 8 B2
Stoke Gifford 43 B5
Stoke Golding 97 B6
Stoke Goldington 83 C5
Stoke Green 48 A2
Stokeham 132 B2
Stoke Hammond 66 A4
Stoke Heath 111 C5
Stoke Holy Cross 104 A3
Stokeinteignhead 13 D4
Stoke Lacy 79 C4
Stoke Lyne 65 A6
Stoke Mandeville 66 B4
Stokenchurch 66 D3
Stoke Newington 49 A6
Stokenham 8 C2
Stoke on Tern 111 C5
Stoke-on-Trent 112 A2
Stoke Orchard 63 A5
Stoke Poges 48 A2
Stoke Prior
Hereford 78 B3
Worcs 80 A2
Stoke Rivers 26 B1
Stoke Rochford 116 C2
Stoke Row 47 A4
Stoke St Gregory 28 C3
Stoke St Mary 28 C2
Stoke St Michael 29 A6
Stoke St Milborough 94 C3
Stokesay 94 C2
Stokesby 121 D6
Stokesley 158 A4
Stoke sub Hamdon 29 D4
Stoke Talmage 66 D2
Stoke Trister 30 C1
Stoke Wake 16 A1
Stolford 28 A2
Stondon Massey 69 C5
Stone Bucks 66 B3
Glos 62 D2
Kent 38 C1
Kent 50 B2
Staffs 112 B3
S Yorks 131 A5
Worcs 95 D6
Stone Allerton 42 D3
Ston Easton 43 D5
Stone Bridge Corner 101 A4
Stonebroom 131 D4
Stone Chair 139 A4
Stone Cross E Sus 22 B4
Kent 53 D5
Stone-edge Batch 42 B3
Stoneferry 151 D4
Stonefield 194 A1
Stonegate E Sus 37 D4
N Yorks 159 A6
Stonegrave 159 D5
Stonehaugh 177 B5
Stonehaven 245 D5
Stonehouse Glos 63 C4
Northumb 177 D4
S Lanark 194 B2
Stone House 155 C6
Stoneleigh 97 D6
Stonely 84 A3
Stoner Hill 33 C6
Stonesby 115 C6
Stonesfield 65 B4
Stone's Green 71 A5
Stone Street Kent 36 A3
Suff 87 D5
Suff 105 C4
Stonethwaite 163 C5
Stoneybreck 285 R4
Stoneyburn 208 D2
Stoney Cross 31 D6
Stoneygate
Aberds 257 C5
Leicester 98 A3
Stoneyhills 70 D3
Stoneykirk 170 B2
Stoney Middleton 130 B2
Stoney Stanton 98 B1
Stoney Stoke 29 B7
Stoney Stratton 29 B6
Stoney Stretton 94 A1
Stoneywood
Aberdeen 245 A5
Falk 207 B5
Stonganess 284 C7
Stonham Aspal 88 B2
Stonnall 96 A3
Stonor 47 A5
Stonton Wyville 99 B4
Stony Cross 79 C5
Stonyfield 264 C2
Stony Stratford 83 C4
Stoodleigh 27 D4
Stopes 130 A2
Stopham 20 A3
Stopsley 67 A7
Stores Corner 89 C4
Storeton 126 A3
Stornoway 288 D5
Storridge 79 C5
Storrington 20 A3
Storrs 154 B2
Storth 154 C3
Storwood 149 C6
Stotfield 266 B3
Stotfold 84 D4
Stottesdon 95 C4
Stoughton Leics 98 A3
Sur 34 A2
W Sus 33 D7
Stoul 235 A6
Stoulton 80 C2
Stourbridge 96 C2
Stourpaine 16 A2
Stourport on Severn 95 D6
Stour Provost 30 C1
Stour Row 30 C2
Stourton Staffs 95 C6
Warks 81 D5
Wilts 30 B1
Stourton Caundle 29 D7
Stove Orkney 282 D7
Shetland 285 L6
Stoven 105 C5
Stow Borders 196 B3
Lincs 116 B3
Lincs 132 A3
Stow Bardolph 102 A2
Stow Bedon 103 B5
Stowbridge 102 A2
Stow cum Quy 85 A7
Stowe 93 D7
Stowe-by-Chartley 112 C4
Stowe Green 62 C1
Stowell 29 C6
Stowford 11 C5
Stowlangtoft 87 A5
Stow Longa 100 D3
Stow Maries 70 D2
Stowmarket 87 B6
Stow-on-the-Wold 64 A2
Stowting 38 A3
Stowupland 87 B6
Straad 203 B5
Strachan 244 C3
Stradbroke 104 D3
Stradishall 86 B3
Stradsett 102 A2
Stragglethorpe 133 D4
Straid 180 B3
Straith 183 D6
Straiton Edin 209 D5
S Ayrs 181 A5
Straloch Aberds 256 D3
Perth 230 B4
Stramshall 113 B4
Strang 152 D3
Stranraer 170 A2
Stratfield Mortimer 47 C4
Stratfield Saye 47 C4
Stratfield Turgis 47 D4
Stratford 49 A6
Stratford St Andrew 89 A4
Stratford St Mary 87 D6
Stratford Sub Castle 31 B5
Stratford Tony 31 C4
Stratford-upon-Avon 81 B4
Strath Highld 261 C4
Highld 281 C4
Strathan Highld 238 C3
Highld 270 B3
Highld 277 B6
Strathaven 194 B2
Strathblane 205 A5
Strathcanaird 271 D4
Strathcarron 249 B6
Strathcoil 225 C5
Strathdon 243 A6
Strathellie 269 C5
Strathkinness 221 C4
Strathmashie House 240 C3
Strathmiglo 220 C2
Strathmore Lodge 280 D3
Strathpeffer 251 A6
Strathrannoch 263 C5
Strathtay 230 C3
Strathvaich Lodge 263 C5
Strathwhillan 191 B6
Strathy 279 B4
Strathyre 217 C5
Stratton Corn 10 A3
Dorset 15 B6
Glos 63 C6
Stratton Audley 65 A7
Stratton on the Fosse 43 D5
Stratton St Margaret 45 A5
Stratton St Michael 104 B3
Stratton Strawless 120 C4
Stravithie 221 C5
Streat 21 A6
Streatham 49 B6
Streatley C Beds 67 A6
W Berks 46 A3
Street Lancs 145 B5
N Yorks 159 A6
Som 29 B4
Street Dinas 110 B2
Street End Kent 52 D3
W Sus 20 C1
Street Gate 179 D4
Streethay 113 D5
Streetlam 157 B7
Streetly 96 B3
Street Lydan 110 B3
Streetly End 86 C2
Strefford 94 C2
Strelley 114 A3
Strensall 149 A5
Stretcholt 28 A2
Strete 8 C2
Stretford 137 D7
Strethall 85 D6
Stretham 101 D7
Strettington 20 B1
Stretton Ches W 127 D4
Stretton
Derbys 130 C3
Rutland 116 D2
Staffs 112 D2
Staffs 113 C6
Warr 127 A6
Stretton Grandison 79 C4
Stretton-on-Dunsmore 97 D7
Stretton-on-Fosse 81 D5
Stretton Sugwas 78 C2
Stretton under Fosse 98 C1
Stretton Westwood 94 B3
Strichen 269 D4
Strines 129 A4
Stringston 28 A1
Strixton 83 A6
Stroat 62 D1
Stromeferry 249 C5
Stromemore 249 C5
Stromness 283 G3
Stronaba 239 D6
Stronachlachar 216 C4
Stronchreggan 237 B4
Stronchrubie 271 C5
Strone Argyll 215 D4
Highld 239 D5
Highld 252 D1
Invclyd 204 A2
Stronmilchan 227 D6
Strontian 236 C2
Strood 51 C4
Strood Green Sur 35 B5
W Sus 34 D3
W Sus 35 C4
Stroud Glos 63 C4
Hants 33 C6
Stroud Green 70 D2
Stroxton 116 B2
Struan Highld 246 A2
Perth 230 B2
Strubby 135 A4
Strumpshaw 104 A4
Strutherhill 194 B2
Struy 251 C5
Stryt-issa 110 A1
Stuartfield 257 B4
Stubbington 19 A4
Stubbins 137 B6
Stubbs Cross 38 B1
Stubbs Green 105 B4
Stubb's Green 104 B3
Stubhampton 30 D3
Stub Place 153 A1
Stubton 115 A6
Stuckgowan 215 B6
Stuckton 31 D5
Stud Grn 48 B1
Studham 67 B6
Studland 17 C4
Studley Warks 80 A3
Wilts 44 B3
Studley Roger 157 D6
Stump Cross 85 C7
Stuntney 102 D1
Sturbridge 112 B2
Sturmer 86 C2
Sturminster Marshall 16 A3
Sturminster Newton 30 D1
Sturry 52 C3
Sturton 142 C1
Sturton by Stow 132 A3
Sturton le Steeple 132 A2
Stuston 104 D2
Stutton N Yorks 148 C3
Suff 88 D2
Styal 128 A3
Styrrup 140 D4
Suainebost 288 A6
Suardail 288 D5
Succoth Aberds 255 C5
Argyll 215 B5
Suckley 79 B5
Suckquoy 283 J5
Sudborough 99 C6
Sudbourne 89 B5
Sudbrook Lincs 116 A2
Mon 43 A4
Sudbrooke 133 B5
Sudbury Derbys 113 B5
London 49 A4
Suff 87 C4
Suddie 252 A2
Sudgrove 63 C5
Suffield Norf 120 B4
N Yorks 160 B3
Sugnall 112 B1
Suladale 258 C3
Sulaisiadar 288 D6
Sulby 152 B3
Sulgrave 82 C2
Sulham 47 B4
Sulhamstead 47 C4
Sulland 282 C6
Sullington 20 A3
Sullom 284 F5
Sullom Voe Oil Terminal 284 F5
Sully 41 E6
Sumburgh 285 N6
Summer Bridge 147 A6
Summercourt 4 B3
Summerfield 119 B4
Summergangs 151 D4
Summer-house 167 D5
Summerleaze 42 A3
Summersdale 20 B1
Summerseat 137 B6
Summertown 65 C6
Summit 138 C2
Sunbury-on-Thames 48 C4
Sundaywell 183 D6
Sunderland
Argyll 200 B2
Cumb 163 A4
T&W 179 D5
Sunderland Bridge 167 B5
Sundhope 196 D2
Sundon Park 67 A6
Sundridge 36 A2
Sunipol 224 A2
Sunk Island 143 B4
Sunningdale 48 C2
Sunninghill 48 C2
Sunningwell 65 C5
Sunniside
Durham 166 B4
T&W 179 D4
Sunnyhurst 137 A5
Sunnylaw 207 A5
Sunnyside 36 C1
Sunton 45 D6
Surbiton 49 C4
Surby 152 D2
Surfleet 117 C5
Surfleet Seas End 117 C5
Surlingham 104 A4
Sustead 120 B3
Susworth 141 C6
Sutcombe 24 D4
Suton 104 B1
Sutors of Cromarty 265 D4
Sutterby 134 B3
Sutterton 117 B5
Sutton Cambs 101 D6
C Beds 84 C4
Kent 39 A5
London 49 C5
Mers 136 D4
Norf 121 C5
Notts 115 B5
Notts 132 A1
N Yorks 140 A2
Oxon 65 C5
Pboro 100 B2
Shrops 95 C5
Shrops 111 B5
Som 29 B6
Staffs 111 C6
Suff 88 C4
Sur 34 B4
S Yorks 140 B3
W Sus 20 A2
Sutton at Hone 50 B2
Sutton Bassett 99 B4
Sutton Benger 44 B3
Sutton Bonington 114 C3
Sutton Bridge 118 C1
Sutton Cheney 97 A7
Sutton Coldfield 96 B4
Sutton Courtenay 65 D6
Sutton Crosses 118 C1
Sutton Grange 157 D6
Sutton Green 34 A3
Sutton Howgrave 157 D7
Sutton In Ashfield 131 D4
Sutton-in-Craven 147 C4
Sutton Ings 151 D4
Sutton in the Elms 98 B2
Sutton Lane Ends 129 B4
Sutton Leach 136 D4
Sutton Maddock 95 A5
Sutton Mallet 28 B3
Sutton Mandeville 30 C3
Sutton Manor 136 D4
Sutton Montis 29 C6
Sutton on Hull 151 D4
Sutton on Sea 135 A5
Sutton-on-the-Forest 149 A4
Sutton on the Hill 113 B6
Sutton on Trent 132 C2
Sutton St Edmund 117 D6
Sutton St James 117 D6
Sutton St Nicholas 78 C3
Sutton Scarsdale 131 C4
Sutton Scotney 32 B3
Sutton under Brailes 81 D6
Sutton-under-Whitestonecliffe 158 C3
Sutton upon Derwent 149 C6
Sutton Valence 37 B6
Sutton Veny 30 A2
Sutton Waldron 30 D2
Sutton Weaver 127 B5
Sutton Wick 43 D4
Swaby 134 B3
Swadlincote 113 D7
Swaffham 103 A4
Swaffham Bulbeck 86 A1
Swaffham Prior 86 A1
Swafield 121 B4
Swainby 158 A3
Swainshill 78 C2
Swainsthorpe 104 A3
Swainswick 43 C6
Swalcliffe 81 D6
Swalecliffe 52 C3
Swallow 142 C3
Swallowcliffe 30 C3
Swallowfield 47 C5
Swallownest 131 A4
Swallows Cross 69 D6
Swanage 17 D4
Swanbister 283 G4
Swanbourne 66 A4
Swan Green
Ches W 128 B2
Suff 104 D3
Swanland 142 A1
Swanley 50 C2
Swanley Village 50 C2
Swanmore 33 D4
Swannington
Leics 114 D2
Norf 120 D3
Swanscombe 50 B3
Swansea
Abertawe 57 C6
Swanton Abbott 121 C4

Swanton Morley 120 D2
Swanton Novers 120 B2
Swanton Street 37 A6
Swanwick Derbys 131 D4
Hants 18 A4
Swarby 116 A3
Swardeston 104 A3
Swarister 284 E7
Swarkestone 114 C1
Swarland 189 C4
Swarland Estate 189 C4
Swarthmoor 153 C3
Swathwick 130 C3
Swaton 116 B4
Swavesey 85 A5
Sway 18 B1
Swayfield 116 C2
Swaythling 32 D3
Sweet Green 79 A4
Sweetham 12 B3
Sweethouse 5 A5
Sweffling 88 A4
Swepstone 114 D1
Swerford 81 D6
Swettenham 128 C3
Swetton 157 D5
Swffryd 60 D4
Swiftsden 37 D5
Swilland 88 B2
Swillington 148 D2
Swimbridge 25 C7
Swimbridge Newland 25 B7
Swinbrook 64 B3
Swinderby 132 C3
Swindon Glos 63 A5
Staffs 95 B6
Swindon 45 A5
Swine 151 D4
Swinefleet 141 A5
Swineshead Bedford 84 A2
Lincs 117 A5
Swineshead Bridge 117 A5
Swiney 275 A6
Swinford Leics 98 D2
Oxon 65 C5
Swingate 114 A3
Swingfield Minnis 39 A4
Swingfield Street 39 A4
Swinhoe 189 A5
Swinhope 143 D4
Swining 284 G6
Swinithwaite 156 C4
Swinnow Moor 147 D6
Swinscoe 113 A5
Swinside Hall 187 B6
Swinstead 116 C3
Swinton Borders 198 B2
Gtr Man 137 C6
N Yorks 157 D6
N Yorks 159 D6
S Yorks 140 D2
Swintonmill 198 B2
Swithland 114 D3
Swordale 264 D1
Swordland 238 C1
Swordly 278 B3
Sworton Heath 128 A1
Swydd-ffynnon 75 B5
Swynnerton 112 B2
Swyre 15 C5
Sychtyn 92 A3
Syde 63 B5
Sydenham London 49 B6
Oxon 66 C3
Sydenham Damerel 11 D5
Syderstone 119 B5
Sydling St Nicholas 15 B6
Sydmonton 46 D2
Syerston 115 A5
Syke 138 B1
Sykehouse 140 B4
Sykes 145 B6
Syleham 104 D3
Sylen 57 B5
Symbister 285 G7
Symington S Ayrs 192 B3
S Lanark 195 C4
Symondsbury 14 B4
Symonds Yat 62 B1
Synod Inn 73 A7
Syre 278 D2
Syreford 63 A6
Syresham 82 C3
Syston Leics 115 D4
Lincs 116 A2
Sytchampton 79 A6
Sywell 83 A5

T

Taagan 262 D2
Tàbost 288 A6
Tabost 288 F4
Tackley 65 A5
Tacleit 288 D2
Tacolneston 104 B2
Tadcaster 148 C3
Taddington 129 B6
Taddiport 25 D5
Tadley 47 C4
Tadlow 85 C4
Tadmarton 81 D6
Tadworth 35 A5
Tafarnau-bach 60 B3
Tafarn-y-gelyn 126 C1
Taff's Well 41 C6
Tafolwern 91 B6
Tai 124 C2
Taibach 40 C2
Tai-bach 109 C6
Taigh a Ghearraidh 287 G2
Tai-mawr 109 A4
Tain Highld 264 B3
Highld 280 B4
Tainant 110 A1
Tainlon 107 A4
Tairbeart Tarbert 288 G2
Tai'r-Bull 60 A1
Tairgwaith 59 D4
Tai-Ucha 125 D5
Takeley 69 A5
Takeley Street 69 A5
Talachddu 77 D4
Talacre 125 A6
Talardd 108 C3
Talaton 13 B5
Talbenny 54 C4
Talbot Green 41 C5
Talbot Village 17 B4
Tale 13 A5
Talerddig 92 A3
Talgarreg 74 C3
Talgarth 77 D5
Talisker 246 A2
Talke 128 D3
Talkin 176 D3
Talladale 261 C6
Talla Linnfoots 195 D6
Tallarn Green 110 A3
Tallentire 163 A4
Talley 58 B3
Tallington 100 A2
Talmine 277 B6
Talog 73 D6
Talsarn 59 C4
Tal-sarn 75 C4
Talsarnau 107 C6
Talskiddy 4 A4
Talwrn Anglesey 123 C4
Wrex 110 A1
Tal-y-bont Ceredig 91 D4
Conwy 124 C2
Gwyn 107 D5
Gwyn 123 C6
Talybont-on-Usk 60 A3
Tal-y-cafn 124 B2
Talygarn 41 C5
Talyllyn 60 A3
Tal-y-llyn 91 B5
Talysarn 107 A4
Talywain 61 C4
Tal-y-wern 91 B6
Tame Bridge 158 A4
Tamerton Foliot 6 A3
Tamworth 97 A5
Tandem 139 B4
Tanden 37 C7
Tandridge 35 A6
Tanerdy 73 D7
Tanfield 178 D3
Tanfield Lea 178 D3
Tangasdal 286 G2
Tangiers 55 C5
Tangley 46 D1
Tanglwst 73 C6
Tangmere 20 B2
Tangwick 284 F4
Tan Hinon 91 D6
Tankersley 139 C6
Tankerton 52 C3
Tan-lan Conwy 124 C2
Gwyn 107 B6
Tannach 281 D5
Tannachie 245 D4
Tannadice 232 C2
Tannington 88 A3
Tansley 130 D3
Tansley Knoll 130 C3
Tansor 100 B2
Tantobie 178 D3
Tanton 168 D3
Tanworth-in-Arden 96 D4
Tan-y-bwlch 107 B6
Tan-y-fron 125 C4
Tan-y-graig Anglesey 123 C5
Gwyn 106 C3
Tanygrisiau 107 B6
Tan-y-groes 73 B5
Tan-y-pistyll 109 C5
Tan-yr-allt 107 A4
Tanyrhydiau 75 B6
Taobh a Chaolais 286 E3
Taobh a' Ghlinne 288 F4
Taobh a Thuath Loch Aineort 286 D3
Taobh a Tuath Loch Baghas-dail 286 D3
Taobh Tuath 287 F4
Taplow 48 A2
Tapton 130 B3
Tarbat Ho. 264 C3
Tarbert Argyll 202 B3
Argyll 202 C1
Argyll 213 D4
Tarbet Argyll 215 B6
Highld 238 C1
Highld 276 D2
Tarbock Green 127 A4
Tarbolton 193 C4
Tarbrax 195 A5
Tardebigge 80 A3
Tarfside 232 A2
Tarland 244 B1
Tarleton 136 A3
Tarlogie 264 B3
Tarlscough 136 B3
Tarlton 63 D5
Tarnbrook 145 B5
Tarporley 127 C5
Tarr 27 B6
Tarrant Crawford 16 A3
Tarrant Gunville 30 D3
Tarrant Hinton 30 D3
Tarrant Keyneston 16 A3
Tarrant Launceston 16 A3
Tarrant Monkton 16 A3
Tarrant Rawston 16 A3
Tarrant Rushton 16 A3
Tarrel 265 B4
Tarring Neville 22 B2
Tarrington 79 C4
Tarsappie 219 B6
Tarskavaig 247 D4
Tarves 256 C3
Tarvie Highld 251 A6
Perth 230 B4
Tarvin 127 C4
Tasburgh 104 B3
Tasley 95 B4
Taston 65 A4
Tatenhill 113 C6
Tathall End 83 C5
Tatham 145 A6
Tathwell 134 A3
Tatling End 48 A3
Tatsfield 36 A2
Tattenhall 127 D4
Tattenhoe 83 D5
Tatterford 119 C5
Tattersett 119 B5
Tattershall 134 D2
Tattershall Bridge 134 D1
Tattershall Thorpe 134 D2
Tattingstone 88 D2
Tatworth 14 A3
Taunton 28 C2
Taverham 120 D3
Tavernspite 56 A1
Tavistock 11 D5
Taw Green 12 B1
Tawstock 25 C6
Taxal 129 B5
Tay Bridge 220 B4
Tayinloan 202 D1
Taymouth Castle 230 D1
Taynish 213 D5
Taynton Glos 62 A3
Oxon 64 B3
Taynuilt 227 C5
Tayport 221 B4
Tayvallich 213 D5
Tealby 142 D3
Tealing 220 A4
Teangue 247 D5
Teanna Mhachair 287 H2
Tebay 155 A5
Tebworth 67 A5
Tedburn St Mary 12 B3
Teddington Glos 80 D2
London 49 B4
Tedstone Delamere 79 B4
Tedstone Wafre 79 B4
Teeton 98 D3
Teffont Evias 30 B3
Teffont Magna 30 B3
Tegryn 73 C5
Teigh 115 D6
Teigncombe 12 C1
Teigngrace 12 D3
Teignmouth 13 D4
Telford 95 A4
Telham 23 A5
Tellisford 44 D2
Telscombe 22 B2
Telscombe Cliffs 22 B1
Templand 184 D3
Temple Corn 10 D2
Glasgow 205 B5
Midloth 196 A2
Temple Balsall 97 D5
Temple Bar Carms 57 A5
Ceredig 75 C4
Temple Cloud 43 D5
Temple Combe 29 C7
Temple Ewell 39 A4
Temple Grafton 80 B4
Temple Guiting 64 A1
Templehall 209 A5
Temple Herdewyke 81 B6
Temple Hirst 140 A4
Temple Normanton 131 C4
Temple Sowerby 165 C4
Templeton Devon 26 D3
Pembs 55 C7
Templeton Bridge 26 D3
Templetown 178 D3
Tempsford 84 B3
Tenbury Wells 78 A3
Tenby Dinbych-y-Pysgod 56 B1
Tendring 71 A5
Tendring Green 71 A5
Ten Mile Bank 102 B2
Tenston 282 F3
Tenterden 37 C6
Terling 70 B1
Ternhill 111 B5
Terregles Banks 174 A2
Terrick 66 C4
Terrington 159 D5
Terrington St Clement 118 D2
Terrington St John 118 D2
Teston 37 A5
Testwood 32 D2
Tetbury 63 D4
Tetbury Upton 63 D4
Tetchill 110 B2
Tetcott 10 B4
Tetford 134 B3
Tetney 143 C5
Tetney Lock 143 C5
Tetsworth 66 C2
Tettenhall 96 B1
Teuchan 257 C5
Teversal 131 C4
Teversham 85 B6
Teviothead 186 C3
Tewel 245 D5
Tewin 68 B2
Tewkesbury 80 D1
Teynham 51 C6
Thackthwaite 163 B4
Thainston 233 A4
Thakeham 21 A4
Thame 66 C3
Thames Ditton 49 C4
Thames Haven 51 A4
Thamesmead 50 A1
Thanington 52 D3
Thankerton 195 C4
Tharston 104 B2
Thatcham 46 C3
Thatto Heath 136 D4
Thaxted 86 D2
The Aird 259 C4
Theakston 157 C7
Thealby 141 B6
Theale Som 29 A4
W Berks 47 B4
The Arms 103 B4
Thearne 150 D3
The Bage 77 C6
The Balloch 218 C3
The Barony 282 E3
Theberton 89 A5
The Bog 94 B1
The Bourne 33 A7
The Braes 247 A4
The Broad 78 A2
The Butts 30 A1
The Camp Glos 63 C5
Herts 67 C7
The Chequer 110 A3
The City 66 D3
The Common 31 B6
The Craigs 263 A6
The Cronk 152 B3
Theddingworth 98 C3
Theddlethorpe All Saints 135 A4
Theddlethorpe St Helen 135 A4
The Dell 105 B5
The Den 204 C3
The Eals 177 A5
The Eaves 62 C2
The Flatt 176 B3
The Four Alls 111 B5
The Garths 284 B8
The Green Cumb 153 B2
Wilts 30 B2
The Grove 174 A2
The Hall 284 D8
The Haven 34 C3
The Heath Norf 120 C3
Suff 88 D2
The Hill 153 B2
The Howe Cumb 154 C3
The Howe IoM 152 E1
The Hundred 78 A3
Thelbridge Barton 26 D2
The Lee 67 C5
The Lhen 152 A3
Thelnetham 103 D6
Thelveton 104 C2
Thelwall 127 A6
The Marsh Powys 93 B7
Wilts 45 A4
Themelthorpe 120 C2
The Middles 179 D4
The Moor 37 D5
The Mumbles Y Mwmbwls 57 D6
The Murray 205 C6
The Neuk 245 C4
Thenford 82 C2
The Oval 43 C6
The Pole of Itlaw 268 D1
The Quarry 62 D3
Therfield 85 D5
The Rhos 55 C6
The Rock 95 A4
The Ryde 68 C2
The Sands 34 B1
The Stocks 37 D7
Thetford Lincs 116 D4
Norf 103 C4
The Throat 47 C6
The Vauld 78 C3
The Wyke 95 A5
Theydon Bois 68 D4
Thickwood 44 B2
Thimbleby Lincs 134 C2
N Yorks 158 B3
Thingwall 126 A2
Thirdpart 204 D1
Thirlby 158 C3
Thirlestane 197 B4
Thirn 157 C6
Thirsk 158 C3
Thirtleby 151 D4
Thistleton Lancs 144 D4
Rutland 116 D2
Thistley Green 102 D2
Thixendale 150 A1
Thockrington 178 B1
Tholomas Drove 101 A5
Tholthorpe 148 A3
Thomas Chapel 55 D7
Thomas Close 164 A2
Thomastown 255 C6
Thompson 103 B5
Thomshill 266 D3
Thong 50 B3
Thongsbridge 139 C4
Thoralby 156 C4
Thoresway 142 D3
Thorganby Lincs 143 D4
N Yorks 149 C5
Thorgill 159 B6
Thorington 105 D5
Thorington Street 87 D6
Thorlby 146 B3
Thorley 69 B4
Thorley Street Herts 69 B4
IoW 18 C2
Thormanby 158 D3
Thornaby-on-Tees 168 D2
Thornage 120 B2
Thornborough Bucks 83 D4
N Yorks 157 D6
Thornbury Devon 11 A5
Hereford 79 B4
S Glos 62 D2
W Yorks 147 D5
Thornby 98 D3
Thorncliffe 129 D5
Thorncombe Dorset 14 A3
Dorset 16 A2

Thorncombe Street 34 B3
Thorncote Green 84 C3
Thorncross 18 C3
Thorndon 88 A2
Thorndon Cross 11 B6
Thorne 141 B4
Thorner 148 C2
Thorne St Margaret 27 C5
Thorney Notts 132 B3
Pboro 101 A4
Thorney Crofts 143 A4
Thorney Green 87 A6
Thorney Hill 17 B5
Thorney Toll 101 A5
Thornfalcon 28 C2
Thornford 29 D6
Thorngumbald 143 A4
Thornham 119 A4
Thornham Magna 104 D2
Thornham Parva 104 D2
Thornhaugh 100 A2
Thornhill Cardiff 41 C6
Cumb 162 D3
Derbys 130 A1
Dumfries 183 C6
Soton 32 D3
Stirling 207 A4
W Yorks 139 B5
Thornhill Edge 139 B5
Thornhill Lees 139 B5
Thornholme 151 A4
Thornley Durham 166 B4
Durham 167 B6
Thornliebank 205 C5
Thorns 86 B3
Thornsett 129 A5
Thorns Green 128 A2
Thornthwaite Cumb 163 B5
N Yorks 147 B5
Thornton Angus 232 D1
Bucks 83 D4
E Yorks 149 C6
Fife 209 A5
Lancs 144 C3
Leics 98 A1
Lincs 134 C2
Mbro 168 D2
Mers 136 C2
Northumb 198 B3
Pembs 55 D5
W Yorks 147 D5
Thornton Curtis 142 B2
Thorntonhall 205 C5
Thornton Heath 49 C6
Thornton Hough 126 A3
Thornton in Craven 146 C3
Thornton-le-Beans 158 B2
Thornton-le-Clay 149 A5
Thornton-le-Dale 160 C2
Thornton le Moor 142 D2
Thornton-le-Moor 158 C2
Thornton-le-Moors 127 B4
Thornton-le-Street 158 C3
Thorntonloch 211 C4
Thorntonpark 198 B3
Thornton Rust 156 C3
Thornton Steward 157 C5
Thornton Watlass 157 C6
Thornwood Common 69 C4
Thornydykes 197 B5
Thoroton 115 A5
Thorp Arch 148 C3
Thorpe Derbys 129 D6
E Yorks 150 C2
Lincs 135 A4
Norf 105 B5
Notts 115 A5
N Yorks 147 A4
Sur 48 C3
Thorpe Abbotts 104 D2
Thorpe Acre 114 C3
Thorpe Arnold 115 C5
Thorpe Audlin 140 B2
Thorpe Bassett 160 D2
Thorpe Bay 51 A6
Thorpe by Water 99 B5
Thorpe Common 88 D3
Thorpe Constantine 97 A5
Thorpe Culvert 135 C4
Thorpe End 121 D4
Thorpe Fendykes 135 C4
Thorpe Green Essex 71 A5
Suff 87 B5
Thorpe Hesley 140 D1
Thorpe in Balne 140 B3
Thorpe in the Fallows 133 A4
Thorpe Langton 99 B4
Thorpe Larches 167 C6
Thorpe-le-Soken 71 A5
Thorpe le Street 150 C1
Thorpe Malsor 99 D5
Thorpe Mandeville 82 C2
Thorpe Market 120 B4
Thorpe Marriot 120 D3
Thorpe Morieux 87 B5
Thorpeness 89 B5
Thorpe on the Hill 133 C4
Thorpe St Andrew 104 A3
Thorpe St Peter 135 C4
Thorpe Salvin 131 A5
Thorpe Satchville 115 D5
Thorpe Thewles 168 C2
Thorpe Tilney 133 D6
Thorpe Underwood 148 B3
Thorpe Waterville 100 C2
Thorpe Willoughby 149 D4
Thorrington 71 A4
Thorverton 13 A4
Thrandeston 104 D2
Thrapston 100 D1
Thrashbush 207 D5
Threapland Cumb 163 A4
N Yorks 146 A3
Threapwood Ches W 110 A3
Staffs 112 A4
Three Ashes 61 A7
Three Bridges 35 C5
Three Burrows 4 C2
Three Chimneys 37 C6
Three Cocks 77 D5
Three Crosses 57 C5
Three Cups Corner 36 D4
Threehammer Common 121 D5
Three Holes 101 A7
Threekingham 116 B3
Three Leg Cross 37 C4
Three Legged Cross 17 A4
Threemile Cross 47 C5
Threemilestone 4 C2
Threemiletown 208 C3
Three Oaks 23 A6
Threlkeld 163 B6
Threshfield 146 A3
Thrigby 121 D6
Thringarth 166 C2
Thringstone 114 D2
Thrintoft 157 B7
Thriplow 85 C6
Throckenholt 101 A5
Throcking 85 D5
Throckley 178 C3
Throckmorton 80 C2
Throphill 178 A3
Thropton 188 C3
Throsk 207 A6
Throwleigh 12 B1
Throwley 52 D1
Thrumpton 114 B3
Thrumster 281 D5
Thrunton 188 B3
Thrupp Glos 63 C4
Oxon 65 B5
Thrushelton 11 C5
Thrussington 115 D4
Thruxton Hants 32 A1
Hereford 78 D2
Thrybergh 140 D2
Thulston 114 B2
Thundergay 202 D3
Thundersley 51 A4
Thundridge 68 B3
Thurcaston 114 D3
Thurcroft 131 A4
Thurgarton Norf 120 B3
Notts 115 A4
Thurgoland 139 C5
Thurlaston Leics 98 B2
Warks 98 D1
Thurlbear 28 C2
Thurlby Lincs 116 D4
Lincs 133 C4
Thurleigh 84 B2
Thurlestone 7 C5
Thurloxton 28 B2
Thurlstone 139 C5
Thurlton 105 B5
Thurlwood 128 D3
Thurmaston 98 A3
Thurnby 98 A3
Thurne 121 D6
Thurnham Kent 37 A6
Lancs 145 B4
Thurning Norf 120 C2
Northants 100 C2
Thurnscoe 140 C2
Thurnscoe East 140 C2
Thursby 175 C6
Thursford 120 B1
Thursley 34 C2
Thurso 280 B3
Thurso East 280 B3
Thurstaston 126 A2
Thurston 87 A5
Thurstonfield 175 C6
Thurstonland 139 B4
Thurton 104 A4
Thurvaston 113 B6
Thuxton 103 A6
Thwaite N Yorks 156 B2
Suff 88 A2
Thwaites 147 C4
Thwaite St Mary 104 B4
Thwaites Brow 147 C4
Thwing 160 D4
Tibbermore 219 B5
Tibberton Glos 62 A3
Telford 111 C5
Worcs 80 B2
Tibenham 104 C2
Tibshelf 131 C4
Tibthorpe 150 B2
Ticehurst 37 C4
Tichborne 33 B4
Tickencote 100 A1
Tickenham 42 B3
Tickhill 140 D3
Ticklerton 94 B2
Ticknall 114 C1
Tickton 150 C3
Tidcombe 45 D6
Tiddington Oxon 66 C2
Warks 81 B5
Tidebrook 36 D4
Tideford 6 B2
Tideford Cross 6 A2
Tidenham 62 D1
Tideswell 129 B6
Tidmarsh 47 B4
Tidmington 81 D5
Tidpit 31 D4
Tidworth 31 A6
Tiers Cross 55 C5
Tiffield 82 B3
Tifty 256 B2
Tigerton 232 B3
Tigh-na-Blair 218 C2
Tighnabruaich 203 A4
Tighnafiline 261 B5
Tigley 7 A6
Tilbrook 84 A2
Tilbury 50 B3
Tilbury Juxta Clare 86 C3
Tile Cross 97 C4
Tile Hill 97 D5
Tilehurst 47 B4
Tilford 34 B1
Tilgate 35 C5
Tilgate Forest Row 35 C5
Tillathrowie 255 C5
Tilley 111 C4
Tillicoultry 208 A2
Tillingham 70 C3
Tillington Hereford 78 C2
W Sus 34 D2
Tillington Common 78 C2
Tillyarblet 232 B3
Tillybirloch 244 B3
Tillycorthie 257 D4
Tillydrine 244 C3
Tillyfour 244 A2
Tillyfourie 244 A3
Tillygarmond 244 C3
Tillygreig 256 D3
Tillykerrie 256 D3
Tilmanstone 53 D5
Tilney All Saints 118 D2
Tilney High End 118 D2
Tilney St Lawrence 118 D2
Tilshead 31 A4
Tilstock 111 B4
Tilston 127 D4
Tilstone Fearnall 127 C5
Tilsworth 67 A5
Tilton on the Hill 99 A4
Timberland 133 D6
Timbersbrook 128 C3
Timberscombe 27 A4
Timble 147 B5
Timperley 128 A2
Timsbury Bath 43 D5
Hants 32 C2
Timsgearraidh 287 A5
Timworth Green 87 A4
Tincleton 16 B1
Tindale 176 D4
Tingewick 82 D3
Tingley 139 A5
Tingrith 84 D2
Tingwall 282 E4
Tinhay 11 C4
Tinshill 147 D6
Tinsley 140 D2
Tintagel 9 C6
Tintern Parva 62 C1
Tintinhull 29 D5
Tintwistle 138 D3
Tinwald 184 D3
Tinwell 100 A2
Tipperty 257 D4
Tipsend 101 B7
Tipton 96 B2
Tipton St John 13 B5
Tiptree 70 B2
Tirabad 59 A5
Tiraghoil 224 D2
Tirley 63 A4
Tirphil 41 A6
Tirril 164 C3
Tir-y-dail 57 A6
Tisbury 30 C3
Tisman's Common 34 C3
Tissington 130 D1
Titchberry 24 C3
Titchfield 18 A4
Titchmarsh 100 D2
Titchwell 119 A4
Tithby 115 B4
Titley 78 A1
Titlington 189 B4
Titsey 36 A2
Tittensor 112 B2
Tittleshall 119 C5
Tiverton Ches W 127 C5
Devon 27 D4
Tivetshall St Margaret 104 C2
Tivetshall St Mary 104 C2
Tividale 96 B2
Tivy Dale 139 C5
Tixall 112 C3
Tixover 99 A6
Toab Orkney 283 G6
Shetland 285 M5
Toadmoor 130 D3
Tobermory 225 A4
Toberonochy 213 B5
Tobha Mor 286 C3
Tobhtarol 288 D2
Tobson 288 D2
Tocher 256 C1
Tockenham 44 B4
Tockenham Wick 44 A4
Tockholes 137 A5
Tockington 43 A5
Tockwith 148 B3
Todber 30 C2
Todding 94 D2
Toddington C Beds 67 A6
Glos 80 D3
Todenham 81 D5
Todhills 175 B6
Todlachie 244 A3
Todmorden 138 A2
Todrig 186 B3
Todwick 131 A4
Toft Cambs 85 B5
Lincs 116 D3
Toft Hill Durham 167 C4
Lincs 134 C2
Toft Monks 105 B5
Toft next Newton 133 A5
Toftrees 119 C5
Tofts 281 B5
Toftwood 120 D1
Togston 189 C5
Tokavaig 247 C5
Tokers Green 47 B5
Tolastadh a Chaolais 288 D2
Tolastadh bho Thuath 288 C6
Tolland 27 B6
Tollard Royal 30 D3
Toll Bar 140 C3
Tollbar End 97 D6
Toll End 96 B2
Toller Fratrum 15 B5
Toller Porcorum 15 B5
Tollerton Notts 115 B4
N Yorks 148 A4
Tollesbury 70 B3
Tolleshunt D'Arcy 70 B3
Tolleshunt Major 70 B3
Toll of Birness 257 C5
Tolm 288 D5
Tolpuddle 16 B1
Tolvah 241 C6
Tolworth 49 C4
Tomatin 253 D4
Tombreck 252 C2
Tomchrasky 239 A6
Tomdoun 239 B5
Tomich Highld 251 D5
Highld 264 C2
Tomich House 252 B1
Tomintoul Aberds 242 C4
Moray 243 A4
Tomnaven 255 C5
Tomnavoulin 254 D3
Tonbridge 36 B3
Tondu 40 C3
Tonfanau 90 B3
Tong Shrops 95 A5
W Yorks 147 D6
Tonge 114 C2
Tongham 34 B1
Tongland 173 C4
Tong Norton 95 A5
Tongue 277 C6
Tongue End 117 D4
Tongwynlais 41 C6
Tonna 40 B2
Ton-Pentre 41 B4
Tonwell 68 B3
Tonypandy 41 B4
Tonyrefail 41 C5
Toot Baldon 65 C6
Toothill 32 D2
Toot Hill 69 C5
Topcliffe 158 D3
Topcroft 104 B3
Topcroft Street 104 B3
Top of Hebers 138 C1
Toppesfield 86 D3
Toppings 137 B6
Topsham 13 C4
Torbay 8 B3
Torbeg 191 C5
Torboll Farm 264 A3
Torbrex 207 A5
Torbryan 8 A2
Torcross 8 C2
Tore 252 A2
Torinturk 202 B3
Torksey 132 B3
Torlum 286 A3
Torlundy 237 B5
Tormarton 43 B6
Tormisdale 200 C1
Tormitchell 181 B4
Tormore 191 B4
Tornagrain 252 B3
Tornahaish 243 B5
Tornaveen 244 B3
Torness 252 D1
Toronto 167 B4
Torpenhow 163 A5
Torphichen 208 C2
Torphins 244 B3
Torpoint 6 B3
Torquay 8 A3
Torquhan 196 B3
Torran Argyll 214 B1
Highld 248 B2
Highld 264 C3
Torrance 205 A6
Torrans 224 D3
Torranyard 204 D3
Torre 8 A3
Torridon 249 A6
Torridon Ho. 249 A5
Torrin 247 B4
Torrisdale 278 B2
Torrisdale-Square 190 B3
Torrish 274 C3
Torrisholme 145 A4
Torroble 272 D3
Torry Aberdeen 245 B6
Aberds 255 C5
Torryburn 208 B3
Torterston 257 B5
Torthorwald 174 A3
Tortington 20 B3
Tortworth 62 D3
Torvaig 259 D4
Torver 154 B1
Torwood 207 B6
Torworth 131 A6
Tosberry 24 C3
Toscaig 249 C4
Toseland 84 A4
Tosside 146 B1
Tostock 87 A5
Totaig Highld 249 D5
Highld 258 C2
Tote 259 D4
Totegan 279 B4
Tothill 135 A4
Totland 18 C2
Totnes 8 A2
Toton 114 B3
Totronald 223 B4
Totscore 258 B3

Tottenham 68 D3
Tottenhill 118 D3
Tottenhill Row 118 D3
Totteridge 68 D2
Totternhoe 67 A5
Tottington 137 B6
Totton 32 D2
Touchen End 48 B1
Tournaig 261 B5
Toux 269 D4
Tovil 37 A5
Toward 203 B6
Towcester 82 C3
Towednack 2 B2
Tower End 118 D3
Towersey 66 C3
Towie Aberds 244 A1
Aberds 268 C3
Towiemore 255 B4
Tow Law 166 B4
Townend 205 A4
Town End Cambs 101 B6
Cumb 154 C3
Towngate 116 D4
Townhead Cumb 164 B3
Dumfries 173 D4
S Ayrs 181 A4
S Yorks 139 C4
Townhead of Greenlaw 173 B5
Townhill 208 B4
Town Row 36 C3
Townsend Bucks 66 C3
Herts 67 C7
Townshend 2 B3
Town Yetholm 187 A7
Towthorpe 149 B5
Towton 148 D3
Towyn 125 B4
Toxteth 126 A3
Toynton All Saints 134 C3
Toynton Fen Side 134 C3
Toynton St Peter 135 C4
Toy's Hill 36 A2
Trabboch 193 C4
Traboe 3 C5
Tradespark Highld 253 A4
Orkney 283 G5
Trafford Park 137 D6
Trallong 59 C6
Tranent 209 C7
Tranmere 126 A3
Trantlebeg 279 C4
Trantlemore 279 C4
Tranwell 178 A3
Trapp 57 A6
Traprain 210 C2
Traquair 196 C2
Trawden 146 D3
Trawsfynydd 108 B2
Trealaw 41 B5
Treales 144 D4
Trearddur 122 C2
Treaslane 258 C3
Trebanog 41 B5
Trebanos 40 A2
Trebartha 10 D3
Trebarwith 9 C6
Trebetherick 9 D5
Treborough 27 B5
Trebudannon 4 A3
Trebullett 10 D4
Treburley 10 D4
Trebyan 5 A5
Trecastle 59 C5
Trecenydd 41 C6
Trecwn 55 A5
Trecynon 41 A4
Tredavoe 2 C2
Treddiog 55 B4
Tredegar 60 C3
Tredington Glos 63 A5
Warks 81 C5
Tredinnick 9 D5
Tredomen 77 D5
Tredunnock 61 D5
Tredustan 77 D5
Treen 2 C1
Treeton 131 A4
Trefasser 72 C1
Trefdraeth 123 C4
Trefecca 77 D5
Trefechan 90 D3
Trefeglwys 92 B3
Trefenter 75 B5
Treffgarne 55 B5
Treffynnon 54 B4
Trefgarn Owen 55 B4
Trefil 60 B3
Trefilan 75 C4
Trefin 54 A4
Treflach 110 C1
Trefnanney 109 D7
Trefnant 125 B5
Trefonen 110 C1
Trefor Anglesey 122 B3
Gwyn 106 B3
Treforest 41 C5
Trefriw 124 C2
Tregadillett 10 C3
Tregaian 123 C4
Tregare 61 B6
Tregaron 75 C5
Tregarth 123 D6
Tregeare 10 C3
Tregeiriog 109 B6
Tregele 122 A3
Tre-Gibbon 60 C1
Tregidden 3 C5
Treglemais 54 B4
Tregole 10 B2
Tregonetha 5 A4
Tregony 4 C4
Tregoss 5 A4
Tregoyd 77 D6
Tregroes 73 B7
Tregurrian 4 A3
Tregynon 93 B4
Trehafod 41 B5
Treharris 41 B5
Treherbert 40 B4
Trekenner 10 D4
Treknow 9 C6
Trelan 3 D5
Trelash 10 B2
Trelassick 4 B3
Trelawnyd 125 B5
Trelech 73 C5
Treleddyd-fawr 54 B3
Trelewis 41 B6
Treligga 9 C6
Trelights 9 D5
Trelill 9 D6
Trelissick 4 D3
Trellech 61 C7
Trelleck Grange 61 C6
Trelogan 125 A6
Trelystan 93 A6
Tremadog 107 B5
Tremail 10 C2
Tremain 73 B5
Tremaine 10 C3
Tremar 6 A1
Trematon 6 B2
Tremeirchion 125 B5
Trenance 4 A3
Trenarren 5 C5
Trench 111 D5
Treneglos 10 C3
Trenewan 5 B6
Trent 29 D5
Trentham 112 A2
Trentishoe 26 A1
Trent Vale 112 A2
Treoes 40 D4
Treorchy Treorci 41 B4
Tre'r-ddôl 91 C4
Trerule Foot 6 B2
Tresaith 73 A5
Tresawle 4 C3
Trescott 95 B6
Trescowe 2 B3
Tresham 62 D3
Tresillian 4 C3
Tresinwen 72 B1
Treskinnick Cross 10 B3
Tresmeer 10 C3
Tresparrett 10 B2
Tresparrett Posts 10 B2
Tressait 230 B2
Tresta Shetland 284 D8
Shetland 285 H5
Treswell 132 B2
Tre-Taliesin 91 C4
Trethosa 4 B4
Trethurgy 5 B5
Tretio 54 B3
Tretire 62 A1
Tretower 60 A3
Treuddyn 126 D2
Trevalga 10 C1
Trevalyn 126 D3
Trevanson 9 D5
Trevarren 4 A4
Trevarrian 4 A3
Trevarrick 5 C4
Trevaughan 56 A1
Tre-vaughan 73 D7
Treveighan 9 D6
Trevellas 4 B2
Treverva 4 D2
Trevethin 61 C4
Trevigro 6 A2
Treviscoe 4 B4
Trevone 9 D4
Trewarmett 9 C6
Trewassa 10 C2
Trewellard 2 B1
Trewen 10 C3
Trewennack 3 C4
Trewern 110 D1
Trewethern 9 D6
Trewidland 6 B1
Trewint Corn 10 B2
Corn 10 C3
Trewithian 4 D3
Trewoofe 2 C2
Trewoon 5 B4
Treworga 4 C3
Treworlas 4 D3
Tre-wyn 61 A5
Treyarnon 9 D4
Treyford W Sus 20 A1
W Sus 33 D7
Trezaise 5 B4
Ty'r-felin-isaf 124 C3
Triangle 138 A3
Triffleton 55 B5
Trimdon 167 B6
Trimdon Colliery 167 B6
Trimdon Grange 167 B6
Trimingham 121 B4
Trimley Lower Street 88 D3
Trimley St Martin 88 D3
Trimley St Mary 88 D3
Trimpley 95 D5
Trimsaran 57 B4
Trimstone 25 A5
Trinafour 229 B6
Trinant 41 A7
Tring 67 B5
Tring Wharf 67 B5
Trinity Angus 233 B4
Jersey P06
Trisant 75 A6
Trislaig 237 B4
Trispen 4 B3
Tritlington 189 D5
Trochry 230 D3
Trodigal 190 C2
Troed-rhiwdalar 76 B3
Troedyraur 73 B6
Troedyrhiw 41 A5
Tromode 152 D3
Trondavoe 284 F5
Troon Corn 3 B4
S Ayrs 192 B3
Trosaraidh 286 E3
Trossachs Hotel 217 D5
Troston 103 D4
Trottiscliffe 50 C3
Trotton 34 D1
Troutbeck Cumb 154 A3
Cumb 164 C1
Troutbeck Bridge 154 A3
Trowbridge 44 D2
Trowell 114 B2
Trow Green 62 C1
Trowle Common 44 D2
Trowley Bottom 67 B6
Trows 197 C5
Trowse Newton 104 A3
Trudoxhill 30 A1
Trull 28 C2
Trumaisgearraidh 287 G3
Trumpan 258 B2
Trumpet 79 D4
Trumpington 85 B6
Trunch 121 B4
Trunnah 144 C3
Truro 4 C3
Trusham 12 C3
Trusley 113 B6
Trusthorpe 135 A5
Trysull 95 B6
Tubney 65 D5
Tuckenhay 8 B2
Tuckhill 95 C5
Tuckingmill 3 A4
Tuddenham 102 D3
Tuddenham St Martin 88 C2
Tudeley 36 B4
Tudhoe 167 B5
Tudorville 62 A1
Tudweiliog 106 C2
Tuesley 34 B2
Tuffley 63 B4
Tufton Hants 32 A3
Pembs 55 B6
Tugby 99 A4
Tugford 94 C3
Tullibardine 218 C4
Tullibody 207 A6
Tullich Argyll 214 A3
Highld 252 D2
Tullich Muir 264 C3
Tulliemet 230 C3
Tulloch Aberds 233 A5
Aberds 256 C3
Perth 219 B5
Tulloch Castle 264 D1
Tullochgorm 214 C2
Tulloes 232 D3
Tullybannocher 218 B2
Tullybelton 219 A5
Tullyfergus 231 D6
Tullymurdoch 231 C5
Tullynessle 244 A2
Tumble 57 A5
Tumby Woodside 134 D2
Tummel Bridge 229 C6
Tunga 288 D5
Tunstall E Yorks 151 D6
Kent 51 C5
Lancs 155 D5
Norf 105 A5
N Yorks 157 B6
Stoke 128 D3
Suff 89 B4
T&W 179 D5
Tunstead Derbys 129 B6
Gtr Man 138 C3
Norf 121 C4
Tunworth 33 A5
Tupsley 78 C3
Tupton 130 C3
Turgis Green 47 D4
Turin 232 C3
Turkdean 64 B2
Tur Langton 99 B4
Turleigh 44 C2
Turn 137 B7
Turnastone 78 D1
Turnberry 192 E2
Turnditch 113 A6
Turners Hill 35 C6
Turners Puddle 16 B2
Turnford 68 C3
Turnhouse 209 C4
Turnworth 16 A2
Turriff 268 D2
Turton Bottoms 137 B6
Turves 101 B5
Turvey 83 B6
Turville 66 D3
Turville Heath 66 D3
Turweston 82 D3
Tushielaw 185 A6
Tutbury 113 C6
Tutnall 96 D2
Tutshill 62 D1
Tuttington 120 C4
Tutts Clump 46 B3
Tuxford 132 B2
Twatt Orkney 282 E3
Shetland 285 H5
Twechar 207 C4
Tweedmouth 198 A3
Tweedsmuir 195 D5
Twelve Heads 4 C2
Twemlow Green 128 C2
Twenty 117 C4
Twerton 43 C6
Twickenham 49 B4
Twigworth 63 A4
Twineham 21 A5
Twinhoe 43 D6
Twinstead 87 D4
Twinstead Green 87 D4
Twiss Green 137 D5
Twiston 146 C2
Twitchen Devon 26 B2
Shrops 94 D1
Two Bridges 11 D7
Two Dales 130 C2
Two Mills 126 B3
Twycross 97 A6
Twyford Bucks 66 A2
Derbys 114 C1
Hants 32 C3
Leics 115 D5
Lincs 116 C2
Norf 120 C2
Wokingham 47 B5
Twyford Common 78 D3
Twynholm 173 C4
Twyning 80 D1
Twyning Green 80 D2
Twynllanan 59 C4
Twynmynydd 57 A6
Twyn-y-Sheriff 61 C6
Twywell 99 D6
Tyberton 78 D1
Tyburn 96 B4
Tycroes 57 A6
Tycrwyn 109 D6
Tydd Gote 118 D1
Tydd St Giles 118 D1
Tydd St Mary 118 D1
Tyddyn-mawr 107 B5
Ty-draw 124 D3
Tye Green Essex 69 C4
Essex 70 A1
Essex 86 D1
Ty-hen Carms 73 D6
Gwyn 106 C1
Tyldesley 137 C5
Tyler Hill 52 C3
Tylers Green 67 D5
Tylorstown 41 B5
Tylwch 92 C3
Ty-mawr 123 B4
Ty Mawr 58 A2
Ty Mawr Cwm 108 A4
Ty-nant Conwy 109 A4
Gwyn 108 C4
Tyncelyn 75 B5
Tyndrum 216 A3
Tyneham 16 C2
Tynehead 196 A2
Tynemouth 179 C5
Tyne Tunnel 179 C5
Tynewydd 40 B4
Tyninghame 210 C3
Tynron 183 C6
Tyn-y-celyn 109 B6
Tyn-y-coed 110 C1
Tyn-y-fedwen 109 B6
Tyn-y-ffridd 109 B6
Tynygongl 123 B5
Tynygraig 75 B5
Tyn-y-graig 76 B4
Ty'n-y-groes 124 B2
Ty'n-y-maes 123 D6
Tyn-y-pwll 123 B4
Ty'n-yr-eithin 75 B5
Tyrie 269 C4
Tyringham 83 C5
Tythecott 25 D5
Tythegston 40 D3
Tytherington Ches E 129 B4
S Glos 43 A5
Som 30 A1
Wilts 30 A3
Tytherleigh 14 A3
Ty-uchaf 109 C5
Tywardreath 5 B5
Tywyn Conwy 124 B2
Gwyn 90 B3

U

Uachdar 286 A3
Uags 249 C4
Ubbeston Green 104 D4
Ubley 43 D4
Uckerby 157 A6
Uckfield 36 D2
Uckington 63 A5
Uddingston 207 D4
Uddington 194 C3
Udimore 23 A6
Udny Green 256 D3
Udny Station 257 D4
Udston 194 A1
Udstonhead 194 B2
Uffcott 45 B5
Uffculme 27 D5
Uffington Lincs 100 A2
Oxon 45 A7
Shrops 111 D4
Ufford Pboro 100 A2
Suff 88 B3
Ufton 81 A6
Ufton Nervet 47 C4
Ugadale 190 C3
Ugborough 7 B5
Uggeshall 105 C5
Ugglebarnby 160 A2
Ughill 139 D5
Ugley 69 A5
Ugley Green 69 A5
Ugthorpe 169 D5
Uidh 286 G2
Uig Argyll 215 D4
Highld 258 B3
Highld 258 C1
Uigen 287 A5
Uigshader 259 D4
Uisken 224 E2
Ulbster 281 D5
Ulceby Lincs 135 B4
N Lincs 142 B3
Ulceby Skitter 142 B3
Ulcombe 37 B6
Uldale 163 A5
Uley 62 D3
Ulgham 189 D5
Ullapool 262 A3
Ullenhall 80 A4
Ullenwood 63 B5
Ulleskelf 148 C4
Ullesthorpe 98 C2
Ulley 131 A4
Ullingswick 78 C3
Ullinish 246 A2
Ullock 162 B3
Ulnes Walton 136 B4
Ulpha 153 A2
Ulrome 151 B4
Ulsta 284 E6
Ulva House 224 C3
Ulverston 154 D1
Ulwell 17 C4
Umberleigh 25 C7
Unapool 271 A5
Unasary 286 D3
Underbarrow 154 B3
Undercliffe 147 D5
Underhoull 284 C7
Underriver 36 A3
Underwood 131 D4
Undy 42 A3
Unifirth 285 H4
Union Cottage 245 C5

Union Mills 152 D3
Union Street 37 C5
Unstone 130 B3
Unstone Green 130 B3
Unthank Cumb 164 B2
Cumb 165 A4
Unthank End 164 B2
Upavon 45 D5
Up Cerne 15 A6
Upchurch 51 C5
Upcott 78 B1
Upend 86 B2
Up Exe 13 A4
Upgate 120 D3
Uphall 208 C3
Uphall Station 208 C3
Upham Devon 12 A3
Hants 32 C4
Uphampton 79 A6
Up Hatherley 63 A5
Uphill 42 D2
Up Holland 136 C4
Uplawmoor 205 C4
Upleadon 62 A3
Upleatham 168 D4
Uplees 52 C1
Uploders 15 B5
Uplowman 27 D5
Uplyme 14 B3
Up Marden 33 D6
Upminster 50 A2
Up Nately 47 D4
Upnor 51 B4
Upottery 14 A2
Upper Affcot 94 C2
Upper Ardchronie 264 B2
Upper Arley 95 C5
Upper Arncott 65 B7
Upper Astrop 82 D2
Upper Badcall 276 D2
Upper Basildon 46 B3
Upper Beeding 21 A4
Upper Benefield 100 C1
Upper Bighouse 279 C4
Upper Boddington 82 B1
Upper Borth 90 D4
Upper Boyndlie 269 C4
Upper Brailes 81 D6
Upper Breakish 247 B5
Upper Breinton 78 C2
Upper Broadheath 79 B6
Upper Broughton 115 C4
Upper Bucklebury 46 C3
Upper Burnhaugh 245 C5
Upperby 175 C7
Upper Caldecote 84 C3
Upper Catesby 82 B2
Upper Chapel 76 C4
Upper Church Village 41 C5
Upper Chute 45 D6
Upper Clatford 32 A2
Upper Clynnog 107 B4
Upper Cumberworth 139 C5
Upper Cwmbran 61 D4
Upper Cwm-twrch 59 D4
Upper Dallachy 267 C4
Upper Dean 84 A2
Upper Denby 139 C5
Upper Denton 176 C4
Upper Derraid 253 C6
Upper Dicker 22 B3
Upper Dovercourt 88 D3
Upper Druimfin 225 A4
Upper Dunsforth 148 A3
Upper Eathie 264 D3
Upper Elkstone 129 D5
Upper End 129 B5
Upper Farringdon 33 B6
Upper Framilode 62 B3
Upper Glenfintaig 239 D6
Upper Gornal 96 B2
Upper Gravenhurst 84 D3
Upper Green Mon 61 B5
W Berks 46 C1
Upper Grove Common 62 A1
Upper Hackney 130 C2
Upper Hale 34 B1
Upper Halistra 258 C2
Upper Halling 50 C3
Upper Hambleton 99 A5
Upper Hardres Court 52 D3
Upper Hartfield 36 C2
Upper Haugh 140 D2
Upper Heath 94 C3
Upper Hellesdon 120 D4
Upper Helmsley 149 B5
Upper Hergest 77 B6
Upper Heyford Northants 82 B3
Oxon 65 A5
Upper Hill 78 B2
Upper Hopton 139 B4
Upper Horsebridge 22 A3
Upper Hulme 129 C5
Upper Inglesham 64 D3
Upper Inverbrough 253 C4
Upper Killay 57 C5
Upper Knockando 254 B2
Upper Lambourn 45 A7
Upper Leigh 112 B4
Upper Lenie 251 D7
Upper Lochton 244 C3
Upper Longdon 113 D4
Upper Lybster 275 A6
Upper Lydbrook 62 B2
Upper Maes-coed 78 D1
Upper Midway 113 C6
Uppermill 138 C2
Upper Milovaig 258 D1
Upper Minety 63 D6
Upper Mitton 95 D6
Upper North Dean 66 D4
Upper Obney 219 A5
Upper Ollach 247 A4
Upper Padley 130 B2
Upper Pollicott 66 B3
Upper Poppleton 149 B4
Upper Quinton 81 C4
Upper Ratley 32 C2
Upper Rissington 64 B3
Upper Rochford 79 A4
Upper Sandaig 238 A1
Upper Sanday 283 G6
Upper Sapey 79 A4
Upper Saxondale 115 B4
Upper Seagry 44 A3
Upper Shelton 84 C1
Upper Sheringham 120 A3
Upper Skelmorlie 204 B2
Upper Slaughter 64 A2
Upper Soudley 62 B2
Uppersound 285 J6
Upper Stondon 84 D3
Upper Stowe 82 B3
Upper Stratton 45 A5
Upper Street Hants 31 D5
Norf 121 D5
Norf 121 D5
Suff 88 D2
Upper Strensham 80 D2
Upper Sundon 67 A6
Upper Swell 64 A2
Upper Tean 112 B4
Upperthong 139 C4
Upperthorpe 141 C5
Upper Tillyrie 219 D6
Upperton 34 D2
Upper Tooting 49 B5
Upper Tote 259 C5
Uppertown Derbys 130 C3
Highld 281 A5
Orkney 283 H5
Upper Town 43 C4
Upper Treverward 93 D6
Upper Tysoe 81 C6
Upper Upham 45 B6
Upper Wardington 82 C1
Upper Weald 83 D4
Upper Weedon 82 B3
Upper Wield 33 B5
Upper Winchendon 66 B3
Upper Witton 96 B3
Upper Woodend 244 A3
Upper Woodford 31 B5
Upper Wootton 46 D3
Upper Wyche 79 C5
Uppingham 99 B5
Uppington 95 A4
Upsall 158 C3
Upshire 68 C4
Up Somborne 32 B2
Upstreet 53 C4
Up Sydling 15 A6
Upthorpe 103 D5
Upton Cambs 100 D3
Ches W 127 C4
Corn 10 A3
Dorset 16 B3
Dorset 16 C1
Hants 32 D2
Hants 46 D1
Leics 97 B6
Lincs 132 A3
Mers 126 A2
Norf 121 D5
Northants 83 A4
Notts 132 B2
Notts 132 D2
Oxon 46 A3
Pboro 100 A3
Slough 48 B2
Som 27 C4
W Yorks 140 B2
Upton Bishop 62 A2
Upton Cheyney 43 C5
Upton Cressett 95 B4
Upton Cross 10 D3
Upton Grey 33 A5
Upton Hellions 12 A3
Upton Lovell 30 A3
Upton Magna 111 D4
Upton Noble 29 B7
Upton Pyne 13 B4
Upton St Leonard's 63 B4
Upton Scudamore 30 A2
Upton Snodsbury 80 B2
Upton upon Severn 79 C6
Upton Warren 80 A2
Upwaltham 20 A2
Upware 102 D1
Upwell 101 A6
Upwey 15 C6
Upwood 101 C4
Uradale 285 K6
Urafirth 284 F5
Urchfont 44 D4
Urdimarsh 78 C3
Ure 284 F4
Ure Bank 157 D7
Urgha 288 H2
Urishay Common 77 D7
Urlay Nook 167 D6
Urmston 137 D6
Urpeth 179 D4
Urquhart Highld 252 A1
Moray 266 C3
Urra 159 A4
Urray 251 A7
Ushaw Moor 167 A5
Usk Brynbuga 61 C5
Usselby 142 D2
Usworth 179 D5
Utkinton 127 C5
Utley 147 C4
Uton 12 B3
Utterby 143 D5
Uttoxeter 113 B4
Uwchmynydd 106 D1
Uxbridge 48 A3
Uyeasound 284 C7
Uzmaston 55 C5

V

Valley 122 C2
Valleyfield 173 C4
Valley Truckle 10 C1
Valsgarth 284 B8
Valtos 259 B5
Van 92 C3
Vange 51 A4
Varteg 61 C4
Vatten 258 D2
Vaul 222 C3
Vaynor 60 B2
Veensgarth 285 J6
Velindre 77 D5
Vellow 27 B5
Veness 282 E6
Venn Green 25 D4
Vennington 94 A1
Venn Ottery 13 B5
Venny Tedburn 12 B3
Ventnor 19 D4
Vernham Dean 46 D1
Vernham Street 46 D1
Vernolds Common 94 C2
Verwood 17 A4
Veryan 4 D4
Vicarage 14 C2
Vickerstown 153 D2
Victoria Corn 5 A4
S Yorks 139 C4
Vidlin 284 G6
Viewpark 207 D5
Vigo Village 50 C3
Vinehall Street 37 D5
Vine's Cross 22 A3
Viney Hill 62 C2
Virginia Water 48 C2
Virginstow 11 B4
Vobster 29 A7
Voe Shetland 284 E5
Shetland 285 G6
Vowchurch 78 D1
Voxter 284 F5
Voy 282 F3

W

Wackerfield 167 C4
Wacton 104 B2
Wadbister 285 J6
Wadborough 80 C2
Waddesdon 66 B3
Waddingham 142 D1
Waddington Lancs 146 C1
Lincs 133 C4
Wadebridge 9 D5
Wadeford 28 D3
Wadenhoe 100 C2
Wadesmill 68 B3
Wadhurst 36 C4
Wadshelf 130 B3
Wadsley 139 D6
Wadsley Bridge 139 D6
Wadworth 140 D3
Waen Denb 125 C4
Denb 125 C6
Waen Fach 109 D7
Waen Goleugoed 125 B5
Wag 274 B4
Wainfleet All Saints 135 D4
Wainfleet Bank 135 D4
Wainfleet St Mary 135 D5
Wainfleet Tofts 135 D4
Wainhouse Corner 10 B2
Wainscott 51 B4
Wainstalls 138 A3
Waitby 155 A6
Waithe 143 C4
Wakefield 139 A6
Wake Lady Green 159 B5
Wakerley 99 B6
Wakes Colne 70 A2
Walberswick 105 D5
Walberton 20 B2
Walbottle 178 C3
Walcot Lincs 116 B3
N Lincs 141 A6
Shrops 94 C1
Swindon 45 A5
Telford 111 D4
Walcote Leics 98 C2
Warks 80 B4
Walcot Green 104 C2
Walcott Lincs 133 D6
Norf 121 B5
Walden 156 C4
Walden Head 156 C3
Walden Stubbs 140 B3
Waldersey 101 A6
Walderslade 51 C4
Walderton 33 D6
Walditch 15 B4
Waldley 113 B5
Waldridge 179 D4
Waldringfield 88 C3
Waldringfield Heath 88 C3
Waldron 22 A3
Wales 131 A4
Walesby Lincs 142 D3
Notts 132 B1
Walford Hereford 62 A1
Hereford 94 D1
Shrops 110 C3
Walford Heath 110 D3
Walgherton 111 A5
Walgrave 99 D5
Walhampton 18 B2
Walkden 137 C6
Walker 179 C4
Walker Barn 129 B4
Walkerburn 196 C2
Walker Fold 145 C6
Walkeringham 141 D5
Walkerith 141 D5
Walkern 68 A2
Walker's Green 78 C3
Walkerville 157 B6
Walkford 17 B6
Walkhampton 7 A4
Walkington 150 D2
Walkley 130 A3
Walk Mill 146 D2
Wall Northumb 177 C7
Staffs 96 A4
Wallaceton 183 D6
Wallacetown S Ayrs 181 A4
S Ayrs 192 C3
Wallands Park 22 A2
Wallasey 136 D2
Wall Bank 94 B3
Wallcrouch 37 C4
Wall Heath 96 C1
Wallingford 47 A4
Wallington Hants 19 A4
Herts 85 D4
London 49 C5
Wallis 55 B6
Walliswood 35 C4
Walls 285 J4
Wallsend 179 C4
Wallston 41 D6
Wall under Heywood 94 B3
Wallyford 209 C6
Walmer 53 D5
Walmer Bridge 136 A3
Walmersley 137 B7
Walmley 96 B4
Walpole 105 D4
Walpole Cross Keys 118 D2
Walpole Highway 118 D2
Walpole Marsh 118 D1
Walpole St Andrew 118 D2
Walpole St Peter 118 D2
Walsall 96 B3
Walsall Wood 96 A3
Walsden 138 A2
Walsgrave on Sowe 97 C6
Walsham le Willows 103 D5
Walshaw 137 B6
Walshford 148 B3
Walsoken 118 D1
Walston 195 B5
Walsworth 84 D4
Walters Ash 66 D4
Walterston 41 D5
Walterstone 61 A5
Waltham Kent 38 A3
NE Lincs 143 C4
Waltham Abbey 68 C3
Waltham Chase 33 D4
Waltham Cross 68 C3
Waltham on the Wolds 115 C6
Waltham St Lawrence 47 B6
Walthamstow 49 A6
Walton Cumb 176 C3
Derbys 130 C3
Leics 98 C2
Mers 136 D2
M Keynes 83 D5
Pboro 100 A3
Powys 77 B6
Som 29 B4
Staffs 112 B2
Suff 88 D3
Telford 111 D4
Warks 81 B5
W Yorks 139 B6
W Yorks 148 C3
Walton Cardiff 80 D2
Walton East 55 B6
Walton-in-Gordano 42 B3
Walton-le-Dale 137 A4
Walton-on-Thames 48 C4
Walton on the Hill Staffs 112 C3
Sur 35 A5
Walton-on-the-Naze 71 A6
Walton on the Wolds 114 D3
Walton-on-Trent 113 D6
Walton West 55 C4
Walwen 126 B2
Walwick 177 B7
Walworth 167 D5
Walworth Gate 167 C5
Walwyn's Castle 55 C4
Wambrook 14 A2
Wanborough Sur 34 B2
Swindon 45 A6
Wandsworth 49 B5
Wangford 105 D5
Wanlockhead 183 A6
Wansford E Yorks 150 B3
Pboro 100 B2
Wanstead 49 A7
Wanstrow 29 A7
Wanswell 62 C2
Wantage 46 A1
Wapley 43 B6
Wappenbury 81 A6
Wappenham 82 C3
Warbleton 22 A4
Warblington 19 A6
Warborough 65 D6
Warboys 101 C5
Warbreck 144 D3

Warbstow 10 B3
Warburton 128 A2
Warcop 165 D5
Warden Kent 52 B2
Northumb 177 C7
Ward End 96 C4
Ward Green 87 A6
Wardhill 282 E7
Wardington 82 C1
Wardlaw 185 A5
Wardle Ches E 127 D6
Gtr Man 138 B2
Wardley 99 A5
Wardlow 130 B1
Wardy Hill 101 C6
Ware Herts 68 B3
Kent 53 C4
Wareham 16 C3
Warehorne 38 B1
Warenford 189 A4
Waren Mill 199 C5
Warenton 199 C5
Wareside 68 B3
Waresley Cambs 84 B4
Worcs 95 D6
Warfield 48 B1
Warfleet 8 B2
Wargrave 47 B5
Warham 119 A6
Warhill 138 D2
Wark Northumb 177 B6
Northumb 198 C2
Warkleigh 26 C1
Warkton 99 D5
Warkworth
Northants 82 C1
Northumb 189 C5
Warlaby 158 B2
Warland 138 A2
Warleggan 5 A6
Warlingham 35 A6
Warmfield 140 A1
Warmingham 128 C2
Warmington
Northants 100 B2
Warks 81 C7
Warminster 30 A2
Warmlake 37 A6
Warmley 43 B5
Warmley Tower 43 B5
Warmonds Hill 83 A6
Warmsworth 140 C3
Warmwell 16 C1
Warndon 80 B1
Warnford 33 C5
Warnham 35 C4
Warninglid 35 D5
Warren Ches E 128 B3
Pembs 55 E5
Warren Heath 88 C3
Warren Row 47 A6
Warren Street 51 D6
Warrington
M Keynes 83 B5
Warr 127 A6
Warsash 18 A3
Warslow 129 D5
Warter 150 B1
Warthermarske 157 D6
Warthill 149 B5
Wartling 23 B4
Wartnaby 115 C5
Warton Lancs 136 A3
Lancs 154 D3
Northumb 188 C3
Warks 97 A5
Warwick 81 A5
Warwick Bridge 176 D2
Warwick on
Eden 176 D2
Wasbister 282 D4
Wasdale Head 163 D4
Washaway 5 A5
Washbourne 8 B1
Wash Common 46 C2
Washfield 27 D4
Washfold 157 A4
Washford 27 A5
Washford Pyne 26 D3
Washingborough
133 B5
Washington
T&W 179 D5
W Sus 21 A4
Wasing 46 C3
Waskerley 166 A3
Wasperton 81 B5
Wasps Nest 133 C5
Wass 159 D4
Watchet 27 A5
Watchfield Oxon 64 D3
Som 28 A3
Watchgate 154 B4
Watchhill 175 D4
Watcombe 8 A3
Watendlath 163 C5
Water Devon 12 C2
Lancs 138 A1
Waterbeach 85 A6
Waterbeck 175 A5
Waterden 119 B5
Water End
E Yorks 149 D6
Herts 67 B6
Herts 68 C2
Waterfall 129 D5
Waterfoot E Renf 205 C5
Lancs 138 A1
Waterford Hants 18 B2
Herts 68 B3
Waterhead Cumb 154 A2
Dumfries 185 C4
Waterheads 196 A1
Waterhouses
Durham 167 A4
Staffs 129 D5
Wateringbury 37 A4
Waterloo
Gtr Man 138 C2
Highld 247 B5
Mers 136 D2
N Lanark 194 A3
Norf 120 D4
Perth 219 A5
Poole 17 B4
Shrops 111 B4
Waterloo Port 123 D4
Waterlooville 19 A5
Watermeetings 184 A2
Watermillock 164 C2
Water Newton 100 B3
Water Orton 97 B4
Waterperry 66 C2
Waterrow 27 C5
Watersfield 20 A3
Waterside
Aberds 257 D5
Blackburn 137 A6
Cumb 175 D5
E Ayrs 182 B2
E Ayrs 205 D4
E Dunb 207 C4
E Renf 205 C5
Water's Nook 137 C5
Waterstock 66 C2
Waterston 55 D5
Water Stratford 82 D3
Waters Upton 111 D5
Water Yeat 154 C1
Watford Herts 67 D7
Northants 82 A3
Watford Gap 96 A4
Wath N Yorks 147 A5
N Yorks 157 D7
N Yorks 159 D5
Wath Brow 162 C3
Wath upon
Dearne 140 C2
Watlington Norf 118 D3
Oxon 66 D2
Watnall 114 A3
Watten 280 C4
Wattisfield 103 D6
Wattisham 87 B6
Wattlesborough
Heath 110 D2
Watton E Yorks 150 B3
Norf 103 A5
Watton at Stone 68 B3
Wattston 207 C5
Wattstown 41 B5
Wauchan 238 D3
Waulkmill
Lodge 283 G4
Waun 91 B6
Waunarlwydd 57 C6
Waunclunda 58 B3
Waunfawr 107 A5
Waungron 57 B5
Waunlwyd 60 C3
Waun-y-clyn 57 B4
Wavendon 83 D6
Waverbridge 175 D5
Waverton
Ches W 127 C4
Cumb 175 D5
Wavertree 126 A3
Wawne 150 D3
Waxham 121 C6
Waxholme 143 A5
Way 53 C5
Wayfield 51 C4
Wayford 14 A4
Waymills 111 A4
Wayne Green 61 B6
Way Village 26 D3
Weachyburn 268 D1
Weald 64 C4
Wealdstone 49 A4
Weardley 148 C1
Weare 42 D3
Weare Giffard 25 C5
Wearhead 165 B6
Weasdale 155 A5
Weasenham All
Saints 119 C5
Weasenham St
Peter 119 C5
Weatherhill 35 B6
Weaverham 127 B6
Weaverthorpe 160 D3
Webheath 80 A3
Wedderlairs 256 C3
Wedderlie 197 A5
Weddington 97 B6
Wedhampton 45 D4
Wedmore 28 A4
Wednesbury 96 B2
Wednesfield 96 A2
Weedon 66 B4
Weedon Bec 82 B3
Weedon Lois 82 C3
Weeford 96 A4
Week 26 D2
Weeke 32 B3
Weekley 99 C5
Week St Mary 10 B3
Weel 150 D3
Weeley 71 A5
Weeley Heath 71 A5
Weem 230 D2
Weeping Cross 112 C3
Weethley Gate 80 B3
Weeting 102 C3
Weeton E Yorks 143 A5
Lancs 144 D3
N Yorks 148 C1
Weetwood Hall 188 A3
Weir 138 A1
Weir Quay 6 A3
Welborne 120 E2
Welbourn 133 D4
Welburn N Yorks 149 A6
N Yorks 159 C5
Welbury 158 A2
Welby 116 B2
Welches Dam 101 C6
Welcombe 24 D3
Weld Bank 137 B4
Weldon 189 D4
Welford Northants 98 C3
W Berks 46 B2
Welford-on-
Avon 81 B4
Welham Leics 99 B4
Notts 132 A2
Welham Green 68 C2
Well Hants 33 A6
Lincs 135 B4
N Yorks 157 C6
Welland 79 C5
Wellbank 221 A4
Welldale 175 B4
Well End 48 A1
Wellesbourne 81 B5
Well Heads 147 D4
Well Hill 50 C1
Welling 50 B1
Wellingborough 83 A5
Wellingham 119 C5
Wellingore 133 D4
Wellington Cumb 162 D3
Hereford 78 C2
Som 27 C6
Telford 111 D5
Wellington Heath 79 C5
Wellington Hill 148 D2
Wellow Bath 43 D6
IoW 18 C2
Notts 131 C6
Wellpond Green 68 A4
Wells 29 A5
Wellsborough 97 A6
Wells Green 128 D1
Wells-Next-The-
Sea 119 A6
Wellswood 8 A3
Well Town 13 A4
Wellwood 208 B3
Welney 102 B1
Welshampton 110 B3
Welsh Bicknor 62 B1
Welsh End 111 B4
Welsh Frankton 110 B2
Welsh Hook 55 B5
Welsh Newton 61 B6
Welshpool Y
Trallwng 93 A6
Welsh St Donats 41 D5
Welton Cumb 164 A1
E Yorks 142 A1
Lincs 133 B5
Northants 82 A2
Welton Hill 133 A5
Welton le
Marsh 135 C4
Welton le Wold 134 A2
Welwick 143 A5
Welwyn 68 B2
Welwyn Garden
City 68 B2
Wem 111 C4
Wembdon 28 B2
Wembley 49 A4
Wembury 7 C4
Wembworthy 12 A1
Wemyss Bay 204 B1
Wenallt Ceredig 75 A5
Gwyn 109 A4
Wendens Ambo 85 D7
Wendlebury 65 B6
Wendling 119 D6
Wendover 66 C4
Wendron 3 B4
Wendy 85 C5
Wenfordbridge 10 D1
Wenhaston 105 D5
Wennington
Cambs 100 D4
Lancs 155 D5
London 50 A2
Wensley Derbys 130 C2
N Yorks 157 C4
Wentbridge 140 B2
Wentnor 94 B1
Wentworth
Cambs 101 D6
S Yorks 140 D1
Wenvoe 41 D6
Weobley 78 B2
Weobley Marsh 78 B2
Wereham 102 A2
Wergs 95 A6
Wern Powys 109 D4
Powys 110 D1
Wernffrwd 57 C5
Wernyrheolydd 61 B5
Werrington Corn 10 C4
Pboro 100 A3
Staffs 112 A3
Wervin 127 B4
Wesham 144 D4
Wessington 130 D3
Westacott 25 B6
West Acre 119 D4
West Adderbury 82 D1
West Allerdean 198 B3
West Alvington 7 C6
West Amesbury 31 A5
West Anstey 26 C3
West Ashby 134 B2
West Ashling 19 A7
West Ashton 44 D2
West Auckland 167 C4
West Ayton 160 C3
West
Bagborough 27 B6
West Barkwith 133 A6
West Barnby 169 D6
West Barns 210 C3
West Barsham 119 B6
West Bay 15 B4
West Beckham 120 B3
West Bedfont 48 B3
West Benhar 208 D1
Westbere 52 C3
West Bergholt 70 A3
West Bexington 15 C5
West Bilney 119 D4
West
Blatchington 21 B5
Westborough 115 A6
Westbourne
Bmouth 17 B4
Suff 88 C2
W Sus 19 A6
West Bowling 147 D5
West Bradford 146 C1
West Bradley 29 B5
West Bretton 139 B5
West Bridgford 114 B3
West Bromwich 96 B3
Westbrook 46 B2
West Buckland
Devon 26 B1
Som 28 C1
West Burrafirth 285 H4
West Burton
N Yorks 156 C4
W Sus 20 A2
Westbury Bucks 82 D3
Shrops 94 A1
Wilts 44 D2
Westbury Leigh 44 D2
Westbury-on-
Severn 62 B3
Westbury on
Trym 43 B4
Westbury-sub-
Mendip 29 A5
West
Butterwick 141 C6
Westby 144 D3
West Byfleet 48 C3
West Caister 121 D7
West Calder 208 D3
West Camel 29 C5
West Challow 46 A1
West
Chelborough 15 A5
West
Chevington 189 D5
West Chiltington 20 A3
West Chiltington
Common 20 A3
West Chinnock 29 D4
West Chisenbury 45 D5
West Clandon 34 A3
West Cliffe 39 A5
Westcliff-on-Sea 51 A5
West Clyne 274 D2
West Clyth 275 A6
West Coker 29 D5
Westcombe 29 B6
West Compton
Dorset 15 B5
Som 29 A5
Westcote 64 A3
Westcott Bucks 66 B3
Devon 13 A5
Sur 35 B4
Westcott Barton 65 A5
West Cowick 140 A4
West Cranmore 29 A6
West Cross 57 D6
West Cullery 245 B4
West Curry 10 B3
West
Curthwaite 175 D6
West Darlochan 190 C2
Westdean 22 C3
West Dean Wilts 31 C6
W Sus 20 A1
West Deeping 100 A3
Westdene 21 B5
West Derby 136 D2
West Dereham 102 A2
West Didsbury 138 D1
West Ditchburn 189 A4
West Down 25 A6
West Drayton
London 48 B3
Notts 132 B2
West Ella 142 A2
West End Bedford 84 B1
E Yorks 150 D2
E Yorks 151 D4
Hants 32 D3
Lancs 137 A6
Norf 103 A5
Norf 121 D7
N Som 42 C3
N Yorks 147 B5
Oxon 65 C5
S Lanark 195 B4
Suff 105 C5
Sur 48 C2
S Yorks 141 C4
Wilts 30 C3
Wilts 44 B3
W Sus 21 A5
West End Green 47 C4
Wester
Aberchalder 252 D1
Wester
Balgedie 219 D6
Wester
Culbeuchly 268 C1
Westerdale
Highld 280 C3
N Yorks 159 A5
Wester
Dechmont 208 D3
Wester Denoon 232 D1
Westerfield
Shetland 285 H5
Suff 88 C2
Wester Fintray 245 A5
Westergate 20 B2
Wester
Gruinards 263 A7
Westerham 36 A2
Westerhope 178 C3
Wester Lealty 264 C2
Westerleigh 43 B6
Wester Milton 253 A5
Wester
Newburn 220 D4
Wester Quarff 285 K6
Wester Skeld 285 J4
Westerton Angus 233 C4
Durham 167 B5
W Sus 20 B1
Westerwick 285 J4
West Farleigh 37 A5
West Felton 110 C2
West Fenton 210 B1
West Ferry 221 A4
Westfield Cumb 162 B2
E Sus 23 A6
Hereford 79 C5
Highld 279 B6
N Lanark 207 C5
Norf 103 A5
W Loth 208 C2
Westfields 15 A7
Westfields of
Rattray 231 D5
West Firle 22 B2
Westgate
Durham 166 B2
N Lincs 141 C5
Norf 119 A5
Norf 119 A6
Westgate on Sea 53 B5
West Ginge 46 A2

West Grafton 45 C6
West Green 47 D5
West Greenskares 268 C2
West Grimstead 31 C6
West Grinstead 35 D4
West Haddlesey 140 A3
West Haddon 98 D3
West Hagbourne 46 A3
West Hagley 96 C2
Westhall Aberds 256 D1
Suff 105 C5
West Hall 176 C3
West Hallam 114 A2
West Halton 141 A7
Westham Dorset 15 D6
E Sus 22 B4
Som 28 A4
West Ham 49 A7
Westhampnett 20 B1
West Handley 130 B3
West Hanney 65 D5
West Hanningfield 70 D1
West Hardwick 140 B2
West Harnham 31 C5
West Harptree 43 D4
West Hatch 28 C2
Westhay 28 A4
Westhead 136 C3
West Head 102 A1
West Heath
Ches E 128 C3
Hants 34 A1
Hants 46 D3
West Helmsdale 274 C4
West Hendred 46 A2
West Heslerton 160 D3
Westhide 78 C3
Westhill Aberds 245 B5
Highld 252 B3
West Hill Devon 13 B5
E Yorks 151 A4
N Som 42 B3
West Hoathly 35 C6
West Holme 16 C2
Westhope
Hereford 78 B2
Shrops 94 C2
West Horndon 50 A3
Westhorpe Lincs 117 B5
Suff 87 A6
West Horrington 29 A5
West Horsley 34 A3
West Horton 198 C4
West Hougham 39 A4
Westhoughton 137 C5
West Houlland 285 H4
Westhouse 155 D5
West-houses 131 D4
Westhumble 35 A4
West Huntington 149 B5
West Hythe 38 B3
West Ilsley 46 A2
Westing 284 C7
West Itchenor 19 A6
West Keal 134 C3
West Kennett 45 C5
West Kilbride 204 D2
West Kingsdown 50 C2
West Kington 44 B2
West Kinharrachie 257 C4
West Kirby 126 A2
West Knapton 160 D2
West Knighton 16 C1
West Knoyle 30 B2
West Kyloe 199 B4
Westlake 7 B5
West Lambrook 28 D4
West Langdon 39 A5
West Langwell 273 D4
West Lavington
Wilts 44 D4
W Sus 34 D1
West Layton 157 A5
West Lea 168 A2
West Leake 114 C3
West Learmouth 198 C2
Westleigh Devon 25 C5
Devon 27 D5
Gtr Man 137 C5
West Leigh 12 A1
Westleton 89 A5
West Lexham 119 D5
Westley Shrops 94 A1
Suff 87 A4
Westley Waterless 86 B2
West Lilling 149 A5
Westlington 66 B3
Westlinton 175 B6
West Linton 195 A6
West Liss 33 C6
West Littleton 43 B6
West Looe 6 B1
West Luccombe 26 A3
West Lulworth 16 C2
West Lutton 150 A2
West Lydford 29 B5
West Lyng 28 C3
West Lynn 118 C3
West Malling 37 A4
West Malvern 79 C5
West Marden 33 D6
West Marina 23 B5
West Markham 132 B2
Westmarsh 53 C4
West Marsh 143 B4
West Marton 146 B2
West Meon 33 C5
West Mersea 71 B4
Westmeston 21 A6
Westmill 68 A3
West Milton 15 B5
Westminster 49 B6
West Minster 51 B6
West Molesey 48 C4
West Monkton 28 C2
West Moors 17 A4
West Morriston 197 B5
Westmuir 232 C1
West Muir 232 B3
Westness 282 E4
West Ness 159 D5
West Newham 178 B2
Westnewton
Cumb 174 D4
Northumb 198 C3
West Newton
E Yorks 151 D4
Norf 118 C3
West Norwood 49 B6
Westoe 179 C5
West Ogwell 12 D3
Weston Bath 43 C6
Ches E 128 D2
Devon 13 C6
Dorset 15 D6
Halton 127 A5
Hants 33 C6
Herts 85 D4
Lincs 117 C5
Northants 82 C2
Notts 132 C2
N Yorks 147 C5
Shrops 94 B3
Shrops 111 C4
Staffs 112 C3
W Berks 46 B1
Weston Beggard 78 C3
Westonbirt 44 A2
Weston by Welland 99 B4
Weston Colville 86 B2
Westoncommon 110 C3
Weston Coyney 112 A3
Weston Favell 83 A4
Weston Green
Cambs 86 B2
Norf 120 D3
Weston Heath 112 D1
Weston Hills 117 C5
Westoning 84 D2
Weston-in-Gordano 42 B3
Weston Jones 111 C6
Weston Longville 120 D3
Weston Lullingfields 110 C3
Weston-on-the-Green 65 B6
Weston-on-Trent 114 C2
Weston Patrick 33 A5
Weston Rhyn 110 B1
Weston-Sub-Edge 80 C4
Weston-super-Mare 42 C2
Weston Turville 66 B4
Weston under Lizard 112 D2
Weston under Penyard 62 A2
Weston under Wetherley 81 A6
Weston Underwood
Derbys 113 A6
M Keynes 83 B5
Westonzoyland 28 B3
West Orchard 30 D2
West Overton 45 C5
Westow 149 A6
West Park 168 B2
West Parley 17 B4
West Peckham 36 A4
West Pelton 179 D4
West Pennard 29 B5
West Pentire 4 A2
West Perry 84 A3
Westport Argyll 190 C2
Som 28 D3
West Putford 25 D4
West Quantoxhead 27 A6
West Rainton 167 A6
West Rasen 133 A5
West Raynham 119 C5
West Retford 132 A1
Westrigg 208 D2
West Rounton 158 A3
West Row 102 D2
West Rudham 119 C5
West Runton 120 A3
Westruther 197 B5
Westry 101 B5
West Saltoun 210 D1
West Sandwick 284 E6
West Scrafton 157 C4
West Sleekburn 179 A4
West Somerton 121 D6
West Stafford 16 C1
West Stockwith 141 D5
West Stoke 20 B1
West Stonesdale 156 A2
West Stoughton 28 A4
West Stour 30 C1
West Stourmouth 53 C4
West Stow 103 D4
West Stowell 45 C5
West Strathan 277 B6
West Stratton 32 A4
West Street 37 A7
West Tanfield 157 D6
West Taphouse 5 A6
West Tarbert 202 B3
West Thirston 189 D4
West Thorney 19 A6
West Thurrock 50 B2
West Tilbury 50 B3
West Tisted 33 C5
West Tofts Norf 103 B4
Perth 219 A6
West Torrington 133 A6
West Town Hants 19 B6
N Som 42 C3
West Tytherley 32 C1
West Tytherton 44 B3
Westville 114 A3
West Walton 118 D1
West Walton Highway 118 D1
Westward 175 D5
Westward Ho! 25 C5
Westwell Kent 38 A1
Oxon 64 C3
Westwell Leacon 38 A1
West Wellow 32 D1
West Wemyss 209 A6
Westwick Cambs 85 A6
Durham 166 D3
Norf 121 C4
West Wick 42 C2
West Wickham
Cambs 86 C2
London 49 C6
West Williamston 55 D6
West Willoughby 116 A2
West Winch 118 D3
West Winterslow 31 B6
West Wittering 19 B6
West Witton 157 C4
Westwood Devon 13 B5
Wilts 44 D2
West Woodburn 177 A6
West Woodhay 46 C1
West Woodlands 30 A1
Westwoodside 141 D5
West Worldham 33 B6
West Worlington 26 D2
West Worthing 21 B4
West Wratting 86 B2
West Wycombe 66 D4
West Wylam 178 C3
West Yell 284 E6
Wetheral 176 D2
Wetherby 148 C3
Wetherden 87 A5
Wetheringsett 88 A2
Wethersfield 86 D3
Wethersta 284 G5
Wetherup Street 88 A2
Wetley Rocks 112 A3
Wettenhall 127 C6
Wetton 129 D6
Wetwang 150 B2
Wetwood 111 B6
Wexcombe 45 D6
Wexham Street 48 A2
Weybourne 120 A3
Weybread 104 C3
Weybridge 48 C3
Weycroft 14 B3
Weydale 280 B3
Weyhill 32 A2
Weymouth 15 D6
Whaddon Bucks 83 D5
Cambs 85 C5
Glos 63 B4
Wilts 31 C5
Whale 164 C3
Whaley 131 B5
Whaley Bridge 129 A5
Whaley Thorns 131 B5
Whaligoe 281 D5
Whalley 146 D1
Whalton 178 A3
Wham 146 A1
Whaplode 117 C6
Whaplode Drove 117 D6
Whaplode St Catherine 117 C6
Wharfe 146 A1
Wharles 144 D4
Wharncliffe Side 139 D5
Wharram le Street 150 A1
Wharton 127 C6
Wharton Green 127 C6
Whashton 157 A5
Whatcombe 16 A2
Whatcote 81 C6
Whatfield 87 C6
Whatley Som 14 A3
Som 30 A1
Whatlington 23 A5
Whatstandwell 130 D3
Whatton 115 B5
Whauphill 171 C6
Whaw 156 A3
Wheatacre 105 B5
Wheatcroft 130 D3
Wheathampstead 68 B1
Wheathill 95 C4
Wheatley Devon 13 B4
Wheatley
Hants 33 A6
Oxon 65 C6
S Yorks 140 C3
W Yorks 138 A3
Wheatley Hill 167 B6
Wheaton Aston 112 D2
Wheddon Cross 27 B4
Wheedlemont 255 D5
Wheelerstreet 34 B2
Wheelock 128 D2
Wheelock Heath 128 D2
Wheelton 137 A5
Wheen 232 A1
Wheldrake 149 C5
Whelford 64 D2
Whelpley Hill 67 C5
Whempstead 68 A3
Whenby 149 A5
Whepstead 87 B4
Wherstead 88 C2
Wherwell 32 A2
Wheston 129 B6
Whetsted 37 B4
Whetstone 98 B2
Whicham 153 B2
Whichford 81 D6
Whickham 179 C4
Whiddon Down 12 B1
Whigstreet 232 D2
Whilton 82 A3
Whimble 11 A4
Whim Farm 195 A7
Whimple 13 B5
Whimpwell Green 121 C5
Whinburgh 103 A6
Whinnieliggate 173 C5
Whinnyfold 257 C5
Whippingham 18 B4
Whipsnade 67 B6
Whipton 13 B4
Whirlow 130 A3
Whisby 133 C4
Whissendine 115 D6
Whissonsett 119 C6
Whistlefield
Argyll 215 C4
Argyll 215 C5
Whistley Green 47 B5
Whiston Mers 136 D3
Northants 83 A5
Staffs 112 A4
Staffs 112 D2
S Yorks 131 A4
Whitbeck 153 B2
Whitbourne 79 B5
Whitburn T&W 179 C6
W Loth 208 D2
Whitburn Colliery 179 C6
Whitby Ches W 126 B3
N Yorks 169 D6
Whitbyheath 126 B3
Whitchurch Bath 43 C5
Bucks 66 A3
Cardiff 41 C6
Devon 11 D5
Hants 32 A3
Hereford 62 B1
Oxon 47 B4
Pembs 54 B3
Shrops 111 A4
Whitchurch Canonicorum 14 B3
Whitchurch Hill 47 B4
Whitcombe 15 C7
Whitcott Keysett 93 C6
Whiteacen 254 B3
Whiteacre Heath 97 B5
Whitebridge 240 A2
Whitebrook 62 C1
Whiteburn 197 B4
Whitecairn 171 B4
Whitecairns 245 A6
Whitecastle 195 B5
Whitechapel 145 C5
Whitecleat 283 G6
White Coppice 137 B5
Whitecraig 209 C6
Whitecroft 62 C2
Whitecross Corn 9 D5
Falk 208 C2
Staffs 112 C2
Whiteface 264 B3
Whitefarland 202 D3
Whitefaulds 192 E2
Whitefield
Gtr Man 137 C7
Perth 219 A6
Whiteford 256 D2
Whitegate 127 C6
Whitehall
Blackburn 137 A5
W Sus 35 D4
Whitehall Village 282 E7
Whitehaven 162 C2
Whitehill 33 B6
Whitehills
Aberds 268 C1
S Lanark 205 C6
Whitehough 129 A5
Whitehouse
Aberds 244 A3
Argyll 202 B3
Whiteinch 205 B5
Whitekirk 210 B2
White Lackington 15 B7
White Ladies Aston 80 B2
Whitelaw 205 D6
Whiteleas 179 C5
Whiteley Bank 19 C4
Whiteley Green 129 B4
Whiteley Village 48 C3
White Lund 144 A4
Whitemans Green 35 D6
White Mill 58 C1
Whitemire 253 A5
Whitemoor 5 B4
Whitemore 128 C3
Whitenap 32 C2
White Ness 285 J5
White Notley 70 B1
Whiteoak Green 64 B4
Whiteparish 31 C6
White Pit 134 B3
White Post 131 D6
Whiterashes 256 D3
White Rocks 61 A6
White Roding 69 B5
Whiterow 281 D5
Whiteshill 63 C4
Whiteside
Northumb 177 C5
W Loth 208 D2
Whitesmith 22 A3
Whitestaunton 28 D2
Whitestone Devon 12 B3
Devon 25 A5
Warks 97 C6
Whitestones 268 D3
Whitestreet Green 87 D5
Whitewall Corner 159 D6
White Waltham 47 B6
Whiteway Glos 63 B5
Glos 63 D4
Whitewell
Aberds 269 C4
Lancs 145 C6
Whitewell Bottom 138 A1
Whiteworks 11 D7
Whitfield Kent 39 A5
Northants 82 D3
Northumb 177 D5
S Glos 62 D2
Whitford Devon 14 B2
Flint 125 B6
Whitgift 141 A6
Whitgreave 112 C2
Whithorn 171 C6
Whiting Bay 191 C6
Whitkirk 148 D2
Whitland 56 A1
Whitletts 192 C3
Whitley N Yorks 140 A3
Reading 47 B5
Wilts 44 C2

Whitley Bay 179 B5
Whitley Chapel 178 D1
Whitley Lower 139 B5
Whitley Row 36 A2
Whitlock's End 96 D4
Whitminster 62 C3
Whitmore 112 A2
Whitnage 27 D5
Whitnash 81 A6
Whitney-on-Wye 77 C6
Whitrigg Cumb 163 A5
Cumb 175 C5
Whitsbury 31 D5
Whitsome 198 A2
Whitson 42 A2
Whitstable 52 C3
Whitstone 10 B3
Whittingham 188 B3
Whittingslow 94 C2
Whittington Glos 63 A6
Lancs 155 D5
Norf 102 B3
Shrops 110 B2
Staffs 95 C6
Staffs 97 A4
Worcs 80 B1
Whittlebury 82 C3
Whittle-le-Woods 137 A4
Whittlesey 101 B4
Whittlesford 85 C6
Whittlestone Head 137 B6
Whitton Borders 187 A6
N Lincs 141 A7
Northumb 188 C3
Powys 77 A6
Shrops 94 D3
Stockton 167 C6
Suff 88 C2
Whittonditch 45 B6
Whittonstall 178 D2
Whitway 46 D2
Whitwell Derbys 131 B5
Herts 68 A1
IoW 18 D4
N Yorks 157 B6
Rutland 99 A6
Whitwell-on-the-Hill 149 A6
Whitwell Street 120 C3
Whitwick 114 D2
Whitwood 140 A2
Whitworth 138 B1
Whixall 111 B4
Whixley 148 B3
Whoberley 97 D6
Whorlton
Durham 166 D4
N Yorks 158 A3
Whygate 177 B5
Whyle 78 A3
Whyteleafe 35 A6
Wibdon 62 D1
Wibsey 147 D5
Wibtoft 98 C1
Wichenford 79 A5
Wichling 37 A7
Wick Bmouth 17 B5
Devon 13 A6
Highld 281 C5
S Glos 43 B6
Shetland 285 K6
V Glam 40 D4
Wilts 31 C5
Worcs 80 C2
W Sus 20 B3
Wicken Cambs 102 D1
Northants 83 D4
Wicken Bonhunt 85 D6
Wickenby 133 A5
Wicken Green Village 119 B5
Wickersley 140 D2
Wickford 70 D1
Wickham Hants 33 D4
W Berks 46 B1
Wickham Bishops 70 B2
Wickhambreux 53 D4
Wickhambrook 86 B3
Wickhamford 80 C3
Wickham Market 88 B4
Wickhampton 105 A5
Wickham St Paul 87 D4
Wickham Skeith 88 A1
Wickham Street
Suff 86 B3
Suff 88 A1
Wick Hill 47 C5
Wicklewood 104 A1
Wickmere 120 B3
Wick St Lawrence 42 C2
Wickwar 43 A6
Widdington 86 D1
Widdrington 189 D5
Widdrington Station 189 D5
Widecombe in the Moor 12 D2
Widegates 6 B1
Widemouth Bay 10 A3
Wide Open 179 B4
Widewall 283 H5
Widford Essex 69 C6
Herts 68 B4
Widham 45 A4
Widmer End 66 D4
Widmerpool 115 C4
Widnes 127 A5
Wigan 137 C4
Wiggaton 13 B6
Wiggenhall St Germans 118 D2
Wiggenhall St Mary Magdalen 118 D2
Wiggenhall St Mary the Virgin 118 D2
Wigginton Herts 67 B5
Oxon 81 D6
Staffs 97 A5
York 149 B4
Wigglesworth 146 B2
Wiggonby 175 C5
Wiggonholt 20 A3
Wighill 148 C3
Wighton 119 B6
Wigley 32 D2
Wigmore Hereford 78 A2
Medway 51 C5
Wigsley 132 B3
Wigsthorpe 100 C2
Wigston 98 B3
Wigthorpe 131 A5
Wigtoft 117 B5
Wigton 175 D5
Wigtown 171 B6
Wigtwizzle 139 D5
Wike 148 C2
Wike Well End 141 B4
Wilbarston 99 C5
Wilberfoss 149 B6
Wilberlee 138 B3
Wilburton 101 D6
Wilby Norf 103 C6
Northants 83 A5
Suff 104 D3
Wilcot 45 C5
Wilcott 110 D2
Wilcrick 42 A3
Wilday Green 130 B3
Wildboarclough 129 C4
Wilden Bedford 84 B2
Worcs 95 D6
Wildhern 46 D1
Wildhill 68 C2
Wildmoor 96 D2
Wildsworth 141 D6
Wilford 114 B3
Wilkesley 111 A5
Wilkhaven 265 B5
Wilkieston 208 D4
Willand 27 D5
Willaston Ches E 128 D1
Ches W 126 B3
Willen 83 C5
Willenhall W Mid 96 B2
W Mid 97 D6
Willerby E Yorks 150 D3
N Yorks 160 D4
Willersey 80 D4
Willersley 77 C7
Willesborough 38 A2
Willesborough Lees 38 A2
Willesden 49 A5
Willett 27 B6
Willey Shrops 95 B4
Warks 98 C1
Willey Green 34 A2
Williamscott 82 C1
Willian 84 D4
Willingale 69 C5
Willingdon 22 B3
Willingham 101 D6
Willingham by Stow 132 A3
Willington Bedford 84 C3
Derbys 113 C6
Durham 167 B4
T&W 179 C5
Warks 81 D5
Willington Corner 127 C5
Willisham Tye 87 B6
Willitoft 149 D6
Williton 27 A5
Willoughbridge 111 A6
Willoughby Lincs 135 B4
Warks 82 A2
Willoughby-on-the-Wolds 115 C4
Willoughby Waterleys 98 B2
Willoughton 142 D1
Willows Grn 69 B7
Willsbridge 43 B5
Willsworthy 11 C6
Wilmcote 81 B4
Wilmington Devon 14 B2
E Sus 22 B3
Kent 50 B2
Wilminstone 11 D5
Wilmslow 128 A3
Wilnecote 97 A5
Wilpshire 145 D6
Wilsden 147 D4
Wilsford Lincs 116 A3
Wilts 31 B5
Wilts 45 D5
Wilsill 147 A5
Wilsley Pound 37 C5
Wilsom 33 B6
Wilson 114 C2
Wilsontown 195 A4
Wilstead 84 C2
Wilsthorpe 116 D3
Wilstone 67 B5
Wilton Borders 186 B3
Cumb 162 C3
N Yorks 160 C2
Redcar 168 D3
Wilts 31 B4
Wilts 45 C6
Wimbish 86 D1
Wimbish Green 86 D2
Wimblebury 112 D4
Wimbledon 49 B5
Wimblington 101 B6
Wimborne Minster 17 B4
Wimborne St Giles 31 D4
Wimbotsham 102 A2
Wimpson 32 D2
Wimpstone 81 C5
Wincanton 29 C7
Wincham 128 B1
Winchburgh 208 C3
Winchcombe 63 A6
Winchelsea 23 A7
Winchelsea Beach 23 A7
Winchester 32 C3
Winchet Hill 37 B5
Winchfield 47 D5
Winchmore Hill
Bucks 67 D5
London 68 D3
Wincle 129 C4
Wincobank 140 D1
Windermere 154 B3
Winderton 81 C6
Windhill 252 B1
Windhouse 284 D6
Windlehurst 129 A4
Windlesham 48 C2
Windley 113 A7
Windmill Hill
E Sus 22 A4
Som 28 D3
Windrush 64 B2
Windsor N Lincs 141 B5
Windsor 48 B2
Windsoredge 63 C4
Windygates 220 D3
Windyknowe 208 D2
Windywalls 197 C6
Wineham 35 D5
Winestead 143 A4
Winewall 146 C3
Winfarthing 104 C2
Winford IoW 19 C4
N Som 43 C4
Winforton 77 C6
Winfrith Newburgh 16 C2
Wing Bucks 66 A4
Rutland 99 A5
Wingate 168 B2
Wingates
Gtr Man 137 C5
Northumb 189 D4
Wingerworth 130 C3
Wingfield C Beds 67 A5
Suff 104 D3
Wilts 44 D2
Wingham 53 D4
Wingmore 38 A3
Wingrave 66 B4
Winkburn 132 D2
Winkfield 48 B2
Winkfield Row 48 B1
Winkhill 129 D5
Winklebury 47 D4
Winkleigh 12 A1
Winksley 157 D6
Winkton 17 B5
Winlaton 178 C3
Winless 281 C5
Winmarleigh 145 C4
Winnal 78 D2
Winnall 32 C3
Winnersh 47 B5
Winscales 162 B3
Winscombe 42 D3
Winsford Ches W 127 C6
Som 27 B4
Winsham 14 A3
Winshill 113 C6
Winskill 164 B3
Winslade 33 A5
Winsley 44 C2
Winslow 66 A3
Winson 64 C1
Winson Grn 96 C3
Winsor 32 D2
Winster Cumb 154 B3
Derbys 130 C2
Winston Durham 166 D4
Suff 88 A2
Winstone 63 C5
Winston Green 88 A2
Winswell 25 D5
Winterborne Clenston 16 A2
Winterborne Herringston 15 C6
Winterborne Houghton 16 A2
Winterborne Kingston 16 B2
Winterborne Monkton 15 C6
Winterborne Stickland 16 A2
Winterborne Whitechurch 16 A2
Winterborne Zelston 16 B2
Winterbourne
S Glos 43 A5
W Berks 46 B2
Winterbourne Abbas 15 B6
Winterbourne Bassett 45 B5
Winterbourne Dauntsey 31 B5
Winterbourne Down 43 B5
Winterbourne Earls 31 B5
Winterbourne Gunner 31 B5
Winterbourne Monkton 45 B5
Winterbourne Steepleton 15 C6
Winterbourne Stoke 31 A4
Winterburn 146 B3
Winter Gardens 51 A4
Winteringham 142 A1
Winterley 128 D2
Wintersett 140 B1
Wintershill 32 D4
Winterton 142 B1
Winterton-on-Sea 121 D6
Winthorpe Lincs 135 C5
Notts 132 D3
Winton Bmouth 17 B4
Cumb 165 D5
N Yorks 158 B3
Wintringham 160 D2
Winwick Cambs 100 C3
Northants 98 D3
Warr 137 D5
Wirksworth 130 D2
Wirksworth Moor 130 D3
Wirswall 111 A4
Wisbech 101 A6
Wisbech St Mary 101 A6
Wisborough Green 34 D3
Wiseton 132 A2
Wishaw N Lanark 194 A2
Warks 97 B4
Wisley 34 A3
Wispington 134 B2
Wissenden 37 B7
Wissett 105 D4
Wistanstow 94 C2
Wistanswick 111 C5
Wistaston 128 D1
Wistaston Green 128 D1
Wiston Pembs 55 C6
S Lanark 195 C4
W Sus 21 A4
Wistow Cambs 101 C4
N Yorks 149 D4
Wiswell 146 D1
Witcham 101 C6
Witchampton 16 A3
Witchford 101 D7
Witham 70 B2
Witham Friary 30 A1
Witham on the Hill 116 D3
Withcall 134 A2
Withdean 21 B6
Witherenden Hill 36 D4
Witheridge 26 D3
Witherley 97 B6
Withern 135 A4
Withernsea 143 A5
Withernwick 151 C4
Withersdale Street 104 C3
Withersfield 86 C2
Witherslack 154 C3
Withiel 5 A4
Withiel Florey 27 B4
Withington Glos 63 B6
Gtr Man 138 D1
Hereford 78 C3
Shrops 111 D4
Staffs 112 B4
Withington Green 128 B3
Withleigh 27 D4
Withnell 137 A5
Withybrook 98 C1
Withycombe 27 A5
Withycombe Raleigh 13 C5
Withyham 36 C2
Withypool 26 B3
Witley 34 C2
Witnesham 88 B2
Witney 65 B4
Wittering 100 A2
Wittersham 37 D6
Witton Angus 232 A3
Worcs 80 A1
Witton Bridge 121 B5
Witton Gilbert 167 A5
Witton-le-Wear 166 B4
Witton Park 167 B4
Wiveliscombe 27 C5
Wivelrod 33 B5
Wivelsfield 35 D6
Wivelsfield Green 35 D6
Wivenhoe 71 A4
Wivenhoe Cross 71 A4
Wiveton 120 A2
Wix 71 A5
Wixford 80 B3
Wixhill 111 C4
Wixoe 86 C3
Woburn 83 D6
Woburn Sands 83 D6
Wokefield Park 47 C4
Woking 34 A3
Wokingham 47 C6
Wolborough 12 D3
Woldingham 35 A6
Wold Newton
E Yorks 160 D4
NE Lincs 143 D4
Wolfclyde 195 C5
Wolferton 118 C3
Wolfhill 219 A6
Wolf's Castle 55 B5
Wolfsdale 55 B5
Woll 186 A3
Wollaston
Northants 83 A6
Shrops 110 D2
Wollaton 114 B3
Wollerton 111 B5
Wollescote 96 C2
Wolsingham 166 B3
Wolstanton 112 A2
Wolston 97 D7
Wolvercote 65 C5
Wolverhampton 96 B2
Wolverley Shrops 110 B3
Worcs 95 D6
Wolverton Hants 46 D3
M Keynes 83 C5
Warks 81 A5
Wolverton Common 46 D3
Wolvesnewton 61 D6
Wolvey 98 C1
Wolviston 168 C2
Wombleton 159 C5
Wombourne 95 B6
Wombwell 140 C1
Womenswold 53 D4
Womersley 140 B3
Wonastow 61 B6
Wonersh 34 B3
Wonson 12 C1
Wonston 32 B3
Wooburn 48 A2
Wooburn Green 48 A2
Woodacott 11 A4
Woodale 156 D4
Woodbank 190 D2
Woodbastwick 121 D5
Woodbeck 132 B2
Woodborough
Notts 115 A4
Wilts 45 D5
Woodbridge
Dorset 29 D7
Suff 88 C3
Woodbury 13 C5
Woodbury Salterton 13 C5

Woodchester 63 C4
Woodchurch Kent 38 B1
Mers 126 A2
Woodcombe 27 A4
Woodcote 47 A4
Woodcott 46 D2
Woodcroft 62 D1
Woodcutts 30 D3
Wood Dalling 120 C2
Woodditton 86 B2
Woodeaton 65 B6
Woodend Cumb 153 A2
Northants 82 C3
W Sus 19 A7
Wood End Herts 68 A3
Warks 96 D4
Warks 97 B5
Wood Enderby 134 C2
Woodend Green 82 C3
Woodfalls 31 C5
Woodfield Oxon 65 A6
S Ayrs 192 C3
Wood Field 35 A4
Woodford Corn 24 D3
Devon 8 B1
Glos 62 D2
Gtr Man 128 A3
London 68 D4
Northants 99 D6
Woodford Bridge 68 D4
Woodford Halse 82 B2
Woodgate Norf 120 D2
W Mid 96 C2
Worcs 80 A2
W Sus 20 B2
Woodgreen 31 D5
Wood Green 68 D3
Woodhall Herts 68 B2
Invclyd 204 A3
N Yorks 156 B3
Woodhall Spa 134 C1
Woodham 48 C3
Woodham Ferrers 70 D1
Woodham Mortimer 70 C2
Woodham Walter 70 C2
Woodhaven 220 B4
Wood Hayes 96 A2
Woodhead 256 C2
Woodhey 137 B6
Woodhill 95 C5
Woodhorn 179 A4
Woodhouse
Leics 114 D3
N Lincs 141 C5
S Yorks 131 A4
W Yorks 140 A1
W Yorks 148 D1
Woodhouse Eaves 114 D3
Woodhouselee 209 D5
Woodhouselees 175 A6
Woodhouse Park 128 A3
Woodhouses 113 D5
Woodhurst 101 D5
Woodingdean 21 B6
Woodkirk 139 A5
Woodland Devon 8 A1
Durham 166 C3
Woodlands
Aberds 245 C4
Dorset 17 A4
Hants 32 D2
Highld 264 D1
N Yorks 148 B2
S Yorks 140 C3
Woodlands Park 47 B6
Woodlands St Mary 46 B1
Woodlane 113 C5
Wood Lanes 129 A4
Woodleigh 7 C6
Woodlesford 139 A6
Woodley Gtr Man 138 D2
Wokingham 47 B5
Woodmancote
Glos 62 D3
Glos 63 A5
Glos 63 C6
W Sus 19 A6
W Sus 21 A5
Woodmancott 33 A4
Woodmansey 150 D3
Woodmansterne 35 A5
Woodminton 31 C4
Woodnesborough 53 D5
Woodnewton 100 B2
Wood Norton 120 C2
Woodplumpton 145 D5
Woodrising 103 A5
Woodseaves
Shrops 111 B5
Staffs 112 C1
Woodsend 45 B6
Woodsetts 131 A5
Woodsford 16 B1
Wood's Green 36 C4
Woodside
Aberdeen 245 B6
Aberds 257 B5
Brack 48 B2
Fife 220 D4
Hants 18 B2
Herts 68 C2
Perth 220 A2
Woodside of Arbeadie 245 C4
Woodstock Oxon 65 B5
Pembs 55 B6
Wood Street
Norf 121 C5
Sur 34 A2
Woodthorpe
Derbys 131 B4
Leics 114 D3
Lincs 135 A4
York 149 C4
Woodton 104 B3
Woodtown Devon 25 C5
Devon 25 C5
Woodvale 136 B2
Woodville 113 D7
Wood Walton 100 C4
Woodyates 31 D4
Woofferton 78 A3
Wookey 29 A5
Wookey Hole 29 A5
Wool 16 C2
Woolacombe 25 A5
Woolage Green 39 A4
Woolaston 62 D1
Woolavington 28 A3
Woolbeding 34 D1
Wooldale 139 C4
Wooler 188 A2
Woolfardisworthy
Devon 12 A3
Devon 24 C4
Woolfords Cottages 195 A5
Woolhampton 46 C3
Woolhope 79 D4
Woolhope Cockshoot 79 D4
Woolland 16 A1
Woollaton 25 D5
Woolley Bath 43 C6
Cambs 100 D3
Corn 24 D3
Derbys 130 C3
W Yorks 139 B6
Woolmere Green 80 A2
Woolmer Green 68 B2
Woolpit 87 A5
Woolscott 82 A1
Woolsington 178 C3
Woolstanwood 128 D1
Woolstaston 94 B2
Woolsthorpe
Lincs 115 B6
Lincs 116 C2
Woolston Devon 7 C6
Shrops 94 C2
Woolston
Shrops 110 C2
Soton 32 D3
Warr 127 A6
Woolstone
M Keynes 83 D5
Oxon 45 A6
Woolton 127 A4
Woolton Hill 46 C2
Woolverstone 88 D2
Woolverton 44 D1
Woolwich 50 B1
Woolwich Ferry 50 B1
Woonton 78 B1
Wooperton 188 A3
Woore 111 A6
Wootten Green 104 D3
Wootton Bedford 84 C2
Hants 17 B6
Hereford 78 B1
Kent 39 A4
N Lincs 142 B2
Northants 83 B4
Oxon 65 B5
Oxon 65 C5
Shrops 94 D2
Shrops 110 C2
Staffs 112 C2
Staffs 113 A5
Wootton Bridge 18 B4
Wootton Common 18 B4
Wootton Courtenay 27 A4
Wootton Fitzpaine 14 B3
Wootton Rivers 45 C5
Wootton St Lawrence 46 D3
Wootton Wawen 81 A4
Worcester 79 B6
Worcester Park 49 C5
Wordsley 96 C1
Worfield 95 B5
Work 282 F5
Workington 162 B2
Worksop 131 B5
Worlaby 142 B2
World's End 46 B2
Worle 42 C2
Worleston 127 D6
Worlingham 105 C5
Worlington 102 D2
Worlingworth 88 A3
Wormald Green 148 A2
Wormbridge 78 D2
Wormegay 118 D3
Wormelow Tump 78 D2
Wormhill 129 B6
Wormingford 87 D5
Worminghall 66 C2
Wormington 80 D3
Worminster 29 A5
Wormit 220 B3
Wormleighton 82 B1
Wormley Herts 68 C3
Sur 34 C2
Wormley West End 68 C3
Wormshill 37 A6
Wormsley 78 C2
Worplesdon 34 A2
Worrall 139 D6
Worsbrough 139 C6
Worsbrough Common 139 C6
Worsley 137 C6
Worstead 121 C5
Worsthorne 146 D2
Worston 146 C1
Worswell 7 C4
Worth Kent 53 D5
W Sus 35 C6
Wortham 104 D1
Worthen 94 A1
Worthenbury 110 A3
Worthing Norf 120 D1
W Sus 21 B4
Worthington 114 C2
Worth Matravers 16 D3
Worting 47 D4
Wortley S Yorks 139 D6
W Yorks 147 D6
Worton N Yorks 156 B3
Wilts 44 D3
Wortwell 104 C3
Wotherton 93 A6
Wotter 7 A4
Wotton 35 B4
Wotton-under-Edge 62 D3
Wotton Underwood 66 B2
Woughton on the Green 83 D5
Wouldham 51 C4
Wrabness 88 D2
Wrafton 25 B5
Wragby Lincs 133 B6
W Yorks 140 B2
Wragholme 143 D5
Wramplingham 104 A2
Wrangbrook 140 B2
Wrangham 256 C1
Wrangle 135 D4
Wrangle Bank 135 D4
Wrangle Lowgate 135 D4
Wrangway 27 D6
Wrantage 28 C3
Wrawby 142 C2
Wraxall Dorset 15 A5
N Som 42 B3
Som 29 B6
Wray 145 A6
Wraysbury 48 B3
Wrayton 155 D5
Wrea Green 144 D3
Wreay Cumb 164 A2
Cumb 164 C2
Wrecclesham 34 B1
Wrekenton 179 D4
Wrelton 159 C6
Wrenbury 111 A4
Wrench Green 160 C3
Wreningham 104 B2
Wrentham 105 C5
Wrenthorpe 139 A6
Wrentnall 94 A2
Wressle E Yorks 149 D6
N Lincs 142 C1
Wrestlingworth 85 C4
Wretham 103 C5
Wretton 102 B2
Wrexham
Wrecsam 126 D3
Wrexham Industrial Estate 110 A2
Wribbenhall 95 D5
Wrightington Bar 136 B4
Wrinehill 111 A6
Wrington 42 C3
Writhlington 43 D6
Writtle 69 C6
Wrockwardine 111 D5
Wroot 141 C5
Wrotham 36 A4
Wrotham Heath 36 A4
Wroughton 45 A5
Wroxall IoW 19 D4
Warks 97 D5
Wroxeter 94 A3
Wroxham 121 D5
Wroxton 81 C7
Wyaston 113 A5
Wyberton 117 A6
Wyboston 84 B3
Wybunbury 111 A6
Wychbold 80 A2
Wych Cross 36 C2
Wyck 33 B6
Wyck Rissington 64 A2
Wycoller 146 D3
Wycomb 115 C5
Wycombe Marsh 66 D4
Wyddial 85 D5
Wye 38 A2
Wyesham 61 B7
Wyfordby 115 D5
Wyke Dorset 30 C1
Shrops 95 A4
Sur 34 A2
W Yorks 139 A4
Wykeham
N Yorks 159 D7
N Yorks 160 C3
Wyken 97 C6
Wyke Regis 15 D6
Wykey 110 C2
Wylam 178 C3
Wylde Green 96 B4
Wyllie 41 B6
Wylye 31 B4
Wymering 19 A5
Wymeswold 115 C4
Wymington 83 A6
Wymondham
Leics 115 D6
Norf 104 A2
Wyndham 40 B4
Wynford Eagle 15 B5
Wyng 283 H4
Wynyard Village 168 C2
Wyre Piddle 80 C2
Wysall 115 C4
Wythall 96 D3
Wytham 65 C5
Wythburn 163 C6
Wythenshawe 128 A3
Wythop Mill 163 B4
Wyton 101 D4
Wyverstone 87 A6
Wyverstone Street 87 A6
Wyville 116 C1
Wyvis Lodge 263 C6

Y

Yaddlethorpe 141 C6
Yafford 18 C3
Yafforth 158 B2
Yalding 37 A4
Yanworth 63 B6
Yapham 149 B6
Yapton 20 B2
Yarburgh 143 D5
Yarcombe 14 A2
Yard 27 B5
Yardley 96 C4
Yardley Gobion 83 C4
Yardley Hastings 83 B5
Yardro 77 B6
Yarkhill 79 C4
Yarlet 112 C3
Yarlington 29 C6
Yarlside 153 D3
Yarm 168 D2
Yarmouth 18 C2
Yarnbrook 44 D2
Yarnfield 112 B2
Yarnscombe 25 C6
Yarnton 65 B5
Yarpole 78 A2
Yarrow 196 D2
Yarrow Feus 196 D2
Yarsop 78 C2
Yarwell 100 B2
Yate 43 A6
Yateley 47 C6
Yatesbury 45 B4
Yattendon 46 B3
Yatton Hereford 78 A2
N Som 42 C3
Yatton Keynell 44 B2
Yaverland 19 C5
Yaxham 120 D2
Yaxley Cambs 100 B3
Suff 104 D2
Yazor 78 C2
Yeading 48 A4
Yeadon 147 C6
Yealand Conyers 154 D4
Yealand Redmayne 154 D4
Yealmpton 7 B4
Yearby 168 C4
Yearsley 159 D4
Yeaton 110 D3
Yeaveley 113 A5
Yedingham 160 D2
Yeldon 84 A2
Yelford 65 C4
Yelland 25 B5
Yelling 85 A4
Yelvertoft 98 D2
Yelverton Devon 7 A4
Norf 104 A3
Yenston 29 C7
Yeoford 12 B2
Yeolmbridge 10 C4
Yeo Mill 26 C3
Yeovil 29 D5
Yeovil Marsh 29 D5
Yeovilton 29 C5
Yerbeston 55 D6
Yesnaby 282 F3
Yetlington 188 C3
Yetminster 29 D5
Yettington 13 C5
Yetts o' Muckhart 219 D5
Y Felinheli 123 D5
Y Ffôr 106 C3
Y-Ffrith 125 A5
Yieldshields 194 A3
Yiewsley 48 A3
Ynysboeth 41 B5
Ynysddu 41 B6
Ynysgyfflog 90 A4
Ynyshir 41 B5
Ynyslas 90 C4
Ynys-meudwy 59 E4
Ynystawe 40 A1
Ynysybwl 41 B5
Yockenthwaite 156 D3
Yockleton 110 D2
Yokefleet 141 A6
Yoker 205 B5
Yonder Bognie 255 B6
York 149 B4
Yorkletts 52 C2
Yorkley 62 C2
York Town 47 C6
Yorton 111 C4
Youlgreave 130 C2
Youlstone 24 D3
Youlthorpe 149 B6
Youlton 148 A3
Young's End 70 B1
Young Wood 133 B6
Yoxall 113 D5
Yoxford 89 A4
Ysbyty-Cynfyn 75 A6
Ysbyty Ifan 108 A3
Ysbyty Ystwyth 75 A6
Ysceifiog 125 B6
Yspitty 57 C5
Ystalyfera 59 E4
Ystrad 41 B4
Ystrad Aeron 75 C4
Ystradfellte 59 D6
Ystradffin 76 C1
Ystradgynlais 59 D4
Ystradmeurig 75 B6
Ystrad-mynach 41 B6
Ystradowen
Carms 59 D4
V Glam 41 D5
Ystumtuen 75 A6
Ythanbank 257 C4
Ythanwells 256 C1
Ythsie 256 C3

Z

Zeal Monachorum 12 A2
Zeals 30 B1
Zelah 4 B3
Zennor 2 B2